Collins
ESSENTIAL ROAD ATLAS
BRITAIN

G000294628

Conten...

Route plannin...

Route planning r...
Restricted motor...
Motorway services information .... x-xi
Orbital motorway maps - M25, Birmingham & M60 .... xii-xiv
Distance chart xv
World Heritage Sites .... xvi-xvii

Urban approach maps (1 mile to 1 inch)   2-32

Symbols used on maps 2
Plymouth 2
Bournemouth 3
Southampton & Portsmouth 4-5
Swansea 6
Cardiff & Newport 7
Bristol 8
Milton Keynes 9
London 10-13
West Midlands 14-15
Coventry 16
Leicester 17
Derby & Nottingham 18-19
Stoke-on-Trent 20
Sheffield 21
Merseyside 22-23
Greater Manchester 24-25
Leeds & Bradford 26-27
Newcastle upon Tyne & Sunderland 28
Middlesbrough 29
Glasgow 30-31
Edinburgh 32

Street maps   33-91

Symbols used on maps   33
Birmingham   34-35
Edinburgh   36-37
Glasgow   38-39
Leeds   40-41
Liverpool   42-43
London   44-45
Manchester   46-47
Birmingham index 48
Edinburgh index   49
Glasgow index   51
Leeds index   52
Liverpool index   54
London index   56
Manchester index 60
Aberdeen   63
Bath   63
Blackpool   64
Bournemouth   64
Bradford   65
Brighton   65
Bristol   66
Cambridge   66
Canterbury   67
Cardiff   67
Carlisle   68
Cheltenham   68
Chester   69
Coventry   69
Derby   70
Dover   70
Dundee   71
Durham   71
Eastbourne   72
Exeter   72
Folkestone   73
Gloucester   73
Guildford   74
Harrogate   74

Hastings   75
Hereford   75
Hull   76
Inverness   76
Leicester   77
Lincoln   77
Middlesbrough   78
Milton Keynes   78
Newcastle upon Tyne 79
Norwich   79
Nottingham   80
Oxford   80
Perth   81
Plymouth   81
Portsmouth   82
Reading   82
Salisbury   83
Scarborough   83
Sheffield   84
Southampton   84
Stoke-on-Trent   85
Stratford-upon-Avon 85
Sunderland   86
Swansea   86
Swindon   87
Torquay   87
Watford   88
Weston-super-Mare 88
Winchester   89
Windsor   89
Worcester   90
York   90

Airport plans
Birmingham International 91
Gatwick   91
Glasgow   91
Heathrow   91
Manchester   91
Stansted   91

Road maps   92-279

Symbols used on maps & key to map pages 92-93
England, Wales & Southern Scotland (3.2 miles to 1 inch) 94-253
Northern Scotland (4.2 miles to 1 inch)   254-279

Index

Collins

Published by Collins
An imprint of HarperCollins Publishers
77-85 Fulham Palace Road, Hammersmith, London W6 8JB

www.harpercollins.co.uk

Printed in China

ISBN 978 0 00 732052 3   Imp 001   XC12494 / CUDN

e-mail: roadcheck@harpercollins.co.uk

Information on fixed speed camera locations provided by PocketGPSWorld.Com Ltd.

With thanks to the Wine Guild of the United Kingdom for help with researching vineyards.

Information regarding blue flag beach awards is current as of summer 2009. For latest information please visit www.blueflag.org.uk

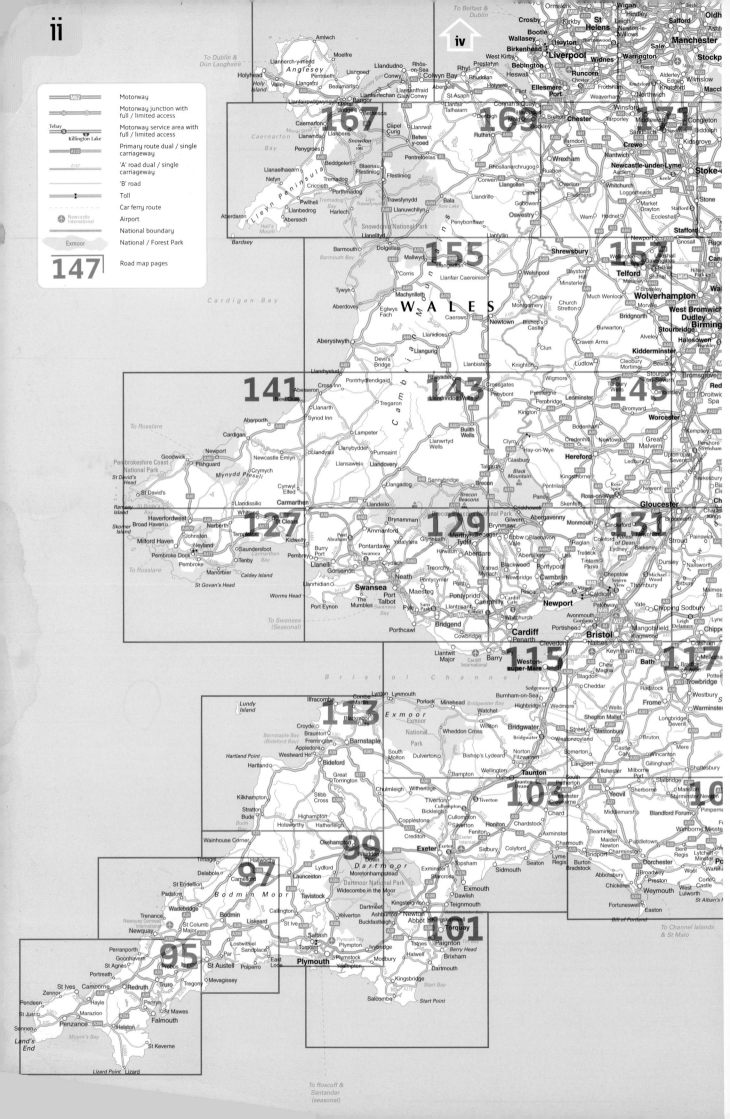

Legend

M62	Motorway
	Motorway junction with full / limited access
Tebay / Killington Lake	Motorway service area with full / limited access
A172	Primary route dual / single carriageway
A167	'A' road dual / single carriageway
	'B' road
	Toll
	Car ferry route
Newcastle International	Airport
	National boundary
Exmoor	National / Forest Park
147	Road map pages

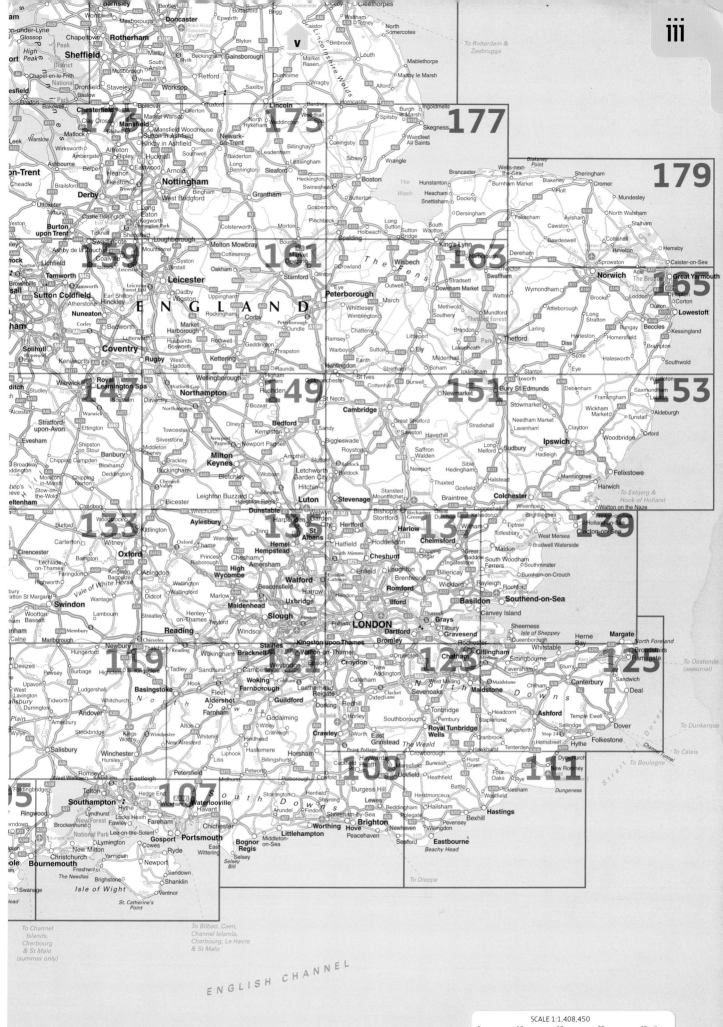

SCALE 1:1,408,450

22 miles to 1 inch / 14 km to 1 cm

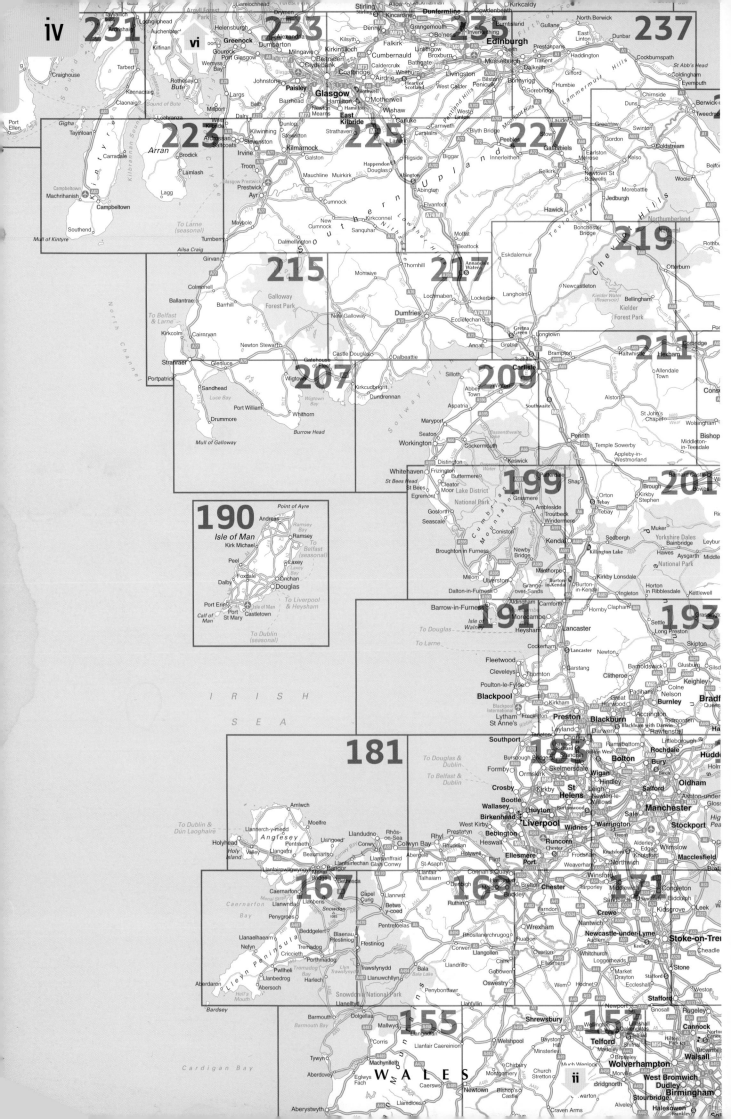

SCALE 1:1,408,450

0 10 20 30 40 miles
0 10 20 30 40 50 60 kilometres
22 miles to 1 inch / 14 km to 1 cm

Legend

M62	Motorway
	Motorway junction with full / limited access
Tebay / Killington Lake	Motorway service area with full / limited access
A172	Primary route dual / single carriageway
A167	'A' road dual / single carriageway
	'B' road
	Toll
	Car ferry route
Newcastle International	Airport
	National boundary
Exmoor	National / Forest Park
147	Road map pages

Map index numbers: 229, 221, 213, 205, 203, 197, 195, 187, 189, 177, 179, 173, 175, 163, 161, 159, 165

NORTH SEA

ENGLAND

iii

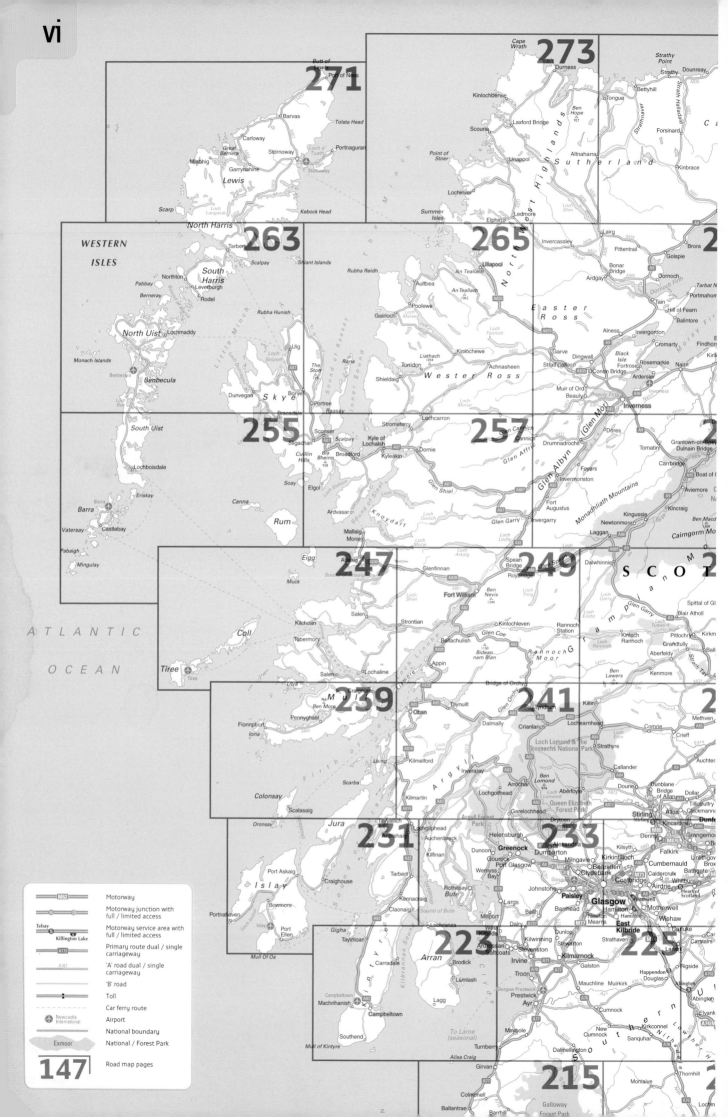

Map page index

271
273
263
265
255
257
247
249
239
241
231
233
225
223
215

WESTERN ISLES

Lewis
North Harris
South Harris
North Uist
Benbecula
South Uist
Barra
Vatersay
Pabaigh
Mingulay

ATLANTIC OCEAN

Skye
Cuillin Hills
Rum
Eigg
Muck
Coll
Tiree
Mull
Iona
Colonsay
Oronsay
Jura
Islay
Arran

NORTH WEST HIGHLANDS
SUTHERLAND
EASTER ROSS
WESTER ROSS

SCOTLAND

Legend

M62	Motorway
	Motorway junction with full / limited access
Tebay / Killington Lake	Motorway service area with full / limited access
A172	Primary route dual / single carriageway
A167	'A' road dual / single carriageway
	'B' road
	Toll
	Car ferry route
Newcastle International	Airport
	National boundary
Exmoor	National / Forest Park
147	Road map pages

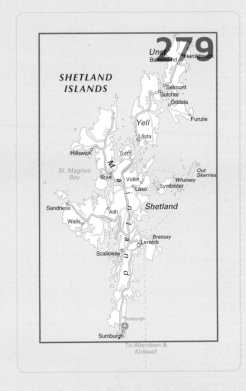

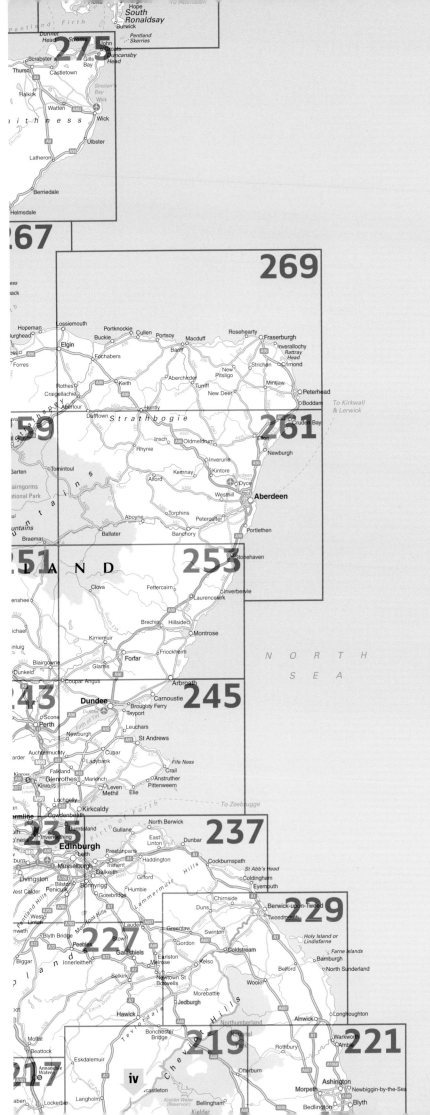

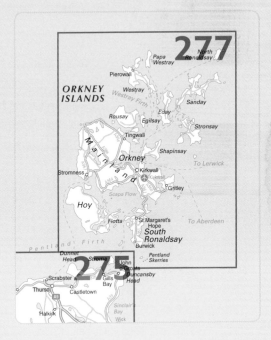

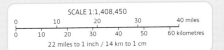

Restricted motorway junctions

A1(M) LONDON TO NEWCASTLE

②
Northbound : No access
Southbound : No exit

③
Southbound : No access

⑤
Northbound : No exit
Southbound : No access
         : No exit

④①
Northbound : No exit to M62 Eastbound

④③
Northbound : No exit to M1 Westbound

Dishforth
Southbound : No access from A168 Eastbound

⑤⑦
Northbound : No access
         : Exit only to A66(M) Northbound
Southbound : Access only from A66(M) Southbound
         : No exit

⑥⑤
Northbound : No access from A1
Southbound : No exit to A1

A3(M) PORTSMOUTH

①
Northbound : No exit
Southbound : No access

④
Northbound : No access
Southbound : No exit

A38(M) BIRMINGHAM

Victoria Road
Northbound : No exit
Southbound : No access

A48(M) CARDIFF

Junction with M4
Westbound : No access from M4 ㉙ Eastbound
Eastbound : No exit to M4 ㉙ Westbound

㉙A
Westbound : No exit to A48 Eastbound
Eastbound : No access from A48 Westbound

A57(M) MANCHESTER

Brook Street
Westbound : No exit
Eastbound : No access

A58(M) LEEDS

Westgate
Southbound : No access
Woodhouse Lane
Westbound : No exit

A64(M) LEEDS

Claypit Lane
Eastbound : No access

A66(M) DARLINGTON

Junction with A1(M)
Northbound : No access from A1(M) Southbound
         : No exit
Southbound : No access
         : No exit to A1(M) Northbound

A74(M) LOCKERBIE

⑱
Northbound : No access
Southbound : No exit

A167(M) NEWCASTLE

Campden Street
Northbound : No exit
Southbound : No access
         : No exit

M1 LONDON TO LEEDS

②
Northbound : No exit
Southbound : No access

④
Northbound : No exit
Southbound : No access

⑥A
Northbound : Access only from M25 ㉑
         : No exit
Southbound : No access
         : Exit only to M25 ㉑

⑦
Northbound : Access only from A414
         : No exit
Southbound : No access
         : Exit only to A414

M1 LONDON TO LEEDS (continued)

⑰
Northbound : No access
         : Exit only to M45
Southbound : Access only from M45
         : No exit

⑲
Northbound : Exit only to M6
Southbound : Access only from M6

㉑A
Northbound : No access
Southbound : No exit

㉓A
Northbound : No access from A453
Southbound : No exit to A453

㉔A
Northbound : No exit
Southbound : No access

㉟A
Northbound : No access
Southbound : No exit

④③
Northbound : No access
         : Exit only to M621
Southbound : No exit
         : Access only from M621

④⑧
Northbound : No exit to A1(M) Southbound
         : Access only from A1(M) Northbound
Southbound : Exit only to A1(M) Southbound
         : No access

M2 ROCHESTER TO CANTERBURY

①
Westbound : No exit to A2 Eastbound
Eastbound : No access from A2 Westbound

M3 LONDON TO WINCHESTER

⑧
Westbound : No access
Eastbound : No exit

⑩
Northbound : No access
Southbound : No exit

⑬
Southbound : No exit to A335 Eastbound
         : No access

⑭
Westbound : No access
Eastbound : No exit

M4 LONDON TO SWANSEA

①
Westbound : No access from A4 Eastbound
Eastbound : No exit to A4 Westbound

②
Westbound : No access from A4 Eastbound
         : No exit to A4 Eastbound
Eastbound : No access from A4 Westbound
         : No exit to A4 Westbound

㉑
Westbound : No access from M48 Eastbound
Eastbound : No exit to M48 Westbound

㉓
Westbound : No exit to M48 Eastbound
Eastbound : No access from M48 Westbound

㉕
Westbound : No access
Eastbound : No exit

㉕A
Westbound : No access
Eastbound : No exit

㉙
Westbound : No access
         : Exit only to A48(M)
Eastbound : Access only from A48(M) Eastbound
         : No exit

㊳
Westbound : No access

㊴
Westbound : No exit
Eastbound : No access
         : No exit

④①
Westbound : No exit
Eastbound : No access

④②
Westbound : No exit to A48
Eastbound : No access from A48

M5 BIRMINGHAM TO EXETER

⑩
Northbound : No exit
Southbound : No access

⑪A
Northbound : No access from A417 Eastbound
Southbound : No exit to A417 Westbound

M6 COVENTRY TO CARLISLE

Junction with M1
Northbound : No access from M1 ⑲ Southbound
Southbound : No exit to M1 ⑲ Northbound

③A
Northbound : No access from M6 Toll
Southbound : No exit to M6 Toll

④
Northbound : No exit to M42 Northbound
         : No access from M42 Southbound
Southbound : No exit to M42
         : No access from M42 Southbound

④A
Northbound : No access from M42 ⑧
         Northbound
         : No exit
Southbound : No access
         : Exit only to M42 ⑧

⑤
Northbound : No access
Southbound : No exit

⑩A
Northbound : No access
         : Exit only to M54
Southbound : Access only from M54
         : No exit

⑪A
Northbound : No exit to M6 Toll
Southbound : No access from M6 Toll

㉔
Northbound : No exit
Southbound : No access

㉕
Northbound : No access
Southbound : No exit

㉚
Northbound : Access only from M61 Northbound
         : No exit
Southbound : No access
         : Exit only to M61 Southbound

㉛A
Northbound : No access
Southbound : No exit

M6 Toll BIRMINGHAM

Ⓣ1
Northbound : Exit only to M42
         : Access only from A4097
Southbound : No access
         : Access only from M42 Southbound

Ⓣ2
Northbound : No exit
         : No access

Ⓣ5
Northbound : No exit
Southbound : No access

Ⓣ7
Northbound : No access
Southbound : No exit

Ⓣ8
Northbound : No access
Southbound : No exit

M8 EDINBURGH TO GLASGOW

⑧
Westbound : No access from M73 ②
         Southbound
         : No access from A8 Eastbound
         : No access from A89 Eastbound
Eastbound : No access from A89 Westbound
         : No exit to M73 ② Northbound

⑨
Westbound : No exit
Eastbound : No access

⑬
Westbound : Access only from M80
Eastbound : Exit only to M80

⑭
Westbound : No exit
Eastbound : No access

⑯
Westbound : No access
Eastbound : No exit

⑰
Eastbound : Access only from A82,
         not central Glasgow
         : Exit only to A82,
         not central Glasgow

⑱
Westbound : No access
Eastbound : No access

⑲
Westbound : Access only from A814 Eastbound
Eastbound : Exit only to A814 Westbound,
         not central Glasgow

M8 EDINBURGH TO GLASGOW (cont)

⑳
Westbound : No access
Eastbound : No exit

㉑
Westbound : No exit
Eastbound : No access

㉒
Westbound : No access
         : Exit only to M77 Southbound
Eastbound : Access only from M77 Northbound
         : No exit

㉓
Westbound : No access
Eastbound : No exit

㉕A
Eastbound : No exit
Westbound : No access

㉘
Westbound : No access
Eastbound : No exit

㉘A
Westbound : No access
Eastbound : No exit

M9 EDINBURGH TO STIRLING

①A
Westbound : No access
Eastbound : No exit

②
Westbound : No exit
Eastbound : No access

③
Westbound : No access
Eastbound : No exit

⑥
Westbound : No access
Eastbound : No exit

⑧
Westbound : No access
Eastbound : No exit

M11 LONDON TO CAMBRIDGE

④
Northbound : No access from A1400 Westbound
         : No exit
Southbound : No access
         : No exit to A1400 Eastbound

⑤
Northbound : No access
Southbound : No exit

⑧A
Northbound : No access
Southbound : No exit

⑨
Northbound : No access
Southbound : No exit

⑬
Northbound : No access
Southbound : No exit

⑭
Northbound : No access from A428 Eastbound
         : No exit to A428 Westbound
         : No exit to A1307
Southbound : No access from A428 Eastbound
         : No access from A1307
         : No exit

M20 LONDON TO FOLKESTONE

②
Westbound : No exit
Eastbound : No access

③
Westbound : No access
         : Exit only to M26 Westbound
Eastbound : Access only from M26 Eastbound
         : No exit

⑪A
Westbound : No exit
Eastbound : No access

M23 LONDON TO CRAWLEY

⑦
Northbound : No exit to A23 Southbound
Southbound : No access from A23 Northbound

⑩A
Southbound : No access from B2036
Northbound : No exit to B2036

Restricted motorway junctions are shown on the maps as:

M25 LONDON ORBITAL MOTORWAY

1B
Clockwise : No access
Anticlockwise : No exit

5
Clockwise : No exit to M26 Eastbound
Anticlockwise : No access from M26 Westbound

Spur of M25 (5)
Clockwise : No access from M26 Westbound
Anticlockwise : No exit to M26 Eastbound

19
Clockwise : No access
Anticlockwise : No exit

21
Clockwise : No access from M1 (6A) Northbound
: No exit to M1 (6A) Southbound
Anticlockwise : No access from M1 (6A) Northbound
: No exit to M1 (6A) Southbound

31
Clockwise : No exit
Anticlockwise : No access

M26 SEVENOAKS

Junction with M25 (5)
Westbound : No exit to M25 Anticlockwise
: No exit to M25 spur
Eastbound : No access from M25 Clockwise
: No access from M25 spur

Junction with M20
Westbound : No access from M20 (3) Eastbound
Eastbound : No exit to M20 (3) Westbound

M27 SOUTHAMPTON TO PORTSMOUTH

4 West
Westbound : No exit
Eastbound : No access

4 East
Westbound : No access
Eastbound : No exit

10
Westbound : No access
Eastbound : No exit

12 West
Westbound : No exit
Eastbound : No access

12 East
Westbound : No access from A3
Eastbound : No exit

M40 LONDON TO BIRMINGHAM

3
Westbound : No access
Eastbound : No exit

7
Eastbound : No exit

8
Northbound : No access
Southbound : No exit

13
Northbound : No access
Southbound : No exit

14
Northbound : No exit
Southbound : No access

16
Northbound : No exit
Southbound : No access

M42 BIRMINGHAM

1
Northbound : No exit
Southbound : No access

7
Northbound : No access
: Exit only to M6 Northbound
Southbound : Access only from M6 Northbound
: No exit

7A
Northbound : No access
: Exit only to M6 Eastbound
Southbound : No access
: No exit

8
Northbound : Access only from M6 Southbound
: No exit
Southbound : Access only from M6 Southbound
: Exit only to M6 Northbound

M45 COVENTRY

Junction with M1
Westbound : No access from M1 (17) Southbound
Eastbound : No exit to M1 (17) Northbound

Junction with A45
Westbound : No exit
Eastbound : No access

M48 CHEPSTOW

M4
Westbound : No exit to M4 Eastbound
Eastbound : No access from M4 Westbound

M49 BRISTOL

18A
Northbound : No access from M5 Southbound
Southbound : No access from M5 Northbound

M53 BIRKENHEAD TO CHESTER

11
Northbound : No access from M56 (15) Eastbound
: No exit to M56 (15) Westbound
Southbound : No access from M56 (15) Eastbound
: No exit to M56 (15) Westbound

M54 WOLVERHAMPTON TO TELFORD

Junction with M6
Westbound : No access from M6 (10A) Southbound
Eastbound : No exit to M6 (10A) Northbound

M56 STOCKPORT TO CHESTER

1
Westbound : No access from M60 Eastbound
: No access from A34 Northbound
Eastbound : No exit to M60 Westbound
: No exit to A34 Southbound

2
Westbound : No access
Eastbound : No exit

3
Westbound : No exit
Eastbound : No access

4
Westbound : No access
Eastbound : No exit

7
Westbound : No access
Eastbound : No exit

8
Westbound : No exit
Eastbound : No access

9
Westbound : No exit to M6 Southbound
Eastbound : No access from M6 Northbound

15
Westbound : No access
: No access from M53 (11)
Eastbound : No exit
: No exit to M53 (11)

M57 LIVERPOOL

3
Northbound : No exit
Southbound : No access

5
Northbound : Access only from A580 Westbound
: No exit
Southbound : No access
: Exit only to A580 Eastbound

M58 LIVERPOOL TO WIGAN

1
Westbound : No access
Eastbound : No exit

M60 MANCHESTER

2
Westbound : No exit
Eastbound : No access

3
Westbound : No access from M56 (1)
: No access from A34 Southbound
: No exit to A34 Northbound
Eastbound : No access from A34 Southbound
: No exit to M56 (1)
: No exit to A34 Northbound

4
Westbound : No access
Eastbound : No exit to M56

M60 MANCHESTER (continued)

5
Westbound : No access from A5103 Southbound
: No exit to A5103 Southbound
Eastbound : No access from A5103 Northbound
: No exit to A5103 Northbound

14
Westbound : No access from A580
: No exit to A580 Eastbound
Eastbound : No access from A580 Westbound
: No exit to A580

16
Westbound : No access
Eastbound : No exit

20
Westbound : No access
Eastbound : No exit

22
Westbound : No access

25
Westbound : No access

26
Westbound : No access
: No exit

27
Westbound : No exit
Eastbound : No access

M61 MANCHESTER TO PRESTON

2
Northbound : No access from A580 Eastbound
: No access from A666
Southbound : No exit to A580 Westbound

3
Northbound : No access from A580 Eastbound
: No access from A666
Southbound : No exit to A580 Westbound

Junction with M6
Northbound : No exit to M6 (30) Southbound
Southbound : No access from M6 (30) Northbound

M62 LIVERPOOL TO HULL

23
Westbound : No exit
Eastbound : No access

32A
Westbound : No exit to A1(M) Southbound

M65 BURNLEY

9
Westbound : No exit
Eastbound : No access

11
Westbound : No access
Eastbound : No exit

M66 MANCHESTER TO EDENFIELD

1
Northbound : No access
Southbound : No exit

Junction with A56
Northbound : Exit only to A56 Northbound
Southbound : Access only from A56 Southbound

M67 MANCHESTER

1
Westbound : No exit
Eastbound : No access

2
Westbound : No access
Eastbound : No exit

M69 COVENTRY TO LEICESTER

2
Northbound : No exit
Southbound : No access

M73 GLASGOW

1
Northbound : No access from A721 Eastbound
Southbound : No exit to A721 Eastbound

2
Northbound : No access from M8 (8) Eastbound
Southbound : No exit to M8 (8) Westbound

3
Northbound : No exit to A80 Southbound
Southbound : No access from A80 Northbound

M74 GLASGOW

2
Westbound : No access
Eastbound : No exit

3
Westbound : No exit
Eastbound : No access

M74 GLASGOW (continued)

7
Northbound : No exit
Southbound : No access

9
Northbound : No exit
: No access

10
Southbound : No access

11
Northbound : No exit
Southbound : No access

12
Northbound : Access only from A70 Northbound
Southbound : Exit only to A70 Southbound

M77 GLASGOW

Junction with M8
Northbound : No exit to M8 (22) Westbound
Southbound : No access from M8 (22) Eastbound

4
Northbound : No exit
Southbound : No access

6
Northbound : No exit to A77
Southbound : No access from A77

7
Northbound : No access
: No exit

8
Northbound : No access
Southbound : No access

M80 STIRLING

3
Southbound : No access

5
Northbound : No access
: No access from M876
Southbound : No exit
: No exit to M876

M90 EDINBURGH TO PERTH

2A
Northbound : No access
Southbound : No exit

7
Northbound : No exit
Southbound : No access

8
Northbound : No access
Southbound : No exit

10
Northbound : No access from A912
: No exit to A912 Southbound
Southbound : No access from A912 Northbound
: No exit to A912

M180 SCUNTHORPE

1
Westbound : No exit
Eastbound : No access

M606 BRADFORD

Straithgate Lane
Northbound : No access

M621 LEEDS

2A
Northbound : No exit
Southbound : No access

5
Northbound : No access
Southbound : No exit

6
Northbound : No access
Southbound : No access

M876 FALKIRK

Junction with M80
Westbound : No exit to M80 (5) Northbound
Eastbound : No access from M80 (5) Southbound

Junction with M9
Westbound : No access
Eastbound : No exit

2
Northbound : No access
Southbound : No exit

X

Motorway services information

All motorway service areas have fuel, food, toilets, disabled facilities and free short-term parking

For further information on motorway services providers:
Moto   www.moto-way.com
Extra   www.extraservices.co.uk
RoadChef   www.roadchef.com
Welcome Break   www.welcomebreak.co.uk
Westmorland   www.westmorland.co.uk

Motorway	Junction	Service provider	Service name	Fuel supplier	Information	Accommodation	Conference facilities	Showers	M&S Simply Food	Costa Coffee	Starbucks	Burger King	KFC	McDonalds	Wimpy
A1(M)	1	Welcome Break	South Mimms	BP	●	●	●					●	●		
	10	Extra	Baldock	Shell	●	●	●	●	●		●		●	●	
	17	Extra	Peterborough	Shell	●	●		●	●				●	●	
	34	Moto	Blyth	Esso	●	●									
	46	Moto	Wetherby	BP				●	●	●	●				
	61	RoadChef	Durham	Athena	●	●	●							●	
	64	Moto	Washington	BP	●	●					●				
A74(M)	16	RoadChef	Annandale Water	Texaco	●	●	●	●			●			●	
	22	Welcome Break	Gretna Green	BP	●	●	●					●	●		
M1	2-4	Welcome Break	London Gateway	Shell	●	●	●	●			●				
	11-12	Moto	Toddington	BP		●		●	●	●	●				
	14-15	Welcome Break	Newport Pagnell	Shell	●	●	●	●			●	●			
	15A	RoadChef	Northampton	BP		●					●				
	16-17	RoadChef	Watford Gap	BP		●		●			●				
	21-21A	Welcome Break	Leicester Forest East	BP	●	●	●	●			●	●			
	22	Moto	Leicester	BP		●					●				
	23A	Moto	Donington Park	BP	●	●		●	●	●	●				
	25-26	Moto	Trowell	BP	●	●		●	●	●	●				
	28-29	RoadChef	Tibshelf	Texaco	●	●		●	●					●	
	30-31	Welcome Break	Woodall	Shell	●	●	●	●			●	●			
	38-39	Moto	Woolley Edge	Esso	●	●		●	●	●	●				
M2	4-5	Moto	Medway	BP		●		●		●	●				
M3	4A-5	Welcome Break	Fleet	Shell	●	●	●	●			●	●			
	8-9	Moto	Winchester	Shell		●			●						
M4	3	Moto	Heston	BP	●	●	●	●	●		●				
	11-12	Moto	Reading	BP	●	●	●	●	●		●				
	13	Moto	Chieveley	BP		●		●	●	●	●				
	14-15	Welcome Break	Membury	Shell	●	●	●	●			●	●			
	17-18	Moto	Leigh Delamere	BP	●	●		●	●	●	●				
	23A	First Motorway	Magor	Esso	●	●		●							
	30	Welcome Break	Cardiff Gate	Total	●										
	33	Moto	Cardiff West	Esso	●	●		●			●				
	36	Welcome Break	Sarn Park	Shell	●	●	●	●							
	47	Moto	Swansea	BP	●	●		●			●				
	49	RoadChef	Pont Abraham	BP	●				●						
M5	3-4	Moto	Frankley	Esso		●		●	●		●				
	8	RoadChef	Strensham (South)	BP		●		●			●			●	●
	8	RoadChef	Strensham (North)	BP	●	●								●	
	13-14	Welcome Break	Michaelwood	BP	●	●	●	●			●				
	19	Welcome Break	Gordano	Shell	●	●	●	●			●				
	21-22	RoadChef	Sedgemoor (South)	Esso	●									●	
	21-22	Welcome Break	Sedgemoor (North)	Shell	●	●	●	●			●				
	24	Moto	Bridgwater	BP	●	●		●							
	25-26	RoadChef	Taunton Deane	Shell	●	●		●			●			●	
	27	Moto	Tiverton	Shell	●	●		●							
	28	Extra	Cullompton	Shell	●										
	29-30	Moto	Exeter	BP	●	●		●			●				
M6	3-4	Welcome Break	Corley	Shell	●	●		●			●	●			
	10-11	Moto	Hilton Park	BP	●	●		●	●	●	●				
	14-15	RoadChef	Stafford (South)	Esso		●		●	●	●	●			●	
	14-15	Moto	Stafford (North)	BP	●	●		●	●	●	●				
	15-16	Welcome Break	Keele	Shell	●						●	●			
	16-17	RoadChef	Sandbach	Esso		●		●			●			●	
	18-19	Moto	Knutsford	BP	●	●		●	●	●	●				
	20	Moto	Lymm	Total	●	●		●			●				
	27-28	Welcome Break	Charnock Richard	Shell	●			●			●	●			
	32-33	Moto	Lancaster	BP	●	●		●			●				
	35A-36	Moto	Burton-in-Kendal (N)	BP	●	●		●			●				
	36-37	RoadChef	Killington Lake (S)	BP	●			●			●				
	38-39	Westmorland	Tebay	Total	●	●	●	●							
	41-42	Moto	Southwaite	Esso	●	●		●			●				
	44-45	Moto	Todhills	BP/Shell		●				●					
M6 Toll	T6-T7	RoadChef	Norton Canes	BP	●	●	●	●			●			●	
M8	4-5	BP	Heart of Scotland	BP		●		●							
M9	9	Moto	Stirling	BP	●	●		●			●				
M11	8	Welcome Break	Birchanger Green	Shell	●	●	●	●				●	●		
M18	5	Moto	Doncaster North	BP	●	●		●			●				
M20	8	RoadChef	Maidstone	Esso	●	●	●	●			●			●	
	11	Stop 24	Stop 24	Shell	●			●			●	●	●		
M23	11	Moto	Pease Pottage	Shell	●			●	●	●	●				
M25	5-6	RoadChef	Clacket Lane	Total	●			●	●		●			●	
	9-10	Extra	Cobham	Shell	●			●			●	●	●		
	23	Welcome Break	South Mimms	BP	●	●	●								
	30	Moto	Thurrock	Esso	●	●		●	●		●				
M27	3-4	RoadChef	Rownhams	Esso	●	●			●						
M40	2	Extra	Beaconsfield	Shell	●		●	●			●	●	●		
	8	Welcome Break	Oxford	BP	●	●	●	●			●	●			
	10	Moto	Cherwell Valley	Esso	●	●		●	●	●	●				
	12-13	Welcome Break	Warwick	BP/Shell	●	●	●	●			●	●			
M42	2	Welcome Break	Hopwood Park	Shell	●			●			●				
	10	Moto	Tamworth	Esso	●	●		●	●	●	●				
M48	1	Moto	Severn View	BP	●			●			●				
M54	4	Welcome Break	Telford	Shell	●	●	●	●			●				
M56	14	RoadChef	Chester	Shell	●	●		●			●				
M61	6-7	First Motorway	Bolton West	BP	●	●		●	●		●				
M62	7-9	Welcome Break	Burtonwood	Shell	●	●	●	●			●	●			
	18-19	Moto	Birch	BP	●	●		●	●	●	●				
	25-26	Welcome Break	Hartshead Moor	Shell	●	●	●	●			●				
	33	Moto	Ferrybridge	Esso	●	●		●			●				
M65	4	Extra	Blackburn with Darwen	Shell	●	●	●	●					●		
M74	4-5	RoadChef	Bothwell (South)	BP			●	●			●				
	5-6	RoadChef	Hamilton (North)	BP	●	●	●	●			●				
	11-12	Cairn Lodge	Happendon	Gulf	●	●		●							
	12-13	Welcome Break	Abington	Shell	●	●	●	●							
M90	6	Moto	Kinross	BP	●	●		●	●	●	●				

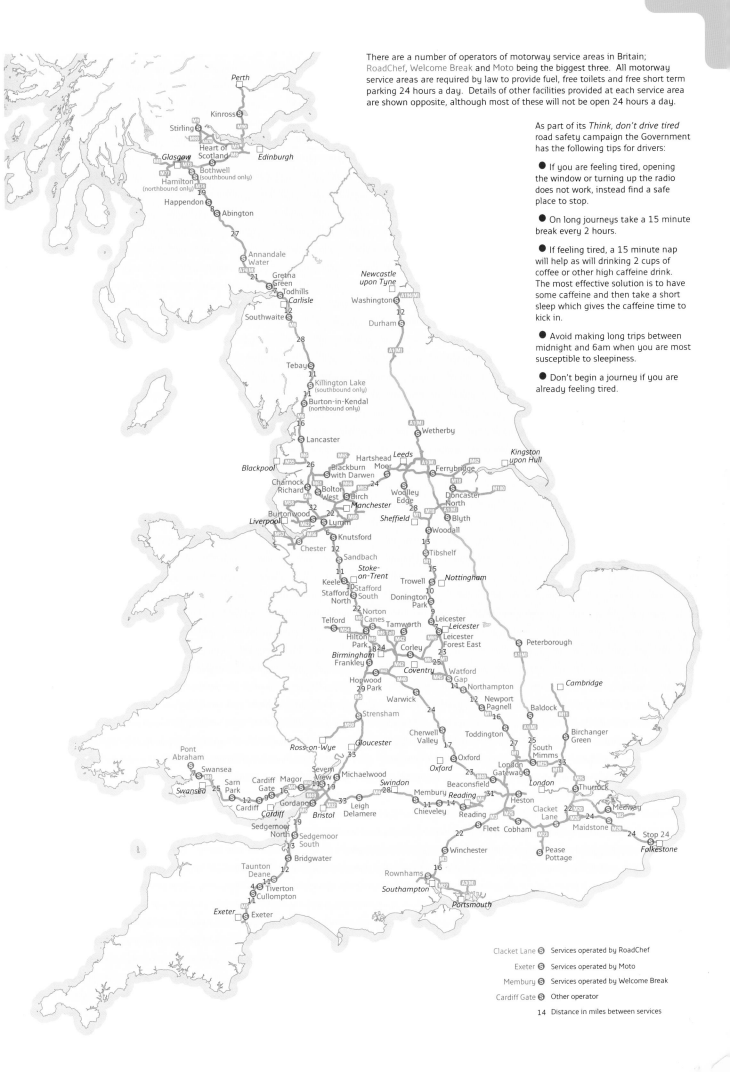

There are a number of operators of motorway service areas in Britain; RoadChef, Welcome Break and Moto being the biggest three. All motorway service areas are required by law to provide fuel, free toilets and free short term parking 24 hours a day. Details of other facilities provided at each service area are shown opposite, although most of these will not be open 24 hours a day.

As part of its *Think, don't drive tired* road safety campaign the Government has the following tips for drivers:

● If you are feeling tired, opening the window or turning up the radio does not work, instead find a safe place to stop.

● On long journeys take a 15 minute break every 2 hours.

● If feeling tired, a 15 minute nap will help as will drinking 2 cups of coffee or other high caffeine drink. The most effective solution is to have some caffeine and then take a short sleep which gives the caffeine time to kick in.

● Avoid making long trips between midnight and 6am when you are most susceptible to sleepiness.

● Don't begin a journey if you are already feeling tired.

Clacket Lane Ⓢ Services operated by RoadChef
Exeter Ⓢ Services operated by Moto
Membury Ⓢ Services operated by Welcome Break
Cardiff Gate Ⓢ Other operator
14 Distance in miles between services

M25 orbital map

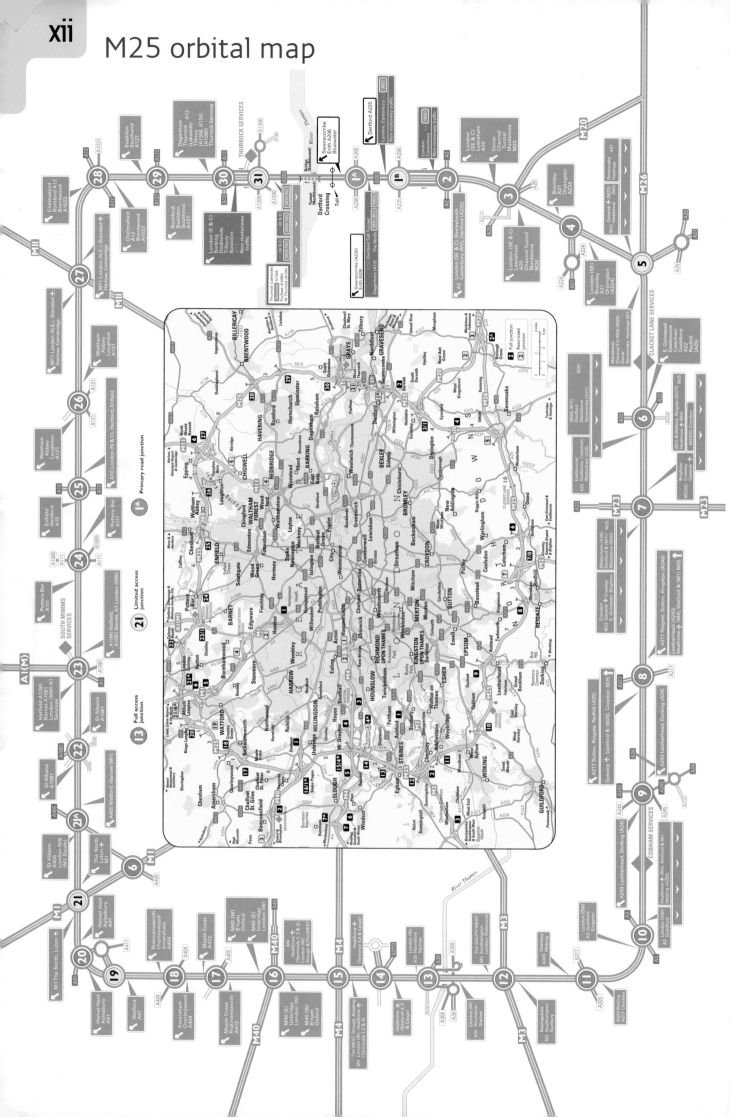

M6 — The SOUTH, B'ham / The S. WEST (M5)
The SOUTH M6 Toll

A5148 Lichfield, (A38) Burton
The SOUTH, Tamworth M6 Toll

A5 Tamworth (M42 North)
The SOUTH, Birmingham Sutton Coldfield M6 Toll

A4601 — A460

A34 — A460
A5195 Brownhills, Burntwood
The SOUTH, Lichfield M6 Toll

A5148

11A — M6 Toll — **T8** — **T7** — **T6** — **T5** — Toll — **T4** — A5

A460 — A5 — Toll — A5 — Toll — A38

A460 (M6 south) Wolverhampton
The NORTH WEST (M6, North) Stafford, telford M6 Toll

A34 Walsall, Cannock A460 Rugeley

A5195 Brownhills, Burntwood
The NORTH WEST (M6 North), Cannock M6 Toll

A38 Burton, Lichfield A5 Tamworth
The NORTH WEST (M6 North), Cannock M6 Toll

NORTON CANES SERVICES

TOLLS

A460 Wolverhampton Cannock

11

A460 Cannock

HILTON PARK SERVICES

A38 Birmingham Sutton Coldfield

M6 Toll London, Coventry, (M6, M42)

A38

10A — M54 — Toll — **T3** — Tolls

M54 NORTH (& MID) WALES Wolverhampton & Telford
The NORTH WEST & Stafford M6

A454 Walsall

A38 Sutton Coldfield
The NORTH WEST Cannock, Lichfield M6 Toll

A446 (M42 North) Coleshill
M6 Toll London, Coventry, (M6, M42(S))

10 — A454

A454 Walsall, W'hampton (Cent. & East)
The North West, Telford (M54), W'hampton (N) M6

A461 Wednesbury
The SOUTH & Birmingham M6

A446 — **T2** — A4091 — A446

A4148

9 — A4148

A461 Wednesbury
The NORTH WEST, Walsall & W'hampton M6

8

M6 Toll

A34 Birmingham (N)
London (M1 & M40) Birmingham (S & Cen.) N.E.C. &

T1 — A446 — M42

A4097

8 — M6 — **7**

A34

A38(M) & A38 B'ham (E, Cen, & NE) & Lichfield
London (M1 & M40) N.E.C & B'ham

A4097 A446 M42 The N. EAST (M1) Tamworth
The NORTH WEST Cannock, Lichfield M6 Toll

9 — M42

M6 London (M1 & M40) Walsall Wolverhampton
The NORTH WEST Walsall Wolverhampton M6

The SOUTH WEST M5 Birmingham (W & S) West Bromwich
The NORTH WEST & Wolverhampton M6

A34 Birmingham (N) & Walsall
The NORTH WEST The SOUTH WEST B'ham (W & S) (M5) M6

M8(N) Birmingham (Cen, E, N, & W)
The NORTH WEST (M5) (M6, South M40) Birmingham (S), N.E.C & London, Coventry

8

A5127 — A38

A452

M42 (M1) & The SOUTH (M40) M42 & M6 M8 LONDON (M1) Coventry N.E.C.

A446 The SOUTH WEST (M5) B'ham (S, N.E.C & London, (S & W) London (N & E) Coventry (N & E) Coventry (S & W)

8 — A41

A41 West Bromwich, Sandwell & B'ham (N & W)
The SOUTH WEST & Birmingham (W & S) M5

6 — A38 — **5** — M6 — **4A** — M6 — **3A**

A4540

A38(M)

Stay in lane through ← markings

M6 & A38(M), A38 B'ham (Cen & NE) ◆ M6 M6

A452 B'ham (E) & Sutton Coldfield
The NORTH WEST & B'ham (Cen, N & W) M6

M6 London (M1), Coventry
The N. WEST (M6 Toll)
The N. EAST (M1), Tamworth

7A — **7** — **4** — M6

A41 West Bromwich & B'ham (NW)
The NORTH (M1 & M6), Birmingham (N), N.E.C. M5

A4123 Birmingham (W) & Dudley
The SOUTH WEST & Birmingham (S) M5

M6 The NORTH WEST, B'ham
The NORTH WEST (M6 Toll) The NORTH EAST (M1) M42

A45 B'ham (S.E.) N.E.C, Coventry (S & W)
The SOUTH WEST (M5), LONDON (M40) Birmingham (SE), Solihull M42

2 — A4123

A4123 Dudley, W'hampton & Sandwell
The NORTH (M1 & M6), Birmingham (N) M5

A456 Kidderminster
The SOUTH WEST & Birmingham (S) M5

A45 B'ham (S.E.) N.E.C, Coventry (S & W)
The NORTH, B'ham (E,N & Cen), Coventry (N & E) M42

6 — A45

A41 Solihull

3 — A456

A456 Birmingham (W & Cen)

FRANKLEY SERVICES

A41 Solihull

A41 — **5** — A4141

A41 Solihull

A38 B'ham (SW) Bromsgrove

A3400 Henley-in-Arden

4 — A38

A38 Birmingham (SW), A491 Stourbridge

M42 London (M40) N.E.C. & M42 & M5 M5 The SOUTH WEST Worcester

A34 Shirley

4 — A3400

M40 London, Warwick, Stratford M42 The SOUTH WEST (M5), Birmingham (S & W)

4A — M42 — **1** — M42 — **2** — M42 — **3** — M42 — **3A**

M42 The NORTH EAST (M1), London (M40) N.E.C. & M42 & M5 M5 The NORTH WEST (M6) B'ham (W, N & Cen)

A441 Birmingham (S)

HOPWOOD PARK SERVICES

A435 B'ham (S), Redditch Evesham

The NORTH M42, Solihull, B'ham (E) N.E.C. & M40 M42 & M40 M40 London Warwick

A38

M5 The NORTH WEST B'ham (W, N & Cen) Stourbridge (M6) M5 The SOUTH WEST Worcester

A38 Bromsgrove

A441 Birmingham (S)

A435 B'ham (S), Redditch Evesham

3 Full access junction   **4A** Limited access junction   **T4** Full access junction M6 Toll   **T1** Limited access junction M6 Toll

Full junction ● Restricted junction

M60 orbital map

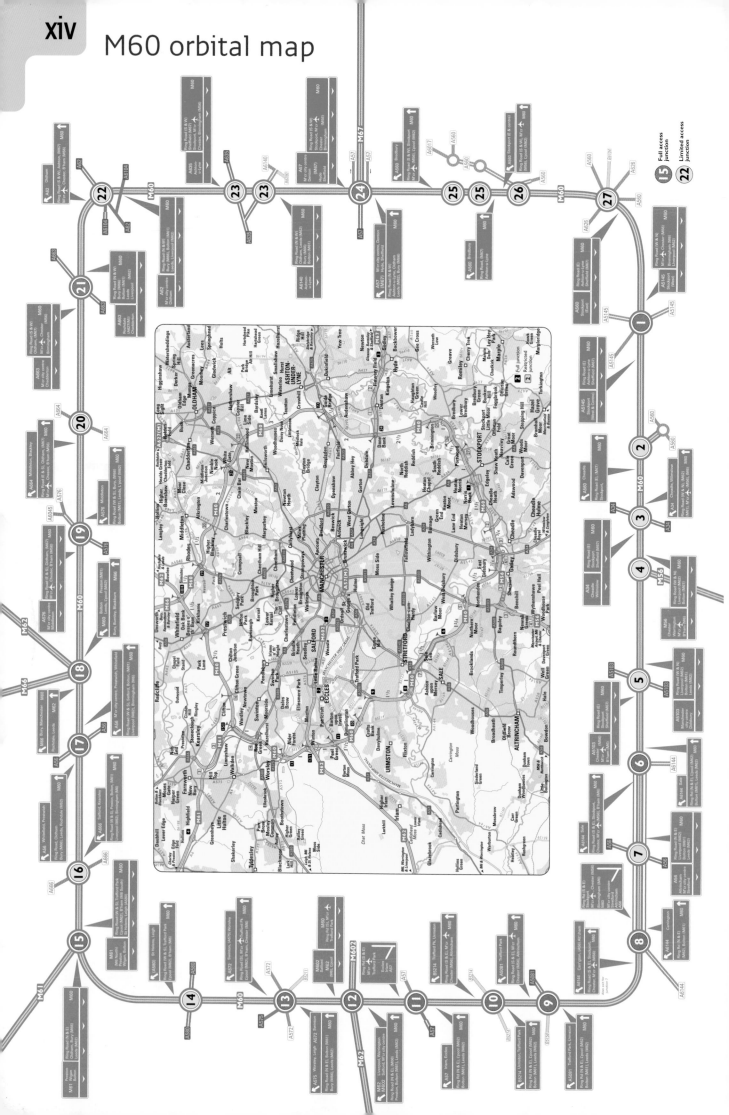

Distances between two selected towns in this table are shown in miles and kilometres.
In general, distances are based on the shortest routes by classified roads.

Distance in kilometres

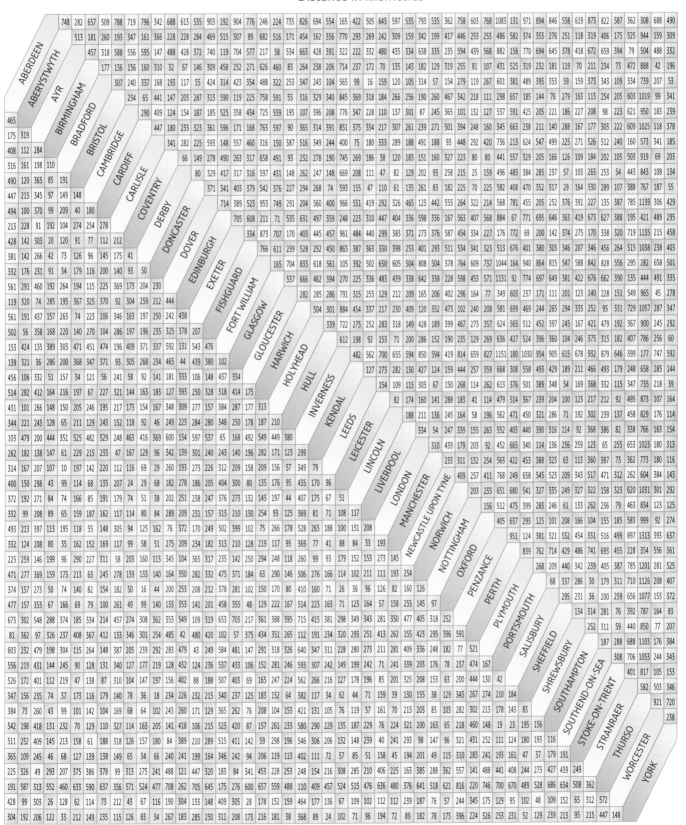

Distance in miles

World Heritage Sites

Through the World Heritage Convention, the United Nations Educational, Scientific and Cultural Organization (UNESCO) seeks to encourage the identification, protection and preservation of cultural and natural heritage around the world. What makes the concept of World Heritage exceptional is its universal application. World Heritage sites belong to all the peoples of the world, irrespective of the territory on which they are located. In 2010 there were 890 sites listed worldwide of which 28 were in the United Kingdom and its overseas territories. The 23 sites within the area of this atlas are described on this page and also indicated on the mapping throughout the atlas by a maroon symbol ★. Together these World Heritage Sites represent the finest examples of Britain's heritage from the ancient monuments of Neolithic times to the Regency splendour of Bath. For more information about World Heritage please visit: http://whc.unesco.org

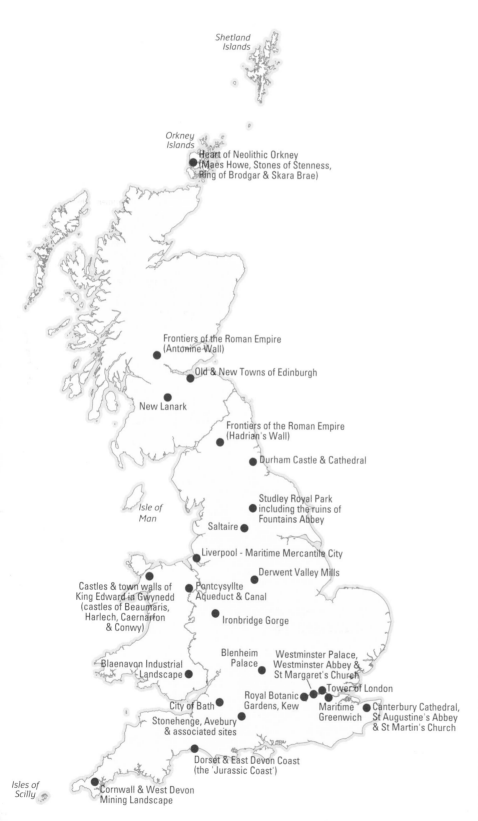

Blaenavon Industrial Landscape *Torfaen*

☎01495 742333 www.world-heritage-blaenavon.org.uk
The industrial landscape around Blaenavon is an outstanding example of the heritage of South Wales as the world's major producer of iron and coal in the 19th century. Evidence of the past can still be seen in the coal and ore mines, quarries, primitive railway system, furnaces, and the social infrastructure of the surrounding community. As an example, Big Pit had been a working coal mine for over 200 years until its closure in 1980. On the surface are colliery workings, reconstructed buildings and the old pit-head baths to explore, but the main attraction is the 300ft (90m) descent in the pit cage to the coal face.

Blenheim Palace *Oxfordshire*

☎01993 811091 www.blenheimpalace.com
A stunning example of English Baroque architecture, Blenheim Palace was built between 1705 and 1722 for John Churchill, 1st Duke of Marlborough following his victory at the Battle of Blenheim and was the birthplace of Sir Winston Churchill. The grounds, landscaped by Lancelot 'Capability' Brown in the 1760s, extend to over 2000 acres (800ha). Internally, the palace is elaborately decorated and furnished and there are several impressive state rooms.

Canterbury Cathedral, St Augustine's Abbey and St Martin's Church *Kent*

☎01227 762862 www.canterbury-cathedral.org
Canterbury cathedral was founded in AD597 by St Augustine, a missionary from Rome, and has been the centre of the English church ever since. Thomas Becket was murdered here in 1170 and the site has since become one of the world's most important centres of pilgrimage.

The architectural styles of the cathedral range from Norman to Perpendicular. The large crypt is the oldest part of the present building and dates from the 11th century. The magnificent nave, comprising tall columns and vaulted arches, was built in the 14th century. Medieval tombs within the cathedral include those of King Henry IV and Edward, the Black Prince.

Nearby are St Martin's Church and St Augustine's Abbey.

Castles and Town Walls of King Edward in Gwynedd

Beaumaris Castle, *Isle of Anglesey*

☎01248 810361 www.cadw.wales.gov.uk
This was the last and largest of Edward I's castles, erected to establish his authority over the Welsh. It was started in 1295 and, although never fully completed, it remains remarkably intact with an outer moat and perfectly symmetrical double concentric walls within.

Caernarfon Castle, *Gwynedd*

☎01286 677617 www.cadw.wales.gov.uk
This castle dominates the town of Caernarfon and has survived in fine condition. Construction was started in 1283 and it was planned both as a royal residence and seat of government. Massive walls run between the 11 great polygonal towers, topped by battlemented wall walks, giving the castle formidable defences. Within the Queen's Tower is the regimental museum of the Royal Welch Fusiliers.

Conwy Castle, *Conwy*

☎01492 592358 www.cadw.wales.gov.uk
Occupying an imposing location over the river in the centre of Conwy town, this castle is one of the most important examples of military architecture in Europe. It was built for Edward I in 1283-9 by 1500 craftsmen. Eight huge drum towers with pinnacled battlements dominate the two wards of the castle.

Harlech Castle, *Gwynedd*

☎01766 780552 www.cadw.wales.gov.uk
Construction of this rugged castle began in 1283, and its protected position, walls and artillery platforms made it stoutly defensible. The castle is concentric, with strong outer walls. The inner walls contained the main living quarters, and the imposing twin-towered gatehouse, with its residential apartments, is one of the main features of the castle.

City of Bath *Bath & North East Somerset*

www.visitbath.co.uk
The location of Britain's only natural hot springs gave Bath its importance as a fashionable resort and tourist attraction. This in turn generated the wealth which enabled the construction of the wonderful Georgian buildings such as the Circus and Royal Crescent.

Cornwall and West Devon Mining Landscape

Cornwall / Devon www.cornish-mining.org.uk
In the early 19th century Cornwall and West Devon produced two thirds of the world's supply of copper. The industry declined in the 1860s but it left a landscape transformed by the deep mines, engine houses and harbours all associated with the rapid growth of pioneering copper and tin mining. The area was designated a World Heritage Site due to its importance in

the British industrial revolution and its significance in the development of mining worldwide.

Derwent Valley Mills *Derbyshire*

☎ 01332 255802 www.derwentvalleymills.org

An area of historic mills dating from the late 18th century stretching 15 miles (24km) from Matlock Bath to Derby. There are numerous sites of historical importance including the complex of mills, workshops and warehouses at Cromford which was the world's first site where water power was successfully harnessed in textile production.

Dorset and East Devon Coast *Dorset / Devon*

www.jurassiccoast.com

This stretch of coastline between Exmouth in the west and Studland in the east is of outstanding geological and palaeontological importance. Coupled with stunning and varied coastal scenery, it is a fine example of the natural landscape.

Durham Castle and Cathedral *Durham*

☎ 0191 386 4266 www.durhamcathedral.co.uk

Dominating the Durham city skyline, this awe-inspiring cathedral, with three massive towers, stands high above the River Wear. The present cathedral was largely built between 1093 and 1133 and is considered to be the greatest piece of Romanesque architecture in Britain. The cathedral contains the tomb of Cuthbert, 7th century Bishop of Lindisfarne, and of the Venerable Bede who wrote about the life of St Cuthbert. Nearby Durham Castle (built 1072), is now part of the university.

Frontiers of the Roman Empire

Hadrian's Wall, *Cumbria & Northumberland*

☎ 01434 322002 www.hadrians-wall.org
www.english-heritage.org.uk

Hadrian's wall is a well preserved and impressive Roman frontier fortification, built between AD122-128 on the orders of Emperor Hadrian. It extends 73 miles (118km) from Bowness-on-Solway to Wallsend. No doubt intended as a symbol of Roman power, it was used to control trade and the movement of people in the region.

Antonine Wall, *mid Scotland*

www.antoninewall.org
www.historic-scotland.org.uk

A 30 mile (60km) long fortification in Scotland started by Emperor Antonious Pius in AD142 as defence against the 'barbarians' of the north. It runs between the Firth of Clyde and the Firth of Forth although much of it has been destroyed over time.

Heart of Neolithic Orkney

Maes Howe, *Orkney*

☎ 01856 761606 www.historic-scotland.gov.uk

This chambered cairn is the finest megalithic (Neolithic) tomb in the British Isles. It consists of a large mound 115ft (35m) in diameter covering a stone-built passage and a large burial chamber.

Ring of Brodgar, *Orkney*

☎ 01855 841815 www.historic-scotland.gov.uk

The Ring of Brodgar (also known as the Ring of Brogar) is a magnificent circle of upright stones, dating back to the Neolithic period. A ditch encloses the stones and is spanned by entrance causeways.

Skara Brae, *Orkney*

☎ 01856 841815 www.historic-scotland.gov.uk

This site contains the best preserved group of Stone Age houses in Western Europe. A storm in 1850 lifted the sand covering the area to reveal the remains of this former fishing village. Ten one-roomed houses joined by covered passages contain their original stone furniture, hearths and drains to provide a remarkable illustration of life in Neolithic times.

Stones of Stenness, *Orkney*

☎ 01856 841815 www.historic-scotland.gov.uk

Dating from around 3100BC, the stones stand 6m (19ft) high and 44 metres (144ft) in diameter and are visible for miles around.

Ironbridge Gorge *Telford & Wrekin*

☎ 01952 884391 www.ironbridge.co.uk

The Iron Bridge was the first bridge in the world to be constructed completely of iron and was at the centre of the industrial revolution in Britain. Ten museums tell the story of the industrial revolution and the part this area played in it. The Blists Hill Victorian Town is an open-air re-creation of a late 19th century working community. The Museum of the Gorge looks at the effects of the revolution on the beautiful gorge itself, and the Broseley Pipeworks, which closed in 1957, is presented as if it were still a working factory. There is also a Museum of Iron, China Museum and Tile Museum, as well as the Bridge and Tollhouse.

Liverpool - Maritime Mercantile City *Merseyside*

www.visitliverpool.com

Originally a fishing village on the River Mersey estuary, Liverpool experienced rapid expansion during the 18th century due to the transatlantic trade in sugar, spices and tobacco as well as the slave trade. It became one of the world's major trading centres. The city was designated a World Heritage Site in recognition of its role in the development of modern dock technology, transport systems and port management.

Maritime Greenwich *Greater London*

☎ 0870 608 2000 www.greenwichwhs.org.uk

Greenwich has a long and interesting history with strong royal and maritime links. The 17th century Royal Naval College, designed by Sir Christopher Wren, is built on the site of the Royal Palace of Greenwich. The National Maritime Museum includes the Palladian style Queen's House designed by Inigo Jones. The Old Royal Observatory, built by Wren in 1675, is the home of Greenwich Mean Time and the world's Prime Meridian – Longitude 0°, where the eastern and western hemispheres meet.

New Lanark *South Lanarkshire*

☎ 01555 661345 www.newlanark.org

Originally founded in 1785 by David Dale and Richard Arkwright as a centre for cotton spinning, New Lanark is now a superb example of a restored industrial village. Dale's son-in-law, Robert Owen, took over the management of the site in 1798 and his belief in the welfare of his workers led to him setting up a cooperative store, a nursery, adult education facilities, decent housing and a social centre for the community of 2500 people. The Institute for the Formation of Character now houses the award winning visitor centre.

Old and New Towns of Edinburgh *Edinburgh*

www.edinburgh.org

Edinburgh grew up around the castle and it still dominates the skyline today. The Royal Mile, consisting of mostly medieval buildings, runs east from the castle to the Palace of Holyroodhouse, through the heart of the Old Town. Numerous narrow streets and alleys lead off it, many with fascinating architecture to explore. The New Town is immediately to the north, separated only by the beautiful Princes Street Gardens. In stark contrast to the Old Town, it is full of spacious terraces and crescents that are some of the finest examples of Georgian town planning in Europe.

Pontcysyllte Aqueduct & Canal *Wrexham*

The Pontcysyllte Canal is 11 miles (18km) long and covers some difficult terrain. The aqueduct, designed by Thomas Telford to carry the canal over the River Dee, was completed in 1805 and is the highest and longest in Britain. The towpath is cantilevered out from the side of the canal trough to allow the canal itself to fill the entire width of the aqueduct piers. The far side of the canal trough has no handrail meaning that boaters have no protection at all from the 126ft (38m) drop!

Royal Botanic Gardens, Kew *Greater London*

☎ 020 8332 5655 www.kew.org

This superb 300 acre (121.5ha) botanic garden was founded in 1759. Kew's reputation as the foremost botanical institution in the world was originally developed by its first two directors, Sir William Hooker (appointed in 1841) and his son Sir Joseph (who succeeded in 1865). The gardens have one of the largest and most diverse collections of plant species in the world. Over 60,000 species are displayed in both formal and informal settings, and in the many greenhouses including the magnificent curved glass Palm House (built in 1848), the Temperate House (completed in 1868), the Princess of Wales Conservatory (1987), and the Davies Alpine House (2006).

Saltaire *West Yorkshire*

☎ 01274 433 678 www.saltairevillage.info

A village located in the Heart of Brontë country with a layout virtually unchanged since it was built in the 19th century by Sir Titus Salt as accommodation for the workers at his woollen mills. The buildings are now in everyday usage as shops, restaurants and pubs. The Salt Mill is now the 1853 Gallery exhibiting the work of local artist David Hockney.

Stonehenge, Avebury and Associated Sites

Stonehenge, *Wiltshire*

☎ 0870 333 1181 www.english-heritage.org.uk

An awe-inspiring prehistoric monument constructed in stages between about 5000 and 3000 years ago. The original purpose is uncertain, but suggestions include an astronomical observatory, temple or other sacred site. Stonehenge was originally a simple bank and ditch. Some centuries later an inner stone circle was added using bluestones from Pembrokeshire. The final, and major building phase around 1500BC brought massive sarsen stones of up to 50 tons (56 tonnes) from the Marlborough Downs 20 miles (32km) away. These were capped by stone lintels to make a continuous outer ring. The central axis aligns with the point of sunrise on Midsummer Day.

Avebury Ring, *Wiltshire*

☎ 01672 539250 www.nationaltrust.org.uk

Around 4500 years old, this is possibly the largest stone circle in Europe, the surviving sarsen stones being enclosed by a substantial earthwork almost 1 mile (1.6km) in circumference. Within this there were two smaller stone circles, though little remains of the more northerly. Information and artefacts uncovered at Avebury Ring can be found in the nearby Alexander Keiller Museum.

Studley Royal Park including the Ruins of Fountains Abbey *North Yorkshire*

☎ 01765 608888 www.fountainsabbey.org.uk

This amazing 800 acres (325ha) park shelters the ruins of over 10 historic buildings. One of these ruins is the imposing remains of a 12th century Cistercian Abbey, with its 15th century tower rising 170ft (52m). The wonderful landscaped gardens contain ornamental lakes and an 18th century Water Garden.

Tower of London *Greater London*

☎ 0844 482 7777 hrp.org.uk/toweroflondon

Dating back to the 11th century, the Tower has been part of London's history for over 900 years. During this time it has had many roles, serving as a royal palace, an arsenal, royal mint, jewel house, royal menagerie and, most notoriously, as a jail and place of execution. The oldest part is the massive rectangular 90ft (27.5m) high White Tower. Originally built as a fortress and residence providing accommodation for the king, today it houses the Royal Armouries' collection. Nearby is the Jewel House, home to the greatest collection of working Crown Jewels in the world. The scaffold site on Tower Green is where seven famous prisoners were executed including Anne Boleyn, Catherine Howard and Lady Jane Grey.

Westminster Palace, Westminster Abbey and St Margaret's Church

Westminster Palace, *Greater London*

☎ 020 7219 4272 www.parliament.uk

More commonly known as the Houses of Parliament and home to the main seat of Government. The original palace was built in the first half of the 11th century by Edward the Confessor and remained the main residence of the monarch until the first half of the 16th century. In 1834 the building was badly damaged by fire and only the crypt, Jewel Tower and Westminster Hall survived. Most of the present building was constructed in Gothic Revival style between 1840 and 1888 and contains 1100 rooms, 100 staircases and over 2 miles (3km) of passages. At the northern end of the building is St Stephens' clock tower, famous for its four clock faces and the 13 ton bell, Big Ben

Westminster Abbey, *Greater London*

☎ 020 7222 5152 www.westminster-abbey.org

Steeped in history, the abbey is the coronation church of all the crowned sovereigns since 1216. Very little of the original Norman structure remains; most of the magnificent Gothic building seen today was built between 1245 and 1272 although the nave, which at 102ft (31m) is the highest in England, was not completed until 1517. The famous west towers, which rise to a height of 225ft (69m) were completed in 1745.

Within the abbey is an impressive array of tombs and memorials to some of Britain's most important figures. Within the chapel of St Edward the Confessor is his great shrine along with the tombs of Henry III, Edward I, Edward III, Richard II and Henry V. Henry VII's Chapel is magnificent and is the final resting place of Henry VII, Mary I and Elizabeth I.

St Margaret's Church, *Greater London*

☎ 020 7654 4840
www.westminster-abbey.org/stmargarets/

Located between Westminster Abbey and the Houses of Parliament, and commonly called 'the parish church of the House of Commons'. The portcullis symbol of the House of Commons can be seen throughout the church and there has been a place reserved for the Speaker of the Commons since 1681.

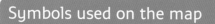

Symbols used on the map

Blue place of interest symbols e.g ★ are listed on page 93

Motorway junction with full / limited access	
Motorway service area	LEICESTER SERVICES
Toll motorway	M6Toll
Primary route dual / single carriageway / junction / service area	A316
'A' road dual / single carriageway	A4054
'B' road dual / single carriageway	B7078
Minor road dual / single carriageway	
Restricted access road	
Road proposed or under construction	
Road tunnel	
Roundabout	
Toll / One way street	

Level crossing	
National Trail / Long Distance Route	Hadrian's Wall Path
Fixed safety camera / fixed average-speed safety camera. Speed shown by number within camera, a V indicates a variable limit.	30 V 30 90
Park and Ride site operated by bus / rail (runs at least 5 days a week)	P&R P&R
Car ferry with destination	Dublin 8hrs
Foot ferry with destination	West Cowes ¾hr
Airport	
Railway line / Railway tunnel / Light railway line	
Railway station / Light rail station	
London Underground / London Overground stations	
Glasgow Subway station	S
Extent of London congestion charging zone	

Notable building	
Hospital	H
Spot height (in metres) / Lighthouse	362 ▲
Built up area	
Woodland / Park	
National Park	
Heritage Coast	
County / Unitary Authority boundary and name	BRISTOL
Area covered by street map	SEE PAGE 88

Urban approach maps

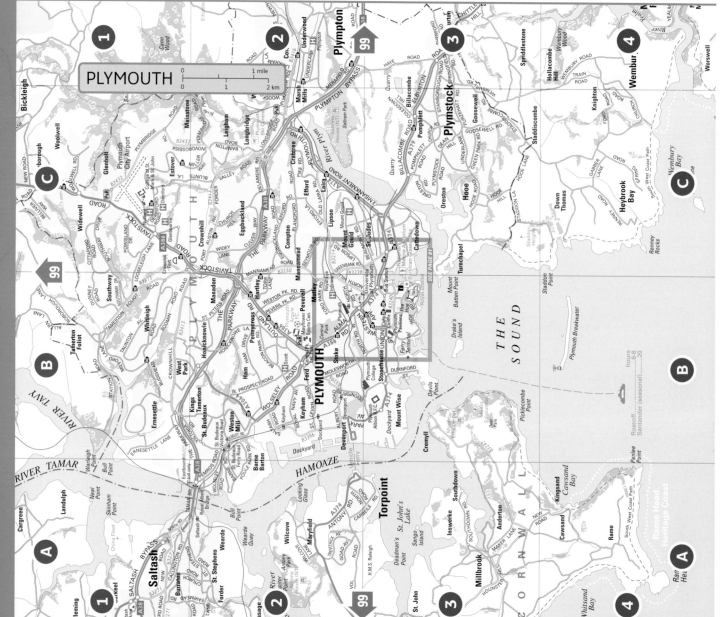

PLYMOUTH

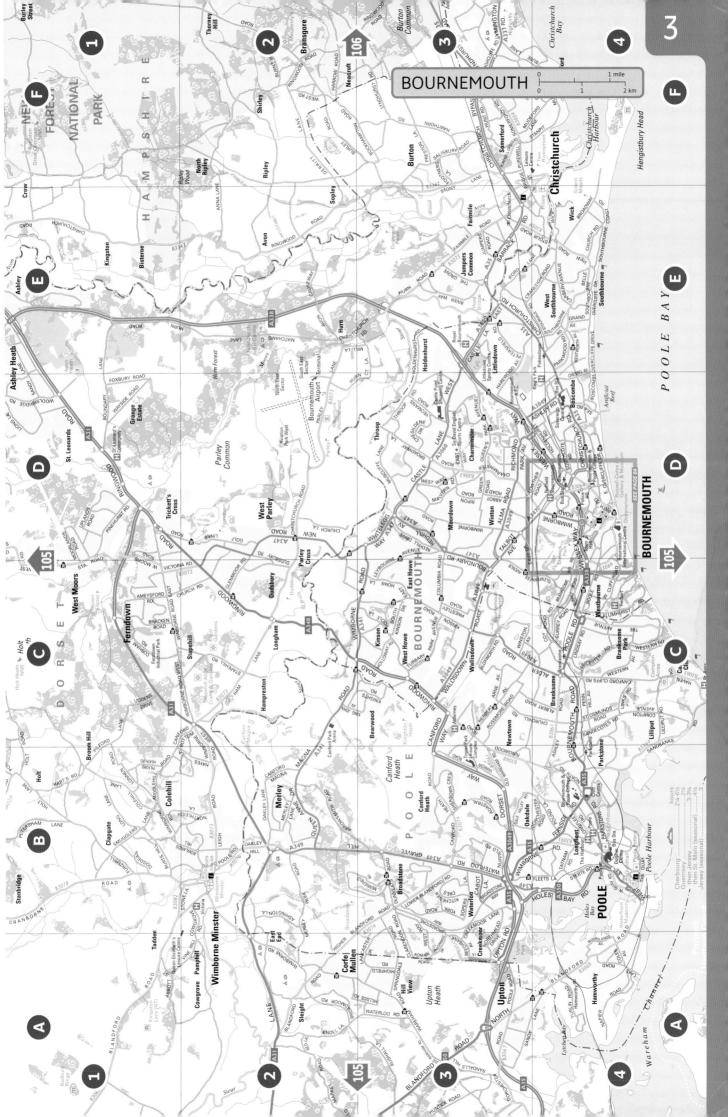

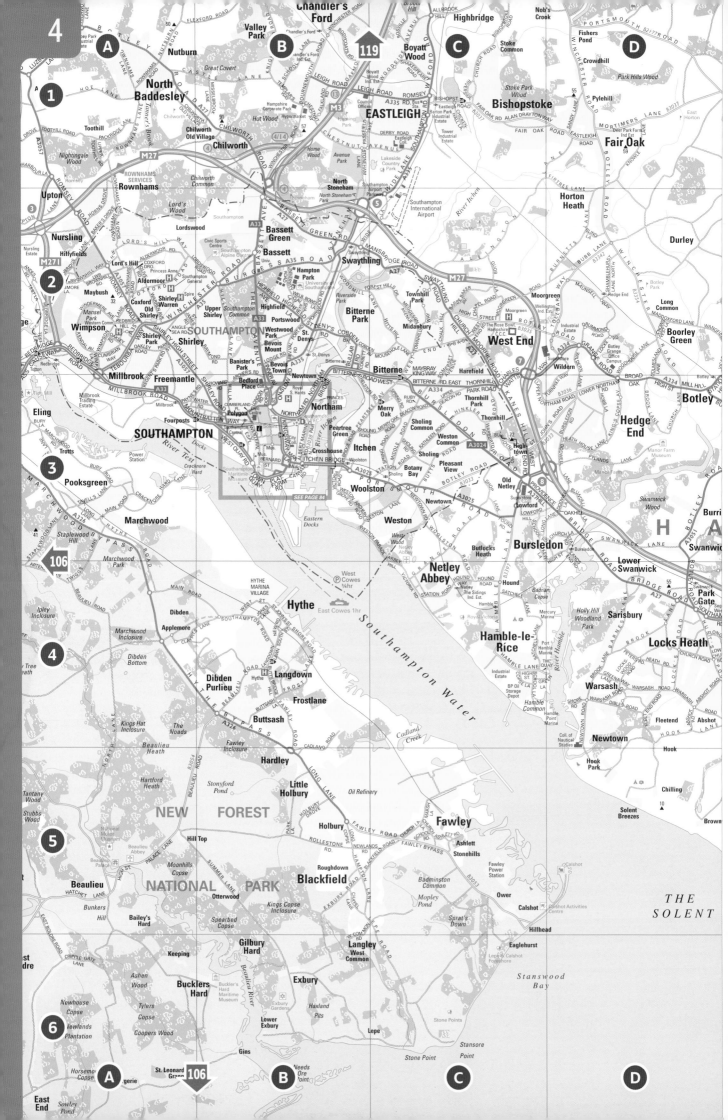

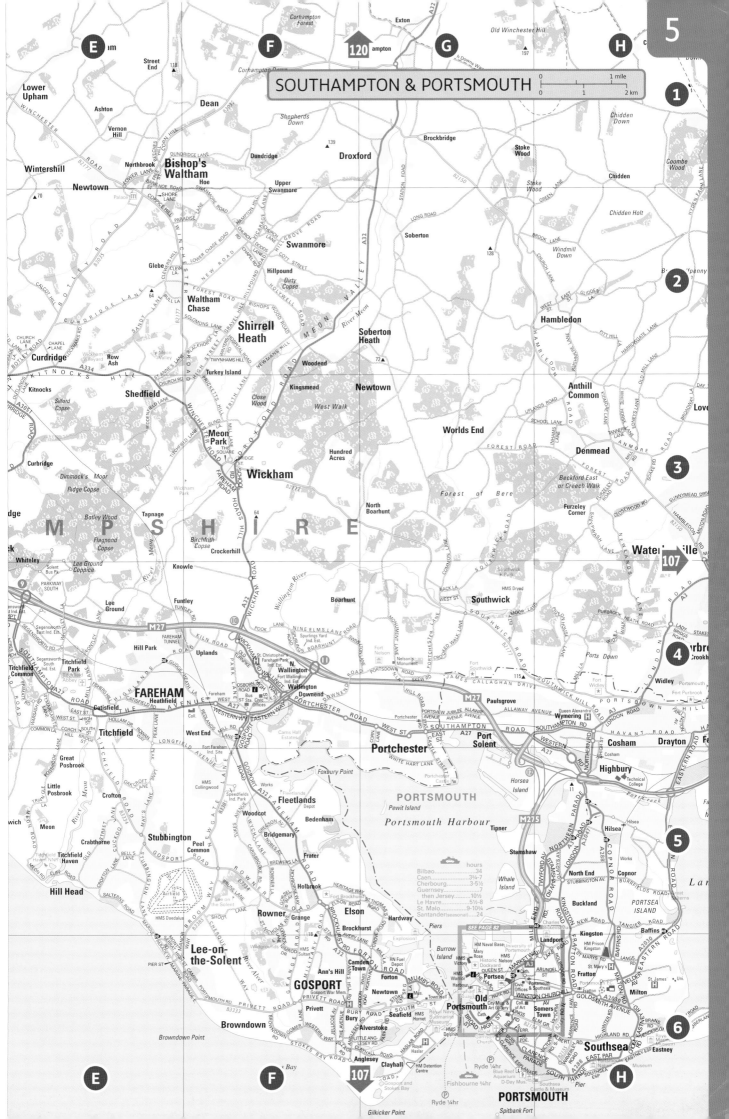

CARDIFF & NEWPORT

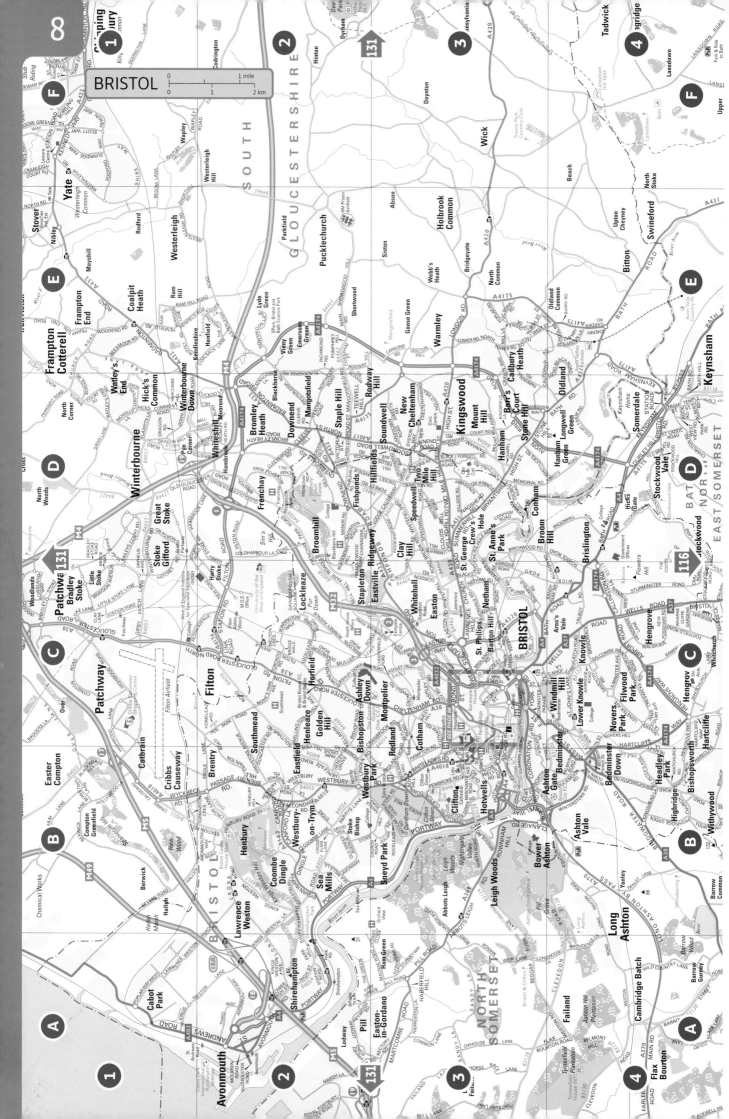

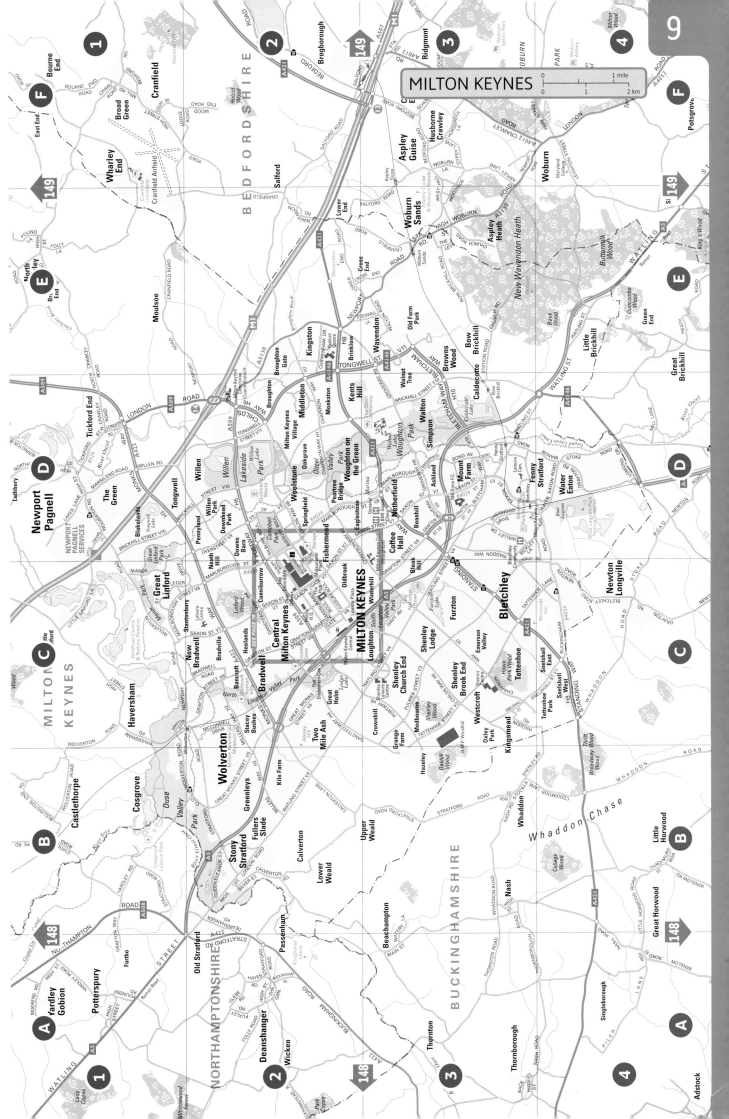

MILTON KEYNES

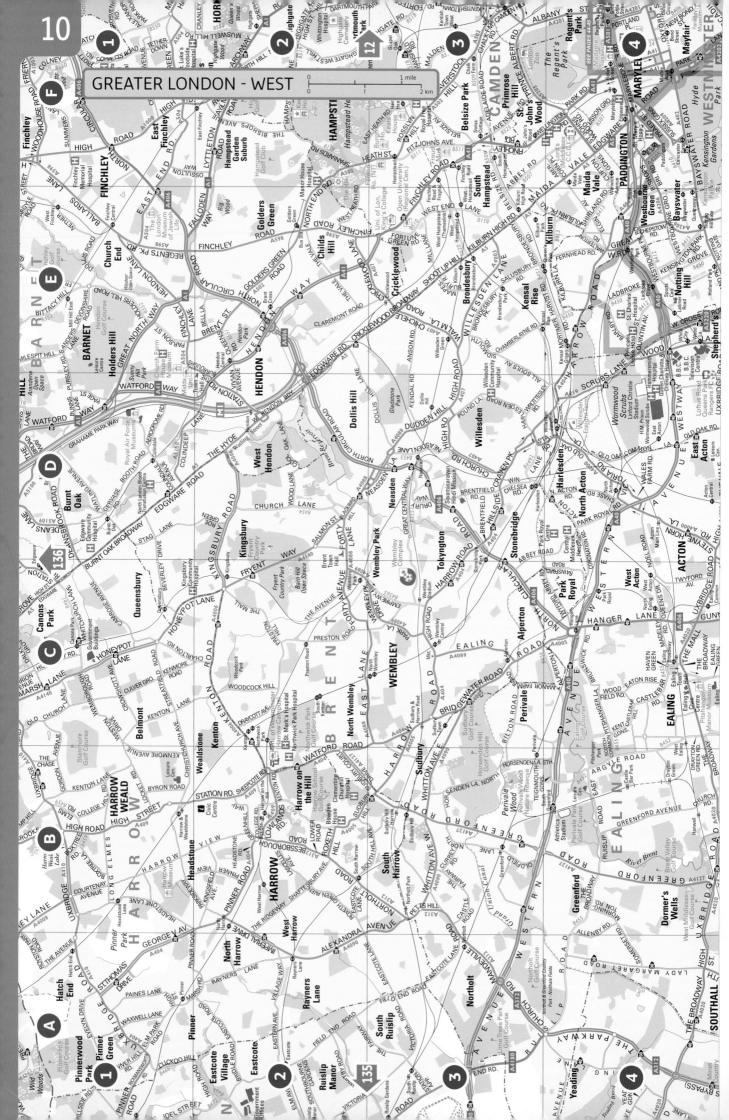

GREATER LONDON - WEST

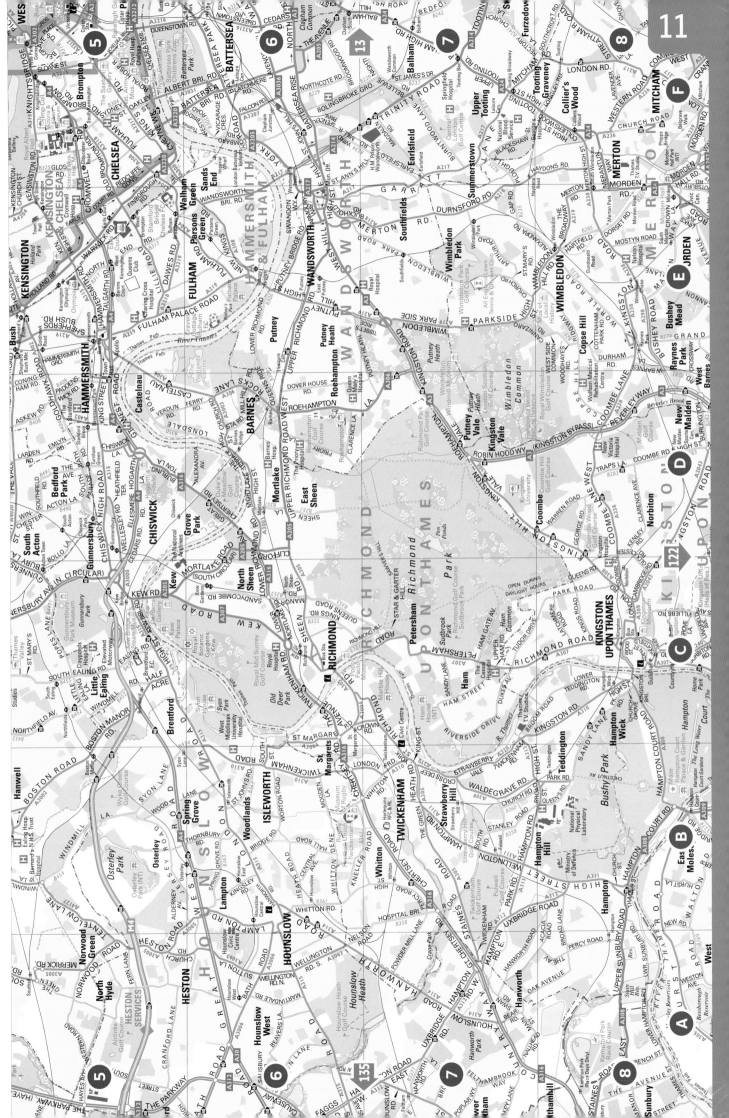

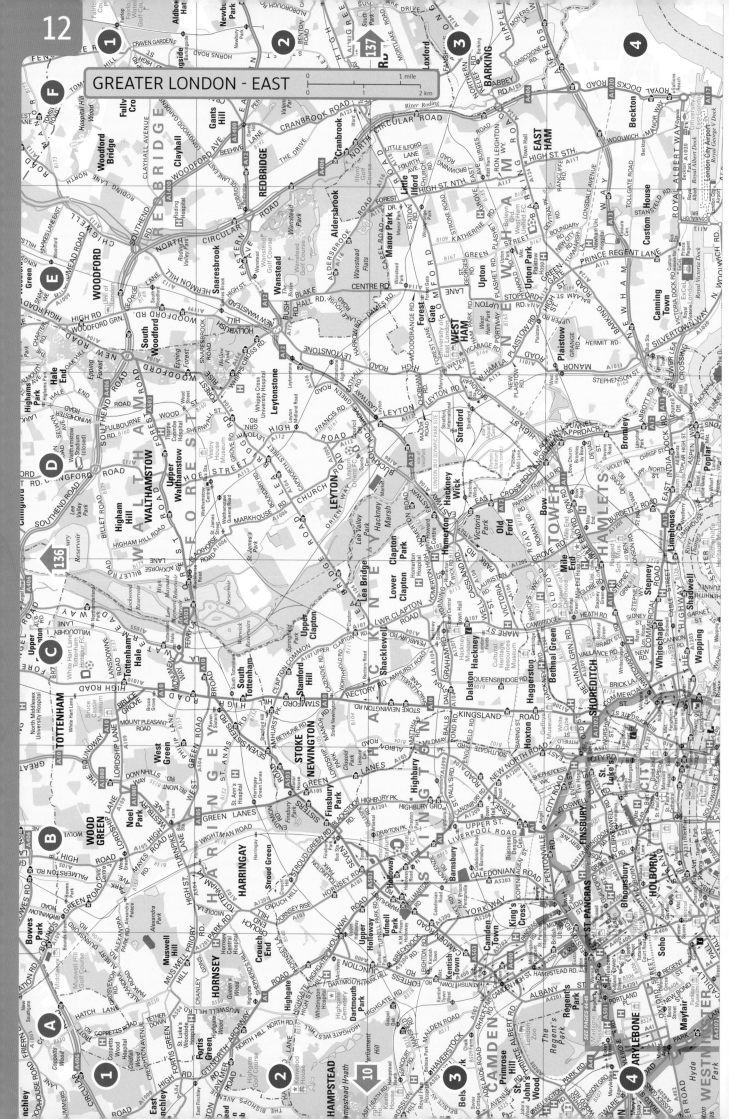

GREATER LONDON - EAST

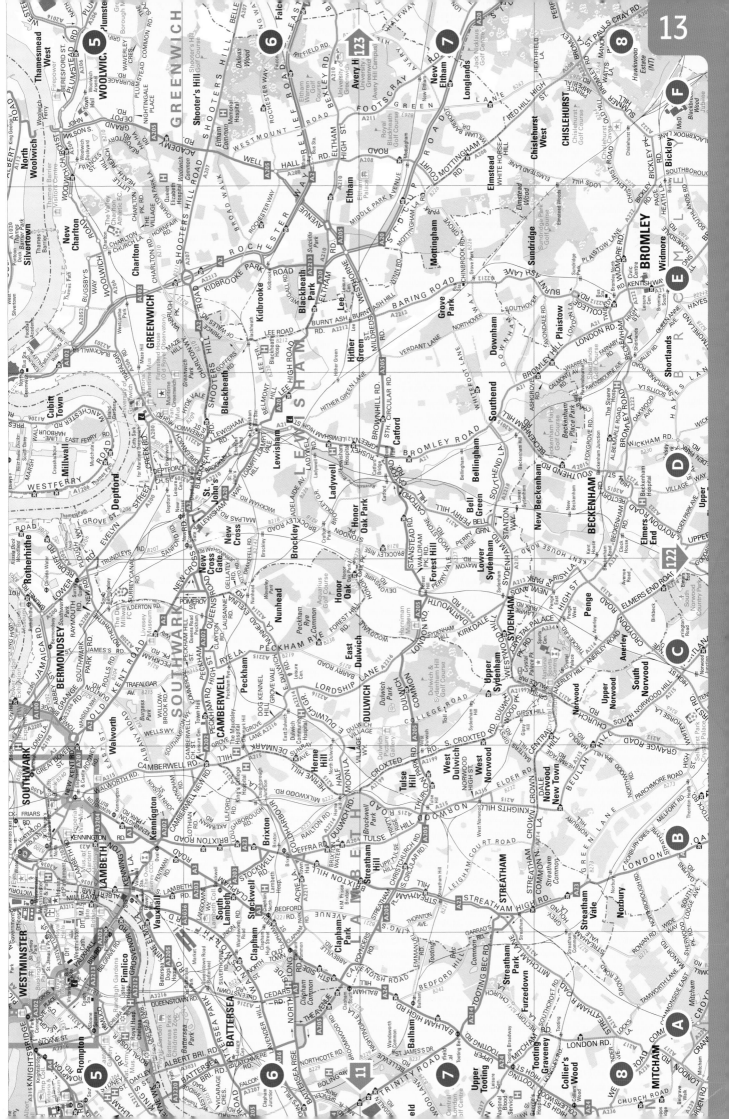

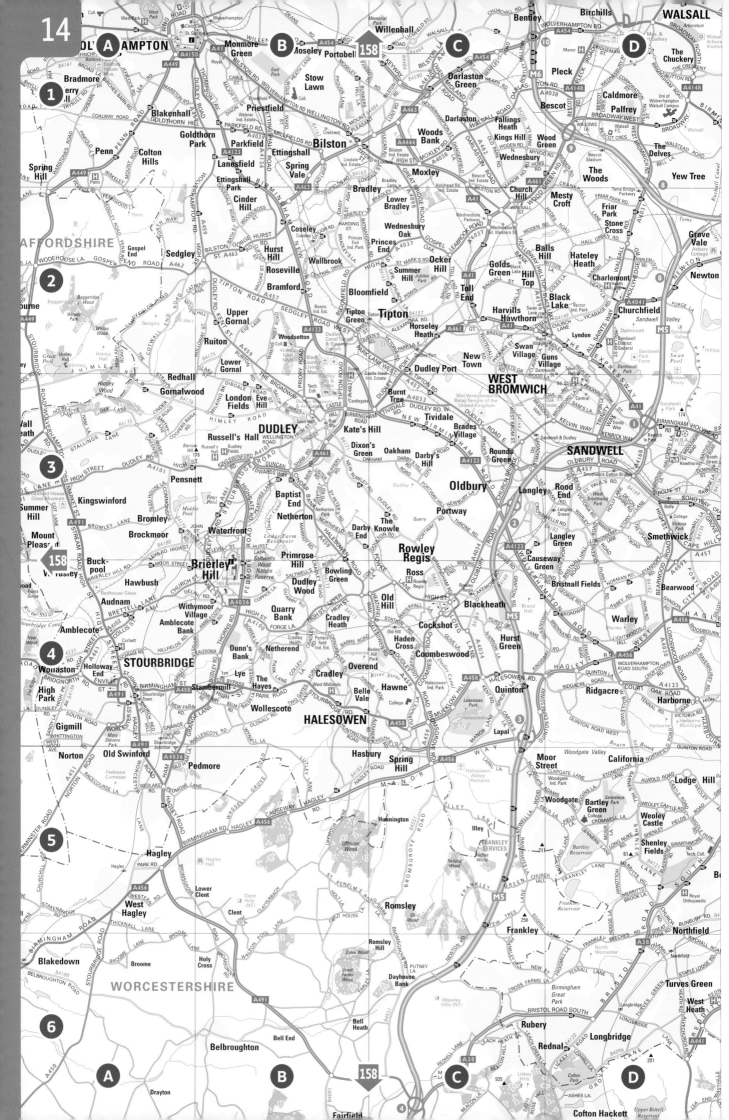

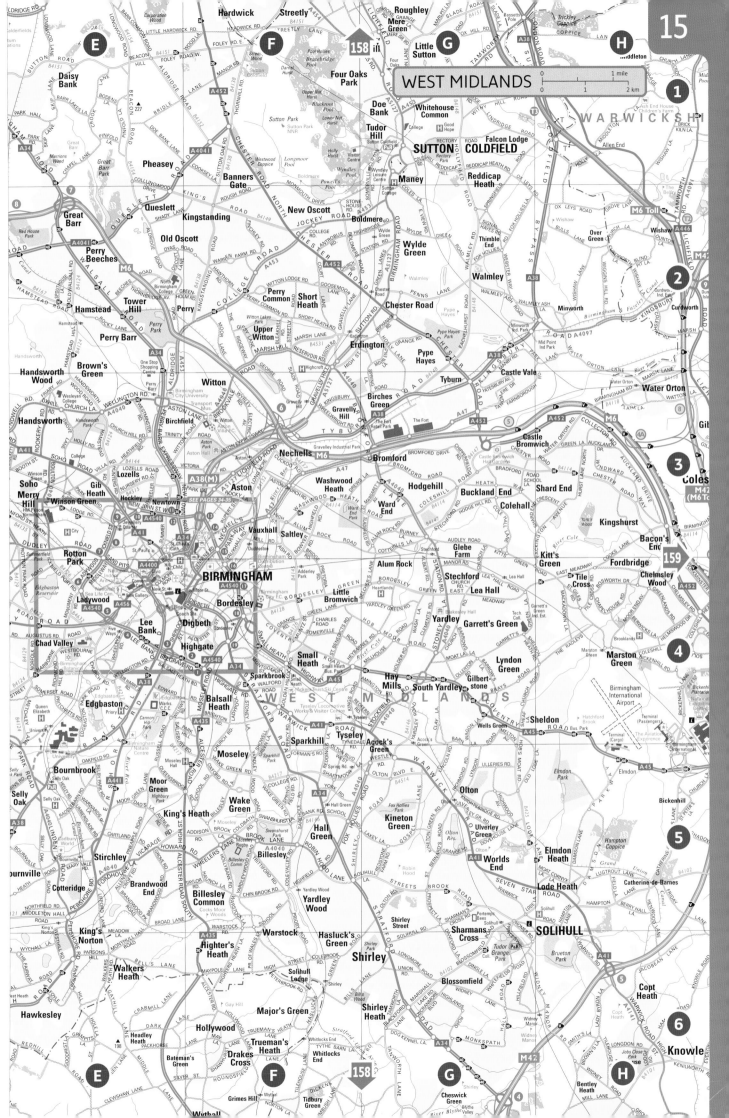

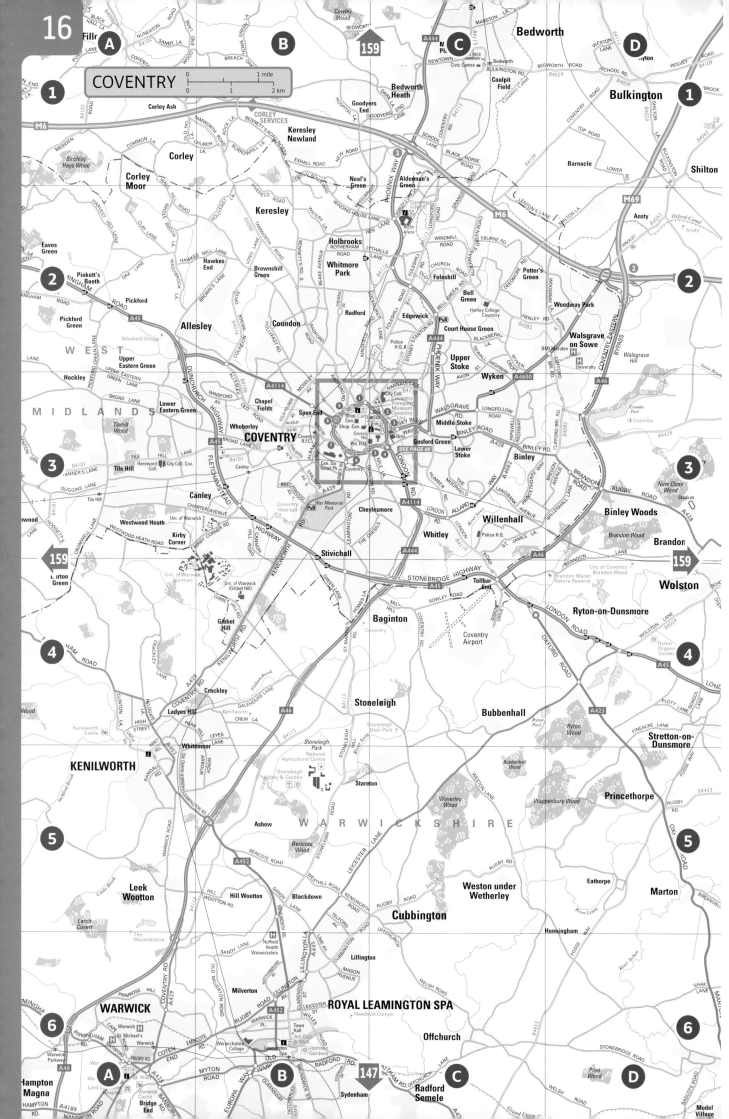

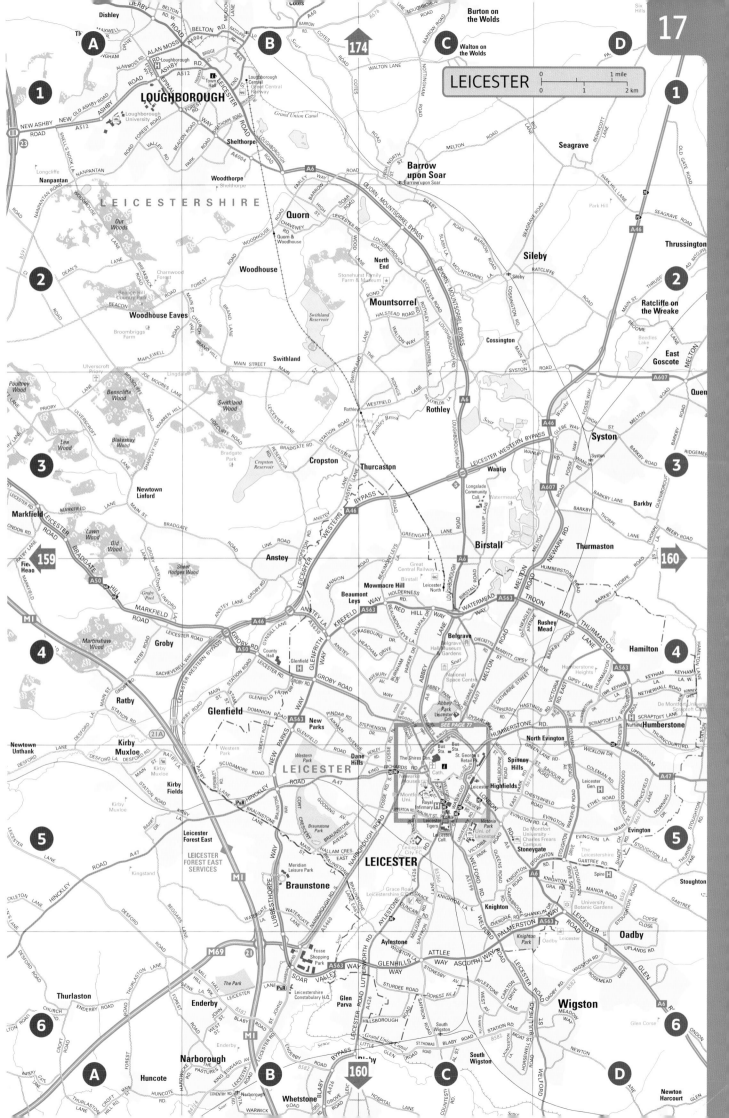

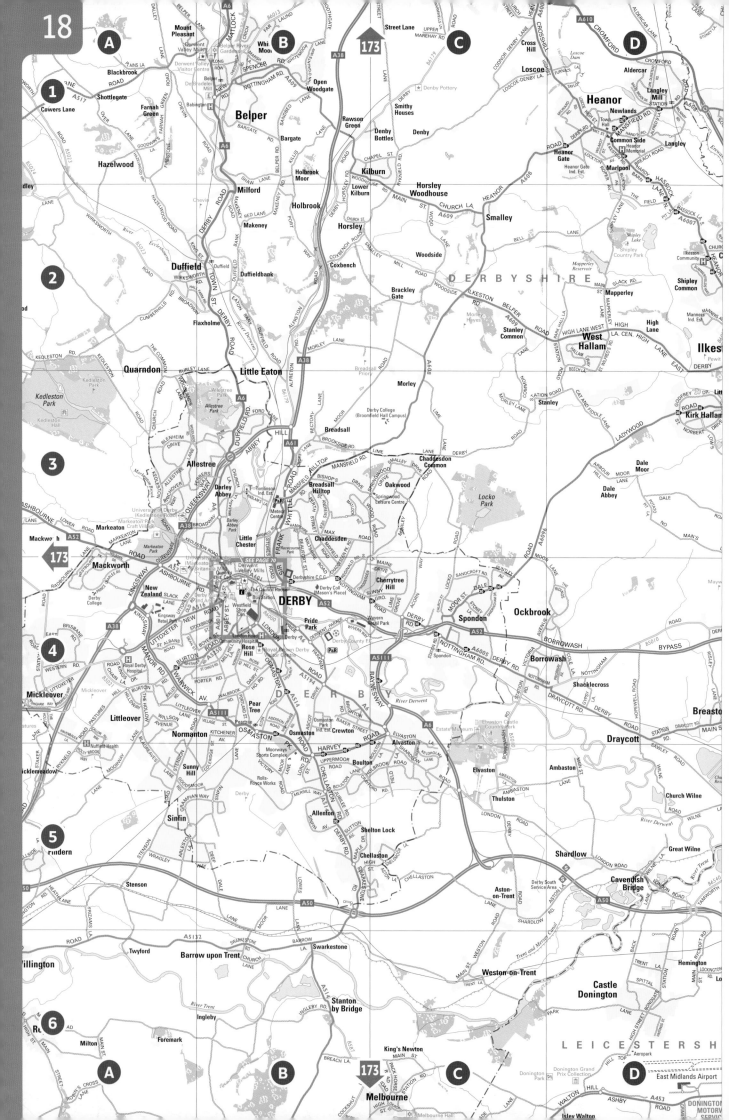

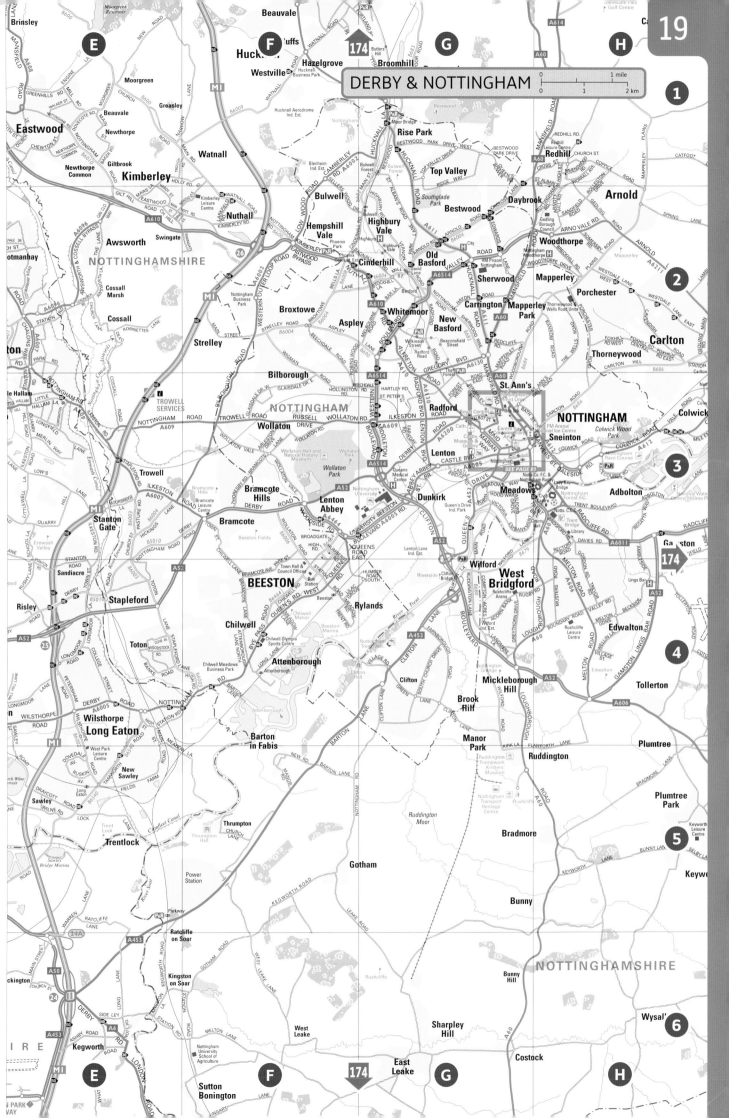

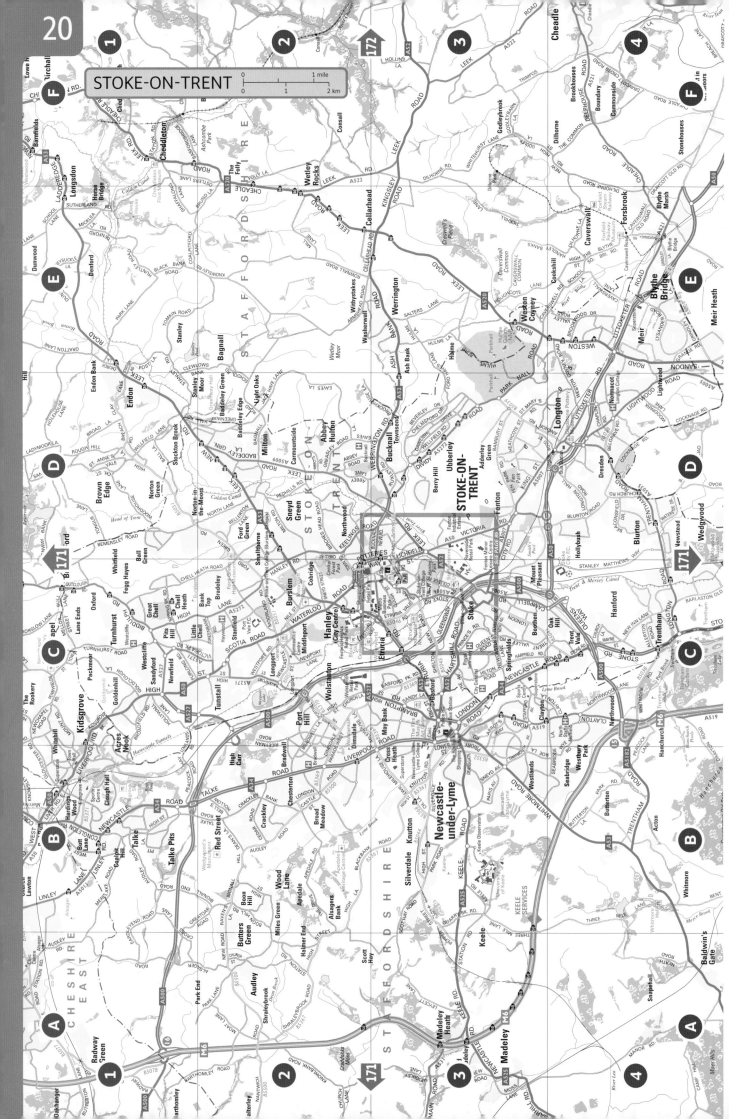

STOKE-ON-TRENT

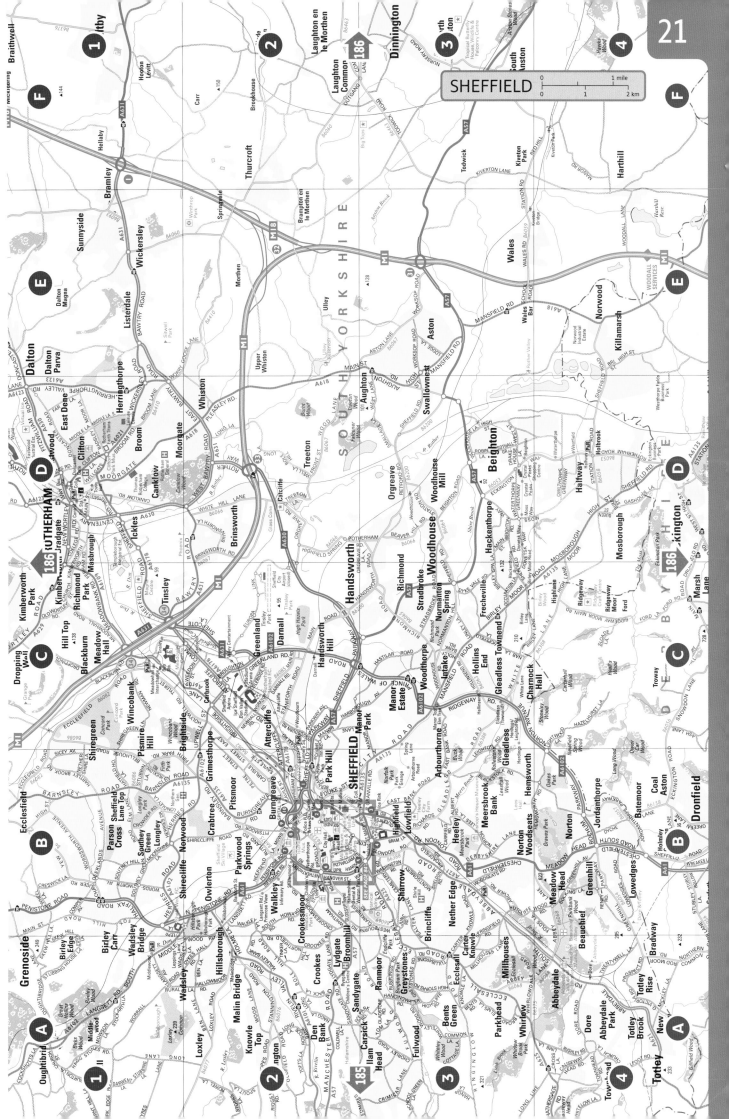

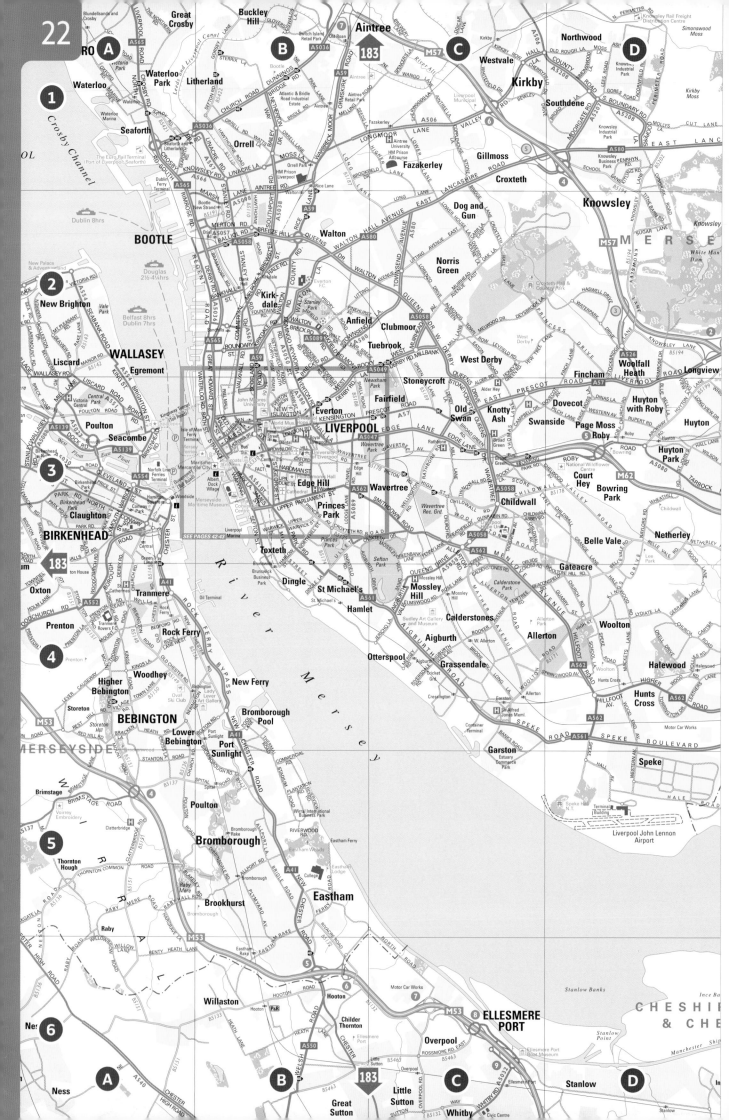

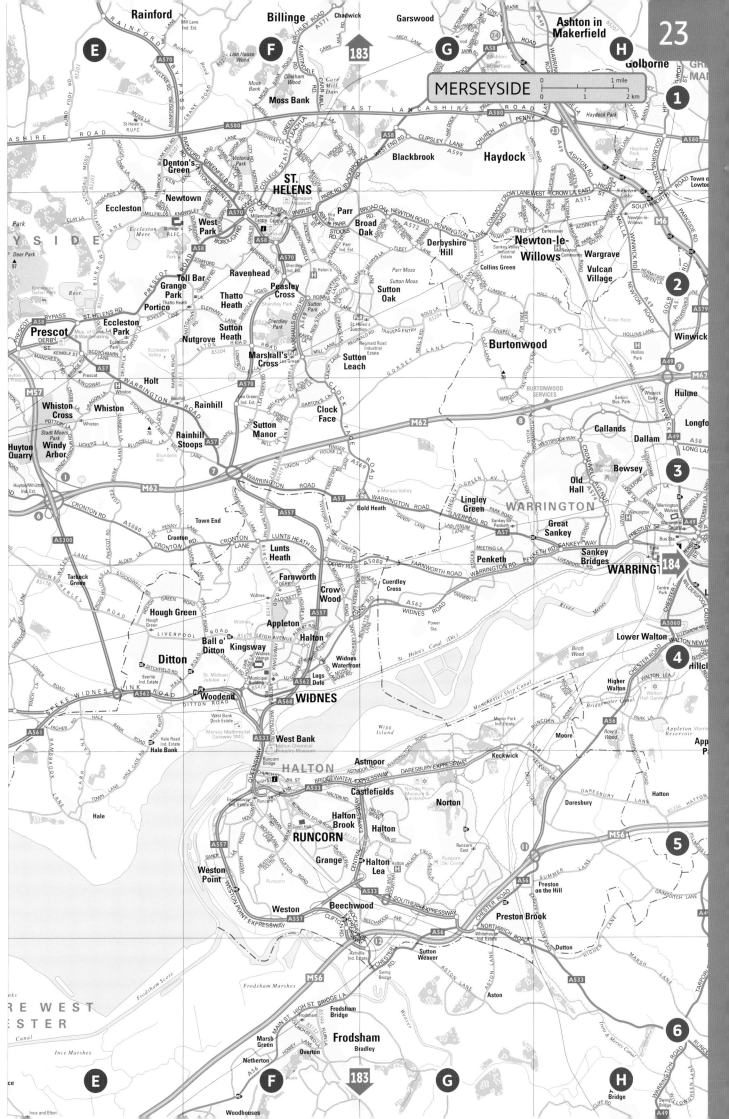

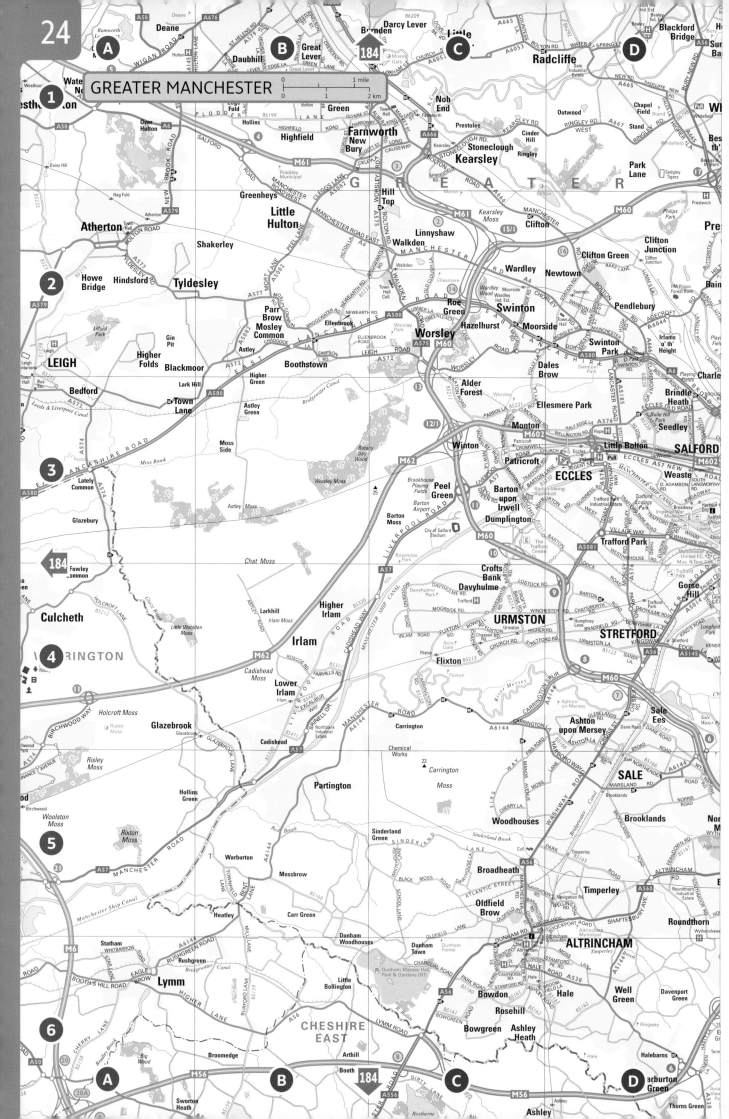

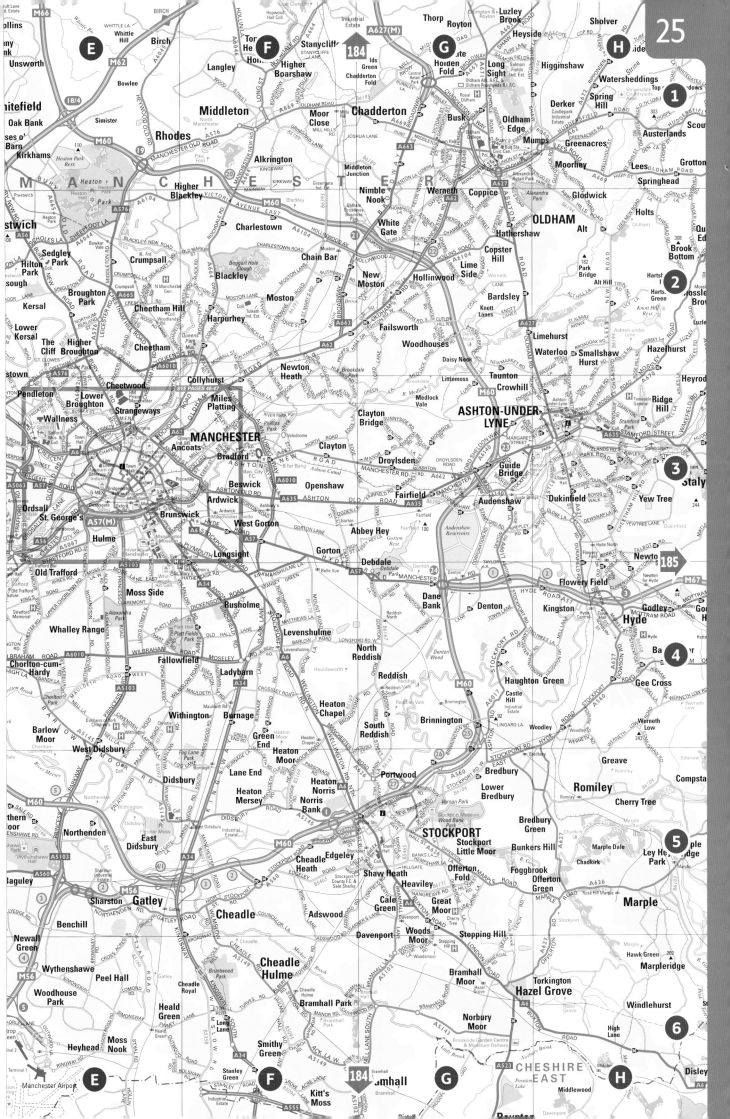

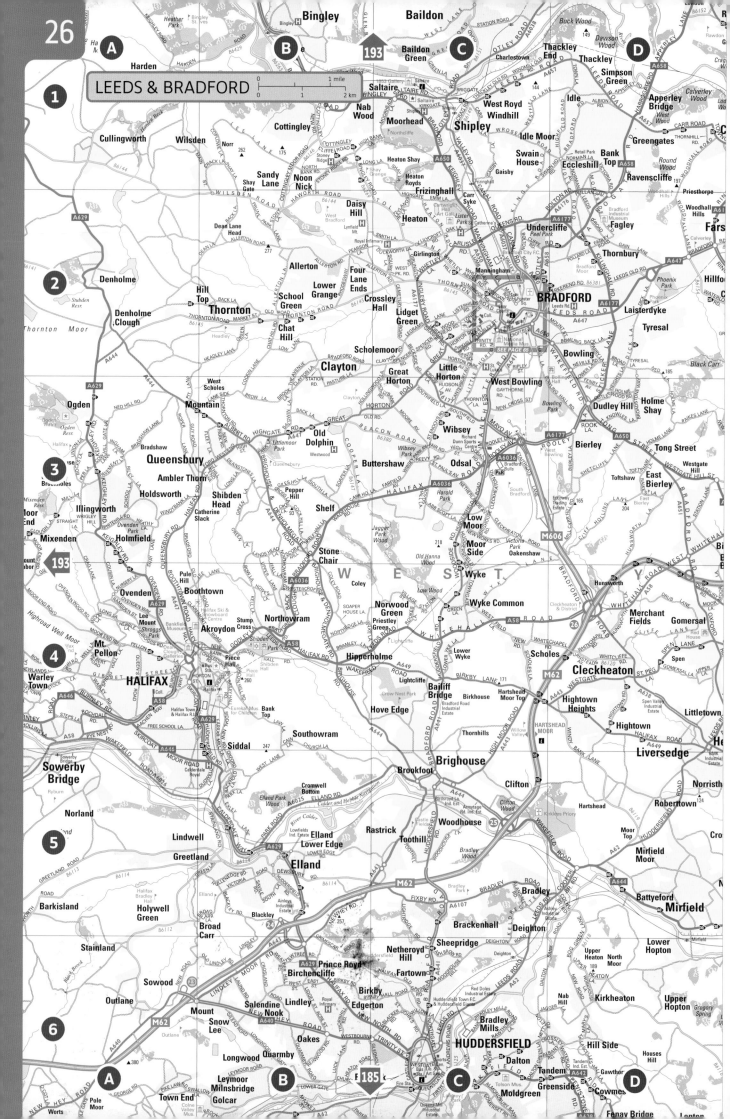

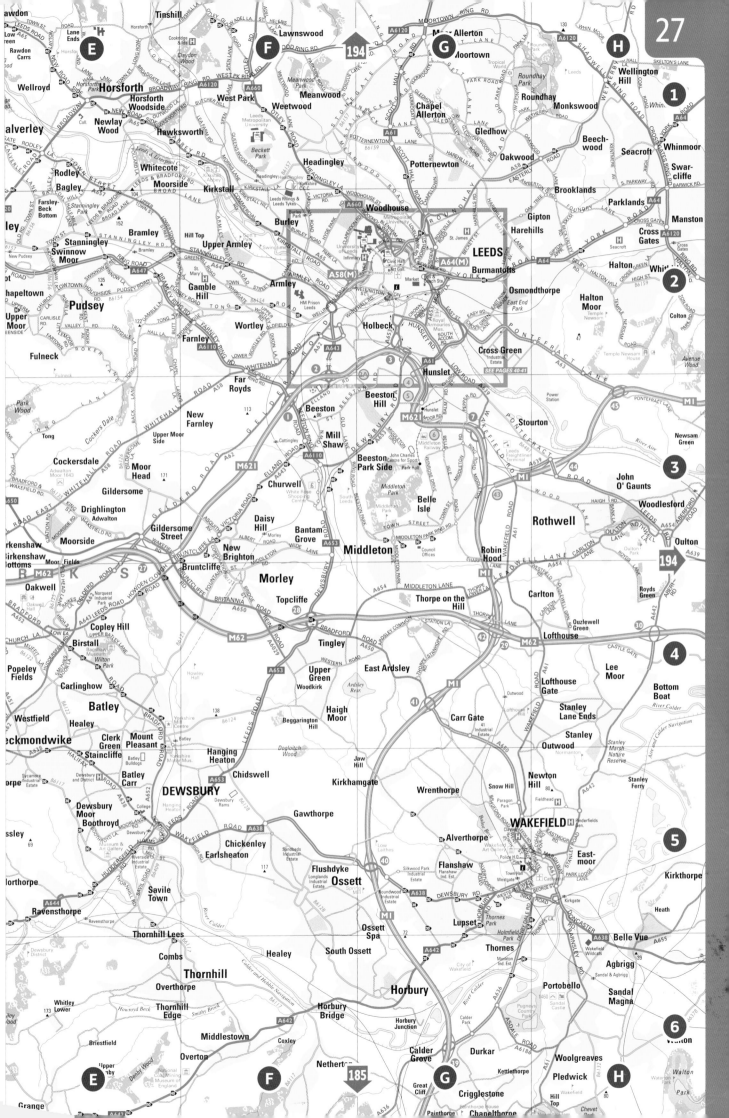

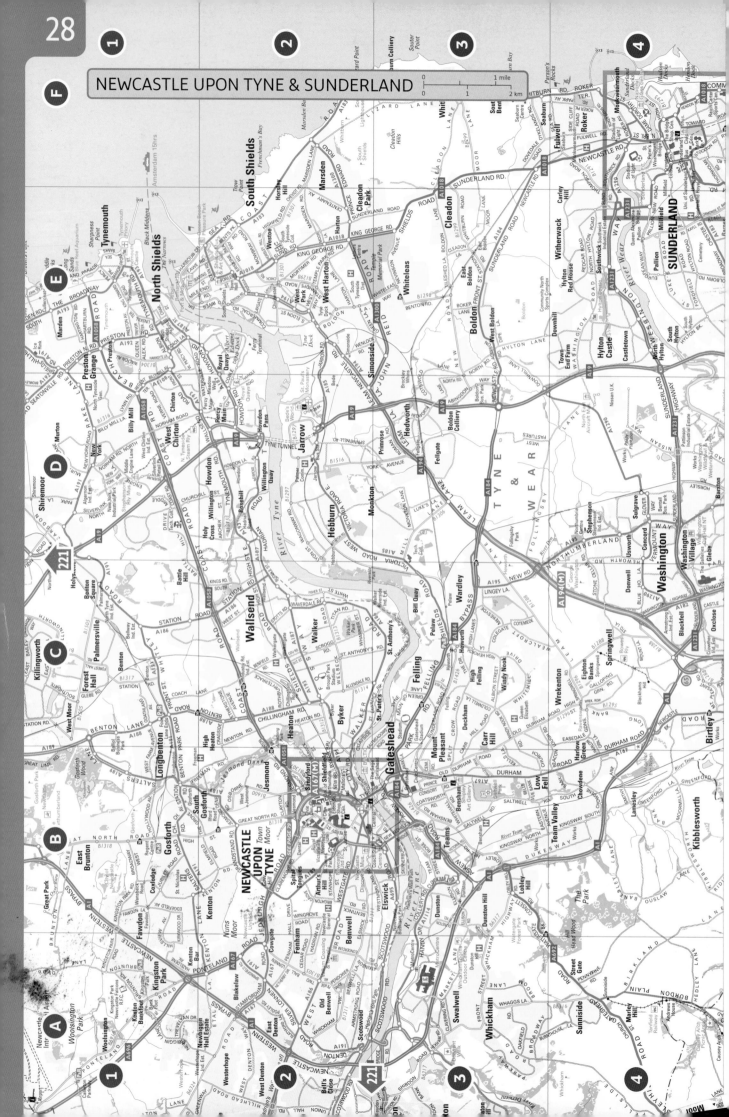

NEWCASTLE UPON TYNE & SUNDERLAND

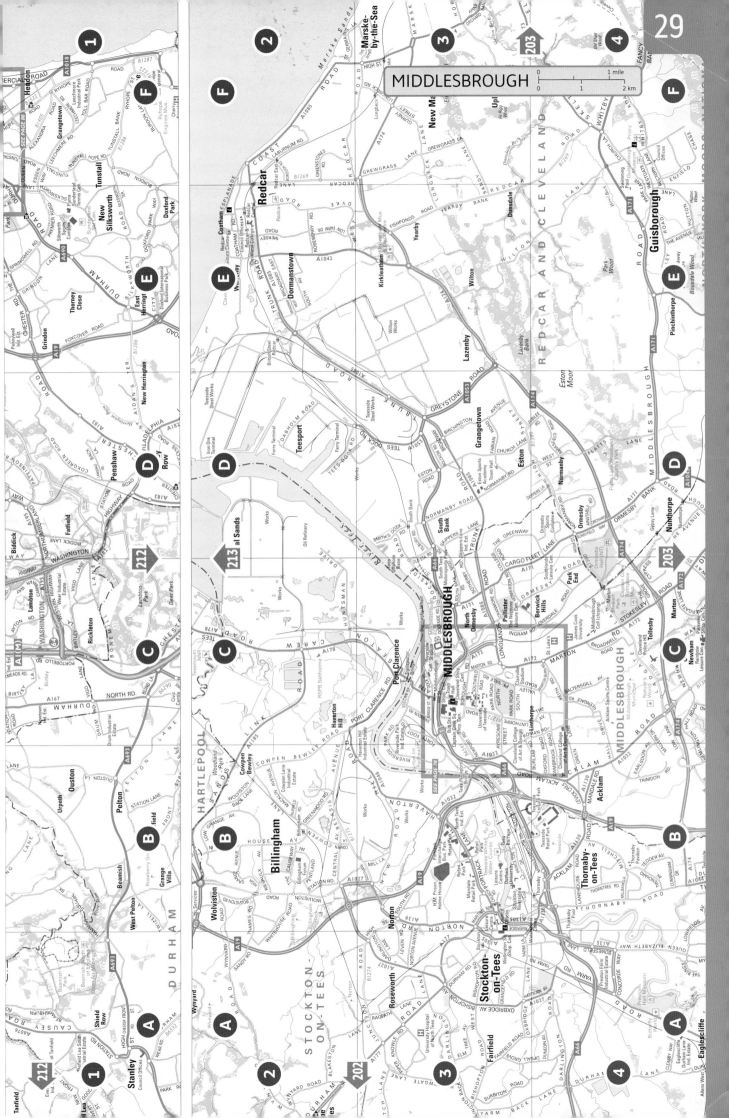

MIDDLESBROUGH

0 ——— 1 mile
0 — 1 — 2 km

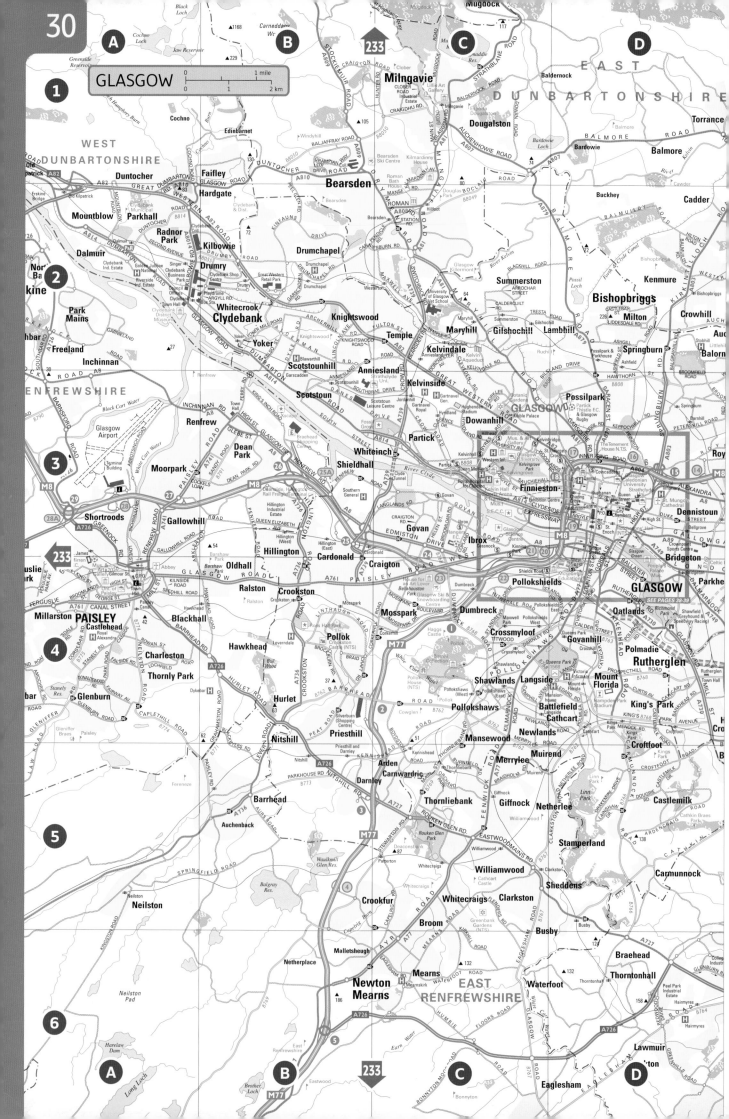

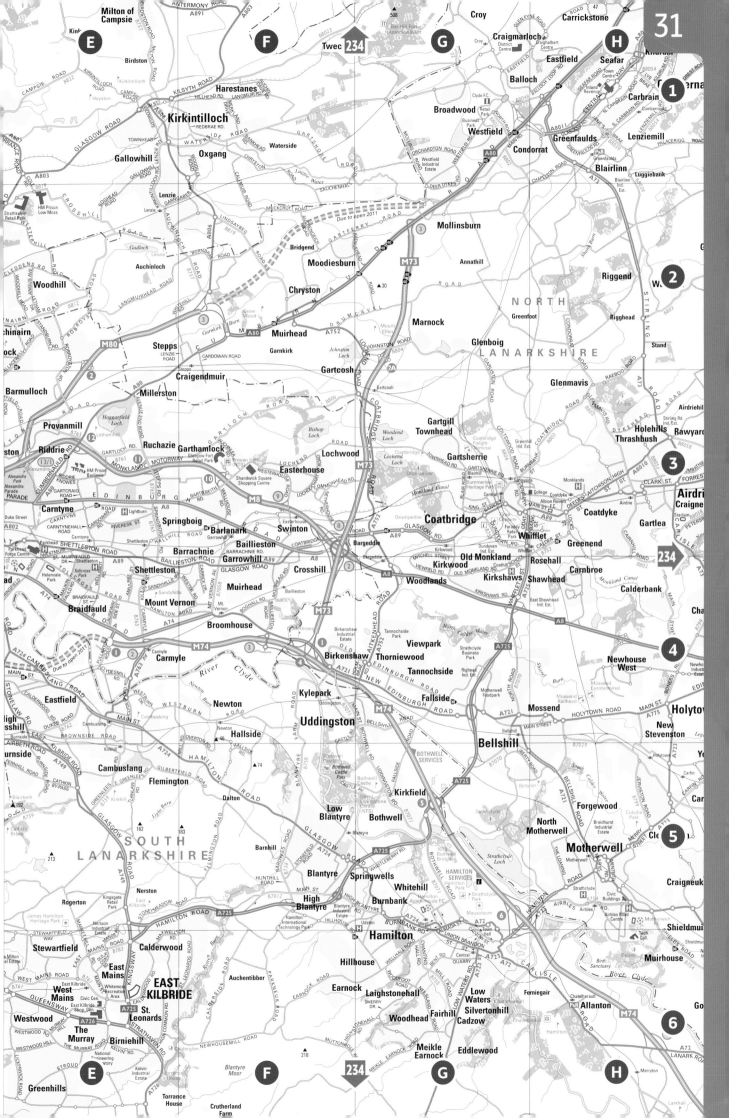

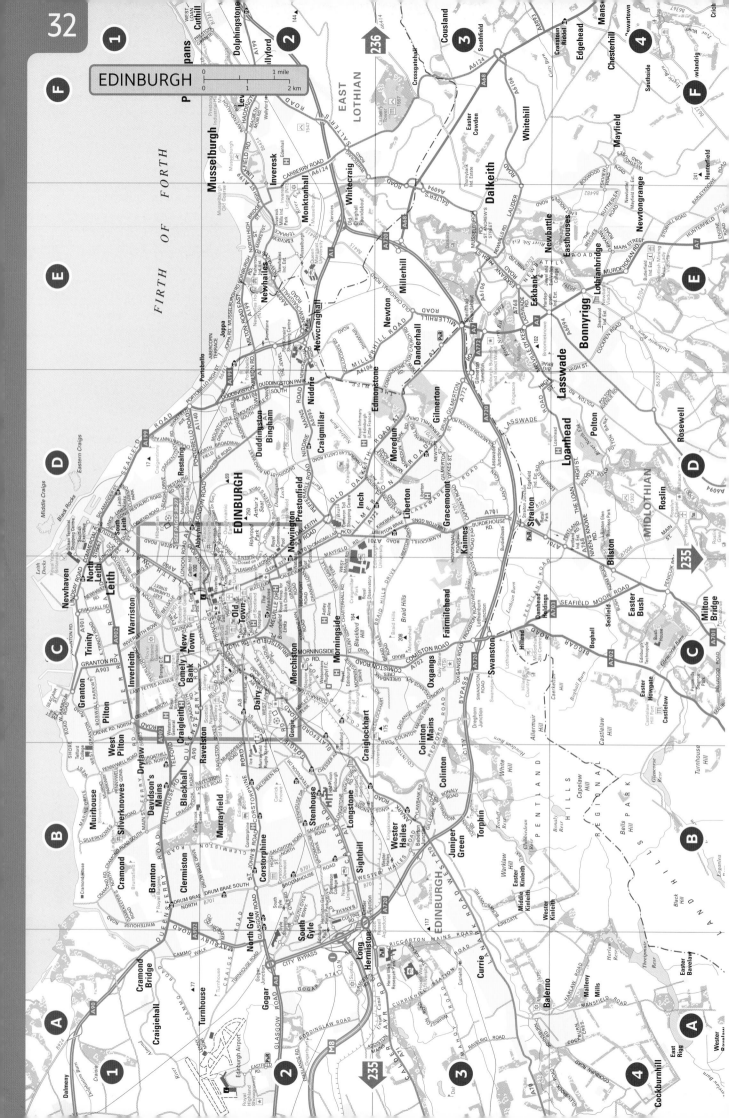

Symbols used on the map

M8	Motorway	Bus / Coach station	⊐JAPAN	Embassy
A4 ❶	Primary route dual / single carriageway / Junction	P&R	Park and Ride site - rail operated (runs at least 5 days a week)	Cinema
A40	'A' road dual / single carriageway		Extent of London congestion charging zone	Cathedral / Church
B507	'B' road dual / single carriageway	Dublin 8hrs	Vehicle / Pedestrian ferry	Mormon	Mosque / Synagogue / Other place of worship
Toll	Other road dual / single carriageway / Toll	P P	Car park		Leisure & tourism
	One way street / Orbital route	Theatre		Shopping
	Access restriction	Major hotel		Administration & law
	Pedestrian street	Public House		Health & welfare
	Street market	Pol	Police station		Education
	Minor road / Track	Lib	Library		Industry / Office
FB	Footpath / Footbridge	PO	Post Office		Other notable building
	Road under construction	Visitor information centre (open all year / seasonally)		Park / Garden / Sports ground
	Main / other National Rail station	Toilet		Cemetery
	London Underground / Overground station			
	Light Rail / Station			

Locator map

Street maps

Aberdeen	63	Leeds index	52
Bath	63	Leicester	77
Birmingham	34-35	Lincoln	77
Birmingham index	48	Liverpool	42-43
Blackpool	64	Liverpool index	54
Bournemouth	64	London	44-45
Bradford	65	London index	56
Brighton	65	Manchester	46-47
Bristol	66	Manchester index	60
Cambridge	66	Middlesbrough	78
Canterbury	67	Milton Keynes	78
Cardiff	67	Newcastle upon Tyne	79
Carlisle	68	Norwich	79
Cheltenham	68	Nottingham	80
Chester	69	Oxford	80
Coventry	69	Perth	81
Derby	70	Plymouth	81
Dover	70	Portsmouth	82
Dundee	71	Reading	82
Durham	71	Salisbury	83
Eastbourne	72	Scarborough	83
Edinburgh	36-37	Sheffield	84
Edinburgh index	49	Southampton	84
Exeter	72	Stoke-on-Trent	85
Folkestone	73	Stratford-upon-Avon	85
Glasgow	38-39	Sunderland	86
Glasgow index	51	Swansea	86
Gloucester	73	Swindon	87
Guildford	74	Torquay	87
Harrogate	74	Watford	88
Hastings	75	Weston-super-Mare	88
Hereford	75	Winchester	89
Hull (Kingston upon Hull)	76	Windsor	89
Inverness	76	Worcester	90
Leeds	40-41	York	90

Airport plans

Birmingham International	91
Gatwick	91
Glasgow	91
Heathrow	91
Manchester	91
Stansted	91

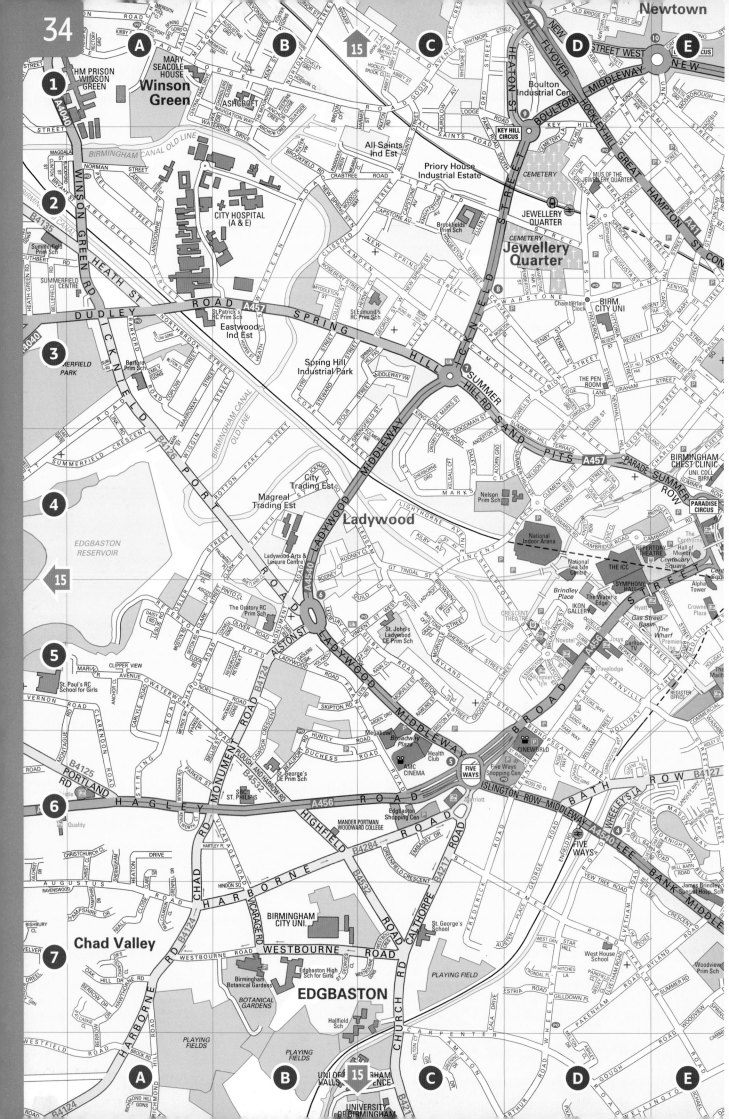

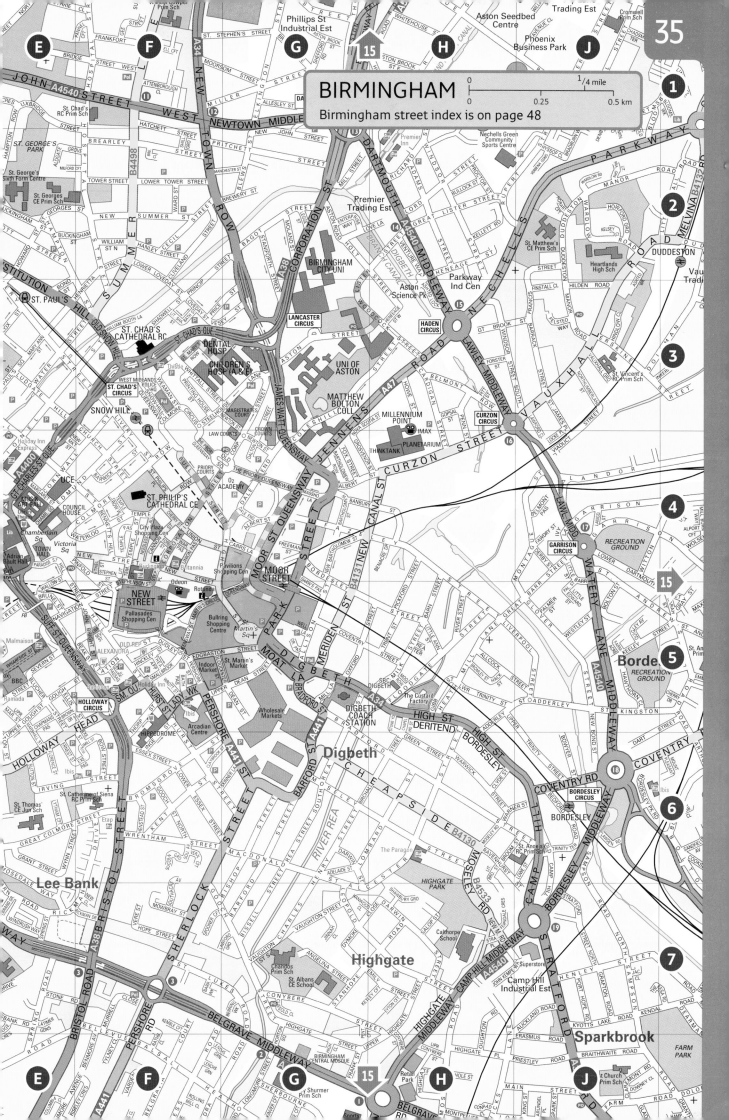

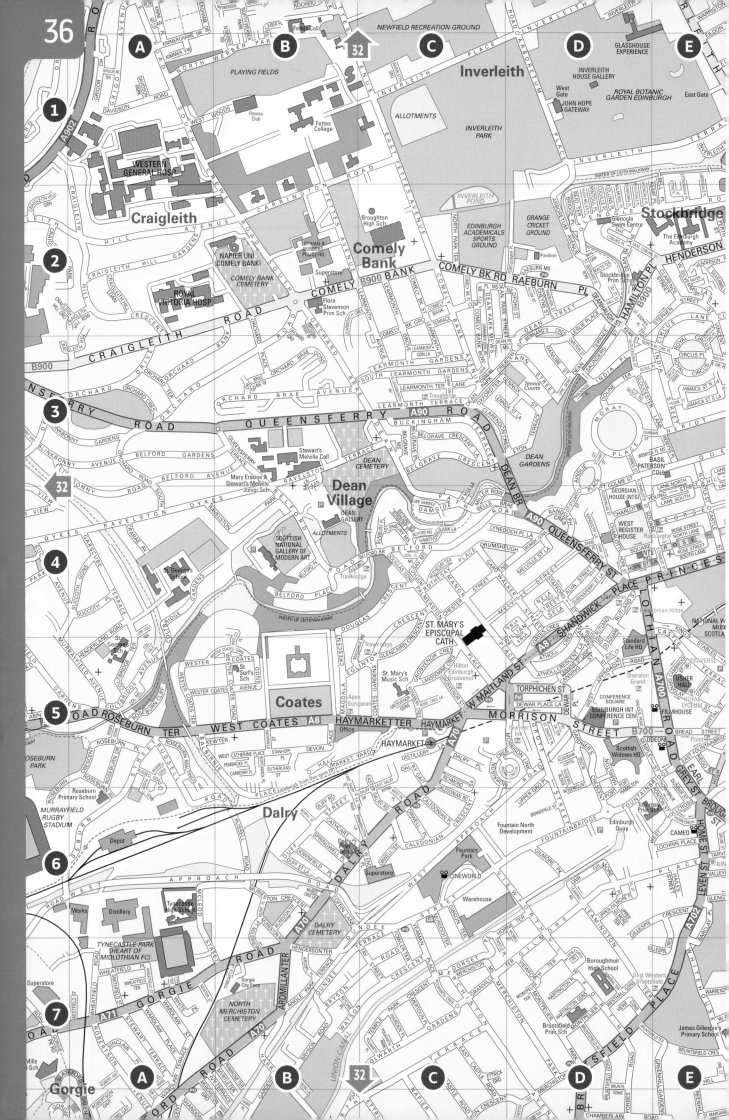

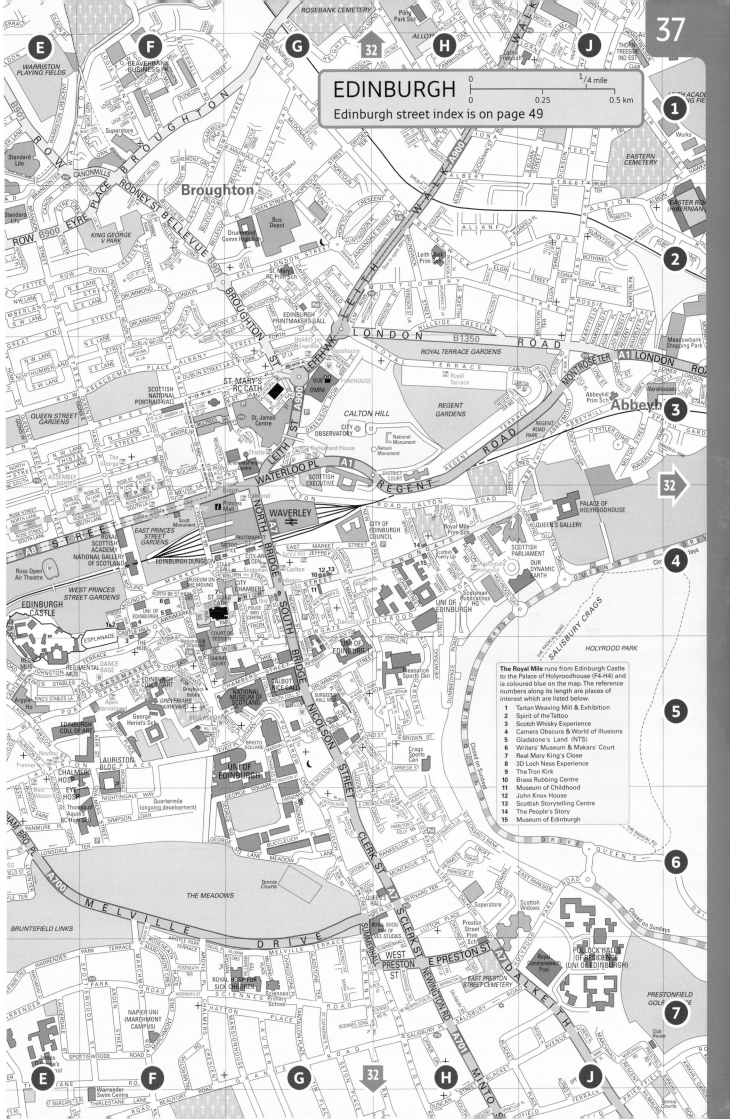

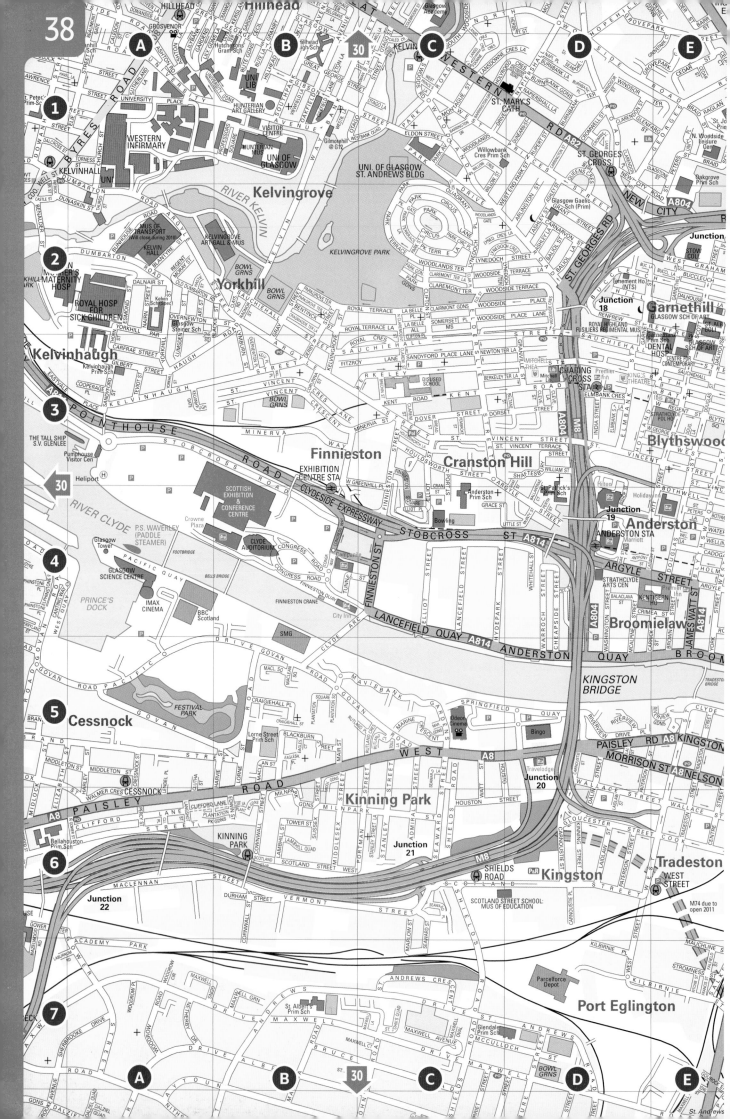

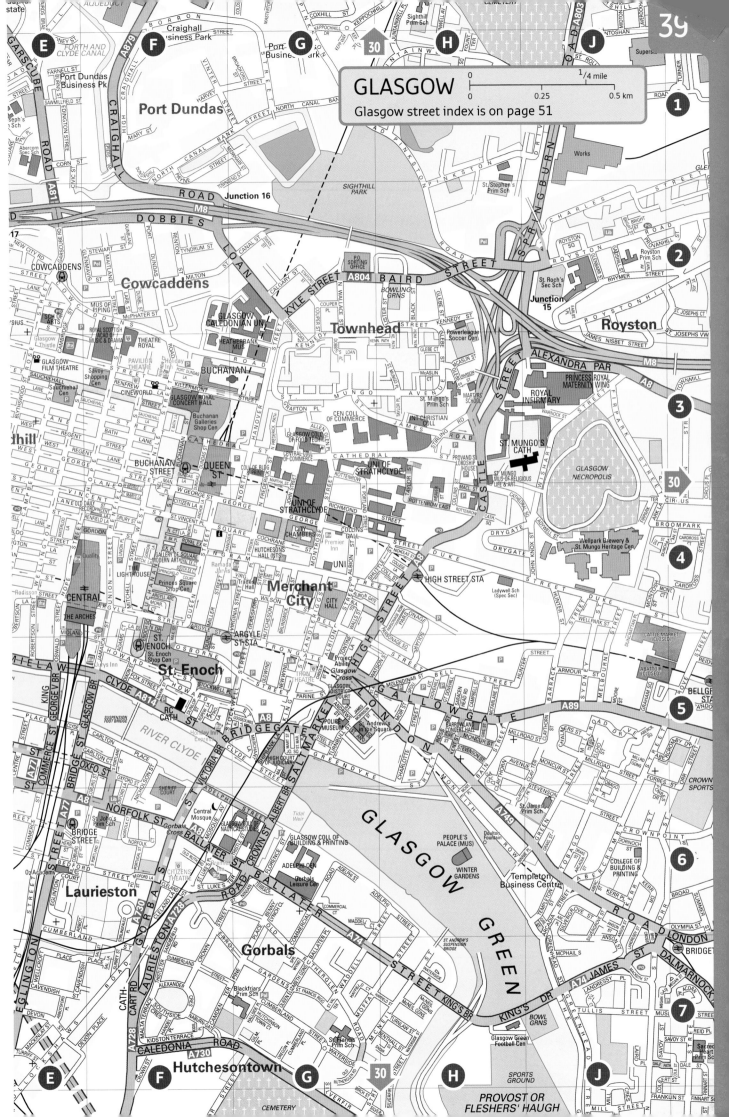

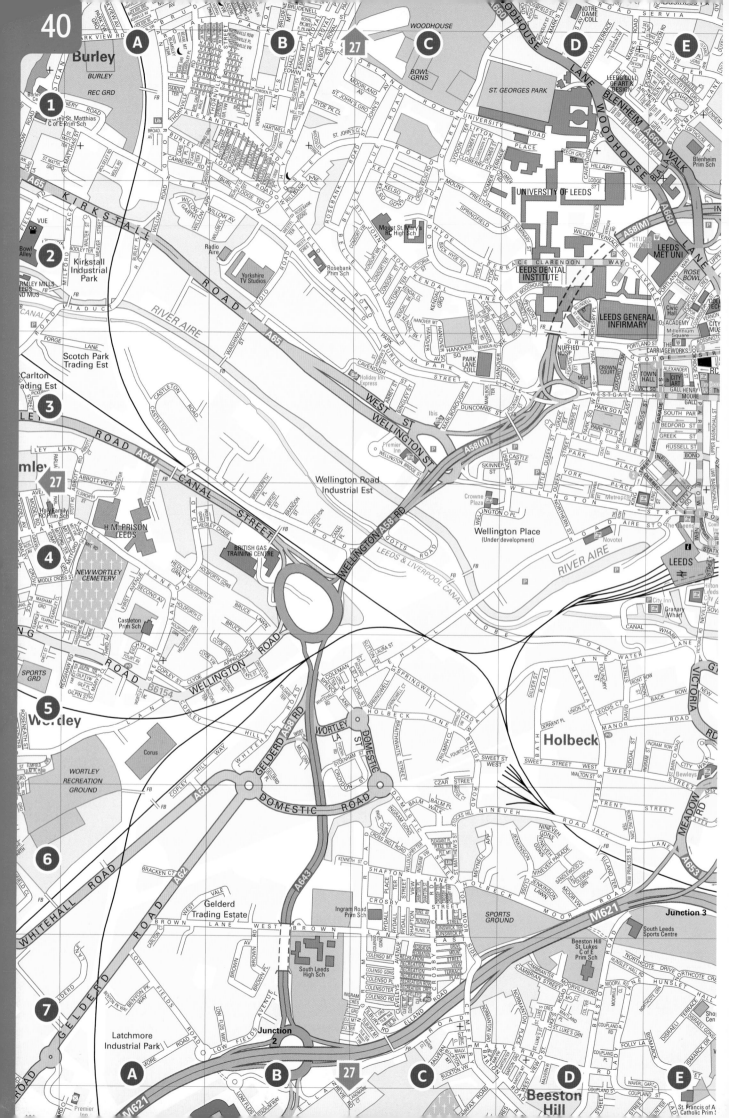

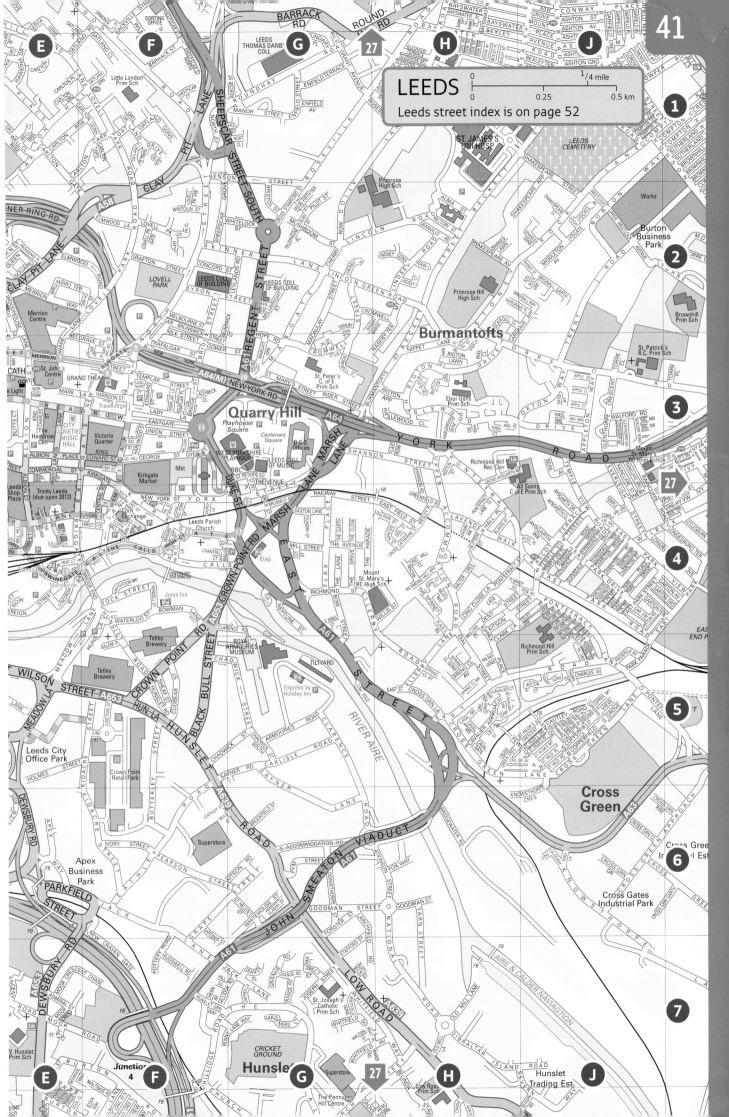

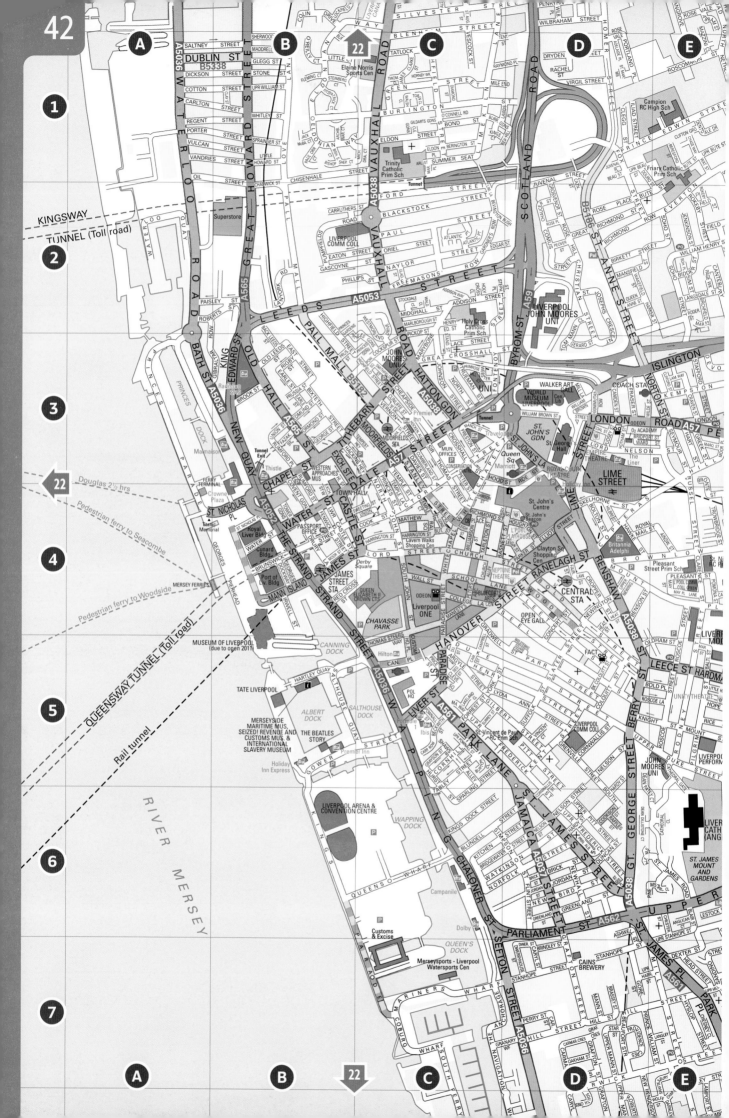

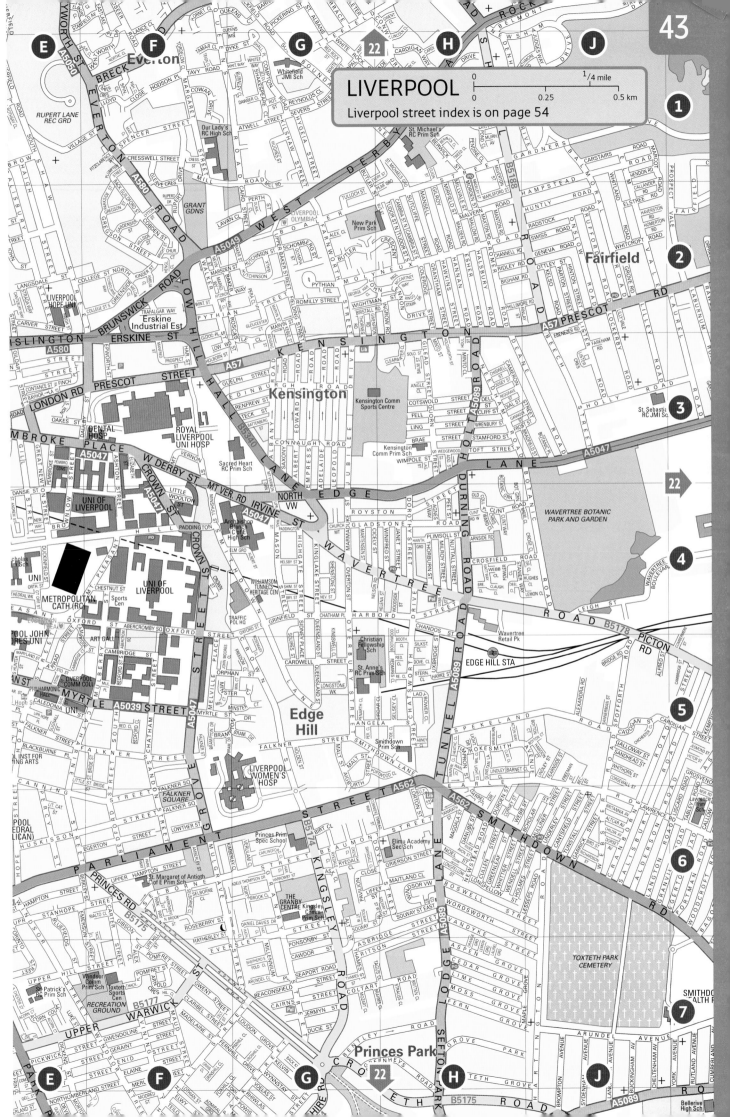

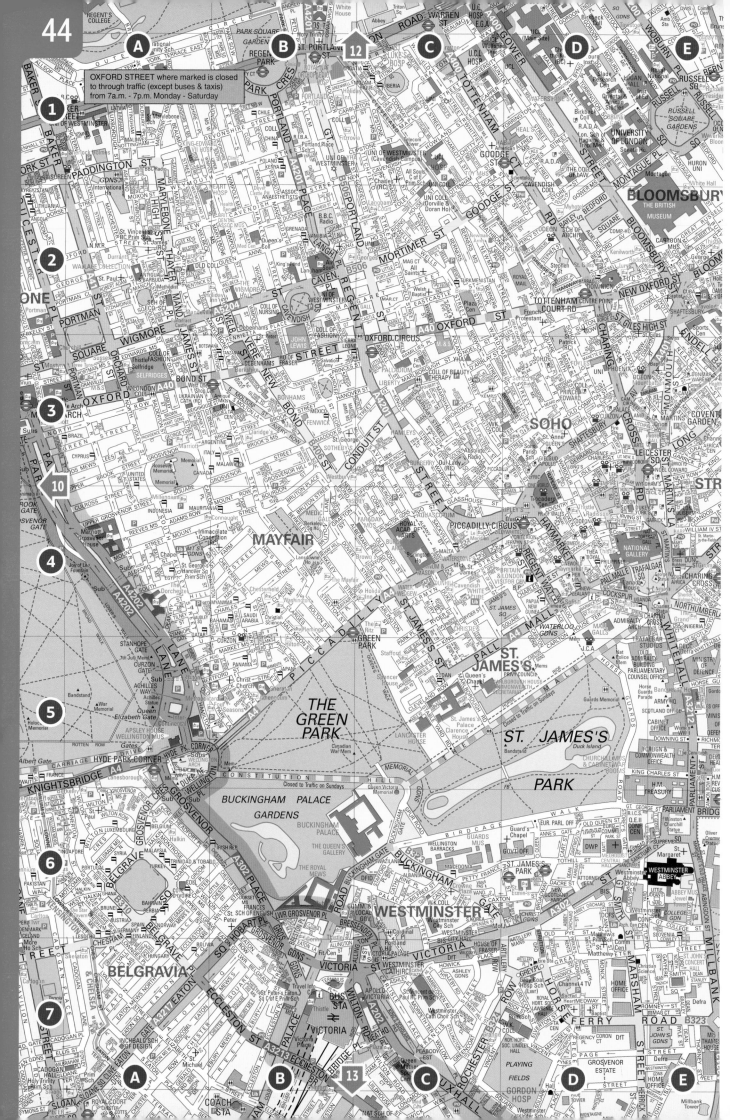

OXFORD STREET where marked is closed to through traffic (except buses & taxis) from 7a.m. - 7p.m. Monday - Saturday

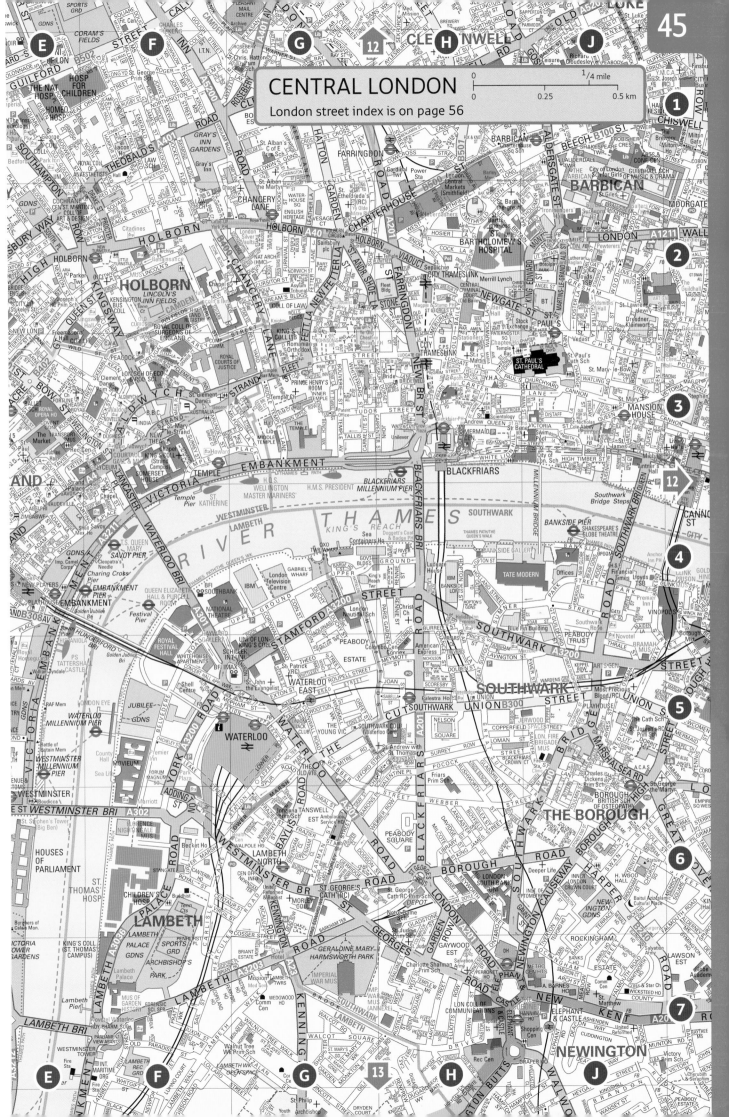

CENTRAL LONDON

London street index is on page 56

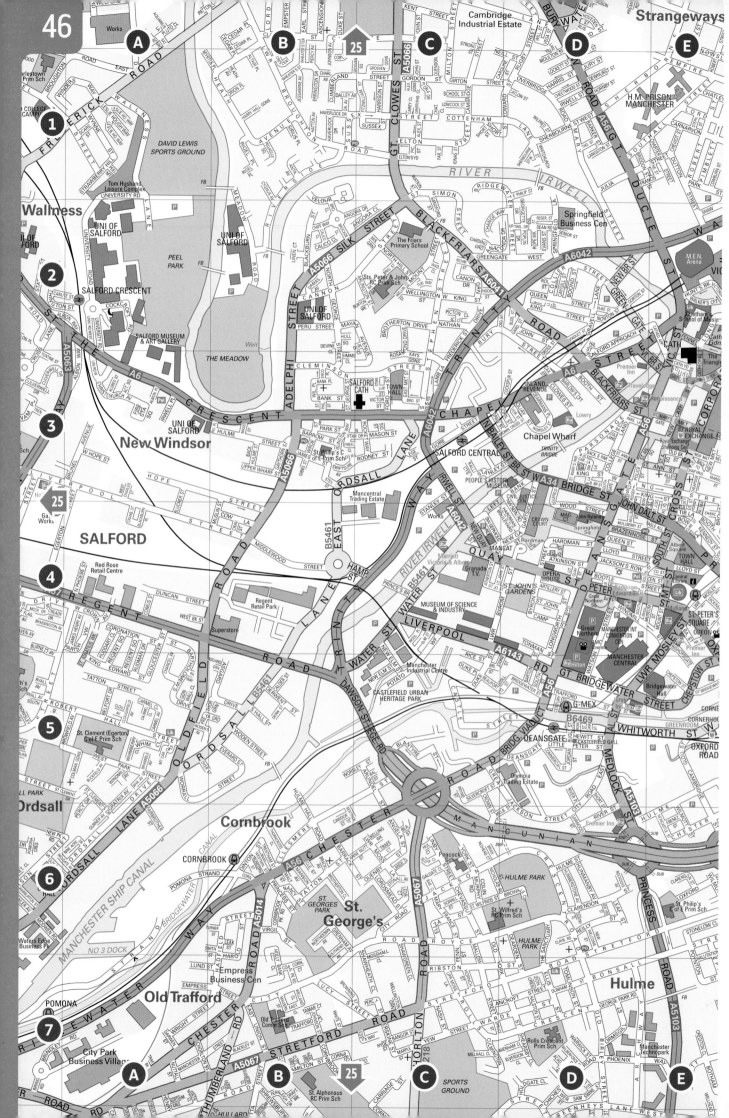

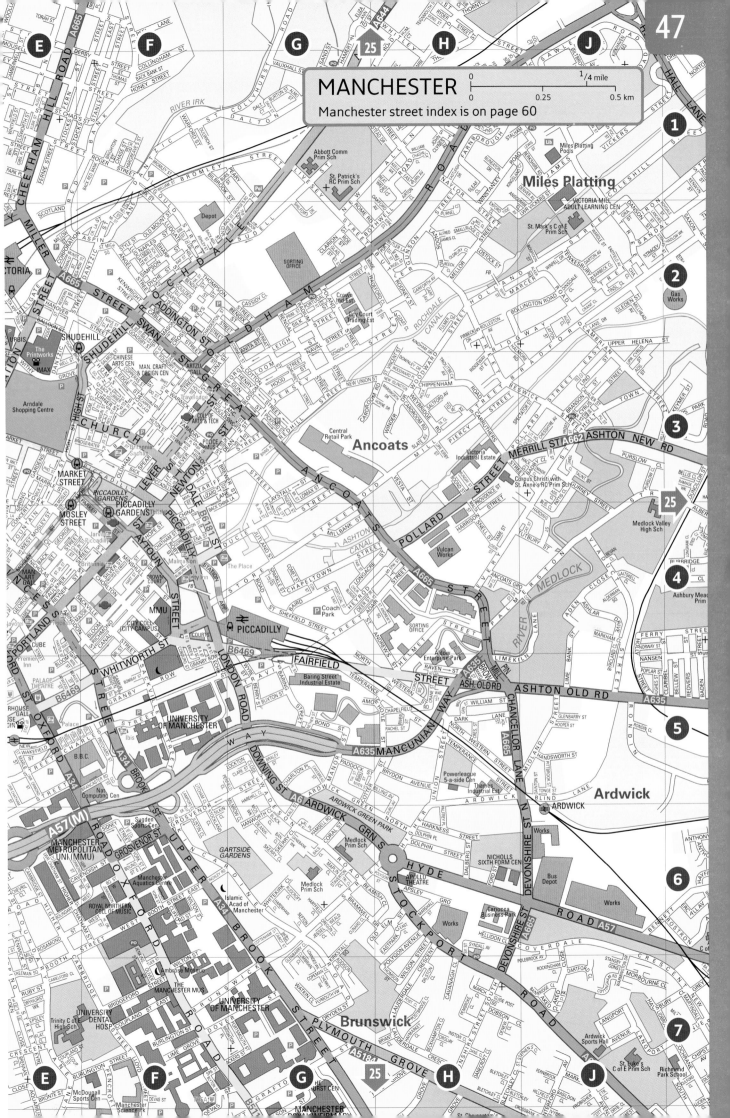

Indexes to street maps

General abbreviations

All	Alley	Chyd	Churchyard	Embk	Embankment	La	Lane	Pl	Place	W	West
App	Approach	Circ	Circus	Est	Estate	Lo	Lodge	Rd	Road	Wf	Wharf
Arc	Arcade	Clo	Close	Flds	Fields	Mans	Mansions	Ri	Rise	Wk	Walk
Av/Ave	Avenue	Cor	Corner	Gdn	Garden	Mkt/Mkts	Market/Markets	S	South	Yd	Yard
Bdy	Broadway	Cres	Crescent	Gdns	Gardens	Ms	Mews	Sq	Square		
Bldgs	Buildings	Ct	Court	Grd	Ground	N	North	St	Street		
Br/Bri	Bridge	Ctyd	Courtyard	Grn	Green	Par	Parade	St.	Saint		
Cen	Central, Centre	Dr	Drive	Gro	Grove	Pas	Passage	Ter	Terrace		
Ch	Church	E	East	Ho	House	Pk	Park	Twr	Tower		

Place names are shown in bold type

Birmingham street index

A
Abbey St 34 C1
Abbey St N 34 C1
Aberdeen St 34 A2
Acorn Gro 34 C4
Adams St 35 H2
Adderley St 35 H5
Adelaide St 35 G6
Albert St 35 G4
Albion St 34 D3
Alcester St 35 G7
Aldgate Gro 35 E2
Alfred Knight Way 34 E6
Allcock St 35 H5
Allesley St 35 G1
Allison St 35 G5
All Saints Rd 34 C1
All Saints St 34 C2
Alston St 34 B5
Anchor Cl 34 A5
Anchor Cres 34 B1
Anderton St 34 C4
Angelina St 35 G7
Ansbro Cl 34 A2
Arden Gro 34 C5
Arthur Pl 34 D4
Ascot Cl 34 A5
Ashted Lock 35 H3
Ashted Wk 35 J2
Ashton Cft 34 C5
Aston 35 H1
Aston Br 35 G1
Aston Brook St 35 G1
Aston Brook St E 35 H1
Aston Expressway 35 G2
Aston Rd 35 H1
Aston St 35 G3
Attenborough Cl 35 F1
Auckland Rd 35 J7
Augusta St 34 D2
Augustine Gro 34 B1
Austen Pl 34 C7
Autumn Gro 34 E1
Avenue Cl 35 J1
Avenue Rd 35 H1

B
Bacchus Rd 34 A1
Bagot St 35 G2
Balcaskie Cl 34 A7
Banbury St 35 G4
Barford Rd 34 A3
Barford St 35 G6
Barn St 35 H5
Barrack St 35 J3
Barrow Wk 35 F7
Barr St 34 D1
Bartholomew Row 35 G4
Bartholomew St 35 G4
Barwick St 35 F4
Bath Pas 35 F5
Bath Row 34 D6
Bath St 35 F3
Beak St 35 F5
Beaufort Gdns 34 A1
Beaufort Rd 34 B6
Bedford Rd 35 J6
Beeches, The 34 D7
Belgrave Middleway 35 F7
Bell Barn Rd 34 D6
Bellcroft 34 C5
Bellevue 35 F7
Bellis St 34 A6
Belmont Pas 35 J4
Belmont Row 35 H3
Benacre Dr 35 H4
Bennett's Hill 35 F4
Benson Rd 34 A1
Berkley St 34 D5
Berrington Wk 35 G7
Birchall St 35 G6
Bishopsgate St 34 D5
Bishop St 35 G7
Bissell St 35 G7
Blews St 35 G2
Bloomsbury St 35 J2
Blucher St 35 E5
Blyton Cl 34 A3
Boar Hound Cl 34 C3
Bodmin Gro 35 J1
Bolton St 35 J5
Bond Sq 34 C3
Bond St 35 E3
Bordesley 35 J5
Bordesley Circ 35 J6
Bordesley Middleway 35 J7
Bordesley Pk Rd 35 J6
Bordesley St 35 G4
Boulton Middleway 34 D1
Bow St 35 F6
Bowyer St 35 J6
Bracebridge St 35 G1
Bradburn Way 35 J2
Bradford St 35 G5
Branston St 34 D2
Brearley Cl 35 F2
Brearley St 35 F2
Bredon Cft 34 B1
Brewery St 35 G2
Bridge St 34 E5
Bridge St W 35 E1
Brindley Dr 34 D4
Brindley Pl 34 D5
Bristol St 35 F7
Broad St 34 D6
Broadway Plaza 34 C6
Bromley St 35 H5
Bromsgrove St 35 F6
Brookfield Rd 34 B2
Brook St 34 E3
Brook Vw Cl 34 E1
Broom St 35 H6
Brough Cl 35 J1
Browning St 34 C5
Brownsea Dr 35 E5
Brunel St 35 E5
Brunswick St 34 D5
Buckingham St 35 E2
Bullock St 35 H2
Bull St 35 F4

C
Cala Dr 34 C7
Calthorpe Rd 34 C7
Cambridge Rd 34 D4
Camden Dr 34 D3
Camden Gro 34 D3
Camden St 34 B2
Camp Hill 35 J7
Camp Hill Middleway 35 H7
Cannon St 35 F4
Capstone Av 34 C2
Cardigan St 35 H3
Carlisle St 34 A2
Carlyle Rd 34 A5
Caroline St 34 E3
Carpenter Rd 34 C7
Carrs La 35 G4
Carver St 34 C3
Cawdor Cres 34 B6
Cecil St 35 F2
Cemetery La 34 D2
Centenary Sq 34 E4
Central Pk Dr 34 A1
Central Sq 34 E5
Chad Rd 34 A7
Chadsmoor Ter 35 J1
Chad Valley 34 A7
Chamberlain Sq 35 E4
Chancellor's Cl 34 A7
Chandlers Cl 34 B1
Chapel Ho St 35 H5
Chapmans Pas 35 E5
Charles Henry St 35 G7
Charlotte Rd 34 D7
Charlotte St 34 E4
Chatsworth Way 34 E6
Cheapside 35 G6
Cherry St 35 F4
Chester St 35 H1
Chilwell Cft 35 F1
Christchurch Cl 34 A6
Church Rd 34 C7
Church St 35 F3
Civic Cl 34 D4
Clare Dr 34 A7
Clarendon Rd 34 A5
Clark St 34 A5
Claybrook St 35 F6
Clement St 34 D4
Clipper Vw 34 A5
Clissold Cl 35 G7
Clissold St 34 B2
Cliveland St 35 F3
Clyde St 35 H6
Colbrand Gro 35 E7
Coleshill St 35 G4
College St 34 B3
Colmore Circ 35 F3
Colmore Row 35 F4
Commercial St 34 E5
Communication Row 34 D6
Constitution Hill 34 E2
Conybere St 35 G7
Cope St 34 B3
Coplow St 34 A3
Cornwall St 35 E4
Corporation St 35 F4
Coveley Gro 34 B1
Coventry Rd 35 J6
Coventry St 35 G5
Cox St 35 E3
Coxwell Gdns 34 B5
Crabtree Rd 34 B2
Cregoe St 34 E6
Crescent, The 34 C1
Crescent Av 34 C1
Cromwell St 35 J1
Crondal Pl 34 D7
Crosby Cl 34 C4
Cumberland St 34 D5
Curzon Circ 35 H3
Curzon St 35 H4

D
Daisy Rd 34 A5
Dale End 35 G4
Daley Cl 34 C4
Dalton St 35 G4
Darnley Rd 34 B5
Dartmouth Circ 35 G1
Dartmouth Middleway 35 G2
Dart St 35 J6
Darwin St 35 G6
Dean St 35 G5
Deeley Cl 34 D7
Denby Cl 35 J2
Derby St 35 J4
Devonshire Av 34 B1
Devonshire St 34 B1
Digbeth 35 G6
Digbeth 35 G5
Dollman St 35 J3
Dover St 34 B1
Duchess Rd 34 B6
Duddeston Manor Rd 35 J2
Dudley St 35 F5
Dymoke Cl 35 G7

E
Edgbaston 34 B7
Edgbaston St 35 F5
Edmund St 35 E4
Edward St 34 D4
Eldon Rd 34 A5
Elkington St 35 G1
Ellen St 34 C3
Ellis St 35 E5
Elvetham Rd 34 D7
Embassy Dr 34 C6
Emily Gdns 34 A3
Emily St 35 G7
Enfield Rd 34 D6
Enterprise Way 35 G2
Ernest St 35 E6
Erskine St 35 J3
Essex St 35 F6
Essington St 34 D5
Estria Rd 34 C7
Ethel St 35 F4
Exeter Pas 35 F6
Exeter St 35 F6
Eyre St 34 B3
Eyton Cft 35 H7

F
Farmacre 35 J5
Farm Cft 34 D1
Farm St 34 D1
Fawdry St 35 J4
Fazeley St 35 G4
Felsted Way 35 J3
Ferndale Cres 35 H7
Finstall Cl 35 J3
Five Ways 34 C6
Fleet St 34 E4
Floodgate St 35 H5
Florence St 35 E6
Ford St 34 C1
Fore St 35 F4
Forster St 35 H3
Foster Gdns 34 B1
Fox St 35 G4
Francis Rd 34 B5
Francis St 35 J3
Frankfort St 35 F1
Frederick Rd 34 C7
Frederick St 34 D3
Freeman St 35 G4
Freeth St 34 B4
Friston Av 34 C6
Fulmer Wk 34 C4

G
Garrison Circ 35 J4
Garrison La 35 J4
Garrison St 35 J4
Gas St 34 D5
Gas St Basin 34 E5
Geach St 35 F1
Gee St 35 F1
George Rd 34 D7
George St 34 D4
George St W 34 C3
Gibb St 35 H5
Gilby Rd 34 C5
Gilldown Pl 34 D7
Glebeland Cl 34 C5
Gloucester St 35 F5
Glover St 35 J5
Gooch St 35 F7
Gooch St N 35 F6
Goode Av 34 C1
Goodman St 34 C4
Gopsal St 35 H3
Gough St 35 E5
Grafton Rd 35 J7
Graham St 34 D3
Grant St 35 E6
Granville St 34 D5
Graston Cl 34 C5
Great Barr St 35 H5
Great Brook St 35 H3
Great Charles St Queensway 35 E4
Great Colmore St 34 E6
Great Hampton Row 34 E2
Great Hampton St 34 D2
Great King St 34 D1
Great King St N 34 E1
Great Lister St 35 H2
Great Tindal St 34 C4
Greenfield Cres 34 C6
Green St 35 H6
Grenfell Dr 34 A7
Grosvenor St 35 G4
Grosvenor St W 34 C5
Guest Gro 34 D1
Guild Cl 34 B5
Guild Cft 35 F1
Guthrie Cl 35 E1

H
Hack St 35 H5
Hadfield Cft 34 E2
Hagley Rd 34 A6
Hall St 34 E3
Hampshire Dr 34 A7
Hampton St 35 E2
Hanley St 35 F2
Hanwood Cl 35 G7
Harborne Rd 34 A7
Harford St 34 E2
Harmer St 34 C2
Harold Rd 34 A5
Hartley Pl 34 A6
Hatchett St 35 F1
Hawthorn Cl 35 J5
Hawthorne Rd 34 A7
Heath Mill La 35 H5
Heath St S 34 B3
Heaton Dr 34 A7
Heaton St 34 D1
Helena St 34 D4
Heneage St 35 H2
Heneage St W 35 H3
Henley St 35 J7
Henrietta St 35 F3
Henstead St 35 F6
Herne Cl 34 C3
Hickman Gdns 34 B5
Highfield Rd 34 B6
Highgate 35 H7
Highgate St 35 G7
High St 35 G4
Hilden Rd 35 J3
Hill St 35 E4
Hinckley St 35 F5
Hindlow Cl 35 J3
Hindon Sq 34 B7
Hingeston St 34 C2
Hitches La 34 D7
Hobart Cft 35 J2
Hobson Cl 34 B1
Hockley Brook Cl 34 B1
Hockley Cl 35 F1
Hockley Hill 34 D1
Hockley St 34 D2
Holland St 34 D4
Holliday Pas 34 E5
Holliday St 34 E5
Holloway Circ 35 F5
Holloway Head 35 E6
Holt St 35 G2
Holywell Cl 34 B5
Hooper St 34 B3
Hope St 35 F7
Hospital St 35 F1
Howard St 35 E2
Howe St 35 H3
Howford Gro 35 J2
Hubert St 35 H1
Hunter's Vale 34 D1
Huntly Rd 34 B6
Hurdlow Av 34 C2
Hurst St 35 F5
Hylton St 34 D2
Hyssop Cl 35 J2

I
Icknield Port Rd 34 A3
Icknield Sq 34 B4
Icknield St 34 C3
Inge St 35 F6
Inkerman St 35 J3
Irving St 35 E6
Islington Row Middleway 34 C6
Ivy La 35 J4

J
Jackson Cl 35 J7
James St 34 E3
James Watt Queensway 35 G3
Jennens Rd 35 G4
Jewellery Quarter 34 D2
Jinnah Cl 35 G7
John Bright St 35 F5
John Kempe Way 35 H7

K
Keeley St 35 J5
Keepers Cl 34 B1
Kellett Rd 35 H2
Kelsall Cft 34 C4
Kelsey Cl 35 J2
Kemble Cft 35 F7
Kendal Rd 35 J7
Kenilworth Ct 34 A6
Kent St 35 F6
Kent St N 34 B1
Kenyon St 34 E3
Ketley Cft 35 G7
Key Hill 34 D2
Key Hill Dr 34 D2
Kilby Av 34 C4
King Edwards Rd 34 D4
Kingston Rd 35 J5
Kingston Row 34 D4
Kirby Rd 34 A1
Knightstone Av 34 C2
Kyotts Lake Rd 35 J7

L
Ladycroft 34 C5
Ladywell Wk 35 F5
Ladywood 34 C4
Ladywood Middleway 34 B5
Ladywood Rd 34 B5
Lancaster Circ 35 G3
Landor St 35 J4
Langdon St 35 J4
Lansdowne St 34 A2
Latimer Gdns 35 E7
Lawden Rd 35 J6
Lawford Cl 35 J3
Lawford Gro 35 G7
Lawley Middleway 35 H3
Ledbury Cl 34 B5
Ledsam St 34 C4
Lee Bk 35 E7
Lee Bk Middleway 34 D6
Lee Cres 34 D7
Lee Mt 34 D7
Lees St 34 B1
Legge La 34 D3
Legge St 35 G2
Lennox St 35 E1
Leopold St 35 G7
Leslie Rd 34 A5
Leyburn Rd 34 C5
Lighthorne Av 34 C4
Link Rd 34 A3
Lionel St 34 E4
Lister St 35 G3
Little Ann St 35 H5
Little Barr St 35 J4
Little Broom St 35 H6
Little Edward St 35 J5
Little Francis Grn 35 J2
Little Shadwell St 35 F3
Liverpool St 35 H5
Livery St 35 F3
Locke Pl 35 J4
Lodge Rd 34 A1
Lombard St 35 G6
Longleat Way 34 D6
Lord St 35 H2
Louisa St 34 D4
Loveday St 35 F3
Love La 35 G2
Lower Dartmouth St 35 J4
Lower Essex St 35 F6
Lower Loveday St 35 F2
Lower Severn St 35 F5

Lower Temple St 35 F4
Lower Twr St 35 F2
Lower Trinity St 35 H5
Lowe St 35 J6
Ludgate Hill 35 E3
Lytham Cft 35 E6

M
Macdonald St 35 G6
Malcolmson Cl 34 A7
Manchester St 35 F2
Margaret St 35 E4
Mariner Av 34 A5
Marroway St 34 A3
Marshall St 35 E5
Mary Ann St 35 E3
Mary St 34 E3
Mason Way 34 E6
Masshouse La 35 G4
Mearse Cl 34 C2
Melton Dr 34 D7
Meredith Pool Cl 34 A1
Meriden St 35 G5
Merryhill Dr 34 A1
Meyrick Wk 34 A6
Middleway Vw 34 C3
Midford Grn 34 E6
Milford Cft 35 E2
Milk St 35 H5
Miller St 35 F1
Mill La 35 G5
Mill St 35 G2
Milton St 35 F1
Moat La 35 G5
Moland St 35 G2
Montague St 35 J4
Monument Rd 34 B6
Moore's Row 35 H5
Moorings, The 34 B1
Moorsom St 35 F1
Moor St Queensway 35 G4
Moreton St 34 C3
Morville St 34 C5
Mosborough Cres 34 E1
Mosedale Way 35 E6
Moseley Rd 35 H6
Moseley St 35 G6
Moss Ho Cl 34 D6
Mostyn Rd 34 A5
Mott St 34 E2
Mowbray St 35 F7
Murrell Cl 35 F7
Musgrave Rd 34 A1
Myddleton St 34 B3

N
Navigation St 35 E5
Navigation Way 34 B1
Nechells Parkway 35 H3
Needless All 35 F4
Nelson St 34 D4
New Bartholomew St 35 G4
Newbold Cft 35 J1

New Bond St 35 J5
New Canal St 35 G4
Newhall Hill 34 D3
Newhall St 34 E3
Newhope Cl 35 F7
New John St 35 G2
New John St W 34 E1
New Mkt St 35 E4
New Moseley Rd 35 H7
New Spring St 34 C2
New Spring St N 34 B2
New St 35 F4
New Summer St 35 F2
Newton St 35 G4
Newtown 34 E1
Newtown Dr 34 D1
Newtown Middleway 35 F1
New Town Row 35 F1
Niall Cl 34 A7
Noel Rd 34 A5
Norman St 34 A2
Northampton St 34 D2
Northbrook St 34 A3
Northumberland St 35 J3
Northwood St 34 D3
Norton St 34 B1
Nova Scotia St 35 G4
Nursery Rd 34 D1

O
Oak Hill Dr 34 A7
Old Br St 34 D1
Old Camp Hill 35 J6
Old Smithy Pl 34 C1
Old Snow Hill 35 F3
Old Sq 35 F4
Oliver Rd 34 B5
Oliver St 35 J1
Oozells St 34 D5
Orchid Dr 35 E1
Orwell Pas 35 G5
Osler St 34 A5
Oxford St 35 G5

P
Paddocks Grn 34 B2
Pakenham Rd 34 D7
Palmer St 35 J5
Palomino Pl 34 B4
Pannel Cft 35 F1
Parade 34 D4
Paradise Circ 34 E4
Paradise St 35 E4
Parker St 34 A6
Parkfield Cl 34 D7
Park Rd 34 C1
Park Rd S 34 C1
Park St 35 G5
Paxton Rd 34 C2
Peel St 34 A2
Pemberton St 34 D2
Penn St 35 H3
Pershore St 35 F5

Pickford St 35 H5
Pinfold St 35 E4
Pinto Cl 34 B5
Pitsford St 34 C2
Pitt St 35 H3
Plough & Harrow Rd 34 B6
Pool St 35 G1
Pope St 34 C3
Port Hope Rd 35 J7
Powell St 34 D3
Power Cres 34 C5
Price St 35 F3
Princip St 35 F3
Printing Ho St 35 F3
Priory Queensway, The 35 G4
Pritchett St 35 F2
Proctor St 35 H2

Q
Quayside 34 B1
Queens Hosp Cl 34 D6
Quigley Av 35 J5

R
Radnor St 34 B1
Radshaw Cl 34 D6
Rake Way 34 D5
Rann Cl 34 C5
Ravenhurst St 35 H6
Rawlins St 34 C5
Rea St 35 G6
Rea St S 35 G6
Rea Ter 35 H5
Rectory Gro 34 A1
Regent Par 34 D3
Regent Pl 34 D3
Regent St 34 D3
Reservoir Retreat 34 B5
Reservoir Rd 34 A5
Richard St 35 H2
Rickman Dr 35 E7
Ridley St 34 E6
River St 35 H5
Rocky La 35 J1
Rodney Cl 34 B4
Rosebery St 34 B2
Roseland Way 34 D6
Rotton Pk St 34 B4
Rupert St 35 H2
Ruston St 34 C5
Ryland Rd 34 D7
Ryland St 34 C5

S
Sadlers Wk 34 B5
St. Andrew's Rd 35 J4
St. Chad's Queensway 35 F3
St. Georges Cl 34 B7
St. Georges St 35 E2
St. Helen's Pas 34 D3
St. James Pl 35 J3
St. James Rd 34 C6

St. Jude's Pas 35 F5
St. Lukes Rd 35 F7
St. Marks Cres 34 C4
St. Marks St 34 C3
St. Martin's Circ Queensway 35 F5
St. Martin's Sq 35 G5
St. Martin's St 34 D6
St. Mary's Row 35 F3
St. Paul's Sq 34 E3
St. Phillips Pl 35 F4
St. Stephen's St 35 F1
St. Vincent St 34 C4
St. Vincent St W 34 B5
Salop St 35 H7
Sampson Rd 35 J7
Sampson Rd N 35 J6
Sand Pits 34 C3
Sandy Way 34 D5
Scotland St 34 D4
Sefton Rd 34 A5
Severn St 35 E5
Shadwell St 35 F3
Shawbury Gro 35 H7
Shaw's Pas 35 G4
Sheepcote St 34 C4
Shefford Rd 35 G1
Shepherds Gdns 34 D6
Sherborne Gro 34 C4
Sherborne St 34 C5
Sheringham 34 A6
Sherlock St 35 F7
Shetland Cl 34 B5
Shillcock Gro 35 F2
Shire Cl 34 A4
Shyltons Cft 34 C5
Skinner La 35 G6
Skipton Rd 34 B5
Sloane St 34 D4
Smallbrook Queensway 35 F5
Smith St 34 E1
Snow Hill Queensway 35 F3
Soho Pool Way 34 B1
Southacre Av 35 F7
South Rd 35 J7
Spencer St 34 D2
Spooner Cft 35 F7
Springbank Rd 34 E7
Springfield St 34 B4
Spring Gro Gdns 34 A1
Spring Hill 34 B3
Spring Hill Pas 34 C3
Spring St 35 E7
Stainsby Av 34 D1
Stanhope Rd 35 G7
Staniforth St 35 G2
Star Hill 34 D7
Station St 35 F5
Steelhouse La 35 F3
Stephenson Pl 35 F5
Stephenson St 35 F4
Steward St 34 B3

Stirling Rd 34 A6
Stoke Way 34 D5
Stone Rd 35 F5
Stone Yd 35 H5
Stour St 34 B3
Stratford Pl 35 H7
Stratford Rd 35 J7
Stratford St N 35 J7
Suffolk St Queensway 35 E5
Sugden Gro 35 F6
Summer Cft 35 F1
Summerfield Rd 34 A3
Summer Hill Rd 34 C3
Summer Hill St 34 D4
Summer Hill Ter 34 D3
Summer La 35 F3
Summer Rd 34 E7
Summer Row 34 E4
Sutton St 35 E6
Swallow St 35 E5

T
Talbot St 34 A1
Temple Pas 35 F4
Temple Row 35 F4
Temple Row W 35 F4
Temple St 35 F4
Tenby St 34 D3
Tenby St N 34 D3
Tennant St 34 D6
Theatre App 35 F5
Theresa Rd 35 J7
Thomas St 35 G1
Thorp St 35 F6
Tower St 35 F2
Townsend Way 34 D4
Trent St 35 H5
Trinity Ter 35 J6

U
Unett St 34 E1
Union Pas 35 F4
Union St 35 F4
Upper Dean St 35 F5
Upper Gough St 35 E6
Upper Marshall St 35 E5
Upper Trinity St 35 H5
Uxbridge St 35 E1

V
Vaughton St 35 G7
Vaughton St S 35 G7
Vauxhall Gro 35 J3
Vauxhall Rd 35 J3
Venture Way 35 H2
Verbena Gdns 35 J2
Vere St 35 F7
Vernolds Cft 35 F6
Vesey St 35 F3
Viaduct St 35 J4
Vicarage Rd 34 B6
Victoria Sq 35 E4

Victor Rd 34 A1
Vittoria St 34 D3
Vyse St 34 D3

W
Walter St 35 J1
Wardlow Rd 35 J2
Ward St 35 F2
Warner St 35 H6
Warstone La 34 C3
Warstone Par E 34 D2
Warwick Pas 35 F4
Warwick St 35 H6
Washington St 34 E5
Waterloo St 35 E4
Waterside Dr 34 A1
Waterside Vw 34 B2
Water St 35 E3
Waterworks Rd 34 A5
Watery La Middleway 35 J4
Weaman St 35 F3
Well La 35 G5
Well St 35 D2
Westbourne Cres 34 C7
Westbourne Gdns 34 B7
Westbourne Rd 34 A7
Western Rd 34 B3
West Grn Cl 34 D7
Westhorpe Gro 34 E1
Westley St 35 J5
Wharf, The 34 E5
Wharf La 34 C1
Wharfside St 35 E5
Wharf St 34 B1
Wheeler St 35 E1
Wheeley's La 34 D6
Whitehouse St 35 H1
Whitmore St 34 C1
Whittall St 35 F3
Wiggin St 34 A4
William Booth La 35 F3
William Henry St 35 J1
William St 34 D6
William St N 35 F2
Willow Gdns 34 A3
Windmill St 35 F6
Windrush Way 35 E7
Windsor St 35 H2
Windsor St S 35 H3
Winson Grn 34 A1
Witton St 35 J4
Woodcock St 35 G3
Woodcote Way 34 B2
Woodview Dr 34 E7
Wrentham St 35 F6
Wrottesley St 35 F5
Wyndham Rd 34 A6
Wynn St 35 E6

Y
Yew Tree Rd 34 D6

Edinburgh street index

A
Abbeyhill 37 J3
Abbeyhill 37 J3
Abbeyhill Cres 37 H4
Abbey La 37 J3
Abbeymount 37 J3
Abbey Strand 37 J4
Abbey St 37 J3
Abercromby Pl 37 F3
Admiral Ter 36 D7
Ainslie Pl 36 D3
Albany La 37 F2
Albany St 37 F3
Albany St La 37 F3
Albert St 37 H1
Albion Gdns 37 J2
Albion Pl 37 J2
Albion Rd 37 J2
Albion Ter 37 J2
Alfred Pl 37 J7
Allanfield 37 H2
Allanfield Pl 37 H2
Allan St 36 D2
Alva Pl 37 J3
Alva St 36 D4
Angle Pk Ter 36 B7
Annandale St 37 G1
Annandale St La 37 G2
Ann St 36 D3
Arboretum Av 36 D2
Arboretum Pl 36 D1

Archibald Pl 37 F6
Arden St 37 F7
Ardmillan Pl 36 B7
Ardmillan Ter 36 B7
Argyle Pk Ter 37 F7
Argyle Pl 37 F7
Arthur St 37 H1
Arthur St La 37 H1
Atholl Cres 36 D5
Atholl Cres La 36 D5
Avondale Pl 36 D1

B
Back Dean 36 B4
Bakehouse Cl 37 H4
Balbirnie Pl 36 A5
Balmoral Pl 36 D2
Bank St 37 F4
Barclay Pl 36 E7
Barony St 37 F2
Beaverbank Pl 37 F1
Beaverhall Rd 37 F1
Bedford St 36 D2
Belford Av 36 A3
Belford Br 36 C4
Belford Gdns 36 A3
Belford Ms 36 C4
Belford Pk 36 B4
Belford Pl 36 B4
Belford Rd 36 B4
Belgrave Cres 36 C3

Belgrave Cres La 36 C3
Belgrave Ms 36 C3
Belgrave Pl 36 C3
Bellevue 37 F2
Bellevue Cres 37 F2
Bellevue Gdns 37 G1
Bellevue Gro 37 G2
Bellevue La 37 F2
Bellevue Pl 37 F2
Bellevue Rd 37 G2
Bellevue St 37 G2
Bellevue Ter 37 F2
Bell Pl 36 E1
Bells Brae 36 C4
Bell's Mills 36 B4
Bernard Ter 37 H6
Blacket Av 37 H7
Blacket Pl 37 H7
Blackfriars St 37 G4
Blackwood Cres 37 H7
Blair St 37 G4
Blandfield 37 G1
Boat Grn 37 F1
Boroughloch 37 G6
Boroughloch Sq 37 G6
Borthwick Pl 36 B5
Bothwell St 37 J2
Bowmont Pl 37 H6
Boyd's Entry 37 G4
Brandfield St 36 D6
Brandon St 37 E2

Brandon Ter 37 E2
Bread St 36 E5
Bridge Pl 36 D2
Briery Bauks 37 H5
Brighton St 37 G5
Bristo Pl 37 F5
Bristo Port 37 F5
Brougham Pl 37 E6
Brougham St 36 E6
Broughton 37 F1
Broughton Mkt 37 F3
Broughton Pl 37 G2
Broughton Pl La 37 G2
Broughton Rd 37 F1
Broughton St 37 G2
Broughton St La 37 G3
Brown's Cl 37 H4
Brown St 37 H5
Brunswick Rd 37 H2
Brunswick St 37 H2
Brunswick St La 37 H2
Brunton Ter 37 J3
Bruntsfield Av 36 D7
Bruntsfield Cres 36 E7
Bruntsfield Gdns 36 D7
Bruntsfield Ter 36 D7
Bryson Rd 36 B7
Buccleuch Pl 37 G6
Buccleuch St 37 G6
Buccleuch Ter 37 G6
Buchanan St 37 H1

Buckingham Ter 36 C3

C
Caledonian Cres 36 C6
Caledonian Pl 36 C6
Caledonian Rd 36 C6
Calton Hill 37 G3
Calton Rd 37 G3
Cambridge Av 37 H1
Cambridge Gdns 37 H1
Cambridge St 36 E5
Campbell's Cl 37 H4
Candlemaker Row 37 F5
Canning St 36 D5
Canning St La 36 D5
Canongate 37 G4
Canon La 37 E2
Canonmills 37 E1
Canon St 37 E1
Carberry Pl 36 B5
Carlton St 36 D3
Carlton Ter 37 H3
Carlton Ter Brae 37 J3
Carlton Ter La 37 H3
Carlton Ter Ms 37 H3
Carlton Wynd 37 H4
Carlyle Pl 37 J3
Carnegie St 37 G5
Carrington Rd 36 B2
Castle Hill 37 F4
Castle St 36 E4

Castle Ter 36 E4
Cathcart Pl 36 B6
Cathedral La 37 G3
Causewayside 37 H7
Chalmers Cres 37 F7
Chalmers St 37 F5
Chambers St 37 F5
Chapel St 37 G5
Charles St 37 G5
Charlotte La 36 D4
Charlotte Sq 36 D4
Chester St 36 C4
Cheyne St 36 D2
Chuckie Pend 36 D5
Circus Gdns 36 E3
Circus La 36 E3
Circus Pl 36 E3
Claremont Bk 37 F2
Claremont Cres 37 F1
Claremont Gro 37 F1
Clarence St 36 E3
Clarendon Cres 36 C3
Clerk St 37 G6
Coates 36 B5
Coates Cres 36 D5
Coates Gdns 36 C5
Cochran Ter 37 G2
Cockburn St 37 F4
Coffin La 36 B6
Collins Pl 36 D2
Coltbridge Av 36 A5

Coltbridge Gdns 36 A5
Coltbridge Millside 36 A5
Coltbridge Ter 36 A5
Coltbridge Vale 36 A5
Colville Pl 36 D2
Comely Bk 36 C2
Comely Bk 36 B2
Comely Bk Av 36 C2
Comely Bk Gro 36 C3
Comely Bk Pl 36 C2
Comely Bk Pl Ms 36 C2
Comely Bk Rd 36 C2
Comely Bk Row 36 C2
Comely Bk St 36 C2
Comely Bk Ter 36 C2
Conference Sq 36 D5
Cornwallis Pl 37 F2
Cornwall St 36 E5
Cowan's Cl 37 G6
Cowgate 37 F5
Cowgatehead 37 F5
Craigleith 36 A2
Craigleith Hill Cres 36 A2
Craigleith Hill Gdns 36 A2
Craigleith Hill Ln 36 A2
Craigleith Hill Row 36 A2
Cranston St 37 G4
Crarae Av 36 A4
Crewe Rd S 36 A1
Crichton St 37 G5
Croft-an-Righ 37 J3
Cumberland St 36 E2
Cumberland St N E La 37 E2
Cumberland St N W La 37 E2
Cumberland St S E La 37 E2
Cumberland St S W La 37 E2
Cumin Pl 37 G7

D
Dalkeith Rd 37 H6
Dalmeny St 37 H1
Dalry 36 B6
Dalry Gait 36 C5
Dalry Pl 36 C5
Dalry Rd 36 B7
Damside 36 C4
Danube St 36 D3
Darnaway St 36 D3
Davidson Pk 36 A1
Davidson Rd 36 A1
Davie St 37 G5
Dean Bk La 36 D2
Dean Br 36 C3
Deanhaugh St 36 D2
Dean Pk Cres 36 C3
Dean Pk Ms 36 C2
Dean Pk St 36 C2
Dean Path 36 C3
Dean St 36 D3
Dean Ter 36 D3
Dean Village 36 B4
Devon Pl 36 B5
Dewar Pl 36 D5
Dewar Pl La 36 D5
Dicksonfield 37 H2
Dickson St 37 J1
Distillery La 36 C5
Dorset Pl 36 C7
Douglas Cres 36 B4
Douglas Gdns 36 C4
Douglas Gdns Ms 36 C4
Doune Ter 36 D3
Downfield Pl 36 B6
Drumdryan St 36 E6
Drummond Pl 37 F2
Drummond St 37 G5
Drumsheugh Gdns 36 C4
Drum Ter 37 J2
Dryden Gait 37 G1
Dryden Gdns 37 G1
Dryden Pl 37 J7
Dryden St 37 G1
Dryden Ter 37 G1
Dublin Meuse 37 F3
Dublin St 37 F2
Dublin St La N 37 F2
Dublin St La S 37 F3
Duff Rd 36 B6
Duff St 36 B6
Duff St La 36 B6
Dumbiedykes Rd 37 H5
Dundas St 37 E2
Dundee St 36 B7
Dundee Ter 36 B7
Dundonald St 37 F2

Dunedin St 37 F1
Dunrobin Pl 36 D2

E
Earl Grey St 36 E5
East Adam St 37 G5
East Castle Rd 36 C7
East Claremont St 37 F2
East Crosscauseway 37 G6
Easter Dalry Dr 36 B6
Easter Dalry Pl 36 B5
Easter Dalry Rigg 36 B6
Easter Dalry Rd 36 C5
Easter Dalry Wynd 36 C6
Easter Rd 37 J3
East Fettes Av 36 C1
East Fountainbridge 36 E5
East London St 37 G2
East Mkt St 37 G4
East Montgomery Pl 37 H2
East Newington Pl 37 H7
East Parkside 37 H6
East Preston St 37 H7
East Preston St La 37 H7
East Sciennes St 37 G7
East Scotland St La 37 F2
East Silvermills La 37 E2
Edina Pl 37 J2
Edina St 37 J2
Edinburgh Quay 36 D6
Eglinton Cres 36 B5
Eildon St 36 E1
Eildon Ter 36 E1
Elder St 37 F3
Elgin St 37 H2
Elgin St N 37 J2
Elgin Ter 37 J2
Elliot St 37 J2
Elm Row 37 G2
Eton Ter 36 D3
Ettrickdale Pl 36 E1
Ettrick Gro 36 C7
Eyre Cres 37 E2
Eyre Pl 37 E2
Eyre Ter 37 E2

F
Fettes Av 36 B2
Fettes Row 37 E2
Findhorn Pl 37 G7
Fingal Pl 37 F7
Forbes St 37 H6
Forres St 36 D3
Forrest Hill 37 F5
Forrest Rd 37 F5
Forth St 37 G3
Fountainbridge 36 D6
Fowler Ter 36 C6
Frederick St 37 E3

G
Gardner's Cres 36 D5
Garscube Ter 36 A4
Gayfield La 37 G2
Gayfield Pl La 37 G2
Gayfield Sq 37 G2
Gayfield St 37 G2
Gayfield St La 37 G2
Gentle's Entry 37 H4
George IV Br 37 F4
George Sq 37 F6
George Sq La 37 F6
George St 36 E4
Gibson Ter 36 C6
Gifford Pk 37 G6
Gillespie Cres 36 D6
Gillespie St 36 D6
Gilmore Pk 36 D6
Gilmore Pl 36 D7
Gilmour St 37 G5
Gladstone Ter 37 G7
Glencairn Cres 36 C5
Glenfinlas St 36 D4
Glengyle Ter 36 E6
Glenogle Rd 36 D2
Glen St 37 E5
Gloucester La 36 D3
Gloucester Pl 36 D3
Gloucester Sq 36 D3
Gloucester St 36 D3
Gorgie Rd 36 A7
Grange Rd 37 F7
Granville Ter 36 C7
Grassmarket 37 F5
Great King St 37 E3
Great Stuart St 36 D4
Greenhill Ct 36 E7
Greenhill Gdns 36 E7
Greenhill Pl 36 E7
Greenhill Ter 36 E7
Greenside La 37 G3
Greenside Row 37 G3

Green St 37 G2
Greyfriars Pl 37 F5
Grigor Av 36 A1
Grigor Dr 36 A1
Grigor Gdns 36 A1
Grigor Ter 36 A1
Grindlay St 36 E5
Grosvenor Cres 36 C5
Grosvenor Gdns 36 C5
Grosvenor St 36 C5
Grove St 36 D5
Gullan's Cl 37 G4
Guthrie St 37 G5

H
Haddon's Ct 37 G5
Hailes St 36 E6
Halmyre St 37 J1
Hamilton Pl 36 D2
Hamilton's Folly Ms 37 H6
Hammermen's Entry 37 H4
Hanover St 37 F3
Harden Pl 36 C7
Hardwell Cl 37 H6
Harrismith Pl 37 J2
Harrison La 36 B7
Harrison Rd 36 B7
Hartington Gdns 36 D7
Hartington Pl 36 D7
Hart St 37 G2
Hatton Pl 37 F7
Haugh St 36 D2
Hawthornbank La 36 C4
Hawthornden Pl 37 H1
Haymarket 36 C5
Haymarket Ter 36 B5
Haymarket Yards 36 B5
Henderland Rd 36 A5
Henderson Pl 37 E2
Henderson Pl La 36 E2
Henderson Row 36 E2
Henderson Ter 36 B7
Heriot Br 37 F5
Heriot Hill Ter 37 F2
Heriot Pl 37 F5
Heriot Row 36 E3
Hermits Cft 37 H6
High Riggs 36 E5
High Sch Wynd 37 G4
High Sch Yards 37 G5
High St 37 F4
Hill Pl 37 G5
Hillside Cres 37 H2
Hillside St 37 H2
Hill Sq 37 G5
Hill St 36 E3
Hill St La N 36 E3
Hill St La S 36 E4
Holyrood Gait 37 H4
Holyrood Pk Rd 37 H7
Holyrood Rd 37 G4
Home St 36 E6
Hope Pk Cres 37 G6
Hope Pk Ter 37 G6
Hope St 36 D4
Hope St La 36 D4
Hopetoun Cres 37 G2
Hopetoun St 37 G2
Horne Ter 36 C6
Horse Wynd 37 J4
Howden St 37 G5
Howe St 37 E3
Hugh Miller Pl 36 D2
Hunter Sq 37 G4
Huntingdon Pl 37 G2
Hutton Rd 37 H4

I
India Pl 36 D3
India St 36 E3
Infirmary St 37 G5
Inverleith 36 C1
Inverleith Gro 36 C1
Inverleith Pl 36 C1
Inverleith Ter 36 D1
Inverleith Ter La 36 E1
Iona St 37 H1
Ivy Ter 36 A7

J
Jamaica St 36 E3
Jamaica St N La 36 E3
Jamaica St S La 36 E3
Jameson Pl 37 H1
Jeffrey St 37 G4
Johnston Ter 37 E5

K
Keir St 37 F5
Kemp Pl 36 D1
Kerr St 36 D2
Kew Ter 36 A5
Kimmerghame Dr 36 A1
Kimmerghame Vw 36 A1

King's Stables La 37 E5
King's Stables Rd 36 E4
Kirkhill Rd 37 J7
Kyle Pl 37 J3

L
Lady Lawson St 37 E5
Lady Menzies Pl 37 J3
Lady Wynd 37 F5
Lamb's Cl 37 H6
Lansdowne Cres 36 C5
Lauderdale St 37 E7
Lauder Rd 37 G7
Lauriston Gdns 37 E5
Lauriston Pk 37 E5
Lauriston Pl 36 E6
Lauriston St 37 E5
Lawnmarket 37 F4
Leamington Rd 36 D6
Leamington Ter 36 D6
Learmonth Av 36 B2
Learmonth Cres 36 B3
Learmonth Gdn La 36 C3
Learmonth Gdns 36 C3
Learmonth Gdns Ms 36 C3
Learmonth Gro 36 C2
Learmonth Pl 36 C2
Learmonth Ter 36 C3
Learmonth Ter La 36 C3
Learmonth Vw 36 C3
Leith St 37 G3
Leith Wk 37 G3
Lennox St 36 C3
Lennox St La 36 C3
Leslie Pl 36 D3
Leven St 36 E6
Leven Ter 37 E6
Liddesdale Pl 36 E1
Little King St 37 G3
Livingstone Pl 37 G7
Lochend Cl 37 H4
Lochrin Pl 36 E6
Logan St 37 F2
Logie Grn Gdns 37 F1
Logie Grn Ln 37 F1
Logie Grn Rd 37 F1
Logie Mill 37 F1
London Rd 37 J3
London St 37 F2
Lonsdale Ter 37 E6
Lorne Pl 37 J1
Lorne Sq 37 J1
Lorne St 37 J1
Lothian Rd 36 D4
Lothian St 37 G5
Lower Gilmore Pl 36 D6
Lower London Rd 37 J3
Lutton Pl 37 H6
Lynedoch Pl La 36 C4
Lyne St 37 J3

M
McDonald Pl 37 G1
McDonald Rd 37 G1
McDonald St 37 G1
Mackenzie Pl 36 D3
McLeod St 36 A6
McNeill St 36 D6
Magdala Cres 36 B5
Magdala Ms 36 B5
Malta Grn 36 D2
Malta Ter 36 D2
Manor Pl 36 C4
Mansionhouse Rd 37 G7
Marchhall Cres 37 J7
Marchhall Pl 37 J7
Marchhall Rd 37 J7
Marchmont Cres 37 F7
Marchmont Rd 37 F6
Marchmont St 37 E7
Market St 37 F4
Marshall's Ct 37 G3
Marshall St 37 G5
Maryfield 37 J3
Maryfield Pl 37 J3
Meadow La 37 G6
Meadow Pl 37 F7
Melgund Ter 37 E6
Melville Dr 37 E6
Melville St 36 C4
Melville St La 36 D4
Melville Ter 37 G7
Merchant St 37 F5
Merchiston Av 36 C7
Merchiston Gro 36 A7
Merchiston Ms 36 C7
Merchiston Pk 36 C7
Mertoun Pl 36 C7
Meuse La 37 F4
Middlefield 37 H1
Millerfield Pl 37 G7
Miller Row 36 C4
Milton St 37 J3
Minto St 37 H7

Moncrieff Ter 37 G7
Montague St 37 H6
Montgomery St 37 G2
Montgomery St La 37 G2
Montpelier 36 D7
Montpelier Pk 36 D7
Montpelier Ter 36 D7
Montrose Ter 37 J3
Moray Pl 36 D3
Morrison Circ 36 C5
Morrison Cres 36 D5
Morrison Link 36 D5
Morrison St 36 C5
Mound, The 37 F4
Mound Pl 37 F4
Multrees Wk 37 F3
Murano Pl 37 H2
Murdoch Ter 36 C6
Murieston Cres 36 B6
Murieston Cres La 36 B6
Murieston La 36 B7
Murieston Pl 36 B6
Murieston Rd 36 B6
Murieston Ter 36 B6
Myrtle Ter 36 B7

N
Napier Rd 36 C7
Nelson St 37 F2
New Arthur Pl 37 H5
Newington Rd 37 H7
New John's Pl 37 H6
New Skinner's Cl 37 G4
New St 37 G4
Newton St 36 A7
Nicolson Sq 37 G5
Nicolson St 37 G5
Niddry St 37 G4
Niddry St S 37 G5
Nightingale Way 37 F6
North Bk St 37 F4
North Br 37 G4
North Castle St 36 D3
North Charlotte St 36 D3
North Clyde St La 37 F3
Northcote St 36 B6
North E Circ Pl 36 E3
North Pk Ter 36 C2
North Richmond St 37 G5
North St. Andrew La 37 F3
North St. Andrew St 37 F3
North St. David St 37 F3
Northumberland Pl La 37 F3
Northumberland St 37 E3
Northumberland St N E La 37 F3
Northumberland St N W La 37 E3
Northumberland St S E La 37 F3
Northumberland St S W La 37 E3
North Werber Pk 36 A1
North Werber Rd 36 B1
North W Circ Pl 36 D3
Norton Pk 37 J2

O
Old Broughton 37 F2
Old Fishmarket Cl 37 G4
Old Tolbooth Wynd 37 H4
Orchard Bk 36 A3
Orchard Brae 36 B2
Orchard Brae Av 36 B3
Orchard Brae Gdns 36 B3
Orchard Brae Gdns W 36 B2
Orchard Brae W 36 B2
Orchard Cres 36 A3
Orchard Dr 36 A3
Orchard Gro 36 B2
Orchard Pl 36 B2
Orchard Rd 36 A3
Orchard Rd S 36 A3
Orchard Ter 36 A3
Orwell Pl 36 C6
Orwell Ter 36 C6
Oxford St 37 H6
Oxford Ter 36 C3

P
Palmerston Pl 36 C4
Panmure Pl 37 E6
Papermill Wynd 37 G1
Parkside St 37 H6
Parkside Ter 37 H6
Parliament Sq 37 F4
Pembroke Pl 36 B5
Perth St 36 E2
Picardy Pl 37 G3
Pilrig Gdns 37 G1
Pilrig Glebe 37 H1
Pleasance 37 G5

Polwarth Cres 36 C7
Polwarth Gdns 36 C7
Polwarth Pk 36 C7
Polwarth Pl 36 C7
Ponton St 36 D6
Portgower Pl 36 D2
Port Hamilton 36 D6
Potterrow 37 G5
Powderhall Rd 37 F1
Priestfield Rd N 37 J7
Primrose Ter 36 B7
Princes St 36 D4

Q
Queen's Dr 37 H5
Queensferry Rd 36 B3
Queensferry St 36 D4
Queensferry St La 36 D4
Queensferry Ter 36 B3
Queen St 36 E3
Queen St Gdns E 37 F3
Queen St Gdns W 37 E3

R
Raeburn Ms 36 D2
Raeburn Pl 36 D2
Raeburn St 36 D2
Ramsay Gdn 37 F4
Ramsay La 37 F4
Randolph Cres 36 D4
Randolph La 36 D4
Randolph Pl 36 D4
Rankeillor St 37 H6
Ravelston Dykes 36 A4
Ravelston Pk 36 A4
Ravelston Ter 36 B4
Regent Pl 37 J3
Regent Rd 37 G3
Regent Ter 37 H3
Regent Ter Ms 37 H3
Register Pl 37 F3
Reid's Cl 37 H4
Reid Ter 36 D2
Richmond La 37 G5
Richmond Pl 37 G5
Richmond Ter 36 C5
Riego St 36 E5
Rillbank Cres 37 G7
Rillbank Ter 37 G7
Rintoul Pl 36 D2
Ritchie Pl 36 B7
Robertson Av 36 A7
Robertson Gait 36 A7
Robertson's Cl 37 G5
Rodney Pl 37 F2
Rodney St 37 F1
Romero Pl 37 J7
Rosebank Cotts 36 D5
Rosebery Cres 36 C5
Rosebery Cres La 36 C5
Roseburn Av 36 A5
Roseburn Cliff 36 A5
Roseburn Dr 36 A5
Roseburn Gdns 36 A5
Roseburn Maltings 36 A5
Roseburn Ter 36 A5
Rosemount Bldgs 36 D6
Roseneath Pl 37 F7
Roseneath St 37 F7
Roseneath Ter 37 F7
Rose St 36 E4
Rose St N La 36 E4
Rose St S La 36 E4
Rossie Pl 37 J2
Rosslyn Cres 37 G1
Rosslyn Ter 37 H1
Rothesay Ms 36 C4
Rothesay Pl 36 C4
Rothesay Ter 36 C4
Roxburgh Pl 37 G5
Roxburgh St 37 G5
Royal Circ 36 E3
Royal Cres 37 F2
Royal Ter 37 G3
Russell Gdns 36 A5
Russell Rd 36 A5
Rutland Ct La 36 D5
Rutland Sq 36 D4
Rutland St 36 D4

S
St. Andrew Sq 37 F3
St. Bernard's Cres 36 D3
St. Bernard's Row 36 D2
St. Catherine's Pl 37 G7
St. Clair Av 37 J1
St. Clair Pl 37 J1
St. Clair Rd 37 J1
St. Clair St 37 J1
St. Colme St 36 D4
St. David's Pl 36 D5
St. David's Ter 36 D5
St. Giles St 37 F4

St. James Pl 37 G3
St. James Sq 37 G3
St. John's Hill 37 H5
St. John St 37 H4
St. Leonard's Bk 37 H6
St. Leonard's Hill 37 H6
St. Leonard's La 37 H6
St. Leonard's St 37 H6
St. Mary's St 37 G4
St. Patrick Sq 37 G6
St. Stephen Pl 36 D2
St. Stephen St 36 D3
St. Vincent St 36 E2
Salisbury Ms 37 H7
Salisbury Pl 37 H7
Salisbury Rd 37 H7
Saunders St 36 D3
Saxe Coburg Pl 36 D2
Saxe Coburg St 36 D2
Sciennes 37 G7
Sciennes Gdns 37 G7
Sciennes Hill Pl 37 G7
Sciennes Ho Pl 37 G7
Sciennes Pl 37 G7
Sciennes Rd 37 F7
Scotland St 37 F2
Semple St 36 D5
Seton Pl 37 G7
Shandwick Pl 36 D5
Shaw's Pl 37 H1
Shaw's St 37 H1
Shaw's Ter 37 H1
Shrub Pl La 37 H1
Sienna Gdns 37 G7

Silvermills 36 E2
Simon Sq 37 G5
Simpson Loan 37 F6
Sinclair Cl 36 A7
Sinclair Gdns 36 A7
Sinclair Pl 36 A7
Sloan St 37 J1
Smithfield St 36 A7
South Br 37 G4
South Charlotte St 36 E4
South Clerk St 37 H6
South Coll St 37 G5
South E Circ Pl 36 E3
South Gray's Cl 37 G4
South Learmonth Av 36 C3
South Learmonth Gdns 36 C3
South Lorne Pl 37 J1
South Oxford St 37 H7
South St. Andrew St 37 F3
South St. David St 37 F3
South Sloan St 37 J1
Spence St 37 J7
Spey St 37 H1
Spey St La 37 H1
Spey Ter 37 H1
Spittal St 36 E5
Spottiswoode Rd 37 E7
Spottiswoode St 37 F7
Spring Gdns 37 J3
Springwell Pl 36 B6
Stafford St 36 D4
Stanhope Pl 36 B5
Stanhope St 36 B5

Stevenlaw's Cl 37 G4
Stewart Ter 36 A7
Stockbridge 36 E2
Succoth Gdns 36 A4
Succoth Pl 36 A4
Summer Bk 37 F2
Summerhall 37 G6
Summerhall Sq 37 H7
Sunbury Ms 36 C4
Sunbury Pl 36 C4
Sunbury St 36 C4
Sunnyside 37 J2
Sutherland St 36 B5
Sylvan Pl 37 G7

T
Tantallon Pl 37 G7
Tarvit St 36 E6
Tay St 36 C7
Temple Pk Cres 36 C7
Terrars Cft 37 H6
Teviotdale Pl 36 D1
Teviot Pl 37 F5
Thirlestane Rd 37 E7
Thistle Pl 36 C7
Thistle St 37 E3
Thistle St N E La 37 F3
Thistle St N W La 37 E3
Thistle St S W La 37 E3
Thornybauk 36 E6
Torphichen St 36 D5
Tron Sq 37 G4
Tynecastle La 36 B7
Tynecastle Ter 36 A7

Tytler Gdns 37 G4

U
Union St 37 G2
Upper Bow 37 F4
Upper Coltbridge Ter 36 A4
Upper Damside 36 C4
Upper Dean Ter 36 D3
Upper Gilmore Pl 36 D6
Upper Gilmore Ter 36 D6
Upper Gray St 37 H7
Upper Gro Pl 36 D6

V
Valleyfield St 36 E6
Veitch's Sq 36 D2
Victoria St 37 F5
Viewcraig Gdns 37 H4
Viewcraig St 37 H5
Viewforth 36 C6
Viewforth Gdns 36 D7
Viewforth Sq 36 D7
Viewforth Ter 36 D7

W
Walker St 36 C4
Wardlaw Pl 36 A7
Wardlaw St 36 A7
Warrender Pk Cres 36 E7
Warrender Pk Rd 36 E7
Warrender Pk Ter 37 E7
Warriston Cres 37 E1
Warriston Rd 37 E1
Washington La 36 B6

Waterloo Pl 37 G3
Watson Cres 36 B7
Waverley Br 37 F4
Waverley Pk 37 J3
Waverley Pk Ter 37 J3
Waverley Pl 37 J3
Wellington St 37 H2
Wemyss Pl 36 E3
Wemyss Pl Ms 36 D3
West Adam St 37 G5
West Annandale St 37 F1
West App Rd 36 D5
West Bow 37 F5
West Bryson Rd 36 B7
West Castle Rd 36 C7
West Catherine Pl 36 B5
West Coates 36 A5
West Coll St 37 G5
West Crosscauseway 37 G6
West End Pl 36 C6
Wester Coates Av 36 A5
Wester Coates Gdns 36 A5
Wester Coates Pl 36 B5
Wester Coates Rd 36 B5
Wester Coates Ter 36 A5
Westfield St 36 A7
Westhall Gdns 36 D7
West Maitland St 36 C5
West Mill La 36 C4
West Montgomery Pl 37 H2
West Newington Pl 37 H7
West Nicolson St 37 G6
West Norton Pl 37 J3
West Pk Pl 36 C6

West Port 37 E5
West Preston St 37 H7
West Register St 37 F3
West Register St La 37 F3
West Richmond St 37 G5
West Scotland St La 37 F2
West Silvermills La 36 E2
West Tollcross 36 E6
West Wds 36 A1
Wheatfield Pl 36 A7
Wheatfield Rd 36 A7
Wheatfield St 36 A7
Wheatfield Ter 36 A7
Whitehouse Ln 36 E7
White Pk 36 A7
William St 36 C5
William St N E La 36 D4
William St N W La 36 D4
William St S E La 36 D4
William St S W La 36 D5
Windmill La 37 G6
Windmill St 37 G6
Windsor St 37 H2
Windsor St La 37 H2

Y
Yeaman Pl 36 C6
York La 37 G3
York Pl 37 F3
Young St 36 D4
Young St La N 36 E4
Young St La S 36 E4

Glasgow street index

A
Abbotsford Pl 39 E7
Abercromby Dr 39 J5
Abercromby Sq 39 J5
Abercromby St 39 J6
Academy Pk 38 A7
Adams Ct La 39 F5
Adelphi St 39 F6
Admiral St 38 C6
Aird's La 39 G5
Albert Br 39 G6
Albert Dr 38 B7
Albion Gate 39 G4
Albion St 39 G5
Alexander Cres 39 F7
Alexandra Par 39 J3
Allen Glen Pl 39 G3
Anchor La 39 F4
Anderston 38 E4
Anderston Quay 38 C5
Anson St 39 J7
Anthony St 38 D4
Arcadia Pl 39 J6
Arcadia St 39 J6
Argyle St 39 F4
Argyll Arc 39 F4
Ark La 39 J4
Arlington St 38 D2
Armour St 39 J5
Arthur St 38 A2
Ashley La 38 D2
Ashley St 38 D2
Ashton La 38 A1
Ashton Rd 38 A1
Auchentoshan Ter 39 J1

B
Bain St 39 H5
Baird St 39 H2
Balaclava St 38 D4
Baliol La 38 D2
Baliol St 38 D2
Ballantrae Ct 38 D4
Ballater Pl 39 G7
Ballater St 39 F6
Bank St 38 B1
Barrack St 39 J5
Barrington Dr 38 C1
Bath La 38 D3
Bath St 38 D3
Beaumont Gate 38 A1
Bedford La 39 F6
Bedford St 39 E6
Bell St 39 G4
Beltane St 38 D3
Benny Lynch Ct 39 G6
Benthall St 39 G7
Bentinck St 38 B2
Berkeley St 38 C3
Berkeley Ter La 38 C3

Binnie Pl 39 H6
Bishop St 38 D4
Blackburn St 38 B5
Blackfriars St 39 G4
Blackie St 38 B3
Black St 39 H2
Blantyre St 38 A2
Blythswoodhill 38 E3
Blythswood Sq 38 E3
Blythswood St 38 E4
Bothwell La 38 E4
Bothwell La (Hillhead) 38 C1
Bothwell St 38 E4
Braid Sq 38 E1
Braid St 38 E1
Breadalbane St 38 C3
Brechin St 38 C3
Bridgegate 39 F5
Bridge St 39 E6
Bridgeton Cross 39 J6
Bright St 39 J2
Broadford St 39 G1
Broomielaw 38 E5
Broompark Dr 39 J4
Brown St 38 E5
Bruce Rd 38 B7
Brunswick St 39 G4
Buccleuch La 38 E2
Buccleuch St 38 D2
Buchanan St 39 F4
Bunhouse Rd 38 A2
Burnbank Gdns 38 D1
Burnbank La 38 D1
Burnbank Pl 38 D1
Burnbank Ter 38 D1
Burns St 39 E1
Bute Gdns 38 B1
Bute La 38 B1

C
Cadogan St 38 E4
Cadzow St 38 D4
Caledonian Cres 38 C1
Caledonia Rd 39 F7
Caledon La 38 A1
Caledon St 38 A1
Calgary St 39 G2
Cambridge St 39 E3
Camden Ter 39 F7
Canal St 39 G2
Candleriggs 39 G5
Cardwell St 39 E7
Carfrae St 38 A3
Carlton Ct 39 F5
Carlton Pl 39 F5
Carnarvon St 38 D2
Carnoustie Pl 38 D6
Carnoustie St 38 D6
Carrick St 38 E5
Carrington St 38 D1

Castle St 39 H4
Cathcart Rd 39 F7
Cathedral Sq 39 H4
Cathedral St 39 F3
Cavendish Pl 39 E7
Cavendish St 39 E7
Cecil St 38 B1
Cedar Ct 38 E1
Cedar St 38 E1
Centre St 38 E6
Cessnock 38 A5
Chalmers St 39 J5
Charles St 39 J2
Charlotte St 39 H5
Cheapside St 38 D5
Chisolm St 39 G5
Church St 38 A2
Circus Dr 39 J4
Citizen La 39 F4
Clairmont Gdns 38 C2
Claremont Pl 38 C2
Claremont St 38 C3
Claremont Ter 38 C2
Claremont Ter La 38 C2
Clarendon Pl 38 D1
Clarendon St 38 D1
Clayslaps Rd 38 B2
Claythorn Av 39 H6
Claythorn Circ 39 H5
Claythorn Pk 39 H6
Claythorn St 39 J5
Claythorn Ter 39 J5
Cleland La 39 F6
Cleland St 39 F6
Cleveland La 38 D3
Cleveland St 38 D3
Clifford La 38 A6
Clifford Pl 38 A6
Clifford St 38 A6
Cliff Rd 38 C1
Clifton Pl 38 C3
Clifton St 38 C2
Clutha St 38 A6
Clyde Arc 38 B5
Clyde Pl 38 E5
Clydeside Expressway 38 B4
Clyde St 39 F5
Cobden Rd 39 J1
Coburg St 39 E6
Cochrane St 39 G4
College La 39 H4
College St 39 G4
Collins St 39 H4
Commerce St 39 E5
Commercial Ct 39 G6
Commercial Rd 39 G7
Congress Rd 38 B4
Congress Way 38 B4
Cook St 38 E6

Cooperage Pl 38 A3
Corn St 39 E1
Cornwall St S 38 B7
Corunna St 38 B3
Couper Pl 39 G2
Couper St 39 G2
Cowan La 38 C1
Cowan St 38 B1
Cowcaddens 39 F2
Cowcaddens Rd 39 E2
Cownwall St 38 B6
Cragmaddie Ter La 38 B2
Craighall Rd 39 F1
Craigiehall Pl 38 B5
Craigiehall St 38 B5
Cranston Hill 38 C3
Cranston St 38 C4
Cressnock St 38 A5
Crimea St 38 D4
Cromwell La 38 D1
Cromwell St 38 D1
Crownpoint Rd 39 J6
Crown St 39 F7
Cumberland Pl 39 G7
Cumberland St 39 E6

D
Dale Path 39 J7
Dalhouse St 38 E3
Dalhousie La 38 E2
Dalintober St 38 D6
Dalmarnock Rd 39 J7
Dalnair St 38 A2
Derby St 38 B3
Devon Pl 39 E7
Devon St 39 E7
Dixon St 39 F5
Dobbies Ln 39 F2
Dobbie's Ln Pl 39 G3
Dornoch St 39 J6
Dorset St 38 C3
Douglas La 38 E3
Douglas St 38 E4
Dover St 38 C3
Drake St 39 J6
Drury St 39 F4
Duke St 39 H4
Dunblane St 39 F2
Dunchattan Pl 39 J5
Dunchattan St 39 J4
Dundashill 39 F1
Dundas La 39 F3
Dundas St 39 F3
Dunearn St 38 D1
Dunlop St 39 F5
Durham St 38 B6

E
Eaglesham Ct 38 B5

Eaglesham Pl 38 B5
Eagle St 39 F1
Earlston Av 39 J2
Earlston Pl 39 J2
East Bath La 39 F3
East Campbell St 39 H5
Edington St 39 E1
Edwin St 38 B6
Eglinton Ct 39 F6
Elcho St 39 J5
Elderslie St 38 C2
Eldon St 38 C1
Elie St 38 A1
Elliot Pl 38 C4
Elliot St 38 C4
Elmbank Cres 38 D3
Elmbank St 38 D3
Elmbank St La 38 D3
Errol Gdns 39 F6
Esmond St 38 A2
Eton La 38 B1
Exchange Pl 39 F4

F
Falfield St 38 E7
Farnell St 39 E1
Finnieston 38 B3
Finnieston Quay 38 B4
Finnieston Sq 38 C3
Finnieston St 38 C4
Firpark St 39 J3
Firpark Ter 39 J4
Fitzroy La 38 B3
Florence St 39 G6
Forbes Dr 39 J6
Forbes St 39 J5
Fountainwell Av 39 H1
Fountainwell Dr 39 H1
Fountainwell Pl 39 H1
Fountainwell Rd 39 H1
Fountainwell Sq 39 H1
Fountainwell Ter 39 H1
Fox St 39 F5
Francis St 38 E7

G
Gadshill St 39 J2
Gallowgate 39 H5
Garnethill 38 E2
Garnethill St 38 E2
Garnet St 38 D3
Garscube Rd 39 E2
Garth St 39 G4
George Sq 39 F4
George St 39 G4
Gibson St 39 H5
Gibson St (Hillhead) 38 B1
Gilbert St 38 A3
Gilmour Pl 39 G7
Gladstone St 38 D1

Glasgow Br 39 F5
Glassford St 39 G4
Glebe Ct 39 H3
Glebe St 39 H2
Glenbarr St 39 J2
Glenfarg St 38 D1
Glenmavis St 39 E2
Gloucester St 38 D6
Goosedubbs 39 G5
Gorbals 39 G7
Gorbals St 39 F7
Gordon La 39 F4
Gordon St 39 F4
Gourock St 38 E7
Govan Rd 38 A5
Grace St 38 C4
Grafton Pl 39 G3
Graham Sq 39 J5
Graignestock St 39 J6
Granby La 38 B1
Grant St 38 D2
Granville St 38 D3
Gray St 38 B3
Great Dovehill 39 H5
Great George St 38 B1
Green, The 39 J7
Greendyke St 39 G5
Greenhead St 39 J6
Green St 39 J6
Grovepark Ct 38 D1
Grovepark Gdns 38 D1

H
Hallside Pl 39 G7
Handel Pl 39 F7
Hanover St 39 F4
Harley St 38 A6
Harvey St 39 F1
Harvie St 38 B5
Hastie St 38 A2
Haugh Rd 38 A3
Hayfield Ct 39 G7
Hayfield St 39 G7
Herbertson St 39 E6
High Craighall Rd 39 F1
High St 39 G5
Hillhead St 38 B1
Hill St 38 D2
Holland St 38 D3
Holm St 38 E4
Holyrood Cres 38 C1
Holyrood Quad 38 D1
Hopehill Rd 39 D1
Hope St 38 E4
Houldsworth La 38 C3
Houldsworth St 38 C3
Houston Pl 38 C5
Houston St 38 C6
Howard St 39 F5
Hunter St 39 H5

Street	Ref
Huntingdon Rd	39 H1
Huntingdon Sq	39 H1
Hutcheson St	39 G5
Hutchesontown	39 G7
Hutchinson Town Ct	39 G7
Hydepark St	38 C5

I

Street	Ref
India St	38 D3
Ingram St	39 G4

J

Street	Ref
Jamaica St	39 F5
James Morrison St	39 G5
James Nisbet St	39 J3
James St	39 J7
James Watt St	38 E5
Jocelyn Sq	39 G5
John Knox St	39 J4
John St	39 G4

K

Street	Ref
Kelvingrove	38 B2
Kelvingrove St	38 B3
Kelvinhaugh	38 A3
Kelvinhaugh Gate	38 A3
Kelvinhaugh Pl	38 B3
Kelvinhaugh St	38 A3
Kelvin Way	38 B2
Kennedy Path	39 G3
Kennedy St	39 G3
Kent Rd	38 C3
Kent St	39 H5
Keppochhill Pl	39 G1
Keppochhill Way	39 G1
Kerr Dr	39 J6
Kerr Pl	39 J6
Kerr St	39 J6
Kidston Pl	39 F7
Kidston Ter	39 F7
Kilbarchan St	39 E6
Kilbirnie Pl	38 D7
Kilbirnie St	38 D7
Killermont St	39 F3
King George V Br	39 E5
King's Br	39 H7
King's Dr	39 H7
Kingston	38 D6
Kingston St	38 E5
King St	39 G5
Kinning Pk	38 B6
Kinning St	38 D6
Kyle St	39 G2

L

Street	Ref
La Belle Allee	38 C2
La Belle Pl	38 C2
Ladywell St	39 J4
Laidlaw St	38 D6
Laird Pl	39 J7
Lambhill Quad	38 B6
Lambhill St	38 B6
Lanark St	39 H5
Lancefield Quay	38 C4
Lancefield St	38 C4
Landressy Pl	39 J7
Landressy St	39 J7
Langshot St	38 A6
Lansdowne Cres	38 C1
Lansdowne Cres La	38 C1
Larbert St	39 F2
Laurieston	39 F6
Laurieston Rd	39 F7
Lendel Pl	38 A6
Lilybank Gdns	38 A1
Lilybank Gdns La	38 A1
Lilybank Ter	38 B1
Lister St	39 H2
Little Dovehill	39 H5
Little St	38 C4
London Rd	39 G5
Lorne St	38 B5
Lumsden St	38 A3
Lymburn St	38 B2
Lynedoch Cres	38 C2
Lynedoch Cres La	38 C2
Lynedoch Pl	38 C2
Lynedoch St	38 C2
Lynedoch Ter	38 D2

M

Street	Ref
Mcalpine St	38 D5
McAslin Ct	39 H3
Mcaslin St	39 H3
McCulloch St	38 C7
Mcfarlane St	39 H5
McIntosh Ct	39 J4
McIntosh St	39 J4
Mcintyre St	38 D4
MacKeith St	39 J7
MacKinlay St	39 E7
Maclean Sq	38 B5
Maclean St	38 B5
Maclennan St	38 A6
Macleod St	39 H4
McNeil Gdns	39 H7
McNeil St	39 G7
McPhail St	39 J7
McPhater St	39 F2
Mair St	38 B5
Maitland St	39 F2
Malta Ter	39 F7
Manresa Pl	39 E1
Marine Cres	38 C5
Marine Gdns	38 C5
Marlow St	38 C7
Martha St	39 G3
Mart St	39 G5
Mary St	39 F1
Mauchline St	38 E7
Mavisbank Gdns	38 B5
Maxwell Av	38 C7
Maxwell Ct	38 B7
Maxwell Dr	38 B7
Maxwell Gdns	38 A7
Maxwell Grn	38 B7
Maxwell La	38 C7
Maxwell Oval	38 C7
Maxwell Rd	38 C7
Maxwell St	39 F5
Megan Gate	39 J7
Megan St	39 J7
Melbourne St	39 J5
Melrose St	38 D1
Merchant City	39 G4
Merchant La	39 G5
Metropole La	39 F5
Middlesex Gdns	38 B6
Middlesex St	38 B6
Middleton St	38 A5
Midland St	39 E4
Midwharf St	39 F1
Miller St	39 F4
Millroad Dr	39 J5
Millroad Gdns	39 J5
Millroad St	39 H5
Milnpark Gdns	38 B6
Milnpark St	38 B6
Milton St	39 F2
Minerva St	38 B3
Minerva Way	38 B3
Mitchell La	39 F4
Mitchell St	39 F4
Moffat St	39 G7
Moir St	39 H5
Molendinar St	39 H5
Moncur St	39 H5
Montague St	38 C1
Monteith Pl	39 H6
Monteith Row	39 H5
Montrose St	39 G4
Moore St	39 J5
Morrison Ct	39 F4
Morrison St	38 D5
Mosque Av	39 F6
Muslin St	39 J7

N

Street	Ref
Naburn Gate	39 F7
Nairn St	38 A2
Napiershall La	38 D1
Napiershall Pl	38 D1
Napiershall St	38 D1
Nelson Mandela Pl	39 F4
Nelson St	38 E5
Netherby Dr	38 A7
New City Rd	38 D2
Newton St	38 D2
Newton Ter La	38 C3
New Wynd	39 G5
Nicholas St	39 H4
Nicholson St	39 F6
Norfolk Ct	39 F6
Norfolk St	39 F6
North Canal Bk	39 G1
North Canal Bk St	39 F1
North Claremount St	38 C2
North Ct	39 F4
North Ct La	39 F4
North Dr	39 F4
North Frederick Path	39 G3
North Frederick St	39 G4
North Gower St	38 A6
North Hanover St	39 G4
North Portland St	39 G4
North St	38 D2
North Wallace St	39 G2

O

Street	Ref
Oakfield Av	38 B1
Oakfield La	38 B1
Oak St	38 D4
Old Dumbarton Rd	38 A2
Old Rutherglen Rd	39 G6
Old Wynd	39 G5
Oregon Pl	39 G7
Orr St	39 J6
Osborne St	39 F5
Oswald St	39 E5
Otago La	38 C1
Otago La N	38 C1
Otago St	38 B1
Overnewton Pl	38 B3
Overnewton Sq	38 A3
Overnewton St	38 A2
Oxford La	39 F6
Oxford St	39 E5

P

Street	Ref
Pacific Dr	38 A5
Pacific Quay	38 A4
Paisley Rd	38 D5
Paisley Rd W	38 C5
Palmerston Pl	38 B3
Parine St	39 G5
Park Av	38 C1
Park Circ	38 C2
Park Circ La	38 C2
Park Circ Pl	38 C2
Park Dr	38 C1
Park Gdns	38 C2
Park Gdns La	38 C2
Park Gate	38 C2
Parkgrove Ter	38 B2
Parkgrove Ter La	38 B2
Park Quad	38 C2
Park Rd	38 C1
Park St S	38 C2
Park Ter	38 C2
Park Ter E La	38 C2
Park Terrrace La	38 C2
Parsonage Row	39 H4
Parsonage Sq	39 H4
Parson St	39 H3
Paterson St	38 D6
Payne St	39 F1
Pembroke St	38 C3
Percy St	38 A6
Perth St	38 D4
Piccadilly St	38 D4
Pine Pl	39 G7
Pinkston Dr	39 H2
Pinkston Rd	39 H1
Pitt St	38 E4
Plantation Pk Gdns	38 A6
Plantation Sq	38 B5
Port Dundas	39 F1
Port Dundas La	39 F3
Port Dundas Rd	39 F2
Port Eglington	38 D7
Portman St	38 C6
Port St	38 C3
Portugal St	39 F6
Possil Rd	39 E1
Professors Sq	38 B1
Provanhill St	39 J2

Q

Street	Ref
Queen Elizabeth Gdns	39 G7
Queens Cres	38 D1
Queen St	39 F4

R

Street	Ref
Radnor St	38 B2
Raglan St	38 E1
Regent Moray St	38 A2
Renfield La	38 E4
Renfield St	39 F4
Renfrew Ct	39 F3
Renfrew La	39 F3
Renfrew St	38 D2
Renton St	39 F2
Rhymer St	39 J2
Richmond St	39 G4
Ritchie St	38 E7
Riverview Dr	38 D5
Riverview Gdns	38 E5
Riverview Pl	38 D5
Robertson La	38 E4
Robertson St	38 E5
Rodney St	39 E1
Ropework La	39 F5
Rose St	38 E3
Ross St	39 H5
Rottenrow	39 G3
Rottenrow E	39 H4
Royal Bk Pl	39 F4
Royal Cres	38 B3
Royal Ex Ct	39 F4
Royal Ex Sq	39 F4
Royal Ter	38 B2
Royal Ter La	38 B2
Royston	39 J2
Roystonhill	39 J2
Royston Rd	39 J2
Royston Sq	39 J2
Rupert St	38 D1
Rutland Ct	38 C5
Rutland Cres	38 C5
Rutland Pl	38 B5

S

Street	Ref
St. Andrews Cres	38 C7
St. Andrew's La	39 G5
St. Andrews Rd	38 C7
St. Andrews Sq	39 G5
St. Andrews St	39 G5
St. Clair St	38 D1
St. Enoch	39 F5
St. Enoch Sq	39 F4
St. Francis Rigg	39 G7
St. Georges Rd	38 D2
St. Georges Rd	38 D2
St. James Rd	39 G3
St. John's Ct	38 B7
St. John's Quad	38 C7
St. Josephs Vw	39 J2
St. Luke's Pl	39 F6
St. Luke's Ter	39 F6
St. Margaret's Pl	39 G5
St. Marys La	39 F4
St. Mungo Av	39 G3
St. Mungo Pl	39 H3
St. Ninian Ter	39 F6
St. Peters La	38 E4
St. Peters St	38 E2
St. Rollox Brae	39 J1
St. Valentine Ter	39 G7
St. Vincent Cres	38 B3
St. Vincent Cres La	38 B3
St. Vincent La	38 E3
St. Vincent Pl	39 F4
St. Vincent St	38 C3
St. Vincent Ter	38 C3
Salisbury La	39 F7
Salisbury St	39 F7
Salkeld St	38 E7
Saltmarket	39 G5
Sandiefield Rd	39 F7
Sandyford Pl La	38 C3
Sandyford St	38 A3
Saracen Head Rd	39 H5
Sauchiehall La	38 E3
Sauchiehall St	38 B2
Savoy St	39 J7
Sawmillfield St	39 E1
Scotland St	38 C6
Scotland St W	38 B6
Scott St	38 E3
Seamore St	38 D1
Seaward La	38 C5
Seaward Pl	38 C6
Seaward St	38 C6
Shaftesbury St	38 D3
Shamrock St	38 E2
Shields Rd	38 C6
Shipbank La	39 G5
Shuttle St	39 G4
Sighthill	39 H1
Silverfir St	39 G7
Silvergrove St	39 J6
Snowdon St	39 G7
Somerset Pl Ms	38 C2
South Ex Ct	39 F4
South Frederick St	39 G4
Southpark Av	38 B1
Southpark La	38 B1
South Portland St	39 F5
Southside Cres	39 F7
South Woodside Rd	38 C1
Spiers Wf	39 F1
Spoutmouth	39 H5
Springburn Rd	39 J2
Springfield Ct	39 F4
Springfield Quay	38 C5
Spring Wynd	39 G7
Stafford St	39 G2
Stanley St	38 C6
Stanley St La	38 C6
Steel St	39 G5
Stevenson St	39 J6
Stewart St	39 F2
Stirlingfauld Pl	39 F7
Stirling Rd	39 H3
Stobcross Rd	38 A3
Stobcross St	38 C4
Stockwell Pl	39 F5
Stockwell St	39 F5
Stromness St	38 E7
Suffolk St	39 H5
Surrey St	39 F7
Sussex St	38 B6
Sutherland La	38 A1
Swan St	39 G2
Sydney St	39 J5

T

Street	Ref
Taylor Pl	39 H3
Taylor St	39 H4
Templeton St	39 J6
Teviot St	38 A3
Thistle St	39 G6
Thistle Ter	39 F7
Thornbank St	38 A3
Thurso St	38 A2
Tobago Pl	39 J5
Tobago St	39 J6
Toll La	38 C5
Tontine La	39 G5
Torness St	38 A1
Tower St	38 B6
Townhead	39 G2
Townsend St	39 F2
Tradeston	38 E6
Tradeston St	38 E6
Trongate	39 G5
Tullis Ct	39 J7
Tullis St	39 J7
Tunnel St	38 B4
Tureen St	39 J5
Turnbull St	39 G5
Turnlaw St	39 H7
Turriff St	39 E7
Tyndrum St	39 F2

U

Street	Ref
Union Pl	39 F4
Union St	39 F4
Unity Pl	38 E1
University Av	38 A1
University Gdns	38 A1
University Pl	38 A1

V

Street	Ref
Vermont St	38 B6
Victoria Br	39 F5
Viewfield La	38 B1
Vinter St	39 F1
Virginia Pl	39 G4
Virginia St	39 G4

W

Street	Ref
Waddell Ct	39 G6
Waddell St	39 G7
Wallace St	38 D5
Walls St	39 G4
Walmer Cres	38 A6
Warnock St	39 J3
Warroch St	38 D5
Washington St	38 D5
Waterloo La	39 E4
Waterloo St	38 E4
Waterside Pl	39 H7
Waterside St	39 G7
Watson St	39 G5
Watt St	38 C6
Weaver St	39 H4
Wellcroft Pl	39 E7
Wellington La	38 E4
Wellington St	39 E4
Wellpark St	39 J4
Westbank La	38 B1
Westbank Quad	38 B1
West Campbell St	38 E4
West End Pk St	38 C2
West George La	38 E3
West George St	38 E3
West Graham St	38 E2
West Greenhill Pl	38 B3
West Nile St	39 F4
West Prince's La	38 C1
West Princes St	38 C1
West Regent La	38 E3
West Regent St	38 E3
West St	38 D7
Whitehall St	38 D4
William St	38 D3
Willowbank Cres	38 C1
Willowbank St	38 C2
Wilson St	39 G4
Windsor St	38 D1
Windsor Ter	38 D1
Wishart St	39 J4
Woodlands Dr	38 C1
Woodlands Gate	38 C2
Woodlands Rd	38 C1
Woodlands Ter	38 C2
Woodrow Circ	38 A7
Woodrow Pl	38 A7
Woodrow Rd	38 A7
Woodside Cres	38 D2
Woodside Pl	38 C2
Woodside Pl La	38 C2
Woodside Ter	38 C2
Woodside Ter La	38 C2

Y

Street	Ref
Yorkhill	38 B2
Yorkhill Par	38 A2
Yorkhill St	38 A3
York St	38 E5

Leeds street index

A

Street	Ref
Abbey St	40 C3
Abbott Ct	40 A3
Abbott Rd	40 A4
Abbott Vw	40 A3
Admiral St	41 E7
Aire St	40 D4
Albion Pl	41 E3
Albion St	41 E3
Alexander St	40 E3
Alexandra Gro	40 B1
Alexandra Rd	40 A1
Alma St	41 H2
Anderson Av	41 H1
Anderson Mt	41 H1
Apex Vw	40 E6
Apex Way	41 E6
Appleton Cl	41 J3
Appleton Ct	41 J3
Appleton Sq	41 J3
Appleton Way	41 J3
Archery Pl	40 D1
Archery Rd	40 D1
Archery St	40 E1
Archery Ter	40 E1
Armley Rd	40 A3
Armouries Rd	41 G5
Artist St	40 B4
Ascot Ter	41 J4
Ashley Av	41 J1
Ashley Rd	41 J1
Ashley Ter	41 J1
Ashton Av	41 J1
Ashton Gro	41 J1
Ashton Mt	41 J1
Ashton Pl	41 J1
Ashton Ter	41 J1
Ashton Vw	41 J1
Ashville Vw	40 A1
Assembly St	41 F4
Atkinson St	41 G6
Autumn Av	40 B1
Autumn Gro	40 B1
Autumn Pl	40 B1
Autumn St	40 B1
Autumn Ter	40 B1
Avenue, The	41 G4
Aysgarth Cl	41 J4

Street	Ref	Street	Ref
Aysgarth Dr	41 J4	Burley Lo Pl	40 B2
Aysgarth Pl	41 J4	Burley Lo Rd	40 A1
Aysgarth Wk	41 J4	Burley Lo St	40 B2
B		Burley Lo Ter	40 B1
Back Ashville Av	40 A1	Burley Pl	40 A2
Back Hyde Ter	40 C2	Burley Rd	40 A1
Back Row	40 E5	Burley St	40 C3
Balm Pl	40 C6	**Burmantofts**	
Balm Wk	40 C6	Burmantofts St	41 H3
Bank St	41 E4	Burton Row	41 G3
Baron Cl	40 C7	Burton St	41 E7
Barrack St	41 F1	Burton Way	41 E7
Barran Ct	41 H1	Butterfield St	41 J2
Barton Gro	40 D7	Butterley St	41 H4
Barton Mt	40 D7	Butts Ct	41 F6
Barton Pl	40 C7	Byron St	41 E3
Barton Rd	40 C7	**C**	
Barton Ter	40 D7	Cain Cl	41 H4
Barton Vw	40 C7	Call La	41 F4
Bath Rd	40 D5	Calls, The	41 F4
Bayswater Vw	41 H1	Calverley St	40 D2
Beamsley Gro	40 A1	Cambrian St	40 D7
Beamsley Mt	40 A1	Cambrian Ter	40 D7
Beamsley Pl	40 A1	Canal Pl	40 B4
Beamsley Ter	40 A1	Canal St	40 A3
Beckett St	41 H3	Canal Wf	40 D4
Bedford St	40 E3	Carberry Pl	40 A1
Beech Gro Ter	40 D1	Carberry Rd	40 A1
Belgrave St	41 E3	Carberry Ter	40 A1
Belinda St	41 H7	Carlisle Rd	41 G5
Belle Vue Rd	40 B2	Carlton Carr	41 E1
Bell St	41 G3	Carlton Ct	40 A7
Belmont Gro	40 D2	Carlton Gdns	41 E1
Benson St	41 F1	Carlton Gate	41 E1
Benyon Pk Way	40 A7	Carlton Gro	41 E1
Berking Av	41 J3	Carlton Hill	41 E1
Bertrand St	40 C6	Carlton Pl	41 E1
Bexley Av	41 H1	Carlton Ri	41 E1
Bexley Gro	41 J1	Carlton Twrs	41 F1
Bexley Mt	41 H1	Carlton Vw	41 E1
Bexley Pl	41 H1	Castle St	40 D3
Bexley Rd	41 J1	Castleton Cl	40 B4
Bexley Ter	41 J1	Castleton Rd	40 A3
Bingley St	40 C3	Cautley Rd	41 J5
Bishopgate St	40 E4	Cavalier App	41 H5
Bismarck Dr	40 E7	Cavalier Cl	41 H5
Bismarck St	40 E7	Cavalier Ct	41 H5
Black Bull St	41 F5	Cavalier Gdns	41 H5
Blackman La	40 E1	Cavalier Gate	41 H5
Blandford Gdns	40 D1	Cavalier Ms	41 H5
Blandford Gro	40 D1	Cavalier Vw	41 H5
Blayds St	41 H4	Cavendish Rd	40 D1
Blayd's Yd	41 E4	Cavendish St	40 C3
Blenheim Av	40 E1	Cemetery Rd	40 C7
Blenheim Ct	40 E1	Central Rd	41 F4
Blenheim Cres	40 E1	Central St	40 D3
Blenheim Gro	40 E1	Chadwick St	41 F5
Blenheim Sq	40 E1	Chadwick St S	41 G5
Blenheim Vw	40 D1	Chantrell Ct	41 F4
Blenheim Wk	40 D1	Charles Av	41 J5
Blundell St	40 D2	Charlton Gro	41 J4
Boar La	40 E4	Charlton Pl	41 J4
Bodley Ter	40 A2	Charlton Rd	41 J4
Bond St	40 E3	Charlton St	41 J4
Boundary Pl	41 G1	Cherry Pl	41 G2
Boundary St	41 G1	Cherry Row	41 G2
Bourse, The	41 E4	Chesney Av	41 F7
Bowling Grn Ter	40 D6	Chiswick St	40 A2
Bowman La	41 F4	Chorley La	40 D2
Bow St	41 G4	Churchill Gdns	40 E1
Bracken Ct	40 A6	Church La	41 F4
Braithwaite St	40 C5	City Sq	40 E4
Brancepeth Pl	40 B4	City Wk	40 E5
Brandon Rd	40 C2	Claremont Av	40 C2
Brandon St	40 B4	Claremont Gro	40 C2
Branksome Pl	40 B1	Claremont Vw	40 C2
Brick St	41 G4	Clarence Rd	41 G5
Bridge Ct	40 C5	Clarendon Pl	40 C1
Bridge End	41 E4	Clarendon Rd	40 C1
Bridge Rd	40 C5	Clarendon Way	40 D2
Bridge St	41 F3	Clark Av	41 J4
Bridgewater Rd	41 H6	Clark Cres	41 J4
Briggate	41 E4	Clark Gro	41 J5
Brignall Garth	41 J2	Clark La	41 H5
Brignall Way	41 H2	Clark Mt	41 J4
Bristol St	41 G2	Clark Rd	41 J5
Britannia St	40 D4	Clark Row	41 J5
Broadway Av	40 A1	Clark Ter	41 J4
Brookfield St	41 G6	Clark Vw	41 J5
Brown Av	40 B7	Clay Pit La	41 E2
Brown La E	40 B6	Cleveleys Av	40 C7
Brown La W	40 A6	Cleveleys Mt	40 C7
Brown Pl	40 B7	Cleveleys Rd	40 C7
Brown Rd	40 B7	Cleveleys St	40 C7
Bruce Gdns	40 B4	Cleveleys Ter	40 C7
Bruce Lawn	40 B4	Cloberry St	40 C1
Brunswick Ct	41 F3	Close, The	41 G4
Brunswick Ter	41 E2	Cloth Hall St	41 F4
Brussels St	41 G4	Clyde App	40 A5
Buckton Cl	40 C7	Clyde Gdns	40 B5
Buckton Mt	40 C7	Clyde Vw	40 A5
Buckton Vw	40 C7	Coleman St	40 C4
Burley	40 A1	Colenso Gdns	40 C7
Colenso Mt	40 B2	Duncombe St	40 C3
Colenso Pl	40 C7	Duxbury Ri	40 E1
Colenso Rd	40 B2	Dyer St	41 F3
Colenso Ter	40 B1	**E**	
Colville Ter	40 A2	East Fld St	41 H4
Commercial St	41 E3	Eastgate	41 F3
Compton Av	41 J1	East King St	41 G4
Compton Cres	41 J1	East Par	41 E3
Compton Gro	41 J1	East Pk Dr	41 J4
Compton Mt	41 J1	East Pk Gro	41 J4
Compton Pl	41 J1	East Pk Mt	41 J4
Compton Rd	41 J1	East Pk Par	41 J4
Compton St	41 J1	East Pk Pl	41 J4
Compton Ter	41 J1	East Pk Rd	41 J4
Compton Vw	41 J1	East Pk Ter	41 J4
Concordia St	41 E4	East Pk Vw	41 J4
Concord St	41 F2	East St	41 G4
Consort St	40 C2	Easy Rd	41 H5
Consort Ter	40 C2	Ebor Mt	40 B1
Consort Vw	40 B2	Ebor Pl	40 B1
Consort Wk	40 C2	Ebor St	40 B1
Constance Gdns	40 E1	Edgware Av	41 H1
Constance Way	40 E1	Edgware Gro	41 H1
Cookridge St	40 E3	Edgware Mt	41 H1
Copley Hill	40 A5	Edgware Pl	41 H1
Copley Hill Way	40 A6	Edgware Row	41 H1
Copley St	40 A5	Edgware St	41 H1
Copperfield Av	41 J5	Edgware Ter	41 H1
Copperfield Cres	41 J5	Edgware Vw	41 H1
Copperfield Gro	41 J5	Edward St	41 F3
Copperfield Mt	41 J5	Edwin Rd	40 B1
Copperfield Pl	41 J5	Eighth Av	40 A5
Copperfield Row	41 J5	Elland Rd	40 C7
Copperfield Ter	41 J5	Elland Ter	40 D6
Copperfield Vw	41 J5	Ellerby La	41 H5
Copperfield Wk	41 J5	Ellerby Rd	41 G4
Copperfield Dr	41 J5	Elmtree La	41 G7
Cotton St	41 G4	Elmwood La	41 F2
Coupland Pl	40 D7	Elmwood Rd	41 E2
Coupland Rd	40 D7	Elsworth St	40 A4
Cowper Av	41 J1	Enfield Av	41 G1
Cowper Cres	41 J1	Enfield St	41 G1
Cowper Rd	41 J1	Enfield Ter	41 G1
Cromer Pl	40 C1	Euston Gro	40 B7
Cromer Rd	40 C1	Euston Mt	40 B7
Cromer St	40 C1	Euston Ter	40 B7
Cromer Ter	40 C2	Everleigh St	41 J3
Cromwell Mt	41 G2	**F**	
Cromwell St	41 G3	Far Cft Ter	40 A5
Crosby Pl	40 C6	Fewston Av	41 H5
Crosby Rd	40 C7	Fewston Ct	41 J5
Crosby St	40 C6	Finsbury Rd	40 D2
Crosby Ter	40 C6	First Av	40 A4
Crosby Vw	40 C6	Firth St	41 G2
Cross Aysgarth Mt	41 H4	Firth Ter	41 G2
Cross Belgrave St	41 F3	Fish St	41 F3
Cross Catherine St	41 H4	Flax Pl	41 G4
Cross Grn	41 J6	Florence Av	41 J1
Cross Grn App	41 J6	Florence Gro	41 J1
Cross Grn Av	41 H5	Florence Mt	41 J1
Cross Grn Cl	41 J6	Florence Pl	41 J1
Cross Grn Cres	41 H5	Florence St	41 J1
Cross Grn Dr	41 J6	Folly La	40 D7
Cross Grn Garth	41 J6	Forster St	41 G6
Cross Grn La	41 H5	Foundry St (Holbeck)	40 D5
Cross Grn Ri	41 J6	Foundry St (Quarry Hill)	41 G2
Cross Grn Way	41 J6	Fountain St	41 E3
Cross Ingram Rd	40 C2	Fourteenth Av	40 A5
Cross Kelso Rd	40 C2	Fourth Ct	40 C5
Cross Mitford Rd	40 A4	Fox Way	41 H6
Cross Stamford St	41 G2	Fraser St	41 J2
Cross York St	41 F4	Frederick Av	41 J5
Crown Ct	40 E4	Front Row	40 D5
Crown Pt Rd	41 F5	Front St	40 D5
Crown St	41 F4	**G**	
Croydon St	40 B5	Gardeners Ct	40 D5
Cudbear St	41 F5	Gargrave App	40 E1
Czar St	40 C5	Gargrave Pl	40 C3
D		Garth, The	41 H2
Danby Wk	40 D2	Garton Av	41 J4
David St	40 D5	Garton Gro	41 J4
Dene Ho Ct	40 E1	Garton Rd	41 J4
Denison Rd	40 C3	Garton Ter	41 J4
Dent St	41 H4	Garton Vw	41 J4
Derwent Pl	40 D5	Gelderd Pl	40 B5
Devon Cl	40 D1	Gelderd Rd	40 A7
Devon Rd	40 D1	George St	41 F3
Dewsbury Rd	41 E6	Gibraltar Island Rd	41 F4
Dial St	41 H5	Gilpin Pl	40 A5
Disraeli Gdns	40 E7	Gilpin St	40 A5
Disraeli Ter	40 E7	Gilpin Ter	40 A5
Dock St	41 F4	Gilpin Vw	40 A5
Dolly La	41 G2	Glasshouse St	41 F6
Dolphin Ct	41 H4	Gledhow Mt	41 H1
Dolphin St	41 H4	Gledhow Pl	41 H1
Domestic Rd	40 B6	Gledhow Rd	41 H1
Domestic St	40 C5	Gledhow Ter	41 H1
Donisthorpe St	41 G6		
Drive, The	41 G4		
Driver Ter	40 B5		
Dudley Way	41 E3		
Duke St	41 F3		
Duncan St	41 E4		

Street	Ref	Street	Ref
Glencoe Vw	40 C3	Ingram Gdns	40 C6
Glensdale Gro	40 E1	Ingram Rd	40 C7
Glensdale Mt	41 J4	Ingram Row	40 E5
Glensdale Rd	41 J4	Ingram St	40 E5
Glensdale St	41 J4	Ingram Vw	40 C6
Glensdale Ter	41 J4	Inner Ring Rd	40 E2
Glenthorpe Av	41 J3	Ivory St	41 F6
Glenthorpe Cres	41 J3	**J**	
Glenthorpe Ter	41 J3	Jack La	40 D6
Globe Rd	40 C4	Jenkinson Cl	40 D6
Gloucester Ter	40 A4	Jenkinson Lawn	40 D6
Goodman St	41 G6	John Smeaton Viaduct	41 G6
Gotts Rd	40 C4	Joseph St	41 G7
Gower St	41 F3	Junction St	41 F5
Grace St	40 D3	**K**	
Grafton St	41 F2	Keeton St	41 H3
Grange Cl	41 G7	Kelsall Av	40 B1
Grange Rd	41 G7	Kelsall Gro	40 B2
Grant Av	41 G1	Kelsall Pl	40 B1
Granville Rd	41 H2	Kelsall Rd	40 B1
Grape St	41 F7	Kelsall Ter	40 B1
Grasmere Cl	40 A5	Kelso Gdns	40 C1
Grassmere Rd	40 A5	Kelso Rd	40 C1
Great George St	40 D3	Kelso St	40 C2
Great Wilson St	40 E5	Kendal Bk	40 C2
Greek St	40 E3	Kendal Cl	40 C2
Greenfield Rd	41 H4	Kendal Gro	40 C2
Green La	40 A5	Kendal La	40 C2
Grosvenor Hill	41 E1	Kendell St	41 F4
H		Kenneth St	40 B6
Hall Gro	40 B1	Kepler Gro	41 H1
Hall La	40 A4	Kepler Mt	41 H1
Hall Pl	41 H4	Kepler Ter	41 H1
Hanover Av	40 C2	Kidacre St	41 F5
Hanover La	40 D3	Kildare Ter	40 B5
Hanover Mt	40 C2	King Charles St	41 E3
Hanover Sq	40 C2	King Edward St	41 F3
Hanover Wk	40 C3	Kings Av	40 B2
Harewood St	41 F3	King's Rd	40 B1
Harold Av	40 A1	Kingston Ter	40 D1
Harold Gro	40 A1	King St	40 D4
Harold Mt	40 A1	Kippax Pl	41 H4
Harold Pl	40 A1	Kirkgate	41 F4
Harold Rd	40 A1	Kirkstall Rd	40 A2
Harold St	40 A1	Kitson Rd	41 G6
Harold Ter	40 A1	Kitson St	41 H4
Harold Vw	40 A1	Knowsthorpe Cres	41 H5
Harold Wk	40 A1	Knowsthorpe La	41 J6
Harper St	41 F4	**L**	
Harrison St	41 F3	Ladybeck Cl	41 F3
Hartwell Rd	40 B1	Lady La	41 F3
Haslewood Cl	41 H3	Lady Pit La	40 D7
Haslewood Ct	41 H3	Lands La	41 E3
Haslewood Dene	41 H3	Lane, The	41 G4
Haslewood Dr	41 H3	Larchfield Rd	41 G6
Haslewood Ms	41 J3	Latchmore Rd	40 A7
Haslewood Pl	41 H3	Laura St	40 C5
Haslewood Sq	41 H3	Lavender Wk	41 H4
Hawkins Dr	41 E1	Leathley Rd	41 F6
Headrow, The	40 D3	Leathley St	41 F6
Heaton's Ct	41 E4	Leicester Cl	40 E1
Hedley Chase	40 A4	Leicester Gro	40 E1
Hedley Gdns	40 A4	Leicester Pl	40 D1
Hedley Grn	40 A4	Leighton St	40 D3
High	41 G7	Leodis Ct	40 D5
High Ct	41 F4	Leylands Rd	41 G2
High Ct La	41 F4	Lifton Pl	40 C1
Hillary Pl	40 D1	Lincoln Grn Rd	41 G2
Hillidge Rd	41 F7	Lincoln Rd	41 G2
Hillidge Sq	41 F7	Lindsey Ct	41 H2
Hill Top Pl	40 B1	Lindsey Gdns	41 H2
Hill Top St	40 B1	Lindsey Rd	41 H2
Hirst's Yd	41 F4	Lisbon St	40 D3
Holbeck	40 D5	Little King St	40 E4
Holbeck La	40 C5	Little Queen St	40 D4
Holbeck Moor Rd	40 C6	Little Woodhouse St	40 D2
Holdforth Cl	40 A4	Livinia Gro	40 E1
Holdforth Gdns	40 A4	Lodge St	40 D1
Holdforth Grn	40 A4	Lofthouse Pl	40 E1
Holdforth Pl	40 A4	Londesboro Gro	41 J4
Holmes St	41 E5	Long Causeway	41 H6
Holroyd St	41 G1	Long Cl La	41 H4
Hope Rd	41 G3	Lord St	40 C5
Howden Gdns	40 B1	Lord Ter	40 B5
Howden Pl	40 B1	Lovell Pk Cl	41 F2
Hudson Rd	41 J1	Lovell Pk Gate	41 F2
Hudswell Rd	41 F7	Lovell Pk Hill	41 F2
Hunslet	41 G7	Lovell Pk Rd	41 F2
Hunslet Grn Way	41 F7	Lovell Pk Vw	41 F2
Hunslet Hall Rd	40 E7	Lower Basinghall St	40 E3
Hunslet La	41 F5	Lower Brunswick St	41 F2
Hunslet Rd	41 F4	Low Flds Av	40 B7
Hyde Pk Cl	40 B1	Low Flds Rd	40 A7
Hyde Pk Rd	40 B1	Low Flds Way	40 B7
Hyde Pl	40 C2	Low Fold	41 G5
Hyde St	40 C2	Low Rd	41 G7
Hyde Ter	40 C2	Low Whitehouse Row	41 G6
I		Ludgate Hill	41 F3
Infirmary St	40 E3	Lyddon Ter	40 C1
Ingram Cl	40 C6	Lydgate	41 J2
Ingram Cres	40 B7		

Lydia St 41 F3

M
Mabgate 41 G3
Mabgate Grn 41 G3
Macaulay St 41 G3
Maitland Pl 40 D7
Maltings Rd 41 F7
Malvern Gro 40 D7
Malvern Ri 40 D7
Malvern Rd 40 C7
Malvern St 40 C7
Malvern Vw 40 C7
Manor Rd 40 D5
Manor St 41 G1
Mark La 41 E3
Marlborough Gdns 40 D1
Marlborough Gro 40 D1
Marlborough St 40 C3
Marlborough Twrs 40 C3
Marshall St 40 D5
Marsh La 41 G4
Maude St 41 F4
May Ter 41 H5
Meadowcroft Ms 41 H4
Meadow La 41 E5
Meadow Rd 40 E6
Melbourne St 41 F2
Merrion Pl 41 F3
Merrion St 41 E3
Merrion Way 41 E2
Meynell App 40 C6
Middleton Av 41 J2
Milford Pl 40 A2
Millgarth St 41 F3
Mill Grn 40 B5
Mill Hill 41 E4
Mill St 41 G4
Millwright St 41 G2
Milner Gdns 41 H5
Milnes St 40 B5
Mitford Rd 40 A4
Mitford Vw 40 A4
Moor Cres 41 E7
Moor Cres Chase 41 E7
Moorland Av 40 B1
Moorland Rd 40 B1
Moor Rd 41 E7
Moorside Maltings 41 E7
Moor Vw 40 D6
Moorville Cl 40 D7
Moorville Ct 40 D7
Moorville Gro 40 D7
Moorville Rd 40 D7
Mount Preston St 40 C2
Mulberry St 41 F6
Mullins Ct 41 H5
Mushroom St 41 G2

N
Naseby Garth 41 G2
Naseby Ter 41 H3
National Rd 41 H6
Navigation Wk 41 F4
Neptune St 41 G4
Neville St 40 E4
New Briggate 41 F3
New Craven Gate 41 F6
New La 40 E5
New Mkt St 41 F4
New Princess St 40 D6
New Sta St 40 E4
New York Rd 41 G3
New York St 41 F4
Nickleby Rd 41 J3

Nile St 41 F3
Nineveh Gdns 40 D6
Nineveh Par 40 D6
Nineveh Rd 40 C6
Nippet La 41 H3
Normanton Gro 40 C7
Normanton Pl 40 D7
Nortech Cl 41 G1
Northcote Cres 40 E7
Northcote Dr 40 D7
Northcote Grn 40 D7
North Ct 41 F3
Northern St 40 D4
North St 41 F3

O
Oak Rd 40 A4
Oatland Cl 41 F1
Oatland Ct 41 F1
Oatland Dr 41 F1
Oatland Gdns 41 F1
Oatland Grn 41 F1
Oatland Hts 41 F1
Oatland La 41 E1
Oatland Rd 41 E1
Oatland Twrs 41 F1
O'Grady Sq 41 H4
Old Mill La 41 H7
Oval, The 41 G7
Oxford Pl 40 D3
Oxford Row 40 D3
Oxley St 41 J4
Oxton Mt 41 J3
Oxton Way 41 J3

P
Parade, The 41 G4
Park Cross St 40 D3
Parkfield St 41 E6
Park La 40 C3
Park Par 41 J5
Park Pl 40 D3
Park Row 40 E3
Park Sq E 40 D3
Park Sq N 40 D3
Park Sq S 40 D3
Park Sq W 40 D3
Park St 40 D3
Park Vw Rd 40 A1
Pearson St 41 F6
Penny La Way 41 F7
Pilot St 41 G2
Pitt Row 41 E4
Place's Rd 41 H4
Plaid Row 41 H3
Playhouse Sq 41 G3
Pleasant Mt 40 C6
Pleasant Pl 40 C6
Pleasant Ter 40 C6
Pontefract Av 41 J4
Pontefract La 41 H3
Pontefract La Cl 41 H4
Pontefract St 41 H4
Portland Cres 40 E2
Portland Gate 40 E2
Portland St 40 D3
Portland Way 40 E2
Pottery Rd 41 F7
Prosper St 41 G2
Providence Pl 41 E2
Pym St 41 G6

Q
Quarry Hill 41 G3
Quebec St 40 D3

Queen Sq 41 E2
Queens Rd 40 B1
Queen St 40 D4

R
Radnor St 40 B5
Railway St 41 G4
Raincliffe Gro 41 J3
Raincliffe Rd 41 J3
Raincliffe St 41 J3
Recreation Cres 40 C7
Recreation Gro 40 C7
Recreation Mt 40 C7
Recreation Pl 40 C7
Recreation Row 40 C7
Recreation St 40 C7
Recreation Ter 40 C7
Recreation Vw 40 C7
Rectory St 41 H2
Redshaw Rd 40 A5
Regent St 41 G3
Regent Ter 40 B1
Rhodes Ter 40 A5
Richmond Hill App 41 H4
Richmond Hill Cl 41 H4
Richmond St 41 G4
Rickard St 40 C5
Rider St 41 G3
Rigton App 41 H3
Rigton Cl 41 H3
Rigton Dr 41 H3
Rigton Grn 41 H3
Rigton Lawn 41 H3
Rigton Ms 41 H3
Rillbank La 40 B2
Roscoe St 41 G1
Rosebank Gdns 40 B2
Rosebank Rd 40 B2
Rosebud Wk 41 G1
Roseville Rd 41 G1
Roseville St 41 H1
Rossington St 40 E3
Roundhay Rd 41 G1
Roxby Cl 41 H2
Royal Pk Av 40 B1
Royal Pk Gro 40 B1
Royal Pk Rd 40 A1
Royal Pk Ter 40 B1
Ruby St 41 G2
Runswick Av 40 C6
Runswick Pl 40 C6
Runswick St 40 C6
Runswick Ter 40 C6
Russell St 40 E3
Rydall Pl 40 C6
Rydall St 40 C6
Rydall Ter 40 C6

S
Sackville St 41 F1
St. Andrew's St 40 C3
St. Barnabas Rd 40 E5
St. Georges Rd 40 D2
St. Helen's St 41 G6
St. Hilda's Av 41 J5
St. Hilda's Cres 41 H5
St. Hilda's Gro 41 J5
St. Hilda's Mt 41 J5
St. Hilda's Pl 41 J5
St. Hilda's Rd 41 J5
St. John's Av 40 C1
St. John's Cl 40 B1
St. John's Gro 40 B1
St. John's Rd 40 B2
St. Luke's Cescent 40 D7

St. Luke's Cres 40 D7
St. Luke's Grn 40 D7
St. Luke's Rd 40 D7
St. Luke's St 40 D7
St. Mark's Av 40 D1
St. Mark's Rd 40 D1
St. Mark's St 40 D1
St. Mary's Cl 40 A5
St. Mary's St 41 G3
St. Matthew's St 40 C6
St. Matthias St 40 A1
St. Matthias Ter 40 A1
St. Paul's St 40 D3
St. Peter's Ct 41 E7
St. Peter's Pl 41 G3
St. Peter's Sq 41 G3
St. Stephen's Ct 41 H3
St. Stephen's Rd 41 H3
Salem Pl 41 F5
Sandlewood Cl 40 D6
Sandlewood Grn 40 D6
Sardinia St 41 F6
Saville Grn 41 J3
Saxton La 41 G4
Sayner La 41 G5
Sayner Rd 41 F5
Scargill Cl 41 H2
Scarth Av 41 J1
Second Av 40 A4
Seminary St 40 D2
Severn Way 41 H7
Shafton La 40 C6
Shafton Pl 40 C6
Shafton St 40 C6
Shafton Vw 40 C6
Shakespeare App 41 H2
Shakespeare Av 41 H2
Shakespeare Cl 41 J2
Shakespeare Gdns 41 J2
Shakespeare Lawn 41 H2
Shakespeare St 41 J1
Shannon Rd 41 H3
Shannon St 41 G3
Sheaf St 41 F5
Sheepscar Ct 41 F1
Sheepscar Gro 41 F2
Sheepscar St N 41 F1
Sheepscar St S 41 F1
Siddal St 40 D5
Sidney St 41 F3
Silver St 40 D5
Skinner La 41 F2
Skinner St 40 C3
Somers St 40 D3
South Accommodation Rd 41 G6
South Par 40 E3
Sovereign St 40 E4
Spence La 40 B5
Spenceley St 40 D1
Spinney, The 41 H4
Spinneyfield Ct 41 H4
Spring Cl Av 41 H5
Spring Cl Gdns 41 H5
Spring Cl St 41 H5
Spring Cl Wk 41 H5
Springfield Mt 40 C2
Spring Gro Ter 40 A1
Spring Gro Vw 40 B1
Spring Gro Wk 40 A1
Springwell Ct 40 C5
Springwell Rd 40 C5
Springwell St 40 C5
Springwell Vw 40 C5
Stafford St 41 G7

Stanley Av 41 J1
Stanley Pl 41 J1
Stanley Rd 41 J1
Stanley Ter 41 J1
Stocks Hill 40 C6
Stoney Rock Gro 41 J2
Stoney Rock La 41 H2
Stott Rd 40 A4
Studio Rd 40 B2
Sutton St 40 C5
Sweet St 40 D5
Sweet St W 40 C5
Swinegate 41 E4
Sydenham Rd 40 B5
Sydenham St 40 B5

T
Telephone Pl 41 G2
Templar La 41 F3
Templar Pl 41 F3
Templar St 41 F3
Temple Vw Gro 41 J4
Temple Vw Pl 41 J4
Temple Vw Rd 41 J3
Temple Vw Ter 41 J4
Thealby Cl 41 G3
Thealby Lawn 41 G3
Thealby Pl 41 G3
Third Av 40 A5
Thirsk Row 40 D4
Thoresby Pl 40 D3
Thornleigh Gdns 41 J5
Thornleigh Gro 41 J5
Thornleigh Mt 41 J5
Thornleigh St 41 J5
Thornleigh Vw 41 J5
Thornville Pl 40 B1
Thornville Rd 40 A1
Thornville Row 40 B1
Thornville St 40 B1
Thornville Vw 40 B1
Tilbury Av 40 C7
Tilbury Gro 40 C7
Tilbury Mt 40 C7
Tilbury Par 40 C7
Tilbury Rd 40 C7
Tilbury Ter 40 C7
Tilbury Vw 40 C7
Tong Rd 40 A5
Top Moor Side 40 C6
Torre Cl 41 J3
Torre Dr 41 J2
Torre Rd 41 H3
Tower Ho St 41 F2
Trafalgar St 41 F3
Trent Rd 41 J3
Trent St 40 D6
Trinity St 41 E3
Triumph Cl 40 C5
Turlow Ct 41 G4

U
Union Pl 40 D5
Union St 41 F3
University Rd 40 C1
Upper Accommodation Rd 41 H3
Upper Basinghall St 40 E3
Upper N St 40 E2
Upper Westlock Av 41 J2

V
Vernon Rd 40 D2
Vernon St 40 E2
Vicar La 41 F3

Victoria Rd 40 E5
Victoria Sq 40 D3
Victoria St 40 C2
Victoria Ter 40 C2
Village Ter 40 A1
Vinery Mt 41 J4
Vinery Pl 41 J4
Vinery St 41 J3
Vinery Ter 41 J4

W
Wade La 41 E3
Walford Gro 41 J3
Walford Rd 41 J3
Walford Ter 41 J3
Walter Cres 41 H4
Walter St 40 A2
Walton St 40 D5
Washington St 40 B3
Water La 40 C5
Waterloo Rd 41 G7
Waterloo St 41 F4
Waverley Garth 40 D7
Weaver St 40 A2
Welbeck Rd 41 J4
Well Cl Ri 41 E1
Wellington Br St 40 C3
Wellington Pl 40 C4
Wellington Rd 40 B4
Wellington St 40 D4
Wesley Pl 41 H4
Westfield Cres 40 B2
Westfield Rd 40 B2
Westfield Ter 40 B2
Westgate 40 D3
Westlock Av 41 J2
West St 40 C3
West Vale 40 A6
Wharf St 41 F4
Whitehall Rd 40 B5
Whitehouse St 41 G7
Whitelock St 41 F2
Whitfield Av 41 G7
Whitfield Gdns 41 G7
Whitfield Pl 41 G7
Whitfield Sq 41 G7
Whitfield Way 41 G7
Willis St 41 H4
Willoughby Ter 40 C6
Willow App 40 A2
Willow Av 40 A2
Willow Cl 40 B2
Willow Garth 40 A2
Willow Rd 40 A2
Willow Ter Rd 40 D2
Wilmington St 41 F1
Winchester St 40 A4
Winfield Gro 40 E1
Winfield Pl 40 E1
Winfield Ter 40 E1
Wintoun St 41 F2
Wolseley Rd 40 A1
Woodhouse La 40 D1
Woodhouse Sq 40 D3
Woodsley Grn 40 B1
Woodsley Rd 40 B2
Wormald Row 41 E3
Wortley La 40 B5
Wortley Pk 40 A5

Y
Yarn St 41 H6
York Pl 40 D3
York Rd 41 H3
York St 41 F4

Liverpool street index

A
Abercromby Sq 43 F4
Abney Cl 43 H5
Acorn Ct 43 E7
Acton Way 43 H5
Adderley St 43 H3
Addison St 42 C2
Addison Way 42 C2
Adelaide Pl 42 D1
Adelaide Rd 43 G4
Adele Thompson Dr 43 F6
Agnes Way 43 H4
Aigburth St 43 G5
Ainsworth St 42 E4
Albany Rd 43 G3
Albert Edward Rd 43 G3
Albert St 43 G4
Alderson Rd 43 J6
Alexandra Cl 43 G2

Alexandra Rd 43 J5
Alex Cl 43 F7
Alfred Ms 42 D6
Alfred St 43 J5
Altcar Av 43 J6
Alt St 43 G6
Amberley St 43 F6
Amelia Cl 43 F2
Amethyst Cl 43 G1
Anchorage, The 42 C7
Angela St 43 G5
Anglezark Cl 43 H3
Anglican Ct 42 E6
Archbishop Warlock Ct 42 B1
Argyle St 42 C5
Arley St 42 C1
Arnold Cres 43 F7
Arnside Rd 43 H4

Arrad St 43 E5
Arundel Av 43 J7
Arundel Cl 43 G7
Asbridge St 43 G7
Ashton St 43 F3
Ashwell St 42 D6
Askham Cl 43 G6
Aspen Gro 43 H7
Atlantic Pt 42 C2
Atwell St 43 G1

B
Back Colquitt St 42 D5
Back Guildford St 43 F1
Back Kelvin Gro 43 G7
Back Leeds St 42 B2
Baker St 43 G2
Baker Way 43 F2
Balmoral Rd 43 J1

Balm St 43 H3
Baltimore St 42 E5
Bannerman St 43 J5
Barnet Cl 43 H5
Basnett St 42 C4
Bath St 42 A3
Battenberg St 43 G3
Bayhorse La 43 E3
Beaconsfield St 43 F7
Beaufort St 42 D7
Beaumont St 43 G6
Beau St 42 D1
Beckwith St 42 C5
Bective St 43 J5
Bedford Cl 43 F5
Bedford St S 43 F6
Beech St 43 J3
Benson St 42 D4
Bentley Rd 43 G7

Beresford St 42 E1
Berington St 42 C1
Berkley St 43 E6
Berry St 42 D5
Berwick Cl 43 H1
Berwick St 43 H1
Bevington Bush 42 C2
Bevington Hill 42 C1
Bidder St 42 E2
Bigham Rd 43 H2
Birchfield St 42 E2
Bird St 43 J6
Birkett St 42 D2
Birstall Rd 43 G2
Birt Cl 43 G6
Bishop Sheppard Ct 42 B1
Bixteth St 42 B3
Blackburne Pl 43 E5

Blackstock St 42 C2
Blair St 42 E6
Blenheim St 42 C1
Bluefields St 43 E6
Blundell St 42 C6
Boaler St 43 G2
Bold Pl 42 D5
Bold St 42 D4
Bolton St 42 D4
Bond St 42 C1
Boothwood Cl 43 H5
Boswell St 43 H6
Botanic Grn 43 H3
Botanic Pl 43 H3
Botanic Rd 43 H3
Boundary La 43 G1
Boyton Ct 43 J5
Bradfield St 43 H3
Brae St 43 H3

Brahms Cl 43 G7
Brampton Dr 43 F5
Brassey St 42 D7
Breames Cl 43 H4
Breck Rd 43 F1
Bremner Cl 43 H4
Brick St 42 D6
Bridge Rd 43 J5
Bridgewater St 42 C6
Bridport St 42 D3
Bright St 43 F2
Brindley St 42 D7
Britannia Av 43 J6
Britten Cl 43 H7
Bronte St 42 E3
Brook St 42 B3
Brownlow Hill 42 D4
Brownlow St 43 E4
Brow Side 43 E1
Brunswick Rd 43 F3
Brunswick St 42 B4
Bryges St 43 G4
Brython St 42 C4
Burlington St 42 C1
Burnley Cl 43 G1
Burroughs Gdns 42 C1
Burrows Ct 42 B1
Burton Cl 42 C5
Bute St 42 D2
Bute St (Edge Hill) 43 H6
Butler Cres 43 G2
Butler St 43 G1
Button St 42 C4
Byrom St 42 D3

C
Cadogan St 43 J5
Caird St 43 G2
Cairns St 43 G7
Caledonia St 43 E5
Callander Rd 43 J2
Cambria St N 43 H2
Cambria St S 43 H2
Cambridge Ct 43 E5
Cambridge St 43 E4
Camden St 42 D3
Cameo Cl 43 G1
Cameron St 43 H3
Campbell St 42 C5
Canada Boul 42 B4
Canning Pl 42 C4
Canning St 43 E5
Cantebury St 42 E2
Cantebury Way 43 E2
Cantsfield St 43 J6
Cardigan St 43 J5
Cardigan Way 43 H1
Cardwell St 43 G5
Carlingford Cl 43 G6
Carlton St 42 A1
Carmarthen Cres 42 D7
Carpenters Row 42 C5
Carruthers St 42 B2
Carstairs Rd 43 J1
Carter St 43 F6
Carver St 43 E2
Caryl St 42 D7
Castle St 42 B4
Catharine St 43 F5
Cathedral Cl 42 E6
Cathedral Gate 42 E5
Cathedral Wk 42 E4
Cawdor St 43 G7
Cazneau St 42 D1
Cedar Gro 43 H7
Celtic St 43 F7
Chadwick St 42 B2
Chaloner St 42 C6
Chandos St 43 H4
Channell Rd 43 H2
Chapel St 42 B4
Chase Way 42 E1
Chatham Pl 43 G4
Chatham St 43 F5
Chatsworth Dr 43 H5
Chaucer St 42 D2
Cheapside 42 C3
Chesney Cl 42 E7
Chesterfield St 42 E6
Chester St 42 E7
Chestnut St 43 F4
Chichester Cl 43 J5
Childwall Av 43 J6
Chisenhale St 42 B1
Chiswell St 43 H3
Christian St 42 D2
Chris Ward Cl 43 H4
Church All 42 C4
Church Mt 43 G4
Church St 42 C4
Churton Ct 43 F2
Cicely St 43 G4
Clarence St 42 E4
Claribel St 43 F7

Claughton Cl 43 H4
Claypole Cl 43 F5
Clay St 42 D7
Clearwater Cl 43 H4
Clegg St 43 F1
Clement Gdns 42 D1
Cleveland Sq 42 C1
Clifford St 42 C5
Cliff St 42 E3
Clifton Gro 43 H3
Clint Rd 42 E1
Clint Rd W 43 H4
Clint Way 43 H4
Coal St 42 D3
Cobden St 43 F2
Coburg Wf 42 C7
Cockspur St 42 C3
Coleridge St 43 H2
College La 42 C4
College St N 43 E2
College St S 43 F2
Colquitt St 42 D5
Coltart Rd 43 G7
Comberme St 43 E7
Commerce Way 43 G6
Commutation Row 42 D3
Compton Rd 43 G1
Comus St 42 D2
Concert St 42 D5
Connaught Rd 43 G3
Contance St 43 E3
Cookson St 42 D6
Cook St 42 C4
Copperas Hill 42 D4
Corinto St 42 E6
Corney St 43 H6
Cornhill 42 C5
Cornwallis St 42 D5
Corsewall St 43 J5
Cotswold St 43 H3
Cotton St 42 A1
Covent Gdn 42 B3
Cowan Dr 43 F1
Cranborne Rd 43 J6
Craven St 42 E3
Cresswell St 43 F1
Cropper St 42 D4
Crosfield Cl 43 J4
Crosfield Rd 43 H4
Crosshall St 42 C3
Crown St 43 F3
Croxteth Gro 43 H7
Croxteth Rd 43 G7
Crump St 42 D6
Cullen St 43 H6
Cumberland St 42 C3
Cunliffe St 42 C3
Custom Ho Pl 42 C5

D
Dale St 42 B4
Daniel Davies Dr 43 G6
Dansie St 43 E4
Danube St 43 H6
Darrel Dr 43 H6
Daulby St 43 F3
Davies St 42 C3
Dawber Cl 43 G1
Dawson St 42 C4
Dean Dillistone Ct 42 D6
Deane Rd 43 H3
Dean Patey Ct 42 D5
Deeley Cl 43 H4
Dell St 43 H3
Denham Dr 43 H1
Denham Way 43 H1
Dentdale Dr 42 E1
Devon St 42 E3
Dexter St 42 E7
Dial St 43 H3
Diamond St 42 C1
Dickens St 43 E7
Dickson St 42 A1
Dombey St 42 C3
Dorothy St 43 H4
Dorrit St 43 E7
Dorset Av 43 J6
Douro St 42 D1
Dovestone Cl 43 H5
Dove St 43 G6
Drury La 42 B4
Dryden St 42 D1
Dublin St 42 A1
Ducie St 43 G7
Duckinfield St 43 E4
Duke St 42 C5
Duncan St 42 D6
Dunkeld Cl 43 F2
Dunstan La 43 G4
Durden St 43 H6
Durning Rd 43 H3

Dwerryhouse St 43 H4
Dyke St 43 H5

E
Earle Rd 43 H3
Earle St 42 B1
East St 42 C5
Eaton St 42 E3
Ebenezer Rd 43 H3
Eden St 42 E1
Edgar St 43 H4
Edge Hill 43 H4
Edge La 42 D3
Edinburgh Rd 43 F2
Edmund St 42 C7
Egerton St 42 C3
Elaine St 43 H2
Eldonian Way 42 C4
Eldon Pl 43 E2
Eldon St 43 F2
Elizabeth St 42 D5
Elliot St 43 G7
Elm Gro 43 E7
Elm Vale 43 G6
Elstree Rd 42 D3
Ember Cres 43 G1
Embledon St 42 D2
Emerson St 42 D5
Empress Rd 43 G3
Enid St 43 E3
Epworth St 42 D6
Erin Cl 42 C4
Erskine St 42 D4
Esher Rd 42 E6
Eversley St 43 H6
Everton Brow 42 C5
Everton Rd 42 D5
Every St 43 J5
Exchange St E 43 H3
Exchange St W

F
Fairclough St 42 D4
Fairfield 43 J2
Falkland St 43 E3
Falkner Sq 43 F6
Falkner St 43 E5
Fareham Rd 43 J3
Farnworth St 43 G2
Fazakerley St 42 B3
Fearnside St 43 J5
Fell St 43 H3
Fenwick St 42 B4
Fern Gro 43 H7
Fernhill Dr 43 F7
Fielding St 43 G2
Field St 42 E2
Finch Pl 42 E3
Finlay St 43 H2
Fishguard Cl 43 F1
Fitzclarence Way 43 F1
Fitzpatrick Ct 42 B1
Fitzroy Way 43 F2
Fleet St 42 D4
Fleming Ct 42 B1
Flint St 42 D6
Fontenoy St 42 C3
Ford St 42 C2
Forrest St 42 C5
Fowler Cl 43 H4
Foxhill Cl 43 F7
Fox St 42 D1
Fraser St 42 D3
Freedom Cl 43 G5
Freeman St 43 J5
Freemasons' Row 42 C2
Frost St 43 H3

G
Galloway St 43 J5
Gannock St 43 H3
Gardenside St 43 F2
Gardners Dr 43 H1
Gardner's Row 42 C2
Garrick St 43 J6
Gascoyne St 42 B2
Geneva Rd 43 J2
George Harrison Cl 43 G2
Georges Dockway 42 B4
George St 42 B3
Geraint St 43 F7
Gerard St 42 D3
Gibraltar Row 42 B3
Gibson St 43 F6
Gilbert St 42 C5
Gildarts Gdns 42 C1
Gildart St 42 E3
Gilead St 43 H3
Gill St 43 E3
Gilroy Rd 43 H7
Gladstone Rd 43 G4
Gladstone St 42 C2
Gleave Cres 43 F1
Glegg St 42 B1

Gloucester Ct 42 D7
Gloucester Pl 43 F1
Gore St
Gower St
Gradwell St 43 H6
Grafton Cres 42 B3
Grafton St 42 B3
Granary Wf 42 B2
Granby St 43 J3
Grantham St 43 H6
Granville Rd 42 C2
Grayson St 43 G5
Great Crosshall St 43 G4
Great George Pl 43 G3
Great George St 42 B3
Great Howard St 43 E6
Great Nelson St 43 F7
Great Newton St 42 B1
Great Orford St 42 C1
Great Richmond St 42 C1
Greek St 43 F3
Greenheys Rd 42 D4
Greenland St 43 F4
Green La 43 J1
Greenleaf St 43 J2
Greenside 43 F1
Green St 43 G6
Gregson St 42 E6
Grenville St S 43 G4
Gresley Cl 43 F7
Grierson St 43 F3
Grinfield St 42 E7
Grinshill Cl 43 F3
Grosvenor St 43 H2
Grove Pk 43 F7
Grove Rd 42 E2
Grove St 43 F1
Guelph St 43 G1
Guion St 42 B3
Gwendoline St 42 B3
Gwenfron Rd
Gwent St

H
Hackins Hey 42 B3
Haigh St 43 E1
Hale St 42 C3
Hall La 43 F3
Halsbury Rd 43 H2
Hampstead Rd 42 B3
Hampton St 43 J5
Hannan Rd 43 H3
Hanover St 42 B4
Harbord St 43 H7
Hardman St 43 F7
Hardy St 43 G2
Harewood St 42 E2
Harker St 42 E3
Harke St 43 H2
Harper St 43 F1
Harrington St 43 F1
Harrowby Cl 42 B1
Harrowby St 43 F2
Hartley Quay 42 A4
Hart St 42 D4
Hatherley Cl 42 D6
Hatherley St 42 C3
Hatton Gdn 42 C2
Haverston Rd 42 C5
Hawdon Ct 43 H4
Hawke St 42 D1
Hawkins St 43 J5
Hawthorn Gro 43 G5
Head St
Heathcote Cl 43 J5
Heathfield St 42 C2
Helena St 43 H3
Helsby St 43 H3
Hendon Rd
Henglers St 43 J5
Henry Edward St 43 H3
Henry St 43 F2
Hewitts Pl 43 H1
Highfield St 42 C2
Highgate St 43 J6
High St 42 B2
Hilbre St 43 J2
Hillaby Cl 43 G2
Hillside St 42 B4
Hill St 42 B3
Hinton St 43 F7
Hockenhall All 42 D3
Hodson Pl 42 B3
Holborn St 43 F6
Holden St 42 C5
Holdsworth St 42 C1
Holly Rd 43 H3
Holmes St 43 H3
Holt Rd 43 E3
Holy Cross Cl 43 H7
Homerton Rd 43 G4
Hood St 42 C2
Hope Pl 43 F1
Hope St 42 B1

Hornby Wk 43 G2
Hotham St 43 F3
Houghton St 42 D7
Houlton St 42 B5
Hughes Cl 42 C4
Hughes St 42 D7
Huntly Rd 42 D6
Hurst St 42 C7
Huskisson St 43 G6
Hutchinson St 43 H2
Hutchinson Wk 43 J6
Hygeia St 42 C5
Hyslop St 42 C3

I
Iliad St 42 B2
Ingrow Rd 42 D1
Irvine St 43 E3
Irwell St 43 E4
Islington 42 D2
Ivatt Way 42 E3

J
Jack McBain Ct 43 G7
Jade Rd 42 D6
Jamaica St 42 D6
James Clarke St 42 B2
James St 42 D1
Janet St 43 G2
Jasmine Cl 42 C1
Jenkinson St 42 D5
Jermyn St 43 J4
Jet Cl 43 H6
John Lennon Dr 43 G4
John Moores Cl 43 F7
Johnson St 43 D1
John St 43 H7
Jordan St 43 J2
Jubilee Dr 43 F6
Judges Dr 43 F3
Judges Way 43 H1
Juvenal Pl 43 F7
Juvenal St 43 G2

K
Keble St 43 F7
Kelso Rd 43 E1
Kelvin Gro 43 C3
Kempston St 43 F3
Kenilworth St 43 H2
Kenley Cl 43 J2
Kensington 43 E6
Kensington St 43 J2
Kent St 43 G3
Kilshaw St 43 G4
Kimberley Cl 43 E5
Kinder St 43 F6
King Edward St 43 G1
Kinglake St 43 D2
Kings Dock St 43 H5
Kingsley Rd 43 F3
Kings Par 43 C4
Kingsway Ct 43 G6
Kingswell Cl 43 F6
Kitchen St 43 B5
Knight St 43 E3

L
Lace St 42 C3
Ladybower Cl 43 J2
Laggan St 43 J5
Lairds Pl 42 D4
Lakeland Cl 43 H2
Lambert Way 43 H4
Lamport St 42 E7
Lance Cl 43 H5
Langley St 42 D4
Langsdale St 43 H4
Langton Rd 43 G4
Lanyork Rd 43 J1
Laurel Gro 43 F2
Lavan Cl 42 C2
Lawrence Rd 42 C5
Lawton St 42 C2
Laxey St 43 B2
Leece St 43 G4
Leeds St 43 B3
Leigh St 42 D4
Leigh St (Edge Hill) 43 F7
Lemon Cl 43 F2
Lemon Gro 42 D7
Leopold Rd 43 J2
Lesseps Rd 42 C3
Lestock St 43 H1
Liffey St 43 F3
Lightwood Dr 43 G5
Lightwood St 43 H3
Lilley Rd 43 H3
Lilly Vale 43 H6
Lime Gro 43 H3
Limekiln La 43 H3
Lime St 42 C2
Lincoln Cl 43 J2
Lindley Cl 42 C3
Lindley St 42 E5

Lindley St 43 J5
Ling St 43 H3
Lister Cres 43 J3
Lister Rd 43 J2
Little Catherine St 43 E6
Little Ct 42 B1
Little Hardman St 42 E5
Little Howard St 42 B1
Little St. Bride St 43 E5
Little Woolton St 43 F4
Liver St 42 C5
Lloyd Cl 43 F1
Lloyd Cl 43 J2
Lockerby Rd 43 H7
Lodge La 42 D3
London Rd 43 H6
Longfellow St 43 G5
Longstone Wk 42 D3
Lord Nelson St 42 C4
Lord St 43 H6
Lorton St 43 F7
Lothian St 43 G7
Loudon Gro 42 B1
Love La 43 B4
Lower Castle St 43 F2
Low Hill 43 F6
Lowther St 43 F3
Low Wd St 43 E7
Luke St 42 D4
Lyceum Pl 42 C5
Lydia Ann St 43 F2
Lytton St

M
Maddrell St 42 B1
Madelaine St 43 F7
Madeley St 43 H1
Magdala St 43 H6
Maitland Cl 43 H6
Malden Rd 43 H2
Mallow Rd 43 H2
Malt St 43 G5
Malvern Rd 43 H2
Manchester St 42 C3
Manesty's La 42 C4
Manfred St 43 F3
Mann Island 42 B4
Mann St 42 D7
Mansell Rd 43 H2
Mansfield St 42 D2
Manton Rd 43 H2
Maple Gro 43 H7
Marathon Cl 43 F1
Marcot Rd 43 J1
Margaret St 43 F1
Mariners Wf 42 C7
Maritime Pl 42 E2
Maritime Way 42 C5
Marlborough St 42 C2
Marlsford St 43 H2
Marmaduke St 43 G4
Marquis St 42 E3
Marsden St 43 F2
Marsden Way 43 F2
Marshall Pl 42 C1
Martensen St 43 G4
Marvin St 43 G2
Marybone 42 C3
Maryland St 43 E5
Mason St 43 G4
Mathew St 42 C4
Maud St 43 F7
Maxton Rd 43 H2
Mayfair Cl 43 H1
May Pl 42 E4
May St 42 E4
Melda St 43 F2
Melville Pl 43 F5
Merlin St 43 F7
Michael Dragonette Ct 42 C1
Midghall St 42 C2
Mile End 42 C1
Millennium Pl 43 G2
Mill La 42 D3
Mill Rd 43 F1
Mill St 42 E7
Millvale St 43 H1
Milroy St 43 H4
Milverton St 43 H1
Minshull St 43 F4
Minster Ct 43 F5
Minto Cl 43 H3
Minto St 43 H3
Mirfield St 43 H2
Molyneux Rd 43 G2
Montgomery Way 43 H1
Moorfields 42 C3
Moor Pl 42 E3
Moor St 42 B4
Morden St 43 H1
Moss Gro 43 H7
Mount Pleasant 42 D4
Mount St 42 E5

Mount Vernon Grn 43 G3
Mount Vernon Rd 43 F4
Mount Vernon St 43 F3
Mozart Cl 43 G7
Muirhead Av 43 H1
Mulberry Pl 43 F5
Mulberry St 43 F5
Mulgrave St 43 F6
Mulliner St 43 J6
Myrtle St 43 E5

N
Navigation Wf 42 C7
Naylor St 42 C2
Needham Rd 43 H3
Nelson Rd 43 G4
Nelson St 43 G4
Netherfield Rd S 42 E1
Nevin St 43 F2
Nevison St 43 G4
New Bird St 42 D6
New Grey Rock Cl 43 G1
Newhall St 42 D6
New Henderson St 42 D7
Newington 42 D4
New Quay 42 B3
New Red Rock Vw 43 G1
Newsham Dr 43 H1
Newstead Rd 43 H6
Newton Way 43 E4
Noel St 43 H6
Norfolk St 42 C6
Norman St 43 E3
Northbrook Cl 43 G6
North Brook St 43 F6
Northcote Cl 43 F1
North John St 42 C3
North St 42 C3
North Vw 43 G4
Norton St 42 D3
Norwood Gro 43 H1
Nuttall St 43 H4

O
Oakes St 43 E3
Oakham St 42 D7
O'Connell Rd 42 C1
Odsey St 43 H3
Oil St 42 A1
Old Coll Pl 43 H4
Old Hall St 42 B3
Oldham St 42 D5
Old Leeds St 42 B3
Olympia St 43 G2
Onslow Rd 43 J2
Opal St 43 G1
Orange Gro 43 H7
O'Reilly Ct 42 B1
Oriel Steet 42 C2
Ormond St 42 B3
Orphan St 43 F5
Orthes St 43 E4
Ottley St 43 J2
Overbury St 43 G4
Overton St 43 G4
Oxendale Cl 43 G6
Oxford St 43 E4
Oxford St E 43 G4

P
Paddington 43 F4
Page Wk 42 E2
Paisley St 42 A2
Pall Mall 42 B2
Paradise St 42 C5
Parker St 42 D4

Park La 42 C5
Park Pl 42 E7
Park Rd 43 E7
Parkside St 43 F2
Park Way 43 F6
Parliament Cl 42 E6
Parliament St 42 D6
Parr St 42 D5
Parton St 43 J2
Paul
   McCartney Way 43 H2
Paul Orr Ct 42 B1
Paul St 42 C2
Pavilion Cl 43 G6
Pear Gro 43 H2
Pearl Way 43 G1
Peet St 43 H4
Pembroke Gdns 43 E3
Pembroke Pl 42 E3
Pembroke St 43 E4
Penarth Cl 43 G5
Pendine Cl 43 H1
Penlinken Dr 43 H1
Penvalley Cres 43 H1
Peover St 42 D2
Pera Cl 43 G2
Percy St 43 E6
Perrygate Cl 43 G5
Perry St 42 D7
Perth St 43 G2
Peter's Arcade 42 C4
Peter St 42 C3
Phillimore Rd 43 H2
Pickop St 42 C3
Pickwick St 43 E7
Picton Rd 43 J5
Pilgrim St 42 E5
Pimhill Cl 43 G7
Pine Ms 42 E6
Pinetop Cl 43 H1
Pitt St 42 D5
Pleasant St 42 E4
Plimsoll St 43 H4
Plumpton St 43 F1
Pomfret St 43 F7
Pomona St 42 E4
Pond Cl 43 H1
Ponsonby St 43 G7
Porter St 42 A1
Portland Pl 42 D1
Portwood Cl 43 G5
Pownall Sq 42 C3
Pownall St 42 C5
Prescot Rd 43 J2
Prescot St 43 F3
Preston St 42 C3
Price St 42 C5
Primrose Hill 42 C3
Prince Albert Ms 42 D6
Prince Edwin St 42 D1
Princes Av 43 F6
Princes Gdns 42 B2
Princes Par 42 A3
Princes Pk 43 G7
Princes Rd 43 F6
Princes St 42 C3
Prince William St 42 D7
Prospect St 43 F3
Providence Cres 42 D7
Prussia St 42 B3
Pudsey St 42 D3
Pumpfields Rd 42 B2
Pythian Cl 43 G2
Pythian St 43 F2

Q
Queen Anne St 42 D2
Queensland St 43 G4
Queens Sq 42 D3
Queens Wf 42 B6
Quorn St 43 H3

R
Rachel St 42 D1
Radstock Rd 43 J2
Raffles St 42 D6
Rainford Gdns 42 C4
Rainford Sq 42 C4
Ranelagh St 42 D4
Raven Cl 43 F2
Raymond Pl 42 C1
Red Cross St 42 B4
Redgrave St 43 H3
Redmires Cl 43 H5
Red Rock St 43 G1
Regent St 42 A1
Renfrew St 43 G3
Renshaw St 42 D4
Reservoir St 43 F1
Reynolds Cl 43 G1
Rialto Cl 43 F6
Rice St 42 E5
Richardson St 43 J6
Richmond Row 42 D2
Richmond St 42 C4
Ridley Rd 43 H2
Rigby St 42 B3
Ringo Starr Dr 43 H2
Ritson St 43 G7
River Avon St 43 H6
Roberts St 42 A2
Roderick St 42 E2
Rodney St 42 E5
Roe St 42 D3
Rokeby Cl 42 E2
Rokeby St 42 E2
Rokesmith Av 43 H5
Romer Rd 43 H2
Romilly St 43 G2
Roscastle Cl 43 G2
Roscoe La 42 D5
Roscoe St 42 E5
Roscommon St 42 D1
Roseberry St 43 F6
Rose Hill 42 D2
Rosemary Cl 43 G4
Rose Pl 42 D2
Rothsay Cl 42 E1
Rothwell St 43 G1
Royal Mail St 42 D4
Royston St 43 G4
Rufford Rd 43 J2
Rumford Pl 42 B3
Rumford St 42 B3
Rupert Dr 43 F2
Russel St 42 E3
Ryedale Cl 43 G6

S
St. Andrew St 42 E4
St. Anne St 42 D2
St. Bride St 43 F5
St. James Pl 42 D6
St. James Rd 42 E6
St. James St 42 D6
St. John's La 42 D3
St. Josephs Cres 42 D2
St. Martins Ms 42 D1
St. Michaels Gro 43 H1
St. Nicholas Pl 42 A4

St. Stephen's Pl 42 C2
Salisbury Rd 43 J6
Salisbury St 42 E1
Salthouse Quay 42 B5
Saltney St 42 A1
Sandhead St 43 J5
Sandino St 42 E7
Sandon St 43 F5
Saxon Cl 43 G1
Saxony Rd 43 G3
Scholar St 43 J6
Schomberg St 43 G2
School La 42 C4
Scotland Rd 42 D2
Seaport Rd 43 G4
Seddon St 42 C5
Seel St 42 C4
Sefton Pk Rd 43 H7
Sefton St 42 C6
Selborne Cl 43 F6
Selborne St 43 F6
Selsey Cl 43 H5
Severs St 43 G1
Seymour St 42 E3
Shakespeare Cl 43 G1
Shallcross Pl 43 G1
Shaws All 42 C5
Shaw St 43 E1
Sheil Rd 43 H1
Shenstone St 43 G4
Shepherd's Fold Cl 43 G4
Sherwood St 42 B1
Shimmin St 43 G4
Sidney Pl 43 G4
Silkstone St 43 H5
Simpson St 42 C6
Sim St 42 E2
Sirdar Cl 43 H5
Sir Thomas St 42 C3
Skelhorne St 42 D4
Slater St 42 D5
Smithdown La 43 F4
Smithdown Rd 43 H6
Smithfield St 42 C3
Soho Pl 42 E2
Soho St 42 E2
Solomon St 43 H3
Solway St E 43 H6
Solway St W 43 G6
South Chester St 42 E7
Southern Cres 42 D7
South Ferry Quay 42 C7
South Hunter St 43 E5
South John St 42 C4
Sparling St 42 C6
Spekeland Rd 43 H5
Spencer St 43 F1
Spindle Cl 43 F1
Spofforth Rd 43 J5
Sprainger St 42 B1
Springfield 42 D2
Squires St 43 G4
Stafford St 42 E3
Stamford St 43 H3
Standish St 42 C3
Stanhope St 42 D7
Stanier Way 43 H4
Stanley St 42 C3
Star St 42 D7
Steinberg Ct 42 B1
Sterndale Cl 43 H5
Stockdale Cl 42 C2
Stone St 42 B1
Stowell St 43 E5
Strada Way 43 E2
Strand, The 42 B4

Strand St 42 B4
Strathmore Rd 43 H1
Strauss Cl 43 H7
Suffolk St 42 D5
Sugnall St 43 E5
Summer Seat 42 C1
Surrey St 42 C5
Sutcliffe St 43 H2
Sweeting St 42 B4
Swindale Cl 43 G6
Swiss Rd 43 J2

T
Tabley St 42 C6
Tace Cl 43 F6
Tagus Cl 43 G7
Tamar Cl 43 F1
Tarleton St 42 C4
Tatlock St 42 C1
Tavy Rd 43 F1
Teck St 43 G3
Teign Cl 43 F1
Tempest Hey 42 B3
Temple Ct 42 C4
Temple La 42 C3
Temple St 42 C1
Tenterden St 42 C1
Thackeray Pl 43 F7
Thames St 43 G7
Thomas St Way 42 C5
Thorburn St 43 H4
Thornes Rd 43 G2
Tichbourne Way 43 F2
Tideswell Cl 43 H5
Timpron St 43 H5
Titchfield St 42 C1
Tithebarn St 42 B3
Tobin Cl 42 C1
Toft St 43 H3
Tom Mann Cl 42 D3
Tordelow Cl 43 F1
Tower Gdns 42 B4
Trafalgar Way 43 F2
Trowbridge St 42 E4
Trueman St 42 C3
Tudor St N 43 H2
Tudor St S 43 H2
Tulloch St 43 G2
Tunnel Rd 43 H5
Tunstall St 43 J6
Tweed St 43 H1
Twomey Cl 42 C1

U
Underley St 43 J6
Union Ct 42 C4
Union St 42 B3
Upper Baker St 43 G2
Upper Beau St 42 D1
Upper Bute St 42 E1
Upper Duke St 42 D5
Upper Frederick St 42 C5
Upper Hampton St 43 F6
Upper Harrington St 43 H3
Upper Hill St 43 E7
Upper Hope Pl 43 E5
Upper Mann St 42 D7
Upper Mason St 43 G4
Upper Newington 42 D4
Upper Parliament St 43 F6
Upper Pitt St 42 D6
Upper Pownall St 42 C5
Upper Stanhope St 43 E6
Upper Warwick St 43 F7
Upper William St 42 B1
Uxbridge St 43 H5

V
Vandries St 42 A1
Vandyke St 43 H6
Vauxhall Rd 42 C2
Vernon St 42 C3
Verulam Cl 43 G6
Victoria St 42 C4
Village St 43 E1
Vincent Ct 42 D5
Vining St 43 F7
Virgil St 42 D1
Voelas St 43 G7
Vronhill Cl 43 G7
Vulcan St 42 A1

W
Wainwright Cl 43 H5
Wakefield St 42 D2
Waldron Cl 42 C2
Walker St 43 F2
Wall St 42 C4
Walsh Cl 42 C1
Wapping 42 C5
Ward St 42 D3
Warwick St 42 E7
Waterloo Quay 42 A2
Water St 42 B4
Watkinson St 42 C6
Watmough St 42 E1
Wavertree Boul 43 J4
Wavertree Rd 43 G4
Webb Cl 43 H4
Webb St 43 H6
Webster Rd 43 J6
Webster St 42 C3
Wedgewood St 43 H3
Wendell St 43 H6
Wentworth Dr 43 F1
West Derby Rd 43 G2
West Derby St 43 F3
Westmorland Dr 42 C2
Whitcroft Rd 43 J2
Whitechapel 42 C4
Whitefield Rd 43 G1
Whitefield Way 43 G1
White Rock Ct 43 G1
White Rock St 43 G1
Whithorn St 43 J5
Whitland Rd 43 J1
Whitley St 42 B1
Whittier St 43 H6
Wightman St 43 G2
Wilde St 42 D3
Wilfer Cl 43 H5
William Brown St 42 D3
William Henry St 42 E2
Williamson St 42 C4
Wimpole St 43 H3
Windsor St 43 E6
Windsor Vw 43 H6
Winifred St 43 H4
Winter St 43 F2
Wolstenholme Sq 42 D7
Woodside St 43 H4
Wood St 42 D4
Wordsworth St 43 H6
Wrayburn St 43 H5
Wrenbury St 43 H3
Wynnstay St 43 G7

Y
Yanwath St 43 H6
York St 42 C5

London street index

A
Abbey Orchard St SW1 44 D6
Abingdon St SW1 44 E6
Achilles Way W1 44 A5
Adam & Eve Ct W1 44 C2
Adams Row W1 44 A4
Adam St WC2 45 E4
Addington St SE1 45 F6
Addle Hill EC4 45 H3
Adelaide St WC2 44 E4
Adeline Pl WC1 44 D2
Adelphi Ter WC2 45 E4
Agar St WC2 44 E4
Air St W1 44 C4
Alaska St SE1 45 G5
Albany W1 44 C4
Albany Ctyd W1 44 C4

Albemarle St W1 44 B4
Albemarle Way EC1 45 H1
Albert Barnes Ho SE1 45 J7
Albion Pl EC1 45 H1
Albion Way EC1 45 J2
Aldburgh Ms W1 44 A2
Aldermanbury EC2 45 J2
Aldermanbury Sq EC2 45 J2
Aldersgate St EC1 45 J2
Alford St W1 44 A4
Aldwych WC2 45 F3
Alfred Ms W1 44 D1
Alfred Pl WC1 44 D1
Allington St SW1 44 C7
All Souls Pl W1 44 B2
Ambassador's Ct SW1 44 C5
Ambrosden Av SW1 44 C7
Amen Cor EC4 45 H3

Amen Ct EC4 45 H2
America St SE1 45 J5
Andrew Borde St WC2 44 D2
Andrewes Ho EC2 45 J2
Andrews Crosse WC2 45 G3
Angel Ct SW1 44 C5
Angel St EC1 45 J2
Apothecary St EC4 45 H3
Apple Tree Yd SW1 44 C4
Apsley Way W1 44 A5
Aquinas St SE1 45 G4
Archer St W1 44 D3
Arches, The WC2 45 E4
Archibald Ms W1 44 A4
Arch St SE1 45 J7
Argyll St W1 44 C3
Aria Ho WC2 45 E2
Arlington St SW1 44 C4

Arne St WC2 45 E3
Arneway St SW1 44 D7
Arrol Ho SE1 45 J7
Artillery Mans SW1 44 D6
Artillery Pl SW1 44 D7
Artillery Row SW1 44 D7
Arundel Gt Ct WC2 45 F3
Arundel St WC2 45 F3
Ashenden SE17 45 J7
Ashentree Ct EC4 45 G3
Ashland Pl W1 44 A1
Ashley Gdns SW1 44 C7
Ashley Pl SW1 44 C7
Astbury Ho SE11 45 G7
Audley Sq W1 44 A4
Austral St SE11 45 H7
Ave Maria La EC4 45 H3
Avery Row W1 44 B3

Avonmouth St SE1 45 J6
Avon Pl SE1 45 J6
Aybrook St W1 44 A2
Aylesbury St EC1 45 H1
Ayres St SE1 45 J5

B
Babmaes St SW1 44 D4
Back Hill EC1 45 G1
Bainbridge St WC1 44 D2
Baker's Ms W1 44 A2
Baker's Row EC1 45 G1
Baker's Yd EC1 45 G1
Balderton St W1 44 A3
Baldwin's Gdns EC1 45 G1
Balfour Ms W1 44 A4
Balfour Pl W1 44 A4
Baltic St E EC1 45 J1

Baltic St W EC1 45 J1
Banbury Ct WC2 44 E3
Bank End SE1 45 J4
Banks Ho SE1 45 J7
Bankside SE1 45 J4
Bankside Lofts SE1 45 H4
Banner St EC1 45 J1
Barbican EC2 45 J2
Barbican, The EC2 45 J1
Barbon Cl WC1 45 E1
Barge Ho St SE1 45 G4
Barkham Ter SE1 45 G6
Barley Mow Pas EC1 45 H2
Barlow Pl W1 44 B4
Barnard's Inn EC1 45 G2
Barons Pl SE1 45 G6
Barrett St W1 44 A3
Barter St WC1 45 E2

Bartholomew Cl EC1 45 J2
Bartholomew Pl EC1 45 J2
Bartlett Ct EC4 45 G2
Bartletts Pas EC4 45 G2
Barton St SW1 44 E6
Bastion Highwalk
  EC2 45 J2
Bateman's Bldgs W1 44 D3
Bateman St W1 44 D3
Bath Ct EC1 45 G1
Bath Ter SE1 45 J7
Bayley St W1 44 D2
Baylis Rd SE1 45 G6
Beak St W1 44 C3
Bear All EC4 45 H2
Bear Gdns SE1 45 J4
Bear La SE1 45 H4
Bear St WC2 44 D4
Beauchamp St EC1 45 G2
Beaumont Ms W1 44 A1
Beaumont St W1 44 A1
Bedford Av WC1 44 D2
Bedfordbury WC2 44 E3
Bedford Ct WC2 44 E4
Bedford Pl WC1 44 E1
Bedford Row WC1 45 F1
Bedford Sq WC1 44 D2
Bedford St WC2 44 E3
Bedford Way WC1 44 D1
Bedlam Ms SE11 45 G7
Beech St EC2 45 J1
Beeston Pl SW1 44 B7
Belgrave Ms N SW1 44 A6
Belgrave Ms S SW1 44 A6
Belgrave Ms W SW1 44 A6
Belgrave Pl SW1 44 A6
Belgrave Sq SW1 44 A6
Belgrave Yd SW1 44 B7
Belgravia SW1 44 A7
Bell Wf La EC4 45 J4
Bell Yd WC2 45 G2
Belvedere Bldgs SE1 45 H6
Belvedere Pl SE1 45 H6
Belvedere Rd SE1 45 F5
Benjamin St EC1 45 H1
Bennet's Hill EC4 45 H3
Bennet St SW1 44 C4
Bennetts Yd SW1 44 D7
Bentinck Ms W1 44 A2
Bentinck St W1 44 A2
Berkeley Sq W1 44 B4
Berkeley St W1 44 B4
Bernard St WC1 44 E1
Berners Ms W1 44 C2
Berners Pl W1 44 C2
Berners St W1 44 C2
Berwick St W1 44 D3
Betterton St WC2 44 E3
Bingham Pl W1 44 A1
Binney St W1 44 A3
Birdcage Wk SW1 44 C6
Bird St W1 44 A3
Bishop's Ct EC4 45 H2
Bishop's Ct WC2 45 G2
Bishops Ter SE11 45 G7
Bittern St SE1 45 J6
Blackburne's Ms W1 44 A3
Blackfriars Br EC4 45 H3
Blackfriars Br SE1 45 H3
Blackfriars Ct EC4 45 H3
Black Friars La EC4 45 H3
Blackfriars Pas EC4 45 H3
Blackfriars Rd SE1 45 H6
Bleeding Heart Yd
  EC1 45 G2
Blenheim St W1 44 B3
Bloomfield Pl W1 44 B3
Bloomsbury WC1 44 D2
Bloomsbury Ct WC1 45 E2
Bloomsbury Pl WC1 45 E1
Bloomsbury Sq WC1 45 E2
Bloomsbury St WC1 44 D2
Bloomsbury Way
  WC1 44 E2
Blore Ct W1 44 D3
Blue Ball Yd SW1 44 C5
Bolsover St W1 44 B1
Bolt Ct EC4 45 G3
Bolton St W1 44 B4
Book Ms WC2 44 D3
Booth La EC4 45 J3
Booth's Pl W1 44 C2
Borough, The SE1 45 J6
Borough High St SE1 45 J6
Borough Rd SE1 45 H6
Borough Sq SE1 45 J6
Boscobel Pl SW1 44 A7
Boswell Ct WC1 45 E1
Boswell St WC1 45 E1
Boundary Row SE1 45 H5
Bourchier St W1 44 D3
Bourdon Pl W1 44 B3
Bourdon St W1 44 B3
Bourlet Cl W1 44 C2

Bourne Est EC1 45 G1
Bouverie St EC4 45 G3
Bow Chyd EC4 45 J3
Bow La EC4 45 J3
Bow St WC2 45 E3
Boyce St SE1 45 F5
Boyfield St SE1 45 H6
Boyle St W1 44 C3
Brackley St EC1 45 J1
Brad St SE1 45 G5
Bread St EC4 45 J3
Bream's Bldgs EC4 45 G2
Bressenden Pl SW1 44 B6
Brewer's Grn SW1 44 D6
Brewers Hall Gdns
  EC2 45 J2
Brewer St W1 44 C3
Briant Est SE1 45 G7
Briant Ho SE1 45 F7
Brick Ct EC4 45 G3
Brick St W1 44 B5
Bride Ct EC4 45 H3
Bride La EC4 45 H3
Bridewell Pl EC4 45 H3
Bridford Ms W1 44 B1
Bridge Pl SW1 44 B7
Bridge St SW1 44 E6
Bridgewater Sq EC2 45 J1
Bridgewater St EC2 45 J1
Bridle La W1 44 C3
Brinton Wk SE1 45 H5
Briset St EC1 45 H1
Britton St EC1 45 H1
Broadbent St W1 44 B3
Broad Ct WC2 45 E3
Broad Sanctuary SW1 44 D6
Broadstone Pl W1 44 A2
Broad Wk W1 44 A4
Broadwall SE1 45 G4
Broadway SW1 44 D6
Broadwick St W1 44 C3
Broad Yd EC1 45 H1
Brockham St SE1 45 J6
Broken Wf EC4 45 J3
Bromley Pl W1 44 C1
Brook Dr SE11 45 G7
Brooke's Ct EC1 45 G1
Brookes Mkt EC1 45 G1
Brooke St EC1 45 G2
Brook's Ms W1 44 B3
Brook St W1 44 A3
Brown Hart Gdns W1 44 A3
Browning Ms W1 44 B2
Brownlow Ms WC1 45 F1
Brownlow St WC1 45 F2
Brunswick Sq WC1 45 E1
Bruton La W1 44 B4
Bruton Pl W1 44 B4
Bruton St W1 44 B4
Brydges Pl WC2 44 E4
Buckingham Arc WC2 45 E4
Buckingham Gate
  SW1 44 C6
Buckingham Ms SW1 44 C6
Buckingham Pl SW1 44 C6
Buckingham St WC2 45 E4
Buckley St SE1 45 G5
Bucknall St WC2 44 D2
Bull Inn Ct WC2 45 E4
Bulstrode Pl W1 44 A2
Bulstrode St W1 44 A2
Burdett St SE1 45 G6
Burgon St EC4 45 H3
Burleigh St WC2 45 F3
Burlington Arc W1 44 C4
Burlington Gdns W1 44 C4
Burrell St SE1 45 H4
Burrows Ms SE1 45 H5
Bury Pl WC1 44 E2
Bury St SW1 44 C4
Butler Pl SW1 44 D6
Byng Pl WC1 44 D1
Bywell Pl W1 44 C2

C

Cadogan La SW1 44 A7
Cahill St EC1 45 J1
Caleb St SE1 45 J5
Cambridge Circ WC2 44 D3
Candover St W1 44 C2
Cannon St EC4 45 J3
Canon Row SW1 44 E6
Canterbury Ho SE1 45 F6
Capener's Cl SW1 44 A6
Capper St WC1 44 C1
Carburton St W1 44 B1
Carey La EC2 45 J2
Carey St WC2 45 F3
Carlisle La SE1 45 F7
Carlisle Pl SW1 44 C7
Carlisle St W1 44 D3
Carlos Pl W1 44 A4
Carlton Gdns SW1 44 D5

Carlton Ho Ter SW1 44 D5
Carlton St SW1 44 D4
Carmelite St EC4 45 G3
Carnaby St W1 44 C3
Carpenter St W1 44 B4
Carrington St W1 44 B5
Carteret St SW1 44 D6
Carter La EC4 45 H3
Carthusian St EC1 45 J1
Carting La WC2 45 E4
Castle Baynard St
  EC4 45 H3
Castlebrook Cl SE11 45 H7
Castle La SW1 44 C6
Castle Yd SE1 45 H4
Cathedral Piazza SW1 44 C7
Cathedral Wk SW1 44 C6
Catherine Pl SW1 44 C6
Catherine St WC2 45 F3
Catherine Wheel Yd
  SW1 44 C5
Catton St WC1 45 F2
Cavendish Ms N W1 44 B1
Cavendish Ms S W1 44 B2
Cavendish Pl W1 44 B2
Cavendish Sq W1 44 B2
Caxton St SW1 44 C6
Cecil Ct WC2 44 D4
Centaur St SE1 45 F6
Centrepoint WC1 44 D2
Chadwick St SW1 44 D7
Chancel St SE1 45 H4
Chancery La WC2 45 G2
Chandos Pl WC2 44 E4
Chandos St W1 44 B2
Chapel Pl W1 44 B3
Chapel St SW1 44 A6
Chaplin Cl SE1 45 G5
Chapone Pl W1 44 D3
Chapter Ho Ct EC4 45 J3
Chapter St SW1 44 D7
Charing Cross SW1 44 D4
Charing Cross Rd
  WC2 44 D2
Charles II St SW1 44 D4
Charles St W1 44 B4
Charlotte Ms W1 44 C1
Charlotte Pl W1 44 C2
Charlotte St W1 44 C1
Charterhouse, The
  EC1 45 H1
Charterhouse Bldgs
  EC1 45 H1
Charterhouse Ms EC1 45 H1
Charterhouse Sq EC1 45 H1
Charterhouse St EC1 45 G2
Cheapside EC2 45 J3
Chenies Ms WC1 44 D1
Chenies St WC1 44 D1
Chequer St EC1 45 J1
Cherry Tree Wk EC1 45 J1
Chesham Cl SW1 44 A7
Chesham Ms SW1 44 A6
Chesham Pl SW1 44 A7
Chesham St SW1 44 A7
Cheshire Ct EC4 45 G3
Chester Cl SW1 44 A6
Chesterfield Gdns W1 44 B4
Chesterfield Hill W1 44 B4
Chesterfield St W1 44 B4
Chester Ms SW1 44 B6
Chester Sq SW1 44 B7
Chester Sq Ms SW1 44 B7
Chester St SW1 44 A6
Chicheley St SE1 45 F5
Chichester Rents
  WC2 45 G2
Chiltern St W1 44 A1
Ching Ct WC2 44 E3
Chiswell St EC1 45 J1
Chitty St W1 44 C1
Christ Ch Pas EC1 45 H2
Church Entry EC4 45 H3
Church Pl SW1 44 C4
Churchyard Row
  SE11 45 H7
Clare Mkt WC2 45 F3
Clarges Ms W1 44 B4
Clarges St W1 44 B4
Clarke's Ms W1 44 A1
Clement's Inn WC2 45 F3
Clement's Inn Pas
  WC2 45 F3
Clennam St SE1 45 J5
Clerkenwell EC1 45 H1
Clerkenwell Grn EC1 45 G1
Clerkenwell Rd EC1 45 G1
Cleveland Ms W1 44 C1
Cleveland Pl SW1 44 C4
Cleveland Row SW1 44 C5
Cleveland St W1 44 C1
Clifford's Inn Pas EC4 45 G3
Clifford St W1 44 C4
Clink St SE1 45 J4
Clipstone Ms W1 44 C1

Clipstone St W1 44 B1
Cliveden Pl SW1 44 A7
Cloak La EC4 45 J3
Cloth Ct EC1 45 H2
Cloth Fair EC1 45 H2
Cloth St EC1 45 J1
Coach & Horses Yd
  W1 44 B3
Coburg Cl SW1 44 C7
Cock La EC1 45 H2
Cockpit Steps SW1 44 D6
Cockpit Yd WC1 45 F1
Cockspur Ct SW1 44 D4
Cockspur St SW1 44 D4
Cole St SE1 45 J6
Coley St WC1 45 F1
College Hill EC4 45 J3
College Ms SW1 44 E6
College St EC4 45 J3
Collinson St SE1 45 J6
Collinson Wk SE1 45 J6
Colnbrook St SE1 45 H7
Colombo St SE1 45 H5
Colonnade WC1 44 E1
Colville Pl W1 44 C2
Computer Pass EC2 45 J2
Concert Hall App SE1 45 F5
Conduit Ct WC2 44 E3
Conduit St W1 44 B3
Cons St SE1 45 G5
Constitution Hill SW1 44 B5
Conway Ms W1 44 C1
Conway St W1 44 C1
Cooper Cl SE1 45 G6
Copeland Ho EC11 45 F7
Copperfield St SE1 45 H5
Coptic St WC1 44 E2
Coral St SE1 45 G6
Coram St WC1 44 E1
Cork St W1 44 C4
Cork St Ms W1 44 C4
Corner Ho St WC2 44 E4
Cornwall Rd SE1 45 G4
Cosmo Pl WC1 45 E1
Cosser St SE1 45 G6
Cottesloe Ms SE1 45 G6
County St SE1 45 J7
Covent Gdn WC2 45 E3
Covent Gdn Mkt WC2 45 E3
Coventry St W1 44 D4
Cowcross St EC1 45 H1
Cowley St SW1 44 E6
Craigs Ct SW1 44 E4
Cramer St W1 44 A2
Cranbourn St WC2 44 D3
Crane Ct EC4 45 G3
Cranfield Row SE1 45 G6
Craven Pas WC2 44 E4
Craven St WC2 44 E4
Crawford Pas EC1 45 G1
Creed La EC4 45 H3
Crescent Row EC1 45 J1
Cripplegate St EC2 45 J1
Cromwell Twr EC2 45 J1
Cross Keys Cl W1 44 A2
Cross Keys Sq EC1 45 J2
Crown Ct EC2 45 J3
Crown Ct WC2 45 E3
Crown Office Row
  EC4 45 G3
Crown Pas SW1 44 C5
Cubitts Yd WC2 45 E3
Cuddington SE17 45 J7
Culross St W1 44 A4
Cursitor St EC4 45 G2
Curzon Gate W1 44 A5
Curzon Sq W1 44 A5
Curzon St W1 44 A5
Cut, The SE1 45 G5
Cypress Pl W1 44 C1

D

Dacre St SW1 44 D6
Dane St WC1 45 F2
Dansey Pl W1 44 D3
Dante Pl SE11 45 H7
Dante Rd SE11 45 H7
D'Arblay St W1 44 C3
Dartmouth St SW1 44 D6
Davidge St SE1 45 H6
Davies Ms W1 44 B3
Davies St W1 44 B3
Deacon Way SE17 45 J7
Dean Bradley St SW1 44 E7
Deanery Ms W1 44 A4
Deanery St W1 44 A4
Dean Farrar St SW1 44 D6
Dean Ryle St SW1 44 E7
Deans Ct EC4 45 H3
Deans Ms W1 44 B2
Dean Stanley St SW1 44 E7
Dean St W1 44 D2
Dean's Yd SW1 44 D6

Dean Trench St SW1 44 E7
Denman St W1 44 D4
Denmark Pl WC2 44 D2
Denmark St WC2 44 D3
Derby Gate SW1 44 E5
Derby St W1 44 A5
Dering St W1 44 B3
Devereux Ct WC2 45 G3
Devonshire Cl W1 44 B1
Devonshire Ms N W1 44 B1
Devonshire Ms S W1 44 B1
Devonshire Ms W W1 44 B1
Devonshire Pl W1 44 A1
Devonshire Pl Ms W1 44 A1
Devonshire Row Ms
  W1 44 B1
Devonshire St W1 44 A1
De Walden St W1 44 A2
Diadem Ct W1 44 D3
Dickens Ms EC1 45 H1
Dickens Sq SE1 45 J6
Disney Pl SE1 45 J5
Disney St SE1 45 J5
Distaff La EC4 45 J3
Doby Ct EC4 45 J3
Dodson St SE1 45 G6
Dolben St SE1 45 H5
Dombey St WC1 45 F1
Doon St SE1 45 G5
Dorrington St EC1 45 G1
Dorrit St SE1 45 J5
Dorset Bldgs EC4 45 H3
Dorset Ms SW1 44 B6
Dorset Ri EC4 45 H3
Doughty Ms WC1 45 F1
Dover St W1 44 B4
Dover Yd W1 44 B4
Downing St SW1 44 E5
Down St W1 44 B5
Down St Ms W1 44 B5
Doyce St SE1 45 J5
D'Oyley St SW1 44 A7
Drake St WC1 45 F2
Draper Ho SE1 45 H7
Drury La WC2 45 E3
Dryden St WC2 45 E3
Duchess Ms W1 44 B2
Duchess St W1 44 B2
Duchy Pl SE1 45 G4
Duchy St SE1 45 G4
Duck La W1 44 D3
Dufferin St EC1 45 J1
Dufour's Pl W1 44 C3
Duke of Wellington Pl
  SW1 44 A5
Duke of York St SW1 44 C4
Duke's Ms W1 44 A2
Duke St SW1 44 C4
Duke St W1 44 A2
Duke's Yd W1 44 A3
Duncannon St WC2 44 E4
Dunns Pas WC1 45 E2
Dunstable Ms W1 44 A1
Durham Ho St WC2 45 E4
Dyer's Bldgs EC1 45 G2
Dyott St WC1 44 E2

E

Eagle Ct EC1 45 H1
Eagle Pl SW1 44 C4
Eagle St WC1 45 F2
Earlham St WC2 44 D3
Earnshaw St WC2 44 D2
Easley's Ms W1 44 A2
Eastcastle St W1 44 C2
East Harding St EC4 45 G2
East Pas EC1 45 H1
East Poultry Av EC1 45 H2
Eaton Gate SW1 44 A7
Eaton La SW1 44 B7
Eaton Ms N SW1 44 A7
Eaton Ms S SW1 44 A7
Eaton Ms W SW1 44 A7
Eaton Pl SW1 44 A7
Eaton Row SW1 44 B6
Eaton Sq SW1 44 B6
Eaton Ter SW1 44 A7
Eaton Ter Ms SW1 44 A7
Ebury Ms SW1 44 B7
Ebury Ms E SW1 44 B7
Ebury St SW1 44 B7
Eccleston Br SW1 44 B7
Eccleston Ms SW1 44 A7
Eccleston Pl SW1 44 B7
Eccleston St SW1 44 B7
Edwards Ms W1 44 A3
Elba Pl SE17 45 J7
Elephant & Castle
  SE1 45 H7
Elephant Rd SE17 45 J7
Elizabeth Ct SW1 44 D7
Elizabeth St SW1 44 A7
Ellington Ho SE1 45 J6

Elliotts Row SE11 45 H7
Elm Ct EC4 45 G3
Elm St WC1 45 F1
Elverton St SW1 44 D7
Ely Ct EC1 45 G2
Ely Pl EC1 45 G2
Embankment Pier
  WC2 45 F4
Embankment Pl WC2 45 E4
Emerald St WC1 45 F1
Emerson St SE1 45 J4
Emery Hill St SW1 44 C7
Emery St SE1 45 G6
Endell St WC2 44 E2
Errol St EC1 45 J1
Essex Ct EC4 45 G3
Essex St WC2 45 G3
Euston Rd NW1 44 B1
Evelyn Yd W1 44 D2
Ewer St SE1 45 J5
Excel Ct WC2 44 D4
Exchange Ct WC2 45 E4
Exeter St WC2 45 E3
Exton St SE1 45 G5
Eyre St Hill EC1 45 G1

F

Falconberg Ct W1 44 D2
Falconberg Ms W1 44 D2
Falcon Ct EC4 45 G3
Falmouth Rd SE1 45 J6
Fann St EC1 45 J1
Fann St EC2 45 J1
Fareham St W1 44 D2
Farm St W1 44 B4
Farnham Pl SE1 45 H5
Farringdon La EC1 45 G1
Farringdon St EC4 45 H2
Faulkner's All EC1 45 H1
Ferrybridge Ho SE11 45 F7
Fetter La EC4 45 G3
Field Ct WC1 45 F2
Fisher St WC1 45 E2
Fitzalan St SE11 45 G7
Fitzhardinge St W1 44 A2
Fitzmaurice Pl W1 44 B4
Fitzroy Ct W1 44 C1
Fitzroy Ms W1 44 C1
Fitzroy Sq W1 44 C1
Fitzroy St W1 44 C1
Fives Ct SE11 45 H7
Flaxman Ct W1 44 D3
Fleet St EC4 45 G3
Flitcroft St WC2 44 D2
Floral St WC2 44 E3
Florin Ct EC1 45 J1
Foley St W1 44 C2
Fore St EC2 45 J2
Fortune St EC1 45 J1
Forum Magnum Sq
  SE1 45 F5
Foster La EC2 45 J2
Foubert's Pl W1 44 C3
Fountain Ct EC4 45 G3
Fountain Sq SW1 44 B7
Fox & Knot St EC1 45 H1
Francis St SW1 44 C7
Frazier St SE1 45 G6
Friars Cl SE1 45 H5
Friar St EC4 45 H3
Friary Ct SW1 44 C5
Friday St EC4 45 J3
Frith St W1 44 D3
Fulwood Pl WC1 45 F2
Furnival St EC4 45 G2
Fynes St SW1 44 D7

G

Gabriel's Wf SE1 45 G4
Gage St WC1 45 E1
Galen Pl WC1 45 E2
Gambia St SE1 45 H5
Ganton St W1 44 C3
Garbutt Pl W1 44 A1
Garden Row SE1 45 H7
Gardners La EC4 45 J3
Garlick Hill EC4 45 J3
Garrick St WC2 44 E3
Garrick Yd WC2 44 E3
Gate Ho Sq SE1 45 J4
Gate St WC2 45 F2
Gaunt St SE1 45 H6
Gayfere St SW1 44 E7
Gaywood Est SE1 45 H7
Gaywood St SE1 45 H7
Gees Ct W1 44 A3
George Ct WC2 45 E4
George Mathers Rd
  SE11 45 H7
George Yd W1 44 A3
Geraldine St SE11 45 H7
Gerald Ms SW1 44 A7
Gerald Rd SW1 44 A7
Gerrard Pl W1 44 D3

Gerrard St W1 **44** D3
Gerridge St SE1 **45** G6
Gilbert Pl WC1 **44** E2
Gilbert St W1 **44** A3
Gildea St W1 **44** B1
Gillingham Row SW1 **44** C7
Gillingham St SW1 **44** B7
Giltspur St EC1 **45** H2
Gladstone St SE1 **45** H6
Glasshill St SE1 **45** H5
Glasshouse St W1 **44** C4
Glasshouse Yd EC1 **45** J1
Globe St SE1 **45** J6
Globe Yd W1 **44** B3
Godliman St EC4 **45** J3
Golden Jubilee Br SE1 **45** F5
Golden Jubilee Br WC2 **45** E4
Golden La EC1 **45** J1
Golden La Est EC1 **45** J1
Golden Sq W1 **44** C3
Goldsmith St EC2 **45** J2
Goodge Pl W1 **44** C2
Goodge St W1 **44** C2
Goodwins Ct WC2 **44** E3
Gordon Sq WC1 **44** D1
Gosfield St W1 **44** C1
Goslett Yd WC2 **44** D3
Goswell Rd EC1 **45** J1
Gough Sq EC4 **45** G2
Gower Ms WC1 **44** D2
Grafton Ms W1 **44** C1
Grafton St W1 **44** B4
Grafton Way W1 **44** C1
Grafton Way WC1 **44** C1
Granby Pl SE1 **45** G6
Grand Av EC1 **45** H1
Grange Ct WC2 **45** F3
Grantham Pl W1 **44** B5
Granville Pl W1 **44** A3
Grape St WC2 **44** E2
Gray's Inn WC1 **45** F1
Gray's Inn Pl WC1 **45** F2
Gray's Inn Sq WC1 **45** G1
Gray St SE1 **45** G6
Gray's Yd W1 **44** A3
Great Arthur Ho EC1 **45** J1
Great Castle St W1 **44** B2
Great Chapel St W1 **44** D2
Great Coll St SW1 **44** E6
Great Dover St SE1 **45** J6
Great George St SW1 **44** D6
Great Guildford St SE1 **45** J4
Great James St WC1 **45** F1
Great Marlborough St W1 **44** C3
Great New St EC4 **45** G2
Great Ormond St WC1 **45** E1
Great Peter St SW1 **44** D7
Great Portland St W1 **44** B1
Great Pulteney St W1 **44** C3
Great Queen St WC2 **45** E3
Great Russell St WC1 **44** D2
Great St. Thomas Apostle EC4 **45** J3
Great Scotland Yd SW1 **44** E5
Great Smith St SW1 **44** D6
Great Suffolk St SE1 **45** H5
Great Sutton St EC1 **45** H1
Great Titchfield St W1 **44** C2
Great Trinity La EC4 **45** J3
Great Turnstile WC1 **45** F2
Great Windmill St W1 **44** D3
Greek Ct W1 **44** D3
Greek St W1 **44** D3
Green Arbour Ct EC1 **45** H2
Greencoat Pl SW1 **44** C7
Greencoat Row SW1 **44** C7
Greenham Cl SE1 **45** G6
Greenhill's Rents EC1 **45** H1
Green's Ct W1 **44** D3
Greenwell St W1 **44** B1
Greet St SE1 **45** G5
Grenville St WC1 **45** E1
Gresham St EC2 **45** J2
Gresse St W1 **44** D2
Greville St EC1 **45** G2
Greycoat Pl SW1 **44** D7
Greycoat St SW1 **44** D7
Greyfriars Pas EC1 **45** H2
Greystoke Pl EC4 **45** G2
Grindal St SE1 **45** G6
Groom Pl SW1 **44** A6
Grosvenor Cotts SW1 **44** A7
Grosvenor Cres SW1 **44** A6
Grosvenor Cres Ms SW1 **44** A6
Grosvenor Est SW1 **44** D7
Grosvenor Gdns SW1 **44** B6
Grosvenor Gdns Ms E SW1 **44** B6

Grosvenor Gdns Ms N SW1 **44** B7
Grosvenor Gdns Ms S SW1 **44** B7
Grosvenor Hill W1 **44** B3
Grosvenor Pl SW1 **44** A6
Grosvenor Sq W1 **44** A3
Grosvenor St W1 **44** B3
Grotto Pas W1 **44** A1
Groveland Ct EC4 **45** J3
Guildhall Yd EC2 **45** J2
Guildhouse St SW1 **44** C7
Guilford Pl WC1 **45** F1
Guilford St WC1 **45** E1
Gunpowder Sq EC4 **45** G2
Gutter La EC2 **45** J2

H
Half Moon Ct EC1 **45** J2
Half Moon St W1 **44** B4
Halkin Arc SW1 **44** A6
Halkin Ms SW1 **44** A6
Halkin Pl SW1 **44** A6
Halkin St SW1 **44** A6
Hallam Ms W1 **44** B1
Hallam St W1 **44** B1
Hamilton Ms W1 **44** B5
Hamilton Pl W1 **44** A5
Ham Yd W1 **44** D3
Hand Ct WC1 **45** F2
Hanging Sword All EC4 **45** G3
Hanover Pl WC2 **45** E3
Hanover Sq W1 **44** B3
Hanover St W1 **44** B3
Hanson St W1 **44** C1
Hanway Pl W1 **44** D2
Hanway St W1 **44** D2
Hare Ct EC4 **45** G3
Hare Pl EC4 **45** G3
Harewood Pl W1 **44** B3
Harley Pl W1 **44** B2
Harley St W1 **44** B2
Harmsworth Ms SE11 **45** H7
Harp All EC4 **45** H2
Harper Rd SE1 **45** J6
Harpur Ms WC1 **45** F1
Harpur St WC1 **45** F1
Hat & Mitre Ct EC1 **45** H1
Hatfields SE1 **45** G4
Hatton Gdn EC1 **45** G1
Hatton Pl EC1 **45** G1
Hatton Wall EC1 **45** G1
Haunch of Venison Yd W1 **44** B3
Hay Hill W1 **44** B4
Hayles St SE11 **45** H7
Haymarket SW1 **44** D4
Haymarket Arc SW1 **44** D4
Hayne St EC1 **45** H1
Hay's Ms W1 **44** B4
Hayward's Pl EC1 **45** H1
Headfort Pl SW1 **44** A6
Heddon St W1 **44** C3
Hedger St SE11 **45** H7
Hen & Chicken Ct EC4 **45** G3
Henrietta Pl W1 **44** B3
Henrietta St WC2 **45** E3
Herald's Pl SE11 **45** H7
Herbal Hill EC1 **45** G1
Hercules Rd SE1 **45** F7
Herrick St SW1 **44** D7
Hertford St W1 **44** B4
High Holborn WC1 **45** E2
High Timber St EC4 **45** J3
Hills Pl W1 **44** C3
Hill St W1 **44** A4
Hind Ct EC4 **45** G3
Hinde St W1 **44** A2
Hindon Ct SW1 **44** C7
Hobart Pl SW1 **44** B6
Holbein Ms SW1 **45** G2
Holborn WC2 **45** F2
Holborn Circ EC1 **45** G2
Holborn Pl WC1 **45** F2
Holborn Viaduct EC1 **45** G2
Holland St SE1 **45** H4
Hollen St W1 **44** D2
Holles St W1 **44** B2
Holmes Ter SE1 **45** G5
Holsworthy Sq WC1 **45** F1
Holyoak Rd SE11 **45** H7
Honey La EC2 **45** J3
Hood Ct EC4 **45** G3
Hop Gdns WC2 **44** E4
Hopkins St W1 **44** C3
Hopton's Gdns SE1 **45** H4
Hopton St SE1 **45** H4
Hornbeam Cl SE11 **45** G7
Horse & Dolphin Yd W1 **44** D3
Horseferry Rd SW1 **44** D7
Horse Guards Av SW1 **44** E5

Horse Guards Rd SW1 **44** D5
Horsemongers Ms SE1 **45** J6
Horse Ride SW1 **44** D5
Hosier La EC1 **45** H2
Houghton St WC2 **45** F3
Howick Pl SW1 **44** C7
Howland Ms E W1 **44** C1
Howland St W1 **44** C1
Hudson's Pl SW1 **44** B7
Huggin Ct EC4 **45** J3
Huggin Hill EC4 **45** J3
Hulme Pl SE1 **45** J6
Hungerford Br SE1 **45** E4
Hungerford Br WC2 **45** E4
Hungerford La WC2 **44** E4
Huntley St WC1 **44** C1
Hunt's Ct WC2 **44** D4
Hutton St EC4 **45** G3
Hyde Pk Cor W1 **44** A5

I
India Pl WC2 **45** F3
Ingestre Pl W1 **44** C3
Ingram Cl SE11 **45** F7
Inigo Pl WC2 **44** E3
Inner Temple La EC4 **45** G3
Invicta Plaza SE1 **45** H4
Ireland Yd EC4 **45** H3
Irving St WC2 **44** D4
Isaac Way SE1 **45** J5
Isabella St SE1 **45** H5
Ivybridge La WC2 **45** E4

J
Jacob's Well Ms W1 **44** A2
James St W1 **44** A2
James St WC2 **45** E3
Jermyn St SW1 **44** C4
Jerusalem Pas EC1 **45** H1
Jervis Ct W1 **44** B3
Joan St SE1 **45** H5
Jockey's Flds WC1 **45** F1
Johanna St SE1 **45** G6
John Adam St WC2 **45** E4
John Carpenter St EC4 **45** H3
John Milton Pass EC2 **45** J3
John Princes St W1 **44** B2
John's Ms WC1 **45** F1
John St WC1 **45** F1
Jones St W1 **44** B4
Jubilee Mkt Hall WC2 **45** E3
Juxon St SE11 **45** F7

K
Kean St WC2 **45** F3
Keeley St WC2 **45** F3
Kell St SE1 **45** H6
Kemble St WC2 **45** F3
Kemp's Ct W1 **44** C3
Kendall Pl W1 **44** A2
Kennet Wf La EC4 **45** J3
Kennington Rd SE1 **45** G6
Kennington Rd SE11 **45** G7
Kenrick Pl W1 **44** A1
Keppel Row SE1 **45** J5
Keppel St WC1 **44** D1
Keyworth Pl SE1 **45** H6
Keyworth St SE1 **45** H6
King Charles St SW1 **44** D5
King Edward St EC1 **45** J2
King Edward Wk SE1 **45** G6
Kinghorn St EC1 **45** J2
King James Ct SE1 **45** H6
King James St SE1 **45** H6
Kingly Ct W1 **44** C3
Kingly St W1 **44** C3
Kings Bench St SE1 **45** H5
Kings Bench Wk EC4 **45** G3
Kingscote St EC4 **45** H3
King's Ms WC1 **45** F1
Kings Pl SE1 **45** J6
King's Reach Twr SE1 **45** G4
King's Scholars' Pas SW1 **44** C7
King St EC2 **45** J3
King St SW1 **44** C5
King St WC2 **44** E3
Kingsway WC2 **45** F2
Kinnerton St SW1 **44** A6
Kirby St EC1 **45** G1
Kirkman Pl W1 **44** D2
Kirk St WC1 **45** F1
Knightrider St EC4 **45** J3

L
Lambeth SE1 **45** F7
Lambeth Br SE1 **45** E7
Lambeth Br SW1 **45** E7
Lambeth Hill EC4 **45** J3
Lambeth Palace Rd SE1 **45** F7
Lambeth Pier SE1 **45** E7

Lambeth Rd SE1 **45** F7
Lambeth Rd SE11 **45** F7
Lambeth Twrs SE11 **45** G7
Lambeth Wk SE1 **45** F7
Lambeth Wk SE11 **45** F7
Lambs Conduit Pas WC1 **45** F1
Lamb's Conduit St WC1 **45** F1
Lamlash St SE11 **45** H7
Lamp Office Ct WC1 **45** F1
Lancashire Ct W1 **44** B3
Lancaster Pl WC2 **45** F3
Lancaster St SE1 **45** H6
Lanesborough Pl SW1 **44** A5
Langham Pl W1 **44** B2
Langham St W1 **44** B2
Langley Ct WC2 **44** E3
Langley St WC2 **44** E3
Lansdowne Row W1 **44** B4
Lansdowne Ter WC1 **45** E1
Lant St SE1 **45** J5
Lauderdale Twr EC2 **45** J1
Launcelot St SE1 **45** G6
Lavington St SE1 **45** H5
Lawrence La EC2 **45** J3
Laystall St EC1 **45** G1
Laytons Bldgs SE1 **45** J5
Lazenby Ct WC2 **44** E3
Leake St SE1 **45** F5
Leather La EC1 **45** G2
Lees Pl W1 **44** A3
Leicester Ct WC2 **44** D3
Leicester Pl WC2 **44** D3
Leicester Sq WC2 **44** D4
Leicester St WC2 **44** D3
Leigh Hunt St SE1 **45** J5
Leigh Pl EC1 **45** G1
Leopards Ct EC1 **45** G1
Leo Yd EC1 **45** H1
Lewisham St SW1 **44** D6
Lexington St W1 **44** C3
Library St SE1 **45** H6
Lily Pl EC1 **45** G1
Limeburner La EC4 **45** H3
Lincoln's Inn WC2 **45** F2
Lincoln's Inn Flds WC2 **45** F2
Lindsey St EC1 **45** H1
Lisle St WC2 **44** D3
Litchfield St WC2 **44** D3
Little Argyll St W1 **44** C3
Little Britain EC1 **45** J2
Little Chester St SW1 **44** A6
Little Coll St SW1 **44** E6
Little Dean's Yd SW1 **44** E6
Little Dorrit Ct SE1 **45** J5
Little Essex St WC2 **45** G3
Little George St SW1 **44** E6
Little Newport St WC2 **44** D3
Little New St EC4 **45** G2
Little Portland St W1 **44** C2
Little Russell St WC1 **44** E2
Little St. James's St SW1 **44** C5
Little Sanctuary SW1 **44** D6
Little Smith St SW1 **44** D6
Little Titchfield St W1 **44** C2
Little Trinity La EC4 **45** J3
Little Turnstile WC1 **45** F2
Livonia St W1 **44** C3
Lollard St SE11 **45** F7
Loman St SE1 **45** H5
Lombard La EC4 **45** G3
London Cen Mkts EC1 **45** H1
London Rd SE1 **45** H6
London Silver Vaults WC2 **45** G2
London Trocadero, The W1 **44** D4
London Wall EC2 **45** J2
Long Acre WC2 **44** E3
Long La EC1 **45** H1
Longridge Ho SE1 **45** J7
Long's Ct WC2 **44** D3
Longstone Ct SE1 **45** J6
Longville Rd SE11 **45** H7
Long Yd WC1 **45** F1
Lord N St SW1 **44** E7
Love La EC2 **45** J2
Lover's Wk W1 **44** A4
Lower Belgrave St SW1 **44** B7
Lower Grosvenor Pl SW1 **44** B6
Lower James St W1 **44** C3
Lower John St W1 **44** C3
Lower Marsh SE1 **45** G6
Lower Rd SE1 **45** G5
Lowndes Cl SW1 **44** A7
Lowndes Ct W1 **44** C3
Lowndes Pl SW1 **44** A7

Ludgate Bdy EC4 **45** H3
Ludgate Circ EC4 **45** H3
Ludgate Hill EC4 **45** H3
Ludgate Sq EC4 **45** H3
Lumley Ct WC2 **45** E4
Lumley St W1 **44** A3
Luxborough St W1 **44** A1
Lyall Ms SW1 **44** A7
Lyall Ms W SW1 **44** A7
Lyall St SW1 **44** A7
Lygon Pl SW1 **44** B7

M
McAuley Cl SE1 **45** G6
Macclesfield St W1 **44** D3
McCoid Way SE1 **45** J6
Macfarren Pl NW1 **44** A1
Macklin St WC2 **45** E2
Mac's Pl EC4 **45** G2
Maddox St W1 **44** B3
Magpie All EC4 **45** G3
Maiden La SE1 **45** J4
Maiden La WC2 **45** E4
Maidstone Bldgs Ms SE1 **45** J5
Malet Pl WC1 **44** D1
Malet St WC1 **44** D1
Mall, The SW1 **44** C5
Maltravers St WC2 **45** F3
Manchester Ms W1 **44** A2
Manchester Sq W1 **44** A2
Manchester St W1 **44** A2
Mandeville Pl W1 **44** A2
Manette St W1 **44** D3
Mansfield Ms W1 **44** B2
Mansfield St W1 **44** B2
Maple Pl W1 **44** C1
Maple St W1 **44** C1
Margaret Ct W1 **44** C2
Margaret St W1 **44** B2
Marigold All SE1 **45** H4
Market Ct W1 **44** C2
Market Ms W1 **44** B5
Market Pl W1 **44** C2
Marlborough Ct W1 **44** C3
Marlborough Rd SW1 **44** C5
Marshall St W1 **44** C3
Marshalsea Rd SE1 **45** J5
Marsham St SW1 **44** D7
Martin Ho SE1 **45** J7
Martlett Ct WC2 **45** E3
Marylebone High St W1 **44** A1
Marylebone La W1 **44** B3
Marylebone Ms W1 **44** B2
Marylebone Pas W1 **44** C2
Marylebone St W1 **44** A2
Masons Arms Ms W1 **44** B3
Mason's Yd SW1 **44** C4
Matthew Parker St SW1 **44** D6
Matthews Yd WC2 **44** E3
Maunsel St SW1 **44** D7
Mayfair W1 **44** B4
Mayfair Pl W1 **44** B4
Mays Ct WC2 **44** E4
Meadow Row SE1 **45** J7
Mead Row SE1 **45** G6
Meard St W1 **44** D3
Medway St SW1 **44** D7
Melbourne Pl WC2 **45** F3
Memel Ct EC1 **45** J1
Memel St EC1 **45** J1
Mepham St SE1 **45** F5
Mercer St WC2 **44** E3
Merrick Sq SE1 **45** J6
Metro Cen Hts SE1 **45** J7
Meymott St SE1 **45** H5
Middlesex Pas EC1 **45** H2
Middle St EC1 **45** J1
Middle Temple EC4 **45** G3
Middle Temple La EC4 **45** G3
Middleton Pl W1 **44** C2
Midford Pl W1 **44** C1
Milcote St SE1 **45** H6
Milford La WC2 **45** F3
Milk St EC2 **45** J3
Millbank SW1 **44** E7
Millbank SW1 **44** E7
Millennium Br EC4 **45** J3
Millennium Br SE1 **45** J3
Miller Wk SE1 **45** G5
Millman Ms WC1 **45** F1
Millman St WC1 **45** F1
Mill St W1 **44** B3
Milroy Wk SE1 **45** H4
Minera Ms SW1 **44** A7
Mint St SE1 **45** J5
Mitre Ct EC2 **45** J2
Mitre Rd SE1 **45** G5
Monck St SW1 **44** D7
Monkton St SE11 **45** G7
Monkwell Sq EC2 **45** J2

Monmouth St WC2 **44** E3
Montague Pl WC1 **44** D1
Montague St EC1 **45** J2
Montague St WC1 **44** E1
Montreal Pl WC2 **45** F3
Montrose Pl SW1 **44** A6
Moor St W1 **44** D3
Morley St SE1 **45** G6
Morpeth Ter SW1 **44** C7
Mortimer Mkt WC1 **44** C1
Mortimer St W1 **44** C2
Morton Pl SE1 **45** G7
Morwell St WC1 **44** D2
Mount Pleasant WC1 **45** F1
Mount Row W1 **44** B4
Mount St W1 **44** A4
Mount St Ms W1 **44** B4
Moxon St W1 **44** A2
Munton Rd SE17 **45** J7
Murphy St SE1 **45** G6
Museum St WC1 **44** E2

N
Nag's Head Ct EC1 **45** J1
Nassau St W1 **44** C2
Neal St WC2 **44** E3
Neal's Yd WC2 **44** E3
Neathouse Pl SW1 **44** C7
Nelson Sq SE1 **45** H5
Newall Ho SE1 **45** J6
New Bond St W1 **44** B3
New Br St EC4 **45** H3
Newburgh St W1 **44** C3
New Burlington Ms W1 **44** C3
New Burlington Pl W1 **44** C3
New Burlington St W1 **44** C3
Newbury St EC1 **45** J2
Newcastle Cl EC4 **45** H2
New Cavendish St W1 **44** B1
New Change EC4 **45** J3
New Compton St WC2 **44** D3
New Fetter La EC4 **45** G2
Newgate St EC1 **45** H2
New Inn Pas WC2 **45** J4
Newington SE1 **45** J7
Newington Causeway SE1 **45** H7
New Inn Pas WC2 **45** F3
New Kent Rd SE1 **45** J7
Newman Pas W1 **44** C2
Newman's Row WC2 **45** F2
Newman St W1 **44** C2
Newman Yd W1 **44** C2
Newnham Ter SE1 **45** G6
New N St WC1 **45** F1
New Oxford St WC1 **44** D2
Newport Ct WC2 **44** D3
Newport Pl WC2 **44** D3
New Row WC2 **44** E3
New Sq WC2 **45** F2
New St Sq EC4 **45** G2
Newton St WC2 **45** E2
New Turnstile WC1 **45** F2
Nicholson St SE1 **45** H5
Nightingale Ms SE11 **45** G7
Noble St EC2 **45** J2
Noel St W1 **44** C3
Norfolk Row SE1 **45** F7
Norris St SW1 **44** D4
North Audley St W1 **44** A3
North Cres WC1 **44** D1
Northington St WC1 **45** F1
North Ms WC1 **45** F1
Northumberland Av WC2 **44** E4
Northumberland St WC2 **44** E4
Norwich St EC4 **45** G2
Nottingham Ct WC2 **44** E3
Nottingham Pl W1 **44** A1
Nottingham St W1 **44** A1
Nottingham Ter NW1 **44** A1

O
Oakden St SE11 **45** G7
Oakey La SE1 **45** G6
Oat La EC2 **45** J2
Odhams Wk WC2 **45** E3
Ogle St W1 **44** C1
Old Bailey EC4 **45** H3
Old Barrack Yd SW1 **44** A5
Old Bond St W1 **44** C4
Old Brewers Yd WC2 **44** E3
Old Bldgs WC2 **45** G2
Old Burlington St W1 **44** C3
Oldbury Pl W1 **44** A1
Old Cavendish St W1 **44** B2
Old Compton St W1 **44** D3
Old Fish St Hill EC4 **45** J3
Old Fleet La EC4 **45** H2

Street	Ref
Old Gloucester St WC1	45 E1
Old Mitre Ct EC4	45 G3
Old N St WC1	45 F1
Old Palace Yd SW1	44 E6
Old Paradise St SE11	45 F7
Old Pk La W1	44 A5
Old Pye St SW1	44 D6
Old Queen St SW1	44 D6
Old Seacoal La EC4	45 H2
Old Sq WC2	45 F2
O'Meara St SE1	45 J5
Onslow St EC1	45 G1
Ontario St SE1	45 H7
Orange St WC2	44 D4
Orange Yd W1	44 D3
Orchard St W1	44 A3
Orde Hall St WC1	45 F1
Orient St SE11	45 H7
Ormond Cl WC1	45 E1
Ormond Ms WC1	45 E1
Ormond Yd SW1	44 C4
Osnaburgh St NW1	44 B1
Ossington Bldgs W1	44 A1
Oswin St SE11	45 H7
Outer Circle NW1	44 A1
Oxendon St SW1	44 D4
Oxford Circ Av W1	44 C3
Oxford St W1	44 C2
Oxo Twr Wf SE1	45 G4
P	
Paddington St W1	44 A1
Pageantmaster Ct EC4	45 H3
Page St SW1	44 D7
Palace Pl SW1	44 C6
Palace St SW1	44 C6
Pall Mall SW1	44 C5
Pall Mall E SW1	44 D4
Palmer St SW1	44 D6
Pancras La EC4	45 J3
Panton St SW1	44 D4
Paris Gdn SE1	45 H4
Park Cres W1	44 B1
Park Cres Ms E W1	44 B1
Park Cres Ms W W1	44 B1
Parker Ms WC2	45 E2
Parker St WC2	45 E2
Park La W1	44 A5
Park Pl SW1	44 C5
Park Sq Ms NW1	44 B1
Park St SE1	45 J4
Park St W1	44 A3
Parliament Sq SW1	44 E6
Parliament St SW1	44 E6
Parliament Vw Apts SE1	45 F7
Passing All EC1	45 H1
Pastor St SE1	45 H7
Paternoster Row EC4	45 J3
Paternoster Sq EC4	45 H3
Paul's Wk EC4	45 H3
Peabody Est EC1	45 J1
Peabody Est SE1	45 G5
Peabody Est SE1	44 C7
Peabody Sq SE1	45 H6
Peabody Trust SE1	45 J5
Pearman St SE1	45 G6
Pear Pl SE1	45 G5
Pear Tree Ct EC1	45 G1
Pemberton Row EC4	45 G2
Pembroke Cl SW1	44 A6
Penhurst Pl SE1	45 F7
Pepper St SE1	45 J5
Percy Ms W1	44 D2
Percy Pas W1	44 C2
Percy St W1	44 D2
Perkin's Rents SW1	44 D6
Perkins Sq SE1	45 J4
Perrys Pl W1	44 D2
Peters Hill EC4	45 J3
Peter's La EC1	45 H1
Peter St W1	44 C3
Petty France SW1	44 C6
Phipp's Ms SW1	44 B7
Phoenix St WC2	44 D3
Piccadilly W1	44 B5
Piccadilly Arc SW1	44 C4
Piccadilly Circ W1	44 D4
Piccadilly Pl W1	44 C4
Pickering Pl SW1	44 C5
Pickwick St SE1	45 J6
Picton Pl W1	44 A3
Pilgrim St EC4	45 H3
Pineapple Ct SW1	44 C6
Pitt's Head Ms W1	44 A5
Playhouse Yd EC4	45 H3
Plaza Shop Cen, The W1	44 C2
Pleydell Ct EC4	45 G3
Pleydell St EC4	45 G3
Plough Pl EC4	45 G2
Plumtree Ct EC4	45 G2
Pocock St SE1	45 H5
Poland St W1	44 C3
Pollen St W1	44 B3
Polperro Ms SE11	45 G7
Pontypool Pl SE1	45 H5
Pooles Bldgs EC1	45 G1
Poppins Ct EC4	45 H3
Porter St SE1	45 J4
Portland Ms W1	44 C3
Portland Pl W1	44 B1
Portman Ms S W1	44 A3
Portman St W1	44 A3
Portpool La EC1	45 G1
Portsmouth St WC2	45 F3
Portugal St WC2	45 F3
Powis Pl WC1	45 E1
Pratt Wk SE11	45 F7
Price's St SE1	45 H5
Priest Ct EC2	45 J2
Primrose Hill EC4	45 G3
Prince's Arc SW1	44 C4
Princes Pl SW1	44 C4
Princess St SE1	45 H7
Princes St W1	44 B3
Princeton St WC1	45 F1
Printers Inn Ct EC4	45 G2
Printer St EC4	45 G2
Procter St WC1	45 F2
Providence Ct W1	44 A3
Prudent Pas EC2	45 J2
Puddle Dock EC4	45 H3
Q	
Quadrant Arc W1	44 C4
Quality Ct WC2	45 G2
Queen Anne Ms W1	44 B2
Queen Anne's Gate SW1	44 D6
Queen Anne St W1	44 B2
Queenhithe EC4	45 J3
Queen's Head Pas EC4	45 J2
Queen Sq WC1	45 E1
Queen Sq Pl WC1	45 E1
Queen St EC4	45 J3
Queen St W1	44 B4
Queen St Pl EC4	45 J4
Queen's Wk SW1	44 C5
Queen's Wk, The SE1	45 F5
Queens Yd W1	44 C1
Queen Victoria St EC4	45 H3
Quilp St SE1	45 J5
R	
Ramillies Pl W1	44 C3
Ramillies St W1	44 C3
Rathbone Pl W1	44 D2
Rathbone St W1	44 C2
Ray St EC1	45 G1
Ray St Br EC1	45 G1
Redcross Way SE1	45 J5
Red Lion Ct EC4	45 G2
Red Lion Sq WC1	45 F2
Red Lion St WC1	45 F1
Red Lion Yd W1	44 A4
Red Pl W1	44 A3
Reeves Ms W1	44 A4
Regency Pl SW1	44 D7
Regency St SW1	44 D7
Regent Pl W1	44 C3
Regent St SW1	44 D4
Regent St W1	44 B2
Remnant St WC2	45 F2
Renfrew Rd SE11	45 H7
Rennie St SE1	45 H4
Rex Pl W1	44 A4
Richardson's Ms W1	44 C1
Richbell Pl WC1	45 F1
Richmond Bldgs W1	44 D3
Richmond Ms W1	44 D3
Richmond Ter SW1	44 E5
Ridgmount Gdns WC1	44 D1
Ridgmount Pl WC1	44 D1
Ridgmount St WC1	44 D1
Riding Ho St W1	44 C2
Risborough St SE1	45 H5
Rising Sun Ct EC1	45 H2
River St EC1	45 H4
Robert Adam St W1	44 A2
Roberts Ms SW1	44 A7
Robert St WC2	45 E4
Rochester Row SW1	44 C7
Rochester St SW1	44 D7
Rockingham Est SE1	45 J7
Rockingham St SE1	45 J7
Rodney Pl SE17	45 J7
Rodney Rd SE17	45 J7
Roger St WC1	45 F1
Rolls Bldgs EC4	45 G2
Rolls Pas EC4	45 G2
Romilly St W1	44 D3
Romney Ms W1	44 A1
Romney St SW1	44 D7
Roscoe St EC1	45 J1
Rose All SE1	45 J4
Rose & Crown Ct EC2	45 J2
Rose & Crown Yd SW1	44 C4
Rosebery Av EC1	45 G1
Rosebery Sq EC1	45 G1
Rose St EC4	45 H2
Rose St WC2	44 E3
Rotherham Wk SE1	45 H5
Rotten Row SW1	44 A5
Roupell St SE1	45 G5
Royal Arc W1	44 C4
Royal Ms, The SW1	44 B6
Royal Opera Arc SW1	44 D4
Royal St SE1	45 F6
Royalty Ms W1	44 D3
Rugby St WC1	45 F1
Rupert Ct W1	44 D3
Rupert St W1	44 D3
Rushworth St SE1	45 H5
Russell Ct SW1	44 C5
Russell Sq WC1	44 E1
Russell St WC2	45 E3
Russia Row EC2	45 J3
Rutherford St SW1	44 D7
Rutland Pl EC1	45 J1
Ryder Ct SW1	44 C4
Ryder St SW1	44 C4
Ryder Yd SW1	44 C4
S	
Sackville St W1	44 C4
Saddle Yd W1	44 B4
Saffron Hill EC1	45 G1
Saffron St EC1	45 G1
Sail St SE11	45 F7
St. Albans Ct EC2	45 J2
St. Albans St SW1	44 D4
St. Alphage Gdns EC2	45 J2
St. Andrew's Hill EC4	45 H3
St. Andrew St EC4	45 G2
St. Anne's Ct W1	44 D3
St. Ann's La SW1	44 D6
St. Ann's St SW1	44 D6
St. Anselm's Pl W1	44 B3
St. Brides Av EC4	45 H3
St. Bride St EC4	45 H2
St. Christopher's Pl W1	44 A2
St. Clement's La WC2	45 F3
St. Cross St EC1	45 G1
St. Ermin's Hill SW1	44 D6
St. Georges Circ SE1	45 H6
St. Georges Ct EC4	45 H2
St. Georges Ms SE1	45 G6
St. Georges Rd SE1	45 G6
St. George St W1	44 B3
St. Giles High St WC2	44 D2
St. Giles Pas WC2	44 D3
St. James's SW1	44 C6
St. James's Mkt SW1	44 D4
St. James's Palace SW1	44 C5
St. James's Pk SW1	44 D5
St. James's Pl SW1	44 C5
St. James's Sq SW1	44 C4
St. James's St SW1	44 C4
St. John's La EC1	45 H1
St. John's Path EC1	45 H1
St. John's Pl EC1	45 H1
St. John's Sq EC1	45 H1
St. John St EC1	45 J2
St. Margaret's Ct SE1	45 J5
St. Margaret's St SW1	44 E6
St. Martin's La WC2	44 E3
St. Martin's-le-Grand EC1	45 J2
St. Martin's Ms WC2	44 E4
St. Martin's Pl WC2	44 E4
St. Martin's St WC2	44 D4
St. Mary's Gdns SE11	45 G7
St. Mary's Wk SE11	45 G7
St. Matthew St SW1	44 D7
St. Olaves Gdns SE11	45 G7
St. Paul's Chyd EC4	45 H3
St. Vincent St W1	44 A2
Salisbury Ct EC4	45 H3
Salisbury Sq EC4	45 H3
Sanctuary, The SW1	44 D6
Sanctuary St SE1	45 J6
Sandell St SE1	45 G5
Sandland St WC1	45 F2
Saperton Wk SE11	45 F7
Sardinia St WC2	45 F3
Savile Row W1	44 C4
Savoy Bldgs WC2	45 F4
Savoy Ct WC2	45 E4
Savoy Hill WC2	45 F4
Savoy Pl WC2	45 E4
Savoy Row WC2	45 F3
Savoy St WC2	45 F3
Savoy Way WC2	45 F4
Sawyer St SE1	45 J5
Scala St W1	44 C1
Scoresby St SE1	45 H5
Scotland Pl SW1	44 E4
Scovell Cres SE1	45 J6
Scovell Rd SE1	45 J6
Secker St SE1	45 G5
Sedding St SW1	44 A7
Sedley Pl W1	44 B3
Sekforde St EC1	45 H1
Serjeants Inn EC4	45 G3
Serle St WC2	45 F2
Sermon La EC4	45 J3
Seymour Ms W1	44 A2
Shaftesbury Av W1	44 D3
Shaftesbury Av WC2	44 D3
Shakespeare Twr EC2	45 J1
Shavers Pl SW1	44 D4
Sheffield St WC2	45 F3
Shelton St WC2	44 E3
Shepherd Mkt W1	44 B4
Shepherd's Pl W1	44 A3
Shepherd St W1	44 B5
Sheraton St W1	44 D3
Sherlock Ms W1	44 A1
Sherwood St W1	44 C3
Shoe La EC4	45 G2
Shorts Gdns WC2	44 E3
Short St SE1	45 G5
Shropshire Pl WC1	44 C1
Sicilian Av WC1	45 E2
Sidford Pl SE1	45 F7
Silex St SE1	45 H6
Silk St EC2	45 J1
Silver Pl W1	44 C3
Silvester St SE1	45 J6
Skinners La EC4	45 J3
Slingsby Pl WC2	44 E3
Smart's Pl WC2	45 E2
Smeaton Ct SE1	45 J7
Smithfield St EC1	45 H2
Smith's Ct W1	44 C3
Smith Sq SW1	44 E7
Smokehouse Yd EC1	45 H1
Snow Hill EC1	45 H2
Snow Hill Ct EC1	45 H2
Soho W1	44 C3
Soho Sq W1	44 D2
Soho St W1	44 D2
Southampton Bldgs WC2	45 G2
Southampton Pl WC1	45 E2
Southampton Row WC1	45 E1
Southampton St WC2	45 E3
South Audley St W1	44 A4
South Cres WC1	44 D2
South Eaton Pl SW1	44 A7
South Molton La W1	44 B3
South Molton St W1	44 B3
South Sq WC1	45 G2
South St W1	44 A4
Southwark SE1	
Southwark Br EC4	45 J4
Southwark Br SE1	45 J4
Southwark Br Rd SE1	45 H6
Southwark St SE1	45 H4
Spanish Pl W1	44 A2
Spenser St SW1	44 C6
Spring Gdns SW1	44 D4
Spur Rd SE1	45 G5
Spur Rd SW1	44 C6
Stable Yd SW1	44 C5
Stable Yd Rd SW1	44 C5
Stacey St WC2	44 D3
Stafford Pl SW1	44 C6
Stafford St W1	44 C4
Staining La EC2	45 J2
Stamford St SE1	45 G5
Stangate SE1	45 F6
Stanhope Gate W1	44 A4
Stanhope Row W1	44 B5
Staple Inn WC1	45 G2
Staple Inn Bldgs WC1	45 G2
Star Yd WC2	45 G2
Station App SE1	45 F5
Stedham Pl WC1	44 E2
Stephen Ms W1	44 D2
Stephen St W1	44 D2
Stew La EC4	45 J3
Stillington St SW1	44 C7
Stone Bldgs WC2	45 F2
Stonecutter St EC4	45 H2
Stones End St SE1	45 J6
Store St WC1	44 D2
Storey's Gate SW1	44 D6
Strand WC2	44 E4
Strand La WC2	45 F3
Stratford Pl W1	44 B3
Stratton St W1	44 B4
Streatham St WC1	44 D2
Strutton Grd SW1	44 D6
Stukeley St WC1	45 E2
Stukeley St WC2	45 E2
Sturge St SE1	45 J5
Sudrey St SE1	45 J6
Suffolk Pl SW1	44 D4
Suffolk St SW1	44 D4
Sullivan Rd SE11	45 G7
Summers St EC1	45 G1
Sumner St SE1	45 H4
Surrey Row SE1	45 H5
Surrey St WC2	45 F3
Sutton La EC1	45 H1
Sutton Row W1	44 D2
Sutton's Way EC1	45 J1
Swallow Pl W1	44 B3
Swallow St W1	44 C4
Swan St SE1	45 J6
Swiss Ct W1	44 D4
Sycamore St EC1	45 J1
T	
Tachbrook Ms SW1	44 C7
Tallis St EC4	45 G3
Tanswell Est SE1	45 G6
Tanswell St SE1	45 G6
Tarn St SE1	45 J7
Tavistock St WC2	45 E3
Telford Ho SE1	45 J7
Temple Av EC4	45 G3
Temple La EC4	45 G3
Temple Pl WC2	45 F3
Temple W Ms SE11	45 H7
Tenison Ct W1	44 C3
Tenison Way SE1	45 G5
Tenterden St W1	44 B3
Terminus Pl SW1	44 B7
Thavies Inn EC1	45 G2
Thayer St W1	44 A2
Theed St SE1	45 G5
Theobald's Rd WC1	45 F1
Thirleby Rd SW1	44 C7
Thomas Doyle St SE1	45 H6
Thorney St SW1	44 E7
Thornhaugh Ms WC1	44 D1
Thornhaugh St WC1	44 D1
Thrale St SE1	45 J4
Three Barrels Wk EC4	45 J4
Three Cups Yd WC1	45 F2
Three Kings Yd W1	44 B3
Tilney St W1	44 A4
Tiverton St SE1	45 J7
Took's Ct EC4	45 G2
Torrington Pl WC1	44 C1
Torrington Sq WC1	44 D1
Tothill St SW1	44 D6
Tottenham Ct Rd W1	44 C1
Tottenham Ms W1	44 C1
Tottenham St W1	44 C2
Toulmin St SE1	45 J6
Tower Ct WC2	44 E3
Tower Royal EC4	45 J3
Tower St WC2	44 D3
Trafalgar Sq SW1	44 D4
Trafalgar Sq WC2	44 D4
Trebeck St W1	44 B4
Treveris St SE1	45 H5
Trig La EC4	45 J3
Trinity Ch Sq SE1	45 J6
Trinity St SE1	45 J6
Trio Pl SE1	45 J6
Trump St EC2	45 J3
Trundle St SE1	45 J5
Tudor St EC4	45 G3
Tufton St SW1	44 D6
Turk's Head Yd EC1	45 H1
Turnagain La EC4	45 H2
Turnmill St EC1	45 G1
Tweezer's All WC2	45 G3
Twyford Pl WC2	45 F2
Tyler's Ct W1	44 D3
U	
Ufford St SE1	45 G5
Ulster Pl NW1	44 B1
Ulster Ter NW1	44 B1
Union Jack Club SE1	45 G5
Union St SE1	45 H5
University St WC1	44 C1
Upper Belgrave St SW1	44 A6
Upper Brook St W1	44 A4
Upper Grosvenor St W1	44 A4
Upper Grd SE1	45 G4
Upper James St W1	44 C3
Upper John St W1	44 C3
Upper Marsh SE1	45 F6
Upper St. Martin's La WC2	44 E3
Upper Tachbrook St SW1	44 C7
Upper Thames St EC4	45 H3
Upper Wimpole St W1	44 B1
V	
Valentine Pl SE1	45 H5
Valentine Row SE1	45 H6
Vandon Pas SW1	44 C6
Vandon St SW1	44 C6
Vane St SW1	44 C7
Vauxhall Br Rd SW1	44 C7
Vere St W1	44 B3
Vernon Pl WC1	45 E2
Verulam Bldgs WC1	45 F1
Verulam St WC1	45 G1
Vesage Ct EC1	45 G2
Victoria Embk EC4	45 F4
Victoria Embk SW1	45 E5
Victoria Embk WC2	45 F4
Victoria Pl SW1	44 B7
Victoria Sq SW1	44 B6
Victoria Sta SW1	44 B7
Victoria St SW1	44 C7
Vigo St W1	44 C4
Villiers St WC2	44 E4
Vincent Sq SW1	44 C7
Vincent St SW1	44 D7
Vine Hill EC1	45 G1
Vine St W1	44 C4
Vine St Br EC1	45 G1
Vine Yd SE1	45 J5
Vintners Ct EC4	45 J3
Virgil St SE1	45 F6
Viscount St EC1	45 J1
W	
Waithman St EC4	45 H3
Walcot Sq SE11	45 G7
Walcott St SW1	44 C7
Walkers Ct W1	44 D3
Wallis All SE1	45 J5
Wallside EC2	45 J2
Walnut Tree Wk SE11	45 G7
Walworth Rd SE1	45 J7
Walworth Rd SE17	45 J7
Wardens Gro SE1	45 J5
Wardour Ms W1	44 C3
Wardour St W1	44 D3
Wardrobe Ter EC4	45 H3
Warner St EC1	45 G1
Warner Yd EC1	45 G1
Warren Ms W1	44 C1
Warren St W1	44 B1
Warwick Ct WC1	45 F2
Warwick Ho St SW1	44 D4
Warwick La EC4	45 H3
Warwick Pas EC4	45 H2
Warwick Row SW1	44 B6
Warwick Sq EC4	45 H2
Warwick St W1	44 C3
Warwick Yd EC1	45 J1
Watergate EC4	45 H3
Watergate Wk WC2	45 E4
Waterhouse Sq EC1	45 G2
Waterloo Br SE1	45 F4
Waterloo Br WC2	45 F4
Waterloo Pl SW1	44 D4
Waterloo Rd SE1	45 G5
Waterloo Sta SE1	45 G5
Water St WC2	45 F3
Watling Ct EC4	45 J3
Watling St EC4	45 J3
Waverton St W1	44 A4
Webber Row SE1	45 G6
Webber St SE1	45 G5
Wedgwood Ho SE11	45 G7
Wedgwood Ms W1	44 D3
Weighhouse St W1	44 A3
Welbeck St W1	44 B2
Welbeck Way W1	44 B2
Well Ct EC4	45 J3
Weller St SE1	45 J5
Wellington St WC2	45 E3
Wells Ms W1	44 C2
Wells St W1	44 C2
Wesley St W1	44 A2
West Cen St WC1	44 E2
West Eaton Pl SW1	44 A7
West Eaton Pl Ms SW1	44 A7
West Halkin St SW1	44 A6
West Harding St EC4	45 G2
Westminster SW1	44 C6
Westminster Br SE1	45 E6
Westminster Br SW1	45 E6
Westminster Br Rd SE1	45 F6
Westminster Gdns SW1	44 E7
Westmoreland St W1	44 A2

West One Shop Cen W1   44 A3
West Poultry Av EC1   45 H2
West Smithfield EC1   45 H2
West Sq SE11   45 H7
West St WC2   44 D3
Weymouth Ms W1   44 B1
Weymouth St W1   44 A2
Wheatley St W1   44 A2
Whetstone Pk WC2   45 F2
Whichcote St SE1   45 G5
Whitcomb St WC2   44 D4
Whitefriars St EC4   45 G3

Whitehall SW1   44 E4
Whitehall Ct SW1   44 E5
Whitehall Gdns SW1   44 E5
Whitehall Pl SW1   44 E5
White Hart St EC4   45 H2
White Horse All EC1   45 H1
White Horse Ms SE1   45 G6
White Horse St W1   44 B5
White Lion Hill EC4   45 H3
White Lyon Ct EC2   45 J1
Whitfield Pl W1   44 C1
Whitfield St W1   44 D2
Whitgift St SE11   45 F7

Whittlesey St SE1   45 G5
Whitworth Ho SE1   45 J7
Wicksteed Ho SE1   45 J7
Wigmore Pl W1   44 B2
Wigmore St W1   44 A3
Wilcox Pl SW1   44 C7
Wild Ct WC2   45 F2
Wild St WC2   45 E3
Wilfred St SW1   44 C6
William IV St WC2   44 E4
Willoughby St WC1   44 E2
Willow Pl SW1   44 C7
Wilton Cres SW1   44 A6

Wilton Ms SW1   44 A6
Wilton Pl SW1   44 A6
Wilton Rd SW1   44 B7
Wilton Row SW1   44 A6
Wilton St SW1   44 B6
Wilton Ter SW1   44 A6
Wimpole Ms W1   44 B1
Wimpole St W1   44 B2
Wincott St SE11   45 G7
Windmill St W1   44 D2
Windmill Wk SE1   45 G5
Windsor Pl SW1   44 C7
Wine Office Ct EC4   45 G2

Winnett St W1   44 D3
Winsley St W1   44 C2
Woburn Sq WC1   44 D1
Wollaston Cl SE1   45 J7
Woodstock Ms W1   44 A2
Woodstock St W1   44 B3
Wood St EC2   45 J3
Wootton St SE1   45 G5

Y
Yarmouth Pl W1   44 B5
York Bldgs WC2   45 E4
York Gate NW1   44 A1

York Pl WC2   45 E4
York Rd SE1   45 F5
Yorkshire Grey Yd WC1   45 F2
York Ter E NW1   44 A1
York Ter W NW1   44 A1

Z
Zoar St SE1   45 J4

Manchester street index

A
Abingdon St   47 E4
Academy Wk   46 D7
Ackers St   47 F7
Acton Sq   46 A3
Adair St   47 G4
Addington St   47 F2
Addison Cl   47 G7
Adelphi St   46 B3
Aden Cl   47 J4
Adlington St   47 H5
Adstone Cl   47 J3
Adswood St   47 J3
Airton Cl   47 H1
Aked Cl   47 J7
Albion Pl   46 A3
Albion St   46 D5
Albion Way   46 A3
Alderman Sq   47 J4
Aldred St   46 A3
Alexander Gdns   46 C1
Alexandra St   46 C1
Alfred James Cl   47 H2
Alker Rd   47 J2
Alley St   46 E3
Almond St   47 G1
Altair Pl   46 B1
Amory St   47 G5
Anaconda Dr   46 C2
Ancoats   47 G3
Ancoats Gro   47 H4
Ancroft St   46 C7
Angela St   46 C6
Angel St   47 F2
Angora Cl   46 B2
Angora Dr   46 B2
Anita St   47 G3
Anne Nuttall St   46 B6
Anscombe Cl   47 H1
Antares Av   46 B1
Apsley Gro   47 H6
Aquarius St   47 E7
Archway   46 D7
Ardwick   47 J5
Ardwick Grn N   47 G5
Ardwick Grn S   47 G5
Arlington St   46 C2
Arnott Cres   46 E7
Artillery St   46 D4
Arundel St   46 C5
Asgard Dr   46 B5
Asgard Grn   46 B5
Ashlar Dr   47 J4
Ashley St   47 F2
Ashton New Rd   47 J3
Ashton Old Rd   47 H5
Aspin La   47 F2
Atherton St   46 C4
Atkinson St   46 D4
Atwood St   47 E5
Auburn St   47 F4
Audlem Cl   47 J2
Augustus St   47 E1
Avenham Cl   46 D7
Aytoun St   47 F4

B
Back Acton St   47 F4
Back Ashley St   47 F2
Back Bk St   47 F1
Back Br St   46 D3
Back China La   47 F4
Back Coll Land   46 D3
Back George St   47 E4
Back Hampson St   47 H1
Back Hulme St   46 B3
Back Junct St   47 G4
Back Piccadilly   47 F3
Back Pool Fold   46 E3
Back Red Bk   47 F1
Back St. George's Rd   47 G2
Back S Par   46 D3
Back Thomas St   47 F3

Back Turner St   47 F3
Badby Cl   47 J3
Bainbridge Cl   47 J7
Baird St   47 G4
Bale St   46 E4
Balloon St   47 E2
Balmforth St   46 C5
Balsam Cl   47 G6
Bangor St   46 C7
Bankmill Cl   47 G6
Bank Pl   46 B3
Bank St   46 B3
Baptist St   47 F2
Barbeck Cl   47 J2
Baring St   47 G5
Barker St   46 D1
Barlow Pl   47 G6
Barlow's Cft   46 D3
Barnett Dr   46 C2
Barrack St   46 B6
Barrhill Cl   46 C6
Barrow St   46 B3
Barton St   46 D5
Basildon Cl   47 J7
Beamish Cl   47 G6
Beattock St   46 C6
Beaufort St   46 C5
Beaver St   47 E5
Beckhampton Cl   47 H7
Bednal Av   47 J1
Beechcroft Cl   47 H2
Belfort Dr   46 A5
Bendix St   47 F2
Bengal St   47 G2
Bennett St   47 J6
Bentinck St   46 B6
Bent St   47 E1
Berkshire Rd   47 J1
Berry St   47 G5
Beswick Row   47 E2
Beswick St   47 H3
Betley St   47 G4
Bevan Cl   47 J4
Bilbrook St   47 F1
Billing Av   47 G5
Binns Pl   47 G3
Birchin La   47 F3
Birchvale Cl   46 D6
Birt St   47 H1
Bishopsgate   46 E4
Blackburn Pl   46 A4
Blackburn St   46 B2
Blackfriars Rd   46 C2
Blackfriars St   46 D3
Blackhill Cl   47 G6
Blackley St   46 B7
Blacklock St   46 E1
Blantyre St   46 C5
Bletchley Cl   47 H7
Blind La   47 J5
Blisworth Cl   47 J3
Bloom St   47 F4
Blossom St   46 D2
Blossom St (Ancoats)   47 G3
Blucher St   46 A4
Blyton St   47 F7
Boad St   47 G4
Bollington Rd   47 H2
Bombay St   47 F5
Bond St   47 G5
Bonsall St   46 D7
Boond St   46 D2
Boond St (Ancoats)   47 H3
Booth St   46 E4
Booth St (Salford)   46 D3
Booth St E   47 F6
Booth St W   47 E7
Bootle St   46 D4
Botham St   46 E7
Bothwell Rd   47 G2
Boundary La   47 E6
Boundary St E   47 F6
Boundary St W   47 E6

Bourdon St   47 J2
Bow La   46 E4
Bow St   46 D4
Brackley Av   46 B6
Bradford Rd   47 H3
Bradleys Ct   47 F3
Braley St   47 G5
Bramble Av   46 A5
Bramwell Dr   47 G6
Brancaster Rd   47 F5
Branson St   47 J3
Brazennose St   46 D4
Brazil St   47 F5
Brennan Cl   47 E7
Brewer St   47 F3
Brian Redhead Ct   46 C6
Brickley St   47 E1
Brick St   47 F3
Briddon St   46 D1
Bridgeford St   47 F7
Bridge St   46 D3
Bridge St W   46 D3
Bridgewater Pl   47 E3
Bridgewater St   46 D5
Bridgewater St (Salford)   46 C5
Bridgewater Viaduct   46 D5
Briggs St   46 C2
Brighton Pl   47 F7
Brighton St   47 F1
Brindle Pl   47 E7
Brocade Cl   46 B2
Brock St   47 G3
Bromley St   47 F1
Bronte St   47 E7
Brook St   47 F5
Brotherton Cl   46 B6
Brotherton Dr   46 C2
Browfield Av   46 A5
Brown Cross St   46 C3
Browning St   46 B7
Browning St (Salford)   46 C3
Brown St   46 E4
Brunel Av   46 A3
Brunswick   47 G7
Brunswick St   47 F7
Bryant Cl   47 H7
Brydon Av   47 H5
Buckfield Av   46 A5
Bugle St   46 D5
Bunsen St   47 F3
Burlington St   47 E7
Burnell Cl   47 H2
Burstock St   47 F1
Burton St   47 G1
Burton Wk   46 B2
Bury St   46 C2
Butler La   47 H2
Butler St   47 H2
Butter La   46 D3
Buxton St   47 G5
Byrcland Cl   47 J5
Byron St   46 D4

C
Cable St   47 F2
Cabot St   47 G6
Cakebread St   47 G5
Calder St   46 B5
Calico Cl   46 B2
Camberwell St   47 E1
Cambrian St   47 J2
Cambridge St   46 E5
Cambridge St (Salford)   46 C1
Camelford Cl   47 E7
Cameron St   46 D5
Canal St   47 F4
Cannon St   46 B2
Canon St   46 E3
Canon Grn Dr   46 C2
Carding Gro   46 C2
Cardroom Rd   47 G3

Carey Cl   46 C1
Carib St   46 D7
Carmel Av   46 A5
Carmel Cl   46 A5
Carnarvon St   46 E1
Caroline St   46 C1
Carpenters La   47 F3
Carriage St   46 C7
Carruthers St   47 H3
Cassidy Cl   47 G2
Castle St   46 C5
Caterham St   47 J4
Cathedral App   46 E2
Cathedral Gates   46 E3
Cathedral St   46 E3
Cathedral Yd   46 E3
Catlow La   47 F3
Catlow St   46 D1
Cavalier St   47 J3
Cavanagh Cl   47 H7
Cavell St   47 F3
Cavendish St   47 E6
Cawdor St   46 B6
Caxton St   46 D3
Caygill St   46 D2
Cedar Pl   46 B1
Central St   46 E4
Century St   46 D5
Chadderton St   47 F2
Chain St   47 E4
Chancel Av   46 A5
Chancellor La   47 H5
Chancery La   47 E4
Change Way   46 C2
Chapelfield Rd   47 H5
Chapel St   46 C3
Chapeltown St   47 G4
Chapel Walks   46 E3
Charles St   47 E5
Charley Av   46 B1
Charlotte St   47 E4
Charlton Pl   47 G5
Charnley Cl   47 J2
Charter St   46 D1
Chase St   47 F1
Chatford Cl   46 C1
Chatham St   47 F4
Chatley St   46 E1
Cheapside   46 E3
Cheetham Hill Rd   46 E2
Cheetwood St   46 D1
Chepstow St   46 E5
Cherryton Wk   47 H2
Chesshyre Av   47 J3
Chester Rd   46 B6
Chester St   46 E6
Chevassut St   46 C6
Cheviot St   46 E1
Chevril Cl   47 E6
Chichester Rd   46 D7
Chiffon Way   46 B2
China La   47 F4
Chippenham Rd   47 H3
Chorlton Rd   46 C7
Chorlton St   47 F4
Chorlton St (Old Trafford)   46 A7
Christchurch Av   46 A3
Churchgate Bldgs   47 G4
Church St   47 F3
Cinder St   47 G2
Cipher St   47 G2
City Rd   46 B7
City Rd E   46 D6
Clarence St   46 E4
Clarendon St   46 D6
Clare St   47 G5
Clarion St   47 G2
Clayburn Rd   46 D6
Cleminson St   46 B3
Cleworth St   46 B6
Clifford St   47 F6
Clifton Gro   46 B7

Clifton St   46 B7
Clive St   47 F2
Cloak St   47 F5
Cloughfield Av   46 A5
Clowes St   46 D3
Cobourg St   47 F4
Coburg Av   46 B1
Cockcroft Rd   46 A2
Cockspur St   46 D3
Coleshill St   47 J1
Colin Murphy Rd   46 C6
College Land   46 D3
Collier St   46 D5
Collier St (Salford)   46 D2
Collingham St   47 F1
Collyhurst Rd   47 G1
Colman Gdns   46 A5
Comet St   47 G4
Commercial St   46 D5
Comus St   46 A4
Concert La   47 E4
Congou St   47 G4
Cooper St   46 E4
Coop St   47 F3
Copeman Cl   47 G7
Copperas St   47 F3
Coral St   47 G6
Cork St   47 J4
Cornbrook   46 B6
Cornbrook   46 B6
Cornbrook Ct   46 B7
Cornbrook Gro   46 B7
Cornbrook Pk Rd   46 B6
Cornbrook St   46 B7
Cornell St   47 G2
Coronation Sq   47 H5
Coronation St   46 A4
Corporation St   46 E3
Cottenham La   46 C1
Cottenham St   47 G6
Cotter St   47 G5
Cottingham Rd   47 J7
Cotton St   47 G3
County St   46 E4
Coupland St   47 E7
Coupland St E   47 F7
Coverdale Cres   47 H6
Cowan St   47 J3
Cowburn St   46 E1
Cow La   46 B4
Cowper St   47 F1
Crabbe St   46 A4
Cranbourne St   46 A4
Crane St   47 H5
Cranfield Cl   47 J2
Craven St   46 B4
Crediton Cl   46 E7
Cresbury St   47 H5
Crescent, The   46 A2
Cross Keys St   47 F2
Crossley Ct   47 J3
Cross St   46 E4
Cross St (Salford)   46 D3
Crown La   47 F2
Crown St   46 C5
Crown St (Salford)   46 C2
Culmington Cl   46 C7
Cumberland St   46 B1
Cumbrian Cl   47 G6
Cunard Cl   47 G6
Cygnus Av   46 B1
Cyrus St   47 J3

D
Dainton Cl   47 J5
Daintry Cl   46 D6
Dalberg St   47 H6
Dale St   47 F3
Dalley Av   46 B1
Dalton Ct   47 G1
Dalton St   47 G1
Damask Av   46 B2
Danebank Wk   47 G6
Danecroft Cl   47 H7

Danson St   47 J2
Dantzic St   47 E3
Dark La   47 H5
Dartford Cl   47 J7
Darton Av   47 J2
Darwen St   46 A7
Davy St   47 G1
Dawson St   46 B5
Dean Rd   46 D2
Deansgate   46 D4
Dean St   47 F3
Deanwater Cl   47 G6
Dearden St   46 D6
Dearmans Pl   46 D3
Deer St   47 G4
Denewell Cl   47 H7
Denver Av   47 J1
Derby St   47 E1
Derwent St   46 B5
Devas St   47 F7
Devine Cl   46 B2
Devonshire St   47 H7
Devonshire St N   47 J6
Devonshire St S   47 H7
Dewhurst St   46 D1
Dickinson St   46 E4
Dilston Cl   47 H7
Dinsdale Cl   47 J2
Dinton St   46 B6
Dobson Cl   47 H7
Dolefield   46 D3
Dolphin Pl   47 H6
Dolphin St   47 H6
Donald St   47 F5
Dorsey St   47 F3
Dover St   47 F7
Downing St   47 G5
Downley Dr   47 H3
Drayton Wk   46 B7
Droitwich Rd   47 H1
Dryden St   47 G2
Dryhurst Wk   47 E7
Ducie St   47 F4
Duke Pl   46 C5
Duke St   46 C5
Duke St (Salford)   46 D2
Dulwich St   47 F1
Duncan St   46 A4
Dun Cl   46 B3
Dunham St   46 D7
Dunlop St   46 D3
Durant St   47 F2
Durling Av   47 H6
Dutton St   46 E1
Dyche St   47 F2
Dyer St   46 A5

E
Eagle St   47 F2
Eastburn Av   47 H1
Eastfield Av   47 J2
Eastleigh Dr   47 H1
East Mkt St   46 C3
East Newton St   47 H2
Eastnor Cl   46 B7
East Ordsall La   46 B4
Eastpark Cl   47 H6
East Philip St   46 D1
East Union St   46 B7
Ebden St   47 F4
Ebenezer St   46 E6
Echo St   47 F5
Eden Cl   47 E7
Edgehill St   47 F3
Edge St   47 F3
Edward St   46 D1
Egerton Rd   46 C5
Egerton St   46 C3
Elbe St   47 H5
Eliza St   46 C6
Ellesmere St   46 B6
Ellis St   46 D7
Elsworth St   47 E1

Elton St 46 C1
Elton's Yd 46 C1
Elverdon Cl 46 D7
Empire St 46 E1
Empress St 46 A7
Encombe Pl 46 B3
Epping St 46 E6
Epsley Cl 47 E7
Epworth St 47 H4
Errington Dr 46 B1
Erskine St 46 C7
Essex St 46 E4
Essex Way 46 C7
Etruria Cl 47 J7
Evans St 46 D2
Everard St 46 B5
Every St 47 H4
Exford Cl 47 H2
Eyre St 47 E7

F
Fairbrother St 46 A6
Fairfield St 47 G5
Fair St 47 G4
Falkland Av 47 J1
Faraday St 47 F3
Farnborough Rd 47 H1
Farrell St 46 C1
Farwood Cl 46 B7
Faulkner St 47 E4
Federation St 47 E2
Fennel St 46 E2
Fenn St 46 C7
Fenwick St 47 E6
Ferdinan St 47 H1
Fernbrook Cl 47 J7
Fernie St 47 E1
Fernleigh Dr 46 B7
Fern St 47 E1
Ferry St 47 J4
Filby Wk 47 J1
Firbeck Dr 47 H2
Firefly Cl 46 B3
Fire Sta Sq 46 A3
Fir St 47 H1
Fitzwilliam St 46 C1
Flatley Cl 47 E7
Flora Dr 46 C1
Ford St 47 H6
Ford St (Salford) 46 C3
Foundry La 47 F3
Fountain St 47 E4
Four Yards 46 E4
Frances St 47 G6
Francis St 46 D1
Frederick St 46 C3
Freeman Sq 47 E7
Freya Gro 46 A5
Frobisher Cl 47 J7
Frost St 47 J3
Fulmer Dr 47 H2

G
Gaitskell Cl 47 J4
Galgate Cl 47 C6
Garden La 46 D3
Garden St 46 D2
Garden Wall Cl 46 A5
Garforth Av 47 H2
Gartside St 46 D4
Garwood St 46 D6
Gateaton St 46 E3
Gaythorn St 46 B3
George Leigh St 47 F3
George Parr Rd 46 D7
George St 47 E4
Georgette Dr 46 D2
Gibbs St 46 B3
Gibson Pl 47 E1
Girton St 46 C1
Glasshouse St 47 G2
Gleden St 47 J2
Glenbarry Cl 47 G7
Glenbarry St 47 J5
Gloucester St 46 E5
Gloucester St (Salford) 46 A5
Goadsby St 47 F2
Gold St 47 F4
Gordon St 46 C1
Gore St 47 F4
Gore St (Salford) 46 C3
Gorton St 46 D2
Goulden St 47 F2
Gould St 47 H1
Grafton St 47 G7
Granby Row 47 F5
Granshaw St 47 J2
Gratrix Av 46 A6
Gravell La 46 D2
Grear Ducie St 46 E2
Great Ancoats St 47 H4
Great Bridgewater St 46 D5
Great Clowes St 46 C1
Great Ducie St 46 D1

Great George St 46 B3
Great Jackson St 46 C5
Great John St 46 C4
Great Marlborough St 47 E5
Greek St 47 F6
Green Gate 46 D2
Greengate W 46 C2
Grenham Av 46 B6
Griffiths Cl 46 C1
Groom St 47 F6
Grosvenor Gdns 46 C1
Grosvenor Sq 46 C1
Grosvenor St 47 F6
Guide Post Sq 47 H7
Gunson St 47 H2
Gun St 47 G3
Gurner Av 46 A6
Gurney St 47 J3

H
Hackleton Cl 47 J3
Hadfield St 46 B7
Half St 46 D2
Halmore Rd 46 E4
Halsbury Cl 47 H2
Halston St 46 D7
Hamerton Rd 47 G1
Hamilton Gro 46 B7
Hamilton St 46 B7
Hampson St 47 H1
Hamsell Rd 47 G6
Handsworth St 47 J5
Hanging Ditch 46 E3
Hanover St 47 E2
Hanworth Cl 47 G6
Harding St 47 J4
Harding St (Salford) 46 D2
Hardman Sq 46 D4
Hardman St 46 D4
Hardshaw Cl 47 G6
Harehill Cl 47 G5
Hare St 46 E3
Hargreave's St 47 F1
Harkness St 47 H6
Harold St 46 B7
Harriett St 47 H2
Harrison St 47 H4
Harrison St (Salford) 46 C1
Harris St 46 D1
Harry Hall Gdns 46 B1
Harter St 47 E4
Hartfield Cl 47 G6
Hart St 47 F4
Hatter St 47 F2
Hatton Av 46 B1
Haverlock Dr 46 B1
Haymarket Cl 47 H7
Heath Av 46 B1
Helga St 47 H1
Hellidon Cl 47 H6
Helmet St 47 H5
Henry St 47 G3
Henry St (Old Trafford) 46 A7
Hewitt St 46 D5
Heyrod St 47 G4
Higher Ardwick 47 H6
Higher Cambridge St 47 E6
Higher Chatham St 47 E6
Higher Ormond St 47 F6
Higher Oswald St 47 F2
Higher York St 47 F6
High St 47 E3
Hillcourt St 47 F6
Hillfield Cl 47 J7
Hillkirk St 47 J3
Hilton St 47 F3
Hinton St 47 G2
Hodson St 46 C2
Holdgate Cl 46 D7
Holkham Cl 47 H3
Holland St 47 H2
Holly Bk Cl 46 B6
Holly St 47 J4
Holt Town 47 J3
Honey St 47 F1
Hood St 47 G3
Hooper St 47 J5
Hope St 46 E4
Hope St (Salford) 46 A3
Hornby St 46 D1
Hornchurch St 46 C7
Horne Dr 47 H3
Houldsworth St 47 F3
Hoyle St 47 H5
Huddart Cl 46 A5
Hughes St 47 J5
Hull Sq 46 B2
Hulme 46 D7
Hulme Ct 46 C6
Hulme Hall Rd 46 B5
Hulme Pl 46 B3

Hulme St 46 D6
Hulme St (Salford) 46 B3
Humberstone Av 46 D6
Hunmanby Av 46 D6
Hunt's Bk 46 E2
Hyde Gro 47 G7
Hyde Pl 47 H7
Hyde Rd 47 H6
Hyde St 46 C7

I
Inchley Rd 47 F6
Instow Cl 47 H7
Ionas St 46 C1
Irk St 47 F1
Iron St 47 J2
Irwell Pl 46 A3
Irwell St 46 D1
Irwell St (Salford) 46 C3
Islington Way 46 B3

J
Jackson Cres 46 C6
Jackson's Row 46 D4
James Henry Av 46 A4
James St 47 J1
James St (Salford) 46 B3
Jenkinson St 47 F6
Jersey St 47 G3
Jerusalem Pl 46 D4
Jessamine Av 46 B1
Jessel Cl 47 G6
Joddrell St 46 D4
John Clynes Av 47 H1
John Dalton St 46 D3
Johnson Sq 47 H1
Johnson St 46 B7
Johnson St (Salford) 46 C3
John St 47 F3
John St (Lower Broughton) 46 C1
John St (Salford) 46 D2
Joiner St 47 F3
Jordan St 46 D5
Joynson Av 46 B1
Julia St 46 D1
Jury St 46 D1
Justin Cl 47 F6
Jutland St 47 G4

K
Kale St 47 G6
Kays Gdns 46 C3
Keele Wk 47 H1
Kelling Wk 46 C6
Kelvin St 47 F3
Kennedy St 46 E4
Kenwright St 47 F2
Kincardine Rd 47 F6
King Edward St 46 A5
Kingham Dr 47 H2
Kingsfold Av 47 H1
Kingsland Cl 47 H1
King St 46 D3
King St (Salford) 46 D2
King St W 46 D3
Kirkgate Cl 47 H2
Kirkhaven Sq 47 J1
Kirkstall Sq 47 G7
Kirkwood Dr 47 H1

L
Lackford Dr 47 H1
Lamb La 46 C3
Lamport Cl 47 F5
Lanchester St 47 J2
Landos Rd 47 H2
Langholme Cl 46 C6
Langport Av 47 J7
Langston St 46 D1
Langston St 47 J2
Lauderdale Cres 47 H7
Laystall St 47 G3
Layton St 47 J2
Leaf St 46 D6
Leak St 46 B6
Ledburn Ct 46 C6
Left Bk 46 C4
Lena St 47 F4
Leslie Hough Way 46 A1
Lever St 47 F3
Lewis St 47 J1
Leycroft St 47 G4
Lidbrook Wk 47 J7
Lime Bk St 47 J5
Lime Gro 47 F7
Limekiln La 47 H5
Linby St 46 C6
Lind St 47 J3
Linen Ct 46 B2
Linsley St 46 C2
Linton Cl 47 H4
Litcham Cl 47 F5
Little Ancoats St 47 F3

Little Holme St 47 J3
Little John St 46 C4
Little Lever St 47 F3
Little Nelson St 47 F2
Little Peter St 46 D5
Little Pit St 47 G3
Little Quay St 46 D4
Liverpool Rd 46 C4
Livesey St 47 G1
Lizard St 47 F3
Lloyd St 46 D4
Lloyd St N 47 F7
Lockett St 46 D1
Lockton Cl 47 G5
Lomax St 47 G3
London Rd 47 F4
Longacre St 47 G4
Long Millgate 46 E2
Longworth St 46 D4
Loom St 47 G3
Lordsmead St 46 C6
Lord St 46 E1
Lostock St 47 H2
Lowcock St 46 C1
Lower Byrom St 46 C4
Lower Chatham St 47 E6
Lower Mosley St 46 D5
Lower Moss La 46 C6
Lower Ormond St 47 E5
Lower Vickers St 47 J2
Lowndes Wk 47 G6
Lucy St 46 B7
Ludgate Hill 47 F2
Ludgate St 47 F2
Luna street 47 F3
Lund St 46 A7
Lupton St 46 C3
Lyceum Pl 47 E6

M
Maidford Cl 47 J3
Major St 47 E4
Makin St 47 E5
Mallard St 47 E5
Mallow St 46 C6
Malta St 47 H3
Malt St 46 B6
Malvern St 46 B7
Manchester St 46 A7
Mancunian Way 46 C6
Mangle St Street 47 F3
Manor St 47 G5
Manson Av 46 B6
Maplin Cl 47 G6
Marble St 47 E3
Marcer Rd 47 H2
Marchmont Cl 47 H7
Market St 46 E3
Markfield Av 47 J7
Markham Cl 47 J4
Marple St 46 C7
Marsden St 46 E3
Marshall St 47 F2
Marshall St (Ardwick) 47 H6
Marsworth Dr 47 H3
Mary France St 46 C6
Mary St 46 D1
Mason St 47 F2
Mason St (Salford) 46 C3
Massey St 46 B3
Mayan Av 46 B2
Mayes St 47 E2
Mayo St 47 H5
Mays St 47 F2
Meadow Rd 46 B1
Medlock St 46 D5
Mellor St 47 H2
Melville St 46 C3
Merrill St 47 H3
Middlewood St 46 B4
Midland St 47 H6
Milk St 46 E3
Millbank St 47 G4
Millbeck St 47 E6
Miller St 47 E2
Mill Grn St 47 H5
Millhall Cl 46 C7
Millhead Av 47 J2
Millow St 47 E2
Milnrow Cl 47 F5
Milton St 47 F2
Mincing St 47 F2
Minshull St 47 F4
Minshull St S 47 F4
Mistletoe Grn 46 C2
Moorhead St 47 G2
Morbourne Cl 47 J7
Mosley St 47 E4
Mosscott Wk 47 G4
Mosshall Cl 46 C7
Moulton St 46 D1

Mouncey St 47 E5
Mount Carmel Cres 46 A5
Mount St 46 E4
Mount St (Salford) 46 C2
Mozart Cl 47 H2
Mulberry St 46 D4
Munday St 47 H3
Munster St 47 E2
Murrey St 47 G3
Museum St 46 E4
Muslin St 46 B4
Myrtle Pl 46 A1

N
Nancy St 46 B6
Nansen St 47 J5
Naples St 47 F2
Nash St 46 C7
Nathan Dr 46 C2
Naval St 47 G3
Naylor St 47 H1
Neild St 47 G5
Neill St 46 C1
Nelson St 47 J1
Nether St 47 G5
New Allen St 47 G2
Newbeck St 47 F2
New Br St 46 D2
Newcastle St 46 E6
New Cath St 46 E3
Newcombe St 46 E1
New Elm St 46 C4
New Gartside St 46 D4
New Islington 47 H3
New Mkt 46 E3
New Mkt St 46 E3
New Mt St 47 F2
New Quay St 46 C4
Newton St 47 F3
New Union St 47 G3
New Vine St 46 D6
New Wakefield St 47 E5
New Welcome St 46 D6
New Windsor 46 A3
Nicholas St 47 E4
Nine Acre Dr 46 A6
Niven St 47 G5
North Bailey St 46 C3
Northdown Av 46 B6
North George St 46 B2
North Hill St 46 C2
North Phoebe St 46 A4
North Star Dr 46 B3
Northumberland Cl 46 A7
Northumberland Cres 46 A7
North Western St 47 G5
North W Services Rd 46 D3
Norton St 46 D2
Norway St 47 J4
Nuneaton Dr 47 H1
Nuttall St 46 A7

O
Oakford Av 47 G1
Oak St 47 F3
Old Bk St 46 E3
Old Birley St 46 D7
Oldbury Cl 47 H2
Old Elm St 47 G6
Oldfield Rd 46 A5
Old Medlock St 46 C4
Old Mill St 47 G3
Old Mt St 47 F2
Oliver St 47 F7
Ordsall Dr 46 A6
Ordsall La 46 A5
Oregon Cl 47 G6
Orion Pl 46 B1
Ormsgill St 46 D7
Orsett Cl 47 H1
Osborne St 47 G1
Oswald St 47 E2
Oswald St (Ancoats) 47 H4
Overbridge Rd 46 D1
Oxford Rd 47 E5
Oxford St 46 E4

P
Paddock St 47 G5
Palfrey Pl 47 H6
Pall Mall 46 E4
Palmerston St 47 H4
Parish Vw 46 A4
Parker St 47 F3
Park Pl 47 E1
Park St 46 E1
Park St (Salford) 46 B3
Parsonage 46 D3
Parsonage La 46 D3

Parsonage Way 46 A5
Paton St 47 F4
Pattishall Cl 47 J4
Peak St 47 G3
Peary St 47 G1
Peel Mt 46 A1
Pegasus Sq 46 B1
Pembroke Cl 47 H7
Pencroft Way 47 F7
Penfield Cl 47 F5
Percy Dr 46 A6
Percy St 46 C7
Peru St 46 B2
Peter St 46 D4
Phoenix St 47 E3
Phoenix Way 46 D7
Piccadilly 47 F3
Pickford St 47 G3
Picton Cl 46 C2
Picton St 46 C1
Piercy Av 46 B1
Piercy St 47 H3
Pigeon St 47 G3
Pimblett St 46 E1
Pine St 47 E4
Pin Mill Brow 47 H5
Pittbrook St 47 J5
Plymouth Gro 47 G7
Plymouth Vw 47 G7
Pochin St 47 J1
Poland St 47 G2
Polebrook Av 47 H7
Police St 46 D3
Pollard St 47 H4
Pollard St E 47 H3
Polygon Av 47 H7
Polygon St 47 G6
Pomona Strand 46 A6
Poplar St 47 J5
Poplin Dr 46 D2
Portland St 47 E5
Portsmouth St 47 G7
Port St 47 F3
Portugal St 47 G2
Portugal St E 47 G4
Postal St 47 G3
Postbridge Cl 47 H7
Potato Wf 46 C5
Poynton St 46 E6
Price St 47 J3
Primrose St 47 G2
Prince's Br 46 C4
Princess Rd 46 D6
Princess St 46 E4
Princess St (Cornbrook) 46 B6
Pritchard St 47 F5
Providence St 47 H4
Pryme St 46 C5
Pump St 47 J3
Purslow Cl 47 J3

Q
Quay St 46 C4
Quay St (Salford) 46 D3
Queen St 46 D4
Queen St (Salford) 46 D2
Quenby St 46 C6
Quendon Av 46 C1

R
Rachel St 47 H5
Radium St 47 G2
Ralli Cts 46 C3
Randerson St 47 G5
Rankin Cl 46 D7
Raven St 47 H5
Reather Wk 47 H1
Red Bk 47 E2
Redfern St 47 E2
Redhill St 47 G3
Red Lion St 47 F3
Regent Sq 46 A5
Reilly St 46 D6
Reservoir St 46 D2
Reyner St 47 E4
Rial Pl 47 E7
Ribston St 46 C7
Rice St 46 C5
Richmond St 47 F4
Richmond St (Salford) 46 C2
Ridgefield 46 D3
Ridgeway St E 47 H3
Ridgway St 47 H3
Riga St 47 F2
Rigel Pl 46 B1
Rigel St 47 H2
Rimworth Dr 47 H1
Ringstead Dr 47 G1
Ripley Cl 47 H4
River Pl 46 D5
Riverside 46 B2
River St 46 D6

Street	Page	Grid
River St (Ardwick)	47	H5
Robert St	46	E1
Roby St	47	F4
Rochdale Rd	47	F2
Rockdove Av	46	D6
Rocket Way	46	C3
Rockingham Cl	47	J7
Rodney St	47	H2
Rodney St (Salford)	46	C3
Roe St	47	G2
Roger St	47	F1
Rolla St	46	D2
Rolleston Av	47	H2
Rolls Cres	46	C7
Roman St	47	F3
Rome Rd	47	G2
Rondin Cl	47	J5
Rondin Rd	47	J5
Rope Wk	46	D2
Rosamond Dr	46	C3
Rosamond St W	47	E6
Rosewell Cl	47	J1
Rostron Av	47	J6
Rowendale St	46	D5
Royce Rd	46	C6
Roydale St	47	J2
Royds Cl	47	J7
Ruby St	47	E7
Rudcroft Cl	47	G6
Rudman Dr	46	A5
Rugby St	46	D1
Runcorn St	46	B6

S

Sackville St	47	E4
Sagar St	46	D1
St. Andrew's Sq	47	H4
St. Andrew's St	47	G4
St. Ann's Sq	46	D3
St. Ann St	46	D3
St. Bartholomew's Dr	46	A4
St. Chad's St	47	E1
St. Clement's Dr	46	A5
St. George's	46	B6
St. Ignatius Wk	46	A5
St. James's Sq	46	E4
St. James St	47	E4
St. John St	46	D4
St. Mary's Gate	46	E3
St. Mary's Parsonage	46	D3
St. Mary's St	46	C3
St. Michael's Sq	47	F2
St. Nicholas Rd	46	C6
St. Philip's St	46	B3
St. Simon St	46	C1
St. Stephen's Cl	47	H7
St. Stephen St	46	C3
St. Thomas St	47	F1
St. Vincent St	47	H3
St. Wilfrids St	46	C6
Salford	46	A4
Salford App	46	D3
Salmon St	47	F3
Saltford Av	47	H3
Salutation St	46	E7
Samouth Cl	47	H2
Sam Swire St	46	D7
Samuel Ogden St	47	F5
Sanctuary, The	46	D7
Sandal St	47	J2
Sandford St	46	C1
Sand St	47	G1
Sawley Rd	47	J1
Scarsdale St	46	A1
School Ct	47	G3
School St	47	F2
School St (Salford)	46	C1
Scotland	47	E2
Scotporth Cl	46	C6
Sefton Cl	47	G6
Senior St	46	D2
Seymour Cl	46	A7
Sharp St	47	F2
Shaw Cres	46	E2
Shawgreen Cl	46	C6
Shawheath Cl	46	C6
Shearsby Cl	46	D7
Sheffield St	47	G4
Sherborne St	46	D1
Sherbourne St W	46	D1
Sherratt St	47	G2
Shetland Rd	47	H1
Shilford Dr	47	G2
Shortcroft St	46	D5
Short St	47	F3
Short St (Salford)	46	C1
Shrewsbury St	46	B7
Shudehill	47	F3
Sidney St	47	F6
Sidney St (Salford)	46	C3
Silkin Cl	47	F6
Silk St	47	G2
Silk St (Salford)	46	B2

Silvercroft St	46	C5
Silver St	47	F4
Simeon St	47	F2
Simms Cl	46	B3
Simpson St	47	F2
Sirius Pl	46	B1
Skerry Cl	47	G6
Skip Pl	47	E1
Slate Av	47	H3
Sleaford Cl	47	H1
Smallridge Cl	47	H2
Smith St	46	A6
Smithy La	46	D3
Snell St	47	H4
Soar St	47	F3
Sorrel St	46	C6
Southall St	46	D4
Southall St (Strangeways)	46	D1
Southend Av	46	B7
Southern St	46	D5
Southgate	46	D3
South Hall St	46	B5
South King St	46	D3
Southmill St	46	E4
South Pump St	47	F4
South W Services Rd	46	C4
Sparkle St	47	G4
Spa St	47	F7
Spaw St	46	C3
Spear St	47	F3
Spectator St	47	H3
Springfield La	46	D2
Springfield Sq	46	D4
Spring Gdns	47	E4
Spruce St	46	C7
Stalham Cl	47	H1
Stanley Rd	46	B7
Stanley St	47	F1
Stanley St (Salford)	46	C4
Stansby Gdns	47	J7
Station App (for Oxford Road Station)	47	E5
Station App (for Piccadilly Station)	47	F4
Staverton Cl	47	G6
Stephen St	46	E1
Stevenson Pl	47	F3
Stevenson Sq	47	F3
Stevenson St	46	B3
Stockland Cl	47	F6
Stockport Rd	47	H6
Stocks St	47	E1
Stocks St E	47	E1
Stonall Av	46	C6
Stonelow Cl	46	E6
Stone St	46	C5
Store St	47	F4
Stracey St	47	J2
Strawberry Hill	46	A1
Stretford Rd	46	B7
Style St	47	F2
Sudbury Cl	46	B7
Sudell St	47	G2
Sussex St	46	B1
Swan St	47	F2
Swiftsure Av	46	B3
Syndall Av	47	H6
Syndall St	47	H6

T

Talgarth Rd	47	G1
Tamar Ct	46	B7
Tame St	47	H4
Tariff St	47	F3
Tasle All	46	D4
Tatton St	46	B6
Tatton St (Salford)	46	A5
Taunton St	47	J3
Tavery Cl	47	H3
Tebutt St	47	G2
Teer St	47	J3
Temperance St	47	G5
Tewkesbury Rd	47	J2
Thirsk St	47	G5
Thomas St	47	F3
Thompson St	47	F2
Thompson St (Strangeways)	46	D1
Thomson St	47	H7
Thor Grn	46	B5
Thornage Dr	47	H1
Thorncross Cl	46	B6
Thornden Rd	47	J1
Thornley Brow	47	E2
Thornton St	47	H1
Tib La	46	E4
Tib St	47	F3
Tideswell Av	47	H2
Tidworth Av	47	H3
Tinsley Cl	47	J2
Tivoli St	46	D4
Todd St	47	E2

Tomlinson St	46	D7
Tonge St	47	J5
Tonman St	46	D4
Torquay Cl	47	H7
Towcester Cl	47	J3
Town Hall La	46	E3
Trafford Bk Rd	46	A7
Trafford Ct	46	C6
Trafford Pl	46	B7
Trafford St	46	D5
Travis St	47	G5
Trentham St	46	B6
Trinity Way	46	B5
Tristam Cl	47	G6
Troutbeck Av	47	H3
Trumpet St	46	D5
Tudbury Way	46	C2
Tuer St	47	F7
Turner St	47	F3
Turner St (Old Trafford)	46	A6
Tutbury St	47	H4
Twillbrook Dr	46	D2

U

Union St	47	F3
Union St (Ardwick)	47	H5
University Rd	46	A2
University Rd W	46	A2
Upper Brook St	47	F6
Upper Cyrus St	47	J3
Upper Helena St	47	J2
Upper Kirby St	47	H3
Upper Moss La	46	C7
Upper Wf St	46	B3

V

Varley St	47	J1
Vauxhall St	47	G1
Velour Cl	46	B1
Vesta St	47	H3
Viaduct St	47	J4
Viaduct St (Salford)	46	D2
Vickers St	47	J1
Victoria Br St	46	D3
Victoria Sta App	46	E2
Victoria St	46	E3
Victor St	47	G1
Victor St (Salford)	46	C3
Virgil St	46	B6

W

Wadeford Cl	47	G2
Wadeson Rd	47	G5
Wadlow Cl	46	C2
Walker's Cft	46	E2
Wallness	46	A1
Wallness La	46	A1
Warde St	46	C7
Wardle St	47	J2
Warford St	47	F1
Warmington Dr	47	J7
Warwick St	47	F3
Warwick St (Hulme)	46	D7
Waterloo St	47	E4
Water St	46	B5
Water St (Ardwick)	47	H5
Watkin Cl	47	G7
Watkin St	46	C1
Watson St	46	D5
Weald Cl	47	G6
Weir St	46	D7
Welland Cl	46	B7
Wellhead Cl	46	E7
Wellington Grn	46	C7
Wellington St	46	C2
Well St	47	E3
West Bk St	46	A4
West Charles St	46	A3
West Crown Av	46	A4
West Hope St	46	A3
West King St	46	C2
Westminster St	46	B6
West Mosley St	47	E4
Weston St	47	J3
West Pk St	46	A5
Weybridge Rd	47	H3
Whalley St	47	H2
Wheater's Cres	46	B1
Wheater's St	46	B1
Wheater's Ter	46	B1
Whimberry Cl	46	A5
Whitchurch St	46	D1
Whitekirk Cl	47	G6
White St	46	B7
Whitfield St	47	E1
Whittle's Cft	47	G4
Whittle St	47	F3
Whitworth St	47	F5
Whitworth St W	46	D5
Wilberforce Cl	46	D7
Wilfred St	46	D1
William Chadwick Cl	47	H1
Williamson St	47	F1

William St	47	H5
Wilmott St	46	E6
Wilson St	47	H7
Wilton Pl	46	B3
Wilton St	47	F6
Winder Dr	47	H3
Windmill Av	46	A5
Windmill St	46	D4
Winfell Dr	47	J2
Winscombe Dr	47	H1
Winser St	47	E5
Winstanley Rd	47	H2
Withy Gro	47	E3
Woden's Av	46	A5
Woden St	46	B5
Woodlark Cl	46	B3
Wood St	46	D4
Woodward Pl	47	H3
Woodward St	47	H3
Woollam Pl	46	C4
Worrall St	46	A5
Worsley St	46	B5
Worsley St (Salford)	46	D3
Wright St	46	A7
Wroe St	46	B3
Wyatt Av	46	A5
Wynne St	46	A1
Wyre St	47	G5

Y

Yew St	46	C7
Yorkshire St	46	D3
York St	47	E3
York St (Hulme)	46	C6
York St (off Charles Street)	47	E5
York St E	47	F6

Z

| Zion Cres | 46 | D7 |

Tourist Information Centre: 23 Union Street
Tel: 01224 288828

Albert Quay	C3	Hutcheon Street	B2
Albert Street	B2	Justice Mill Lane	B3
Alburg Road	B3	King's Crescent	C1
Albyn Place	A3	King Street	C1
Argyll Place	A2	Langstane Place	B3
Ashgrove Road	A1	Leadside Road	B2
Ashgrove Road West	A1	Leslie Terrace	B1
Ash-hill Drive	A1	Links Road	C2
Ashley Road	A3	Linksfield Road	C1
Back Hilton Road	A1	Loch Street	B2
Baker Street	B2	Maberly Street	B2
Beach Boulevard	C2	Market Street	C3
Bedford Place	B1	Menzies Road	C3
Bedford Road	B1	Merkland Road East	C1
Beechgrove Terrace	A2	Mid Stocket Road	A2
Belgrave Terrace	A2	Mile-end Avenue	A2
Berryden Road	B1	Miller Street	C2
Blaikie's Quay	C3	Mount Street	B2
Bon-Accord Street	B3	Nelson Street	B1
Bonnymuir Place	A2	North Esplanade East	C3
Bridge Street	B2	North Esplanade West	C3
Brighton Place	A3	Orchard Street	C1
Cairncry Road	A1	Osborne Place	A3
Canal Road	B1	Palmerston Road	C3
Carden Place	A3	Park Road	C1
Carlton Place	A3	Park Street	C2
Cattofield Place	A1	Pittodrie Place	C1
Causewayend	B1	Pittodrie Street	C1
Chapel Street	B2	Powis Place	B2
Claremont Street	A3	Powis Terrace	B1
Clifton Road	A1	Queens Road	A3
College Bounds	C1	Queens Terrace	A3
College Street	C3	Regent Quay	C2
Commerce Street	C2	Rosehill Crescent	A1
Commercial Quay	C3	Rosehill Drive	A1
Constitution Street	C2	Rosemount Place	A2
Cornhill Drive	A1	Rose Street	B2
Cornhill Road	A1	Rubislaw Terrace	B3
Cornhill Terrace	A1	St. Swithin Street	A3
Cotton Street	C2	Schoolhill	B2
Cromwell Road	A3	Seaforth Road	C1
Desswood Place	A3	Sinclair Road	C3
Devonshire Road	A3	Skene Square	B2
Elmbank Terrace	B1	Skene Street	B2
Esslemont Avenue	B2	South Crown Street	B3
Ferryhill Road	B3	South Esplanade West	B3
Fonthill Road	B3	Spital	C1
Forest Road	A3	Springbank Terrace	B3
Forest Avenue	A3	Spring Gardens	B2
Fountainhall Road	A2	Stanley Street	A3
Froghall Terrace	B1	Sunnybank Road	B1
Gallowgate	C2	Sunnyside Road	B1
George Street	B1	Union Glen	B3
Gillespie Crescent	A1	Union Grove	A3
Gladstone Place	A3	Union Street	B3
Golf Road	C1	Urquhart Road	C2
Gordondale Road	A2	Victoria Bridge	C3
Great Southern Road	B3	Victoria Road	C3
Great Western Road	A3	Walker Road	C3
Guild Street	C3	Waterloo Quay	C2
Hamilton Place	A2	Waverley Place	B3
Hardgate	B3	Well Place	C3
Hilton Drive	A1	Westburn Drive	A1
Hilton Place	A1	Westburn Road	A2
Hilton Street	A1	West North Street	C2
Holburn Road	B3	Whitehall Place	A2
Holburn Street	B3	Whitehall Road	A2
Holland Street	B1	Willowbank Road	B3

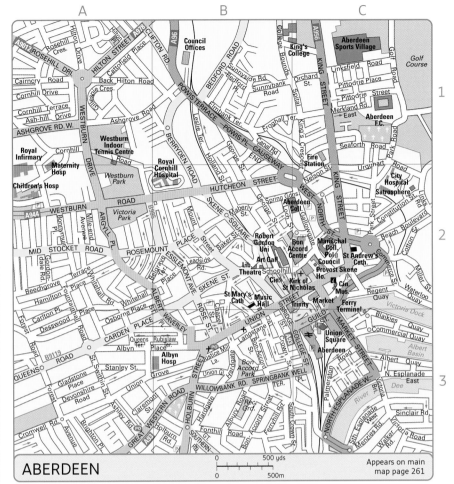

ABERDEEN

0   500 yds

0   500m

Appears on main
map page 261

Tourist Information Centre: Abbey Chambers, Abbey Churchyard
Tel: 0906 711 2000

Ambury	A3	Pierrepont Street	B3
Archway Street	C3	Pulteney Gardens	C3
Argyle Street	B2	Pulteney Mews	C1
Avon Street	A2	Pulteney Road	C2
Barton Street	A2	Queen Street	A2
Bath Street	B2	Quiet Street	A1
Bathwick Hill	C1	Rossiter Road	B3
Beau Street	B2	Royal Crescent	A1
Bennett Street	A1	St. James's Parade	A2
Bridge Street	B2	St. John's Road	B1
Broad Quay	A3	St. Marks Road	B3
Broad Street	B1	Sawclose	A2
Broadway	C3	Southgate Street	B3
Brock Street	A1	Spring Crescent	C3
Chapel Row	A2	Stall Street	B2
Charles Street	A2	Sutton Street	C1
Charlotte Street	A1	Sydney Place	C1
Cheap Street	B2	The Circus	A1
Claverton Street	B3	Union Street	B2
Corn Street	A3	Upper Borough Walls	A2
Daniel Street	C1	Walcot Street	B1
Darlington Street	C1	Wells Road	A3
Dorchester Street	B3	Westgate Buildings	A2
Edward Street	C1	Westgate Street	A2
Excelsior Street	C3	Wood Street	A1
Ferry Lane	C2	York Street	B2
Gay Street	A1		
George Street	A1		
Grand Parade	B2		
Great Pulteney Street	C1		
Green Park Road	A2		
Green Street	B1		
Grove Street	B1		
Henrietta Gardens	C1		
Henrietta Mews	C1		
Henrietta Road	B1		
Henrietta Street	B1		
Henry Street	B2		
High Street	B2		
Holloway	A3		
James Street West	A2		
John Street	A1		
Kingsmead East	A2		
Kingsmead Square	A2		
Lansdown Road	B1		
Laura Place	B1		
Lime Grove	C2		
Lime Grove Gardens	C2		
Lower Borough Walls	B2		
Lower Bristol Road	A3		
Magdalen Avenue	A3		
Manvers Street	B3		
Milk Street	A2		
Milsom Street	B1		
Monmouth Place	A1		
Monmouth Street	A2		
Newark Street	B3		
New Bond Street	B2		
New King Street	A2		
New Orchard Street	B2		
New Street	B2		
North Parade	B2		
North Parade Road	C2		
Old King Street	A1		
Orange Grove	B2		
Paragon	B1		

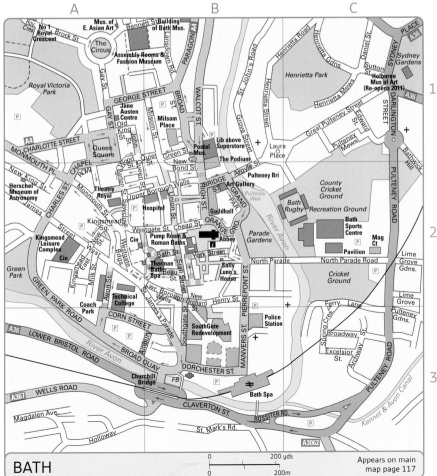

BATH

0   200 yds

0   200m

Appears on main
map page 117

Blackpool   Bournemouth

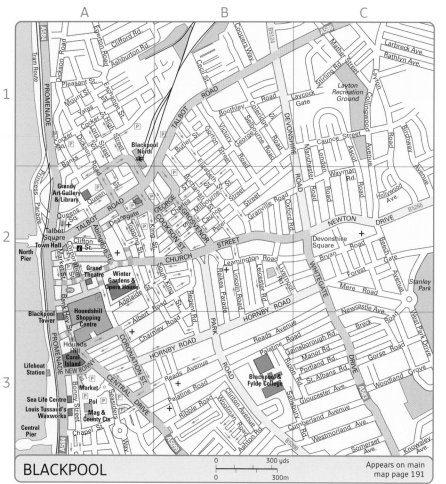

BLACKPOOL

0   300 yds
0   300m

Appears on main map page 191

Tourist Information Centre: 1 Clifton Street
Tel: 01253 478222

Abingdon Street	A2	Manor Road	C3
Adelaide Street	A2	Market Street	A2
Albert Road	A3	Mather Street	C1
Ascot Road	C1	Mere Road	C2
Ashburton Road	A1	Milbourne Street	B2
Ashton Road	B3	Mount Street	A1
Bank Hey Street	A2	New Bonny Street	A3
Banks Street	A1	Newcastle Avenue	C2
Beech Avenue	C2	Newton Drive	C2
Birchway Avenue	C1	Oxford Road	B2
Bonny Street	A3	Palatine Road	B3
Boothley Road	B1	Park Road	B3
Breck Road	C3	Peter Street	B2
Bryan Road	C2	Pleasant Street	A1
Buchanan Street	B2	Portland Road	C3
Butler Street	B1	Princess Parade	A2
Caunce Street	B2/C1	Promenade	A1
Cecil Street	B1	Queens Square	A2
Central Drive	A3	Queen Street	A2
Chapel Street	A3	Rathlyn Avenue	C1
Charles Street	B2	Reads Avenue	B3
Charnley Road	A3	Regent Road	B2
Church Street	B2	Ribble Road	B3
Clifford Road	A1	Ripon Road	B3
Clifton Street	A2	St. Albans Road	C3
Clinton Avenue	B3	Salisbury Road	C3
Cocker Square	A1	Seasiders Way	A3
Cocker Street	A1	Selbourne Road	B1
Coleridge Road	B1	Somerset Avenue	C3
Collingwood Avenue	C1	South King Street	B2
Cookson Street	B2	Stirling Road	C1
Coopers Way	B1	Talbot Road	A2/B1
Coronation Street	A3	Talbot Square	A2
Corporation Street	A2	Topping Street	A2
Cumberland Avenue	C3	Victory Road	B1
Deansgate	A2	Wayman Road	C2
Devonshire Road	B1	Westmorland Avenue	C3
Devonshire Square	C2	West Park Drive	C2
Dickson Road	A1	Whitegate Drive	C2/C3
Egerton Road	A1	Woodland Grove	C3
Elizabeth Street	B1	Woolman Road	B3
Exchange Street	A1	Yates Street	A1
Forest Gate	C2		
Gainsborough Road	B3		
George Street	B2/B1		
Gloucester Avenue	C3		
Gorse Road	C3		
Gorton Street	B1		
Granville Road	B2		
Grosvenor Street	B2		
High Street	A1		
Hollywood Avenue	C2		
Hornby Road	A3		
Hounds Hill	A3		
King Street	A2		
Knowsley Avenue	C3		
Larbreck Avenue	C1		
Laycock Gate	C1		
Layton Road	C1		
Leamington Road	B2		
Leicester Road	B2		
Lincoln Road	B2		
Liverpool Road	B2		
London Road	C1		
Lord Street	A1		
Manchester Road	C1		

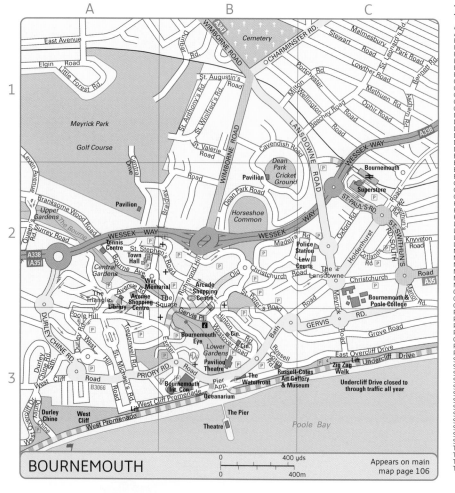

BOURNEMOUTH

0   400 yds
0   400m

Appears on main map page 106

Undercliff Drive closed to through traffic all year

Tourist Information Centre: Westover Road
Tel: 0845 05 11 700

Ascham Road	C1	Undercliff Drive	C3
Avenue Road	A2	Wellington Road	C1
Bath Road	B3	Wessex Way	A2/C1
Beechey Road	C1	West Cliff Promenade	A3
Bennett Road	C1	West Cliff Road	A3
Bourne Avenue	A2	West Hill Road	A3
Braidley Road	B2	West Overcliff Drive	A3
Branksome Wood Road	A2	West Promenade	A3
Cavendish Road	B1	Westover Road	B3
Central Drive	A1	Wimborne Road	B2
Charminster Road	B1		
Christchurch Road	C2		
Cotlands	C2		
Dean Park Road	B2		
Dunbar Road	B1		
Durley Chine	A3		
Durley Chine Road	A3		
Durley Chine Road South	A3		
Durley Road	A3		
East Avenue	A1		
East Overcliff Drive	C3		
Elgin Road	A1		
Exeter Road	B3		
Gervis Place	B3		
Gervis Road	C3		
Grove Road	C3		
Hinton Road	B3		
Holdenhurst Road	C2		
Knyveton Road	C2		
Lansdowne Road	B1		
Leven Avenue	A1		
Little Forest Road	A1		
Lowther Road	C1		
Madeira Road	B2		
Malmesbury Park Road	C1		
Manor Road	C2		
Methuen Road	C1		
Meyrick Road	C2		
Milton Road	B1		
Old Christchurch Road	B2		
Ophir Road	C1		
Oxford Road	C2		
Pier Approach	B3		
Poole Hill	A3		
Portchester Road	C1		
Priory Road	A3		
Queen's Road	A2		
Richmond Hill	B2		
Russell Cotes Road	B3		
St. Augustin's Road	B1		
St. Anthony's Road	B1		
St. Leonard's Road	C1		
St. Michael's Road	A3		
St. Pauls' Road	C2		
St. Peter's Road	B2		
St. Stephen's Road	B2		
St. Swithun's Road	C2		
St. Swithun's Road South	C2		
St. Valerie Road	B1		
St. Winifred's Road	B1		
Stewart Road	C1		
Surrey Road	A2		
The Lansdowne	C2		
The Square	B2		
The Triangle	A2		
Tregonwell Road	A3		

Tourist Information Centre: City Hall, Centenary Square
Tel: 01274 433678

Akam Road	A1	John Street	A2
Ann Place	A3	Kirkgate	B2
Ashgrove	A3	Leeds Road	C2
Balme Street	B1	Little Horton Lane	A3
Bank Street	B2	Lower Kirkgate	B2
Baptist Place	A1	Lumb Lane	A1
Barkerend Road	C1	Manchester Road	B3
Barry Street	A2	Manningham Lane	A1
Bolling Road	C3	Mannville Terrace	A3
Bolton Road	C1	Manor Row	B1
Brearton Street	A1	Melbourne Place	A3
Bridge Street	B2	Midland Road	B1
Britannia Street	B3	Moody Street	C3
Broadway	B2	Morley Street	A3
Burnett Street	C2	Neal Street	A3
Caledonia Street	B3	Nelson Street	B3
Canal Road	B1	North Parade	B1
Captain Street	C1	North Street	C1
Carlton Street	A2	North Wing	C1
Carter Street	C3	Nuttall Road	C1
Centenary Square	B2	Otley Road	C1
Chain Street	A1	Paradise Street	A1
Channing Way	B2	Park Road	B3
Chapel Street	C2	Peckover Street	C2
Charles Street	B2	Prince's Way	B2
Cheapside	B2	Prospect Street	C3
Chester Street	A3	Radwell Drive	A3
Churchbank	C2	Rawson Place	B1
Claremont	C1	Rawson Road	A1
Croft Street	B3	Rebecca Street	A1
Darfield Street	A1	Rouse Fold	C3
Darley Street	B1	Russell Street	A3
Drake Street	B2	Salem Street	B1
Drewton Road	A1	Sawrey Place	A3
Dryden Street	C3	Sedgwick Close	A1
Duke Street	B1	Sharpe Street	B3
Dyson Street	A1	Shipley Airedale Road	C1
East Parade	C2	Simes Street	A1
Edmund Street	A3	Snowden Street	A1
Edward Street	C3	Sunbridge Road	A1
Eldon Place	A1	Sylhet Close	A1
Fairfax Street	C3	Ternhill Road	B3
Filey Street	C2	Tetley Street	A2
Fitzwilliam Street	C3	The Tyrls	B2
Fountain Street	A1	Thornton Road	A2
George Street	C2	Trafalgar Street	A1
Godwin Street	B2	Trinity Road	A3
Gracechurch Street	A1	Tumbling Hill Street	A2
Grafton Street	A3	Valley Road	B1
Grattan Road	A2	Vaughan Street	A1
Great Horton Road	A3	Vicar Lane	C2
Grove Terrace	A3	Vincent Street	A2
Guy Street	C3	Wakefield Road	C3
Hall Ings	B2	Wapping Road	C1
Hall Lane	C3	Water Lane	A2
Hallfield Road	A1	Westgate	A1
Hamm Strasse	B1	Wigan Street	A2
Hammerton Street	C2		
Hanover Square	A1		
Harris Street	C2		
Heap Lane	C1		
Houghton Place	A1		
Howard Street	A3		
Hustlergate	B2		
Ivegate	B2		
James Street	B2		

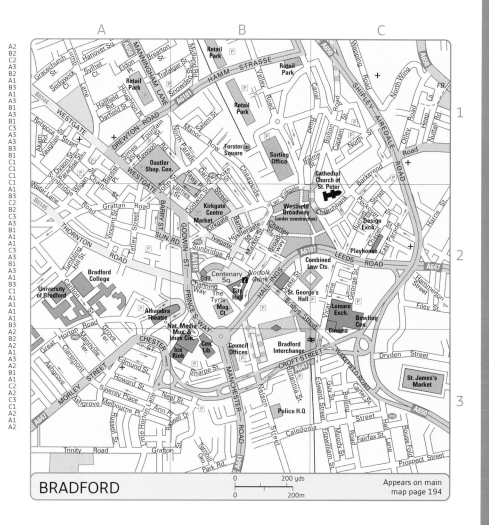

BRADFORD

0   200 yds
0   200m

Appears on main
map page 194

Tourist Information Centre: Royal Pavilion Shop,
4-5 Pavilion Buildings   Tel: 0906 711 2255

Addison Road	A1	Southover Street	C2
Albion Hill	C2	Springfield Road	B1
Beaconsfield Road	B1	Stafford Road	A1
Brunswick Square	A2	Stanford Road	B1
Buckingham Place	B1	Sussex Street	C2
Buckingham Road	B2	Terminus Road	B2
Carlton Hill	C2	The Lanes	B3
Cheapside	B2	The Upper Drive	A1
Church Street	B2	Trafalgar Street	B2
Churchill Square	B3	Union Road	C1
Clifton Hill	A2	Upper Lewes Road	C1
Clyde Road	B1	Upper North Street	A2
Davigdor Road	A1	Upper Rock Gardens	C3
Ditchling Rise	B1	Viaduct Road	B1
Ditchling Road	C1	Victoria Road	A2
Dyke Road	B2	Waterloo Street	A2
Dyke Road Drive	B1	Wellington Road	C1
Eastern Road	C3	West Drive	C2
Edward Street	C3	West Street	B3
Elm Grove	C1	Western Road	A2
Fleet Street	B2	Wilbury Crescent	A1
Florence Road	B1	York Avenue	A2
Freshfield Road	C3	York Place	C2
Furze Hill	A2		
Gloucester Road	B2		
Grand Junction Road	B3		
Hamilton Road	B1		
Hanover Street	C2		
Highdown Road	A1		
Holland Road	A2		
Hollingdean Road	C1		
Howard Place	B1		
Islingword Road	C1		
John Street	C2		
King's Road	A3		
Lansdowne Road	A2		
Lewes Road	C1		
London Road	B1		
Lyndhurst Road	A1		
Madeira Drive	C3		
Marine Parade	C3		
Montefiore Road	A1		
Montpelier Road	A2		
New England Road	B1		
New England Street	B1		
Nizells Avenue	A1		
Norfolk Terrace	A2		
North Road	B2		
North Street	B2		
Old Shoreham Road	A1		
Old Steine	C3		
Park Crescent Terrace	C1		
Park Street	C2		
Port Hall Road	A1		
Preston Circus	B1		
Preston Road	B1		
Preston Street	A3		
Prince's Crescent	C1		
Queen's Park Road	C2		
Queen's Road	B2		
Richmond Place	C2		
Richmond Road	C1		
Richmond Street	C2		
Richmond Terrace	C2		
St. James's Street	C3		
Somerhill Road	A2		

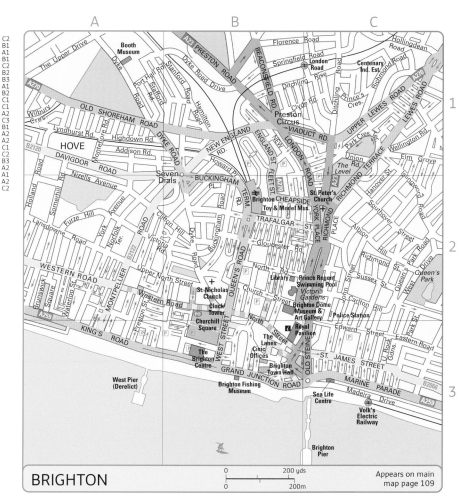

BRIGHTON

0   200 yds
0   200m

Appears on main
map page 109

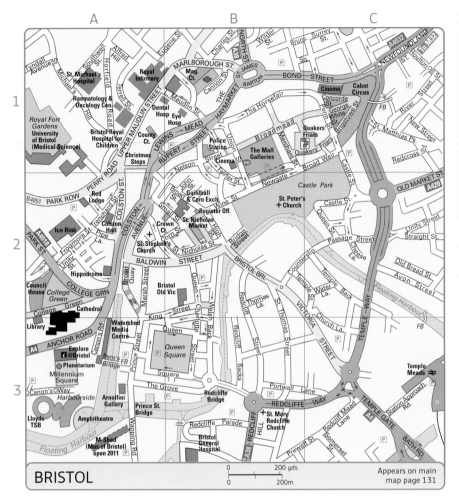

BRISTOL

Appears on main
map page 131

Tourist Information Centre: Explore@Bristol, Anchor Road
Tel: 0906 711 2191

Alfred Hill	A1	Redcliffe Bridge	B3
Anchor Road	A3	Redcliffe Parade	B3
Avon Street	C2	Redcliff Hill	B3
Baldwin Street	A2	Redcliff Mead Lane	C3
Bath Road	C3	Redcliff Street	B2
Bond Street	B1	Redcross Street	C1
Bridge Street	B2	River Street	C1
Brigstowe Street	C1	Rupert Street	A1
Bristol Bridge	B2	St. James Barton	B1
Broadmead	B1	St. Matthias Park	C1
Broad Quay	A2	St. Michael's Hill	A1
Broad Street	B2	St. Nicholas Street	B2
Broad Weir	C1	St. Thomas Street	B2
Brunswick Square	B1	Small Street	A2
Cannon Street	B1	Somerset Street	C3
Canon's Road	A3	Southwell Street	A1
Canon's Way	A3	Station Approach Road	C3
Castle Street	C2	Straight Street	C2
Charles Street	B1	Surrey Street	C1
Cheese Lane	C2	Temple Back	C2
Christmas Steps	A1	Temple Gate	C3
Church Lane	C2	Temple Street	B2
College Green	A2	Temple Way	C3
Colston Avenue	A2	Terrell Street	A1
Colston Street	A2	The Grove	A3
Concorde Street	C1	The Haymarket	B1
Corn Street	C1	The Horsefair	B1
Countership	B2	Thomas Lane	B2
Eugene Street	A1	Trenchard Street	A2
Fairfax Street	B1	Tyndall Avenue	A1
Frogmore Street	A2	Union Street	B1
George White Street	C1	Unity Street	A2
High Street	B2	Unity Street	C2
Horfield Road	A1	Upper Maudlin Street	A1
Houlton Street	C1	Victoria Street	B2
John Street	B2	Wapping Road	A3
King Street	A2	Water Lane	B2
Lewins Mead	A1	Welsh Back	B2
Lower Castle Street	C1	Wilder Street	B1
Lower Maudlin Street	B1	Wine Street	B2
Marlborough Street	B1		
Marsh Street	A2		
Merchant Street	B1		
Nelson Street	B1		
Newfoundland Street	C1		
Newgate	B2		
New Street	C1		
North Street	B1		
Old Bread Street	C2		
Old Market Street	C2		
Park Row	A2		
Park Street	A2		
Passage Street	C2		
Penn Street	C1		
Pero's Bridge	A3		
Perry Road	A2		
Pipe Lane	A2		
Portwall Lane	B3		
Prewett Street	B3		
Prince Street	A3		
Prince Street Bridge	C1		
Quakers' Friars	B1		
Queen Charlotte Street	B2		
Queen Square	A3		
Queen Street	C2		
Redcliff Backs	B3		

CAMBRIDGE

Appears on main
map page 150

Tourist Information Centre: Wheeler Street
Tel: 0871 226 8006

Adam and Eve Street	C2	Tenison Road	C3
Alpha Road	B1	Tennis Court Road	B2
Aylestone Road	C1	Trinity Street	B2
Barton Road	A3	Trumpington Road	B3
Bateman Street	B3	Trumpington Street	B3
Belvior Road	C1	Union Road	B3
Brookside	B3	Victoria Avenue	B1
Burleigh Street	C2	Victoria Road	B1
Carlyle Road	B1	West Road	A2
Castle Street	A1		
Chesterton Lane	B1		
Chesterton Road	B1		
Clarendon Street	C2		
De Freville Avenue	C1		
Devonshire Road	C3		
Downing Street	B2		
East Road	C2		
Eden Street	C2		
Elizabeth Way	C1		
Emmanuel Road	B2		
Fen Causeway, The	A3		
Glisson Road	C3		
Gonville Place	C3		
Granchester Street	A3		
Grange Road	A3		
Gresham Road	C3		
Hamilton Road	C1		
Harvey Road	C3		
Hills Road	C3		
Humberstone Road	C1		
Huntingdon Road	A1		
Jesus Lane	B2		
King's Parade	B2		
King Street	B2		
Lensfield Road	B3		
Madingley Road	A1		
Magdalene Bridge Street	B1		
Maids Causeway	B2		
Market Street	B2		
Mawson Road	C3		
Millington Road	A3		
Mill Road	C3		
Montague Road	C1		
Newmarket Road	C1		
Newnham Road	A3		
Norfolk Street	C2		
Panton Street	B3		
Parker Street	B2		
Park Parade	B1		
Parkside	C2		
Park Terrace	B2		
Pembroke Street	B2		
Queen's Road	A2		
Regent Street	B2		
Regent Terrace	B2		
St. Andrew's Street	B2		
St. Barnabas Road	C3		
St. John's Street	B2		
St. Matthew's Street	C2		
St. Paul's Road	C3		
Searce Street	A1		
Sidgwick Avenue	A3		
Sidney Street	B2		
Silver Street	A3		
Station Road	C3		
Storey's Way	A1		

Tourist Information Centre: 12-13 Sun Street, The Buttermarket
Tel: 01227 378100

Best Lane	B2	Watling Street	B2
Borough Northgate	B1	Whitehall Gardens	A2
Broad Street	C1	Whitehall Road	A2
Burgate	B2	Wincheap	A3
Castle Row	A3	York Road	A3
Castle Street	A3		
College Road	C1		
Cossington Road	C3		
Craddock Road	C1		
Dover Street	C2		
Edgar Road	C1		
Ersham Road	C3		
Forty Acres Road	A1		
Gordon Road	A3		
Havelock Street	C1		
Hawk's Lane	B2		
High Street	B2		
Ivy Lane	C2		
King Street	B1		
Kirby's Lane	A1		
Lansdown Road	B3		
Longport	C2		
Lower Bridge Street	C2		
Lower Chantry Lane	C2		
Marlowe Avenue	B3		
Martyrs' Field Road	A3		
Mead Way	A2		
Military Road	C1		
Monastery Street	C2		
New Dover Road	C3		
North Holmes Road	C1		
North Lane	A1		
Nunnery Fields	C3		
Oaten Hill	C3		
Old Dover Road	C3		
Orchard Street	A1		
Oxford Road	B3		
Palace Street	B2		
Pin Hill	A3		
Pound Lane	A1		
Puckle Lane	C3		
Rheims Way	A2		
Rhodaus Town	B3		
Roper Road	A1		
Rose Lane	B2		
St. Dunstan's Street	A1		
St. George's Lane	B2		
St. George's Place	C2		
St. George's Street	B2		
St. Gregory's Road	C1		
St. Margarets Street	B2		
St. Peter's Lane	B1		
St. Peter's Place	A2		
St. Peter's Street	A1		
St. Radigund's Street	B1		
St. Stephen's Road	B1		
Simmonds Road	A3		
Station Road East	A3		
Station Road West	A1		
Stour Street	A2		
The Causeway	B1		
The Friar's	B2		
Tourtel Road	C1		
Tudor Road	A3		
Union Street	C1		
Upper Bridge Street	B3		

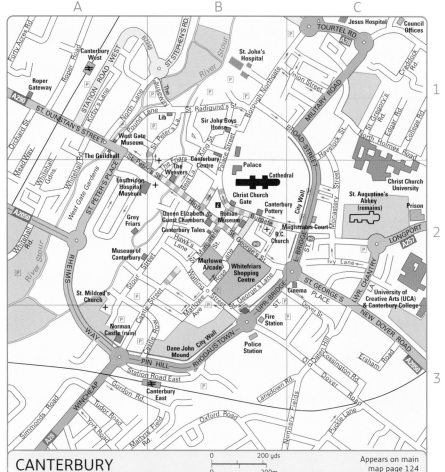

CANTERBURY

0 200 yds
0 200m

Appears on main map page 124

Tourist Information Centre: The Old Library, Trinity Street
Tel: 0870 1211 258

Adam Street	C3	Moira Terrace	C2
Albany Road	C1	Moy Road	C1
Allerton Street	A3	Museum Avenue	B1
Arran Place	C1	Neville Street	A2
Arran Street	C1	Newport Road	C2
Basil Place	B1	Newport Road Lane	C2
Bedford Street	C1	Ninian Park Road	A3
Boulevard de Nantes	B2	North Road	A1
Bridge Street	B3	Oxford Lane	C2
Brook Street	A3	Park Grove	B2
Bute Street	B3	Park Place	B1
Bute Terrace	B3	Park Street	B3
Castle Street	A2	Partridge Road	C1
Cathays Terrace	B1	Penarth Road	B3
Cathedral Road	A2	Pendyris Street	A3
Celerity Drive	C3	Pitman Street	A2
Central Link	C3	Planet Street	C2
Charles Street	B2	Queen Street	B2
Churchill Way	C2	Rhymney Street	B1
City Road	C1	Richard Street	B1
Clare Road	A3	Richmond Road	C1
Clare Street	A2	Ryder Street	A2
Claude Road	C1	St. Mary Street	B3
Coburn Street	B1	St. Peters Street	C2
College Road	B2	Salisbury Road	B1
Colum Road	A1	Schooner Way	C3
Corbett Road	B1	Senghennydd Road	B1
Cornwall Street	A3	Stafford Road	A3
Cottrell Road	C1	Strathnairn Street	C1
Cowbridge Road East	A2	Stuttgarter Strasse	A2
Craddock Street	A3	Taffs Mead Embankment	B3
Craiglee Drive	C3	Talbot Street	A2
Croft Street	C1	Thesiger Street	B1
Crwys Road	B1	The Parade	C2
Cyfartha Street	C1	The Walk	C1
De Burgh Street	A2	Tudor Street	C3
Despenser Street	A3	Tyndall Street	C3
Duke Street	B2	Wedmore Road	A3
Dumfries Place	C2	Wells Street	A3
Ellen Street	C3	West Grove	C2
Elm Street	C1	Westgate Street	B2
Fanny Street	B1	Windsor Place	B2
Fitzhamon Embankment	A3	Windsor Road	C2
Flora Street	B1	Wood Street	B3
Glossop Road	C2	Woodville Road	B1
Gordon Road	C1	Wordsworth Avenue	C1
Greyfriars Road	B2	Working Street	B2
Hamilton Street	A2	Wyeverne Road	B1
Harriet Street	B1		
Herbert Street	C3		
High Street	B2		
Hirwain Street	B1		
Keppoch Street	C1		
Kingsway	B2		
Lewis Street	A2		
Longcross Street	C2		
Maindy Road	A1		
Mardy Street	A3		
Mark Street	A2		
Merches Gardens	A3		
Merthyr Street	B1		
Meteor Street	C2		
Mill Lane	B3		
Minny Street	B1		
Miskin Street	B1		
Moira Place	C2		

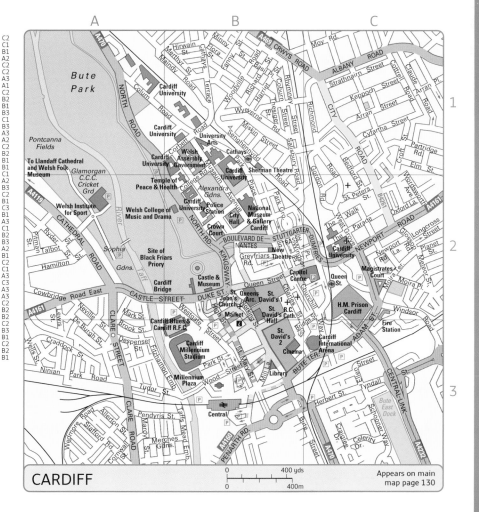

CARDIFF

0 400 yds
0 400m

Appears on main map page 130

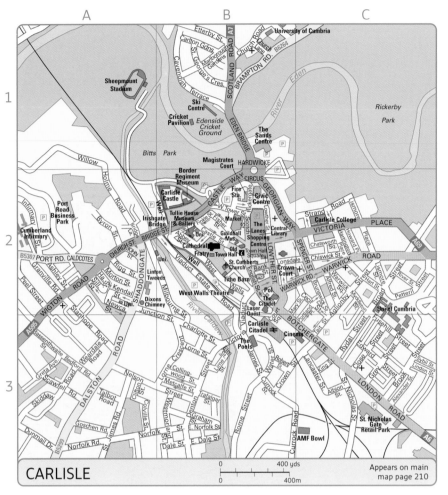

CARLISLE

Appears on main map page 210

Appears on main map page 210

Tourist Information Centre: Old Town Hall, Green Market
Tel: 01228 625600

Abbey Street	B2	Lancaster Street	C3
Aglionby Street	C2	Lime Street	B3
Albion Street	C3	Lindon Street	C3
Alexander Street	C3	Lismore Place	C2
Alfred Street	C2	Lismore Street	C2
Ashley Street	A2	London Road	C3
Bank Street	B2	Lonsdale	B2
Bassenthwaite Street	A3	Lorne Crescent	B3
Bedford Road	A3	Lorne Street	B3
Botchergate	B3	Lowther Street	B2
Brampton Road	B1	Marlborough Gardens	B1
Bridge Lane	A2	Mary Street	B2
Bridge Street	A2	Metcalfe Street	B3
Broad Street	C2	Milbourne Street	A2
Brook Street	C3	Morton Street	A2
Brunswick Street	C2	Myddleton Street	C2
Byron Street	A2	Nelson Street	A3
Caldcotes	A2	Newcastle Street	A2
Carlton Gardens	B1	Norfolk Road	A3
Castle Street	B2	Norfolk Street	A3
Castle Way	B2	Peel Street	A2
Cavendish Terrace	B1	Petteril Street	C2
Cecil Street	C2	Port Road	A2
Charlotte Street	B3	Portland Place	C3
Chatsworth Square	C2	Rickergate	B2
Chiswick Street	C2	Rigg Street	A2
Church Lane	B1	River Street	C2
Church Road	B1	Robert Street	B3
Church Street	A2	Rome Street	B3
Clifton Street	A3	Rydal Street	B3
Close Street	C3	St. George's Crescent	B1
Collingwood Street	B3	St. James Road	A3
Colville Street	A3	St. Nicholas Street	C3
Crown Street	B3	Scawfell Road	A3
Currock Road	B3	Scotch Street	B2
Currock Street	B3	Scotland Road	B1
Dale Street	B3	Shaddongate	A2
Denton Street	B3	Silloth Street	A2
Dunmail Drive	A3	Skiddaw Road	A3
East Dale Street	B3	Spencer Street	C2
East Norfolk Street	B3	Stanhope Road	A2
Eden Bridge	B1	Strand Road	C2
Edward Street	C3	Sybil Street	C3
Elm Street	B3	Tait Street	C3
English Street	B2	Talbot Road	A3
Etterby Street	B1	Trafalgar Street	B3
Finkle Street	B2	Viaduct Estate Road	B2
Fisher Street	B2	Victoria Place	C2
Fusehill Street	C3	Victoria Viaduct	B3
Georgian Way	B2	Warwick Road	B2
Goschen Road	A3	Warwick Square	C2
Graham Street	B3	Water Street	B3
Granville Road	A2	Weardale Road	A3
Greta Avenue	A3	West Tower Street	B2
Grey Street	C3	West Walls	B2
Hardwicke Circus	B1	Westmorland Street	B3
Hart Street	C2	Wigton Road	A2
Hartington Place	C2	Willow Holme Road	A1
Hawick Street	A2		
Howard Place	C2		
Infirmary Street	A2		
James Street	B3		
John Street	A2		
Junction Street	A2		
Kendal Street	A2		
King Street	C3		

CHELTENHAM

Appears on main map page 146

Appears on main map page 146

Tourist Information Centre: 77 Promenade
Tel: 01242 522878

Albany Road	A3	Portland Street	B2
Albert Road	C1	Prestbury Road	C1
Albion Street	B2	Princes Road	A3
All Saints Road	C2	Priory Street	C3
Andover Road	A3	Promenade	B2
Arle Avenue	A1	Rodney Road	B2
Ashford Road	A3	Rosehill Street	C3
Bath Parade	B2	Royal Well Road	B2
Bath Road	B3	St. George's Place	B2
Bayshill Road	A2	St. George's Road	A2
Berkeley Street	B2	St. James Street	B2
Brunswick Street	B1	St. Johns Avenue	B2
Carlton Street	C2	St. Margaret's Road	B1
Central Cross Drive	C1	St. Paul's Road	B1
Christchurch Road	A2	St. Paul's Street North	B1
Churchill Drive	C3	St. Paul's Street South	B1
Clarence Road	B1	St. Stephen's Road	A3
College Lawn	B3	Sandford Mill Road	C3
College Road	B3	Sandford Road	B3
Cranham Road	C3	Sherborne Street	C2
Douro Road	A2	Southgate Drive	C3
Dunalley Street	B1	Strickland Road	C3
Eldon Road	C2	Suffolk Road	A3
Evesham Road	B1	Suffolk Square	A3
Fairview Road	C2	Sun Street	A1
Folly Lane	B1	Swindon Road	A1
Gloucester Road	A2	Sydenham Road	C2
Grafton Road	A3	Sydenham Villas Road	C3
Hales Road	C3	Tewkesbury Road	A1
Hanover Street	B1	Thirlestaine Road	B3
Hayward's Road	C3	Tivoli Road	A3
Henrietta Street	B2	Townsend Street	A1
Hewlett Road	C2	Vittoria Walk	B3
High Street	B1	Wellington Road	B1
Honeybourne Way	A1	West Drive	B1
Hudson Street	B1	Western Road	A2
Imperial Square	B2	Whaddon Road	C1
Keynsham Road	B3	Winchcombe Street	B2
King Alfred Way	C3	Windsor Street	C1
King's Road	C2		
Lansdown Crescent	A3		
Lansdown Road	A3		
London Road	C3		
Lypiatt Road	A3		
Malvern Road	A2		
Market Street	A1		
Marle Hill Parade	B1		
Marle Hill Road	B1		
Millbrook Street	A1		
Montpellier Spa Road	B3		
Montpellier Street	A3		
Montpellier Terrace	A3		
Montpellier Walk	A3		
New Street	A2		
North Place	B2		
North Street	B2		
Old Bath Road	C3		
Oriel Road	B2		
Overton Road	A2		
Painswick Road	A2		
Parabola Road	A2		
Park Place	A3		
Park Street	A1		
Pittville Circus	C1		
Pittville Circus Road	C2		
Pittville Lawn	C1		

CHESTER

Tourist Information Centre: Town Hall, Northgate Street
Tel: 01244 402111

Bath Street	C2	Queen's Park Road	B3
Bedward Row	A2	Queen's Road	C1
Black Diamond Street	B1	Queen Street	B2
Black Friars	A3	Raymond Street	A1
Bold Square	B2	Russel Street	C2
Boughton	C2	St. Anne Street	B1
Bouverie Street	A1	St. George's Crescent	C3
Bridge Street	B2	St. John's Road	C3
Brook Street	B1	St. John Street	B2
Canal Street	A1	St. Martins Way	A1
Castle Drive	A3	St. Oswalds Way	B1
Charles Street	B1	St. Werburgh Street	B2
Cheyney Road	A1	Seller Street	C2
Chichester Street	A1	Sibell Street	C1
City Road	C2	Souter's Lane	B3
City Walls Road	A2	Stanley Street	A2
Commonhall Street	A2	Station Road	C1
Cornwall Street	B1	Steam Mill Street	C2
Crewe Street	C1	Talbot Street	B1
Cuppin Street	A3	The Bars	C2
Dee Hills Park	C2	The Groves	B3
Dee Lane	C2	Trafford Street	B1
Deva Terrace	C2	Union Street	B3
Duke Street	B3	Upper Northgate Street	A1
Eastgate Street	B2	Vicar's Lane	B2
Edinburgh Way	C3	Victoria Crescent	C3
Egerton Street	B1	Victoria Place	B2
Elizabeth Crescent	C3	Victoria Road	A1
Foregate Street	B2	Walker Street	C1
Forest Street	B2	Walpole Street	A1
Francis Street	C1	Walter Street	B1
Frodsham Street	B2	Watergate Street	A2
Garden Lane	A1	Water Tower Street	A2
George Street	B1	Weaver Street	A2
Gloucester Street	B1	White Friars	A3
Grey Friars	A3	York Street	B2
Grosvenor Park Terrace	C2		
Grosvenor Road	A3		
Grosvenor Street	A3		
Handbridge	B3		
Hoole Road	B1		
Hoole Way	B1		
Hunter Street	A2		
King Street	A2		
Leadworks Lane	C2		
Lightfoot Street	C1		
Louise Street	A1		
Love Street	B2		
Lower Bridge Street	B3		
Lower Park Road	C3		
Mill Street	C2		
Milton Street	B1		
Newgate Street	B2		
Nicholas Street	A2		
Nicholas Street Mews	A2		
Northern Pathway	C3		
Northgate Avenue	B1		
Northgate Street	A2		
Nun's Road	A3		
Old Dee Bridge	B3		
Pepper Street	B3		
Phillip Street	C1		
Prince's Avenue	C1		
Princess Street	A2		
Queen's Avenue	C1		
Queen's Drive	C3		

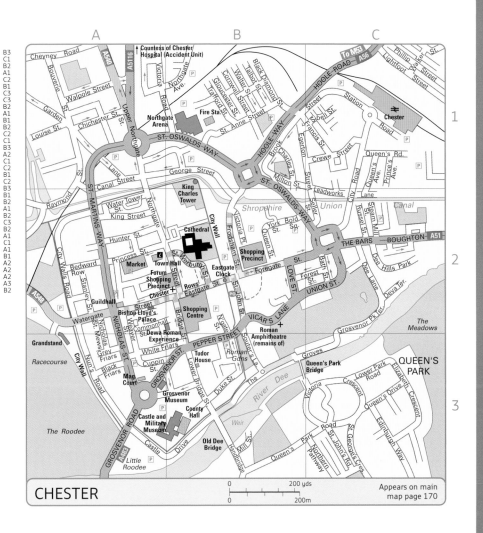

CHESTER

0 — 200 yds
0 — 200m

Appears on main map page 170

COVENTRY

Tourist Information Centre: St. Michael's Tower, Coventry Cathedral Tel: 024 7622 7264

Abbott's Lane	A1	New Union Street	B2
Acacia Avenue	C3	Norfolk Street	A2
Albany Road	A3	Oxford Street	C2
Alma Street	C2	Park Road	B3
Asthill Grove	B3	Parkside	B3
Barker's Butts Lane	A1	Primrose Hill Street	C1
Barras Lane	A2	Priory Street	B2
Berry Street	C1	Puma Way	B3
Bishop Street	B1	Quarryfield Lane	C3
Blythe Road	C1	Queen's Road	A3
Bond Street	A2	Queen Street	C1
Bramble Street	C2	Queen Victoria Road	A2
Bretts Close	C1	Quinton Road	B3
Broadway	A3	Radford Road	A1
Burges	B2	Raglan Street	C2
Butts Road	A2	Regent Street	A3
Cambridge Street	C1	Ringway Hill Cross	A2
Canterbury Street	C1	Ringway Queens	A2
Clifton Street	C1	Ringway Rudge	A2
Colchester Street	C1	Ringway St. Johns	B3
Cornwall Road	C3	Ringway St. Nicholas	B1
Corporation Street	B2	Ringway St. Patricks	B3
Coundon Road	A1	Ringway Swanswell	B1
Coundon Street	A1	Ringway Whitefriars	C2
Cox Street	C2	St. Nicholas Street	B1
Croft Road	A2	Sandy Lane	B1
Drapers Fields	B1	Seagrave Road	C3
Earl Street	B2	Silver Street	B1
East Street	C2	Sky Blue Way	C2
Eaton Road	B3	South Street	C2
Fairfax Street	B2	Spencer Avenue	A3
Far Gosford Street	C2	Spon Street	A2
Foleshill Road	B1	Srathmore Avenue	B3
Fowler Road	A1	Stoney Road	B3
Gordon Street	A3	Stoney Stanton Road	B1
Gosford Street	C2	Swanswell Street	B1
Greyfriars Road	A2	The Precinct	B2
Gulson Road	C2	Tomson Avenue	A1
Hales Street	B2	Trinity Street	B2
Harnall Lane East	C1	Upper Hill Street	A2
Harnall Lane West	B1	Upper Well Street	B2
Harper Road	C2	Vauxhall Street	C2
Harper Street	B2	Vecqueray Street	C2
Hertford Street	B2	Victoria Street	C1
Hewitt Avenue	A1	Vine Street	C1
High Street	B2	Warwick Road	A2
Hill Street	A2	Waveley Road	A2
Holyhead Road	A2	Westminster Road	A3
Hood Street	C2	White Street	B1
Howard Street	B1	Windsor Street	A2
Jordan Well	B2	Wright Street	C1
King William Street	C1		
Lamb Street	B2		
Leicester Row	B1		
Leigh Street	C1		
Little Park Street	B3		
London Road	C3		
Lower Ford Street	C2		
Market Way	B2		
Meadow Street	A2		
Michaelmas Road	A3		
Middleborough Road	A1		
Mile Lane	B3		
Mill Street	A1		
Minster Road	A2		
Much Park Street	B2		

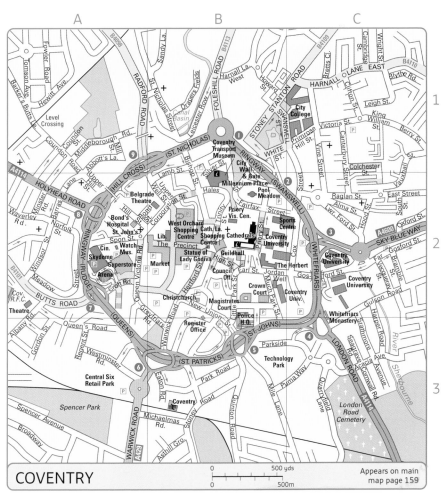

COVENTRY

0 — 500 yds
0 — 500m

Appears on main map page 159

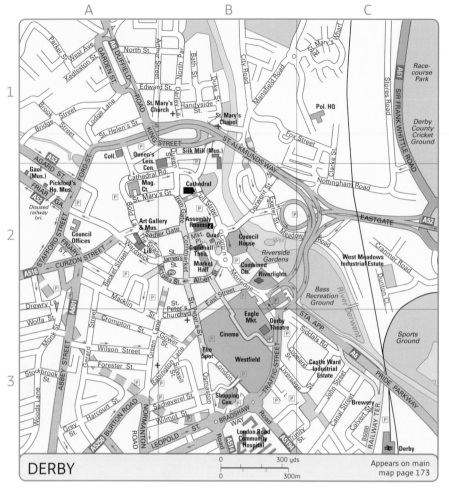

DERBY

```
      A              B              C
```

Scale: 0 — 300 yds / 0 — 300m

Appears on main map page 173

Tourist Information Centre: Assembly Rooms, Market Place
Tel: 01332 255802

Abbey Street	A3
Agard Street	A1
Albert Street	B2
Arthur Street	A1
Babington Lane	A3
Bath Street	B1
Becket Street	A2
Bold Lane	A2
Bradshaw Way	B3
Bridge Street	A1
Brook Street	A1
Burton Road	A3
Calvert Street	C3
Canal Street	C3
Cathedral Road	A2
City Road	B1
Clarke Street	C2
Copeland Street	B3
Cornmarket	B2
Corporation Street	B2
Cranmer Road	C2
Crompton Street	A3
Curzon Street	A2
Darley Lane	B1
Derwent Street	B2
Drewry Lane	A2
Duffield Road	A1
Duke Street	B1
Dunton Close	C2
Eastgate	C2
East Street	B2
Edward Street	A1
Exeter Street	B2
Ford Street	A2
Forester Street	A3
Fox Street	B1
Friar Gate	A2
Friary Street	A2
Full Street	B2
Garden Street	A1
Gerard Street	A3
Gower Street	A3
Green Lane	A3
Grey Street	A3
Handyside Street	B1
Harcourt Street	A3
Iron Gate	B2
John Street	C3
Kedleston Street	A1
King Street	A1
Leopold Street	A3
Liversage Street	B3
Lodge Lane	A1
London Road	B3
Macklin Street	A2
Mansfield Road	B1
Market Place	B2
Meadow Road	B2
Monk Street	A3
Morledge	B2
Normanton Road	A3
North Parade	B1
North Street	A1
Nottingham Road	C2
Osmaston Road	B3
Parker Street	A1
Pride Parkway	C3
Queen Street	B1
Railway Terrace	C3
Sacheverel Street	A3
Sadler Gate	B2
St. Alkmunds Way	B1
St. Helen's Street	A1
St. James Street	B2
St. Mary's Gate	A2
St. Mary's Wharf Road	C1
St. Peter's Churchyard	B3
St. Peter's Street	B2
Siddals Road	C3
Sir Frank Whittle Road	C1
Sitwell Street	B3
Stafford Street	A2
Station Approach	C2
Stockbrook Street	A3
Stores Road	C1
The Strand	A2
Traffic Street	B3
Trinity Street	B3
Victoria Street	A2
Wardwick	A2
West Avenue	A1
Wilmot Street	A3
Wilson Street	A3
Wolfa Street	A3
Woods Lane	A3

DOVER

```
      A              B              C
```

Scale: 0 — 500 yds / 0 — 500m

Appears on main map page 125

Tourist Information Centre: Old Town Gaol, Biggin Street
Tel: 01304 205108

Astor Avenue	A2
Barton Road	A1
Beaconsfield Avenue	A1
Beaconsfield Road	A1
Belgrave Road	A2
Biggin Street	B2
Bridge Street	B2
Brookfield Avenue	A1
Buckland Avenue	A1
Cannon Street	B2
Canons Gate Road	B2
Castle Avenue	B1
Castle Hill Road	B2
Castle Street	B2
Cherry Tree Avenue	A1
Citadel Road	A3
Clarendon Place	A2
Clarendon Street	A2
Connaught Road	B1
Coombe Valley Road	A2
Dover Road	C1
Durham Hill	B2
Eaton Road	A2
Edred Road	A2
Elms Vale Road	A2
Folkestone Road	A2
Frith Road	B1
Godwyne Road	B2
Green Lane	A1
Guston Road	B1
Heathfield Avenue	A1
High Street	B2
Hillside Road	A1
Jubilee Way	C1
Ladywell	B2
Limekiln Street	B3
London Road	A1
Longfield Road	A2
Maison Dieu Road	B2
Marine Parade	B2
Mayfield Avenue	A1
Military Road	B2
Mount Road	A3
Napier Road	B1
Noah's Ark Road	A2
Northbourne Avenue	A2
North Military Road	A2
Old Charlton Road	B1
Old Folkestone Road	A3
Oswald Road	A1
Park Avenue	B1
Pencester Road	B2
Priory Hill	A2
St. Radigund's Road	A1
Salisbury Road	B1
Snargate Street	B3
South Road	A2
Stanhope Road	B1
The Viaduct	B3
Tower Street	A2
Townwall Street	B2
Union Street	B3
Upper Road	C1
York Street	B2

Dundee

Tourist Information Centre: Discovery Point, Discovery Quay
Tel: 01382 527527

Adelaide Place	A1
Albany Terrace	A1
Albert Street	C2
Alexander Street	B1
Ann Street	B2
Arbroath Road	C2
Arklay Street	C1
Arklay Terrace	C1
Arthurstone Terrace	C2
Barrack Road	A2
Blackness Road	A2
Blinshall Street	A2
Brewery Lane	A2
Brook Street	A2
Broughty Ferry Road	C2
Brown Street	A2
Bruce Street	A1
Byron Street	A1
Canning Street	B1
City Square	B3
Clepington Road	C1
Constitution Road	B2
Constitution Street	B1
Court Street	C1
Cowgate Street	B2
Dens Road	B1
Douglas Street	A2
Dudhope Street	A1
Dudhope Terrace	C1
Dundonald Street	C2
Dura Street	C2
East Dock Street	C2
East Marketgait	B2
Fairbairn Street	B1
Greenmarket	B3
Guthrie Street	A2
Hawkhill	A2
High Street	B3
Hill Street	B1
Hilltown	B1
Kenmore Terrace	A1
Killin Avenue	A1
Kinghorne Road	A1
King Street	B2
Larch Street	A2
Law Crescent	A1
Lawside Avenue	A1
Law Street	A1
Leng Street	A1
Lochee Road	A2
Lower Princes Street	C2
Mains Road	B1
Main Street	B1
Meadowside	B2
Morgan Street	C2
Murraygate	B2
Nelson Street	B2
Nethergate	A3
North Marketgait	A2
Perth Road	A3
Polepark Road	A2
Princes Street	C2
Riverside Drive	A3
Roseangle	A3
Rosebank Road	B2
Seagate	B2
South Marketgait	B3
South Tay Street	A3
Strathmartine Road	B1
Tannadice Street	B1
Tay Road Bridge	B3
Trades Lane	B2
Upper Constitution Street	A1
Victoria Road	B2
Victoria Street	C2
Ward Road	A2
West Marketgait	A2
West Port	A2
William Street	C2

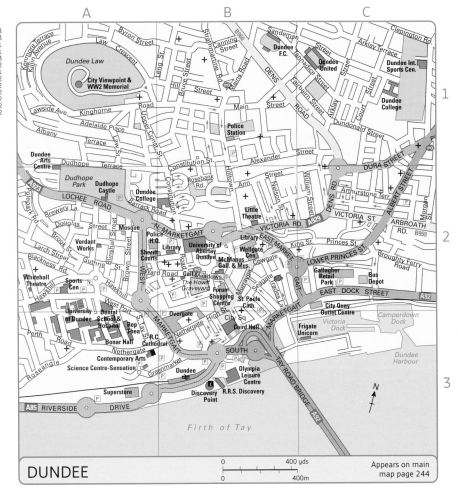

DUNDEE

Appears on main map page 244

Durham

Tourist Information Centre: 2 Millennium Place
Tel: 0191 384 3720

Aykley Heads	A1
Church Street	B3
Clay Lane	A3
Claypath	B2
Crossgate	B2
Crossgate Peth	A3
Darlington Road	A3
Dryburn Road	A1
Durham Road	A1
Fieldhouse Lane	A1
Framwelgate	B2
Framwelgate Peth	B1
Framwelgate Waterside	B2
Gilesgate	C2
Great North Road	A1
Green Lane	C2
Grove Street	B3
Hallgarth Street	C3
Hawthorn Terrace	A2
Leazes Road	B2
Margery Lane	B3
Market Place	B2
Millburngate Bridge	B2
Newcastle Road	A1
New Elvet	B2
North Bailey	B2
North End	A1
North Road	B2
Old Elvet	C2
Pity Me Bypass	A1
Potters Bank	A3
Quarryheads Lane	B3
Providence Row	B2
Redhills Lane	A2
St. Monica Grove	A2
Sidegate	B2
Silver Street	B2
South Bailey	B3
South Road	B3
South Street	B3
Southfield Way	A1
Stockton Road	B3
Sutton Street	B2
The Avenue	A3
Toll House Road	A2
Western Hill	A2
Whinney Hill	C3
Whitesmocks	A1

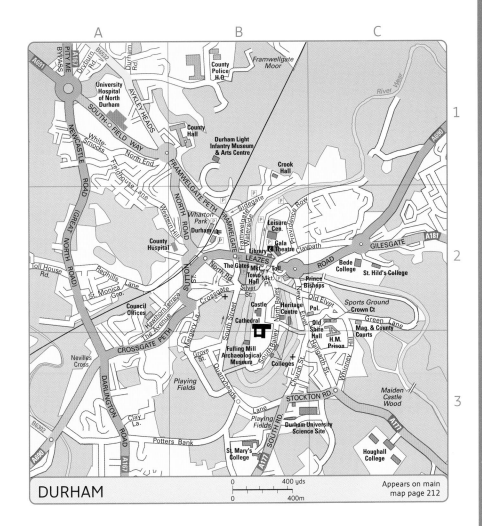

DURHAM

Appears on main map page 212

Eastbourne   Exeter

Edinburgh street map on pages 36-37

EASTBOURNE

Tourist Information Centre: 3 Cornfield Road
Tel: 0871 663 0031

Arlington Road	A2	The Avenue	B2
Arundel Road	B1	The Goffs	A1
Ashford Road	B2/C2	Trinity Trees	C2
Avondale Road	C1	Upper Avenue	B1
Bedfordwell Road	B1	Upperton Lane	B2
Belmore Road	C1	Upperton Road	A1
Blackwater Road	B3	Watts Lane	A1
Borough Lane	A1	Whitley Road	A1
Bourne Street	C2	Willingdon Road	A1
Carew Road	A1/B1	Winchcombe Road	C1
Carlisle Road	A3		
Cavendish Avenue	C1		
Cavendish Place	C2		
College Road	B3		
Commercial Road	B2		
Compton Place Road	A2		
Compton Street	B3		
Cornfield Terrace	B2		
Denton Road	A3		
Devonshire Place	B2		
Dittons Road	A2		
Dursley Road	C2		
Enys Road	B1		
Eversfield Road	B1		
Fairfield Road	A3		
Firle Road	C1		
Furness Road	B3		
Gaudick Road	A3		
Gilbert Road	C1		
Gildredge Road	B2		
Gorringe Road	B1		
Grand Parade	C3		
Grange Road	B3		
Grassington Road	B3		
Grove Road	B2		
Hartfield Road	B1		
Hartington Place	C2		
High Street	A1		
Hyde Gardens	B2		
King Edward's Parade	B3		
Langney Road	C2		
Lewes Road	B1		
Marine Parade	C2		
Mark Lane	B2		
Meads Road	A3		
Melbourne Road	C1		
Mill Gap Road	A1		
Mill Road	A1		
Moat Croft Road	A1		
Moy Avenue	C1		
Ratton Road	A1		
Royal Parade	C2		
Saffrons Park	A3		
Saffrons Road	A2		
St. Anne's Road	A1		
St. Leonard's Road	B2		
Seaside	C2		
Seaside Road	C2		
Selwyn Road	A1		
Silverdale Road	B3		
South Street	B2		
Southfields Road	A2		
Station Parade	B2		
Susan's Road	C2		
Sydney Road	C2		
Terminus Road	B2		

Appears on main map page 110

0   200 yds
0   200m

EXETER

Tourist Information Centre: Dix's Field
Tel: 01392 665700

Albion Street	A3	St. James' Road	C1
Alphington Street	A3	St. Leonard's Road	C3
Barnfield Road	B2	Sidwell Street	B2
Bartholomew Street West	A2	Southernhay East	B2
Bedford Street	B2	South Street	B2
Belmont Road	C1	Spicer Road	C2
Blackboy Road	C1	Station Road	A1
Blackall Road	B1	Streatham Drive	A1
Bonhay Road	A2	Streatham Rise	A1
Buller Road	A3	The Quay	B3
Church Road	A3	Thornton Hill	B1
Clifton Hill	C1	Topsham Road	B3
Clifton Road	C2	Velwell Road	A1
Clifton Street	C2	Victoria Street	C1
College Road	C2	Water Lane	B3
Commercial Road	B3	Well Street	C1
Cowick Street	A3	West Avenue	B1
Cowley Bridge Road	A1	Western Road	A2
Danes Road	B1	Western Way	C2
Denmark Road	C2	Wonford Road	C3
Devonshire Place	C1	York Road	B1
Dix's Field	B2		
East Grove Road	C3		
Elmside	C1		
Exe Street	A2		
Fore Street	B2		
Haldon Road	A2		
Haven Road	B3		
Heavitree Road	C2		
Hele Road	A1		
High Street	B2		
Holloway Street	B3		
Hoopern Street	B1		
Howell Road	B1		
Iddesleigh Road	C1		
Iron Bridge	A2		
Isca Road	B3		
Jesmond Road	C1		
Longbrook Street	B1		
Looe Road	A1		
Lyndhurst Road	C3		
Magdalen Road	C2		
Magdalen Street	B3		
Marlborough Road	C3		
Matford Avenue	C3		
Matford Lane	C3		
Mount Pleasant Road	C1		
New Bridge Street	A3		
New North Road	A1/B1		
North Street	B2		
Okehampton Road	A3		
Okehampton Street	A3		
Old Tiverton Road	C1		
Oxford Road	C1		
Paris Street	B2		
Paul Street	B2		
Pennsylvania Road	B1		
Portland Street	C2		
Prince of Wales Road	A1		
Princesshay	B2		
Prospect Park	C1		
Queen's Road	A3		
Queen Street	B2		
Radford Road	C3		
Richmond Road	A2		
St. David's Hill	A1		

Appears on main map page 102

0   400 yds
0   400m

Tourist Information Centre: Discover Folkestone,
20 Bouverie Place. Tel: 01303 258594

Alder Road	B2	Westbourne Gardens	A3
Archer Road	C2	Wingate Road	B1
Bathurst Road	A2	Wood Avenue	C1
Beatty Road	C1	Wilton Road	A2
Black Bull Road	B2		
Bournemouth Road	B2		
Bouverie Road West	A3		
Bradstone Road	B2		
Broadfield Road	A2		
Broadmead Road	B2		
Brockman Road	B2		
Canterbury Road	C1		
Castle Hill Avenue	B3		
Cheriton Gardens	B3		
Cheriton Road	A2/B2		
Cherry Garden Avenue	A1		
Christ Church Road	B3		
Churchill Avenue	B1		
Clifton Crescent	A3		
Coniston Road	A1		
Coolinge Road	B2		
Cornwallis Avenue	A2		
Dawson Road	B2		
Dixwell Road	A3		
Dolphins Road	B1		
Dover Hill	C1		
Dover Road	C1		
Downs Road	B1		
Earles Avenue	A3		
Foord Road	B2		
Godwyn Road	A3		
Grimston Avenue	A3		
Grimston Gardens	A3		
Guildhall Street	B2		
Guildhall Street North	B2		
Harbour Way	C2		
Hill Road	C1		
Ivy Way	C1		
Joyes Road	C1		
Linden Crescent	B2		
Links Way	A1		
Lower Sandgate Road	A3		
Lucy Avenue	A1		
Manor Road	B3		
Marine Parade	B3		
Marshall Street	C1		
Mead Road	B2		
Old High Street	C3		
Park Farm Road	B1		
Pavilion Road	B2		
Radnor Bridge Road	C2		
Radnor Park Avenue	A2		
Radnor Park Road	B2		
Radnor Park West	A2		
Sandgate Hill	A3		
Sandgate Road	B3		
Shorncliffe Road	A2		
Sidney Street	C2		
The Leas	B3		
The Stade	C3		
The Tram Road	C2		
Tontine Street	C2		
Turketel Road	A3		
Tyson Road	C1		
Wear Bay Crescent	C2		
Wear Bay Road	C1		

FOLKESTONE

| 0 | 200 yds |
| 0 | 200m |

Appears on main
map page 125

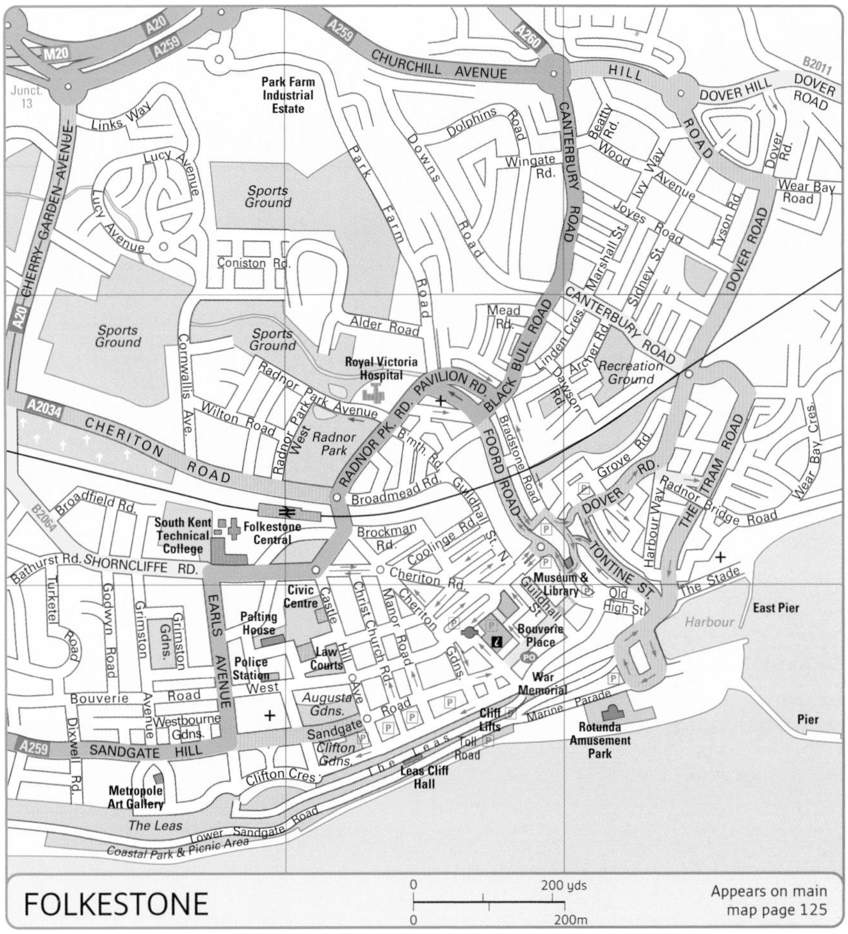

Tourist Information Centre: 28 Southgate Street
Tel: 01452 396572

Adelaide Street	B3	St. Oswald's Road	A1
Alexandra Road	B1	Secunda Way	A3
Alfred Street	C2	Severn Road	A2
Alma Place	A3	Seymour Road	A3
Alvin Street	B1	Southgate Street	A2
Archdeacon Street	A1	Spa Road	A2
Argyll Road	C1	Stanley Road	B3
Askwith Road	C3	Station Road	B2
Barnwood Road	C1	Stroud Road	A3
Barton Street	B2	The Quay	A2
Black Dog Way	B1	Tredworth Road	B3
Bristol Road	A3	Trier Way	A3
Brunswick Road	B2	Upton Street	B3
Bruton Way	B2	Vicarage Road	C3
Calton Road	B3	Victoria Street	B2
Castle Meads Way	A1	Wellington Street	B2
Cecil Road	A3	Westgate Street	A1
Cheltenham Road	C1	Weston Road	A3
Churchill Road	A3	Wheatstone Road	B3
Clifton Road	A3	Willow Avenue	C3
Conduit Street	B3	Worcester Street	B1
Coney Hill Road	C3		
Dean's Way	B1		
Denmark Road	B1		
Derby Road	B2		
Estcourt Road	B1		
Eastern Avenue	C3		
Eastgate Street	B2		
Frampton Road	A3		
Gouda Way	A1		
Great Western Road	B2		
Greyfriars	B2		
Hatherley Road	B3		
Heathville Road	B1		
Hempsted Lane	A2		
Henry Road	B1		
High Street	B3		
Hopewell Street	B3		
Horton Road	C2		
Howard Street	B3		
India Road	C2		
King Edward's Avenue	B3		
Kingsholm Road	B1		
Lansdown Road	B1		
Linden Road	A3		
Llanthony Road	A2		
London Road	B1		
Lower Westgate Street	A1		
Marlborough Road	C3		
Merevale Road	C1		
Metz Way	B2		
Midland Road	B3		
Millbrook Street	B2		
Myers Road	C2		
Northgate Street	B2		
Oxford Road	B1		
Oxstalls Lane	C1		
Painswick Road	C3		
Park Road	B2		
Parkend Road	B3		
Pitt Street	B1		
Quay Street	A2		
Regent Street	B3		
Robinson Road	A3		
Ryecroft Street	B3		
St. Ann Way	A3		

GLOUCESTER

| 0 | 500 yds |
| 0 | 500m |

Appears on main
map page 132

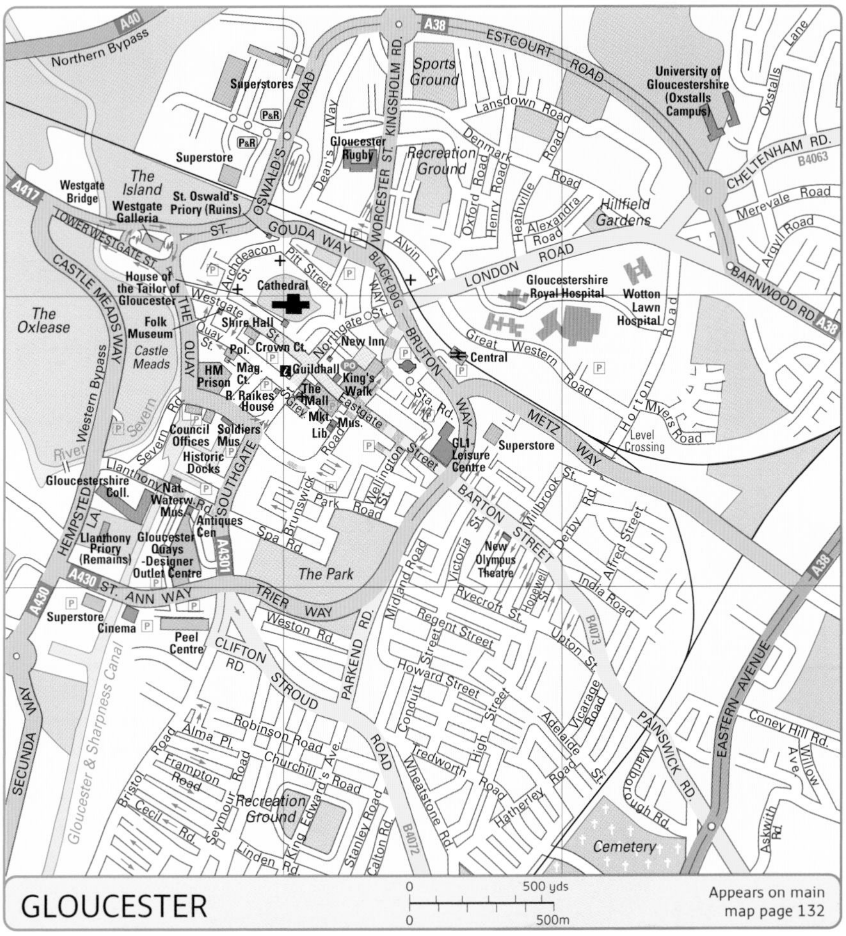

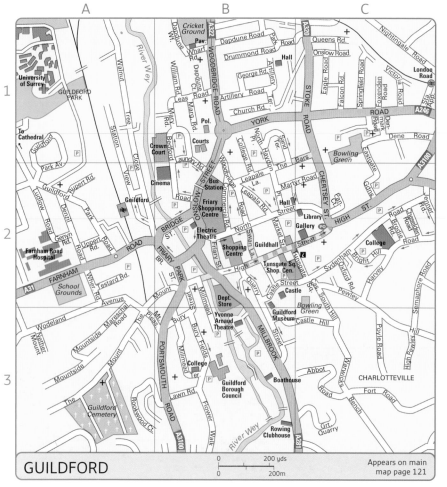

GUILDFORD

Appears on main map page 121

0 — 200 yds
0 — 200m

Tourist Information Centre: 14 Tunsgate
Tel: 01483 444333

Abbot Road	C3	Portsmouth Road	B3
Artillery Road	B1	Poyle Road	C3
Artillery Terrace	B1	Quarry Street	B2
Bedford Road	B1	Queens Road	C1
Bridge Street	B2	Rookwood Court	A3
Bright Hill	C2	Rupert Road	A2
Brodie Road	C2	Sand Terrace	B1
Bury Fields	B3	Semaphore Road	C3
Bury Street	B3	South Hill	C2
Castle Hill	C3	Springfield Road	C1
Castle Square	C2	Station Approach	C1
Castle Street	B2	Station View	A1
Chertsey Street	C1	Stoke Road	C1
Cheselden Road	C2	Swan Lane	B2
Commercial Road	B2	Sydenham Road	C2
Dapdune Court	B1	Testard Road	A2
Dapdune Road	B1	The Bars	B2
Dapdune Wharf	B1	The Mount	A3
Dene Road	C1	Tunsgate	C2
Denmark Road	C1	Upperton Road	A2
Denzil Road	A2	Victoria Road	C1
Drummond Road	B1	Walnut Tree Close	A1
Eagle Road	C1	Warwicks	C3
Eastgate Gardens	C1	Wharf Road	B1
Falcon Road	C1	Wherwell Road	A2
Farnham Road	A2	William Road	B1
Flower Walk	B3	Wodeland Avenue	A3
Fort Road	C3	Woodbridge Road	B1
Foxenden Road	C1	York Road	B1
Friary Bridge	B2		
Friary Street	B2		
Genyn Road	A2		
George Road	B1		
Great Quarry	C3		
Guildford Park Avenue	A1		
Guildford Park Road	A2		
Harvey Road	C2		
Haydon Place	B1		
High Pewley	C3		
High Street	B2/C2		
Laundry Road	B1		
Lawn Road	B3		
Leap Lane	B2		
Leas Road	B1		
Ludlow Road	A2		
Mareschal Road	A3		
Margaret Road	B1		
Market Street	B2		
Martyr Road	B2		
Mary Road	B1		
Millbrook	B3		
Millmead	B2		
Millmead Terrace	B3		
Mount Pleasant	A3		
Mountside	A3		
Nether Mount	A3		
Nightingale Road	C1		
North Place	B1		
North Street	B2		
Onslow Road	C1		
Onslow Street	B2		
Oxford Road	C2		
Pannells Court	C2		
Park Road	B1		
Park Street	B2		
Pewley Hill	C2		

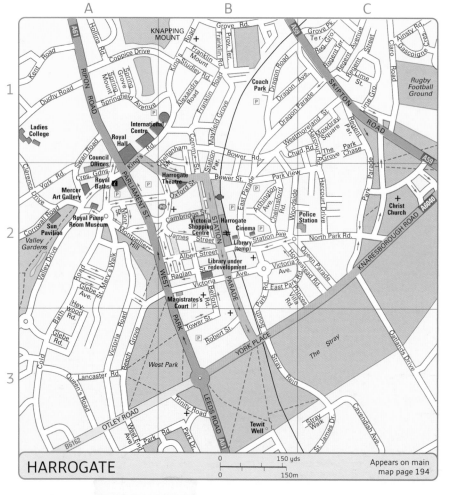

HARROGATE

Appears on main map page 194

0 — 150 yds
0 — 150m

Tourist Information Centre: Royal Baths, Crescent Road
Tel: 0845 389 3223

Ainsty Road	C1	Regent Grove	C1
Albert Street	B2	Regent Parade	C1
Alexandra Road	B1	Regent Street	C1
Arthington Avenue	B2	Regent Terrace	C1
Beech Grove	A3	Ripon Road	A1
Belford Road	B2	Robert Street	B3
Bower Road	B1	St. James Drive	C3
Bower Street	B2	St. Mary's Walk	A3
Cambridge Street	B2	Skipton Road	C1
Cavendish Avenue	C3	South Park Road	B3
Chelmsford Road	B2	Springfield Avenue	A1
Cheltenham Mount	B1	Spring Grove	A1
Chudleigh Road	C1	Spring Mount	A1
Clarence Drive	A2	Station Avenue	B2
Claro Road	C1	Station Parade	B2
Cold Bath Road	A3	Stray Rein	B3
Commercial Street	B1	Stray Walk	C3
Coppice Drive	A1	Studley Road	B1
Cornwall Road	A2	Swan Road	A2
Crescent Gardens	A2	The Grove	C1
Dragon Avenue	B1	Tower Street	B3
Dragon Parade	B1	Trinity Road	B3
Dragon Road	B1	Valley Drive	A2
Duchy Road	A1	Victoria Avenue	B2
East Parade	B2	Victoria Road	A3
East Park Road	B2	West End Avenue	A3
Franklin Mount	B1	West Park	B2
Franklin Road	B1	Woodside	B2
Gascoigne Crescent	C1	York Place	B3
Glebe Avenue	A3	York Road	A2
Glebe Road	A3		
Grove Park Terrace	C1		
Grove Road	B1		
Harcourt Drive	C2		
Harcourt Road	C1		
Heywood Road	A3		
Hollins Road	A1		
Homestead Road	B2		
James Street	B2		
Kent Road	A1		
King's Road	A2		
Knaresborough Road	C2		
Lancaster Road	A3		
Leeds Road	B3		
Lime Grove	C1		
Lime Street	C1		
Mayfield Grove	B1		
Montpellier Hill	A2		
Montpellier Street	A2		
Mowbray Square	C1		
North Park Road	B2		
Oatlands Drive	C3		
Otley Road	A3		
Oxford Street	B2		
Park Chase	C1		
Park Drive	B3		
Park Parade	C2		
Park Road	A3		
Park View	B2		
Parliament Street	A2		
Princes Villa Road	B3		
Providence Terrace	B1		
Queen Parade	C2		
Queen's Road	A3		
Raglan Street	B2		
Regent Avenue	C1		

Tourist Information Centre: Queens Square, Priory Meadow
Tel: 0845 274 1001

Albert Road	B3
All Saints Street	C2
Amherst Road	A2
Ashburnham Road	C2
Ashford Road	A1
Ashford Way	A1
Baldslow Road	B2
Beaconsfield Road	B1
Bembrook Road	C2
Bohemia Road	A2
Braybrooke Road	B2
Broomsgrove Road	C1
Cambridge Road	A3
Castle Hill Road	B3
Castle Street	B3
Chiltern Drive	C1
Church Road	A3
Collier Road	C2
Cornwallis Terrace	A3
Croft Road	C2
De Cham Road	A3
Denmark Place	B3
Downs Road	B1
East Parade	C3
Elphinstone Road	B1
Eversfield Place	A3
Falaise Road	A3
Farley Bank	C1
Fearon Road	B1
Fellows Road	C1
Frederick Road	C1
Freshwater Avenue	A1
George Street	C3
Harold Place	B3
Harold Road	C2
High Street	C2
Hillside Road	A1
Hoad's Wood Road	B1
Hughenden Road	B1
Laton Road	B1
Linley Drive	B1
Linton Road	A2
Lower Park Road	A2
Magdalen Road	A3
Malvern Way	C1
Marine Parade	C3
Milward Road	B2
Mount Pleasant Road	B1
Old London Road	C2
Park Avenue	A1
Park Crescent	A1
Park View	A1
Park Way	A1
Parker Road	B1
Parkstone Road	A1
Pelham Place	B3
Priory Avenue	B2
Priory Road	C2
Queen's Road	B2
Robertson Street	B3
Rock-a-Nore Road	C3
St. George's Road	C2
St. Helen's Down	B1
St. Helen's Park Road	B2
St. Helen's Road	A1
St. John's Road	A3

St. Margaret's Road	A3
St. Mary's Road	B2
St. Mary's Terrace	B2
St. Thomas's Road	C2
Thanet Way	A1
The Bourne	C2
Upper Park Road	A2
Vicarage Road	B2
Warrior Square	A3
Wellington Road	B2
White Rock	A3
Woodbrook Road	B1
Wykeham Road	A2

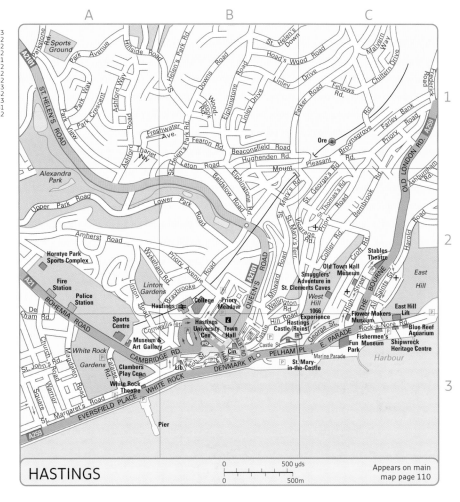

HASTINGS

0   500 yds
0   500m

Appears on main
map page 110

Tourist Information Centre: 1 King Street
Tel: 01432 268430

Aubrey Street	B2
Barrs Court Road	C1
Barton Road	A2
Barton Yard	A2
Bath Street	C2
Belmont Avenue	A3
Berrington Street	B2
Bewell Street	B2
Blackfriars Street	B1
Blueschool Street	B1
Brewers Passage	B2
Bridge Street	B2
Broad Street	B2
Canonmoor Street	A1
Cantilupe Street	C2
Castle Street	B2
Catherine Street	C2
Central Avenue	C2
Church Street	B2
Commercial Road	C1
Commercial Street	B2
Coningsby Street	B1
East Street	B2
Edgar Street	B1
Eign Gate	B2
Eign Street	A2
Ferrers Street	B2
Friars Street	A2
Gaol Street	C2
Green Street	C3
Grenfell Road	C3
Greyfriars Avenue	A3
Greyfriars Bridge	B2
Grove Road	C3
Harold Street	C3
High Street	B2
High Town	B2
King Street	B2
Kyrle Street	C2
Maylord Street	B2
Mill Street	C3
Monkmoor Street	C1
Moorfield Street	A1
Moor Street	B1
Mostyn Street	A1
Nelson Street	C3
Newmarket Street	B1
Park Street	C3
Penhaligon Way	A1
Plough Lane	A1
Portland Street	A1
Quay Street	B2
Ryeland Street	A2
St. Guthlac Street	C2
St. James Road	C3
St. Martin's Avenue	B3
St. Martin's Street	B3
St. Owen Street	C2
Station Approach	C1
Station Road	A2
Stonebow Road	C1
Symonds Street	C2
The Atrium	B1
Turner Street	C3
Union Street	B2
Union Walk	C1

Vaughan Street	C2
Victoria Street	A2
West Street	B2
Widemarsh Street	B2
Wye Street	B3

HEREFORD

0   250 yds
0   250m

Appears on main
map page 145

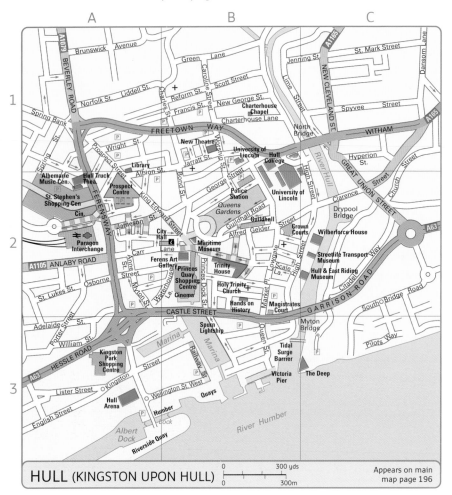

Appears on main
map page 196

HULL (KINGSTON UPON HULL)

0 — 300 yds
0 — 300m

Tourist Information Centre: 1 Paragon Street
Tel: 0844 811 2070

Adelaide Street	A3
Albion Street	A2
Alfred Gelder Street	B2
Anlaby Road	A2
Anne Street	A2
Beverley Road	A1
Bond Street	B2
Brunswick Avenue	A1
Caroline Street	B1
Carr Lane	A2
Castle Street	B2
Charles Street	B1
Charterhouse Lane	B1
Church Street	C2
Citadel Way	C2
Clarence Street	C2
Cleveland Street	C1
Dansom Lane	C1
English Street	A3
Ferensway	A2
Francis Street	B1
Freetown Way	A1
Garrison Road	C2
George Street	B2
Great Union Street	C1
Green Lane	B1
Guildhall Road	B2
Hessle Road	A3
High Street	C1
Hyperion Street	C1
Jameson Street	A2
Jarratt Street	B1
Jenning Street	B1
King Edward Street	A2
Kingston Street	A3
Liddell Street	A1
Lime Street	B1
Lister Street	A3
Lowgate	B2
Market Place	B2
Myton Street	A2
New Cleveland Street	C1
New George Street	B1
Norfolk Street	A1
North Bridge	B1
Osborne Street	A2
Pilots Way	C3
Porter Street	A3
Princes Dock Street	B2
Prospect Street	A1
Queen Street	B3
Reform Street	B1
St. Lukes Street	A2
St. Mark Street	C1
Scale Lane	B2
Scott Street	B1
Scott Street Bridge	B1
South Bridge Road	C2
Spring Bank	A1
Spring Street	A2
Spyvee Street	C1
Waterhouse Lane	A2
Wellington Street West	A3
William Street	A3
Witham	C1
Worship Street	B1
Wright Street	A1

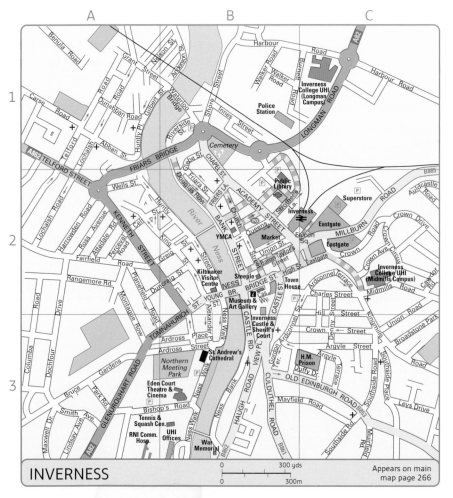

Appears on main
map page 266

INVERNESS

0 — 300 yds
0 — 300m

Tourist Information Centre: Castle Wynd
Tel: 0845 22 55 121

Abban Street	A1	Lochalsh Road	A1
Academy Street	B2	Longman Road	C1
Alexander Place	B2	Maxwell Drive	A3
Anderson Street	B1	Mayfield Road	B3
Ardconnel Street	B3	Midmills Road	C2
Ardconnel Terrace	C2	Millburn Road	C2
Ardross Place	B3	Montague Row	A2
Ardross Street	B3	Muirfield Road	C3
Argyle Street	C3	Nelson Street	A1
Argyle Terrace	C3	Ness Bank	B3
Attadale Road	A2	Ness Bridge	B2
Auldcastle Road	C2	Ness Walk	B3
Bank Street	B2	Old Edinburgh Road	B3
Baron Taylor's Street	B2	Park Road	A3
Benula Road	A1	Perceval Road	A2
Bishop's Road	A3	Planefield Road	A2
Bridge Street	B2	Queensgate	B2
Broadstone Park	C3	Rangemore Road	A2
Bruce Gardens	A3	Riverside Street	B1
Burnett Road	C1	Ross Avenue	A2
Carse Road	A1	Shore Street	B1
Castle Road	B2	Smith Avenue	A3
Castle Street	B2	Southside Place	C3
Castle Wynd	B2	Southside Road	C3
Cawdor Road	C2	Stephen's Brae	C2
Celt Street	A2	Strother's Lane	B2
Chapel Street	B1	Telford Road	A1
Charles Street	C2	Telford Street	A1
Church Street	B2	Tomnahurich Street	A3
Columba Road	A3	Union Road	C3
Crown Avenue	C2	Union Street	B2
Crown Circus	C2	View Place	B3
Crown Drive	C2	Walker Road	B1
Crown Road	C2	Waterloo Bridge	B1
Crown Street	C3	Wells Street	A2
Culduthel Road	B3	Young Street	B2
Denny Street	C3		
Dochfour Drive	A3		
Douglas Row	B1		
Duffy Drive	B3		
Duncraig Street	A2		
Eastgate	C2		
Fairfield Road	A2		
Falcon Square	C2		
Friars Bridge	A1		
Friars Lane	B2		
Friars Street	B2		
Gilbert Street	A1		
Glebe Street	B1		
Glen Urquhart Road	A3		
Gordon Terrace	B3		
Grant Street	A1		
Greig Street	A2		
Harbour Road	B1		
Harrowden Road	A2		
Haugh Road	B3		
High Street	B2		
Hill Street	C2		
Hontly Place	A1		
Huntly Street	A2		
Innes Street	B1		
Kenneth Street	A2		
Kingsmills Road	C2		
King Street	A2		
Leys Drive	C3		
Lindsay Avenue	A3		

Tourist Information Centre: 7-9 Every Street, Town Hall Square
Tel: 0844 888 5181

Abbey Street	B1	Market Place South	B2
Albion Street	B2	Market Street	B2
All Saints Road	A2	Mill Lane	A3
Aylestone Road	B3	Millstone Lane	B2
Bassett Street	A1	Montreal Road	C1
Bath Lane	A2	Morledge Street	C2
Bedford Street North	C1	Narborough Road	A3
Belgrave Gate	B1	Narborough Road North	A2
Bell Lane	C1	Nelson Street	C3
Belvoir Street	B2	Newarke Close	A3
Braunstone Gate	A2	Newarke Street	B2
Burgess Street	B1	Northgate Street	A1
Burleys Way	B1	Ottawa Road	C1
Byron Street	B1	Oxford Street	B2
Cank Street	B2	Pasture Lane	A1
Castle Street	A2	Peacock Lane	B2
Charles Street	C2	Pocklingtons Walk	B2
Christow Street	C1	Prebend Street	C3
Church Gate	B1	Princess Road East	C3
Clarence Street	B1	Pringle Street	A1
Clyde Street	C1	Queen Street	C2
College Street	C2	Regent Road	B3
Colton Street	C2	Regent Street	C3
Conduit Street	C2	Repton Street	A1
Crafton Street East	C1	Rutland Street	C2
Cravan Street	A1	Samuel Street	C2
De Montfort Street	C3	Sanvey Gate	A1
Deacon Street	B3	Saxby Street	C3
Dryden Street	B1	Slater Street	A1
Duns Lane	A2	Soar Lane	A1
Dunton Street	A1	South Albion Street	C2
Eastern Boulevard	A3	Southampton Street	C2
Friar Lane	B2	Sparkenhoe Street	C2
Friday Street	B1	St. George Street	C2
Frog Island	A1	St. George's Way	C2
Gallowtree Gate	B2	St. John's Street	B1
Gaul Street	A3	St. Margaret's Way	A1
Glebe Street	C2	St. Matthew's Way	C1
Gotham Street	C3	St. Nicholas Circle	A2
Granby Street	B2	Swain Street	C2
Grange Lane	B3	Swan Street	A1
Grasmere Street	A3	Taylor Road	C1
Great Central Street	A1	Thames Street	B1
Halford Street	B2	The Gateway	A3
Havelock Street	B3	The Newarke	A2
Haymarket	B1	Tigers Way	B3
High Street	B2	Tower Street	B3
Highcross Street	A1	Tudor Road	A1
Hobart Street	C2	Ullswater Street	A3
Horsfair Street	B2	University Road	C3
Humberstone Gate	B2	Upperton Road	A3
Humberstone Road	C1	Vaughan Way	A1
Infirmary Road	B3	Vestry Street	C2
Jarrom Street	A3	Walnut Street	A3
Jarvis Street	A2	Waterloo Way	C3
Kamloops Crescent	C1	Welford Road	B2
Kent Street	C1	Wellington Street	B2
King Richard's Road	A2	West Street	B3
King Street	B2	Western Boulevard	A3
Lancaster Road	B3	Western Road	A3
Lee Street	B1	Wharf Street North	C1
Lincoln Street	C2	Wharf Street South	C1
London Road	C3	Wilberforce Road	A3
Loseby Lane	B2	Windermere Street	A3
Lower Brown Street	B2	Woodboy Street	C1
Manitoba Road	C1	Yeoman Street	B2
Mansfield Street	B1	York Road	B2

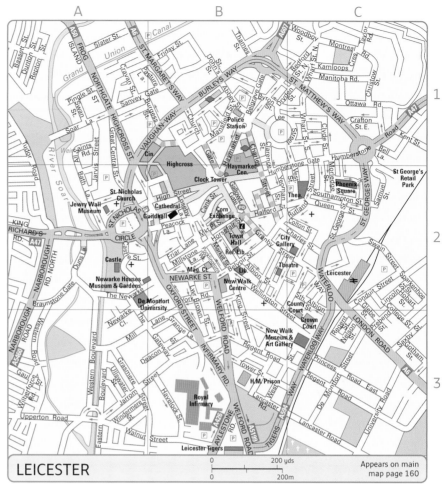

LEICESTER

0 200 yds
0 200m

Appears on main
map page 160

Tourist Information Centre: 9 Castle Hill
Tel: 01522 873000

Alexandra Terrace	A2	Spa Road	C3
Baggholme Road	C2	St. Anne's Road	C2
Bailgate	B1	St. Giles Avenue	C1
Beaumont Fee	B2	St. Mark Street	B3
Beevor Street	A3	St. Mary's Street	B3
Brayford Way	A3	St. Rumbold Street	B2
Brayford Wharf North	A2	Stamp End	C3
Broadgate	B2	Steep Hill	B2
Broadway	B1	The Avenue	A2
Bruce Road	C1	Tritton Road	A3
Burton Road	A1	Union Row	A2
Canwick Road	B3	Upper Lindum Street	C2
Carholme Road	A2	Upper Long Leys Road	A1
Carline Road	A1	Vere Street	B1
Carr Street	A2	Vine Street	C2
Cheviot Street	C2	Waterside North	B3
Church Lane	B1	Waterside South	B3
Clasketgate	B2	West Parade	A2
Croft Street	B2	Westgate	B1
Cross Street	B3	Wigford Way	B2
Curle Avenue	C1	Wilson Street	A2
Drury Lane	B2	Winn Street	C2
East Gate	B2	Wragby Road	C1
Firth Road	A3	Yarborough Road	A1
George Street	C3		
Great Northern Terrace	B3		
Greetwell Close	C1		
Greetwell Road	C2		
Gresham Street	A2		
Hampton Street	A2		
Harvey Street	A2		
High Street	B3		
John Street	C2		
Langworthgate	B1		
Lee Road	C1		
Lindum Road	B2		
Lindum Terrace	C2		
Long Leys Road	A1		
Mainwaring Road	C1		
Mill Road	A1		
Milman Road	C2		
Monks Road	C2		
Monson Street	B3		
Moor Street	A1		
Mount Street	A1		
Nettleham Road	B1		
Newland	A2		
Newland Street West	A2		
Newport	B1		
Northgate	B1		
Orchard Street	A2		
Pelham Bridge	B3		
Portland Street	B3		
Portland Street	B3		
Pottergate	B2		
Queensway	C1		
Rasen Lane	B1		
Richmond Road	A2		
Ripon Street	B3		
Rope Walk	A3		
Rosemary Lane	B2		
Ruskin Avenue	C1		
Saltergate	B2		
Sewell Road	C2		
Silver Street	B2		
Sincil Bank	B3		

LINCOLN

0 200 yds
0 200m

Appears on main
map page 187

Middlesbrough   Milton Keynes

Manchester street map on pages 46-47

MIDDLESBROUGH

Tourist Information Centre: Town Hall, Albert Road
Tel: 01642 729700

Street	Grid	Street	Grid
Abingdon Road	B2	Roman Road	A3
Aire Street	A2	Roseberry Road	C2
Albert Road	B1	Saltwells Road	C2
Ayresome Green Lane	A2	Scotts Road	C1
Ayresome Street	A2	Sheperdson Way	C1
Beech Grove Road	B3	Snowdon Road	B1
Belle Vue Grove	C3	Southfield Road	B2
Bishopton Road	B3	Southwell Road	B3
Borough Road	B1/C3	St. Barnabas Road	A2
Breckon Hill Road	C2	Surrey Street	A2
Bridge Street East	B1	Sycamore Road	B3
Bridge Street West	B1	The Avenue	B3
Burlam Road	A3	The Crescent	A3
Cambridge Road	A3	The Vale	A3
Cannon Park Way	A1	Thornfield Road	A3
Cannon Street	A1	Union Street	A2
Cargo Fleet Road	C1	Valley Road	B3
Chipchase Road	A3	Victoria Road	B2
Clairville Road	B2	Victoria Street	A1
Clive Road	A2	Westbourne Grove	C2
Corporation Road	B1	Westbourne Road	A3
Crescent Road	A2	Westminster Road	B3
Cumberland Road	B3	Wilson Street	B1
Deepdale Avenue	B3	Woodlands Road	B2
Derwent Street	A2		
Dockside Road	B1/C1		
Douglas Street	C2		
Eastbourne Road	B3		
Emerson Avenue	B3		
Forty Foot Road	A1		
Grange Road	B1		
Granville Road	B2		
Gresham Road	A2		
Harford Street	A2		
Harrow Road	A3		
Hartington Road	A1		
Heywood Street	A2		
Highfield Road	C3		
Holwick Road	A1		
Hudson Quay	C1		
Hutton Road	C2		
Ingram Road	C2		
Keith Road	B3		
Lansdowne Road	C2		
Linthorpe Road	B3		
Longford Street	A2		
Longlands Road	C2		
Marsh Street	A1		
Marton Burn Road	B3		
Marton Road	C2/C3		
Newport Road	A1/B1		
North Ormesby Road	C1		
Nut Lane	C2		
Orchard Road	A3		
Overdale Road	C3		
Oxford Road	A3		
Park Lane	B2		
Park Road North	B2		
Park Road South	B2		
Park Vale Road	B2		
Parliament Road	A2		
Portman Street	B2		
Princes Road	A2		
Reeth Road	A3		
Riverside Park Road	A1		
Rockcliffe Road	A3		

Appears on main map page 213

MILTON KEYNES

Street	Grid
Avebury Boulevard	B2/C1
Boycott Avenue	B3
Bradwell Common Boulevard	A1
Bradwell Road	A3
Burnham Drive	A1
Chaffron Way	C3
Childs Way	A3/C2
Conniburrow Boulevard	B1
Dansteed Way	A1
Deltic Avenue	A2
Elder Gate	A2
Evans Gate	B3
Fennel Drive	B1
Fishermead Boulevard	C2
Fulwoods Drive	C3
Gibsons Green	A1
Glovers Lane	A1
Grafton Gate	A2
Grafton Street	A1/B3
Gurnards Avenue	C2
Hampstead Gate	A1
Harrier Drive	C3
Leys Road	A3
Lloyds	C3
Mallow Gate	B1
Marlborough Street	C1
Mayditch Place	A1
Midsummer Boulevard	B2/C1
Oldbrook Boulevard	B3
Patriot Drive	A2
Pentewan Gate	C2
Portway	B2/C1
Precedent Drive	A2
Quinton Drive	A1
Redland Drive	A3
Saxon Gate	B2
Saxon Street	B1/C3
Secklow Gate	C1
Silbury Boulevard	B2/C1
Skeldon Gate	C1
Snowdon Drive	B3
Stainton Drive	A1
Strudwick Drive	C3
Trueman Place	C3
Underwood Place	B3
Witan Gate	B2

Appears on main map page 149

Tourist Information Centre: 8-9 Central Arcade
Tel: 0191 277 8000

Albert Street	C2	Pitt Street	A2
Ancrum Street	A1	Portland Road	C1
Argyle Street	C2	Portland Terrace	C1
Askew Road	C3	Pottery Lane	A3
Barrack Road	A1	Quarryfield Road	C3
Barras Bridge	B1	Quayside	C3
Bath Lane	A2	Queen Victoria Road	B1
Bigg Market	B2	Railway Street	A3
Blackett Street	B2	Redheugh Bridge	A3
Byron Street	C1	Richardson Road	A1
Chester Street	C1	Rye Hill	A3
City Road	C2	St. James Boulevard	A3
Claremont Road	B1	St. Mary's Place	B1
Clarence Street	C2	St. Thomas Street	B1
Clayton Street	B2	Sandyford Road	B1/C1
Clayton Street West	A3	Scotswood Road	A3
Corporation Street	A2	Skinnerburn Road	B3
Coulthards Lane	C3	South Shore Road	C3
Crawhall Road	C2	Stanhope Street	A2
Dean Street	B2	Starbeck Avenue	C1
Diana Street	A2	Stodart Street	C1
Elswick East Terrace	A3	Stowell Street	A2
Eskdale Terrace	C1	Strawberry Place	A2
Essex Close	A3	Summerhill Grove	A2
Falconar Street	C1	Swing Bridge	B3
Forth Banks	B3	The Close	B3
Forth Street	A3	Tyne Bridge	C3
Gallowgate	A2	Union Street	C2
Gateshead Highway	C3	Warwick Street	C1
George Street	A3	Wellington Street	A2
Gibson Street	C2	West Street	C3
Grainger Street	B2	Westgate Road	A2
Grantham Road	C1	Westmorland Road	A3
Grey Street	B2	Windsor Terrace	B1
Hanover Street	B3	York Street	A2
Hawks Road	C3		
Helmsley Road	C1		
High Street	C3		
Hillgate	C3		
Howard Street	C2		
Hunters Road	A1		
Ivy Close	A3		
Jesmond Road	C1		
Jesmond Road West	B1		
John Dobson Street	B2		
Kelvin Grove	C1		
Kyle Close	A3		
Lambton Street	C3		
Mansfield Street	A2		
Maple Street	A3		
Maple Terrace	A3		
Market Street	B2		
Melbourne Street	C2		
Mill Road	C3		
Neville Street	A3		
New Bridge Street	C2		
Newgate Street	B2		
Northumberland Road	B2		
Northumberland Street	B1		
Oakwellgate	C3		
Orchard Street	B3		
Oxnam Crescent	A1		
Park Terrace	B1		
Percy Street	B2		
Pilgrim Street	B2		
Pipewellgate	B3		

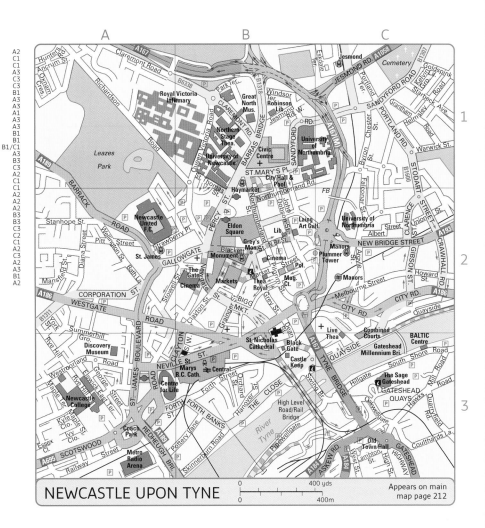

NEWCASTLE UPON TYNE

0   400 yds
0   400m

Appears on main map page 212

Tourist Information Centre: The Forum, Millennium Plain
Tel: 01603 213999

Albion Way	C3	Queens Road	B3
All Saints Green	B3	Rampant Horse Street	B3
Ashby Street	B3	Recorder Road	C2
Bakers Road	A1	Red Lion Street	B2
Bank Plain	B2	Riverside	C3
Barker Street	A1	Riverside Road	C2
Barn Road	A2	Rosary Road	C2
Barrack Street	B1	Rose Lane	B2
Bedford Street	B2	Rouen Road	B3
Ber Street	B3	Rupert Street	A3
Bethel Street	A2	Russell Street	A1
Bishopbridge Road	C2	St. Andrew's Street	B2
Bishopgate	C2	St. Augustine's Street	A1
Botolph Street	B1	St. Benedict's Street	A2
Brazen Gate	B3	St. Crispin's Road	A1
Britannia Road	C1	St. Faiths Lane	B2
Brunswick Road	A3	St. George's Street	B1
Bullclose Road	B1	St. Giles Street	A2
Canary Way	C3	St. James Close	C1
Carrow Hill	C3	St. Leonards Road	C2
Carrow Road	C3	St. Martin's Road	A1
Castle Meadow	B2	St. Stephen's Road	A3
Chapel Field Road	A2	St. Stephen's Street	B3
Chapelfield North	A2	Silver Road	B1
City Road	B3	Silver Street	B1
Clarence Road	C3	Southwell Road	B3
Colegate	B1	Surrey Street	B3
Coslany Street	A2	Sussex Street	A1
Cowgate	B1	Theatre Street	A2
Dereham Road	A2	Thorn Lane	B3
Duke Street	B1	Thorpe Road	C2
Earlham Road	A2	Tombland	B2
Edward Street	B1	Trinity Street	A3
Elm Hill	B2	Trory Street	A2
Fishergate	B1	Union Street	A3
Gas Hill	C1	Unthank Road	A3
Grapes Hill	A2	Vauxhall Street	A3
Grove Avenue	A3	Victoria Street	A3
Grove Road	A3	Wensum Street	B1
Grove Walk	A3	Wessex Street	A3
Gurney Road	C1	Westwick Street	A1
Hall Road	B3	Wherry Road	C3
Hardy Road	C3	Whitefriars	B1
Heathgate	C1	Wodehouse Street	B1
Heigham Street	A1	York Street	A3
Horns Lane	B3		
Ipswich Road	A3		
Ketts Hill	C1		
King Street	B3		
Koblenz Avenue	C3		
Lothian Street	A1		
Lower Clarence Road	C2		
Magdalen Street	B1		
Magpie Road	B1		
Market Avenue	B2		
Marlborough Road	B1		
Mountergate	B2		
Mousehold Street	C1		
Newmarket Road	A3		
Newmarket Street	A3		
Oak Street	A1		
Orchard Street	A1		
Palace Street	B2		
Pitt Street	B1		
Pottergate	A2		
Prince of Wales Road	B2		

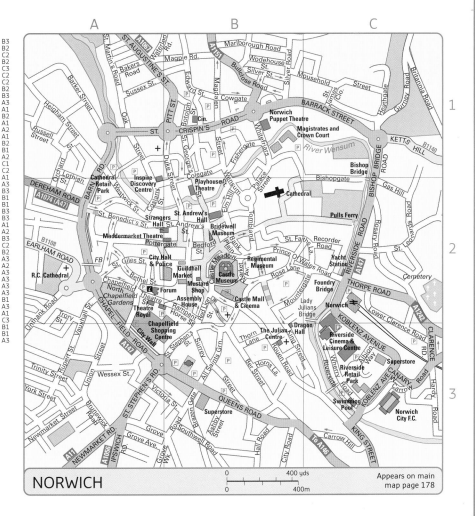

NORWICH

0   400 yds
0   400m

Appears on main map page 178

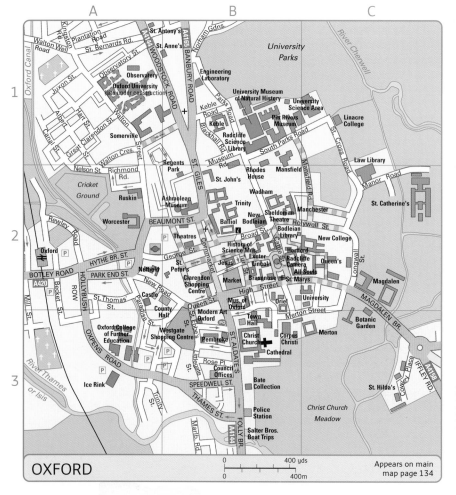

NOTTINGHAM

0 — 400 yds
0 — 400m

Appears on main map page 173

Street	Grid	Street	Grid
Abbotsford Drive	B1	Maid Marian Way	A2
Albert Street	B2	Mansfield Road	B1
Angel Row	A2	Manvers Street	C2
Barker Gate	C2	Market Street	B2
Bath Street	C1	Middle Pavement	B2
Beacon Hill Rise	C1	Milton Street	B1
Bellar Gate	C2	Mount Street	A2
Belward Street	C2	North Church Street	B1
Bridlesmith Gate	B2	North Sherwood Street	B1
Broad Street	B2	Park Row	A2
Brook Street	C1	Park Terrace	A2
Burton Street	A1	Park Valley	A2
Canal Street	B3	Peel Street	A1
Carlton Street	B2	Pelham Street	B2
Carrington Street	B3	Pennyfoot Street	C2
Castle Boulevard	A3	Peveril Drive	A3
Castle Gate	B2	Pilcher Gate	B2
Castle Meadow Road	A3	Plantagenet Street	C1
Castle Road	A3	Popham Street	B3
Chapel Bar	A2	Poplar Street	C2
Chaucer Street	A1	Queens Road	B3
Cheapside	B2	Queen Street	B2
City Link	C3	Regent Street	A2
Clarendon Street	A1	Robin Hood Street	C1
Cliff Road	B3	Roden Street	C1
Clumber Street	B2	St. Ann's Well Road	C1
College Street	A2	St. James Street	A2
Collin Street	B3	St. Mary's Gate	B2
Cranbrook Street	C2	St. Peter's Gate	B2
Cromwell Street	A1	Shakespeare Street	A1
Curzon Street	B1	Shelton Street	B1
Derby Road	A2	Sneinton Road	C2
Dryden Street	A1	South Parade	B2
Fisher Gate	C2	South Sherwood Street	B1
Fishpond Drive	A3	Southwell Road	C2
Fletcher Gate	B2	Station Street	B3
Forman Street	B2	Stoney Street	C2
Friar Lane	A2	Talbot Street	A1
Gedling Street	C2	The Great Northern Close	C3
George Street	B2	The Rope Walk	A2
Gill Street	A1	Union Road	B1
Glasshouse Street	B1	Upper Parliament Street	A2
Goldsmith Street	A1	Victoria Street	B2
Goose Gate	C2	Warser Gate	B2
Hamilton Drive	A3	Waverley Street	A1
Hampden Street	A1	Wheeler Gate	B2
Handel Street	C2	Wilford Street	A3
Heathcote Street	B2	Wollaton Street	A2
High Pavement	B2	Woolpack Lane	C2
Hockley	C2		
Hollowstone	C2		
Hope Drive	A3		
Huntingdon Drive	A2		
Huntingdon Street	B1		
Instow Rise	C1		
Kent Street	B1		
King Edward Street	B2		
King Street	B2		
Lamartine Street	C1		
Lenton Road	A3		
Lincoln Street	B2		
Lister Gate	B3		
London Road	C3		
Long Row	B2		
Low Pavement	B2		
Lower Parliament Street	B2		

OXFORD

0 — 400 yds
0 — 400m

Appears on main map page 134

Street	Grid
Albert Street	A1
Banbury Road	B1
Beaumont Street	A2
Becket Street	A2
Blackhall Road	B1
Botley Road	A2
Broad Street	B2
Canal Street	A1
Cattle Street	B2
Cornmarket	B2
Cowley Place	C3
Folly Bridge	B3
George Street	A2
Great Clarendon Street	A1
Hart Street	A1
High Street	B2
Hollybush Row	A2
Holywell Street	B2
Hythe Bridge Street	A2
Iffley Road	C3
Juxon Street	A1
Keble Road	B1
Kingston Road	A1
Littlegate Street	B3
Longwall Street	C2
Magdalen Bridge	C2
Manor Road	C2
Mansfield Road	C1
Marlborough Road	B3
Merton Street	B3
Mill Street	A2
Museum Road	B1
Nelson Street	A2
New Road	A2
Norham Gardens	B1
Observatory Street	A1
Oxpens Road	A3
Paradise Street	A2
Park End Street	A2
Parks Road	B1
Plantation Road	A1
Queen Street	B2
Rewley Road	A2
Richmond Road	A2
Rose Place	B3
St. Aldate's	B3
St. Bernards Road	A1
St. Cross Road	C1
St. Ebbe's Street	B3
St. Giles	B1
St. Thomas' Street	A2
South Parks Road	B1
Speedwell Street	B3
Thames Street	B3
Trinity Street	A3
Turl Street	B2
Walton Crescent	A1
Walton Street	A1
Walton Well Road	A1
Woodstock Road	A1

Tourist Information Centre: Lower City Mills, West Mill Street
Tel: 01738 450600

Abbot Crescent	A3	Shore Road	C3
Abbot Street	A3	South Methven Street	B2
Albany Terrace	A1	South Street	B2
Atholl Street	B1	Strathmore Street	C1
Balhousie Street	B1	Stuart Avenue	A3
Barossa Place	B1	Tay Street	C2
Barossa Street	B1	Victoria Street	B2
Barrack Street	B1	Watergate	C2
Bowerswell Road	C2	Whitefriars Crescent	A2
Caledonian Road	B2	Whitefriars Street	A2
Canal Street	B2	William Street	B2
Cavendish Avenue	A3	Wilson Street	A3
Charlotte Street	B1	Young Street	A3
Clyde Place	A3	York Place	A2
Darnhall Drive	A3		
Dundee Road	C2		
Dunkeld Road	A1		
Edinburgh Road	B3		
Feus Road	A1		
Friar Street	A3		
George Street	C2		
Glasgow Road	A2		
Glover Street	A2		
Gowrie Street	C1		
Gray Street	A2		
Graybank Road	A2		
Hay Street	B1		
High Street	B2		
Isla Road	C1		
Jeanfield Road	A2		
King's Place	B3		
King James Place	B3		
King Street	B2		
Kinnoull Street	B1		
Kinnoull Terrace	C2		
Knowelea Place	A3		
Leonard Street	B2		
Lochie Brae	C1		
Long Causeway	A1		
Main Street	C1		
Manse Road	C2		
Marshall Place	B3		
Melville Street	B1		
Mill Street	B2		
Milne Street	B2		
Murray Crescent	A3		
Needless Road	A3		
New Row	B2		
North Methven Street	B1		
Park Place	A3		
Perth Bridge	C1		
Pickletullum Road	A2		
Pitcullen Terrace	C1		
Pitheavlis Crescent	A3		
Princes Street	C3		
Priory Place	B3		
Queen Street	A3		
Queens Bridge	C2		
Raeburn Park	A3		
Riggs Road	A2		
Rose Crescent	A2		
Rose Terrace	B1		
St. Catherines Road	A1		
St. John Street	C2		
St. Leonard's Bank	B3		
Scott Street	B2		

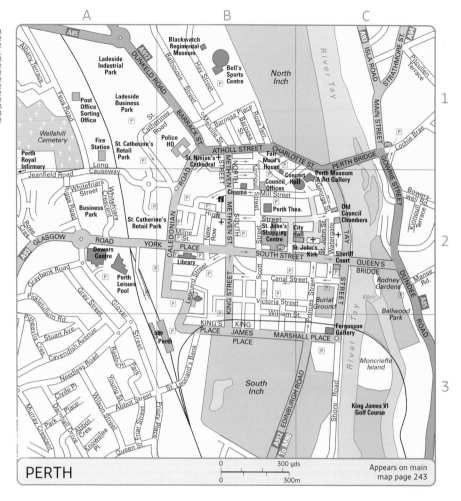

PERTH

Tourist Information Centre: Plymouth Mayflower Centre,
3-5 The Barbican Tel: 01752 306330

Alexandra Road	C1	North Street	B2
Alma Road	A1	Notte Street	B3
Armada Street	B2	Oxford Street	A2
Armada Way	B2	Pentillie Road	B1
Ashford Road	C1	Ponsonby Road	A1
Barbican Approach	C3	Princess Street	B3
Beaumont Road	C2	Queen's Road	C1
Beechwood Avenue	B1	Royal Parade	B2
Belgrave Road	C1	Salisbury Road	C2
Bretonside	B2	Saltash Road	A1
Buckwell Street	B3	Seaton Avenue	B1
Camden Street	B2	Seymour Avenue	C2
Cattledown Road	C3	Southside Street	B3
Cecil Street	A2	Stoke Road	A2
Central Park Avenue	A1	Stuart Road	A1
Charles Street	B2	Sutton Road	C2
Citadel Road	A3	Sydney Street	A2
Clarence Place	A2	Teats Hill Road	C3
Cliff Road	A3	The Crescent	A3
Clifton Place	B1	Tothill Avenue	C2
Clovelly Road	C3	Tothill Road	C2
Cobourg Street	B2	Union Street	A2
Coleridge Road	C1	Vauxhall Street	B3
Connaught Avenue	C1	West Hoe Road	A3
Cornwall Street	B2	Western Approach	A2
Dale Road	B1	Whittington Street	A1
De-La-Hay Avenue	A1	Wilton Street	A2
Desborough Road	C2	Wyndham Street	A2
Drake Circus	B2		
East Street	A3		
Ebrington Street	B2		
Elliot Street	A3		
Embankment Road	C2		
Exeter Street	B2		
Ford Park Road	B1		
Furzehill Road	C1		
Gdynia Way	C3		
Glen Park Avenue	B1		
Grand Parade	A3		
Greenbank Avenue	C2		
Greenbank Road	C1		
Grenville Road	C2		
Harwell Street	A2		
Hill Park Crescent	B1		
Hoe Road	B3		
Houndiscombe Road	B1		
James Street	B2		
King Street	A2		
Knighton Road	C2		
Lipson Hill	C1		
Lipson Road	C2		
Lisson Grove	C1		
Lockyer Street	B3		
Looe Street	B2		
Madeira Road	B3		
Manor Road	A2		
Martin Street	A3		
Mayflower Street	B2		
Millbay Road	A3		
Mount Gould Road	C1		
Mutley Plain	B1		
New George Street	A2		
North Cross	B2		
North Hill	B2		
North Road East	B2		
North Road West	A2		

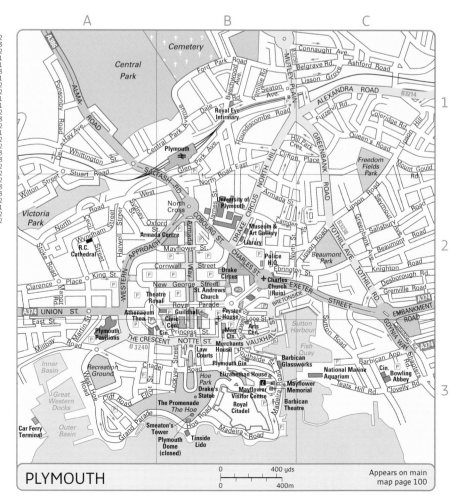

PLYMOUTH

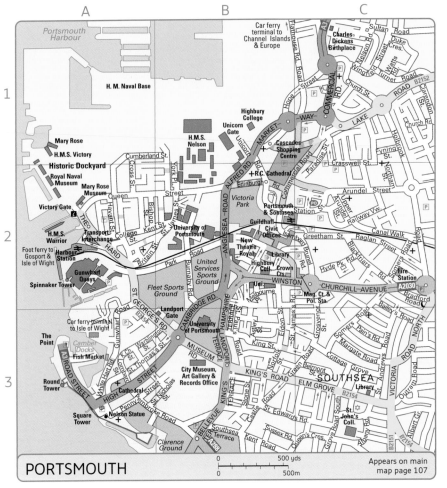

PORTSMOUTH

Appears on main map page 107

Tourist Information Centre: The Hard
Tel: 023 9282 6722

Albany Road	C3	Penny Street	A3
Albert Grove	C3	Queen's Crescent	C3
Alfred Road	B2	Queen Street	A2
Anglesea Road	B2	Raglan Street	C2
Arundel Street	C2	Railway View	C2
Astley Street	B3	St. Andrews Road	C3
Bailey's Road	C2	St. Edward's Road	B3
Bellevue Terrace	B3	St. George's Road	A2
Belmont Street	C3	St. James Road	B3
Bishop Street	A1	St. James Street	B2
Blackfriars Road	C2	St. Paul's Road	B3
Bradford Road	C2	St. Thomas's Street	A2
Britain Street	A2	Somers Road	C2
Broad Street	A3	Southsea Terrace	B3
Burnaby Road	B2	Station Street	C2
Cambridge Road	B3	Stone Street	B3
Canal Walk	C2	Sultan Road	C1
Castle Road	B3	Sussex Street	B3
Church Road	C1	The Hard	A2
Church Street	C1	Turner Road	C1
Clarendon Street	C1	Unicorn Road	B1
College Street	A2	Upper Arundel Street	C2
Commercial Road	B2	Victoria Road North	C3
Cottage Grove	C3	Warblington Street	A3
Crasswell Street	C1	Watts Road	C1
Cross Street	A1	White Hart Road	A3
Cumberland Street	A1	Wingfield Street	C1
Duke Crescent	C1	Winston Churchill Avenue	B2
Edinburgh Road	B2	York Place	B2
Eldon Street	B3		
Elm Grove	C3		
Flathouse Road	C1		
Fyning Street	C1		
Green Road	B3		
Greetham Street	C2		
Grosvenor Street	C3		
Grove Road South	C3		
Gunwharf Road	A3		
Hampshire Terrace	B3		
Havant Street	A2		
High Street	A3		
Holbrook Road	C1		
Hope Street	B1		
Hyde Park Road	C2		
Isambard Brunel Road	B2		
Kent Road	B3		
Kent Street	A1		
King Charles Street	A3		
King's Road	B3		
King's Terrace	B3		
King Street	B3		
Lake Road	C1		
Landport Terrace	B3		
Lombard Street	A3		
Margate Road	C3		
Market Way	B1		
Melbourne Place	B2		
Museum Road	B3		
Nelson Road	C1		
Norfolk Street	B3		
Northam Street	C2		
Outram Road	C3		
Pain's Road	C3		
Paradise Street	C2		
Park Road	B2		
Pembroke Road	A3		

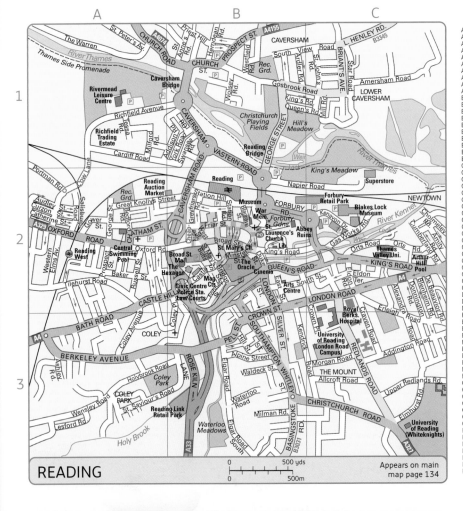

READING

Appears on main map page 134

Addington Road	C3	Lesford Road	A3
Addison Road	A1	London Road	C2
Alexandra Road	C2	London Street	B2
Allcroft Road	C3	Lower Henley Road	C1
Alpine Street	B3	Mill Road	B3
Amersham Road	C1	Milford Road	A1
Amity Road	A2	Milman Road	B3
Ardler Road	B1	Minster Street	B2
Ashley Road	A3	Morgan Road	C3
Audley Street	A2	Napier Road	B2
Baker Street	A2	Orts Road	C2
Basingstoke Road	B3	Oxford Road	A2
Bath Road	A3	Pell Street	B3
Bedford Road	A2	Portman Road	A1
Berkeley Avenue	A3	Priest Hill	B1
Blagrave Street	B2	Prospect Street *Caversham*	B1
Blenheim Road	C2	Prospect Street *Reading*	A2
Briant's Avenue	C1	Queen's Road *Caversham*	B1
Bridge Street	B2	Queen's Road *Reading*	B2
Broad Street	B2	Richfield Avenue	A1
Cardiff Road	A1	Rose Kiln Lane	B3
Castle Hill	A2	Russell Street	A2
Castle Street	B2	St. Anne's Road	B1
Catherine Street	A2	St. John's Road	C1
Caversham Road	B2	St. Mary's Butts	B2
Chatham Street	A2	St. Peters Avenue	B2
Cheapside	B2	St. Saviours Road	A3
Cholmeley Road	C2	Silver Street	B3
Christchurch Road	C3	South Street	B2
Church Road	A1	Southampton Street	B3
Church Street	B1	South View Road	B1
Coley Avenue	A3	Star Road	C1
Coley Place	B2	Station Hill	B2
Cow Lane	A2	Station Road	B2
Craven Road	C3	Swansea Road	B1
Crown Place	C2	Tessa Road	A1
Crown Street	B3	The Warren	A1
Cumberland Road	C2	Tilehurst Road	A3
Curzon Street	A2	Upper Redlands Road	C3
De Beauvoir Road	C2	Vastern Road	B1
Donnington Road	C2	Waldek Street	B3
Duke Street	B2	Waterloo Road	B3
East Street	B2	Wensley Road	A3
Eldon Road	C2	Western Elms Avenue	A2
Eldon Terrace	C2	Westfield Road	B1
Elgar Road	B3	West Street	B2
Elgar Road South	B3	Whitley Street	B3
Elmhurst Road	C3	Wolsey Road	B1
Erleigh Road	C2	York Road	B1
Fobney Street	B2		
Forbury Road	B2		
Friar Street	B2		
Gas Work Road	C2		
George Street *Caversham*	B1		
George Street *Reading*	A2		
Gosbrook Road	B1		
Gower Street	A2		
Great Knollys Street	A2		
Greyfriars Road	B2		
Hemdean Road	B1		
Hill Street	B3		
Hollybrook Road	A3		
Kenavon Drive	C2		
Kendrick Road	B3		
King's Road *Caversham*	B1		
King's Road *Reading*	B2		

Salisbury

Tourist Information Centre: Fish Row
Tel: 01722 334956

Street	Grid
Albany Road	B1
Ashley Road	A1
Avon Terrace	A1
Barnard Street	C2
Bedwin Street	B1
Belle Vue Road	B1
Bishops Walk	B3
Blackfriars Way	C3
Blue Boar Row	B2
Bourne Avenue	C1
Bourne Hill	C1
Bridge Street	B2
Brown Street	B2
Butcher Row	B2
Carmelite Way	B3
Castle Street	B1
Catherine Street	B2
Chipper Lane	B2
Churchfields Road	A2
Churchill Way East	C2
Churchill Way North	B1
Churchill Way South	C3
Churchill Way West	A1
Clifton Road	A1
College Street	C1
Crane Bridge Road	A2
Crane Street	B2
De Vaux Place	B3
Devizes Road	A1
Elm Grove Road	C2
Endless Street	B1
Estcourt Road	C1
Exeter Street	B3
Fairview Road	C1
Fisherton Street	A2
Fowlers Hill	C2
Fowlers Road	C2
Friary Lane	C3
Gas Lane	A1
Gigant Street	C2
Greencroft Street	C1
Hamilton Road	B1
High Street	B2
Ivy Street	B2
Kelsey Road	C1
Laverstock Road	C2
Manor Road	C1
Marsh Lane	A1
Meadow Road	A1
Milford Hill	C2
Milford Street	B2
Mill Road	A2
Millstream Approach	B1
Minster Street	B2
New Canal	B2
New Street	B2
North Walk	B3
Park Street	C1
Pennyfarthing Street	B2
Queens Road	B1
Rampart Road	C2
Rollestone Street	B1
St. Ann Street	C3
St. John's Street	B2
St. Marks Road	C1
St. Paul's Road	A1

Street	Grid
Salt Lane	B2
Scots Lane	B2
Silver Street	B2
Southampton Road	C3
Swaynes Close	B1
Tollgate Road	C2
Trinity Street	C2
Wain-a-long Road	C1
West Walk	B3
Wilton Road	A1
Winchester Street	B2
Windsor Road	A2
Wyndham Road	B1
York Road	A1

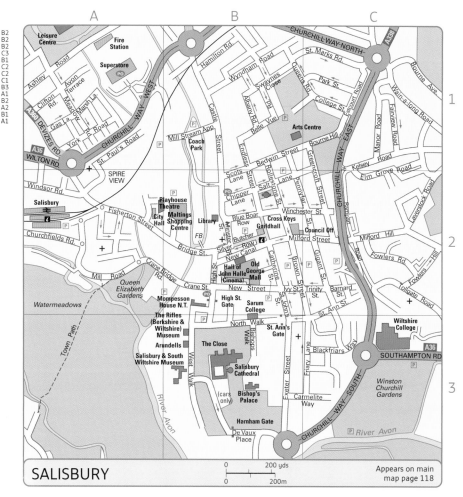

SALISBURY

0   200 yds
0   200m

Appears on main map page 118

Scarborough

Tourist Information Centre: Brunswick Shopping Centre,
Unit 15a, Westborough Tel: 01723 383636

Street	Grid
Aberdeen Walk	B2
Albion Road	B3
Ashville Avenue	A2
Avenue Road	A3
Belmont Road	B3
Candler Street	A2
Castle Road	B2
Chatsworth Gardens	A1
Columbus Ravine	A2
Commercial Street	A3
Cross Street	B2
Dean Road	A2
Eastborough	B2
Esplanade	B3
Falconers Rd	B2
Falsgrave Road	A3
Foreshore Road	B2
Franklin Street	A2
Friargate	B2
Friarsway	B2
Garfield Road	A2
Gladstone Road	A2
Gladstone Street	A2
Gordon Street	A2
Grosvenor Road	B3
Highfield	A3
Hoxton Road	A2
Longwestgate	C2
Manor Road	A2
Marine Drive	C1
Mayville Avenue	A2
Moorland Road	A1
New Queen Street	B1
Newborough	B2
North Marine Road	B1
North Street	B2
Northstead Manor Drive	A1
Northway	A2
Norwood Street	A2
Oak Road	A3
Peasholm Crescent	A1
Peasholm Drive	A1
Peasholm Road	A1
Prince Of Wales Terrace	B3
Princess Street	C2
Prospect Road	A2
Queen Street	B2
Queen's Parade	B1
Raleigh Street	A2
Ramshill Road	B3
Roscoe Street	A3
Rothbury Street	A2
Royal Albert Drive	B1
Royal Avenue	B3
Sandside	C2
Seamer Road	A3
St. James Road	A3
St. John's Avenue	A3
St. John's Road	A3
St. Thomas Street	B2
Tollgate	B1
Trafalgar Road	A1
Trafalgar Square	B1
Trafalgar Street West	A2
Trinity Road	A3
Valley Bridge Parade	B3

Street	Grid
Valley Bridge Road	B2
Valley Road	A3
Vernon Road	B2
Victoria Park Mount	A1
Victoria Road	A3
Victoria Street	B2
West Street	B3
Westborough	A3
Westbourne Grove	B3
Westover Road	A3
Westwood	B3
Westwood Road	A3
Weydale Avenue	A1
Wykeham Street	A3

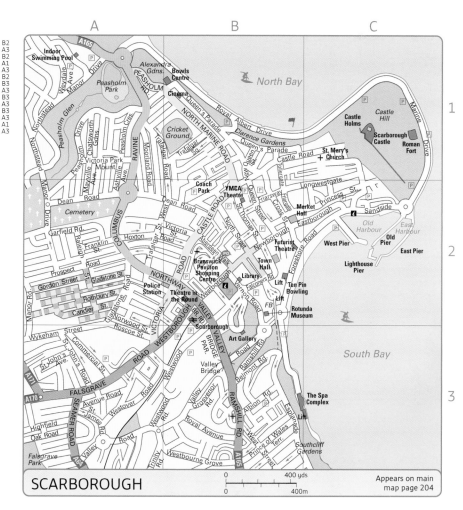

SCARBOROUGH

0   400 yds
0   400m

Appears on main map page 204

SHEFFIELD

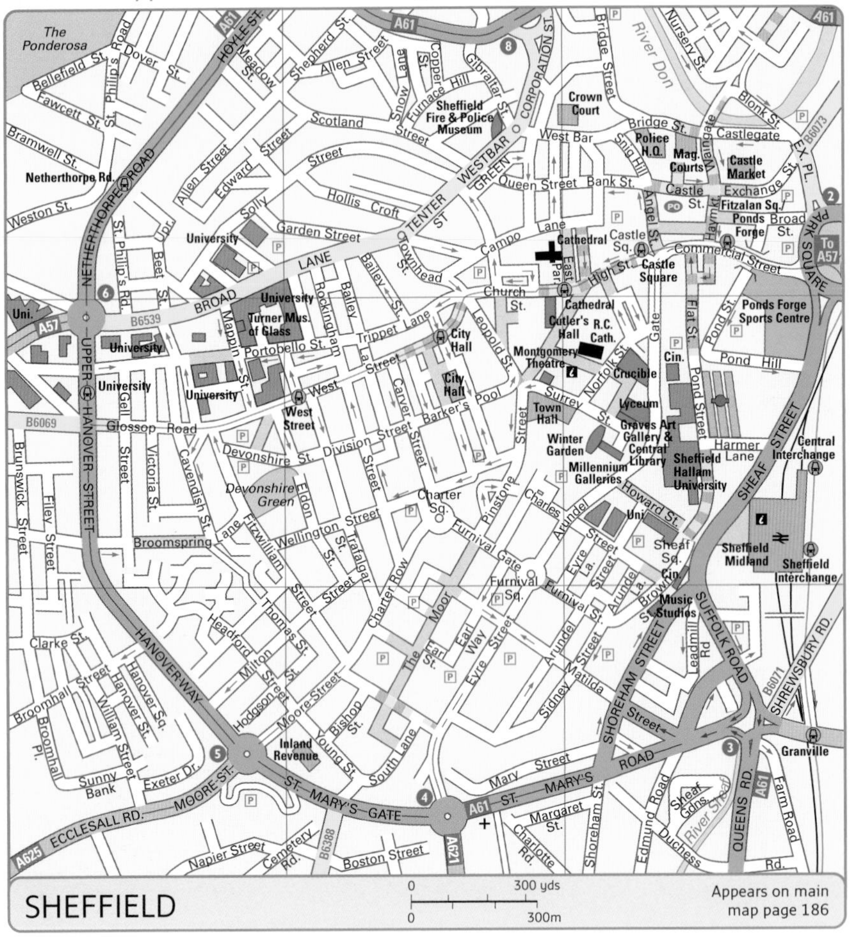

Tourist Information Centre: 14 Norfolk Row
Tel: 0114 221 1900

Appears on main map page 186

SOUTHAMPTON

Tourist Information Centre: 9 Civic Centre Road
Tel: 023 8083 3333

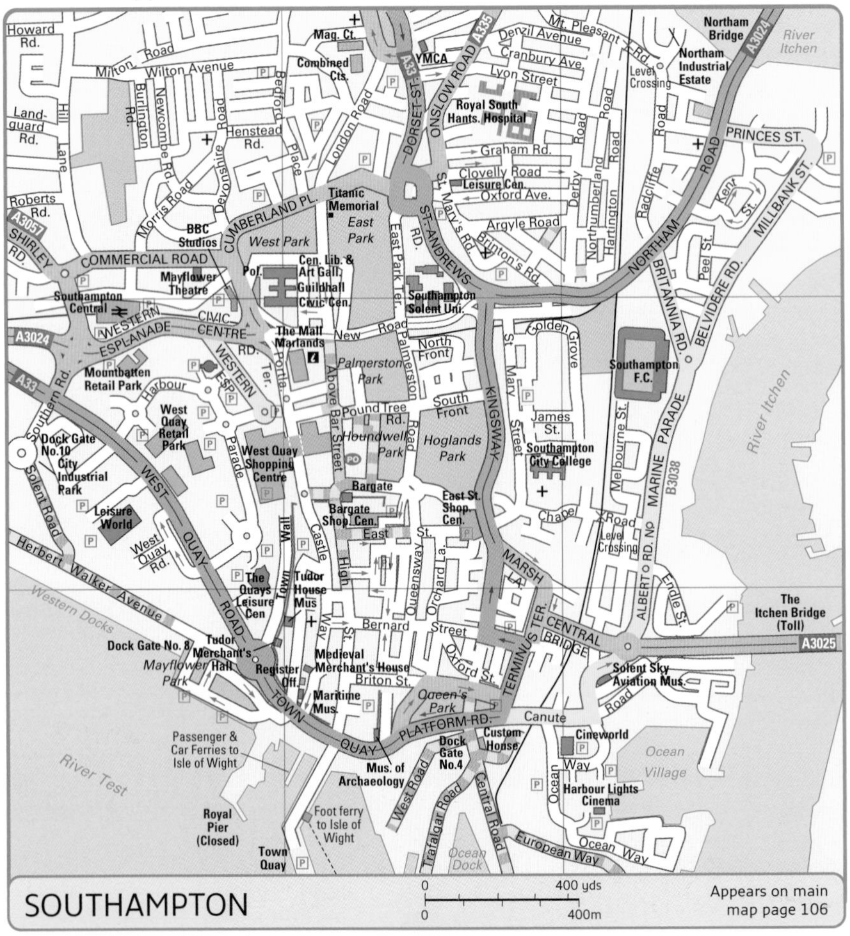

Appears on main map page 106

Tourist Information Centre: Victoria Hall, Bagnall Street, Hanley Tel: 01782 236000

Albion Street	B1
Ashford Street	B2
Avenue Road	B2
Aynsley Road	B2
Bedford Road	B2
Bedford Street	A2
Belmont Road	A1
Beresford Street	B2
Berry Hill Road	C2
Boon Avenue	A3
Botteslow Street	C1
Boughey Road	B3
Broad Street	B1
Bucknall New Road	C1
Bucknall Old Road	C1
Cauldon Road	B2
Cemetery Road	A2
Church Street	B3
Clough Street	A1
College Road	B2
Commercial Road	C1
Copeland Street	B3
Dewsbury Road	C3
Eagle Street	C1
Eastwood Road	C1
Elenora Street	B3
Etruria Road	A1
Etruria Vale Road	A1
Etruscan Street	A2
Festival Way	A1
Forge Lane	A1
Garner Street	A2
Glebe Street	B3
Greatbatch Avenue	A3
Hanley	B1
Hartshill Road	A3
Hill Street	A3
Honeywall	A3
Howard Place	B2
Ivy House Road	C1
Leek Road	B3
Lichfield Street	C1
Liverpool Road	B3
Lordship Lane	B3
Lytton Street	B3
Manor Street	C3
Marsh Street	B1
Newlands Street	B2
North Street	A2
Old Hall Street	B1
Oxford Street	A3
Parliament Row	B1
Potteries Way	B1
Potters Way	C1
Prince's Road	A3
Quarry Avenue	A3
Quarry Road	A3
Queen's Road	A3
Queensway	A2
Rectory Road	B2
Regent Road	B2
Richmond Street	A3
Ridgway Road	B2
Seaford Street	B2
Shelton New Road	A2
Shelton Old Road	A3
Snow Hill	B2
Stafford Street	B1
Station Road	B3
Stoke	B3
Stoke Road	B3
Stone Street	A3
Stuart Road	C2
Sun Street	B1
The Parkway	B2
Trentmill Road	C2
Victoria Road	C2
Warner Street	B1
Waterloo Road	C1
Wellesley Street	B2
Wellington Road	C1
West Avenue	A3
Westland Street	A3
Yoxall Avenue	A3

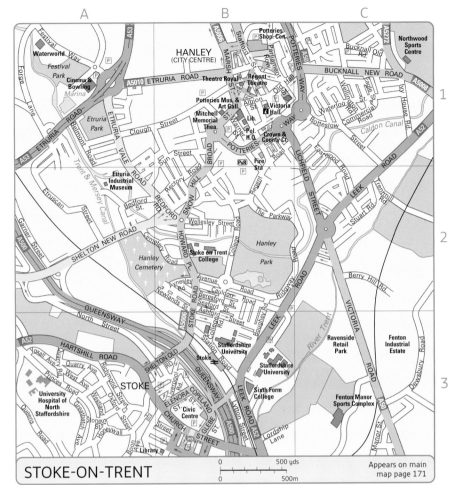

STOKE-ON-TRENT

Appears on main map page 171

Tourist Information Centre: Bridgefoot Tel: 0870 160 7930

Albany Road	A2
Alcester Road	A1
Arden Street	A1
Avonside	B3
Banbury Road	C2
Bancroft Place	C2
Birmingham Road	A1
Brewery Street	B1
Bridgefoot	C2
Bridge Street	B2
Bridgeway	C2
Bridgetown Road	C3
Broad Street	A3
Broad Walk	A3
Bull Street	A3
Chapel Lane	B2
Chapel Street	B2
Cherry Orchard	A3
Chestnut Walk	A2
Church Street	B2
Clopton Bridge	C2
Clopton Road	B1
College Lane	B3
College Street	B3
Ely Street	B2
Evesham Place	A3
Evesham Road	A3
Great William Street	B1
Greenhill Street	A2
Grove Road	A2
Guild Street	B1
Henley Street	B1
High Street	B2
Holtom Street	A3
John Street	B1
Kendall Avenue	B1
Maidenhead Road	B1
Mansell Street	A1
Meer Street	B2
Mill Lane	B3
Mulberry Street	B1
Narrow Lane	A3
New Street	B3
Old Town	A3
Old Town Square	A3
Old Tramway Walk	C3
Orchard Way	A3
Payton Street	B1
Red Lion Court	B2
Rother Street	A2
Ryland Street	B3
St. Andrews Crescent	A2
St. Gregory's Road	B1
Sanctus Drive	A3
Sanctus Road	A3
Sanctus Street	A3
Sandfield Road	A3
Scholar's Lane	A2
Seven Meadow Road	A3
Shakespeare Street	B1
Sheep Street	B2
Shipston Road	C3
Shottery Road	A2
Shrieve's Walk	B2
Southern Lane	B3
Station Road	A1
Swan's Nest Lane	C2
The Waterways	A1
Tiddington Road	C2
Trinity Street	B3
Tyler Street	B1
Union Street	B2
Warwick Court	B1
Warwick Crescent	C1
Warwick Road	C1
Waterside	B2
Welcombe Road	C1
Westbourne Grove	A2
Western Road	A1
West Street	A3
Wharf Road	A1
Windsor Street	B2
Wood Street	B2

STRATFORD-UPON-AVON

Appears on main map page 147

Sunderland Swansea

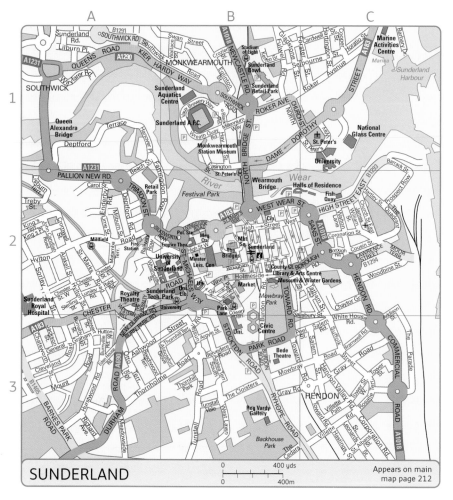

SUNDERLAND

Appears on main map page 212

0   400 yds
0   400m

Tourist Information Centre: 50 Fawcett Street
Tel: 0191 553 2000

Abbotsford Grove	B3	Lime Street	A2
Addison Street	C3	Livingstone Road	B2
Aiskell Street	A3	Lumley Road	A2
Argyle Street	B3	Matamba Terrace	A2
Ashwood Street	A3	Milburn Street	A2
Azalea Terace South	B3	Millennium Way	B1
Barnes Park Road	A3	Moor Terrace	C2
Barrack Street	C1	Mount Road	A3
Beach Street	A2	Mowbray Road	B3
Beechwood Terrace	A3	New Durham Road	A3
Belvedere Road	B3	Newcastle Road	B1
Black Road	B1	North Bridge Street	B1
Borough Road	B2/C2	Otto Terrace	A3
Bramwell Road	C3	Pallion New Road	A2
Brougham Street	B2	Park Lane	B2
Burdon Road	B3	Park Road	B3
Burn Park Road	A3	Peel Street	B3
Burnaby Street	A3	Prospect Row	C2
Burnville Road	A3	Queens Road	A1
Carol Street	A2	Raby Road	A2
Chatsworth Street	A3	Railway Row	A2
Chaytor Grove	C2	Roker Avenue	B1/C1
Chester Road	A2	Rosalie Terrace	C3
Chester Street	A2	Ryhope Road	B3
Church Street East	C2	St. Albans Street	C3
Church Street North	B1	St. Leonards Street	C3
Cleveland Road	A3	St. Marks Road	A2
Commercial Road	C3	St. Mary's Way	B2
Cooper Street	C1	St. Michaels Way	B2
Coronation Street	C2	St. Peter's Way	C1
Corporation Road	C3	Salem Road	C3
Cousin Street	C2	Salem Street	C3
Cromwell Street	A2	Salisbury Street	B2
Crozier Street	B1	Sans Street	C2
Dame Dorothy Street	B1	Selbourne Street	B1
Deptford Road	A2	Silksworth Row	A2
Deptford Terrace	A1	Sorley Street	A2
Durham Road	A3	Southwick Road	A1
Easington Street	B1	Southwick Road	B1
Eden House Road	A3	Stewart Street	A3
Eglinton Street	B1	Stockton Road	B3
Enderby Road	A2	Suffolk Street	C3
Farringdon Row	A1	Sunderland Road	A1
Forster Street	C1	Swan Street	B1
Fox Street	A3	Tatham Street	C2
Fulwell Road	B1	The Cedars	B3
General Graham Street	A3	The Cloisters	B3
Gladstone Street	B1	The Parade	C3
Gray Road	B3/C3	The Quadrant	C2
Hanover Place	A1	The Royalty	A2
Hartington Street	C1	Thornhill Park	B3
Hartley Street	C2	Thornhill Terrace	B3
Hastings Street	C3	Thornholme Road	A3
Hay Street	B1	Toward Road	B2/C3
Hendon Road	C2	Tower Street	C3
Hendon Valley Road	C3	Tower Street West	C3
High Street East	C2	Trimdon Street	A2
High Street West	B2	Tunstall Road	B3
Holmeside	B2	Tunstall Vale	B3
Horatio Street	C1	Vaux Brewery Way	B1
Hurstwood Road	A3	Villette Road	C3
Hutton Street	A3	Vine Place	B2
Hylton Road	A2	Wallace Street	B2
Hylton Road	A2	West Lawn	B3
Jackson Street	A3	West Wear Street	B2
James William Street	C2	Western Hill	A2
Kenton Grove	B1	Wharncliffe Street	A2
Kier Hardy Way	A1	White House Road	C3
King's Place	A2	Woodbine Street	C2
Lawrence Street	C2	Wreath Quay Road	B1

SWANSEA

Appears on main map page 128

0   500 yds
0   500m

Tourist Information Centre: Plymouth Street
Tel: 01792 468321

Aberdyberthi Street	C1	Mount Pleasant	B2
Albert Row	B3	Mumbles Road	A3
Alexandra Road	B2	Neath Road	C1
Argyle Street	A3	Nelson Street	B3
Baptist Well Place	B1	New Cut Road	C2
Baptist Well Street	B1	New Orchard Street	B1
Beach Street	A3	Nicander Parade	A2
Belgrave Lane	A3	Norfolk Street	A2
Belle Vue Way	B2	North Hill Road	B1
Berw Road	A1	Orchard Street	B2
Berwick Terrace	B1	Oxford Street	A3
Bond Street	A3	Oystermouth Road	A3
Brooklands Terrace	A2	Page Street	B2
Brunswick Street	A3	Pant-y-Celyn Road	A2
Brynmor Crescent	A3	Park Terrace	B1
Brynmor Road	A3	Pedrog Terrace	A1
Burrows Place	C3	Penlan Crescent	A2
Cambrian Place	C3	Pentre Guinea Road	C1
Carig Crescent	A1	Pen-y-Craig Road	A1
Carlton Terrace	B2	Picton Terrace	B2
Carmarthen Road	B1	Powys Avenue	A1
Castle Street	B2	Princess Way	B2
Clarence Terrace	B3	Quay Parade	C2
Colbourne Terrace	B1	Rhondda Street	A2
Constitution Hill	A2	Rose Hill	A2
Creidiol Road	A1	St. Elmo Avenue	C1
Cromwell Street	A2	St. Helen's Avenue	A3
Cwm Road	C1	St. Helen's Road	A3
De La Beche Street	B2	St. Mary Street	B2
Delhi Street	C2	Singleton Street	B3
Dillwyn Street	B3	Somerset Place	C3
Dyfatty Street	B1	South Guildhall Road	A3
Dyfed Avenue	A2	Strand	C2
Earl Street	A2	Taliesyn Road	A2
East Burrows Road	C3	Tan-y-Marian Road	A1
Eigen Crescent	A1	Tegid Road	A1
Emlyn Road	A1	Teilo Crescent	A1
Fabian Way	C2	Terrace Road	A2
Fairfield Terrace	A2	The Kingsway	B2
Ffynone Drive	A2	Townhill Road	A1
Ffynone Road	A2	Trawler Road	B3
Foxhole Road	C1	Villiers Street	C1
Glamorgan Street	B3	Vincent Street	A3
Gors Avenue	A1	Walter Road	A3
Granagwen Road	B1	Watkin Street	B2
Grove Place	B2	Waun-Wen Road	B1
Gwent Road	A1	Wellington Street	B3
Gwili Terrace	A1	West Way	B3
Hanover Street	A2	Westbury Street	A3
Heathfield	B2	Western Street	A3
Hewson Street	A2	William Street	B3
High Street	B2	Windmill Terrace	C1
High View	B1	York Street	C3
Islwyn Road	A1		
Kilvey Road	C1		
Kilvey Terrace	C2		
King Edward's Road	A3		
King's Road	B3		
Llangyfelach Road	B1		
Long Ridge	B1		
Mackworth Street	C2		
Maesteg Street	C1		
Mansel Street	A2		
Mayhill Road	A1		
Milton Terrace	B2		
Morris Lane	C2		

Tourist Information Centre: 37 Regent Street
Tel: 01793 530328

Albion Street	A3
Bath Road	B3
Beatrice Street	B1
Beckhampton Street	C2
Birch Street	A2
Bridge Street	B2
Broad Street	C1
Canal Walk	B2
Caulfield Road	C1
Church Place	A2
Cirencester Way	C1
Clifton Street	B3
Commercial Road	B2
County Road	C1
Cricklade Street	C3
Curtis Street	B2
Dean Street	A2
Drove Road	C3
Eastcott Hill	B3
Edmund Street	B2
Elmina Road	C1
Euclid Street	C2
Faringdon Road	A2
Farnsby Street	B2
Fleet Street	B2
Fleming Way	B2
Gladstone Street	C1
Goddard Avenue	B3
Great Western Way	A1
Grosvenor Road	A3
Groundwell Road	C2
Hawksworth Way	A1
High Street	C3
Holbrook Way	B2
Hythe Road	B3
Islington Street	B2
Jennings Street	A2
Kemble Drive	A1
Kent Road	B3
Kingshill Street	A3
Lansdown Road	B3
Manchester Road	B1
Market Street	B2
Milford Street	B2
Milton Road	B2
Morris Street	A1
Newburn Crescent	A2
Newcombe Drive	A1
North Star Avenue	B1
Ocotal Way	C1
Okus Road	A3
Park Lane	A2
Penzance Drive	A2
Plymouth Street	C2
Princes Street	C2
Queen Street	B2
Radnor Street	A3
Redcliffe Street	A2
Regent Street	B2
Rodbourne Road	A1
Rosebery Street	C1
Spring Gardens	C2
Stafford Street	B3
Station Road	B1
Swindon Road	B3
The Parade	B2
Upham Road	C3
Victoria Road	C2
Westcott Place	A3
Western Street	C3
William Street	A3
York Road	C2

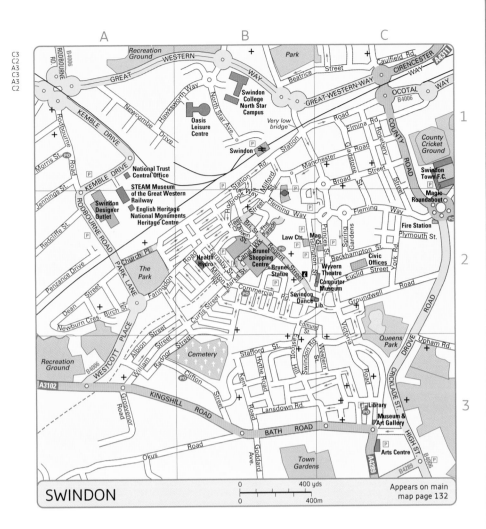

SWINDON

0   400 yds
0   400m

Appears on main
map page 132

Tourist Information Centre: Vaughan Parade
Tel: 0870 70 70 010

Abbey Road	B2
Ash Hill Road	B1
Avenue Road	A2
Bampfylde Road	A2
Barton Road	A1
Belgrave Road	A2
Belmont Road	C1
Braddons Hill Road East	C2
Bridge Road	A2
Bronshill Road	B1
Brunswick Square	B1
Carlton Road	C1
Cary Parade	C3
Cedars Road	C2
Chestnut Avenue	A2
Cockington Lane	A3
Croft Road	B2
Crownhill Park	A1
Dunmere Road	C1
East Street	A1
Ellacombe Church Road	C1
Ellacombe Road	B1
Falkland Road	A2
Falkland Road	A2
Fleet Street	B2
Forest Road	B1
Goshen Road	A2
Hatfield Road	B1
Hennapyn Road	A3
Higher Warberry Road	C2
Hillesdon Road	C2
Kenwyn Road	C1
Lower Warberry Road	C2
Lucius Street	A2
Lymington Road	B1
Mallock Road	A2
Market Street	B2
Marnham Road	C1
Meadfoot Lane	C3
Meadfoot Road	C3
Middle Warberry Road	C2
Mill Lane	A2
Newton Road	A1
Old Mill Road	A2
Old Mill Road	A3
Parkfield Road	B1
Parkhill Road	C3
Prince's Road	C2
Princes Road East	C2
Quinta Road	C1
Rathmore Road	A3
Reddenhill Road	C1
Rosehill Road	C2
Sanford Road	A2
Seaway Lane	A3
Shedden Hill	B2
Sherwell Lane	A2
Solsbro Road	A3
South Street	A2
St. Lukes Road	B2
St. Marychurch Road	B1
St. Michael's Road	A1
Stitchill Road	C2
Strand	C3
Teignmouth Road	A1
The King's Drive	A2
Thurlow Road	B1
Tor Hill Road	B2
Torbay Road	A3
Torwood Gardens Road	C3
Torwood Street	C3
Union Street	B2
Upton Hill	B1
Upton Road	A1
Vanehill Road	C3
Victoria Parade	C3
Walnut Road	A3
Warbro Road	C1
Warren Road	B2
Windsor Road	C1

TORQUAY

0   400 yds
0   400m

Appears on main
map page 101

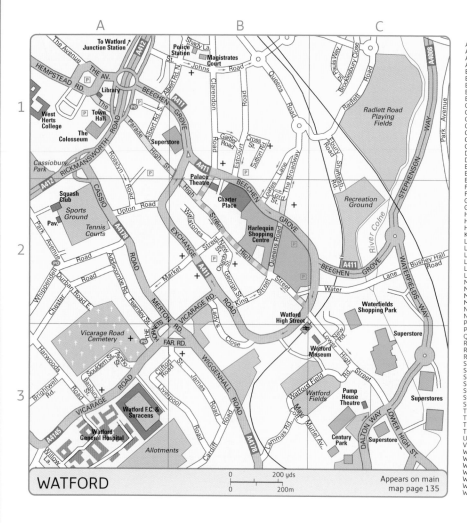

WATFORD

0   200 yds
0   200m

Appears on main map page 135

Addiscombe Road	A2
Albert Road North	A1
Albert Road South	A1
Aynho Street	A3
Banbury Street	A3
Beechen Grove	A1/C2
Brightwell Road	A3
Brocklesbury Close	C1
Bushey Hall Road	C2
Cardiff Road	B3
Cassio Road	A2
Chester Road	A2
Church Street	B2
Clarendon Road	B1
Clifton Road	A3
Cross Street	B1
Dalton Way	C3
Durban Road East	A2
Ebury Road	C1
Estcourt Road	B1
Exchange Road	A2
Farraline Road	A3
Fearnley Street	A2
Garlet Road	B1
George Street	A2
Harwoods Road	A3
Hempsted Road	A1
High Street	A1/B2
King Street	B2
Lady's Close	B2
Lammas Road	B3
Liverpool Road	A3
Loates Lane	B2
Lord Street	B2
Lower High Street	C3
Market Street	A2
May Cottages	B3
Merton Road	A2
Muriel Avenue	B3
New Road	C3
New Street	B2
Park Avenue	C1
Park Avenue	A2
Queens Road	B1/B2
Radlett Road	C1
Rickmansworth Road	A2
Rosslyn Road	A1
Shaftesbury Road	C1
Souldern Street	A3
St. James Road	B3
St. Johns Road	A1
St. Pauls Way	C1
Stephenson Way	C2
Sutton Road	B1
The Avenue	A1
The Broadway	B2
The Hornets	A3
The Parade	A1
Upton Road	A2
Vicarage Road	A3/B2
Water Lane	C2
Waterfields Way	C2
Watford Field Road	B3
Wellstones	B2
Whippendell Road	A2
Wiggenhall Road	B3
Willow Lane	A3

WESTON-SUPER-MARE

0   400 yds
0   400m

Appears on main map page 115

Tourist Information Centre: Beach Lawns
Tel: 01934 888800

Addicott Road	B3		Stafford Road	C2
Albert Avenue	B3		Station Road	B2
Alexandra Parade	B2		Sunnyside Road	B3
Alfred Street	B2		Swiss Road	C2
All Saints Road	B1		The Centre	B2
Amberey Road	C3		Trewartha Park	C1
Arundell Road	B1		Upper Church Road	A1
Ashcombe Gardens	C1		Walliscote Road	B3
Ashcombe Road	C2		Waterloo Street	B2
Atlantic Road	A1		Whitecross Road	B3
Baker Street	B2		Winterstoke Road	C3
Beach Road	B3			
Beaconsfield Road	B2			
Birnbeck Road	A1			
Boulevard	B2			
Brendon Avenue	C1			
Bridge Road	C2			
Brighton Road	B3			
Bristol Road	B1			
Carlton Street	B2			
Cecil Road	B1			
Clarence Road North	B3			
Clarendon Road	C2			
Clevedon Road	B3			
Clifton Road	B3			
Drove Road	C3			
Earlham Grove	C2			
Ellenborough Park North	B3			
Ellenborough Park South	B3			
Exeter Road	B3			
George Street	B2			
Gerard Road	B1			
Grove Park Road	B1			
High Street	B2			
Highbury Road	A1			
Hildesheim Bridge	B2			
Hill Road	C1			
Jubilee Road	B2			
Kenn Close	C3			
Kensington Road	C3			
Knightstone Road	A1			
Langford Road	C3			
Lewisham Grove	C2			
Locking Road	C2			
Lower Bristol Road	C1			
Lower Church Road	A1			
Manor Road	C1			
Marchfields Way	C3			
Marine Parade	B3			
Meadow Street	B2			
Milton Road	C2			
Montpelier	B1			
Neva Road	B2			
Norfolk Road	C3			
Oxford Street	B2			
Queen's Road	B1			
Rectors Way	C3			
Regent Street	B2			
Ridgeway Avenue	B3			
Royal Crescent	A1			
St. Paul's Road	B3			
Sandford Road	C2			
Severn Road	B3			
Shrubbery Road	A1			
South Road	A1			
Southside	B1			

Tourist Information Centre: Guildhall, High Street
Tel: 01962 840500

Alison Way	A1
Andover Road	A1
Archery Lane	A2
Bar End Road	C3
Barfield Close	C3
Beaufort Road	A3
Beggar's Lane	C2
Blue Ball Hill	C2
Bridge Stret	C2
Broadway	B2
Canon Street	B3
Chesil Street	C3
Christchurch Road	A3
City Road	A1
Clifton Hill	A2
Clifton Road	A1
Clifton Terrace	A2
Colebrook Street	B2
College Street	B3
College Walk	B3
Compton Road	A3
Cranworth Road	A1
Culver Road	B3
Domum Road	C3
Durngate	C2
East Hill	C3
Eastgate Street	C2
Easton Lane	C1
Ebden Road	C1
Edgar Road	A3
Elm Road	A1
Fairfield Road	A1
Friarsgate	B2
Gordon Road	B1
Great Minster Street	B2
Hatherley Road	A1
High Street	B2
Hyde Abbey Road	B1
Hyde Close	B1
Hyde Street	B1
Jewry Street	B2
King Alfred Place	B1
Kingsgate Street	B3
Little Minster Street	B2
Lower Brook Street	B2
Magdalen Hill	C2
Market Lane	B2
Middle Brook Street	B2
Middle Road	A2
Milland Road	C3
North Walls	A1
Parchment Street	B2
Park Avenue	B1
Peninsula Square	A2
Portal Road	C3
Quarry Road	C3
Romans' Road	A3
Romsey Road	A2
St. Catherine's Road	C3
St. Cross Road	A3
St. George's Street	B2
St. James Lane	A2
St. James Villas	A3
St. John's Street	C2
St. Michael's Road	A3
St. Paul's Hill	A1
St. Peter Street	B2
St. Swithun Street	B3
St. Thomas Street	B3
Saxon Road	B1
Silver Hill	B2
Southgate Street	A3
Staple Gardens	B2
Station Road	A1
Step Terrace	A2
Stockbridge Road	A1
Sussex Street	A2
Swan Lane	B1
Symond's Street	B3
Tanner Street	B2
The Square	B2
Tower Street	A2
Union Street	C2
Upper Brook Street	B2
Upper High Street	A2
Wales Street	C2
Water Lane	C2
Wharf Hill	C3
Worthy Lane	A1

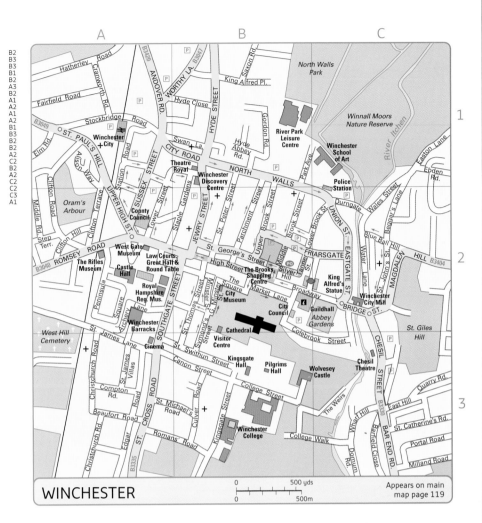

WINCHESTER

0 ___ 500 yds
0 ___ 500m

Appears on main
map page 119

Tourist Information Centre: Old Booking Hall, Central Station
Tel: 01753 743900

Adelaide Square	C3
Albert Street	A2
Alexandra Road	B3
Alma Road	B2/B3
Arthur Road	B2
Barry Avenue	B1
Bexley Street	B2
Bolton Avenue	B3
Bolton Crescent	B3
Bolton Road	B3
Bulkeley Avenue	A3
Castle Hill	C2
Charles Street	B2
Clarence Crescent	B2
Clarence Road	A2
College Crescent	A3
Dagmar Road	B2
Datchet Road	C1
Frances Road	B3
Goslar Way	A2
Goswell Road	B2
Green Lane	A2
Grove Road	B2
Helston Lane	A2
High Street (Eton)	B1
High Street (Windsor)	C2
Imperial Road	A3
King Edward VII Avenue	C3
Kings Road	C3
Meadow Lane	B1
Mill Lane	A1
Osborne Road	B3
Oxford Road	B2
Park Street	C2
Parsonage Lane	A2
Peascod Street	B2
Peel Close	A3
Princess Avenue	A3
Romney Lock Road	C1
St. Leonards Road	B3
St. Marks Road	B2
Sheet Street	C2
South Meadow Lane	B1
Springfield Road	A3
Stovell Road	A1
Thames Street	C1
The Long Walk	C3
Upcroft	A3
Vansittart Road	B2
Victoria Street	B2
Victor Road	B3
Westmead	A3
Windsor & Eton Relief Road	A2
York Avenue	A3
York Road	A3

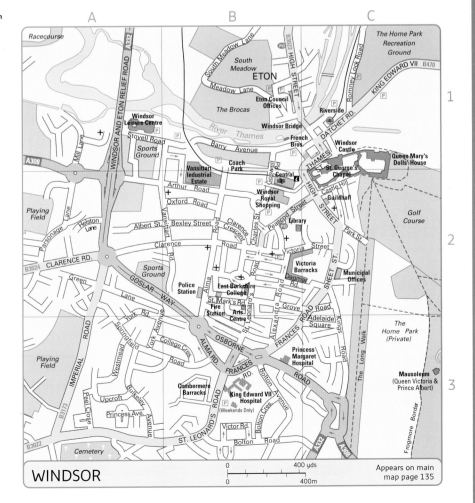

WINDSOR

0 ___ 400 yds
0 ___ 400m

Appears on main
map page 135

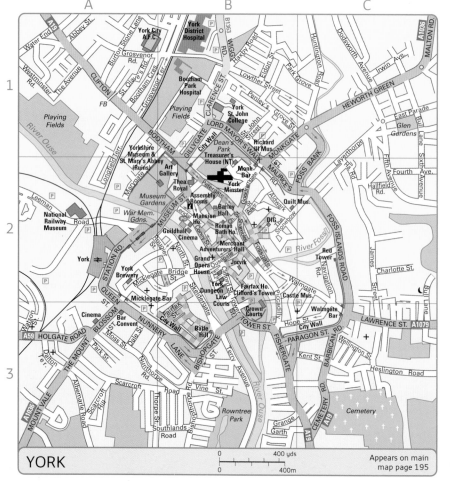

WORCESTER

Tourist Information Centre: The Guildhall, High Street
Tel: 01905 726311

Street	Grid		Street	Grid
Albany Terrace	A1		Sherriff Street	C1
Albert Road	C3		Shrub Hill	C2
Angel Place	A2		Shrub Hill Road	C2
Angel Street	B2		Sidbury	B3
Arboretum Road	B1		Southfield Street	B1
Back Lane South	A1		Spring Hill	C2
Bath Road	B3		Stanley Road	C3
Bridge Street	A2		Tallow Hill	C2
Britannia Road	A1		Tennis Walk	A1
Britannia Square	A1		The Butts	A2
Broad Street	A2		The Cross	B2
Carden Street	B3		The Moors	A1
Castle Street	A2		The Shambles	B2
Charles Street	B3		The Tything	A1
Chestnut Street	B1		Tolladine Road	C1
Chestnut Walk	B1		Trinity Street	B2
City Walls Road	B2		Upper Tything	A1
Cole Hill	C3		Vincent Road	C3
College Street	B3		Washington Street	B1
Compton Road	C3		Westbury Street	B1
Copenhagen Street	A3		Wyld's Lane	C3
Croft Road	A2			
Deansway	A2			
Dent Close	C3			
Dolday	A2			
Farrier Street	A2			
Foregate Street	B2			
Fort Royal Hill	C3			
Foundry Street	B3			
Friar Street	B3			
George Street	C2			
Grand Stand Road	A2			
High Street	B2			
Hill Street	C2			
Hylton Road	A2			
Infirmary Walk	A2			
Kleve Walk	B3			
Lansdowne Crescent	B1			
Lansdowne Walk	C1			
London Road	B3			
Loves Grove	A1			
Lowesmoor	B2			
Lowesmoor Place	B2			
Midland Road	C3			
Moor Street	A1			
Newport Street	A2			
New Road	A3			
New Street	B2			
Northfield Street	B1			
North Quay	A2			
Padmore Street	B2			
Park Street	B3			
Park Street	C3			
Pheasant Street	B2			
Pump Street	B3			
Rainbow Hill	B1			
Richmond Hill	C3			
St. Martin's Gate	B2			
St. Mary's Street	A1			
St. Oswalds Road	A1			
St. Paul's Street	B2			
Sansome Street	B2			
Sansome Walk	B1			
Severn Street	B3			
Severn Terrace	A1			
Shaw Street	A2			

200 yds / 200m

Appears on main map page 146

YORK

Tourist Information Centre: De Grey Rooms, Exhibition Square
Tel: 01904 550099

Street	Grid		Street	Grid
Abbey Street	A1		Paragon Street	B3
Albermarle Road	A3		Park Grove	B1
Aldwark	B2		Park Street	A3
Barbican Road	C3		Penley's Grove Street	B1
Bishopthorpe Road	B3		Petergate	B2
Bishopgate Street	B3		Piccadilly	B2
Blossom Street	A3		Queen Street	A2
Bootham	A1		Rougier Street	A2
Bootham Crescent	A1		St. Andrewgate	B2
Bridge Street	B2		St. John Street	B1
Bull Lane	C1/C2		St. Maurice's Road	B2
Burton Stone Lane	A1		St. Olave's Road	A1
Cemetery Road	C3		Scarcroft Hill	A3
Charlotte Street	C2		Scarcroft Road	A3
Church Street	B2		Shambles	B2
Clarence Street	B1		Sixth Avenue	C1
Clifford Street	B2		Skeldergate	B2
Clifton	A1		Southlands Road	A3
Coney Street	B2		Station Road	A2
Dale Street	A3		Terry Avenue	B3
Dalton Terrace	A3		The Avenue	A1
Dodsworth Avenue	C1		The Mount	A3
East Parade	C1		The Stonebow	B2
Eldon Street	B1		Thorpe Street	A3
Fairfax Street	B3		Tower Street	B2
Fifth Avenue	C1		Vine Street	B3
Fishergate	B3		Walmgate	B2
Foss Bank	B1		Water End	A1
Fossgate	B2		Watson Street	A3
Foss Islands Road	C2		Wellington Street	C3
Fourth Avenue	C2		Westminster Road	A1
Gillygate	B1		Wigginton Road	B1
Goodramgate	B2			
Grange Garth	B3			
Grosvenor Road	A1			
Grosvenor Terrace	A1			
Hallfield Road	C2			
Haxby Road	B1			
Heslington Road	C3			
Heworth Green	C1			
Holgate Road	A3			
Hope Street	B3			
Huntington Road	C1			
Irwin Avenue	C1			
James Street	B2			
Kent Street	C3			
Lawrence Street	C3			
Layerthorpe	C2			
Leeman Road	A2			
Lendal	B2			
Longfield Terrace	A2			
Lord Mayor's Walk	B1			
Lowther Street	B1			
Malton Road	C1			
Marygate	A2			
Maurices Road	A2			
Micklegate	A2			
Monkgate	B1			
Moss Street	A3			
Mount Vale	A3			
Museum Street	B2			
Navigation Road	C2			
North Street	B2			
Nunnery Lane	A3			
Nunthorpe Road	A3			
Ousegate	B2			

400 yds / 400m

Appears on main map page 195

Key to map symbols   🅿 Short stay car park   🅿 Mid stay car park   🅿 Long stay car park   🅿 Other car park   ▭ Airport terminal building

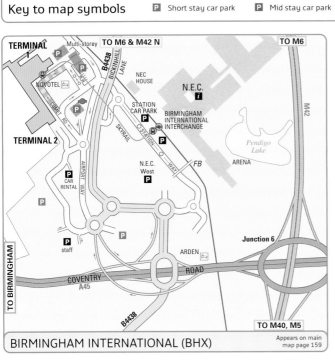

BIRMINGHAM INTERNATIONAL (BHX)
Appears on main map page 159

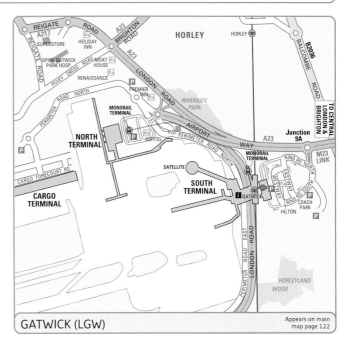

GATWICK (LGW)
Appears on main map page 122

GLASGOW (GLA)
Appears on main map page 233

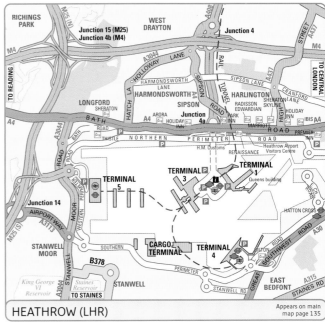

HEATHROW (LHR)
Appears on main map page 135

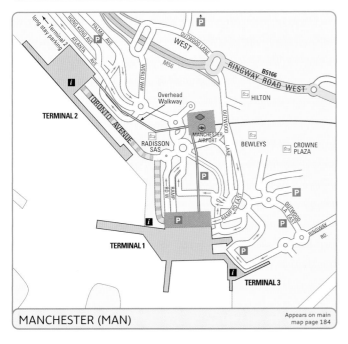

MANCHESTER (MAN)
Appears on main map page 184

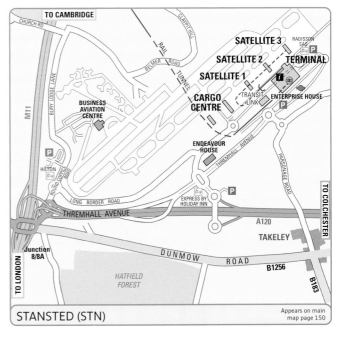

STANSTED (STN)
Appears on main map page 150

Symbols used on the map

M5 Motorway

M6 Toll Toll motorway

8 9 Motorway junction with full / limited access
(in congested areas there is just a numbered symbol)

Maidstone
Birch
Sarn
Motorway service area with off road / full / limited access

A556 Primary route dual / single carriageway

S 24 hour service area on primary route

Peterhead Primary route destination
Primary route destinations are places of major traffic importance linked by the primary route network. They are shown on a green background on direction signs.

A30 'A' road dual / single carriageway

B1403 'B' road dual / single carriageway

Minor road

Road with restricted access

Roads with passing places

Road proposed or under construction

33 Multi-level junction with full / limited access (with junction number)

Roundabout

4 Road distance in miles between markers

Road tunnel

Steep hill (arrows point downhill)

Toll Level crossing / Toll

Car ferry route with journey times
St. Malo 8hrs

Railway line / station / tunnel

South Downs Way National Trail / Long Distance Route

---

30 V Fixed safety camera
Speed limit shown by a number within the camera, a V indicates a variable limit.

30 30 Fixed average-speed safety camera
Speed limit shown by a number within the camera.

✈ ✈ Airport with / without scheduled services

H Heliport

P&R **P&R** Park and Ride site operated by bus / rail
(runs at least 5 days a week)

Built up area

□ □ □ Town / Village / Other settlement

Hythe Seaside destination

National boundary

KENT County / Unitary Authority boundary and name

Heritage Coast

National Park

Regional / Forest Park boundary

Woodland

Danger Zone Military range

·468 ▲941 Spot / Summit height (in metres)

Lake / Dam / River / Waterfall

Canal / Dry canal / Canal tunnel

Beach / Lighthouse

SEE PAGE 3 Area covered by urban area map

	0	150	300	500	700	900	metres
Land height reference bar
water	0	490	985	1640	2295	2950	feet

Reading our maps

Park & Ride
Sites are shown that operate at least 5 days a week. Bus operated sites have a yellow symbol and rail operated sites a pink symbol.

Distances
Blue numbers give distances in miles between junctions shown with a blue marker

Multi-level junctions
Non-motorway junctions where slip roads are used to access the main roads

Motorway service area

World Heritage site
Places of interest defined by UNESCO as special on a world scale.

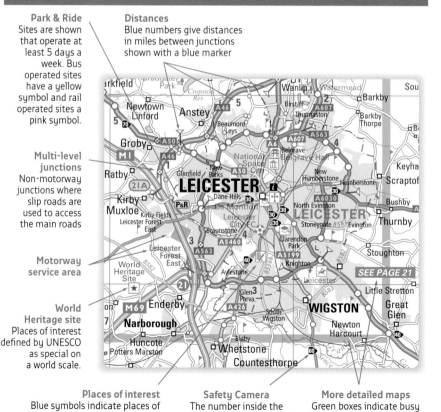

Places of interest
Blue symbols indicate places of interest. See the section to the right for the different types of feature represented on the map.

Safety Camera
The number inside the camera shows the speed limit at the camera location.

More detailed maps
Green boxes indicate busy built-up-areas where more detailed mapping is available.

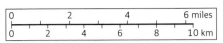

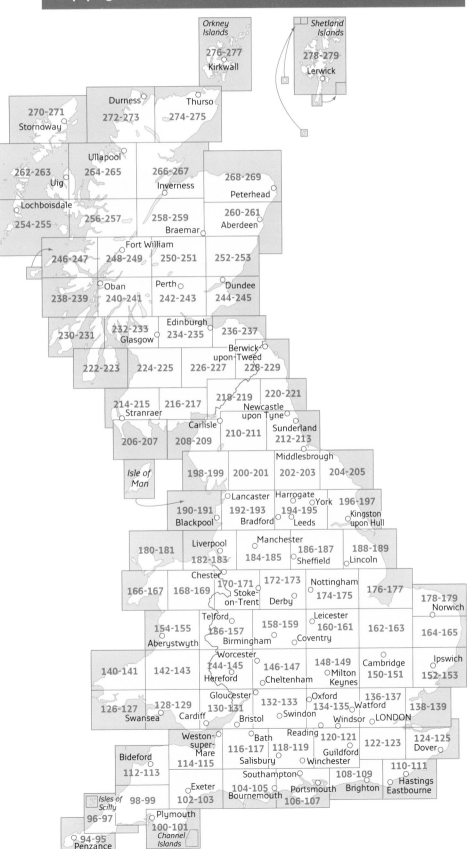

Places of interest

A selection of tourist detail is shown on the mapping. It is advisable to check with the local tourist information centre regarding opening times and facilities available.

Any of the following symbols may appear on the map in maroon ★ which indicates that the site has World Heritage status.

_i_	Tourist information centre (open all year)
_i_	Tourist information centre (open seasonally)
m	Ancient monument
	Aquarium
	Aqueduct / Viaduct
	Arboretum
1643	Battlefield
	Blue flag beach
Å	Camp site / Caravan site
	Castle
	Cave
	Country park
	County cricket ground
	Distillery
	Ecclesiastical feature
	Event venue
	Farm park
	Garden
	Golf course
	Historic house
	Historic ship
	Major football club
£	Major shopping centre / Outlet village
	Major sports venue
	Motor racing circuit
	Mountain bike trail
	Museum / Art gallery
	Nature reserve (NNR indicates a National Nature Reserve)
	Racecourse
	Rail Freight Terminal
	Ski slope (artificial / natural)
	Spotlight nature reserve (Best sites for access to nature)
	Steam railway centre / preserved railway
	Surfing beach
	Theme park
	University
	Vineyard
	Wildlife park / Zoo
★	Other interesting feature
(NT) (NTS)	National Trust / National Trust for Scotland property

Map scale

A scale bar appears at the bottom of every page to help with distances.

0		2		4		6 miles
0	2	4	6	8	10 km	

England, Wales & Southern Scotland are at a scale of 1:200,000 or 3.2 miles to 1 inch
Northern Scotland is at a scale of 1:263,158 or 4.2 miles to 1 inch.

Map pages

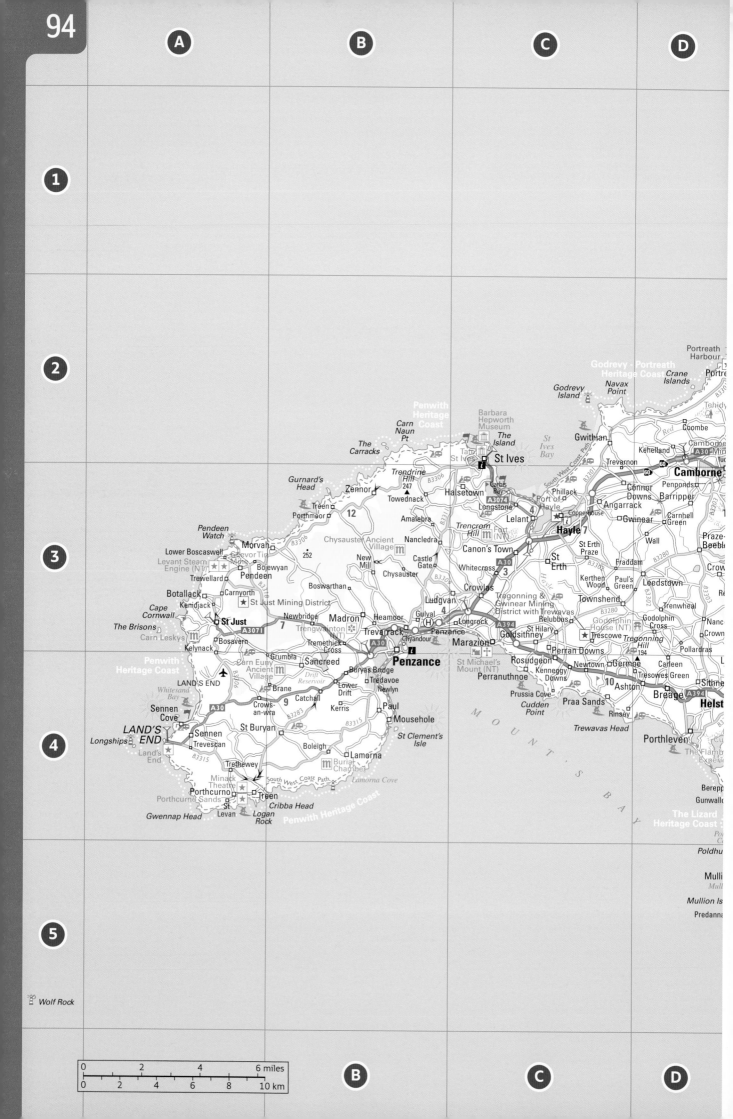

Portreath
Harbour

Godrevy - Portreath
Heritage Coast   Crane
Navax   Islands
Godrevy   Point   Portre
Island
Tehidy

Penwith   Red   Coombe
Heritage   Barbara   Gwithian   Cambor
Coast   Hepworth   Kehelland   A30
Carn   Museum   St   Trevarnon   60   Camborne
Naun   The   Ives   60
Pt   Island   Bay   Phillack   Connor   Penponds
The   St Ives   Downs   Barripper
Carracks   Carbis   Port of   Angarrack
Trendrine   Bay   Hayle   Coppernouse   Gwinear   Carnhell
Gurnard's   Hill   Longstone   4   Hayle 7   Green
Head   Zennor   247   Halsetown   Lelant   Wall   Praze-
Towednack   A3074   St Erth   Beebl
Treen   Amalebra   Trencrom   Praze   Fraddam   Crow
Porthmeor   12   Hill   Canon's Town   St   Kerthen   Paul's
Nancledra   Fort   Erth   Wood   Green   Leedstown
Pendeen   Chysauster Ancient   (NT)   A30   Townshend   B3303
Watch   New   Village   Whitecross   3   B3280   Trenwheal
Lower Boscaswell   Mill   Castle   Crowlas   Tregonning &   Godolphin
Morvah   252   Gate   Gwinear Mining   House (NT)   Cross   Nanc
Levant Steam   Trevor Tin   Chysauster   Ludgvan   District with Trewavas   Trescowe   Tregonning   Crown
Engine (NT)   Bojewyan   Boswarthan   4   Relubbus   St Hilary   Hill   Pollardras
Trewellard   Pendeen   St Just Mining District   Heamoor   Gulval   Longrock   A394   194
Botallack   Carnyorth   Newbridge   Madron   Trevarrack   Penzance   Goldsithney   Perran Downs   Carleen
Kenidjack   7   Trengwainton   A30   Marazion   Rosudgeon   Newtown   Germoe   Sithne
Cape   St Just   Tremethick   (NT)   Chyandour   St Michael's   Perranuthnoe   Kenneggy   Tresowes Green   Breage
Cornwall   A3071   Cross   Mount (NT)   Downs   10   Ashton   A394
The Brisons   Bosaven   Grumbla   Burvas Bridge   Prussia Cove   Rinsey   Helst
Carn Leskys   Kelynack   Sancreed   Tredavoe   Cudden   Praa Sands
Carn Euny   Drift   Lower   Newlyn   Point
Penwith   Ancient   Reservoir   Drift   M   O   Trewavas Head
Heritage Coast   Village   Brane   Catchall   Kerris   Paul   U   Porthleven
Whitesand   9   Mousehole   N   The Flamb
Bay   LAND'S END   Crows-   T   Expe
Sennen   an-wra   St Clement's   '
Cove   St Buryan   Boleigh   Isle   S
LAND'S   Sennen   Lamorna   Berepp
Longships   END   Trevescan   Boleigh   Burial   Gunwallo
Land's   Lamorna   Chamber   B   Mulli
End   Trethewey   A
Minack   Y   Poldhu
Theatre   Treen   Mulli
Porthcurno   St   Logan   South West Coast Path   Lamorna Cove   The Lizard   Mullion Is
Porthcurno Sands   Levan   Rock   Heritage Coast   Predann
Gwennap Head   Cribba Head   Penwith Heritage Coast   Po
C

Wolf Rock

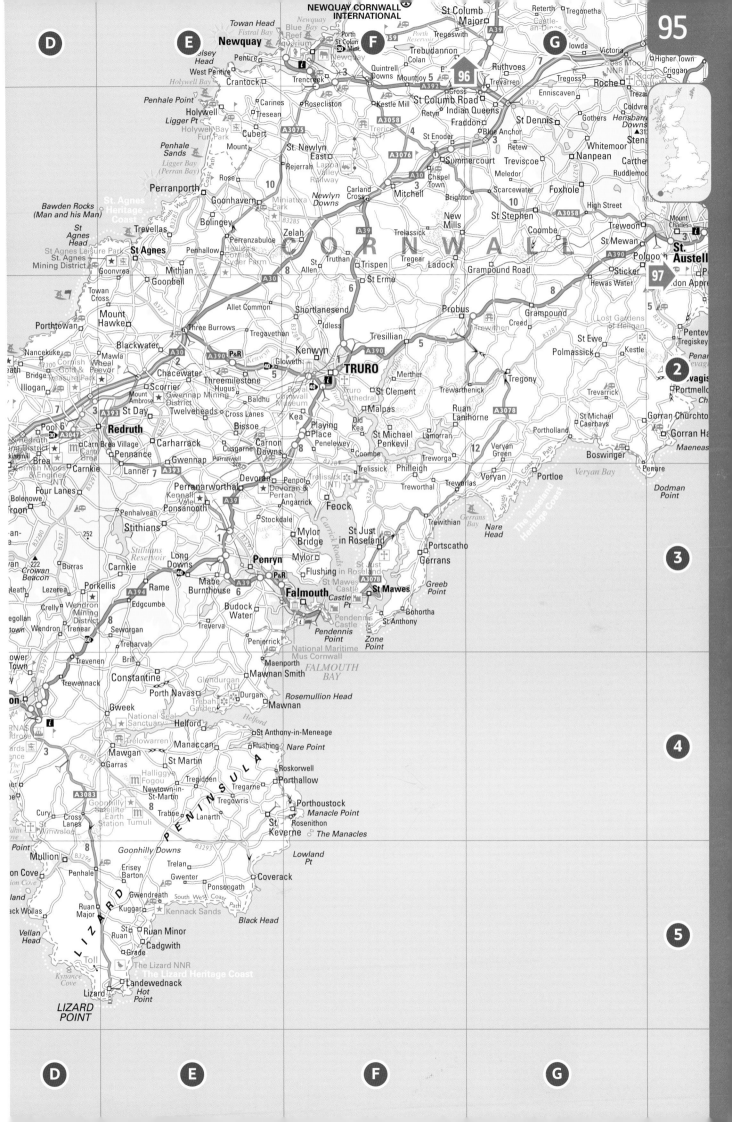

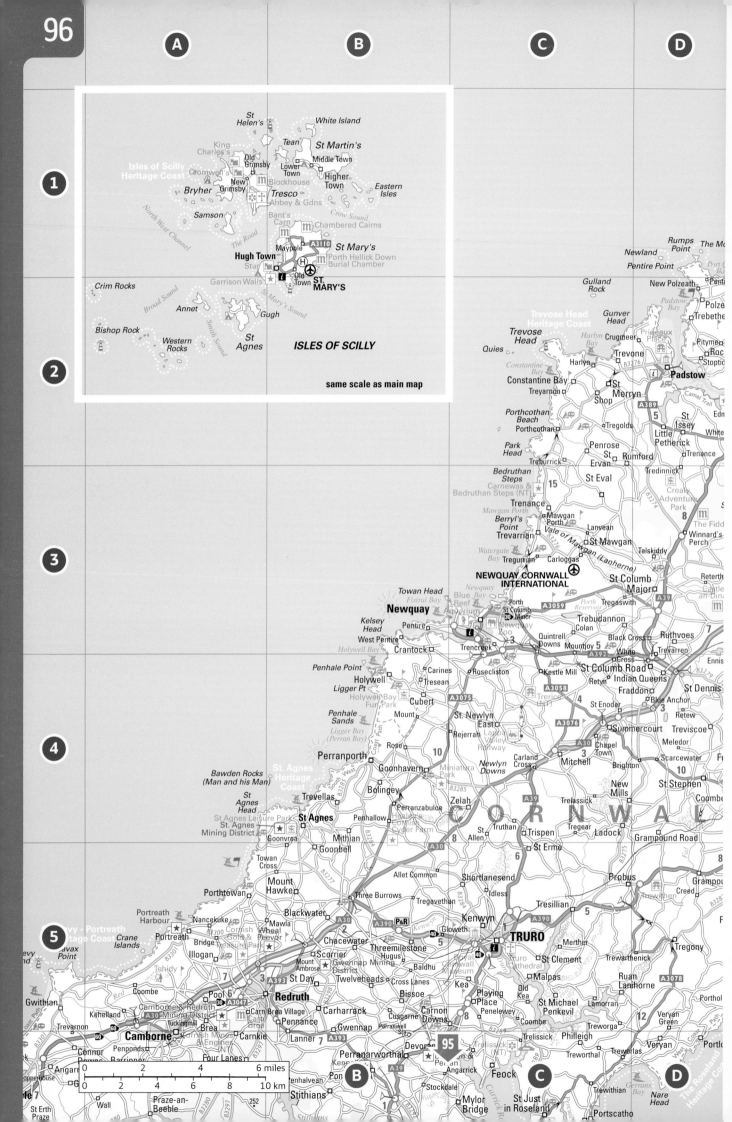

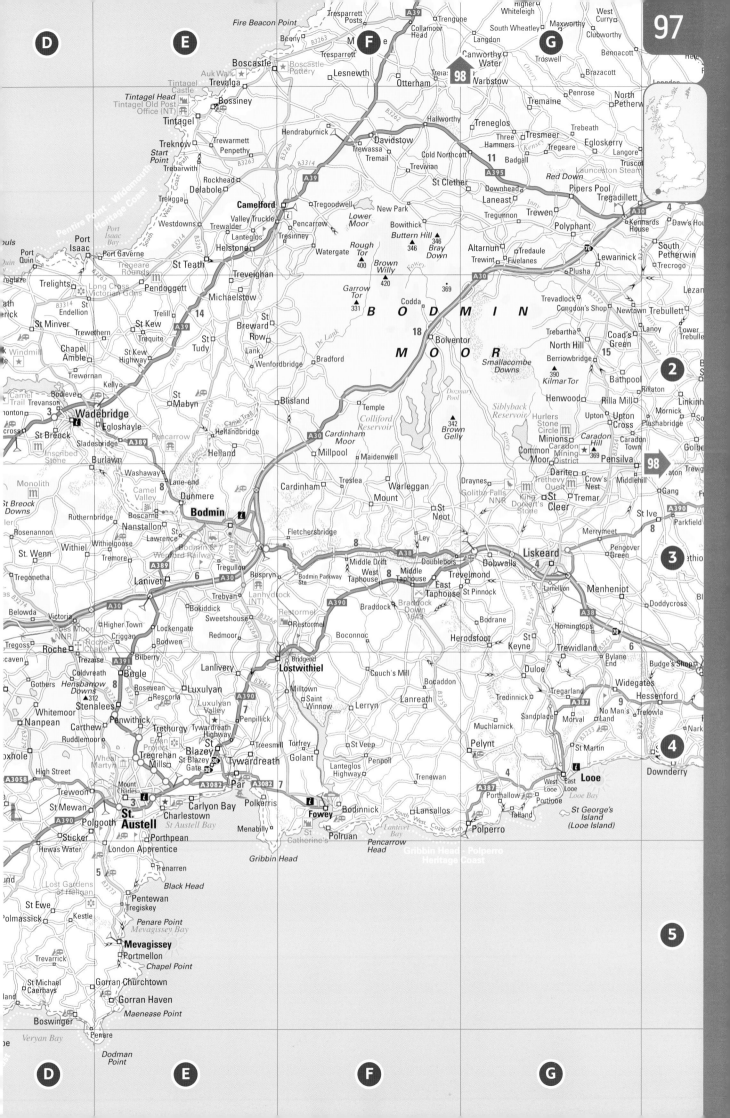

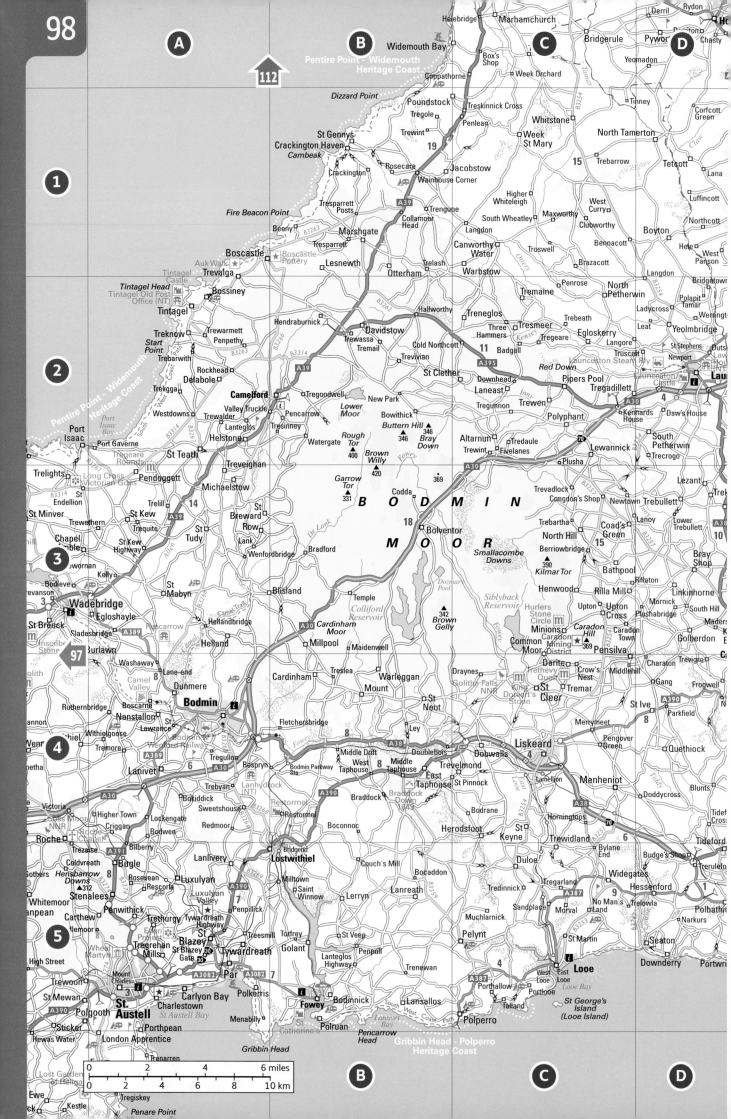

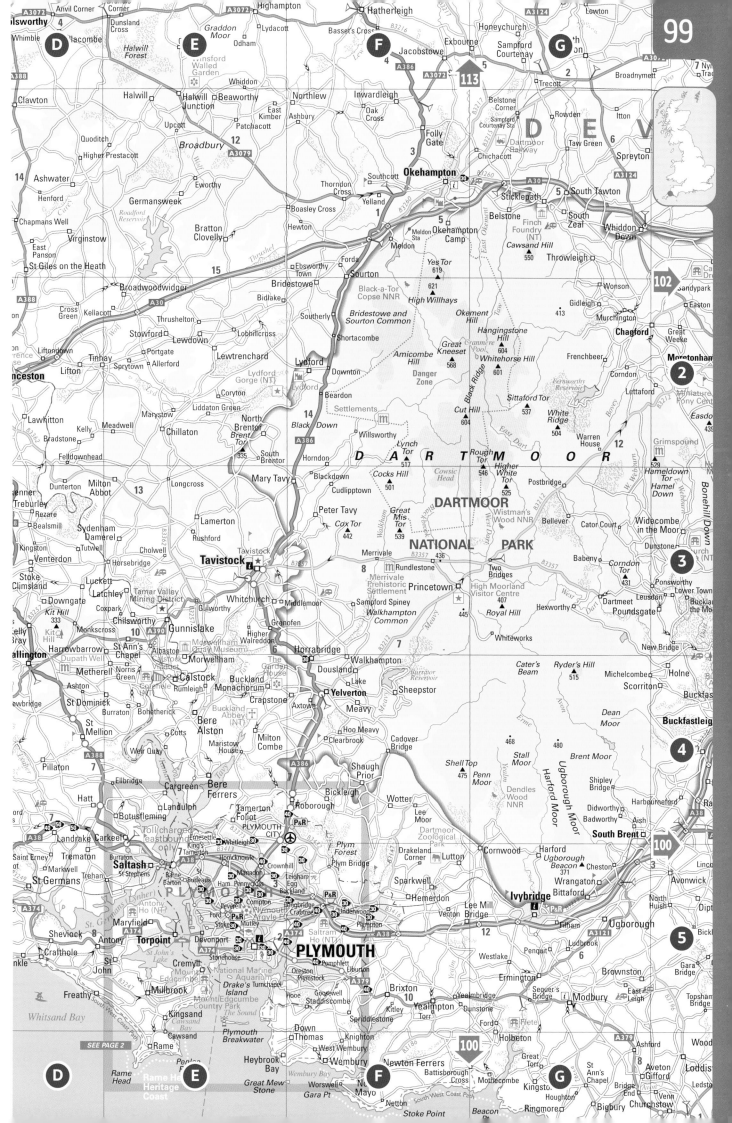

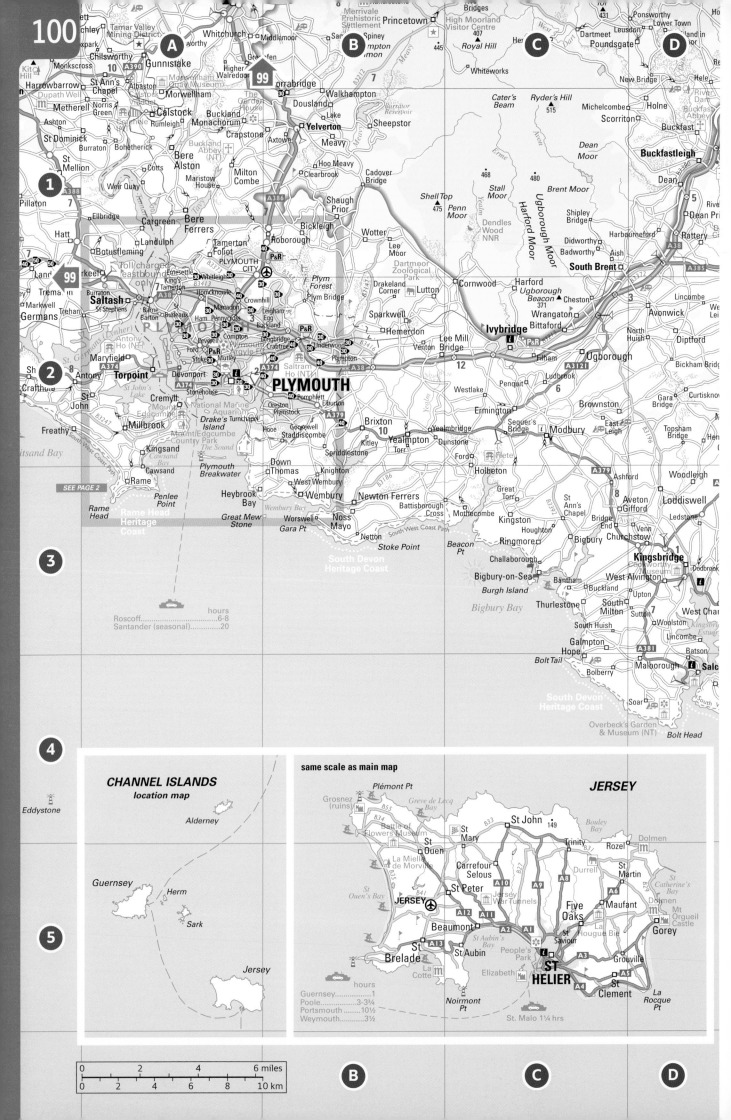

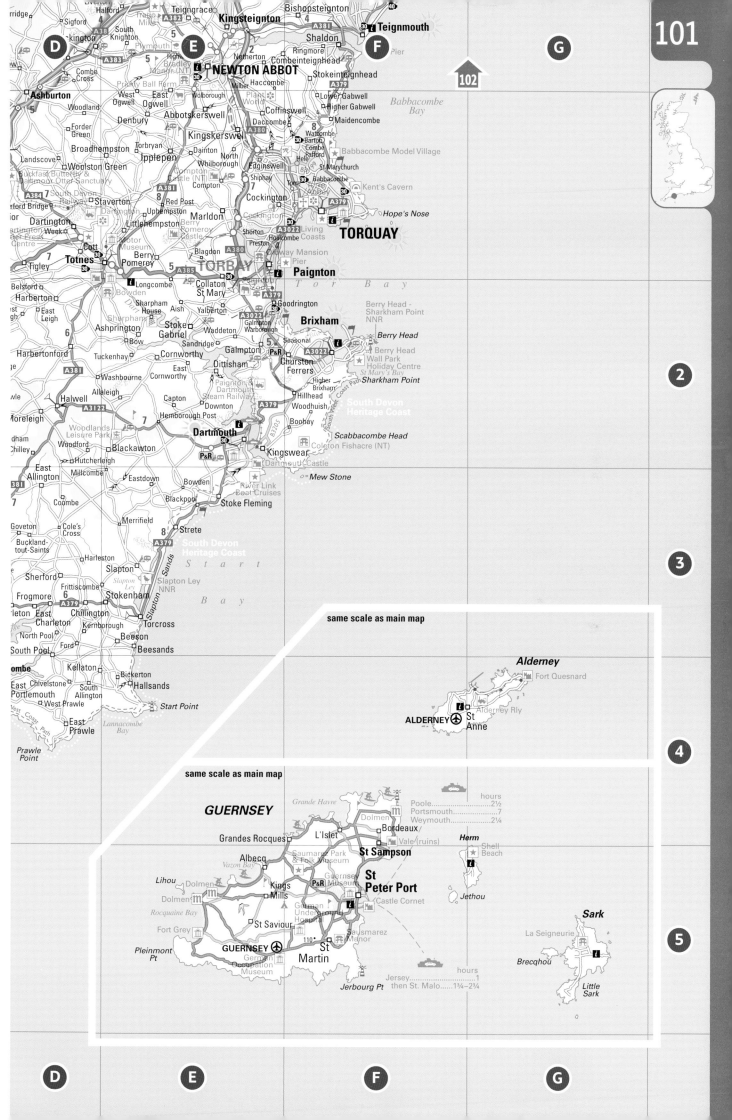

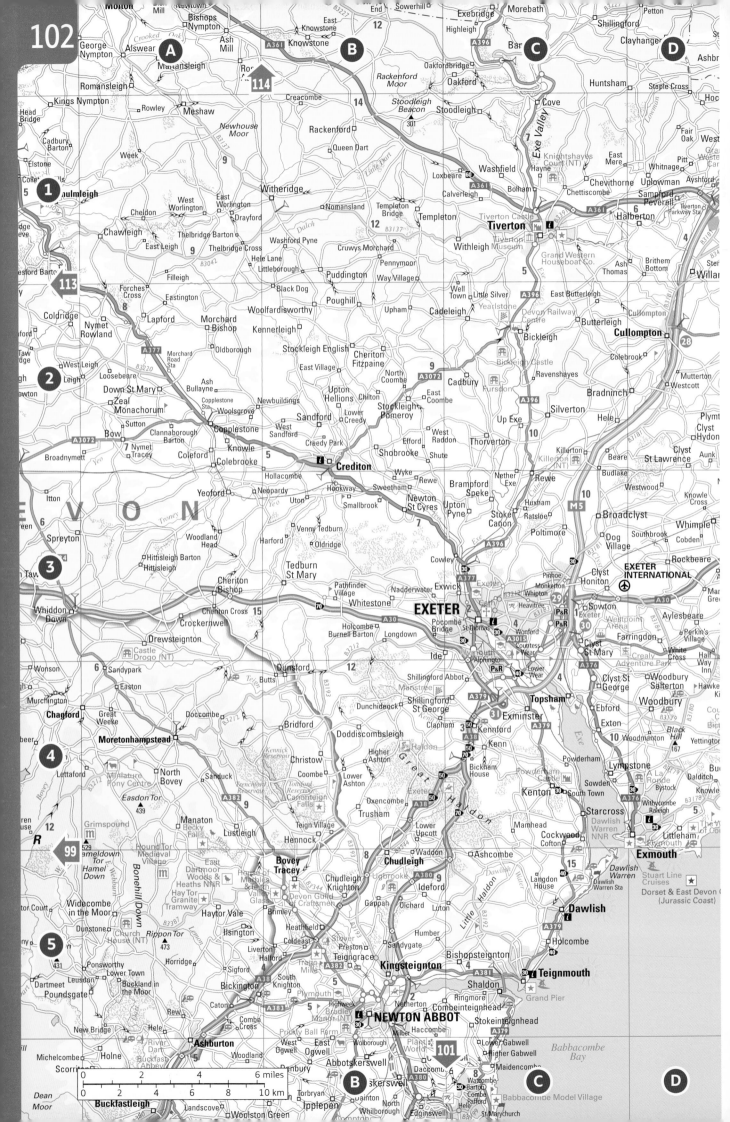

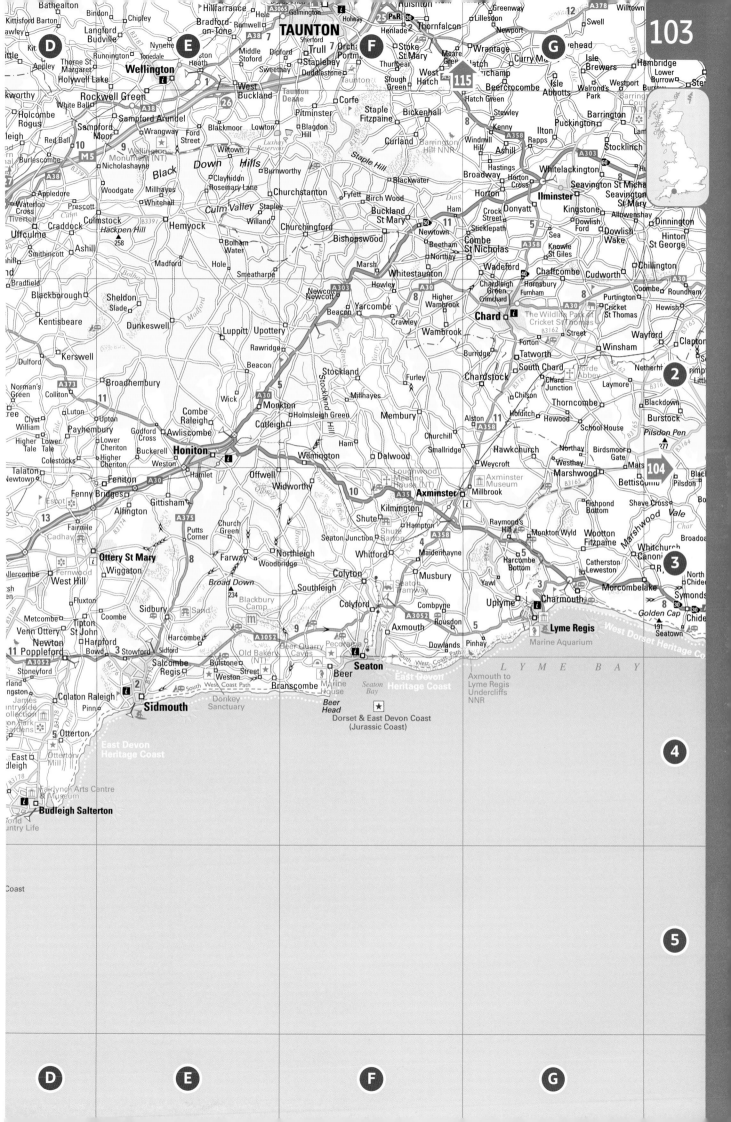

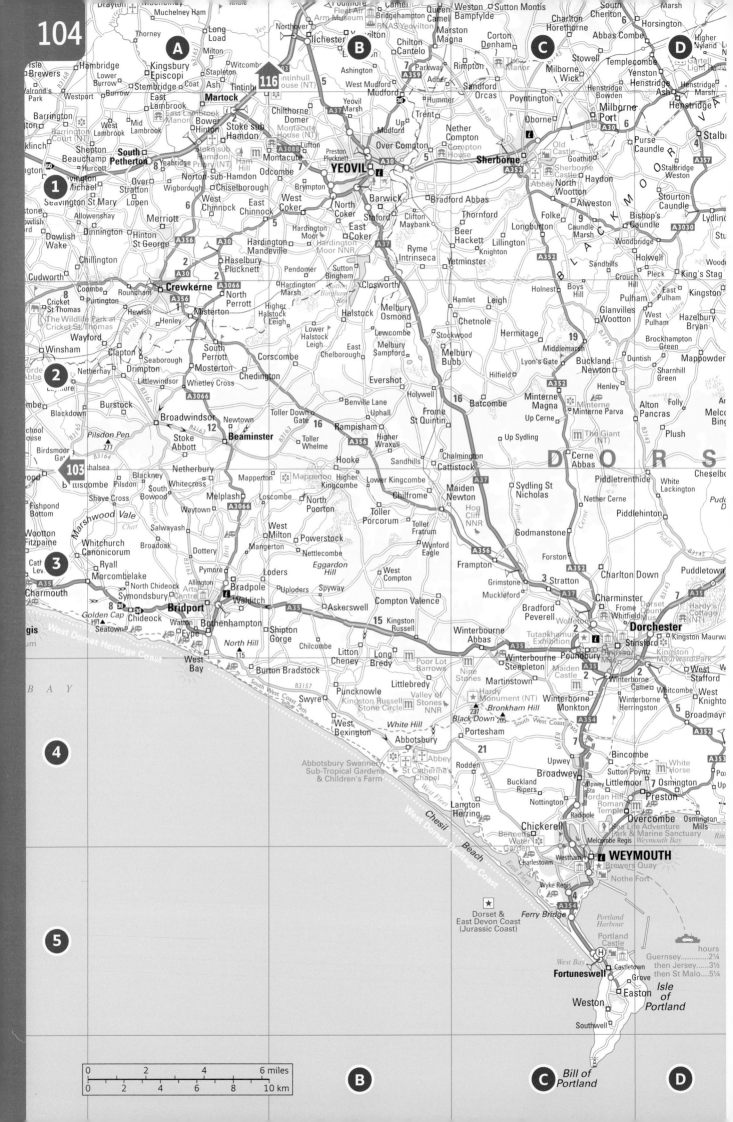

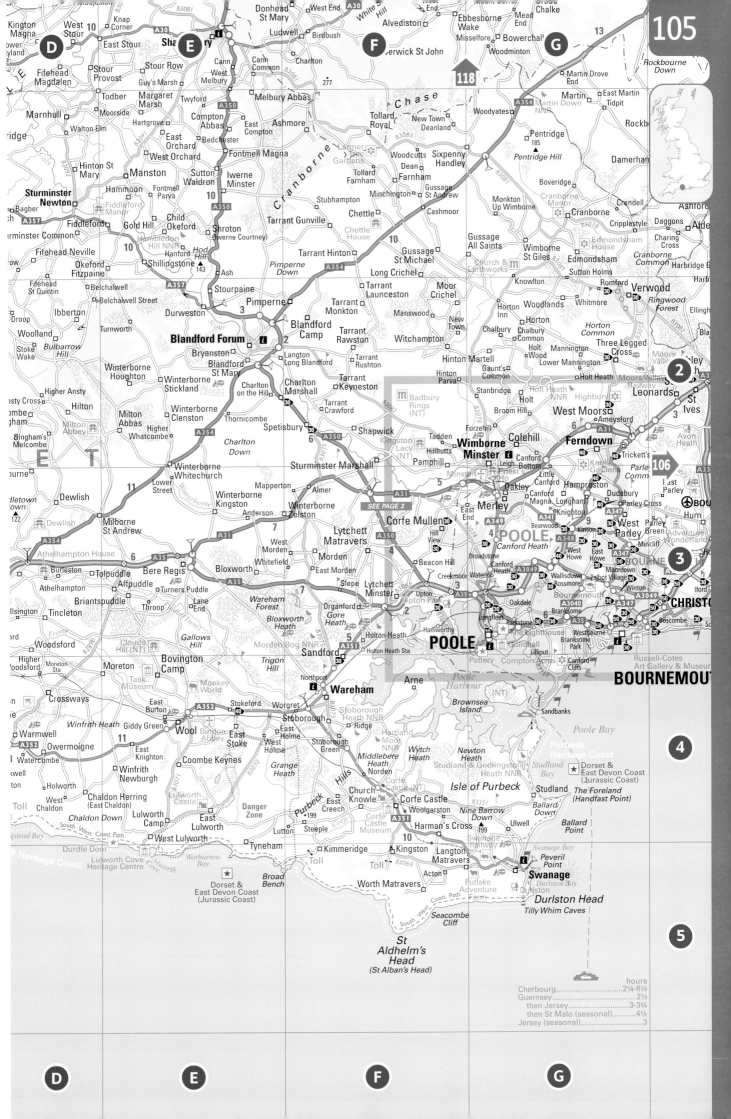

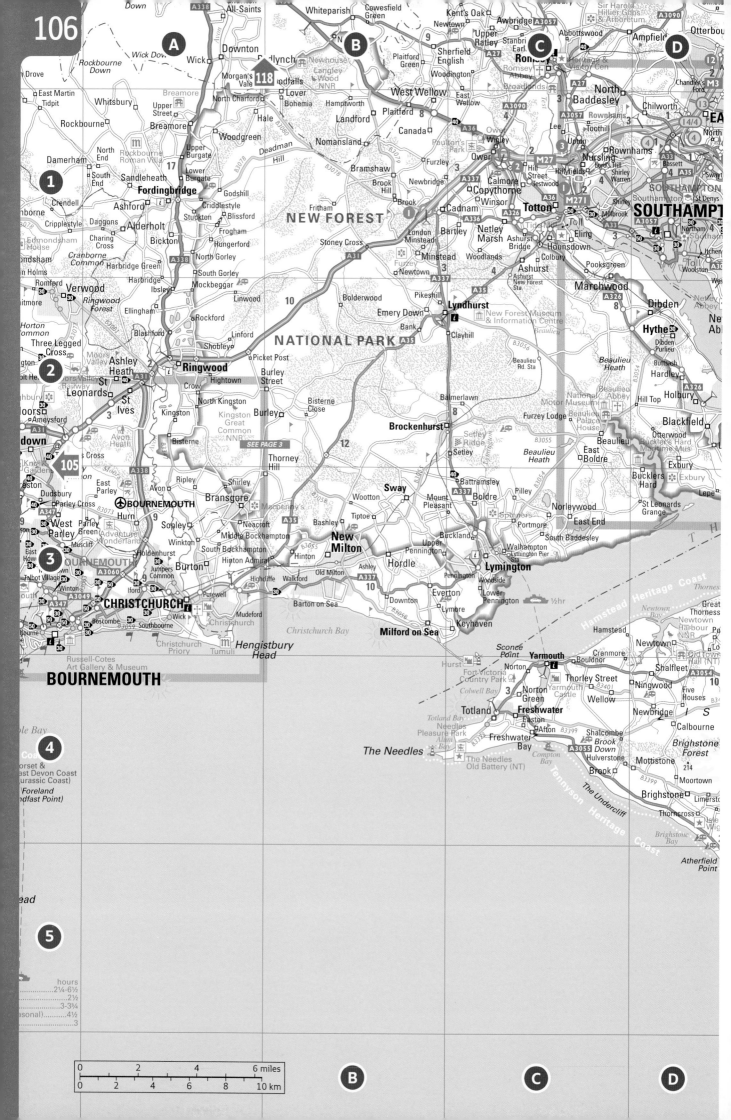

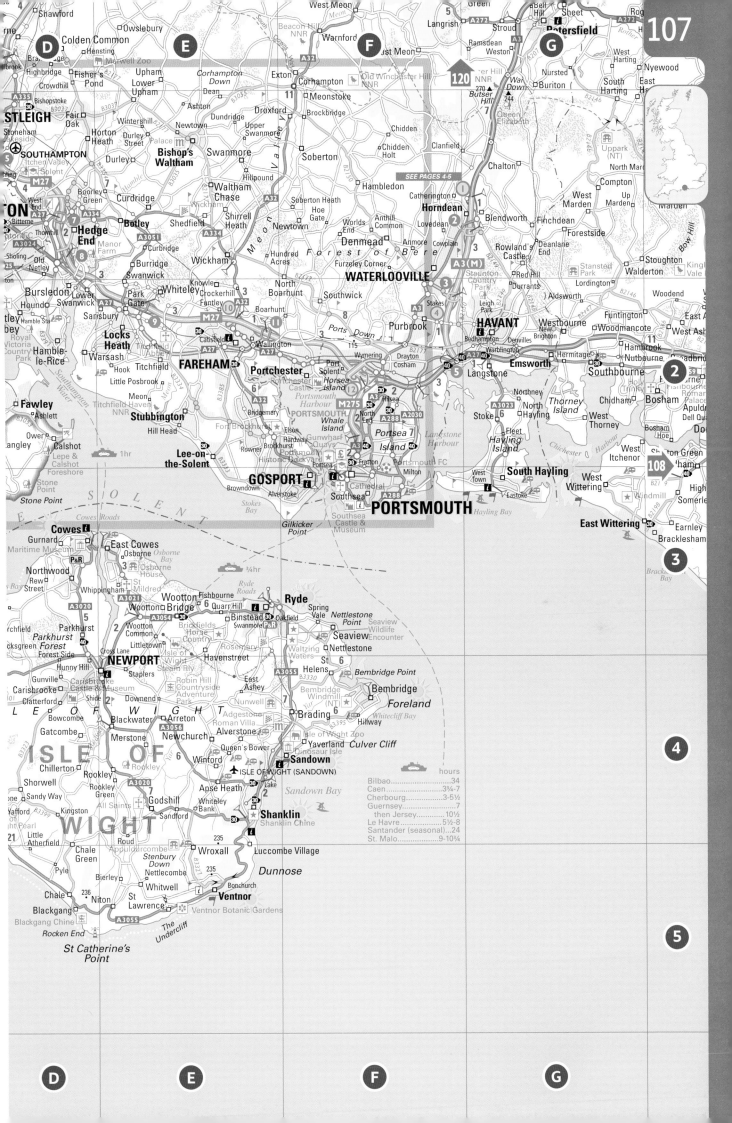

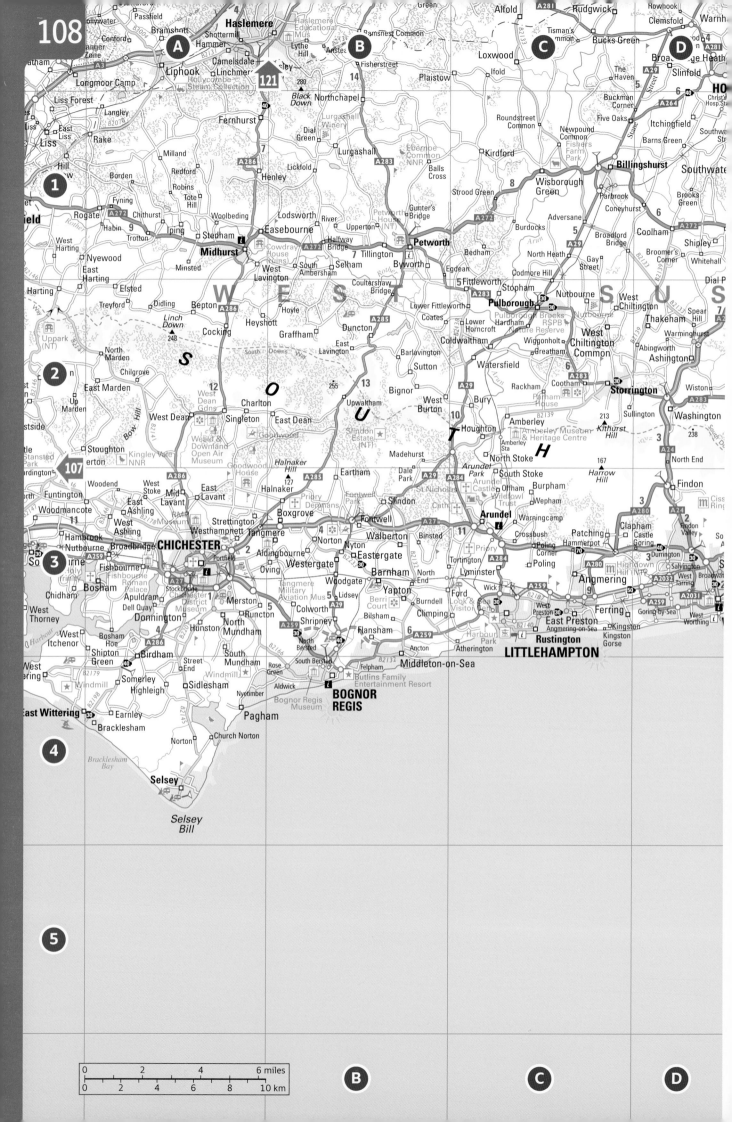

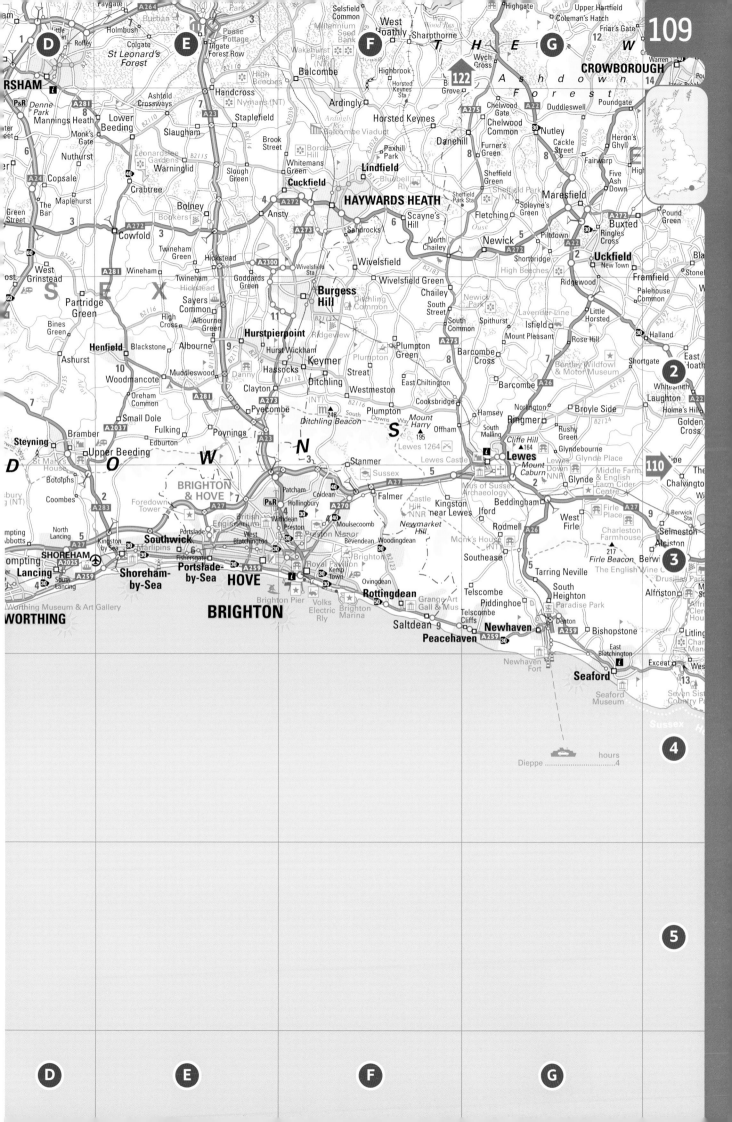

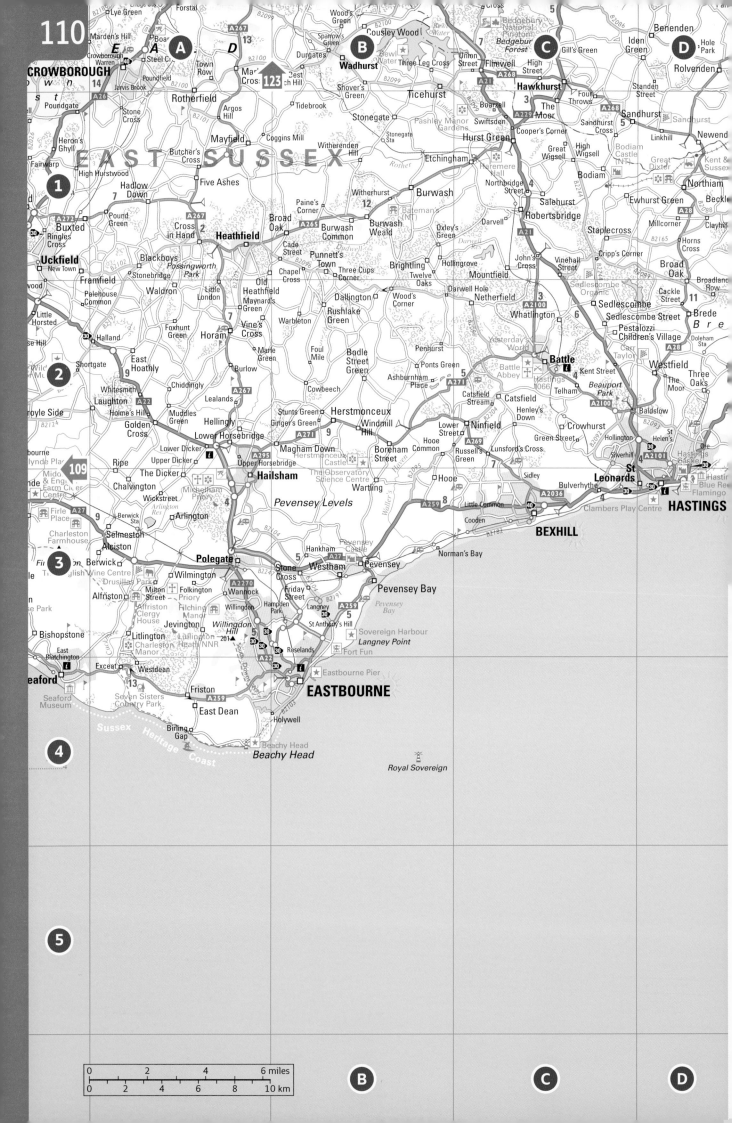

Channel Tunnel terminal maps

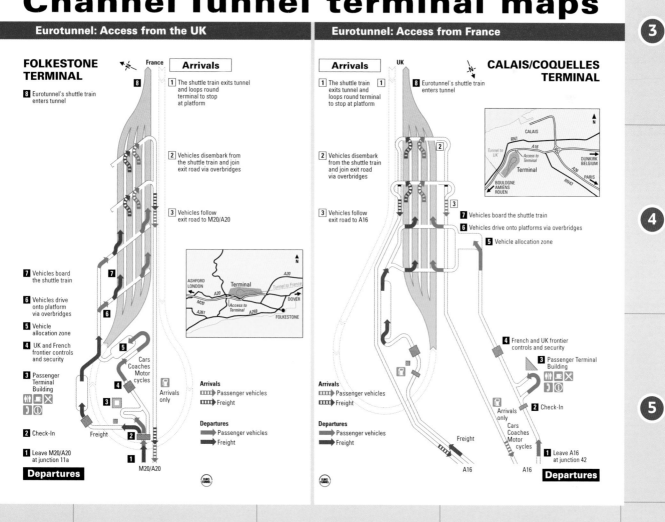

Eurotunnel: Access from the UK

FOLKESTONE TERMINAL

8 Eurotunnel's shuttle train enters tunnel

Arrivals

1 The shuttle train exits tunnel and loops round terminal to stop at platform

2 Vehicles disembark from the shuttle train and join exit road via overbridges

3 Vehicles follow exit road to M20/A20

7 Vehicles board the shuttle train

6 Vehicles drive onto platform via overbridges

5 Vehicle allocation zone

4 UK and French frontier controls and security

3 Passenger Terminal Building

2 Check-In

1 Leave M20/A20 at junction 11a

Departures

Cars Coaches Motor cycles

Arrivals only

M20/A20

Freight

Arrivals
Passenger vehicles
Freight

Departures
Passenger vehicles
Freight

ASHFORD LONDON — Terminal — Tunnel to France — DOVER — Access to Terminal — FOLKESTONE

Eurotunnel: Access from France

Arrivals

1 The shuttle train exits tunnel and loops round terminal to stop at platform

2 Vehicles disembark from the shuttle train and join exit road via overbridges

3 Vehicles follow exit road to A16

8 Eurotunnel's shuttle train enters tunnel

CALAIS/COQUELLES TERMINAL

CALAIS — RN1 — A16 — Tunnel to UK — Terminal — Access to Terminal — DUNKIRK BELGIUM — A26 — PARIS — RN43 — BOULOGNE AMIENS ROUEN

7 Vehicles board the shuttle train

6 Vehicles drive onto platforms via overbridges

5 Vehicle allocation zone

4 French and UK frontier controls and security

3 Passenger Terminal Building

2 Check-In

Arrivals only

Cars Coaches Motor cycles

1 Leave A16 at junction 42

Departures

Freight

A16

Arrivals
Passenger vehicles
Freight

Departures
Passenger vehicles
Freight

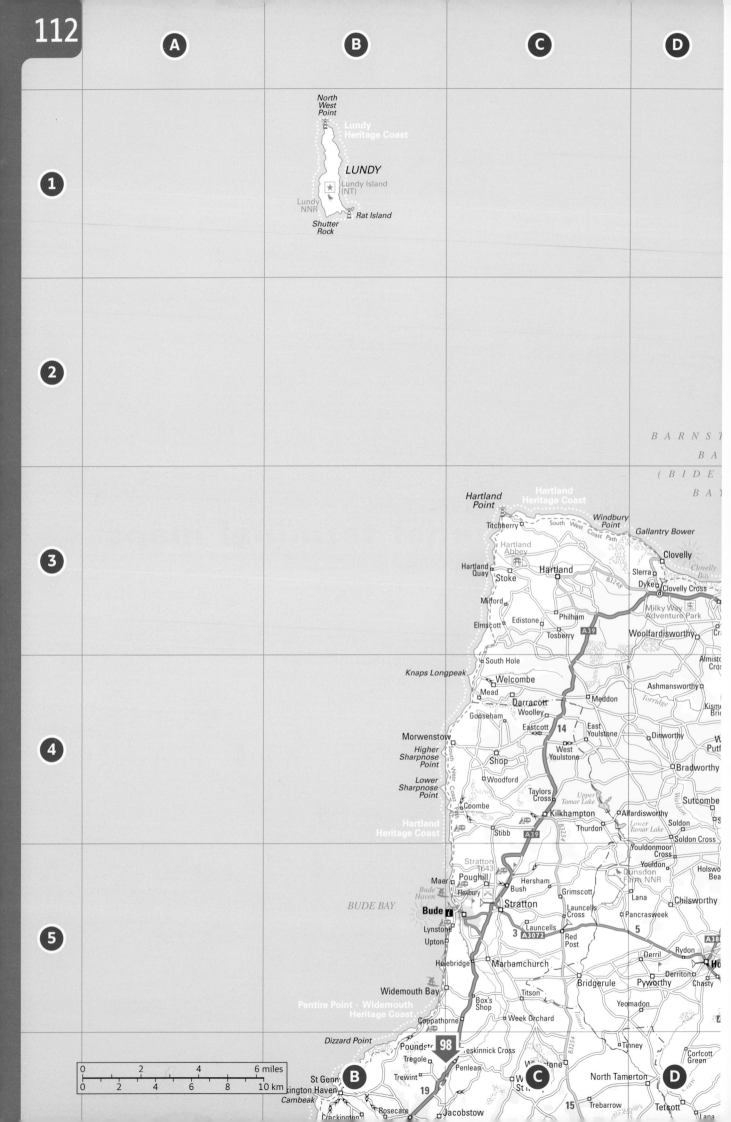

A   B   C   D

1

2

3

4

5

North West Point

Lundy Heritage Coast

LUNDY

Lundy Island (NT)

Lundy NNR

★

Rat Island

Shutter Rock

BARNST...
BA...
(BIDE...
BAY...

Hartland Point

Hartland Heritage Coast

Windbury Point   *Gallantry Bower*

Titchberry   *South West Coast Path*

Clovelly
Clovelly Bay

Hartland Abbey

Hartland Quay   Stoke   **Hartland**   Slerra

Dyke   Clovelly Cross

Milford   B3248

Milky Way Adventure Park

Edistone   Philham   A39   Cr...

Elmscott   Tosberry   **Woolfardisworthy**

South Hole   Almisto... Cros...

Knaps Longpeak   **Welcombe**   Ashmansworthy

Mead   Darracott   Meddon   *Torridge*

Gooseham   Woolley   East Youlstone   Dinworthy   Kism.. Bri...

Morwenstow   Eastcott   14

Higher Sharpnose Point   Shop   West Youlstone   Bradworthy

Woodford

Lower Sharpnose Point   Taylors Cross   *Upper Tamar Lake*   Sutcombe

Coombe   Kilkhampton   Alfardisworthy   Soldon   W...

Hartland Heritage Coast   B3254   Thurdon   *Lower Tamar Lake*   Soldon Cross

Stibb   A39   Youldonmoor Cross

Stratton 1643   Youldon   Holsw... Bea...

Dunsdon Farm NNR

Maer   Poughill   Hersham Bush   Lana   Chilsworthy

Bude Haven   Flexbury   Grimscott

BUDE BAY   **Bude**   **Stratton**   Launcells Cross   Pancrasweek

Lynstone   3   A3072   5

Upton   Launcells   Red Post   Derril   Rydon   A38

Helebridge   **Marhamchurch**   Bridgerule   Pyworthy   Derriton   Chasty   H...

Titson   Yeomadon

Widemouth Bay   Box's Shop   Week Orchard   Tinney

Pentire Point - Widemouth Heritage Coast   Corfcott Green

Dizzard Point   Coppathorne   98   ...eskinnick Cross   W...   **North Tamerton**

Poundst...   Tregole   **C**   W... St...   Tetcott

St Genn...   **B**   Trewint   Penlean   15   Trebarrow

...kington Haven   19   Lana

Cambeak   Rosecare   **Jacobstow**

Crackington

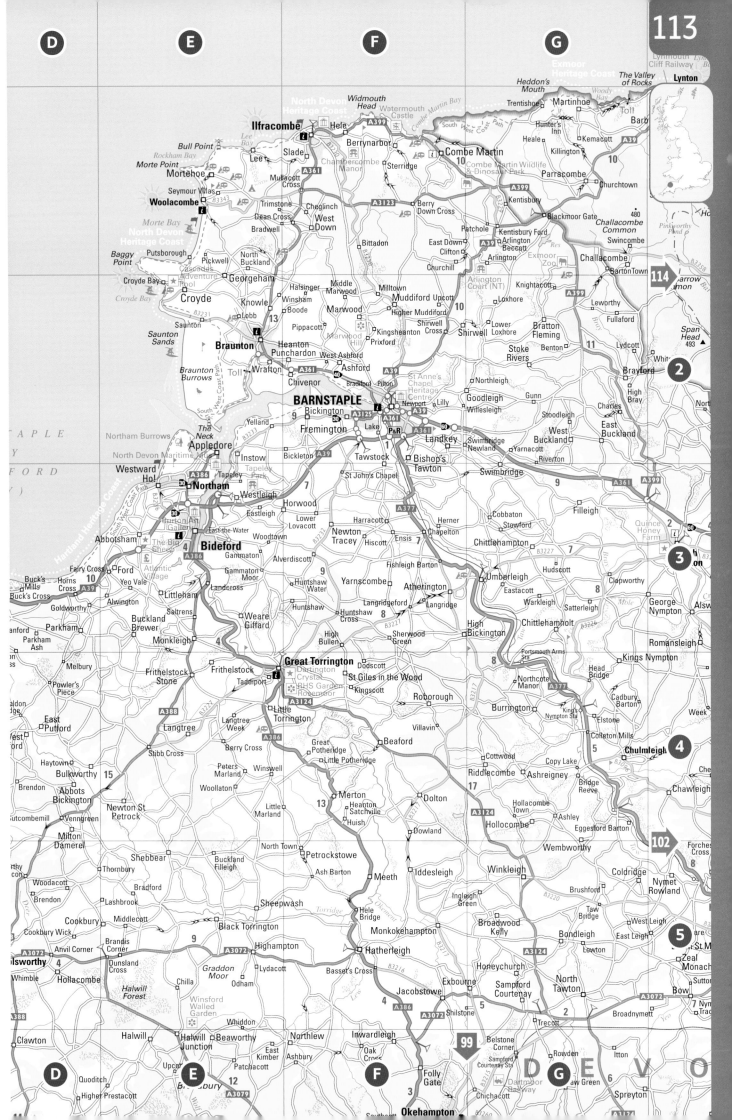

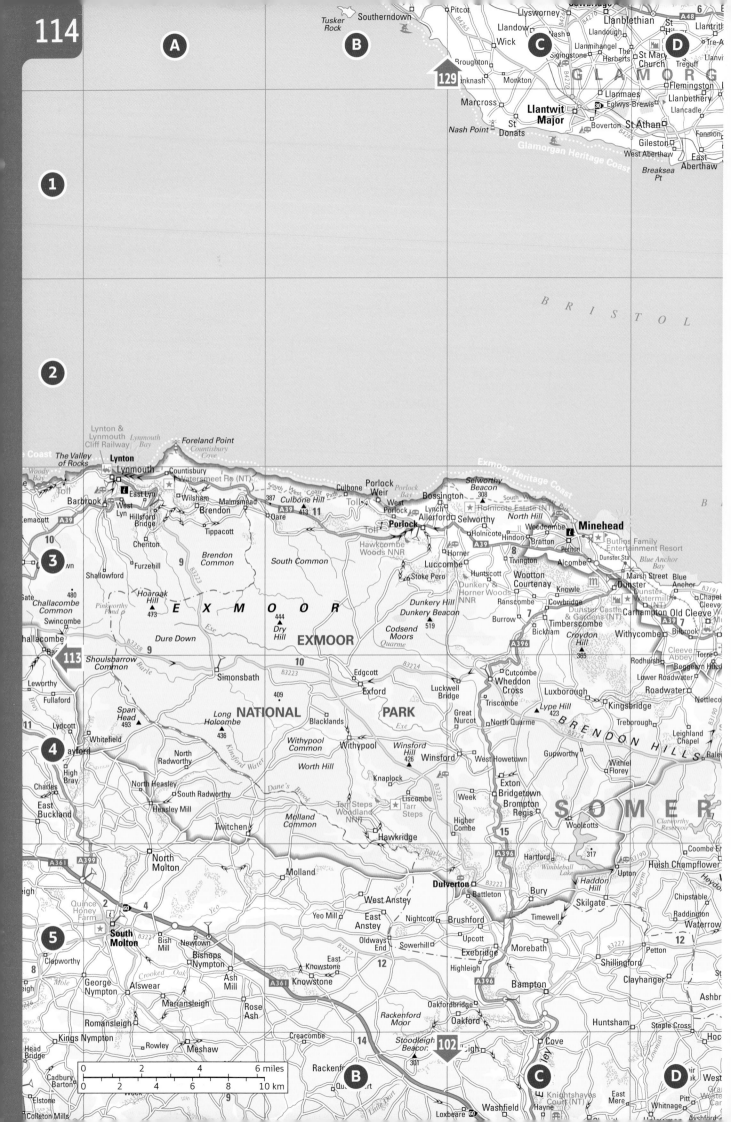

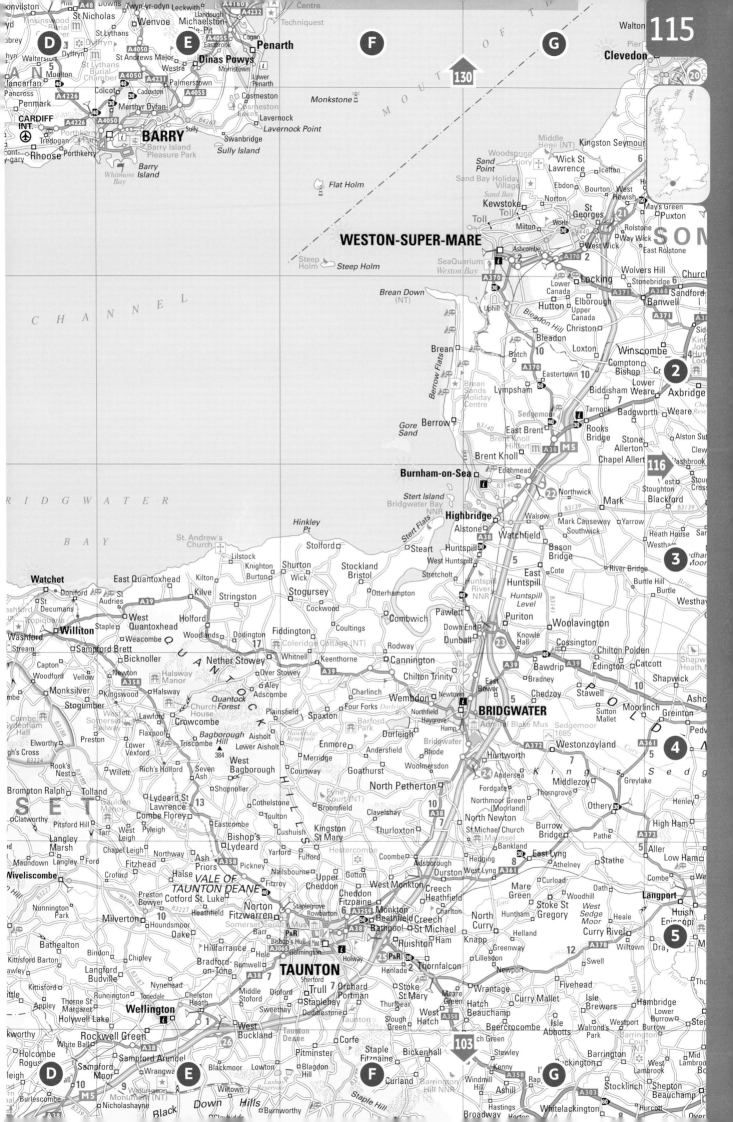

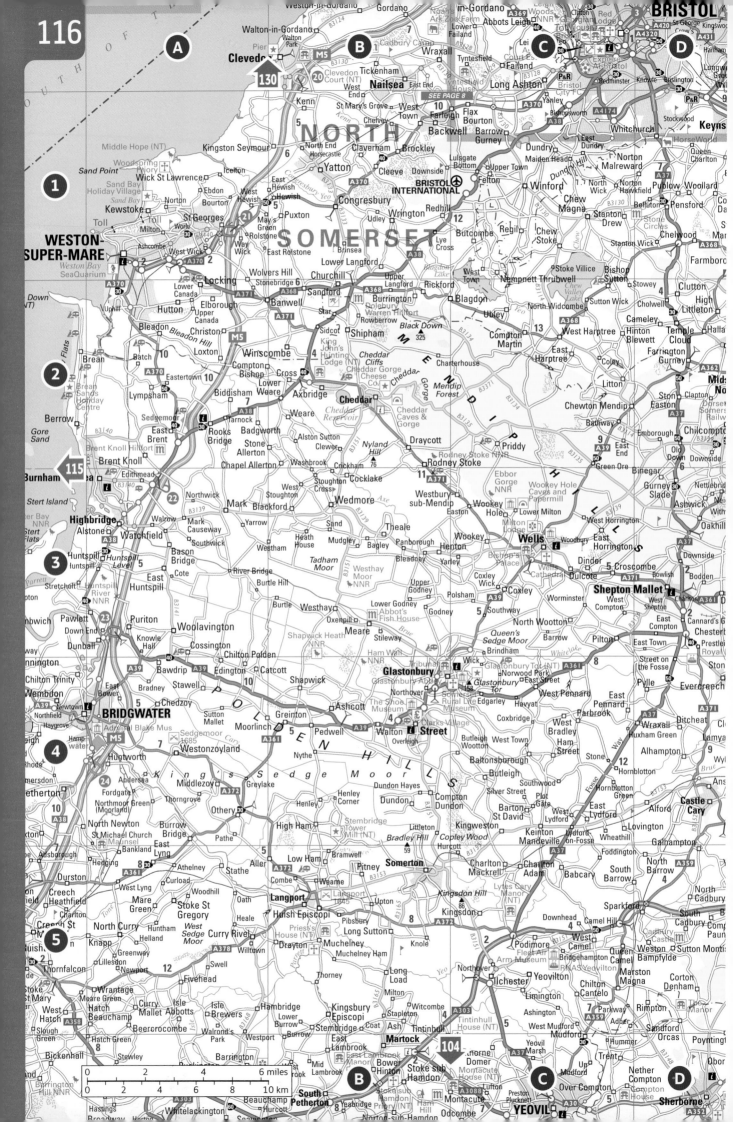

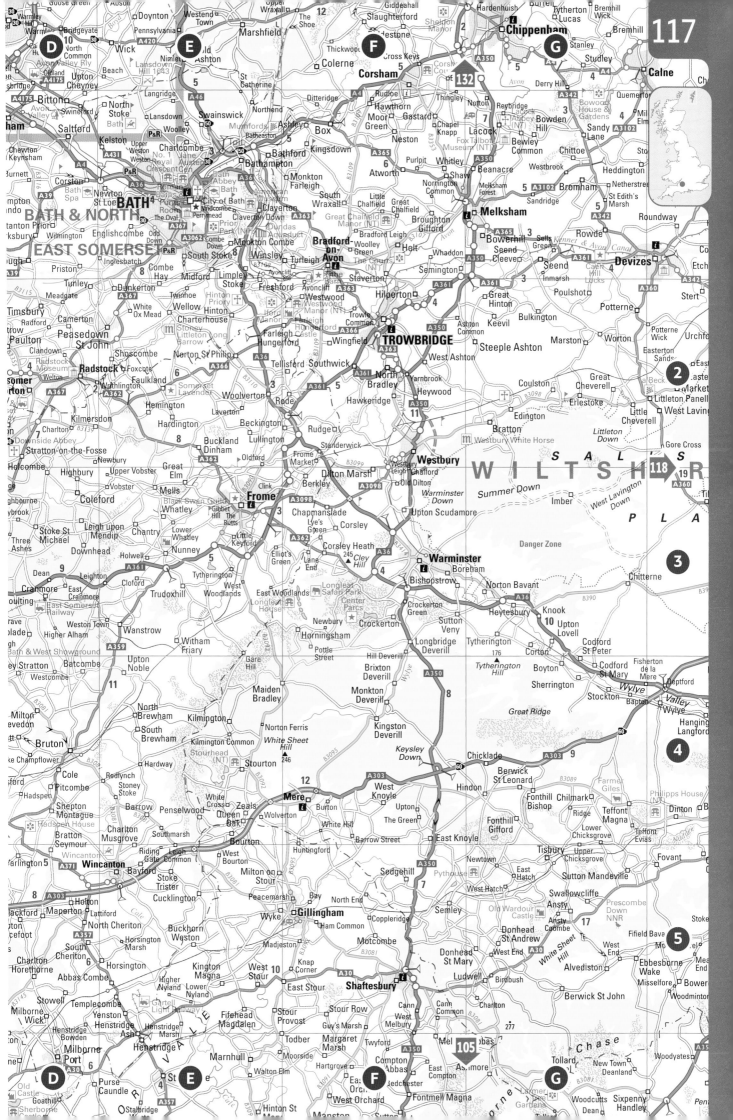

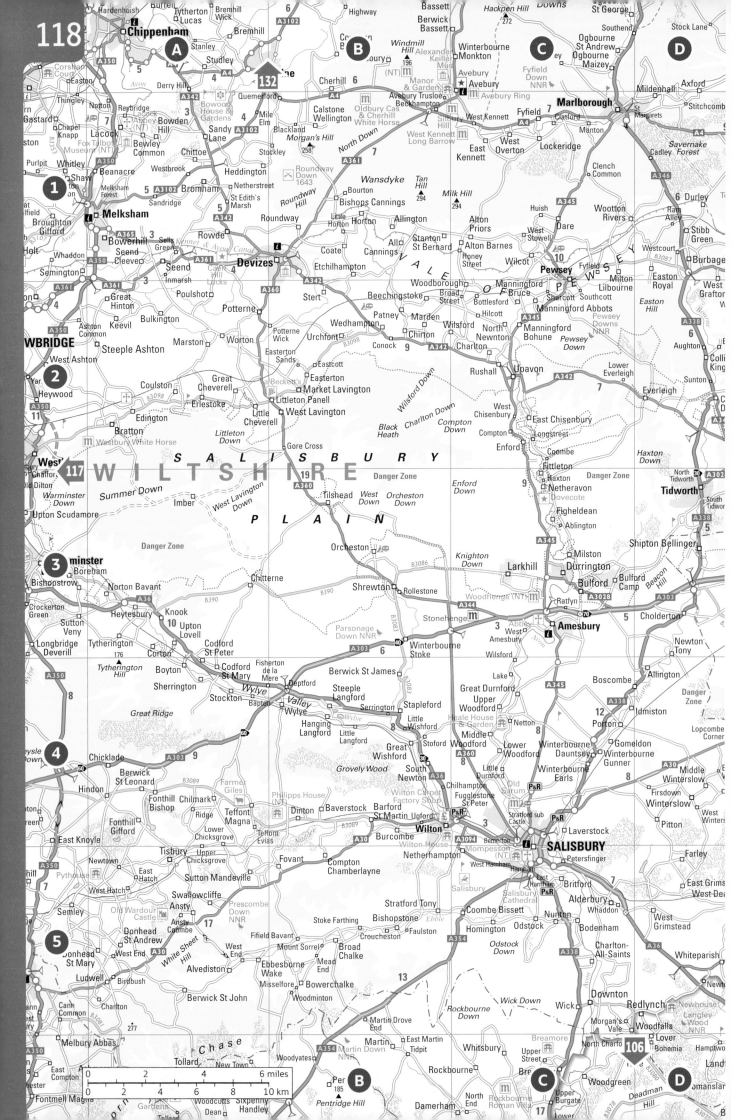

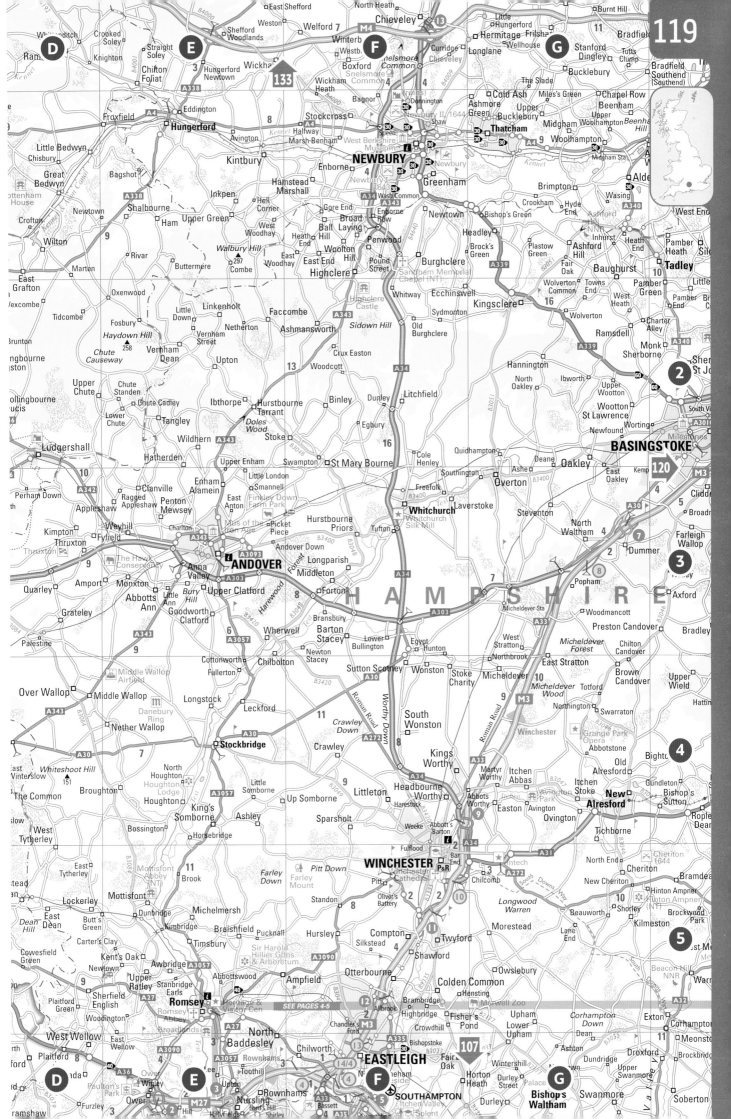

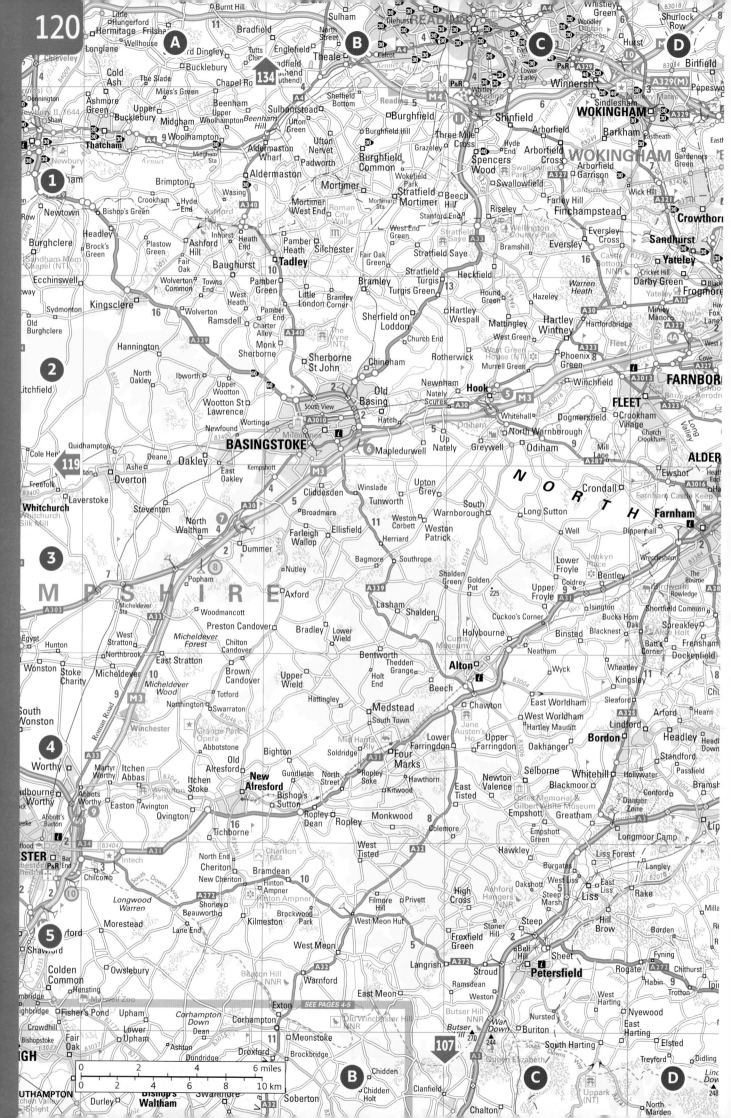

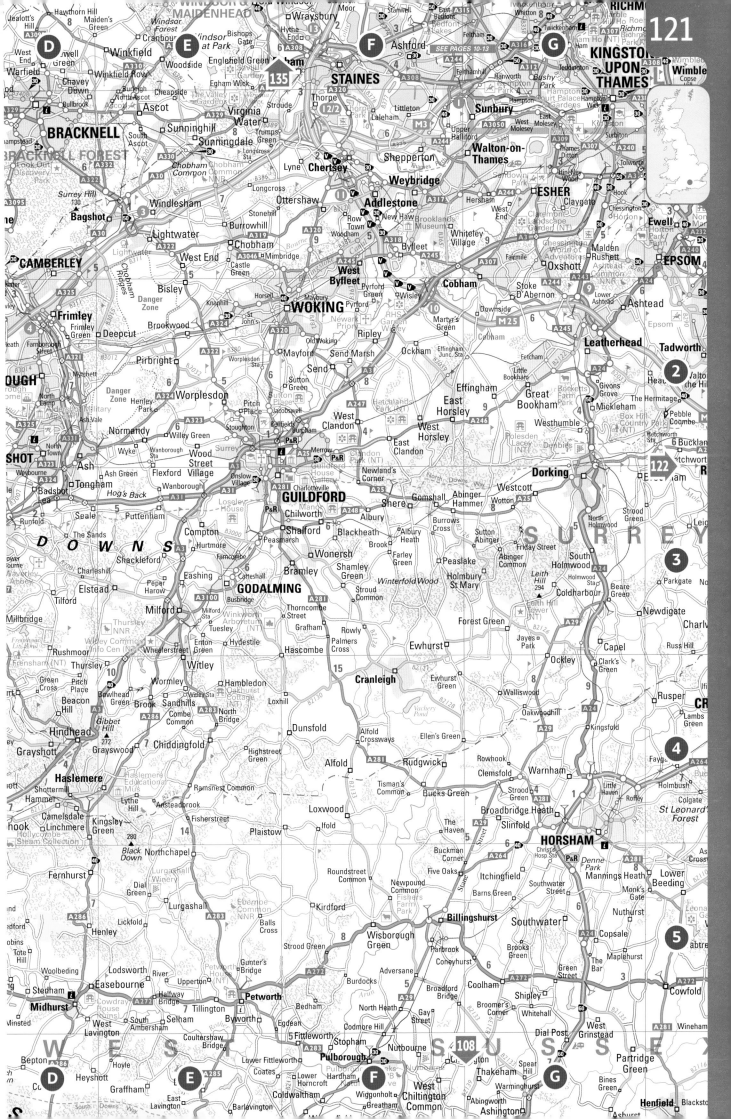

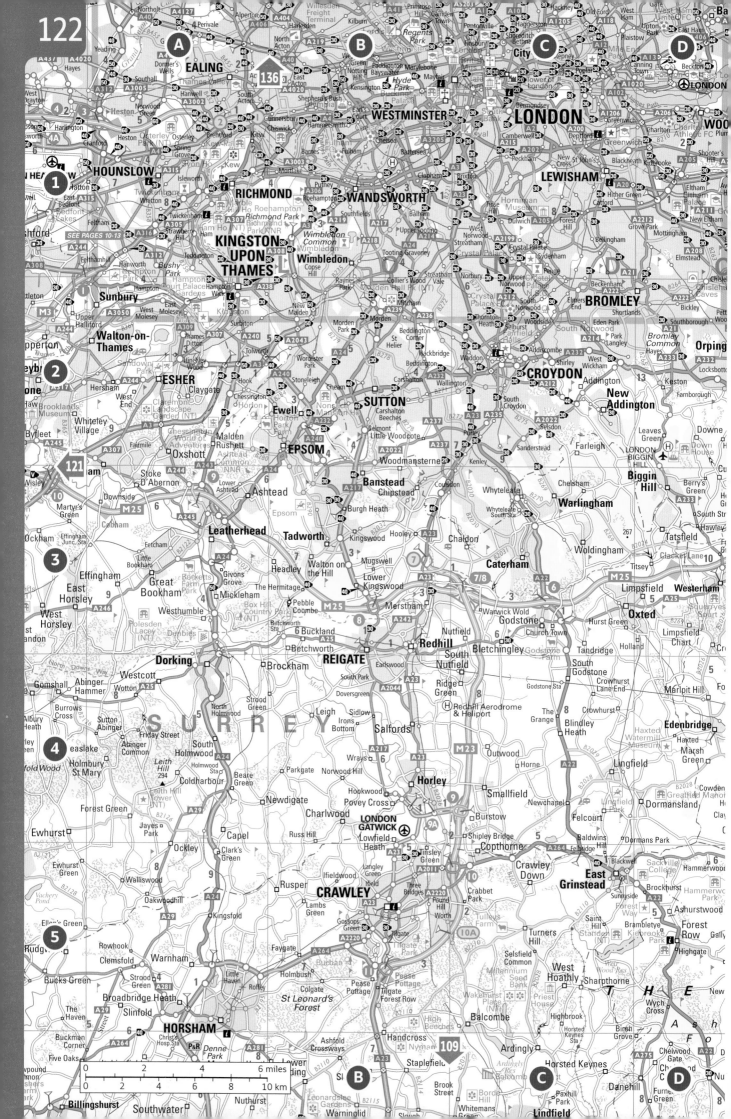

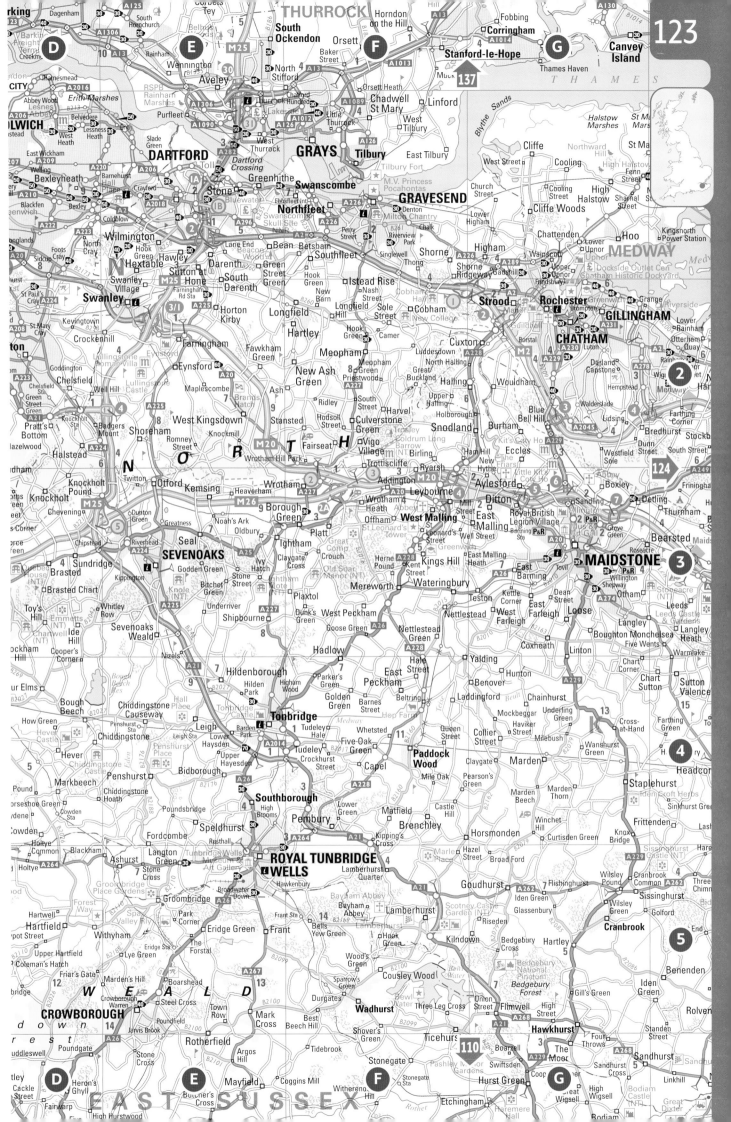

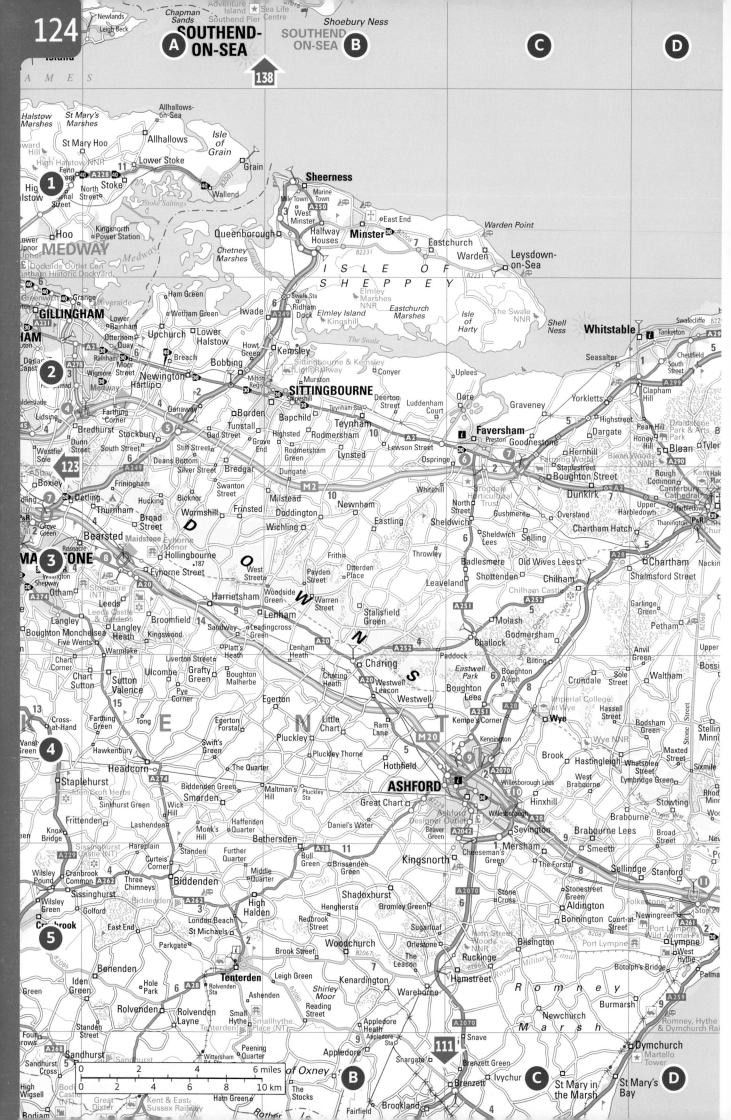

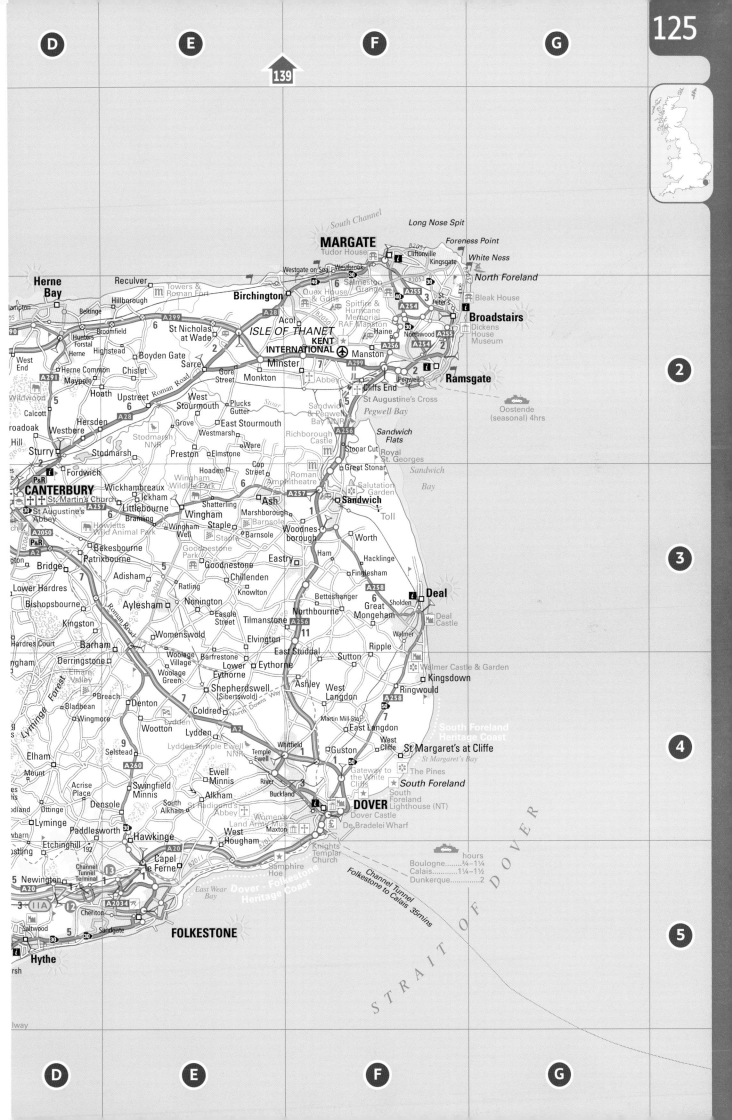

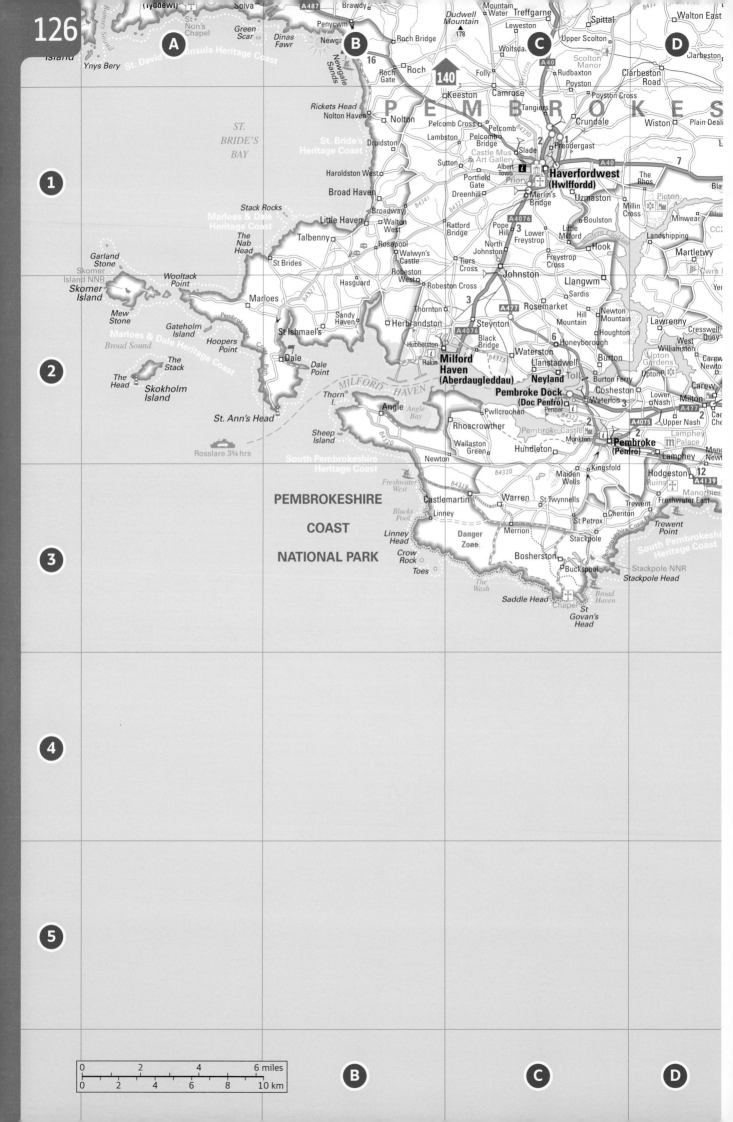

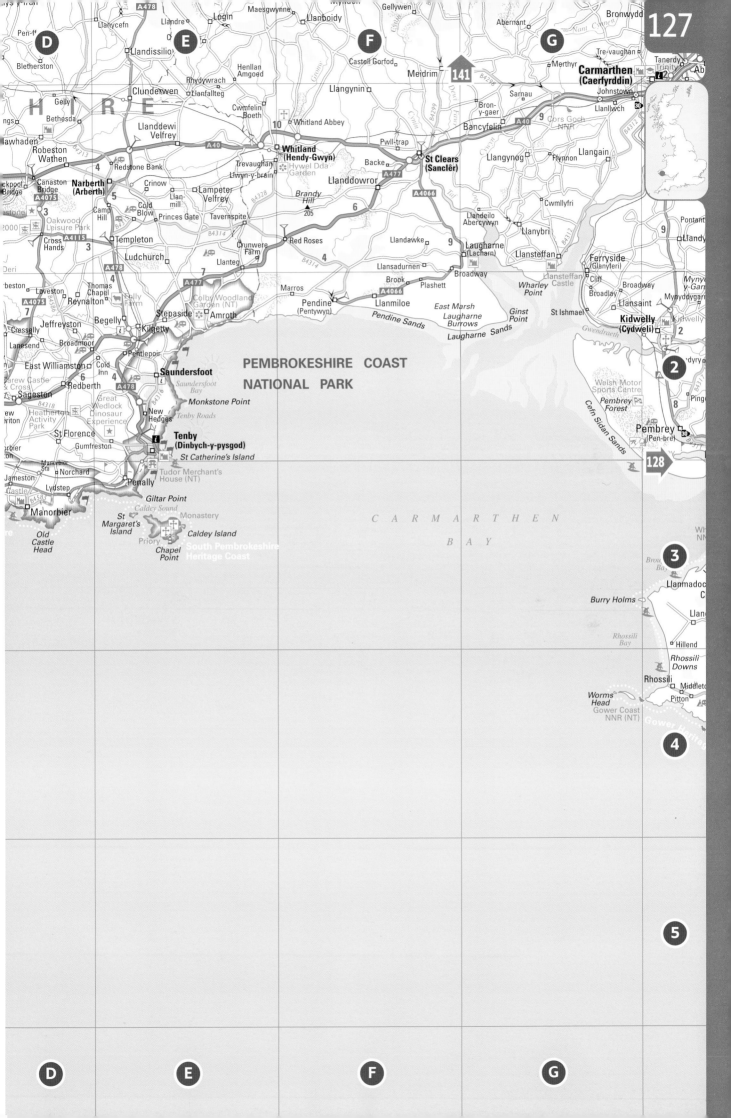

PEMBROKESHIRE COAST NATIONAL PARK

CARMARTHEN BAY

South Pembrokeshire Heritage Coast

Gower Coast NNR (NT)

Gower Heritage

141

128

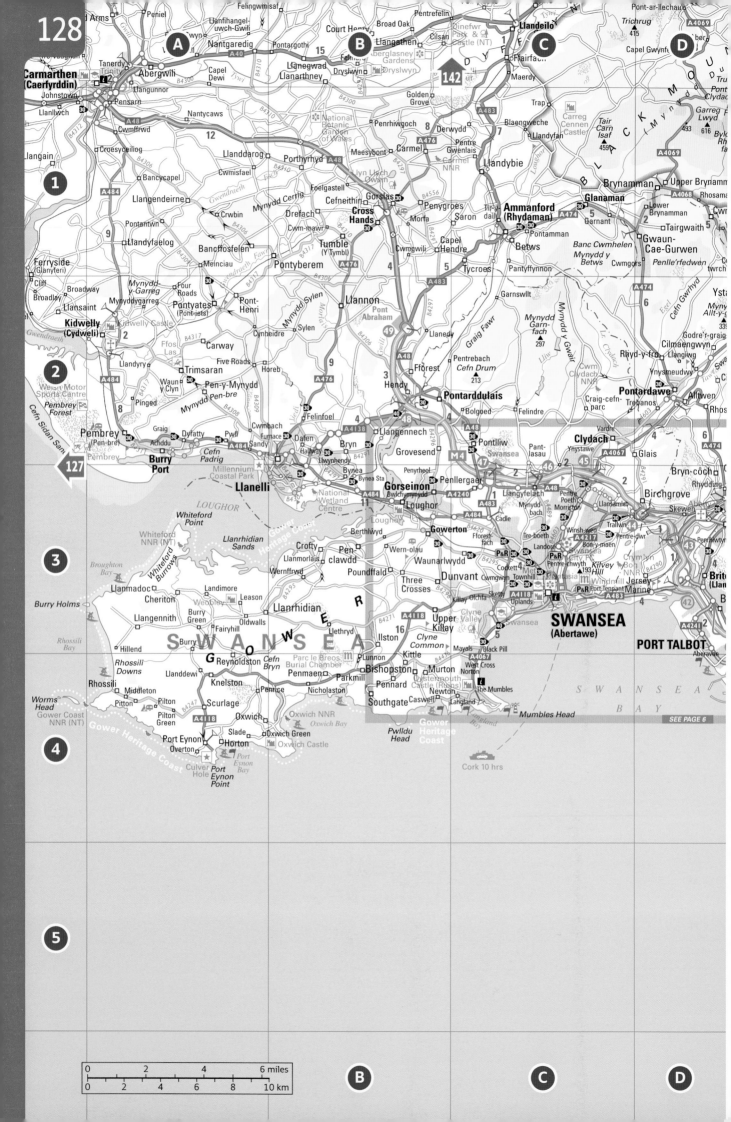

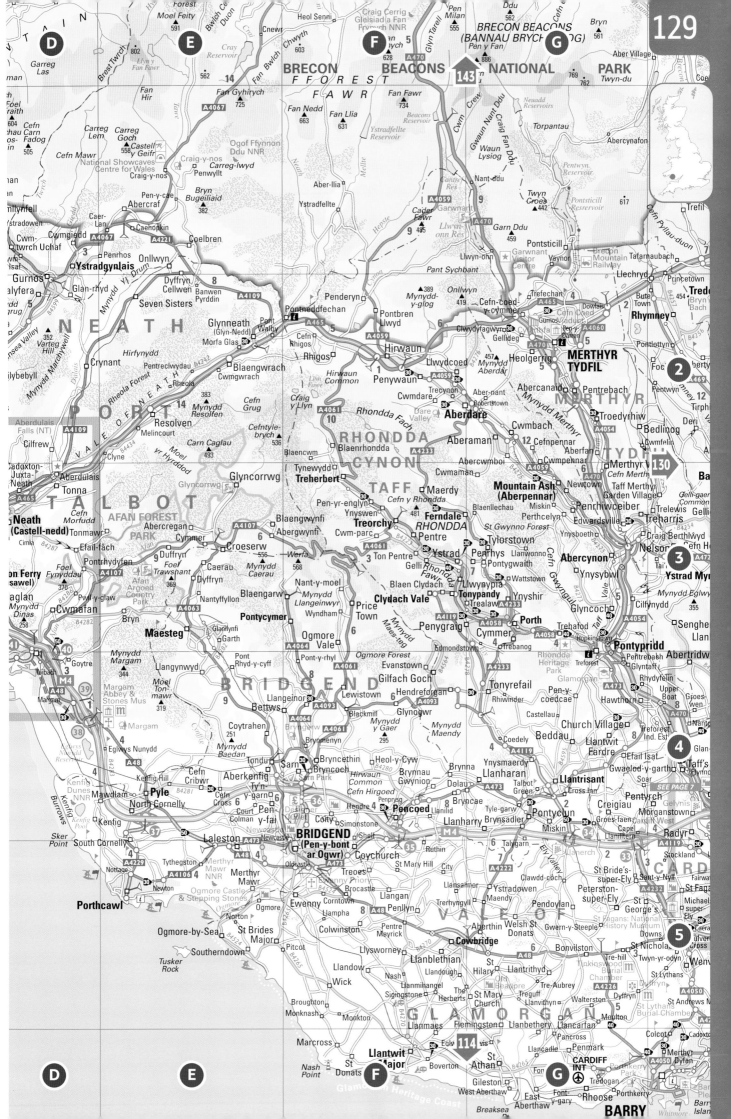

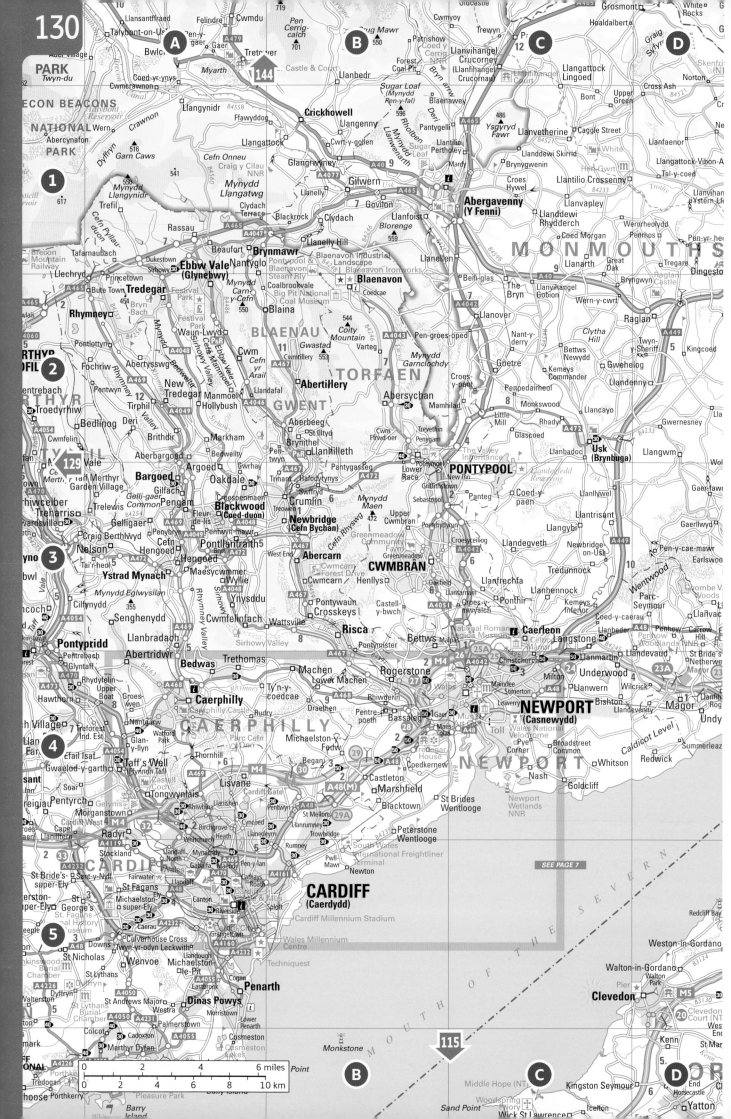

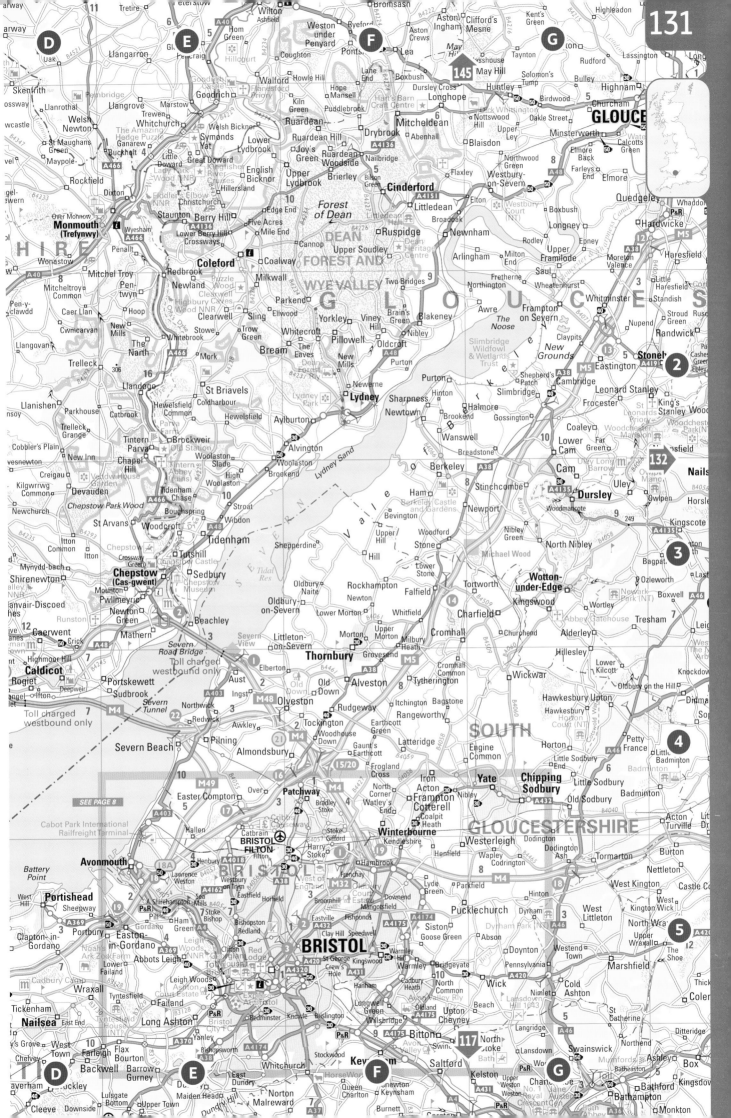

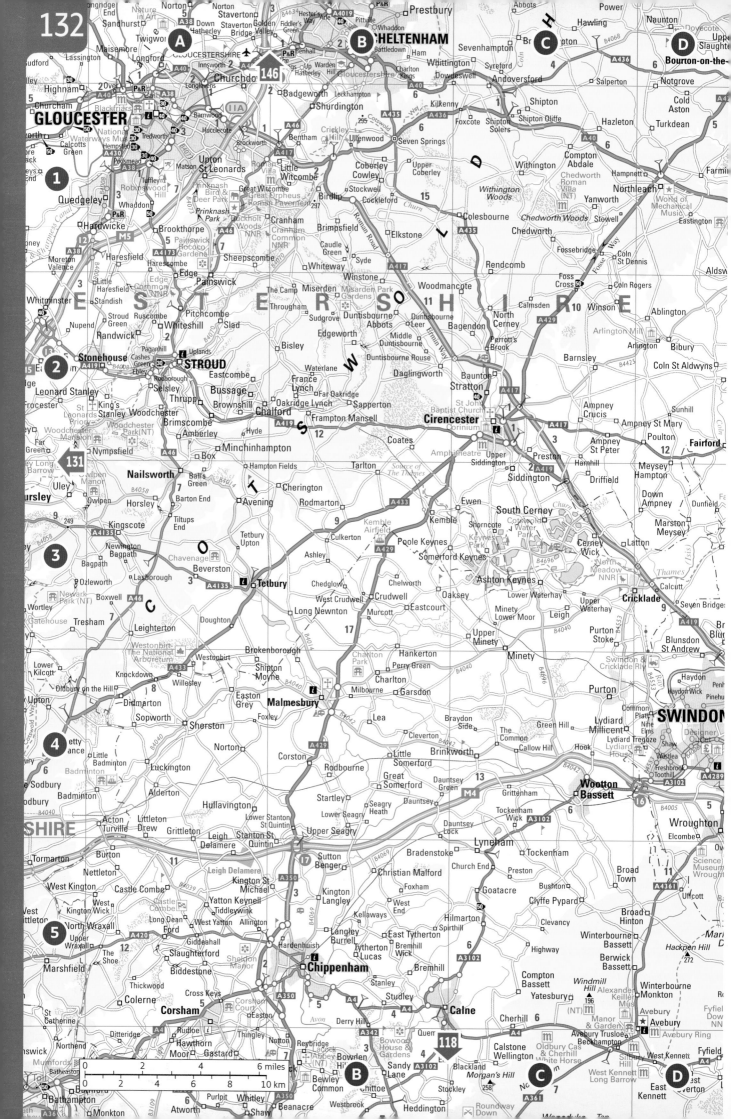

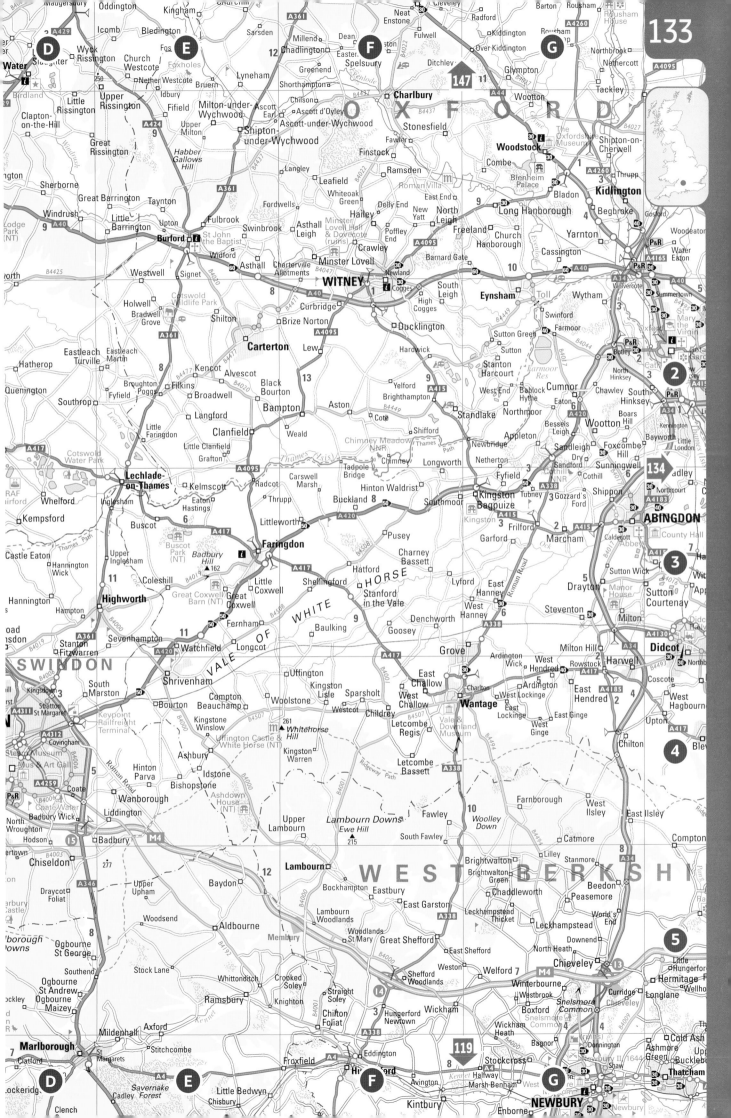

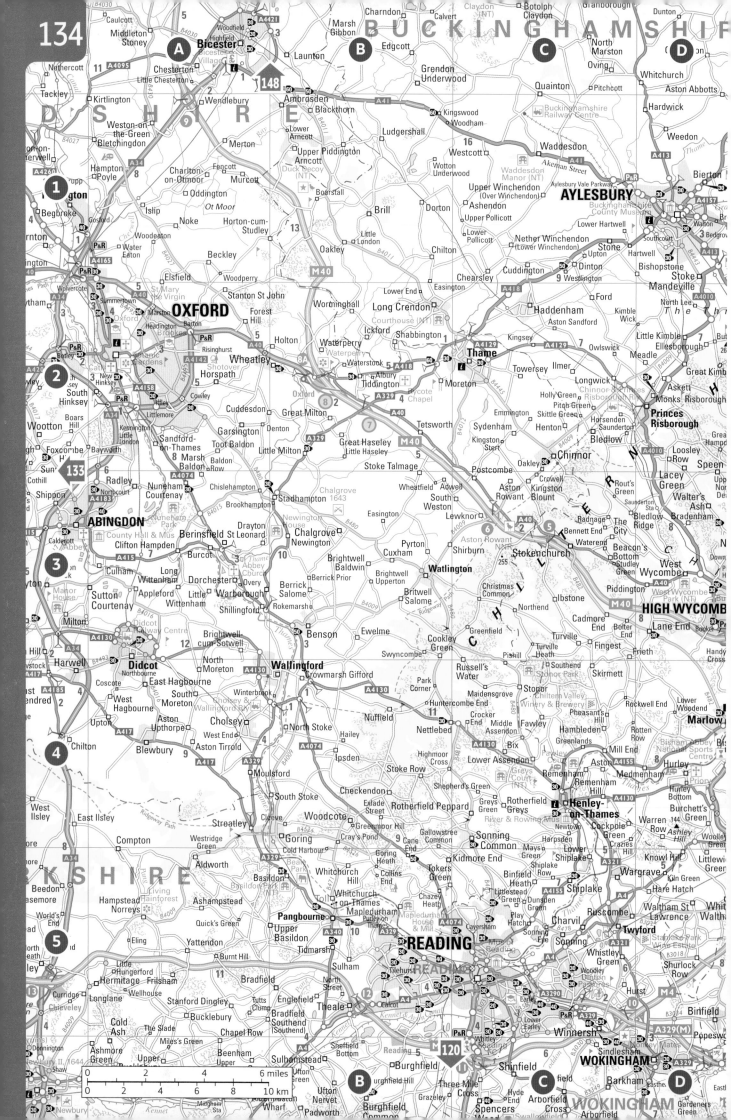

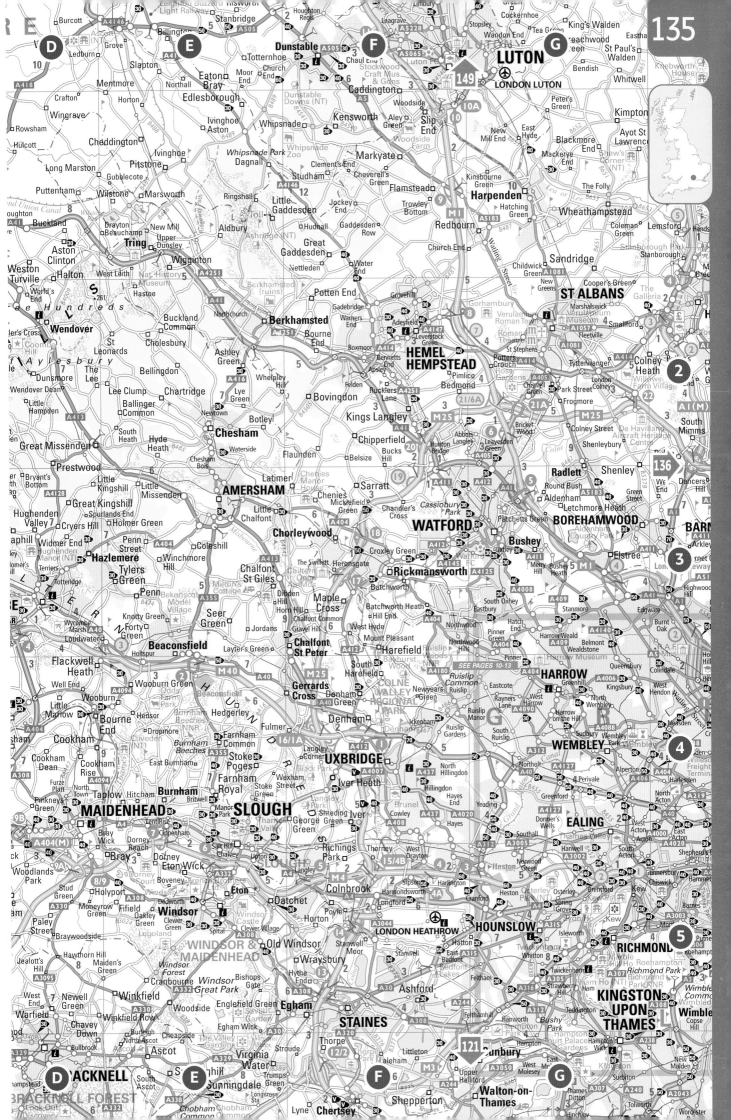

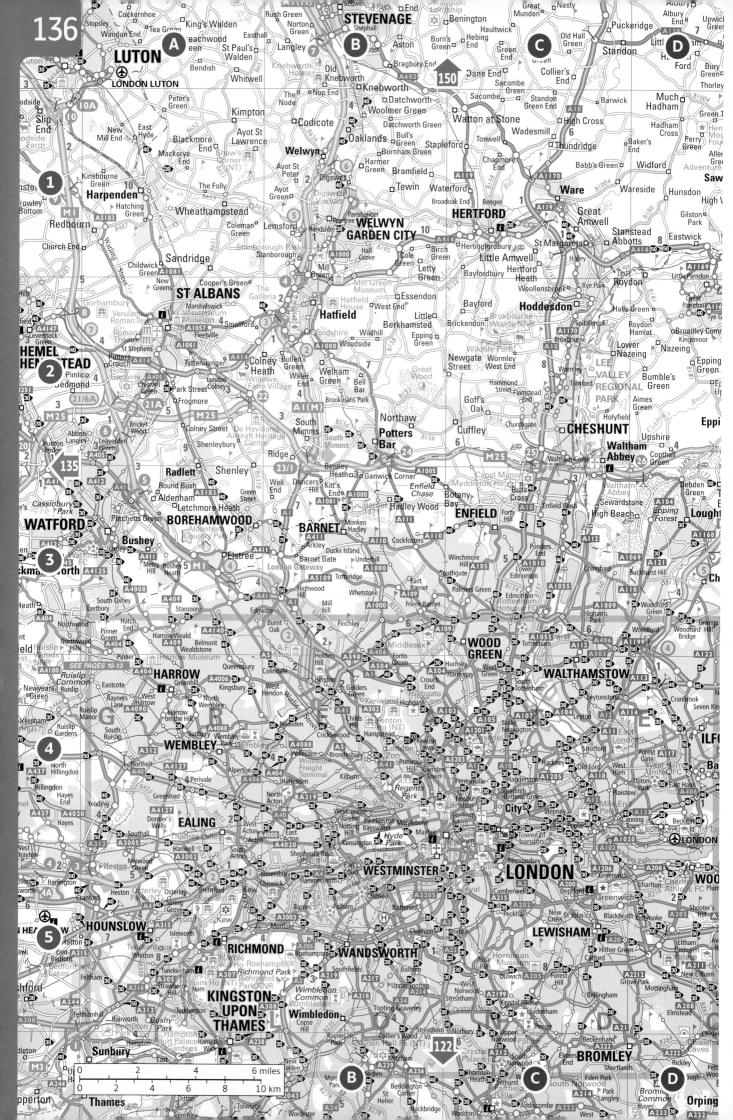

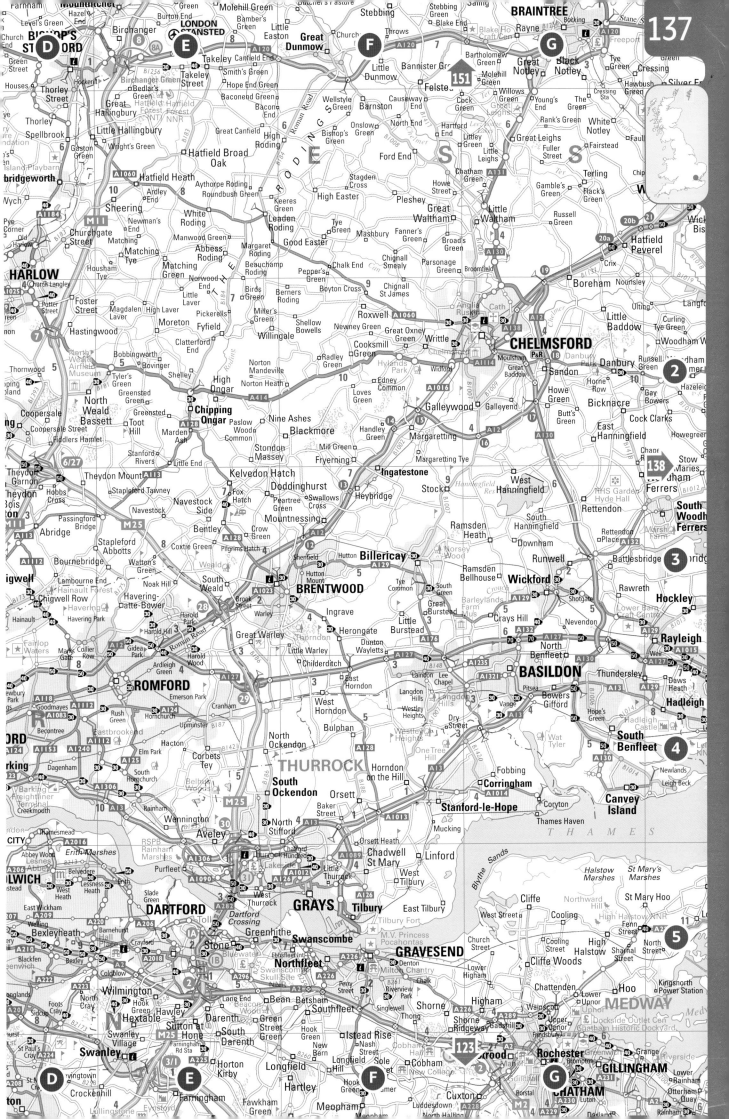

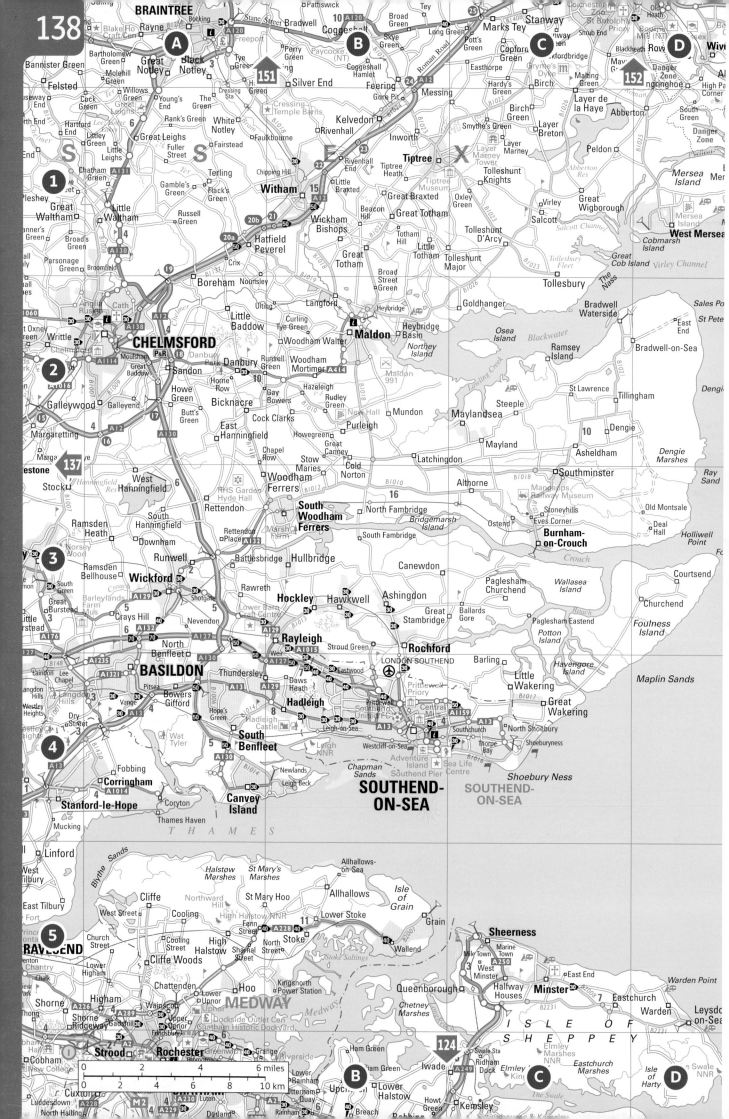

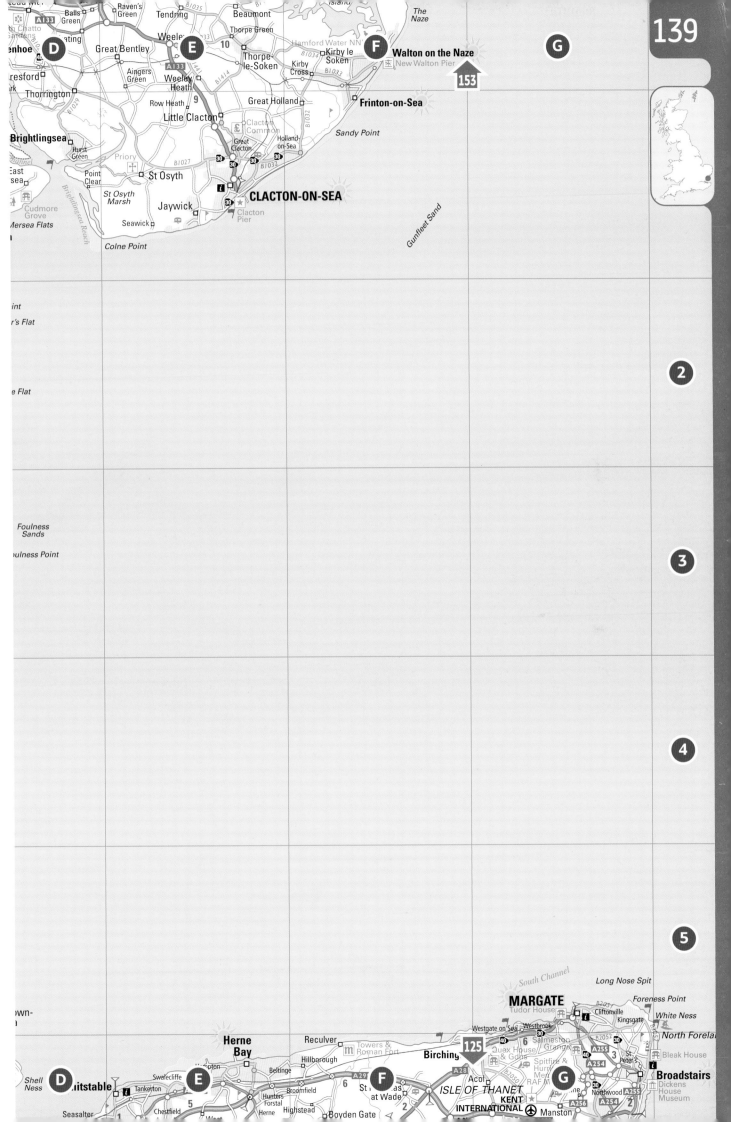

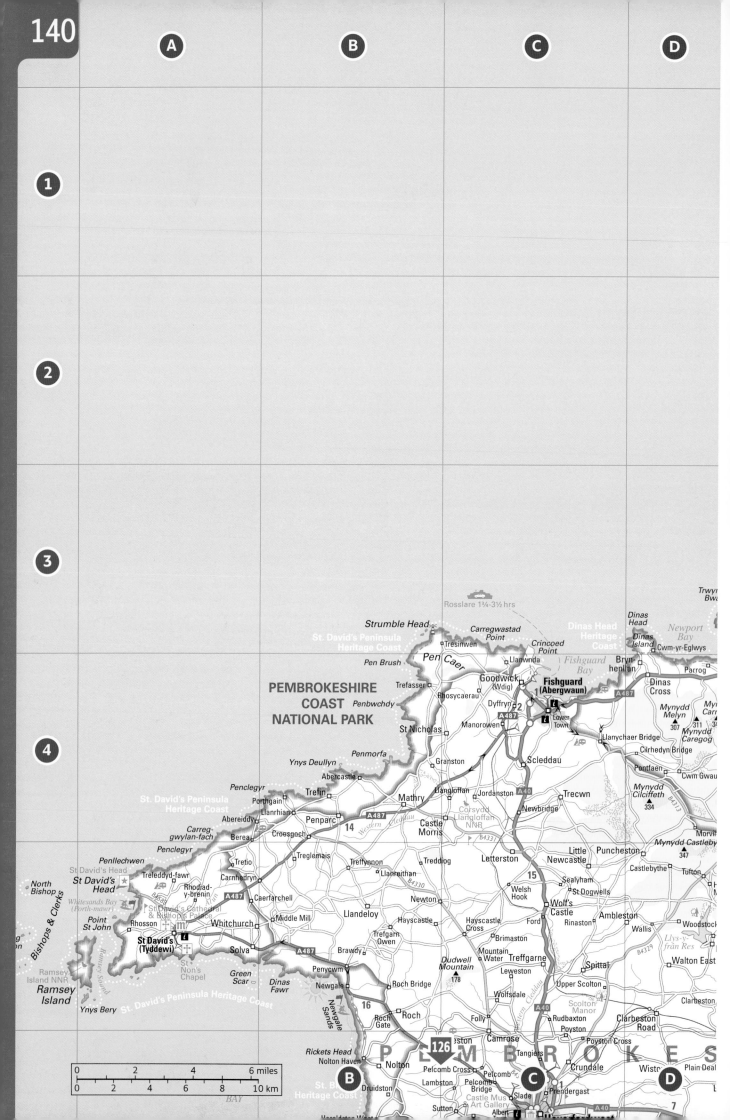

A B C D

1

2

3

Rosslare 1¾-3½ hrs

Strumble Head

Carregwastad
Point

Dinas Head
Heritage
Coast

Dinas
Head

Trwyn
Bwa

St. David's Peninsula
Heritage Coast

Tresinwen

Crincoed
Point

Dinas
Island

Cwm-yr-Eglwys

Newport
Bay

Pen Brush

Pen Caer

Llanwnda

Fishguard
Bay

Bryn-
henllan

Parrog

PEMBROKESHIRE
COAST
NATIONAL PARK

Trefasser

Goodwick
(Wdig)

Fishguard
(Abergwaun)

Dinas
Cross

Penbwchdy

Rhosycaerau

Dyffryn

Lower
Town

Mynydd
Melyn

Myr
Carr

307

4

St Nicholas

Manorowen

311

Mynydd
Caregog

Penmorfa

Llanychaer Bridge

Cilrhedyn Bridge

347

Ynys Deullyn

Granston

Scleddau

Pontfaen

Cwm Gwau

Abercastle

Penclegyr

Llangloffan

Jordanston

Trecwn

Mynydd
Cilciffeth
334

Trefin

Mathry

Newbridge

Morvi

Porthgain

Penparc

Castle
Morris

Corsydd
Llangloffan
NNR

Mynydd Castleby
347

Llanrhian

Croesgoch

Letterston

Little
Newcastle

Puncheston

Abereiddy

Carreg-
gwylan-fach

Berea

Treglemais

Treffynnon

Treddiog

Castlebythe

Tufton

Penclegyr

Tretio

Llanreithan

15

Sealyham

St Dogwells

Welsh
Hook

Ambleston

Woodstoc

Penllechwen

St David's Head

Treleddyd-fawr

Carnhedryn

Newton

Wolf's
Castle

Rinaston

Wallis

Llys-y-
frân Res

North
Bishop

St David's
Head

Rhodiad-
y-brenin

Caerfarchell

Hayscastle

Hayscastle
Cross

Ford

Whitesands Bay
(Porth-mawr)

St David's Cathedral
& Bishop's Palace

Llandeloy

Brimaston

Walton East

Point
St John

Rhosson

Middle Mill

Trefgarn
Owen

Mountain
Water

Treffgarne

Spittal

Bishops & Clerks

Whitchurch

Brawdy

Dudwell
Mountain
178

Leweston

Upper Scolton

Clarbeston

St David's
(Tyddewi)

Solva

Penycwm

Roch Bridge

Wolfsdale

Ramsey
Island NNR

St
Non's
Chapel

Green
Scar

Dinas
Fawr

Newgale

Roch

Folly

Scolton
Manor

Clarbeston
Road

Ramsey
Island

St. David's Peninsula Heritage Coast

Newgale
Sands

16

Roch
Gate

Rudbaxton

Poyston

Ynys Bery

Camrose

Poyston Cross

Rickets Head

126

Tangiers

Plain Deal

Nolton Haven

Nolton

PEMBROKES

Pelcomb Cross

Pelcomb

Crundale

Wisto

PEMBROKES

Druidston

Lambston

Pelcomb
Bridge

Slade

St. B
Heritage Coast

Castle Mus
& Art Gallery

Sutton

Albert

Prendergast

7

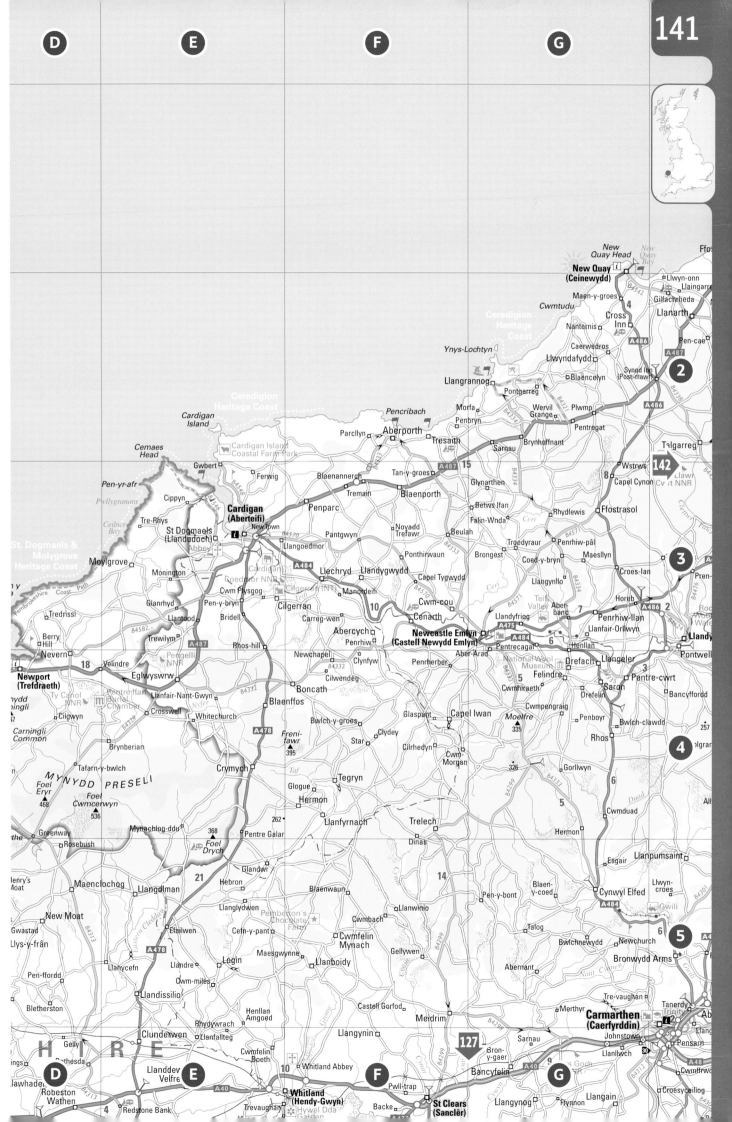

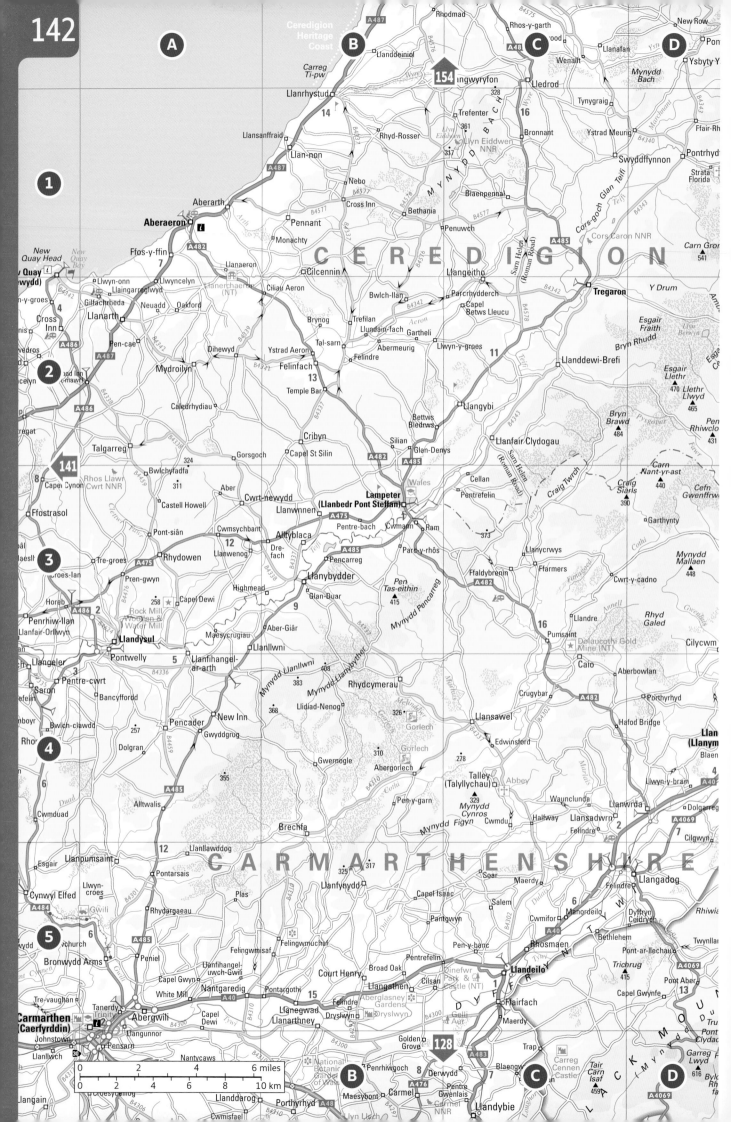

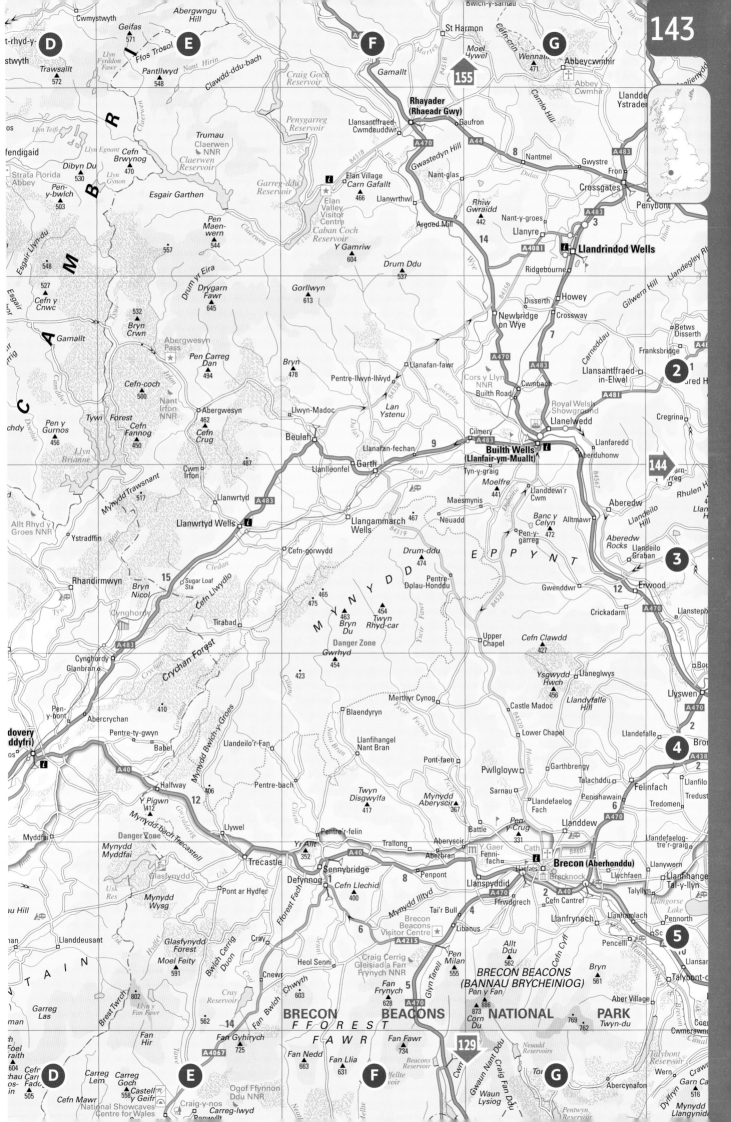

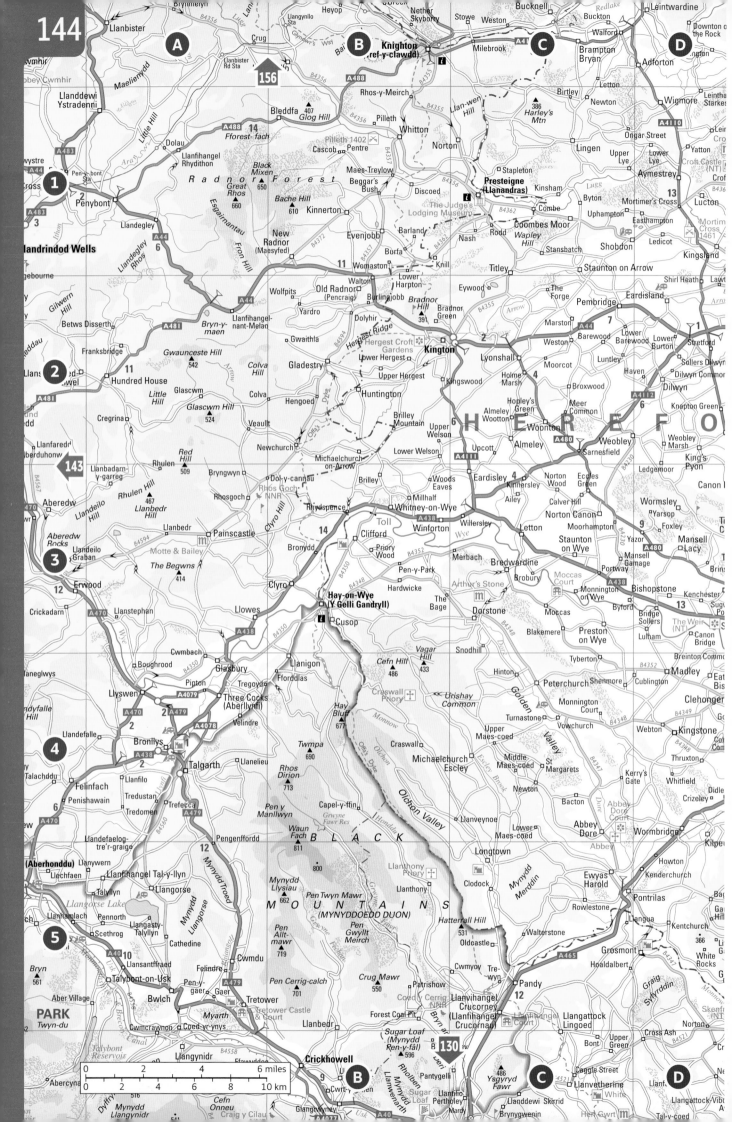

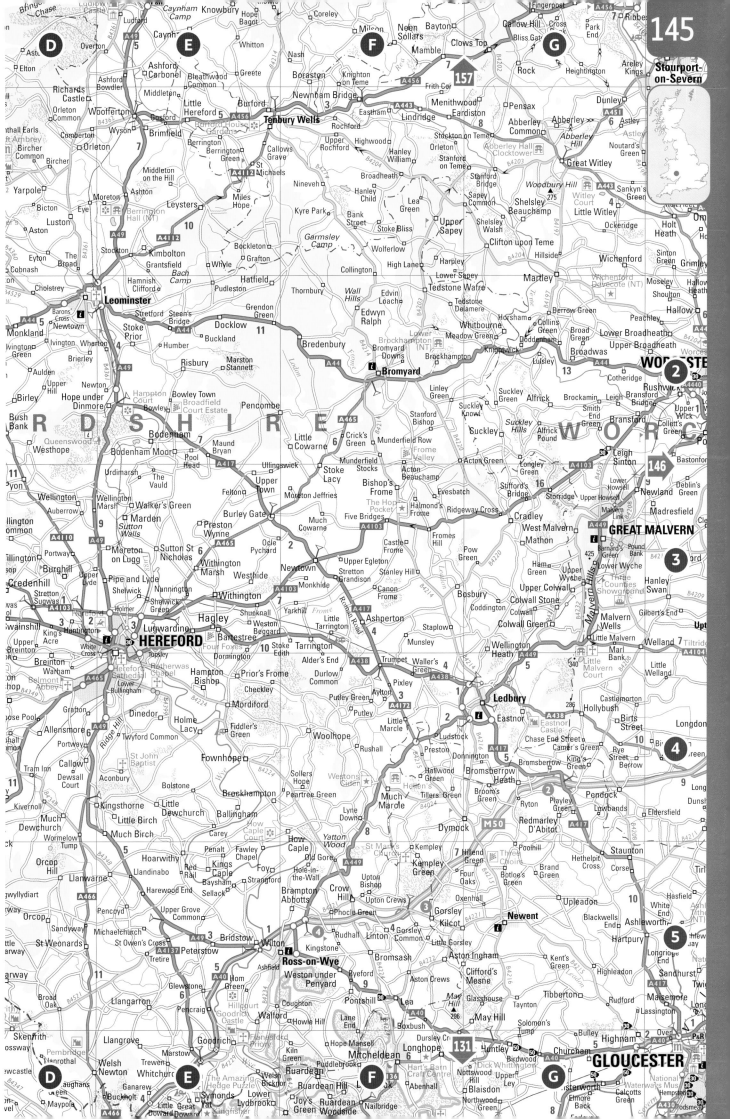

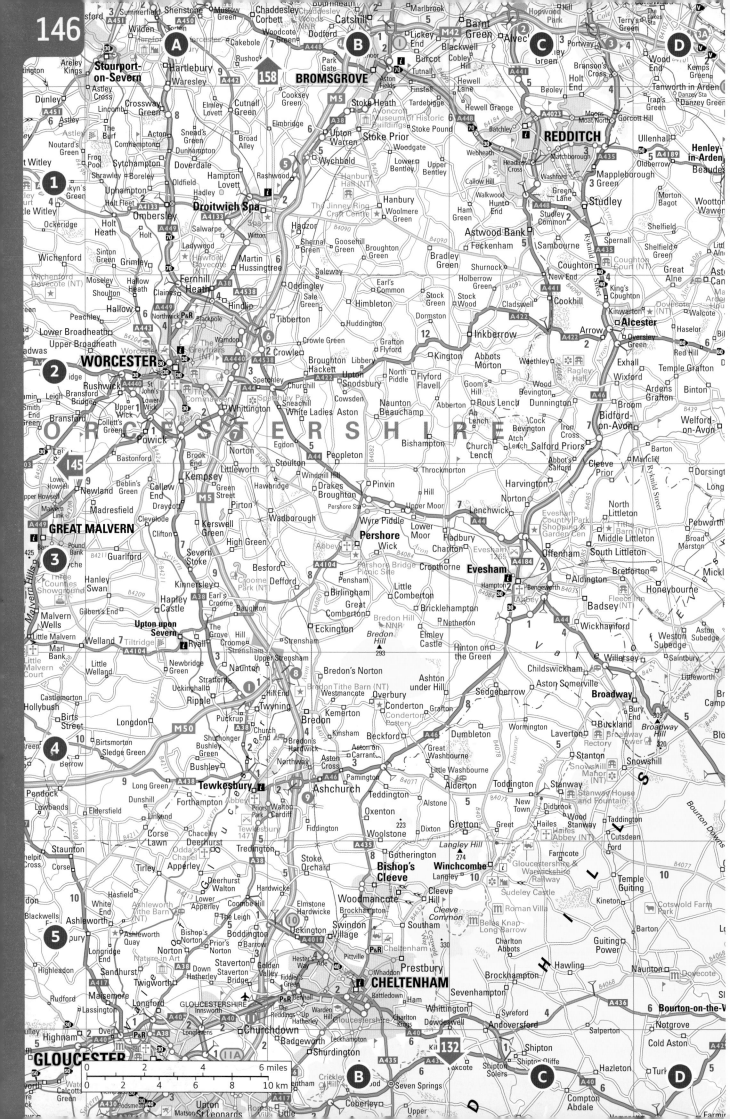

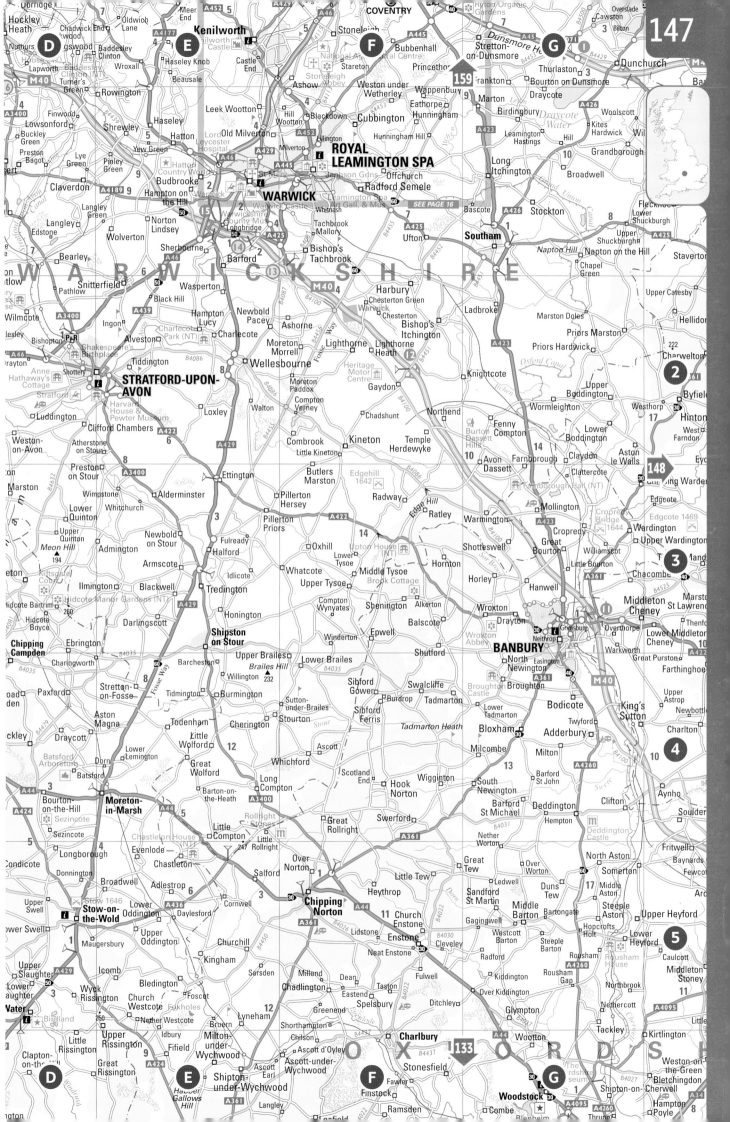

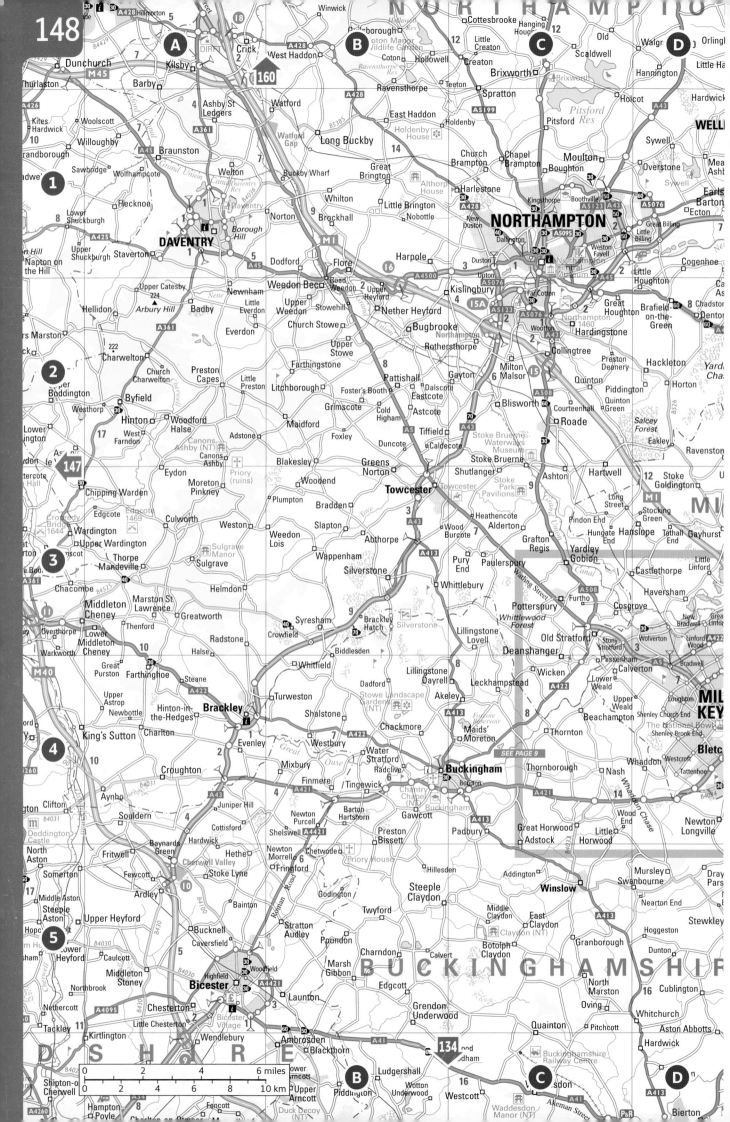

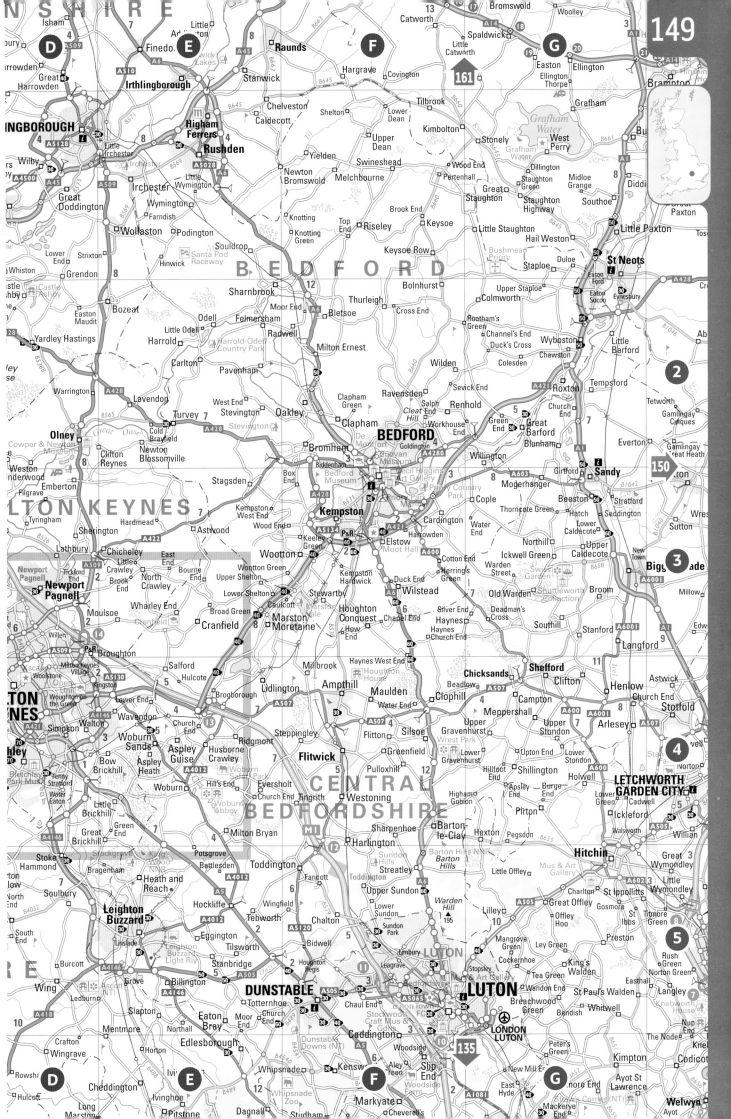

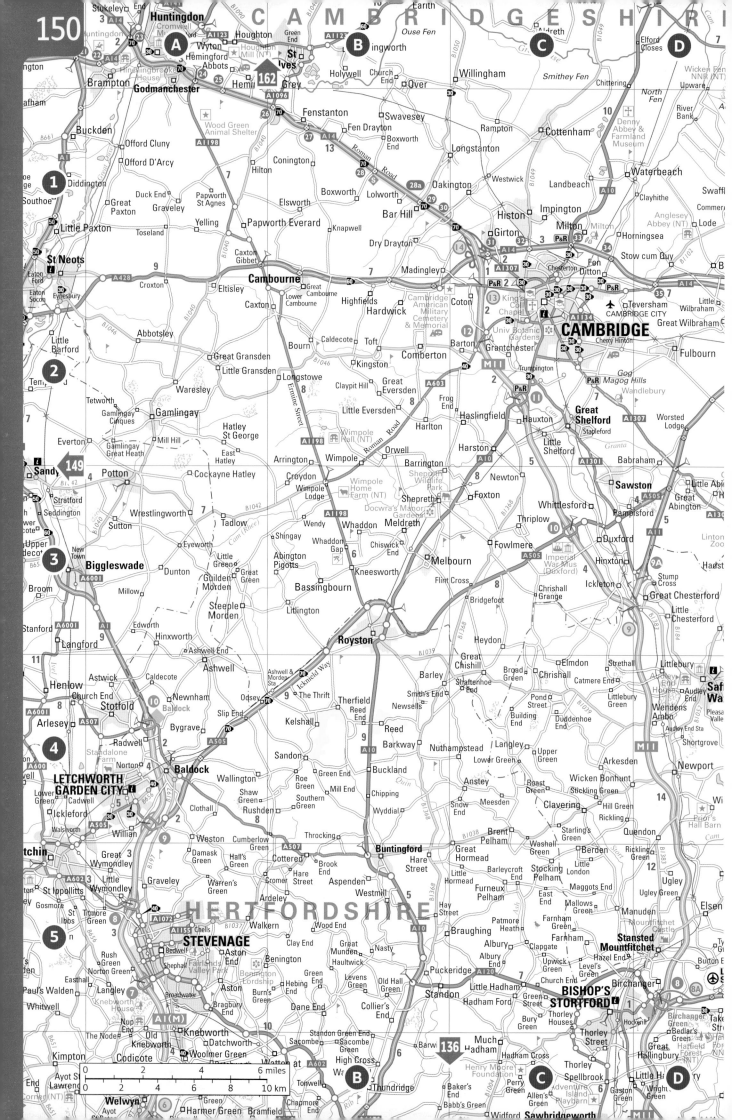

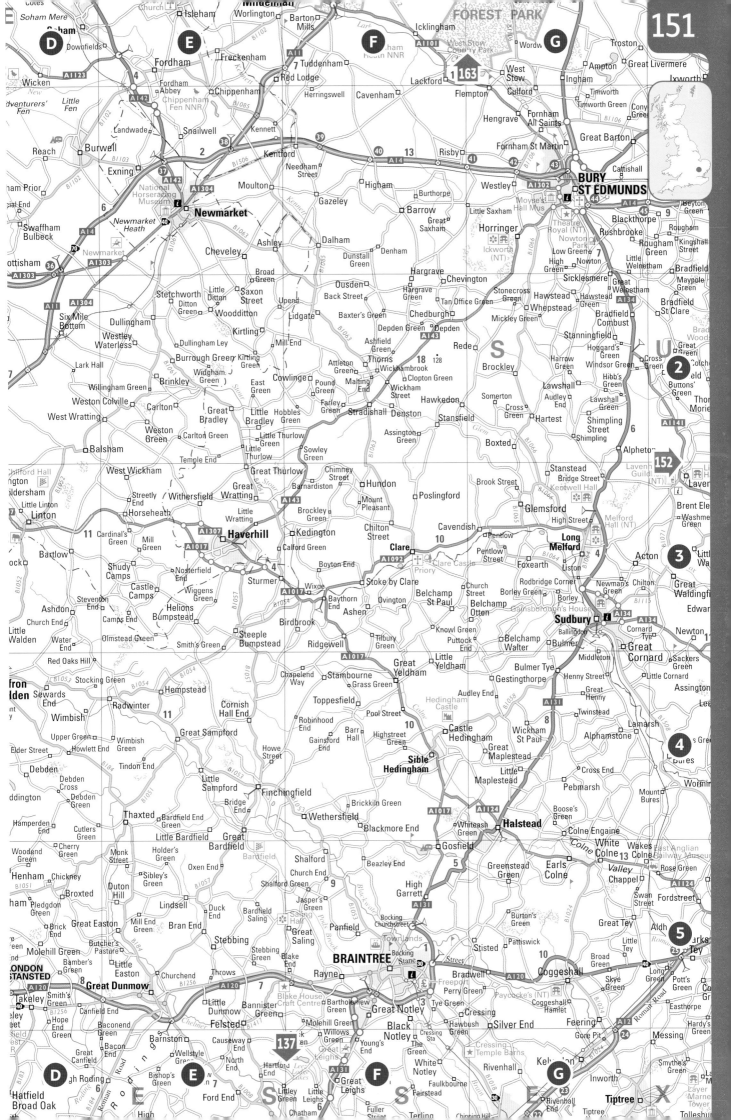

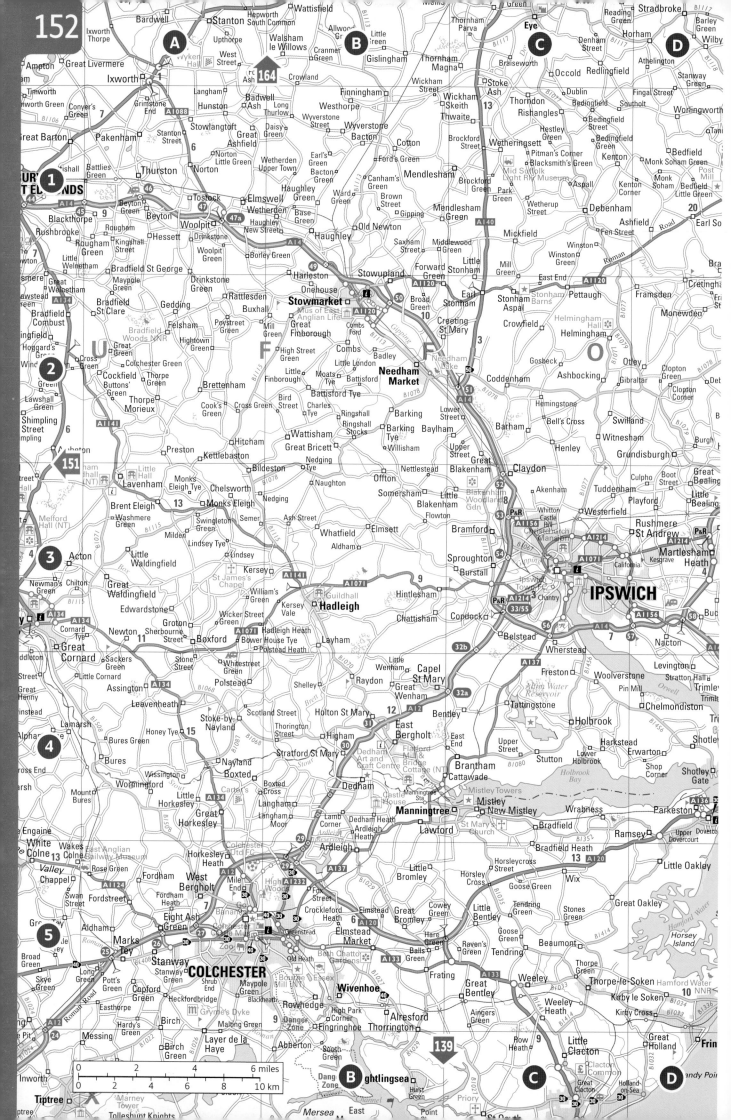

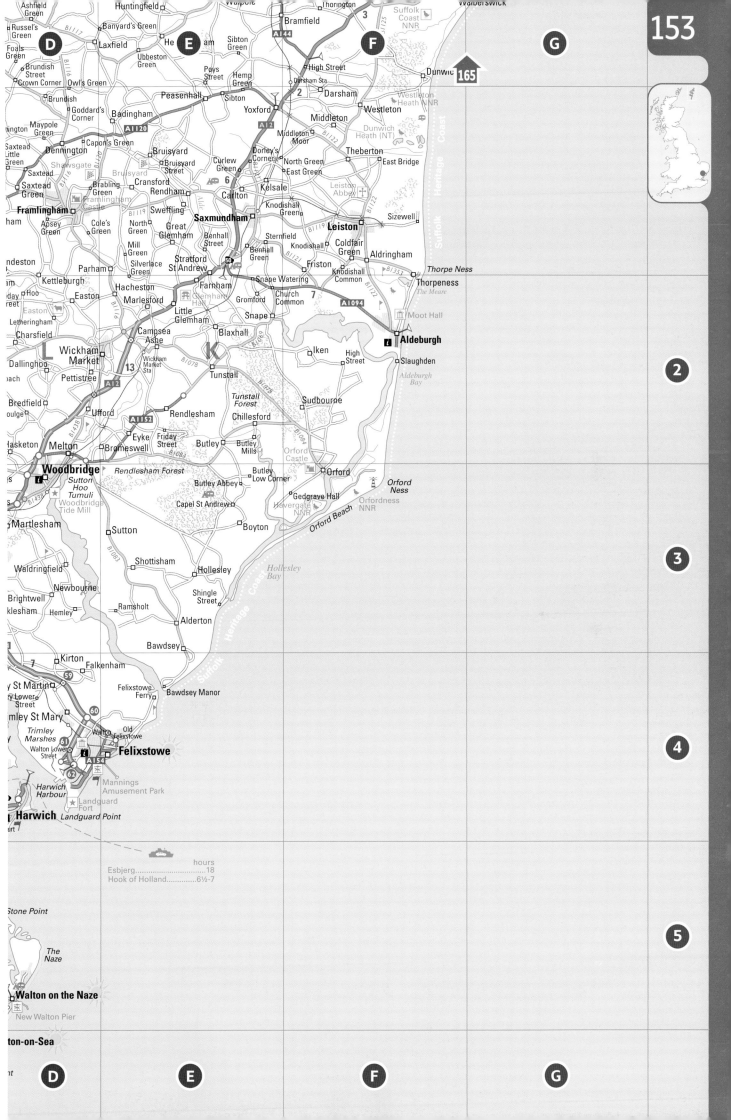

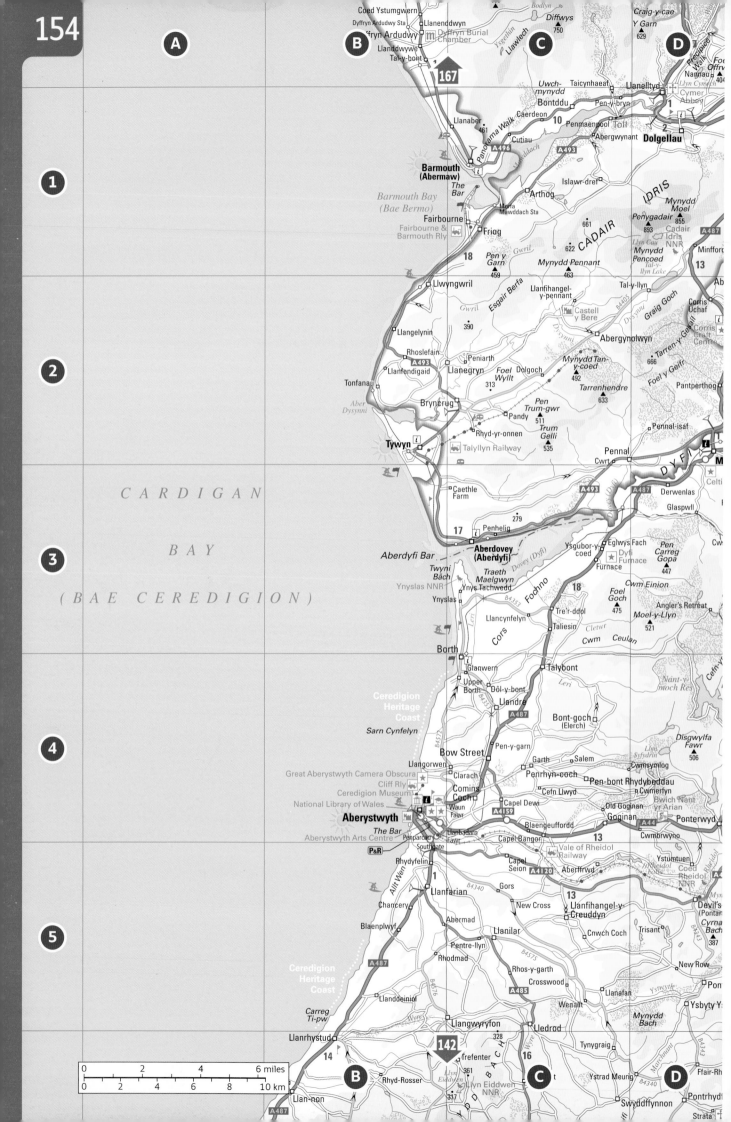

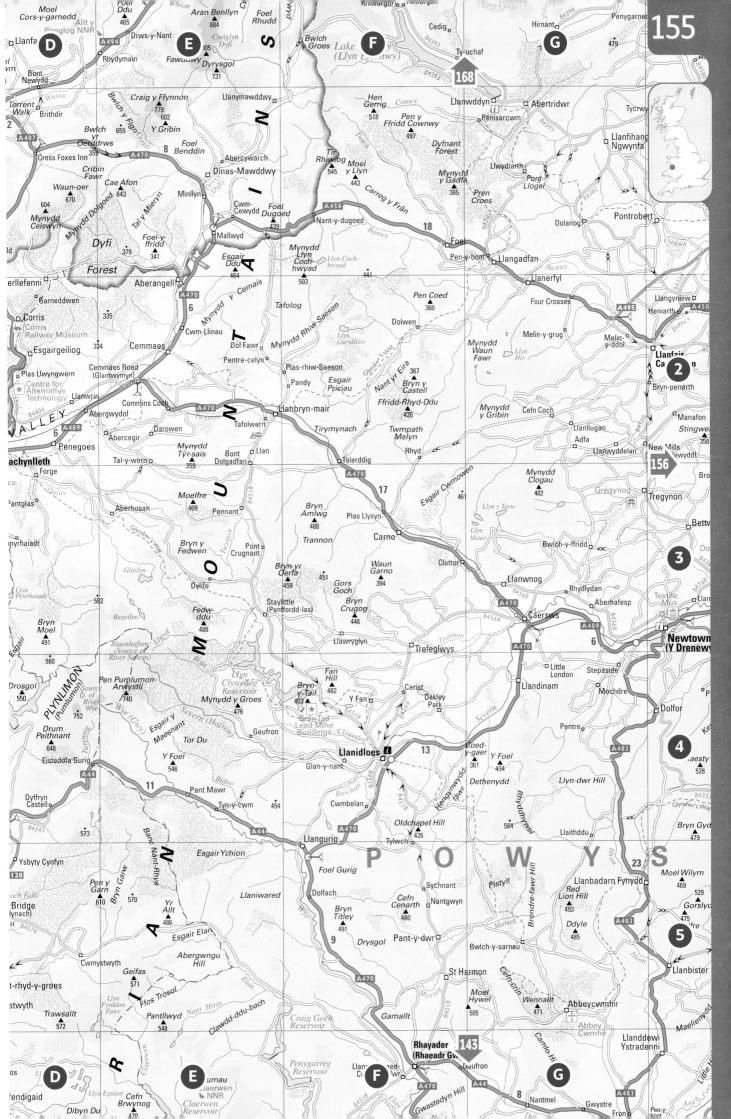

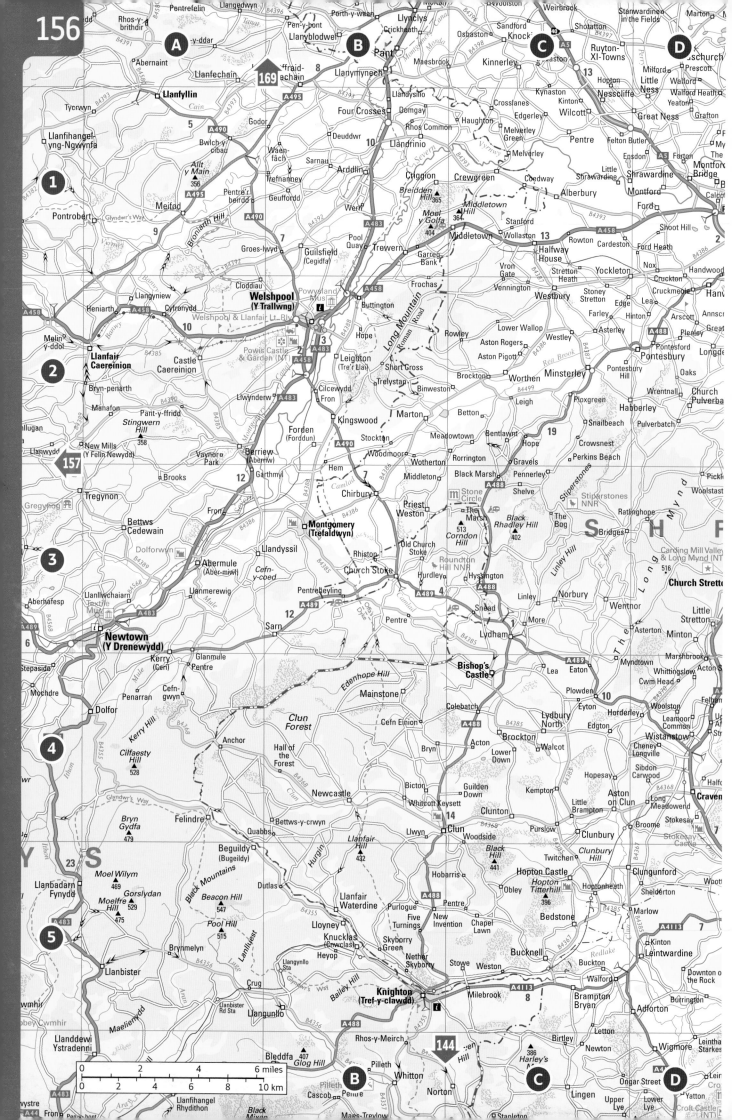

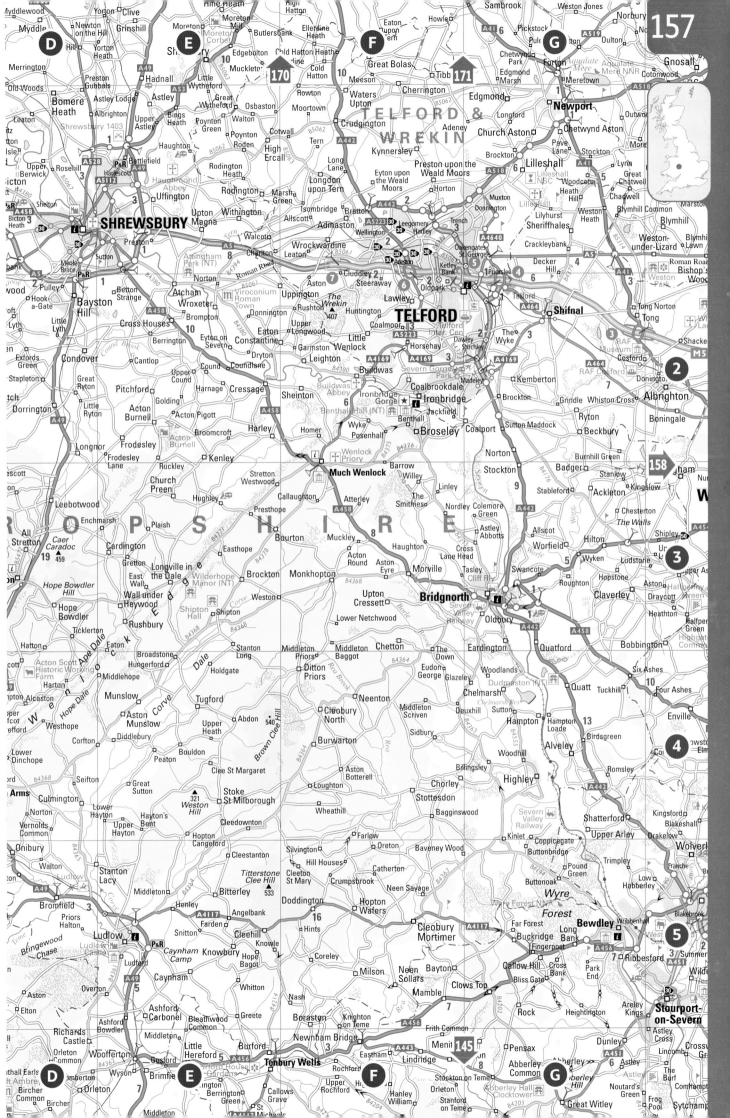

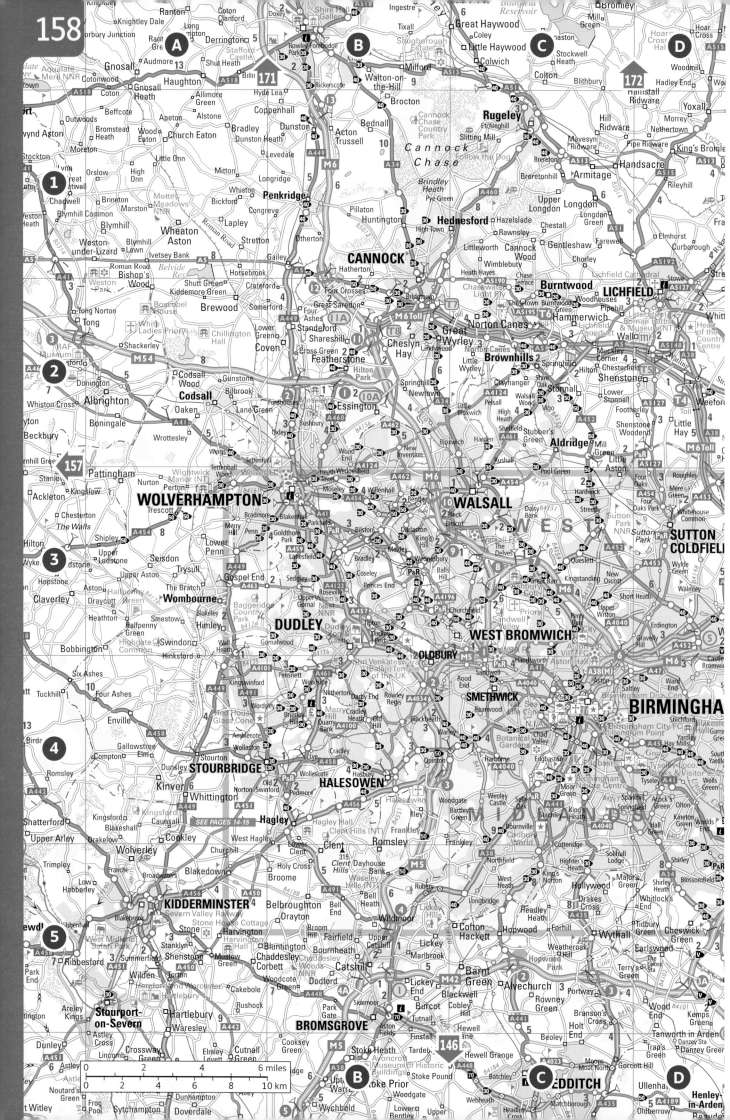

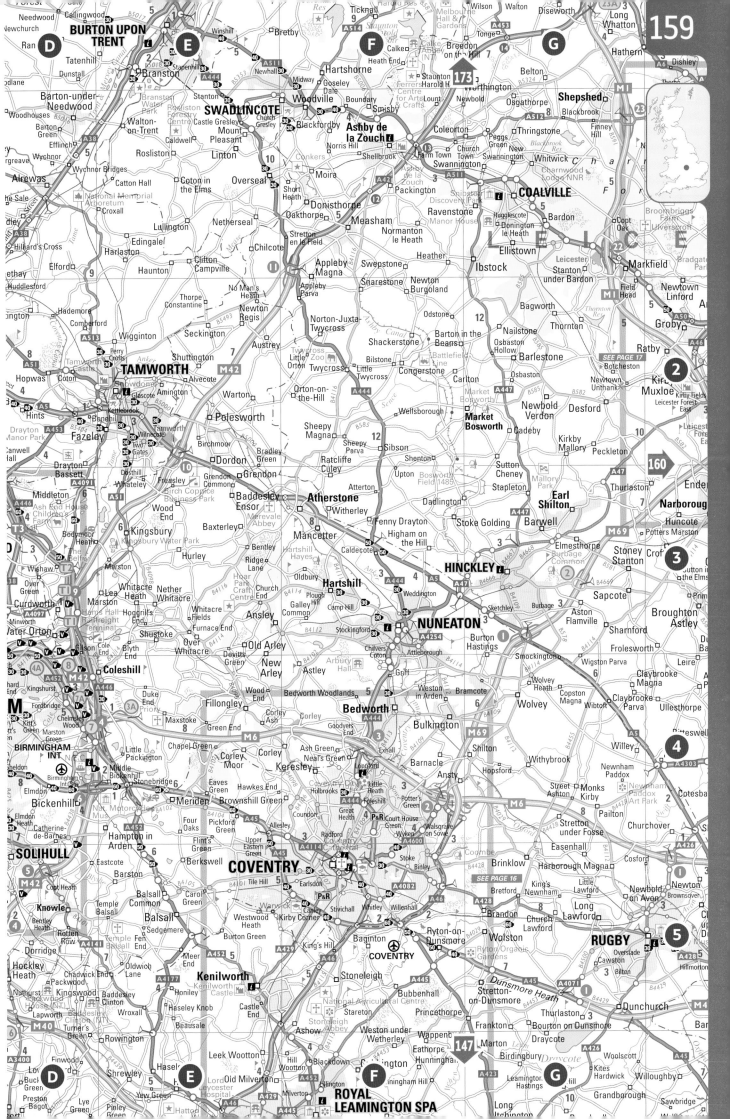

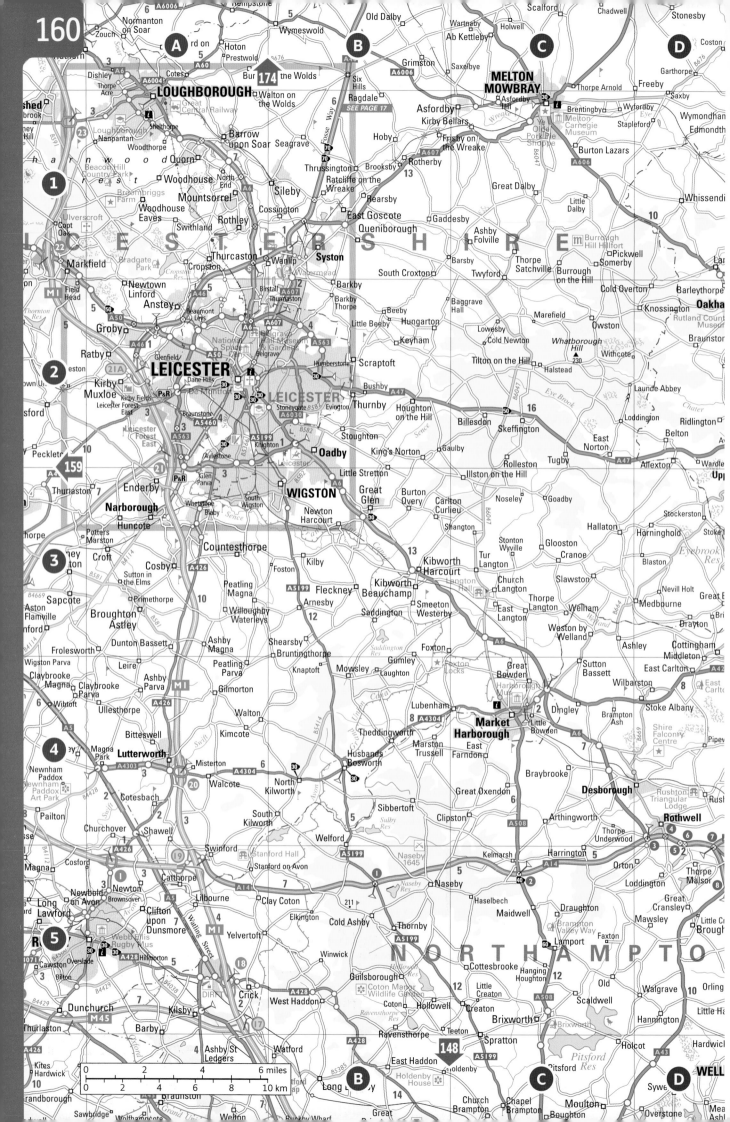

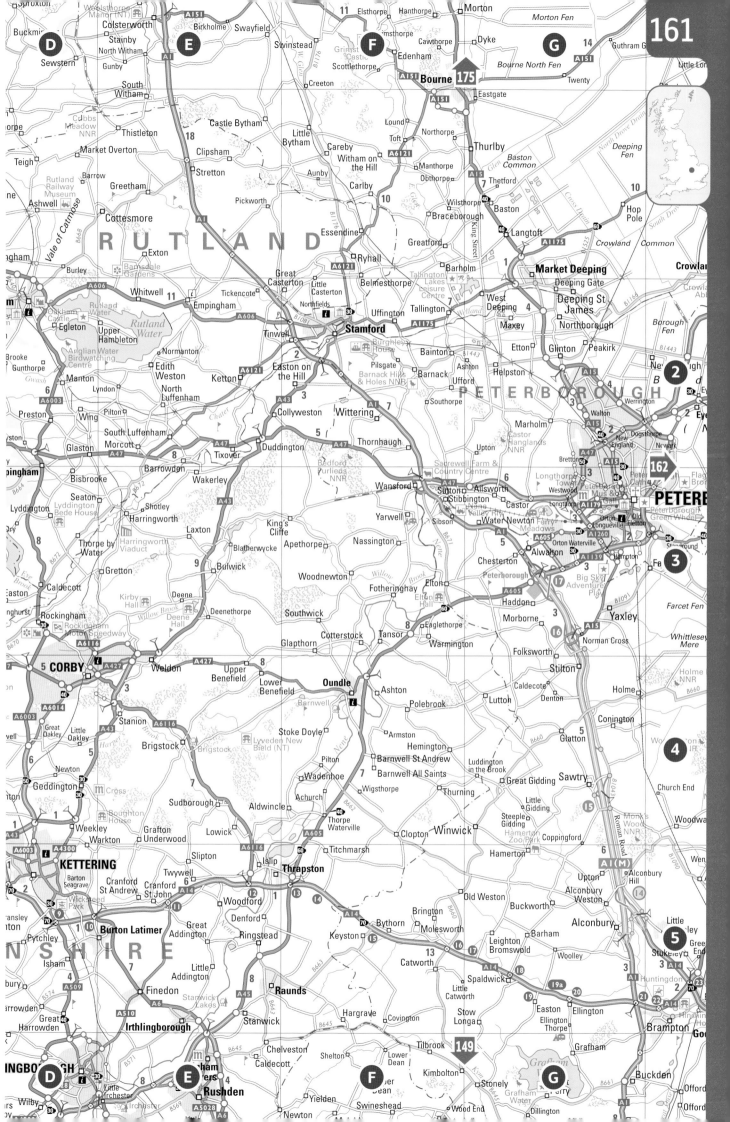

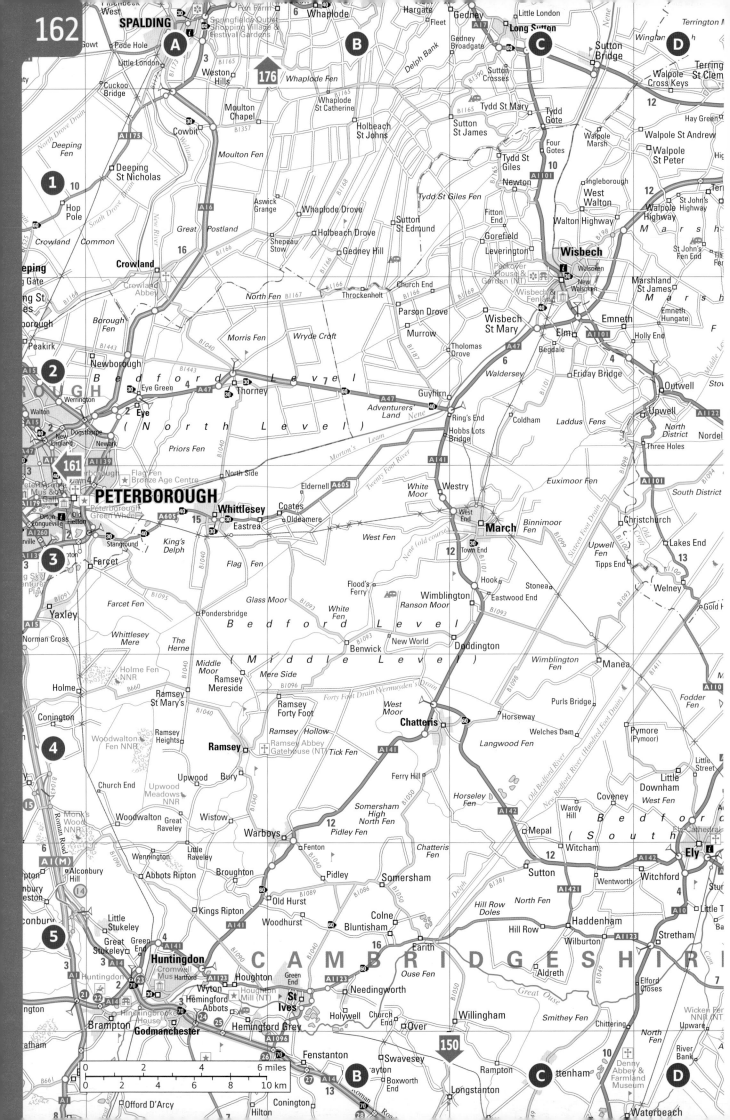

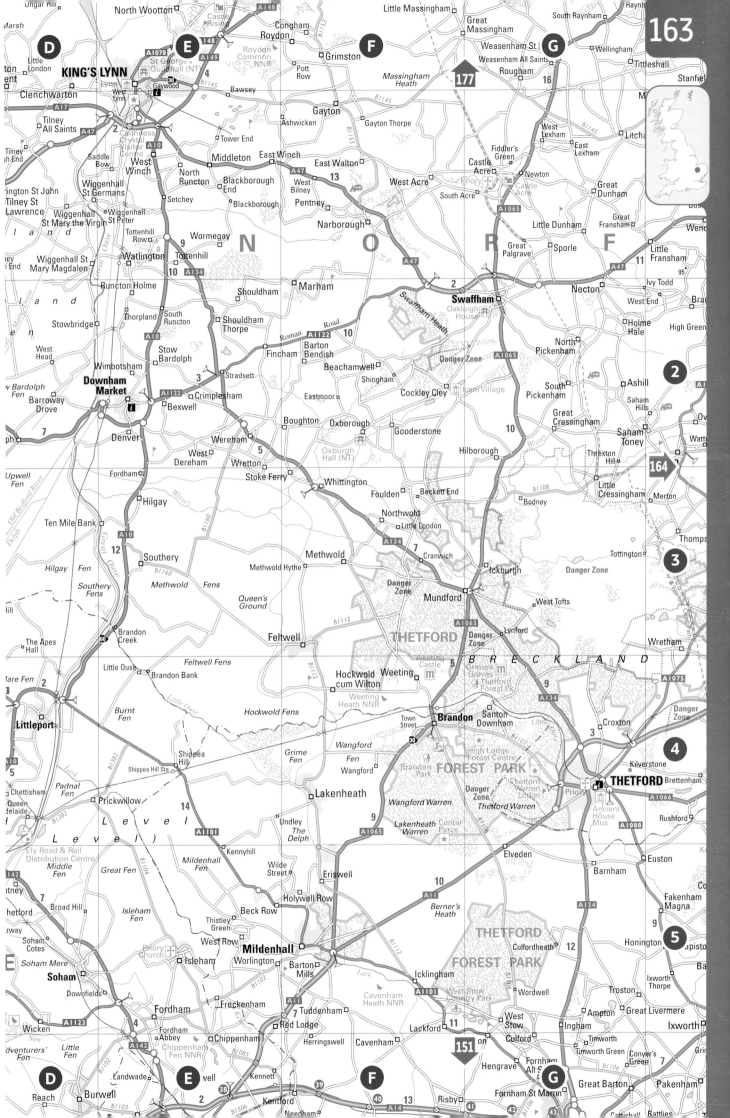

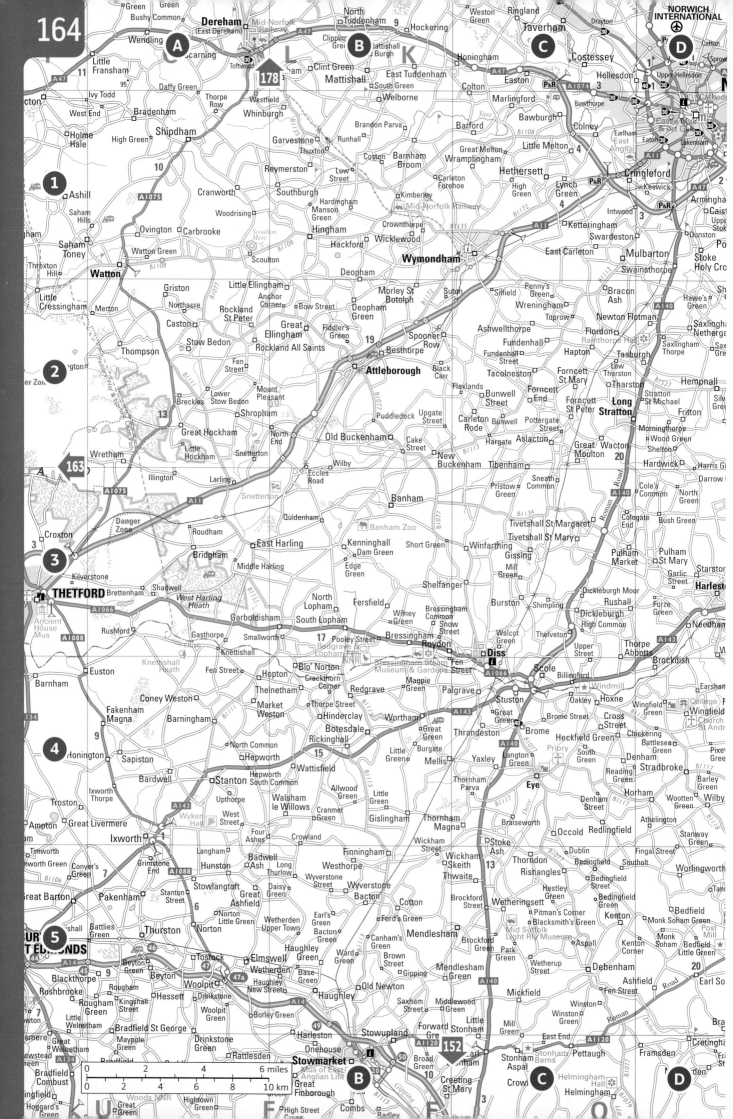

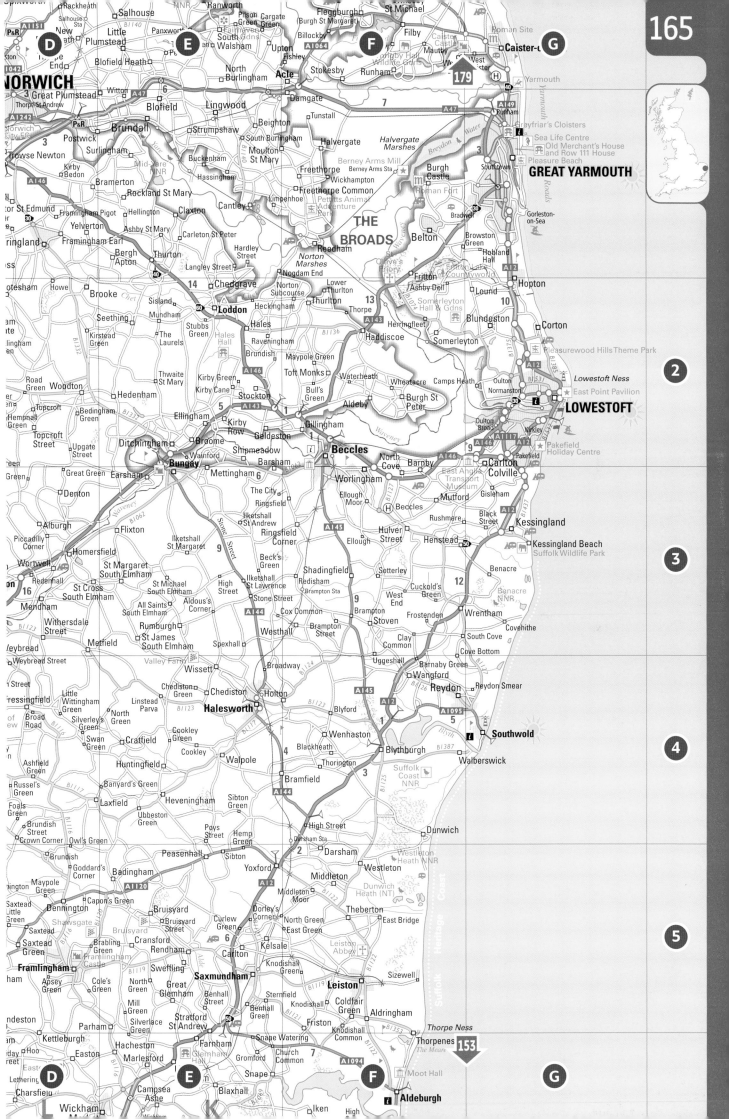

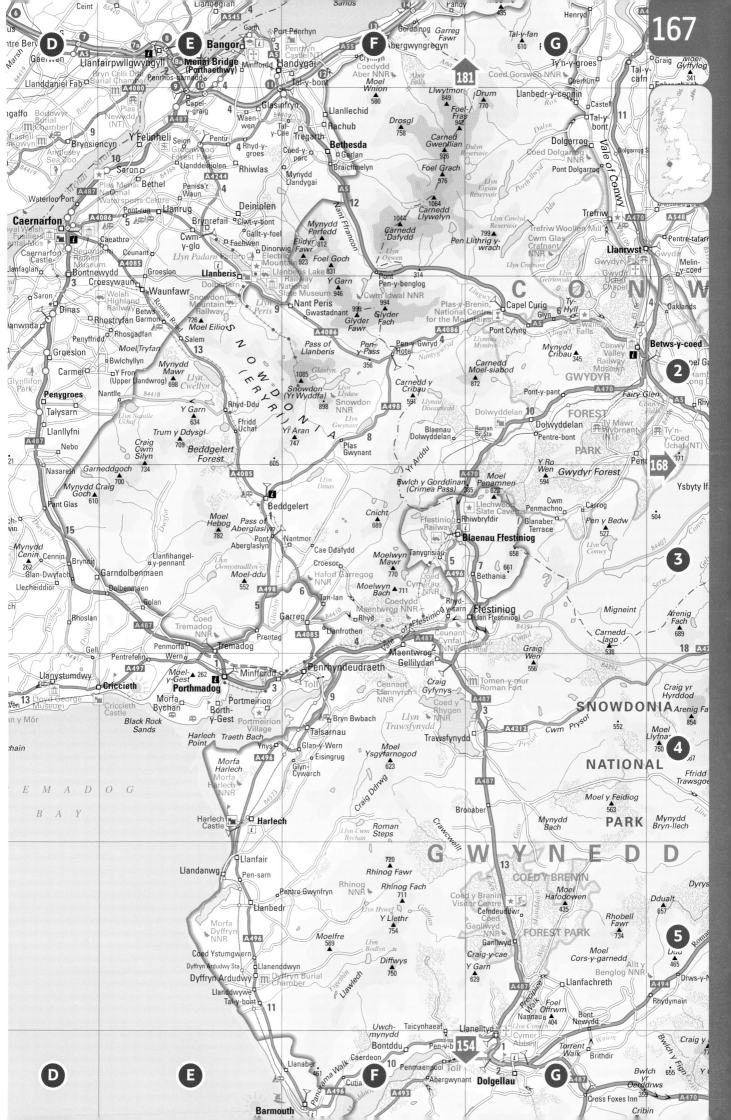

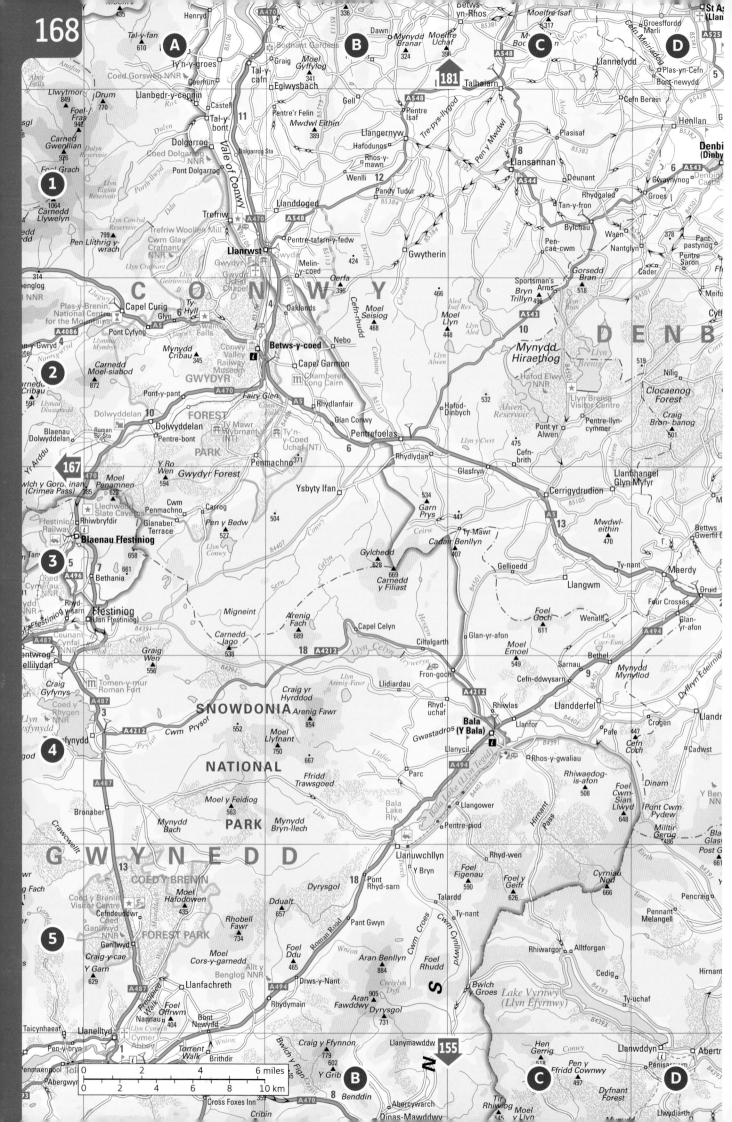

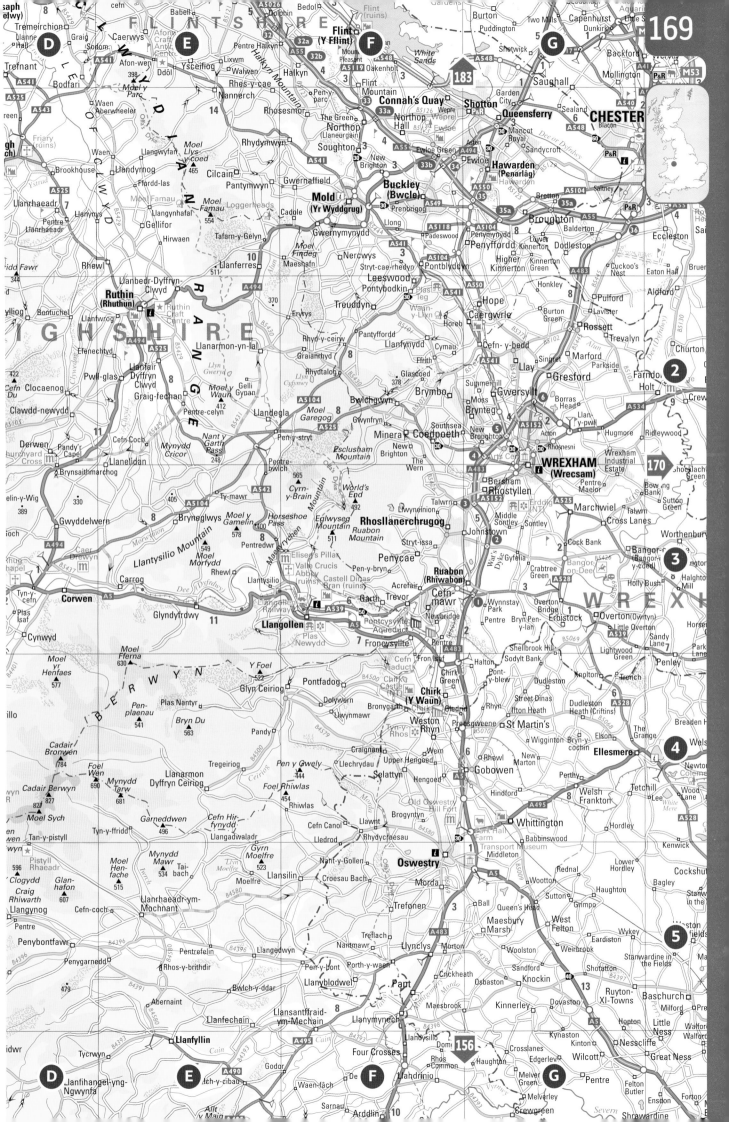

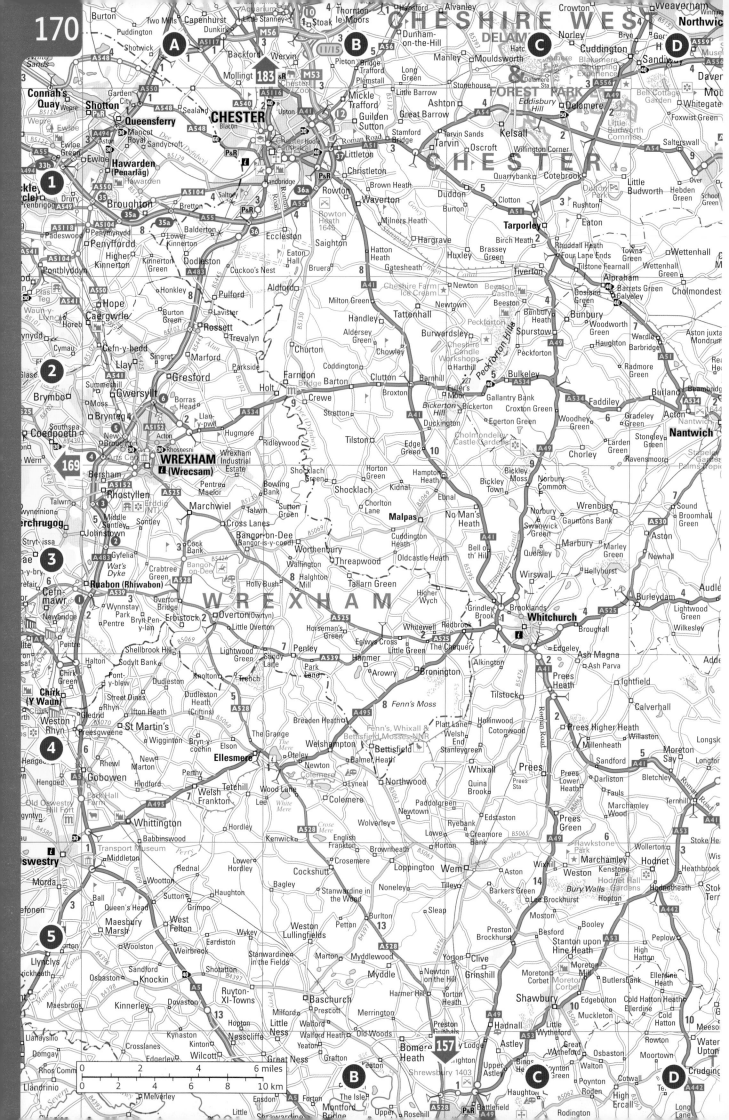

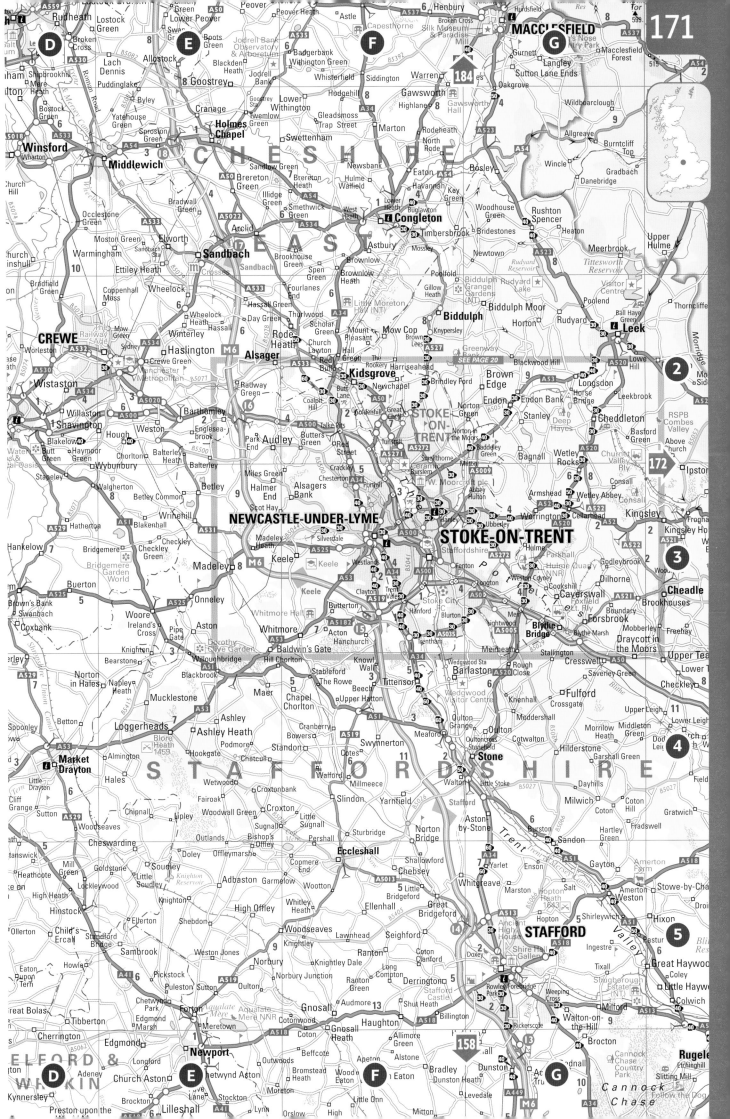

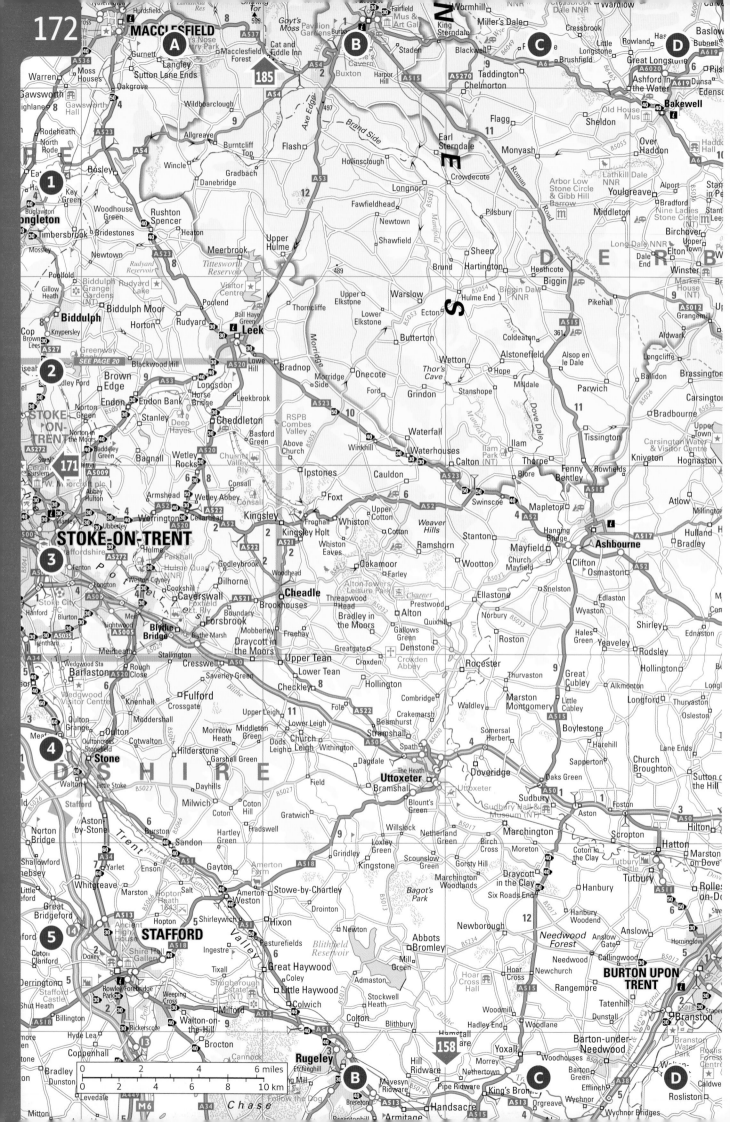

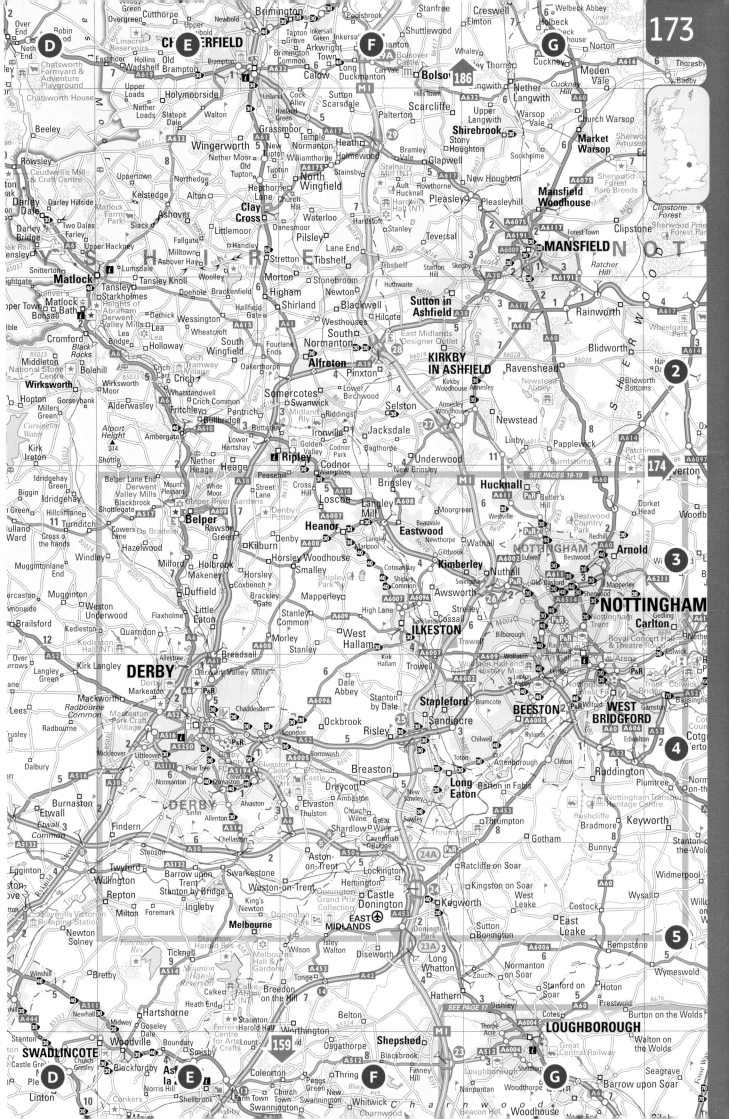

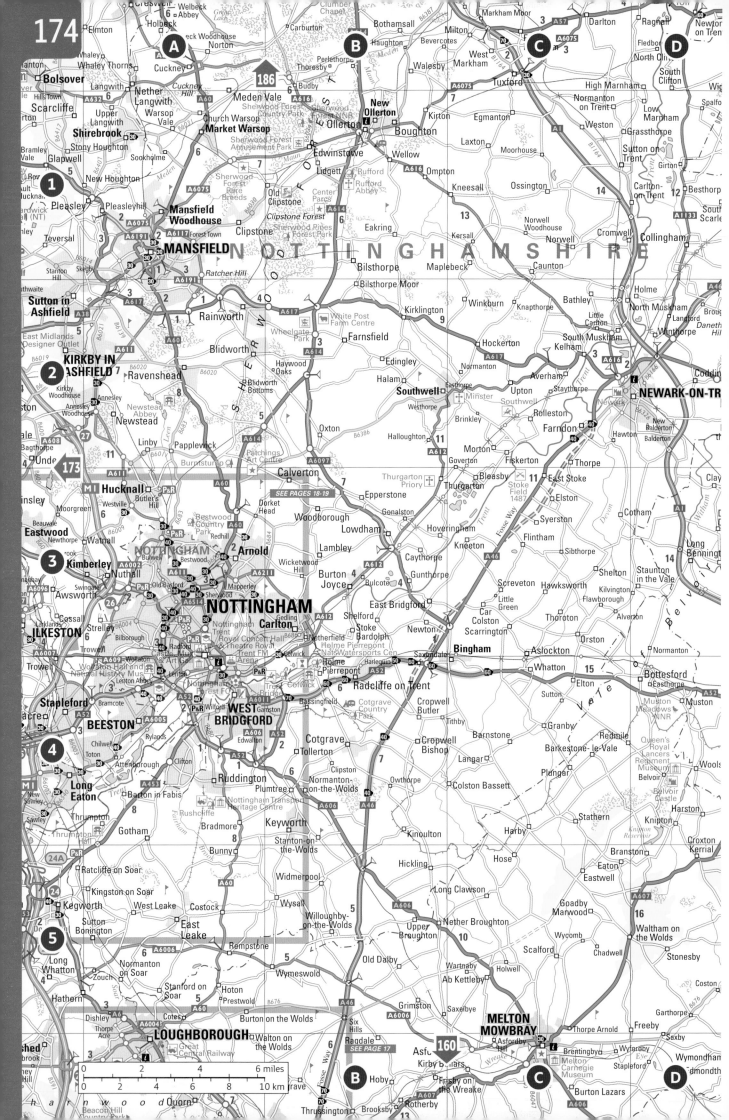

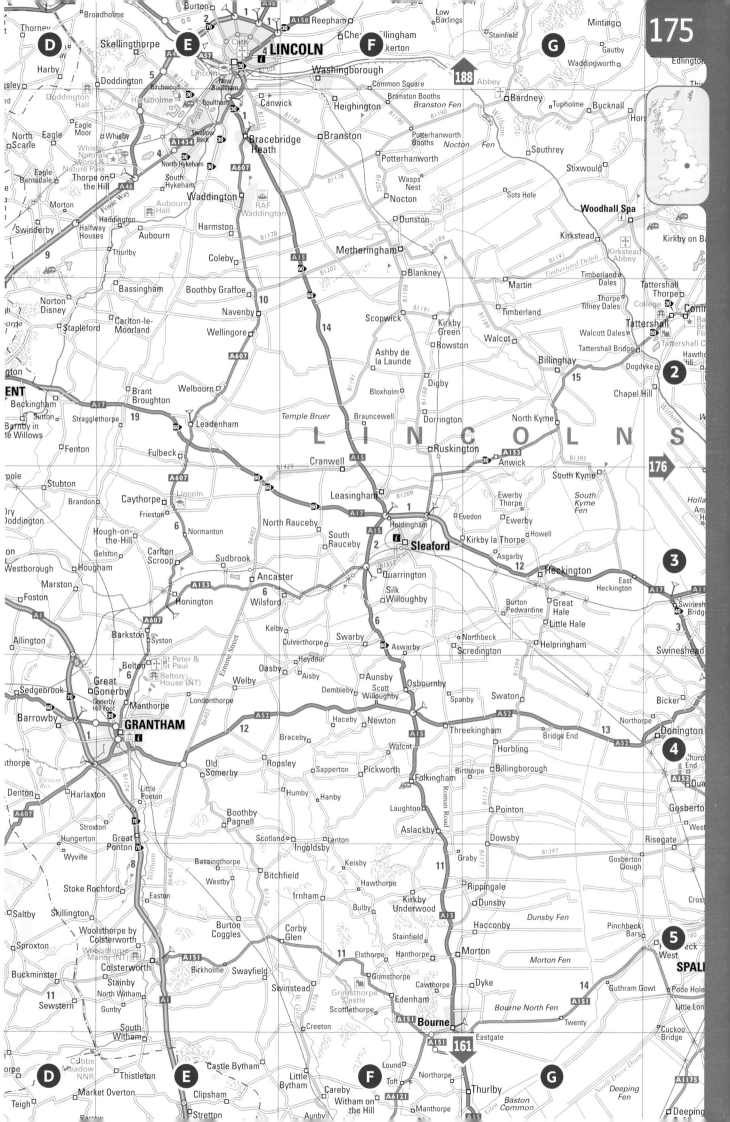

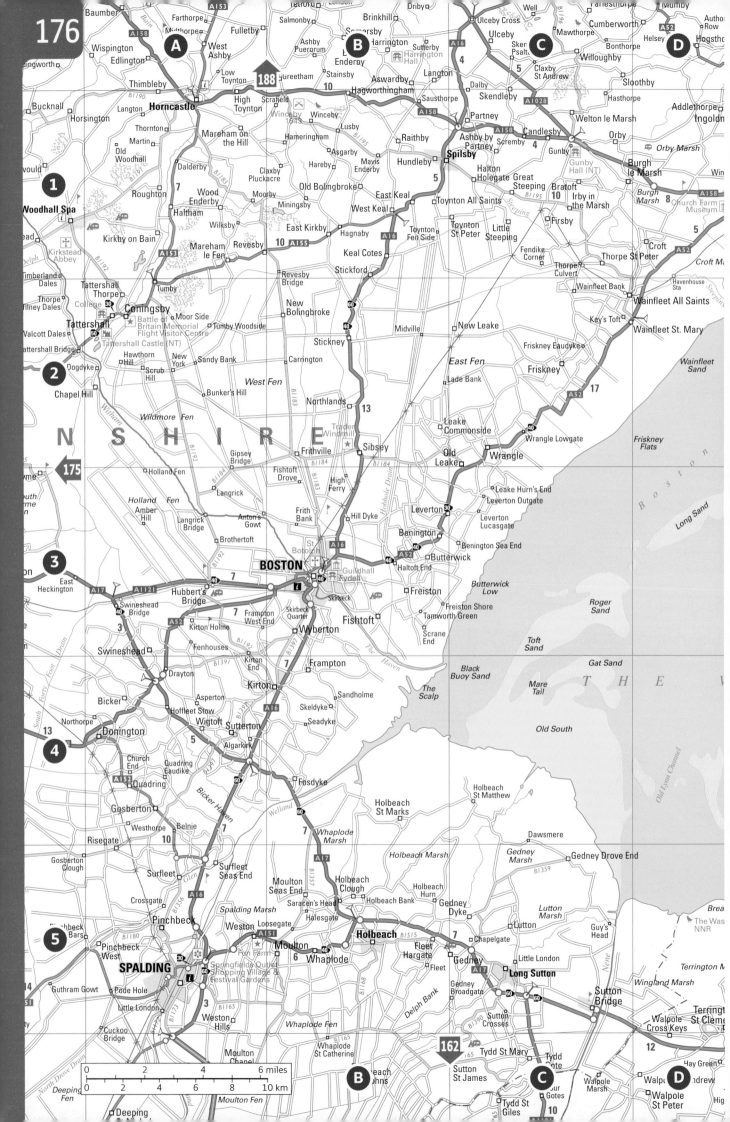

D Ch t Leonards

E

F

G

2

189

Ingoldmells Point
Fantasy Island

Butlins Family
Entertainment Resort

Skegness Water
Leisure Park

thorpe · Seathorne

ells

Skegness

Natureland
Seal Sanctuary

rsh · Seacroft

Gibraltar
Point NNR

· Gibraltar

Gibraltar Pt

D e e p s

L y n n   D e e p s

North Norfolk
Heritage Coast

Scolt Head
Island
NNR

Holkham
Bay

Holme Dunes
NNR

Brancaster Bay

Nurton

Creek

3

Holme next the Sea

Thornham

A149

Titchwell

Brancaster
Staithe

Brancaster

Burnham
Deepdale

i

17

Burnham
Norton

Burnham
Overy Staithe

Burnham
Overy Town

Holkham Bay
NNR

Holkham

Wells-ne

i

Burnham
Market

Sea Life Centre

Ringstead

Peddars Way &
Norfolk Coast Path

B1355

Burnham Thorpe

B1105

Hunstanton

Creake
Abbey

Wight

Wells &
Walsingham
Lt. Rly

W A S H

Summerfield

B1153

North
Creake

Egmere

Shireham
Museum

Shrine of Our Lady
of Walsingham

Norfolk
Lavender

40

Heacham

Eaton

Sedgeford

Docking

B1454

B1155

Stanhoe

South
Creake

North
Barsh

Hough
St Gil

Seal Sand

13

Snettisham

Southgate

A149

Fring

B1454

Bircham
Newton

Great Bircham

B1153

Barmer

B1355

Barmer

Syderstone

West
Barsham

East
Barsham

4

Sculthorpe

Peter Black
Sand

Ingoldisthorpe

Shernborne

Bircham
Tofts

Bagthorpe

B1454

Dersingham

B1440

Anmer

Houghton Hall

Tattersett

A148

Dunton

Shereford

178

Faken

Bulldog
Sand

Dersingham
Bog NNR

Sandringham
House

Sandringham

New Houghton

East Rudham

17

West Rudham

Coxford

Tatterford

Hempton

Toftrees

Fakeni

st Sand

Wolferton

West Newton

Babingley

Flitcham

B1440

Peddars Way & Norfolk Coast Path

B1153

Helhoughton

West Raynham

A1065

East
Raynham

Colkirk

5

Ongar Hill

Castle Rising

St Mary
Magdalene
Chapel

Harpley

Whissonsett

Marsh

Trinity
Hospital

Castle
Rising

A148

Hillington

Little Massingham

Great
Massingham

South Raynham

Weasenham St Peter

Wellingham

Godwick

Horningtoft

North Wootton

South
Wootton

A1078

A148

Congham

Roydon

B1153

Roydon
Common
NNR

Grimston

Weasenham All Saints

Rougham

16

Tittleshall

Stanfiel

Little
London

A149

St George's
Guildhall (NT)

KING'S LYNN

i

Clenchwarton

A17

30

West
Lynn

Gaywood

Caithness
Crystal Visitor
Centre

Pott
Row

Massingham
Heath

163

Mileham

4

B1145

Bawsey

Gayton

Tilney
h End

A47

A10

Tower End

Litcham

D

E

F

G

Tilney
ints

Saddle
Bow

West
Winch

Middleton

East Winch

East Walton

Ashwicken

n Thorpe

Fiddler's
Green

Castle
Acre

East
Lexham

Longh

Bitteri

A47

North

Newton

Reeston

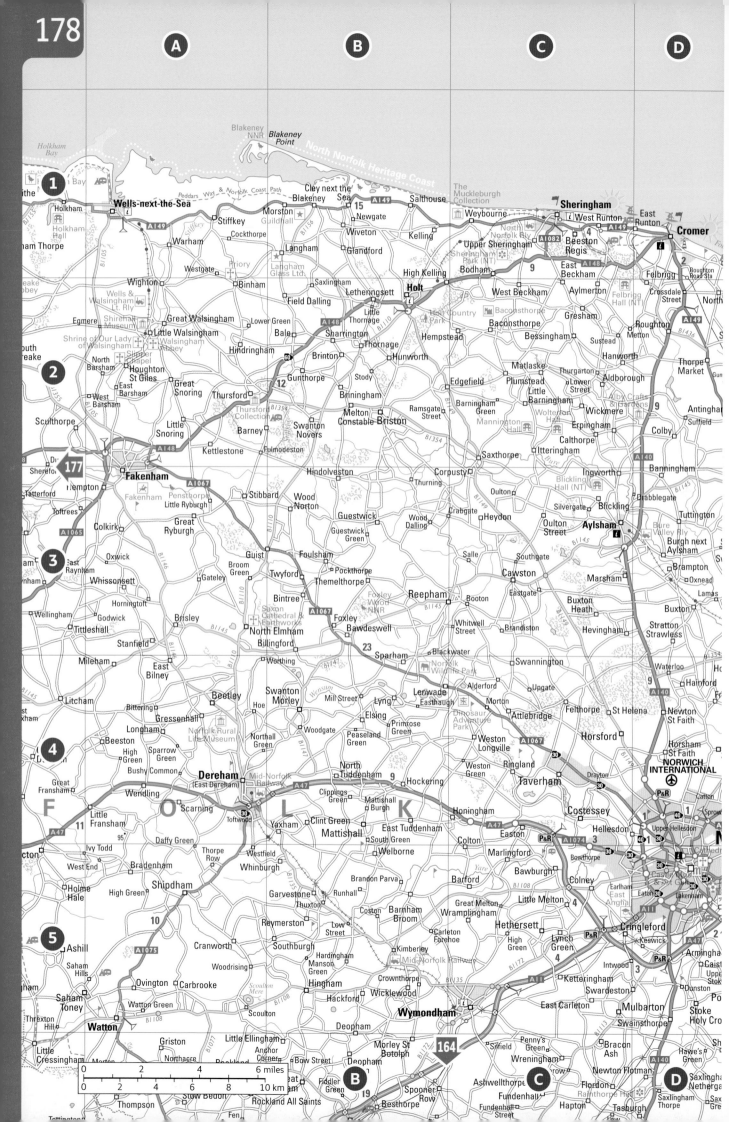

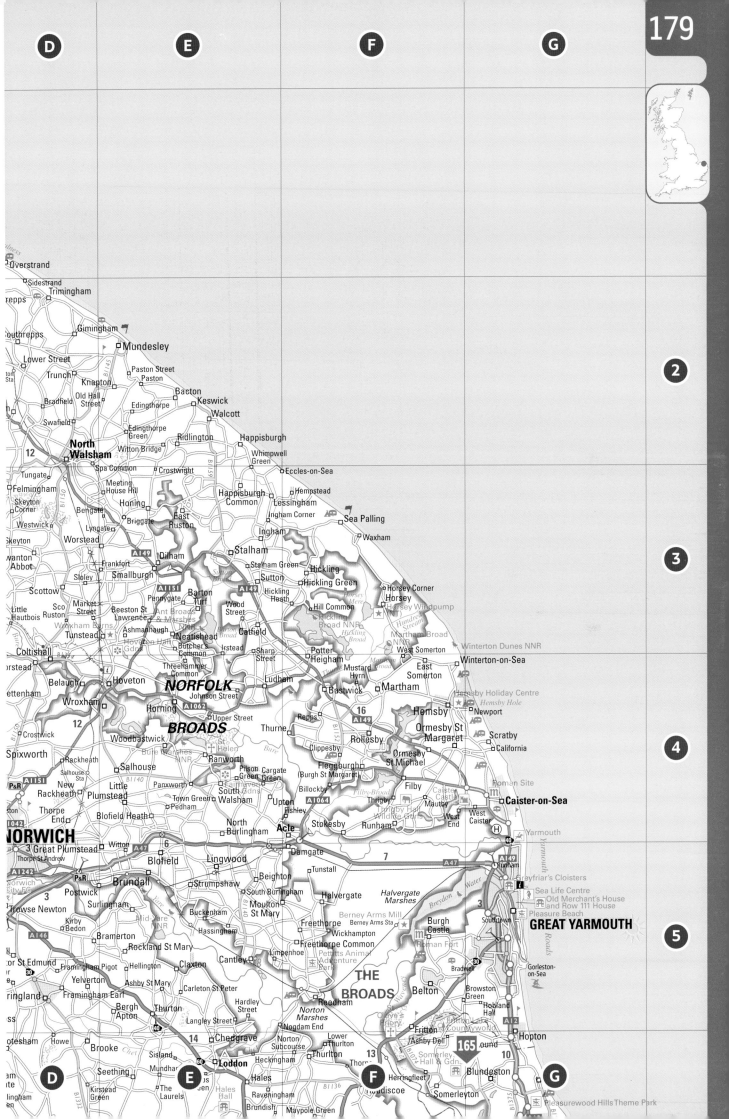

D E F G

2

3

4

5

Overstrand
Sidestrand Trimingham
repps
Southrepps Gimingham
Mundesley
Lower Street
Trunch Knapton Paston Street
Paston
Old Hall Bacton
Bradfield Street Keswick
Swafield Edingthorpe Walcott
North Edingthorpe Ridlington Happisburgh
12 Walsham Green Witton Bridge Whimpwell
Spa Common Crostwight Green Eccles-on-Sea
Tungate Meeting Happisburgh Hempstead
Felmingham House Hill Common Lessingham
Skeyton Honing Ingham Corner Sea Palling
Corner Bengate East Ingham Waxham
Westwick Lyngate Briggate Ruston Stalham
Skeyton Worstead Dilham Stalham Green Hickling
Swanton Frankfort Sloley Sutton Hickling Green Horsey Corner
Abbot Smallburgh Barton Hickling Hill Common Horsey Horsey Windpump
Scottow Pennygate Turf Heath Wood
Little Sco Market Beeston St Street Horsey West Somerton
Hautbois Ruston Street Lawrence Ashmanhaugh Catfield Broad NNR Martham Broad
Tunstead Neatishead Butcher's Irstead Potter Mustard NNR Winterton Dunes NNR
Coltishall Common Sharp Heigham Hyrn East Winterton-on-Sea
Threehammer Street Ludham Bastwick Somerton Martham
Belaugh Common Johnson Street NORFOLK Hemsby Holiday Centre
Hoveton Horning BROADS Thurne Repps Hemsby Hole
Wroxham Woodbastwick Upper Street 16 Rollesby Newport
12 Crostwick Horning Clippesby Ormesby St Scratby
Spixworth Rackheath Salhouse Pilson Cargate Fleggburgh Ormesby Margaret California
New Little Green Green St Michael Filby
Rackheath Plumstead Panxworth South Billockby Thrigby Caister Castle Roman Site
Thorpe Walsham Upton A1064 Mautby Caister-on-Sea
End Pedham Town Green Fishley Stokesby Runham West West Caister
NORWICH Blofield Heath North Acle End
Great Plumstead Witton Burlingham Damgate 7 Runham Yarmouth
Thorpe St Andrew Blofield Lingwood Tunstall Greyfriar's Cloisters
Postwick Brundall Beighton Sea Life Centre
Surlingham Strumpshaw South Burlingham Halvergate Southtown Old Merchant's House
Trowse Newton Moulton Halvergate and Row 111 House
Kirby Buckenham St Mary Marshes Berney Arms Mill Burgh GREAT YARMOUTH
Bedon Bramerton Hassingham Freethorpe Berney Arms Sta Castle 3
Rockland St Mary Wickhampton Roman Fort
St Edmund Hellington Claxton Cantley Freethorpe Common Bradwell Gorleston-on-Sea
Yelverton Ashby St Mary Limpenhoe Pettitts Animal Browston
Framingham Pigot Carleton St Peter Adventure Belton Green
Framingham Earl Bergh Hardley Park THE Hobland
Thurton Apton Street Reedham BROADS Hopton
Langley Street Norton Olive's Fritton Hound
Howe Chedgrave Marshes Priory Ashby Dell 165
Brooke 14 Sisland Nogdam End Somerleyton 10
Seething Mundham Loddon Lower 13 Hall & Gdn. Blundeston
Kirstead The Heckingham Thurlton Herringfleet
Green Laurels Hales Thurlton Thorn Haddiscoe Somerleyton
Ravenningham Pleasurewood Hills Theme Park
Brundish Maypole Green

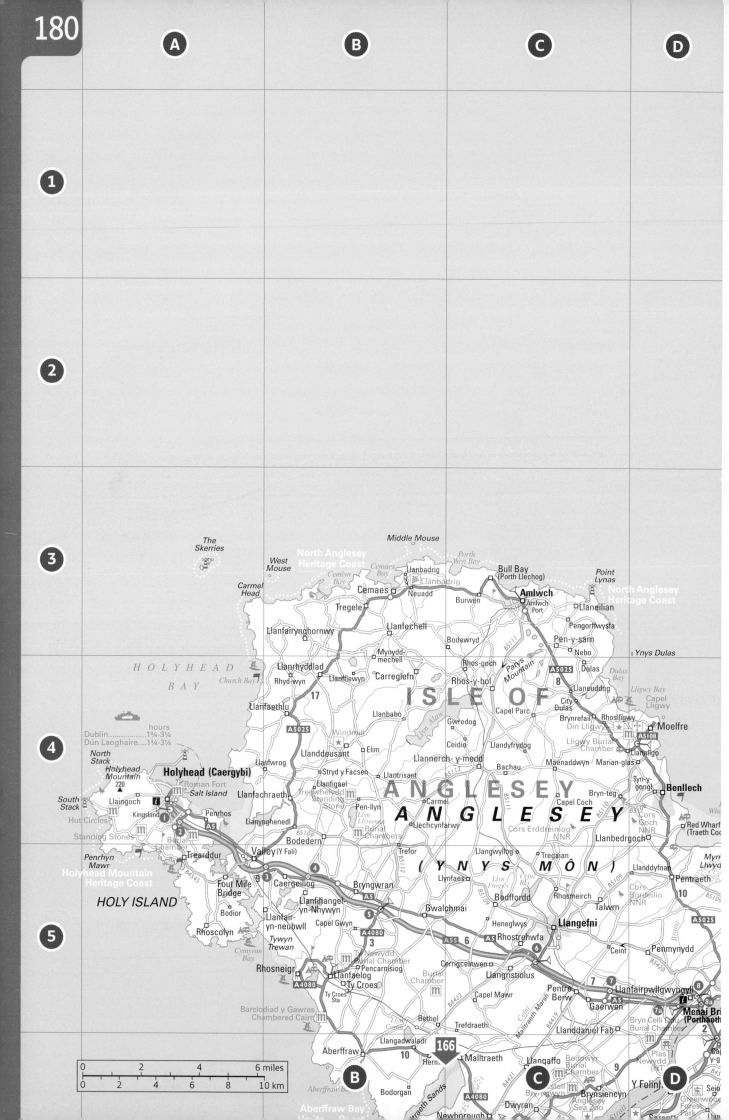

A B C D

1

2

3

The Skerries

Middle Mouse

West Mouse

North Anglesey Heritage Coast

Porth Wen Bay

Cemaes Bay

Bull Bay (Porth Llechog)

Point Lynas

North Anglesey Heritage Coast

Carmel Head

Cemlyn Bay

Llanbadrig

Llanbadrig

Amlwch

Amlwch Port

Llaneilian

Cemaes

Neuadd

Burwen

Pengorffwysfa

Tregele

Llanfechell

Bodewryd

Pen-y-sarn

Llanfairynghornwy

Mynydd-mechell

Rhos-goch

Nebo

Parys Mountain

Ynys Dulas

HOLYHEAD BAY

Llanrhyddlad

Rhyd-wyn

Llanflewyn

Carreglefn

Rhos-y-bol

A5025

Dulas

8

Dulas Bay

Lligwy Bay

Capel Lligwy

Church Bay

ISLE OF

Llaneuddog

17

Llanfaethlu

Llanbabo

Gwredog

Capel Parc

City Dulas

Brynrefail

Rhoslligwy

Din Lligwy

Moelfre

A5108

Ceidio

Llandyfrydog

Lligwy Burial Chamber

Llanallgo

Llanddeusant

Elim

Llannerch-y-medd

Bachau

Maenaddwyn

Marian-glas

North Stack

Holyhead Mountain 220

Dublin................1¾-3¼

Dún Laoghaire....1¾-3¼ hours

Llanfwrog

Stryd y Facsen

Llantrisant

ANGLESEY

Bryn-teg

Tyn-y-gongl

Benllech

South Stack

Holyhead (Caergybi)

Roman Fort Salt Island

Llanfachraeth

Tregwehelyth Standing Stone

Pen-llyn

ANGLESEY

Capel Coch

Hut Circles

Llaingoch

Kingsland

Penrhos

A5

Llanynghenedl

Llanfigael

Pen-y-sarn

Llywenan Burial Chambers

Llechcynfarwy

Cors Erddreiniog NNR

Goch

Llanbedrgoch

Red Wharf Bay (Traeth Coch)

Standing Stones

Burial Chamber

Treaddur

Valley (Y Fali)

Bodedern

B5109

Trefor

Llangwyllog

Tregaian

Penrhyn Mawr

Holyhead Mountain Heritage Coast

Four Mile Bridge

Caergeiliog

4

Bryngwran

Llanfaes

Llyn Frogwy

Cefni Res

Llanddyfnan

Pentraeth

Mynydd Llwydi

10

HOLY ISLAND

Bodior

9 3

Llanfihangel-yn-Nhywyn

A5

Gwalchmai

(YNYS MÔN)

Bodffordd

Rhosmeirch

Talwrn

Rhoscolyn

Llanfair-yn-neubwll

Capel Gwyn

5

A55 6

Rhostrehwfa

A5025

Cymyran Bay

Tywyn Trewan

Ty Newydd Burial Chamber

3

Heneglwys

A5

Llangefni

Ceint

Penmynydd

Rhosneigr

Pencarnisiog

Cerrigceinwen

Llangristiolus

7 7

Llanfairpwllgwyngyll

8

A4080

Llanfaelog

Ty Croes

Capel Mawr

Burial Chamber

6

Pentre Berw

Gaerwen

7a

Menai Br (Porthaeth

Barclodiad y Gawres Chambered Cairn

Ty Croes Sta

Bethel

Capel Mawr

B4421

Plas Newydd (NT)

2

Aberffraw

Llangadwaladr

166

Malltraeth

Trefdraeth

Maltraeth Marsh

Llanqaffo

Bodowyr Burial Chamber

9

Llanddaniel Fab

Bryn Celli Ddu Burial Chamber

Y Felin

Aberffraw Bay

Bodorgan

Malltraeth Sands

A4080

Bryngwran

Anglesey Sea Zoo

Greenwood Forest Park

Aberffraw Bay Heritage Coast

Newborough

Dwyran

Sdraerp

B C D

0   2   4   6 miles
0   2   4   6   8   10 km

A   B   C   D

1

2

181

3

4

Birkenhead to   hours
Belfast.....................8
Dublin..................7-7¼
Liverpool to   hours
Douglas..........2½-4¼
Dublin.......................8

LIVERPOOL

BAY

West
Hoyle
Bank

East
Hoyle
Bank

Meols
Sta

Hoylake

Royal
Liverpool

Manor Road Sta

Hoylake Sta

A553

Hilbre Island

West Kirby Sta

West Kirby

Grange

Frankby

A5114

Caldy

B5140

Irb
Hi

A540

Thurstaston

*Dawpool
Bank*

Welsh Channel

Prestatyn
Sands
Holiday
Centre

Point of
Ayr

Talacre

Llawndy

Mostyn Bank

Flynnongroyw

Prestatyn

Sky
Tower

A548

Efrith

Gronant

Gwespyr

Pen-y-ffordd

Rhyl

SeaQuarium

Rhyl Sun Centre

30

30

B5119

Meliden
(Gallt Melyd)

A547

Llanasa

Gwaenysgor

Trelogan

A548

Mostyn Quay

Glan-y-don

Mostyn

East
Hoyle
Bank

Kinmel Bay
(Bae Cinmel)

2

A525

Bodrhyddan
Hall

Tan-yr-
allt

Gop
Hill 8

Axton

Whitford
(Chwitffordd)

10

40

Llannerch-y-Môr

Holywell Bank

Greenfield Valley

wyn Bay
(e Colwyn)

22

10

23

*Abergele
Roads*

Pensarn

A548

5

Towyn

Plas
Llwyd

Morfa
Rhuddlan

Rhuddlan

6

Trelawnyd

A5151

Mèn
Achwyfan

Pantasaph
Friary

St Winifred's Holy Well & Chap

Greenfield
(Maes-Glas)

Llanddulas

A547

23a

30

5

Abergele

A55

24

St George

Pengwern

Cwm

Ochr-
y-foel

Rhuddlan
Cas & Twt Hill

Dyserth

3

Marian
Cwm

Hyn
Helyg

Lloc

5026

Gorsedd

Carmel

Basingwerk
Abbey

1

30

Walwen

A5026

Bagillt

Holywell (Treffynnon)

Bedol

Llysfaen

Rhyd-y-foel

24a

Bodelwyddan

27

A525

B5429

Roman

A55

Road

31

Pantasaph

Calcoed

Brynford

Dolphin

Babell

Walwen

Whelston

*Bagillt
Bank*

Llanelian-
yn-Rhos

owen

25

26

27

27a

28

Rhuallt

29

A548

Betws-
yn-Rhos

6

St Asaph
(Llanelwy)

6

Pen-y-
cefn

Pantasaph

Calcoed

A5026

A548

5

Dawn

324

Moelfre Isaf

317

Groesffordd
Marli

B538

Tremeirchion

Graig

Sodom

Caerwys

Babell

Ysceifiog

Lixwm

Walwen

Flint
(Y Fflint)

Mount Pleasant

A55

32a

Mynydd
Branar

396

Moelfre Uchaf

Mynydd
Bodrochwyn

Cefn Meiriadog

B5381

Llannerch
Hall

A525

Afon-wen

Ddôl

Moel
y Parc
398

Pentre Halkyn

Halkyn

32b

4

3

Llannefydd

Plas-yn-Cefn

Trefnant

Afonwen
Croft and
Antique
Centre

14

Rhosesmor

The Green
urgain

Pen-y-
parc

33

A548

Llanfair Talhaiarn

Cefn
Berain

Bont-newydd

A541

Bodfari

VALE OF CLWYD

Nannerch

B5123

rthop
Soughton

A541

Pentre
Isaf

A544

Tre-pys-llygod

B528

B5429

A525

Green

A543

168

Cilcain 4

Llandyrnog

30

Brig

Elwy

Hanllan

Llansannan

B5382

Pen

Friary
(ruins)

Waen

Llangwyfan

Moel
Llys-y-coed

Rhydymwyn

Deunant

Denbigh
(Dinbych)

A543

6

A 45

0   2   4   6 miles

0 2 4 6 8 10 km

B   C   D

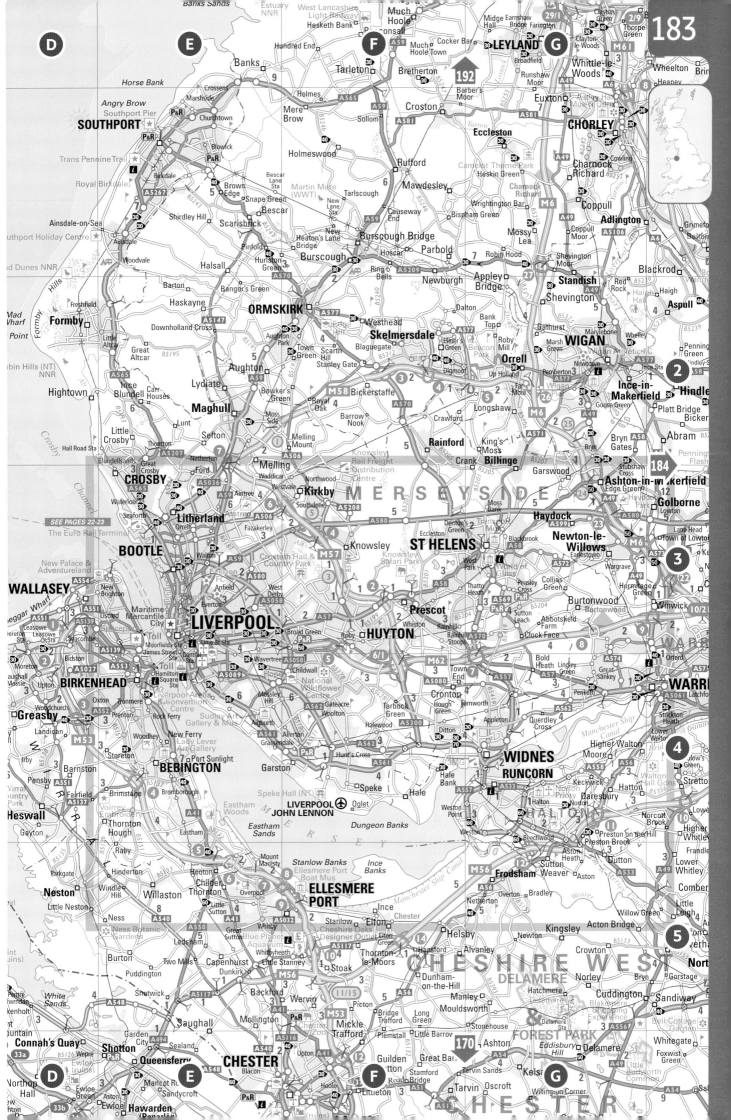

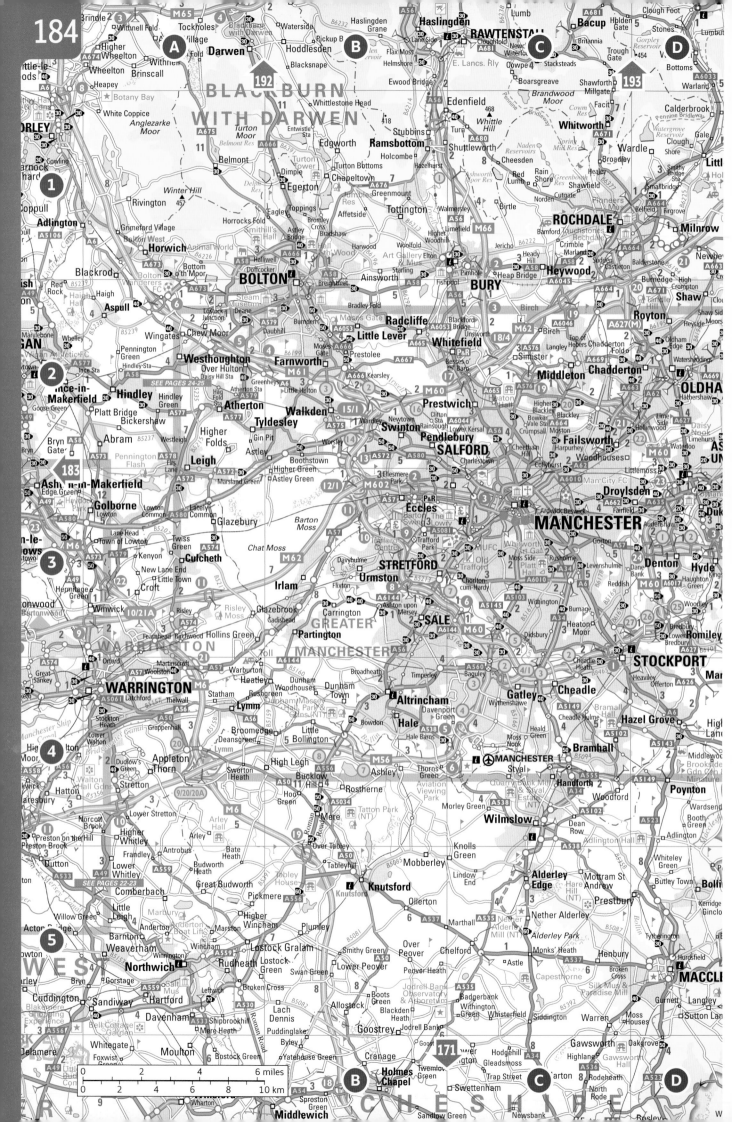

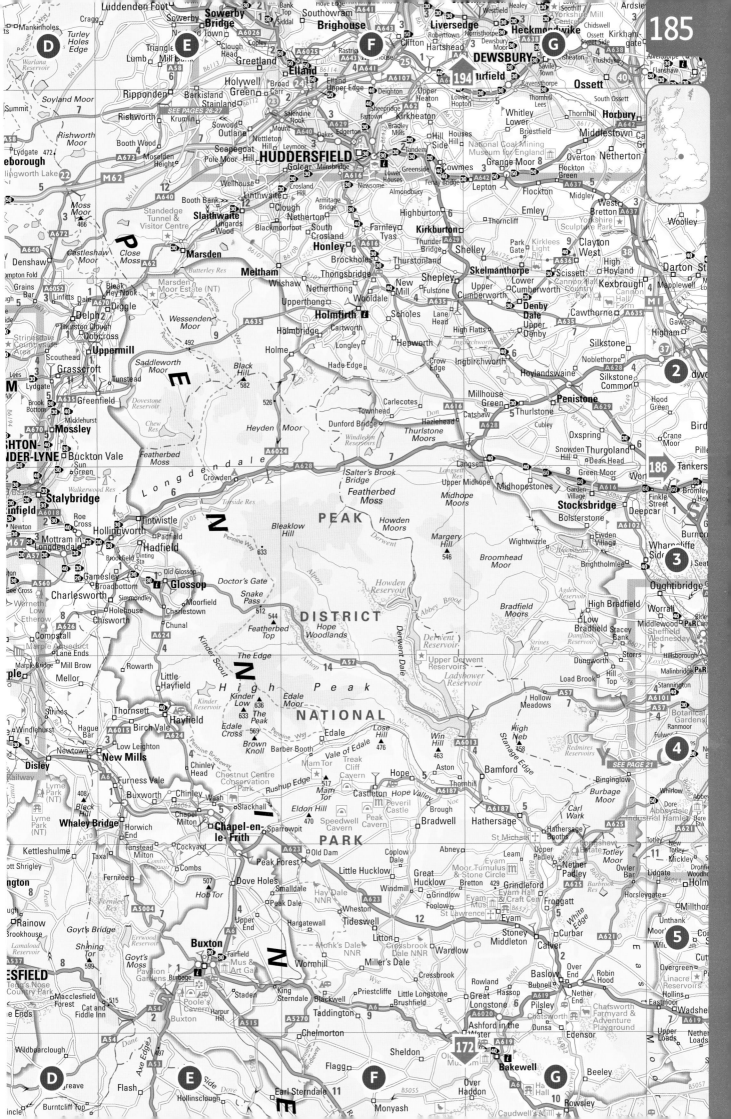

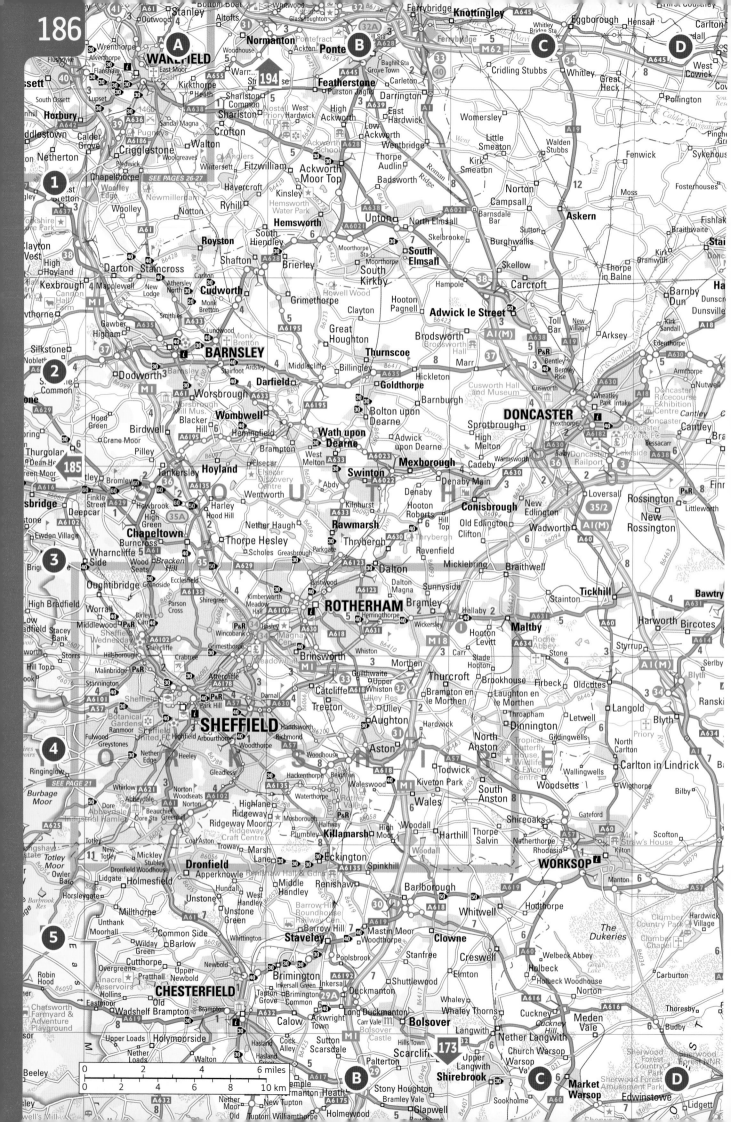

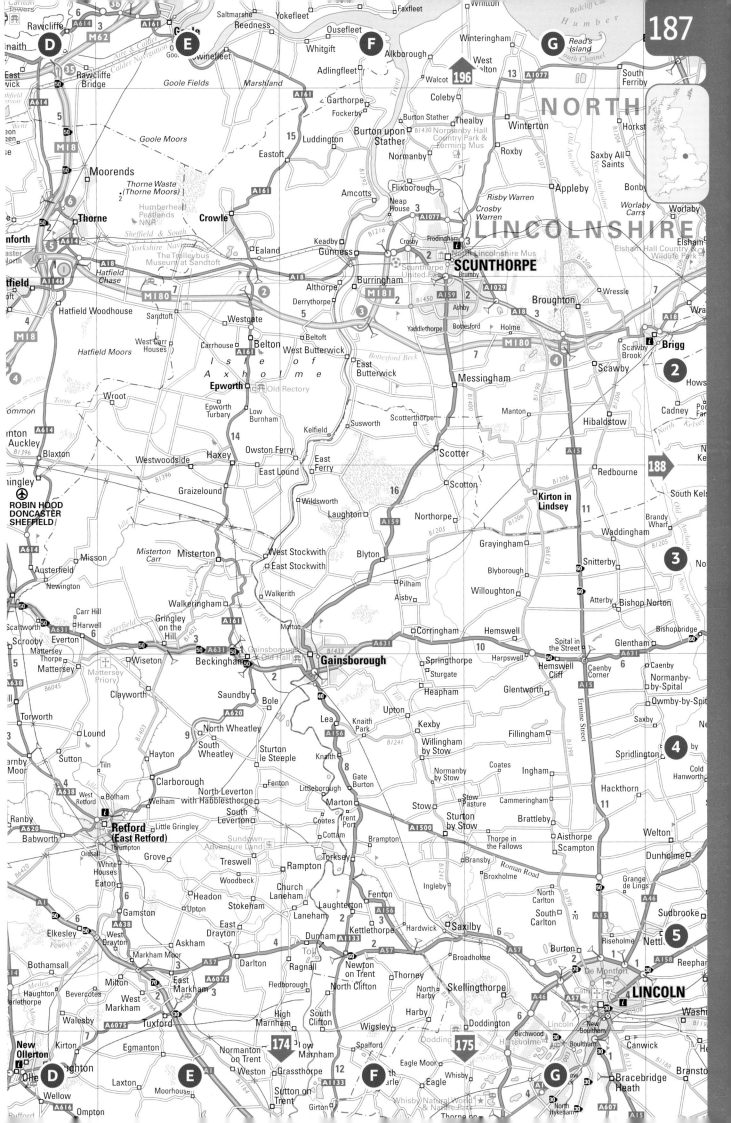

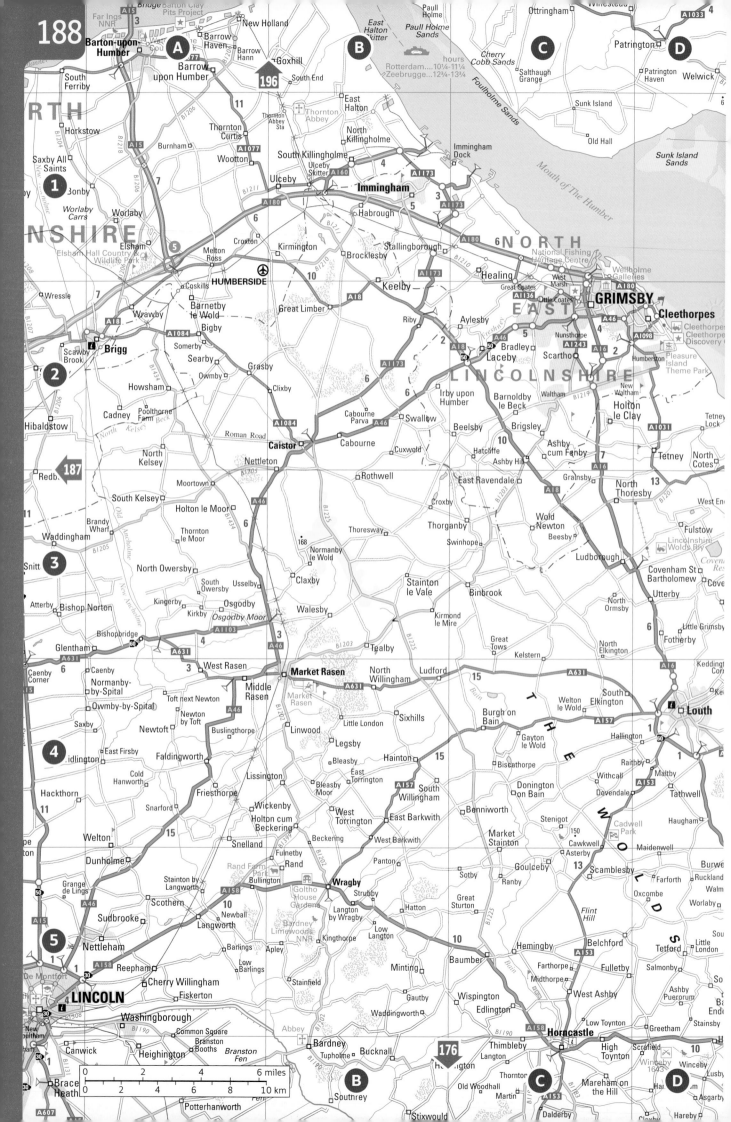

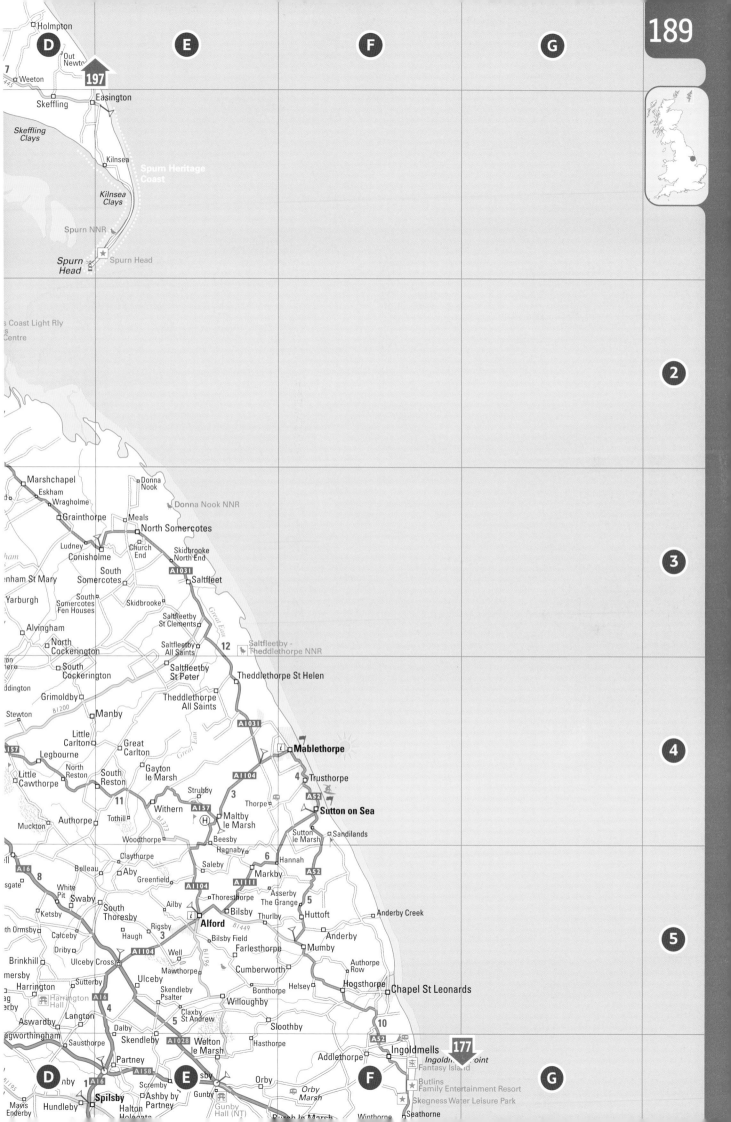

D **E** **F** **G**

Holmpton
Out Newton
197
Weeton
Easington
Skeffling
Skeffling Clays
Kilnsea
Spurn Heritage Coast
Kilnsea Clays
Spurn NNR
Spurn Head
Spurn Head

Coast Light Rly
Centre

2

Marshchapel
Eskham
Donna Nook
Wragholme
Donna Nook NNR
Grainthorpe
Meals
North Somercotes
Ludney
Conisholme
Church End
Skidbrooke North End
nham St Mary
South Somercotes
A1031
Saltfleet
Yarburgh
South Somercotes Fen Houses
Skidbrooke
Alvingham
Saltfleetby St Clements
North Cockerington
Saltfleetby All Saints
12
Saltfleetby - Theddlethorpe NNR

3

South Cockerington
Saltfleetby St Peter
Theddlethorpe St Helen
Grimoldby
B1200
Manby
Theddlethorpe All Saints
Stewton
Little Carlton
A1031
Legbourne
Great Carlton
A157
North Reston
Gayton le Marsh
i 7 Mablethorpe
Little Cawthorpe
South Reston
A1104
4 Trusthorpe
Strubby
11
Withern
3
Thorpe
A52
Muckton
Authorpe
Tothill
A157
Maltby le Marsh
H
Beesby
Sutton on Sea
B1373
Woodthorpe
Hagnaby
Sutton le Marsh
Sandilands

4

Claythorpe
Saleby
6 Hannah
Belleau
Aby
Greenfield
Markby
A52
gate
8
White Pit
Swaby
A16
Ailby
A104
Thoresthorpe
Asserby
5
Anderby Creek
South Thoresby
Rigsby
i
Bilsby
The Grange
Huttoft
Ketsby
Calceby
Haugh
3
Alford
Thurlby
Driby
Bilsby Field
Anderby
Brinkhill
Ulceby Cross
A1104
Well
Farlesthorpe
Mumby
mersby
Sutterby
Mawthorpe
Cumberworth
Helsey
Authorpe Row
Harrington
Ulceby
Skendleby Psalter
Bonthorpe
Hogsthorpe
Chapel St Leonards
erby
Harrington Hall
A16
Willoughby
Aswardby
Langton
4
Claxby St Andrew
Sloothby
10
gworthingham
Dalby
5
Welton le Marsh
Hasthorpe
A52
Sausthorpe
Skendleby
A1028
Addlethorpe
Ingoldmells
177
Partney
Ingold Point
Fantasy Island
nby
A16
A158
Scremby
sby
Orby
Orby Marsh
Butlins Family Entertainment Resort
Spilsby
Ashby by Partney
Gunby
Skegness Water Leisure Park
Hundleby
Halton Holegate
Gunby Hall (NT)
Winthorpe
Seathorne
Mavis Enderby

5

D **E** **F** **G**

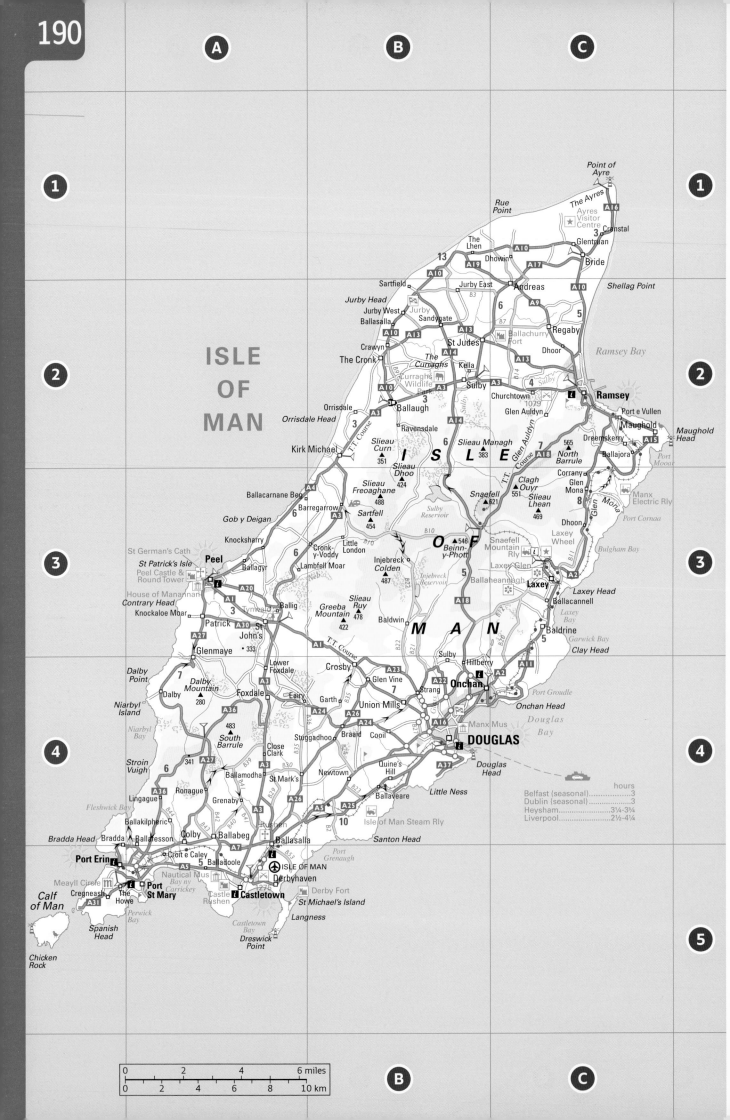

ISLE OF MAN

Point of Ayre

The Ayres

Rue Point

Ayres Visitor Centre

A16

Cranstal

Glentruan

3

Bride

Shellag Point

The Lhen

13

A19

Dhowin

A10

A17

Sartfield

Jurby East

B3

Andreas

A10

Ramsey Bay

6

A9

5

Jurby Head

Jurby West

Jurby

Sandygate

Ballasalla

A10

A13

A13

Ballachurry Fort

Regaby

B7

Dhoor

Crawyn

St Judes

A14

Keila

A13

Port e Vullen

The Cronk

The Curraghs

Sulby

A3

4

Sulby

Ramsey

Maughold

Orrisdale

Curraghs Wildlife Park

A10

Churchtown

1079

Glen Auldyn

Dreemskerry

A15

Maughold Head

Orrisdale Head

Ballaugh

3

Ravensdale

A14

Slieau Managh

383

565

North Barrule

A18

7

Corrany

Ballajora

Port Mooar

Kirk Michael

Slieau Curn 351

Slieau Dhoo 424

ISLE

Snaefell 621

Clagh Ouyr 551

Slieau Lhean 469

Glen Mona

8

Dhoon

Manx Electric Rly

Ballacarnane Beg

Slieau Freoaghane 488

Sulby Reservoir

OF

Glen Mona

Port Cornaa

Gob y Deigan

Barregarrow

A4

6

Sartfell 454

B10

Snaefell Mountain Rly

Laxey Wheel

Bulgham Bay

St German's Cath

Knocksharry

Cronk-y-Voddy

Little London

Beinn-y-Phott 546

Snaefell

5

Laxey Glen

St Patrick's Isle

Peel

6

B70

Injebreck Colden 487

F

Ballaheannagh

Laxey

Laxey Head

Peel Castle & Round Tower

Ballagyr

Lambfell Moar

Nab

Injebreck Reservoir

B21

A18

Ballacannell

House of Manannan

Ballig

Greeba Mountain 422

Slieau Ruy 478

Baldwin

M

A

N

Baldrine

Contrary Head

A1

Tynwald

B22

B26

5

Laxey Bay

Knockaloe Moar

3

Garwick Bay

Patrick

A30

St John's

T.T. Course

Sulby

Clay Head

A27

· 333

Crosby

A23

Hillberry

A2

A11

Glenmaye

A1

Glen Vine

A22

Onchan

Dalby Point

7

Lower Foxdale

Garth

7

Strang

Port Groudle

Niarbyl Island

Dalby Mountain 280

Foxdale

A3

Fairy

B35

Union Mills

A16

Onchan Head

Dalby

A36

Crosby

A24

Braaid

Cooil

Manx Mus

Douglas Bay

483

South Barrule

A27

A24

Stuggadhoo

DOUGLAS

Stroin Vuigh

6

341

Ballamodha

B39

B30

Newtown

Quine's Hill

A37

Douglas Head

Niarbyl Bay

A36

Ronague

St Mark's

B29

A26

A23

Ballaveare

Little Ness

Fleshwick Bay

Grenaby

A3

A5

A25

10

Isle of Man Steam Rly

Santon Head

Lingague

B44

Rushen

Ballakilpheric

Colby

Ballabeg

Ballasalla

Port Grenaugh

Bradda Head

Bradda

Ballafesson

A7

Croit e Caley

A5

Balladoole

Port Grenaugh

Port Erin

Meayll Circle

Croit e Caley

5

ISLE OF MAN

Derbyhaven

Calf of Man

Cregneash

The Howe

Port St Mary

Nautical Mus

Bay ny Carrickey

Castle Rushen

Castletown

Derby Fort

A31

St Michael's Island

Perwick Bay

Castletown Bay

Langness

Spanish Head

Dreswick Point

Chicken Rock

hours

Belfast (seasonal)..................3

Dublin (seasonal)..................3

Heysham..................3¼-3¾

Liverpool..................2½-4¼

| 0 | 2 | 4 | 6 miles |
| 0 | 2 | 4 | 6 | 8 | 10 km |

D   **E**   **F**   **G**

Sands

Great Urswick

Dalton-in-Furness

Little Urswick   Bardsea

Humphrey Head Point

Stainton with Adgar
Newto

Scales   9   Baycliff

Hawcoat

A5087

199

North Walney NNR

Gleaston   Aldingl

Abbey   Furness

Dendron

Newbarns Abbey

North Scale

Roose

Leece   Newbiggin

M O R E C A M

Dock Museum

Roosecote

Vickerstown

4   Roose

Cartmel Wharf

BARROW-IN-FURNESS

B A Y

Tummer
Hill Scar

A590

Roosebeck

1

Biggar

Rampside

Mort
Bank

Isle of
Walney

Roa Island

Sheep
Island

Foulney Island

Yeoman
Wharf

Piel

South End

Piel Island

Piel Bar

Lancaster Sound

Hilpsford Point

A589   Sandylands

3

Heysham

A683

Douglas 3¼-3¾hrs

Middleton

Heysham Lake

Sunderland
Bank

2

Sunderland

Sunderland

2

Lo
Up

Larne 8hrs

Bernard
Wharf

Cockersand
Abbey

North
Wharf

Pilling Lane

La

192

22

Rossall
Point

Knott End-on-Sea

Fisher's Row

Freeport

Preesall

Pilling   Stake Pool

Scronkey

Fleetwood

Stalmine

aglan

3

Moor End

Hale Nook

3

A587

Burn
Naze

Staynall

Cold
Row

Sower Carr

A585

Trunnah

Stanah

Out Rawcliffe

Ra
Ro

40

Hambleton

Cleveleys

Little
Bispham

Little
Thornton

Whin Lane End

Thornton

Norbreck

Skippool

Larbreck   Toll

Gre

Bispham

Carleton

2   Little
Singleton

Little
Eccleston

Copp

A584   A587

Warbreck

A586

Singleton

Elsw

North Shore

Normoss

Poulton-le-Fylde

Thistleton

BLACKPOOL

Hardhorn
Newton

B5266

A585

BLACKPOOL

Layton

Staining

Greenhalgh

Esprick

Blackpool Zoo

Wh

Blackpool Tower

Great
Marton

Weeton

3

dlar

Sea Life Centre

Mythop

Moor
Side

South Shore

Mereside

4

South Pier

Blackpool

Great
Plumpton

Wesha

Blackpool Pleasure Beach

Common
Edge

Little
Plumpton

Westby

Ki

Squires
Gate

Peel

Lower
Ballam

Wrea Green

Blackpool Holiday Centre

4

**BLACKPOOL
INTERNATIONAL**

Higher
Ballam

Moss
Side

Bryning

Hall Cross

St Anne's

Hey Houses

LYTHAM ST ANNE'S

Ansdell

Warton

Fairhaven

Saltcotes

Warton
Bank

Salter's
Bank

Royal Lytham
& St. Anne's

Lytham

10

A584

Ribble

Banks Sands

Ribble
Estuary
NNR

West Lancas
Light Ra

Hesketh Ba

5

Hundred End

Banks

Ta

Horse Bank

Crossens

Holmes

183

ry Brow

Marshside

Mere
Brow

B5246

SOUTHPORT

Southport Pier

Churchtown

P&R

Blowick

Holmeswood

Trans Pennine Trail

P&R

D   **E**   **F**   **G**

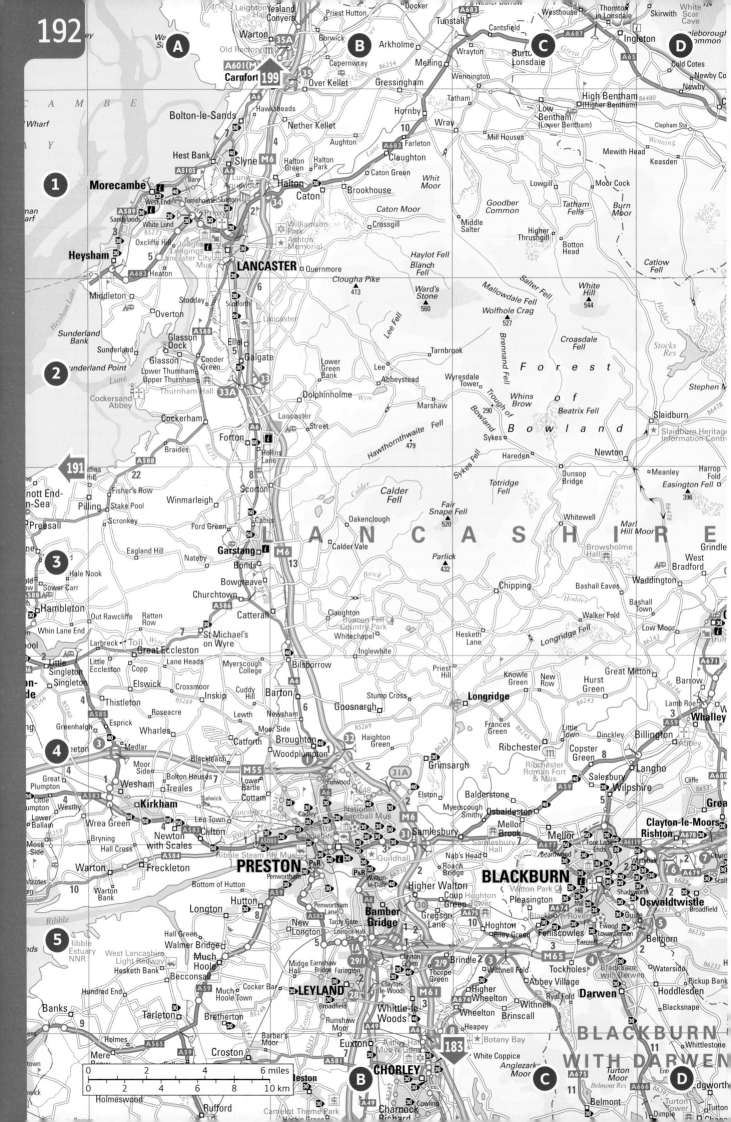

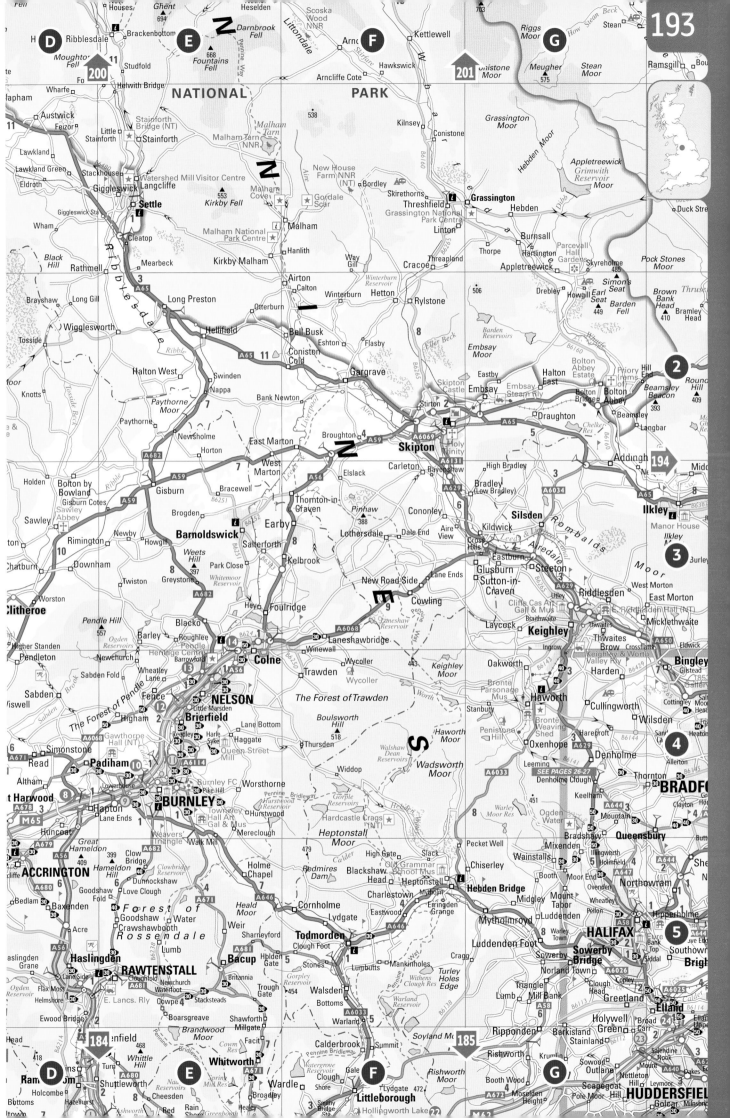

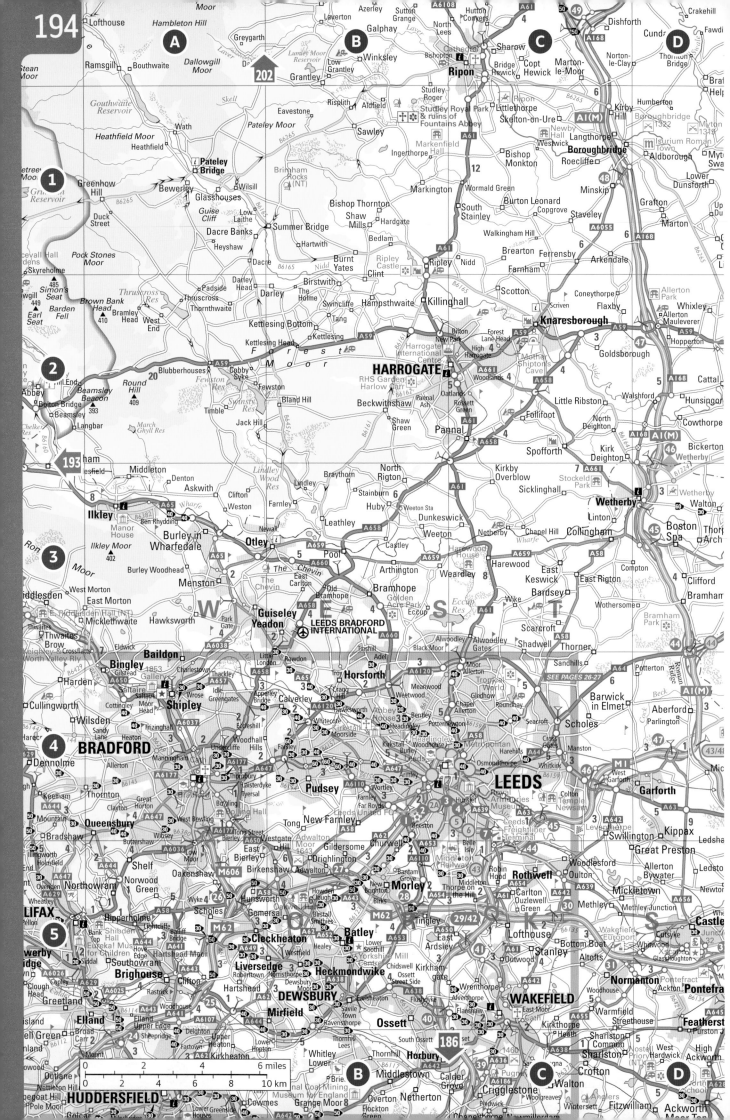

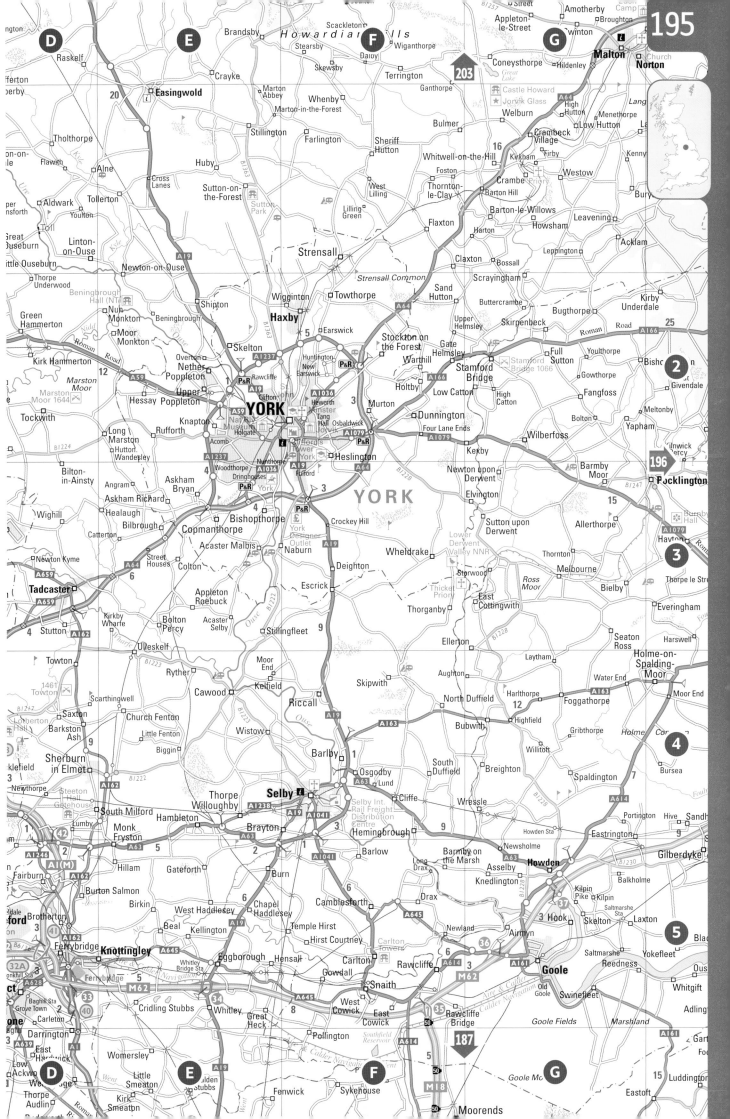

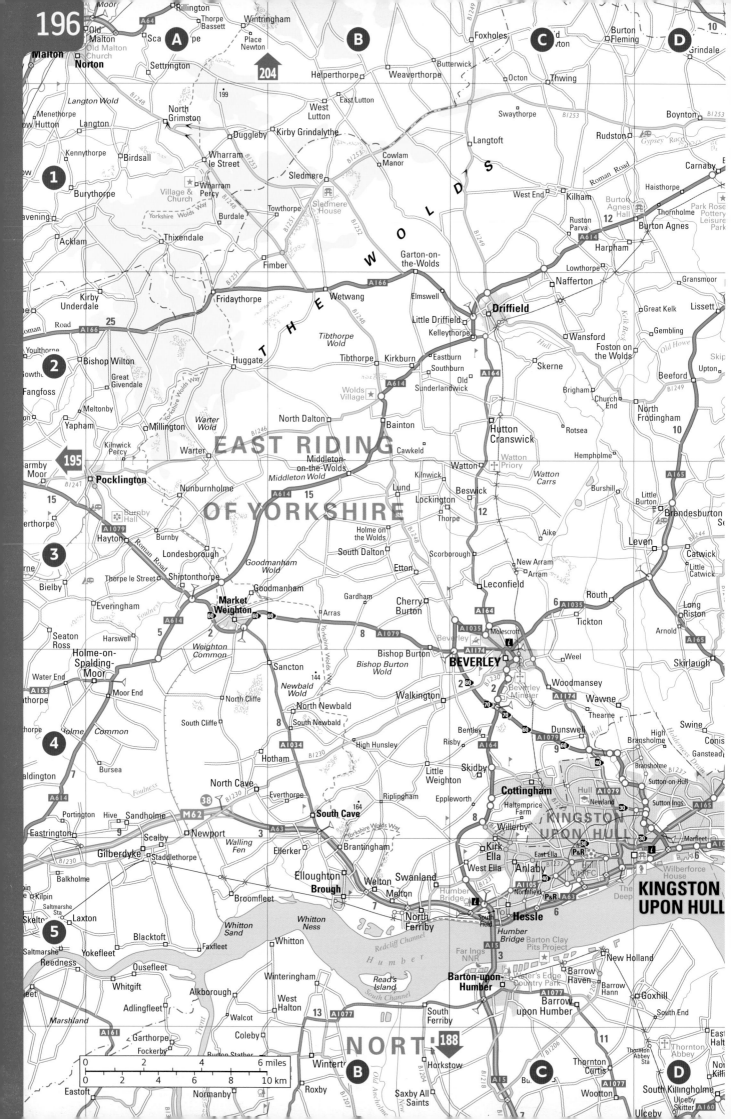

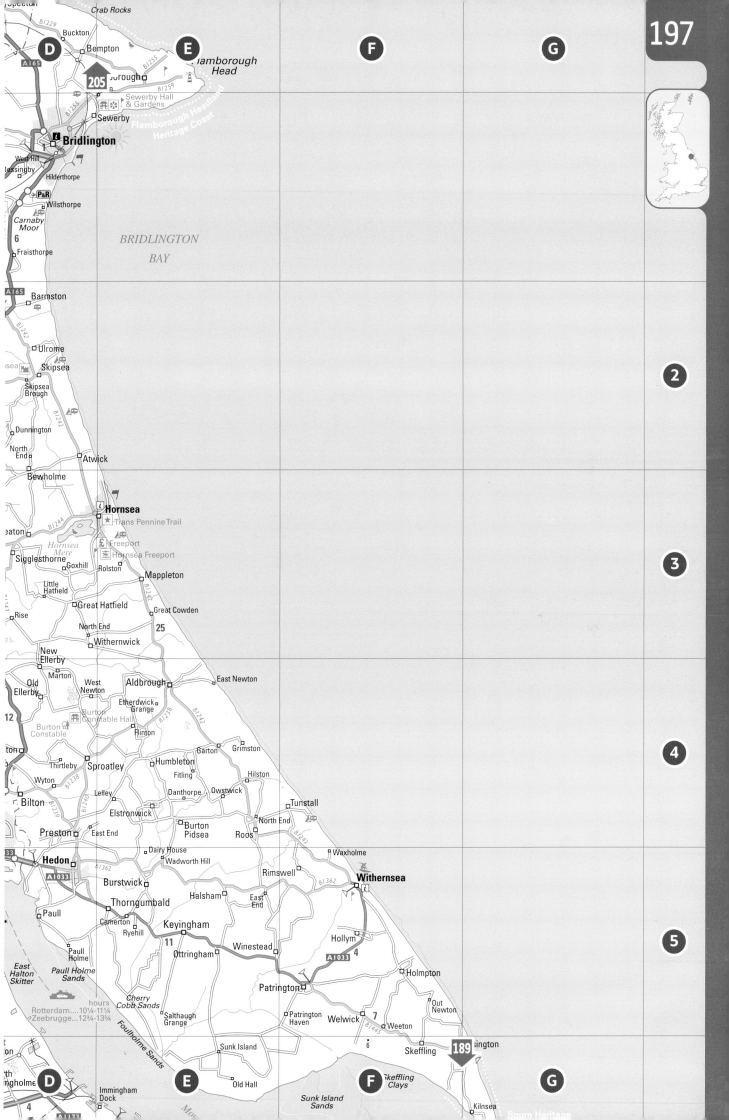

D

Crab Rocks

B1229 Buckton
Bempton
E
Flamborough Head
A165
orough
B1259
205
Sewerby Hall & Gardens
Sewerby
Flamborough Headland Heritage Coast

West Hill
Bessingby
Bridlington
Hilderthorpe

P&R
Wilsthorpe
Carnaby Moor
6
Fraisthorpe

BRIDLINGTON BAY

F

G

A165
Barmston
B1242

Ulrome
Skipsea
sea
Skipsea Brough
B1242

Dunnington
North End
Atwick
Bewholme

2

eaton
Hornsea
Trans Pennine Trail
Hornsea Mere
Freeport
Hornsea Freeport
Sigglesthorne
Goxhill
Rolston
Mappleton
Little Hatfield
B1242
Great Hatfield
Great Cowden
Rise
North End
25
Withernwick

3

New Ellerby
Marton
West Newton
Aldbrough
East Newton
Old Ellerby
Etherdwick Grange
B1238
B1242
12
Burton Constable Hall
Burton Constable
Flinton
Garton
Grimston
ton
Thirtleby
Sproatley
Humbleton
Fitling
Hilston
Wyton
B1238
Lelley
Danthorpe
Owstwick
Bilton
B1239
B1240
Elstronwick
Tunstall
Preston
East End
Burton Pidsea
Roos
North End
B1242

4

Dairy House
Waxholme
Hedon
B1362
Wadworth Hill
A1033
Rimswell
B1362
Withernsea
Burstwick
Thorngumbald
Halsham
East End
Paull
Camerton
Keyingham
Hollym
Ryehill
11
A1033
Paull Holme
Ottringham
Winestead
4
East Halton Skitter
Paull Holme Sands
Holmpton
hours
Rotterdam....10¼-11¼
Zeebrugge...12¾-13¾
Cherry Cobb Sands
Patrington
Out Newton
Salthaugh Grange
Patrington Haven
Welwick
7
Weeton
B1445
6
Foulholme Sands
Sunk Island
Skeffling
189
ington

5

D
ngholme
4
A1173
Immingham Dock
E
Old Hall
Mon
Sunk Island Sands
F
Skeffling Clays
G
Kilnsea
Soum Heritage

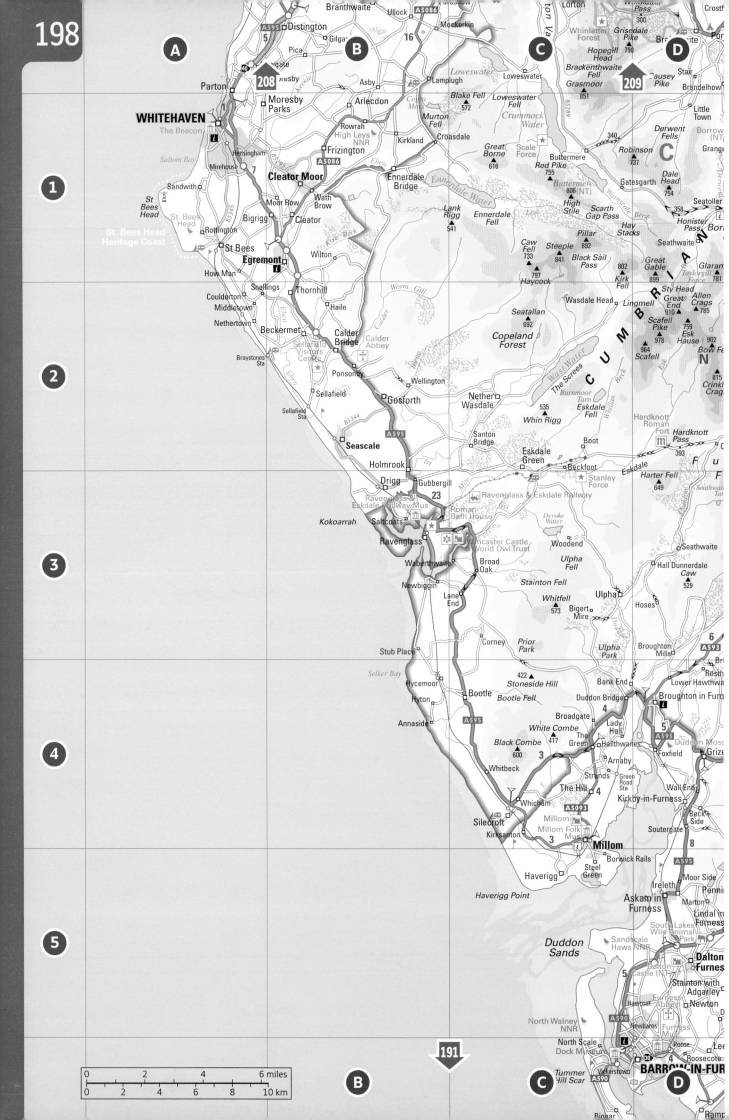

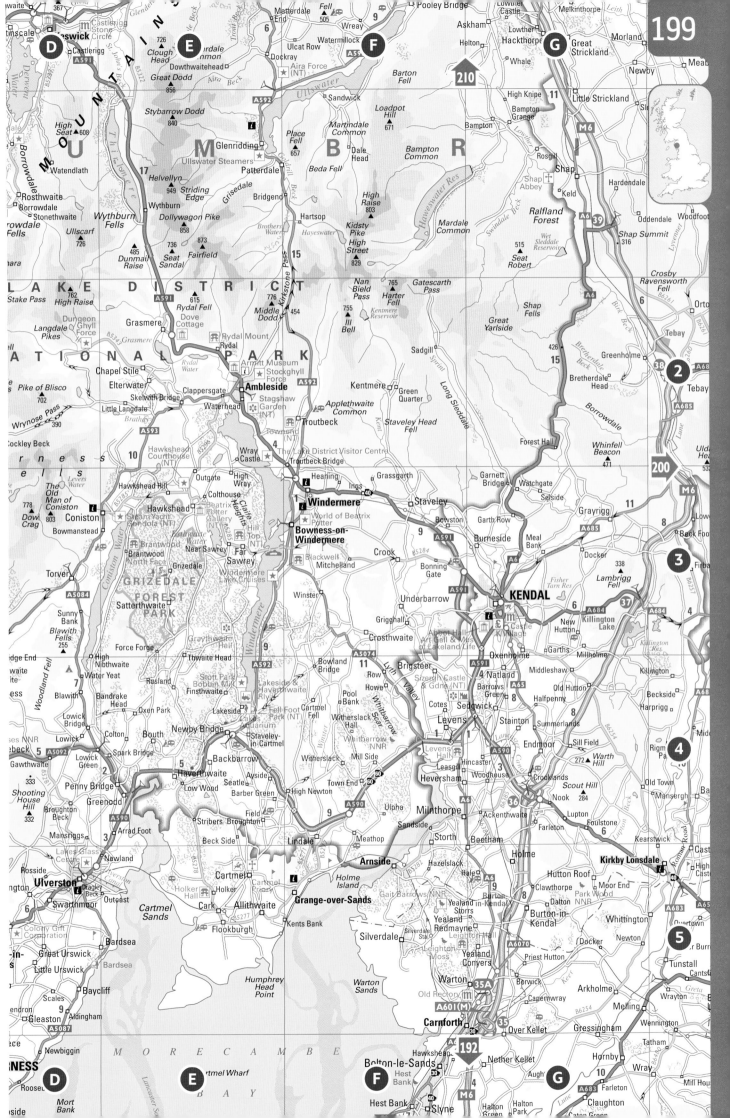

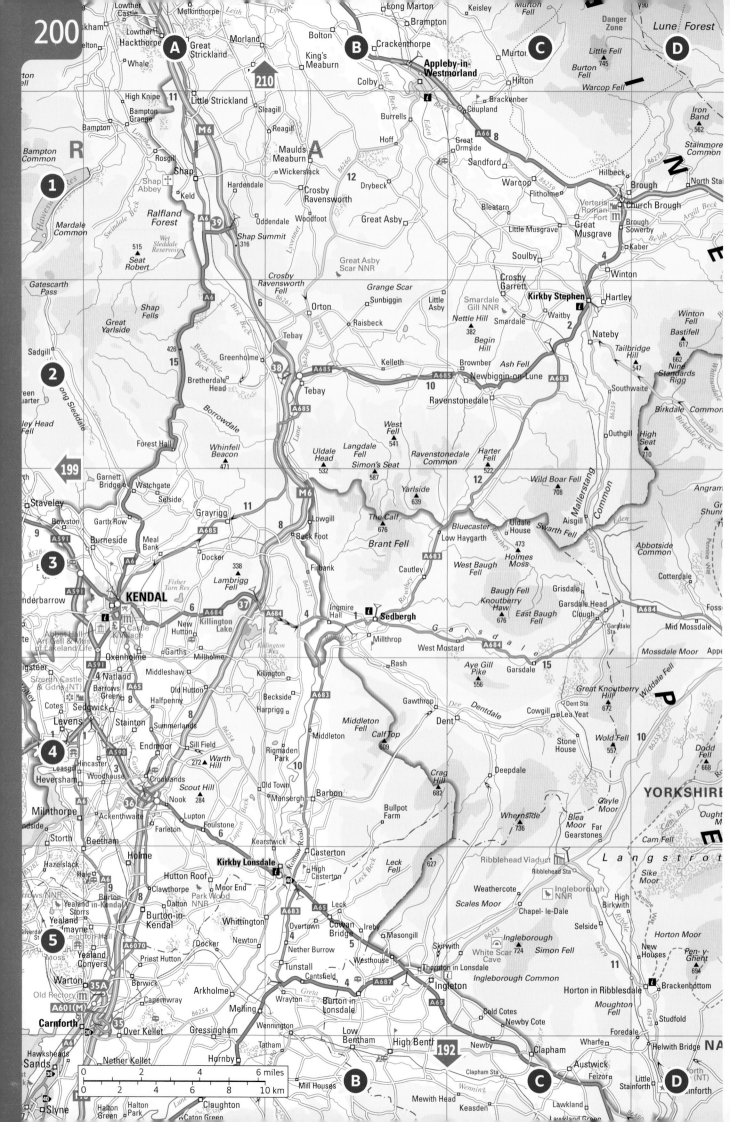

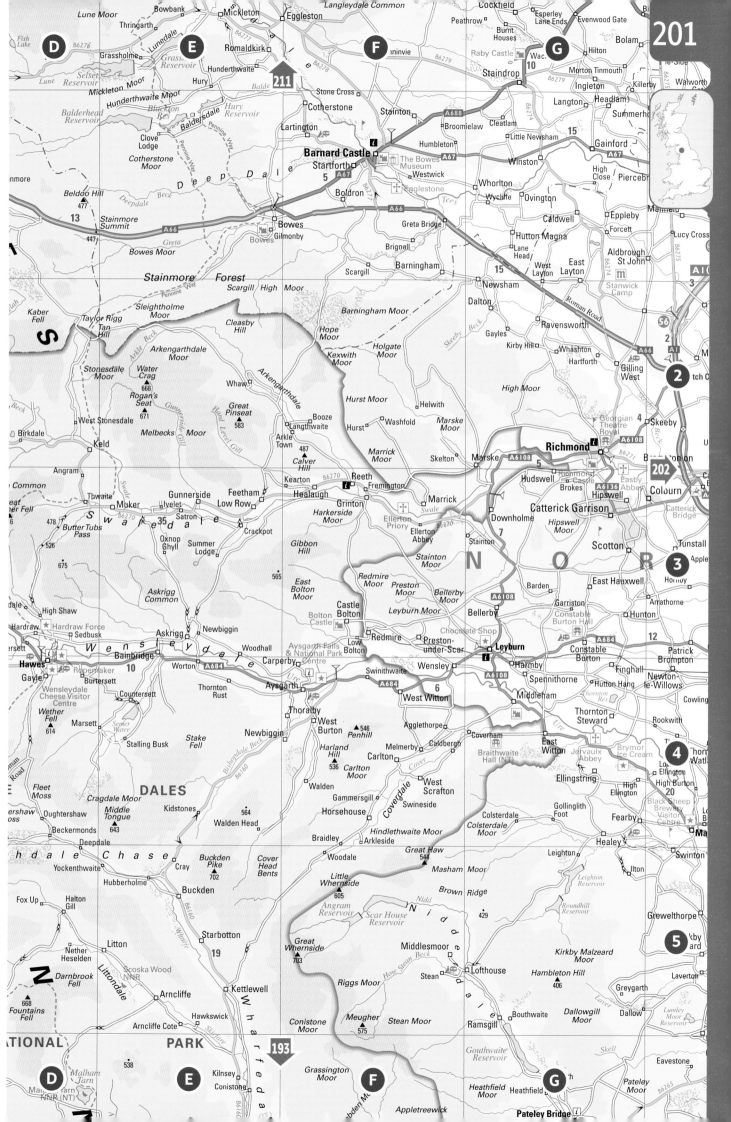

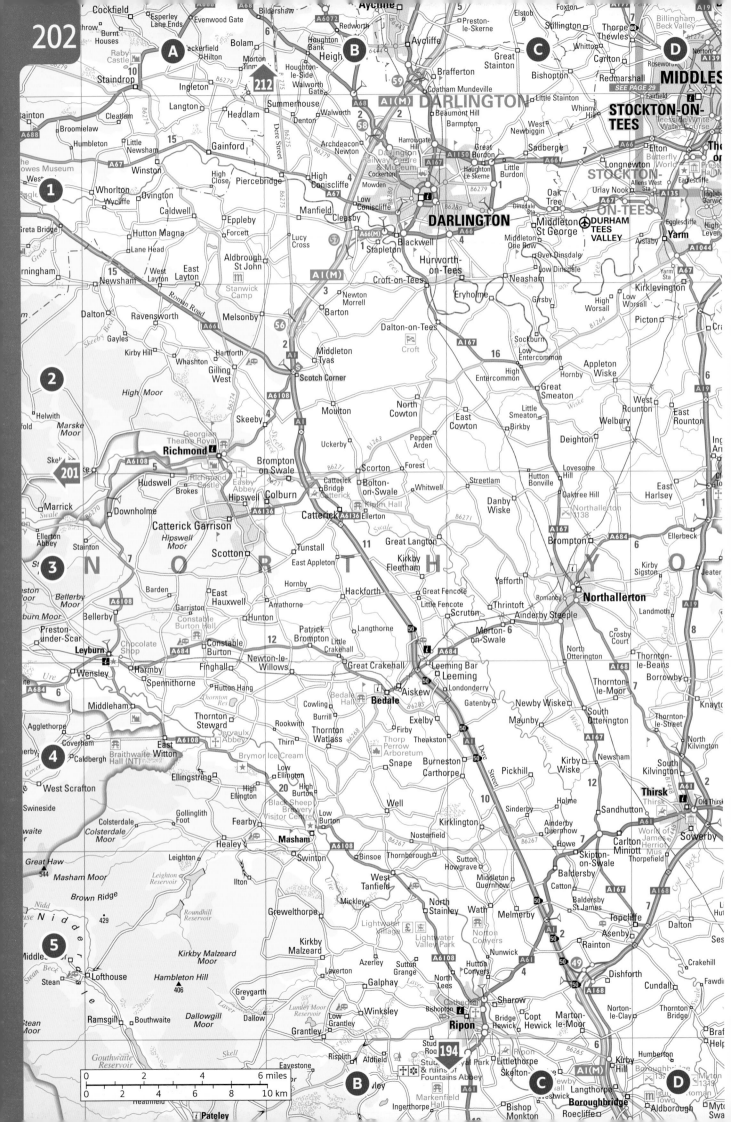

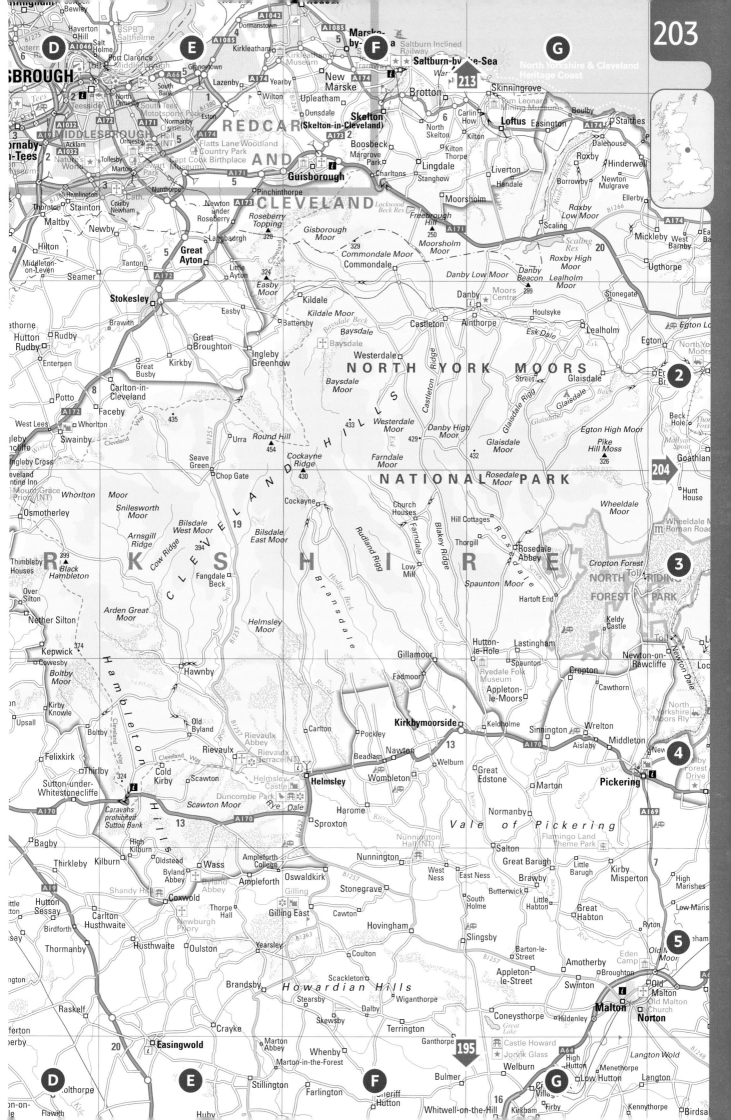

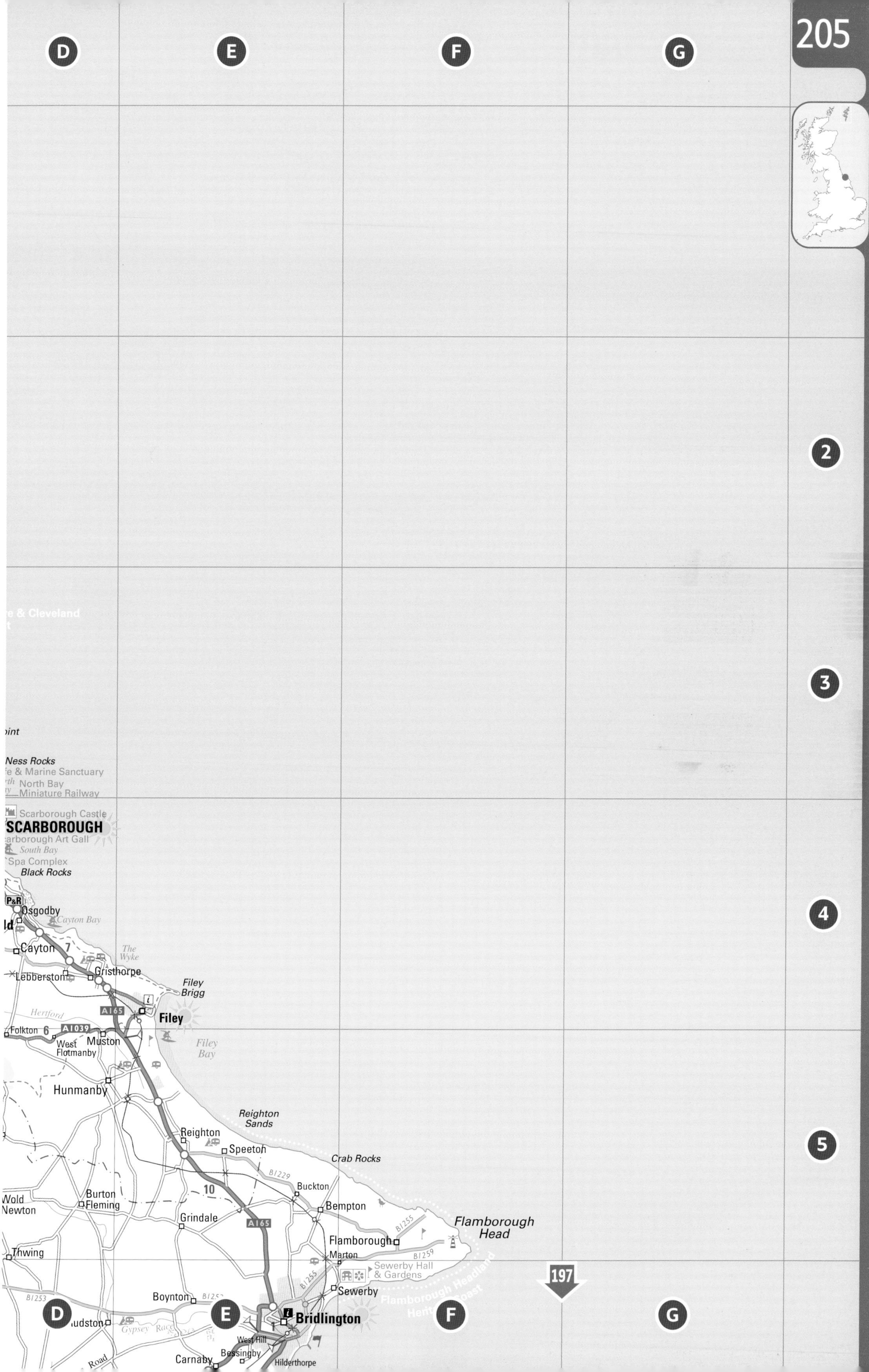

D E F G

197

2

3

4

5

...point

Ness Rocks
...fe & Marine Sanctuary
...rth North Bay
...y Miniature Railway

🏰 Scarborough Castle
SCARBOROUGH
...arborough Art Gall
⚓ *South Bay*
Spa Complex
Black Rocks

P&R
...ld 🔵Osgodby
Cayton Bay
🔵Cayton 7
🔵
Lebberston 🔵 🔵Gristhorpe
The Wyke
Hertford **A165** *Filey Brigg*
i
🔵Folkton 6 **A1039** **Filey**
🔵 West Muston
Flotmanby *Filey Bay*
Hunmanby

Reighton Sands
🔵Reighton
🔵 🔵Speeton
Crab Rocks
B1229
Wold 🔵Buckton
Newton Burton
Fleming 🔵Bempton
🔵Grindale **A165** *Flamborough Head*
B1255
🔵Thwing 🔵Flamborough
🔵Marton
Sewerby Hall
& Gardens
B1255
Boynton 🔵 *B1253* 🔵Sewerby
B1253 *Flamborough Headland*
...udston i **Bridlington** *Heritage Coast*
Gypsey Race West Hill
🔵Bessingby
Carnaby Hilderthorpe

D E F G

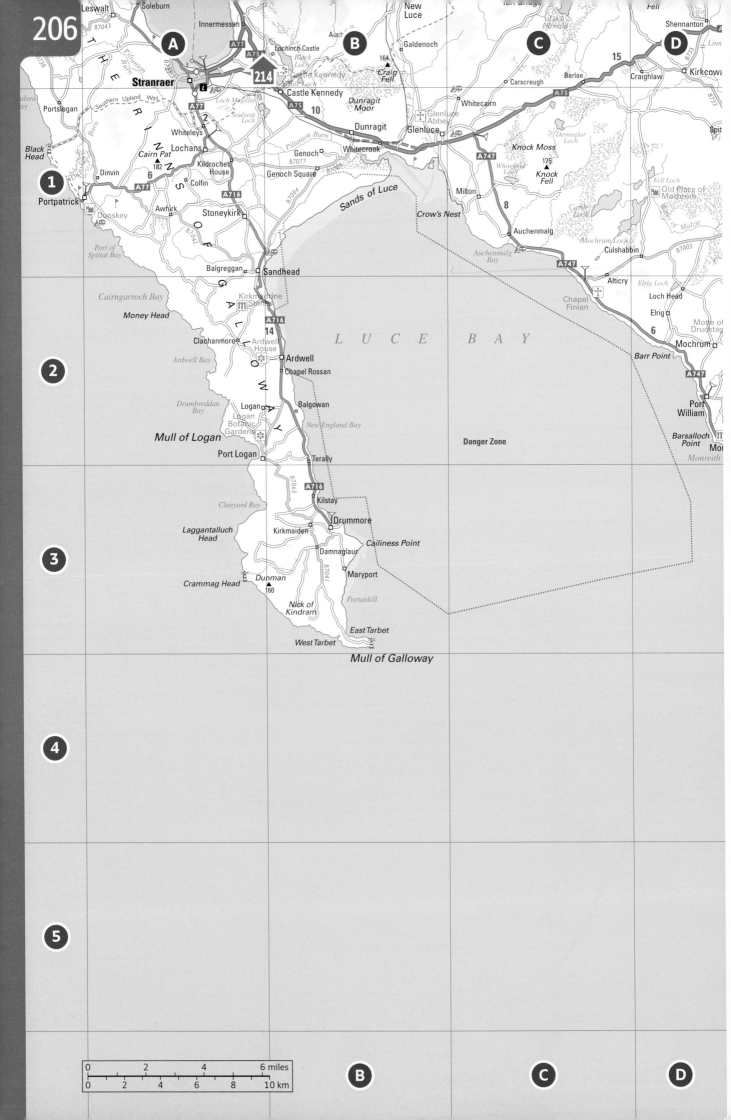

Leswalt · Soleburn
Innermessan
New Luce
Fell

A · **B** · **C** · **D**

Shennanton

Galdenoch
Craig Fell · 164
Carscreugh
Barlae
Craiglaw · 15
Kirkeowan

Stranraer · 214
Castle Kennedy
Lochinch Castle
Dunragit Moor
Glenluce Abbe
Whitecairn
A75

Portslogan
Loch Magillie
Soulseat Loch
Castle Kennedy
Dunragit
Glenluce
Knock Moss
175 · Knock Fell
Dernaglar Loch
Spit

Black Head
Whiteleys · Lochans
Genoch
Whitecrook
Genoch Square
Whitefield Loch
Old Place of Mochrum
Fell Loch

1 Portpatrick · Dinvin · Cairn Pat · 182 · Kildrochet House · Colfin · B7077 · B7084
Milton
A747 · 8
Auchenmalg

Dunskey · Awhirk
Stoneykirk
Sands of Luce
Crow's Nest
Auchenmalg Bay
A747
Culshabbin
B7005

Port of Spittal Bay
Balgreggan · Sandhead
Alticry
Elrig Loch
Loch Head

2 Cairngarroch Bay
Money Head
Kirkmadrine Stones
A716 · 14
Ardwell House
Clachanmore · Ardwell
Chapel Rossan
Ardwell Bay
L U C E   B A Y
Chapel Finian
Elrig
6
Motte of Druchtag
Mochrum
Barr Point

Drumbreddan Bay
Logan
Logan Botanic Gardens
Balgowan
New England Bay
Port William
Barsalloch Point
Mull of Logan
Port Logan
Terally
Danger Zone
Monreith

3 Clanyard Bay
Kilstay
A716
Laggantalluch Head
Kirkmaiden
Drummore
Cailiness Point
Crammag Head
Damnaglaur
Dunman · 160
Maryport
Nick of Kindram
Portankill
East Tarbet
West Tarbet
Mull of Galloway

4

5

0   2   4   6 miles
0 2 4 6 8 10 km

B · **C** · **D**

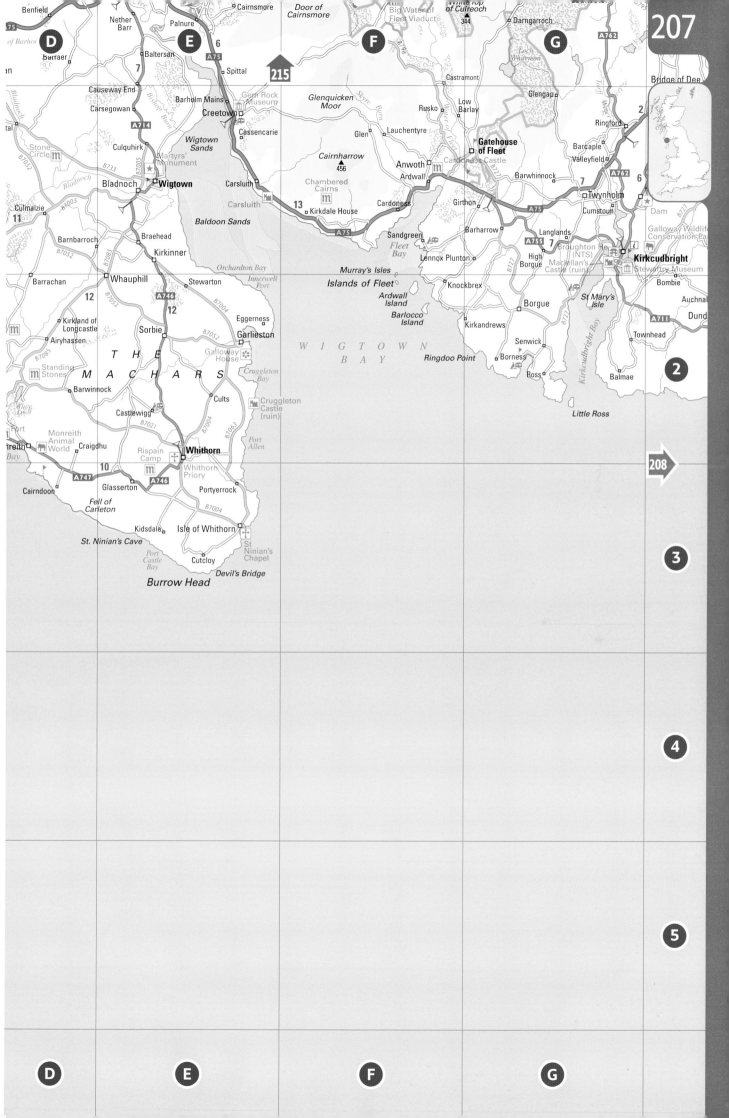

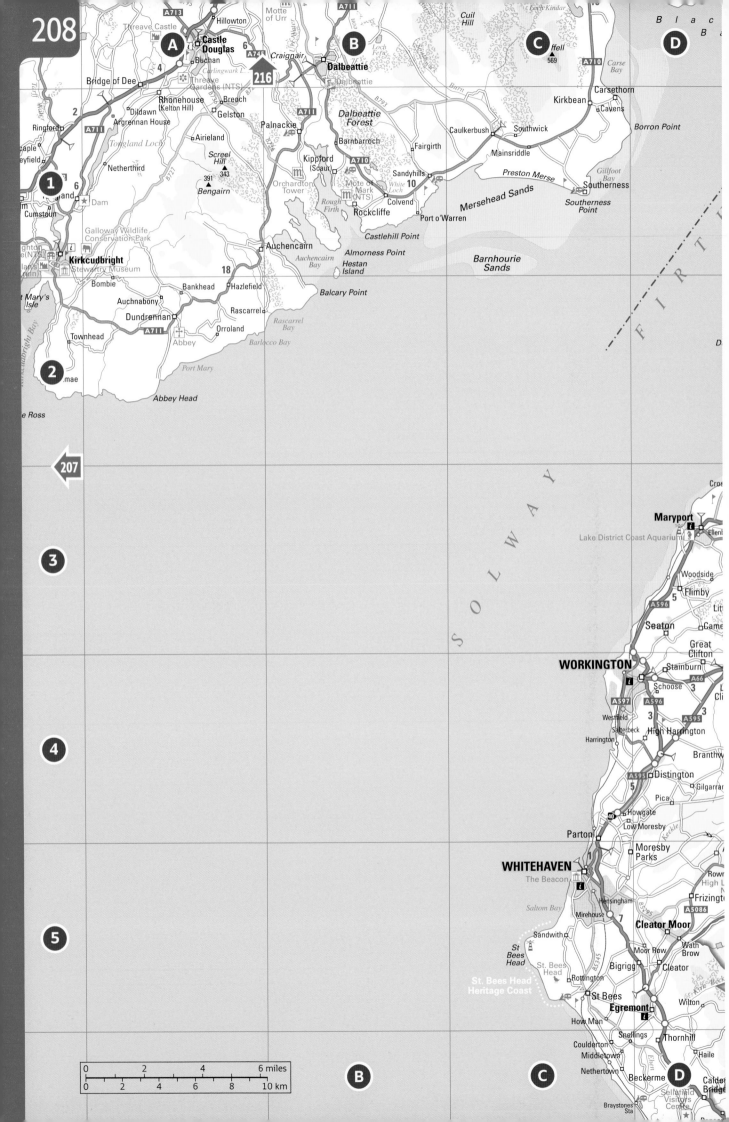

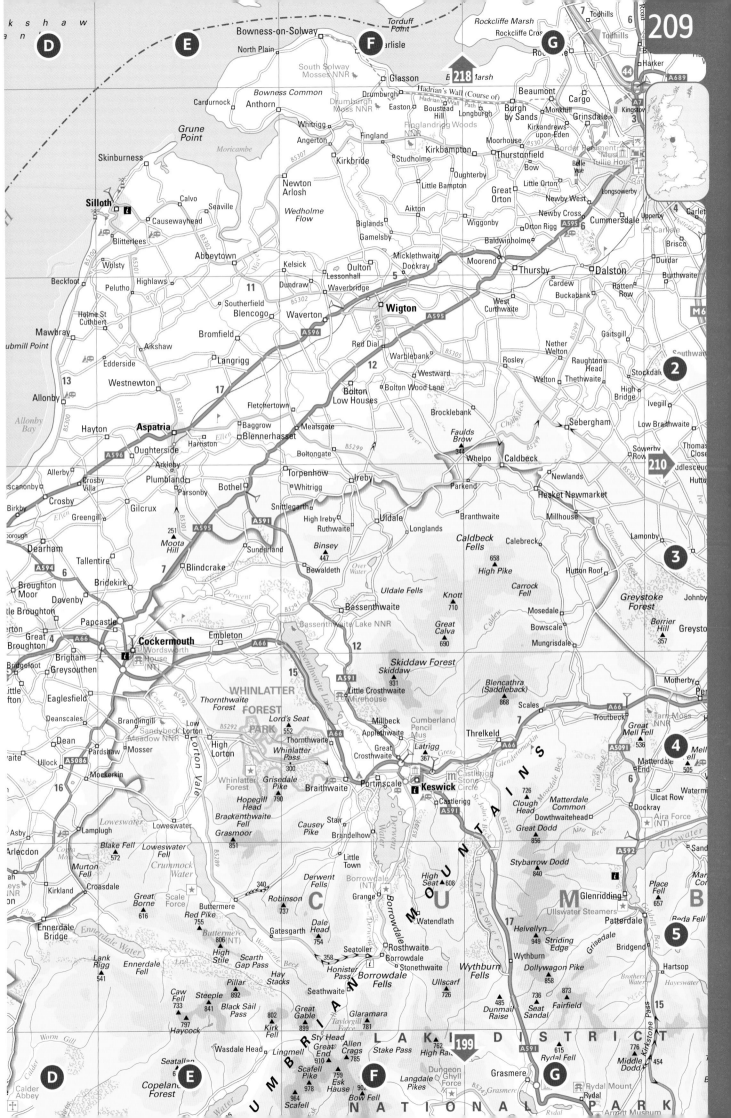

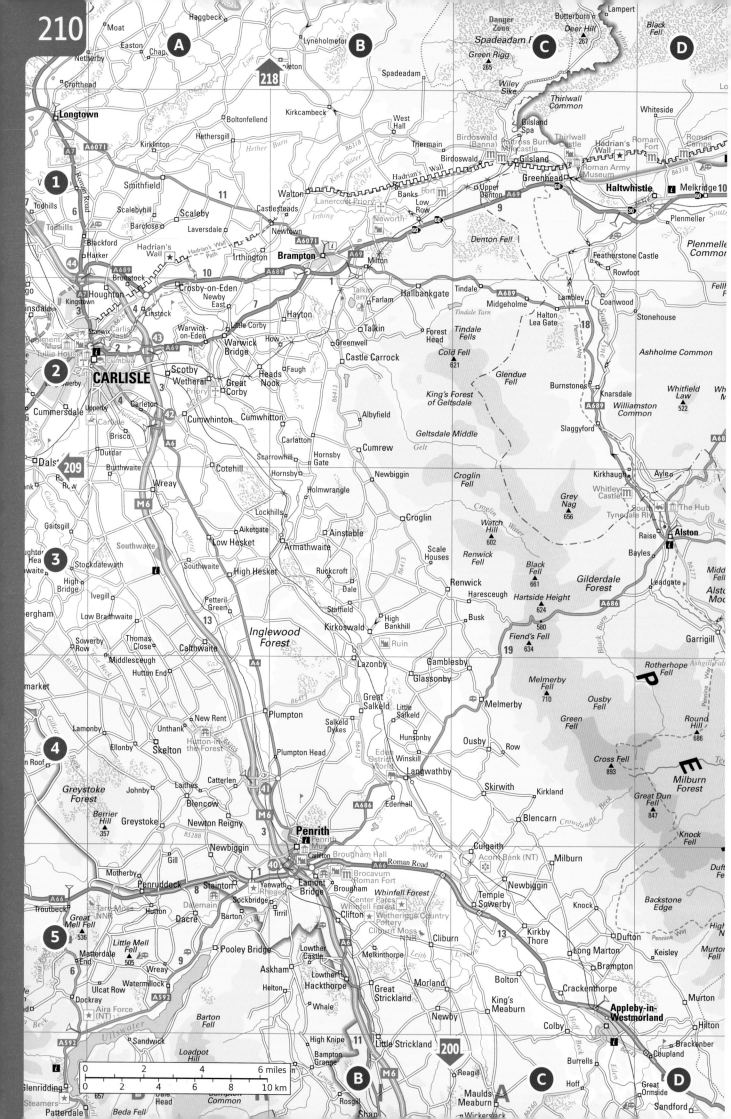

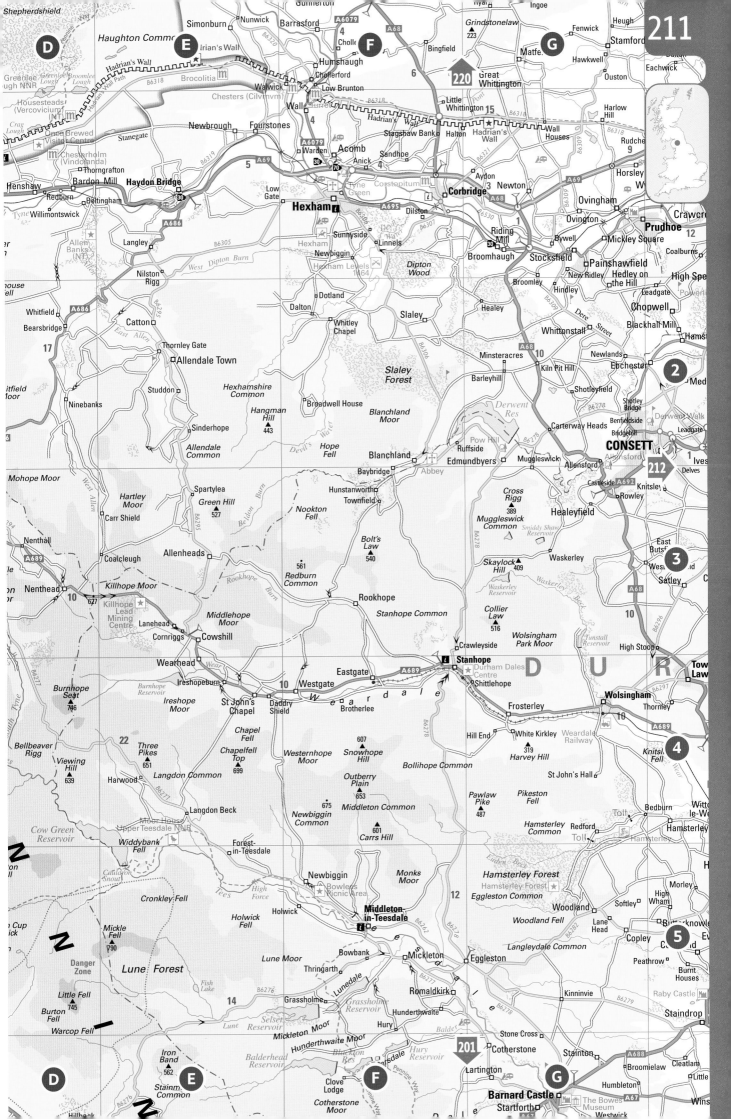

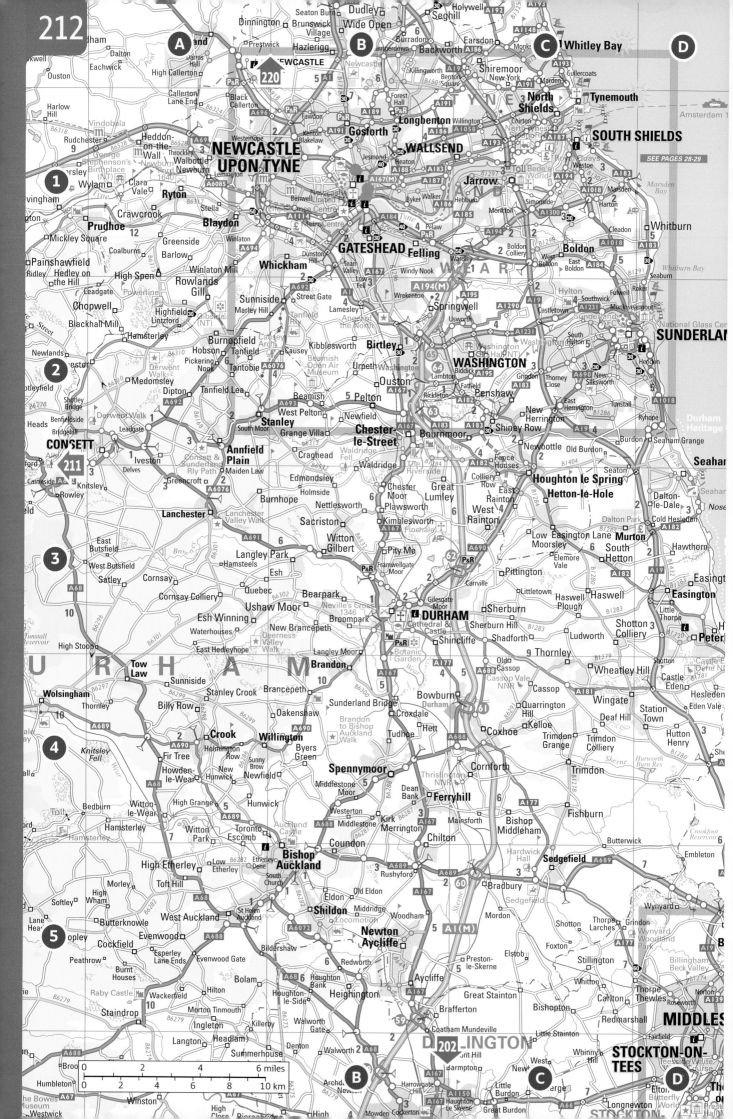

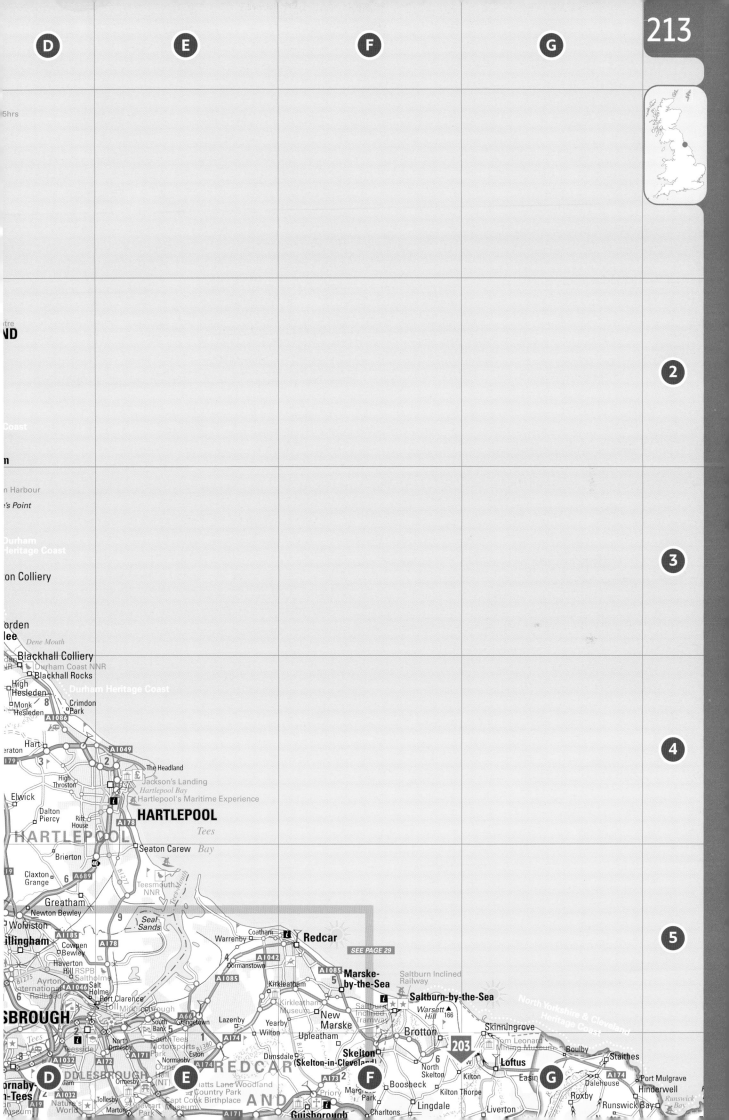

D **E** **F** **G**

5hrs

ND

Coast

n

n Harbour

e's Point

Durham
Heritage Coast

on Colliery

orden
lee *Dene Mouth*

Blackhall Colliery
Durham Coast NNR
Blackhall Rocks
High
Hesleden
Monk 8 Crimdon
Hesleden Park

Durham Heritage Coast

Hart A1086

A1049
eraton
A79 3
High The Headland
Throston Jackson's Landing
Hartlepool Bay
Hartlepool's Maritime Experience
Elwick
Dalton A178
Piercy Rift **HARTLEPOOL**
House *Tees*
HARTLEPOO *Bay*
Seaton Carew
Brierton
40
Claxton 6 A689
Grange
Greatham
Newton Bewley
Wolviston 9 Seal
Sands
illingham A1185 A178
Cowpen Coatham
Bewley Warrenby **Redcar**
Haverton A1042
Hill RSPB Dormanstown SEE PAGE 29
B1275 Saltholme A1085 A1085
Ayrton Salt Marske-
International Holme Kirkleatham 5 by-the-Sea
Railroad A1046 Port Clarence Saltburn Inclined
6 Toll Middlesbrough Railway
Kirkleatham **Saltburn-by-the-Sea**
SBROUGH South Grangetown Museum Saltburn *North Yorkshire & Cleveland*
Bank 5 Lazenby Yearby New Inclined *Heritage Coast*
North South Tees Marske Tramway Warsett 166 Skinningrove
2 Ormesby Motorsports Wilton Upleatham Brotton Hill
Park B1380 203
A1032 Normanby **REDCAR** A173 2 **Loftus** Tom Leonard
A72 A171 Dunsdale **Skelton** 6 Boulby Staithes
ornaby- A1032 Hall (Skelton-in-Cleveland) North Mining Museum
n-Tees A19 E (NT) F Skelton Kilton Easin G
dam Watts Lane Woodland Margrove Boosbeck Kilton Thorpe Roxby Dalehouse Hinderwell
Nature's Country Park Priory Lingdale Liverton Port Mulgrave
World Tollesby Capt Cook Birthplace A173 Runswick Bay
Stewart Museum **AND** Charltons *Runswick*
Park Marton **Guisborough** *Bay*

D **E** **F** **G**

2

3

4

5

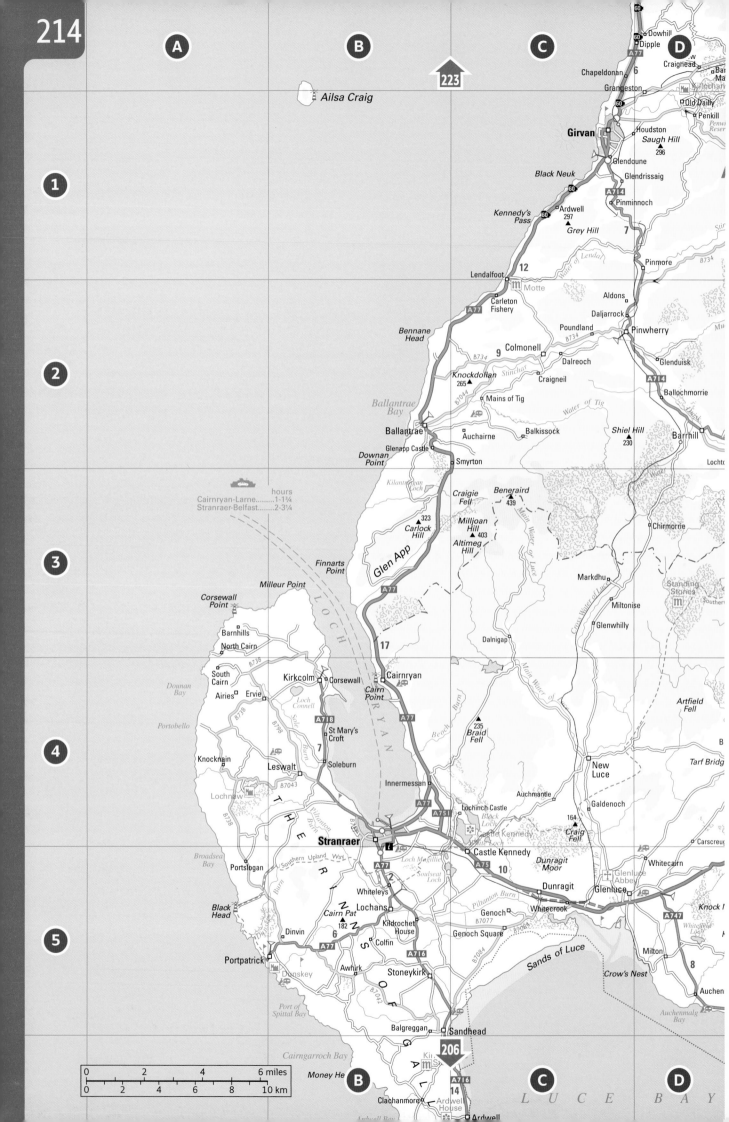

223

Ailsa Craig

60 Dowhill
Dipple
A77
Chapeldonan
6
Craighead
Grangeston
60
Old Daily
Penkill
Penw...
Reser...

Girvan
Houdston
Saugh Hill
296
Glendoune
Black Neuk
Glendrissaig
60
A714
Pinminnoch
Kennedy's Pass
Ardwell
297
60
Grey Hill
7
Pinmore
B73A
12
Lendalfoot
Water of Lendal
Motte
Pinwherry
A77
Carleton Fishery
Aldons
Daljarrock
Poundland
Bennane Head
B734
Colmonell
Dalreoch
Glenduisk
9
Craigneil
A714
Knockdolian
265
Stinchar
Ballochmorrie
B744
Mains of Tig
Water of Tig
Ballantrae Bay
Auchairne
Balkissock
Shiel Hill
230
Barrhill
Ballantrae
Glenapp Castle
Smyrton
Lochto...
Downan Point
Craigie Fell
Beneraird
439
Kilantringan Loch
Milljoan Hill
403
Chirmorrie
323
Carlock Hill
Altimeg Hill
Main Water or Luce

**Cairnryan–Larne.........1–1¼ hours
Stranraer–Belfast........2–3¼**

Finnarts Point
Glen App
Markdhu
Standing Stones
Milleur Point
A77
Miltonise
17
Glenwhilly
Corsewall Point
Dalnigap
Barnhills
North Cairn
Cross Water of Luce
South Cairn
B738
Cairnryan
Cairn Point
Artfield Fell
Kirkcolm
Corsewall
Dounan Bay
Airies
Ervie
Loch Connell
Beoch Burn
235
Braid Fell
Portobello
B798
A718
7
Tarf Bridg...
St Mary's Croft
Knocknain
Soleburn
New Luce
Leswalt
A77
Auchmantle
B7043
Lochnaw
Innermessan
Galdenoch
A751
Lochinch Castle
Black Loch
164
Piltanton Burn
B7...
Craig Fell
Carscreu...
Stranraer
White Loch
Castle Kennedy
Broadsea Bay
Southern Upland Way
A77
Loch Magillie
Whitecairn
Portslogan
A75
10
Dunragit Moor
Glenluce Abbey
Soulseat Loch
Dunragit
Glenluce
Solway Burn
2
Whiteleys
Whitecrook
Black Head
Lochans
Genoch
A747
Cairn Pat
Dinvin
182
Kildrochet House
Genoch Square
B7077
Milton
6
Whitefiel...
Loch...
A77
Colfin
A716
Sands of Luce
Portpatrick
Awhirk
Crow's Nest
8
Dunskey
Stoneykirk
Auchen...
B7042
Port of Spittal Bay
Auchenmalg Bay
Balgreggan
Sandhead
206
Cairngarroch Bay
A716
14
Money He...
Clachanmore
Ardwell House
Ardwell

L U C E   B A Y

0   2   4   6 miles
0   2   4   6   8   10 km

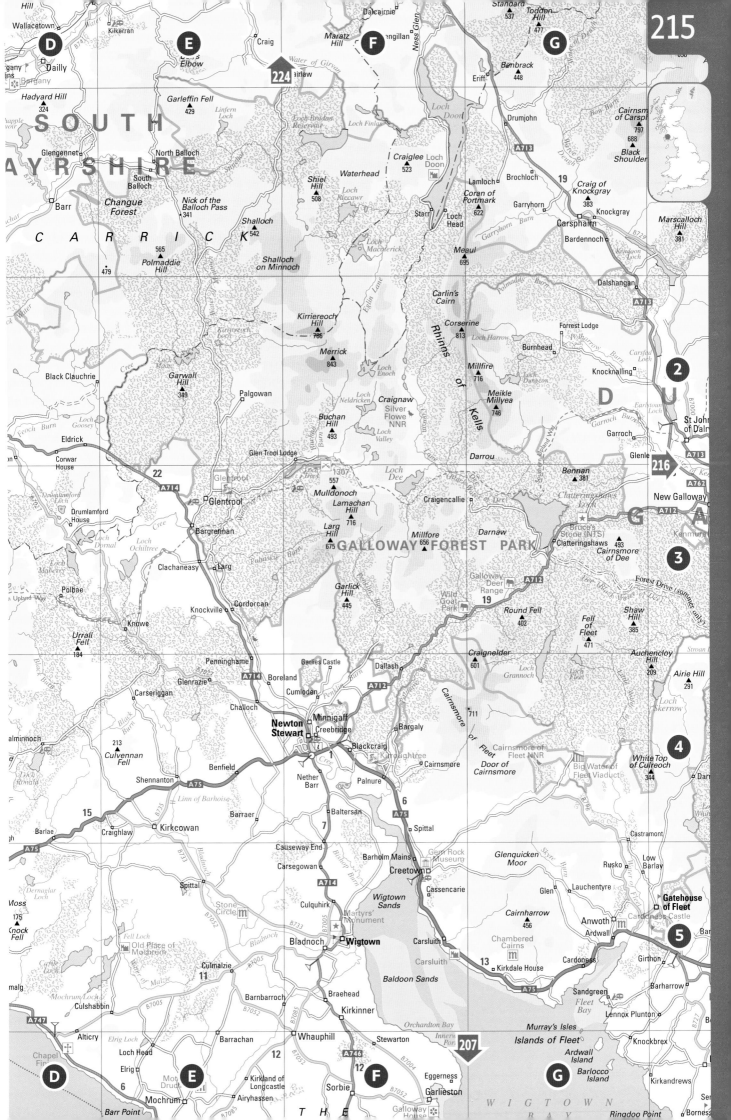

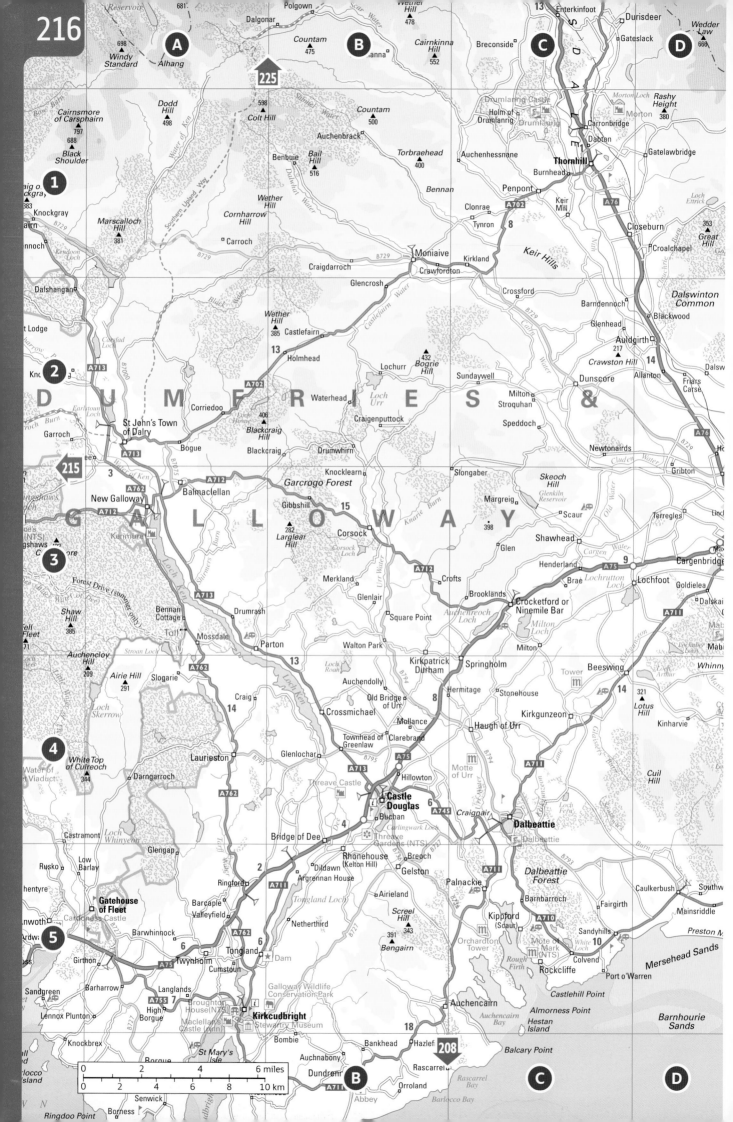

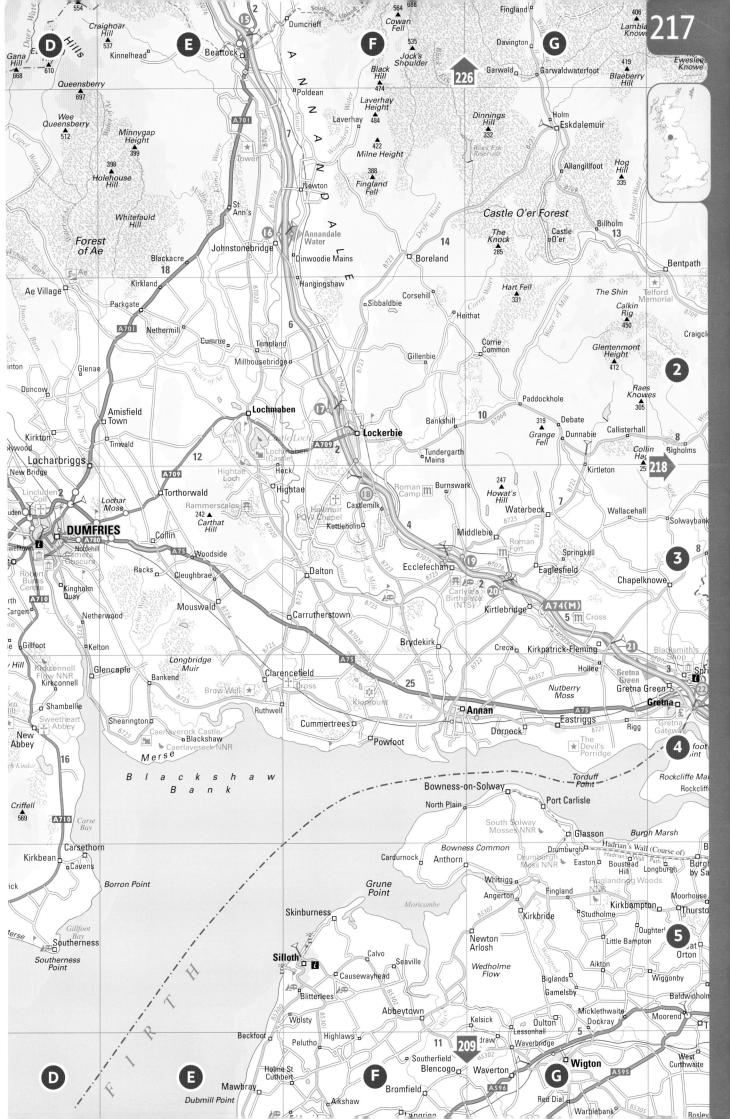

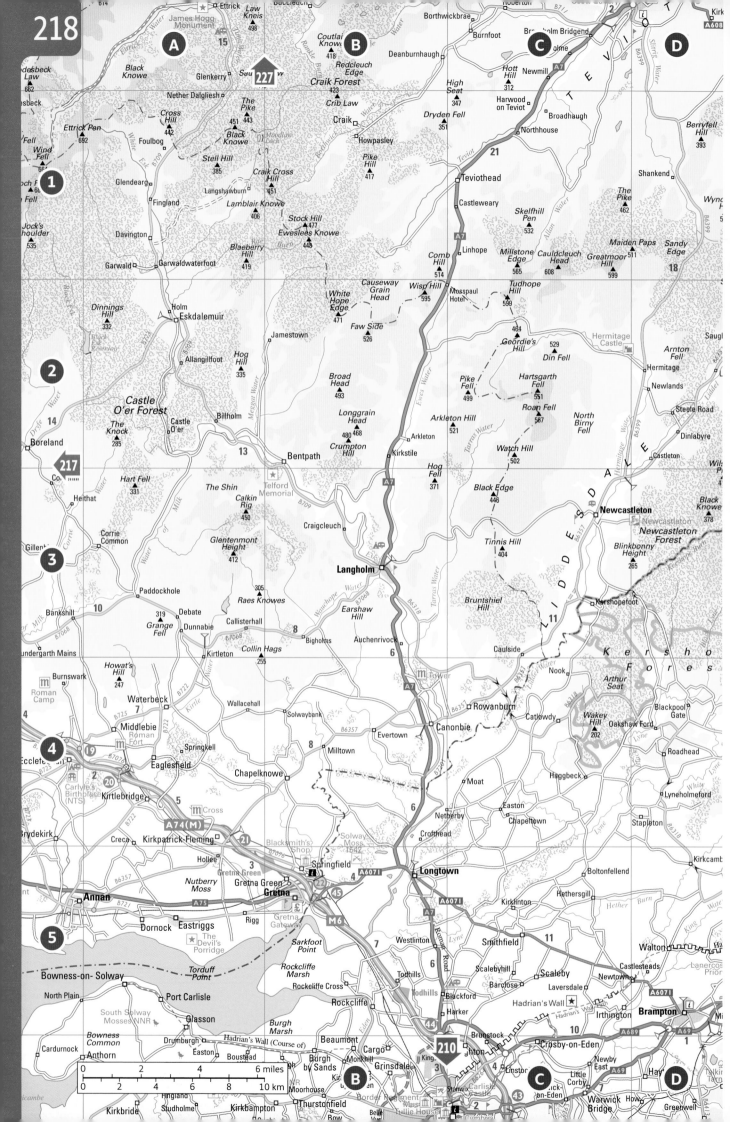

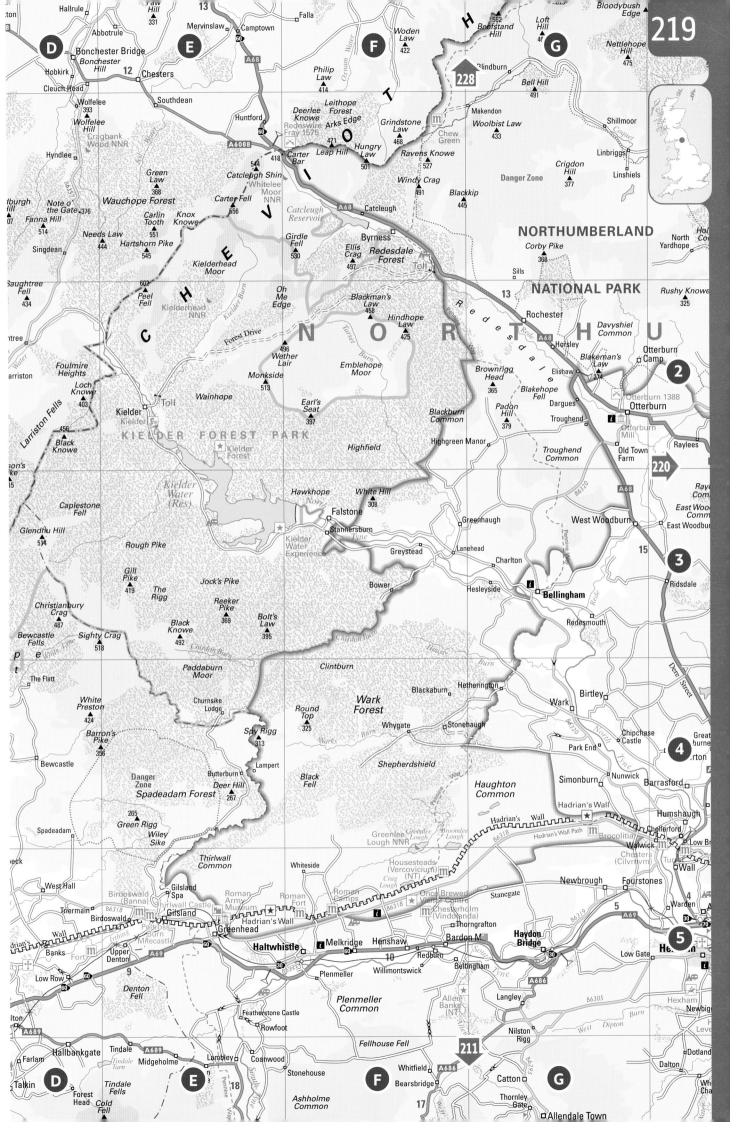

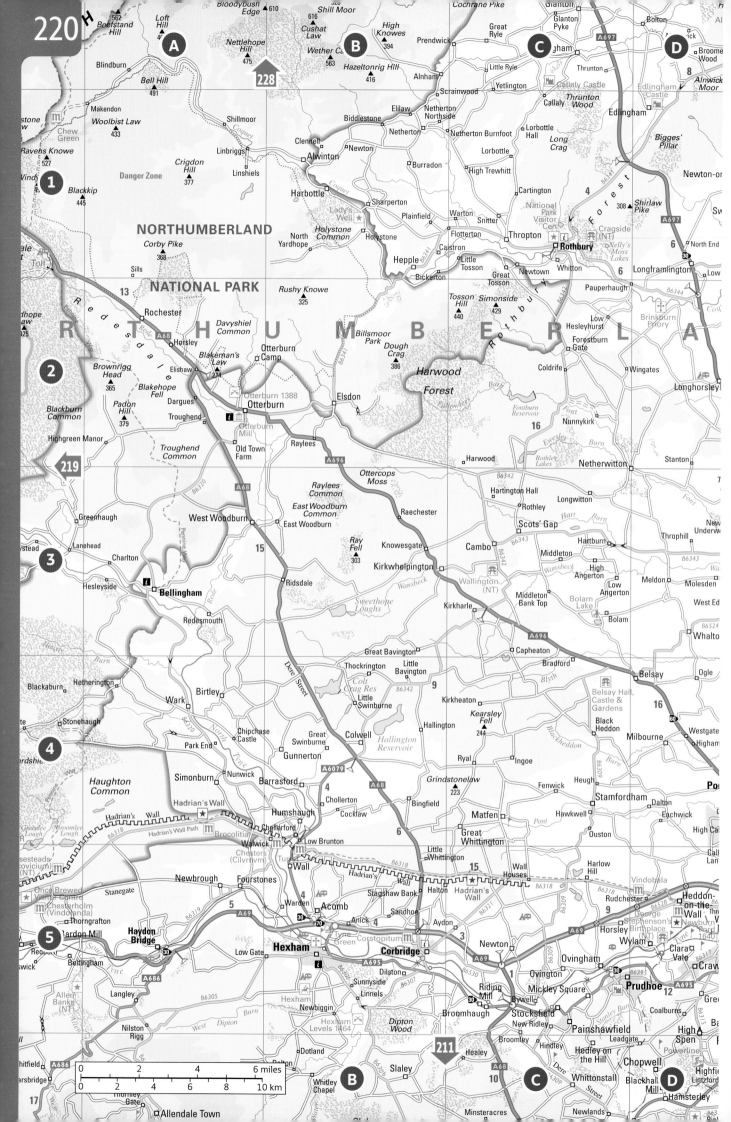

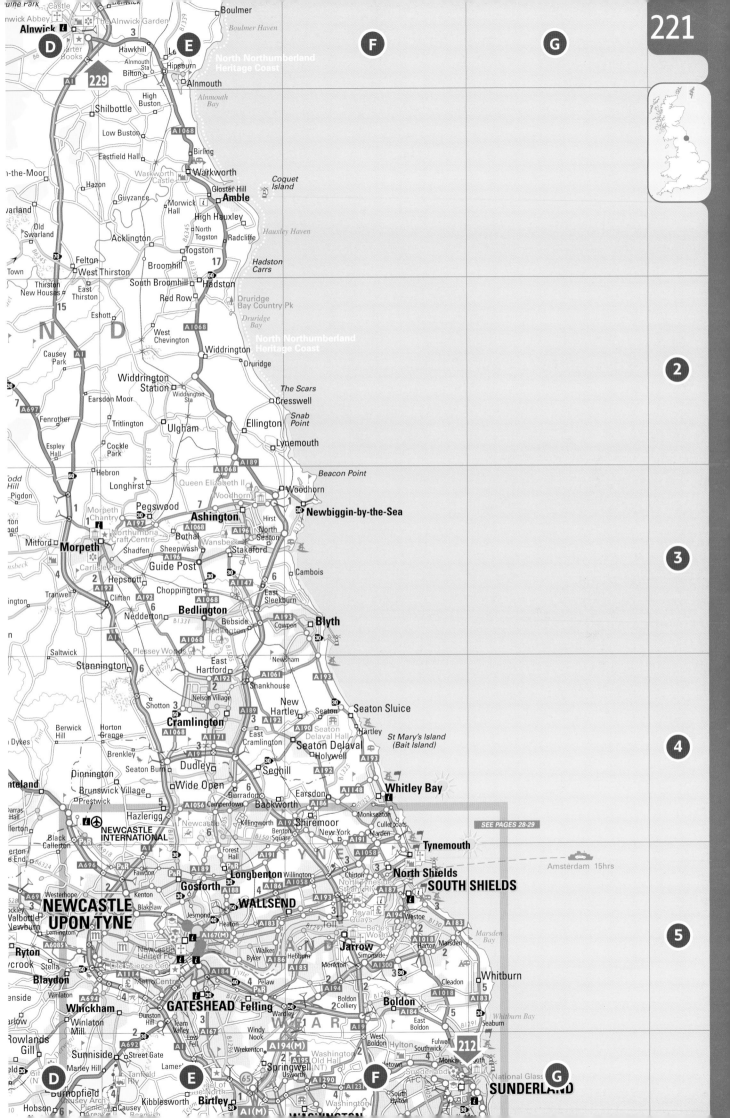

A B C D

Escart Farm

Ronachan
Corriechrevie
Loch Ciaran

West Tarbert Bay
East Tarbert Bay

B farbert
Ballo
Crossaig

C Bhan
Ardailly
100
Druimyeon Bay
Loch Garasdale

Auchinafaud
248
Cnoc an t-Samhlaidh
264
Cour Bay
Cour

Rhunahaorine Point
Cruach Mhic-Gougain
R

Gigha
Ardminish
Ardminish Bay
A83
Rhunahaorine

16

Achamore Gardens

Craro Island
¼ hr
Cnoc Reamhar
203
Sunadale

2¼ hrs
Tayinloan
285
Narachan Hill

Y

1

Killean
Grogport
Whitefarland

Cara Island
329
Deucheran Hill

Mull of Cara
Beacharr
Cruach Mhic-an-t- Saoir
364
Cruach nan Gabhar
354
Carradale Forest

Grob Bagh
T
Diollaid Mhòr
362

Muasdale
Achaglass

33

Glenacardoch Point
Belloch
Arnicle
Beinn Bhreac
426
Rhonadale
Carradale

A83
Beinn an Tuirc
454
Dippen
Carradale Garden

2

Glenbarr
Torrisdale
Carradale Bay

Barr Water
Bord Mòr
408

Bellochantuy Bay
Whitestone

Meall Buidhe
374

Bellochantuy
N
Abbey (ruins)
Saddell

Killocraw
Lussa Loch
Corrylach
Saddell Forest
Bunlarie
Saddell Bay

Sgreadan Hill
397

13

Tangy Loch
Ballochgair

Tangy
Ugadale Point

Westport
Skeroblingarry
Drumgarve
Glen Lussa

3

Low Ballevain
Calliburn
Peninver
Ardnacross Bay

Machrihanish Bay
Kilchenzie
A83
I

East Darlochan
Drumore

CAMPBELTOWN
Kilmichael
Campbeltown (Ceann Loch Chille Chiarain)
Davaar Island

Machrihanish
Machrihanish Water
Dalivaddy
Witchburn
Davaar

Drumlemble
B843
6
Kilkerran
Glenramskill
New Orleans

Chiscan
Knocknaha
Beinn Ghuilean
352

Earadale Point
The Slate
385
Oatfield
Kilchrist

K

Cnoc Moy
446
Conie Water
Killellan
Arinarach Hill
312

4

Rubha Dùin Bhàin
Largybaan
10
Glen Kerran
Feochaig
Ru Stafnish

273
Cnoc Odhar
277
Sheanachie

Cnoc Reamhar
Glen Breackerie
Conie Glen
Brecklate

Strone Glen
Keprigan
Kildavie

Beinn na Lice
428
Carrine
Southend
Macharioch
Polliwilline Bay

South Point
Garveld
Keil

Feorlan
Carskey Bay

Mull of Kintyre
Borgadelmore Point
Sanda Sound
Sheep Island

5

Sanda Island

0   2   4   6 miles
0   2   4   6   8   10 km

B C D

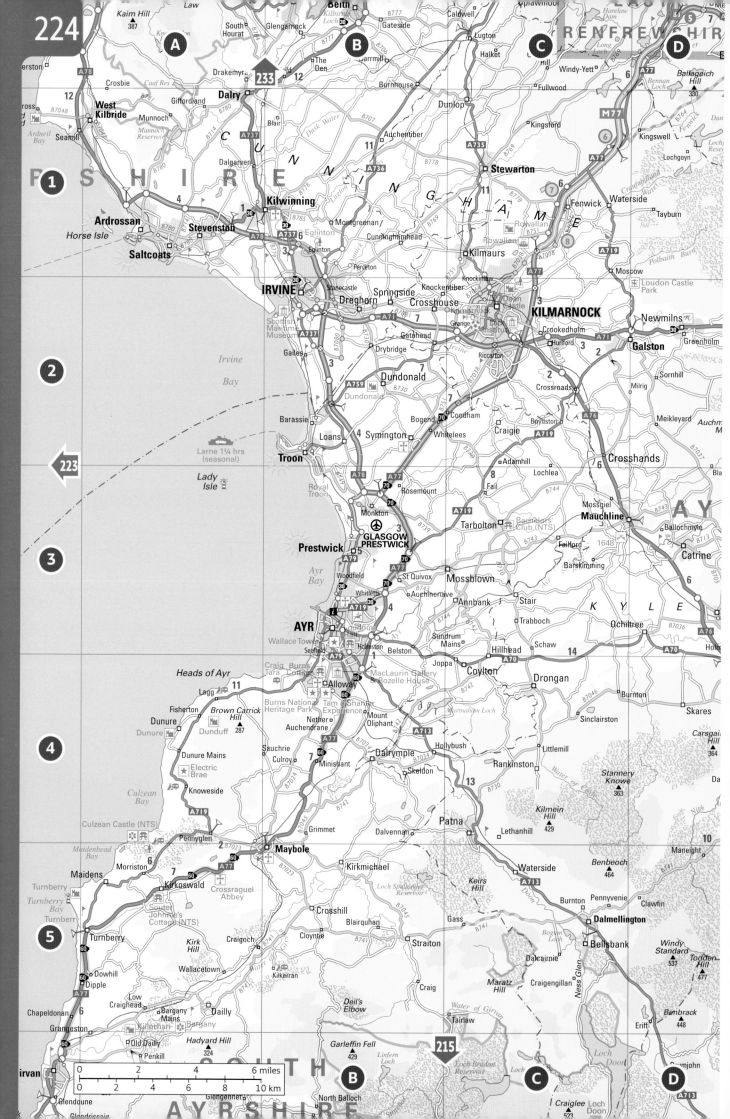

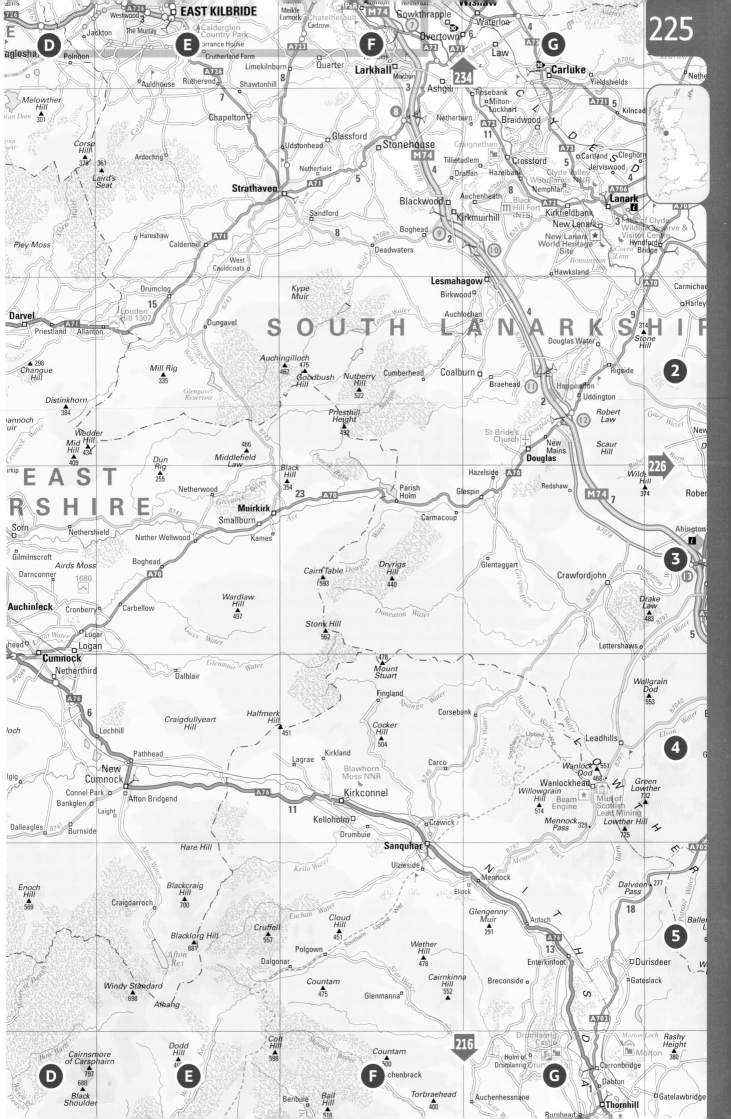

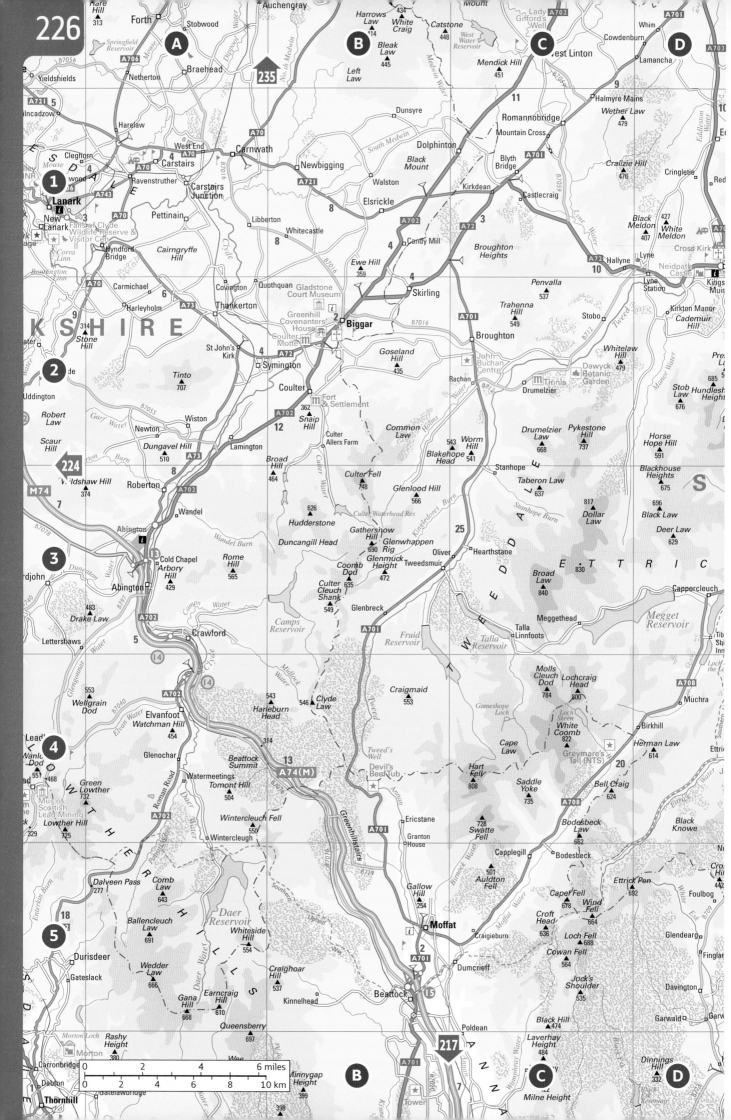

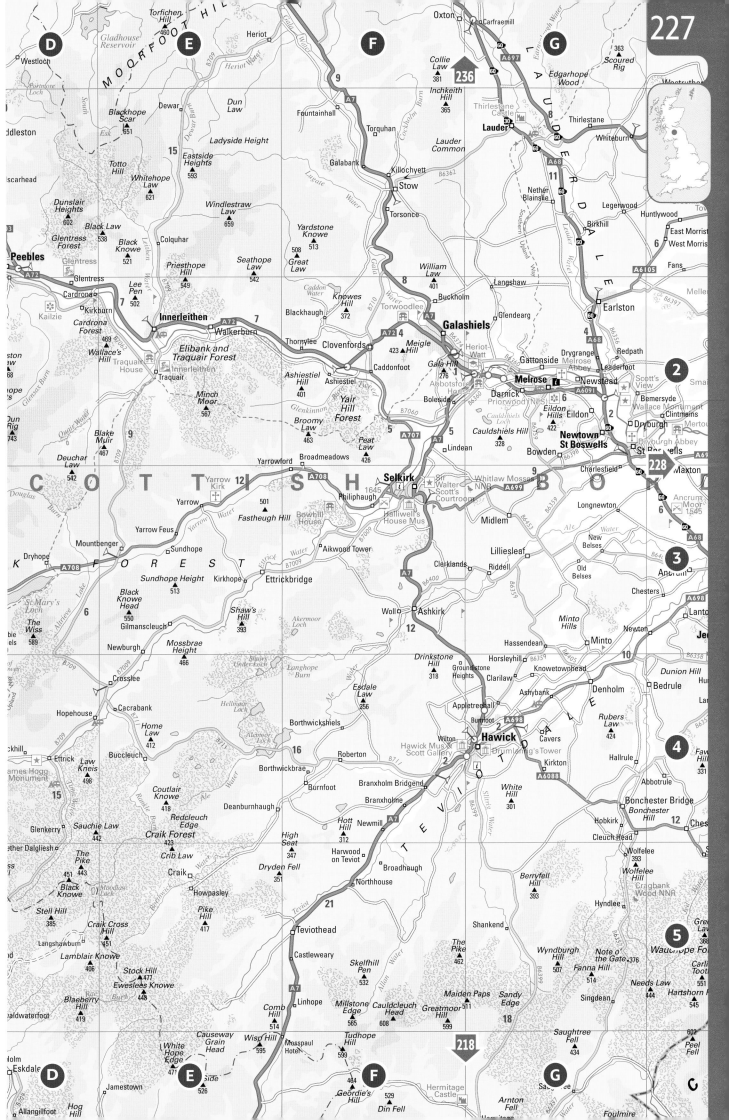

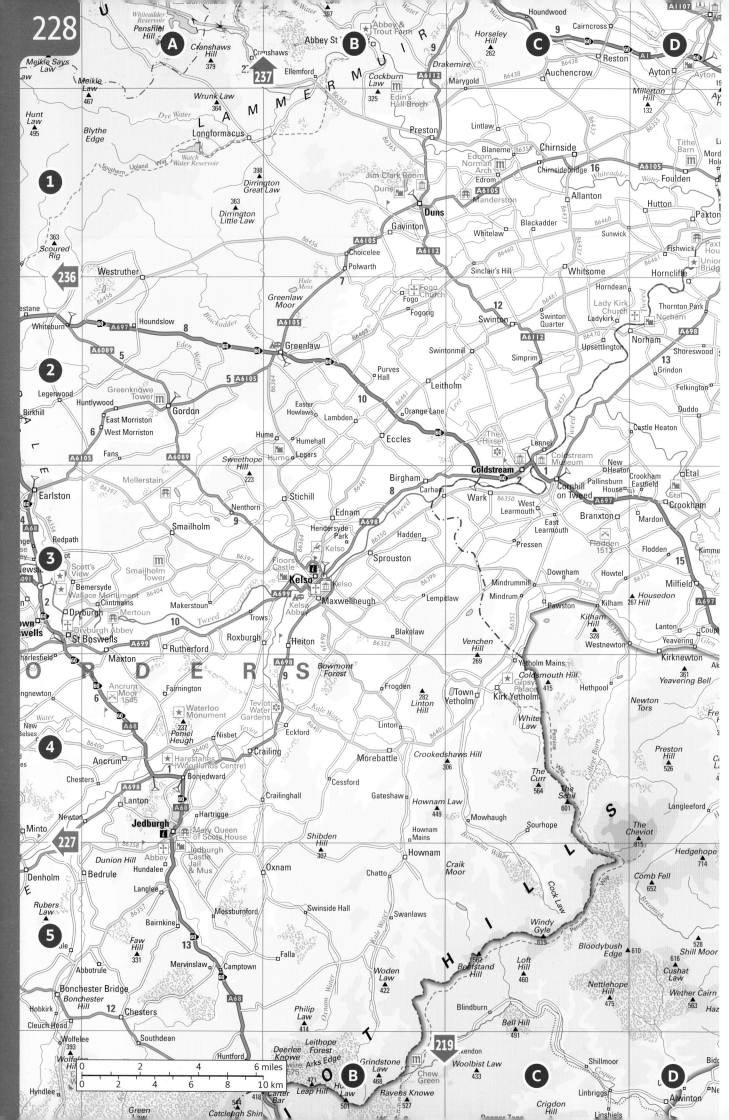

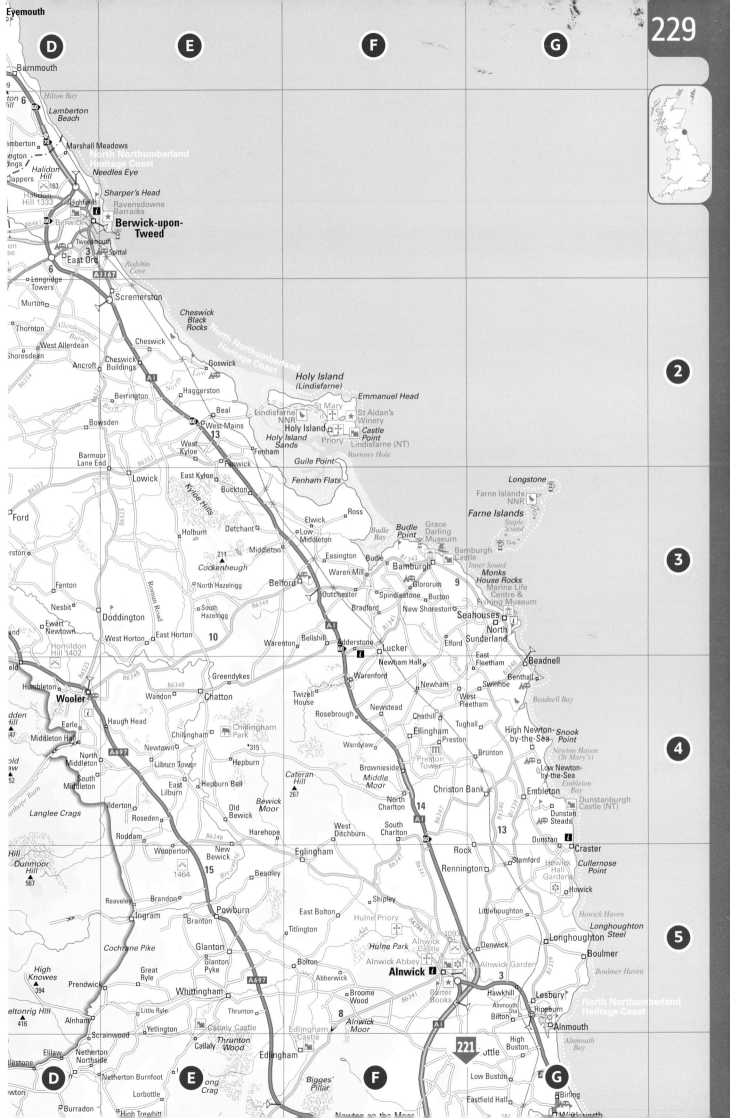

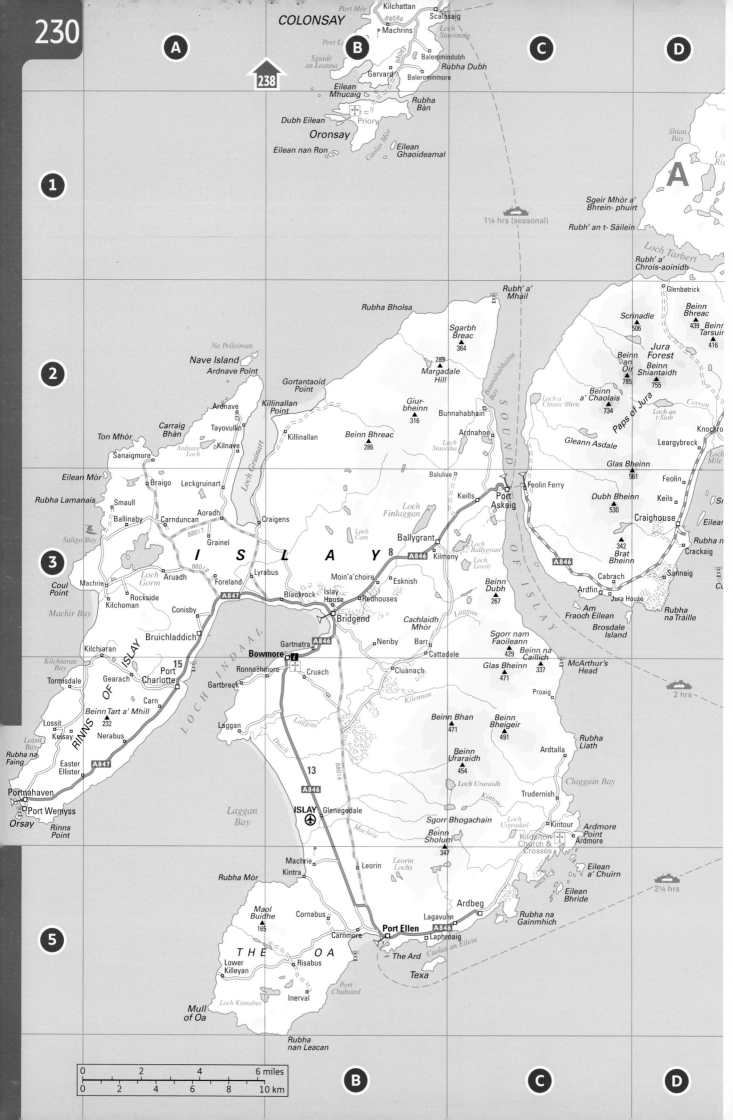

COLONSAY

Port Mòr   Kilchattan
Scalasaig
Machrins
88086

Port Le
Sguide
an Leanna
88085
Baleromindubh
Garvard   Rubha Dubh
Balerominmore
Eilean
Mhucaig   Rubha
Bàn
Dubh Eilean
Priory
Oronsay
Eilean nan Ron
Caolas Mòr   Eilean
Ghaoideamal

Shian
Bay
Loch
Ris

238

1¼ hrs (seasonal)

Sgeir Mhòr a'
Bhrein- phuirt
Rubh' an t- Sàilein

Loch Tarbert

Rubh' a'
Chrois-aoinidh

Rubh' a'
Mhàil

Rubha Bholsa

Glenbatrick

Beinn
Bhreac
Beinn
Tarsuin
416

Scrinadle
506

Sgarbh
Breac
364

283

Margadale
Hill

Jura
Forest

Beinn
an
Oir
785

Beinn
Shiantaidh
755

Na Peileirean

Nave Island

Giur-
bheinn
316

Ardnave Point

Loch a'
Chnuic Bhric

Beinn
a' Chaolais
734

Paps of Jura

Loch an
t-Siob

Bunnahabhain

Ardnave
Killinallan
Point

Beinn Bhreac
286

Ardhoe

Gleann Asdale

Corran

Knockro

Carraig
Bhàn

Tayovullin

Killinallan

Glas Bheinn
561

Feolin

Leargybreck

Loch
Mile

Ton Mhòr

Kilnave

Ardnave
Loch

Loch
Staoisha

Balulive

Sr

Sanaigmore

Eilean Mòr

Braigo   Leckgruinart

Loch Gruinart

Keills   Port
Askaig
Feolin Ferry

Dubh Bheinn
530

Keils

Craighouse

Rubha Lamanais

Smaull

Aoradh

Craigens

Ballygrant

Brat
Bheinn
342

Eilean

Saligo Bay   Ballinaby   Carnduncan

Grainel

Loch
Cam

8   A846   Kilmeny

Loch
Ballygrant

Cabrach   Rubha n
Crackaig

Loch
Gorm

I S L A Y

Lyrabus

Moin'a'choire

Loch
Lossit

Beinn
Dubh
267

Ardfin   Jura House

Rubha
na Tràille   Cu

Machrie   Aruadh

Foreland

Blackrock

Esknish

Am
Fraoch Eilean

Cu

Coul
Point

B8018

Rockside
Kilchoman

Conisby

Islay
House

Redhouses

Cachlaidh
Mhòr

Sgorr nam
Faoileann
429

Brosdale
Island

Bridgend   Laggan

Beinn na
Caillich

Rubha
na Tràille

Machir Bay   A847

Bruichladdich

Gartnatra   A846   Neriby

Barr

Beinn
Dubh
267

Kilchiaran

Port
Charlotte   15

Bowmore

Ronnachmore   Cruach   Cluanach   Cattadale

Glas Bheinn
471   McArthur's
Head

Tormisdale   Gearach

Gartbreck

Kilchiaran
Bay

Carn

Laggan

Laggan

Kilennan   Proaig

2 hrs

Beinn Tart a' Mhill
232   Nerabus

Duich   13   B8016

Beinn Bhan
471

Beinn
Bheigeir
491

Rubha
Liath

Lossit
Bay

Lossit
Kelsay

Beinn
Uraraidh
454

Ardtalla

Rubha na
Faing

R I N N S   O F   I S L A Y

A846

Loch Uraraidh

Claggain Bay

Easter
Ellister

Laggan
Bay

ISLAY   Glenegedale

Machrie

Trudernish

Portnahaven

Port Wemyss   Orsay   Rinns
Point

Sgorr Bhogachain

Loch
Uigeadail   Kintour

Ardmore
Point
Ardmore

Beinn
Sholum
347

Kilnaughton
Church &
Crosses

Machrie   Kintra

Leorin

Leorin
Lochs

Rubha Mòr

Eilean
a' Chuirn

Maol
Buidhe
165

Cornabus

Ardbeg

Lagavulin

Rubha na
Gainmhich

2¼ hrs

T H E   O A

Carnmore   Port Ellen   A846   Laphroaig

Eilean
Bhride

Lower
Killeyan

Risabus   Inerval

The Ard   Caolas an Eilein

Texa

Port
Chubaird

Mull
of Oa   Loch Kinnabus

Rubha
nan Leacan

A   B   C   D

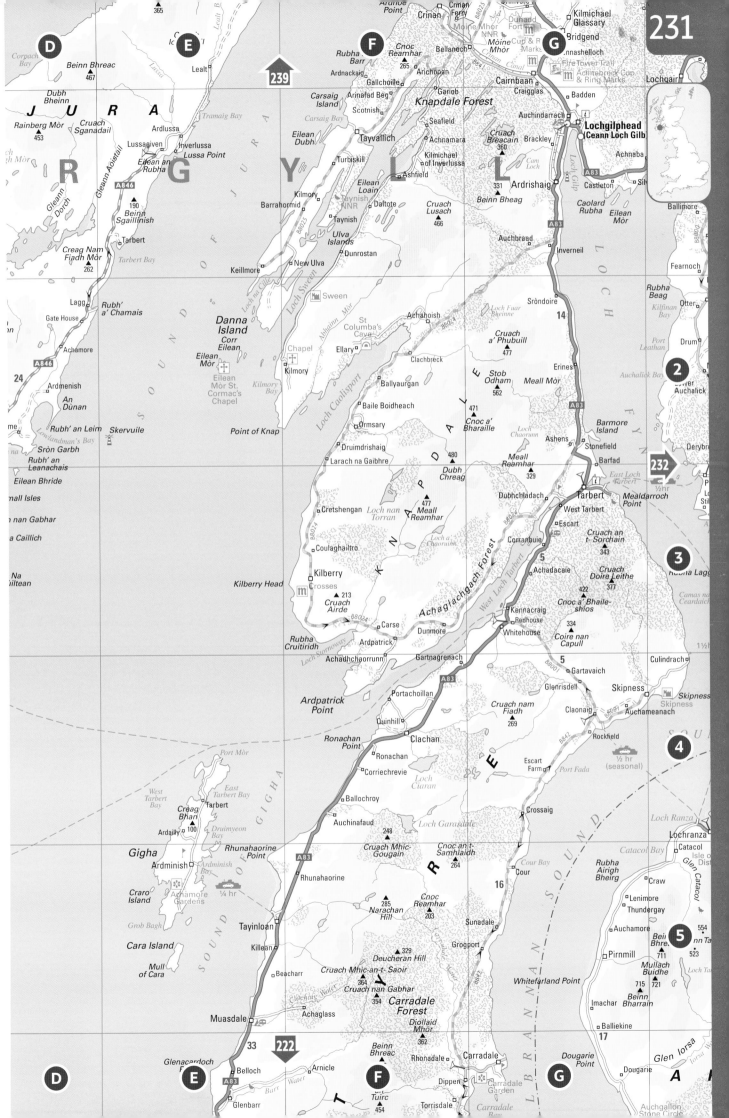

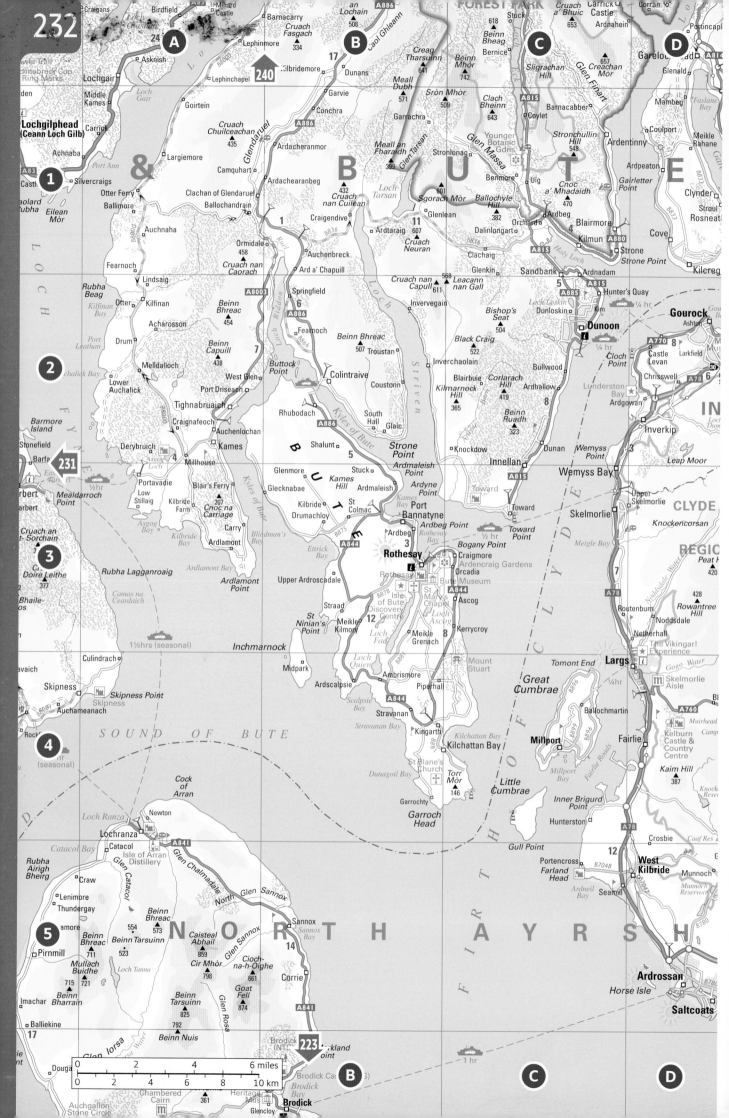

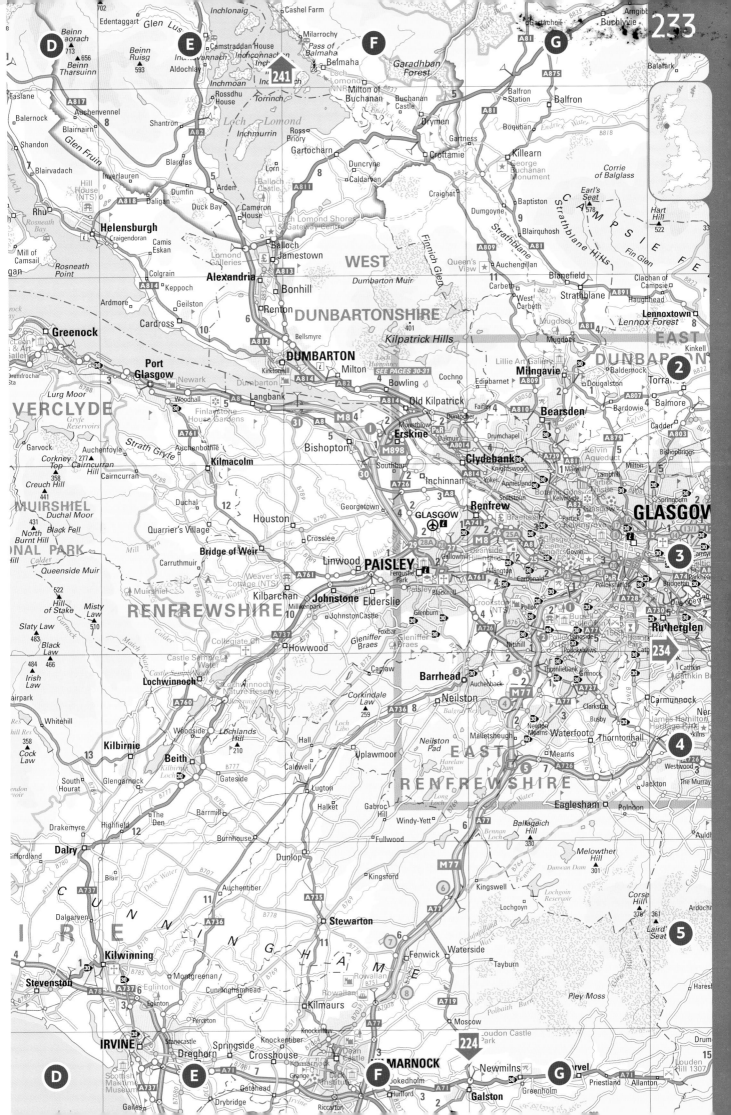

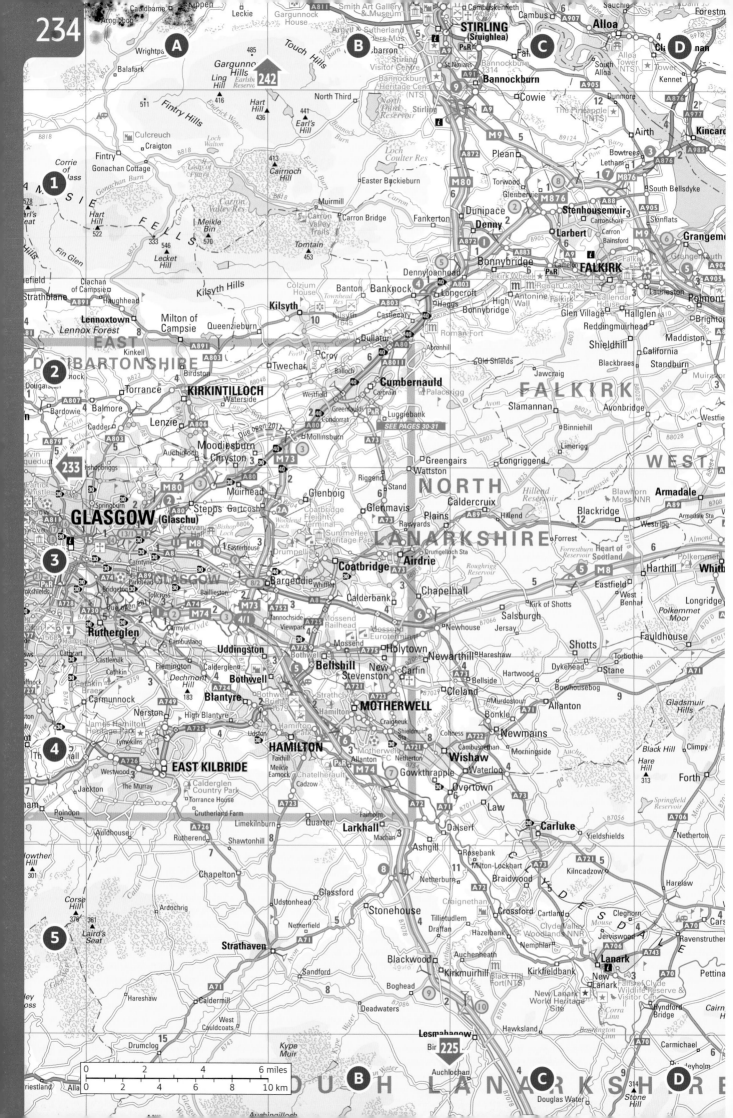

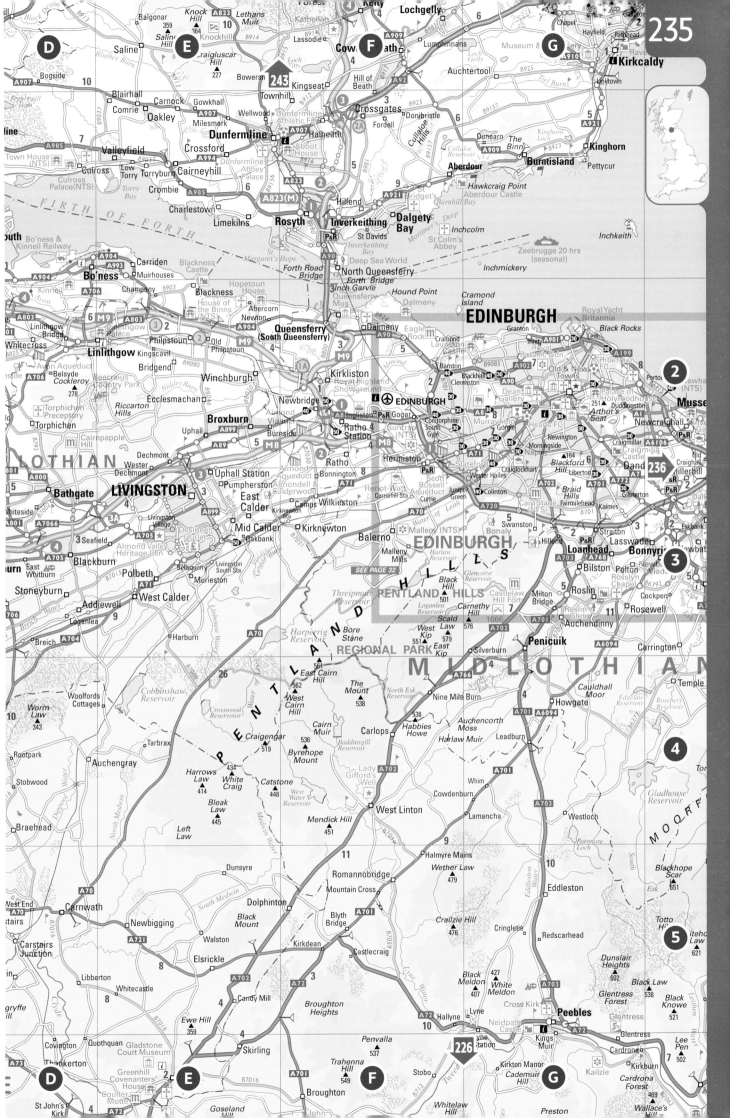

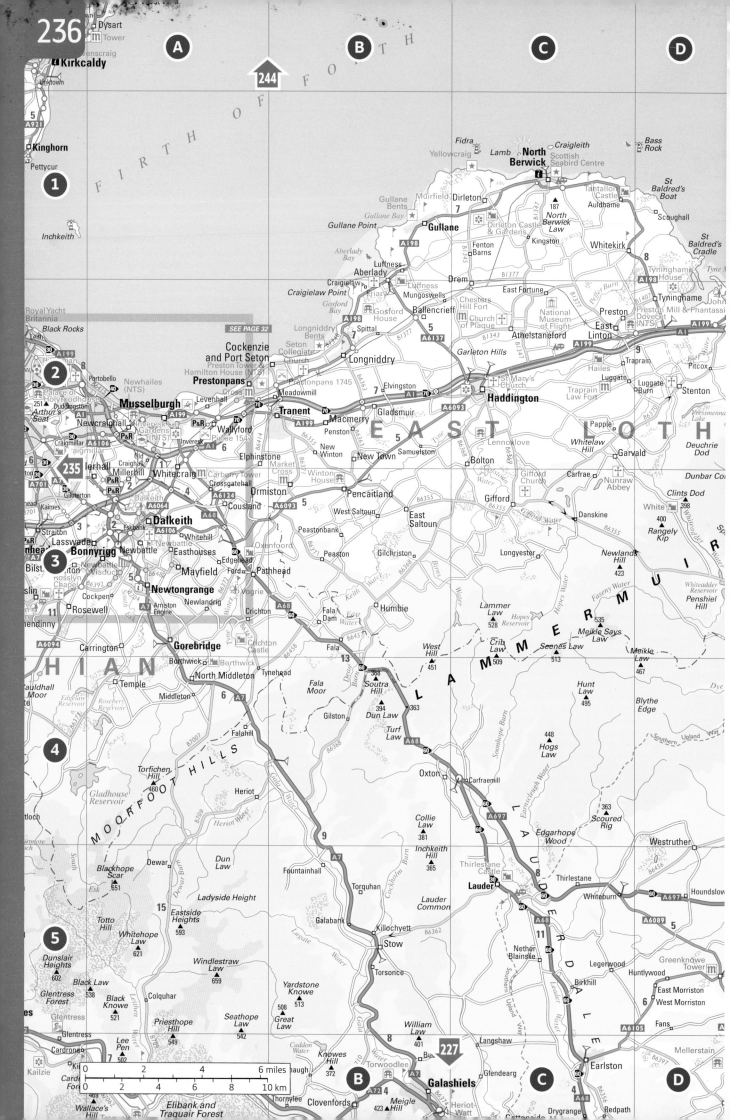

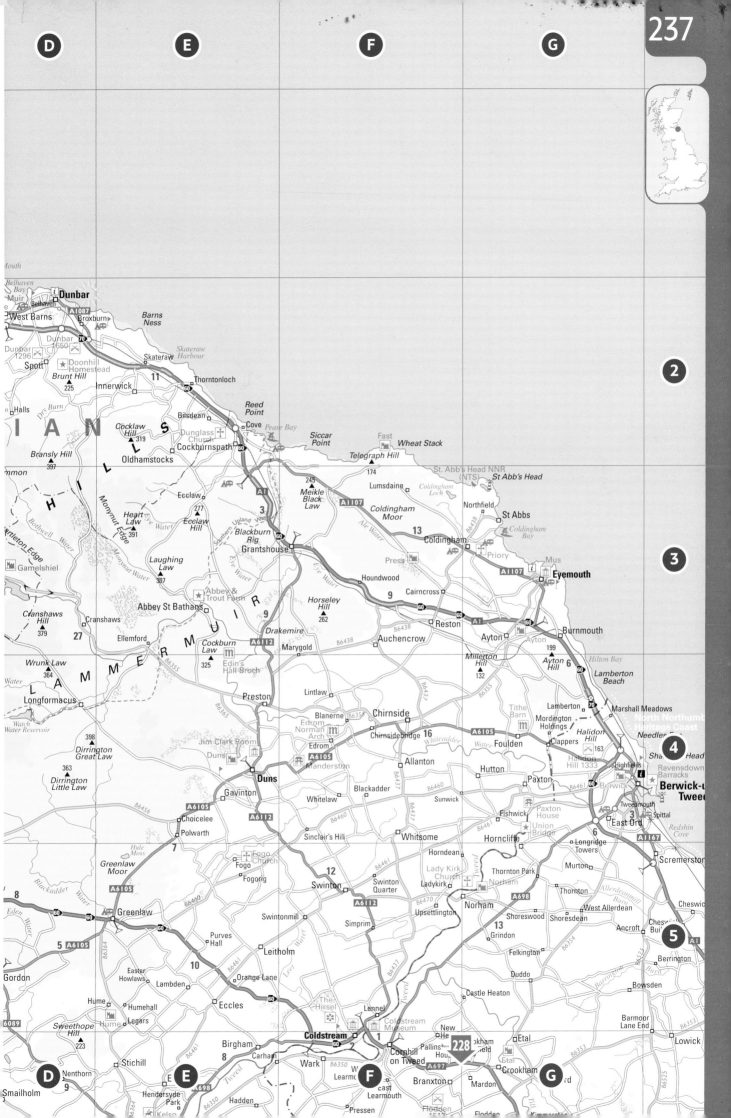

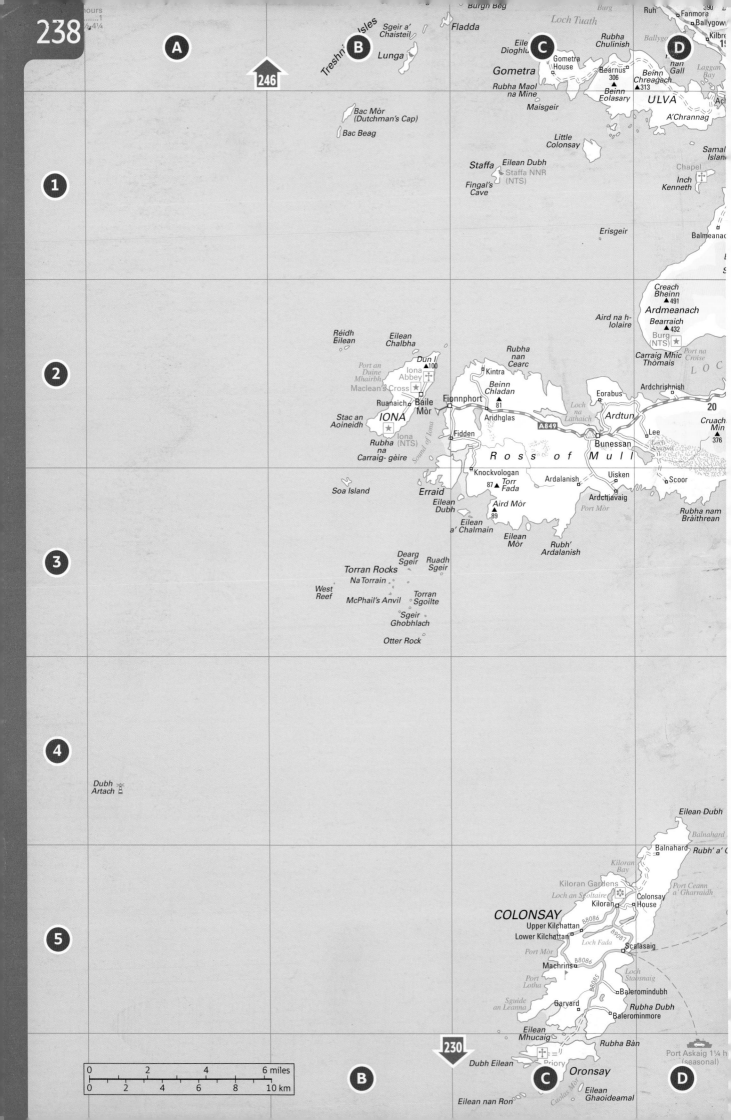

246

A

B

Treshnish Isles
Sgeir a' Chaisteil
Fladda
Lunga

Eile Dioghlu
Gometra House
C
Rubha Chulinish
Bearnus
Beinn 306
Chreagach
▲313
Beinn
Folsary

Burgh Beg
Burg
Ruh
Fanmore
Ballygow

Loch Tuath
Ballygo
Kilbre

D
nan Gall
Laggan
Bay

Gometra
Rubha Maol
na Mine

ULVA
A'Chrannag
Ach

Maisgeir

Bac Mòr
(Dutchman's Cap)
Bac Beag

Little
Colonsay

Samal
Islan

1

Staffa
Fingal's
Cave
Eilean Dubh
Staffa NNR
(NTS)

Chapel
Inch
Kenneth

Erisgeir

Balmeanac

Réidh
Eilean
Eilean
Chalbha
Port an
Duine
Mhairbh
Maclean's Cross
Ruanaich
Baile
Mòr
Dun I
▲100
Iona
Abbey

Fionnphort

Rubha
nan
Cearc
Kintra
Beinn
Chladan
▲81
Aridhglas

Creach
Bheinn
▲491
Ardmeanach
Bearraich
▲432
Burg
(NTS)
Carraig Mhic
Thòmais

Aird na h-
Iolaire

2

Stac an
Aoineadh
IONA
Rubha
na (NTS)
Carraig-gèire
Iona

Fidden

Soa Island

Erraid

A849
Eorabus
Loch
na
Lathaich

Ardtun

Ardchrishnish

20

LOC

Cruach
Min
▲376

Bunessan

Eilean
Dubh
Eilean
a' Chalmain
Knockvologan
87 ▲ Torr
Fada
Aird Mòr
▲89
Eilean
Mòr
Rubh'
Ardalanish
Ardalanish
Ross of Mull
Uisken
Ardchiavaig
Port Mòr
Scoor

Rubha nam
Bràithrean

3

Dearg
Sgeir
Ruadh
Sgeir
Torran Rocks
Na Torran
West
Reef
McPhail's Anvil
Torran
Sgoilte
Sgeir
Ghobhlach
Otter Rock

4

Dubh
Artach

Eilean Dubh
Balnahard

Balnahard
Rubh' a' C

Kiloran
Bay

Port Ceann
a' Gharraidh

Kiloran Gardens
Loch an Sgoltaire
Kiloran
COLONSAY
Upper Kilchattan
Lower Kilchattan
Port Mòr
Machrins
B8086
B8087
Garvard
Sguide
an Leanna
Colonsay
House
B8086
Loch Fada
Scalasaig
B8085
B8083
Loch
Stapsnaig
Balerominodubh
Rubha Dubh
Balerominmore

5

Eilean
Mhucaig
Dubh Eilean
Priory
Oronsay
Eilean nan Ron
Eilean
Ghaoideamal
Caolas Mòr
Rubha Bàn

Port Askaig 1¼ h
(seasonal)

230

| 0 | | 2 | | 4 | | 6 miles |
| 0 | 2 | 4 | 6 | 8 | | 10 km |

B

C

D

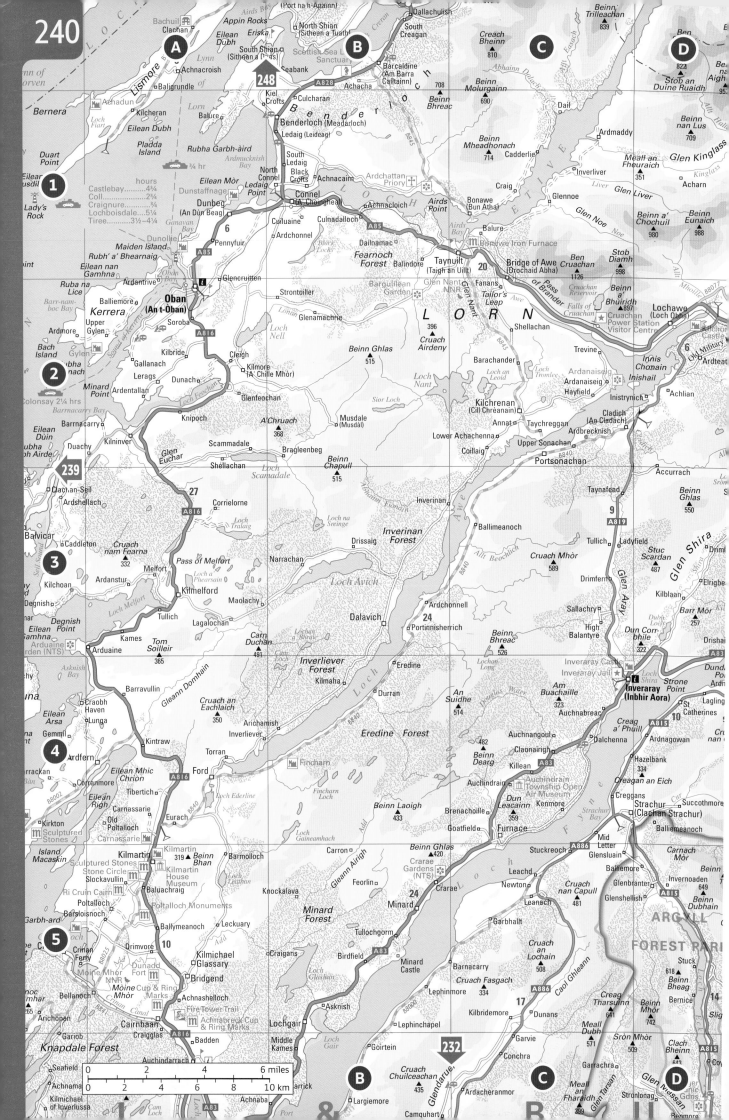

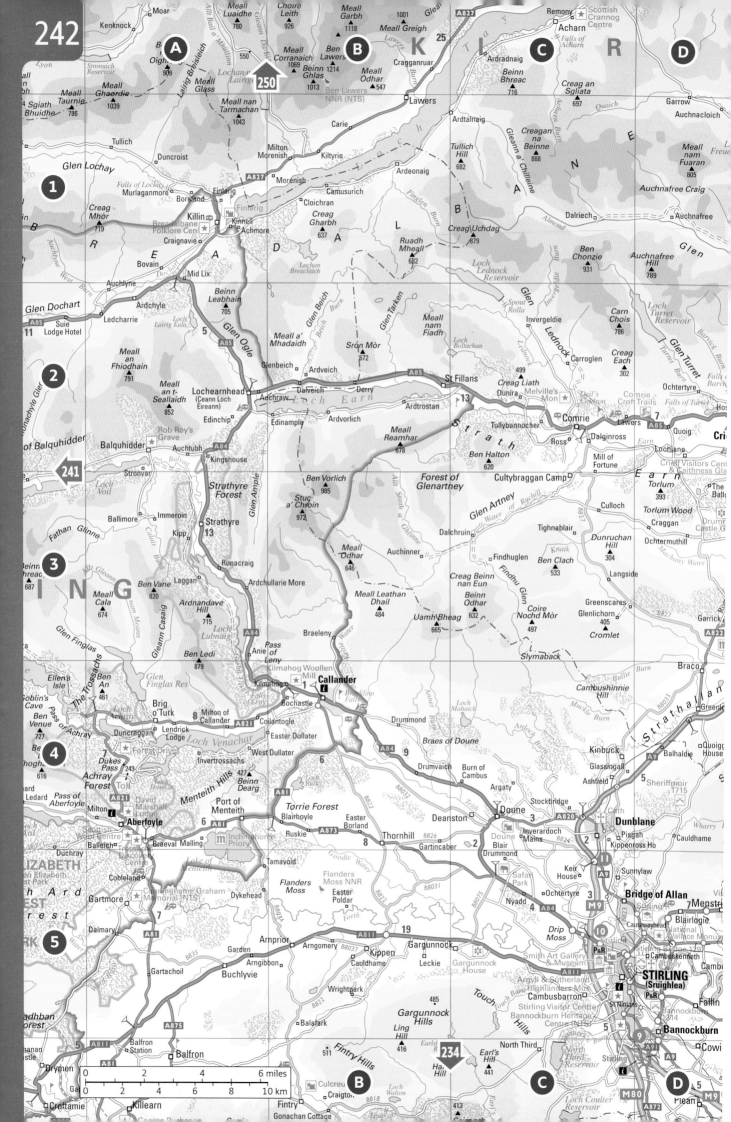

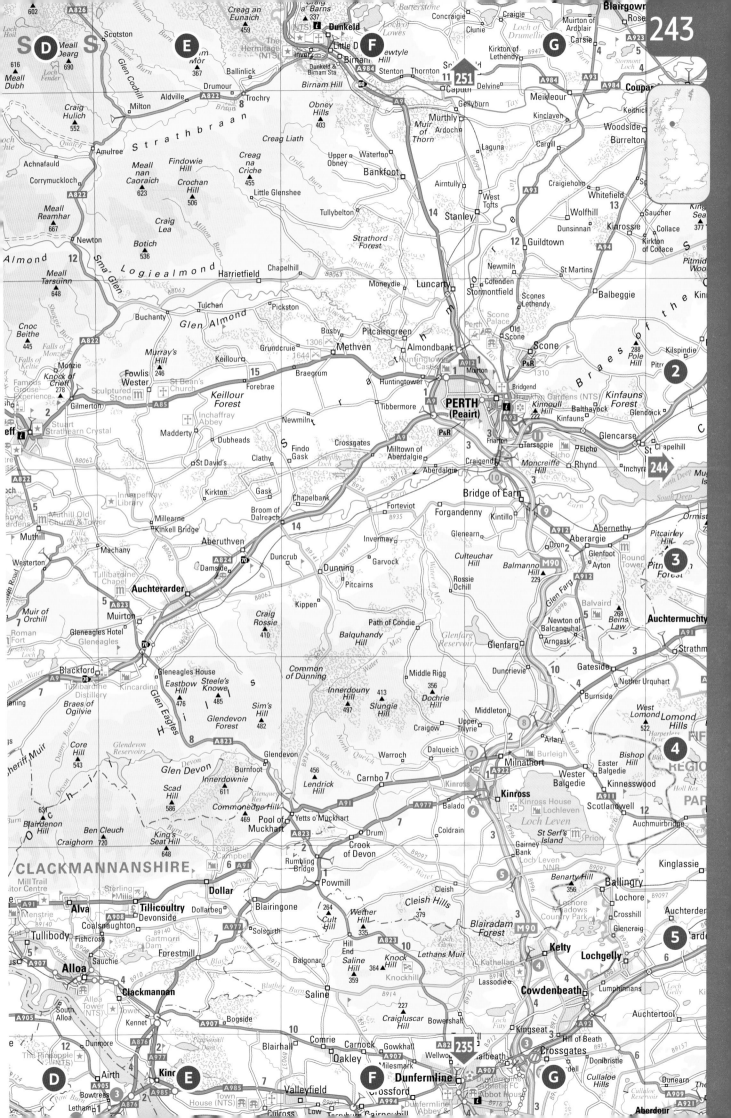

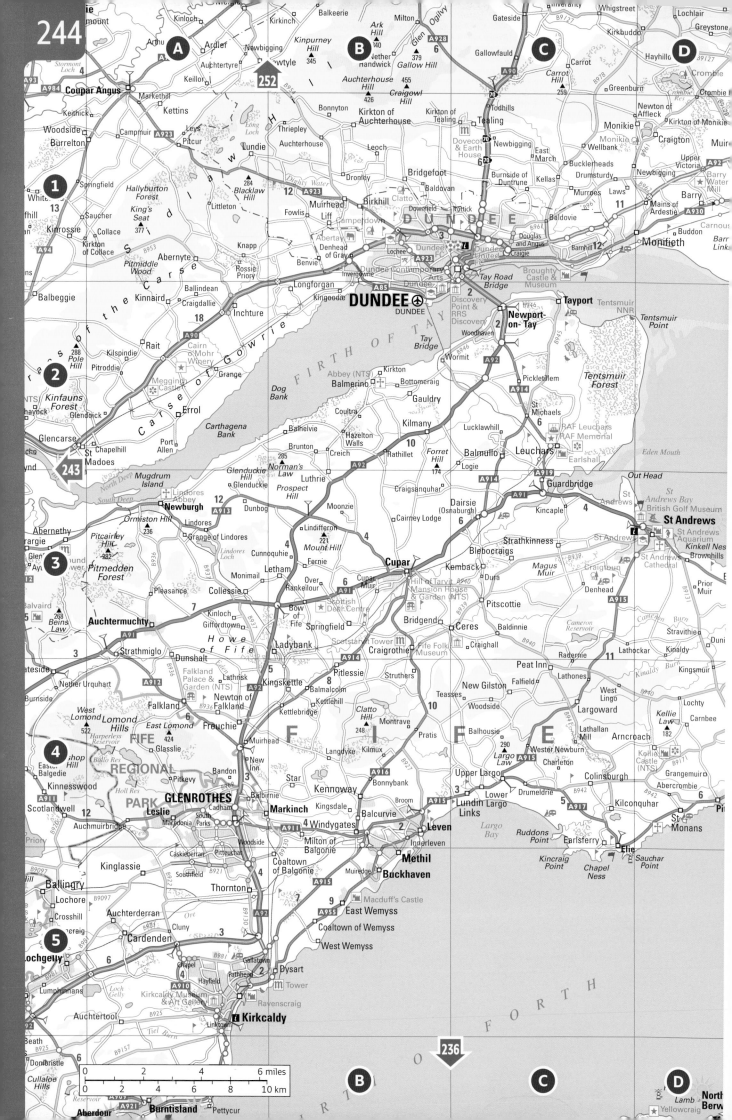

Reudiol
Denhead of
birlot
St Vigeans
Marywell
Meg's
Craig
Carmyll
D
Guyn
B9127
Carlingheugh
Bay
The Deil's Heid
E
Arbirlot
Arbroath Abbey
F
G
Bonnyton
Easter
Knox
A92
Arbroath
Elliot
6
253
rum
Salmond's Muir
2
Panbride
East Haven
Drum
Carnoustie
stie!

Buddon Ness

✳ Bell Rock
🚩 (Inchcape)

2

Buddo Ness
Babbet Ness
Boarhills
10 A917
Kingsbarns
Cambo
Estate
Cambo
Ness
North
Carr
3
Kenly Water
Tullybothy Craigs
Craighead
no
Wormiston
Fife Ness
Kippo Burn
B940
Airdrie
B9171
Crail
B9131
4
West Ness
Spalefield
A917
Innergellie
4
Kilrenny
Cellardyke
Anstruther
Scottish Fisheries Museum
ttenweem

North Ness
Isle of May NNR
Isle of May
Chapel
South Ness

5

Craig
D
Bass Rock
E
F
G
rick
Scottish
Seabird
Centre

237

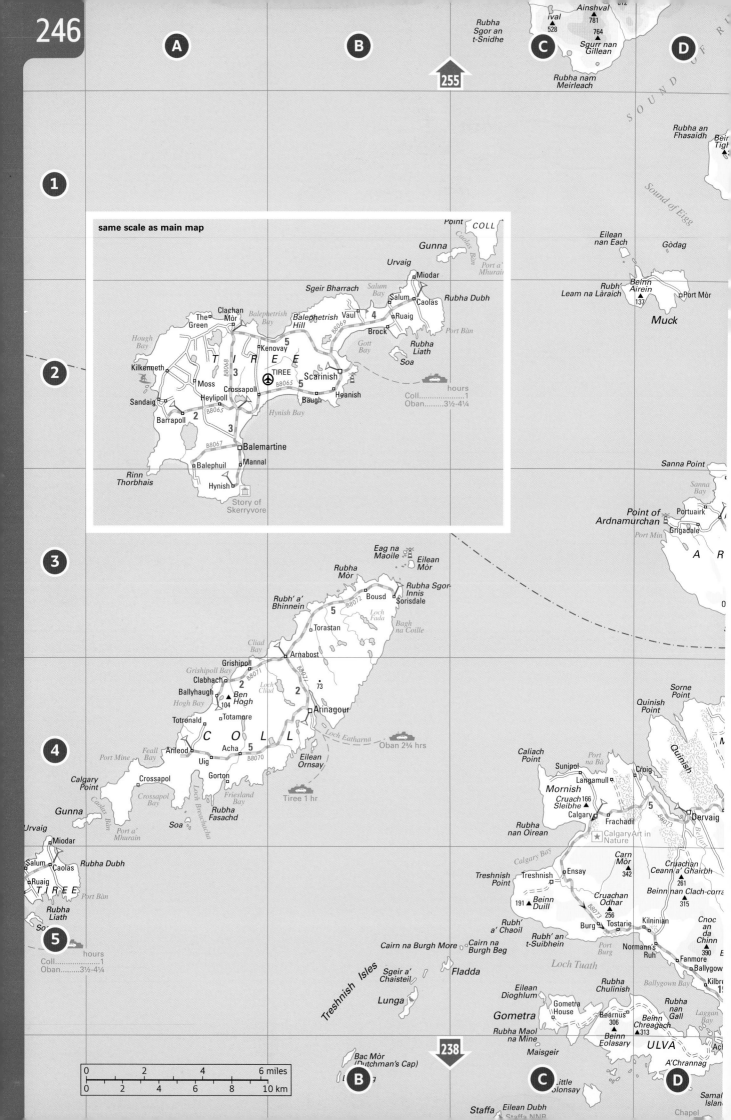

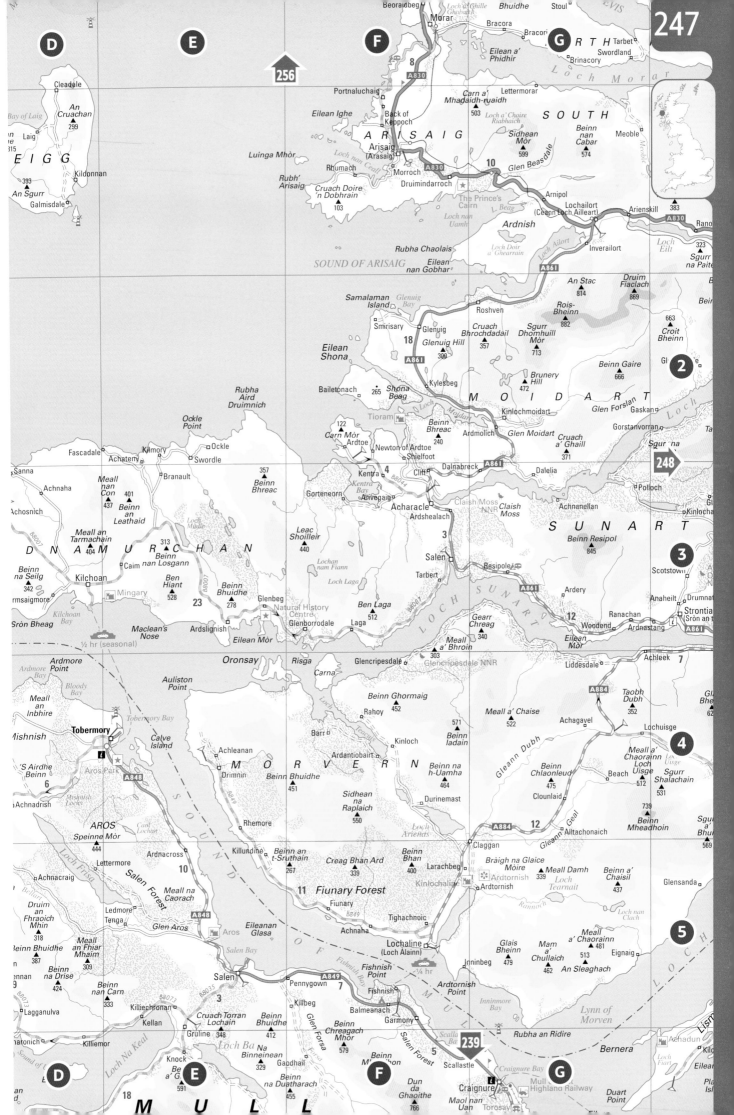

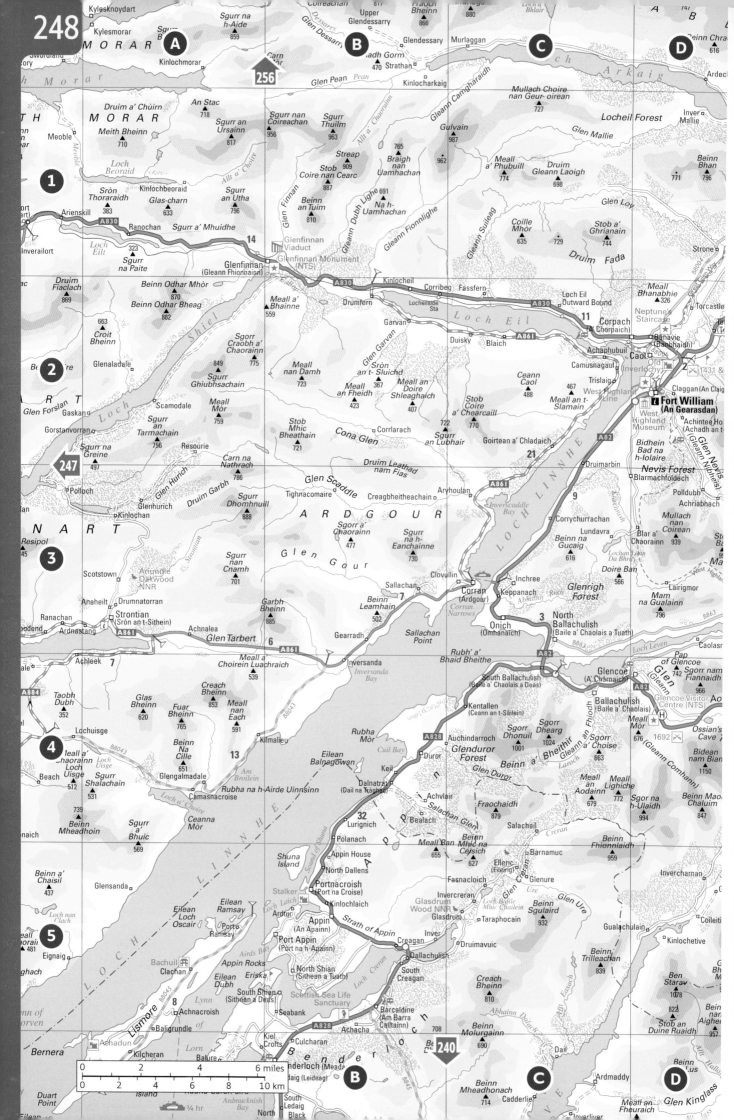

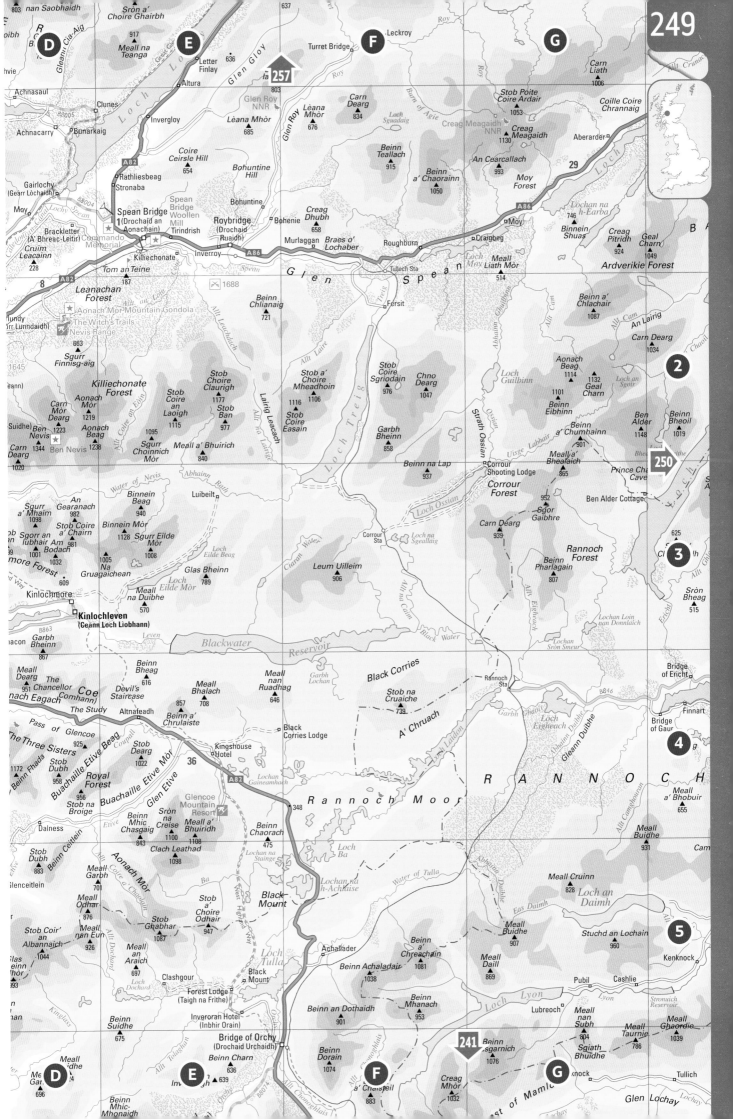

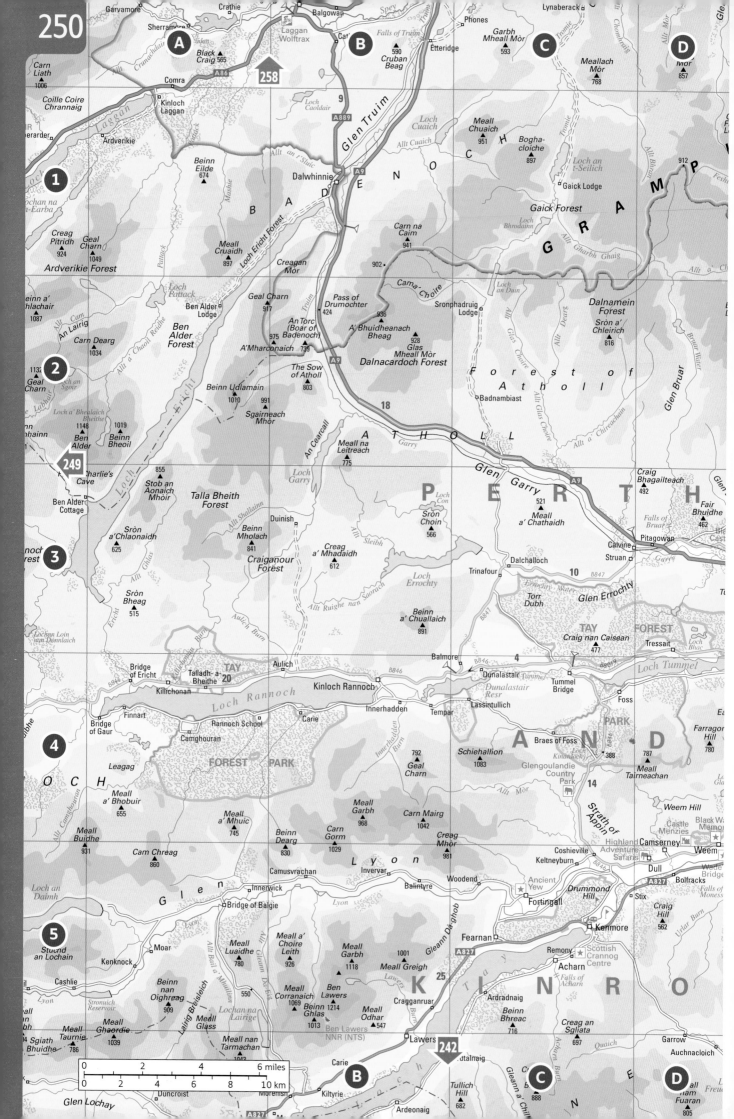

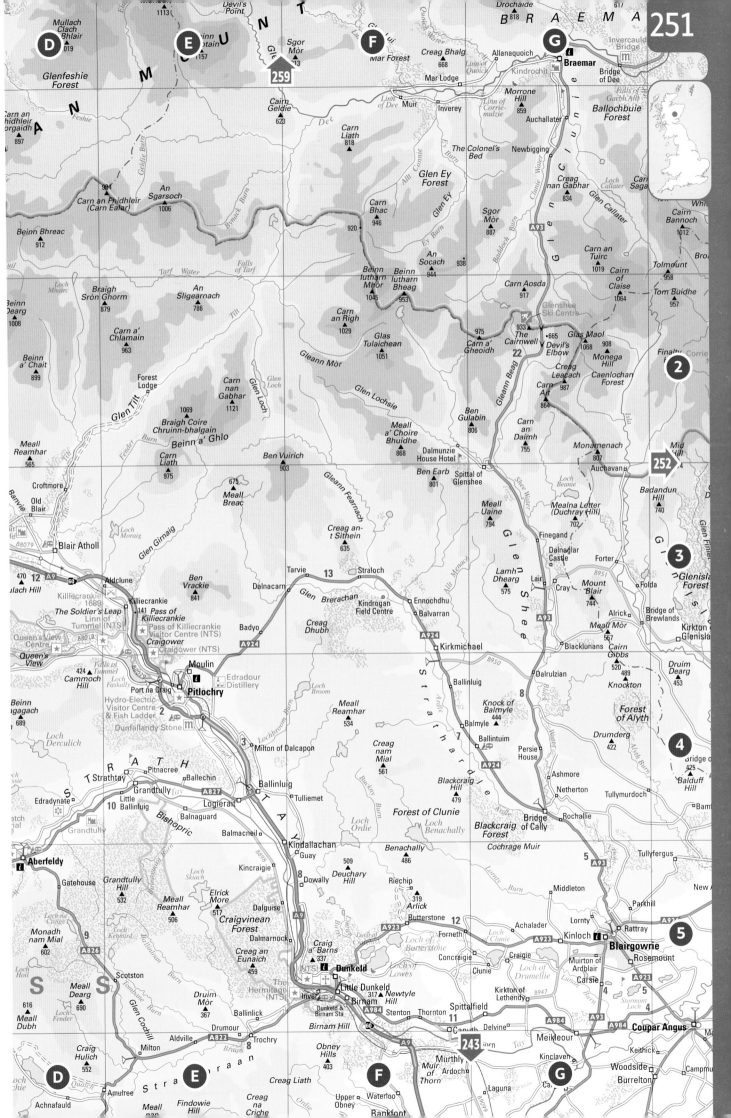

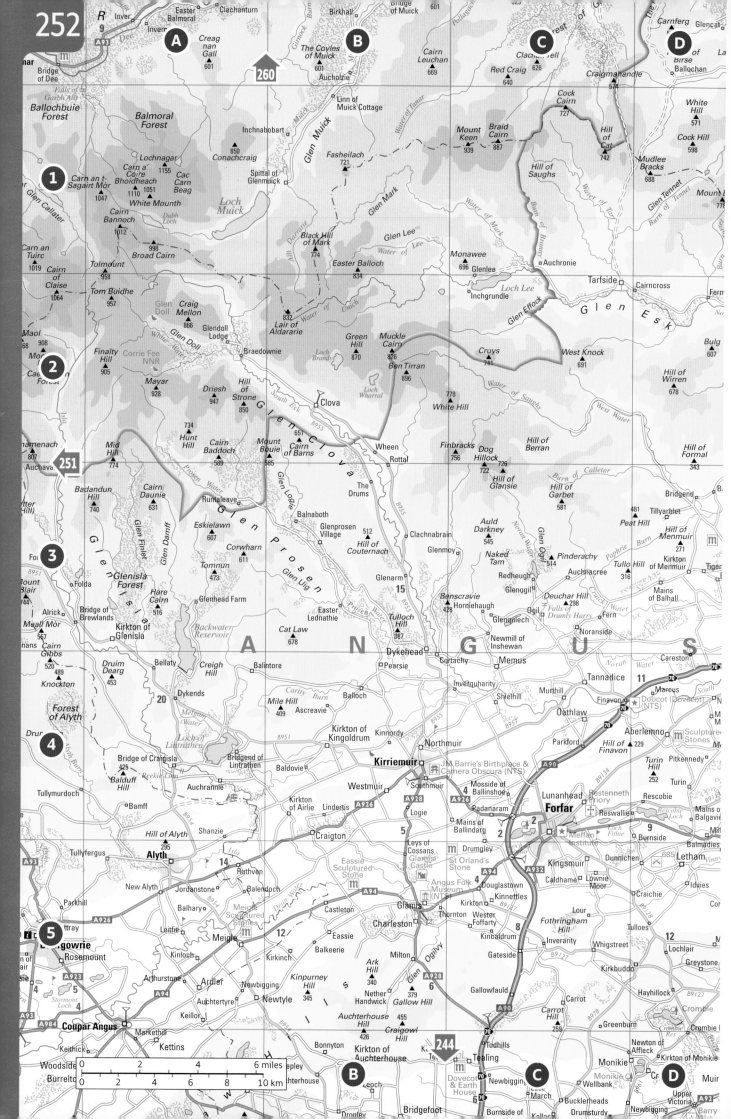

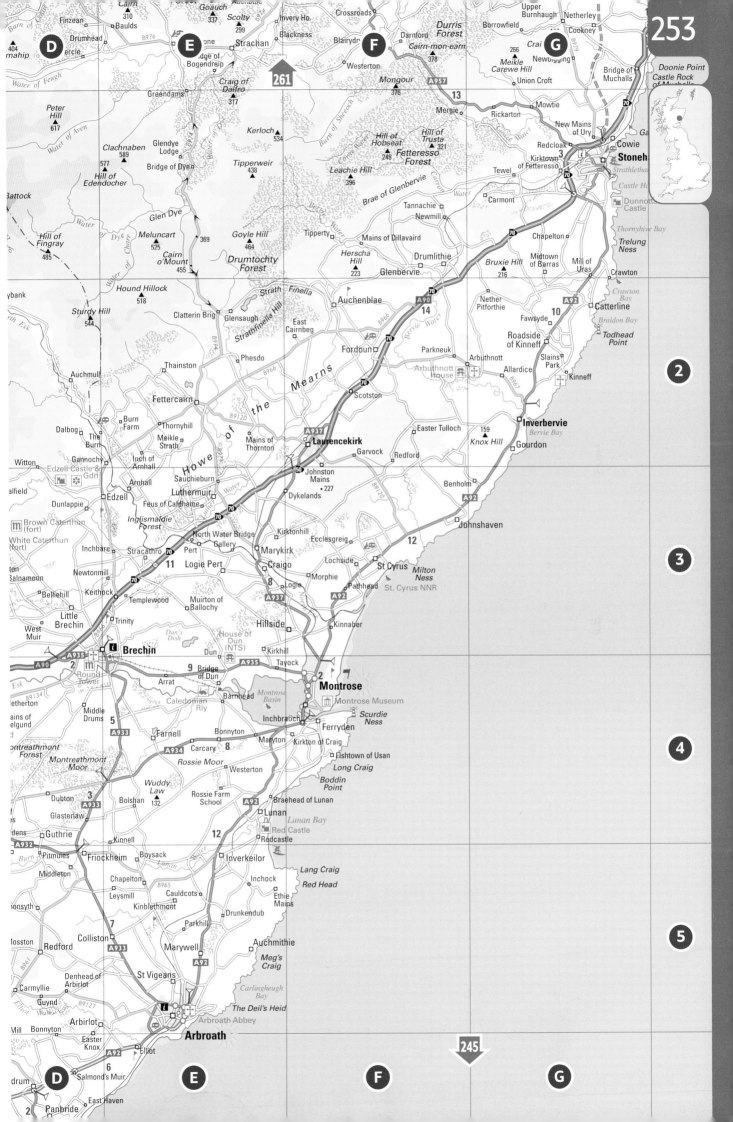

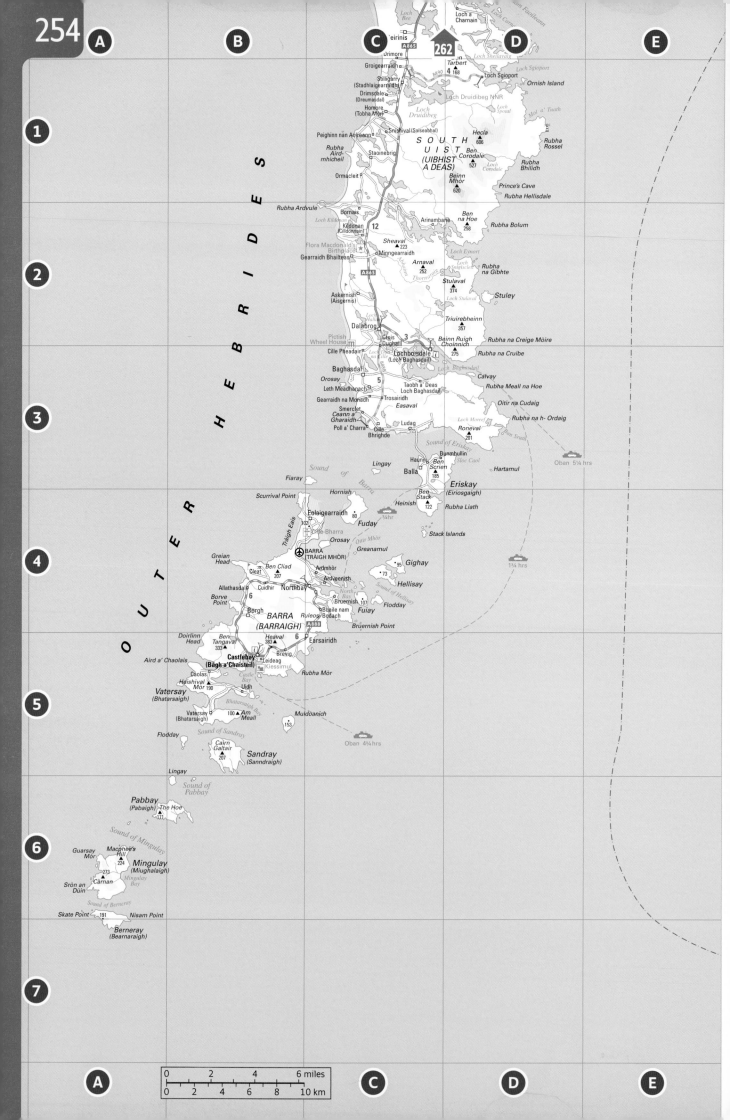

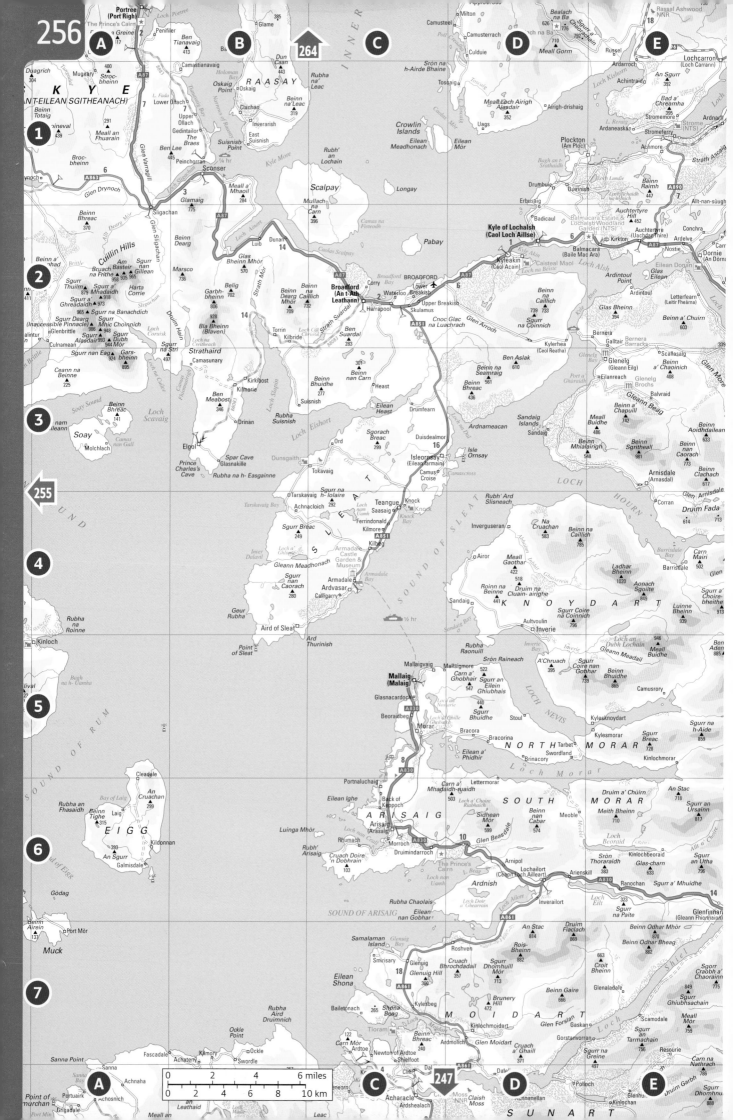

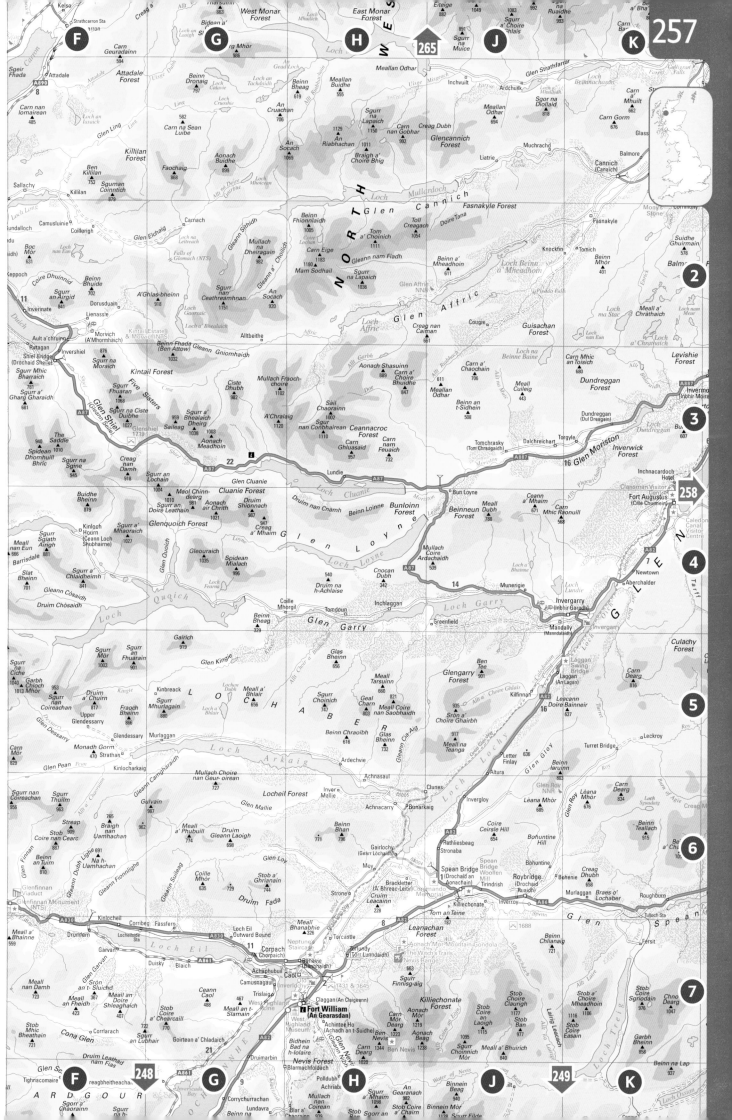

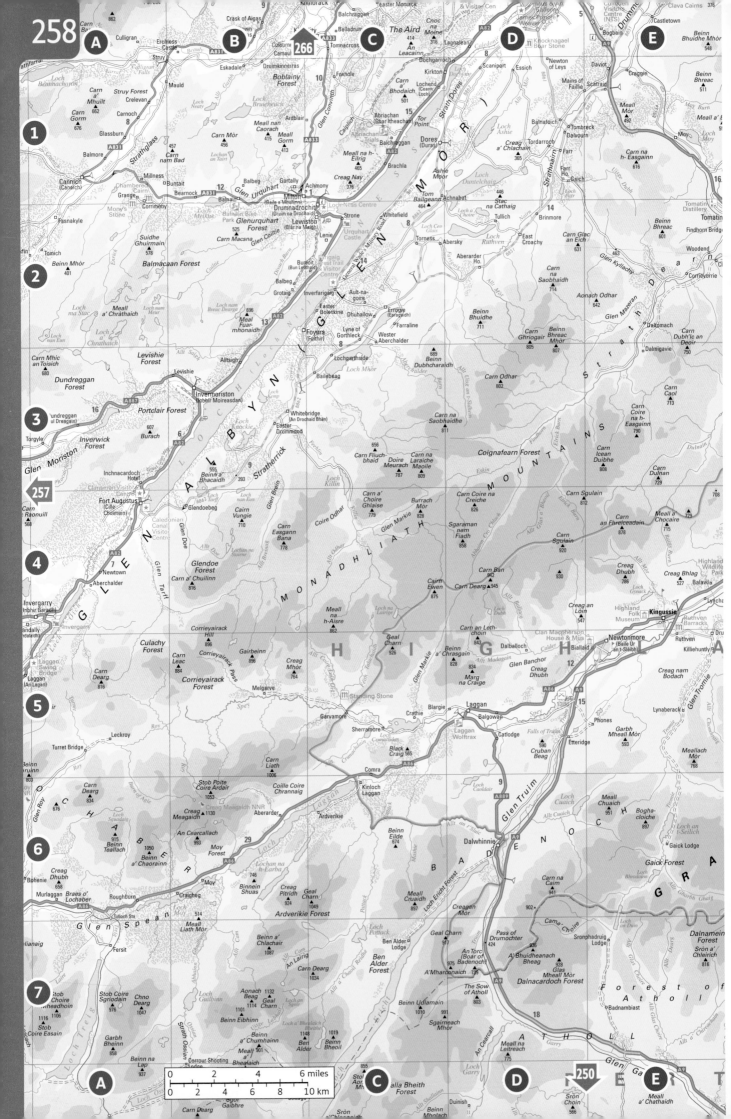

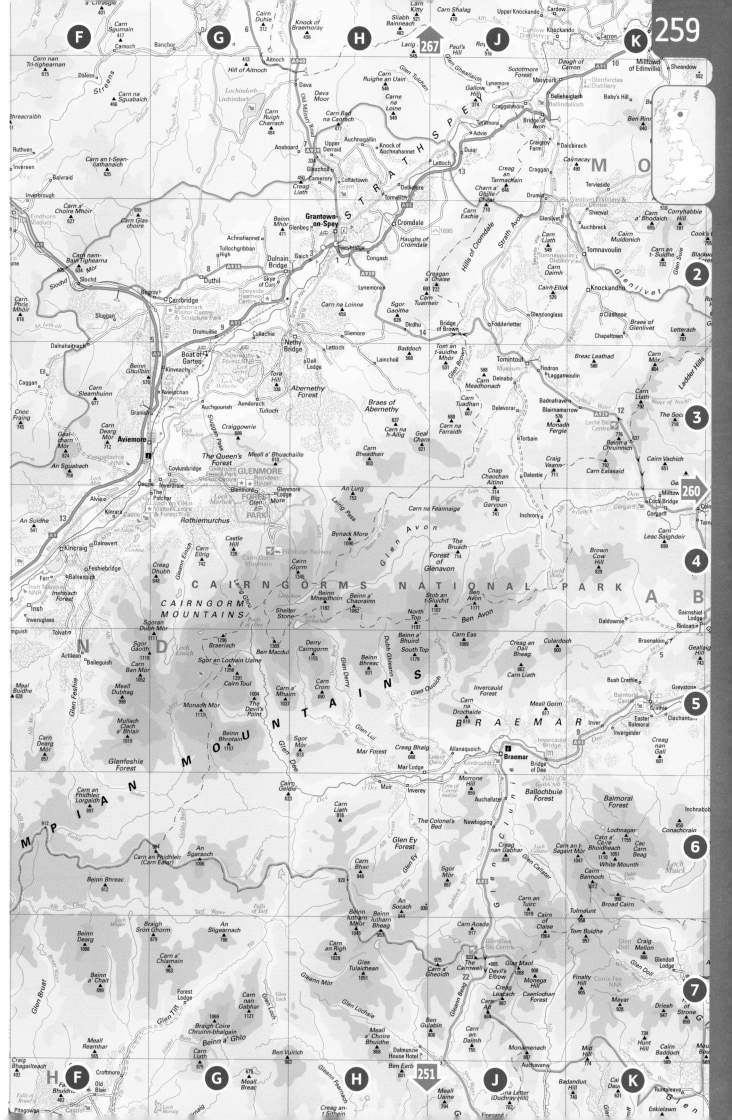

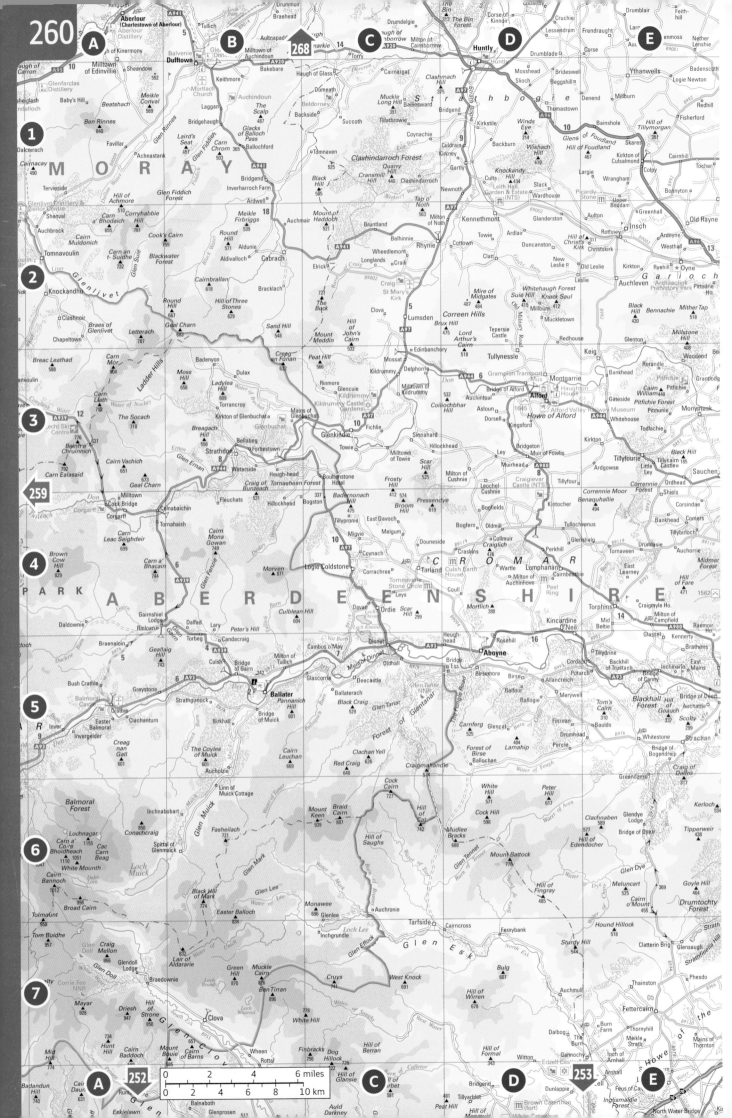

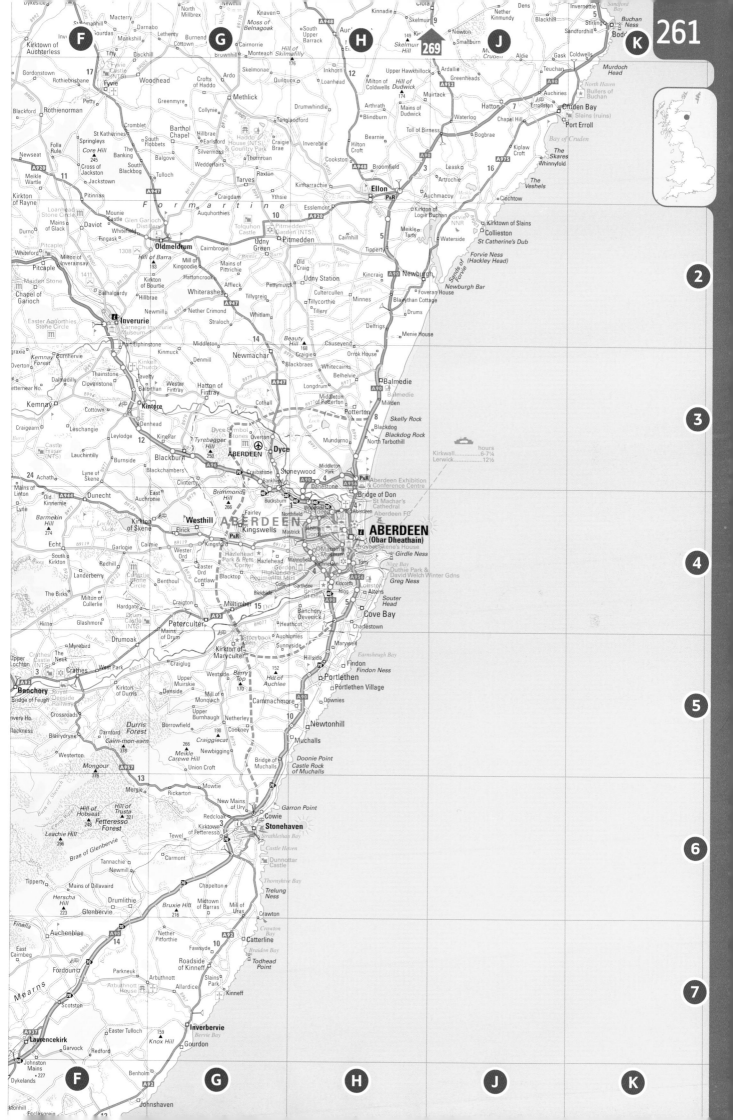

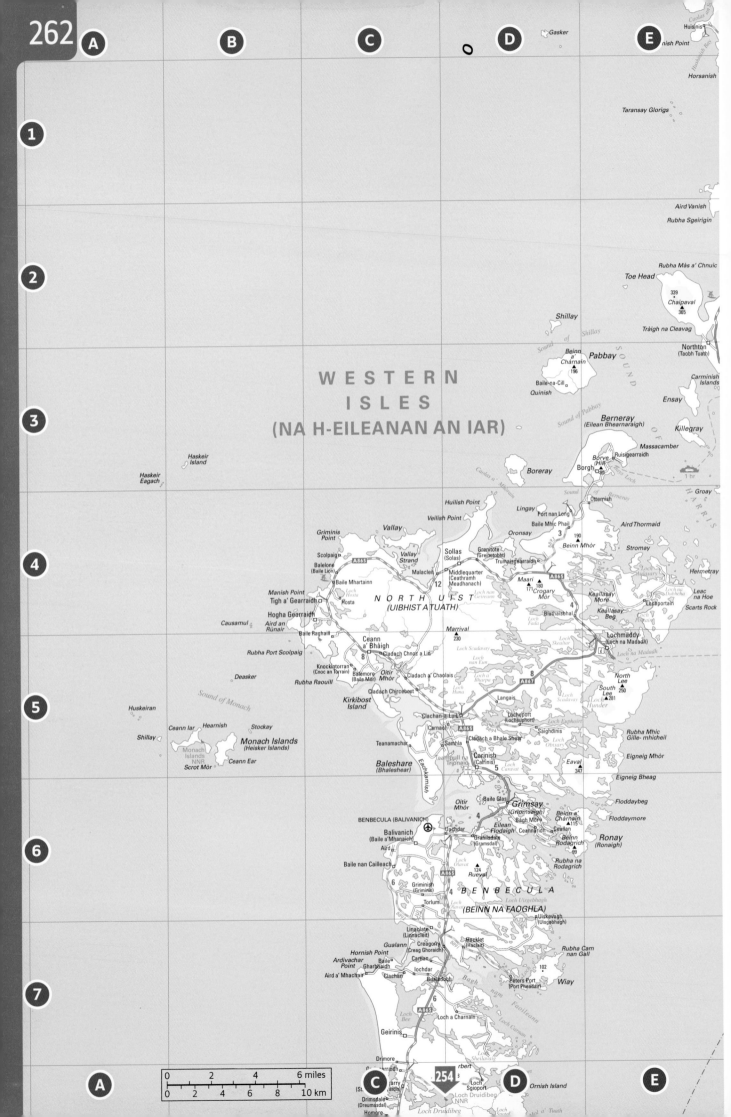

A   B   C   D   E

1

2

3

WESTERN
ISLES
(NA H-EILEANAN AN IAR)

4

5

6

7

Haskeir
Island

Haskeir
Eagach

Gasker

Huisinis
Uinish Point

Horsanish

Taransay Glorigs

Aird Vanish

Rubha Sgeirigin

Rubha Màs a' Chnuic

Toe Head

339
Chaipaval
365

Shillay

Tràigh na Cleavag

Sound of Shillay

Beinn
a'
Chàrnain
196

Pabbay

Northton
(Taobh Tuath)

Carminish
Islands

Baile-na-Cill

Quinish

Ensay

Killegray

Sound of Pabbay

Berneray
(Eilean Bhearnaraigh)

Massacamber

Boreray

Caolas a' Mhòrain

Borve
Hill

Borgh

Ruisigearraidh

Sound
of
Berneray

Groay

1 hr

HARRIS

Huilish Point

Veilish Point

Griminis
Point

Valley

Lingay

Port nan Long

Aird Thormaid

Stromay

Hermetray

Uternish

Oronsay

Baile Mhic Phail

Scolpaig

Valley
Strand

Sollas
(Solas)

A865

Granitote
(Greinetobht)

3

Beinn Mhòr

190

A865

Loch
Aulasary

Leac
na Hoe

Balelone
(Baile Lión)

Malaclett

Middlequarter
(Ceathramh
Meadhanach)

Trumaisgearraidh

Maari

180

4

Keallasay
More

Loch
Dubhcha

Scarts Rock

Baile Mhartainn

12

Crogary
Mòr

Blathaisbhal

Keallasay
Beg

Loch
Portain

Manish Point

Tigh a' Gearraidh

Loch
Hosta

171

NORTH UIST
(UIBHIST A TUATH)

Lochportain

Hosta

Loch nan
Geireann

Loch
Fada

4

Hogha Gearraidh

Causamul

Aird an
Rùnair

Baile Raghaill

Ceann
a' Bhàigh

Cladach Chnoc a Lìn

Marrival
230

Loch Scadavay

Lochmaddy
(Loch na Madadh)

Rubha Port Scolpaig

Deasker

8

Knockintorran
(Cnoc an Torrain)

Balemore
(Baile Mòr)

Oitir
Mhòr

Cladach a' Chaolais

Loch
nan Eun

Loch a
Bharpa

8

North
Lee

Loch na Madadh

Rubha Raouill

Cladach Chircebost

Loch
Huna

A867

South
Lee
250

281

Huskeiran

Sound of Monach

Kirkibost
Island

Cladach Chircebost

Langais

Loch Scadavay

Rubha Mhic
Gille- mhicheil

Shillay

Ceann Iar

Hearnish

Stockay

Clachan-a-Luib

Carnach

A865

Cladach a Bhale Shear

Saighdinis

Locheport
(Lochèuphort)

Loch
Obisary

Loch Eupheirt

Eigneig Mhòr

Monach Islands
(Heisker Islands)

Teanamachar

Samhla

Carinish
(Cairinis)

Eaval
347

Eigneig Bheag

Monach
Islands
NNR

Ceann Ear

Scrot Mòr

Baleshare
(Bhaleshear)

Teampull na Trionaid

5

Loch
Caravat

Floddaybeg

Floddaymore

Eachkamish

Oitir
Mhòr

Baile Glas

Grimsay
(Griomsaigh)

Bàgh Mòr

Beinn a'
Chàrnain
115

Ronay
(Ronaigh)

BENBECULA (BALIVANICH)

Uachdar

Eilean
Flodaigh

Ceannaridh

Ceallan

Beinn
Rodagrich
49

Balivanich
(Baile a'Mhanaich)

Gramisdale
(Gramsdall)

Rubha na
Rodagrich

Aird

Baile nan Cailleach

Loch
Olavat

124
Rueval

Griminish
(Griminis)

A865

BENBECULA
(BEINN NA FAOGHLA)

Loch Uisgebhagh

Uiskevagh
(Uisgebhagh)

Torlum

Loch
Olavat

Rubha Cam
nan Gall

Linaclate
(Lionacleit)

Gualann

Creagorry
(Creag Ghoraidh)

Hacklet
(Haclait)

Hornish Point

Baile
Gharbhaidh

Carnan

Ardivachar
Point

Iochdar

102

Wiay

Aird a' Mhachair

Clachan

Bhalaigh

Peters Port
(Port Pheadair)

Bagh nam Faoileann

7

A865

6

Loch Bee

Loch a Charnain

Loch Sgiopoirt

Loch Druidibeg
NNR

Drimore

254

rbert

Ornish Island

Geirinis

Loch
Sheilabhaig

A   B   C   D   E

0   2   4   6 miles
0   2   4   6   8   10 km

Drimsdale
(Dreumasdal)

Homore

St.

arraidh

Loch Druidibeg

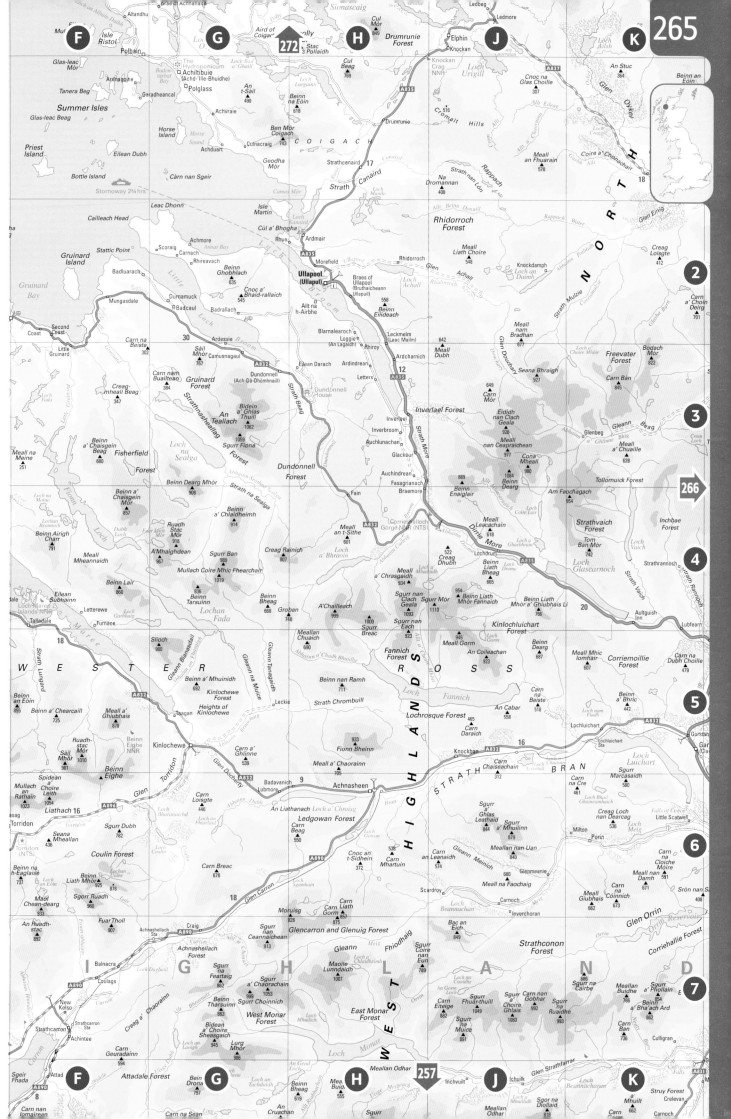

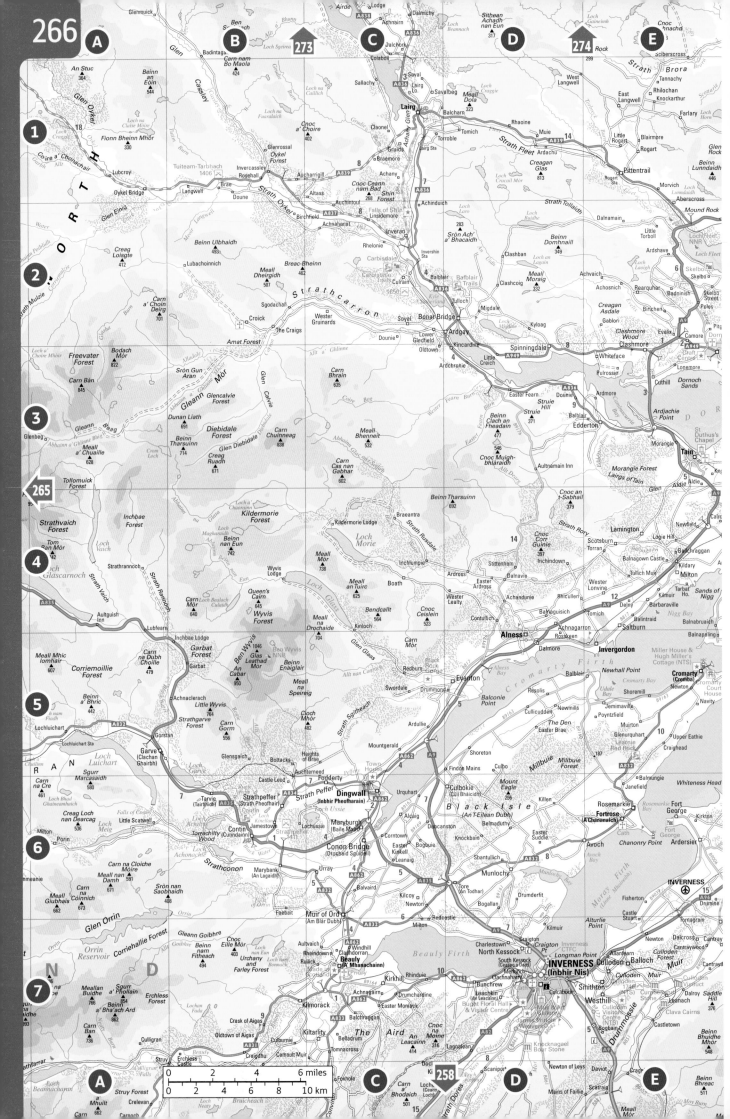

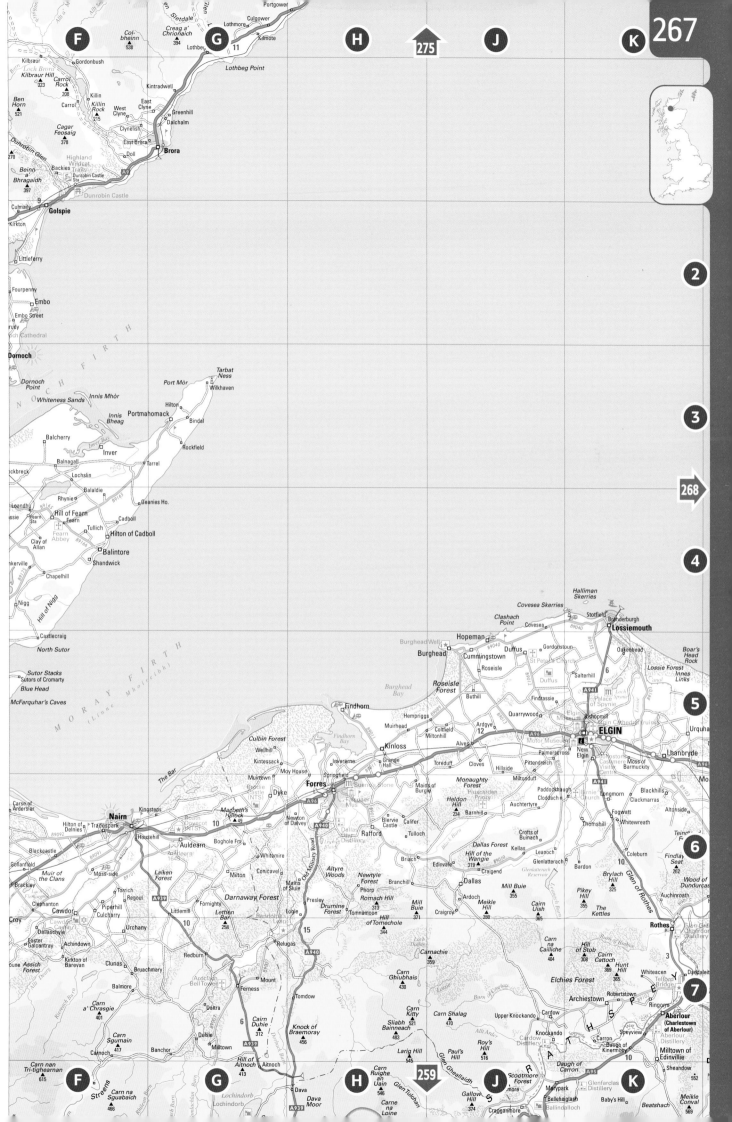

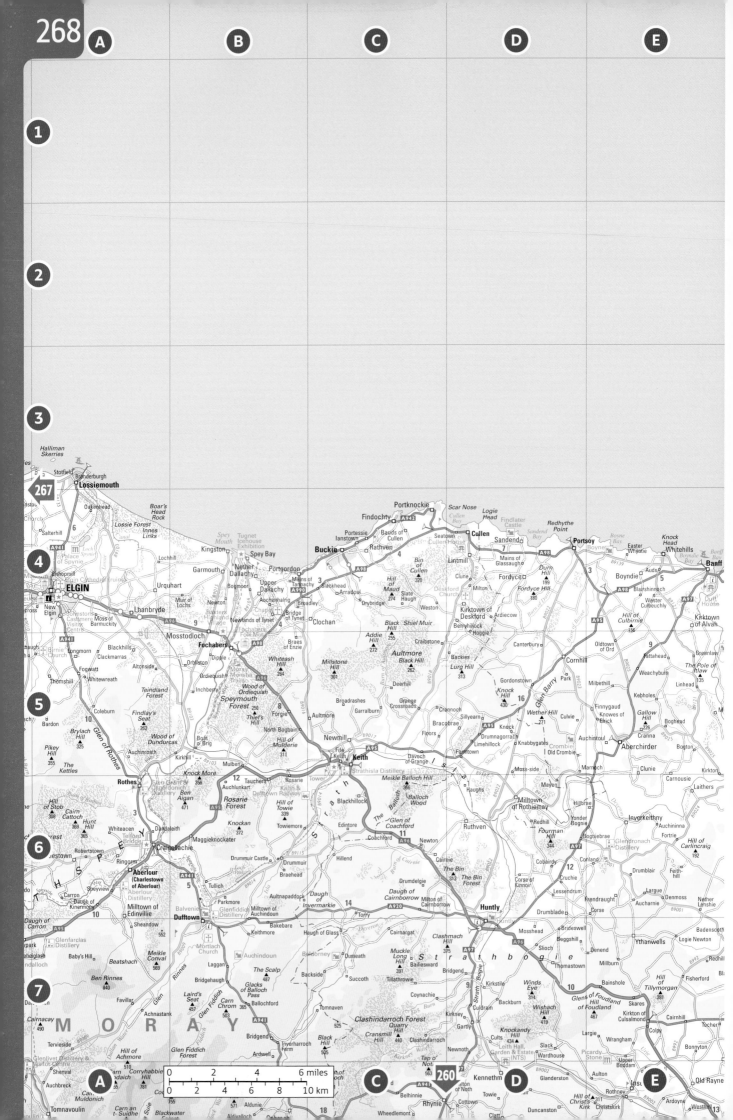

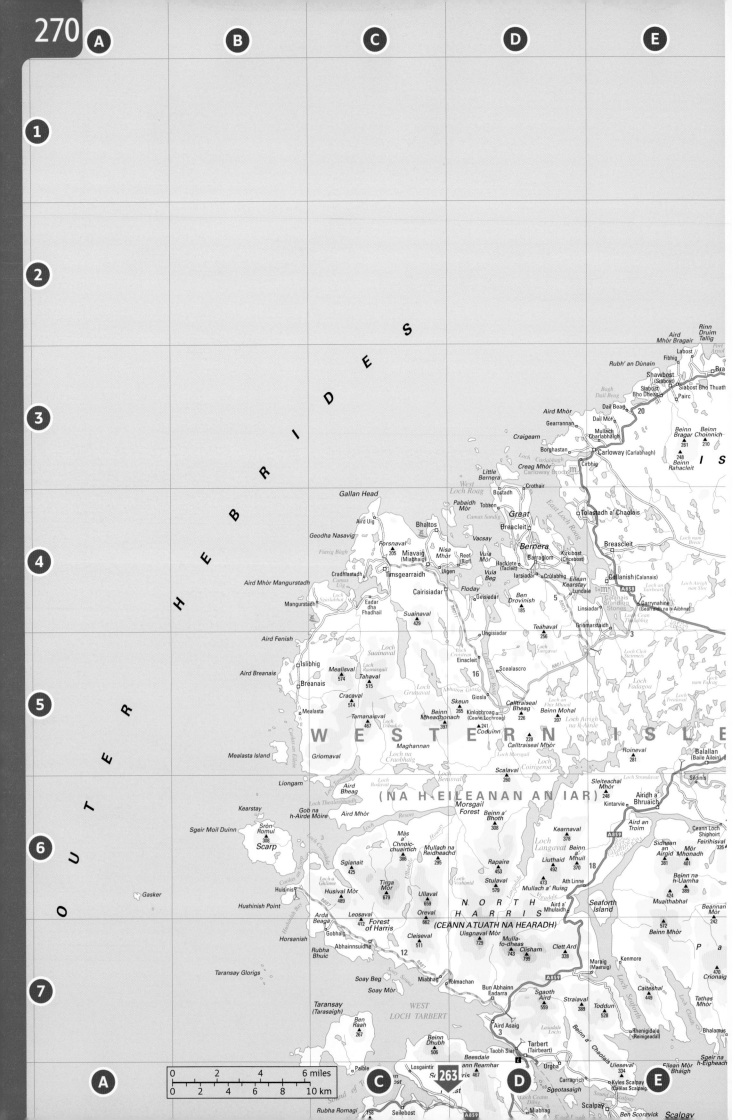

A   B   C   D   E

1

2

HEBRIDES

3

Aird Mhòr Bragair
Rinn Druim Tallig
Aird Mhòr Bragair
Port Arnol
Labost
Fibhig
Bra
Rubh' an Dùnain
Shawbost
(Siabost)
Siabost
(Siabost)
Bagh
Dail Beag
Siabost Bho Thuath
Siabost
Bho Dheas
Pairc
Dail Beag
20
Aird Mhòr
Dail Mòr
Beinn
Bragar 261
Beinn
Choinnich 210
Gearrannan
Mullach
Charlabhaigh
Craigeam
248
Beinn
Rahacleit
Borghastan
Carloway (Carlabhagh)
Loch
Carlabhagh
I S
Creag Mhòr
Cirbhig
Carloway Broch
Little
Bernera
West
Loch Roag
Bostadh
Gallan Head
Tobson
Crothair
Tolastadh a' Chaolais
Pabaidh
Mòr
Camas Sandig
Great
Breacleit
Breascleit
Aird Uig
Bhaltos
Loch nam
Breac
Geodha Nasavig
Vacsay
Bernera
Forsnaval
205
Nisa
Mhòr
Reet
(Riof)
Vuia
Mòr
Kirkibost
(Circebost)
A858
Fiavig Bàgh
Miavaig
(Miabhaig)
Hacklete
(Tacleit)
Barraglom
Callanish (Calanais)
Cradhlastadh
Uigen
Vuia
Beg
Iarsiadar
Eilean
Kearstay
Loch Airigh
nan Sloc
Aird Mhòr Mangurstadh
Tarmsgearraidh
Floday
Crùlabhig
Lundale
Calanais
Standing
Stones
Garrynahine
(Gearraidh na h-Aibhne)
Camas
Uig
Cairisiadar
Geisiadar
Linsiadar
Mangurstadh
Eadar
dha
Fhadhail
Ben
Drovinish
185
5
A858
Loch an
Tairbeairt
Loch Ceann
Thulabhig
Suainaval
429
Teahaval
256
Griomarstaidh
3
4

Aird Fenish
Ungisiadar
Loch
Croistean
Loch Clett
Steimreis
Loch
Suainaval
Loch
Tungavat
Islibhig
Mealisval
574
Einacleit
Aird Breanais
Loch
Raonasgail
Tahaval
515
Scealascro
16
B8011
Loch
Fadagoa
Breanais
Cracaval
514
Loch
Grimavat
Giosla
Skeun
265
Calltraiseal
Bheag
Beinn Mohal
207
Loch Trealaval
Mealasta
Tamanaisval
467
Beinn
Mheadhonach
397
Kinlochroag
(Ceann Lochroag)
226
Loch Airigh
na h-Airde
Beinn
nam Fajeau
Coduinn
241
Calltraiseal Mhòr
228
Roineval
281
Balallan
(Baile Ailein)
Maghannan
Loch na
Craobhaig
Loch Morsgail
Loch
Coirigerod
Scalaval
260
Griomaval
W E S T E R N   I S L E
Mealasta Island
Liongam
Loch
Benisval
(N A   H - E I L E A N A N   A N   I A R)
Sleiteachal
Mhòr
248
Sildinis
Loch Strandavat
Aird
Bheag
Morsgail
Forest
Airidh a'
Bhruaich
Kearstay
Gob na
h-Airde Mòire
Aird Mhòr
Beinn a'
Bhoth
308
Kintarvie
Aird an
Troim
A859
Ceann Loch
Shiphoirt
Feirihisval
326
Sgeir Moil Duinn
Sròn
Romul
308
Scarp
Màs
a'
Chnoic-
chuairtich
386
Mullach na
Reidheachd
295
Kearnaval
378
Loch
Langavat
Sidhean
an
Airgid
381
Mòr
Mhonadh
401
Sgianait
425
Beinn
a'
Mhuil
18
Beinn na
h-Uamha
424
389
Gasker
Rapaire
453
Liuthaid
370
Loch
Voshimid
Stulaval
579
Ath Linne
473
Muaithabhal
Tirga
Mòr
679
Ullaval
659
Mullach a' Ruisg
Seaforth
Island
Beannan
Mòr
242
Huisinis
Husival Mòr
489
N O R T H
Aird a'
Mhulaidh
Hushinish Point
Leosaval
412
Oreval
Forest
of Harris
H A R R I S
Beinn Mhòr
572
Arda
Beaga
662
(CEANN A TUATH NA HEARADH)
P a
Horsanish
Gobhain
Abhainnsuidhe
Uisgnaval Mòr
729
Mulla-
fo-dheas
743
Clett Ard
328
Rubha
Bhuic
12
Cleiseval
511
Clisham
799
Crionaig
Taransay Glorigs
Soay Beg
Maraig
(Maaruig)
Kenmore
470
Kyles Scalpay
Caiteshal
449
Tathas
Mhòr
Taransay
(Tarasaigh)
Soay Mòr
Miabhag
Tolmachan
WEST
LOCH TARBERT
Bun Abhainn
Eadarra
Sgaoth
Aird
559
Straiaval
389
Toddun
528
Rhenigidale
(Reinigeadal)
Ben
Raah
267
Beinn
Dhubh
506
Aird Asaig
3
Laxadale
Lochs
Beinn a'
Chaolais
Loch Seaforth
Bhlaman
Taobh Siar
Tarbert
(Tairbeart)
Beesdale
Paible
Losgaintir
ann Reamhar
Sa
263
Urgha
Carragrich
Ueseval
334
Sgeir na
h-Eigheach
O U T E R
Rubha Romagi
Seilebost
158
Miabhag
Sgeotasaigh
Kyles Scalpay
Caolas Scalpaig
Eilean Mòr
Bhàigh
Ben Scoravick
Scalpay

A   C   D   E

0   2   4   6 miles
0 2 4 6 8   10 km

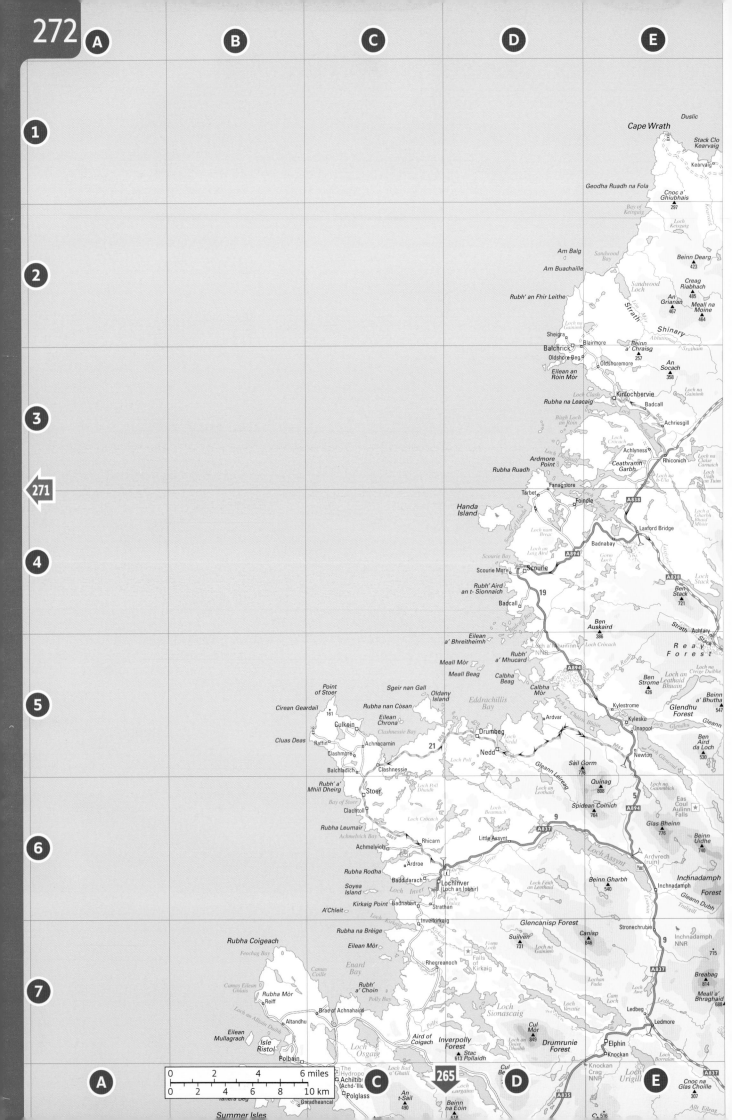

A   B   C   D   E

1

2

3

271

4

5

6

7

Cape Wrath

Duslic

Stack Clo
Kearvaig

Kearvaig

Geodha Ruadh na Fola

Cnoc a'
Ghiubhais
297

Bay of
Keisgaig

Loch
Keisgaig

Am Balg

Am Buachaille

Sandwood
Bay

Beinn Dearg
423

Rubh' an Fhir Leithe

Sandwood
Loch

Strath

Creag
Riabhach
485

An
Grianan
467

Meall na
Moine
464

Sheigra

Balchrick

Blairmore

Oldshore Beg

Eilean an
Ròin Mòr

Oldshoremore

Beinn
a' Chraisg
257

An
Socach
358

Shinary

Kinlochbervie

Loch Clash

Rubha na Leacaig

Badcall

Achriesgill

Loch na
Gainimh

Bàgh Loch
an Ròin

Achlyness

Loch na
Claise
Carnaich

Ardmore
Point

Rubha Ruadh

Ceathramh
Garbh

Rhiconich

Loch
Crocach

Loch na
Uidh
nam Tuim

Fanagmore

Tarbet

Handa
Island

Loch nam
Breac

Foindle

A838

Loch na
Gharbh
Bhad
Mhòir

Laxford Bridge

South of Handa

Loch an
Laig Aird

Badnabay

Loch
Laxford

Scourie Bay

A894

Gorm
Loch

A838

Loch
Stack

Scourie More

Scourie

19

Ben
Stack
721

Rubh' Aird
an t- Sionnaich

Badcall

Ben
Auskaird
386

Strath Achfary

Reay

Forest

Eilean
a' Bhreitheimh

Rubh'
a' Mhucard

Loch a' Mhuillinn
NNR

Loch Crocach

A894

Ben
Strome
426

Loch na
Leathaid
Bhuain

Loch na
Creige Duibhe

Meall Mòr

Meall Beag

Calbha
Beag

Calbha
Mòr

Beinn
a' Bhutha
547

Point
of Stoer

Sgeir nan Gall

Oldany
Island

Eddrachillis
Bay

Kylestrome

Kylesku

Glendhu
Forest

Cirean Geardail
161

Rubha nan Còsan

Unapool

Gleann

Cluas Deas

Raffin

Eilean
Chrona

Clashnessie Bay

Ardvar

Newton

Ben
Aird
da Loch
530

Culkein

Achnacarnin

Drumbeg

Loch
Nedd

Sàil Gorm
776

Clashmore

21

Nedd

Balchladich

Clashnessie

Loch Poll

Gleann Leireag

Quinag
808

Loch na
Gainmhich

Eas
Coul
Aulinn
Falls

Rubh' a'
Mhill Dheirg

Stoer

Loch Poll
Dhuaidh

Spidean Còinich
764

5

A894

Bay of Stoer

Clachtoll

Loch Crocach

Loch
Beannach

Ardvreck
(ruin)

Glas Bheinn
776

Beinn
Uidhe
740

Rubha Leumair

Achmelvich Bay

Rhicarn

Little Assynt

A837

9

Loch Assynt

Inchnadamph

Forest

Achmelvich

Inver

Beinn Gharbh
540

Inchnadamph

Ardroe

Baddidarrach

Lochinver
(Loch an Inbhir)

Loch Feòir
an Leothaid

Gleann Dubh

Rubha Rodha

Soyea
Island

Loch Inver

Kirkaig Point

Badnaban

Strathan

Stronechrubie

A'Chleit

Inverkirkaig

Glencanisp Forest

Canisp
846

Inchnadamph
NNR

715

Rubha na Brèige

Rubha Coigach

Eilean Mòr

Rhegreanoch

Falls of
Kirkaig

Suilven
731

9

A837

Breabag
814

Feochag Bay

Fionn
Loch

Loch na
Gainimh

Lochan
Fada

Meall a'
Bhraghaid
688

Enard
Bay

Rubh'
a' Choin

Polly Bay

Ledbeg

Camas Eilean
Ghlais

Rubha Mòr

Reiff

Loch
Sionascaig

Loch
Veyatie

Cam
Loch

Loch Awe

Ledmore

Altandhu

Polly

A837

Eilean
Mullagrach

Isle
Ristol

Cùl
Mòr
849

Drumrunie
Forest

Elphin

Loch
Borralan

Polbain

Aird of
Coigach

Inverpolly
Forest

Stac
613 Pollaidh

Cùl Be

Loch an
Doire
Dhuibh

Knockan

Cnoc na Glas Choille
307

The
Hydropo

Achiltibu

Achd-'Ille

Polglass

An
t-Sàil

Beinn
na Eoin
490

Glencanisp Forest

Knockan
Crag
NNR

Cnoc an
t-Sagairt

Loch
Urigill

A835

A837

Tanera Beg

Garadheancal

Summer Isles

A   C   D   E

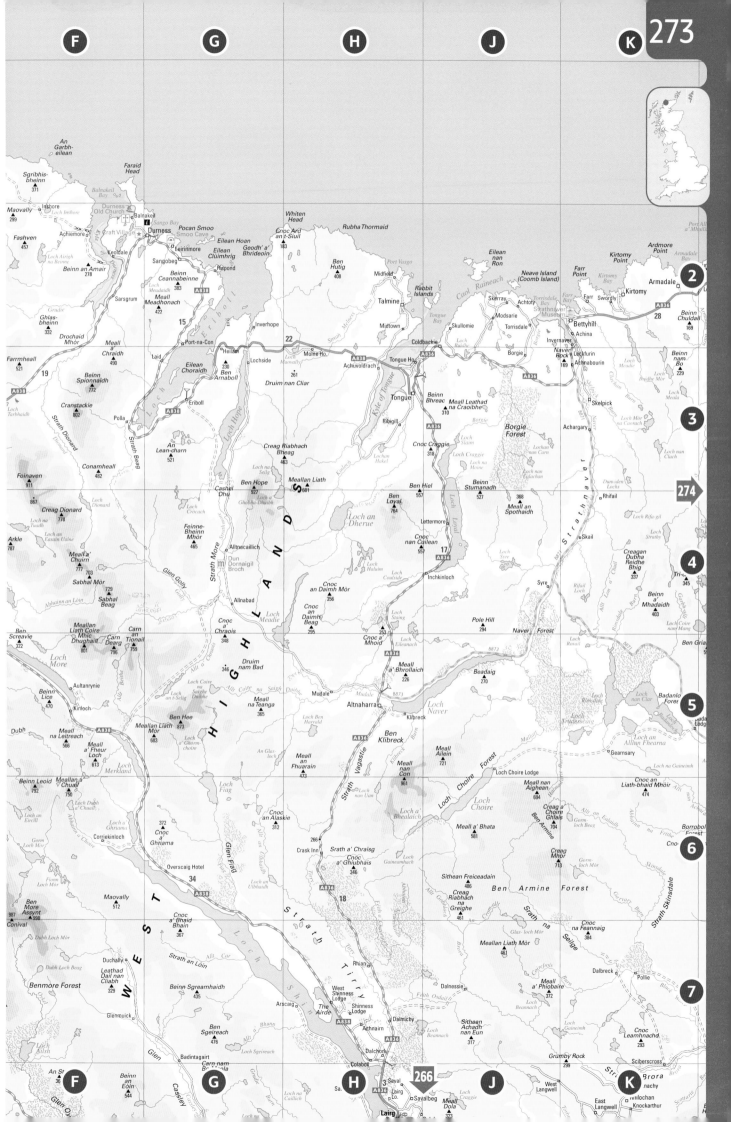

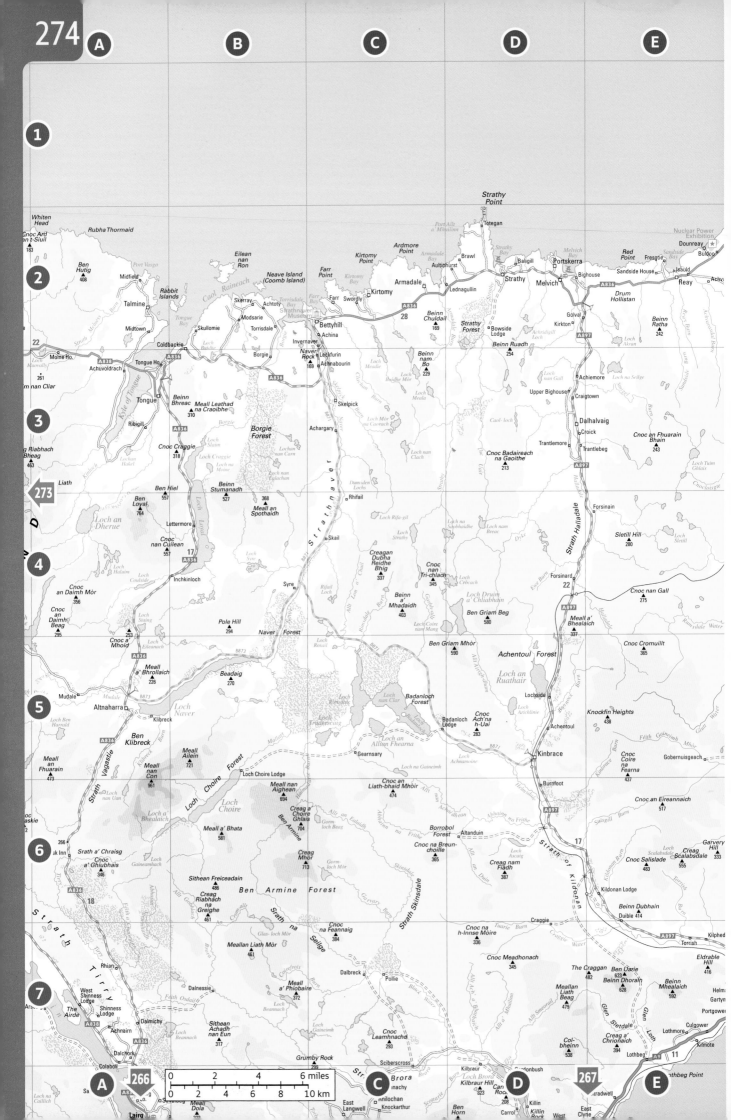

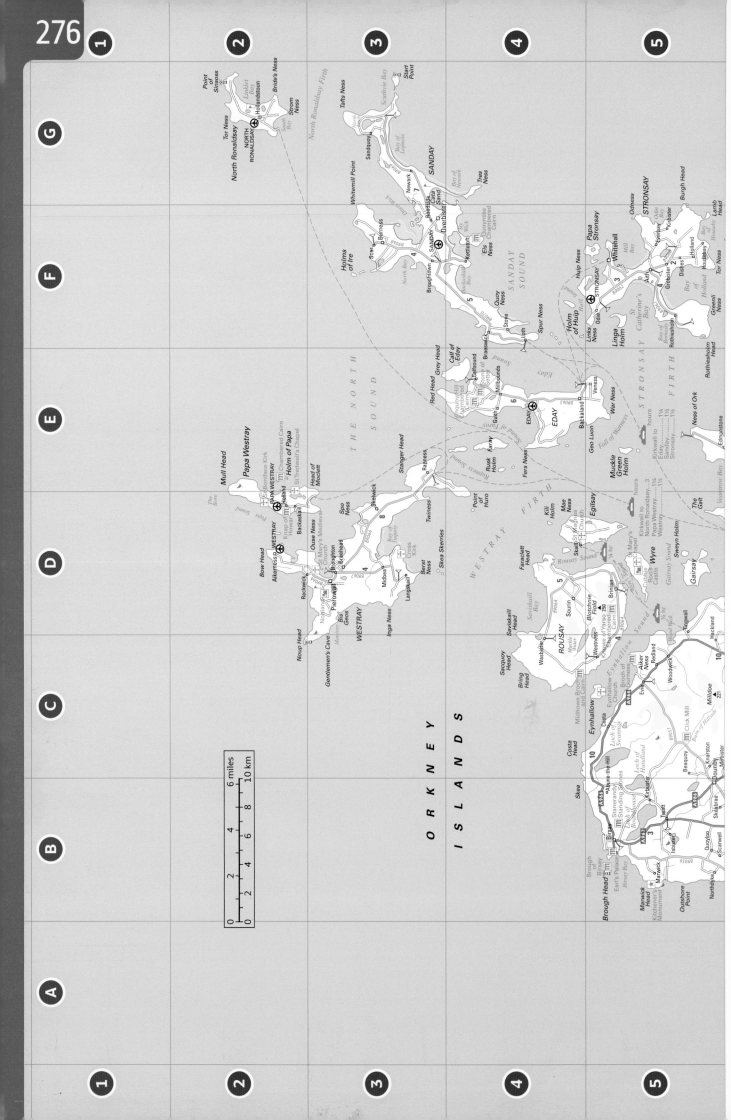

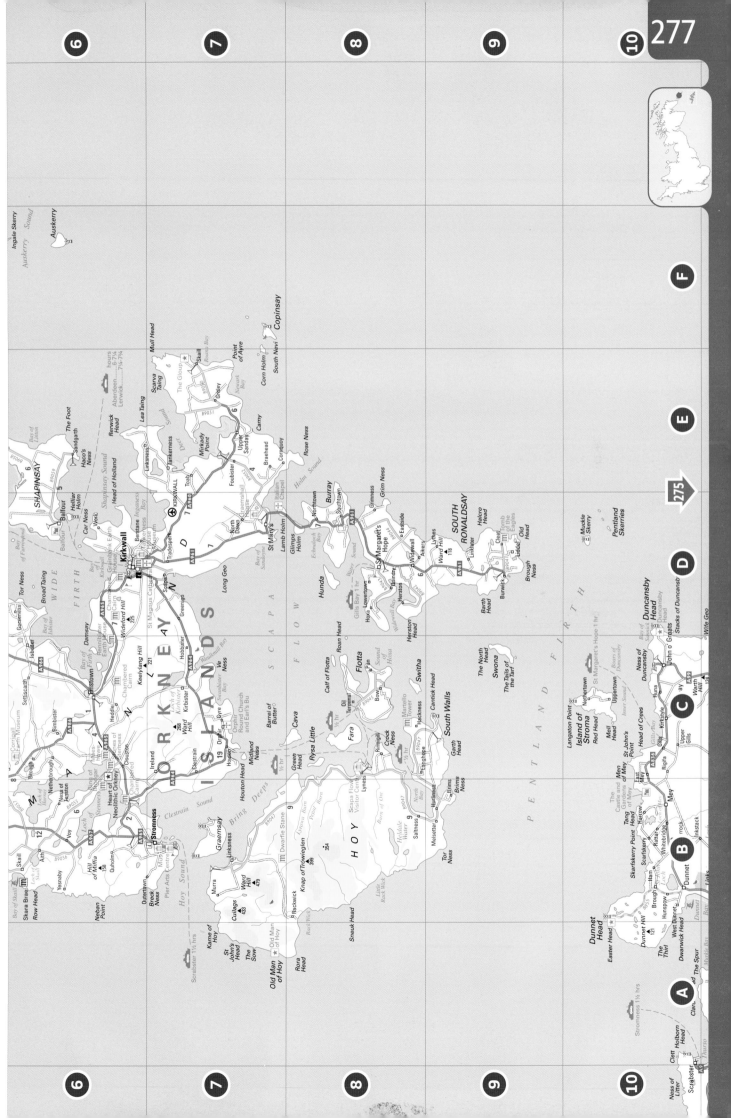

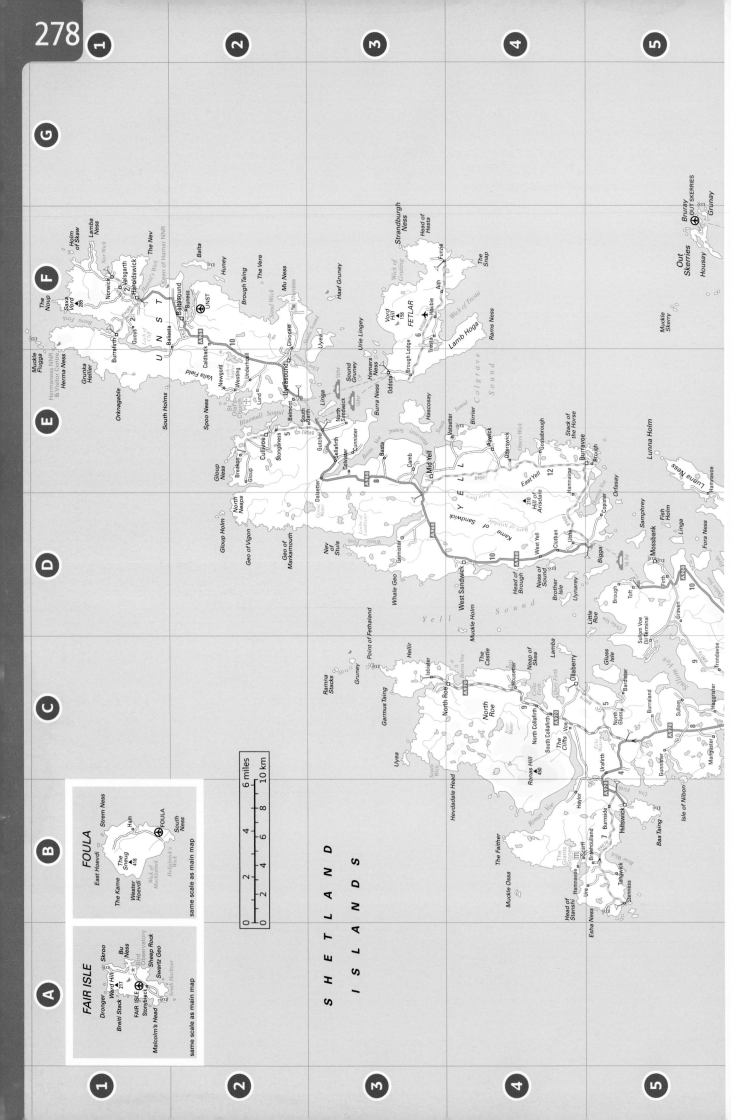

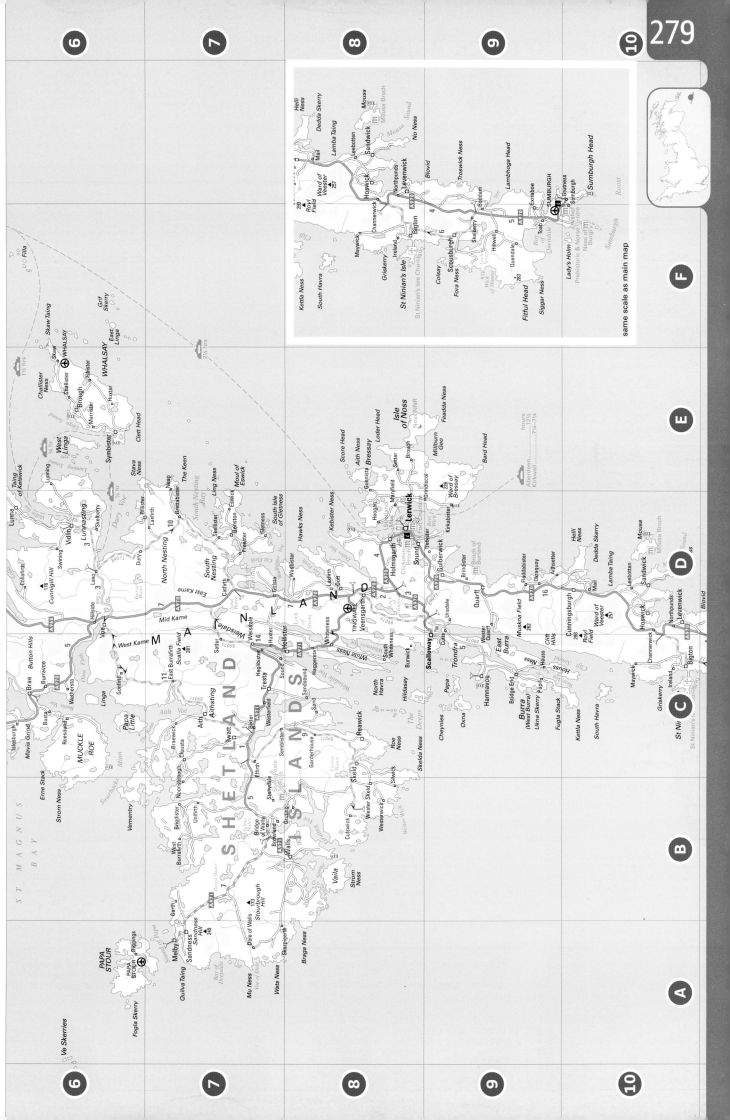

Place and place of interest names are followed by a **page number** and a grid reference in black type. The feature can be found on the map somewhere within the grid square shown.

Where two or more places have the same name the abbreviated *county* or *unitary authority* names are shown to distinguish between them. A list of these abbreviated names appears below.

The top 1000 most visited places of interest are shown within the index in blue type. Their postcode information is supplied after the county names to aid integration with satnav systems.

A&B	Argyll & Bute
Aber	Aberdeenshire
B&H	Brighton & Hove
B&NESom	Bath & North East Somerset
B'burn	Blackburn with Darwen
B'pool	Blackpool
BGwent	Blaenau Gwent
Bed	Bedford
Bourne	Bournemouth
BrackF	Bracknell Forest
Bucks	Buckinghamshire
Caerp	Caerphilly
Cambs	Cambridgeshire
Carmar	Carmarthenshire
CenBeds	Central Bedfordshire
Cere	Ceredigion
Chanl	Channel Islands
ChesE	Cheshire East
ChesW&C	Cheshire West & Chester
Corn	Cornwall
Cumb	Cumbria
D&G	Dumfries & Galloway
Darl	Darlington
Denb	Denbighshire
Derbys	Derbyshire
Dur	Durham
EAyr	East Ayrshire
EDun	East Dunbartonshire
ELoth	East Lothian
ERenf	East Renfrewshire
ERid	East Riding of Yorkshire
ESuss	East Sussex
Edin	Edinburgh
Falk	Falkirk
Flints	Flintshire
Glas	Glasgow
Glos	Gloucestershire
GtLon	Greater London
GtMan	Greater Manchester
Gwyn	Gwynedd
Hants	Hampshire
Hart	Hartlepool
Here	Herefordshire
Herts	Hertfordshire
High	Highland
Hull	Kingston upon Hull
Invcly	Inverclyde
IoA	Isle of Anglesey
IoM	Isle of Man
IoS	Isles of Scilly
IoW	Isle of Wight
Lancs	Lancashire
Leic	Leicester
Leics	Leicestershire
Lincs	Lincolnshire
MK	Milton Keynes
MTyd	Merthyr Tydfil
Med	Medway
Mersey	Merseyside
Middl	Middlesbrough
Midlo	Midlothian

Mon	Monmouthshire
N'hants	Northamptonshire
N'umb	Northumberland
NAyr	North Ayrshire
NELincs	North East Lincolnshire
NLan	North Lanarkshire
NLincs	North Lincolnshire
NPT	Neath Port Talbot
NSom	North Somerset
NYorks	North Yorkshire
Norf	Norfolk
Nott	Nottingham
Notts	Nottinghamshire
Ork	Orkney
Oxon	Oxfordshire
P&K	Perth & Kinross
Pembs	Pembrokeshire

Peter	Peterborough
Plym	Plymouth
Ports	Portsmouth
R&C	Redcar & Cleveland
RCT	Rhondda Cynon Taff
Read	Reading
Renf	Renfrewshire
Rut	Rutland
S'end	Southend-on-Sea
SAyr	South Ayrshire
SGlos	South Gloucestershire
SLan	South Lanarkshire
SYorks	South Yorkshire
ScBord	Scottish Borders
Shet	Shetland

Shrop	Shropshire
Slo	Slough
Som	Somerset
Soton	Southampton
Staffs	Staffordshire
Stir	Stirling
Stock	Stockton-on-Tees
Stoke	Stoke-on-Trent
Suff	Suffolk
Surr	Surrey
Swan	Swansea
Swin	Swindon
T&W	Tyne & Wear
Tel&W	Telford & Wrekin
Thur	Thurrock
VGlam	Vale of Glamorgan

W&M	Windsor & Maidenhead
W'ham	Wokingham
WBerks	West Berkshire
WDun	West Dunbartonshire
WIsles	Western Isles (Na h-Eileanan an Iar)
WLoth	West Lothian
WMid	West Midlands
WSuss	West Sussex
WYorks	West Yorkshire
Warks	Warwickshire
Warr	Warrington
Wilts	Wiltshire
Worcs	Worcestershire
Wrex	Wrexham

1	Bath & North East Somerset
2	Blaenau Gwent
3	Bournemouth
4	Bracknell Forest
5	Bridgend
6	Bristol
7	Caerphilly
8	Cardiff
9	Clackmannanshire
10	Darlington
11	Dundee
12	East Dunbartonshire
13	East Renfrewshire
14	Glasgow
15	Halton
16	Hartlepool
17	Inverclyde
18	Luton
19	Merthyr Tydfil
20	Middlesbrough
21	Monmouthshire
22	Neath Port Talbot
23	Newport
24	North Lanarkshire
25	Plymouth
26	Poole
27	Portsmouth
28	Reading
29	Redcar And Cleveland
30	Renfrewshire
31	Rhondda Cynon Taff
32	Slough
33	South Gloucestershire
34	Southampton
35	Stockton-on-tees
36	Telford & Wrekin
37	Torfaen
38	Vale Of Glamorgan
39	Warrington
40	West Dunbartonshire
41	Windsor & Maidenhead
42	Wokingham

1853 Gallery WYorks BD18 3LA 26 C1

A

Ab Kettleby 174 C5
Ab Lench 146 C2
Abbas Combe 117 E5
Abberley 145 G1
Abberley Common 145 G1
Abberton Essex 138 D1
Abberton Worcs 146 B2
Abberwick 229 F5
Abbess Roding 137 E1
Abbey Dore 144 C4
Abbey Hulton 171 G3
Abbey St. Bathans 237 E3
Abbey Village 192 C5
Abbey Wood 137 D5
Abbeycwmhir 155 G5
Abbeydale 186 A4
Abbeystead 192 B2
Abbeytown 209 E1
Abbotrule 228 A3
Abbots Bickington 113 D4
Abbots Bromley 172 B5
Abbots Langley 135 F2
Abbots Leigh 131 E5
Abbots Morton 146 C2
Abbots Ripton 162 A5
Abbot's Salford 146 C2
Abbots Worthy 119 F4
Abbotsbury 104 B4
Abbotsbury Swannery, Subtropical Gardens & Children's Farm Dorset DT3 4JG 104 B4
Abbotsfield Farm 183 G3
Abbotsham 113 E3
Abbotskerswell 101 E1
Abbotsley 150 A2
Abbotstone 119 G4
Abbotts Ann 119 E3
Abbott's Barton 119 F4
Abbottswood 119 E5
Abdon 157 E4
Abdy 186 B3
Abenhall 131 F1
Aber 142 A3
Aber Village 144 A5
Aberaeron 142 A1
Aberaman 129 G2
Aberangell 155 E2
Aber-Arad 141 G3
Aberarder 249 G1
Aberarder House 258 D2
Aberargie 243 G2
Aberarth 142 A1
Aberavon 129 D3
Aber-banc 141 G5
Aberbargoed 130 A2
Aberbeeg 130 B2
Aberbowlan 142 C4
Aberbran 143 F5
Abercanaid 129 G2
Abercarn 130 B3
Abercastle 140 B4
Abercegir 155 E2
Aberchalder 257 K4
Aberchirder 268 E5
Abercorn 235 E2
Abercraf 129 E1
Abercregan 129 E3
Abercrombie 244 D4
Abercrychan 143 D4
Abercwmboi 129 G2
Abercych 141 F3
Abercynafon 129 G1
Abercynon 129 G3
Abercywarch 155 E1
Aberdalgie 243 F2
Aberdare 129 F2
Aberdaron 166 A5
Aberdeen (Obar Dheathain) 261 H4
Aberdeen Airport 261 G3
Aberdeen Art Gallery AB10 1FQ 63 Aberdeen
Aberdeen Exhibition & Conference Centre Aberdeen AB23 8BL 261 H3
Aberdesach 166 D2
Aberdour 235 F1
Aberdovey (Aberdyfi) 154 C2
Aberduhonw 143 G2
Aberdulais 129 D3
Aberedw 143 G3
Abereiddy 140 A4
Abererch 166 C4
Aberfan 129 G2
Aberfeldy 251 D5
Aberffraw 166 C1
Aberffrwd 154 C5
Aberford 194 D4
Aberfoyle 242 A4
Abergavenny (Y Fenni) 130 B1
Abergele 182 A5
Aber-Giâr 142 B3
Abergorlech 142 B4
Abergwesyn 143 E2
Abergwili 142 A5
Abergwydol 155 D2
Abergwynant 154 C1
Abergwynfi 129 E3
Abergwyngregyn 181 E5
Abergynolwyn 154 C2
Aberhafesp 155 G3
Aberhosan 155 E3
Aberkenfig 129 E4
Aberlady 236 B1
Aberlemno 252 D4
Aberllefenni 155 E1
Aber-llia 129 F1
Aberlour (Charlestown of Aberlour) 267 K7
Abermad 154 B5
Abermeurig 142 A3
Abermule (Aber-miwl) 156 A3
Abernaint 169 E5

Abernant Carmar 141 G5
Aber-nant RCT 129 G2
Abernethy 243 G3
Abernyte 244 A1
Aberporth 141 F2
Aberscross 266 E2
Abersky 243 C2
Abersoch 166 C5
Abersychan 130 B2
Aberthin 129 G5
Abertillery 130 B2
Abertridwr Caerp 130 A4
Abertridwr Powys 155 G1
Abertysswg 130 A2
Aberuthven 243 E3
Aberyscir 143 F5
Aberystwyth 154 B4
Aberystwyth Arts Centre Cere SY23 3DE 154 B4
Abhainnsuidhe 270 C7
Abingdon 133 G3
Abinger Common 121 G3
Abinger Hammer 121 F3
Abington 226 A3
Abington Pigotts 150 B3
Abingworth 108 C2
Ablington Glos 132 D2
Ablington Wilts 118 C3
Abney 185 F5
Above Church 172 B2
Aboyne 260 D5
Abram 184 A2
Abriachan (Obar Itheachan) 258 C1
Abridge 137 D3
Abronhill 234 B2
Abson 131 G5
Abthorpe 148 B3
Abune-the-Hill 276 B5
Aby 189 E5
Acaster Malbis 195 E3
Acaster Selby 195 E3
Accrington 193 D5
Accurrach 240 C2
Acha 246 A4
Achacha 248 B5
Achadacaie 231 G3
Achadh Mòr 271 F5
Achadh-chaorrunn 231 F4
Achadunan 241 E3
Achagavel 247 G4
Achaglass 231 F5
Achahoish 231 F2
Achalader 251 G5
Achallader 249 F5
Achamore 231 D2
Achandunie 266 D4
Achany 266 C1
Achaphubuil 248 C2
Acharacle 247 F3
Achargary 274 C3
Acharn A&B 240 D1
Acharn P&K 250 C5
Acharonich 239 D1
Acharosson 232 A2
Achateny 247 E2
Achath 261 F3
Achavanich 275 G4
Achduart 265 G1
Achentoul 274 D5
Achfary 272 E5
Achgarve 264 E2
Achiemore High 273 F2
Achiemore High 274 D3
Achies 275 G3
A'Chill 255 H4
Achiltibuie (Achd-'Ille-Bhuidhe) 265 G1
Achina 274 C2
Achindown 267 F7
Achinduich 266 C2
Achingills 275 G2
Achintee 265 F7
Achintee House (Achadh an t-Suidhe) 248 D2
Achintraid 256 E1
Achlean 259 F5
Achleanan 247 E4
Achleek 247 G4
Achlian 240 D2
Achlyness 272 E3
Achmelvich 272 C6
Achmony 258 C1
Achmore High 256 E1
Achmore High 265 G2
Achmore Stir 242 A1
Achnaba 232 A1
Achnabat 258 C1
Achnabourin 274 C3
Achnacairn 240 B1
Achnacarnin 272 C5
Achnacarry 249 D1
Achnaclerach 266 B5
Achnacloich A&B 240 B1
Achnacloich High 256 B4
Achnaclyth 275 F5
Achnacraig 247 D5
Achnacroish 248 A5
Achnadrish 246 D4
Achnafalnich 241 E2
Achnafauld 243 D1
Achnagairn 266 C7
Achnagarron 266 D4
Achnaha High 247 D5
Achnaha High 247 D3
Achnahanat 266 C2
Achnahannet 259 G2
Achnairn 273 H7
Achnalea 248 A1
Achnamara 231 F1
Achnanellan 247 G5
Achnasaul 248 C1
Achnasheen 265 H6
Achnashelloch 240 B5
Achnastank 259 K1
Achorn 275 G5
Achosnich High 266 E2
Achosnich High 246 D3
Achreamie 275 F2
Achriabhach 248 D3
Achriesgill 272 E3

Achtoty 273 J2
Achurch 161 F4
Achuvoldrach 273 H3
Achvaich 266 E2
Achvarasdal 274 E2
Achvlair 248 B3
Achvraie 265 G1
Ackenthwaite 199 G4
Ackergill 275 J3
Acklam Middl 203 D1
Acklam NYorks 195 G1
Ackleton 157 G3
Acklington 221 E1
Ackton 194 D5
Ackworth Moor Top 186 B1
Acle 179 F4
Acock's Green 158 D4
Acol 125 F2
Acomb N'umb 211 F1
Acomb York 195 E2
Aconbury 145 E4
Acre 193 D5
Acrefair 169 F3
Acrise Place 125 D4
Acton ChesE 170 D2
Acton Dorset 105 F5
Acton GtLon 136 A4
Acton Shrop 156 C4
Acton Staffs 171 F3
Acton Suff 151 G3
Acton Worcs 146 A1
Acton Wrex 170 A2
Acton Beauchamp 145 F2
Acton Bridge 183 G5
Acton Burnell 157 E2
Acton Green 145 F2
Acton Pigott 157 E2
Acton Round 157 F3
Acton Scott 157 D4
Acton Trussell 158 B1
Acton Turville 132 A4
Adamhill 224 C2
Adbaston 171 E5
Adber 116 C5
Adderbury 147 G4
Adderley 171 D4
Adderstone 229 F3
Addiewell 235 D3
Addingham 193 G3
Addington Bucks 148 C5
Addington GtLon 122 C2
Addington Kent 123 F3
Addiscombe 122 C2
Addlestone 121 F1
Addlethorpe 176 C5
Adel 194 B4
Adeney 157 G1
Adeyfield 135 F2
Adfa 155 G2
Adforton 156 D5
Adisham 125 E3
Adlestrop 147 E5
Adlingfleet 196 A5
Adlington ChesE 184 D4
Adlington Lancs 183 G1
Admaston Staffs 172 B5
Admaston Tel&W 157 F1
Admington 147 E3
Adsborough 115 F5
Adscombe 115 E4
Adstock 148 C4
Adstone 148 A2
Adventure Island S'end SS1 1EE 138 B4
Adventure Wonderland Dorset BH23 6BA 3 D2
Adversane 121 F5
Advie 259 J1
Adwalton 194 B5
Adwell 134 B3
Adwick le Street 186 C2
Adwick upon Dearne 186 B2
Adziel 269 H5
Ae Village 217 D2
Afan Argoed Country Park NPT SA13 3HG 129 E3
Affetside 184 B1
Affleck 261 G2
Affpuddle 105 E3
Afon Wen 166 D4
Afon-wen 182 C5
Africa Alive! Suff NR33 7TF 165 G2
Afton 106 C4
Afton Bridgend 225 E4
Agglethorpe 201 F4
Aigburth 183 E4
Aiginis 271 G4
Aike 196 C3
Aikerness 276 D3
Aikers 277 D8
Aiketgate 210 A3
Aikshaw 209 E2
Aikton 209 F1
Ailby 189 E5
Ailey 143 C3
Ailsworth 161 G3
Aimes Green 136 D2
Aimster 275 G2
Ainderby Quernhow 202 C4
Ainderby Steeple 202 C3
Aingers Green 152 C5
Ainsdale 183 E1
Ainsdale-on-Sea 183 E1
Ainstable 210 B3
Ainsworth 184 B1
Ainthorpe 203 G2
Aintree 183 E3
Aird WIsles 262 C6
Aird WIsles 271 H4
Aird a' Mhachair 262 C7
Aird a' Mhulaidh 270 D6
Aird Asaig 270 D7
Aird Dhail 271 G1

Aird Leimhe 263 G3
Aird Mhige 263 G2
Aird Mhighe 263 F3
Aird of Sleat 256 B4
Aird Thunga 271 G4
Aird Uig 270 C4
Airdrie Fife 245 D2
Airdrie NLan 234 B3
Aire View 193 F3
Airidh a' Bhruaich 270 E6
Airieland 216 B5
Airies 214 A4
Airigh-drishaig 256 D1
Airmyn 195 G5
Airntully 243 F1
Airor 256 D4
Airth 234 C1
Airton 193 F2
Airyhassen 207 D2
Aisby Lincs 187 F3
Aisby Lincs 175 F4
Aisgill 200 C3
Aish Devon 100 C1
Aish Devon 101 E2
Aisholt 115 E4
Aiskew 202 B4
Aislaby NYorks 204 B2
Aislaby NYorks 203 G4
Aislaby Stock 202 D1
Aisthorpe 187 G4
Aith Ork 277 B6
Aith Ork 276 F5
Aith Shet 279 C7
Aith Shet 278 F3
Aithsetter 279 D9
Aitnoch 259 G1
Akeld 229 D4
Akeley 148 C4
Akenham 152 C3
Albaston 99 E3
Albecq 101 E5
Alberbury 156 C1
Albert Park TS1 3LB 78 Middlesbrough
Albert Town 126 C1
Albourne 109 E2
Albourne Green 109 E2
Albrighton Shrop 158 A1
Albrighton Shrop 157 D1
Alburgh 165 D2
Albury Herts 150 C5
Albury Oxon 134 B2
Albury Surr 121 F3
Albury End 150 C5
Alby Heath 121 F3
Alcaig 266 C6
Alcaston 157 A4
Alcester 146 C2
Alciston 110 A3
Alcombe 114 C3
Alconbury 161 G5
Alconbury Hill 161 G5
Alconbury Weston 161 G5
Aldborough Norf 178 C3
Aldborough NYorks 194 D1
Aldbourne 133 E5
Aldbrough 197 E4
Aldbrough St. John 202 B1
Aldbury 135 E2
Aldclune 251 E3
Aldeburgh 153 F2
Aldeby 165 F2
Aldenham 136 A3
Aldenham Country Park Herts WD6 3AT 136 A3
Alderbury 118 C5
Alderford 178 C4
Alderholt 106 A1
Alderley 131 G3
Alderley Edge 184 C5
Aldermaston 119 G1
Aldermaston Wharf 120 B1
Alderminster 147 E3
Alderney 101 G4
Alderney Airport 101 F4
Alder's End 145 F4
Aldersey Green 170 B2
Aldershot 121 D2
Alderton Glos 146 B4
Alderton N'hants 148 C3
Alderton Suff 153 E3
Alderton Wilts 132 A4
Alderwasley 173 E2
Aldfield 194 B1
Aldford 170 B2
Aldham Essex 152 A5
Aldham Suff 152 B3
Aldie Aber 269 J6
Aldie High 266 E3
Aldingbourne 108 B3
Aldingham 199 D5
Aldington Kent 124 C5
Aldington Worcs 146 C3
Aldivalloch 260 C2
Aldochlay 241 F5
Aldons 214 C2
Aldous's Corner 165 E3
Aldreth 162 C5
Aldridge 158 C2
Aldringham 153 F1
Aldsworth Glos 133 D2
Aldsworth WSuss 107 G2
Aldunie 260 C2
Aldwark Derbys 172 D2
Aldwark NYorks 195 D1
Aldwick 108 B4
Aldwincle 161 F4
Aldworth 134 A5
Alexandra Palace GtLon N22 7AY 12 A1
Alexandria 233 E2
Aley 115 E4
Aley Green 135 F1
Alfardisworthy 112 C4
Alfington 103 E3
Alfold 121 F4
Alfold Crossways 121 F4
Alford Aber 260 D3
Alford Lincs 189 E5

Alford Som 116 D4
Alfreton 173 F2
Alfrick 145 G2
Alfrick Pound 145 G2
Alfriston 110 A3
Algarkirk 176 A4
Alhampton 116 D4
Alkborough 196 A5
Alkerton 147 F3
Alkham 125 E4
Alkington 170 C4
Alkmonton 172 C4
All Cannings 118 B1
All Saints South Elmham 165 E2
All Stretton 157 D3
Allaleigh 101 E3
Allanaquoich 259 J5
Allancreich 260 D5
Allanfearn 266 E7
Allangillfoot 218 A2
Allanton D&G 216 B2
Allanton EAyr 225 E2
Allanton NLan 234 C4
Allanton ScBord 237 F4
Allanton SLan 234 B4
Allardice 253 G2
Allathasdal 254 B4
Allbrook 119 F5
Allanton 211 E2
Allendale Town 211 E2
Allenheads 211 E3
Allen's Green 137 D1
Allensford 211 G2
Allensmore 145 D4
Allenton 173 E4
Aller 116 B5
Allerby 209 D3
Allercombe 102 D3
Allerford Devon 99 E2
Allerford Som 114 C3
Allerston 204 B4
Allerthorpe 195 G3
Allerton Mersey 183 F4
Allerton WYorks 194 A4
Allerton Bywater 194 D5
Allerton Mauleverer 194 D2
Allesley 159 E4
Allestree 173 E4
Allet Common 96 B5
Allexton 160 D2
Allgreave 171 G1
Allhallows 124 A1
Allhallows-on-Sea 124 A1
Alligin Shuas 264 E6
Allimore Green 158 A1
Allington Dorset 104 A3
Allington Lincs 175 D3
Allington Wilts 118 D4
Allington Wilts 118 B1
Allington Wilts 132 A5
Allithwaite 199 E5
Allnabad 273 G4
Alloa 243 D5
Allonby 209 D2
Allostock 184 B5
Alloway 224 B4
Allowenshay 103 G1
Allscot 157 G3
Allscott 157 F1
Allt na h-Airbhe 265 H2
Alltachonaich 247 G4
Alltbeithe 257 F1
Alltforgan 168 C5
Alltmawr 143 G3
Alltnacaillich 273 G4
Alltsigh 258 B3
Alltwalis 142 A4
Alltwen 128 D2
Alltyblaca 142 B3
Allwood Green 164 B4
Almeley 144 C2
Almeley Wootton 144 C2
Almer 105 F3
Almington 171 E4
Alminstone Cross 113 D3
Almondbank 243 F2
Almondbury 185 F1
Almondell & Calderwood Country Park WLoth EH52 5PE 235 E3
Almondsbury 131 F4
Alne 195 D1
Alness 266 D5
Alnham 229 D5
Alnmouth 229 G5
Alnwick 229 F5
Alnwick Garden, The N'umb NE66 1YU 229 F5
Alperton 136 A4
Alphamstone 151 G4
Alpheton 151 G2
Alphington 102 C3
Alport 172 D1
Alpraham 170 C2
Alresford 152 B5
Alrewas 159 D1
Alrick 251 G3
Alsager 171 E2
Alsagers Bank 171 F3
Alsop en le Dale 172 C2
Alston Cumb 210 D3
Alston Devon 103 G2
Alston Sutton 116 B2
Alstone Glos 146 B4
Alstone Som 116 A3
Alstone Staffs 158 A1
Alstonefield 172 C2
Alswear 114 A5
Alt 184 D2
Altandhu 272 B7
Altanduin 274 D6
Altarnun 97 G1
Altass 266 C2
Altens 261 H4
Alterwall 275 H2
Altham 193 D4
Althorne 138 C3
Althorp House N'hants NN7 4HQ 148 B1

Althorpe 187 F2
Alticry 215 D5
Altnafeadh 249 E4
Altnaharra 273 H5
Altofts 194 C5
Alton Derbys 173 E1
Alton Hants 120 C4
Alton Staffs 172 B3
Alton Barnes 118 C1
Alton Pancras 104 D2
Alton Priors 118 C1
Alton Towers Leisure Park Staffs ST10 4DB 172 B3
Alton Water Reservoir Suff IP9 2RY 152 C4
Altonside 267 K6
Altrincham 184 B4
Altura 257 J5
Alva 243 D5
Alvanley 183 F5
Alvaston 173 E4
Alvechurch 158 C5
Alvecote 159 E2
Alvediston 118 A5
Alveley 157 G4
Alverdiscott 113 F3
Alverstoke 107 F3
Alverstone 107 E4
Alverthorpe 194 C5
Alverton 174 C3
Alves 267 J5
Alvescot 133 E2
Alveston SGlos 131 F4
Alveston Warks 147 E2
Alvie 259 F4
Alvingham 189 D3
Alvington 131 F2
Alwalton 161 G3
Alweston 104 C1
Alwington 113 E3
Alwinton 220 B1
Alwoodley 194 C3
Alwoodley Gates 194 C3
Alyth 252 A5
Amalebra 94 B3
Amatnatua 266 B2
Ambaston 173 F4
Amber Hill 176 A3
Ambergate 173 E2
Amberley Glos 132 A2
Amberley WSuss 108 C2
Amble 221 E1
Amblecote 158 A4
Ambleside 199 E2
Ambleston 140 D5
Ambrismore 232 B4
Ambrosden 134 B1
Amcotts 187 F1
Amersham 135 E3
Amerton 171 G5
Amerton Farm Staffs ST18 0LA 171 G5
Amesbury 118 C3
Ameysford 105 G2
Amington 159 E2
Amisfield Town 217 E2
Amlwch 180 C3
Amlwch Port 180 C3
Ammanford (Rhydaman) 128 C1
Amotherby 203 G5
Ampfield 119 E5
Ampleforth 203 E5
Ampleforth College 203 E5
Ampney Crucis 132 C2
Ampney St. Mary 132 C2
Ampney St. Peter 132 C2
Amport 119 E3
Ampthill 149 F3
Ampton 163 G5
Amroth 127 E2
Amulree 243 D1
Anaboard 259 H1
Anaheilt 248 A3
Ancaster 175 E3
Anchor 156 A4
Anchor Corner 164 B2
Ancroft 237 F5
Ancrum 228 A4
Ancton 108 B3
Anderby 189 F5
Anderby Creek 189 F5
Andersea 116 A4
Andersfield 115 F4
Anderson 105 E3
Anderton 184 A5
Anderton Boat Lift ChesW&C CW9 6FW 184 A5
Andover 119 E3
Andover Down 119 E3
Andoversford 132 C1
Andreas 190 C2
Anelog 166 A5
Anerley 183 E3
Anfield 183 E3
Angarrack 94 C3
Angarrick 95 E3
Angelbank 157 E5
Angerton 209 F1
Angle 126 B2
Anglers Country Park WYorks WF4 2EB 186 A1
Angler's Retreat 154 D3
Anglesey (Ynys Môn) 180 B4
Anglesey Abbey Cambs CB25 9EJ 150 D1
Angmering 108 C3
Angmering-on-Sea 108 C3
Angram NYorks 195 E3
Angram NYorks 201 D3
Anick 211 F1
Anie 242 A3
Animal World & Butterfly House GtMan BL1 5UG 184 A1
Ankerville 267 F4
Anlaby 196 C5
Anmer 177 F5
Anmore 107 F1
Anna Valley 119 E3
Annan 217 F4

Annaside 198 B4
Annat A&B 240 D1
Annat High 264 E6
Annbank 224 C3
Anne Hathaway's Cottage Warks CV37 9HH 147 D2
Annesley 173 G2
Annesley Woodhouse 173 F2
Annfield Plain 212 A2
Anniesland 233 G3
Annscroft 157 D2
Ansdell 191 G5
Ansford 116 D4
Ansley 159 E3
Anslow 172 C5
Anslow Gate 172 C5
Ansteadbrook 121 E4
Anstey Herts 150 C4
Anstey Leics 160 A2
Anstruther 245 D4
Ansty Warks 159 F4
Ansty Wilts 118 A5
Ansty WSuss 109 F1
Ansty Coombe 118 A5
Ansty Cross 105 D2
Anthill Common 107 F1
Anthorn 209 E1
Antingham 179 D2
Anton's Gowt 176 A3
Antony 99 D5
Antrobus 184 A5
Anvil Corner 113 D5
Anvil Green 124 D4
Anwick 175 G2
Anwoth 215 G5
Aonach Mòr Mountain Gondola & Nevis Range Ski Centre High PH33 6SW 249 D2
Aoradh 230 A3
Apethorpe 161 F3
Apeton 158 A1
Apley 188 B5
Apperknowle 186 A5
Apperley 146 A5
Apperley Bridge 194 A4
Appersett 201 D3
Appin (An Apainn) 248 B5
Appin House 248 B5
Appleby 187 G1
Appleby Magna 159 F1
Appleby Parva 159 F2
Appleby-in-Westmorland 210 C5
Applecross 264 D7
Appledore Devon 113 E2
Appledore Devon 103 D1
Appledore Kent 111 E1
Appledore Heath 124 B5
Appleford 134 A3
Appleshaw 119 E3
Applethwaite 209 F4
Appleton Halton 183 G4
Appleton Oxon 133 G2
Appleton Roebuck 195 E3
Appleton Thorn 184 A4
Appleton Wiske 202 C2
Appleton-le-Moors 203 G4
Appleton-le-Street 203 G5
Appletreehall 227 G4
Appletreewick 193 G1
Appley 115 G3
Appley Bridge 183 G2
Apse Heath 107 E4
Apsey Green 153 D1
Apsley 135 F2
Apsley End 149 G4
Apuldram 108 A3
Arbeia Roman Fort & Museum T&W NE33 2BB 28 T&W
Arbirlot 253 D5
Arborfield 120 C1
Arborfield Cross 120 C1
Arborfield Garrison 120 C1
Arbourthorne 186 A4
Arbroath 253 E5
Arbuthnott 253 F2
Archdeacon Newton 202 B1
Archiestown 267 K7
Arclid 171 E1
Ard a' Chapuill 232 B1
Ardacheranbeg 232 B1
Ardacheranmor 232 B1
Ardachoil 239 G1
Ardachu 266 D2
Ardailly 231 E4
Ardalanish 238 C3
Ardallie 261 J1
Ardanaiseig 240 C2
Ardaneaskan 256 E1
Ardanstur 240 A3
Ardantiobairt 247 F4
Ardantrive 240 A2
Ardarroch 264 E7
Ardbeg A&B 232 B3
Ardbeg A&B 230 C5
Ardbeg A&B 232 C1
Ardblair 258 C1
Ardbrecknish 240 C2
Ardcharnich 265 H3
Ardchiavaig 238 C3
Ardchonnel 240 B1
Ardchonnell 240 B3
Ardchrishnish 238 D2
Ardchronie 266 D3
Ardchuilk 257 J1
Ardchullarie More 242 A3
Ardchyle 242 A2
Arddlin 156 B1
Ardechvie 257 H5
Ardeley 150 B5
Ardelve 256 E2
Arden 233 E1
Ardencaple House 239 G3
Ardens Grafton 146 D2
Ardentallan 240 A2
Ardentinny 232 C1
Ardeonaig 242 B1

Ardersier **266** E6
Ardery **247** G3
Ardessie **265** G3
Ardfad **239** G3
Ardfern **240** A4
Ardfin **230** C3
Ardgartan **241** E4
Ardgay **266** D2
Ardgenavan **241** D3
Ardgour (Corran) **248** C3
Ardgowan **232** D2
Ardgowse **260** E3
Ardgye **267** J5
Ardhallow **232** C2
Ardheslaig **264** D6
Ardiecow **268** D4
Ardinamar **239** G3
Ardindrean **265** H3
Ardingly **109** F1
Ardington **133** G4
Ardington Wick **133** G4
Ardintoul **256** E2
Ardkinglas House **241** D3
Ardlair **260** D2
Ardlamont **232** A3
Ardleigh **152** B5
Ardleigh Green **137** E4
Ardleigh Heath **152** B4
Ardleish **241** F3
Ardler **252** A5
Ardley **148** A5
Ardley End **137** E1
Ardlui (Àird Laoigh) **241** F3
Ardlussa **231** E1
Ardmaddy **240** C1
Ardmair **265** H2
Ardmaleish **232** B3
Ardmay **241** E4
Ardmenish **231** D2
Ardmhòr **254** C4
Ardminish **231** E5
Ardmolich **247** G2
Ardmore *A&B* **230** C4
Ardmore *A&B* **239** G2
Ardmore *A&B* **233** E2
Ardmore *High* **266** E3
Ardnackaig **239** G5
Ardnacross **247** E5
Ardnadam **232** C1
Ardnadrochit **239** G1
Ardnagoine **265** F1
Ardnagowan **240** D4
Ardnahein **241** D5
Ardnahoe **230** C2
Ardnarff **256** E1
Ardnastang **248** A3
Ardnave **230** A2
Ardno **241** D4
Ardo **261** G1
Ardoch *D&G* **225** G5
Ardoch *Moray* **267** J6
Ardoch *P&K* **243** F1
Ardochrig **234** A5
Ardoyne **260** E2
Ardpatrick **231** F3
Ardpeaton **232** D1
Ardradnaig **250** C5
Ardrishaig **231** G1
Ardroe **272** C6
Ardross **266** D4
Ardrossan **232** D5
Ardscalpsie **232** B4
Ardshave **266** E2
Ardshealach **247** F3
Ardshellach **239** G3
Ardsley **186** A2
Ardslignish **247** E3
Ardtalla **230** C4
Ardtalnaig **242** C1
Ardtaraig **232** B1
Ardteatle **240** D2
Ardtoe **247** F2
Ardtornish **247** G5
Ardtrostan **242** B2
Ardtur **248** B5
Arduaine **240** A3
Ardullie **266** C5
Ardura **239** F1
Ardvar **272** D5
Ardvasar **256** C4
Ardveenish **254** C4
Ardveich **242** B2
Ardverikie **250** A1
Ardvorlich *A&B* **241** F3
Ardvorlich *P&K* **242** B2
Ardwall **215** G5
Ardwell *D&G* **206** B2
Ardwell *Moray* **260** B1
Ardwell *SAyr* **214** C1
Ardwick **184** C3
Areley Kings **158** A5
Arford **120** D4
Argaty **242** C4
Argoed **130** A3
Argoed Mill **143** F1
Argos Hill **110** A1
Argrennan House **216** B5
Argyll & Sutherland Highlanders Museum *Stir* FK8 1EH **242** C5
Arichamish **240** B4
Arichastlich **241** E1
Arichonan **239** G5
Aridhglas **238** C2
Arienskill **247** G1
Arileod **246** A4
Arinacrinachd **264** D6
Arinafad Beg **231** F1
Arinagour **246** B4
Arinambane **254** C2
Arisaig (Àrasaig) **247** F1
Arivegaig **247** F3
Arkendale **194** C1
Arkesden **150** C4
Arkholme **199** G5
Arkle Town **201** F2
Arkleby **209** E3
Arkleside **201** F4
Arkleton **218** B2
Arkley **136** B3
Arksey **186** C2
Arkwright Town **186** B5
Arlary **243** G4
Arle **146** B5
Arlecdon **208** D5
Arlesey **149** G4
Arleston **157** F1
Arley **184** A4
Arlingham **131** G1
Arlington *Devon* **113** G1
Arlington *ESuss* **110** A3
Arlington *Glos* **132** D2
Arlington Beccott **113** G1
Armadale *High* **274** C2
Armadale *High* **256** C4
Armadale *WLoth* **234** D3
Armathwaite **210** B3
Arminghall **179** D5
Armitage **158** C1
Armitage Bridge **185** F1
Armley **194** B4
Armscote **147** E3
Armshead **171** G3
Armston **161** F4
Armthorpe **186** D2
Arnabost **246** B3
Arnaby **198** C4
Arncliffe **201** E5
Arncliffe Cote **201** E5
Arncroach **244** D4
Arne **105** F4
Arnesby **160** B3
Arngask **243** G3
Arngibbon **242** B5
Arngomery **242** B5
Arnhall **253** E3
Arnicle **222** C2
Arnipol **247** G1
Arnisdale (Arnasdal) **256** E3
Arnish **264** B7
Arniston Engine **236** A3
Arnol **271** F3
Arnold *ERid* **196** D3
Arnold *Notts* **173** G3
Arnolfini Gallery BS1 4QA **66** Bristol
Arnprior **242** B5
Arnside **199** F5
Aros Experience *High* IV51 9EU **263** K7
Arowry **170** B4
Arrad Foot **199** E4
Arradoul **268** C4
Arram **196** C3
Arran **223** E2
Arras **196** B3
Arrat **253** E4
Arrathorne **202** B3
Arreton **107** E4
Arrington **150** B2
Arrivain **241** E1
Arrochar **241** F4
Arrow **146** C2
Arscaig **273** H7
Arscott **156** D2
Arthington **194** B3
Arthingworth **160** C4
Arthog **154** C1
Arthrath **261** H1
Arthurstone **252** A5
Artrochie **261** J1
Aruadh **230** A3
Arundel **108** C3
Arundel Castle *WSuss* BN18 9AB **108** C3
Arundel Cathedral (R.C.) *WSuss* BN18 9AY **108** C3
Aryhoulan **248** C3
Asby **209** D4
Ascog **232** C3
Ascot **121** E1
Ascott **147** F4
Ascott d'Oyley **133** F1
Ascott Earl **133** E1
Ascott-under-Wychwood **133** F1
Ascreavie **252** B4
Asenby **202** D5
Asfordby **160** C1
Asfordby Hill **160** C1
Asgarby *Lincs* **176** B1
Asgarby *Lincs* **175** G3
Ash *Dorset* **105** E1
Ash *Kent* **125** E3
Ash *Kent* **123** F2
Ash *Som* **116** B5
Ash *Surr* **121** D2
Ash Barton **113** F5
Ash Bullayne **102** A2
Ash Green *Surr* **121** E3
Ash Green *Warks* **159** F4
Ash Magna **170** C4
Ash Mill **114** A5
Ash Parva **170** C4
Ash Priors **115** E5
Ash Street **152** B3
Ash Thomas **102** D1
Ash Vale **121** D2
Ashampstead **134** A5
Ashbocking **152** C2
Ashbourne **172** C3
Ashbrittle **115** D5
Ashburnham Place **110** B2
Ashburton **101** D1
Ashbury *Devon* **99** F1
Ashbury *Oxon* **133** E4
Ashby **187** F2
Ashby by Partney **176** C1
Ashby cum Fenby **188** C2
Ashby de la Launde **175** F2
Ashby de la Zouch **159** F1
Ashby Dell **165** F2
Ashby Folville **160** C1
Ashby Hill **188** C2
Ashby Magna **160** A3
Ashby Parva **160** A4
Ashby Puerorum **188** D5
Ashby St. Ledgers **148** A1
Ashby St. Mary **179** E5
Ashchurch **146** B4
Ashcombe *Devon* **102** C5
Ashcombe *NSom* **116** A1
Ashcott **116** B4
Ashdon **151** D3
Ashe **119** G3
Asheldham **138** C2
Ashen **151** F3
Ashenden **124** A5
Ashendon **134** C1
Ashens **231** G2
Ashfield *A&B* **231** F1
Ashfield *Here* **145** E5
Ashfield *Stir* **242** C4
Ashfield *Suff* **152** D1
Ashfield Green *Suff* **165** D4
Ashfield Green *Suff* **151** F2
Ashfold Crossways **109** E1
Ashford *Devon* **100** C3
Ashford *Devon* **113** F2
Ashford *Hants* **106** A1
Ashford *Kent* **124** C4
Ashford *Surr* **135** F5
Ashford Bowdler **157** E5
Ashford Carbonel **157** E5
Ashford Hill **119** G1
Ashford in the Water **185** F5
Ashgill **234** B4
Ashiestiel **227** F2
Ashill *Devon* **103** D1
Ashill *Norf* **163** G2
Ashill *Som* **103** G1
Ashingdon **138** B3
Ashington *N'umb* **221** E3
Ashington *Som* **116** C5
Ashington *WSuss* **108** D2
Ashkirk **227** F3
Ashlett **107** D2
Ashleworth **146** A5
Ashleworth Quay **146** A5
Ashley *Cambs* **151** E1
Ashley *ChesE* **184** B4
Ashley *Devon* **113** G4
Ashley *Glos* **132** B3
Ashley *Hants* **119** E4
Ashley *Hants* **106** B3
Ashley *Kent* **125** F4
Ashley *N'hants* **160** C3
Ashley *Staffs* **171** E4
Ashley *Wilts* **117** F1
Ashley Down **131** E5
Ashley Green **135** E2
Ashley Heath *Dorset* **106** A2
Ashley Heath *Staffs* **171** E4
Ashmanhaugh **179** E3
Ashmansworth **119** F2
Ashmansworthy **112** D4
Ashmolean Museum *Oxon* OX1 2PH **80** Oxford
Ashmore *Dorset* **105** F1
Ashmore *P&K* **251** G4
Ashmore Green **119** G1
Ashorne **147** F2
Ashover **173** E1
Ashover Hay **173** E1
Ashow **159** F5
Ashperton **145** F3
Ashprington **101** E2
Ashreigney **113** G4
Ashridge Estate *Herts* HP4 1LX **135** E1
Ashtead **121** G2
Ashton *ChesW&C* **170** C1
Ashton *Corn* **94** D4
Ashton *Corn* **99** D4
Ashton *Hants* **107** E1
Ashton *Here* **145** E1
Ashton *Invcly* **232** D2
Ashton *N'hants* **161** F4
Ashton *N'hants* **148** C3
Ashton *Peter* **161** G2
Ashton Common **117** F2
Ashton Court Estate *NSom* BS41 9JN **8** B3
Ashton Keynes **132** C3
Ashton under Hill **146** B4
Ashton upon Mersey **184** B3
Ashton-in-Makerfield **183** G3
Ashton-under-Lyne **184** D3
Ashurst *Hants* **106** C1
Ashurst *Kent* **123** E5
Ashurst *WSuss* **109** D2
Ashurst Bridge **106** C1
Ashurstwood **122** D5
Ashwater **99** D1
Ashwell *Herts* **150** A4
Ashwell *Rut* **161** D1
Ashwell End **150** A3
Ashwellthorpe **164** C2
Ashwick **116** D3
Ashwicken **163** F1
Ashybank **227** G4
Askam in Furness **198** D5
Askern **186** C1
Askernish (Aisgernis) **254** C2
Askerswell **104** B3
Askett **134** D2
Askham *Cumb* **210** B5
Askham *Notts* **187** E5
Askham Bryan **195** E3
Askham Richard **195** E3
Asknish **240** B5
Askrigg **201** E3
Askwith **194** A3
Aslackby **175** F4
Aslacton **164** C2
Aslockton **174** C3
Asloun **260** D3
Aspall **152** C1
Aspatria **209** E2
Aspenden **150** B5
Asperton **176** A4
Aspley Guise **149** E4
Aspley Heath **149** E4
Aspull **184** A2
Asselby **195** G5
Asserby **189** E5
Assington **152** A4
Assington Green **151** F2
Astbury **171** F1
Astcote **148** B2
Asterby **188** C5
Asterley **156** C2
Asterton **156** D3
Asthall **133** E1
Asthall Leigh **133** F1
Astle **184** C5
Astley *GtMan* **184** B2
Astley *Shrop* **157** E1
Astley *Warks* **159** F4
Astley *Worcs* **145** G1
Astley Abbotts **157** G3
Astley Bridge **184** B1
Astley Cross **146** A1
Astley Green **184** B3
Astley Lodge **157** E1
Aston *ChesE* **170** D3
Aston *ChesW&C* **183** G5
Aston *Derbys* **185** F4
Aston *Derbys* **172** C4
Aston *Flints* **170** A1
Aston *Here* **157** D5
Aston *Here* **145** D1
Aston *Herts* **150** A5
Aston *Oxon* **133** F2
Aston *Shrop* **170** C5
Aston *Shrop* **158** A3
Aston *Staffs* **171** E3
Aston *SYorks* **186** B4
Aston *Tel&W* **157** F2
Aston *W'ham* **134** C4
Aston *WMid* **158** C4
Aston Abbotts **148** D5
Aston Botterell **157** F4
Aston Cantlow **146** D2
Aston Clinton **135** D1
Aston Crews **145** F5
Aston Cross **146** B4
Aston End **150** A5
Aston Eyre **157** F3
Aston Fields **146** B1
Aston Flamville **159** G3
Aston Heath **183** G5
Aston Ingham **145** F5
Aston juxta Mondrum **171** D2
Aston le Walls **147** G2
Aston Magna **147** D4
Aston Munslow **157** E4
Aston on Carrant **146** B4
Aston on Clun **156** C4
Aston Pigott **156** C2
Aston Rogers **156** C2
Aston Rowant **134** C3
Aston Sandford **134** C2
Aston Somerville **146** C4
Aston Subedge **146** D3
Aston Tirrold **134** A4
Aston Upthorpe **134** A4
Aston-by-Stone **171** G4
Aston-on-Trent **173** F5
Astwick **150** A4
Astwood **149** E3
Astwood Bank **146** C1
Aswarby **175** F3
Aswardby **189** D5
Aswick Grange **162** B1
Atch Lench **146** C2
Atcham **157** E2
Ath Linne **270** D6
Athelhampton **105** D3
Athelington **164** D4
Athelney **116** A5
Athelstaneford **236** C2
Atherington *Devon* **113** F3
Atherington *WSuss* **108** C3
Athersley North **186** A2
Atherstone **159** F3
Atherstone on Stour **147** E2
Atherton **184** A2
Atlow **172** D3
Attadale **257** F1
Attenborough **173** G4
Atterby **187** G3
Attercliffe **186** A4
Atterley **157** F3
Atterton **159** F3
Attingham Park *Shrop* SY4 4TP **157** E1
Attleborough *Norf* **164** B2
Attleborough *Warks* **159** F3
Attlebridge **178** C4
Attleton Green **151** F2
Atwick **197** D2
Atworth **117** F1
Auberrow **145** D3
Aubourn **175** E1
Auch **241** F1
Auchairne **214** C2
Auchallater **251** G1
Auchameanach **231** G4
Auchamore **231** G5
Aucharnie **268** E6
Aucharrigill **266** B1
Auchattie **260** E5
Auchavan **251** G3
Auchbraad **231** G1
Auchbreck **259** K2
Auchenback **233** G4
Auchenblae **253** F2
Auchenbothie **233** E2
Auchenbrack **216** B1
Auchenbreck **232** B1
Auchencairn **216** B5
Auchencrow **237** F3
Auchendinny **235** G3
Auchendolly **216** B4
Auchenfoyle **233** E2
Auchengillan **233** G1
Auchengray **235** D4
Auchenhalrig **268** B4
Auchenheath **234** C5
Auchenhessnane **216** C1
Auchenlochan **232** A2
Auchenmalg **214** D5
Auchenrivock **218** B3
Auchentiber **233** E5
Auchenvennel **233** D1
Auchessan **241** G2
Auchgourish **259** G3
Auchinafaud **231** F4
Auchincruive **224** B3
Auchindarrach **231** G1
Auchindarroch **248** C4
Auchindrain **240** C4
Auchindrean **265** H3
Auchininna **268** E6
Auchinleck **224** D3
Auchinloch **234** A2
Auchinner **242** B3
Auchinroath **267** K6
Auchintoul *Aber* **260** D3
Auchintoul *Aber* **268** E5
Auchintoul *High* **266** C2
Auchiries **261** J1
Auchleven **260** E2
Auchlochan **225** G2
Auchlunachan **265** H3
Auchlunies **261** G5
Auchlunkart **268** B6
Auchlyne **242** A2
Auchmacoy **261** H1
Auchmair **260** B2
Auchmantle **214** C4
Auchmithie **253** E5
Auchmuirbridge **244** A4
Auchmull **253** D2
Auchnabony **208** A2
Auchnabreac **240** C4
Auchnacloich **242** D1
Auchnacraig **239** G1
Auchnacree **252** C3
Auchnafree **242** D1
Auchnagallin **259** H1
Auchnagatt **269** H6
Auchnaha **232** A1
Auchnangoul **240** C4
Aucholzie **260** B5
Auchorrie **260** E4
Auchrannie **252** A4
Auchraw **242** A2
Auchreoch **241** F2
Auchronie **252** C1
Auchterarder **243** E3
Auchtercairn **264** E4
Auchterderran **244** A5
Auchterhouse **244** B1
Auchtermuchty **244** A3
Auchterneed **266** B6
Auchtertool **244** A5
Auchtertyre *Angus* **252** A5
Auchtertyre (Uachdar Thire) *High* **256** E2
Auchtertyre *Moray* **267** J6
Auchtertyre *Stir* **241** F2
Auchtubh **242** A2
Auckengill **275** J2
Auckley **186** D2
Audenshaw **184** D3
Audlem **171** D3
Audley **171** E2
Audley End *Essex* **150** D4
Audley End *Essex* **151** G4
Audley End *Suff* **151** G2
Audmore **171** F5
Auds **268** E4
Aughton *ERid* **195** G4
Aughton *Lancs* **183** E2
Aughton *Lancs* **192** B1
Aughton *SYorks* **186** B4
Aughton *Wilts* **118** D2
Aughton Park **183** F2
Auldearn **267** G6
Aulden **145** D2
Auldgirth **216** D2
Auldhame **236** C1
Auldhouse **234** A4
Aulich **250** B4
Ault a'chruinn **257** F2
Ault Hucknall **173** F1
Aultanrynie **273** F5
Aultbea (An t-Allt Beithe) **264** E3
Aultgrishan **264** D3
Aultguish Inn **265** K4
Aultibea **275** F6
Aultiphurst **274** D2
Aultmore **268** C5
Ault-na-goire **258** C2
Aultnamain Inn **266** D3
Aultnapaddock **268** B6
Aulton **260** E2
Aultvaich **266** C7
Aultvoulin **256** D4
Aunby **161** F1
Aundorach **259** G3
Aunk **102** D2
Aunsby **175** F4
Auquhorthies **261** G2
Aust **131** E4
Austerfield **187** D3
Austrey **159** E2
Austwick **193** D1
Authorpe **189** E4
Authorpe Row **189** F5
Avebury **132** D5
Avebury Trusloe **118** B1
Aveley **137** E4
Avening **132** A3
Averham **174** C2
Avery Hill **136** D5
Aveton Gifford **100** C3
Aviation Viewing Park *GtMan* M90 1QX **25** E6
Avielochan **259** G3
Aviemore **259** F3
Avington *Hants* **119** G4
Avington *WBerks* **119** E1
Avoch **266** D6
Avon **106** A3
Avon Dassett **147** G2
Avon Heath Country Park *Dorset* BH24 2DA **3** E1
Avon Valley Railway *SGlos* BS30 6HD **8** E4
Avonbridge **234** D2
Avoncliff **117** F2
Avonmouth **131** E5
Avonwick **100** D2
Awbridge **119** E5
Awhirk **214** B5
Awkley **131** E4
Awliscombe **103** E2
Awre **131** G2
Awsworth **173** F3
Axbridge **116** B2
Axford *Hants* **120** B3
Axford *Wilts* **133** E5
Axminster **103** F3
Axmouth **103** F3
Axton **182** C4
Axtown **100** B1
Aycliffe **212** B5
Aydon **211** G1
Aylburton **131** F2
Ayle **210** D3
Aylesbeare **102** D3
Aylesbury **134** D1
Aylesby **188** C2
Aylesford **123** G3
Aylesham **125** E3
Aylestone **160** A2
Aylmerton **178** C2
Aylsham **178** C3
Aylton **145** F4
Aymestrey **144** D1
Aynho **148** A4
Ayot Green **136** B1
Ayot St. Lawrence **136** A1
Ayot St. Peter **136** B1
Ayr **224** B3
Aysgarth **201** F4
Aysgarth Falls & National Park Centre *NYorks* DL8 3TH **201** F4
Ayshford **102** D1
Ayside **199** E4
Ayston **161** D2
Aythorpe Roding **137** E1
Ayton *P&K* **243** G3
Ayton *ScBord* **237** G3
Aywick **278** E4
Azerley **202** B5

B

Babbacombe **101** F1
Babbacombe Model Village *Torbay* TQ1 3LA **101** F1
Babbinswood **170** A4
Babb's Green **136** C1
Babcary **116** C5
Babel **143** E4
Babell **182** C5
Babeny **99** G3
Bablock Hythe **133** G2
Babraham **150** D2
Babworth **187** D4
Baby's Hill **259** K1
Bac **271** G3
Bachau **180** C4
Back of Keppoch **247** F1
Back Street **151** F2
Backaland **276** E4
Backaskaill **276** D2
Backbarrow **199** E4
Backburn **260** D1
Backe **127** F1
Backfolds **269** J5
Backford **183** F5
Backhill **261** F1
Backhill of Clackriach **269** H6
Backhill of Trustach **260** E5
Backies *High* **267** F1
Backies *Moray* **268** D5
Backlass **275** H3
Backside **260** C1
Backwell **116** B1
Backworth **221** E4
Bacon End **137** E1
Baconend Green **137** E1
Baconsthorpe **178** C2
Bacton *Here* **144** C4
Bacton *Norf* **179** E2
Bacton *Suff* **152** B1
Bacton Green **152** B1
Bacup **193** E5
Badachro **264** D4
Badanloch Lodge **274** C5
Badavanich **265** H6
Badbea **275** F7
Badbury **133** D4
Badbury Wick **133** D4
Badby **148** A2
Badcall *High* **272** D4
Badcall *High* **272** E3
Badcaul **265** G2
Baddeley Green **171** G2
Badden **231** G1
Baddesley Clinton **159** D5
Baddesley Clinton *Warks* B93 0DQ **159** D5
Baddesley Ensor **159** E3
Baddidarach **272** C6
Badenscoth **261** F1
Badenyon **260** B3
Badgall **97** G1
Badger **157** G3
Badgerbank **184** C5
Badgers Mount **123** D2
Badgeworth **132** B1
Badgworth **116** A2
Badicaul **256** D2
Badingham **153** E1
Badintagairt **273** G7
Badlesmere **124** C3
Badley **152** B2
Badlipster **275** H4
Badluarach **265** F2
Badminton **132** A4
Badnaban **272** C6
Badnabay **272** E4
Badnafrave **259** K3
Badnagie **275** G5
Badnambiast **250** C2
Badninish **266** E2
Badrallach **265** G2
Badsey **146** C3
Badshot Lea **121** D3
Badsworth **186** B1
Badwell Ash **152** A1
Badworthy **100** C1
Badyo **251** E3
Bag Enderby **189** D5
Bagber **105** D1
Bagby **203** D4
Bagendon **132** C2
Baggeridge Country Park *Staffs* DY3 4HB **14** A2
Bagginswood **157** F4
Baggrave Hall **160** B2
Baggrow **209** E2
Bàgh Mòr **262** D6
Baghasdal **254** C3
Bagillt **182** D5
Baginton **159** F5
Baglan **128** D3
Bagley *Shrop* **170** B5
Bagley *Som* **116** B3
Bagmore **120** B3
Bagnall **171** G2
Bagnor **119** F1
Bagpath **132** A3
Bagshot *Surr* **121** E1
Bagshot *Wilts* **119** E1
Bagstone **131** F4
Bagthorpe *Norf* **177** F4
Bagthorpe *Notts* **173** F2
Baguley **184** C4
Bagworth **159** G2
Bagwyllydiart **144** D5
Baildon **194** A4
Baile an Truiseil **271** F2
Baile Boidheach **231** F2
Baile Gharbhaidh **262** C7
Baile Glas **262** D6
Baile Mhartainn **262** C4
Baile Mhic Phail **262** D4
Baile Mòr **238** B2
Baile nan Cailleach **262** C6
Baile Raghaill **262** C5
Bailebeag **258** C3
Baileguish **259** F5
Baile-na-Cille **262** D3
Bailetonach **247** F2
Bailiesward **260** C1
Bailiff Bridge **194** A5
Baillieston **234** A3
Bainbridge **201** E3
Bainsford **234** C1
Bainshole **260** E1
Bainton *ERid* **196** B2
Bainton *Oxon* **148** A5
Bainton *Peter* **161** F2
Bairnkine **228** A5
Bakebare **260** B1
Baker Street **137** F4
Baker's End **136** C1
Bakewell **172** D1
Bala (Y Bala) **168** C4
Balachuirn **264** B7
Balado **243** F4
Balafark **242** B5
Balaldie **267** F4
Balallan (Baile Ailein) **270** E5
Balavil **258** E4
Balbeg *High* **258** B1
Balbeg *High* **258** B2
Balbeggie **243** G2
Balbirnie **244** A4
Balbithan **261** F3
Balblair *High* **266** E5
Balblair *High* **266** C2
Balblair *High* **266** E3
Balby **186** C2
Balcharn **266** C1
Balcherry **267** F3
Balchers **269** F5
Balchladich **272** C5
Balchraggan *High* **266** C7
Balchraggan *High* **258** C1
Balchrick **272** D3
Balcombe **122** C5
Balcurvie **244** B4
Baldernock **233** G2
Baldersby **202** C5
Baldersby St. James **202** C5
Balderstone *GtMan* **184** D1
Balderstone *Lancs* **192** C4
Balderton *ChesW&C* **170** A1
Balderton *Notts* **174** D2
Baldhu **96** B5
Baldinnie **244** C3
Baldock **150** A4
Baldon Row **134** A2
Baldovan **244** B1
Baldovie *Angus* **252** B4
Baldovie *Dundee* **244** C1
Baldrine **190** C3
Baldslow **110** C2
Baldwin **190** B3
Baldwinholme **209** G1
Baldwin's Gate **171** E3
Baldwins Hill **122** C5
Bale **178** B2
Balelone (Baile Lion) **262** C4
Balemartine **246** A2
Balemore (Baile Mòr) **262** C5
Balendoch **252** A5
Balephuil **246** A2
Balerno **235** F3
Balernock **233** D1
Baleromindubh **238** C5
Balerominmore **238** C5
Baleshare (Bhaleshear) **262** C5
Balevulin **239** D2
Balfield **252** D3
Balfour *Aber* **260** D5
Balfour *Ork* **277** D6
Balfron **233** G1
Balfron Station **233** G1
Balgonar **243** F5
Balgove **261** G1
Balgowan *D&G* **206** B2
Balgowan *High* **258** D5
Balgown **263** J5
Balgreen **269** F5

Balgreggan 214 B5
Balgy 264 E6
Balhaldie 242 D4
Balhalgardy 261 F2
Balham 136 B5
Balhary 252 A5
Balhelvie 244 B2
Balhousie 244 C4
Baligill 274 D2
Balindore 240 B1
Balintore Angus 252 A4
Balintore High 267 F4
Balintraid 266 E4
Balintyre 250 B5
Balivanich (Baile a'Mhanaich) 262 C6
Balkeerie 252 A5
Balkholme 195 G5
Balkissock 214 C2
Ball 170 A5
Ball Haye Green 171 G2
Ball Hill 119 F1
Balla 254 C2
Ballabeg 190 A4
Ballacannell 190 C3
Ballacarnane Beg 190 A3
Ballachulish (Baile a' Chaolais) 248 C4
Balladoole 190 A5
Ballafesson 190 A4
Ballagyr 190 A3
Ballajora 190 C2
Ballakilpheric 190 A4
Ballamodha 190 A4
Ballantrae 242 A4
Ballards Gore 138 C3
Ballasalla IoM 190 A4
Ballasalla IoM 190 B2
Ballater 260 B5
Ballaterach 260 C5
Ballaugh 190 B2
Ballaveare 190 B4
Ballchraggan 266 E4
Ballechin 251 E4
Balleich 242 A4
Ballencrieff 236 B2
Ballidon 172 D2
Balliekine 231 G5
Balliemeanoch 240 D4
Balliemore A&B 240 D5
Balliemore A&B 240 A2
Ballig 190 A3
Ballimeanoch 240 C3
Ballimore A&B 232 A1
Ballimore Stir 242 A3
Ballinaby 230 A3
Ballindean 244 A2
Ballingdon 151 G3
Ballinger Common 135 E2
Ballingham 145 E4
Ballingry 243 G5
Ballinlick 251 E5
Ballinluig P&K 251 E4
Ballinluig P&K 251 E5
Ballintuim 251 G4
Balloch Angus 252 B4
Balloch High 266 E7
Balloch NLan 234 B2
Balloch WDun 233 E1
Ballochan 260 D5
Ballochandrain 232 A1
Ballochford 260 B1
Ballochgair 222 C3
Ballochmartin 232 C4
Ballochmorrie 214 D2
Ballochmyle 224 D3
Ballochroy 231 F4
Ballogie 260 D5
Balls Cross 121 E5
Balls Green Essex 152 B5
Ball's Green Glos 132 A3
Balls Hill 158 B3
Ballyaurgan 231 F2
Ballygown 246 D5
Ballygrant 230 B3
Ballyhaugh 246 A4
Ballymeanoch 240 A5
Ballymichael 223 E2
Balmacara (Baile Mac Ara) 256 E2
Balmaclellan 216 A3
Balmacneil 251 E4
Balmadies 253 D5
Balmae 207 G2
Balmaha 241 G5
Balmalcolm 244 B4
Balmaqueen 263 K4
Balmeanach A&B 247 F5
Balmeanach A&B 238 D1
Balmedie 261 H3
Balmedie Country Park Aber AB23 8XG 261 H3
Balmer Heath 170 B4
Balmerino 244 B2
Balmerlawn 106 C2
Balminnoch 215 D4
Balmore EDun 234 A2
Balmore High 267 F4
Balmore High 257 K1
Balmore High 263 H7
Balmore P&K 250 D4
Balmullo 244 C2
Balmungie 266 E6
Balmyle 251 F4
Balnaboth 252 B3
Balnabruaich 266 E4
Balnacra 265 F7
Balnafoich 258 D1
Balnagall 267 F3
Balnagown Castle 266 E4
Balnaguisich 266 D4
Balnahard A&B 238 D5
Balnahard A&B 239 D1
Balnain 258 B1
Balnakeil 273 F2
Balnaknock 263 K5
Balnamoon 252 D3
Balnapaling 266 E5
Balnespick 259 F4

Balquhidder 242 A2
Balsall 159 E5
Balsall Common 159 E5
Balsall Heath 158 C4
Balscote 147 F3
Balsham 151 D2
Baltasound 278 F2
Balterley 171 E2
Balterley Heath 171 E2
Baltersan 251 F4
Balthangie 269 G5
Balthayock 243 G2
Baltonsborough 116 C4
Baluachraig 240 A5
Balulive 230 C3
Balure A&B 240 C1
Balure A&B 240 A1
Balvaird 266 C6
Balvarran 251 F3
Balvicar 239 G3
Balvraid High 256 E3
Balvraid High 259 F1
Bamber Bridge 192 B5
Bamber's Green 151 D5
Bamburgh 229 F3
Bamburgh Castle N'umb NE69 7DF 229 F3
Bamff 252 A4
Bamford Derbys 185 G4
Bamford GtMan 184 C1
Bampton Cumb 199 G1
Bampton Devon 114 C5
Bampton Oxon 133 F2
Bampton Grange 199 G1
Banavie (Banbhaidh) 248 D2
Banbury 147 G3
Banbury Museum Oxon OX16 2PQ 147 G4
Bancffosfelen 128 A1
Banchor 267 F5
Banchory 261 F5
Banchory Devenick 261 H4
Bancycapel 128 A1
Bancyfelin 127 G1
Bancyffordd 142 A4
Bandon 244 A4
Bandrake Head 199 E4
Banff 268 E4
Bangor 181 D5
Bangor-on-Dee (Bangor-is-y-coed) 170 A3
Bangor's Green 183 E2
Banham 164 B3
Banham Zoo Norf NR16 2HE 164 B3
Bank 106 B2
Bank End 198 C4
Bank Newton 193 F2
Bank Street 165 F1
Bank Top Lancs 183 G2
Bank Top WYorks 194 A5
Bankend 217 E4
Bankfoot 243 F1
Bankglen 225 D4
Bankhead Aber 260 E3
Bankhead Aber 260 E4
Bankhead Aberdeen 261 G3
Bankhead D&G 208 A2
Bankland 116 A5
Banknock 234 B2
Banks Cumb 210 B1
Banks Lancs 191 G5
Bankshill 217 F2
Banningham 178 D3
Bannister Green 151 E5
Bannockburn 242 D5
Banstead 122 B3
Bantam Grove 194 B5
Bantham 100 C3
Banton 234 B2
Banwell 116 A2
Banwen Pyrddin 129 E2
Banyard's Green 165 E4
Bapchild 124 B2
Baptiston 233 G1
Bapton 118 A4
Bar End 119 F5
Bar Hill 150 B1
Barachander 240 C2
Barassie 224 B2
Barbaraville 266 E4
Barber Booth 185 F4
Barber Green 199 E4
Barber's Moor 183 F1
Barbican Arts & Conference Centre GtLon EC2Y 8DS 45 J1
Barbon 200 B4
Barbridge 170 D2
Barbrook 114 A3
Barby 160 B5
Barcaldine (Am Barra Calltainn) 248 B5
Barcaple 216 A5
Barcheston 147 E4
Barclose 210 A1
Barcombe 109 G2
Barcombe Cross 109 G2
Barden 202 A3
Barden Park 123 G4
Bardennoch 216 C2
Bardfield End Green 151 E4
Bardfield Saling 151 F5
Bardister 278 C5
Bardney 175 G1
Bardon Leics 159 G1
Bardon Moray 267 K6
Bardon Mill 211 D1
Bardowie 233 G2
Bardsea 199 D5
Bardsey 194 C3
Bardsey Island (Ynys Enlli) 166 A5
Bardwell 164 A4
Bare 192 A1
Barewood 144 C2
Barfad 231 F3
Barford Norf 178 C5
Barford Warks 147 E1
Barford St. John 147 G3

Barford St. Martin 118 B4
Barford St. Michael 147 G4
Barfrestone 125 E3
Bargaly 215 F3
Bargany Mains 224 A5
Bargeddie 234 A3
Bargrennan 215 E3
Barham Cambs 161 G5
Barham Kent 125 E3
Barham Suff 152 C2
Barharrow 216 A5
Barholm 161 F1
Barholm Mains 215 F5
Barkby 160 B2
Barkby Thorpe 160 B2
Barkers Green 170 C5
Barkestone-le-Vale 174 C4
Barkham 120 C1
Barking GtLon 136 D4
Barking Suff 152 B2
Barking Tye 152 B2
Barkisland 193 G5
Barkston 175 E3
Barkston Ash 195 D4
Barkway 150 B4
Barland 144 B1
Barlaston 171 F4
Barlavington 108 B2
Barlborough 186 B5
Barlby 195 F4
Barlestone 159 G2
Barley Herts 150 B4
Barley Lancs 193 E3
Barley Green 164 D4
Barleycroft End 150 C5
Barleyhill 211 G2
Barleythorpe 160 D2
Barling 138 C4
Barlings 188 A5
Barlow Derbys 186 A5
Barlow NYorks 195 F5
Barlow T&W 212 A1
Barmby Moor 195 G3
Barmby on the Marsh 195 F5
Barmer 177 G4
Barmolloch 240 A5
Barmoor Lane End 229 E3
Barmouth (Abermaw) 154 C1
Barmpton 202 C1
Barmston 197 D2
Barnaby Green 165 F4
Barnacabber 232 C1
Barnacarry 240 B5
Barnack 161 F2
Barnacle 159 F4
Barnamuc 248 C5
Barnard Castle 201 F1
Barnard Gate 133 G1
Barnardiston 151 F3
Barnard's Green 145 G3
Barnbarroch D&G 215 D5
Barnbarroch D&G 216 C5
Barnburgh 186 B2
Barnby 165 F3
Barnby Dun 186 D2
Barnby in the Willows 175 D2
Barnby Moor 187 D4
Barndennoch 216 C2
Barne Barton 100 A2
Barnehurst 137 E5
Barnes 136 B5
Barnes Street 123 F4
Barnet 136 B3
Barnet Gate 136 B3
Barnetby le Wold 188 A2
Barney 178 A2
Barnham Suff 163 G5
Barnham WSuss 108 B3
Barnham Broom 178 B5
Barnhead 253 E4
Barnhill ChesW&C 170 B2
Barnhill Dundee 244 C1
Barnhill Moray 267 J6
Barnhills 214 A3
Barningham Dur 201 F1
Barningham Suff 164 A4
Barningham Green 178 C2
Barnoldby le Beck 188 C2
Barnoldswick 193 E3
Barns Green 121 G5
Barnsdale Bar 186 C1
Barnsley Glos 132 C2
Barnsley SYorks 186 A2
Barnsole 125 E3
Barnstaple 113 F2
Barnston Essex 137 F1
Barnston Mersey 183 D4
Barnstone 174 C4
Barnt Green 158 C5
Barnton ChesW&C 184 A5
Barnton Edin 235 F2
Barnwell All Saints 161 F4
Barnwell Country Park N'hants PE8 5PB 161 F4
Barnwell St. Andrew 161 F4
Barnwood 132 A1
Barons' Cross 145 D2
Barr A&B 230 B3
Barr High 247 F4
Barr SAyr 215 D1
Barr Som 115 D5
Barr Hall 151 F4
Barra (Barraigh) 254 B4
Barra (Tràigh Mhòr) Airport 254 B4
Barrachan 207 E2
Barrackan 239 G4
Barraer 215 E4
Barraglom 270 D4
Barrahormid 231 F1
Barran 241 D2
Barrapol 246 A2
Barrasford 220 B4
Barravullin 240 A4
Barregarrow 190 B3
Barrets Green 170 C2

Barrhead 233 F4
Barrhill 214 D2
Barrington Cambs 150 B3
Barrington Som 103 G1
Barripper 94 D3
Barrisdale 256 E4
Barrmill 233 E4
Barrnacarry 240 A2
Barrock 275 H1
Barrow Glos 146 A5
Barrow Lancs 192 D4
Barrow Rut 161 D1
Barrow Shrop 157 F2
Barrow Som 117 E5
Barrow Suff 151 F1
Barrow Gurney 116 C1
Barrow Haven 196 C5
Barrow Hill 186 B5
Barrow Nook 183 F2
Barrow Street 117 F4
Barrow upon Humber 196 C5
Barrow upon Soar 160 A1
Barrow upon Trent 173 E5
Barroway Drove 163 D2
Barrowby 175 D4
Barrowcliff 204 D4
Barrowden 161 E2
Barrowford 193 E4
Barrow-in-Furness 191 F1
Barrows Green 199 G4
Barry Angus 244 D1
Barry VGlam 115 E1
Barry Island Pleasure Park VGlam CF62 5TR 115 E1
Barsby 160 B1
Barsham 165 E3
Barskimming 224 C3
Barsloisnoch 240 A5
Barston 159 E5
Bartestree 145 E3
Barthol Chapel 261 G1
Bartholomew Green 151 F5
Barthomley 171 E2
Bartley 106 C1
Bartley Green 158 C4
Bartlow 151 D3
Barton Cambs 150 C2
Barton ChesW&C 170 B2
Barton Cumb 210 A3
Barton Glos 146 C5
Barton Lancs 192 B4
Barton Lancs 183 E2
Barton NYorks 202 B2
Barton Oxon 134 A2
Barton Torbay 101 F1
Barton Warks 146 D2
Barton Bendish 163 F2
Barton End 132 A3
Barton Green 159 D1
Barton Hartshorn 148 B4
Barton Hill 195 G1
Barton in Fabis 173 E2
Barton in the Beans 159 F2
Barton Mills 163 F5
Barton on Sea 106 B3
Barton St. David 116 C4
Barton Seagrave 161 D5
Barton Stacey 119 F3
Barton Town 113 G1
Barton Turf 179 E3
Bartongate 147 G4
Barton-le-Clay 149 F4
Barton-le-Street 203 G5
Barton-le-Willows 195 G1
Barton-on-the-Heath 147 E4
Barton-under-Needwood 159 D1
Barton-upon-Humber 196 C5
Barvas (Barabhas) 271 F1
Barway 162 D5
Barwell 159 G3
Barwhinnock 216 A5
Barwick Herts 136 C1
Barwick Som 104 B1
Barwick in Elmet 194 C4
Barwinnock 207 E3
Baschurch 170 B5
Bascote 147 G1
Base Green 152 B1
Basford Green 171 G2
Bashall Eaves 192 C3
Bashall Town 192 D3
Bashley 106 B3
Basildon Essex 137 G4
Basildon WBerks 134 B5
Basingstoke 120 B2
Baslow 185 G5
Bason Bridge 116 A3
Bassaleg 130 B4
Bassenthwaite 209 F3
Basset's Cross 113 F5
Bassett 106 D1
Bassingbourn 150 B3
Bassingfield 174 B4
Bassingham 175 E2
Bassingthorpe 175 E5
Basta 278 E3
Baston 161 G1
Bastonford 146 A2
Bastwick 179 F4
Batavaime 241 G1
Batch 116 A2
Batchley 146 C1
Batchworth 135 F3
Batchworth Heath 135 F3
Batcombe Dorset 104 C2
Batcombe Som 117 D4
Bate Heath 184 A5
Bath 117 E1
Bath Abbey B&NESom BA1 1LT 63 Bath
Bathampton 117 E1

Bathealton 115 D5
Batheaston 117 E1
Bathford 117 E1
Bathgate 235 D3
Bathley 174 C2
Bathpool Corn 97 G2
Bathpool Som 115 F5
Bathway 116 C2
Batley 194 B5
Batsford 147 D4
Batson 100 D4
Battersby 203 E2
Battersea 136 B5
Battersea Cats & Dogs Home GtLon SW8 4AA 13 A5
Battersea Park Children's Zoo GtLon SW11 4NJ 13 A5
Battisborough Cross 100 C3
Battisford 152 B2
Battisford Tye 152 B2
Battle ESuss 110 C2
Battle Powys 143 G4
Battle Abbey ESuss TN33 0AD 110 C2
Battledown 146 B5
Battlefield 157 E1
Battlesbridge 137 G3
Battlesden 149 E5
Battlesea Green 164 D4
Battleton 114 C5
Battles Green 152 A1
Battramsley 106 C3
Batt's Corner 120 D3
Bauds of Cullen 268 C4
Baugh 246 B2
Baughton 146 A4
Baughurst 119 G1
Baulds 260 E5
Baulking 133 F3
Baumber 188 C5
Baunton 132 C2
Baveney Wood 157 F5
Baverstock 118 B4
Bawburgh 178 C5
Bawdeswell 178 B3
Bawdrip 116 A4
Bawdsey 153 E3
Bawsey 163 E1
Bawtry 187 D3
Baxenden 193 D5
Baxterley 159 E3
Baxter's Green 151 F2
Baxters Highland Village Moray IV32 7LD 268 B4
Bay 263 H6
Baybridge 211 F3
Baycliff 199 D5
Baydon 133 E5
Bayford Herts 136 C2
Bayford Som 117 E5
Bayfordbury 136 C1
Bayham Abbey 123 F5
Bayles 210 C3
Baylham 152 C2
Baynards Green 148 A5
Baysham 145 E5
Bayston Hill 157 D2
Bayswater 136 B4
Baythorn End 151 F3
Baythorpe 176 A3
Bayton 157 F5
Bayworth 134 A2
Beach High 247 G4
Beach SGlos 131 G5
Beachampton 148 C4
Beachamwell 163 F2
Beacharr 231 F2
Beachley 131 E3
Beacon Devon 103 E2
Beacon Devon 103 F2
Beacon Fell Country Park Lancs PR3 2NL 192 B3
Beacon Hill Dorset 105 F3
Beacon Hill Essex 138 C1
Beacon Hill Surr 121 D4
Beacon Hill Country Park Leics LE12 8SR 17 A2
Beacon Park, Up Holland Lancs WN8 7RU 183 G2
Beacon's Bottom 134 C3
Beaconsfield 135 E3
Beacravik 263 G2
Beadlam 203 F4
Beadlow 149 G4
Beadnell 229 G4
Beaford 113 F4
Beal N'umb 229 E3
Beal NYorks 195 E5
Bealach 248 A4
Beale Park WBerks RG8 9NH 134 B5
Beambridge 170 D2
Beamhurst 172 B4
Beaminster 104 A2
Beamish 212 B2
Beamish, North of England Open Air Museum Dur DH9 0RG 29 A1
Beamsley 193 G2
Bean 137 E5
Beanacre 118 A1
Beanley 229 E5
Beaquoy 276 C5
Beardon 99 F2
Beardwood 192 C5
Beare 102 C3
Beare Green 121 G3
Bearley 147 D1
Bearnie 261 H1
Bearnock 258 B1
Bearpark 212 B3
Bearsbridge 211 D2
Bearsden 233 G2
Bearsted 123 G3

Bearstone 171 E4
Bearwood Poole 105 G3
Bearwood WMid 158 C4
Beatles Story Mersey L3 4AD 42 B5
Beattock 226 B5
Beauchamp Roding 137 E1
Beauchief 186 A4
Beaudesert 147 D1
Beaufort 130 A1
Beaulieu 106 C2
Beaulieu: National Motor Museum, Abbey & Palace House Hants SO42 7ZN 4 A5
Beauly (A' Mhanachainn) 266 C7
Beaumaris (Biwmares) 181 E5
Beaumont Chanl 100 C5
Beaumont Cumb 209 G1
Beaumont Essex 152 C5
Beaumont Hill 202 B1
Beaumont Leys 160 A2
Beausale 159 E5
Beauvale 173 F3
Beauworth 119 G5
Beaver Green 124 B4
Beaworthy 99 E1
Bebington 183 E4
Bebside 221 E3
Beccles 165 F2
Beccles Heliport 165 F3
Becconsall 192 A5
Beck Foot 200 B3
Beck Hole 204 B2
Beck Row 163 E5
Beck Side Cumb 198 D4
Beck Side Cumb 199 E4
Beckbury 157 G2
Beckenham 122 C2
Beckering 188 B4
Beckermet 198 B2
Beckermonds 201 D4
Beckett End 163 F3
Beckfoot Cumb 198 C3
Beckfoot Cumb 209 D2
Beckford 146 B4
Beckhampton 118 B1
Beckingham Lincs 175 D2
Beckingham Notts 187 E4
Beckington 117 F2
Beckley ESuss 111 D1
Beckley Oxon 134 A1
Beck's Green 165 E3
Beckside 200 B4
Beckton 136 D4
Beckwithshaw 194 B2
Becontree 137 D4
Bedale 202 B4
Bedburn 211 G4
Bedchester 105 E1
Beddau 129 G4
Beddgelert 167 E3
Beddingham 109 G3
Beddington 122 B2
Beddington Corner 122 B2
Bedfield 152 D1
Bedfield Little Green 152 D1
Bedford 149 F3
Bedgebury Cross 123 G5
Bedgrove 134 D1
Bedham 121 F5
Bedhampton 107 G2
Bedingfield 152 C1
Bedingfield Street 152 C1
Bedingham Green 165 D2
Bedlam Lancs 193 E5
Bedlam NYorks 194 B1
Bedlar's Green 150 D5
Bedlington 221 E3
Bedlinog 129 G2
Bedminster 131 E5
Bedmond 135 F2
Bednall 158 B1
Bedrule 228 A5
Bedstone 156 C5
Bedwas 130 A4
Bedwell 150 A5
Bedwellty 130 A2
Bedworth 159 F4
Bedworth Woodlands 159 F4
Beeby 160 B2
Beech Hants 120 B4
Beech Staffs 171 F4
Beech Hill 120 B1
Beechingstoke 118 B2
Beechwood 183 G4
Beecraigs Country Park WLoth EH49 6PL 235 D2
Beedon 133 G5
Beeford 196 D2
Beeley 173 D1
Beelsby 188 C2
Beenham 119 G1
Beeny 97 F1
Beer 103 F4
Beer Hackett 104 C1
Beercrocombe 116 A5
Beesands 101 E4
Beesby Lincs 189 E4
Beesby NELincs 188 C3
Beeson 101 E3
Beeston CenBeds 149 G3
Beeston ChesW&C 170 C2
Beeston Norf 178 A4
Beeston Notts 173 F4
Beeston WYorks 194 B4
Beeston Regis 178 C1
Beeston St. Lawrence 179 E3
Beeswing 216 C4
Beetham Cumb 199 F5
Beetham Som 103 F1
Beetley 178 A4
Beffcote 158 A1

Began 130 B4
Begbroke 133 G1
Begdale 162 C2
Begelly 127 E2
Beggar's Bush 144 B1
Beggearn Huish 114 D4
Beggshill 260 D1
Beguildy (Bugeildy) 156 A5
Beighton Norf 179 E5
Beighton SYorks 186 B4
Beili-glas 130 C2
Bekesbourne 125 D3
Bekonscot Model Village Bucks HP9 2PL 135 E3
Belaugh 179 D4
Belbroughton 158 B5
Belchalwell 105 D2
Belchalwell Street 105 D2
Belchamp Otten 151 G3
Belchamp St. Paul 151 F3
Belchamp Walter 151 G3
Belchford 188 C5
Belfield 184 D1
Belford 229 F3
Belgrave 160 A2
Belhaven 237 D2
Belhelvie 261 H3
Belhinnie 260 C2
Bell Bar 136 B2
Bell Busk 193 F2
Bell End 158 B5
Bell Heath 158 B5
Bell Hill 120 C5
Bell o' th' Hill 170 C3
Bellabeg 260 B3
Belladrum 266 C7
Bellanoch 240 A5
Bellaty 252 A4
Belle Isle 194 C4
Belle Vue 209 G1
Belleau 189 E5
Belleheiglash 259 J1
Bellerby 202 A3
Bellever 99 G3
Bellfields 121 F2
Belliehill 253 D3
Bellingdon 135 E2
Bellingham GtLon 136 C5
Bellingham N'umb 220 A3
Belloch 222 B2
Bellochantuy 222 B2
Bell's Cross 152 C2
Bells Yew Green 123 F5
Bellsbank 224 C5
Bellshill N'umb 229 F3
Bellshill NLan 234 B3
Bellside 234 C4
Bellsmyre 233 F2
Bellsquarry 235 E3
Belluton 116 C1
Belmaduthy 266 D6
Belmesthorpe 161 F1
Belmont B'burn 184 A1
Belmont GtLon 122 B3
Belmont GtLon 136 A3
Belmont Shet 278 E2
Belnie 176 A4
Belowda 97 D3
Belper 173 E3
Belper Lane End 173 E3
Belsay 220 D4
Belsford 101 D2
Belsize 135 F2
Belstead 152 C3
Belston 224 B3
Belstone 99 G1
Belstone Corner 99 G1
Belsyde 235 D2
Belthorn 192 D5
Beltinge 125 D2
Beltingham 211 D1
Beltoft 187 F2
Belton Leics 173 F5
Belton Lincs 175 E4
Belton NLincs 187 E2
Belton Norf 179 F5
Belton Rut 160 C2
Belton House Lincs NG32 2LS 175 E4
Beltring 123 F4
Belvedere 137 D5
Belvoir 174 D4
Bembridge 107 F4
Bemersyde 227 G2
Bemerton 118 C4
Bempton 205 E5
Ben Alder Cottage 249 G3
Ben Alder Lodge 250 A2
Ben Rhydding 194 A3
Benacre 165 G3
Benbecula (Beinn na Faoghla) 262 D6
Benbecula (Balivanich) Airport 262 C6
Benbuie 216 B1
Benderloch (Meadarloch) 240 B1
Bendish 149 G5
Benenden 124 A5
Benfield 215 E4
Benfieldside 211 G2
Bengate 179 E3
Bengeo 136 C1
Bengeworth 146 C3
Benhall 146 B5
Benhall Green 153 E1
Benhall Street 153 E1
Benholm 253 F2
Beningbrough 195 E2
Benington Herts 150 A5
Benington Lincs 176 B3
Benington Sea End 176 C3
Benllech 180 D4
Benmore A&B 232 A1
Benmore Stir 241 G2
Bennacott 98 C1
Bennan Cottage 216 A3
Bennett End 134 C3
Bennetts End 135 F2
Benniworth 188 C4
Benover 123 G4

Benson 134 B3
Benston 279 D7
Benthall N'umb 229 G4
Benthall Shrop 157 F2
Bentham 132 B1
Benthoul 261 G4
Bentlawnt 156 C2
Bentley ERid 196 C4
Bentley Essex 137 E3
Bentley Hants 120 B3
Bentley Suff 152 C4
Bentley SYorks 186 C2
Bentley Warks 159 E3
Bentley WMid 158 B3
Bentley WYorks 194 A4
Bentley Heath
   Herts 136 B3
Bentley Heath
   WMid 159 D5
Benton 113 G2
Benton Square 221 F4
Bentpath 218 B2
Bentworth 120 B3
Benvie 244 B1
Benville Lane 104 B2
Benwell 212 B1
Benwick 162 B3
Beoley 146 C1
Beoraidbeg 256 C5
Bepton 108 A2
Berden 150 C5
Bere Alston 100 A1
Bere Ferrers 100 A1
Bere Regis 105 E3
Berea 140 A4
Berepper 95 D4
Bergh Apton 179 E5
Berinsfield 134 A3
Berkeley 131 F3
Berkhamsted 135 E2
Berkley 117 F3
Berkswell 159 E5
Bermondsey 136 C5
Bernera 256 C5
Berneray (Eilean
   Bhearnaraigh) 262 E3
Berners Roding 137 F2
Bernice 240 C5
Bernisdale 263 K6
Berrick Prior 134 B3
Berrick Salome 134 B3
Berriedale 275 G6
Berriew (Aberriw) 156 A2
Berrington N'umb 229 E2
Berrington Shrop 157 E2
Berrington Worcs 145 E1
Berrington Green 145 E1
Berriowbridge 97 G2
Berrow Som 115 F2
Berrow Worcs 145 G4
Berrow Green 145 G2
Berry Cross 113 E4
Berry Down Cross 113 F1
Berry Hill Glos 131 F2
Berry Hill Pembs 141 D3
Berry Pomeroy 101 E1
Berryhillock 268 D4
Berrynarbor 113 F1
Berry's Green 122 D3
Bersham 170 A3
Berstañe 277 D6
Berthlwyd 128 B3
Berwick 110 A3
Berwick Bassett 132 D5
Berwick Hill 221 D4
Berwick St. James 118 B4
Berwick St. John 118 A3
Berwick St. Leonard 118 A3
Berwick-upon-
   Tweed 237 G4
Bescar 183 E1
Bescot 158 C3
Besford Shrop 170 C5
Besford Worcs 146 B3
Bessacarr 186 D2
Bessels Leigh 133 G2
Besses o' th' Barn 184 C2
Bessingby 197 D1
Bessingham 178 C2
Best Beech Hill 123 F5
Besthorpe Norf 164 B2
Besthorpe Notts 174 D1
Bestwood 173 G3
Bestwood Country Park
   Notts NG6 8UF 19 G1
Beswick ERid 196 C3
Beswick GtMan 184 C3
Betchworth 122 B3
Bethania Cere 142 B1
Bethania Gwyn 168 A3
Bethel Gwyn 167 E1
Bethel Gwyn 168 C4
Bethel IoA 180 B5
Bethersden 124 B5
Bethesda Gwyn 167 F1
Bethesda Pembs 127 D1
Bethlehem 142 C5
Bethnal Green 136 C4
Betley 171 E3
Betley Common 171 E3
Betsham 137 F5
Betteshanger 125 F3
Bettiscombe 103 G3
Bettisfield 170 B4
Betton Shrop 156 C2
Betton Shrop 171 D4
Betton Strange 157 E2
Bettws Bridgend 129 F4
Bettws Newport 130 B3
Bettws Bledrws 142 B2
Bettws Cedewain 156 A3
Bettws Gwerfil
   Goch 168 D3
Bettws Newydd 130 C2
Bettws-y-crwyn 156 B4
Bettyhill 274 C2
Betws Cere 141 G3
Betws Disserth 144 A2
Betws Garmon 167 E2
Betws Ifan 141 G3
Betws-y-coed 168 A2

Betws-yn-Rhos 182 A5
Beulah Cere 141 F3
Beulah Powys 143 F2
Bevendean 109 F3
Bevercotes 187 D5
Beverley 196 C4
Beverston 132 A3
Bevington 131 F3
Bewaldeth 209 F3
Bewcastle 219 D4
Bewdley 157 G5
Bewerley 194 A1
Bewholme 197 D2
Bewl Water ESuss
   TN3 8JH 123 F5
Bewley Common 118 A1
Bexhill 110 C3
Bexley 137 D5
Bexleyheath 137 D5
Bexwell 163 E2
Beyton 152 A1
Beyton Green 152 A1
Bhalamus 270 D4
Bhaltos 270 C4
Biallaid 258 E5
Bibury 132 D2
Bicester 148 A5
Bickenhall 103 F1
Bickenhill 159 D4
Bicker 176 A4
Bickershaw 184 A2
Bickerstaffe 183 F2
Bickerton
   ChesW&C 170 C2
Bickerton Devon 101 E4
Bickerton N'umb 220 B1
Bickerton NYorks 195 D2
Bickford 158 A1
Bickham 114 C3
Bickham Bridge 100 D2
Bickham House 102 C4
Bickington Devon 113 F2
Bickington Devon 102 A5
Bickleigh Devon 100 B1
Bickleigh Devon 102 C2
Bickleton 113 F2
Bickley 122 D2
Bickley Moss 170 C3
Bickley Town 170 C3
Bicknacre 137 G2
Bicknoller 115 E4
Bicknor 124 A3
Bickton 106 A1
Bicton Here 145 D1
Bicton Shrop 156 D1
Bicton Shrop 156 B4
Bicton Heath 157 D1
Bicton Park Gardens
   Devon EX9 7BJ 103 D4
Bidborough 123 E4
Biddenden 124 A5
Biddenden Green 124 A4
Biddenham 149 F3
Biddestone 132 A5
Biddick 212 C2
Biddisham 116 A2
Biddlesden 148 B3
Biddlestone 220 B1
Biddulph 171 F2
Biddulph Moor 171 G2
Bideford 113 E2
Bidford-on-Avon 146 D2
Bidlake 99 E2
Bidston 183 D3
Bidwell 149 F5
Bielby 195 G3
Bieldside 261 G4
Bierley IoW 107 E5
Bierley WYorks 194 A4
Bierton 134 D1
Big Pit National Coal
   Museum Torfaen
   NP4 9XP 130 A4
Big Sand 264 D4
Big Sheep, The Devon
   EX39 5AP 113 E3
Big Sky Adventure Play
   Peter PE2 7BU 161 G3
Bigbury 100 D3
Bigbury-on-Sea 100 C3
Bigby 188 A2
Bigert Mire 198 C3
Biggar Cumb 191 E1
Biggar SLan 226 A2
Biggin Derbys 173 D3
Biggin Derbys 172 C2
Biggin NYorks 195 E4
Biggin Hill 122 D3
Biggin Hill Airport 122 D3
Biggings 279 A6
Biggleswade 149 G3
Bigholms 218 B3
Bighouse 274 D2
Bighton 120 B4
Biglands 209 F1
Bignor 108 B2
Bigrigg 208 D5
Bigton 279 C10
Bilberry 97 E4
Bilborough 173 G3
Bilbrook Som 114 D3
Bilbrook Staffs 158 A2
Bilbrough 195 E3
Bilbster 275 H3
Bilby 186 D4
Bildershaw 212 A5
Bildeston 152 A3
Billericay 137 F3
Billesdon 160 C2
Billesley 146 D2
Billholm 218 A2
Billingborough 175 G4
Billinge 183 G3
Billingford Norf 164 C4
Billingford Norf 178 B3
Billingham 213 D5
Billinghay 175 G2
Billingley 186 B2
Billingshurst 121 F5
Billingsley 157 G4
Billington CenBeds 149 E5
Billington Lancs 192 D4

Billington Staffs 171 F5
Billister 279 D6
Billockby 179 F4
Billy Row 212 A4
Bilsborrow 192 B4
Bilsby 189 E5
Bilsby Field 189 E5
Bilsdean 237 E2
Bilsham 108 B3
Bilsington 124 C5
Bilson Green 131 F1
Bilsthorpe 174 B1
Bilsthorpe Moor 174 B2
Bilston Midlo 235 G3
Bilston WMid 158 B3
Bilstone 159 F2
Bilting 124 C4
Bilton ERid 197 D4
Bilton N'umb 229 G5
Bilton NYorks 194 C2
Bilton Warks 159 G5
Bilton-in-Ainsty 195 D3
Bimbister 277 C6
Binbrook 188 C3
Bincombe 104 C4
Bindal 267 G3
Bindon 115 E5
Binegar 116 D3
Bines Green 109 E2
Binfield 134 D5
Binfield Heath 134 C5
Bingfield 220 B4
Bingham 174 C4
Bingham's
   Melcombe 105 D2
Bingley 194 A4
Bings Heath 157 E1
Binham 178 A2
Binley Hants 119 F1
Binley WMid 159 F5
Binniehill 234 C2
Binsoe 202 B5
Binstead 107 E3
Binsted Hants 120 C3
Binsted WSuss 108 B3
Binton 146 D2
Bintree 178 B3
Binweston 156 C2
Birch Essex 152 A5
Birch GtMan 184 C2
Birch Cross 172 C4
Birch Green Essex 138 C1
Birch Green Herts 136 B1
Birch Grove 109 G1
Birch Heath 170 C1
Birch Vale 185 E4
Birch Wood 103 F1
Bircham Newton 177 F4
Bircham Tofts 177 F4
Birchanger 150 D5
Bircher 145 D1
Bircher Common 145 D1
Birchfield 266 B2
Birchgrove Cardiff 130 A4
Birchgrove Swan 128 D3
Birchington 125 F2
Birchmoor 159 E2
Birchover 172 D1
Birchwood Lincs 175 E1
Birchwood Warr 184 A3
Bircotes 186 D3
Bird Street 152 B2
Birdbrook 151 F3
Birdbush 118 A5
Birdfield 240 B5
Birdforth 203 D5
Birdham 108 A3
Birdingbury 147 G1
Birdland, Bourton-on-
   the-Water Glos
   GL54 2BN 147 D5
Birdlip 132 B1
Birdoswald 210 C1
Birds Green 137 E2
Birdsall 196 A1
Birdsgreen 157 G4
Birdsmoor Gate 103 G2
Birdston 234 A2
Birdwell 186 A2
Birdwood 131 G1
Birgham 228 C3
Birichen 266 E2
Birkby Cumb 209 D3
Birkby NYorks 202 C2
Birkdale Mersey 183 E1
Birkdale NYorks 201 D2
Birkenhead 183 E4
Birkenhills 269 F6
Birkenshaw 194 B5
Birkhall 260 B5
Birkhill Angus 244 B1
Birkhill ScBord 236 C5
Birkhill ScBord 226 D4
Birkholme 175 E5
Birkin 195 E5
Birks 194 B5
Birkwood 225 G2
Birley 145 D2
Birley Carr 186 A3
Birling Kent 123 F5
Birling N'umb 221 E1
Birling Gap 110 A4
Birlingham 146 B3
Birmingham 158 C4
Birmingham Botanical
   Gardens WMid
   B15 3TR 34 B7
Birmingham City Museum
   & Art Gallery WMid
   B3 3DH 35 E4
Birmingham International
   Airport 159 D4
Birnam 251 F5
Birsay 276 B5
Birse 260 D5
Birsemore 260 D5
Birstall 160 A3
Birstall Smithies 194 B5
Birstwith 194 B2
Birthorpe 175 G4

Birtle 184 C1
Birtley Here 144 C1
Birtley N'umb 220 A4
Birtley T&W 212 B1
Birts Street 145 G4
Birtsmorton 146 A4
Bisbrooke 161 D3
Biscathorpe 188 C4
Bish Mill 114 A5
Bisham 135 D4
Bishampton 146 B2
Bishop Auckland 212 B5
Bishop Burton 196 B3
Bishop Middleham 212 C4
Bishop Monkton 194 C1
Bishop Norton 187 G3
Bishop Sutton 116 C2
Bishop Thornton 194 B1
Bishop Wilton 195 G2
Bishopbridge 188 A3
Bishopbriggs 234 A2
Bishopmill 267 K5
Bishops Cannings 118 B1
Bishop's Castle 156 C4
Bishop's Caundle 104 C1
Bishop's Cleeve 146 B5
Bishop's Frome 145 F3
Bishops Gate 135 E5
Bishop's Green
   Essex 137 F1
Bishop's Green
   Hants 119 G1
Bishop's Hull 115 F5
Bishop's Itchington 147 F2
Bishop's Lydeard 115 E5
Bishop's Norton 146 A5
Bishops Nympton 114 A5
Bishop's Offley 171 F5
Bishop's Stortford 150 C5
Bishop's Sutton 120 B4
Bishop's Tachbrook 147 F1
Bishop's Tawton 113 F2
Bishop's Waltham 107 E1
Bishop's Wood 158 A2
Bishopsbourne 125 D3
Bishopsteignton 102 C5
Bishopston Bristol 131 E5
Bishopston Swan 128 B4
Bishopstone Bucks 134 D1
Bishopstone ESuss 109 G3
Bishopstone Here 144 D3
Bishopstone Swin 133 E4
Bishopstone Wilts 118 B5
Bishopstrow 117 F3
Bishopswood 103 F1
Bishopsworth 116 C1
Bishopthorpe 195 E3
Bishopton Darl 212 C5
Bishopton NYorks 202 B5
Bishopton Renf 233 F2
Bishopton Warks 147 D2
Bishton 130 C4
Bisley Glos 132 B2
Bisley Surr 121 E2
Bispham 191 G4
Bispham Green 183 F1
Bissoe 96 B5
Bisterne 106 A2
Bisterne Close 106 B2
Bitchet Green 123 E3
Bitchfield 175 E5
Bittadon 113 F1
Bittaford 100 C2
Bittering 178 A4
Bitterley 157 E5
Bitterne 107 D1
Bitteswell 160 A4
Bitton 117 D1
Bix 134 C4
Bixter 279 C7
Blaby 160 A3
Black Bourton 133 E2
Black Bridge 126 C2
Black Callerton 212 A1
Black Carr 164 B2
Black Clauchrie 215 D2
Black Corries Lodge 249 D4
Black Country Living
   Museum WMid
   DY1 4SQ 14 C3
Black Crofts 248 B2
Black Cross 96 D3
Black Dog 102 B2
Black Heddon 220 C4
Black Hill 147 E2
Black Marsh 156 C3
Black Moor 194 B3
Black Mount 249 E5
Black Notley 151 F5
Black Park Country
   Park Bucks
   SL3 6DR 135 F4
Black Pill 128 C3
Black Sheep Brewery
   Visitor Centre NYorks
   HG4 4EN 202 B4
Black Street 165 G3
Black Swan Guild,
   Frome Som
   BA11 1BB 117 E3
Black Torrington 113 E5
Blackacre 217 E1
Blackadder 237 E4
Blackawton 101 E2
Blackborough
   Devon 103 D2
Blackborough Norf 163 E1
Blackborough End 163 E1
Blackboys 110 A1
Blackbraes Aber 261 G3
Blackbraes Falk 234 D2
Blackbrook Derbys 173 E3
Blackbrook Leics 159 G1
Blackbrook Mersey 183 G3
Blackbrook Staffs 171 E4
Blackburn Aber 261 G3
Blackburn B'burn 192 C5
Blackburn WLoth 235 D3
Blackbushe 120 C2
Blackcastle 267 F6

Blackchambers 261 F3
Blackcraig D&G 215 F4
Blackcraig D&G 216 B2
Blackden Heath 184 B5
Blackdog 261 H3
Blackdown Devon 99 F3
Blackdown Dorset 103 G2
Blackdown Warks 147 F1
Blacker Hill 186 A2
Blackfen 137 D5
Blackfield 106 D2
Blackford Aber 261 F1
Blackford Cumb 218 B5
Blackford P&K 243 D4
Blackford Som 117 D5
Blackford Som 116 B3
Blackford Bridge 184 C2
Blackfordby 159 F1
Blackgang 107 D5
Blackgang Chine
   IoW PO38 2HN 107 D5
Blackhall Edin 235 G2
Blackhall Renf 233 F3
Blackhall Colliery 213 D4
Blackhall Rocks 213 D4
Blackham 123 D5
Blackheath Essex 152 B5
Blackheath GtLon 136 C5
Blackheath Suff 165 F4
Blackheath Surr 121 F3
Blackheath WMid 158 B4
Blackhill Aber 269 J5
Blackhill Aber 269 J6
Blackhillock 268 C6
Blackhills 267 K6
Blackland 118 B1
Blacklands 114 B4
Blackleach 192 A4
Blackley 184 C2
Blacklunans 251 G3
Blackmill 129 F4
Blackmoor Hants 120 C4
Blackmoor Som 103 E1
Blackmoor Gate 113 G1
Blackmoorfoot 185 E1
Blackmore 137 F2
Blackmore End
   Essex 151 F4
Blackmore End
   Herts 136 A1
Blackness Aber 260 E5
Blackness Falk 235 E2
Blackness High 275 H5
Blacknest 120 C3
Blackney 104 A3
Blacko 193 E4
Blackpole 146 A2
Blackpool B'pool 191 G4
Blackpool Devon 101 E3
Blackpool Bridge 127 D1
Blackpool Gate 218 D4
Blackpool International
   Airport 191 G4
Blackpool Piers B'pool
   FY4 1BB 191 G4
Blackpool Pleasure
   Beach B'pool
   FY4 1PL 191 G4
Blackpool Tower
   FY1 4BJ 64 Blackpool
Blackpool Zoo
   B'pool FY3 8PP 191 G4
Blackridge 234 C3
Blackrock A&B 230 B3
Blackrock Mon 130 B1
Blackrod 184 A1
Blackshaw 217 E4
Blackshaw Head 193 F5
Blacksmith's Green 152 C1
Blacksnape 192 D5
Blackstone 109 E2
Blackthorn 134 B1
Blackthorpe 152 A1
Blacktoft 196 A5
Blacktop 261 G4
Blacktown 130 B4
Blackwater Corn 96 B5
Blackwater Hants 120 D2
Blackwater IoW 107 E4
Blackwater Norf 178 B3
Blackwater Som 103 F1
Blackwaterfoot 223 E3
Blackwell Darl 202 B1
Blackwell Derbys 185 F5
Blackwell Derbys 173 F2
Blackwell Warks 147 E3
Blackwell Worcs 158 B5
Blackwell WSuss 122 C5
Blackwells End 145 G5
Blackwood (Coed-duon)
   Caerp 130 A3
Blackwood D&G 216 D2
Blackwood SLan 234 B5
Blackwood Hill 171 G2
Blacon 170 A1
Bladbean 125 D4
Bladnoch 215 F5
Bladon 133 G1
Blaen Clydach 129 F3
Blaenannerch 141 F3
Blaenau
   Dolwyddelan 167 F2
Blaenau Ffestiniog 167 F3
Blaenavon 130 B2
Blaenawey 130 B1
Blaencelyn 141 G2
Blaencwm 129 F2
Blaendyryn 143 F4
Blaenffos 141 E4
Blaengarw 129 F3
Blaengeuffordd 154 C4
Blaengweche 128 C1
Blaengwrach 129 E2
Blaengwynfi 129 E3
Blaenllechau 129 G3
Blaenos 143 D4
Blaenpennal 142 C1
Blaenplwyf 154 B5
Blaenporth 141 F3
Blaenrhondda 129 F2

Blaenwaun 141 F5
Blaen-y-coed 141 G5
Blagdon NSom 116 B2
Blagdon Torbay 101 E1
Blagdon Hill 103 F1
Blaguegate 183 F2
Blaich 248 C2
Blaina 130 A2
Blair 233 E5
Blair Atholl 251 E3
Blair Castle P&K
   PH18 5TL 251 D3
Blair Drummond 242 C5
Blair Drummond Safari &
   Adventure Park Stir
   FK9 4UR 242 B4
Blairannaich 241 F4
Blairbuie 232 C2
Blairgowrie 251 G5
Blairhall 235 E1
Blairhoyle 242 B4
Blairhullichan 241 G4
Blairingone 243 E5
Blairkip 224 D2
Blairlogie 242 D5
Blairmore A&B 232 C1
Blairmore High 266 E1
Blairmore High 272 D3
Blairnairn 233 E1
Blairpark 232 D4
Blairquhan 224 B5
Blairquhosh 233 G1
Blair's Ferry 232 A3
Blairshinnoch 268 E4
Blairskaithmore 241 G4
Blairvadach 233 D1
Blairydryne 261 F5
Blaisdon 131 G1
Blake End 151 F5
Blake House Craft
   Centre Essex
   CM77 6RA 151 F5
Blakebrook 158 A5
Blakedown 158 A5
Blakelaw ScBord 228 B3
Blakelaw T&W 212 B1
Blakeley 158 A3
Blakelow 171 D2
Blakemere 144 C3
Blakemere Shopping
   Experience ChesW&C
   CW8 2EB 183 G5
Blakeney Glos 131 F2
Blakeney Norf 178 B1
Blakenhall ChesE 171 E3
Blakenhall WMid 158 B3
Blakeshall 158 A4
Blakesley 148 B2
Blanchland 211 F2
Bland Hill 194 B2
Blandford Camp 105 F2
Blandford Forum 105 E2
Blandford St. Mary 105 E2
Blanefield 233 G2
Blanerne 237 F4
Blankney 175 F1
Blantyre 234 A4
Blar a' Chaorainn 248 D3
Blargie 258 D5
Blarglas 233 E1
Blarmachfoldach 248 C3
Blarnalearoch 265 H2
Blashford 106 A2
Blaston 160 D3
Blathaisbhal 262 D4
Blatherwycke 161 E3
Blawith 199 D3
Blaxhall 153 E2
Blaxton 187 D2
Blaydon 212 A1
Bleadney 116 B3
Bleadon 116 A2
Bleak Hey Nook 185 E2
Blean 124 D2
Bleasby Lincs 188 B4
Bleasby Notts 174 C3
Bleasby Moor 188 B4
Bleatarn 200 C1
Bleathwood
   Common 145 E1
Blebocraigs 244 C3
Bleddfa 144 B1
Bledington 147 E5
Bledlow 134 C2
Bledlow Ridge 134 C3
Blencarn 210 C4
Blencogo 209 E2
Blencow 210 A4
Blendworth 107 G1
Blenheim Palace Oxon
   OX20 1PX 133 G1
Blennerhasset 209 E3
Blervie Castle 267 H6
Bletchingdon 134 A1
Bletchingley 122 C3
Bletchley MK 149 D4
Bletchley Shrop 170 D4
Bletherston 141 D5
Bletsoe 149 F2
Blewbury 134 A4
Blickling 178 C3
Blickling Hall Norf
   NR11 6NF 178 C3
Blidworth 173 G2
Blidworth Bottoms 173 G2
Blindburn Aber 261 H1
Blindburn N'umb 228 C5
Blindcrake 209 E3
Blindley Heath 122 C4
Blisland 97 F2
Bliss Gate 157 G5
Blissford 106 A1
Blisworth 148 C2
Blithbury 172 B5
Blitterlees 209 E1
Blo' Norton 164 B4
Blockley 147 D4
Blofield 179 E5
Blofield Heath 179 E4
Blore 172 C3

Blossomfield 158 D5
Blount's Green 172 B4
Blowick 183 E1
Bloxham 147 G4
Bloxholm 175 F2
Bloxwich 158 B2
Bloxworth 105 E3
Blubberhouses 194 A2
Blue Anchor Corn 96 D4
Blue Anchor Som 114 D3
Blue Bell Hill 123 G2
Blue Planet Aquarium,
   Ellesmere Port
   ChesW&C
   CH65 9LF 183 E5
Blue Reef Aquarium
   ESuss TN34 3DW
   75 Hastings
Blue Reef Aquarium,
   Newquay Corn
   TR7 1DU 96 C3
Blue Reef Aquarium,
   Southsea Ports
   PO5 3PB 5 G6
Blue Reef Aquarium,
   Tynemouth T&W
   NE30 4JF 28 E1
Bluebell Railway WSuss
   TN22 3QL 109 F1
Bluewater 137 E5
Blundellsands 183 E3
Blundeston 165 G2
Blunham 149 G2
Blunsdon
   St. Andrew 132 D4
Bluntington 158 A5
Bluntisham 162 B5
Blunts 98 D4
Blurton 171 F3
Blyborough 187 G3
Blyford 165 F4
Blymhill 158 A1
Blymhill Common 157 G1
Blymhill Lawn 158 A1
Blyth N'umb 221 F3
Blyth Notts 186 D4
Blyth Bridge 235 F5
Blyth End 159 E3
Blythburgh 165 F4
Blythe Bridge 171 G3
Blythe Marsh 171 G3
Blyton 187 F3
Boarhills 245 D3
Boarhunt 107 F2
Boars Hill 133 G2
Boarsgrave 193 E3
Boarshead 123 E5
Boarstall 134 B1
Boarzell 110 C1
Boasley Cross 99 F1
Boat o' Brig 268 B5
Boat of Garten 259 G3
Boath 266 C4
Bobbing 124 A2
Bobbington 158 A3
Bobbingworth 137 E2
Bocaddon 97 F4
Bochastle 242 B4
Bocketts Farm Park
   Surr KT22 9BS 121 G2
Bockhampton 133 F5
Bocking 151 F5
Bocking
   Churchstreet 151 F5
Bockleton 145 E1
Boconnoc 97 F3
Boddam Aber 269 K6
Boddam Shet 279 C11
Bodden 116 C3
Boddington 146 A5
Bodedern 180 B4
Bodelwyddan 182 B5
Bodenham Here 145 E2
Bodenham Wilts 118 C5
Bodenham Moor 145 E2
Bodesbeck 226 C5
Bodewryd 180 C3
Bodfari 182 B5
Bodffordd 180 C5
Bodfuan 166 C4
Bodham 178 C1
Bodiam 110 C1
Bodiam Castle ESuss
   TN32 5UA 110 C1
Bodicote 147 G4
Bodieve 97 D2
Bodinnick 97 F4
Bodior 180 A5
Bodle Street Green 110 B2
Bodleian Library
   Oxon OX1 3BG
   80 Oxford
Bodmin 97 E3
Bodnant Garden Conwy
   LL28 5RE 181 G5
Bodney 163 G3
Bodorgan 166 C1
Bodrane 97 G3
Bodsham Green 124 C4
Bodwen 97 E3
Bodymoor Heath 159 D3
Bogallan 266 D6
Bogbain 266 E7
Bogbrae 261 J1
Bogbuie 266 C6
Bogend 224 B2
Bogfern 260 D4
Bogfields 260 D4
Bogfold 269 G5
Boghead Aber 268 C5
Boghead EAyr 225 G3
Boghead SLan 234 B5
Boghole Farm 267 G6
Bogmoor 268 B4
Bogniebrae 268 D6
Bognor Regis 108 B4
Bograxie 261 F3
Bogroy 259 G2
Bogside 243 E5
Bogston 260 B4
Bogton 268 E5
Bogue 216 A2

Bohemia 106 B1
Bohenie 249 E1
Bohetherick 100 A1
Bohuntine 249 E1
Boirseam 263 F3
Bojewyan 94 A3
Bokiddick 97 E3
Bolam Dur 212 A5
Bolam N'umb 220 C3
Bolam Lake Country
Park N'umb
NE20 0HE 220 C3
Bolberry 100 C4
Bold Heath 183 G4
Bolderwood 106 B2
Boldon 212 C1
Boldon Colliery 212 C1
Boldre 106 C3
Boldron 201 F1
Bole 187 F4
Bolehill 173 D2
Boleigh 94 B4
Bolenowe 95 D3
Boleside 227 F2
Bolfracks 250 D5
Bolgoed 128 C2
Bolham Devon 102 C1
Bolham Notts 187 E4
Bolham Water 103 E1
Bolingey 96 B4
Bollington 184 D5
Bolney 109 E1
Bolnhurst 149 E3
Bolshan 253 E4
Bolsover 186 B5
Bolsterstone 185 G3
Bolstone 145 E4
Boltby 203 D4
Bolter End 134 C3
Bolton Cumb 210 C5
Bolton ELoth 236 C2
Bolton ERid 195 G2
Bolton GtMan 184 B2
Bolton N'umb 229 F5
Bolton Abbey 193 G2
Bolton Abbey Estate
NYorks
BD23 6EX 193 G2
Bolton Bridge 193 G2
Bolton by Bowland 193 D3
Bolton Houses 192 A4
Bolton Low Houses 209 F2
Bolton Museum &
Art Gallery GtMan
BL1 1SE 184 B2
Bolton Percy 195 E3
Bolton Priory NYorks
BD23 6EX 193 G2
Bolton upon
Dearne 186 B2
Bolton Wood Lane 209 F2
Boltonfellend 210 A1
Boltongate 209 F2
Bolton-le-Sands 192 A1
Bolton-on-Swale 202 B3
Bolventor 97 F2
Bombie 208 A2
Bomere Heath 157 D1
Bonar Bridge 266 D2
Bonawe (Bun Atha) 240 C1
Bonby 188 A1
Boncath 141 F4
Bonchester Bridge 227 G4
Bonchurch 107 E5
Bondleigh 113 G5
Bonds 192 A3
Bonehill 159 D2
Bo'ness 235 D1
Bonhill 233 E2
Boningale 158 A2
Bonjedward 228 A4
Bonkle 234 C4
Bonning Gate 199 F3
Bonnington Edin 235 F3
Bonnington Kent 124 C5
Bonnybank 244 B4
Bonnybridge 234 C1
Bonnykelly 269 G5
Bonnyrigg 236 A3
Bonnyton Aber 260 E1
Bonnyton Angus 245 D1
Bonnyton Angus 253 E4
Bonnyton Angus 244 B1
Bonsall 173 D2
Bont 130 C1
Bont Dolgadfan 155 E2
Bont Newydd 168 A5
Bontddu 154 C1
Bont-goch (Elerch) 154 C4
Bonthorpe 189 E5
Bont-newydd
Conwy 182 B5
Bontnewydd Gwyn 167 D1
Bontuchel 169 D2
Bonvilston 129 G5
Bon-y-maen 128 C3
Boode 113 F2
Boohay 101 F2
Booker 134 D3
Booley 170 C5
Boor 264 E3
Boorley Green 107 E1
Boosbeck 203 F1
Boose's Green 151 G4
Boot 198 C2
Boot Street 152 D3
Booth 193 G5
Booth Bank 185 E1
Booth Green 184 D4
Booth Wood 185 E1
Boothby Graffoe 175 E2
Boothby Pagnell 175 E4
Boothstown 184 B2
Boothville 148 C1
Bootle Cumb 198 C4
Bootle Mersey 183 E3
Booton 178 C3
Boots Green 184 B5
Booze 201 F2
Boquhan 233 G1
Boraston 157 F5

Bordeaux 101 F4
Borden Kent 124 A2
Borden WSuss 120 D5
Bordley 193 F2
Bordon 120 C4
Boreham Essex 137 G2
Boreham Wilts 117 F3
Boreham Street 110 B2
Borehamwood 136 A3
Boreland D&G 217 F1
Boreland D&G 215 E4
Boreland Stir 242 A1
Boreley 146 A1
Boreraig 263 G6
Borgh WIsles 262 E3
Borgh WIsles 254 B4
Borghastan 270 D3
Borgie 273 J3
Borgue D&G 207 G2
Borgue High 275 G6
Borley 151 G3
Borley Green Essex 151 G3
Borley Green Suff 152 A1
Bornais 254 C1
Borness 207 G3
Bornisketaig 263 J4
Borough Green 123 F3
Boroughbridge 194 C1
Borras Head 170 A2
Borrowash 173 F4
Borrowby NYorks 203 G1
Borrowby NYorks 202 D4
Borrowdale 209 F5
Borrowfield 261 G5
Borstal 123 G2
Borth 154 C4
Borthwick 236 A4
Borthwickbrae 227 F4
Borthwickshiels 227 F4
Borth-y-Gest 167 D2
Borve (Borgh)
WIsles 271 G2
Borwick 199 G5
Borwick Rails 198 C5
Bosavern 94 A3
Bosbury 145 F3
Boscarne 97 E3
Boscastle 98 A1
Boscastle Pottery Corn
PL35 0HE 98 A1
Boscombe Bourne 106 A3
Boscombe Wilts 118 D4
Bosham 108 A3
Bosham Hoe 108 A3
Bosherston 126 C3
Bosley 171 G1
Bossall 195 G1
Bossiney 97 E1
Bossingham 125 D4
Bossington Hants 119 E4
Bossington Som 114 B3
Bostadh 270 D4
Bostock Green 171 D1
Boston 176 B3
Boston Spa 194 D3
Boswarthan 94 B3
Boswinger 97 D5
Bosworth Battlefield
Country Park Leics
CV13 0AD 159 G2
Botallack 94 A3
Botanic Garden
Oxon OX1 4AZ
80 Oxford
Botany Bay 136 C3
Botany Bay Lancs
PR6 9AF 184 A1
Botcheston 159 G2
Botesdale 164 B4
Bothal 221 E3
Bothamsall 187 D5
Bothel 209 E3
Bothenhampton 104 A3
Bothwell 234 B4
Botley Bucks 135 E2
Botley Hants 107 E1
Botley Oxon 133 G2
Botloe's Green 145 G5
Botolph Claydon 148 C5
Botolphs 109 D3
Botolph's Bridge 124 D5
Bottacks 266 B5
Bottesford Leics 174 D4
Bottesford NLincs 187 F2
Bottisham 150 D1
Bottlesford 118 C2
Bottom Boat 194 C5
Bottom of Hutton 192 A5
Bottom o'th'Moor 184 A1
Bottomcraig 244 B2
Bottoms 193 F5
Botton Head 192 C1
Botusfleming 100 A1
Botwnnog 166 B4
Bough Beech 123 E4
Boughrood 144 A4
Boughspring 131 E3
Boughton N'hants 148 C1
Boughton Norf 163 F2
Boughton Notts 174 B1
Boughton Aluph 124 C4
Boughton Lees 124 C4
Boughton Malherbe 124 A4
Boughton
Monchelsea 123 G3
Boughton Street 124 C3
Boulby 203 G1
Bouldnor 106 C4
Bouldon 157 E4
Boulge 153 D2
Boulmer 229 G5
Boulston 126 C1
Boultenstone Hotel 260 C3
Boultham 175 E1
Boundary Derbys 159 F1
Boundary Staffs 171 G3
Bourn 150 B2
Bourne 175 F5
Bourne End Bucks 135 D4
Bourne End
CenBeds 149 E3

Bourne End Herts 135 F2
Bournebridge 137 E3
Bournemouth 105 G3
Bournemouth
Airport 106 A3
Bournemouth International
Centre BH2 5BH 64
Bournemouth
Bournheath 158 B5
Bournmoor 212 C2
Bournville 158 C4
Bourton Bucks 148 C4
Bourton Dorset 117 E4
Bourton NSom 116 A1
Bourton Oxon 133 D3
Bourton Shrop 157 E3
Bourton Wilts 118 B1
Bourton on
Dunsmore 159 G5
Bourton-on-the-Hill 147 D4
Bourton-on-
the-Water 147 D5
Bousd 246 B3
Boustead Hill 209 F1
Bouth 199 E4
Bouthwaite 202 A5
Bovain 242 A1
Boveney 135 E5
Boveridge 105 G1
Boverton 114 C1
Bovey Tracey 102 A2
Bovingdon 135 F2
Bovingdon Green 135 D4
Bovinger 137 E2
Bovington Camp 105 E4
Bow Cumb 209 G1
Bow Devon 102 A2
Bow Devon 101 E2
Bow Ork 277 C8
Bow Brickhill 149 E4
Bow of Fife 244 B3
Bow Street Cere 154 C4
Bow Street Norf 164 B2
Bowbank 211 F5
Bowburn 212 C4
Bowcombe 107 D4
Bowd 103 E3
Bowden Devon 101 E3
Bowden ScBord 227 G2
Bowden Hill 118 A1
Bowdon 184 B4
Bower 219 F3
Bower Hinton 104 A1
Bower House Tye 152 A3
Bowerchalke 118 B5
Bowerhill 118 A1
Bowermadden 275 H2
Bowers 171 F4
Bowers Gifford 137 G4
Bowershall 243 F5
Bowertower 275 H2
Bowes 201 E1
Bowgreave 192 A4
Bowhousebog 234 C4
Bowithick 97 F1
Bowker's Green 183 F2
Bowland Bridge 199 F4
Bowley 145 E2
Bowley Town 145 E2
Bowlhead Green 121 E4
Bowling WDun 233 F2
Bowling WYorks 194 A4
Bowling Bank 170 A3
Bowlish 116 D3
Bowmanstead 199 E3
Bowmore 230 B3
Bowness-on-
Solway 218 A5
Bowness-on-
Windermere 199 F3
Bowood House &
Gardens Wilts
SN11 0LZ 118 A1
Bowscale 209 G3
Bowsden 237 G5
Bowside Lodge 274 D2
Bowston 199 F3
Bowthorpe 178 C5
Bowtrees 234 D1
Box Glos 132 A2
Box Wilts 117 F1
Box End 149 F3
Boxbush Glos 131 G1
Boxbush Glos 145 G5
Boxford Suff 152 A3
Boxford WBerks 133 G5
Boxgrove 108 B3
Boxley 123 G3
Boxmoor 135 F2
Box's Shop 112 C5
Boxted Essex 152 A4
Boxted Suff 151 G2
Boxted Cross 152 A4
Boxwell 132 A3
Boxworth 150 B1
Boxworth End 150 B1
Boyden Gate 125 E2
Boydston 224 C2
Boylestone 172 C4
Boyndie 268 E4
Boynton 196 D1
Boys Hill 104 C2
Boysack 253 E5
Boyton Corn 98 D1
Boyton Suff 153 E3
Boyton Wilts 118 A4
Boyton Cross 137 F2
Boyton End 151 F3
Bozeat 149 E2
Braaid 190 B4
Braal Castle 275 G2
Brabling Green 153 D1
Brabourne 124 C4
Brabourne Lees 124 C4
Brabster 275 J2
Bracadale 255 J1
Braceborough 161 F1
Bracebridge Heath 175 E1
Braceby 175 F4
Bracewell 193 E3
Brackenber 200 C1
Brackenbottom 200 D5

Brackenfield 173 E2
Brackens 269 F5
Bracklach 260 B2
Bracklamore 269 G5
Bracklesham 108 A4
Brackletter (A' Bhreac-
Leitir) 249 D1
Brackley A&B 231 G1
Brackley High 267 F6
Brackley N'hants 148 A4
Brackley Gate 173 E3
Brackley Hatch 148 B3
Bracknell 121 C1
Braco 242 D4
Bracobrae 268 D5
Bracon Ash 164 C2
Bracora 256 D5
Bracorina 256 D5
Bradbourne 172 D2
Bradbury 212 C5
Bradda 190 A4
Braddock 97 F3
Bradenham Bucks 134 D3
Bradenham Norf 178 A5
Bradenstoke 132 C5
Bradfield Devon 103 D2
Bradfield Essex 152 C4
Bradfield Norf 179 D2
Bradfield WBerks 134 B5
Bradfield Combust 151 G2
Bradfield Green 171 D2
Bradfield Heath 152 C5
Bradfield St. Clare 152 A2
Bradfield St. George 152 A1
Bradfield Southend
(Southend) 134 A5
Bradford Corn 97 F2
Bradford Derbys 172 D1
Bradford Devon 113 F4
Bradford N'umb 220 C4
Bradford N'umb 229 F3
Bradford WYorks 194 A4
Bradford Abbas 104 B1
Bradford Cathedral
Church of St. Peter
WYorks BD1 4EH
65 Bradford
Bradford Leigh 117 F1
Bradford Peverell 104 C3
Bradford-on-Avon 117 F1
Bradford-on-Tone 115 E5
Bradgate Park Leics
LE6 0HE 17 B3
Bradiford 113 F2
Brading 107 F4
Bradley ChesW&C 183 G5
Bradley Derbys 172 D3
Bradley Hants 120 B3
Bradley NELincs 188 C2
Bradley (Low Bradley)
NYorks 193 G3
Bradley Staffs 158 A1
Bradley WMid 158 B3
Bradley Fold 184 B2
Bradley Green
Warks 159 E2
Bradley Green
Worcs 146 B1
Bradley in the
Moors 172 B3
Bradley Mills 185 F1
Bradley Stoke 131 F4
Bradmore Notts 173 G4
Bradmore WMid 158 A3
Bradney 116 A4
Bradninch 102 D2
Bradnop 172 B2
Bradnor Green 144 B3
Bradpole 104 A3
Bradshaw GtMan 184 B1
Bradshaw WYorks 193 G4
Bradstone 99 D2
Bradwall Green 171 E1
Bradwell Derbys 185 F4
Bradwell Devon 113 E1
Bradwell Essex 151 G5
Bradwell MK 148 D4
Bradwell Norf 179 G5
Bradwell Grove 133 D2
Bradwell Waterside 138 C2
Bradwell-on-Sea 138 D2
Bradworthy 112 D4
Brae D&G 216 C2
Brae High 266 B1
Brae Shet 279 C6
Brae of Achnahaird 272 C7
Braeantra 266 C4
Braedownie 252 A2
Braefoot 269 F6
Braegrum 243 F2
Braehead D&G 215 F5
Braehead Moray 268 B6
Braehead Ork 277 F7
Braehead Ork 276 D3
Braehead SLan 225 G2
Braehead SLan 235 D4
Braehead of Lunan 253 E4
Braehoulland 278 B5
Braeleny 242 B3
Braemar 259 J5
Braemore High 266 C1
Braemore High 275 F5
Braemore High 265 H4
Braenaloin 259 K5
Braes of Enzie 268 B5
Braes of Foss 250 C4
Braes of Ullapool
(Bruthaichean Ullapuil)
265 H2
Braeswick 276 F4
Braeval 242 A4
Braewick 279 C7
Brafferton Darl 212 B5
Brafferton NYorks 202 D5
Brafield-on-the-
Green 148 D2
Bragar 270 E3
Bragbury End 150 A5
Bragenham 149 E5
Bragleenbeg 240 B2

Braichmelyn 167 F1
Braides 192 A2
Braidley 201 F4
Braidwood 234 C5
Braigo 230 A3
Brailsford 173 D3
Brain's Green 131 F2
Braintree 151 F5
Braiseworth 164 C4
Braishfield 119 E5
Braithwaite Cumb 209 F4
Braithwaite SYorks 186 D1
Braithwaite
WYorks 193 G3
Braithwell 186 C3
Bramber 109 D2
Brambletye 122 D5
Brambridge 119 E5
Bramcote Notts 173 G4
Bramcote Warks 159 G4
Bramdean 120 B5
Bramerton 179 D5
Bramfield Herts 136 B1
Bramfield Suff 165 E4
Bramford 152 C3
Bramhall 184 C4
Bramham 194 D3
Bramhope 194 B3
Bramley Hants 120 B2
Bramley Surr 121 F3
Bramley SYorks 186 B3
Bramley Corner 120 B2
Bramley Head 194 A2
Bramley Vale 173 F1
Bramling 125 E3
Brampford Speke 102 C3
Brampton Cambs 162 A5
Brampton Cumb 210 B3
Brampton Cumb 210 C5
Brampton Derbys 186 A5
Brampton Lincs 187 F5
Brampton Norf 178 D3
Brampton Suff 165 F3
Brampton Abbotts 145 F5
Brampton Ash 160 C4
Brampton Bryan 156 C4
Brampton en le
Morthen 186 B4
Brampton Street 165 F3
Brampton Valley Way
Country Park N'hants
NN6 9DG 160 C5
Bramshall 172 B4
Bramshaw 106 B1
Bramshill 120 C1
Bramshott 120 D4
Bramwell 116 B5
Bran End 151 E5
Branault 247 E3
Brancaster 177 F3
Brancaster Staithe 177 F3
Brancepeth 212 B4
Branchill 267 H6
Brand Green 145 G5
Brandelhow 209 F4
Branderburgh 267 K4
Brandesburton 196 D3
Brandeston 152 D1
Brandis Corner 113 E5
Brandiston 178 C3
Brandlingill 209 E4
Brandon Dur 212 B4
Brandon Lincs 175 E3
Brandon N'umb 229 E5
Brandon Suff 163 F4
Brandon Warks 159 G5
Brandon Bank 163 E4
Brandon Creek 163 E3
Brandon Park Suff
IP27 0SU 163 F4
Brandon Parva 178 B5
Brandon to Bishop
Auckland Walk Dur
DH7 7RJ 212 B4
Brandsby 203 E5
Brandy Wharf 188 A3
Brane 94 B4
Branksome 105 G3
Branksome Park 105 G3
Bransbury 119 F3
Bransby 187 F5
Branscombe 103 E4
Bransford 145 G2
Bransford Bridge 146 A2
Bransgore 106 A3
Bransholme 196 D4
Branson's Cross 158 C5
Branston Leics 174 D5
Branston Lincs 175 F1
Branston Staffs 172 D5
Branston Booths 175 F1
Branston Water Park Staffs
DE14 3EZ 172 D5
Brant Broughton 175 E2
Brantham 152 C4
Branthwaite Cumb 209 F3
Branthwaite Cumb 209 E4
Brantingham 196 B5
Branton N'umb 229 E5
Branton SYorks 186 D2
Brantwood 199 E3
Branxholm
Bridgend 227 F4
Branxholme 227 F4
Branxton 228 C3
Brassey Green 170 C1
Brassington 172 D2
Brasted 123 D3
Brasted Chart 123 D3
Brathens 260 E5
Bratoft 176 C1
Bratton Som 114 C3
Bratton Tel&W 157 F1
Bratton Wilts 118 A2
Bratton Clovelly 99 E2
Bratton Fleming 113 G2
Bratton Seymour 117 D5
Braughing 150 B5
Braunston N
hants 148 A1

Braunston Rut 160 D2
Braunstone 160 A2
Braunton 113 E2
Brawby 203 G5
Brawdy 140 B5
Brawith 203 E2
Brawl 274 D2
Brawlbin 275 F3
Bray 135 E5
Bray Shop 98 D3
Bray Wick 135 D5
Braybrooke 160 C4
Braydon Side 132 C4
Brayford 113 G2
Brayshaw 193 D2
Braythorn 194 B3
Brayton 195 F4
Braywoodside 135 D5
Brazacott 98 C1
Brea 96 A5
Breach Kent 125 D4
Breach Kent 124 A2
Breachwood Green 149 G5
Breacleit 270 D4
Breaden Heath 170 B4
Breadsall 173 E4
Breadstone 131 G2
Breage 96 A4
Breakon 278 E2
Breamore 106 A1
Brean 115 F2
Breanais 270 B5
Brearton 194 C1
Breascleit 270 E4
Breaston 173 F4
Brechfa 142 B4
Brechin 253 E3
Breckles 164 A2
Brecon
(Aberhonddu) 143 G5
Brecon Beacons Visitor
Centre Powys
LD3 8ER 143 F5
Breconside 225 G5
Bredbury 184 D3
Brede 110 D2
Bredenbury 145 F2
Bredfield 153 D2
Bredgar 124 A2
Bredhurst 123 G2
Bredon 146 B4
Bredon's Hardwick 146 B4
Bredon's Norton 146 B4
Bredwardine 144 C3
Breedon on the Hill 173 F5
Breibhig 271 G2
Breich 235 D3
Breightmet 184 B2
Breighton 195 G4
Breinton 145 D4
Breinton Common 145 D4
Bremhill 132 B5
Bremhill Wick 132 B5
Brenachoille 240 C4
Brenchley 123 F4
Brendon Devon 114 A3
Brendon Devon 113 E5
Brendon Devon 113 D5
Brenkley 221 E4
Brent Eleigh 152 A3
Brent Knoll 116 A2
Brent Pelham 150 C4
Brentford 136 A5
Brentingby 160 C1
Brentwood 137 E3
Brenzett 111 F1
Brenzett Green 111 F1
Breoch 216 B5
Brereton 158 C1
Brereton Green 171 E1
Brereton Heath 171 F1
Breretonhill 158 C1
Bressay 279 E8
Bressingham 164 B3
Bressingham
Common 164 B3
Bressingham Steam
Museum & Gardens
Norf IP22 2AA 164 B3
Bretby 173 D5
Bretford 159 G5
Bretforton 146 C3
Bretherdale Head 199 G2
Bretherton 192 A5
Brettabister 279 D7
Brettenham Norf 164 A3
Brettenham Suff 152 A2
Bretton Derbys 185 F5
Bretton Flints 170 A1
Bretton Peter 161 G2
Brevig 254 B5
Brewood 158 A2
Briach 267 H6
Briantspuddle 105 E3
Brick End 151 D5
Brickendon 136 C2
Bricket Wood 136 A2
Brickkiln Green 151 F4
Bricklehampton 146 B3
Bride 190 C1
Brideswell 260 D1
Bridestowe 99 F2
Bridfordt 102 B4
Bridge Cumb 198 D4
Bridge Kent 125 D3
Bridge End Devon 100 D3
Bridge End Essex 151 E4
Bridge End Lincs 175 G4
Bridge End Shet 279 C9
Bridge Hewick 202 C5
Bridge o'Ess 260 D5
Bridge of Alford 260 D3
Bridge of Allan 242 C5
Bridge of Avon 259 J1

Bridge of Awe
(Drochaid Abha) 240 C1
Bridge of Balgie 250 A5
Bridge of
Bogendreip 260 E5
Bridge of
Brewlands 251 G3
Bridge of Brown 259 J2
Bridge of Cally 251 G4
Bridge of Canny 260 E5
Bridge of Craigisla 252 A4
Bridge of Dee Aber 259 J5
Bridge of Dee Aber 260 D5
Bridge of Dee D&G 216 B4
Bridge of Don 261 H4
Bridge of Dun 253 E4
Bridge of Dye 253 E1
Bridge of Earn 243 G3
Bridge of Ericht 250 A4
Bridge of Feugh 260 E5
Bridge of Forss 275 F2
Bridge of Gairn 260 B5
Bridge of Gaur 250 A4
Bridge of Muchalls 261 G5
Bridge of Muick 260 B5
Bridge of Orchy (Drochaid
Urchaidh) 241 E1
Bridge of Tynet 268 B4
Bridge of Walls 279 B7
Bridge of Weir 233 F3
Bridge Reeve 113 G4
Bridge Sollers 144 D3
Bridge Street 151 G3
Bridge Trafford 183 F5
Bridgefoot Angus 244 B1
Bridgefoot Cambs 150 C3
Bridgefoot Cumb 209 D4
Bridgehampton 116 C5
Bridgehaugh 260 B1
Bridgehill 211 G2
Bridgemary 107 E2
Bridgemere 171 E3
Bridgend A&B 230 B3
Bridgend A&B 240 A5
Bridgend Aber 260 D1
Bridgend Aber 260 D1
Bridgend Angus 252 D3
Bridgend (Pen-y-bont ar
Ogwr) Bridgend 129 F5
Bridgend Corn 97 F4
Bridgend Cumb 199 F1
Bridgend Fife 244 B3
Bridgend Moray 260 B1
Bridgend P&K 243 G2
Bridgend WLoth 235 E2
Bridgend of
Lintrathen 252 A4
Bridgerule 112 C5
Bridges 156 C3
Bridgeton Aber 260 D3
Bridgeton Glas 234 A3
Bridgetown Corn 98 D2
Bridgetown Som 114 C4
Bridgewater Hall,
Manchester GtMan
M2 3WS 46 B4
Bridgeyate 131 F5
Bridgham 164 A3
Bridgnorth 157 G3
Bridgnorth Cliff
Railway Shrop
WV16 4AH 157 G3
Bridgtown 158 B2
Bridgwater 115 F4
Bridlington 197 D1
Bridport 104 A3
Bridstow 145 E5
Brierfield 193 E4
Brierley Glos 131 F1
Brierley Here 145 D2
Brierley SYorks 186 B1
Brierley Hill 158 B4
Brierton 213 D5
Briestfield 185 G1
Brig o'Turk 242 A4
Brigg 188 A2
Briggate 179 E3
Briggswath 204 B2
Brigham Cumb 209 D3
Brigham ERid 196 C2
Brighouse 194 A5
Brighstone 106 C4
Brightgate 173 D2
Brighthampton 133 F2
Brightholmlee 185 G3
Brightling 110 B1
Brightlingsea 139 D1
Brighton B&H 109 F3
Brighton Corn 96 D4
Brighton Centre, The
B&H BN1 2GR
65 Brighton
Brighton Museum &
Art Gallery B&H
BN1 1EE 65 Brighton
Brighton Pier B&H
BN2 1TW 65 Brighton
Brightons 234 D2
Brightwalton 133 G5
Brightwalton Green 133 G5
Brightwell 152 D3
Brightwell Baldwin 134 B3
Brightwell
Upperton 134 B3
Brightwell-cum-
Sotwell 134 A3
Brignall 201 F1
Brigsley 188 C2
Brigsteer 199 F4
Brigstock 161 E4
Brill Bucks 134 B1
Brill Corn 95 E4
Brilley 144 B3
Brilley Mountain 144 B2
Brimaston 140 C5
Brimfield 145 E1
Brimington 186 B5
Brimington
Common 186 B5
Brimley 102 A5
Brimpsfield 132 B1
Brimpton 119 G1

Brims 277 B9
Brimscombe 132 A2
Brimstage 183 E4
Brinacora 256 D5
Brindham 116 C3
Brindister *Shet* 279 D9
Brindister *Shet* 279 B7
Brindle 192 B5
Brindley Ford 171 F2
Brineton 158 A1
Bringhurst 160 D3
Brington 161 F5
Brinian 276 D5
Briningham 178 B2
Brinkhill 189 D5
Brinkley *Cambs* 151 E2
Brinkley *Notts* 174 C2
Brinklow 159 E5
Brinkworth 132 C4
Brinmore 258 D2
Brinscall 192 C5
Brinsea 116 B1
Brinsley 173 F3
Brinsop 144 B3
Brinsworth 186 B3
Brinton 178 B2
Brisco 210 A2
Brisley 178 A3
Brislington 131 F5
Brissenden Green 124 B5
Bristol 131 E5
Bristol Cathedral
  BS1 5TJ 66 Bristol
Bristol City Museum &
  Art Gallery *Bristol*
  BS8 1RL 8 B3
Bristol Filton
  Airport 131 E4
Bristol International
  Airport 116 C1
Bristol Zoo *Bristol*
  BS8 3HA 8 B3
Briston 178 B2
Britain At War Experience
  GtLon SE1 2TF 12 C4
Britannia 193 E5
Britford 118 C5
Brithdir *Caerp* 130 A2
Brithdir *Gwyn* 155 D1
Brithem Bottom 102 D1
British Empire &
  Commonwealth Museum
  BS1 6QH 66 Bristol
British Library
  (St. Pancras) *GtLon*
  NW1 2DB 12 B4
British Museum *GtLon*
  WC1B 3DG 44 E2
Briton Ferry
  (Llansawel) 129 D3
Britwell 135 E4
Britwell Salome 134 B3
Brixham 101 E2
Brixton *Devon* 100 B2
Brixton *GtLon* 136 C5
Brixton Deverill 117 F4
Brixworth 160 C5
Brixworth Country Park
  N'hants
  NN6 9DG 160 C5
Brize Norton 133 E2
Broad Alley 146 A1
Broad Blunsdon 133 D3
Broad Campden 147 D4
Broad Carr 185 E1
Broad Chalke 118 B5
Broad Ford 123 G5
Broad Green
  Cambs 151 E2
Broad Green
  CenBeds 149 E3
Broad Green *Essex* 151 G5
Broad Green *Essex* 150 C4
Broad Green
  Mersey 183 F3
Broad Green *Suff* 152 B2
Broad Green *Worcs* 145 G2
Broad Haven 126 B1
Broad Hill 163 D5
Broad Hinton 132 D5
Broad Laying 119 F1
Broad Marston 146 D3
Broad Oak *Carmar* 142 B5
Broad Oak *Cumb* 198 C3
Broad Oak *ESuss* 110 A3
Broad Oak *ESuss* 110 B1
Broad Oak *Here* 145 D5
Broad Road 165 D4
Broad Street *ESuss* 111 D2
Broad Street *Kent* 124 A3
Broad Street *Kent* 124 D5
Broad Street *Wilts* 118 C4
Broad Street Green 138 B2
Broad Town 132 C5
Broadbottom 185 D3
Broadbridge 108 A3
Broadbridge Heath 121 G4
Broadclyst 102 C3
Broadfield *Lancs* 192 D5
Broadfield *Lancs* 192 B5
Broadford (An t-Ath
  Leathann) 256 C2
Broadford Airport 256 C2
Broadford Bridge 121 F5
Broadgate 198 C4
Broadhaugh 227 F5
Broadhaven 275 J3
Broadheath *GtMan* 184 B4
Broadheath *Worcs* 145 F1
Broadhembury 103 E2
Broadhempston 101 E1
Broadholme 187 F5
Broadland Row 110 D2
Broadlay 127 G2
Broadley *Lancs* 184 C1
Broadley *Moray* 268 B4
Broadley Common 136 D2
Broadmayne 104 D4
Broadmeadows 227 F2
Broadmere 120 B3
Broadmoor 127 D2
Broadnymett 102 A2

Broadoak *Dorset* 104 A3
Broadoak *Glos* 131 F1
Broadoak *Kent* 125 D2
Broadoak End 136 C1
Broadrashes 268 C5
Broad's Green 137 F2
Broadsea 269 H4
Broadstairs 125 F2
Broadstone *Poole* 105 G3
Broadstone *Shrop* 157 E4
Broadstreet
  Common 130 C4
Broadwas 145 G2
Broadwater *Herts* 150 A5
Broadwater *WSuss* 108 D3
Broadwater Down 123 E5
Broadwaters 158 A5
Broadway *Carmar* 127 G2
Broadway *Carmar* 127 F1
Broadway *Pembs* 126 B1
Broadway *Som* 103 G1
Broadway *Suff* 165 E4
Broadwell *Glos* 147 E5
Broadwell *Oxon* 133 E2
Broadwell *Warks* 147 G1
Broadwell House 211 F2
Broadwey 104 C4
Broadwindsor 104 A2
Broadwood Kelly 113 G5
Broadwoodwidger 99 E2
Brobury 144 C3
Brocastle 129 F5
Brochel 264 B7
Brochloch 215 G1
Brock 246 B2
Brockamin 145 G2
Brockbridge 107 F1
Brockdish 164 D4
Brockenhurst 106 B2
Brockford Green 152 C1
Brockford Street 152 C1
Brockhall 148 B1
Brockham 121 G3
Brockhampton
  Glos 146 C5
Brockhampton
  Glos 146 B5
Brockhampton
  Here 145 E4
Brockhampton
  Here 145 F2
Brockhampton
  Green 104 D2
Brockholes 185 F1
Brockhurst *Hants* 107 E2
Brockhurst *WSuss* 122 D5
Brocklebank 210 C2
Brockley *NSom* 116 B1
Brockley *Suff* 151 G2
Brockley Green 151 F3
Brock's Green 119 F1
Brockton *Shrop* 157 E3
Brockton *Shrop* 157 G2
Brockton *Shrop* 156 C3
Brockton *Shrop* 156 C5
Brockton *Tel&W* 157 G1
Brockweir 131 E2
Brockwood Park 120 B5
Brockworth 132 A1
Brocton 158 B1
Brodick 223 F2
Brodsworth 186 C2
Brogborough 149 E4
Brogden 193 E3
Brogyntyn 169 F4
Broken Cross
  ChesE 184 C5
Broken Cross
  ChesW&C 184 A5
Brokenborough 132 B4
Brokes 202 A3
Bromborough 183 E4
Brome 164 C4
Brome Street 164 C4
Bromeswell 153 E2
Bromfield *Cumb* 209 E2
Bromfield *Shrop* 157 D5
Bromham *Bed* 149 F2
Bromham *Wilts* 118 A1
Bromley *GtLon* 136 D2
Bromley *SYorks* 186 A4
Bromley Cross 184 B1
Bromley Green 124 B5
Brompton *Med* 123 G2
Brompton *NYorks* 202 C3
Brompton *NYorks* 204 C4
Brompton *NYorks* 193 F2
Brompton *ScBord* 226 C2
Brompton *Shrop* 157 D5
Brompton on Swale 202 B3
Brompton Ralph 115 D4
Brompton Regis 114 C4
Bromsash 145 F5
Bromsberrow 145 G4
Bromsberrow
  Heath 145 G4
Bromsgrove 158 B5
Bromstead Heath 158 A1
Bromyard 145 F2
Bromyard Downs 145 F2
Bronaber 168 A4
Brondesbury 136 B4
Brongest 141 G3
Bronington 170 B4
Bronllys 144 A3
Bronnant 142 C1
Bronté Weaving Shed
  WYorks
  BD22 8EP 193 G4
Bronwydd Arms 142 A5
Bronydd 144 B3
Bron-y-gaer 127 G1
Brongarth 169 F4
Bronygarth 169 F4
Brook *Carmar* 127 F2
Brook *Hants* 106 B1
Brook *Hants* 119 E5
Brook *IoW* 106 C1
Brook *Kent* 124 C4
Brook *Surr* 121 G4
Brook *Surr* 121 F3
Brook Bottom 185 D2
Brook End *Bed* 149 F1

Brook End *Herts* 150 B5
Brook End *MK* 149 E3
Brook End *Worcs* 146 A3
Brook Hill 106 B1
Brook Street *Essex* 137 E3
Brook Street *Kent* 124 B5
Brook Street *Suff* 151 G3
Brook Street *WSuss* 109 F1
Brooke *Norf* 165 D2
Brooke *Rut* 160 D2
Brookend *Glos* 131 E3
Brookend *Glos* 131 F2
Brookfield 185 E3
Brookhampton 134 B3
Brookhouse *ChesE* 184 D5
Brookhouse *Denb* 169 D1
Brookhouse *Lancs* 192 B1
Brookhouse *SYorks* 186 C4
Brookhouse Green 171 F1
Brookhouses 171 G1
Brookland 111 E1
Brooklands *D&G* 216 C3
Brooklands *Shrop* 170 C3
Brooklands Museum *Surr*
  KT13 0QN 121 F1
Brookmans Park 136 B2
Brooks 156 A4
Brooks Green 121 G5
Brooksby 160 B1
Broom *CenBeds* 149 G3
Broom *Fife* 244 B2
Broom *Warks* 146 C2
Broom Green 178 A3
Broom Hill *Dorset* 105 G2
Broom Hill *Worcs* 158 B5
Broom of Dalreach 243 F3
Broomcroft 157 E2
Broome *Norf* 165 E2
Broome *Shrop* 156 D5
Broome *Worcs* 158 B5
Broome Wood 229 F5
Broomedge 184 B4
Broomer's Corner 121 G5
Broomfield *Aber* 261 H1
Broomfield *Essex* 137 G1
Broomfield *Kent* 125 D2
Broomfield *Kent* 124 A3
Broomfield *Som* 115 F4
Broomfleet 196 A4
Broomhall Green 170 D3
Broomhaugh 211 G1
Broomhead 269 H4
Broomhill *Bristol* 131 F5
Broomhill *N'umb* 221 E1
Broomielaw 201 F1
Broomley 211 G1
Broompark 212 B3
Broom's Green 145 G4
Brora 267 G1
Broseley 157 F2
Brotherlee 211 F4
Brothertoft 176 A3
Brotherton 195 D5
Brotton 203 F1
Broubster 275 F2
Brough *Cumb* 200 C1
Brough *Derbys* 185 F4
Brough *ERid* 196 B5
Brough *High* 275 H1
Brough *Notts* 174 D2
Brough *Ork* 277 C6
Brough *Shet* 279 E8
Brough *Shet* 278 D5
Brough *Shet* 279 E6
Brough *Shet* 278 E5
Brough Lodge 278 E3
Brough Sowerby 200 C1
Broughall 170 C3
Brougham 210 B5
Brougham Hall *Cumb*
  CA10 2DE 210 B5
Broughton *Bucks* 134 D1
Broughton *Cambs* 162 A5
Broughton *Flints* 170 A1
Broughton *Hants* 119 E4
Broughton *Lancs* 192 B4
Broughton *MK* 149 D3
Broughton *N'hants* 160 D5
Broughton *NLincs* 187 G2
Broughton *NYorks* 203 G5
Broughton *NYorks* 193 F2
Broughton *Ork* 276 D3
Broughton *Oxon* 147 G4
Broughton *ScBord* 226 C2
Broughton *VGlam* 129 F5
Broughton Astley 160 A3
Broughton Beck 199 D4
Broughton Gifford 117 F1
Broughton Green 146 B1
Broughton Hackett 146 B2
Broughton in
  Furness 198 D4
Broughton Mills 198 D3
Broughton Moor 209 D3
Broughton Poggs 133 E2
Broughtown 276 F3
Broughty Ferry 244 C1
Browland 279 B7
Brown Candover 119 G4
Brown Edge *Lancs* 183 E1
Brown Edge *Staffs* 171 G2
Brown Heath 170 B1
Brown Lees 171 F2
Brown Street 152 B1
Brownber 200 B1
Browndown 107 E3
Brownheath 170 B5
Brownhill 269 G6
Brownhills *Fife* 244 D3
Brownhills *WMid* 158 C2
Brownieside 229 F4
Brownlow 171 F1
Brownlow Heath 171 F1
Brown's Bank 170 D3
Brownsea Island *Dorset*
  BH13 7EE 105 G4
Brownshill 132 A2

Brownshill Green 159 F4
Brownsover 160 A5
Brownston 100 C2
Browston Green 179 F5
Broxa 204 C3
Broxbourne 136 C2
Broxburn *ELoth* 237 D2
Broxburn *WLoth* 235 E2
Broxholme 187 G5
Broxted 151 D5
Broxton 170 B2
Broxwood 144 C2
Broyle Side 109 G2
Bruachmary 267 F7
Bruan 275 J5
Brue (Brù) 271 F3
Bruera 170 B1
Bruern 147 E5
Bruernish 254 C4
Bruichladdich 230 A3
Bruisyard 153 E1
Bruisyard Street 153 E1
Brumby 187 G1
Brund 172 C1
Brundall 179 E5
Brundish *Norf* 165 E2
Brundish *Suff* 153 D1
Brundish Street 165 D4
Brunswick Village 221 E4
Bruntingthorpe 160 B3
Bruntland 260 C2
Brunton *Fife* 244 B2
Brunton *N'umb* 229 F4
Brunton *Wilts* 118 D2
Brushfield 185 F5
Brushford *Devon* 113 G5
Brushford *Som* 114 C5
Bruton 117 D4
Bryanston 105 E2
Bryant's Bottom 135 D3
Brydekirk 217 F3
Brymbo 169 F2
Brymor Ice Cream *NYorks*
  HG4 4PG 202 A4
Brympton 104 B1
Bryn *Caerp* 130 A3
Bryn *Carmar* 128 B2
Bryn *ChesW&C* 184 A5
Bryn *GtMan* 183 G2
Bryn *NPT* 129 E3
Bryn *Shrop* 156 B4
Bryn Bach Country
  Park *BGwent*
  NP22 3AY 130 A2
Bryn Bwbach 167 F4
Bryn Gates 183 G2
Bryn Pen-y-lan 170 A3
Brynamman 128 D1
Brynberian 141 E4
Bryncae 129 F4
Bryncethin 129 F4
Bryncir 167 D3
Bryncoch *Bridgend* 129 F4
Bryn-côch *NPT* 128 D3
Bryncroes 166 B4
Bryncrug 154 C2
Bryneglwys 169 E3
Brynford 182 C5
Bryngwran 180 B5
Bryngwyn *Mon* 130 C2
Bryngwyn *Powys* 144 A3
Bryn-henllan 140 D4
Brynhoffnant 141 G2
Bryning 192 A4
Brynithel 130 B2
Brynmawr *BGwent* 130 A1
Bryn-mawr *Gwyn* 166 B4
Brynmelyn 156 A5
Brynmenyn 129 F4
Brynna 129 F4
Brynnau Gwynion 129 F4
Brynog 142 B2
Bryn-penarth 156 A2
Brynrefail *Gwyn* 167 E1
Brynrefail *IoA* 180 C4
Brynsadler 129 G4
Brynsaithmarchog 169 D2
Brynsiencyn 167 D1
Bryn-teg *IoA* 180 C4
Brynteg *Wrex* 170 A2
Bryn-y-cochin 170 A4
Brynygwenin 130 C1
Bryn-y-maen 181 G5
Buaile nam Bodach 254 C4
Bualadubh 262 C7
Bualintur 255 K2
Bualnaluib 264 E2
Bubbenhall 159 F5
Bubnell 185 G5
Bubwith 195 G4
Buccleuch 227 E4
Buchan 216 B4
Buchanan Castle 233 F1
Buchanhaven 269 K6
Buchanty 243 E2
Buchlyvie 242 A5
Buckabank 209 G2
Buckby Wharf 148 B1
Buckden *Cambs* 149 G1
Buckden *NYorks* 201 E5
Buckenham 179 E5
Buckerell 103 E2
Buckfast 100 D1
Buckfast Abbey *Devon*
  TQ11 0EE 100 D1
Buckfastleigh 100 D1
Buckhaven 244 B5
Buckholm 227 F2
Buckholt 131 E1
Buckhorn Weston 117 E5
Buckhurst Hill 136 D3
Buckie 268 C4
Buckies 275 G2
Buckingham 148 B4
Buckingham Palace *GtLon*
  SW1A 1AA 44 B6
Buckland *Bucks* 135 D1
Buckland *Devon* 100 C3
Buckland *Glos* 146 C4
Buckland *Hants* 106 C3
Buckland *Here* 145 E2

Buckland *Herts* 150 B4
Buckland *Kent* 125 F4
Buckland *Oxon* 133 F3
Buckland *Surr* 122 B3
Buckland Brewer 113 E3
Buckland Common 135 E2
Buckland Dinham 117 E2
Buckland Filleigh 113 E5
Buckland in the
  Moor 102 A5
Buckland
  Monachorum 100 A1
Buckland Newton 104 C2
Buckland Ripers 104 C4
Buckland St. Mary 103 F1
Buckland-tout-
  Saints 101 D3
Bucklebury 134 A5
Bucklerheads 244 C1
Bucklers Hard 106 D3
Bucklesham 152 D3
Buckley (Bwcle) 169 F1
Buckley Green 147 D1
Bucklow Hill 184 B4
Buckman Corner 121 G5
Buckminster 175 D5
Bucknall *Lincs* 188 C5
Bucknall *Stoke* 171 G3
Bucknell *Oxon* 148 A5
Bucknell *Shrop* 156 C5
Buckridge 157 G5
Buck's Cross 112 D3
Bucks Green 121 F4
Bucks Hill 135 F2
Bucks Horn Oak 120 D3
Buck's Mills 113 D3
Bucksburn 261 G4
Buckspool 126 C3
Buckton *ERid* 205 E5
Buckton *Here* 156 C5
Buckton *N'umb* 229 F3
Buckton Vale 185 D2
Buckworth 161 G5
Budbrooke 147 E1
Budby 186 D5
Buddon 244 D1
Bude 112 C5
Budge's Shop 98 D5
Budlake 102 C2
Budle 229 F3
Budleigh Salterton 103 D4
Budock Water 95 E3
Budworth Heath 184 A5
Buerton 171 D3
Bugbrooke 148 B2
Buglawton 171 F1
Bugle 97 E4
Bugthorpe 195 G2
Building End 150 C4
Buildwas 157 F2
Builth Road 143 G2
Builth Wells (Llanfair-
  ym-Muallt) 143 G2
Bulby 175 G1
Bulcote 174 B3
Buldoo 274 E2
Bulford 118 C3
Bulford Camp 118 C3
Bulkeley 170 C2
Bulkington *Warks* 159 F4
Bulkington *Wilts* 118 A2
Bulkworthy 113 D4
Bull Bay
  (Porth Llechog) 180 C3
Bull Green 124 B5
Bullbridge 173 E2
Bullbrook 121 D1
Bullen's Green 136 B2
Bulley 131 G1
Bullington 188 A5
Bullpot Farm 200 B4
Bulls Cross 136 C3
Bull's Green *Herts* 136 B1
Bull's Green *Norf* 165 F2
Bullwood 232 C2
Bulmer *Essex* 151 G3
Bulmer *NYorks* 195 F1
Bulmer Tye 151 G4
Bulphan 137 E4
Bulstone 103 E4
Bulverhythe 110 C3
Bulwark 269 H6
Bulwell 173 G3
Bulwick 161 E3
Bumble's Green 136 D2
Bun Abhainn
  Eadarra 270 D7
Bun's Green 150 B5
Bun Abhainn
  Eadarra 270 D7
Bun Loyne 257 J4
Bunarkaig 249 D1
Bunbury 170 C2
Bunbury Heath 170 C2
Bunchrew 266 D7
Bundalloch 256 E2
Buness 278 F2
Bunessan 238 C2
Bungay 165 E3
Bunker's Hill 176 A2
Bunlarie 222 C2
Bunloit
  (Bun Leothaid) 258 C2
Bunmhullin 254 C3
Bunnahabhain 230 C2
Bunny 173 G5
Buntait 257 K1
Buntingford 150 B5
Bunwell 164 C2
Bunwell Street 164 C2
Burbage *Derbys* 185 E5
Burbage *Leics* 159 G3
Burbage *Wilts* 118 D1
Burbage Common *Leics*
  LE10 3DD 159 G3
Burchett's Green 134 D4
Burcombe 118 B4
Burcot *Oxon* 134 A3
Burcot *Worcs* 158 B5
Burcott 149 D5
Burdale 196 A1
Burdocks 121 F5
Burdon 212 C2
Burdrop 147 F4

Buckland *Herts* 150 B4
Bures 152 A4
Bures Green 152 A4
Burfa 144 B1
Burford *Oxon* 133 E1
Burford *Shrop* 145 E1
Burg 246 C5
Burgate 164 B4
Burgates 120 C5
Burge End 149 G4
Burgess Hill 109 F2
Burgh 152 D2
Burgh by Sands 209 G1
Burgh Castle 179 F5
Burgh Heath 122 B3
Burgh le Marsh 176 C1
Burgh next
  Aylsham 178 D3
Burgh on Bain 188 C4
Burgh St. Margaret
  (Fleggburgh) 179 F4
Burgh St. Peter 165 F2
Burghclere 119 F1
Burghead 267 J5
Burghfield
  Common 120 B1
Burghfield 120 B1
Burghfield Hill 120 B1
Burghill 144 B2
Burghwallis 186 C1
Burham 123 G2
Buriton 120 C5
Burland 170 D2
Burlawn 97 D3
Burleigh 121 E1
Burlescombe 103 D1
Burleston 105 D3
Burley *Hants* 106 B2
Burley *Rut* 161 D2
Burley Gate 145 E3
Burley in
  Wharfedale 194 A3
Burley Street 106 B2
Burley Woodhead 194 A3
Burleydam 170 D2
Burlingjobb 144 B2
Burlow 110 A2
Burlton 170 B5
Burmarsh 124 D5
Burmington 147 E4
Burn 195 E5
Burn Farm 253 E2
Burn Naze 191 G3
Burn of Cambus 242 C4
Burnage 184 C3
Burnaston 173 D4
Burnby 196 A3
Burncross 186 A3
Burndell 108 B3
Burnden 184 B2
Burnedge 184 D1
Burnend 269 G6
Burneside 199 G3
Burness 276 F3
Burneston 202 C4
Burnett 117 D1
Burnfoot *P&K* 243 E4
Burnfoot *ScBord* 227 G4
Burnfoot *ScBord* 227 G4
Burnham *Bucks* 135 E4
Burnham Deepdale 177 G3
Burnham Green 136 B1
Burnham Market 177 G3
Burnham Norton 177 G3
Burnham Overy
  Staithe 177 G3
Burnham Overy
  Town 177 G3
Burnham Thorpe 177 G3
Burnham-on-
  Crouch 138 C2
Burnham-on-Sea 116 A3
Burnhaven 269 K6
Burnhead *D&G* 215 G3
Burnhead *D&G* 216 C1
Burnhervie 261 F3
Burnhill Green 157 G2
Burnhope 212 A3
Burnhouse 233 E4
Burniston 204 D3
Burnley 193 E4
Burnmouth 237 G3
Burnopfield 212 A2
Burn's Green 150 B5
Burns National Heritage
  Park *SAyr*
  KA7 4PQ 224 B4
Burnsall 193 G1
Burnside *Aber* 261 F3
Burnside *EAyr* 225 D4
Burnside *Fife* 243 G4
Burnside *Shet* 278 B5
Burnside *WLoth* 235 E2
Burnside of
  Duntrune 244 C1
Burnstones 210 C2
Burnswark 217 F3
Burnt Hill 134 A5
Burnt Houses 212 A5
Burnt Oak 136 B3
Burnt Yates 194 B1
Burntcliff Top 171 G1
Burntisland 235 G1
Burnton *EAyr* 224 C4
Burnton *EAyr* 224 C5
Burntwood 158 C2
Burntwood Green 158 C2
Burnworthy 103 E1
Burpham *Surr* 121 F2
Burpham *WSuss* 108 C3
Burra 279 C9
Burradon *N'umb* 220 B1
Burradon *T&W* 221 E4
Burrafirth 278 F1
Burraland 278 C5
Burras 95 D3
Burraton *Corn* 100 A1
Burraton *Corn* 100 A1
Burravoe *Shet* 278 E5

Burravoe *Shet* 279 C6
Burray 277 D8
Burrells 200 B1
Burrell Collection
  Glas G43 1AT 30 C4
Burrelton 244 A1
Burridge *Devon* 103 G2
Burridge *Hants* 107 E1
Burrill 202 B4
Burringham 187 F2
Burrington *Devon* 113 G4
Burrington *Here* 156 D5
Burrington *NSom* 116 B2
Burrough Green 151 E2
Burrough on the
  Hill 160 C1
Burrow *Som* 114 C3
Burrow *Som* 104 A1
Burrow Bridge 116 A4
Burrowhill 121 E3
Burrows Cross 121 F3
Burry 128 A3
Burry Green 128 A3
Burry Port 128 A2
Burscough 183 F1
Burscough Bridge 183 F1
Bursea 196 A4
Burshill 196 C3
Bursledon 107 D2
Burslem 171 F3
Burstall 152 C3
Burstock 104 A2
Burston *Norf* 164 C3
Burston *Staffs* 171 G4
Burstow 122 C4
Burstwick 197 E5
Burtersett 201 D4
Burthorpe 151 F1
Burthwaite 210 A3
Burtle 116 B3
Burtle Hill 116 A3
Burton *ChesW&C* 183 E5
Burton *ChesW&C* 170 C2
Burton *Dorset* 106 A3
Burton *Lincs* 187 G5
Burton *N'umb* 229 F3
Burton *Pembs* 126 C2
Burton *Som* 115 E3
Burton *Wilts* 132 A5
Burton *Wilts* 117 F4
Burton Agnes 196 D1
Burton Bradstock 104 A4
Burton Coggles 175 E5
Burton End 150 D5
Burton Ferry 126 C2
Burton Fleming 205 D5
Burton Green
  Warks 159 E5
Burton Green *Wrex* 170 A2
Burton Hastings 159 G4
Burton in Lonsdale 200 B5
Burton Joyce 174 B3
Burton Latimer 161 E5
Burton Lazars 160 C1
Burton Leonard 194 C1
Burton on the
  Wolds 173 G5
Burton Overy 160 B3
Burton Pedwardine 175 G3
Burton Pidsea 197 E4
Burton Salmon 195 D5
Burton Stather 187 F1
Burton upon
  Stather 187 F1
Burton upon Trent 172 D5
Burton-in-Kendal 199 G5
Burton's Green 151 G5
Burtonwood 183 G3
Burwardsley 170 C2
Burwarton 157 F4
Burwash 110 B1
Burwash Common 110 B1
Burwash Weald 110 B1
Burwell *Cambs* 151 D1
Burwell *Lincs* 189 D5
Burwen 180 C3
Burwick *Ork* 277 D9
Burwick *Shet* 279 C8
Bury *Cambs* 162 A4
Bury *GtMan* 184 C1
Bury *Som* 114 C5
Bury *WSuss* 108 C2
Bury End 146 C4
Bury Green 150 C5
Bury St. Edmunds 151 G1
Buryas Bridge 94 B4
Burythorpe 195 G1
Busbridge 121 E3
Busby *ERenf* 233 G4
Busby *P&K* 243 G1
Buscot 133 E3
Bush 112 C5
Bush Bank 145 D2
Bush Crathie 259 K5
Bush Green 164 D3
Bushbury 158 B2
Bushby 160 B2
Bushey 136 A3
Bushey Heath 136 A3
Bushley 146 A4
Bushley Green 146 A4
Bushton 132 C5
Bushy Common 178 A4
Business Design Centre,
  Islington *GtLon*
  N1 0QH 12 B3
Busk 210 C3
Buslingthorpe 188 A4
Bussage 132 A2
Busta 279 C6
Butcher's Common 179 E3
Butcher's Cross 110 A1
Butcher's Pasture 151 E5
Butcombe 116 C1
Bute 232 B3
Bute Town 130 A2
Buthill 267 J5
Butleigh 116 C4
Butleigh Wootton 116 C4
Butler's Cross 134 D2
Butler's Hill 173 G3
Butlers Marston 147 F3

Butlersbank 170 C5
Butley 153 E2
Butley Abbey 153 E3
Butley Low Corner 153 E3
Butley Mills 153 E2
Butley Town 184 D5
Butt Green 171 D2
Butt Lane 171 F2
Butterburn 219 E4
Buttercrambe 195 G2
Butterknowle 212 A5
Butterleigh 102 C2
Butterley 173 F2
Buttermere *Cumb* 209 E5
Buttermere *Wilts* 119 E1
Butters Green 171 F2
Buttershaw 194 A4
Butterstone 251 F5
Butterton *Staffs* 172 B2
Butterton *Staffs* 171 F3
Butterwick *Dur* 212 C5
Butterwick *Lincs* 176 B3
Butterwick *NYorks* 204 C5
Butterwick *NYorks* 203 G5
Buttington 156 B2
Buttonbridge 157 G5
Buttonoak 157 G5
Buttons' Green 152 A2
Butts 102 B4
Butt's Green *Essex* 137 G2
Butt's Green
Hants 119 D5
Buttsash 106 D2
Buxhall 152 B2
Buxted 109 G1
Buxton *Derbys* 185 E5
Buxton *Norf* 178 D3
Buxton Heath 178 C3
Buxworth 185 E4
Bwlch 144 A5
Bwlch-clawdd 141 G4
Bwlch-derwin 167 D3
Bwlchgwyn 169 F2
Bwlch-llan 142 B2
Bwlchnewydd 141 G5
Bwlchtocyn 166 C5
Bwlch-y-cibau 156 A1
Bwlch-y-ddar 169 E5
Bwlchyfadfa 142 A3
Bwlch-y-ffridd 155 G3
Bwlch-y-groes 141 F4
Bwlchyllyn 167 E2
Bwlchymynydd 128 B3
Bwlch-y-sarnau 155 G5
Byers Green 212 B4
Byfield 148 A2
Byfleet 121 F1
Byford 144 C3
Bygrave 150 A4
Byker 212 B1
Byland Abbey 203 E5
Bylane End 97 G4
Bylchau 168 C1
Byley 171 E1
Bynea 128 B3
Byrness 219 F3
Bystock 102 D4
Bythorn 161 F5
Byton 144 C1
Bywell 211 G1
Byworth 121 E5

C

Cabharstadh 271 F5
Cabourne 188 B2
Cabourne Parva 188 B2
Cabrach *A&B* 230 C3
Cabrach *Moray* 260 B2
Cabus 192 A3
Cackle Street
ESuss 110 D2
Cackle Street
ESuss 109 G1
Cacrabank 227 E4
Cadboll 267 F4
Cadbury 102 C2
Cadbury Barton 113 G4
Cadbury Heath 131 F5
Cadbury World *WMid*
B30 1JR 15 E5
Cadder 234 A2
Cadderlie 240 C1
Caddington 135 F1
Caddleton 239 G3
Caddonfoot 227 F2
Cade Street 110 B1
Cadeby *Leics* 159 G2
Cadeby *SYorks* 186 C2
Cadeleigh 102 C2
Cader 168 D1
Cadgwith 95 E5
Cadham 244 A4
Cadishead 184 B3
Cadle 128 C3
Cadley *Lancs* 192 B4
Cadley *Wilts* 118 D1
Cadmore End 134 C3
Cadnam 106 B1
Cadney 188 A2
Cadole 169 F1
Cadover Bridge 100 B1
Cadoxton 115 E1
Cadoxton-Juxta-
Neath 129 D3
Cadwell 149 G4
Cadwst 168 D4
Cadzow 234 B4
Cae Ddafydd 167 F3
Caeathro 167 E1
Caehopkin 129 E1
Caen 275 F7
Caenby 188 A4
Caenby Corner 187 G4
Caer Llan 131 D2
Caerau *Bridgend* 129 E3
Caerau *Cardiff* 130 A5
Caerdeon 154 C1
Caerfarchell 140 A5
Caergeiliog 180 B5
Caergwrle 170 A2
Caerhun 181 F5
Caer-Lan 129 E1
Caerleon 130 C3
Caernarfon 167 D1
Caernarfon Castle *Gwyn*
LL55 2AY 167 D1
Caerphilly 130 A4
Caersws 155 G3
Caerwedros 141 G2
Caerwent 131 D3
Caerwys 182 C5
Caethle Farm 154 C3
Caggan 259 F3
Caggle Street 130 C1
Caim *High* 247 E3
Caim *IoA* 181 E4
Caio 142 C4
Cairisiadar 270 C4
Cairminis 263 F3
Cairnargat 260 C1
Cairnbaan 240 A5
Cairnbeathie 260 D4
Cairnbrogie 261 G2
Cairnbulg 269 J4
Cairncross *Angus* 252 D2
Cairncross *ScBord* 237 F3
Cairncurran 233 E3
Cairndoon 207 D3
Cairndow 241 D3
Cairness 269 J4
Cairney Lodge 244 B3
Cairneyhill 235 E1
Cairngorm Mountain *High*
PH22 1RB 259 G4
Cairnhill *Aber* 261 H2
Cairnhill *Aber* 260 E1
Cairnie *Aber* 261 G4
Cairnie *Aber* 268 C6
Cairnorrie 269 G6
Cairnryan 214 B4
Cairnsmore 215 F4
Caister-on-Sea 179 G4
Caistor 188 B2
Caistor St. Edmund 178 D5
Caistron 220 B1
Caithness Crystal Visitor
Centre *Norf*
PE30 4NE 163 E1
Cake Street 164 B2
Cakebole 158 A5
Calbost 271 G6
Calbourne 106 D4
Calceby 189 D5
Calcoed 182 C5
Calcot 134 B5
Calcott *Kent* 125 D2
Calcott *Shrop* 156 D1
Calcotts Green 131 G1
Calcutt 132 D3
Caldarvan 233 F1
Caldback 278 F2
Caldbeck 209 G3
Caldbergh 201 F4
Caldecote *Cambs* 150 B2
Caldecote *Cambs* 161 G4
Caldecote *Herts* 150 A4
Caldecote *N'hants* 148 B2
Caldecote *Warks* 159 F3
Caldecott *N'hants* 149 E1
Caldecott *Oxon* 133 G3
Caldecott *Rut* 161 D3
Calder Bridge 198 B2
Calder Grove 186 A1
Calder Mains 275 F3
Calder Vale 192 B3
Calderbank 234 B3
Calderbrook 184 D1
Caldercruix 234 C3
Calderglen 234 A4
Calderglen Country Park
SLan G75 0QZ 31 E6
Caldermill 234 A5
Caldey Island 127 E3
Caldhame 252 C5
Caldicot 131 D4
Caldwell *Derbys* 159 E1
Caldwell *ERenf* 233 F4
Caldwell *NYorks* 202 A1
Caldy 182 D4
Calebreck 209 G3
Caledrhydiau 142 A2
Calford Green 151 E3
Calfsound 276 E4
Calgary 246 C4
Califer 267 H6
California *Falk* 234 D2
California *Norf* 179 G4
California *Suff* 152 D3
California Country Park
W'ham
RG40 4HT 120 C1
Calke 173 E5
Calke Abbey *Derbys*
DE73 7LE 173 E5
Callakille 264 C6
Callaly 220 C1
Callander 242 B4
Callanish (Calanais) 270 E4
Callaughton 157 F3
Callerton Lane End 212 A1
Calliburn 222 C3
Calligarry 256 C4
Callington 99 D4
Callingwood 172 C5
Callisterhall 218 A3
Callow 145 D4
Callow End 146 A3
Callow Hill *Wilts* 132 C4
Callow Hill *Worcs* 157 G5
Callow Hill *Worcs* 146 C1
Callows Grave 145 E1
Calmore 106 C1
Calmsden 132 C2
Calne 132 B5
Calow 186 B5
Calrossie 266 E4
Calshot 107 D2
Calstock 100 A1
Calstone
Wellington 118 B1
Calthorpe 178 C2
Calthwaite 210 A3
Calton *NYorks* 193 F2
Calton *Staffs* 172 C2
Calveley 170 C2
Calver 185 G5
Calver Hill 144 C3
Calverhall 170 D4
Calverleigh 102 C1
Calverley 194 B4
Calvert 148 B5
Calverton *MK* 148 C4
Calverton *Notts* 174 B3
Calvine 250 C3
Calvo 209 E1
Cam 131 G3
Camasnacroise 248 A4
Camastianavaig 256 B1
Camasunary 256 B3
Camault Muir 266 C7
Camb 278 E3
Camber 111 E2
Camberley 121 D1
Camberwell 136 C5
Camblesforth 195 F5
Cambo 220 C3
Cambois 221 F3
Camborne 95 D3
Cambourne 150 B2
Cambridge *Cambs* 150 C2
Cambridge *Glos* 131 G2
Cambridge American
Military Cemetery &
Memorial *Cambs*
CB23 7PH 150 B2
Cambridge City
Airport 150 C2
Cambridge University
Botanic Garden *Cambs*
CB2 1JF 150 C2
Cambus 243 D5
Cambus o'May 260 C5
Cambusbarron 242 C5
Cambuskenneth 242 D5
Cambuslang 234 A3
Cambusnethan 234 C4
Camden Town 136 B4
Camel Hill 116 C5
Camel Trail *Corn*
PL27 7AL 97 D2
Cameley 116 D2
Camelford 97 F1
Camelon 234 C1
Camelot Theme Park
Lancs PR7 5LP 183 G1
Camelsdale 121 D4
Camer 123 F2
Cameron House 233 E1
Camerory 259 H1
Camer's Green 145 G4
Camerton
B&NESom 117 D2
Camerton *Cumb* 208 D3
Camerton *ERid* 197 E5
Camghouran 250 A4
Camis Eskan 233 E1
Cammachmore 261 H5
Cammeringham 187 G4
Camore 266 E2
Camp Hill *Pembs* 127 E1
Camp Hill *Warks* 159 F3
Campbeltown (Ceann Loch
Chille Chiarain) 222 C3
Campbeltown
Airport 222 B3
Camperdown 221 E4
Camperdown Country
Park *Dundee*
DD2 4TF 244 B1
Campmuir 244 A1
Camps 235 F3
Camps End 151 E3
Camps Heath 165 G2
Campsall 186 C1
Campsea Ashe 153 E2
Campton 149 G4
Camptown 228 A5
Camquhart 232 A1
Camrose 140 C5
Camserney 250 D5
Camstraddan
House 241 F5
Camus Croise 256 C3
Camus-luinie 257 F2
Camusnagaul *High* 248 C2
Camusnagaul *High* 265 G3
Camusrory 256 E5
Camusteel 264 D7
Camusterrach 264 D7
Camusurich 242 B1
Camusvrachan 250 B5
Canada 106 B1
Canaston Bridge 127 D1
Candacraig 260 B5
Candlesby 176 C1
Candy Mill 235 E5
Cane End 134 B5
Canewdon 138 B3
Canfield End 151 D5
Canford Bottom 105 G2
Canford Cliffs 105 G4
Canford Heath 105 G3
Canford Magna 105 G3
Canham's Green 152 B1
Canisbay 275 J1
Canley 159 F5
Cann 117 F5
Cann Common 117 F5
Canna 255 H4
Cannard's Grave 116 D3
Cannich (Canaich) 257 K1
Canning Town 136 D4
Cannington 115 F4
Cannock 158 B2
Cannock Wood 158 C1
Cannon Hall Country Park
SYorks S75 4AT 185 G2
Cannon Hall Farm *SYorks*
S75 4AT 185 G2
Cannon Hill Park *WMid*
B13 8RD 15 E4
Cannop 131 F1
Canon Bridge 144 D3
Canon Frome 145 F3
Canon Pyon 145 D3
Canonbie 218 B4
Canons Ashby 148 A2
Canon's Town 94 C3
Canterbury *Aber* 268 D5
Canterbury *Kent* 124 D3
Canterbury Cathedral
Kent CT1 2EH
67 Canterbury
Canterbury Tales, The
Kent CT1 2TG
67 Canterbury
Cantley *Norf* 179 E5
Cantley *SYorks* 186 D2
Cantlop 157 E2
Canton 130 A5
Cantray 266 E7
Cantraydoune 266 E7
Cantraywood 266 E7
Cantsfield 200 B5
Canvey Island 137 G4
Canwell Hall 158 D2
Canwick 175 E1
Canworthy Water 98 C1
Caol 248 D2
Caolas *A&B* 246 B2
Caolas *WIsles* 254 B5
Caolasnacon 248 D3
Capel *Kent* 123 F4
Capel *Surr* 121 G3
Capel Bangor 154 C4
Capel Betws Lleucu 142 C2
Capel Carmel 166 A5
Capel Celyn 168 B3
Capel Coch 180 C4
Capel Curig 168 A2
Capel Cynon 141 G3
Capel Dewi *Carmar* 142 A5
Capel Dewi *Cere* 154 C4
Capel Dewi *Cere* 142 A3
Capel Garmon 168 B2
Capel Gwyn
Carmar 142 A5
Capel Gwyn *IoA* 180 B5
Capel Gwynfe 142 D5
Capel Hendre 128 B1
Capel Isaac 142 B5
Capel Iwan 141 F4
Capel le Ferne 125 E5
Capel Llanilltern 129 G4
Capel Mawr 180 C5
Capel Parc 180 C4
Capel St. Andrew 153 E3
Capel St. Mary 152 B4
Capel St. Silin 142 B2
Capel Seion 154 C5
Capel Tygwydd 141 F3
Capeluchaf 166 D3
Capelulo 181 F5
Capel-y-ffin 144 B4
Capel-y-graig 167 E1
Capenhurst 183 E5
Capernwray 199 G5
Capheaton 220 C3
Caplaw 233 F4
Capon's Green 153 D1
Cappercleuch 226 D3
Capplegill 226 C5
Capstone 123 G2
Capton *Devon* 101 E2
Capton *Som* 115 D4
Caputh 251 F5
Car Colston 174 C3
Caradon Town 97 G2
Carbellow 225 E3
Carbeth 233 G2
Carbis Bay 94 C3
Carbost *High* 263 K7
Carbost *High* 255 J1
Carbrain 234 B2
Carbrooke 178 A5
Carburton 186 D5
Carcary 253 E4
Carco 225 F4
Carcroft 186 C1
Cardenden 244 A5
Cardeston 156 C1
Cardew 209 G2
Cardiff
(Caerdydd) 130 A5
Cardiff Bay Visitor Centre
Cardiff CF10 4PA 7 C4
Cardiff Castle & Museum
CF10 3RB 67 Cardiff
Cardiff International
Airport 115 D1
Cardiff Millennium
Stadium CF10 1GE
67 Cardiff
Cardigan (Aberteifi) 141 E3
Cardinal's Green 151 E3
Cardington *Bed* 149 F3
Cardington *Shrop* 157 E3
Cardinham 97 F3
Cardno 269 H4
Cardonald 233 G3
Cardoness 215 G5
Cardow 267 J7
Cardrona 227 D2
Cardross 233 E2
Cardurnock 209 E1
Careby 161 F1
Careston 252 D4
Carew 126 D2
Carew Cheriton 126 D2
Carew Newton 126 D2
Carey 145 E4
Carfin 234 B4
Carfrae 236 C3
Carfraemill 236 C4
Cargate Green 179 E4
Cargen 217 D3
Cargenbridge 217 D3
Cargill 243 G1
Cargo 209 G1
Cargreen 100 A1
Carham 228 B3
Carhampton 114 D3
Carharrack 96 B5
Carie *P&K* 250 B4
Carie *P&K* 242 B1
Carines 96 B4
Carinish (Cairinis) 262 D5
Carisbrooke 107 D4
Carisbrooke Castle &
Museum *IoW*
PO30 1XY 107 D4
Cark 199 E5
Carkeel 100 A1
Carland Cross 96 C4
Carlatton 210 B2
Carlby 161 F1
Carlecotes 185 F2
Carleen 94 D4
Carleton *Cumb* 210 A2
Carleton *Cumb* 210 B5
Carleton *Lancs* 191 G3
Carleton *NYorks* 193 F3
Carleton *WYorks* 195 D5
Carleton Fishery 214 C2
Carleton Forehoe 178 B5
Carleton Rode 164 C2
Carleton St. Peter 179 E5
Carlin How 203 G1
Carlisle 210 A2
Carlisle Cathedral
Cumb CA3 8TZ
68 Carlisle
Carlisle Park,
Morpeth *N'umb*
NE61 1YD 221 D3
Carloggas 96 C3
Carlops 235 F4
Carloway
(Càrlabhagh) 270 E3
Carlton *Bed* 149 E2
Carlton *Cambs* 151 E2
Carlton *Leics* 159 F2
Carlton *Notts* 174 B3
Carlton *NYorks* 195 F5
Carlton *NYorks* 201 F4
Carlton *NYorks* 203 F4
Carlton *Stock* 212 C5
Carlton *Suff* 153 E1
Carlton *SYorks* 186 A1
Carlton *WYorks* 194 C5
Carlton Colville 165 G2
Carlton Curlieu 160 B3
Carlton Green 151 E2
Carlton Husthwaite 203 D5
Carlton in Lindrick 186 C4
Carlton Miniott 202 C4
Carlton Scroop 175 E3
Carlton-in-
Cleveland 203 E2
Carlton-le-
Moorland 175 E2
Carlton-on-Trent 174 D1
Carluke 234 C4
Carlyon Bay 97 E4
Carmacoup 225 F3
Carmarthen
(Caerfyrddin) 142 A5
Carmel *Carmar* 128 B1
Carmel *Flints* 182 C5
Carmel *Gwyn* 167 D2
Carmel *IoA* 180 B4
Carmichael 226 A2
Carmont 253 G1
Carmunnock 233 G4
Carmyle 234 A3
Carmyllie 253 D5
Carn 230 A4
Carn Brea Village 96 A5
Carn Dearg 264 D4
Carnaby 196 D1
Carnach *High* 257 G2
Carnach *High* 265 G2
Carnach *WIsles* 262 D5
Carnan 262 C7
Carnassarie 240 A4
Carnbee 244 D4
Carnbo 243 F4
Carndu 256 E2
Carnduncan 230 A3
Carnforth 199 F5
Carnhedryn 140 B5
Carnhell Green 94 D3
Carnichal 269 H5
Carnkie *Corn* 95 D3
Carnkie *Corn* 95 E3
Carnmore 230 B5
Carno 155 F3
Carnoch *High* 257 K1
Carnoch *High* 265 J6
Carnoch *High* 267 F7
Carnock 235 E1
Carnon Downs 96 C5
Carnousie 268 E5
Carnoustie 245 D1
Carntyne 234 A3
Carnwath 235 D5
Carnyorth 94 A3
Carol Green 159 E5
Carperby 201 F4
Carr 186 C3
Carr Hill 187 D3
Carr Houses 183 E2
Carr Shield 211 E3
Carr Vale 186 B5
Carradale 222 D2
Carragrich 263 G2
Carrbridge 259 G2
Carrefour Selous 100 C5
Carreglefn 180 B4
Carreg-wen 141 F3
Carrhouse 187 E2
Carrick 232 A1
Carrick Castle 241 D5
Carriden 235 E1
Carrine 222 B5
Carrington *GtMan* 184 B3
Carrington *Lincs* 176 B2
Carrington *Midlo* 236 A3
Carroch 216 A1
Carrog *Conwy* 168 A3
Carrog *Denb* 169 E3
Carroglen 242 C2
Carrol 267 F1
Carron *A&B* 240 B5
Carron *Falk* 234 C1
Carron *Moray* 267 K7
Carron Bridge 234 B1
Carronbridge 216 C1
Carronshore 234 C1
Carrot 252 C5
Carrow Hill 130 D3
Carrutherstown 217 F3
Carruthmuir 233 E3
Carrville 212 C3
Carry 232 A3
Carsaig 239 E2
Carscreugh 214 D4
Carse 231 F3
Carse of Ardersier 267 F6
Carsegowan 215 F5
Carseriggan 215 E4
Carsethorn 217 D5
Carsgoe 275 G2
Carshalton 122 B2
Carshalton Beeches 122 B2
Carsie 251 G5
Carsington 173 D2
Carsington Water *Derbys*
DE6 1ST 172 D2
Carsluith 215 F5
Carsphairn 215 G1
Carstairs 234 D5
Carstairs Junction 235 D5
Carswell Marsh 133 F3
Carter's Clay 119 E5
Carterton 133 E2
Carterway Heads 211 G2
Carthew 97 E4
Carthorpe 202 C4
Cartington 220 C1
Cartland 234 C5
Cartmel 199 E5
Cartmel Fell 199 F4
Cartworth 185 F2
Carway 128 A2
Cascades Adventure
Pool *Devon*
EX33 1NZ 113 E2
Cascob 144 B1
Cashel Farm 241 G5
Cashes Green 132 A2
Cashlie 249 G5
Cashmoor 105 F1
Caskieberran 244 A4
Cassencarie 215 F5
Cassington 133 G1
Cassop 212 C4
Castell 168 A1
Castell Gorfod 141 F5
Castell Howell 142 A3
Castellau 129 G4
Castell-y-bwch 130 B3
Casterton 200 B5
Castle Acre 163 G1
Castle Ashby 149 D2
Castle Bolton 201 F3
Castle Bromwich 158 D4
Castle Bytham 161 E1
Castle Caereinion 156 A2
Castle Camps 151 E3
Castle Carrock 210 B2
Castle Cary 116 D4
Castle Combe 132 A5
Castle Donington 173 F5
Castle Douglas 216 B4
Castle Drogo *Devon*
EX6 6PB 102 A3
Castle Eaton 132 D3
Castle Eden 212 D4
Castle Eden Dene National
Nature Reserve *Dur*
SR8 1NJ 212 D4
Castle End 159 E5
Castle Frome 145 F3
Castle Gate 94 B3
Castle Goring 108 D3
Castle Green 121 E1
Castle Gresley 159 E1
Castle Heaton 237 G5
Castle Hedingham 151 F4
Castle Hill *Kent* 123 F4
Castle Hill *Suff* 152 C3
Castle Howard *NYorks*
YO60 7DA 195 G1
Castle Kennedy 214 C5
Castle Leod 266 B6
Castle Levan 232 D2
Castle Madoc 143 G4
Castle Morris 140 C4
Castle O'er 218 A2
Castle Rising 177 E5
Castle Semple Water
Country Park *Renf*
PA12 4HJ 233 E4
Castle Stuart 266 E7
Castlebay (Bàgh
a'Chaisteil) 254 B5
Castlebythe 140 D5
Castlecary 234 B2
Castlecraig *High* 267 F5
Castlecraig *ScBord* 235 F5
Castlefairn 216 B2
Castleford 194 D5
Castlemartin 126 C3
Castlemilk *D&G* 217 F3
Castlemilk *Glas* 234 A4
Castlemorton 145 G4
Castlerigg 209 F4
Castleside 211 G3
Castlesteads 210 B1
Castlethorpe 148 C3
Castleton *A&B* 231 G1
Castleton *Aber* 269 F5
Castleton *Angus* 252 B5
Castleton *Derbys* 185 F4
Castleton *GtMan* 184 C1
Castleton *Newport* 130 B4
Castleton *NYorks* 203 F2
Castleton *ScBord* 218 D2
Castletown *Dorset* 104 C5
Castletown *High* 275 G2
Castletown *High* 266 E7
Castletown *IoM* 190 A5
Castletown *T&W* 212 C2
Castleweary 227 F5
Castlewigg 207 E2
Castley 194 B3
Caston 164 A2
Castor 161 G3
Castramont 215 G4
Caswell 128 B4
Cat & Fiddle Inn 185 E5
Catacol 232 A5
Catbrain 131 E4
Catbrook 131 E2
Catchall 94 B4
Catcleugh 219 F1
Catcliffe 186 B4
Catcott 116 A4
Caterham 122 C3
Catfield 179 E3
Catfirth 279 D7
Catford 136 C5
Catforth 192 A4
Cathays 130 A5
Cathcart 233 G3
Cathedine 144 A5
Catherine-de-
Barnes 159 D4
Catherington 107 F1
Catherston
Leweston 103 G3
Catherton 157 F5
Cathkin 234 A4
Catisfield 107 E2
Catlodge 258 D5
Catlowdy 218 C4
Catmere End 150 C4
Catmore 133 G4
Caton *Devon* 102 A5
Caton *Lancs* 192 B1
Caton Green 192 B1
Cator Court 99 G3
Catrine 224 D3
Catsfield 110 C2
Catsfield Stream 110 C2
Catshaw 185 G2
Catshill 158 B5
Cattadale 230 B3
Cattal 194 D2
Cattawade 152 B4
Catterall 192 B3
Catterick 202 B3
Catterick Bridge 202 B3
Catterick Garrison 202 A3
Catterlen 210 A4
Catterline 253 G2
Catterton 195 E3
Catteshall 121 E3
Catthorpe 160 A5
Cattishall 151 G1
Cattistock 104 B2
Catton *N'umb* 211 E2
Catton *Norf* 178 D4
Catton *NYorks* 202 C5
Catton Hall 159 E1
Catwick 196 D3
Catworth 161 F5
Caudle Green 132 B1
Caudwell's Mill & Craft
Centre *Derbys*
DE4 2EB 173 D1
Caulcott *CenBeds* 149 F3
Caulcott *Oxon* 148 A5
Cauldcots 253 E5
Cauldhame *Stir* 242 B5
Cauldhame *Stir* 242 D4
Cauldon 172 B3
Caulkerbush 216 D5
Caulside 218 C3
Caundle Marsh 104 C1
Caunsall 158 A4
Caunton 174 C1
Causeway End
D&G 215 F4
Causeway End
Essex 137 F1
Causeway End
Lancs 183 F1
Causewayhead
Cumb 209 E1
Causewayhead
Stir 242 D5
Causey 212 B2
Causey Arch Picnic Area
Dur NE16 5EG 28 A4
Causey Park 221 D2
Causeyend 261 H3
Cautley 200 B3
Cavendish 151 G3
Cavendish Bridge 173 F5
Cavenham 151 F1
Cavens 217 D5
Cavers 227 G4
Caversfield 148 A5
Caversham 134 C5
Caverswall 171 G3
Cawdor 267 F6
Cawkeld 196 B2
Cawkwell 188 C4
Cawood 195 E4
Cawsand 100 A3
Cawston *Norf* 178 C3
Cawston *Warks* 159 G5
Cawthorn 203 G4
Cawthorne 185 G2
Cawthorpe 175 F5
Cawton 203 F5
Caxton 150 B2
Caxton Gibbet 150 A1
Caynham 157 E5
Caythorpe *Lincs* 175 E3
Caythorpe *Notts* 174 B3
Cayton 205 D4
CC2000 *Pembs*
SA67 8DD 127 D1
Ceallan 262 D6
Ceann a' Bhàigh
WIsles 262 C5
Ceann a' Bhàigh
WIsles 263 F3
Ceann Loch
Shiphoirt 270 E6
Ceannaridh 262 D6
Cearsiadar 271 F6
Cedig 168 C5
Cefn Berain 168 C1
Cefn Canol 169 F4
Cefn Cantref 143 G5
Cefn Coch *Denb* 169 E2
Cefn Coch *Powys* 155 G2
Cefn Cribwr 129 E4
Cefn Cross 129 E4
Cefn Einion 156 B4

Cefn Hengoed **130** A3
Cefn Llwyd **154** C4
Cefn Rhigos **129** F2
Cefn-brith **168** C2
Cefn-caer-Ferch **166** D3
Cefn-coch **169** E5
Cefn-coed-y-
cymmer **129** G2
Cefn-ddwysarn **168** C4
Cefndeuddwr **168** A5
Cefneithin **128** B1
Cefn-gorwydd **143** F3
Cefn-gwyn **156** A4
Cefn-mawr **169** F3
Cefnpennar **129** G2
Cefn-y-bedd **170** A2
Cefn-y-pant **141** E5
Ceidio **180** C5
Ceidio Fawr **166** B4
Ceint **180** C5
Cellan **142** C3
Cellardyke **245** D4
Cellarhead **171** G3
Cemaes **180** B3
Cemmaes **155** E2
Cemmaes Road
(Glantwymyn) **155** E2
Cenarth **141** F3
Cennin **167** D3
Centre for Life
T&W NE1 4EP
79 Newcastle upon Tyne
Ceramica Stoke
ST6 3DS **20** C2
Ceres **244** C3
Cerist **155** F4
Cerne Abbas **104** C2
Cerney Wick **132** C3
Cerrigceinwen **180** C5
Cerrigydrudion **168** C3
Cessford **228** B4
Ceunant **167** E1
Chaceley **146** A4
Chacewater **96** B5
Chackmore **148** B4
Chacombe **147** G3
Chad Valley **158** C4
Chadderton **184** D2
Chadderton Fold **184** C2
Chaddesden **173** E4
Chaddesley Corbett **158** A5
Chaddleworth **133** G5
Chadlington **147** F5
Chadshunt **147** F2
Chadstone **149** D2
Chadwell Leics **174** C5
Chadwell Shrop **157** G1
Chadwick End **159** E5
Chaffcombe **103** G2
Chafford Hundred **137** F5
Chagford **102** A4
Chailey **109** F2
Chainhurst **123** G4
Chalbury **105** G2
Chalbury Common **105** G2
Chaldon **122** C3
Chaldon Herring (East
Chaldon) **105** D4
Chale **107** D5
Chale Green **107** D4
Chalfont Common **135** F3
Chalfont St. Giles **135** F3
Chalfont St. Peter **135** F3
Chalford Glos **132** A2
Chalford Wilts **117** F3
Chalgrove **134** B3
Chalk **137** F5
Chalk End **137** F1
Challaborough **100** C3
Challacombe **113** G1
Challister **279** E6
Challoch **215** E4
Challock **124** C3
Chalmington **104** B2
Chalton CenBeds **149** F5
Chalton Hants **107** G1
Chalvey **135** E5
Chalvington **110** A3
Champany **235** E2
Chancery **154** B5
Chandler's Cross **135** F3
Chandler's Ford **119** F5
Channel Islands **100** A5
Channerwick **279** D10
Chantry Som **117** E3
Chantry Suff **152** C3
Chapel **244** A5
Chapel Allerton
Som **116** B2
Chapel Allerton
WYorks **194** C4
Chapel Amble **97** D2
Chapel Brampton **148** C1
Chapel Chorlton **171** F4
Chapel Cleeve **114** D3
Chapel Cross **110** B1
Chapel End **149** F3
Chapel Green
Warks **159** E4
Chapel Green
Warks **147** G1
Chapel Haddlesey **195** E5
Chapel Hill Aber **261** J1
Chapel Hill Lincs **176** A2
Chapel Hill Mon **131** E2
Chapel Hill NYorks **194** C3
Chapel Knapp **117** F1
Chapel Lawn **156** C5
Chapel Leigh **115** E5
Chapel Milton **185** E4
Chapel of Garioch **261** F2
Chapel Rossan **206** B2
Chapel Row Essex **137** G2
Chapel Row
WBerks **119** G1
Chapel St. Leonards **189** F5
Chapel Stile **199** E2
Chapel Town **96** C4
Chapelbank **243** F3
Chapeldonan **223** G5

Chapelend Way **151** F4
Chapel-en-le-Frith **185** E4
Chapelgate **176** C5
Chapelhall **234** B3
Chapelhill High **267** F4
Chapelhill P&K **244** A2
Chapelhill P&K **243** F1
Chapel-le-Dale **200** C5
Chapelthorpe **186** A1
Chapelknowe **218** B4
Chapelton Aber **253** G1
Chapelton Angus **253** E5
Chapelton Devon **113** F3
Chapelton SLan **234** A5
Chapelton B'burn **184** B1
Chapelton Cumb **218** C4
Chapelton Moray **259** K2
Chapelton WSuss **186** A3
Chapmans Well **99** D1
Chapmanslade **117** F3
Chapmore End **136** C1
Chappel **151** G3
Charaton **98** D4
Chard **103** G2
Chard Junction **103** G2
Chardleigh Green **103** G1
Chardstock **103** G2
Charfield **131** G3
Charing **124** B4
Charing Cross **106** A1
Charing Heath **124** B4
Charingworth **147** D4
Charlbury **133** F1
Charlcombe **117** E1
Charlcote **147** E2
Charles **113** G2
Charles Tye **152** B2
Charlesfield **227** G3
Charleshill **121** D3
Charleston **252** B5
Charlestown Aber **269** J4
Charlestown
Aberdeen **261** H4
Charlestown Corn **97** E4
Charlestown
Derbys **185** E3
Charlestown
Dorset **104** C5
Charlestown Fife **235** E1
Charlestown
GtMan **184** C2
Charlestown High **264** E4
Charlestown High **266** D7
Charlestown
WYorks **194** A4
Charlestown
WYorks **193** F1
Charlestown of Aberlour
(Aberlour) **267** K7
Charlesworth **185** E3
Charleton **244** C4
Charlinch **115** F4
Charlotteville **121** F3
Charlton GtLon **136** D5
Charlton Hants **119** E3
Charlton Herts **149** G5
Charlton N'hants **148** A4
Charlton N'umb **220** A3
Charlton Oxon **133** G4
Charlton Som **117** D2
Charlton Som **116** D3
Charlton Som **115** F5
Charlton Tel&W **157** F1
Charlton Wilts **118** A5
Charlton Wilts **132** B4
Charlton Wilts **118** C2
Charlton Worcs **146** C3
Charlton WSuss **108** A2
Charlton Abbots **146** C5
Charlton Adam **116** C5
Charlton Down **104** C3
Charlton
Horethorne **117** D5
Charlton Kings **146** B5
Charlton Mackrell **116** C5
Charlton Marshall **105** E2
Charlton Musgrove **117** E5
Charlton on the Hill **105** E2
Charlton-All-Saints **118** C5
Charlton-on-
Otmoor **134** A1
Charltons **203** F1
Charlwood **122** B4
Charminster **104** C3
Charmouth **103** G3
Charndon **148** B5
Charney Bassett **133** F3
Charnock Richard **183** G1
Charsfield **153** D2
Chart Corner **123** G4
Chart Sutton **124** A4
Charter Alley **119** G2
Charterhouse **116** B2
Charterville
Allotments **133** F2
Chartham **124** D3
Chartham Hatch **124** D3
Chartridge **135** E2
Chartwell
Kent TN16 1PS **123** D3
Charvil **134** C5
Charwelton **148** A2
Chase End Street **145** G4
Chase Terrace **158** C2
Chasetown **158** C2
Chastleton **147** E5
Chasty **112** D4
Chatburn **193** D3
Chatcull **171** E4
Chatham **124** A2
Chatham Green **137** G2
Chatham Historic
Dockyard Med
ME4 4TZ **123** G2
Chathill **229** E5
Chatsworth Farmyard &
Adventure Playground
Derbys
DE45 1PP **185** G5

Chatsworth House Derbys
DE45 1PP **185** G5
Chattenden **137** G5
Chatteris **162** B4
Chattisham **152** B3
Chatton **229** E4
Chaul End **149** F5
Chavey Down **121** D1
Chawleigh **102** A1
Chawston **149** G2
Chawton **120** C4
Chazey Heath **134** B5
Cheadle GtMan **184** C4
Cheadle Staffs **172** B4
Cheadle Heath **184** C4
Cheadle Hulme **184** C4
Cheam **122** B2
Cheapside **121** E1
Chearsley **134** C1
Checkendon **134** B4
Checkley ChesE **171** E3
Checkley Here **145** E4
Checkley Staffs **172** B4
Checkley Green **171** E3
Chedburgh **151** F2
Cheddar **116** B2
Cheddar Caves & Gorge
Som BS27 3QF **116** B2
Cheddington **135** E1
Cheddleton **171** G2
Cheddon Fitzpaine **115** F5
Chedglow **132** B3
Chedgrave **165** E2
Chedington **104** A2
Chediston **165** E4
Chediston Green **165** E4
Chedworth **132** C1
Chedzoy **116** A4
Cheesden **184** C1
Cheeseman's Green **124** C5
Cheetham Hill **184** C2
Cheglinch **113** F1
Cheldon **102** A1
Chelford **184** C5
Chellaston **173** E4
Chells **150** A4
Chelmarsh **157** G4
Chelmondiston **152** D4
Chelmorton **172** C1
Chelmsford **137** G2
Chelmsford Cathedral
Essex CM1 1TY **137** G2
Chelmsley Wood **159** D4
Chelsea **136** B5
Chelsfield **123** D2
Chelsham **122** C3
Chelston Heath **115** E5
Chelsworth **152** A3
Cheltenham **146** B5
Chelveston **149** E1
Chelvey **116** B1
Chelwood **116** D1
Chelwood Common **109** G1
Chelwood Gate **109** G1
Chelworth **132** B3
Cheney Longville **156** D4
Chenies **135** F3
Chepstow
(Cas-gwent) **131** E3
Cherhill **132** C5
Cherington Glos **132** B3
Cherington Warks **147** E4
Cheriton Devon **114** A3
Cheriton Hants **119** G5
Cheriton Kent **125** D5
Cheriton Pembs **126** C3
Cheriton Som **114** A3
Cheriton Bishop **102** A3
Cheriton Cross **102** A3
Cheriton Fitzpaine **102** B2
Cherrington **171** D5
Cherry Burton **196** B3
Cherry Green **151** D5
Cherry Hinton **150** C2
Cherry Willingham **188** A5
Chertsey **121** F1
Cheselbourne **105** D3
Chesham **135** E2
Chesham Bois **135** E2
Cheshunt **136** C2
Cheslyn Hay **158** B2
Chessington **121** G1
Chessington World of
Adventures GtLon
KT9 2NE **121** G1
Chestall **158** C1
Chester **170** B1
Chester Cathedral
ChesW&C CH1 2HU
69 Chester
Chester Moor **212** B3
Chester Zoo ChesW&C
CH2 1LH **183** F5
Chesterblade **117** D3
Chesterfield
Derbys **186** A5
Chesterfield Staffs **158** D2
Chester-le-Street **212** B2
Chesters ScBord **228** A5
Chesters ScBord **228** A4
Chesterton Cambs **150** C1
Chesterton Cambs **161** G3
Chesterton Oxon **148** A5
Chesterton Shrop **157** G3
Chesterton Staffs **171** F3
Chesterton Warks **147** F2
Chesterton Green **147** F2
Chestfield **124** D2
Cheston **100** C2
Cheswardine **171** E5
Cheswick **229** E2
Cheswick Buildings **229** E2
Cheswick Green **158** D5
Chetnole **104** C2
Chettiscombe **102** C1
Chettisham **162** D4

Chettle **105** F1
Chetton **157** F3
Chetwode **148** B5
Chetwynd Aston **157** G1
Chetwynd Park **171** E5
Cheveley **151** E1
Chevening **123** D3
Cheverell's Green **135** F1
Chevin Forest Park WYorks
LS21 3JL **194** B3
Chevington **151** F2
Chevithorne **102** C1
Chew Magna **116** C1
Chew Moor **184** A2
Chew Stoke **116** C1
Chewton
Keynsham **116** D1
Chewton Mendip **116** C2
Chichacott **99** G1
Chicheley **149** E3
Chichester Cathedral WSuss
PO19 1PX **108** A3
Chickerell **104** C4
Chickering **164** D4
Chicklade **118** A4
Chicksands **149** G4
Chidden **107** F1
Chidden Holt **107** F1
Chiddingfold **121** E4
Chiddingly **110** A2
Chiddingstone **123** D4
Chiddingstone
Causeway **123** E4
Chiddingstone
Hoath **123** D4
Chideock **104** A3
Chidham **107** G2
Chidswell **194** B5
Chieveley **133** G5
Chignall St. James **137** F2
Chignall Smealy **137** F1
Chigwell **136** D3
Chigwell Row **137** D3
Chilbolton **119** E3
Chilcomb **119** G5
Chilcombe **104** B3
Chilcompton **117** D2
Chilcote **159** E1
Child Okeford **105** E1
Childer Thornton **183** E5
Childerditch **137** F4
Childrey **133** F4
Child's Ercall **170** D5
Childs Hill **136** B4
Childswickham **146** C4
Childwall **183** F4
Childwick Green **136** A1
Chilfrome **104** B3
Chilgrove **108** A2
Chilham **124** C3
Chilhampton **118** B4
Chilla **113** E5
Chillaton **99** E2
Chillenden **125** E3
Chillerton **107** D4
Chillesford **153** E2
Chilley **101** D2
Chillingham **229** E4
Chillington Devon **101** D3
Chillington Som **103** G1
Chilmark **118** A4
Chilson Oxon **133** F1
Chilson Som **103** G2
Chilsworthy Corn **99** E3
Chilsworthy Devon **112** D5
Chilthorne Domer **104** B1
Chilton Bucks **134** B1
Chilton Devon **102** B2
Chilton Dur **212** B5
Chilton Oxon **133** G4
Chilton Suff **151** G3
Chilton Candover **119** G4
Chilton Cantelo **116** C5
Chilton Foliat **133** F5
Chilton Polden **116** A4
Chilton Street **151** F3
Chilton Trinity **115** F4
Chilvers Coton **159** F3
Chilwell **173** G4
Chilworth Hants **106** D1
Chilworth Surr **121** F3
Chimney **133** F2
Chimney Street **151** F3
Chineham **120** B2
Chingford **136** C3
Chinley **185** E4
Chinley Head **185** E4
Chinnor **134** C2
Chipchase Castle **220** A4
Chipley **115** E5
Chipnall **171** E4
Chippenham
Cambs **151** E1
Chippenham Wilts **132** B5
Chipperfield **135** F2
Chipping Herts **150** B4
Chipping Lancs **192** C3
Chipping Campden **147** D4
Chipping Hill **138** B1
Chipping Norton **147** F5
Chipping Ongar **137** E2
Chipping Sodbury **131** G4
Chipping Warden **147** G3
Chipstable **115** D5
Chipstead Kent **123** D3
Chipstead Surr **122** B3
Chirbury **156** B3
Chirk (Y Waun) **169** F4
Chirk Green **169** F4
Chirmorrie **214** D3
Chirnside **237** F4
Chirnsidebridge **237** F4
Chirton T&W **212** C1
Chirton Wilts **118** B2
Chisbury **119** D1
Chiscan **222** B4
Chiselborough **104** A1
Chiseldon **133** D5
Chiserley **193** G5
Chislehampton **134** A3

Chislehurst **136** D5
Chislet **125** E2
Chiswell Green **136** A2
Chiswick **136** B5
Chiswick End **150** B3
Chisworth **185** D3
Chithurst **120** D5
Chittering **162** C5
Chitterne **118** A3
Chittlehamholt **113** G3
Chittlehampton **113** G3
Chittoe **118** A1
Chivelstone **101** D4
Chivenor **113** F2
Chobham **121** E1
Choicelee **237** E4
Cholderton **118** D3
Chollerford **220** B4
Chollerton **220** B4
Cholmondeston **170** D2
Cholsey **134** A4
Cholstrey **145** D2
Cholwell
B&NESom **116** D2
Cholwell Devon **99** E3
Chop Gate **203** E3
Choppington **221** E3
Chopwell **212** A2
Chorley ChesE **170** C2
Chorley Lancs **183** G1
Chorley Shrop **157** F4
Chorley Staffs **158** C1
Chorleywood **135** F3
Chorlton **171** E2
Chorlton Lane **170** B3
Chorlton-cum-
Hardy **184** C3
Chowley **170** B2
Chrishall **150** C4
Chrishall Grange **150** C3
Chriswell **232** D1
Christ Church Oxon
OX1 1DP **80** Oxford
Christchurch
Cambs **162** C3
Christchurch
Dorset **106** A3
Christchurch
Newport **130** C4
Christian Malford **132** B5
Christleton **170** B1
Christmas Common **134** C3
Christon **129** G4
Christon Bank **229** G4
Christow **102** B4
Christskirk **260** E2
Chryston **234** A2
Chudleigh **102** B5
Chudleigh Knighton **102** B5
Chulmleigh **113** G4
Chunal **185** E3
Church **192** D5
Church Aston **157** G1
Church Brampton **148** C1
Church Brough **200** C1
Church Broughton **172** D4
Church Charwelton **148** A2
Church Common **153** A2
Church Crookham **120** C2
Church Eaton **158** A1
Church End Cambs **162** B2
Church End Cambs **162** B5
Church End Cambs **162** A4
Church End
CenBeds **149** G4
Church End
CenBeds **149** E5
Church End
CenBeds **149** G2
Church End
CenBeds **149** E4
Church End
CenBeds **149** E4
Church End ERid **196** C2
Church End Essex **151** D3
Church End Essex **151** F5
Church End Glos **146** A4
Church End Hants **120** B2
Church End Herts **136** A1
Church End Herts **150** A1
Church End Lincs **176** A4
Church End Lincs **189** E3
Church End Warks **159** E3
Church End Wilts **132** C5
Church End Essex **151** E3
Church Enstone **147** F5
Church Fenton **195** E4
Church Green **103** E3
Church Gresley **159** E1
Church
Hanborough **133** G1
Church Hill
ChesW&C **170** C1
Church Hill Derbys **173** F1
Church Houses **203** F3
Church Knowle **105** F4
Church Laneham **187** F5
Church Langley **137** D2
Church Langton **160** C3
Church Lawford **159** G5
Church Lawton **171** F2
Church Leigh **172** B4
Church Lench **146** C2
Church Mayfield **172** C3
Church Minshull **171** D1
Church Norton **108** A4
Church of St. Mary-
in-Castro Kent
CT16 1HU **70** Dover
Church Preen **157** E3
Church Pulverbatch **156** D2
Church Stoke **156** B3
Church Stowe **148** B2
Church Street
Essex **151** F3
Church Street Kent **137** G5
Church Stretton **157** D3
Church Town Leics **159** F1
Church Town Surr **122** C3
Church Village **129** G4
Church Warsop **173** G1

Church Westcote **147** E5
Church Wilne **173** F4
Churcham **131** G1
Churchdown **132** A1
Churchend Essex **138** D3
Churchend Essex **151** E5
Churchend SGlos **131** G3
Churchfield **158** C3
Churchgate **136** C2
Churchgate Street **137** D1
Churchill Devon **113** F1
Churchill Devon **113** F1
Churchill NSom **116** B2
Churchill Oxon **147** E5
Churchill Worcs **146** A5
Churchill Museum &
Cabinet War Rooms
GtLon SW1A 2AQ **44** D5
Churchingford **103** F1
Churchover **160** A4
Churchstanton **103** E1
Churchstow **100** D3
Churchtown Devon **113** G1
Churchtown IoM **190** C2
Churchtown Lancs **192** A3
Churchtown
Mersey **183** E1
Churnsike Lodge **219** E4
Churston Ferrers **101** F2
Churt **121** D4
Churton **170** B2
Churwell **194** B5
Chute Cadley **119** E2
Chute Standen **119** E2
Chwilog **166** D4
Chyandour **94** B3
Chysauster **94** B3
Cilan Uchaf **166** B5
Cilcain **169** E1
Cilcennin **142** B1
Cilcewydd **156** B2
Cilfrew **129** D2
Cilfynydd **129** G3
Cilgerran **141** E3
Cilgwyn Carmar **142** D4
Cilgwyn Pembs **141** D4
Ciliau Aeron **142** B2
Cille Bhrighde **254** C3
Cille Pheadair **254** C3
Cilmaengwyn **128** D2
Cilmery **143** G2
Cilrhedyn **141** F4
Cilrhedyn Bridge **140** D4
Cilsan **142** B5
Ciltalgarth **168** B3
Cilwendeg **141** F4
Cilybebyll **128** D2
Cilycwm **143** D3
Cimla **129** D3
Cinderford **131** F1
Cippenham **135** E4
Cippyn **141** E3
Cirbhig **270** D3
Cirencester **132** C2
City GtLon **136** C4
City VGlam **129** F5
City Airport **136** D4
City Dulas **180** C4
Clabhach **246** A4
Clachaig **232** C1
Clachan A&B **241** D3
Clachan A&B **248** A5
Clachan A&B **231** F4
Clachan High **256** B1
Clachan WIsles **262** C7
Clachan Mòr **246** A2
Clachan of
Campsie **234** A2
Clachan of
Glendaruel **232** A1
Clachan-a-Luib **262** D5
Clachandhu **239** D1
Clachaneasy **215** E3
Clachanmore **206** A2
Clachan-Seil **239** G3
Clachanturn **259** K5
Clachbreck **231** F2
Clachnabrain **252** B3
Clachnaharry **266** D7
Clachtoll **272** C6
Clackmannan **243** E5
Clackmarras **267** K6
Clacton Pier Essex
CO15 1QX **139** E1
Clacton-on-Sea **139** E1
Cladach a Bhale
Shear **262** C5
Cladach Chircebost **262** C5
Cladach Chnoc a
Lin **262** C5
Cladich
(An Cladach) **240** C2
Cladswell **146** C2
Claggan (An Claigeann)
High **248** C2
Claggan High **247** G5
Claigan **263** H6
Claines **146** A2
Clambers Play Centre
ESuss TN34 1LD
75 Hastings
Clandown **117** D2
Clanfield Hants **107** G1
Clanfield Oxon **133** E2
Clannaborough
Barton **102** A2
Clanville **119** E3
Claonaig **231** G4
Claonairigh **240** C4
Claonel **266** C1
Clapgate **150** C5
Clapham Bed **149** F2
Clapham Devon **102** B4
Clapham GtLon **136** B5
Clapham NYorks **192** D1
Clapham WSuss **108** C3
Clapham Green **149** F2
Clapham Hill **124** D2
Clappers **237** G4
Clappersgate **199** E2

Clapton Som **104** A2
Clapton Som **116** D2
Clapton-in-
Gordano **131** D5
Clapton-on-the-Hill **133** D1
Clapworthy **113** G3
Clara Vale **212** A1
Clarach **154** C4
Clarbeston **141** D5
Clarbeston Road **140** D5
Clarborough **187** E4
Clardon **275** G2
Clare **151** F3
Clare Castle Country Park
Suff CO10 8NJ **151** F3
Clarebrand **216** B4
Claremont Landscape
Garden Surr
KT10 9JG **121** G1
Clarencefield **217** E4
Clarilaw **227** G4
Clark's Green **121** G4
Clarkston **233** G4
Clashban **266** D2
Clashcoig **266** D2
Clashdorran **266** C7
Clashgour **249** E4
Clashindarroch **260** C1
Clashmore High **266** E3
Clashmore High **272** C5
Clashnessie **272** C5
Clashnoir **259** K2
Clatford **118** C1
Clathy **243** E2
Clatt **260** D2
Clatter **155** F3
Clattercote **147** G3
Clatterford **107** D4
Clatterford End **137** E2
Clatterin Brig **253** E2
Clatteringshaws **215** G3
Clatworthy **115** D4
Claughton Lancs **192** B1
Claughton Lancs **192** B3
Clavelshay **115** F4
Claverdon **147** D1
Claverham **116** B1
Clavering **150** C4
Claverley **157** G3
Claverton **117** E1
Claverton Down **117** E1
Clawdd-côch **129** G5
Clawdd-newydd **169** D2
Clawfin **224** D5
Clawthorpe **199** G5
Clawton **99** D1
Claxby **188** B3
Claxby Pluckacre **176** B1
Claxby St. Andrew **189** E5
Claxton Norf **179** E5
Claxton NYorks **195** F1
Claxton Grange **213** D5
Clay Common **165** F3
Clay Coton **160** A5
Clay Cross **173** E1
Clay End **150** B5
Clay Hill **131** F5
Clay of Allan **267** F4
Claybrooke Magna **159** G4
Claybrooke Parva **159** G4
Claydene **123** D4
Claydon Oxon **147** G2
Claydon Suff **152** C3
Claygate Kent **123** G4
Claygate Surr **121** G1
Claygate Cross **123** F3
Clayhanger Devon **114** D5
Clayhanger WMid **158** C2
Clayhidon **103** E1
Clayhill ESuss **110** D1
Clayhill Hants **106** C2
Clayhithe **150** D1
Clayock **275** G3
Claypit Hill **150** B2
Claypits **131** G2
Claypole **174** D3
Claythorpe **189** E5
Clayton Staffs **171** F3
Clayton SYorks **186** B2
Clayton WSuss **109** F2
Clayton WYorks **194** A4
Clayton Green **192** B5
Clayton West **185** G1
Clayton-le-Moors **192** D4
Clayton-le-Woods **192** B5
Clayworth **187** E4
Cleadale **247** E4
Cleadon **212** C1
Clearbrook **100** B1
Clearwell **131** E2
Cleasby **202** B1
Cleat Ork **277** D9
Cleat WIsles **254** B4
Cleatlam **202** A1
Cleatop **193** E1
Cleator **208** D5
Cleator Moor **208** D5
Cleckheaton **194** A5
Clee St. Margaret **157** E4
Cleedownton **157** E4
Cleehill **157** E5
Cleestanton **157** E5
Cleethorpes **188** D2
Cleethorpes Discovery
Centre NELincs
DN35 0AG **188** D2
Cleeton St. Mary **157** F5
Cleeve NSom **116** B1
Cleeve Oxon **134** B4
Cleeve Hill **146** B5
Cleeve Prior **146** C3
Cleghorn **234** C5
Clehonger **145** D4
Cleigh **240** A2
Cleish **243** F5
Cleland **234** B4
Clement's End **135** F1
Clemsfold **121** G4
Clench Common **118** C1
Clenchwarton **177** D5
Clennell **220** B1
Clent **158** B5

Clent Hills
 Worcs DY9 9JR **14** B5
Cleobury Mortimer **157** F5
Cleobury North **157** F4
Clephanton **267** F6
Clerklands **227** G3
Clestrain **277** C7
Clermiston **235** F2
Cleuch Head **227** G4
Cleughbrae **217** E3
Clevancy **132** C5
Clevedon **130** B3
Cleveland Tontine
 Inn **202** D3
Cleveley **147** F5
Cleveleys **191** G3
Clevelode **146** A3
Cleverton **132** B4
Clewer **116** B2
Clewer Green **135** E5
Clewer Village **135** E5
Cley next the Sea **178** B1
Cliburn **210** B5
Cliddesden **120** B3
Cliff Carmar **127** G2
Cliff High **247** F3
Cliff End **111** D2
Cliff Grange **170** D4
Cliffe Lancs **192** D4
Cliffe Med **137** G5
Cliffe NYorks **195** F4
Cliffe Woods **137** G5
Clifford Here **144** B3
Clifford WYorks **194** D3
Clifford Chambers **147** D2
Clifford's Mesne **145** F5
Clifford's Tower
 YO1 9SA **90** York
Cliffs End **125** F2
Clifton Bristol **131** E5
Clifton CenBeds **149** G4
Clifton Cumb **210** B5
Clifton Derbys **172** C3
Clifton Devon **113** F1
Clifton Lancs **192** A4
Clifton N'umb **221** E3
Clifton Nott **173** G4
Clifton NYorks **194** A3
Clifton Oxon **147** G5
Clifton Stir **241** F1
Clifton SYorks **186** C3
Clifton Worcs **146** A3
Clifton WYorks **194** A5
Clifton York **195** E2
Clifton Campville **159** E1
Clifton Hampden **134** A4
Clifton Maybank **104** B1
Clifton Park Museum
 SYorks S65 2AA **21** D1
Clifton Reynes **149** E2
Clifton upon
 Dunsmore **160** C4
Clifton upon Teme **145** G1
Cliftonville **125** F1
Climping **108** C3
Climpy **234** D4
Clink **117** E3
Clint **194** B2
Clint Green **178** B4
Clinterty **261** G3
Clintmains **228** A3
Clippesby **179** F4
Clippings Green **178** B4
Clipsham **161** E1
Clipston N'hants **160** C4
Clipston Notts **174** B4
Clipstone **173** G1
Clitheroe **192** D3
Clive **170** C5
Cliveden Bucks
 SL6 0JA **135** E4
Clivocast **278** E3
Clixby **188** B2
Clocaenog **169** D2
Clochan **268** C4
Clochtow **261** J1
Clock Face **183** G3
Clockhill **269** G6
Cloddach **267** J6
Cloddiau **156** A2
Clodock **144** C5
Cloford **117** E3
Cloichran **242** B1
Clola **269** J6
Clonrae **216** C1
Clophill **149** F4
Clopton **161** F4
Clopton Corner **152** D2
Clopton Green Suff **151** F2
Clopton Green Suff **152** A2
Close Clark **190** A4
Closeburn **216** C1
Closworth **104** B1
Clothall **150** A4
Clothan **278** D4
Clotton **170** C1
Clough Cumb **200** C3
Clough GtMan **184** D1
Clough GtMan **184** D1
Clough WYorks **185** E1
Clough Foot **193** F5
Clough Head **193** G5
Cloughton **204** D3
Cloughton
 Newlands **204** D3
Clounlaid **247** G4
Clousta **279** C7
Clouston **277** C6
Clova Aber **260** C2
Clova Angus **252** B2
Clove Lodge **201** E1
Clovelly **112** D3
Clovelly Cross **112** D3
Clovelly Village Devon
 EX39 5TA **112** D3
Clovenfords **227** F2
Clovenstone **261** F3
Cloves **267** J5
Clow Bridge **193** E5
Clowne **186** B5

Clows Top **157** G5
Cloyntie **224** B5
Cluanach **230** B4
Clubworthy **98** C1
Cluddley **157** F1
Cluer (Cliuthar) **263** G2
Clumber Country Park
 Notts S80 3AZ **186** D5
Clun **156** B4
Clunas **267** F7
Clunbury **156** C4
Clunderwen **127** E1
Clune High **258** E2
Clune Moray **268** D4
Clunes **249** E1
Clungunford **156** C5
Clunie Aber **268** E5
Clunie P&K **251** G5
Clunton **156** C4
Cluny **244** A5
Clutton B&NESom **116** D2
Clutton ChesW&C **170** B2
Clwt-y-bont **167** E1
Clwydyfagwyr **129** G2
Clydach Mon **130** B3
Clydach Swan **128** C2
Clydach Terrace **130** A1
Clydach Vale **129** F3
Clydey **141** F4
Clyffe Pypard **132** C5
Clynder **232** D1
Clyne **129** E2
Clynelish **267** F1
Clynfyw **141** F4
Clynnog-fawr **166** D3
Clyro **144** B3
Clyst Honiton **102** C3
Clyst Hydon **102** D2
Clyst St. George **102** C4
Clyst St. Lawrence **102** D2
Clyst St. Mary **102** C4
Clyst William **103** D2
Cnewr **143** E5
Cnoc **271** G4
Cnwch Coch **154** C5
Coachford **268** C6
Coad's Green **97** G2
Coal Aston **186** A5
Coalbrookdale **157** F2
Coalbrookvale **130** A2
Coalburn **225** G2
Coalburns **212** A1
Coalcleugh **211** E3
Coaley **131** G2
Coalmoor **157** F2
Coalpit Heath **131** F4
Coalpit Hill **171** F2
Coalport **157** F2
Coalsnaughton **243** E5
Coaltown of
 Balgonie **244** B5
Coaltown of
 Wemyss **244** B5
Coalville **159** G1
Coalway **131** E1
Coanwood **210** C2
Coast **265** F2
Coat **116** B5
Coatbridge **234** B3
Coate Swin **133** D4
Coate Wilts **118** B1
Coates Cambs **162** B3
Coates Glos **132** B2
Coates Lincs **187** G4
Coates Notts **187** F4
Coates WSuss **108** B2
Coatham **213** E5
Coatham
 Mundeville **212** B5
Cobairdy **268** D6
Cobbaton **113** G3
Cobbler's Plain **131** D2
Cobby Syke **194** A2
Cobden **102** D3
Coberley **132** B1
Cobhall Common **145** D4
Cobham Kent **123** D4
Cobham Surr **121** G1
Cobleland **242** A5
Cobley Hill **158** C5
Cobnash **145** D1
Coburty **269** H4
Cochno **233** F2
Cock Alley **173** F1
Cock Bank **170** A3
Cock Bevington **146** C2
Cock Bridge **259** K4
Cock Clarks **138** B2
Cock Green **137** G1
Cock Marling **111** D2
Cockayne **203** F3
Cockayne Hatley **150** A3
Cockburnspath **237** E2
Cockenzie & Port
 Seton **236** B2
Cocker Bar **192** B5
Cockerham **192** A4
Cockermouth **209** E3
Cockernhoe **149** G5
Cockerton **202** B1
Cockett **128** C3
Cockfield Dur **212** A5
Cockfield Suff **152** A2
Cockfosters **136** B3
Cocking **108** A2
Cockington Country
 Park Torbay
 TQ2 6XA **101** E4
Cocklake **116** B3
Cocklaw **220** B4
Cockleford **132** B1
Cockle Park **221** E2
Cockleford **103** F3
Cockley Beck **198** D2
Cockley Cley **163** F2
Cockpen **236** A3
Cockpole Green **134** C4
Cockshutt **170** B5
Cockthorpe **178** A1
Cockwood Devon **102** C4
Cockwood Som **115** F3

Cockyard **185** E4
Codda **97** F2
Coddenham **152** C2
Coddington
 ChesW&C **170** B2
Coddington Here **145** G3
Coddington Notts **174** D2
Codicote **136** B1
Codmore Hill **108** C2
Codnor **173** F3
Codnor Park **173** F2
Codrington **131** G5
Codsall **158** A2
Codsall Wood **158** A2
Coed Morgan **130** C1
Coed Ystumgwern **167** E5
Coedcae **130** B2
Coedely **129** G4
Coedkernew **130** B4
Coedpoeth **169** F2
Coedway **156** C1
Coed-y-bryn **141** G2
Coed-y-caerau **130** C3
Coed-y-paen **130** C3
Coed-y-parc **167** F1
Coed-yr-ynys **144** A5
Coelbren **129** E1
Coffinswell **101** E1
Cofton **102** C4
Cofton Hackett **158** C5
Cogan **130** A5
Cogenhoe **148** D1
Cogges **133** F2
Coggeshall **151** G5
Coggeshall Hamlet **151** G5
Coggins Mill **110** A1
Cóig Peighinnean **271** H1
Coilantogle **242** A4
Coileitir **248** D5
Coilessan **241** E4
Coillaig **240** C2
Coille Mhorgil **257** G4
Coille-righ **257** F3
Coillore **255** J1
Coity **129** F4
Col **271** G4
Col Uarach **271** G4
Colaboll **273** H7
Colan **96** C3
Colaton Raleigh **103** D4
Colbost **263** H7
Colburn **202** B3
Colbury **106** C1
Colby Cumb **210** C5
Colby IoM **190** A4
Colby Norf **178** D2
Colchester **152** A5
Colchester Castle Museum
 Essex CO1 1TJ **152** A5
Colchester Green **152** A2
Colchester Zoo Essex
 CO3 0SL **152** A5
Colcot **115** E1
Cold Ash **119** G1
Cold Ashby **160** B5
Cold Ashton **131** G5
Cold Aston **132** D1
Cold Blow **127** E1
Cold Brayfield **149** E2
Cold Chapel **226** A3
Cold Cotes **200** C5
Cold Hanworth **188** A4
Cold Harbour **134** B4
Cold Hatton **170** D5
Cold Hatton Heath **170** D5
Cold Hesledon **212** D3
Cold Higham **148** B2
Cold Inn **127** E2
Cold Kirby **203** E4
Cold Newton **160** C2
Cold Northcott **97** G1
Cold Norton **138** B2
Cold Overton **160** D2
Cold Row **191** G3
Coldbackie **273** J2
Coldbeck **200** C2
Coldblow **137** E5
Coldean **109** F3
Coldeast **102** B5
Colden **193** F5
Colden Common **119** F5
Coldfair Green **153** F1
Coldham **162** C2
Coldharbour Glos **131** E2
Coldharbour Surr **121** G3
Coldingham **237** G3
Coldrain **243** F4
Coldred **125** E4
Coldrey **120** C3
Coldridge **113** G5
Coldrife **220** C2
Coldstream **228** C3
Coldvreath **97** D4
Coldwaltham **108** C2
Coldwells **269** K6
Cole **117** D4
Cole End **159** D4
Cole Green **136** B1
Cole Henley **119** F2
Colebatch **156** C4
Colebrook **102** D2
Colebrooke **102** A2
Coleburn **267** K6
Coleby Lincs **175** E1
Coleby NLincs **187** F1
Coleford Devon **102** A2
Coleford Glos **131** E1
Coleford Som **117** D3
Colegate End **164** C3
Colehill **105** G2
Coleman Green **136** A1
Coleman's
 Hatch **122** D5
Colemere **170** B4
Colemore **120** C4
Colemore Green **157** G3
Colenden **243** G2
Coleorton **159** G1
Colerne **132** A5
Cole's Common **164** D3
Cole's Cross **101** D3

Cole's Green **153** D1
Colesbourne **132** C1
Colesden **149** G2
Coleshill Bucks **135** E3
Coleshill Oxon **133** E3
Coleshill Warks **159** E4
Colestocks **103** D2
Coley B&NESom **116** C2
Coley Staffs **172** B5
Colfin **214** B5
Colgate **122** B5
Colgrain **233** E2
Colinsburgh **244** C4
Colintraive **232** B2
Colkirk **178** A3
Coll **246** A5
Collace **244** A1
Collafirth **279** D6
Collamoor Head **98** B1
Collaton St. Mary **101** E1
Collessie **244** A3
Colleton Mills **113** G4
Collett's Green **146** A2
Collier Row **137** E3
Collier's End **150** B5
Collier's Wood **136** B5
Collier Street **123** G4
Colliery Row **212** C3
Collieston **261** J2
Collin **217** E3
Collingbourne
 Ducis **118** D2
Collingbourne
 Kingston **118** D2
Collingham Notts **174** D1
Collingham WYorks **194** C3
Collington **145** F1
Collingtree **148** C2
Collins End **134** B5
Collins Green
 Warr **183** G3
Collins Green
 Worcs **145** G2
Colliston **253** E5
Colliton **103** D2
Collmuir **260** D4
Collycroft **159** F4
Collyhurst **184** C2
Collynie **261** G1
Collyweston **161** E2
Colmonell **214** C2
Colmworth **149** G2
Coln Rogers **132** C2
Coln St. Aldwyns **132** D2
Coln St. Dennis **132** C1
Colnabaichin **259** K4
Colnbrook **135** F5
Colne Cambs **162** B5
Colne Lancs **193** E4
Colne Engaine **151** G4
Colney **178** C5
Colney Heath **136** B2
Colney Street **136** A2
Colonsay **238** C5
Colonsay House **238** C5
Colony Gift Corporation
 Cumb LA12 0LD **199** D5
Colpy **260** E1
Colquhar **235** J1
Colsterdale **202** A4
Colsterworth **175** E5
Colston Bassett **174** C4
Colston Hall
 BS1 5AR **66** Bristol
Coltfield **267** J5
Colthouse **199** E3
Coltishall **179** D4
Coltness **234** C4
Colton Cumb **199** E4
Colton Norf **178** C5
Colton NYorks **195** E3
Colton Staffs **172** B5
Colton WYorks **194** C4
Colva **144** B2
Colvend **216** C5
Colvister **278** E3
Colwall **145** G3
Colwall Green **145** G3
Colwall Stone **145** G3
Colwell **220** B4
Colwich **172** B5
Colwick **174** B3
Colwinston **129** F5
Colworth **108** B3
Colwyn Bay
 (Bae Colwyn) **181** G5
Colyford **103** F3
Colyton **103** F3
Combe Here **144** C1
Combe Oxon **133** G1
Combe Som **116** B5
Combe WBerks **119** E1
Combe Common **121** E4
Combe Cross **102** A5
Combe Down **117** E1
Combe Florey **115** E4
Combe Hay **117** E2
Combe Martin **113** F1
Combe Martin Wildlife &
 Dinosaur Park Devon
 EX34 0NG **113** F1
Combe Pafford **101** F1
Combe Raleigh **103** E2
Combe St. Nicholas **103** G1
Combeinteignhead **102** B5
Comberbach **184** A5
Comberford **159** D2
Comberton Cambs **150** B2
Comberton Here **145** D1
Combpyne **103** F3
Combridge **172** B4
Combrook **147** F2
Combs Derbys **185** E5
Combs Suff **152** B2
Combs Ford **152** B2
Combwich **115** F3
Comer **241** F4
Comers **260** E4
Comhampton **146** A1
Comins Coch **154** C4

Commercial End **151** D1
Commins Coch **155** E2
Common Edge **191** G4
Common Moor **97** G2
Common Platt **132** C4
Common Side **186** A5
Common Square **188** A5
Commondale **203** F1
Commonside **172** D3
Compstall **185** D3
Compton Devon **101** E1
Compton Hants **119** F5
Compton Plym **100** A2
Compton Staffs **158** A4
Compton Surr **121** E3
Compton WBerks **134** A5
Compton WSuss **107** G1
Compton Wilts **118** C2
Compton
 Beauchamp **133** E4
Compton Bishop **116** A2
Compton
 Chamberlayne **118** B5
Compton Dundon **116** B4
Compton Martin **116** C2
Compton
 Pauncefoot **116** D5
Compton Valence **104** B3
Compton Verney **147** F2
Compton Wynyates **147** F3
Comra **258** C5
Comrie Fife **235** E1
Comrie P&K **242** C2
Conchra A&B **232** B1
Conchra High **256** E2
Concraigie **251** G5
Conder Green **192** A2
Conderton **146** B4
Condicote **146** D5
Condorrat **234** B2
Condover **157** D2
Coney Weston **164** A4
Coneyhurst **121** G5
Coneysthorpe **203** G5
Coneythorpe **194** C2
Conford **120** D4
Congash **259** H2
Congdon's Shop **97** G2
Congerstone **159** F2
Congham **177** F5
Congleton **171** F1
Congresbury **116** B1
Congreve **158** B1
Conham **131** F5
Conicaval **267** G6
Coningsby **176** A2
Conington Cambs **161** G4
Conington Cambs **150** B1
Conisbrough **186** C3
Conisby **230** A3
Conisholme **189** E3
Coniston Cumb **199** E3
Coniston ERid **197** D4
Coniston Cold **193** F2
Conistone **193** F1
Connah's Quay **169** F1
Connel
 (A' Choingheal) **240** B1
Connel Park **225** E4
Connor Downs **94** C3
Conock **118** B2
Conon Bridge (Drochaid
 Sgùideil) **266** C6
Cononish **241** F2
Cononley **193** F3
Cononsyth **253** D5
Consall **171** G3
Consett **212** A2
Constable Burton **202** A3
Constantine **95** E4
Constantine Bay **96** C2
Contin
 (Cunndainn) **266** B6
Contlaw **261** G4
Contullich **266** D4
Conwy **181** F5
Conwy Castle Conwy
 LL32 8LD **181** F5
Conyer **124** B2
Conyer's Green **151** G1
Cooden **110** C3
Coodham **224** C2
Cookbury **113** E5
Cookbury Wick **113** D5
Cookham **135** D4
Cookham Dean **135** D4
Cookham Rise **135** D4
Cookhill **146** C2
Cookley Suff **165** E4
Cookley Worcs **158** A4
Cookley Green
 Oxon **134** B3
Cookley Green Suff **165** E4
Cookney **261** G5
Cook's Green **152** A2
Cooksbridge **109** F2
Cooksey Green **146** B1
Cookshill **171** G3
Cooksmill Green **137** F2
Cookston **261** H1
Coolham **121** G5
Cooling **137** G5
Cooling Street **137** G5
Coombe Corn **97** D4
Coombe Corn **112** D4
Coombe Corn **96** A5
Coombe Corn **96** C5
Coombe Devon **101** D3
Coombe Devon **102** D3
Coombe Devon **103** D3
Coombe Som **115** F5
Coombe Som **104** A3
Coombe Wilts **118** C2
Coombe Bissett **118** C5

Coombe Country Park
 Works CV3 2AB **16** D3
Coombe End **114** D5
Coombe Hill **146** A5
Coombe Keynes **105** E4
Coombes **109** D3
Coombes Moor **144** C1
Cooper's Corner
 ESuss **110** C1
Cooper's Corner
 Kent **123** D4
Cooper's Green **136** A2
Coopersale **137** D2
Coopersale Street **137** D2
Cootham **108** C2
Cop Street **125** E3
Copdock **152** C3
Copford Green **152** A5
Copgrove **194** C1
Copister **278** D5
Cople **149** G3
Copley Dur **211** G5
Copley WYorks **193** G5
Coplow Dale **185** F5
Copmanthorpe **195** E3
Copmere End **171** F5
Copp **192** A4
Coppathorne **112** C5
Coppenhall **158** B1
Coppenhall Moss **171** E2
Copperhouse **94** C3
Coppicegate **157** G4
Coppingford **161** G4
Coppleridge **117** F5
Copplestone **102** A2
Coppull **183** G1
Coppull Moor **183** G1
Copsale **121** G5
Copse Hill **122** B2
Copster Green **192** C4
Copston Magna **159** G4
Copt Heath **159** D5
Copt Hewick **202** C5
Copt Oak **159** G1
Copthall Green **136** D2
Copthorne **122** C5
Copy Lake **113** G4
Copythorne **106** C1
Coralhill **269** J4
Corbets Tey **137** E4
Corbridge **211** F1
Corby **161** D4
Corby Glen **175** F5
Corcrach **260** E5
Coreley **157** F5
Corfcott Green **98** D1
Corfe **103** F1
Corfe Castle **105** F4
Corfe Castle Dorset
 BH20 5EZ **105** F4
Corfe Mullen **105** F3
Corfton **157** D4
Corgarff **259** K4
Corhampton **120** B5
Corley **159** E4
Corley Ash **159** E4
Corley Moor **159** E4
Corn Exchange Cambs
 CB2 3QB **66** Cambridge
Cornabus **230** B5
Cornard Tye **152** A3
Corndon **99** G2
Corney **198** C3
Cornforth **212** C4
Cornhill **268** D5
Cornhill on Tweed **228** C3
Cornholme **193** F5
Cornish Gold & Treasure
 Park Corn
 TR16 4HN **96** A5
Cornish Hall End **151** E4
Cornquoy **277** E7
Cornriggs **211** E3
Cornsay **212** A3
Cornsay Colliery **212** A3
Corntown High **266** C6
Corntown VGlam **129** F5
Cornwell **147** E5
Cornwood **100** C2
Cornworthy **101** E2
Corpach
 (A' Chorpaich) **248** D2
Corpusty **178** C3
Corrachree **260** C4
Corran A&B **241** E5
Corran High **256** E4
Corran (Ardgour)
 High **248** C3
Corranbuie **231** G3
Corranmore **239** G4
Corrany **190** C3
Cornbeg **248** B2
Corrie **232** B5
Corrie Aber **268** E6
Corrie Common **218** A3
Corriechrevie **231** F4
Corriecravie **223** E3
Corriedoo **216** A2
Corriekinloch **273** F6
Corrielorne **240** A3
Corrievorrie **258** E1
Corrimony **257** K1
Corringham Lincs **187** F3
Corringham Thur **137** G4
Corris **155** D2
Corris Uchaf **154** D2
Corrour Shooting
 Lodge **249** G3
Corrow **241** D4
Corry **256** C2
Corrychurrachan **248** C3
Corrylach **222** C2
Corrymuckloch **243** D1
Corsback **275** H1
Corscombe **104** B2
Corse Aber **268** E6
Corse Glos **145** G5
Corse Lawn **146** A4
Corse of Kinnoir **268** D6
Corsebank **225** G4

Corsegight **269** G5
Corsehill **217** F2
Corsewall **214** B4
Corsham **132** A5
Corsindae **260** E4
Corsley **117** F3
Corsley Heath **117** F3
Corsock **216** B3
Corston B&NESom **117** D1
Corston Wilts **132** B4
Corstorphine **235** F2
Cortachy **252** B4
Corton Suff **165** G2
Corton Wilts **118** A3
Corton Denham **116** D5
Corwar House **215** D2
Corwen **169** D2
Coryton Devon **99** E2
Coryton Thur **137** G4
Cosby **160** A3
Coscote **134** A4
Coseley **158** B3
Cosford Shrop **157** G2
Cosford Warks **160** A5
Cosgrove **148** C3
Cosham **107** F2
Cosheston **126** D2
Coshieville **250** C5
Coskills **188** A2
Cosmeston **115** E1
Cosmeston Lakes Country
 Park VGlam
 CF64 5UY **115** E1
Cossall **173** F3
Cossington Leics **160** B1
Cossington Som **116** A3
Costa **276** C5
Costessey **178** C4
Costock **173** G5
Coston Leics **174** D5
Coston Norf **178** B5
Cote Oxon **133** F2
Cote Som **116** A3
Cotebrook **170** C1
Cotehill **210** B2
Cotes Cumb **199** F4
Cotes Leics **173** G5
Cotes Staffs **171** F5
Cotesbach **160** A4
Cotford St. Luke **115** E4
Cotgrave **174** B4
Cothall **261** G3
Cotham **174** C3
Cothelstone **115** E4
Cotheridge **145** G2
Cotherstone **201** F1
Cothill **133** G3
Cotleigh **103** F2
Cotmanhay **173** F3
Coton Cambs **150** C2
Coton N'hants **160** B5
Coton Staffs **171** G4
Coton Staffs **159** D2
Coton Staffs **171** F5
Coton Clanford **171** F5
Coton Hill **171** G4
Coton in the Clay **172** C5
Coton in the Elms **159** E1
Cotonwood Shrop **170** C4
Cotonwood Staffs **171** F5
Cotswold Water Park Glos
 GL7 6DF **132** C3
Cotswold Wildlife Park Oxon
 OX18 4JP **133** E2
Cott **101** D1
Cottam Lancs **192** A4
Cottam Notts **187** F4
Cottartown **259** H1
Cottenham **150** C1
Cotterdale **200** D3
Cottered **150** B5
Cotteridge **158** C5
Cotterstock **161** F3
Cottesbrooke **160** C5
Cottesmore **161** E1
Cottingham ERid **196** C4
Cottingham
 N'hants **160** D3
Cottingley **194** A4
Cottisford **148** A4
Cotton Staffs **172** B3
Cotton Suff **152** B1
Cotton End **149** F3
Cottonworth **119** E4
Cottown Aber **260** D2
Cottown Aber **269** G6
Cottown Aber **261** F3
Cotts **100** A1
Cottwood **113** G4
Cotwall **171** F1
Cotwalton **171** G4
Couch's Mill **97** F4
Coughton Here **145** E5
Coughton Warks **146** C1
Cougie **257** J2
Coulaghailtro **231** F3
Coulags **265** F7
Coulby Newham **203** E1
Coulderton **198** A2
Coull **260** D4
Coulport **232** D1
Coulsdon **122** B3
Coulston **118** A2
Coulter **226** B2
Coultershaw Bridge **108** B2
Coultings **115** F3
Coulton **203** F5
Coultra **244** B2
Cound **157** E2
Coundlane **157** E2
Coundon Dur **212** B5
Coundon WMid **159** F4
Countersett **201** E4
Countess Wear **102** C4
Countesthorpe **160** A3
Countisbury **114** A3
Coup Green **192** B5
Coupar Angus **252** A5
Coupland Cumb **200** C1
Coupland N'umb **228** D3
Cour **231** G5
Court Colman **129** E4

Court Henry **142** B5
Court House Green **159** F4
Court-at-Street **124** C5
Courtauld Institute of Art
  Gallery *GtLon*
  WC2R 0RN **45** F3
Courteenhall **148** C2
Courtsend **138** D3
Courtway **115** F4
Cousland **236** A3
Cousley Wood **123** F5
Coustonn **232** B2
Cove *A&B* **232** D1
Cove *Devon* **102** C1
Cove *Hants* **120** D2
Cove *High* **264** E2
Cove *ScBord* **237** E2
Cove Bay **261** H4
Cove Bottom **165** F3
Covehithe **165** G3
Coven **158** B2
Coveney **162** C4
Covenham
  St. Bartholomew **188** D3
Covenham St. Mary **188** D3
Coventry **159** F4
Coventry Airport **159** F5
Coventry Cathedral *WMid*
  CV1 5AB **69** Coventry
Coventry Transport Museum
  WMid CV1 1JD
  69 Coventry
Coverack **95** E5
Coverham **202** A4
Covesea **267** J4
Covingham **133** D4
Covington *Cambs* **161** F5
Covington *SLan* **226** A2
Cowan Bridge **200** B5
Cowbeech **110** B2
Cowbit **162** A1
Cowbridge *Som* **114** C3
Cowbridge *VGlam* **129** F5
Cowden **123** D4
Cowden Pound **123** D4
Cowdenbeath **243** G5
Cowdenburn **235** G4
Cowers Lane **173** E3
Cowes **107** D3
Cowesby **203** D4
Cowesfield Green **119** D5
Cowey Green **152** B5
Cowfold **109** E1
Cowgill **200** C4
Cowie *Aber* **253** G1
Cowie *Stir* **234** C1
Cowlam Manor **196** B1
Cowley *Devon* **102** C3
Cowley *Glos* **132** B1
Cowley *GtLon* **135** F4
Cowley *Lancs* **183** G1
Cowley *Oxon* **134** A2
Cowling *Lancs* **183** G1
Cowling *NYorks* **193** F3
Cowling *NYorks* **202** B4
Cowlinge **151** F2
Cowmes **185** F1
Cowpe **193** E5
Cowpen **221** E5
Cowpen Bewley **213** D5
Cowplain **107** F1
Cowsden **146** B2
Cowshill **211** E3
Cowthorpe **194** D2
Cox Common **165** E3
Coxbank **171** D3
Coxbench **173** E3
Coxbridge **116** C4
Coxford **177** G5
Coxheath **123** G3
Coxhoe **212** C4
Coxley **116** C3
Coxley Wick **116** C3
Coxpark **99** E3
Coxtie Green **137** E3
Coxwold **203** E5
Coychurch **129** F5
Coylet **232** C1
Coylton **224** C4
Coylumbridge **259** G3
Coynach **260** C4
Coynachie **260** C1
Coytrahen **129** E4
Crabbet Park **122** C5
Crabgate **178** B3
Crabtree *Plym* **100** B2
Crabtree *SYorks* **186** A4
Crabtree *WSuss* **109** E1
Crabtree Green **170** A3
Crackaig **230** D3
Crackenthorpe **210** C5
Crackington **98** B1
Crackington Haven **98** B1
Crackley **171** F2
Crackleybank **157** G1
Crackpot **201** E3
Crackthorn Corner **164** B4
Cracoe **193** F1
Craddock **103** D1
Cradhlastadh **270** C4
Cradley *Here* **145** G3
Cradley *WMid* **158** B4
Cradley Heath **158** B4
Crafthole **99** D5
Crafton **135** D1
Cragg **193** G5
Cragg Hill **194** B4
Craggan *Moray* **259** J1
Craggan *P&K* **242** D3
Cragganmore **259** J1
Cragganruar **250** B3
Craggie *High* **258** E1
Craggie *High* **274** D7
Craghead **212** B2
Cragside *N'umb*
  NE65 7PX **220** C1
Craibstone
  Aberdeen **261** G3
Craibstone *Moray* **268** C5
Craichie **252** D5
Craig *A&B* **240** C1
Craig *A&B* **239** E1
Craig *D&G* **216** A4

Craig *High* **264** D5
Craig *High* **265** G7
Craig *SAyr* **224** B5
Craig Berthlwyd **129** G3
Craigans **240** A5
Craigbeg **249** G1
Craigcleuch **218** B3
Craigdallie **244** A2
Craigdam **261** G1
Craigdarroch *D&G* **216** B1
Craigdarroch *EAyr* **225** E5
Craigdhu *D&G* **207** D2
Craigdhu *High* **266** B7
Craigearn **261** F3
Craigellachie **267** K7
Craigellie **269** J4
Craigencallie **215** G2
Craigend *Moray* **267** J6
Craigend *P&K* **243** G2
Craigendive **232** B1
Craigendoran **233** E1
Craigengillan **224** C5
Craigenputtock **216** B2
Craigens **230** A3
Craighall **244** C3
Craighat **233** F1
Craighead *Fife* **245** E3
Craighead *High* **266** E5
Craighlaw **215** E4
Craighouse **230** D3
Craigie *Aber* **261** H3
Craigie *Dundee* **244** C1
Craigie *P&K* **251** G5
Craigie *SAyr* **224** C2
Craigie Brae **261** G1
Craigieburn **226** C5
Craigieholm **243** G1
Craigielaw **236** B2
Craiglockhart **235** G2
Craiglug **261** G5
Craigmaud **269** G5
Craigmillar **235** G2
Craigmore **232** C2
Craigmyle House **260** E4
Craignafeoch **232** A2
Craignant **169** F4
Craignavie **242** A1
Craigneuk **234** B4
Craignure **239** G1
Craigo **253** E3
Craigoch **224** A5
Craigrothie **244** B3
Craigroy **267** J6
Craigrory Farm **259** J1
Craigruie **241** G2
Craigsanquhar **244** B3
Craigton *Aberdeen* **261** G4
Craigton *Angus* **244** D1
Craigton *Angus* **252** B5
Craigton *High* **266** D7
Craigton *Stir* **234** A1
Craigtown **274** D3
Craig-y-nos **129** E1
Craik *Aber* **260** C2
Craik *ScBord* **227** E5
Crail **245** E4
Crailing **228** A4
Crailinghall **228** A4
Crakehill **202** D5
Crakemarsh **172** B4
Crambe **195** G1
Cramlington **221** E4
Cramond **235** F2
Cranage **171** E1
Cranberry **171** F4
Cranbourne **135** E5
Cranbrook
  Common **123** G5
Crane Moor **186** A2
Cranfield **149** E3
Cranford *Devon* **112** D3
Cranford *GtLon* **136** A5
Cranford St. Andrew **161** E5
Cranford St. John **161** E5
Cranham *Glos* **132** A1
Cranham *GtLon* **137** E4
Crank **183** G3
Cranleigh **121** F4
Cranmer Green **164** B4
Cranmore *IoW* **106** C4
Cranmore *Som* **117** D3
Cranna **268** E5
Crannoch **268** C5
Cranoe **160** C3
Cransford **153** E1
Cranshaws **237** D3
Cranstal **190** C1
Crantock **96** B3
Cranwell **175** F3
Cranwich **163** F3
Cranworth **178** A5
Craobh Haven **239** G4
Crapstone **100** B1
Crarae **240** B5
Crask Inn **273** H6
Crask of Aigas **266** B7
Craskins **260** D4
Craster **229** G5
Craswall **144** B4
Crateford **158** B2
Cratfield **165** E4
Crathes **261** F5
Crathie *Aber* **259** K5
Crathie *High* **258** C5
Crathorne **202** D2
Craven Arms **156** D4
Craw **231** G5
Crawcrook **212** A1
Crawford *Lancs* **183** F2
Crawford *SLan* **226** A3
Crawfordjohn **225** G3
Crawfordton **216** B1
Crawick **225** F4

Crawley *Devon* **103** F2
Crawley *Hants* **119** F4
Crawley *Oxon* **133** F1
Crawley *WSuss* **122** B5
Crawley Down **122** C5
Crawleyside **211** F3
Crawshawbooth **193** E5
Crawton **253** G2
Crawyn **190** B2
Cray *NYorks* **201** E5
Cray *P&K* **251** G3
Cray *Powys* **143** E5
Crayke **203** E5
Crays Hill **137** G3
Crazies Hill **134** C4
Creacombe **102** B1
Creagan **239** G2
Creagbheitheachain
  248 B3
Creagorry
  (Creag Ghoraidh) **262** C7
Crealy Adventure
  Park Devon
  Devon EX5 1DR **102** C3
Creamore Bank **170** C4
Creaton **160** C5
Creca **218** A4
Credenhill **145** D3
Crediton **102** B2
Creebridge **215** F4
Creech Heathfield **115** F5
Creech St. Michael **115** F5
Creed **96** D5
Creedy Park **102** B2
Creekmoor **105** F3
Creekmouth **137** D4
Creeting St. Mary **152** B2
Creeton **175** F5
Creetown **215** F5
Creggans **240** B4
Cregneash **190** A5
Cregrina **144** A2
Creich **244** B2
Creigau **131** D2
Creigiau **129** G4
Crelevan **257** K1
Crelly **95** D3
Cremyll **100** A2
Crendell **105** G1
Cressage **157** E2
Cressbrook **185** F5
Cresselly **127** D2
Cressing **151** G5
Cresswell *N'umb* **221** E2
Cresswell *Staffs* **171** G4
Cresswell Quay **127** D2
Creswell **186** C5
Cretingham **152** D2
Cretshengan **231** F3
Crewe *ChesE* **171** E1
Crewe *ChesW&C* **170** B2
Crewe Green **171** E2
Crewgreen **156** C1
Crewkerne **104** A2
Crew's Hole **131** F5
Crewton **173** E4
Crianlarich (A'Chrion-
  Làraich) **241** F2
Cribbs Causeway **131** E4
Cribyn **142** B2
Criccieth **167** D4
Crich **173** E2
Crich Carr **173** E2
Crich Common **173** E2
Crich Tramway Village
  Derbys DE4 5DP **173** E2
Crichie **269** H6
Crichton **236** A3
Crick *Mon* **131** D3
Crick *N'hants* **160** A5
Crickadarn **143** G3
Cricket Hill **120** D1
Cricket St. Thomas **103** G2
Crickham **116** B3
Crickheath **169** F5
Crickhowell **130** B1
Cricklade **132** D3
Cricklewood **136** B4
Cridling Stubbs **195** E5
Crieff **243** D2
Criftins (Dudleston
  Heath) **170** A4
Criggan **97** E3
Criggion **156** B1
Crigglestone **186** A1
Crimble **184** C1
Crimchard **103** G2
Crimdon Park **213** D4
Crimond **269** J5
Crimonmogate **269** J5
Crimplesham **163** E2
Crinan **239** G5
Crinan Ferry **239** G5
Cringleford **178** C5
Cringletie **235** G5
Crinow **127** E1
Cripplestyle **105** G1
Cripp's Corner **110** C1
Crix **137** G1
Crizeley **144** D4
Croalchapel **216** D1
Croasdale **209** D5
Crock Street **103** G1
Crockenhill **123** E2
Crocker End **134** C4
Crockerhill **107** E2
Crockernwell **102** A3
Crockerton **117** F3
Crockerton Green **117** F3
Crocketford
  (Ninemile Bar) **216** C3
Crockey Hill **195** F3
Crockham Hill **122** D3

Crockhurst Street **123** F4
Crockleford Heath **152** B5
Croes Hywel **130** C1
Croesau Bach **169** F5
Croeserw **129** E3
Croesgoch **140** B4
Croes-lan **141** G3
Croesor **167** F3
Croespenmaen **130** A3
Croesyceiliog
  Carmar **128** A1
Croesyceiliog
  Torfaen **130** C3
Croesywaun **167** E2
Croford **115** E5
Croft *Here* **145** D1
Croft *Leics* **160** A3
Croft *Lincs* **176** D1
Croft *Warr* **184** A3
Croftamie **233** F1
Crofthead **218** B4
Croftmore **251** D2
Crofton *Wilts* **119** D1
Crofton *WYorks* **186** A1
Croft-on-Tees **202** B2
Crofts **216** B3
Crofts of Benachielt **275** G5
Crofts of Buinach **267** J6
Crofts of Haddo **261** G1
Crofty **128** B3
Crogen **168** D4
Croggan **239** G2
Croglin **210** B3
Croick *High* **266** C3
Croick *High* **274** D3
Croig **246** D4
Crois Dughaill **254** C3
Croit e Caley **190** A5
Cromarty (Cromba) **266** E5
Crombie **235** E1
Crombie Country Park
  Angus DD5 3QL **252** D5
Crombie Mill **244** D1
Cromblet **261** F1
Cromdale **259** H2
Cromer *Herts* **150** A5
Cromer *Norf* **178** D1
Cromford **173** D2
Cromhall **131** F3
Cromhall Common **131** F3
Cromor **271** G5
Crompton Fold **185** D1
Cromwell **174** C1
Cronberry **225** E3
Crondall **120** C3
Cronk-y-Voddy **190** B3
Cronton **183** F4
Crook *Cumb* **199** F3
Crook *Dur* **212** A4
Crook of Devon **243** F4
Crooked Soley **133** F5
Crookedholm **224** C2
Crookham *N'umb* **228** D3
Crookham *WBerks* **119** G1
Crookham Eastfield **228** D3
Crookham Village **120** C2
Crooklands **199** G4
Cropredy **147** G3
Cropston **160** A1
Cropthorne **146** B3
Cropton **203** G4
Cropwell Bishop **174** B4
Cropwell Butler **174** B4
Crosbie **232** D5
Crosbost **271** F5
Crosby *Cumb* **209** D3
Crosby *IoM* **190** B4
Crosby *Mersey* **183** E3
Crosby *NLincs* **187** F1
Crosby Court **202** C3
Crosby Garrett **200** C3
Crosby
  Ravensworth **200** B1
Crosby Villa **209** D3
Crosby-on-Eden **210** A2
Croscombe **116** C3
Crosemere **170** B5
Crosland Hill **185** F1
Cross *Som* **116** B2
Cross (Cros) *Wlsles* **271** H1
Cross Ash **130** D1
Cross Bank **157** G5
Cross End *Bed* **149** F2
Cross End *Essex* **151** G4
Cross Foxes Inn **155** E1
Cross Gates **194** C4
Cross Green *Devon* **99** D2
Cross Green *Staffs* **158** B2
Cross Green *Suff* **152** A2
Cross Green *Suff* **151** G2
Cross Green *Suff* **151** G2
Cross Hands
  Carmar **128** B1
Cross Hands
  Pembs **127** D1
Cross Hill **173** F3
Cross Hills **193** G3
Cross Houses **157** E2
Cross in Hand **110** A1
Cross Inn *Cere* **141** G2
Cross Inn *Cere* **142** B1
Cross Inn *RCT* **129** G4
Cross Keys **132** A5
Cross Lane **107** E3
Cross Lane Head **157** G3
Cross Lanes *Corn* **96** B5
Cross Lanes *Corn* **96** B5
Cross Lanes *NYorks* **195** E1
Cross Lanes *Wrex* **170** A3
Cross of Jackston **261** F1
Cross o'th'hands **173** D3
Crossaig **231** G4
Crossapol **246** A4
Crossapoll **246** A2
Cross-at-Hand **123** G4
Crossbush **108** C3
Crosscanonby **209** D3
Crossdale Street **178** D2
Crossens **183** E1

Crossflatts **194** A3
Crossford *D&G* **216** D2
Crossford *Fife* **235** E1
Crossford *SLan* **234** C5
Crossgate *Lincs* **176** A5
Crossgate *Staffs* **171** G4
Crossgatehall **236** A3
Crossgates *Fife* **235** F1
Crossgates *NYorks* **204** D4
Crossgates *P&K* **243** F2
Crossgates *Powys* **143** G1
Crossgill **192** B1
Crosshands **224** C2
Crosshill *Fife* **243** G5
Crosshill *SAyr* **224** B5
Crosshouse **224** B2
Crosskeys **130** B3
Crosskirk **275** B3
Crosslanes **156** C1
Crosslee *Renf* **233** F3
Crosslee *ScBord* **227** E4
Crossmichael **216** B3
Crossmoor **192** A4
Crossroads *Aber* **261** F5
Crossroads *EAyr* **224** C2
Crossway *Mon* **130** D1
Crossway *Powys* **143** G2
Crossway Green
  Mon **131** E3
Crossway Green
  Worcs **146** A1
Crossways *Dorset* **105** D4
Crossways *Glos* **131** E1
Crosswell **141** E4
Crosswood **142** C1
Crosthwaite **199** F3
Croston **183** F1
Crostwick **179** D4
Crostwight **179** E3
Crothair **270** D4
Crouch **123** F3
Crouch End **136** B4
Crouch Hill **104** D1
Croucheston **118** B5
Croughton **148** A4
Crovie **269** G4
Crow **106** A2
Crow Edge **185** F2
Crow Green **137** E3
Crow Hill **145** F1
Crowan **94** D3
Crowborough **123** E5
Crowborough
  Warren **123** E5
Crowcombe **115** E4
Crowdecote **172** C1
Crowden **185** E3
Crowdhill **119** F5
Crowell **134** C3
Crowfield *N'hants* **148** B3
Crowfield *Suff* **152** C2
Crowhurst *ESuss* **110** C2
Crowhurst *Surr* **122** C4
Crowhurst Lane End **122** C4
Crowland *Lincs* **162** A1
Crowland *Suff* **164** B4
Crowlas **94** C3
Crowle *NLincs* **187** E1
Crowle *Worcs* **146** B2
Crowle Green **146** B2
Crowmarsh Gifford **134** B4
Crown Corner **165** D4
Crownhill **100** A2
Crownthorpe **178** B5
Crowntown **94** D3
Crow's Nest **97** G3
Crows-an-wra **94** A4
Crowsnest **156** C2
Crowthorne **120** D1
Crowton **183** G5
Croxall **159** E1
Croxby **188** B3
Croxdale **212** B4
Croxden **172** B4
Croxley Green **135** F3
Croxteth Country Park
  Mersey L12 0HB **22** C2
Croxteth Hall *Mersey*
  L12 0HB **22** C2
Croxton *Cambs* **150** A2
Croxton *NLincs* **188** A1
Croxton *Norf* **163** G4
Croxton *Staffs* **171** E4
Croxton Green **170** C2
Croxton Kerrial **174** D5
Croxtonbank **171** E4
Croy *High* **266** E7
Croy *NLan* **234** B2
Croyde **113** E2
Croyde Bay **113** E2
Croydon *Cambs* **150** B3
Croydon *GtLon* **122** C2
Cruach **230** B4
Cruchie **268** D6
Cruckmeole **156** D2
Cruckton **156** D1
Cruden Bay **261** J1
Crudgington **157** F1
Crudwell **132** B3
Crug **156** A5
Crugmeer **96** D2
Crugybar **142** C4
Crùlabhig **270** D4
Crumlin **130** B3
Crumpsall **184** C2
Crumpsbrook **157** F5
Crundale *Kent* **124** C4
Crundale *Pembs* **126** C1
Crunwere Farm **127** E1
Crutherland Farm **234** A4
Cruwys Morchard **102** B1
Crux Easton **119** F2
Crwbin **128** A1
Cryers Hill **135** D3
Crymlyn **181** E5
Crymych **141** E4
Crynant **129** D2
Crystal Palace **136** C5
Crystal Palace Park
  GtLon SE20 8DT **13** C7
Cuaig **264** D6
Cubbington **147** F1
Cubert **96** B4

Cubley **185** G2
Cublington *Bucks* **148** D5
Cublington *Here* **144** D4
Cuckfield **109** E1
Cucklington **117** E5
Cuckney **186** C5
Cuckold's Green **165** F3
Cuckoo Bridge **176** A5
Cuckoo's Corner **120** C3
Cuckoo's Nest **170** A1
Cuddesdon **134** A2
Cuddington *Bucks* **134** C1
Cuddington
  ChesW&C **183** G5
Cuddington Heath **170** B3
Cuddy Hill **192** A4
Cudham **123** D2
Cudlipptown **99** F3
Cudmore Grove Country
  Park *Essex*
  CO5 8UE **152** C1
Cudworth *Som* **103** G1
Cudworth *SYorks* **186** A2
Cuerdley Cross **183** G4
Cuffley **136** C2
Cuidhaseadair **271** H2
Cuidhir **254** B4
Cuidrach **263** J6
Cuil-uaine **240** B1
Cuilmuich **241** D5
Cuil-uaine **240** B1
Culag **241** D5
Culbo **266** D5
Culbokie
  (Cùil Bhàicidh) **266** D6
Culbone **114** B3
Culburnie **266** B7
Culcabock **266** D7
Culcharan **240** B1
Culcharry **267** F6
Culcheth **184** A3
Culdrain **260** D1
Culduie **264** D7
Culford **151** G1
Culfordheath **163** G5
Culgaith **210** C5
Culgower **274** E7
Culham **134** A2
Culindrach **232** A4
Culkein **272** C5
Culkerton **132** B3
Cullachie **259** G2
Cullen **268** D4
Cullercoats **221** F4
Cullicudden **266** D5
Culligran **265** K7
Cullingworth **193** G4
Cullipool **239** G3
Cullivoe **278** E2
Culloch **242** C3
Culloden **266** E7
Cullompton **102** D2
Culmaily **267** F2
Culmalzie **215** E5
Culmington **157** D4
Culmstock **103** E1
Culnacraig **265** G1
Culnadalloch **240** B1
Culnaknock **264** B5
Culnamean **255** K2
Culpho **152** D3
Culquhirk **215** F5
Culrain **266** C2
Culroy **224** B4
Culsh **260** C3
Culshabbin **215** E5
Culswick **279** B8
Culter Allers Farm **226** B2
Cultercullen **261** H2
Cults *Aber* **260** D1
Cults *Aberdeen* **261** G4
Cults *D&G* **207** E2
Cultybraggan
  Camp **242** C2
Culverhouse Cross **130** A5
Culverstone Green **123** F2
Culverthorpe **175** F3
Culvie **268** D5
Culworth **148** A3
Culzean Castle & Country
  Park *SAyr*
  KA19 8LE **224** A4
Cumberhead **225** F2
Cumberlow Green **150** B4
Cumbernauld **234** B2
Cumbernauld **189** F5
Cuminestown **269** G6
Cumloden **215** F4
Cummersdale **209** G1
Cummertrees **217** F4
Cummingston **267** J5
Cumnock **225** D3
Cumnor **133** G2
Cumrew **210** B3
Cumrue **217** E2
Cumstoun **216** A5
Cumwhinton **210** A2
Cumwhitton **210** B2
Cundall **202** D5
Cunninghamhead **233** E5
Cunningsburgh **279** D10
Cunnister **278** E3
Cunnoquhie **244** B3
Cupar **244** B3
Cupar Muir **244** B3
Curbar **185** G5
Curborough **158** D1
Curbridge *Hants* **107** E1
Curbridge *Oxon* **133** F2
Curdridge **107** E1
Curdworth **159** D3
Curland **103** E1
Curler Green **153** E1
Curling Tye Green **138** B2
Curload **116** A5
Curridge **133** G5
Currie **235** F3
Curry Mallet **116** A5
Curry Rivel **116** A5
Curteis' Corner **124** A5
Curtisden Green **123** G4
Curtisknowle **100** D2

Cury **95** D4
Cusgarne **96** B5
Cushnie **269** F4
Cushuish **115** E4
Cusop **144** B3
Cusworth **186** C2
Cutcloy **207** E3
Cutcombe **114** C4
Cutgate **184** C1
Cuthill **266** E3
Cutiau **154** C1
Cutlers Green **151** D4
Cutnall Green **146** A1
Cutsdean **146** C4
Cutsyke **194** D5
Cutthorpe **186** A5
Cutts **279** D9
Cuttyhill **269** J5
Cuxham **134** B3
Cuxton **123** G2
Cuxwold **188** B2
Cwm *BGwent* **130** A2
Cwm *Denb* **182** B5
Cwm Ffrwd-oer **130** B2
Cwm Gwaun **140** D4
Cwm Head **156** D4
Cwm Irfon **143** E3
Cwm Penmachno **168** A3
Cwm Plysgog **141** E3
Cwmafan **129** D3
Cwmaman **129** G3
Cwmann **142** B3
Cwmbach *Carmar* **141** F5
Cwmbach *Carmar* **128** A2
Cwmbach *Powys* **144** A4
Cwmbach *Powys* **143** G2
Cwmbach *RCT* **129** G2
Cwmbelan **155** F4
Cwmbrwyno **154** D5
Cwmbrân **130** B3
Cwmbrwyno **154** D5
Cwmcarn **130** B3
Cwmcarvan **131** D2
Cwm-Cewydd **155** E1
Cwm-cou **141** F3
Cwmcrawnon **130** A1
Cwmdare **129** F2
Cwmdu *Carmar* **142** C4
Cwmdu *Powys* **144** A5
Cwmduad **141** G4
Cwmerfyn **154** D4
Cwmfelin **129** G2
Cwmfelin Boeth **127** E1
Cwmfelin Mynach **141** F5
Cwmfelinfach **130** A3
Cwmffrwd **128** A1
Cwmgiedd **129** E1
Cwmgors **128** D1
Cwmgwili **128** B1
Cwmgwrach **129** E2
Cwmgwyn **128** C3
Cwmhiraeth **141** G4
Cwmifor **142** C5
Cwmisfael **128** A1
Cwm-Llinau **155** E2
Cwmllyfri **127** G1
Cwmllynfell **128** D1
Cwm-mawr **128** B1
Cwm-miles **141** E5
Cwm-Morgan **141** F4
Cwm-parc **129** F3
Cwmpengraig **141** G4
Cwmpennar **129** G2
Cwmsychbant **142** A3
Cwmsymlog **154** C4
Cwmtillery **130** B2
Cwm-twrch Isaf **129** D1
Cwm-twrch Uchaf **129** D1
Cwm-y-glo **167** E1
Cwmyoy **144** C5
Cwm-yr-Eglwys **140** D3
Cwmyrhaiadr **155** D3
Cwmystwyth **155** D5
Cwrt **154** C2
Cwrt-newydd **142** A3
Cwrt-y-cadno **142** C3
Cwrt-y-gollen **130** B2
Cyffylliog **169** D2
Cyfronydd **156** A2
Cymau **169** F2
Cymmer *NPT* **129** E3
Cymmer *RCT* **129** G3
Cyncoed **130** A4
Cynghordy **143** E4
Cynheidre **128** A2
Cynwyd **169** D3
Cynwyl Elfed **141** G5

D

Dabton **216** C1
Daccombe **101** F1
Dacre *Cumb* **210** A5
Dacre *NYorks* **194** A1
Dacre Banks **194** A1
Daddry Shield **211** E4
Dadford **148** B4
Dadlington **159** G3
Dafen **128** B2
Daffy Green **178** A5
Dagdale **172** B4
Dagenham **137** D4
Daggons **106** A1
Daglingworth **132** B2
Dagnall **135** E1
Dail **240** C1
Dail Beag **270** E3
Dail Mòr **270** E3
Dailly **224** A5
Dailnamac **240** B1
Dainton **101** E1
Dairsie (Osnaburgh) **244** C3
Dairy House Yard **197** E3
Daisy Bank **158** C3
Daisy Green **152** B1
Dalabrog **254** C2
Dalavich **240** B3
Dalballoch **258** D5
Dalbeattie **216** C4
Dalblair **225** E3
Dalbog **253** D2
Dalbreck **274** C7
Dalbury **173** D4
Dalby *IoM* **190** A4

Dalby *Lincs* **176** C1
Dalby *NYorks* **203** F5
Dalby Forest Drive *NYorks* YO18 7LT **204** B4
Dalcairnie **224** C5
Dalchalloch **250** C3
Dalchalm **267** G1
Dalchenna **240** C4
Dalchirach **259** J1
Dalchork **273** H7
Dalchreichart **257** J3
Dalchruin **242** C3
Dalcross **266** E7
Dalderby **176** A1
Dalditch **102** D4
Daldownie **259** K4
Dale *Cumb* **210** B3
Dale *GtMan* **185** D2
Dale *Pembs* **126** B2
Dale Abbey **173** F4
Dale End *Derbys* **172** D1
Dale End *NYorks* **193** F3
Dale Head **199** F1
Dale of Walls **279** A7
Dale Park **108** B2
Dalehouse **203** G1
Dalelia **247** G3
Daless **259** F1
Dalestie **259** J3
Dalfad **260** B4
Dalganachan **275** F4
Dalgarven **233** D5
Dalgety Bay **235** F1
Dalgig **225** D4
Dalginross **242** C2
Dalgonar **225** F5
Dalguise **251** E5
Dalhalvaig **274** D3
Dalham **151** F1
Daligan **233** E1
Dalinlongart **232** C1
Dalivaddy **222** B3
Daljarrock **214** C2
Dalkeith **236** A3
Dallachulish **248** B5
Dallas **267** J6
Dallaschyle **267** F7
Dallash **215** F4
Dalleagles **225** D4
Dallinghoo **153** D2
Dallington *ESuss* **110** B2
Dallington *N'hants* **148** C1
Dallow **202** A5
Dalmadilly **261** F3
Dalmally (Dail Mhàilidh) **241** D2
Dalmarnock **251** F5
Dalmary **242** A5
Dalmellington **224** C5
Dalmeny **235** F2
Dalmichy **273** H7
Dalmigavie **258** E3
Dalmore **266** D5
Dalmuir **233** F2
Dalmunzie House Hotel **251** F2
Dalnabreck **247** G3
Dalnacarn **251** F3
Dalnaglar Castle **251** G3
Dalnaha **239** F2
Dalnahaitnach **259** F3
Dalnamain **266** E2
Dalnatrat (Dail na Tràghad) **248** B4
Dalnavert **259** F4
Dalnavie **266** D4
Dalness **249** D4
Dalnessie **273** J7
Dalnigap **214** C3
Dalqueich **243** F4
Dalreoch **214** C2
Dalriech **242** C1
Dalroy **266** E7
Dalrulzian **251** G4
Dalry **233** D5
Dalrymple **224** B4
Dalscote **148** B2
Dalserf **234** B4
Dalsetter **278** E3
Dalshangan **215** G2
Dalskairth **216** D3
Dalston **209** G1
Dalswinton **216** D2
Daltomach **258** E2
Dalton *Cumb* **199** G5
Dalton *D&G* **217** F3
Dalton *Lancs* **183** F2
Dalton *N'umb* **220** D4
Dalton *N'umb* **211** F2
Dalton *NYorks* **202** D5
Dalton *NYorks* **202** A2
Dalton *SYorks* **186** B3
Dalton Magna **186** B3
Dalton Piercy **213** D4
Dalton-in-Furness **198** D5
Dalton-le-Dale **212** D3
Dalton-on-Tees **202** B2
Daltote **231** F1
Daltra **267** G7
Dalveich **242** B2
Dalvennan **224** B4
Dalvourn **258** D1
Dalwhinnie **250** B1
Dalwood **103** F2
Dam Green **164** B3
Damask Green **150** A5
Damerham **106** A1
Damgate **179** F5
Damnaglaur **206** B3
Damside **243** E3
Danaway **124** A2
Danbury **137** G2
Danby **203** G2
Danby Wiske **202** C3
Dancers Hill **136** B3
Dandaleith **267** K7
Danderhall **236** A3
Dane Bank **184** D3
Dane End **150** B5
Dane Hills **160** A2
Danebridge **171** G1
Danehill **109** G1
Danesmoor **173** F1
Danestone **261** H3
Daniel's Water **124** B4
Danskine **236** C3
Danthorpe **197** E4
Danzey Green **146** D1
Darby End **158** B4
Darby Green **120** D1
Darenth **137** E5
Daresbury **183** G4
Darfield **186** B2
Dargate **124** C2
Dargues **220** A2
Darite **97** G3
Darland **123** G2
Darlaston **158** B3
Darley **194** B2
Darley Bridge **173** D1
Darley Dale **173** D1
Darley Head **194** A2
Darley Hillside **173** D1
Darlingscott **147** E3
Darlington **202** B1
Darliston **170** C4
Darlton **187** E5
Darnabo **269** F6
Darnall **186** A4
Darnconner **225** D3
Darnford **261** F5
Darngarroch **216** A4
Darnick **227** G2
Darowen **155** E2
Darra **269** F6
Darracott **112** C4
Darras Hall **221** D4
Darrington **186** B1
Darrow Green **165** D3
Darsham **153** F1
Dartfield **269** J5
Dartford **137** E5
Dartington **101** D1
Dartington Cider Press Centre *Devon* TQ9 6TQ **101** D1
Dartington Crystal Ltd. *Devon* EX38 7AN **113** E4
Dartmeet **99** G3
Dartmouth **101** E2
Darton **186** A1
Darvel **225** D2
Darvell **110** C1
Darwell Hole **110** B2
Darwen **192** C5
Datchet **135** E5
Datchworth **136** B1
Datchworth Green **136** B1
Daubhill **184** A2
Daugh of Kinermony **267** K7
Dauntsey **132** B4
Dauntsey Green **132** B4
Dauntsey Lock **132** B4
Dava **259** H1
Davaar **222** C4
Davan **260** C4
Davenham **184** A5
Davenport Green **184** C4
Daventry **148** A1
Daventry Country Park *N'hants* NN11 2JB **148** A1
David Marshall Lodge *Stir* FK8 3SX **242** A4
Davidstow **97** F1
Davington **226** D5
Daviot *Aber* **261** F2
Daviot *High* **258** E1
Davoch of Grange **268** C5
Davyhulme **184** B3
Dawley **157** F2
Dawlish **102** C5
Dawn **181** G5
Daws Heath **138** B4
Daw's House **98** D2
Dawsmere **176** C4
Day Green **171** E2
Dayhills **171** G4
Dayhouse Bank **158** B5
Daylesford **147** E5
Ddôl **182** C5
Deadman's Cross **149** G3
Deadwaters **234** B5
Deaf Hill **212** C4
Deal **125** F3
Deal Hall **138** D3
Dean *Cumb* **209** D4
Dean *Devon* **100** D1
Dean *Dorset* **105** F1
Dean *Hants* **107** E1
Dean *Oxon* **147** F5
Dean *Som* **117** D3
Dean Bank **212** B4
Dean Castle & Country Park *EAyr* KA3 1XB **224** C2
Dean Cross **113** F1
Dean Gallery *Edin* EH4 3DS **36** B4
Dean Head **185** G2
Dean Prior **100** D1
Dean Row **184** C4
Dean Street **123** G3
Deanburnhaugh **227** E4
Deane *GtMan* **184** A2
Deane *Hants* **119** G2
Deanland **105** F1
Deanlane End **107** G1
Deans Bottom **124** A2
Deanscales **209** D4
Deansgreen **184** A4
Deanshanger **148** C4
Deanston **242** C4
Dearham **209** D3
Debach **152** D2
Debate **218** A3
Debden **151** D4
Debden Cross **151** D4
Debden Green *Essex* **151** D4
Debden Green *Essex* **136** D3
Debenham **152** C1
Deblin's Green **146** A3
Dechmont **235** E2
Decker Hill **157** G1
Deddington **147** G4
Dedham **152** B4
Dedham Heath **152** B4
Dedworth **135** E5
Deecastle **260** C5
Deene **161** E3
Deenethorpe **161** E3
Deep, The HU1 4DP **76** Kingston upon Hull
Deep Sea World, North Queensferry *Fife* KY11 1JR **235** F1
Deepcar **185** G3
Deepcut **121** E2
Deepdale *Cumb* **200** C4
Deepdale *NYorks* **201** D5
Deeping Gate **161** G2
Deeping St. James **161** G2
Deeping St. Nicholas **162** A1
Deepweir **131** D4
Deerhill **268** C5
Deerhurst **146** A5
Deerhurst Walton **146** A5
Deerness Valley Walk *Dur* DH7 7RJ **212** A3
Deerton Street **124** B2
Defford **146** B3
Defynnog **143** F5
Deganwy **181** F5
Degnish **239** G3
Deighton *NYorks* **202** C2
Deighton *WYorks* **185** F1
Deighton *York* **195** F3
Deiniolen **167** E1
Delabole **97** E1
Delamere **170** C1
Delavorar **259** J3
Delfrigs **261** H2
Dell Lodge **259** H3
Dell Quay **108** A3
Delliefure **259** H1
Delly End **133** F1
Delnabo **259** J3
Delny **266** E4
Delph **185** D2
Delphorrie **260** C3
Delves **212** A3
Delvine **251** G5
Dembleby **175** F4
Denaby **186** B3
Denaby Main **186** B3
Denbies Wine Estate *Surr* RH5 6AA **121** G2
Denbigh (Dinbych) **168** D1
Denbury **101** E1
Denby **173** E3
Denby Dale **185** G2
Denby Pottery *Derbys* DE5 8NX **18** C1
Denchworth **133** F3
Dendron **198** D5
Denend **260** E1
Denford **161** E5
Dengie **138** C2
Denham *Bucks* **135** F4
Denham *Suff* **164** C4
Denham *Suff* **151** F1
Denham Green **135** F4
Denham Street **164** C4
Denhead *Aber* **261** F3
Denhead *Aber* **269** J5
Denhead *Fife* **244** C3
Denhead of Arbirlot **253** D5
Denhead of Gray **244** B1
Denholm **227** G4
Denholme **193** G4
Denholme Clough **193** G4
Denio **166** C4
Denmead **107** F1
Denmill **261** G3
Denmoss **268** E6
Dennington **153** D1
Denny **234** C1
Dennyloanhead **234** C1
Denshaw **185** D1
Denside **261** G5
Densole **125** E4
Denston **151** F2
Denstone **172** B3
Dent **200** C4
Denton *Cambs* **161** G4
Denton *Darl* **202** B1
Denton *ESuss* **109** G3
Denton *GtMan* **184** D3
Denton *Kent* **125** E4
Denton *Kent* **137** F5
Denton *Lincs* **175** D4
Denton *N'hants* **148** D2
Denton *Norf* **165** D3
Denton *NYorks* **194** A3
Denton *Oxon* **134** A2
Denton's Green **183** F3
Denver **163** E2
Denvilles **107** G2
Denwick **229** G5
Deopham **178** B5
Deopham Green **164** B2
Depden **151** F2
Depden Green **151** F2
Deptford *GtLon* **136** C5
Deptford *Wilts* **118** B4
Derby **173** E4
Derby City Museum & Art Gallery DE1 1BS **70** Derby
Derbyhaven **190** A5
Dereham (East Dereham) **178** A4
Dererach **239** E2
Deri **130** A2
Derril **112** D5
Derringstone **125** E4
Derrington **171** F5
Derriton **112** D5
Derry **242** B2
Derry Hill **132** B5
Derrythorpe **187** F2
Dersingham **177** E4
Dervaig **246** D4
Derwen **169** D2
Derwenlas **154** D3
Derwent Walk Country Park *Dur* NE16 3BN **28** A3
Derwydd **128** C1
Derybruich **232** A2
Desborough **160** D4
Desford **159** G2
Detchant **229** E3
Dethick **173** E2
Detling **123** G3
Deuddwr **156** B1
Deunant **168** C1
Deuxhill **157** F4
Devauden **131** D3
Devil's Bridge (Pontarfynach) **154** D5
Devitts Green **159** E3
Devizes **118** B1
Devon Guild of Craftsmen *Devon* TQ13 9AF **102** B5
Devonport **100** A2
Devonside **243** E5
Devoran **95** E3
Dewar **236** A5
Dewlish **105** D3
Dewsall Court **145** D4
Dewsbury **194** B5
Dewsbury Moor **194** B5
Dhiseig **239** D1
Dhoon **190** C3
Dhoor **190** C2
Dhowin **190** C1
Dhuhallow **258** C2
Dial Green **121** E5
Dial Post **109** D2
Dibden **106** D2
Dibden Hill **135** E3
Dibden Purlieu **106** D2
Dick Institute *EAyr* KA1 3BU **224** C2
Dickleburgh **164** C3
Dickleburgh Moor **164** C3
Didbrook **146** C4
Didcot **134** A3
Diddington **149** G1
Diddlebury **157** E4
Didley **145** D4
Didling **108** A2
Didmarton **132** A4
Didsbury **184** C3
Didworthy **100** C1
Digby **175** F2
Digg **263** K5
Diggle **185** E2
Digmoor **183** F2
Digswell **136** B1
Dihewyd **142** A2
Dildawn **216** B5
Dilham **179** E3
Dilhorne **171** G3
Dillington **149** G1
Dilston **211** F1
Dilton Marsh **117** F3
Dilwyn **144** D2
Dilwyn Common **144** D2
Dimple **184** B1
Dinas *Carmar* **141** F4
Dinas *Gwyn* **167** D2
Dinas *Gwyn* **166** B4
Dinas Cross **140** D4
Dinas Dinlle **166** D2
Dinas Powys **130** A5
Dinas-Mawddwy **155** E1
Dinckley **192** C4
Dinder **116** C3
Dinedor **145** E4
Dingestow **131** D1
Dingley **160** C4
Dingwall (Inbhir Pheofharain) **266** C6
Dinlabyre **218** D2
Dinnet **260** C5
Dinnington *Som* **104** A1
Dinnington *SYorks* **186** C4
Dinnington *T&W* **221** E4
Dinorwig **167** E1
Dinosaur Adventure Park *Norf* NR9 5JW **178** C4
Dinosaur Museum, Dorchester *Dorset* DT1 1EW **104** C3
Dinton *Bucks* **134** C1
Dinton *Wilts* **118** B4
Dinton Pastures Country Park *W'ham* RG10 0TH **134** C5
Dinvin **214** B5
Dinwoodie Mains **217** F1
Dinworthy **112** D4
Dipford **115** F5
Dippen *A&B* **222** C2
Dippen *NAyr* **223** F3
Dippenhall **120** D3
Dipple *Moray* **268** B5
Dipple *SAyr* **224** A5
Diptford **100** D2
Dipton **212** A2
Dirdhu **259** H2
Dirleton **236** C1
Discoed **144** B1
Discovery Museum *T&W* NE1 4JA **79** Newcastle upon Tyne
Diseworth **173** F5
Dishes **276** F5
Dishforth **202** C5
Dishley **173** G5
Disley **185** D4
Diss **164** C3
Disserth **143** G2
Distington **208** D4
Ditcheat **116** D4
Ditchingham **165** E2
Ditchley **147** F5
Ditchling **109** F2
Ditteridge **117** F1
Dittisham **101** E2
Ditton *Halton* **183** F4
Ditton *Kent* **123** G3
Ditton Green **151** E2
Ditton Priors **157** F4
Dixton *Glos* **146** B4
Dixton *Mon* **131** E1
Dobcross **185** D2
Dobwalls **97** G3
Doccombe **102** A4
Dochgarroch **258** D1
Dock Museum, Barrow-in-Furness *Cumb* LA14 2PW **191** E1
Dockenfield **120** D3
Docker *Cumb* **199** G3
Docker *Lancs* **199** G5
Docking **177** F4
Docklow **145** E2
Dockray *Cumb* **209** G4
Dockray *Cumb* **209** F1
Dodbrooke **100** D3
Doddenham **145** G2
Doddinghurst **137** E3
Doddington *Cambs* **162** C3
Doddington *Kent* **124** B3
Doddington *Lincs* **187** G5
Doddington *N'umb* **229** D3
Doddington *Shrop* **157** F5
Doddiscombsleigh **102** B4
Doddycross **98** D4
Dodford *N'hants* **148** B1
Dodford *Worcs* **158** B5
Dodington *SGlos* **131** G4
Dodington *Som* **115** E3
Dodington Ash **131** G5
Dodleston **170** A1
Dods Leigh **172** B4
Dodscott **113** F4
Dodworth **186** A2
Doehole **173** E2
Doffcocker **184** A1
Dog Village **102** C3
Dogdyke **176** A2
Dogmersfield **120** C2
Dogsthorpe **162** A2
Dol Fawr **155** E2
Dolanog **155** G1
Dolau *Powys* **144** A1
Dolau *RCT* **129** G4
Dolbenmaen **167** E3
Doley **171** E5
Dolfach **155** F5
Dolfor **156** A4
Dolgarreg **142** D4
Dolgarrog **168** A1
Dolgellau **154** D1
Dolgoch **154** C2
Dolgran **142** A4
Doll **267** F1
Dollar **243** E5
Dollarbeg **243** E5
Dolphin **182** C5
Dolphinholme **192** B2
Dolphinton **235** F5
Dolton **113** F4
Dolwen *Conwy* **181** G5
Dolwen *Powys* **155** F2
Dolwyddelan **168** A2
Dôl-y-bont **154** C4
Dol-y-cannau **144** A3
Dolyhir **144** B2
Dolywern **169** F4
Domgay **156** B1
Doncaster **186** C2
Doncaster Racecourse Exhibition Centre *SYorks* DN2 6BB **186** D2
Donhead St. Andrew **118** A5
Donhead St. Mary **118** A5
Donibristle **235** F1
Doniford **115** D3
Donington *Lincs* **176** A4
Donington *Shrop* **158** A2
Donington le Heath **159** G1
Donington on Bain **188** C4
Donisthorpe **159** F1
Donkey Sanctuary, Salcombe Regis *Devon* EX10 0NU **103** E4
Donna Nook **189** E3
Donnington *Glos* **147** D5
Donnington *Here* **145** G4
Donnington *Shrop* **157** E2
Donnington *Tel&W* **157** G1
Donnington *WBerks* **119** F1
Donnington *WSuss* **108** A3
Donyatt **103** G1
Dorchester *Dorset* **104** C3
Dorchester *Oxon* **134** A3
Dorchester Abbey *Oxon* OX10 7HH **134** A3
Dordon **159** E2
Dore **186** A4
Dores (Duras) **258** C1
Dorket Head **173** G3
Dorking **121** G3
Dorley's Corner **153** E1
Dormans Park **122** C4
Dormansland **122** D4
Dormanstown **213** E5
Dormer's Wells **136** A4
Dormington **145** E3
Dormston **146** B2
Dorn **147** E4
Dorney **135** E5
Dorney Reach **135** E5
Dornie (An Dòrnaidh) **256** E2
Dornoch **266** E3
Dornock **218** A5
Dorrery **275** F3
Dorridge **159** D5
Dorrington *Lincs* **175** F2
Dorrington *Shrop* **157** D2
Dorsell **260** D3
Dorsington **146** D3
Dorstone **144** C3
Dorton **134** B1
Dorusduain **257** F2
Dosthill **159** E3
Dotland **211** F2
Dottery **104** A3
Doublebois **97** F3
Dougalston **233** G2
Dougarie **223** D2
Doughton **132** A3
Douglas *IoM* **190** B4
Douglas *SLan* **225** G2
Douglas & Angus **244** C1
Douglas Water **225** G2
Douglastown **252** C5
Doulting **116** D3
Dounby **276** B5
Doune *A&B* **241** F5
Doune *A&B* **241** F3
Doune *High* **259** F3
Doune *High* **266** B1
Doune *Stir* **242** C4
Dounepark **269** F4
Douneside **260** C4
Dounie *High* **266** D3
Dounie *High* **266** C2
Dounreay **274** E2
Dousland **100** B1
Dovaston **170** A5
Dove Holes **185** E5
Dovenby **209** D3
Dovendale **188** D4
Dover **125** F4
Dover Castle *Kent* CT16 1HU **70** Dover
Dovercourt **152** D4
Doverdale **146** A1
Doveridge **172** C4
Doversgreen **122** B4
Dowally **251** F5
Dowdeswell **146** C5
Dowhill **224** A5
Dowlais **129** G2
Dowland **113** F4
Dowlands **103** F3
Dowlish Ford **103** G1
Dowlish Wake **103** G1
Down Ampney **132** D3
Down End **116** A3
Down Hatherley **146** A5
Down St. Mary **102** A2
Down Thomas **100** B3
Downderry **98** D5
Downe **122** D2
Downend *IoW* **107** E4
Downend *SGlos* **131** F5
Downend *WBerks* **133** G5
Downfield **244** B1
Downfields **163** E5
Downgate **99** D3
Downham *Essex* **137** G3
Downham *Lancs* **193** D3
Downham *N'umb* **228** C3
Downham Market **163** E2
Downhead *Corn* **97** G1
Downhead *Som* **117** D3
Downhead *Som* **116** C5
Downholland Cross **183** E2
Downholme **202** A3
Downies **261** H5
Downley **135** D3
Downs **130** A5
Downside *NSom* **116** B1
Downside *Som* **116** D3
Downside *Som* **116** D2
Downside *Surr* **121** G2
Downton *Devon* **99** F2
Downton *Devon* **101** E2
Downton *Hants* **106** B3
Downton *Wilts* **118** C5
Downton on the Rock **156** D5
Dowsby **175** G5
Dowthwaitehead **209** G4
Doxey **171** G5
Doynton **131** G5
Drabblegate **178** D3
Draethen **130** B4
Draffan **234** B5
Dragley Beck **199** D5
Drakeland Corner **100** B2
Drakelow **158** A4
Drakemyre **233** D4
Drakes Broughton **146** B3
Drakes Cross **158** C5
Draughton *N'hants* **160** C5
Draughton *NYorks* **193** G2
Drax **195** F5
Draycot Foliat **133** D5
Draycote **147** G1
Draycott *Derbys* **173** F4
Draycott *Glos* **147** D4
Draycott *Shrop* **158** A3
Draycott *Som* **116** B2
Draycott *Worcs* **146** A3
Draycott in the Clay **172** C5
Draycott in the Moors **171** G4
Drayford **102** A1
Draynes **97** G3
Drayton *Leics* **160** D3
Drayton *Lincs* **176** A4
Drayton *Norf* **178** C4
Drayton *Oxon* **147** G3
Drayton *Oxon* **133** G3
Drayton *Ports* **107** F2
Drayton *Som* **116** B5
Drayton *Warks* **147** D2
Drayton *Worcs* **158** B5
Drayton Bassett **159** D2
Drayton Beauchamp **135** E1
Drayton Manor Park *Staffs* B78 3TW **159** D2
Drayton Parslow **148** D5
Drayton St. Leonard **134** A3
Drebley **193** G2
Dreemskerry **190** C2
Dreenhill **126** C1
Drefach *Carmar* **141** G4
Drefach *Carmar* **128** B1
Dre-fach *Cere* **142** B3
Drefelin **141** G4
Dreghorn **224** B2
Drem **236** C2
Drewsteignton **102** A3
Driby **189** D5
Driffield *ERid* **196** C2
Driffield *Glos* **132** C3
Drigg **198** B3
Drighlington **194** B5
Drimfern **240** C3
Drimlee **240** D3
Drimnin **247** E4
Drimore **262** C7
Drimpton **104** A2
Drimsdale (Dreumasdal) **254** C1
Drimsynie **241** D4
Drimvore **240** A5
Drinan **256** B3
Dringhouses **195** E2
Drinisiader **263** G2
Drinkstone **152** A1
Drinkstone Green **152** A1
Drishaig **241** D3
Drissaig **240** B3
Drointon **172** B5
Droitwich Spa **146** A1
Dron **243** G3
Dronfield **186** A5
Dronfield Woodhouse **186** A5
Drongan **224** C4
Dronley **244** B1
Droop **105** D2
Dropmore **135** E4
Droxford **107** F1
Droylsden **184** D3
Druid **168** D3
Druidston **126** B1
Druimarbin **248** C2
Druimavuic **248** C5
Druimdrishaig **231** F2
Druimindarroch **247** F1
Druimkinnerras **258** B1
Drum *A&B* **232** A2
Drum *P&K* **243** F4
Drumachloy **232** B3
Drumbeg **272** D5
Drumblade **268** D6
Drumblair **268** E6
Drumbuie *D&G* **225** F4
Drumbuie *High* **256** D1
Drumburgh **209** F1
Drumchapel **233** G2
Drumchardine **266** C7
Drumchork **264** E3
Drumclog **225** E2
Drumdelgie **268** C6
Drumderfit **266** D6
Drumeldrie **244** C4
Drumelzier **226** C2
Drumfearn **256** C3
Drumfern **248** B2
Drumgarve **222** C3
Drumgley **252** C4
Drumguish **258** E5
Drumhead **260** E5
Drumin **259** J1
Drumine **266** E6
Drumjohn **215** G1
Drumlamford House **215** D3
Drumlasie **260** E4
Drumlemble **222** B4
Drumlithie **253** F1
Drummond *High* **266** D5
Drummond *Stir* **242** B4
Drummore **206** B3
Drummuir **268** B6
Drummuir Castle **268** B6
Drumnadrochit (Druim na Drochaid) **258** C2
Drumnagorrach **268** D5
Drumnatorran **248** A3
Drumoak **261** F5
Drumore **222** C3
Drumour **243** E1
Drumpellier Country Park *NLan* ML5 1RX **31** G3
Drumrash **216** A3
Drumrunie **265** H1
Drums **261** H2
Drumsturdy **244** C1
Drumuie **263** K7
Drumuillie **259** G2
Drumvaich **242** B4
Drumwhindle **261** H1
Drumwhirn **216** B2
Drunkendub **253** E5
Druridge **221** E2
Druridge Bay Country Park *N'umb* NE61 5BX **221** E2
Drury **169** F1
Drusillas Park *ESuss* BN26 5QS **110** A3
Drws-y-nant **168** B5
Dry Doddington **174** D3
Dry Drayton **150** B1
Dry Harbour **264** C6
Dry Sandford **133** G2
Dry Street **137** F4
Drybeck **200** B1
Drybridge *Moray* **268** C4
Drybridge *NAyr* **224** B2
Drybrook **131** F1
Dryburgh **227** G2
Drygrange **227** G2
Dryhope **227** D3
Drymen **233** F1
Drymuir **269** H6
Drynoch **255** K1
Dryslwyn **142** B5
Dryton **157** E2
Duachy **240** A2
Dubford **269** F4
Dubhchladach **231** G3
Dubheads **243** E2
Dublin **152** C1
Dubton **253** D4
Duchal **233** E3
Duchally **273** F7
Duchray **241** G4

Duck Bay 233 E1
Duck End Bed 149 F3
Duck End Cambs 150 A1
Duck End Essex 151 E4
Duck Street 194 A1
Duckington 170 B2
Ducklington 133 F2
Duckmanton 186 B5
Duck's Cross 149 G2
Ducks Island 136 B3
Duddenhoe End 150 C4
Duddingston 235 G2
Duddington 161 E2
Duddleswell 109 G1
Duddo 237 G5
Duddon 170 C1
Duddon Bridge 198 C4
Dudleston 170 A4
Dudleston Heath
  (Criftins) 170 A4
Dudley T&W 221 E4
Dudley WMid 158 B3
Dudley Port 158 B3
Dudley Zoo & Castle
  WMid DY1 4QB 14 B3
Dudsbury 105 G3
Duffield 173 E3
Duffryn 129 E3
Dufftown 260 B1
Dufton 210 C5
Duggleby 196 A1
Duiar 259 J1
Duible 274 E6
Duilletter 241 D2
Duinish 250 B3
Duirinish 256 D1
Duisdealmor 256 D3
Duisky 248 C2
Duke End 159 E4
Dukestown 130 A1
Dukinfield 184 D3
Dulas 180 C4
Dulax 260 B3
Dulcote 116 C3
Dulford 103 D2
Dull 250 D5
Dullatur 234 B2
Dullingham 151 E2
Dullingham Ley 151 E2
Dulnain Bridge 259 G2
Duloe Bed 149 G2
Duloe Corn 97 G4
Dulsie 267 G7
Dulverton 114 C5
Dulwich 136 C5
Dulwich Picture Gallery
  GtLon SE21 7AD 13 C7
Dumbarton 233 E2
Dumbleton 146 C4
Dumcrieff 226 C5
Dumfin 233 E1
Dumfries 217 D3
Dumgoyne 233 G1
Dummer 119 G3
Dun 253 E4
Dunach 240 A2
Dunalastair 250 C4
Dunan A&B 232 C2
Dunan High 256 B2
Dunans 240 C5
Dunball 116 A3
Dunbar 237 D2
Dunbeath 275 G5
Dunbeg
  (An Dùn Beag) 240 A1
Dunblane 242 C4
Dunbog 244 A3
Dunbridge 119 E5
Duncanston Aber 260 D2
Duncanston High 266 C6
Dunchideock 102 B4
Dunchurch 159 G5
Duncote 148 B2
Duncow 217 D2
Duncraggan 242 A4
Duncrievie 243 G4
Duncroist 242 A1
Duncrub 243 F3
Duncryne 233 F1
Duncton 108 B2
Dundee 244 C1
Dundee Airport 244 B2
Dundee Contemporary Arts
  DD1 4DY 71 Dundee
Dundon 116 B4
Dundon Hayes 116 B4
Dundonald 224 B2
Dundonnell (Ach-Dà-
  Dhòmhnaill) 265 G3
Dundraw 209 F2
Dundreggan
  (Dul Dreagain) 257 K3
Dundrennan 208 A2
Dundridge 107 E1
Dundry 116 C1
Dunearn 235 G1
Dunecht 261 F4
Dunfield 132 D3
Dunford Bridge 185 F2
Dungate 124 B3
Dungavel 225 E2
Dungworth 185 G3
Dunham 187 E5
Dunham Massey Hall,
  Park & Gardens GtMan
  WA14 4SJ 24 C6
Dunham Town 184 B4
Dunham
  Woodhouses 184 B4
Dunham-on-the-
  Hill 183 F5
Dunhampton 146 A1
Dunholme 188 A5
Dunino 244 D3
Dunipace 234 C1
Dunira 242 C1
Dunkeld 251 F5

Dunkerton 117 E2
Dunkeswell 103 E2
Dunkeswick 194 C3
Dunkirk ChesW&C 183 E5
Dunkirk Kent 124 C3
Dunk's Green 123 F3
Dunlappie 253 D3
Dunley Hants 119 F2
Dunley Worcs 145 G1
Dunlop 233 F5
Dunloskin 232 C2
Dunmere 97 E3
Dunmore A&B 231 F3
Dunmore Falk 234 C1
Dunn 235 G1
Dunn Street 123 G2
Dunnabie 218 A3
Dunnet 275 H1
Dunnichen 252 C5
Dunning 243 F3
Dunnington ERid 197 D2
Dunnington Warks 146 C2
Dunnington York 195 F2
Dunnockshaw 193 E5
Dunoon 232 C1
Dunragit 214 C5
Dunrostan 231 F1
Duns 237 E4
Duns Tew 147 G5
Dunsa 185 G5
Dunsby 175 G5
Dunscore 216 C2
Dunscroft 187 D2
Dunsdale 203 F1
Dunsden Green 134 C5
Dunsfold 121 F3
Dunsford 102 B4
Dunshalt 244 A3
Dunshill 146 A4
Dunsinnan 243 G1
Dunsland Cross 113 E5
Dunsley NYorks 204 B1
Dunsley Staffs 158 A4
Dunsmore 135 D2
Dunsop Bridge 192 C2
Dunstable 149 F5
Dunstable Downs CenBeds
  LU6 2GY 149 F5
Dunstall 172 C5
Dunstall Green 151 F1
Dunstan 229 G5
Dunstan Steads 229 G4
Dunster 114 C3
Dunster Castle & Gardens
  Som TA24 6SL 114 C3
Dunston Lincs 175 F1
Dunston Norf 178 D5
Dunston Staffs 158 B1
Dunston Hill 212 B1
Dunstone Devon 102 A5
Dunstone Devon 100 B4
Dunsville 187 D2
Dunswell 196 C4
Dunsyre 235 E5
Dunterton 99 D3
Duntisbourne
  Abbots 132 B2
Duntisbourne Leer 132 B2
Duntisbourne
  Rouse 132 B2
Duntish 104 C2
Duntocher 233 F2
Dunton Bucks 148 D5
Dunton CenBeds 150 A3
Dunton Norf 177 G4
Dunton Bassett 160 A3
Dunton Green 123 E3
Dunton Wayletts 137 F3
Duntulm 263 K4
Dunure 224 A4
Dunure Mains 224 A4
Dunvant 128 B3
Dunvegan 263 H7
Dunvegan Castle High
  IV55 8WF 263 H7
Dunwich 165 F4
Dura 244 C3
Durdar 210 A2
Durgan 95 E4
Durgates 123 F5
Durham 212 B3
Durham Cathedral
  DH1 3EH 70 Durham
Durham Dales Centre Dur
  DL13 2FJ 211 G4
Durham Tees Valley
  Airport 202 C1
Durinemast 247 F4
Durisdeer 225 G5
Durleigh 115 F4
Durley Hants 107 E1
Durley Wilts 118 D1
Durley Street 107 E1
Durlow Common 145 F4
Durlston Country
  Park Dorset
  BH19 2JL 105 G5
Durnamuck 265 G2
Durness 273 G2
Durno 261 F2
Duror 248 B4
Durran A&B 240 B4
Durran High 275 G2
Durrants 107 G2
Durrington Wilts 118 C3
Durrington WSussex 108 D3
Dursley 131 G3
Dursley Cross 131 F1
Durston 115 F4
Durweston 105 E2
Dury 279 D6
Duston 148 C1
Duthie Park & David Welch
  Winter Gardens Aberdeen
  AB11 7TH 261 H4
Duthil 259 F2
Dutlas 156 B5
Duton Hill 151 E5
Dutson 99 D1
Dutton 183 G5
Duxford 150 C4

Dwygyfylchi 181 F5
Dwyran 166 D1
Dyce 261 G3
Dyfatty 128 A2
Dyffryn Bridgend 129 E3
Dyffryn Pembs 140 C4
Dyffryn VGlam 129 G5
Dyffryn Ardudwy 167 E5
Dyffryn Castell 155 F3
Dyffryn Ceidrych 142 D5
Dyffryn Cellwen 129 E1
Dyke Devon 112 D3
Dyke Lincs 175 G5
Dyke Moray 267 G6
Dykehead Angus 252 B3
Dykehead NLan 234 C4
Dykehead Stir 242 A5
Dykelands 253 F3
Dykends 252 A4
Dykeside 269 F6
Dylan Thomas Centre
  SA1 1RR 86 Swansea
Dylife 155 E3
Dymchurch 111 G1
Dymock 145 G4
Dyrham 131 G5
Dysart 244 B5
Dyserth 182 B5

E

Eachwick 220 D4
Eadar dha Fhadhail 270 C4
Eagland Hill 192 A3
Eagle 175 D1
Eagle Barnsdale 175 D1
Eagle Moor 175 D1
Eaglescliffe 202 D1
Eaglesfield Cumb 209 D4
Eaglesfield D&G 218 A4
Eaglesham 233 G4
Eaglethorpe 161 F3
Eagley 184 B1
Eairy 190 A4
Eakley 148 D2
Eakring 174 B1
Ealand 187 E1
Ealing 136 A4
Eamont Bridge 210 B5
Earby 193 F3
Earcroft 192 C5
Eardington 157 G3
Eardisland 144 D2
Eardisley 144 C3
Eardiston Shrop 170 A5
Eardiston Worcs 145 F1
Earith 162 B5
Earl Shilton 159 G3
Earl Soham 152 D1
Earl Sterndale 172 C1
Earl Stonham 152 C2
Earle 229 D4
Earlestown 183 G3
Earley 134 C5
Earlham 178 C5
Earlish 263 J5
Earls Barton 149 D1
Earls Colne 151 G5
Earl's Common 146 B2
Earl's Court 136 B5
Earls Court Exhibition
  Centre GtLon
  SW5 9TA 11 E5
Earl's Croome 146 A3
Earl's Green 152 B1
Earlsdon 159 F5
Earlsferry 244 C4
Earlsford 261 G1
Earlsheaton 194 B5
Earlston 227 G2
Earlswood Mon 131 D3
Earlswood Surr 122 B4
Earlswood Warks 158 D5
Earnley 108 A4
Earnshaw Bridge 192 B5
Earsairidh 254 C5
Earsdon 221 F4
Earsdon Moor 221 D2
Earsham 165 E3
Earsham Street 164 D4
Earswick 195 F2
Eartham 108 B3
Earthcott Green 131 F4
Easby 203 F1
Easebourne 121 D5
Easenhall 159 G5
Eashing 121 E3
Easington Bucks 134 B1
Easington Dur 213 D3
Easington ERid 189 D1
Easington N'umb 229 F3
Easington Oxon 134 B3
Easington Oxon 147 G4
Easington R&C 203 G1
Easington Colliery 212 D3
Easington Lane 212 C3
Easingwold 195 E1
Easole Street 125 E3
Eassie 252 B5
East Aberthaw 114 D1
East Acton 136 B4
East Allington 101 D3
East Anstey 114 B5
East Anton 119 E3
East Appleton 202 B3
East Ashey 107 E4
East Ashling 108 A3
East Ayton 204 C4
East Barkwith 188 B4
East Barming 123 G3
East Barnby 204 B1
East Barnet 136 B3
East Barsham 178 A3
East Beckham 178 C2
East Bedfont 135 F5
East Bergholt 152 B4
East Bierley 194 B5
East Bilney 178 A4

East Blatchington 109 G4
East Boldon 212 C1
East Boldre 106 C2
East Bolton 229 F5
East Bower 116 A4
East Brent 116 A2
East Bridge 153 F1
East Bridgford 174 B3
East Brora 267 G1
East Buckland 113 G2
East Budleigh 103 D4
East Burnham 135 E4
East Burra 279 C9
East Burrafirth 279 C7
East Burton 105 E4
East Butsfield 212 A3
East Butterleigh 102 C2
East Butterwick 187 F2
East Cairnbeg 253 F2
East Calder 235 E3
East Carleton 178 C5
East Carlton
  N'hants 160 D4
East Carlton
  WYorks 194 B3
East Carlton Countryside
  Park N'hants
  LE16 8YF 160 D4
East Chaldon (Chaldon
  Herring) 105 D4
East Challow 133 F4
East Charleton 101 D3
East Chelborough 104 B2
East Chiltington 109 F2
East Chinnock 104 A1
East Chisenbury 118 C2
East Clandon 121 F2
East Claydon 148 C5
East Clyne 267 G1
East Clyth 275 H5
East Coker 104 B1
East Compton
  Dorset 105 E1
East Compton Som 116 D3
East Coombe 102 B2
East Cornworthy 101 E2
East Cottingwith 195 G3
East Cowes 107 E3
East Cowick 195 F5
East Cowton 202 C2
East Cramlington 221 E4
East Cranmore 117 D3
East Creech 105 F4
East Croachy 258 D2
East Darlochan 222 B3
East Davoch 260 C4
East Dean ESuss 110 A4
East Dean Hants 119 D5
East Dean WSuss 108 B2
East Dereham
  (Dereham) 178 A4
East Down 113 F1
East Drayton 187 E5
East Ella 196 C5
East End ERid 197 D4
East End ERid 197 E5
East End Essex 138 D2
East End Hants 119 F1
East End Hants 106 C3
East End Herts 150 C5
East End Kent 124 A5
East End Kent 124 B1
East End MK 149 E3
East End NSom 131 D5
East End Oxon 133 F5
East End Poole 105 F3
East End Som 116 C2
East End Suff 152 C4
East End Suff 152 C2
East Farleigh 123 G3
East Farndon 160 C4
East Ferry 187 F3
East Firsby 188 A4
East Fleetham 229 G4
East Fortune 236 C2
East Garston 133 F5
East Ginge 133 G4
East Goscote 160 B1
East Grafton 119 D1
East Green Suff 153 E1
East Green Suff 151 F2
East Grimstead 118 D5
East Grinstead 122 C5
East Guldeford 111 E1
East Haddon 148 B1
East Hagbourne 134 A4
East Halton 188 C1
East Ham 136 D4
East Hanney 133 G3
East Hanningfield 137 G2
East Hardwick 186 B1
East Harling 164 A3
East Harlsey 202 D3
East Harnham 118 C5
East Harptree 116 C2
East Hartford 221 E4
East Harting 107 G1
East Hatch 118 A5
East Hatley 150 A2
East Hauxwell 202 A3
East Haven 245 D1
East Heckington 175 G3
East Hedleyhope 212 A3
East Helmsdale 275 F7
East Hendred 133 G4
East Herrington 212 C2
East Heslerton 204 C5
East Hewish 116 B1
East Hoathly 110 A2
East Holme 105 E4
East Horndon 137 F4
East Horrington 116 C3
East Horsley 121 F2
East Horton 229 E3
East Howe 105 G3
East Huntspill 116 A3
East Hyde 136 A1
East Ilsley 133 G4
East Keal 176 B1
East Kennett 118 C1
East Keswick 194 C3

East Kilbride 234 A4
East Kimber 99 E1
East Kirkby 176 B1
East Knapton 204 B5
East Knighton 105 E4
East Knowstone 114 B5
East Knoyle 117 F4
East Kyloe 229 E3
East Lambrook 104 A1
East Lancashire Railway
  Lancs BL9 0EY 193 E5
East Langdon 125 F4
East Langton 160 C3
East Langwell 266 C1
East Lavant 108 A3
East Lavington 108 B2
East Layton 202 A1
East Leake 173 G5
East Learmouth 228 C3
East Learney 260 E4
East Leigh Devon 102 A2
East Leigh Devon 102 A1
East Leigh Devon 101 D2
East Leigh Devon 100 C2
East Lexham 163 G1
East Lilburn 229 E4
East Linton 236 C2
East Liss 120 C5
East Lockinge 133 G3
East Looe 97 G4
East Lound 187 E2
East Lulworth 105 E4
East Lutton 196 B1
East Lydford 116 C4
East Lyn 114 A3
East Lyng 116 A5
East Mains 260 E5
East Malling 123 G3
East Malling Heath 123 F3
East March 244 C1
East Marden 108 A2
East Markham 187 E5
East Martin 105 G1
East Marton 193 F2
East Meon 120 B5
East Mere 102 C1
East Mersea 139 D1
East Mey 275 J1
East Midlands
  Airport 173 F5
East Molesey 121 G1
East Moor 194 C1
East Morden 105 F3
East Morriston 236 D5
East Morton 194 A3
East Ness 203 F5
East Newton 197 E4
East Norton 160 C2
East Oakley 119 G2
East Ogwell 102 B5
East Orchard 105 E1
East Ord 237 G4
East Panson 99 D1
East Parley 106 A3
East Peckham 123 F4
East Pennard 116 C4
East Point Pavilion,
  Lowestoft Suff
  NR33 0AP 165 G2
East Portlemouth 100 D4
East Prawle 101 D4
East Preston 108 C3
East Pulham 104 D2
East Putford 113 D4
East Quantoxhead 115 E3
East Rainton 212 C3
East Ravendale 188 C3
East Raynham 177 G5
East Retford
  (Retford) 187 E4
East Rigton 194 C3
East Rolstone 116 A1
East Rounton 202 D2
East Row 204 B1
East Rudham 177 G5
East Runton 178 D1
East Ruston 179 E3
East Saltoun 236 B3
East Shefford 133 F5
East Sleekburn 221 E3
East Somerton 179 F4
East Stockwith 187 F3
East Stoke Dorset 105 E4
East Stoke Notts 174 C3
East Stour 117 E5
East Stourmouth 125 E2
East Stratton 119 G3
East Street 116 C4
East Studdal 125 F4
East Suisnish 256 B1
East Taphouse 97 F3
East Thirston 221 D2
East Tilbury 137 F5
East Tisted 120 C4
East Torrington 188 B4
East Town 116 D3
East Tuddenham 178 B4
East Tytherley 119 D5
East Tytherton 132 B5
East Village 102 B2
East Wall 157 E3
East Walton 163 F1
East Wellow 119 E5
East Wemyss 244 B5
East Whitburn 235 D3
East Wickham 137 D5
East Williamston 127 D2
East Winch 163 F1
East Winterslow 118 D4
East Wittering 107 G3
East Witton 202 A4
East Woodburn 220 B3
East Woodhay 119 F1
East Woodlands 117 E3
East Worldham 120 C4
East Worlington 102 A1
East Youlstone 112 C4
Eastacott 113 G3
Eastbourne 110 B4
Eastbourne Pier
  ESuss BN21 3EL
  72 Eastbourne

Eastbrook 130 A5
Eastburn ERid 196 B2
Eastburn WYorks 193 G3
Eastbury Herts 136 A3
Eastbury WBerks 133 F5
Eastby 193 G2
Eastchurch 124 B1
Eastcombe Glos 132 A2
Eastcombe Som 115 E4
Eastcote GtLon 136 A4
Eastcote N'hants 148 B2
Eastcote WMid 159 D5
Eastcott Corn 112 C4
Eastcott Wilts 118 B2
Eastcourt 132 B3
Eastdown 101 E3
Eastend 159 E1
Easter Ardross 266 D4
Easter Balgedie 243 G4
Easter Balmoral 259 K5
Easter Boleskine 258 C2
Easter Borland 242 B4
Easter Brae 266 D5
Easter Buckieburn 234 B1
Easter Compton 131 E4
Easter Drummond 258 B3
Easter Dullater 242 B4
Easter Ellister 230 A4
Easter Fearn 266 D3
Easter Galcantray 267 F7
Easter Howlaws 237 E5
Easter Kinkell 266 C6
Easter Knox 235 D1
Easter Lednathie 252 B3
Easter Moniack 266 C7
Easter Ord 261 G4
Easter Poldar 242 B5
Easter Skeld (Skeld) 279 C8
Easter Suddie 266 D6
Easter Tulloch 253 F2
Easter Whyntie 268 E4
Eastergate 108 B3
Easterhouse 234 A3
Easterton 118 B2
Easterton Sands 118 B2
Eastertown 116 A2
Eastfield NLan 234 C3
Eastfield NYorks 204 D4
Eastfield Hall 221 E1
Eastgate Dur 211 F4
Eastgate Lincs 161 G1
Eastgate Norf 178 C3
Easthall 150 A5
Eastham Mersey 183 E4
Eastham Worcs 145 F1
Easthampstead 121 D1
Easthampton 144 D1
Easthaugh 178 B4
Eastheath 120 D1
Easthope 157 E2
Easthorpe Essex 152 A5
Easthorpe Leics 174 D4
Easthorpe Notts 174 C2
Easthouses 236 A3
Easting Devon 102 A2
Easting Glos 132 B3
Easting Gloss 131 G2
Eastleach Martin 133 E2
Eastleach Turville 133 E2
Eastleigh Devon 113 E3
Eastleigh Hants 106 D1
Eastling 124 B3
Eastmoor Derbys 186 A5
Eastmoor Norf 163 F2
Eastney 107 F3
Eastnor 145 G4
Eastoft 187 F1
Eastoke 107 G3
Easton Cambs 161 G5
Easton Cumb 218 C4
Easton Cumb 209 F1
Easton Devon 102 A4
Easton Dorset 104 C5
Easton Hants 119 G4
Easton IoW 106 C4
Easton Lincs 175 E5
Easton Norf 178 C4
Easton Som 116 C3
Easton Suff 153 D2
Easton Wilts 132 A5
Easton Grey 132 A4
Easton Maudit 149 D2
Easton on the Hill 161 F2
Easton Royal 118 D1
Easton-in-Gordano 131 E5
Eastrea 162 A3
Eastriggs 218 A5
Eastrington 195 G4
Eastry 125 F3
Eastside 277 D8
East-the-Water 113 E3
Eastville 131 F1
Eastwell 174 C5
Eastwick 136 D1
Eastwood Notts 173 F3
Eastwood S'end 138 B4
Eastwood SYorks 186 B3
Eastwood
  WYorks 193 F5
Eastwood End 162 C3
Eathorpe 147 F1
Eaton ChesE 171 F1
Eaton ChesW&C 170 C1
Eaton Leics 174 C5
Eaton Norf 178 D5
Eaton Norf 177 E4
Eaton Oxon 133 G2
Eaton Shrop 157 E3
Eaton Shrop 156 C4
Eaton Bishop 144 D4
Eaton Bray 149 E5
Eaton Constantine 157 F2
Eaton Ford 149 G2
Eaton Hall 170 B1
Eaton Hastings 133 E3
Eaton Socon 149 G2
Eaton upon Tern 171 D5
Eaves Green 159 E4
Eavestone 194 B1
Ebberston 204 B4
Ebbesborne Wake 118 A5

Ebbw Vale
  (Glynebwy) 130 A2
Ebchester 212 A2
Ebdon 116 A1
Ebford 102 C4
Ebley 132 A2
Ebnal 170 B3
Ebost 255 J1
Ebrington 147 D3
Ebsworthy Town 99 F1
Ecchinswell 119 F2
Ecclaw 237 E3
Ecclefechan 217 F3
Eccles GtMan 184 B3
Eccles Kent 123 G3
Eccles ScBord 237 E5
Eccles Green 144 C3
Eccles Road 164 B2
Ecclesfield 186 A3
Ecclesgreig 253 F3
Eccleshall 171 F5
Eccleshill 194 A4
Ecclesmachan 235 E2
Eccles-on-Sea 179 F3
Eccleston
  ChesW&C 170 B1
Eccleston Lancs 183 G1
Eccleston Mersey 183 F3
Eccup 194 B3
Echt 261 F4
Eckford 228 B4
Eckington Derbys 186 B5
Eckington Worcs 146 B3
Ecton N'hants 148 D1
Ecton Staffs 172 B2
Edale 185 F4
Eday 276 E4
Eday Airfield 276 E4
Edburton 109 E2
Edderside 209 E2
Edderton 266 E3
Eddington 119 E1
Eddleston 235 G5
Eden Camp NYorks
  YO17 6RT 204 B5
Eden Park 122 C2
Eden Project Corn
  PL24 2SG 97 E4
Eden Vale 212 D4
Edenbridge 122 D4
Edendonich 241 D2
Edenfield 184 B1
Edenhall 210 B4
Edenham 175 F5
Edensor 185 G5
Edentaggart 241 F5
Edenthorpe 186 D2
Edern 166 B4
Edgarley 116 C4
Edgbaston 158 C4
Edgcote 148 A3
Edgcott Bucks 148 B5
Edgcott Som 114 B4
Edgcumbe 95 E3
Edge Glos 132 A2
Edge Shrop 156 C2
Edge End 131 E1
Edge Green
  ChesW&C 170 B2
Edge Green GtMan 183 G3
Edge Green Norf 164 B3
Edgebolton 170 C5
Edgefield 178 B2
Edgehead 236 A3
Edgeley 170 C3
Edgerley 156 C1
Edgerton 185 F1
Edgeworth 132 B2
Edginswell 101 E1
Edgmond 157 G1
Edgmond Marsh 171 E5
Edgton 156 C4
Edgware 136 B3
Edgworth 184 B1
Edinample 242 B2
Edinbanchory 260 C3
Edinbane 263 J6
Edinbarnet 233 G2
Edinburgh 235 G2
Edinburgh Airport 235 F2
Edinburgh Castle Edin
  EH1 2NG 37 E4
Edinburgh Zoo Edin
  EH12 6TS 32 B2
Edinchip 242 A2
Edingale 159 E1
Edingley 174 B2
Edingthorpe 179 E2
Edingthorpe Green 179 E2
Edington Som 116 A4
Edington Wilts 118 A2
Edintore 268 C6
Edinvale 267 J6
Edistone 112 C3
Edith Weston 161 E2
Edithmead 116 A3
Edlaston 172 C3
Edlesborough 135 E1
Edlingham 220 D1
Edlington 188 C5
Edmondsham 105 G1
Edmondsley 212 B3
Edmondstown 129 G3
Edmondthorpe 161 D1
Edmonstone 276 E5
Edmonton Corn 97 D2
Edmonton GtLon 136 C3
Edmundbyers 211 G2
Ednam 228 B3
Ednaston 172 D3
Edney Common 137 F2
Edra 251 F4
Edradynate 251 D4
Edrom 237 F4
Edstaston 170 C4
Edstone 147 D1
Edvin Loach 145 F2
Edwalton 173 G4
Edwardstone 152 A3
Edwardsville 129 G3
Edwinsford 142 C4
Edwinstowe 174 B1

Edworth **150** A3
Edwyn Ralph **145** F2
Edzell **253** E3
Efail Isaf **129** G4
Efail-fâch **129** D3
Efailnewydd **166** C4
Efailwen **141** E5
Efenechtyd **169** G2
Effirth **279** C7
Efflinch **159** D1
Efford **102** B2
Egbury **119** F2
Egdon **146** B2
Egerton GtMan **184** B1
Egerton Kent **124** B4
Egerton Forstal **124** A4
Egerton Green **170** C2
Egg Buckland **100** A2
Eggborough **195** E5
Eggerness **207** E2
Eggesford Barton **113** G4
Eggington **148** A5
Egginton **173** D5
Egglescliffe **202** D1
Eggleston **211** F5
Egham **135** F5
Egham Wick **135** E5
Egilsay **276** D5
Egleton **161** D2
Eglingham **229** F5
Eglinton **233** E5
Egloshayle **97** E2
Egloskerry **97** G1
Eglwys Cross **170** B3
Eglwys Fach **154** C3
Eglwys Nunydd **129** E4
Eglwys-Brewis **114** D1
Eglwyswrw **141** E4
Egmanton **174** C1
Egmere **178** A2
Egremont **208** D5
Egton **204** B2
Egton Bridge **204** B2
Egypt **119** F3
Eigg **247** D1
Eight Ash Green **152** A5
Eignaig **247** G5
Eil **259** F3
Eildon **227** G2
Eilean Darach **265** H3
Eilean Donan Castle High
    IV40 8DX **256** E2
Eilean Shona **247** F2
Einacleit **270** D5
Eisgean **271** F6
Eisingrug **167** F4
Eisteddfa Gurig **155** D4
Elan Valley Visitor Centre
    Powys LD6 5HP **143** F1
Elan Village **143** F1
Elberton **131** F4
Elborough **116** A2
Elburton **100** B2
Elcombe **132** B4
Elder Street **151** D4
Eldernell **162** B3
Eldersfield **145** G4
Elderslie **233** F3
Eldon **212** B5
Eldrick **215** D2
Eldroth **193** D1
Eldwick **194** A3
Elemore Vale **212** C3
Elford N'umb **229** F3
Elford Staffs **159** D1
Elford Closes **162** D5
Elgin **267** K5
Elgol **256** B3
Elham **125** D4
Elie **244** C4
Elilaw **220** B1
Elim **180** B4
Eling Hants **106** C1
Eling W'Berks **134** A5
Eling Tide Mill Hants
    SO40 9HF **4** A3
Eliock **245** G1
Elishader **263** K5
Elishaw **220** A2
Elkesley **187** D5
Elkington **160** B5
Elkstone **132** B1
Elland **194** A5
Elland Upper Edge **194** A5
Ellary **231** F2
Ellastone **172** C3
Ellbridge **100** A1
Ellel **192** A2
Ellemford **237** E3
Ellenabeich **239** G3
Ellenborough **208** D3
Ellenhall **171** F5
Ellen's Green **121** F4
Ellerbeck **202** D3
Ellerby **203** G1
Ellerdine **170** D5
Ellerdine Heath **170** D5
Elleric (Eileing) **248** C5
Ellerker **196** B5
Ellerton ERid **195** G3
Ellerton NYorks **202** B3
Ellerton Shrop **171** E5
Ellerton Abbey **201** F3
Ellesborough **134** D2
Ellesmere **170** A4
Ellesmere Park **184** B3
Ellesmere Port **183** F5
Ellingham Hants **106** A2
Ellingham N'umb **229** F4
Ellingham Norf **165** E2
Ellingstring **202** A4
Ellington Cambs **161** G5
Ellington N'umb **221** E2
Ellington Thorpe **161** G5
Elliot **245** E1
Elliot's Green **117** E3
Ellisfield **120** B3

Ellistown **159** G1
Ellon **261** H1
Ellonby **210** A4
Ellough **165** F3
Ellough Moor **165** F3
Elloughton **196** B5
Ellwood **131** E2
Elm **162** C2
Elm Park **137** E4
Elmbridge **146** B1
Elmdon Essex **150** C4
Elmdon WMid **159** D4
Elmdon Heath **159** D4
Elmers End **122** C2
Elmer's Green **183** F2
Elmesthorpe **159** G3
Elmhurst **158** D1
Elmley Castle **146** B3
Elmley Lovett **146** A1
Elmore **131** G1
Elmore Back **131** G1
Elmscott **112** C3
Elmsett **152** B3
Elmstead Essex **152** B5
Elmstead GtLon **136** D5
Elmstead Market **152** B5
Elmstone
    Hardwicke **146** B5
Elmswell ERid **196** B2
Elmswell Suff **152** A1
Elmton **186** C5
Elphin **272** E7
Elphinstone **236** A2
Elrick Aber **261** G4
Elrick Moray **260** C1
Elrig **206** D2
Elringbeag **240** D3
Elsdon **220** B2
Elsecar **186** A2
Elsecar Heritage Centre
    SYorks S74 8HJ **186** A3
Elsenham **150** D5
Elsfield **134** A1
Elsham **188** A1
Elsing **178** B4
Elslack **193** F3
Elstead **121** E3
Elsted **108** A2
Elsthorpe **175** F5
Elstob **212** C5
Elston Lancs **192** B4
Elston Notts **174** C3
Elstone **113** G4
Elstow **149** F3
Elstree **136** A3
Elstronwick **197** E4
Elswick **192** A4
Elsworth **150** B1
Elterwater **199** E2
Eltham **136** D5
Eltisley **150** A2
Elton Cambs **161** F3
Elton ChesW&C **183** F5
Elton Derbys **172** D1
Elton Glos **131** G1
Elton GtMan **184** B1
Elton Here **157** D5
Elton Notts **174** C4
Elton Stock **202** D1
Elton Green **183** F5
Elvanfoot **226** A4
Elvaston **173** F4
Elvaston Castle Country Park
    Derbys DE72 3EP **18** C4
Elveden **163** G5
Elvingston **236** B2
Elvington Kent **125** E3
Elvington York **195** G3
Elwick Hart **213** D4
Elwick N'umb **229** F3
Elworth **171** E1
Elworthy **115** D4
Ely Cambs **162** D5
Ely Cardiff **130** A5
Emberton **149** D3
Emberton Country Park
    MK MK46 5FJ **149** D2
Embleton Cumb **209** E3
Embleton Hart **212** D5
Embleton N'umb **229** G4
Embo **267** F6
Embo Street **267** F6
Emborough **116** D2
Embsay **193** G2
Embsay Steam Railway
    NYorks
    BD23 6AF **193** G2
Emerson Park **137** E4
Emery Down **106** B2
Emley **185** G1
Emmington **134** C2
Emmington **134** C2
Emneth **162** D2
Emneth Hungate **162** D2
Empingham **161** E2
Empshott **120** C4
Empshott Green **120** C4
Emsworth **107** G2
Enborne **119** F1
Enborne Row **119** F1
Enchmarsh **157** E3
Enderby **160** A3
Endmoor **199** G4
Endon **171** G2
Endon Bank **171** G2
Enfield **136** C3
Enfield Wash **136** C3
Enford **118** C2
Engine Common **131** F4
Englefield **134** B5
Englefield Green **135** E5
Englesea-brook **171** E2
English Bicknor **131** E1
English Frankton **170** B5
Englishcombe **117** E1
Enham Alamein **119** E3
Enmore **115** F4
Ennerdale
    Bridge **209** D5

Enniscaven **97** D4
Ennochdhu **251** F3
Ensay **246** C5
Ensdon **156** D1
Ensay **196** A4
Ensis **113** F3
Enson **171** G5
Enstone **147** F5
Enterkinfoot **225** G5
Enterpen **203** D2
Enton Green **121** E3
Enville **158** A4
Eolaigearraidh **254** C4
Eorabus **238** C2
Eorodal **271** H1
Eoropaidh **271** H1
Epney **131** G1
Epperstone **174** B3
Epping **137** D2
Epping Green
    Essex **136** D2
Epping Green
    Herts **136** B2
Epping Upland **136** D2
Eppleby **202** A1
Eppleworth **196** C4
Epsom **122** B2
Epwell **147** F3
Epworth **187** E2
Epworth Turbary **187** E2
Erbistock **170** A3
Erbusaig **256** D2
Erchless Castle **266** B7
Erdington **158** D3
Eredine **240** B3
Eriboll **273** G3
Ericstane **226** B4
Eridge Green **123** E5
Eriff **224** D5
Erines **231** G2
Erisey Barton **95** E5
Eriskay
    (Eiriosgaigh) **254** C3
Eriswell **163** F5
Erith **137** E5
Erlestoke **118** A2
Ermington **100** C2
Ernesettle **100** A1
Erpingham **178** C2
Erringden Grange **193** F5
Errogie (Earagaidh) **258** C2
Errol **244** A2
Errollston **261** J1
Erwarton **152** D4
Erwood **143** G3
Eryholme **202** C2
Eryrys **169** F2
Escart **231** G3
Escart Farm **231** G4
Escomb **212** B5
Escrick **195** F3
Esgair **141** G5
Esgairgeiliog **155** D2
Esgyryn **181** G5
Esh **212** A3
Esh Winning **212** A3
Esher **121** G1
Eshott **221** E2
Eshton **193** F2
Eskadale **258** B1
Eskbank **236** A2
Eskdale Green **198** C2
Eskdalemuir **218** A2
Esknish **230** B3
Esperley Lane Ends **212** A5
Espley Hall **221** D2
Esprick **192** A4
Essendine **161** F1
Essendon **136** B2
Essich **258** D1
Essington **158** B2
Esslemont **261** H2
Eston **203** E1
Eswick **279** D7
Etal **228** D3
Etchilhampton **118** B1
Etchingham **110** C1
Etchinghill Kent **125** D5
Etchinghill Staffs **158** C1
Etherdwick Grange **197** E4
Etherley Dene **212** A5
Etherow Country Park
    GtMan SK6 5JQ **25** H5
Ethie Mains **253** E5
Eton **135** E5
Eton Wick **135** E5
Etteridge **258** D5
Ettiley Heath **171** E1
Ettington **147** E3
Etton ERid **196** B3
Etton Peter **161** G2
Ettrick **227** D4
Ettrickbridge **227** E3
Ettrickhill **227** D4
Etwall **173** D4
Eudon George **157** F4
Eurach **240** A4
Eureka! Museum for
    Children WYorks
    HX1 2NE **26** B4
Euston **163** G5
Euxton **183** G1
Evanstown **129** F4
Evedon **175** F3
Evelix **266** E2
Evenjobb **144** B1
Evenley **148** A4
Evenlode **147** E5
Evenwood **212** A5
Evenwood Gate **212** A5
Everbay **276** F5
Evercreech **116** D4
Everdon **148** A2
Everingham **196** A3
Everleigh **118** D2
Everley High **275** J2
Everley NYorks **204** C4
Eversholt **149** E4
Evershot **104** B2

Eversley **120** C1
Eversley Cross **120** C1
Everthorpe **196** B4
Everton CenBeds **150** A2
Everton Hants **106** B3
Everton Mersey **183** E3
Everton Notts **187** D3
Evertown **218** B4
Eves Corner **138** C3
Evesbatch **145** F3
Evesham **146** C3
Evesham Country Park
    Shopping & Garden
    Centre Worcs
    WR11 4TP **146** C3
Evie **276** C5
Evington **160** B2
Ewart Newtown **229** D3
Ewden Village **185** G3
Ewell **122** B2
Ewell Minnis **125** E4
Ewelme **134** B3
Ewen **132** C3
Ewenny **129** F5
Ewerby **175** G3
Ewerby Thorpe **175** G3
Ewhurst **121** F3
Ewhurst Green
    ESuss **110** C1
Ewhurst Green
    Surr **121** F4
Ewloe **170** A1
Ewloe Green **169** F1
Ewood **192** C5
Ewood Bridge **193** D5
Eworthy **99** E1
Ewshot **120** D3
Ewyas Harold **144** C5
Exbourne **113** G5
Exbury **106** D2
Exbury Gardens Hants
    SO45 1AZ **4** B6
Exceat **110** A4
Exebridge **114** C5
Exelby **202** B4
Exeter **102** C3
Exeter Cathedral Devon
    EX1 1HS **72** Exeter
Exeter International
    Airport **102** C3
Exford **114** C4
Exfords Green **157** D2
Exhall Warks **146** D2
Exhall Warks **159** F4
Exlade Street **134** B4
Exminster **102** C4
Exmouth **102** D4
Exnaboe **279** F9
Exning **151** E1
Explore-At-Bristol
    BS1 5DB **66** Bristol
Exton Devon **102** C4
Exton Hants **120** B5
Exton Rut **161** E1
Exton Som **114** C4
Exwick **102** C3
Eyam **185** G5
Eydon **148** A3
Eye Here **145** D1
Eye Peter **162** A2
Eye Suff **164** C4
Eye Green **162** A2
Eyemouth **237** G3
Eyeworth **150** A3
Eyhorne Street **124** A3
Eyke **153** E2
Eynesbury **149** G2
Eynort **255** J2
Eynsford **123** E2
Eynsham **133** G2
Eype **104** A3
Eyre **263** K6
Eythorne **125** E4
Eyton Here **145** D1
Eyton Shrop **156** C4
Eyton on Severn **157** E2
Eyton upon the Weald
    Moors **157** F1
Eywood **144** C2

F

Faccombe **119** E2
Faceby **203** D2
Fachwen **167** E1
Facit **184** C1
Faddiley **170** C2
Fadmoor **203** F4
Faebait **266** B6
Faifley **233** G2
Fail **224** C3
Failand **131** E5
Failford **224** C3
Failsworth **184** C2
Fain **265** H4
Fair Isle **278** A1
Fair Isle Airstrip **278** A1
Fair Oak Devon **102** D1
Fair Oak Hants **107** D1
Fair Oak Hants **119** G1
Fair Oak Green **120** B1
Fairbourne **154** C1
Fairburn **195** D5
Fairfield Derbys **185** E5
Fairfield GtMan **184** D3
Fairfield Kent **111** E1
Fairfield Stock **202** D1
Fairfield Worcs **158** B5
Fairfield Halls, Croydon
    GtLon CR9 1DG **122** C2
Fairford **132** D2
Fairgirth **216** C5
Fairhaven **191** G5
Fairhill **234** B4
Fairholm **234** B4
Fairlands Valley Park Herts
    SG2 0BL **150** A5
Fairlie **232** D4
Fairlight **111** D2
Fairlight Cove **111** D2
Fairmile Devon **103** D3
Fairmile Surr **121** G1

Fairmilehead **235** G3
Fairnington **228** A4
Fairoak **171** E4
Fairseat **123** F2
Fairstead **137** G1
Fairwarp **109** G1
Fairwater **130** A5
Fairy Cross **113** E3
Fairyhill **128** A3
Fakenham **178** A3
Fakenham Magna **164** A4
Fala **236** B3
Fala Dam **236** B3
Falahill **236** A4
Faldingworth **188** A4
Falfield Fife **244** C4
Falfield SGlos **131** F3
Falin-Wnda **141** G3
Falkenham **153** D4
Falkirk **234** C1
Falkirk Wheel Falk
    FK1 4RS **234** C1
Falkland **244** A4
Falla **228** B5
Fallgate **173** E1
Fallin **242** D5
Falmer **109** F3
Falmouth **95** F3
Falsgrave **204** D4
Falston **219** F3
Famous Grouse Experience,
    Glenturret Distillery
    P&K PH7 4HA **243** D2
Fanagmore **272** D4
Fanans **240** C2
Fancott **149** F5
Fangdale Beck **203** E3
Fangfoss **195** G2
Fankerton **234** B1
Fanmore **246** D5
Fanner's Green **137** F1
Fans **236** D5
Fantasy Island Lincs
    PE25 1RH **177** D1
Far Cotton **148** C2
Far Forest **157** G5
Far Gearstones **200** C4
Far Green **131** G2
Far Moor **183** G2
Far Oakridge **132** B2
Far Royds **194** B4
Far Sawrey **199** E3
Farcet **162** A3
Farden **157** E5
Fareham **107** E2
Farewell **158** C1
Faringdon **133** E3
Farington **192** B5
Farlam **210** B2
Farlary **266** E1
Farleigh NSom **116** C1
Farleigh Surr **122** C2
Farleigh Hungerford **117** F2
Farleigh Wallop **120** B3
Farlesthorpe **189** E5
Farleton Cumb **199** G4
Farleton Lancs **192** B1
Farley Derbys **173** D1
Farley Shrop **156** C2
Farley Staffs **172** B3
Farley Wilts **118** D5
Farley Green Suff **151** F2
Farley Green Surr **121** F3
Farley Hill **120** C1
Farleys End **131** G1
Farlington **195** F1
Farlow **157** F4
Farm Town **159** F1
Farmborough **117** D1
Farmcote **146** C5
Farmington **132** D1
Farmoor **133** G2
Farmtown **268** D5
Farnborough
    GtLon **122** D2
Farnborough
    Hants **121** D2
Farnborough
    Warks **147** G3
Farnborough
    W'Berks **133** G4
Farnborough Street **121** D2
Farncombe **121** E3
Farndish **149** E1
Farndon ChesW&C **170** B2
Farndon Notts **174** C2
Farne Islands **229** G3
Farnell **253** E4
Farnham Dorset **105** F1
Farnham Essex **150** C5
Farnham NYorks **194** C1
Farnham Suff **153** E1
Farnham Surr **120** D3
Farnham Common **150** C5
Farnham Green **150** C5
Farnham Royal **135** E4
Farningham **123** E2
Farnley NYorks **194** B3
Farnley WYorks **194** B4
Farnley Tyas **185** F1
Farnsfield **174** B2
Farnworth GtMan **184** B2
Farnworth
    Halton **183** G4
Farr High **274** C2
Farr High **258** D1
Farr High **259** F4
Farr House **258** D1
Farraline **258** C2
Farrington **102** D3
Farrington
    Gurney **116** D2
Farsley **194** B4
Farthing Corner **124** A2
Farthing Green **124** A4
Farthinghoe **148** A4
Farthingstone **148** B2
Farthorpe **188** C5
Fartown **185** F1
Farway **103** E3
Fasag **264** E6

Fasagrianach **265** H3
Fascadale **247** E2
Fashion Museum
    B&NESom
    BA1 2QH **63** Bath
Faslane **232** D1
Fasnacloich **248** C5
Fasnakyle **257** K2
Fassfern **248** D1
Fatfield **212** C2
Fattahead **268** E5
Faugh **210** B2
Fauldhouse **234** D3
Faulkbourne **137** G1
Faulkland **117** E2
Fauls **170** C4
Faulston **118** B5
Faversham **124** C2
Favillar **259** K1
Fawdington **202** D5
Fawdon **212** B1
Fawfieldhead **172** B1
Fawkham Green **123** E2
Fawler **133** F1
Fawley Bucks **134** C4
Fawley Hants **107** D2
Fawley W'Berks **133** F4
Fawley Chapel **145** E5
Fawsyde **253** G2
Faxfleet **196** A5
Faxton **160** C5
Faygate **122** B5
Fazakerley **183** E3
Fazeley **159** D2
Fearby **202** A4
Fearn **267** F4
Fearnan **250** C5
Fearnbeg **264** D6
Fearnhead **184** A3
Fearnmore **264** D5
Fearnoch A&B **232** B2
Fearnoch A&B **232** A1
Featherstone
    Staffs **158** B2
Featherstone
    WYorks **194** D5
Featherstone Castle **210** C1
Feckenham **146** C1
Feering **151** G5
Feetham **201** E3
Feith-hill **268** E6
Feizor **193** D1
Felbridge **122** C5
Felbrigg **178** D2
Felcourt **122** C4
Felden **135** F2
Felhampton **156** D4
Felindre Carmar **142** D4
Felindre Carmar **142** B5
Felindre Carmar **141** G4
Felindre Carmar **142** C4
Felindre Cere **142** B2
Felindre Powys **156** A4
Felindre Powys **144** A5
Felindre Swan **128** C2
Felinfach Cere **142** B2
Felinfach Powys **143** G4
Felinfoel **128** B2
Felingwm Isaf **142** B5
Felingwmisaf **142** B5
Felingwmuchaf **142** B5
Felixkirk **203** D4
Felixstowe **153** D4
Felixstowe Ferry **153** E4
Felkington **237** G5
Felldownhead **99** D2
Felling **212** B1
Fellonmore **239** F2
Felmersham **149** E2
Felmingham **179** D3
Felpham **108** B4
Felsham **152** A2
Felsted **151** E5
Feltham **136** A5
Felthamhill **136** A5
Felthorpe **178** C4
Felton Here **145** E3
Felton NSom **116** C1
Felton Butler **156** C1
Feltwell **163** F3
Fen Ditton **150** C1
Fen Drayton **150** B1
Fen End **159** E5
Fen Street Norf **164** A2
Fen Street Norf **164** B4
Fen Street Suff **164** A4
Fen Street Suff **152** A4
Fenay Bridge **185** F1
Fence **193** E4
Fence Houses **212** C2
Fencott **134** A1
Fendike Corner **176** C1
Fenham **229** F2
Fenhouses **176** A3
Feniscowles **192** C5
Feniton **103** E3
Fenn Street **137** G5
Fenni-fach **143** F5
Fenny Bentley **172** C2
Fenny Bridges **103** E3
Fenny Compton **147** G2
Fenny Drayton **159** F3
Fenny Stratford **149** D4
Fenrother **221** D2
Fenstanton **150** B1
Fenton Cambs **162** B5
Fenton Lincs **187** F5
Fenton Lincs **175** D2
Fenton Notts **187** E4
Fenton Stoke **171** F3
Fenton Barns **236** C1
Fenwick EAyr **233** F5
Fenwick Lincs **187** F3
Fenwick N'umb **220** C4
Fenwick N'umb **229** E2
Fenwick SYorks **186** C1
Feochaig **222** C4
Feock **95** F3
Feolin **230** C3
Feolin Ferry **230** C3
Feorlan **222** B5
Feorlin **240** B5

Ferens Art Gallery
    HU1 3RA
    76 Kingston upon Hull
Ferguslie Park **233** F3
Feriniquarrie **263** G6
Fern **252** C3
Ferndale **129** F3
Ferndown **105** G2
Ferness **267** G7
Fernham **133** E3
Fernhill Heath **146** A2
Fernhurst **121** D5
Fernie **244** B3
Fernilea **255** J1
Fernilee **185** E5
Fernybank **252** D2
Fernsby **194** C1
Ferrers Centre for Arts &
    Crafts Leics
    LE65 1RU **173** E5
Ferrindonald **256** C4
Ferring **108** C3
Ferrybridge **195** D5
Ferryden **253** F4
Ferryhill **162** B4
Ferryside
    (Glanyferi) **127** G1
Fersfield **164** B3
Fersit **249** F2
Ferwig **141** E3
Feshiebridge **259** F4
Festival Park BGwent
    NP23 8PP **130** A2
Fetcham **121** G2
Fetlar **278** F3
Fetlar Airport **278** F3
Fetcham **121** G2
Fettercairn **253** E2
Fetterangus **269** H5
Fetternear House **261** F3
Feus of Caldhame **253** E3
Fewcott **148** A5
Fewston **194** A2
Ffairfach **142** C5
Ffair-Rhos **142** D1
Ffaldybrenin **142** C3
Ffarmers **142** C3
Ffawyddog **130** B1
Ffestiniog
    (Llan Ffestiniog) **168** A3
Ffestiniog Railway Gwyn
    LL49 9NF **167** F3
Ffordd-las Denb **169** E1
Fforddlas Powys **144** B4
Fforest **128** B2
Fforest-fach **128** C3
Ffostrasol **141** G3
Ffos-y-ffin **142** A1
Ffridd Uchaf **167** E2
Ffrith Denb **182** B4
Ffrith Flints **169** F2
Ffrwdgrech **143** F5
Ffynnon **127** G1
Ffynnongroyw **182** C4
Fibhig **270** E3
Fichlie **260** C3
Fidden **238** C2
Fiddington Glos **146** B4
Fiddington Som **115** F3
Fiddleford **105** E1
Fiddler's Green
    Glos **146** B5
Fiddler's Green
    Here **145** E4
Fiddler's Green
    Norf **163** G1
Fiddler's Green
    Norf **163** F3
Fiddlers Hamlet **137** D2
Field **172** B4
Field Broughton **199** E4
Field Dalling **178** B2
Field Head **159** G2
Fife Keith **268** C5
Fifehead Magdalen **117** E5
Fifehead Neville **105** D1
Fifehead
    St. Quintin **105** D1
Fifield Oxon **133** E1
Fifield W&M **135** E5
Fifield Bavant **118** B5
Figheldean **118** C3
Filby **179** F4
Filey **205** E4
Filgrave **149** D3
Filham **100** C2
Filkins **133** E2
Filleigh Devon **113** G3
Filleigh Devon **102** A1
Fillingham **187** G4
Fillongley **159** E4
Filmore Hill **120** B5
Filton **131** F5
Fimber **196** A1
Finavon **252** C4
Fincham **163** E2
Finchampstead **120** C1
Finchdean **107** G1
Finchingfield **151** E4
Finchley **173** E4
Findern **173** E4
Findhorn **267** H5
Findhorn Bridge **259** F2
Findhuglen **242** C3
Findo Gask **243** F2
Findochty **268** C4
Findon Aber **261** H5
Findon WSuss **108** D3
Findon Mains **266** D5
Findon Valley **108** D3
Findrassie **267** J5
Findron **259** J3
Finedon **161** E5
Finegland **251** G3
Fingal Street **164** D4
Fingask **261** F2
Fingerpost **157** G5
Fingest **134** C3
Finghall **202** A4
Fingland Cumb **209** F1
Fingland D&G **226** D5
Fingland D&G **225** F4

293

Finglesham 125 F3
Fingringhoe 152 B5
Finkle Street 186 A3
Finlarig 242 A1
Finmere 148 B4
Finnart A&B 241 E5
Finnart P&K 250 A4
Finney Hill 159 G1
Finningham 152 B1
Finningley 187 D3
Finnygaud 268 E5
Finsbay
 (Fionnsbhagh) 263 F3
Finsbury 136 C4
Finstall 158 B5
Finsthwaite 199 E4
Finstock 133 F1
Finstown 277 C6
Fintry Aber 269 F5
Fintry Stir 234 A1
Finwood 147 D1
Finzean 260 D5
Fionnphort 238 B2
Fir Tree 212 A4
Firbank 200 B3
Firbeck 186 C4
Firby NYorks 202 B4
Firby NYorks 195 G1
Firgrove 184 D1
Firs Lane 184 A2
Firsby 176 C1
Firsdown 118 D4
Firth 278 D5
Fishbourne IoW 107 E3
Fishbourne WSuss 108 A3
Fishburn 212 C4
Fishcross 243 E5
Fisherford 260 E1
Fishers Farm Park WSuss
 RH14 0EG 121 F5
Fisher's Pond 119 F5
Fisher's Row 192 A3
Fishersgate 109 E3
Fisherstreet 121 E4
Fisherton High 266 E6
Fisherton SAyr 224 A4
Fisherton de la
 Mere 118 A4
Fishguard
 (Abergwaun) 140 C4
Fishlake 187 D1
Fishleigh Barton 113 F3
Fishley 179 F4
Fishnish 247 F5
Fishpond Bottom 103 G3
Fishponds 131 F5
Fishpool 184 C2
Fishtoft 176 B3
Fishtoft Drove 176 B3
Fishtown of Usan 253 F4
Fishwick 237 G4
Fiskerton Lincs 188 A5
Fiskerton Notts 174 C2
Fitling 197 E4
Fittleton 118 C3
Fittleworth 108 C2
Fitton End 162 C1
Fitz 156 D1
Fitzhead 115 E5
Fitzroy 115 E5
Fitzwilliam 186 B1
Fitzwilliam Museum
 Cambs CB2 1RB
 66 Cambridge
Fiunary 247 F5
Five Acres 131 E1
Five Ash Down 109 G1
Five Ashes 110 A1
Five Bridges 145 F3
Five Houses 106 D4
Five Lanes 130 D3
Five Oak Green 123 F4
Five Oaks Chanl 100 C5
Five Oaks WSuss 121 F5
Five Roads 128 A2
Five Turnings 156 B5
Five Wents 124 A3
Fivehead 116 A5
Fivelanes 97 G1
Flack's Green 137 G1
Flackwell Heath 135 D4
Fladbury 146 B3
Fladdabister 279 D9
Flagg 172 C1
Flambards Experience, The
 Corn TR13 0QA 95 D4
Flamborough 205 F5
Flamingo Land Theme
 Park NYorks
 YO17 6UX 203 G4
Flamingo Park,
 Hastings ESuss
 TN34 3AR 110 D3
Flamstead 135 F1
Flamstead End
 136 C4
Flansham 108 B3
Flanshaw 194 C5
Flasby 193 F2
Flash 172 B1
Flashader 263 J6
Flask Inn 204 C2
Flatts Lane Woodland
 Country Park R&C
 TS6 0NN 29 D4
Flaunden 135 F2
Flawborough 174 C3
Flawith 195 D1
Flax Bourton 116 C1
Flax Moss 193 D5
Flaxby 194 C2
Flaxholme 173 E3
Flaxlands 164 C2
Flaxley 131 F1
Flaxpool 115 E4
Flaxton 195 F1
Fleckney 160 B3
Flecknoe 148 A1
Fledborough 187 F5
Fleet Hants 120 D2
Fleet Hants 107 G2
Fleet Lincs 176 B5

Fleet Air Arm Museum
 Som BA22 8HT 116 C5
Fleet Hargate 176 B5
Fleetville 136 A2
Fleetwood 191 G3
Fleggburgh (Burgh St.
 Margaret) 179 F4
Flemingston 129 G5
Flemington 234 A4
Flempton 151 G1
Fleoideabhagh 263 F3
Flesherin 271 H4
Fletchersbridge 97 F3
Fletchertown 209 F2
Fletching 109 G1
Fleuchats 260 B4
Fleur-de-lis 130 A3
Flexbury 112 C5
Flexford 121 E2
Flimby 208 D3
Flimwell 123 E5
Flint (Y Fflint) 182 D5
Flint Cross 150 C3
Flint Mountain 182 D5
Flintham 174 C3
Flinton 197 E4
Flint's Green 159 E4
Flishinghurst 123 G5
Flitcham 177 F5
Flitholme 200 C1
Flitton 149 F4
Flitwick 149 F4
Flixborough 187 F1
Flixton GtMan 184 B3
Flixton NYorks 204 D5
Flixton Suff 165 E3
Flockton 185 G1
Flockton Green 185 G1
Flodden 228 D3
Flodigarry 263 K4
Flood's Ferry 162 B3
Flookburgh 199 E5
Floors 268 C5
Flordon 164 C2
Flore 148 B1
Flotta 277 C8
Flotterton 220 B4
Flowton 152 B3
Flushdyke 194 B5
Flushing Aber 269 J6
Flushing Corn 95 F3
Flushing Corn 95 E4
Fluxton 103 D3
Flyford Flavell 146 B2
Foals Green 165 D4
Fobbing 137 G4
Fochabers 268 B5
Fochriw 130 A2
Fockerby 187 F1
Fodderletter 259 J2
Fodderty 266 C6
Foddington 116 C5
Foel 155 F1
Foelgastell 128 B1
Foggathorpe 195 G4
Fogo 237 E5
Fogorig 237 E5
Fogwatt 267 K6
Foindle 274 D4
Folda 251 G3
Fole 172 B2
Foleshill 159 F4
Folke 104 C1
Folkestone 125 E5
Folkingham 175 F4
Folkington 110 A3
Folksworth 161 G4
Folkton 205 D5
Folla Rule 261 F1
Follifoot 194 C2
Folly Dorset 104 D2
Folly Pembs 140 C5
Folly Farm, Begelly Pembs
 SA68 0XA 127 E2
Folly Gate 99 F1
Fonmon 115 D1
Fonthill Bishop 118 A4
Fonthill Gifford 118 A4
Fontmell Magna 105 E1
Fontmell Parva 105 E1
Fontwell 108 B3
Font-y-gary 115 D1
Foolow 185 F5
Footherley 158 D2
Foots Cray 137 D5
Forbestown 260 B3
Force Forge 199 E3
Force Green 122 D3
Forcett 202 A1
Forches Cross 102 A2
Ford A&B 240 A4
Ford Bucks 134 C2
Ford Devon 100 C2
Ford Devon 113 E3
Ford Devon 101 D3
Ford Glos 146 C5
Ford Mersey 183 E3
Ford Midlo 236 A3
Ford N'umb 229 D3
Ford Pembs 140 C5
Ford Plym 100 A2
Ford Shrop 156 D1
Ford Som 115 D5
Ford Staffs 172 B2
Ford Wilts 132 A5
Ford WSuss 108 B3
Ford End 137 F1
Ford Green 192 A3
Ford Heath 156 D1
Ford Street 103 E1
Forda 99 F1
Fordbridge 159 D4
Fordcombe 123 E4
Fordell 235 F1
Forden (Fforddun) 156 B2
Forder Green 101 D1
Fordgate 116 A4
Fordham Cambs 163 E5
Fordham Essex 152 A5
Fordham Norf 163 E3
Fordham Abbey 151 E1
Fordham Heath 152 A5

Fordhouses 158 B2
Fordingbridge 106 A1
Fordon 205 D5
Fordoun 253 F2
Ford's Green 152 B1
Fordstreet 152 A5
Fordwells 133 F1
Fordwich 125 D3
Fordyce 268 D4
Forebrae 243 E2
Forebridge 171 G5
Foredale 193 E1
Foreland 230 A3
Foremark 173 E5
Foremark Reservoir Derbys
 DE65 6EG 173 E5
Forest 202 B2
Forest Coal Pit 144 B5
Forest Gate 136 D4
Forest Green 121 G3
Forest Hall Cumb 199 G2
Forest Hall T&W 212 B1
Forest Hill Oxon 134 A2
Forest Lane Head 194 C2
Forest Lodge (Taigh na
 Frithe) A&B 249 G5
Forest Lodge P&K 251 E2
Forest Row 122 D5
Forest Side 107 D4
Forest Town 173 G1
Forestburn Gate 220 C2
Forest-in-Teesdale 211 E5
Forestmill 243 E5
Forestside 107 G1
Forfar 252 C4
Forfar Loch Country Park
 Angus DD8 1BT 252 C4
Forgandenny 243 F3
Forge 155 D3
Forgie 268 B5
Forhill 158 C5
Formby 183 D2
Forncett End 164 C2
Forncett St. Mary 164 C2
Forncett St. Peter 164 C2
Forneth 251 F5
Fornham All Saints 151 G1
Fornham St. Martin 151 G1
Fornighty 267 G6
Forres 267 H6
Forrest 234 C3
Forrest Lodge 215 G2
Forsbrook 171 G3
Forse 275 H5
Forsinain 274 E4
Forsinard 274 D4
Forston 104 C3
Fort Augustus (Cille
 Chuimein) 257 K4
Fort Fun, Eastbourne
 ESuss BN22 7LQ 110 B3
Fort George 266 E6
Fort William
 (An Gearasdan) 248 D2
Forter 251 F3
Forteviot 243 F3
Forth 234 D4
Forthampton 146 A4
Fortingall 250 C5
Fortis Green 136 B4
Forton Hants 119 F3
Forton Lancs 192 A2
Forton Shrop 156 D1
Forton Som 103 G2
Forton Staffs 171 E5
Fortrie 268 E6
Fortrose
 (A'Chananaich) 266 E6
Fortuneswell 104 C5
Forty Green 135 E3
Forty Hill 136 C3
Forward Green 152 B2
Fosbury 119 E2
Foscot 147 E5
Fosdyke 176 B4
Foss 250 C4
Foss Cross 132 C2
Fossdale 201 D3
Fossebridge 132 C1
Foster Street 137 D2
Fosterhouses 186 D1
Foster's Booth 148 B2
Foston Derbys 172 C4
Foston Leics 160 B3
Foston Lincs 175 D3
Foston NYorks 195 F1
Foston on the
 Wolds 196 D2
Fotherby 188 D3
Fotheringhay 161 F3
Foubister 277 E7
Foul Mile 110 B2
Foula 278 B1
Foula Airstrip 278 B1
Foulbog 226 D5
Foulden Norf 163 F3
Foulden ScBord 237 G4
Foulness Island 138 D3
Foulridge 193 E3
Foulsham 178 B3
Foulstone 199 G4
Foulzie 269 F4
Fountainhall 236 B5
Four Ashes Staffs 158 B2
Four Ashes Staffs 158 A4
Four Ashes Suff 164 A4
Four Crosses
 Denb 168 D3
Four Crosses
 Powys 156 B1
Four Crosses
 Powys 155 G3
Four Crosses
 Staffs 158 B2
Four Elms 123 D4
Four Forks 115 F4
Four Gotes 162 C1
Four Lane Ends
 B'burn 192 C5

Four Lane Ends
 ChesW&C 170 C1
Four Lane Ends
 York 195 F2
Four Lanes 95 D3
Four Marks 120 B4
Four Mile Bridge 180 A5
Four Oaks Glos 145 D1
Four Oaks WMid 159 D1
Four Oaks WMid 158 D3
Four Oaks Park 158 D3
Four Roads 128 A2
Four Throws 110 C1
Fourlane Ends 173 E2
Fourlanes End 171 F2
Fourpenny 267 F2
Fourstones 211 E1
Fovant 118 B5
Foveran House 261 H2
Fowey 97 F4
Fowlis 244 B1
Fowlis Wester 243 E2
Fowlmere 150 C3
Fownhope 145 E4
Fox Hatch 137 E3
Fox Lane 121 D2
Fox Street 152 B5
Fox Up 201 D5
Foxbar 233 F3
Foxcombe Hill 133 G2
Foxcote Glos 132 C1
Foxcote Som 117 E2
Foxdale 190 A4
Foxearth 151 G3
Foxfield 198 D4
Foxham 132 B5
Foxhole Corn 97 D4
Foxhole High 258 C1
Foxholes 204 D5
Foxhunt Green 110 A2
Foxley N'hants 148 B2
Foxley Norf 178 B3
Foxley Wilts 132 A4
Foxt 172 B3
Foxton Cambs 150 C3
Foxton Dur 212 C5
Foxton Leics 160 B3
Foxton Locks Leics
 LE16 7RA 160 B4
Foxwist Green 170 D1
Foy 145 E5
Foyers (Foithir) 258 B2
Frachadil 246 C4
Fraddam 94 C3
Fraddon 96 D4
Fradley 159 D1
Fradswell 171 G4
Fraisthorpe 197 D1
Framfield 109 G1
Framingham Earl 179 D5
Framingham Pigot 179 D5
Framlingham 153 D1
Frampton Dorset 104 C3
Frampton Lincs 176 B4
Frampton Cotterell 131 F4
Frampton Mansell 132 B2
Frampton on
 Severn 131 G2
Frampton West
 End 176 A3
Framsden 152 D2
Framwellgate Moor 212 B3
France Lynch 132 B2
Frances Green 192 C4
Franche 158 A5
Frandley 184 A5
Frankby 182 D4
Frankfort 179 E3
Frankley 158 B4
Franksbridge 144 A2
Frankton 159 G5
Frant 123 E5
Fraserburgh 269 H4
Frating 152 B5
Fratton 107 F2
Freasley 159 E3
Freathy 99 D5
Freckenham 163 E5
Freckleton 192 A5
Freeby 174 D5
Freefolk 119 F3
Freeland 133 G1
Freester 279 D7
Freethorpe 179 F5
Freethorpe
 Common 179 F5
Freiston 176 B3
Freiston Shore 176 B3
Fremington Devon 113 F2
Fremington NYorks 201 F3
French Brothers Cruises
 W&M SL4 5JH 135 E5
French Brothers Cruises
 PE12 6JU 176 A5
Frenchbeer 99 G2
Frendraught 268 E6
Frenich 241 G4
Frensham 120 D3
Fresgoe 274 E2
Freshbrook 132 D4
Freshfield 183 D2
Freshford 117 E2
Freshwater 106 C4
Freshwater Bay 106 C4
Freshwater East 126 D3
Fressingfield 165 D4
Freston 152 C4
Fretherne 131 G2
Frettenham 178 D4
Freuchie 244 A4
Freystrop Cross 126 C1
Friars, The, Aylesford Kent
 ME20 7BX 123 G3
Friars Carse 216 D2
Friar's Gate 123 D5
Friarton 243 G2
Friday Bridge 162 C2
Friday Street ESuss 110 B3
Friday Street Suff 152 D2

Friday Street Suff 153 E2
Friday Street Surr 121 G3
Fridaythorpe 196 A2
Friern Barnet 136 B3
Friesthorpe 188 A4
Frieston 175 E3
Frieth 134 C3
Frilford 133 G3
Frilsham 134 A5
Frimley 121 D2
Frimley Green 121 D2
Frindsbury 123 G2
Fring 177 F5
Fringford 148 B5
Friningham 124 A3
Frinsted 124 A3
Frinton-on-Sea 139 F1
Friockheim 253 D5
Friog 154 C1
Frisby on the
 Wreake 160 B1
Friskney 176 C2
Friskney
 Eaudyke 176 C2
Friston ESuss 110 A4
Friston Suff 153 F1
Fritchley 173 E2
Frith 124 B3
Frith Bank 176 B3
Frith Common 145 F1
Fritham 106 B3
Frithelstock 113 E4
Frithelstock
 Stone 113 E4
Frithville 176 B2
Frittenden 124 A4
Frittiscombe 101 E3
Fritton Norf 164 D2
Fritton Norf 179 F5
Fritwell 148 A5
Frizinghall 194 A4
Frizington 208 D5
Frocester 131 G2
Frochas 156 B2
Frodesley 157 E2
Frodesley Lane 157 E2
Frodingham 187 F1
Frodsham 183 G5
Frog End 150 C2
Frog Pool 145 G1
Frogden 228 B4
Froggatt 185 G5
Froghall 172 B3
Frogham 106 A1
Frogland Cross 131 F4
Frogmore Devon 101 D3
Frogmore Hants 120 D2
Frogmore Herts 136 A2
Frogwell 98 D4
Frolesworth 160 A3
Frome 117 E3
Frome Market 117 F2
Frome St. Quintin 104 B2
Frome Whitfield 104 C3
Fromes Hill 145 F3
Fron Gwyn 166 C4
Fron Powys 156 B2
Fron Powys 143 G1
Fron Powys 156 A3
Fron Isaf 169 F3
Froncysyllte 169 F3
Fron-goch 168 C4
Frosterley 211 G4
Frostenden 165 F3
Frosterley 211 G4
Frotoft 276 D5
Froxfield 119 E1
Froxfield Green 120 C5
Fruitmarket Gallery Edin
 EH1 1DF 37 G4
Fryerning 137 F2
Fugglestone
 St. Peter 118 C4
Fulbeck 175 E2
Fulbourn 150 D2
Fulbrook 133 E1
Fulflood 119 F5
Fulford Som 115 F5
Fulford Staffs 171 G4
Fulford York 195 F3
Fulham 136 B5
Fulking 109 E2
Full Sutton 195 G2
Fullaford 113 G2
Fuller Street 137 G1
Fuller's Moor 170 C3
Fullerton 119 E4
Fulletby 188 C5
Fullwood 233 F4
Fulmer 135 F4
Fulmodeston 178 A2
Fulnetby 188 A5
Fulready 147 E3
Fulstow 188 D3
Fulstow 185 F2
Fulwell Oxon 147 F5
Fulwell T&W 212 C2
Fulwood Lancs 192 B4
Fulwood SYorks 186 A4
Fun Farm, Spalding Lincs
 PE12 6JU 176 A5
Fundenhall 164 C2
Fundenhall
 Street 164 C2
Funtington 108 A3
Funtley 107 E2
Funzie 278 F2
Furley 103 F2
Furnace A&B 240 C4
Furnace Carmar 128 B2
Furnace Cere 154 C3
Furnace High 265 F4
Furnace End 159 E3
Furner's Green 109 G1
Furness Vale 185 E4
Furneux Pelham 150 C5
Furnham 103 G2
Further Quarter 124 A5
Furtho 148 C3
Furze Green 164 D3
Furze Platt 135 D4
Furzehill Devon 114 A3
Furzehill Dorset 105 G2
Furzeley Corner 107 F1

Furzey Lodge 106 C2
Furzley 106 B1
Fyfett 103 F1
Fyfield Essex 137 E2
Fyfield Glos 133 E2
Fyfield Hants 119 D3
Fyfield Oxon 133 G3
Fyfield Wilts 118 C1
Fyfield Wilts 118 C1
Fylingthorpe 204 C2
Fyning 120 C5
Fyvie 261 F1

G

Gabalfa 130 A5
Gabhsunn Bho
 Dheas 271 G2
Gabhsunn Bho
 Thuath 271 G2
Gablon 266 E2
Gabroc Hill 233 F4
Gaddesby 160 B1
Gaddesden Row 135 F1
Gadebridge 135 F2
Gadshill 137 G5
Gaer Newport 130 B4
Gaer Powys 144 A5
Gaer-fawr 130 D3
Gaerllwyd 130 D3
Gaerwen 180 C5
Gagingwell 147 G5
Gaich High 259 H2
Gaich High 258 D1
Gaick Lodge 250 C1
Gailes 224 B2
Gailey 158 B1
Gainford 202 A1
Gainsborough 187 F3
Gainsford End 151 F4
Gairloch
 (Gearrloch) 264 D4
Gairlochy (Geàrr
 Lòchaidh) 249 D1
Gairney Bank 243 G5
Gairnshiel Lodge 259 K4
Gaitsgill 209 G2
Galabank 236 B5
Galashiels 227 F2
Galdenoch 214 C4
Gale 184 D1
Galgate 192 A2
Galhampton 116 D5
Gallanach 240 A2
Gallantry Bank 170 C2
Gallatown 244 A5
Galley Common 159 F3
Galleyend 137 G2
Galleywood 137 G2
Gallowfauld 252 C5
Gallowhill 233 F3
Gallows Green 172 B3
Gallowstree
 Common 134 B4
Gallowstree Elm 158 A4
Galltair 256 E2
Gallt-y-foel 167 E1
Gallypot Street 123 D5
Galmington 115 F5
Galmisdale 247 D1
Galmpton Devon 100 C3
Galmpton Torbay 101 E2
Galmpton
 Warborough 101 E2
Galphay 202 B5
Galston 224 C2
Galtrigill 263 G6
Gamble's Green 137 G1
Gamblesby 210 C4
Gamelsby 209 F1
Gamesley 185 E3
Gamlingay 150 A2
Gamlingay Cinques 150 A2
Gamlingay Great
 Heath 150 A2
Gammaton 113 E3
Gammaton Moor 113 E3
Gammersgill 201 F4
Gamrie 269 F4
Gamston Notts 187 E5
Gamston Notts 174 B4
Ganarew 131 E1
Ganavan 240 A1
Ganllwyd 168 A5
Gannochy 253 E2
Ganstead 197 D4
Ganthorpe 203 F5
Ganton 204 D5
Ganwick Corner 136 B3
Gaodhail 239 F1
Gappah 102 B5
Gara Bridge 100 D3
Garabal 241 E3
Garadheancal 265 F1
Garbat 266 C5
Garbhallt 240 C5
Garboldisham 164 B3
Garden 242 A5
Garden City 170 A1
Garden Village 185 G3
Gardeners Green 120 D1
Gardenstown 269 F4
Garderhouse 279 C8
Gardham 196 B3
Gare Hill 117 E3
Garelochhead 241 E5
Garford 133 G3
Garforth 194 D4
Gargrave 193 F2
Gargunnock 242 C5
Gariob 231 F2
Garlic Street 164 D3
Garlieston 207 E2
Garlies Castle 215 F4
Garlinge Green 124 D3
Garlogie 261 F4
Garmelow 171 F5
Garmond 269 G5

Garmony 247 F5
Garmouth 268 B4
Garmston 157 F2
Garnant 128 C1
Garndolbenmaen 167 D3
Garneddwen 155 D2
Garnett Bridge 199 G3
Garnfadryn 166 B4
Garnswllt 128 C2
Garrabost 271 H4
Garrachra 232 B1
Garralburn 268 C5
Garras 95 E4
Garreg 167 F3
Garreg Bank 156 B1
Garrick 242 C3
Garrigill 210 D3
Garriston 202 A3
Garroch 215 G3
Garrochty 232 B4
Garros 263 K5
Garrow 242 C1
Garryhorn 215 G1
Garrynahine (Gearraidh na
 h-Aibhne) 270 E4
Garsdale 200 C4
Garsdale Head 200 C3
Garsdon 132 B4
Garshall Green 171 G4
Garsington 134 A2
Garstang 192 A3
Garston 183 F4
Garswood 183 G3
Gartachoil 242 A5
Gartally 258 B1
Gartavaich 231 G4
Gartbreck 230 A4
Gartcosh 234 A3
Garth Bridgend 129 E3
Garth Cere 154 C4
Garth Gwyn 181 D5
Garth IoM 190 B4
Garth Powys 143 F3
Garth Shet 279 B7
Garth Wrex 169 F3
Garth Row 199 G3
Garthbrengy 143 G3
Garthdee 261 H4
Gartheli 142 B2
Garthmyl 156 A3
Garthorpe Leics 174 D5
Garthorpe NLincs 187 F1
Garths 199 G3
Garthynty 142 D3
Gartincaber 242 B4
Gartly 260 D1
Gartmore 242 A5
Gartnagrenach 231 F4
Gartnatra 230 B3
Gartness 233 G1
Gartocharn 233 F1
Garton 197 E4
Garton-on-the-
 Wolds 196 B1
Gartymore 275 F7
Garvald 236 C2
Garvamore 258 C5
Garvan 248 B2
Garvard 238 C5
Garve (Clachan
 Ghairbh) 265 K5
Garveld 222 B5
Garvestone 178 B5
Garvie 232 B1
Garvock Aber 253 F2
Garvock Invcly 233 D2
Garvock P&K 243 F3
Garwald 226 D4
Garwaldwaterfoot 226 D5
Garway 145 D5
Garway Hill 144 D5
Gask Aber 269 J6
Gask Aber 269 F6
Gask P&K 243 E3
Gaskan 248 A1
Gass 224 C5
Gastard 117 F1
Gasthorpe 164 A3
Gaston Green 137 E1
Gatcombe 107 D4
Gate Burton 187 F4
Gate Helmsley 195 F2
Gate House 231 D2
Gateacre 183 F4
Gateford 186 C4
Gateforth 195 E5
Gatehead 224 B2
Gatehouse 231 D2
Gatehouse of Fleet 216 A5
Gatelawbridge 216 D1
Gateley 178 A3
Gatenby 202 C4
Gatesgarth 209 E5
Gateshaw 228 B4
Gateshead 212 B1
Gatesheath 170 B1
Gateside Angus 252 C5
Gateside Fife 243 G4
Gateside NAyr 233 E4
Gateslack 225 G5
Gathurst 183 G2
Gatley 184 C4
Gattonside 227 G2
Gaufron 143 F1
Gaulby 160 B2
Gauldry 244 B2
Gauntons Bank 170 C3
Gaunt's Common 105 G2
Gaunt's Earthcott 131 F4
Gautby 188 B5
Gavinton 237 E4
Gawber 186 A2
Gawcott 148 B4
Gawsworth 184 C5
Gawthorp 200 B4
Gawthwaite 199 D4
Gay Bowers 137 G2
Gay Street 121 F5
Gaydon 147 F2

Gayhurst 148 D3
Gayle 201 D4
Gayles 202 A2
Gayton Mersey 183 D4
Gayton N'hants 148 C2
Gayton Norf 163 F1
Gayton Staffs 171 G5
Gayton le Marsh 189 E4
Gayton le Wold 188 C4
Gayton Thorpe 163 F1
Gaywood 177 E5
Gazeley 151 F2
Geanies House 267 F4
Gearach 230 A4
Gearnsary 274 C5
Gearradh 248 B3
Gearraidh Bhailteas 254 C2
Gearraidh Bhaird 271 F5
Gearraidh na
Monadh 254 C3
Gearrannan 270 D3
Geary 263 H5
Gedding 152 A2
Geddington 161 D4
Gedintailor 256 B1
Gedling 174 B3
Gedney 176 C5
Gedney Broadgate 176 C5
Gedney Drove End 176 C5
Gedney Dyke 176 C5
Gedney Hill 162 B1
Gee Cross 185 D3
Geilston 233 E2
Geirinis 262 C7
Geisiadar 270 D4
Geldeston 165 E2
Gell Conwy 168 B1
Gell Gwyn 167 D4
Gelli 129 F3
Gelli Aur Country
Park Carmar
SA32 8LR 142 C5
Gelli Gynan 169 E2
Gellideg 129 G2
Gellifor 169 E1
Gelligaer 130 A3
Gellilydan 167 F4
Gellioedd 168 C3
Gelly 127 D1
Gellyburn 243 F1
Gellywen 141 F5
Gelston D&G 216 B5
Gelston Lincs 175 E3
Gembling 196 D2
Gemmil 239 G4
Genoch 214 C5
Genoch Square 214 C5
Gentleshaw 158 C1
Geocrab 263 G2
George Green 135 F4
George Nympton 114 A5
Georgeham 113 E2
Georgetown 233 F3
Gerlan 167 F1
Germansweek 99 E1
Germoe 94 C4
Gerrans 95 F3
Gerrards Cross 135 F4
Gerston 275 G3
Gestingthorpe 151 G4
Geuffordd 156 B1
Geufron 155 E4
Gibbet Hill 117 E3
Gibbshill 216 B3
Gibraltar Lincs 177 D2
Gibraltar Suff 152 C2
Gibraltar Point National
Nature Reserve Lincs
PE24 4SU 177 D2
Gibside T&W
NE16 6BG 212 A2
Giddeahall 132 A5
Giddy Green 105 E4
Gidea Park 137 E4
Gidleigh 99 G2
Giffnock 233 G4
Gifford 236 C3
Giffordland 233 D5
Giffordtown 244 A3
Giggleswick 193 E1
Gigha 231 E5
Gilberdyke 196 A5
Gilbert's End 146 A3
Gilchriston 236 B3
Gilcrux 209 E3
Gildersome 194 B5
Gildingwells 186 C4
Gilesgate Moor 212 B3
Gileston 114 D1
Gilfach 130 A3
Gilfach Goch 129 F4
Gilfachrheda 142 A2
Gilgarran 208 D4
Gill 210 A5
Gillamoor 203 F4
Gillen 263 H5
Gillenbie 217 F2
Gillfoot 217 D3
Gilling East 203 F5
Gilling West 202 A2
Gillingham Dorset 117 F5
Gillingham Med 123 G2
Gillingham Norf 165 F2
Gillivoan 275 G5
Gillock 275 H3
Gillow Heath 171 F2
Gills 275 J1
Gill's Green 123 G5
Gilmanscleuch 227 E3
Gilmerton Edin 235 G3
Gilmerton P&K 243 D2
Gilmilnscroft 225 D3
Gilmonby 201 E1
Gilmorton 160 A4
Gilsland 210 A5
Gilsland Spa 210 A5
Gilson 159 D3
Gilstead 194 A4
Gilston 236 B4
Gilston Park 136 D1
Giltbrook 173 F3

Gilwern 130 B1
Gimingham 179 D2
Gin Pit 184 A2
Ginclough 185 D5
Ginger's Green 110 B2
Giosla 270 D5
Gipping 152 B1
Gipsey Bridge 176 A3
Girlsta 279 D7
Girsby 202 C2
Girtford 149 G3
Girthon 216 A5
Girton Cambs 150 C1
Girton Notts 174 D1
Girvan 214 C1
Gisburn 193 E3
Gisburn Cotes 193 E3
Gisleham 165 G3
Gislingham 164 B4
Gissing 164 C3
Gittisham 103 E3
Givons Grove 121 G2
Glackour 265 H3
Gladestry 144 B2
Gladsmuir 236 B2
Glaic 232 B2
Glais 128 D2
Glaisdale 203 G2
Glaister 223 E2
Glame 264 B7
Glamis 252 B5
Glamis Castle Angus
DD8 1QJ 252 B5
Glan Conwy 168 B2
Glanaber Terrace 168 A3
Glanaman 128 C1
Glanbran 143 E4
Glan-Denys 142 B2
Glandford 178 B1
Glan-Duar 142 B3
Glandwr 141 E5
Glan-Dwyfach 167 D3
Glangrwyney 130 B1
Glanllynfi 129 E3
Glanmule 156 A3
Glan-rhyd NPT 129 D2
Glanton 229 E5
Glanton Pyke 229 E5
Glanvilles Wootton 104 C2
Glanwern 154 C4
Glanwydden 181 G4
Glan-y-don 182 C5
Glan-y-llyn 130 A4
Glan-y-nant 155 F4
Glan-yr-afon
Gwyn 168 C3
Glan-yr-afon
Gwyn 168 D3
Glan-yr-afon IoA 181 E4
Glan-y-Wern 167 F4
Glapthorn 161 F3
Glapwell 173 F1
Glasahoile 241 G4
Glasbury 144 A4
Glaschoil 259 H1
Glascoed Mon 130 C2
Glascoed Wrex 169 F2
Glascorrie 260 C5
Glascote 159 E2
Glascwm 144 A2
Glasdrum 248 C5
Glasfryn 168 C2
Glasgow (Glaschu) 233 G3
Glasgow Airport 233 F3
Glasgow Botanic
Garden Glas
G12 0UE 30 C3
Glasgow Prestwick
Airport 224 B3
Glasgow Royal Concert Hall
Glas G2 3NY 39 F3
Glasgow Science Centre
Glas G51 1EA 38 A4
Glashmore 261 F4
Glasinfryn 167 E1
Glasnacardoch 256 C5
Glasnakille 256 B3
Glaspant 141 F4
Glaspwll 154 D3
Glass Studio, Eastbourne
Pier ESuss
BN21 3EL 110 B4
Glassburn 257 K1
Glassel 260 E5
Glassenbury 123 G5
Glasserton 207 E3
Glassford 234 B5
Glasshouse 145 G5
Glasshouses 194 A1
Glassingall 242 C4
Glasslie 244 A4
Glasson Cumb 218 A5
Glasson Lancs 192 A2
Glasson Dock 192 A2
Glassonby 210 B4
Glasterlaw 253 D4
Glaston 161 D2
Glastonbury 116 B4
Glastonbury Abbey Som
BA6 9EL 116 C4
Glatton 161 G4
Glazebrook 184 A3
Glazebury 184 A3
Glazeley 157 G4
Gleadless 186 A4
Gleadsmoss 171 F1
Gleann Tholastaidh 271 H3
Gleaston 199 E5
Gledhow 194 C4
Gledrid 169 F4
Glemsford 151 G3
Glen D&G 216 C3
Glen D&G 215 G5
Glen Auldyn 190 C3
Glen Mona 190 C3
Glen Parva 160 A3
Glen Trool Lodge 215 F2
Glen Village 234 C2
Glen Vine 190 B4

Glenae 217 D2
Glenaladale 248 A2
Glenald 241 E5
Glenamachrie 240 B2
Glenapp Castle 214 B2
Glenarm 252 B3
Glenbarr 222 B2
Glenbatrick 230 D2
Glenbeg High 265 K3
Glenbeg High 259 H2
Glenbeg High 247 F3
Glenbeich 242 B2
Glenbervie Aber 253 F1
Glenbervie Falk 234 C1
Glenboig 234 B3
Glenborrodale 247 F3
Glenbranter 240 D5
Glenbreck 226 B3
Glenbrittle 255 K2
Glenburn 233 F3
Glenbyre 239 E2
Glencaple 217 D4
Glencarse 243 G2
Glencat 260 D5
Glenceitlin 248 D5
Glencloy 223 F2
Glencoe
(A' Chàrnaich) 248 D4
Glencoe Visitor Centre
High PH49 4LA 248 D4
Glenconglass 259 J2
Glencraig 243 G5
Glencripesdale 247 F4
Glencrosh 216 B2
Glencruitten 240 A2
Glencuie 260 C2
Glendearg D&G 226 D5
Glendearg ScBord 227 G2
Glendessary 257 F5
Glendevon 243 E4
Glendoebeg 258 B4
Glendoick 244 A2
Glendoll Lodge 252 A2
Glendoune 214 C1
Glendrissaig 214 C1
Glenduckie 244 A3
Glenduisk 214 D2
Glendye Lodge 253 E1
Gleneagles Hotel 243 E3
Gleneagles House 243 E4
Glenearn 243 G3
Glenegedale 230 B4
Glenelg
(Gleann Eilg) 256 E3
Glenfarg 243 G3
Glenfeochan 240 A2
Glenfield 160 A2
Glenfinnan (Gleann
Fhionnainn) 248 B1
Glenfoot 243 G3
Glengalmadale 248 A4
Glengap 216 A5
Glengarnock 233 E4
Glengarrisdale 239 F5
Glengennet 215 D1
Glengolly 275 G2
Glengrasco 263 K7
Glengyle 241 F3
Glenhead 216 C2
Glenhead Farm 252 A3
Glenhurich 248 A3
Gleniffer Braes Country Park
Renf PA2 8TE 30 A4
Glenkerry 227 D4
Glenkiln 223 F2
Glenkin 232 C1
Glenkindie 260 C3
Glenlair 216 B3
Glenlatterach 267 K6
Glenlean 232 B1
Glenlee Angus 252 C2
Glenlee D&G 216 A2
Glenlichorn 242 C3
Glenlivet 259 J2
Glenlochar 216 B4
Glenluce 214 C5
Glenmallan 241 E5
Glenmanna 225 F5
Glenmavis 234 B3
Glenmaye 190 A4
Glenmore A&B 194 B3
Glenmore High 263 K7
Glenmore High 256 B2
Glenmore Forest Park
Visitor Centre High
PH22 1QY 259 G3
Glenmore Lodge 259 G4
Glenmoy 252 C3
Glenmuick 273 F7
Glennoe 240 C1
Glenochar 226 A4
Glenogil 252 C3
Glenprosen
Village 252 B3
Glenquiech 252 C3
Glenramskill 222 C4
Glenrazie 215 E4
Glenridding 209 G5
Glenrisdell 231 G4
Glenrossal 266 B1
Glenrothes 244 A4
Glensanda 248 A5
Glensaugh 253 E2
Glensgaich 266 B5
Glenshalg 260 D4
Glenshellish 240 D5
Glensluain 240 C5
Glentaggart 225 G2
Glentham 188 A3
Glenton 260 E2
Glentress 227 D2
Glentress Forest ScBord
EH45 8NB 235 G5
Glentrool 215 F3
Glentruan 190 C1
Glentworth 187 G4
Glenuachdarach 263 K6
Glenuig 247 F2
Glenure 248 C5
Glenurquhart 266 E5
Glenwhilly 214 C3

Glespin 225 G3
Gletness 279 D7
Glewstone 145 E5
Glinton 161 G2
Glogue 141 F4
Glooston 160 C3
Glororum 229 F3
Glossop 185 E3
Gloster Hill 221 E1
Gloucester 132 A1
Gloucester Cathedral
Glos GL1 2LR
73 Gloucester
Gloucester Historic
Docks Glos GL1 2ER
73 Gloucester
Gloucestershire
Airport 146 A5
Gloucestershire &
Warwickshire Railway
Glos GL54 5DT 146 B5
Gloup 278 D2
Gloweth 96 B5
Glusburn 193 G3
Glympton 147 G5
Glyn 168 A2
Glyn Ceiriog 169 F4
Glynarthen 141 G3
Glyncoch 129 G3
Glyncorrwg 129 E3
Glyn-Cywarch 167 F4
Glynde 109 G3
Glyndebourne 109 G2
Glyndyfrdwy 169 E3
Glynneath
(Glyn-Nedd) 129 E2
Glynogwr 129 F4
Glyntaff 129 G4
Gnosall 171 F5
Gnosall Heath 171 F5
Go Bananas, Colchester
Essex CO1 1BX 152 A5
Goadby 160 C3
Goadby Marwood 174 C5
Goatacre 132 C5
Goatfield 240 C4
Goathill 104 C1
Goathland 204 B2
Goathurst 115 F4
Gobernuisgeach 274 E5
Gobhaig 270 C7
Gobowen 170 A4
Godalming 121 E3
Goddard's Corner 153 D1
Goddards Green 109 E1
Godden Green 123 D3
Godford Cross 103 E2
Godington 148 B5
Godleybrook 171 G3
Godmanchester 162 A5
Godmanstone 104 C3
Godmersham 124 C3
Godney 116 B3
Godolphin Cross 94 D3
Godor 156 B1
Godre'r-graig 129 D2
Godshill Hants 106 A1
Godshill IoW 107 E4
Godstone 122 C3
Godstone Farm Surr
RH9 8LX 122 C3
Godwick 178 A3
Goetre 130 C2
Goff's Oak 136 C2
Gogar 235 F2
Gogarth 181 F4
Goginan 154 C4
Goirtean a'
Chladaich 248 C2
Goirtein 232 A1
Golan 167 E3
Golant 97 F4
Golberdon 98 D3
Golborne 184 A3
Golcar 185 F1
Gold Hill Cambs 162 D3
Gold Hill Dorset 105 E2
Goldcliff 130 C4
Golden Acre Park
WYorks
LS16 8BQ 194 B3
Golden Cross 110 A2
Golden Green 123 F4
Golden Grove 128 B1
Golden Pot 120 C3
Golden Valley
Derbys 173 F2
Golden Valley Glos 146 B5
Goldenhill 171 F2
Golders Green 136 B4
Goldhanger 138 C2
Goldielea 216 D3
Golding 157 E2
Goldington 149 F2
Goldsborough
NYorks 204 B1
Goldsborough
NYorks 194 C2
Goldsithney 94 C3
Goldstone 171 E5
Goldthorn Park 158 B3
Goldthorpe 186 B2
Goldworthy 113 D3
Goleulong 2000 Lightship,
Cardiff Cardiff
CF10 4PA 7 C4
Golford 123 G5
Gollanfield 267 F6
Gollinglith Foot 202 A4
Golspie 267 F2
Golval 274 D2
Gomeldon 118 C4
Gomersal 194 B5
Gometra 246 C5
Gometra House 246 C5
Gomshall 121 F3
Gonachan Cottage 234 A1
Gonalston 174 B3
Gonerby Hill Foot 175 E4
Gonfirth 279 C6
Good Easter 137 F1

Gooderstone 163 F2
Goodleigh 113 G2
Goodmanham 196 A3
Goodmayes 137 D4
Goodnestone Kent 125 E3
Goodnestone Kent 124 C2
Goodrich 131 E1
Goodrington 101 E2
Goodshaw 193 E5
Goodshaw Fold 193 E5
Goodwick (Wdig) 140 C4
Goodworth Clatford 119 E3
Goodyers End 159 F4
Goole 195 G5
Goom's Hill 146 C2
Goonbell 96 B5
Goonhavern 96 B4
Goonvrea 96 B5
Goose Green Essex 152 C5
Goose Green Essex 152 C5
Goose Green
GtMan 183 G2
Goose Green Kent 123 F3
Goose Green SGlos 131 F5
Goose Pool 145 D4
Gooseham 112 C4
Goosehill Green 146 B1
Goosewell 100 B2
Goosey 133 F3
Goosnargh 192 B4
Goostrey 184 B5
Gorcott Hill 146 C1
Gordon 236 D5
Gordonbush 267 F1
Gordonstoun 267 J5
Gordonstown Aber 268 D5
Gordonstown Aber 261 F1
Gore Cross 118 B2
Gore End 119 F1
Gore Pit 138 B1
Gore Street 125 E2
Gorebridge 236 A3
Gorefield 162 C1
Gorey 100 C3
Gorgie 235 G2
Gorgie City Farm Edin
EH11 2LA 36 B7
Goring 134 B4
Goring Heath 134 B5
Goring-by-Sea 108 D3
Gorllwyn 141 G4
Gornalwood 158 B3
Gorrachie 269 F5
Gorran Churchtown 97 D5
Gorran Haven 97 E5
Gors 154 C5
Gorsedd 182 C5
Gorseinon 128 B3
Gorseness 277 D6
Gorseybank 173 D2
Gorsgoch 142 A2
Gorslas 128 B1
Gorsley 145 F5
Gorsley Common 145 F5
Gorstage 184 A5
Gorstan 265 K5
Gorstanvorran 248 A2
Gorsty Hill 172 C5
Gorten 239 G1
Gortenbuie 239 E1
Gorteneorn 247 F3
Gorton GtMan 184 C3
Gosbeck 152 C2
Gosberton 176 A4
Gosberton Clough 175 G5
Goseley Dale 173 E5
Gosfield 151 F5
Gosford Here 145 E1
Gosford Oxon 134 A1
Gosforth Cumb 198 B2
Gosforth T&W 212 B1
Gosland Green 170 C2
Gosmore 149 G5
Gospel End 158 A3
Gosport 107 F3
Gossabrough 278 E4
Gossington 131 G2
Gossops Green 122 B5
Goswick 229 E2
Gotham 173 G4
Gotherington 146 B5
Gothers 97 D4
Gott 279 D8
Gotton 115 F4
Gourdas 269 F6
Gourdon 253 G2
Gourock 232 D2
Govan 233 G3
Goverton 174 C2
Goveton 101 D3
Govilon 130 B1
Gowanhill 269 J4
Gowdall 195 F5
Gowerton 128 B3
Gowkhall 235 E1
Gowkthrapple 234 B4
Gowthorpe 195 G2
Goxhill ERid 197 D4
Goxhill NLincs 196 D5
Goytre 129 E4
Gozzard's Ford 133 G3
Grabhair 271 F6
Graby 175 F4
Gradbach 171 G1
Grade 95 E5
Gradeley Green 170 C2
Graffham 108 B2
Grafham Cambs 149 G1
Grafham Surr 121 F3
Grafham Water Cambs
PE28 0BH 149 G1
Grafton Here 145 D4
Grafton NYorks 194 D1
Grafton Oxon 133 E2
Grafton Shrop 156 D1
Grafton Worcs 145 E1
Grafton Worcs 146 B4

Grafton Flyford 146 B2
Grafton Regis 148 C3
Grafton Underwood 161 E4
Grafty Green 124 A4
Graianrhyd 169 F2
Graig Carmar 128 A2
Graig Conwy 181 G5
Graig Denb 182 B5
Graig-fechan 169 E2
Grain 124 A1
Grainel 230 A3
Grainhow 269 G6
Grains Bar 185 D2
Grainsby 188 C3
Grainthorpe 189 D3
Graizelound 187 E3
Gramisdale
(Gramsdal) 262 D6
Grampound 96 D5
Grampound Road 96 D4
Granborough 148 C5
Granby 174 C4
Grand Pier, Teignmouth
Devon
TQ14 8BB 102 C5
Grandborough 147 G1
Grandes Rocques 101 F4
Grandtully 251 E4
Grange Cumb 209 F5
Grange EAyr 224 C2
Grange High 257 K1
Grange Med 123 G2
Grange Mersey 182 D4
Grange P&K 244 A2
Grange Crossroads 268 C5
Grange de Lings 187 G5
Grange Hall 267 H5
Grange Hill 136 D3
Grange Moor 185 G1
Grange of Lindores 244 A3
Grange Villa 212 B2
Grangehall 172 D2
Grangemill 172 D2
Grangemouth 234 D1
Grangemuir 244 D4
Grange-over-Sands 199 F5
Grangetown
Cardiff 130 A5
Grangetown R&C 213 E5
Granish 259 G3
Gransmoor 196 D2
Granston 140 B4
Grantchester 150 C2
Grantham 175 E4
Grantley 202 B5
Grantlodge 261 F3
Granton 235 G2
Granton House 226 B5
Grantown-on-Spey 259 H2
Grantsfield 145 E1
Grantshouse 237 F3
Grappenhall 184 A4
Grasby 188 A2
Grasmere 199 E2
Grasscroft 185 D2
Grassendale 183 E4
Grassgarth 199 F3
Grassholme 211 F5
Grassington 193 G1
Grassmoor 173 F1
Grassthorpe 174 C1
Grateley 119 D3
Gratwich 172 B4
Gravel Hill 135 F3
Gravelly Bank 173 D5
Graven 278 D5
Graveney 124 C2
Gravesend 137 F5
Grayingham 187 G3
Grayrigg 199 G3
Grays 137 F5
Grayshott 121 D4
Grayswood 121 E4
Grazeley 120 B1
Greasbrough 186 B3
Greasby 183 D4
Great Aberystwyth Camera
Obscura Cere
SY23 2DN 154 B4
Great Abington 150 D3
Great Addington 161 E5
Great Alne 146 D2
Great Altcar 183 E2
Great Amwell 136 C1
Great Asby 200 B1
Great Ashfield 152 A1
Great Ayton 203 E1
Great Baddow 137 G2
Great Bardfield 151 E4
Great Barford 149 G2
Great Barr 158 C3
Great Barrow 170 B1
Great Barton 151 G1
Great Barugh 203 G5
Great Bavington 220 B3
Great Bealings 152 D3
Great Bedwyn 119 D1
Great Bentley 152 C5
Great Bernera 270 D4
Great Billing 148 D1
Great Bircham 177 F4
Great Blakenham 152 C2
Great Bolas 170 D5
Great Bookham 121 G2
Great Bourton 147 G3
Great Bowden 160 C4
Great Bradley 151 E2
Great Braxted 138 B1
Great Bricett 152 B2
Great Brickhill 149 E4
Great Bridgeford 171 F5
Great Brington 148 B1
Great Bromley 152 B5
Great Broughton
Cumb 209 D3
Great Broughton
NYorks 203 E2

Great Buckland 123 F2
Great Budworth 184 A5
Great Burdon 202 C1
Great Burstead 137 F3
Great Busby 203 E2
Great Cambourne 150 B2
Great Canfield 137 E1
Great Canney 138 B2
Great Carlton 189 E4
Great Casterton 161 F2
Great Chalfield 117 F1
Great Chart 124 B4
Great Chatwell 157 G1
Great Chell 171 F2
Great Chesterford 150 D3
Great Cheverell 118 A2
Great Chishill 150 C4
Great Clacton 139 E1
Great Clifton 208 D4
Great Coates 188 C2
Great Comberton 146 B3
Great Corby 210 A2
Great Cornard 151 G3
Great Cowden 197 E3
Great Coxwell 133 E3
Great Crakehall 202 B4
Great Cransley 160 D5
Great Cressingham 163 G2
Great Crosby 183 E2
Great Crosthwaite 209 F4
Great Cubley 172 C4
Great Cumbrae 232 C4
Great Dalby 160 C1
Great Doddington 149 D1
Great Doward 131 E1
Great Dunham 163 G1
Great Dunmow 151 E5
Great Durnford 118 C4
Great Easton Essex 151 E5
Great Easton Leics 160 D3
Great Eccleston 192 A3
Great Edstone 203 G4
Great Ellingham 164 B2
Great Elm 117 E3
Great Eversden 150 B2
Great Fencote 202 B3
Great Finborough 152 B2
Great Fransham 163 G1
Great Gaddesden 135 F1
Great Gidding 161 G4
Great Givendale 196 A2
Great Glemham 153 E1
Great Glen 160 B3
Great Gonerby 175 D4
Great Gransden 150 A2
Great Green
Cambs 150 A3
Great Green Norf 165 D3
Great Green Suff 152 A2
Great Green Suff 164 C4
Great Habton 203 G5
Great Hale 175 G4
Great Hall Hants
SO23 8UJ
89 Winchester
Great Hallingbury 137 E1
Great Hampden 134 D2
Great Harrowden 161 D5
Great Harwood 192 D4
Great Haseley 134 B2
Great Hatfield 197 D3
Great Haywood 172 B5
Great Heath 159 F4
Great Heck 195 E5
Great Henny 151 G4
Great Hinton 118 A2
Great Hockham 164 A2
Great Holland 139 F1
Great Horkesley 152 A4
Great Hormead 150 C4
Great Horton 194 A4
Great Horwood 148 C4
Great Houghton
N'hants 148 C2
Great Houghton
SYorks 186 B2
Great Hucklow 185 F5
Great Kelk 196 D2
Great Kimble 134 D2
Great Kingshill 135 D3
Great Langton 202 B3
Great Leighs 137 G1
Great Limber 188 B2
Great Linford 148 D3
Great Livermere 163 G5
Great Longstone 185 G5
Great Lumley 212 B3
Great Lyth 157 D2
Great Malvern 145 G3
Great Maplestead 151 G4
Great Marton 191 G4
Great Massingham 177 F5
Great Melton 178 C5
Great Milton 134 B2
Great Missenden 135 D2
Great Mitton 192 D4
Great Mongeham 125 F3
Great Moulton 164 C2
Great Munden 150 B5
Great Musgrave 200 C1
Great Ness 156 D1
Great Notley 151 F5
Great Nurcot 114 C4
Great Oak 130 C2
Great Oakley Essex 152 C5
Great Oakley
N'hants 161 D4
Great Offley 149 G5
Great Orme Tramway
Conwy
LL30 2HG 181 F4
Great Ormside 200 C1
Great Orton 209 G1
Great Ouseburn 194 D1
Great Oxendon 160 C4
Great Oxney Green 137 F2
Great Palgrave 163 G1
Great Parndon 136 D2
Great Paxton 150 A1
Great Plumpton 191 G4
Great Plumstead 179 E5

Great Ponton 175 E4
Great Potheridge 113 F4
Great Preston 194 C5
Great Purston 148 A4
Great Raveley 162 A4
Great Rissington 133 D1
Great Rollright 147 F4
Great Ryburgh 178 A3
Great Ryle 229 E5
Great Ryton 229 E5
Great St. Mary's Church
   Cambs CB2 3PQ
   66 Cambridge
Great Saling 151 F5
Great Salkeld 210 B4
Great Sampford 151 E4
Great Sankey 183 G4
Great Saredon 158 B2
Great Saxham 151 F1
Great Shefford 133 F5
Great Shelford 150 C2
Great Smeaton 202 C2
Great Snoring 178 A2
Great Somerford 132 B4
Great Stainton 212 C5
Great Stambridge 138 C3
Great Staughton 149 G1
Great Steeping 176 C1
Great Stonar 125 F3
Great Strickland 210 B5
Great Stukeley 162 A5
Great Sturton 188 C5
Great Sutton
   ChesW&C 183 E5
Great Sutton *Shrop* 157 E4
Great Swinburne 220 B4
Great Tew 147 F5
Great Tey 151 G5
Great Thorness 107 D3
Great Thurlow 151 E3
Great Torr 100 C3
Great Torrington 113 E4
Great Tosson 220 C1
Great Totham
   Essex 138 B1
Great Totham
   Essex 138 B1
Great Tows 188 C3
Great Urswick 199 D5
Great Waldingfield 152 A3
Great Walsingham 178 A2
Great Waltham 137 F1
Great Warley 137 E3
Great Washbourne 146 B4
Great Weeke 102 A4
Great Welnetham 151 G2
Great Wenham 152 B4
Great Whittington 220 C4
Great Wigborough 138 C1
Great Wigsell 110 C3
Great Wilbraham 150 D2
Great Wilne 173 E5
Great Wishford 118 B4
Great Witcombe 132 B1
Great Witley 145 G1
Great Wolford 147 E4
Great Wratting 151 E3
Great Wymondley 150 A5
Great Wyrley 158 B2
Great Wytheford 157 E3
Great Yarmouth 179 G5
Great Yeldham 151 F4
Greatford 161 F1
Greatgate 172 B3
Greatham *Hants* 120 C4
Greatham *Hart* 213 D5
Greatham *WSuss* 108 C2
Greatness 123 E3
Greatstone-on-Sea 111 F1
Greatworth 148 A3
Green 169 D1
Green Cross 121 D4
Green End *Bed* 149 G2
Green End *Bucks* 149 E4
Green End *Cambs* 162 A5
Green End *Cambs* 162 B5
Green End *Herts* 150 B5
Green End *Herts* 150 B4
Green End *Warks* 159 E4
Green Hammerton 195 D2
Green Hill 132 C4
Green Lane 146 C1
Green Moor 185 G3
Green Ore 116 C2
Green Quarter 199 F2
Green Street *ESuss* 110 C2
Green Street *Herts* 136 A3
Green Street *Herts* 150 C5
Green Street *Worcs* 146 A3
Green Street
   WSuss 121 G5
Green Street Green
   GtLon 123 D2
Green Street Green
   Kent 137 E5
Green Tye 136 D1
Greenburn 252 C5
Greencroft 212 A3
Greendams 253 E1
Greendykes 229 E4
Greenend 137 E5
Greenfaulds 234 B2
Greenfield *CenBeds* 149 F4
Greenfield (Maes-Glas)
   Flints 182 C5
Greenfield *GtMan* 185 G2
Greenfield *High* 257 J4
Greenfield *Lincs* 189 E5
Greenfield *Oxon* 134 C3
Greenford 136 A4
Greengairs 234 B2
Greengates 194 A4
Greengill 209 E3
Greenhalgh 192 A4
Greenham 119 F1
Greenhaugh 219 F3
Greenhead 210 C1
Greenheads 261 J1
Greenheys 184 B2
Greenhill *GtLon* 136 A4

Greenhill *High* 267 G1
Greenhill *SYorks* 186 A4
Greenhithe 137 E5
Greenholm 224 D2
Greenholme 199 G2
Greenhow Hill 194 A1
Greenigo 277 D7
Greenland 275 H2
Greenlands 134 C4
Greenlaw *Aber* 268 E5
Greenlaw *ScBord* 237 E5
Greenloaning 242 D4
Greenmeadow 130 B3
Greenmoor Hill 134 B4
Greenmount 184 B1
Greenmyre 261 G3
Greenock 233 D2
Greenodd 199 E4
Greens Norton 148 B3
Greenside *T&W* 212 A1
Greenside *WYorks* 185 F1
Greenstead 152 B5
Greenstead Green 151 G5
Greensted 137 E2
Greensted Green 137 E2
Greenway *Pembs* 141 D4
Greenway *Som* 116 A5
Greenwell 210 B2
Greenwich 136 C5
Greenwood Forest Park,
   Y Felinheli *Gwyn*
   LL56 4QN 167 E1
Greet 146 C4
Greete 157 E5
Greetham *Lincs* 188 D5
Greetham *Rut* 161 E1
Greetland 193 G3
Gregson Lane 192 B5
Greinton 116 B4
Grenaby 190 A4
Grendon *N'hants* 149 D1
Grendon *Warks* 159 E3
Grendon Common 159 E3
Grendon Green 145 E2
Grendon
   Underwood 148 B5
Grenitote
   (Greinetobht) 262 D4
Grenofen 99 E3
Grenoside 186 A3
Greosabhagh 263 G2
Gresford 170 A2
Gresham 178 C2
Greshornish 263 J6
Gress (Griais) 271 G3
Gressenhall 178 A4
Gressingham 192 B1
Greta Bridge 201 F1
Gretna 218 B5
Gretna Green 218 B5
Gretton *Glos* 146 C4
Gretton *N'hants* 161 E3
Gretton *Shrop* 157 E3
Grewelthorpe 202 B5
Greygarth 202 A5
Greylake 116 A4
Greys Green 134 C4
Greysouthen 209 D4
Greystead 219 F3
Greystoke 210 A4
Greystone *Aber* 259 K5
Greystone *Angus* 252 D5
Greystone *Lancs* 193 E3
Greystones 186 A4
Greywell 120 C2
Gribthorpe 195 G4
Gribton 216 D2
Griff 159 F4
Griffithstown 130 B3
Grigadale 246 D3
Griggnall 199 F3
Grimeford Village 184 A1
Grimesthorpe 186 A3
Grimethorpe 186 B2
Griminish (Griminis) 262 C6
Grimister 278 D3
Grimley 146 A1
Grimmet 224 B4
Grimness 277 D8
Grimoldby 189 D4
Grimpo 170 A5
Grimsargh 192 B4
Grimsay
   (Griomsaigh) 262 D6
Grimsbury 147 G3
Grimsby 188 C2
Grimscote 148 B2
Grimscott 112 C5
Grimshader
   (Griomsiadar) 271 G4
Grimsthorpe 175 F5
Grimston *ERid* 197 E4
Grimston *Leics* 174 B5
Grimston *Norf* 177 F5
Grimstone 104 C3
Grimstone End 152 A1
Grinacombe Moor 99 E1
Grindale 205 E5
Grindiscol 279 D9
Grindle 158 A2
Grindleford 185 G5
Grindleton 193 D3
Grindley 172 B5
Grindley Brook 170 C3
Grindlow 185 F5
Grindon *N'umb* 237 G5
Grindon *Staffs* 172 B2
Grindon *Stock* 212 C5
Grindon *T&W* 212 C2
Gringley on the Hill 187 E3
Grinsdale 209 G1
Grinshill 170 C5
Grinton 201 F3
Griomarstaidh 270 E4
Grisdale 200 D3
Grishipoll 246 A4
Gristhorpe 205 D4
Griston 164 A2
Gritley 277 E7
Grittenham 132 C4
Grittleton 132 A5
Grizebeck 198 D4

Grizedale 199 E3
Grizedale Forest Park
   Cumb LA22 0QJ 199 E3
Grobister 276 E5
Groby 160 A2
Groes 168 D1
Groes-faen 129 G4
Groesffordd 166 B4
Groesffordd Marli 182 B5
Groeslon *Gwyn* 167 D2
Groeslon *Gwyn* 167 E1
Groes-lwyd 156 B1
Groes-wen 130 A4
Grogport 231 G5
Groigearraidh 254 C1
Gromford 153 E2
Groombridge 123 E5
Groombridge Place Gardens
   Kent TN3 9QG 123 E5
Grosmont *Mon* 144 D5
Grosmont *NYorks* 204 B2
Grotaig 258 B2
Groton 152 A3
Groundistone
   Heights 227 F4
Grouville 100 C5
Grove *Bucks* 149 E5
Grove *Dorset* 104 C5
Grove *Kent* 125 E2
Grove *Notts* 187 E5
Grove *Oxon* 133 G3
Grove End 124 A2
Grove Green 123 G3
Grove Park 136 D5
Grove Town 195 E5
Grovehill 135 F2
Grovesend *SGlos* 131 F4
Grovesend *Swan* 128 B2
Gruids 266 C1
Grula 255 J2
Gruline 247 E5
Grumbla 94 B4
Grundcruie 243 F2
Grundisburgh 152 D2
Gruting 279 B8
Grutness 279 G10
Guay 251 F5
Gubbergill 198 B3
Gubblecote 135 E1
Guernsey 101 F5
Guernsey Airport 101 E5
Guestling Green 111 D2
Guestling Thorn 111 D2
Guestwick 178 B3
Guestwick Green 178 B3
Guide 192 D5
Guide Post 221 E3
Guilden Down 156 C4
Guilden Morden 150 A3
Guilden Sutton 170 B1
Guildford 121 E3
Guildford House Gallery
   Surr GU1 3AJ
   74 Guildford
Guildtown 243 G1
Guilsborough 160 B5
Guilsfield (Cegidfa) 156 B1
Guilthwaite 186 B4
Guisborough 203 F1
Guiseley 194 A3
Guist 178 B3
Guith 276 E4
Guiting Power 146 C5
Gulberwick 279 D9
Gullane 236 B1
Gullane Bents *ELoth*
   EH31 2AZ 236 B1
Gulval 94 B3
Gulworthy 99 E3
Gumfreston 127 E2
Gumley 160 B3
Gunby *Lincs* 175 D5
Gunby *Lincs* 176 C1
Gundleton 120 B4
Gunn 113 G2
Gunnerside 201 E3
Gunnerton 220 B4
Gunness 187 F1
Gunnislake 99 E3
Gunnista 279 E8
Gunnister 278 C5
Gunstone 158 A2
Gunter's Bridge 121 E5
Gunthorpe *Norf* 178 B2
Gunthorpe *Notts* 174 B3
Gunthorpe *Rut* 161 D2
Gunville 107 D4
Gunwalloe 95 D4
Gupworthy 114 C4
Gurnard 107 D3
Gurnett 184 D5
Gurney Slade 116 D3
Gurnos *MTyd* 129 G2
Gurnos *Powys* 129 D2
Gushmere 124 C3
Gussage All Saints 105 G1
Gussage St. Andrew 105 F1
Gussage St. Michael 105 F1
Guston 125 F4
Gutcher 278 E3
Guthram Gowt 175 G5
Guthrie 253 D4
Guyhirn 162 B2
Guy's Head 176 C4
Guy's Marsh 117 F5
Guyzance 221 E1
Gwaelod-y-garth 130 A4
Gwaenysgor 182 B4
Gwaithla 144 B2
Gwalchmai 180 B5
Gwastad 140 D5
Gwastadnant 167 F2
Gwaun-Cae-
   Gurwen 128 D1
Gwaunysgor 168 D1
Gwbert 141 E3

Gweek 95 E4
Gwehelog 130 C2
Gwenddwr 143 G3
Gwendreath 95 E5
Gwennap 96 B5
Gwenter 95 E5
Gwernaffield 169 F1
Gwernesney 130 D2
Gwernogle 142 B2
Gwernymynydd 169 F1
Gwern-y-Steeple 129 G5
Gwersyllt 170 A2
Gwespyr 182 C4
Gwinear 94 C3
Gwithian 94 C3
Gwredog 180 C4
Gwyddelwern 169 D3
Gwyddgrug 142 A4
Gwynfryn 169 F2
Gwystre 143 G1
Gwytherin 168 B3
Gyfelia 170 A3
Gyre 277 C7
Gyrn Goch 166 D3

H

H.M.S. Belfast *GtLon*
   SE1 2JH 12 C4
H.M.S. Victory PO1 3PX
   82 Portsmouth
H.M.S. Warrior PO1 3QX
   82 Portsmouth
Habberley 156 C2
Habin 120 D5
Haccombe 102 B5
Hacconby 175 G5
Haceby 175 F4
Hacheston 153 E2
Hackbridge 122 B2
Hackenthorpe 186 B4
Hackford 178 B5
Hackforth 202 B3
Hackland 276 C5
Hackleton 148 D2
Hacklinge 125 F3
Hackness *NYorks* 204 C3
Hackness *Ork* 277 C8
Hackthorn 187 G4
Hackthorpe 210 B5
Hacton 137 E4
Hadden 228 B3
Haddenham
   Bucks 134 C2
Haddenham
   Cambs 162 C5
Haddington *ELoth* 236 C2
Haddington *Lincs* 175 E1
Haddiscoe 165 F2
Haddo Country Park *Aber*
   AB41 7EQ 261 G1
Haddon 161 G3
Hade Edge 185 F2
Hademore 159 D2
Hadfield 185 E3
Hadham Cross 136 D1
Hadham Ford 150 C5
Hadleigh *Essex* 138 B4
Hadleigh *Suff* 152 B3
Hadleigh Castle Country
   Park *Essex*
   SS7 2PP 138 B4
Hadleigh Heath 152 A3
Hadley *Tel&W* 157 F1
Hadley *Worcs* 146 A1
Hadley End 172 C5
Hadley Wood 136 B3
Hadlow 123 F4
Hadlow Down 110 A1
Hadnall 170 C5
Hadspen 117 D4
Hadstock 151 D3
Hadston 221 E2
Hadzor 146 B1
Haffenden Quarter 124 A4
Hafod Bridge 142 B5
Hafod-Dinbych 168 B2
Hafodunos 168 B1
Hafodyrynys 130 B3
Haggate 193 E4
Haggbeck 218 C4
Haggersta 279 C8
Haggerston *GtLon* 136 C4
Haggerston *N'umb* 229 E2
Haggrister 278 C5
Haggs 234 B2
Hagley *Here* 145 E3
Hagley *Worcs* 158 B4
Hagnaby *Lincs* 176 B1
Hagnaby *Lincs* 189 E5
Hague Bar 185 D4
Hagworthingham 176 B1
Haigh 184 A2
Haigh Hall Country Park
   GtMan
   WN2 1PE 183 G2
Haighton Green 192 B4
Hail Weston 149 G1
Haile 198 B2
Hailes 146 C4
Hailey *Herts* 136 C1
Hailey *Oxon* 134 B4
Hailey *Oxon* 134 B4
Hailsham 110 A3
Haimer 275 G2
Hainault 137 D3
Hainault Forest Country
   Park *Essex*
   IG7 4QN 137 D3
Haine 125 F2
Hainford 178 D4
Hainton 188 B5
Haisthorpe 196 D1
Hakin 126 B2
Halam 174 B2
Halbeath 235 F1
Halberton 102 D1
Halcro 275 H2

Hale *Cumb* 199 G5
Hale *GtMan* 184 B4
Hale *Halton* 183 F4
Hale *Hants* 106 A1
Hale *Surr* 120 D3
Hale Bank 183 F4
Hale Barns 184 B4
Hale Nook 191 G3
Hale Street 123 F4
Hales *Norf* 165 E2
Hales *Staffs* 171 E4
Hales Green 172 C3
Hales Place 124 D3
Halesgate 176 B5
Halesowen 158 B4
Halesworth 165 E4
Halewood 183 F4
Half Way Inn 102 D3
Halford *Devon* 102 B5
Halford *Shrop* 156 D4
Halford *Warks* 147 E3
Halfpenny 199 G4
Halfpenny Green 158 A3
Halfway *Carmar* 142 C4
Halfway *Carmar* 128 B2
Halfway *Powys* 143 E4
Halfway *SYorks* 186 B4
Halfway *WBerks* 119 F1
Halfway Bridge 121 E5
Halfway House 156 C1
Halfway Houses
   Kent 124 B1
Halfway Houses
   Lincs 175 D1
Halghton Mill 170 B3
Halifax 193 G3
Halistra 263 H6
Halket 233 F4
Halkirk 275 G3
Halkyn 182 C5
Hall 233 F4
Hall Cross 192 A5
Hall Dunnerdale 198 D3
Hall Green *ChesE* 171 F2
Hall Green *Lancs* 192 A5
Hall Green *WMid* 158 D4
Hall Grove 136 B1
Halland 110 A2
Hallaton 160 C3
Hallatrow 116 D2
Hallbankgate 210 B2
Hallen 131 E4
Hallfield Gate 173 E2
Hallglen 234 C2
Halling 123 G2
Hallington *Lincs* 188 D4
Hallington *N'umb* 220 B4
Halliwell 184 A1
Halloughton 174 B2
Hallow 146 A2
Hallow Heath 146 A2
Hallrule 227 G4
Halls 183 E1
Hall's Green *Essex* 136 D2
Hall's Green *Herts* 150 A5
Hallsands 101 E4
Hallthwaites 198 C4
Hallwood Green 145 F4
Hallworthy 97 F1
Hallyne 235 F5
Halmer End 171 E3
Halmond's Frome 145 F3
Halmore 131 F2
Halmyre Mains 235 F5
Halnaker 108 B3
Halsall 183 E1
Halse *N'hants* 148 A3
Halse *Som* 115 E5
Halsetown 94 C3
Halsham 197 E5
Halsinger 113 F2
Halstead *Essex* 151 G4
Halstead *Kent* 123 D2
Halstead *Leics* 160 C2
Halstock 104 B2
Halsway 115 E4
Haltcliffe Farm 196 C4
Haltham 176 A1
Haltoft End 176 B3
Halton *Bucks* 135 D1
Halton *Halton* 183 G4
Halton *Lancs* 192 B1
Halton *N'umb* 211 F1
Halton *Wrex* 170 A4
Halton East 193 F2
Halton Gill 201 D5
Halton Green 192 B1
Halton Holegate 176 C1
Halton Lea Gate 210 C2
Halton Park 192 B1
Halton West 193 E2
Haltwhistle 210 D1
Halvergate 179 F5
Halwell 101 D2
Halwill 99 E1
Halwill Junction 99 E1
Ham *Devon* 103 F2
Ham *Glos* 131 F3
Ham *Glos* 146 B5
Ham *GtLon* 136 A5
Ham *High* 275 H1
Ham *Kent* 125 F3
Ham *Plym* 100 A2
Ham *Shet* 278 A1
Ham *Som* 115 F5
Ham *Som* 103 F1
Ham *Wilts* 119 E1
Ham Common 117 F5
Ham Green *Here* 145 G3
Ham Green *Kent* 124 A2
Ham Green *Kent* 111 D1
Ham Green *NSom* 131 E5
Ham Green *Worcs* 146 C1
Ham Hill 123 F2
Ham Hill Country Park
   Som TA14 6RW 104 A1
Ham Street 116 C4
Hambleden 134 C4
Hambledon *Hants* 107 F3
Hambledon *Surr* 121 E4

Hamble-le-Rice 107 D2
Hambleton *Lancs* 191 G3
Hambleton *NYorks* 195 E4
Hambridge 116 A5
Hambrook *SGlos* 131 F5
Hambrook *WSuss* 107 G2
Hameringham 176 B1
Hamerton 161 G5
Hamilton 234 B4
Hamlet *Devon* 103 E3
Hamlet *Dorset* 104 B2
Hammer 121 D4
Hammerpot 108 C3
Hammersmith 136 B5
Hammersmith Apollo
   GtLon W6 9QH 11 E5
Hammerwich 158 C2
Hammerwood 122 D5
Hammond Street 136 C2
Hammoon 105 E1
Hamnavoe *Shet* 278 C9
Hamnavoe *Shet* 279 D6
Hamnavoe *Shet* 278 D4
Hamnavoe *Shet* 278 D5
Hamnish Clifford 145 E2
Hamp 115 F4
Hampden Park 110 B3
Hampden Park Stadium
   Glas G42 9BA 30 C4
Hamperden End 151 D4
Hampnett 132 D1
Hampole 186 C2
Hampreston 105 G3
Hampstead 136 B4
Hampstead
   Norreys 134 A5
Hampsthwaite 194 B2
Hampton *Devon* 103 F3
Hampton *GtLon* 121 G1
Hampton *Kent* 125 D2
Hampton *Peter* 161 G3
Hampton *Shrop* 157 G4
Hampton *Swin* 133 D3
Hampton *Worcs* 146 C3
Hampton Bishop 145 E4
Hampton Court Palace &
   Garden *GtLon*
   KT8 9AU 11 B8
Hampton Fields 132 A3
Hampton Heath 170 B3
Hampton in Arden 159 E4
Hampton Loade 157 G4
Hampton Lovett 146 A1
Hampton Lucy 147 E2
Hampton on the
   Hill 147 E1
Hampton Poyle 134 A1
Hampton Wick 121 G1
Hamptworth 106 B1
Hamsey 109 G2
Hamstall Ridware 158 D1
Hamstead 106 C3
Hamstead Marshall 119 F1
Hamsteels 212 A3
Hamsterley *Dur* 212 A4
Hamsterley *Dur* 212 A2
Hamsterley Forest *Dur*
   DL13 3NL 211 G5
Hamstreet 124 C5
Hamworthy 105 F3
Hanbury *Staffs* 172 C5
Hanbury *Worcs* 146 B1
Hanbury Woodend 172 C5
Hanby 175 F4
Hanchurch 171 F3
Handa Island 272 D4
Handale 203 G1
Handbridge 170 B1
Handcross 122 B5
Handforth 184 C4
Handley *ChesW&C* 170 B2
Handley *Derbys* 173 E1
Handley Green 137 F2
Handsacre 158 C1
Handside 136 B1
Handsworth *SYorks* 186 B4
Handsworth *WMid* 158 C3
Handwoodbank 156 D1
Handy Cross 135 D3
Hanford *Dorset* 105 E1
Hanford *Stoke* 171 F3
Hanging Bridge 172 C3
Hanging Houghton 160 C5
Hanging Langford 118 B4
Hangingshaw 217 F2
Hanham 131 F5
Hankelow 171 D3
Hankerton 132 B3
Hankham 110 B3
Hanley 171 F3
Hanley Castle 146 A3
Hanley Child 145 F1
Hanley Swan 146 A3
Hanley William 145 F1
Hanlith 193 F1
Hanmer 170 B4
Hannah 189 E5
Hannington
   Hants 119 G2
Hannington
   N'hants 160 D5
Hannington *Swin* 133 D3
Hannington Wick 133 D3
Hanslope 148 D3
Hanthorpe 175 F5
Hanwell *GtLon* 136 A4
Hanwell *Oxon* 147 G3
Hanwood 156 D2
Hanworth *GtLon* 136 A5
Hanworth *Norf* 178 C2
Happisburgh 179 E2
Happisburgh
   Common 179 E3
Hapsford 183 F5
Hapton *Lancs* 193 D4
Hapton *Norf* 164 C2
Harberton 101 D2
Harbertonford 101 D2
Harbledown 124 D3
Harborne 158 C4
Harborough Magna 159 G5
Harbost (Tabost) 271 H1

Harbottle 220 B1
Harbour Park Amusements,
   Littlehampton *WSuss*
   BN17 5LL 108 C3
Harbourneford 100 D1
Harbridge 106 A1
Harbridge Green 106 A1
Harburn 235 E3
Harbury 147 F2
Harby *Leics* 174 C4
Harby *Notts* 187 F5
Harcombe 103 E3
Harcombe Bottom 103 G3
Harden *WMid* 158 C2
Harden *WYorks* 193 G4
Hardendale 199 G1
Hardenhuish 132 B5
Hardgate *Aber* 261 F4
Hardgate *NYorks* 194 B1
Hardham 108 C2
Hardhorn 191 G4
Hardingham 178 B5
Hardingstone 148 C2
Hardington 117 E2
Hardington
   Mandeville 104 B1
Hardington Marsh 104 B2
Hardington Moor 104 B1
Hardley 106 C2
Hardley Street 179 E5
Hardmead 149 E3
Hardraw 201 D3
Hardstoft 173 F1
Hardway *Hants* 107 F2
Hardway *Som* 117 E4
Hardwick *Bucks* 134 D1
Hardwick *Cambs* 150 B2
Hardwick *Lincs* 187 F5
Hardwick *N'hants* 149 D1
Hardwick *Norf* 164 D2
Hardwick *Oxon* 133 F2
Hardwick *Oxon* 148 A5
Hardwick *SYorks* 186 B4
Hardwick *WMid* 158 C3
Hardwick Hall *Derbys*
   S44 5QJ 173 F1
Hardwick Hall Country Park,
   Sedgefield *Dur*
   TS21 2EH 212 C5
Hardwick Village 186 D5
Hardwicke *Glos* 146 B5
Hardwicke *Glos* 131 G1
Hardwicke *Here* 144 B3
Hardy's Green 152 A5
Hare Green 152 B5
Hare Hatch 134 D5
Hare Street *Herts* 150 B5
Hare Street *Herts* 150 B5
Hareby 176 B1
Harecroft 193 G4
Hareden 192 C3
Harefield 135 F3
Harehill 172 C4
Harehills 194 C4
Harehope 229 E4
Harelaw 234 D5
Hareplain 124 A5
Haresceugh 210 C3
Harescombe 132 A1
Haresfield 132 A1
Hareshaw *NLan* 234 D3
Hareshaw *SLan* 234 A5
Harestock 119 F4
Harewood 194 C3
Harewood End 145 E5
Harewood House *WYorks*
   LS17 9LG 194 C3
Harford *Devon* 100 C2
Harford *Devon* 102 B3
Hargate 164 C2
Hargatewall 185 F5
Hargrave *ChesW&C* 170 B1
Hargrave *N'hants* 161 F5
Hargrave *Suff* 151 F2
Hargrave Green 151 F2
Harker 218 B5
Harkstead 152 C4
Harlaston 159 E1
Harlaxton 175 D4
Harle Syke 193 E4
Harlech 167 E4
Harlech Castle *Gwyn*
   LL46 2YH 167 E4
Harlequin 174 B4
Harlescott 157 E1
Harlesden 136 B4
Harleston *Devon* 101 D3
Harleston *Norf* 164 D3
Harleston *Suff* 152 B1
Harlestone 148 C1
Harley *Shrop* 157 E2
Harley *SYorks* 186 A3
Harleyholm 226 A2
Harlington
   CenBeds 149 F4
Harlington *GtLon* 135 F5
Harlosh 263 H7
Harlow 136 D2
Harlow Hill 211 G1
Harlthorpe 195 G4
Harlton 150 B2
Harlyn 96 C2
Harman's Cross 105 F4
Harmby 202 A4
Harmer Green 136 B1
Harmer Hill 170 B5
Harmondsworth 135 F5
Harmston 175 E1
Harnage 157 E2
Harnham 118 C5
Harnhill 132 C2
Harold Hill 137 E3
Harold Park 137 E3
Harold Wood 137 E3
Haroldston West 126 B1
Haroldswick 278 F1
Harome 203 F4
Harpenden 136 A1
Harpford 103 D3
Harpham 196 C1
Harpley *Norf* 177 F5
Harpley *Worcs* 145 F1

Harpole **148** B1
Harprigg **200** B4
Harpsdale **275** G3
Harpsden **134** C4
Harpswell **187** G4
Harpur Hill **185** E5
Harpurhey **184** C2
Harracott **113** F3
Harrietfield **243** E2
Harringay **136** C4
Harrington *Cumb* **208** C4
Harrington *Lincs* **189** D5
Harrington *N'hants* **160** C5
Harringworth **161** E3
Harris **255** J5
Harris Green **164** D2
Harris Museum & Art
  Gallery, Preston *Lancs*
  PR1 2PP **192** B5
Harriseahead **171** F2
Harriston **209** E2
Harrogate **194** C2
Harrogate International
  Centre *NYorks* HG1 5LA
  74 Harrogate
Harrold **149** E2
Harrold-Odell Country Park
  Bed MK43 7DS **149** E2
Harrop Fold **192** D3
Harrow *GtLon* **136** A4
Harrow *High* **275** H1
Harrow Green **151** G2
Harrow Museum *GtLon*
  HA2 6PX **10** B1
Harrow on the Hill **136** A4
Harrow Weald **136** A3
Harrowbarrow **99** E3
Harrowden **149** F3
Harrowgate Hill **202** B1
Harry Stoke **131** F5
Harston *Cambs* **150** C2
Harston *Leics* **174** D4
Harswell **196** A3
Hart **213** D4
Hartburn **220** C3
Hartest **151** G2
Hartfield *ChesW&C* **184** A5
Hartfield *High* **264** D7
Hartford *Cambs* **162** A5
Hartford
  ChesW&C **184** A5
Hartford *Som* **114** C4
Hartford End **137** F1
Hartfordbridge **120** C2
Hartforth **202** A2
Hartgrove **105** E1
Harthill *ChesW&C* **170** C2
Harthill *NLan* **234** D3
Harthill *SYorks* **186** B4
Hartington **172** C1
Hartington Hall **220** C3
Hartland **112** C3
Hartland Quay **112** C3
Hartlebury **158** A5
Hartlepool **213** E4
Hartlepool's Maritime
  Experience *Hart*
  TS24 0XZ **213** E4
Hartley *Cumb* **200** C4
Hartley *Kent* **123** F2
Hartley *Kent* **123** G5
Hartley *N'umb* **221** F4
Hartley Green **171** G5
Hartley Mauditt **120** C4
Hartley Wespall **120** B5
Hartley Wintney **120** C2
Hartlington **193** G2
Hartlip **124** A2
Hartoft End **203** G3
Harton *NYorks* **195** G1
Harton *Shrop* **157** D4
Harton *T&W* **212** C1
Hartpury **146** A5
Hartrigge **228** A4
Hartshead **194** A5
Hartshill **159** F3
Hartsholme Country Park
  Lincs LN6 0EY **175** E1
Hartshorne **173** E2
Hartsop **199** F1
Hartwell *Bucks* **134** C1
Hartwell *ESuss* **123** D5
Hartwell *N'hants* **148** C2
Hartwith **194** B1
Hartwood **234** C4
Harvel **123** F2
Harvington *Worcs* **146** C3
Harvington *Worcs* **158** A5
Harwell *Notts* **187** D3
Harwell *Oxon* **133** G4
Harwich **152** D4
Harwood *Dur* **211** E4
Harwood *GtMan* **184** B1
Harwood *N'umb* **220** C2
Harwood Dale **204** C3
Harwood on
  Teviot **227** F5
Harworth **186** D3
Hasbury **158** B4
Hascombe **121** F3
Haselbech **160** C5
Haselbury
  Plucknett **104** A1
Haseley **147** E1
Haseley Knob **159** E5
Haselor **146** C2
Hasfield **146** A5
Hasguard **126** B2
Haskayne **183** E2
Hasketon **153** D2
Hasland **173** E1
Hasland Green **173** E1
Haslemere **121** E4
Haslingden **193** D5
Haslingden Grane **193** D5
Haslingfield **150** C2
Haslington **171** E2
Hassall **171** E2
Hassall Green **171** E2
Hassell Street **124** C1

Hassendean **227** G3
Hassingham **179** E5
Hassocks **109** F2
Hassop **185** G5
Haster **275** J3
Hasthorpe **176** C1
Hastigrow **275** H2
Hastingleigh **124** C4
Hastings *ESuss* **110** D3
Hastings *Som* **103** G1
Hastings Fishermen's
  Museum *ESuss*
  TN34 3DW **75** Hastings
Hastingwood **137** D2
Hastoe **135** E4
Haswell **212** C3
Haswell Plough **212** C3
Hatch *CenBeds* **149** G3
Hatch *Hants* **120** B5
Hatch Beauchamp **116** A5
Hatch End **136** A4
Hatch Green **103** G1
Hatching Green **136** A1
Hatchmere **183** G5
Hatcliffe **188** C2
Hatfield *Here* **145** E2
Hatfield *Herts* **136** B2
Hatfield *SYorks* **187** D2
Hatfield Broad Oak **137** E1
Hatfield Heath **137** E1
Hatfield House *Herts*
  AL9 5NF **136** B2
Hatfield
  Woodhouse **187** D2
Hatford **133** F3
Hatherden **119** E2
Hatherleigh **113** F5
Hatherop **132** D2
Hathersage **185** G4
Hathersage Booths **185** G4
Hathershaw **184** D2
Hatherton *ChesE* **171** D3
Hatherton *Staffs* **158** B1
Hatley St. George **150** A2
Hatt **99** D4
Hattingley **120** B4
Hatton *Aber* **261** J1
Hatton *Derbys* **172** D5
Hatton *GtLon* **136** A5
Hatton *Lincs* **188** B5
Hatton *Shrop* **157** D3
Hatton *Warks* **147** E1
Hatton *Warr* **183** G4
Hatton Country World
  Warks
  CV35 8XA **147** E1
Hatton Heath **170** B1
Hatton of Fintray **261** G3
Hattoncrook **261** G2
Haugh **189** E5
Haugh Head **229** E4
Haugh of Glass **260** C1
Haugh of Urr **216** C4
Haugham **188** D4
Haughhead **234** A2
Haughley **152** B1
Haughley Green **152** B1
Haughley New
  Street **152** B1
Haughs **268** D6
Haughton *ChesE* **170** C2
Haughton *Notts* **187** D5
Haughton *Powys* **156** C1
Haughton *Shrop* **157** F3
Haughton *Shrop* **157** E1
Haughton *Shrop* **170** A5
Haughton *Staffs* **171** F5
Haughton Green **184** D3
Haughton
  Le Skerne **202** C1
Haultwick **150** B5
Haunn **254** C3
Haunton **159** E1
Hauxton **150** C2
Havannah **171** F1
Havant **107** G2
Haven **144** D2
Havenstreet **107** E3
Havercroft **186** A1
Haverfordwest
  (Hwlffordd) **126** C1
Haverhill **151** E3
Haverigg **198** C5
Havering Park **137** D3
Havering-atte-
  Bower **137** E3
Haversham **148** D3
Haverthwaite **199** E4
Haverton Hill **213** D1
Haviker Street **123** G4
Havyat **116** C2
Hawarden
  (Penarlâg) **170** A1
Hawbridge **146** B3
Hawbush Green **151** F5
Hawcoat **198** D5
Hawes **201** D4
Hawe's Green **164** D2
Hawick **227** G4
Hawkchurch **103** G2
Hawkedon **151** F2
Hawkenbury *Kent* **123** E5
Hawkenbury *Kent* **124** A4
Hawkeridge **117** F2
Hawkerland **103** D4
Hawkes End **159** E4
Hawkesbury **131** G4
Hawkesbury
  Upton **131** G4
Hawkhill **229** G5
Hawkhurst **123** G5
Hawkinge **125** E4
Hawkley **120** C5
Hawkridge **114** B4
Hawkshead **199** E3
Hawkshead Hill **199** E3
Hawksheads **192** A1
Hawksland **234** B5
Hawkswick **201** E5

Hawksworth
  Notts **174** C3
Hawksworth
  WYorks **194** A3
Hawksworth
  WYorks **194** B4
Hawkwell *Essex* **138** B3
Hawkwell *N'umb* **220** C4
Hawley *Hants* **121** D2
Hawley *Kent* **137** E5
Hawley's Corner **122** D3
Hawling **146** C5
Hawnby **203** E4
Haworth **193** G4
Hawstead **151** G2
Hawstead Green **151** G2
Hawthorn *Dur* **212** D3
Hawthorn *Hants* **120** B4
Hawthorn *RCT* **130** A4
Hawthorn *Wilts* **117** F1
Hawthorn Hill
  BrackF **135** D5
Hawthorn Hill
  Lincs **176** A2
Hawthorpe **175** F5
Hawton **174** C2
Haxby **195** F2
Haxey **187** E2
Haxted **122** D4
Haxton **118** C3
Hay Green **162** D1
Hay Mills **158** D4
Hay Street **150** B5
Haydon *Dorset* **104** C1
Haydon *Swin* **132** D4
Haydon Bridge **211** E1
Haydon Wick **132** D4
Haye **99** D3
Hayes *GtLon* **135** F4
Hayes *GtLon* **122** C2
Hayes End **135** F4
Hayfield *A&B* **240** C2
Hayfield *Derbys* **185** E4
Hayfield *Fife* **244** A5
Hayfield *High* **275** F2
Haygrove **115** F4
Hayhillock **252** D5
Hayle **94** C3
Hayling Island **107** G2
Haymoor Green **171** D2
Hayne **102** C1
Haynes **149** G3
Haynes Church End **149** F3
Haynes West End **149** F3
Hay-on-Wye (Y Gelli
  Gandryll) **144** B3
Hayscastle **140** B5
Hayscastle Cross **140** C5
Hayton *Cumb* **210** B2
Hayton *Cumb* **209** E2
Hayton *ERid* **196** A3
Hayton *Notts* **187** E4
Hayton's Bent **157** E4
Haytor Vale **102** A5
Haytown **113** D4
Hayward Gallery
  GtLon SE1 8XZ **45** F4
Haywards Heath **109** F1
Haywood Oaks **174** B2
Hazel End **150** C5
Hazel Grove **184** D4
Hazel Street **123** F5
Hazelbank *A&B* **240** C4
Hazelbank *SLan* **234** C5
Hazelbury Bryan **104** D2
Hazeleigh **138** B2
Hazeley **120** C2
Hazelhurst **184** B1
Hazelside **225** G3
Hazelslack **199** F5
Hazelslade **158** C1
Hazelwood *Derbys* **173** E3
Hazelwood *GtLon* **122** D2
Hazlefield **208** A2
Hazlehead
  Aberdeen **261** G4
Hazlehead *SYorks* **185** F2
Hazlemere **135** D3
Hazlerigg **221** E4
Hazleton **132** C1
Hazon **221** D1
Heacham **177** E4
Head Bridge **113** G4
Headbourne
  Worthy **119** F4
Headcorn **124** A4
Headingley **194** B4
Headington **134** A2
Headlam **202** A1
Headless Cross **146** C1
Headley *Hants* **120** D4
Headley *Hants* **119** G1
Headley *Surr* **122** B3
Headley Down **120** D4
Headley Heath **158** C5
Headon **187** E5
Heads Nook **210** A2
Heady Hill **184** C1
Heage **173** E2
Healaugh *NYorks* **201** F3
Healaugh *NYorks* **195** E3
Heald Green **184** C4
Heale *Devon* **113** G1
Heale *Som* **116** A5
Healey *Lancs* **184** C1
Healey *N'umb* **211** G2
Healey *NYorks* **202** A4
Healey *WYorks* **194** B5
Healeyfield **211** G2
Healey's Cornish Cyder Farm
  Corn TR4 9LW **96** B4
Healing **188** C1
Heamoor **94** B3
Heaning **199** F3
Heanish **246** B2
Heanor **173** F3
Heanton
  Punchardon **113** F4
Heanton Satchville **113** F4
Heap Bridge **184** C1
Heapey **192** C5

Heapham **187** F4
Hearn **120** D4
Heart of the Country
  Centre *Staffs*
  WS14 9QR **158** D2
Hearthstead **226** C3
Heasley Mill **114** A4
Heast **256** C3
Heath *Cardiff* **130** A4
Heath *Derbys* **173** F1
Heath *WYorks* **186** A1
Heath & Reach **149** E5
Heath End *Derbys* **173** E5
Heath End *Hants* **119** G1
Heath End *Hants* **119** F1
Heath End *Surr* **120** D3
Heath Hayes **158** C1
Heath Hill **157** G1
Heath House **116** B4
Heath Town **158** B3
Heathbrook **170** D5
Heathcot **261** G4
Heathcote *Derbys* **172** C1
Heathcote *Shrop* **171** D5
Heathencote **148** C3
Heather **159** F1
Heatherton Activity Park
  Pembs
  SA70 8RJ **127** D4
Heathfield *Devon* **102** B5
Heathfield *ESuss* **110** A1
Heathfield *NYorks* **194** A1
Heathfield *Som* **115** D5
Heathrow Airport **135** F5
Heathton **158** A3
Heatley **184** B4
Heaton *Lancs* **192** A1
Heaton *Staffs* **171** G1
Heaton *T&W* **212** B1
Heaton *WYorks* **194** A4
Heaton Moor **184** C3
Heaton Park *GtMan*
  M25 2SW **25** F1
Heaton's Bridge **183** F1
Heaverham **123** E3
Heaviley **184** D4
Heavitree **102** C3
Hebburn **212** C1
Hebden **193** G1
Hebden Bridge **193** F5
Hebden Green **170** D1
Hebing End **150** B5
Hebron *Carmar* **141** E5
Hebron *N'umb* **221** D3
Heck **217** E2
Heckfield **120** C1
Heckfield Green **164** C4
Heckfordbridge **152** A5
Heckingham **165** E2
Heckington **175** G3
Heckmondwike **194** B5
Heddington **118** A1
Heddle **277** C6
Heddon-on-the-
  Wall **212** A1
Hedenham **165** E2
Hedge End **107** D1
Hedgerley **135** E4
Hedging **116** A5
Hedley on the Hill **211** G2
Hednesford **158** C1
Hedon **197** D5
Hedsor **135** E4
Heeley **186** A4
Heglibister **279** C7
Heighington *Darl* **212** B5
Heighington *Lincs* **175** F1
Heightington **157** G5
Heights of Brae **266** C5
Heilam **273** G3
Heithat **217** F2
Heiton **228** B3
Hele *Devon* **113** F1
Hele *Devon* **102** C2
Hele *Devon* **99** D1
Hele *Devon* **102** A5
Hele *Som* **115** E5
Hele *Torbay* **101** F1
Hele Bridge **113** F5
Hele Lane **102** A1
Helebridge **112** C5
Helensburgh **233** D1
Helford **95** E4
Helhoughton **177** G5
Helions Bumpstead **151** E3
Hell Corner **119** E1
Hellaby **186** C3
Helland *Corn* **97** E2
Helland *Som* **116** A5
Hellandbridge **97** E2
Hellesdon **178** D4
Hellidon **148** A2
Hellifield **193** E2
Hellingly **110** A2
Hellington **179** E5
Hellister **279** C8
Helmdon **148** A3
Helmingham **152** C2
Helmington Row **212** A4
Helmsdale **275** F7
Helmshore **193** D5
Helmsley **203** F4
Helperby **194** D1
Helperthorpe **204** C5
Helpringham **175** G3
Helpston **161** G2
Helsby **183** F5
Helsey **189** F5
Helston **95** D4
Helstone **97** E1
Helton **210** B5
Helwith **201** F2
Helwith Bridge **193** E1
Hem **156** B2
Hemborough Post **101** E2
Hemel Hempstead **135** F2
Hemerdon **100** B2
Hemingbrough **195** F4
Hemingby **188** C5
Hemingfield **186** A2

Hemingford Abbots **162** A5
Hemingford Grey **162** A5
Hemingstone **152** C2
Hemington *Leics* **173** F5
Hemington
  N'hants **161** F4
Hemington *Som* **117** E2
Hemley **153** D3
Hemlington **203** D1
Hemp Green **153** E1
Hempholme **196** C3
Hempnall **164** D2
Hempnall Green **164** D2
Hempriggs House **275** J4
Hempriggs **267** J5
Hempstead *Essex* **151** E4
Hempstead *Med* **123** G2
Hempstead *Norf* **179** F3
Hempstead *Norf* **178** C2
Hempsted **132** A1
Hempton *Norf* **178** A3
Hempton *Oxon* **147** G4
Hemsby **179** F4
Hemswell **187** G3
Hemswell Cliff **187** G4
Hemsworth **186** B1
Hemyock **103** E1
Henbury *Bristol* **131** E5
Henbury *ChesE* **184** C5
Henderland **216** C3
Hendersyde Park **228** B3
Hendon *GtLon* **136** B4
Hendon *T&W* **212** C2
Hendraburnick **97** F1
Hendre *Bridgend* **129** F4
Hendre *Gwyn* **166** C4
Hendreforgan **129** F4
Hendy **128** B2
Heneglwys **180** C5
Henfield *SGlos* **131** F5
Henfield *WSuss* **109** E2
Henford **99** D1
Hengherst **124** B5
Hengoed *Caerp* **130** A3
Hengoed *Powys* **144** B2
Hengoed *Shrop* **169** F4
Hengrave **151** G1
Henham **150** D5
Heniarth **156** A2
Henlade **115** F5
Henley *Dorset* **104** C2
Henley *Shrop* **157** E5
Henley *Som* **116** B4
Henley *Som* **104** A2
Henley *Suff* **152** C2
Henley *WSuss* **121** D5
Henley Corner **116** B4
Henley Park **121** E2
Henley-in-Arden **147** D1
Henley's Down **110** C2
Henllan *Carmar* **141** G3
Henllan *Denb* **168** D1
Henllan Amgoed **141** E5
Henllys **130** B3
Henlow **149** G4
Hennock **102** B4
Henny Street **151** G4
Henryd **181** F5
Henry's Moat **140** D5
Hensall **195** E5
Henshaw **211** D1
Hensingham **208** C5
Henstead **165** F3
Hensting **119** F5
Henstridge Ash **104** D1
Henstridge Bowden **117** D5
Henstridge Marsh **117** E5
Henton *Oxon* **134** C2
Henton *Som* **116** B3
Henwood **97** G3
Heogan **279** D8
Heol Senni **143** F5
Heolgerrig **129** G2
Heol-y-Cyw **129** F4
Hepburn **229** E4
Hepburn Bell **229** E4
Hepple **220** B1
Hepscott **221** E3
Hepthorne Lane **173** F1
Heptonstall **193** F5
Hepworth *Suff* **164** A4
Hepworth *WYorks* **185** F2
Hepworth South
  Common **164** A4
Herbrandston **126** B2
Hereford **145** E3
Hereford Cathedral
  Here HR1 2NG
  75 Hereford
Heriot **236** A4
Heritage Motor Centre,
  Gaydon *Warks*
  CV35 0BJ **147** F2
Herm **101** G5
Hermiston **235** F2
Hermitage *D&G* **216** B4
Hermitage *Dorset* **104** C2
Hermitage *ScBord* **218** D2
Hermitage *WBerks* **134** A5
Hermitage *WSuss* **107** G2
Hermitage Green **184** A3
Hermon *Carmar* **141** G4
Hermon *IoA* **166** C1
Hermon *Pembs* **141** F4
Herne **125** D2
Herne Bay **125** D2
Herne Common **125** D2
Herne Pound **123** F3
Herner **113** F3
Hernhill **124** C2
Herodsfoot **97** G3
Herongate **137** F3
Heron's Ghyll **109** G1
Heronsgate **135** F3
Herriard **120** B3
Herringfleet **165** F2
Herring's Green **149** F3
Herringswell **151** F1
Herringthorpe **186** B3

Hersden **125** D2
Hersham *Corn* **112** C5
Hersham *Surr* **121** G1
Herstmonceux **110** B2
Herston **277** D8
Hertford **136** C1
Hertford Heath **136** C1
Hertingfordbury **136** C1
Hesket Newmarket **209** G3
Hesketh Bank **192** A5
Hesketh Lane **192** C3
Heskin Green **183** G1
Hesleden **212** D4
Hesleyside **220** A3
Heslington **195** F2
Hessay **195** E2
Hessenford **98** D5
Hessett **152** A1
Hessle **196** C5
Hest Bank **192** A1
Hester's Way **146** B5
Hestley Green **152** C1
Heston **136** A5
Heswall **183** D4
Hethe **148** A5
Hethelpit Cross **145** G5
Hetherington **220** A4
Hethersett **178** C5
Hethersgill **210** A1
Hethpool **228** C4
Hett **212** B4
Hetton **193** F2
Hetton-le-Hole **212** C3
Heugh **220** C4
Heugh-head *Aber* **260** B3
Heugh-head *Aber* **260** D5
Heveningham **165** E4
Hever **123** D4
Hever Castle & Gardens
  Kent
  TN8 7NG **123** D4
Heversham **199** F4
Hevingham **178** C3
Hewas Water **97** D5
Hewell Grange **146** C1
Hewell Lane **146** C1
Hewelsfield **131** E2
Hewelsfield
  Common **131** E2
Hewish *NSom* **116** B1
Hewish *Som* **104** A2
Hewood **103** G2
Heworth **195** F2
Hexham **211** F1
Hexham Abbey *N'umb*
  NE46 3NB **211** F1
Hextable **137** E5
Hexthorpe **186** C2
Hexton **149** G4
Hexworthy **99** G3
Hey **193** E3
Hey Houses **191** G5
Heybridge *Essex* **137** F3
Heybridge *Essex* **138** B2
Heybridge Basin **138** B2
Heybrook Bay **100** A3
Heydon *Cambs* **150** C3
Heydon *Norf* **178** C3
Heydour **175** F4
Heylipoll **246** A2
Heylor **278** B4
Heysham **192** A1
Heyshaw **194** A1
Heyshott **108** A2
Heyside **184** D2
Heytesbury **118** A3
Heythrop **147** F5
Heywood *GtMan* **184** C1
Heywood *Wilts* **117** F2
Hibaldstow **187** G2
Hibb's Green **151** G2
Hickleton **186** B2
Hickling *Norf* **179** F3
Hickling *Notts* **174** B5
Hickling Green **179** F3
Hickling Heath **179** F3
Hickstead **109** E1
Hidcote Bartrim **147** D3
Hidcote Boyce **147** D3
Hidcote Manor Garden
  Glos GL55 6LR **147** D3
High Ackworth **186** B1
High Angerton **220** C3
High Balantyre **240** C5
High Bankhill **210** B3
High Beach **136** D3
High Bentham (Higher
  Bentham) **192** C1
High Bickington **113** F3
High Birkwith **200** C5
High Blantyre **234** A4
High Bonnybridge **234** C2
High Borgue **216** A5
High Borve **271** G2
High Bradfield **185** G3
High Bradley **193** G3
High Bransholme **196** D4
High Bray **113** G2
High Bridge **209** G2
High Brooms **123** E4
High Bullen **113** F3
High Burton **202** B4
High Buston **221** E1
High Callerton **221** D4
High Casterton **200** B5
High Catton **195** G2
High Close **202** A1
High Cogges **133** F2
High Common **164** C3
High Coniscliffe **202** B1
High Crompton **184** D2
High Cross *Hants* **120** C5
High Cross *Herts* **136** C1
High Easter **137** F1
High Ellington **202** A4
High Entercommon **202** C2
High Ercall **157** E1
High Etherley **212** A5
High Ferry **176** B3

High Flatts **185** F2
High Garrett **151** F5
High Gate **193** F5
High Grange **212** A4
High Green *Norf* **178** C5
High Green *Norf* **178** A4
High Green *Norf* **178** A5
High Green *SYorks* **151** G1
High Green *SYorks* **186** A3
High Green *Worcs* **146** A3
High Halden **124** A5
High Halstow **137** G5
High Ham **116** B4
High Harrington **208** D4
High Harrogate **194** C2
High Hatton **170** D5
High Hauxley **221** E1
High Hawsker **204** C2
High Heath *Shrop* **170** D5
High Heath *WMid* **158** C2
High Hesket **210** A3
High Hesleden **213** D4
High Hoyland **185** G1
High Hunsley **196** B4
High Hurstwood **109** G1
High Hutton **195** G1
High Ireby **209** F3
High Kelling **178** B2
High Kilburn **203** E5
High Kingthorpe **204** B4
High Knipe **199** G1
High Lane *Derbys* **173** F3
High Lane *GtMan* **185** D4
High Lane *Worcs* **145** F1
High Laver **137** E2
High Legh **184** B4
High Leven **203** D1
High Littleton **116** D2
High Lodge Forest Centre
  Suff IP27 0AF **163** D4
High Lorton **209** E4
High Marishes **204** B5
High Marnham **187** F5
High Melton **186** C2
High Moor **186** B4
High Moorland Visitor
  Centre, Princetown *Devon*
  PL20 6QF **99** F3
High Newton **199** F4
High Newton-by-the-
  Sea **229** G4
High Nibthwaite **199** D3
High Offley **171** E5
High Ongar **137** E2
High Onn **158** A1
High Park Corner **152** B5
High Roding **137** F1
High Shaw **201** D3
High Spen **212** A1
High Stoop **212** A3
High Street *Corn* **97** D4
High Street *Kent* **123** G5
High Street *Suff* **153** F2
High Street *Suff* **165** E5
High Street *Suff* **165** F4
High Street *Suff* **151** G3
High Street Green **152** B5
High Throston **213** D4
High Town **158** B1
High Toynton **176** A1
High Trewhitt **220** C1
High Wham **212** A5
High Wigsell **110** C1
High Woods Country Park
  Essex CO4 5JR **152** B5
High Woolaston **131** E3
High Worsall **202** C2
High Wray **199** E3
High Wych **137** D1
High Wycombe **135** D3
Higham *Derbys* **173** E2
Higham *Kent* **137** G5
Higham *Lancs* **193** E4
Higham *Suff* **151** F1
Higham *Suff* **152** B4
Higham *SYorks* **186** A2
Higham Dykes **220** D3
Higham Gobion **149** G4
Higham on the Hill **159** F3
Higham Wood **123** F4
Highampton **113** F5
Highams Park **136** C3
Highbridge *Hants* **119** F5
Highbridge *Som* **116** A3
Highbrook **122** C5
Highburton **185** F1
Highbury **117** D3
Highclere **119** F1
Highcliffe **106** B3
Higher Alham **117** D3
Higher Ansty **105** D2
Higher Ashton **102** B4
Higher Ballam **191** G4
Higher Bentham (High
  Bentham) **192** C1
Higher Blackley **184** C2
Higher Brixham **101** F2
Higher Cheriton **103** E2
Higher Combe **114** C4
Higher Folds **184** A2
Higher Gabwell **101** F1
Higher Green **184** B3
Higher Halstock
  Leigh **104** B2
Higher Kingcombe **104** B3
Higher Kinnerton **170** A1
Higher Muddiford **113** F2
Higher Nyland **117** E5
Higher Prestacott **99** D1
Higher Standen **193** D3
Higher Tale **103** D2
Higher Thrushgill **192** C1
Higher Town *Corn* **97** E3
Higher Town *IoS* **96** B1
Higher Walreddon **99** E3
Higher Walton
  Lancs **192** B5
Higher Walton
  Warr **183** G4
Higher Wambrook **103** F2
Higher Whatcombe **105** E2

297

Higher Wheelton **192** C5
Higher Whiteleigh **98** C1
Higher Whitley **185** F4
Higher Wincham **184** A5
Higher Woodhill **184** B1
Higher Woodsford **105** D4
Higher Wraxall **104** B2
Higher Wych **156** B2
Highfield *ERid* **195** G4
Highfield *NAyr* **233** E4
Highfield *Oxon* **148** A5
Highfield *SYorks* **186** A4
Highfield *T&W* **212** D4
Highfields *Cambs* **150** B2
Highfields *N'umb* **237** G4
Highgate *ESuss* **122** D5
Highgate *GtLon* **136** B4
Highgreen Manor **220** A2
Highlane *ChesE* **171** F1
Highlane *Derbys* **186** B4
Highlaws **209** E2
Highleadon **145** G5
Highleigh *Devon* **114** C5
Highleigh *WSuss* **108** A4
Highley **157** G4
Highmead **142** B3
Highmoor Cross **134** B4
Highmoor Hill **131** D4
Highnam **131** G1
Highstead **125** E2
Highsted **124** B2
Highstreet **124** C2
Highstreet Green
    Essex **151** F4
Highstreet Green
    Surr **121** E4
Hightae **217** E3
Highter's Heath **158** C5
Hightown *Hants* **106** A2
Hightown *Mersey* **183** D2
Hightown Green **152** A2
Highway **132** C5
Highweek **102** B5
Highwood **145** F1
Highwood Hill **136** B3
Highworth **133** E3
Hilborough **163** G2
Hilcote **173** F2
Hilcott **118** C2
Hilden Park **123** E4
Hildenborough **123** E4
Hildersham **150** D3
Hilderstone **171** G4
Hilderthorpe **197** D1
Hilfield **104** C2
Hilgay **163** E3
Hill *SGlos* **131** F3
Hill *Warks* **147** G1
Hill *Worcs* **146** B3
Hill Brow **120** C5
Hill Chorlton **171** E4
Hill Common **179** F3
Hill Cottages **203** G3
Hill Croome **146** A3
Hill Deverill **117** F3
Hill Dyke **176** B3
Hill End *Dur* **211** G4
Hill End *Fife* **243** F5
Hill End *Glos* **146** A4
Hill End *GtLon* **135** F3
Hill End *NYorks* **193** G3
Hill Green **150** C4
Hill Head **107** E2
Hill Houses **157** F5
Hill Mountain **126** C2
Hill of Beath **235** F1
Hill of Fearn **267** E4
Hill Ridware **158** C1
Hill Row **162** C5
Hill Side **185** F1
Hill Street **106** C4
Hill Top *Hants* **106** D2
Hill Top *SYorks* **186** B3
Hill Top *SYorks* **185** G4
Hill View **105** F3
Hill Wootton **147** F1
Hillam **195** E5
Hillbeck **200** C1
Hillberry **190** B4
Hillborough **125** E2
Hillbrae *Aber* **268** E6
Hillbrae *Aber* **261** F3
Hillbrae *Aber* **261** G1
Hillbutts **105** F2
Hillclifflane **173** D3
Hillend *Aber* **268** C6
Hillend *Fife* **235** F1
Hillend *Midlo* **235** G3
Hillend *NLan* **234** C3
Hillend *Swan* **128** A3
Hillend Green **145** G5
Hillersland **131** E1
Hillesden **148** B5
Hillesley **131** G4
Hillfarrance **115** E5
Hillfoot End **149** G4
Hillhead *Devon* **101** F2
Hillhead *SAyr* **224** C3
Hillhead of
    Auchentumb **269** H5
Hillhead of Cocklaw **269** J6
Hilliard's Cross **159** D1
Hilliclay **275** G2
Hillingdon **135** F4
Hillington *Glas* **233** G3
Hillington *Norf* **177** F5
Hillmorton **160** A5
Hillockhead *Aber* **260** B4
Hillockhead *Aber* **260** C3
Hillowton **216** B4
Hillpound **107** E1
Hill's End **149** E4
Hills Town **173** F1
Hillside *Aber* **261** H5
Hillside *Angus* **253** F3
Hillside *Moray* **267** J5
Hillside *Shet* **279** D6
Hillside *Worcs* **145** G1
Hillswick **278** B5

Hillway **107** F4
Hillwell **279** F9
Hillyfields **106** C1
Hilmarton **132** C3
Hilperton **117** F2
Hilsea **107** F2
Hilston **197** E4
Hilton *Cambs* **150** A1
Hilton *Cumb* **210** D5
Hilton *Derbys* **172** D4
Hilton *Dorset* **105** D2
Hilton *Dur* **212** A5
Hilton *High* **267** G3
Hilton *Shrop* **157** G3
Hilton *Staffs* **158** C2
Hilton *Stock* **203** D1
Hilton Croft **261** H1
Hilton of Cadboll **267** F4
Hilton of Delnies **267** F6
Himbleton **146** B2
Himley **158** A3
Himley Hall & Park
    WMid DY3 4DF **14** A2
Hincaster **199** G4
Hinchley Wood **121** G1
Hinckley **159** G3
Hinderclay **164** B4
Hinderton **183** E5
Hinderwell **203** G5
Hindford **170** A4
Hindhead **120** D4
Hindley *GtMan* **184** A2
Hindley *N'umb* **211** G2
Hindley Green **184** A2
Hindlip **146** A2
Hindolveston **178** B3
Hindon *Som* **114** C3
Hindon *Wilts* **118** A4
Hindringham **178** A2
Hingham **178** B4
Hinksford **158** A4
Hinstock **171** D5
Hintlesham **152** B3
Hinton *Glos* **131** F2
Hinton *Hants* **106** B3
Hinton *Here* **144** C4
Hinton *N'hants* **148** A3
Hinton *SGlos* **131** G5
Hinton *Shrop* **156** D2
Hinton Admiral **106** B3
Hinton Ampner **119** G5
Hinton Blewett **116** C2
Hinton
    Charterhouse **117** E2
Hinton Martell **105** G2
Hinton on the
    Green **146** C3
Hinton Parva
    Dorset **105** G2
Hinton Parva *Swin* **133** E4
Hinton St. George **104** A1
Hinton St. Mary **105** D1
Hinton Waldrist **133** F3
Hinton-in-the-
    Hedges **148** A4
Hints *Shrop* **157** F5
Hints *Staffs* **159** D2
Hinwick **149** E1
Hinxhill **124** C4
Hinxton **150** C3
Hinxworth **150** A4
Hipperholme **194** A5
Hipsburn **229** G5
Hipswell **202** A3
Hirn **261** F4
Hirnant **221** E3
Hirst **221** E3
Hirst Courtney **195** F5
Hirwaen **169** E1
Hirwaun **129** F2
Hiscott **113** F3
Histon **150** C1
Hitcham *Bucks* **135** E4
Hitcham *Suff* **152** A2
Hitchin **149** G5
Hither Green **136** C5
Hittisleigh **102** A3
Hittisleigh Barton **102** A3
Hive **196** A4
Hixon **172** B5
Hoaden **125** E3
Hoaldalbert **144** D5
Hoar Cross **172** C5
Hoar Park Craft Centre
    Warks
    CV10 0QU **159** E3
Hoarwithy **145** E5
Hoath **125** E2
Hobarris **156** C5
Hobbies Green **151** F2
Hobbs Cross **137** D3
Hobbs Lots Bridge **162** B2
Hobkirk **227** G4
Hobson **212** A2
Hoby **160** B1
Hockerill **150** C5
Hockering **178** B4
Hockerton **174** C2
Hockley **138** B3
Hockley Heath **159** D5
Hockliffe **149** E5
Hockwold cum
    Wilton **163** F4
Hockworthy **102** D1
Hoddesdon **136** C2
Hoddlesden **192** D5
Hodgehill **171** F1
Hodgeston **126** D3
Hodnet **170** D5
Hodnetheath **170** D5
Hodson **133** D4
Hodthorpe **186** C5
Hoe **178** A4
Hoe Gate **107** F1
Hoff **200** B1
Hoffleet Stow **176** A4
Hoggard's Green **151** G2
Hoggeston **148** D5
Hoggie **268** D5

Hoggrill's End **159** E3
Hogha Gearraidh **262** C4
Hoghton **192** C5
Hognaston **172** D2
Hogsthorpe **189** F5
Holbeach **176** B5
Holbeach Bank **176** B5
Holbeach Clough **176** B5
Holbeach Drove **162** B2
Holbeach Hurn **176** B5
Holbeach St. Johns **162** B1
Holbeach St. Marks **176** B4
Holbeach
    St. Matthew **176** C4
Holbeck **186** C5
Holbeck
    Woodhouse **186** C5
Holberrow Green **146** C2
Holbeton **100** C2
Holborough **123** G2
Holbrook *Derbys* **173** E3
Holbrook *Suff* **152** C4
Holbrooks **159** F4
Holburn **229** E3
Holbury **106** D2
Holcombe *Devon* **102** C5
Holcombe *GtMan* **184** B1
Holcombe *Som* **117** D3
Holcombe Burnell
    Barton **102** B3
Holcombe Rogus **103** D1
Holcot **148** C1
Holden **193** D3
Holden Gate **193** E5
Holdenby **148** B1
Holdenhurst **106** A3
Holder's Green **151** E5
Holders Hill **136** B4
Holdgate **157** E4
Holdingham **175** F3
Holditch **103** G2
Hole **103** E1
Hole Park **124** A5
Holehouse **185** E3
Hole-in-the-Wall **145** F4
Holford **115** E3
Holgate **195** E2
Holker **199** E5
Holkham **178** A1
Hollacombe *Devon* **113** D5
Hollacombe *Devon* **102** B2
Hollacombe Town **113** G4
Holland *Ork* **276** B1
Holland *Ork* **276** F5
Holland *Surr* **122** D3
Holland Fen **176** A3
Holland-on-Sea **139** E1
Hollandstoun **276** G2
Hollee **218** A5
Hollesley **153** E3
Hollicombe **101** F1
Hollingbourne **124** A3
Hollingbury **109** F3
Hollingrove **110** B1
Hollington *Derbys* **172** D4
Hollington *ESuss* **110** C2
Hollington *Staffs* **172** B4
Hollingworth **185** E3
Hollins **186** A5
Hollins Green **184** A3
Hollins Lane **192** A4
Hollinsclough **172** B1
Hollinwood *GtMan* **184** D2
Hollinwood *Shrop* **170** C4
Hollocombe **113** G4
Hollow Meadows **185** G4
Holloway **173** E2
Hollowell **160** B5
Holly Bush **170** B5
Holly End **162** C2
Holly Green **134** C2
Hollybush *Caerp* **130** A2
Hollybush *EAyr* **224** B4
Hollybush *Worcs* **145** G4
Hollyhurst **170** C3
Hollym **197** F5
Hollywater **120** D4
Hollywood **158** C5
Holm *D&G* **218** A2
Holm (Tolm) *WIsles* **271** G4
Holm of Drumlanrig **216** C1
Holmbridge **185** F2
Holmbury St. Mary **121** G3
Holmbush **122** B5
Holme *Cambs* **161** G4
Holme *Cumb* **199** G5
Holme *NLincs* **187** G2
Holme *Notts* **174** D2
Holme *NYorks* **202** C4
Holme *WYorks* **185** F2
Holme Chapel **193** E5
Holme Hale **163** G2
Holme Lacy **145** E4
Holme Marsh **144** C2
Holme next the Sea **177** F3
Holme on the
    Wolds **196** B3
Holme Pierrepont **174** B4
Holme St. Cuthbert **209** E2
Holme-on-Spalding-
    Moor **196** A4
Holmer **145** E3
Holmer Green **135** E3
Holmes **183** F1
Holmes Chapel **171** E1
Holme's Hill **110** A2
Holmesfield **186** A5
Holmeswood **183** F1
Holmewood **173** F1
Holmfield **193** G5
Holmfirth **185** F2
Holmhead *D&G* **216** B2
Holmhead *EAyr* **225** D3
Holmpton **197** F5
Holmrook **198** B2
Holmsgarth **279** D8
Holmside **212** B3
Holmsleigh Green **103** F2
Holmston **224** B3
Holmwrangle **210** B3
Holne **100** D1
Holnest **104** C1

Holnicote **114** C3
Holsworthy **112** D5
Holsworthy Beacon **113** D5
Holt *Dorset* **105** G2
Holt *Norf* **178** B2
Holt *Wilts* **117** F1
Holt *Wrex* **170** B2
Holt *Worcs* **146** A1
Holt End *Hants* **120** B4
Holt End *Worcs* **146** C1
Holt Fleet **146** A1
Holt Heath *Dorset* **105** G2
Holt Heath *Worcs* **146** A1
Holt Wood **105** G2
Holtby **195** F2
Holton *Oxon* **134** B2
Holton *Som* **117** D5
Holton *Suff* **165** F4
Holton cum
    Beckering **188** B4
Holton Heath **105** F3
Holton le Clay **188** C2
Holton le Moor **188** A3
Holton St. Mary **152** B4
Holtspur **135** E4
Holtye **123** D5
Holtye Common **123** D5
Holway **115** F5
Holwell *Dorset* **104** C1
Holwell *Herts* **149** G4
Holwell *Leics* **174** C5
Holwell *Oxon* **133** E2
Holwell *Som* **117** D5
Holwick **211** F5
Holworth **105** D4
Holy Cross **158** B5
Holy Island *IoA* **180** A5
Holy Island (Lindisfarne)
    N'umb **229** F2
Holy Trinity Church,
    Skipton *NYorks*
    BD23 1NJ **193** F3
Holy Trinity Church,
    Stratford-upon-Avon
    Warks CV37 6BG
    85 Stratford-upon-Avon
Holybourne **120** C3
Holyfield **136** C2
Holyhead
    (Caergybi) **180** A4
Holymoorside **173** E1
Holyport **135** E5
Holystone **220** B1
Holytown **234** B3
Holywell *Cambs* **162** B5
Holywell *Corn* **96** B4
Holywell *Dorset* **104** B2
Holywell *ESuss* **110** B3
Holywell (Treffynnon)
    Flints **182** C5
Holywell *N'umb* **221** F4
Holywell Bay Fun Park
    Corn TR8 5PW **96** B4
Holywell Green **185** E1
Holywell Lake **115** E5
Holywell Row **163** F5
Holywood **216** D2
Hom Green **145** E5
Homer **157** F2
Homersfield **165** D3
Homington **118** C5
Homore
    (Tobha Mòr) **254** C1
Honey Hill **124** D2
Honey Street **118** C1
Honey Tye **152** A4
Honeyborough **126** C2
Honeybourne **146** D3
Honeychurch **113** G5
Honiley **159** E5
Honing **179** E3
Honingham **178** C4
Honington *Lincs* **175** E3
Honington *Suff* **164** A4
Honington *Warks* **147** E3
Honiton **103** E2
Honkley **170** A2
Honley **185** F1
Hoo
    (Tobha Mòr) **254** C1
Hoo *Med* **123** G1
Hoo *Suff* **153** D2
Hoo Green **184** B4
Hoo Meavy **100** B1
Hood Green **186** A2
Hood Hill **186** A3
Hooe *ESuss* **110** B3
Hooe *Plym* **100** B2
Hooe Common **110** B2
Hook *Cambs* **162** C3
Hook *ERid* **195** G5
Hook *GtLon* **121** G1
Hook *Hants* **120** C2
Hook *Hants* **107** E2
Hook *Pembs* **126** C1
Hook *Wilts* **132** C4
Hook Green *Kent* **123** F5
Hook Green *Kent* **123** F2
Hook Green *Kent* **137** F5
Hook Green *Kent* **137** G5
Hook Norton **147** F4
Hook-a-Gate **157** D2
Hooke **104** B2
Hookgate **171** E4
Hookway **102** B3
Hookwood **122** B4
Hoole **170** B1
Hooley **122** B3
Hoop **131** E2
Hooton **183** E5
Hooton Levitt **186** C3
Hooton Pagnell **186** B2
Hooton Roberts **186** B3
Hop Farm, The *Kent*
    TN12 6PY **123** F3
Hop Pocket, The *Here*
    WR6 5BT **145** F3
Hope *Derbys* **185** F4
Hope *Devon* **100** C4
Hope *Flints* **170** A2
Hope *Powys* **156** B2

Hope *Shrop* **156** C2
Hope *Staffs* **172** C2
Hope Bagot **157** E5
Hope Bowdler **157** D3
Hope End Green **151** D5
Hope Mansell **131** F1
Hope under
    Dinmore **145** E2
Hopehouse **227** D4
Hopeman **267** J5
Hope's Green **137** G4
Hopesay **156** C4
Hopkinstown **129** G3
Hopley's Green **144** C2
Hopperton **194** D2
Hopsford **159** G4
Hopstone **157** G3
Hopton *Derbys* **173** D2
Hopton *Norf* **165** G2
Hopton *Shrop* **170** A5
Hopton *Shrop* **170** C5
Hopton *Staffs* **171** G5
Hopton *Suff* **164** A4
Hopton Cangeford **157** E4
Hopton Castle **156** C5
Hopton Wafers **157** F5
Hoptonheath **156** C5
Hopwas **159** D2
Hopwood **158** C5
Horam **110** A2
Horbling **175** G4
Horbury **185** G1
Horden **212** D3
Horderley **156** D3
Hordle **106** B3
Hordley **170** A4
Horeb *Carmar* **128** A2
Horeb *Cere* **141** G3
Horeb *Flints* **169** F2
Horfield **131** E5
Horham **164** D4
Horkesley Heath **152** A5
Horkstow **187** F3
Horley *Oxon* **147** G3
Horley *Surr* **122** B4
Horn Hill **135** F3
Hornblotton **116** C4
Hornblotton Green **116** C4
Hornby *Lancs* **192** B1
Hornby *NYorks* **202** B3
Hornby *NYorks* **202** C2
Horncastle **176** A1
Hornchurch **137** E4
Horncliffe **237** F3
Horndean *Hants* **107** G1
Horndean *ScBord* **237** G5
Horndon **99** F2
Horndon on the Hill **137** F4
Horne **122** C4
Horne Row **137** G2
Horner **114** B3
Horniehaugh **252** C4
Horninghold **160** D3
Horninglow **172** D5
Horningsea **150** C1
Horningsham **117** F3
Horningtoft **178** A3
Horningtops **97** G3
Horns Cross *Devon* **113** D3
Horns Cross *ESuss* **110** D1
Hornsbury **103** G1
Hornsby **210** B3
Hornsby Gate **210** B2
Hornsea **197** E3
Hornsea Freeport *ERid*
    HU18 1UT **197** E3
Hornsey **136** C4
Hornton **147** F3
Horrabridge **100** B1
Horridge **102** A5
Horringer **151** G1
Horrocks Fold **184** B1
Horse Bridge **171** G2
Horse Bridge *Hants* **119** E4
Horsebridge *Devon* **99** E3
Horsebridge *Hants* **119** E4
Horsebrook **158** A1
Horsecastle **116** B1
Horsehay **157** F2
Horseheath **151** E3
Horsehouse **201** F4
Horsell **121** E2
Horseman's Green **170** B3
Horsenden **134** C2
Horseshoe Green **123** D4
Horseway **162** C4
Horsey **179** F3
Horsey Corner **179** F3
Horsford **178** C4
Horsforth **194** B4
Horsham *Worcs* **145** G2
Horsham *WSuss* **121** G4
Horsham St. Faith **178** D4
Horsington *Lincs* **175** G1
Horsington *Som* **117** E5
Horsington Marsh **117** E5
Horsley *Derbys* **173** E3
Horsley *Glos* **132** A3
Horsley *N'umb* **211** G1
Horsley *N'umb* **220** B2
Horsley Cross **152** C5
Horsley Woodhouse **173** E3
Horsleycross Street **152** C5
Horsleygate **186** A5
Horsleyhill **227** G4
Horsmonden **123** F4
Horspath **134** A2
Horstead **179** D4
Horsted Keynes **109** F1
Horton *Bucks* **135** E1
Horton *Dorset* **105** G2
Horton *Lancs* **193** E3
Horton *N'hants* **148** D2
Horton *SGlos* **131** G4
Horton *Shrop* **170** B5
Horton *Som* **103** G1
Horton *Staffs* **171** G2
Horton *Swan* **128** A4
Horton *Tel&W* **157** F1

Horton *W&M* **135** F5
Horton *Wilts* **118** B1
Horton Cross **103** G1
Horton Grange **221** E4
Horton Green **170** B3
Horton Heath **107** D1
Horton in
    Ribblesdale **200** D3
Horton Inn **105** G2
Horton Kirby **123** E2
Horton Park Farm *Surr*
    KT19 8PT **121** G1
Horton-cum-
    Studley **134** B1
Horwich **184** A1
Horwich End **185** E4
Horwood **113** F3
Hoscar **183** F1
Hose **174** C5
Hoses **198** D3
Hosh **243** D2
Hosta **262** C4
Hoswick **279** D10
Hotham **196** A4
Hothfield **124** B4
Hoton **173** G5
Houbie **278** F3
Houdston **214** C1
Hough **171** E1
Hough Green **183** F4
Hougham **175** D3
Hough-on-the-Hill **175** E3
Houghton *Cambs* **162** A5
Houghton *Cumb* **210** A2
Houghton *Devon* **100** C3
Houghton *Hants* **119** E4
Houghton *Pembs* **126** C2
Houghton *WSuss* **108** C2
Houghton Bank **212** B5
Houghton Conquest **149** F3
Houghton Green **123** D4
Houghton le Spring **212** C3
Houghton on the
    Hill **160** B2
Houghton Regis **149** F5
Houghton St. Giles **178** A2
Houghton-le-Side **212** B5
Houlsyke **203** G2
Hound **107** D2
Hound Green **120** C2
Houndslow **236** D5
Houndsmoor **115** E5
Houndwood **237** F3
Hounsdown **106** C1
Hounslow **136** A5
House of Marbles & Teign
    Valley Glass *Devon*
    TQ13 9DS **102** B4
Housebay **276** F5
Househill **267** F6
Houses Hill **185** F1
Housesteads Roman
    Fort *N'umb*
    NE47 6NN **211** D1
Housetter **278** C4
Housham Tye **137** E1
Houss **279** C9
Houston **233** F3
Houstry **275** G5
Houstry of Dunn **275** H3
Houton **277** C7
Hove **109** E3
Hove Edge **194** A5
Hoveringham **174** B3
Hoveton **179** E4
Hovingham **203** F5
How **210** B2
How Caple **145** F4
How End **149** F3
How Green **123** D4
How Man **208** C5
Howbrook **186** A3
Howden **195** G5
Howden Clough **194** B5
Howden-le-Wear **212** A4
Howe *Cumb* **199** F4
Howe *High* **275** J2
Howe *Norf* **165** D2
Howe *NYorks* **202** C4
Howe Green *Essex* **137** G2
Howe Green *Essex* **151** E4
Howe of Teuchar **269** F6
Howe Street *Essex* **137** F1
Howe Street *Essex* **151** E4
Howegreen **138** B2
Howell **175** G3
Howey **143** G2
Howgate *Cumb* **208** C4
Howgate *Midlo* **235** G4
Howgill *Lancs* **193** E3
Howgill *NYorks* **193** G2
Howick **229** G5
Howle **171** D5
Howle Hill **145** F5
Howlett End **151** D4
Howley **103** F2
Hownam **228** B5
Hownam Mains **228** B4
Howpasley **227** E5
Howsham *NLincs* **188** A2
Howsham *NYorks* **195** G1
Howt Green **124** A2
Howtel **228** C3
Howton **144** D5
Howwood **233** F3
Hoxa **277** D8
Hoxne **164** D4
Hoy *High* **275** H2
Hoy *Ork* **277** B8
Hoylake **182** D4
Hoyland **186** A2
Hoylandswaine **185** G2
Hoyle **108** B2
Hubberholme **201** E5
Hubbert's Bridge **176** A3
Huby *NYorks* **195** E1
Huby *NYorks* **194** B3
Hucclecote **132** A1
Hucking **124** A3
Hucknall **173** G3
Huddersfield **185** F1

Huddington **146** B2
Huddlesford **158** D2
Hudnall **135** F1
Hudscott **113** G3
Hudswell **202** A3
Huggate **196** A2
Hugglescote **159** G1
Hugh Town **96** B1
Hughenden Valley **135** D3
Hughley **157** E3
Hugmore **170** A2
Hugus **96** B5
Huish *Devon* **113** F4
Huish *Wilts* **118** C1
Huish Champflower **114** D5
Huish Episcopi **116** B5
Huisinis **270** B6
Hulcote **149** E4
Hulcott **135** D1
Hull **196** D5
Hulland **172** D3
Hulland Ward **173** D3
Hullavington **132** A4
Hullbridge **138** B3
Hulme **171** G3
Hulme End **172** C2
Hulme Walfield **171** F1
Hulver Street **165** F3
Hulverstone **106** C4
Humber *Devon* **102** B5
Humber *Here* **145** E2
Humber Bridge Country
    Park *ERid*
    HU13 0LN **196** C5
Humberside Airport **188** A1
Humberston **188** D2
Humberstone **160** B2
Humberton **194** D1
Humbie **236** B3
Humbleton *Dur* **201** F1
Humbleton *ERid* **197** E4
Humbleton *N'umb* **229** D4
Humby **175** F4
Hume **237** E5
Humehall **237** E5
Hummer **104** B1
Humshaugh **220** B4
Huna **275** J1
Huncoat **193** D4
Huncote **160** A3
Hundalee **228** A5
Hundall **186** A5
Hunderthwaite **211** F5
Hundleby **176** B1
Hundleton **126** C2
Hundon **151** F3
Hundred Acres **107** E1
Hundred End **192** A5
Hundred House **144** A2
Hungarton **160** B2
Hungate End **148** C3
Hungerford *Hants* **106** A1
Hungerford *Shrop* **157** E4
Hungerford *WBerks* **119** E1
Hungerford
    Newtown **133** F5
Hungerton **175** D5
Hunglader **263** J4
Hunmanby **205** D5
Hunningham **147** F1
Hunningham Hill **147** F1
Hunny Hill **107** D4
Hunsdon **136** D1
Hunsingore **194** D2
Hunslet **194** C4
Hunsonby **210** B4
Hunspow **275** H1
Hunstanton **177** E3
Hunstanworth **211** F3
Hunston *Suff* **152** A1
Hunston *WSuss* **108** A3
Hunsworth **194** A5
Hunt End **146** C1
Hunt House **204** B3
Huntercombe End **134** B4
Hunters Forstal **125** D2
Hunter's Quay **232** C2
Hunterston **232** C4
Huntford **219** E1
Huntham **116** A5
Huntingdon **162** A5
Huntingfield **165** E4
Huntingford **117** F4
Huntington *Here* **144** B2
Huntington *Here* **145** D3
Huntington *Staffs* **158** B1
Huntington *Tel&W* **157** F2
Huntington *York* **195** F2
Huntingtower **243** F2
Huntley **131** G1
Huntly **260** D1
Huntlywood **236** D5
Hunton *Hants* **119** F3
Hunton *Kent* **123** G4
Hunton *NYorks* **202** A3
Hunton Bridge **135** F2
Hunt's Cross **183** F4
Huntscott **114** C3
Huntsham **114** D5
Huntshaw **113** F3
Huntshaw Cross **113** F3
Huntshaw Water **113** F3
Huntspill **116** A3
Huntworth **116** A4
Hunwick **212** A4
Hunworth **178** B2
Hurcott *Som* **116** C5
Hurcott *Som* **103** G1
Hurdley **156** B3
Hurdsfield **184** D5
Hurley *W&M* **134** D4
Hurley *Warks* **159** E3
Hurley Bottom **134** D4
Hurlford **224** C2
Hurliness **277** B9
Hurlston Green **183** E1
Hurn **106** A3
Hurst *NYorks* **201** F2
Hurst *W'ham* **134** C5
Hurst Green *Essex* **139** D1

Hurst Green *ESuss* 110 C1
Hurst Green *Lancs* 192 C4
Hurst Green *Surr* 122 C3
Hurst Wickham 109 E2
Hurstbourne
Tarrant 119 E2
Hurstpierpoint 109 E2
Hurstwood 193 E4
Hurtmore 128 E3
Hurworth-on-Tees 202 C1
Hury 211 F5
Husabost 263 G6
Husbands
Bosworth 160 B4
Husthwaite 203 E5
Huthwaite 173 F2
Huttoft 189 F5
Hutton *Cumb* 210 A5
Hutton *Essex* 137 E3
Hutton *Lancs* 192 A5
Hutton *NSom* 116 A2
Hutton *ScBord* 237 G4
Hutton Bonville 202 C2
Hutton Buscel 204 C4
Hutton Conyers 202 C5
Hutton Cranswick 196 C2
Hutton End 210 A4
Hutton Hang 202 A4
Hutton Henry 212 D4
Hutton Magna 202 A1
Hutton Mount 137 F3
Hutton Mulgrave 204 B2
Hutton Roof *Cumb* 199 G5
Hutton Roof *Cumb* 209 G3
Hutton Rudby 203 D2
Hutton Sessay 203 D5
Hutton Wandesley 195 E2
Hutton-le-Hole 203 G3
Huxham 102 C3
Huxham Green 116 C4
Huxley 170 C1
Huxter *Shet* 279 C7
Huxter *Shet* 279 E6
Huyton 183 F3
Hyde *Glos* 132 A2
Hyde *GtMan* 184 D3
Hyde End *W'ham* 120 C1
Hyde End *WBerks* 119 G4
Hyde Heath 135 E2
Hyde Lea 158 B1
Hydestile 121 E3
Hylands Park *Essex*
CM2 8WQ 137 F2
Hyndford Bridge 234 D5
Hyndlee 227 G5
Hynish 246 A3
Hyssington 156 C3
Hythe *Hants* 106 D2
Hythe *Kent* 125 D5
Hythe End 135 D5
Hythie 269 J5
Hyton 198 B4

I
Ianstown 268 C4
Iarsiadar 270 D4
Ibberton 105 D2
Ible 172 D2
Ibsley 106 A2
Ibstock 159 G1
Ibstone 134 C3
Ibthorpe 119 E2
Ibworth 119 G2
Icelton 116 A1
Ickburgh 163 G3
Ickford 134 B2
Ickham 125 E3
Ickleford 149 G4
Icklesham 111 E3
Ickleton 150 C3
Icklingham 163 F5
Ickwell Green 149 G3
Icomb 147 E5
Idbury 147 E5
Iddesleigh 113 F5
Ide 102 C3
Ide Hill 123 D3
Ideford 102 B5
Iden 111 E1
Iden Green *Kent* 123 G5
Iden Green *Kent* 124 A5
Idle 194 A4
Idless 96 C5
Idlicote 147 E3
Idmiston 118 C4
Idridgehay 173 D3
Idridgehay Green 173 D3
Idrigil 263 J5
Idstone 133 E4
Iffley 134 A2
Ifield 122 B5
Ifieldwood 122 B5
Ifold 121 F4
Iford *Bourne* 106 A3
Iford *ESuss* 109 G3
Ifton 131 D4
Ifton Heath 170 A4
Ightfield 170 C4
Ightham 123 E3
Ightham Mote *Kent*
TN15 0NT 123 E3
Iken 153 F2
Ilam 172 C2
Ilchester 116 C5
Ilderton 229 E4
Ilford 136 D4
Ilfracombe 113 F1
Ilkeston 173 F3
Ilketshall
St. Andrew 165 E3
Ilketshall
St. Lawrence 165 E3
Ilketshall
St. Margaret 165 E3
Ilkley 194 A3
Illey 158 B4

Illidge Green 171 E1
Illington 164 A3
Illingworth 193 G5
Illogan 96 A5
Illston on the Hill 160 C3
Ilmer 134 C2
Ilmington 147 E3
Ilminster 103 G1
Ilsington *Devon* 102 A5
Ilsington *Dorset* 105 D3
Ilston 128 B3
Ilton *NYorks* 202 A5
Ilton *Som* 103 G1
Imachar 231 G5
Imber 118 A3
Immeroin 242 A3
Immingham 188 B2
Immingham Dock 188 C1
Imperial War Museum,
Duxford *Cambs*
CB22 4QR 150 C3
Imperial War Museum,
London *GtLon*
SE1 6HZ 45 G7
Imperial War Museum
North *GtMan*
M17 1TZ 24 D3
Impington 150 C1
Ince 183 F5
Ince Blundell 183 E2
Ince-in-Makerfield 183 G2
Inch Kenneth 238 D1
Inch of Arnhall 253 E2
Inchbare 253 E1
Inchberry 268 B5
Inchbraoch 253 F4
Inchgrundle 252 C2
Inchindown 266 D4
Inchinnan 233 F3
Inchkinloch 273 J4
Inchlaggan 257 H4
Inchlumpie 266 C4
Inchmarlo 260 E5
Inchmarnock 232 B4
Inchnabobart 252 B1
Inchnacardoch
Hotel 257 K3
Inchnadamph 272 E6
Inchock 253 E5
Inchree 248 C3
Inchrory 259 J4
Inchture 244 A2
Inchvuilt 257 J1
Inchyra 243 G2
Indian Queens 96 D4
Inerval 230 B5
Ingatestone 137 F3
Ingbirchworth 185 G3
Ingerthorpe 194 B1
Ingestre 171 G5
Ingham *Lincs* 187 G4
Ingham *Norf* 179 E3
Ingham *Suff* 163 G5
Ingham Corner 179 E3
Ingleborough 162 C3
Ingleby *Derbys* 173 E5
Ingleby *Lincs* 187 F5
Ingleby Arncliffe 202 D2
Ingleby Barwick 202 D1
Ingleby Cross 202 D2
Ingleby Greenhow 203 E2
Ingleigh Green 113 G5
Inglesbatch 117 E1
Inglesham 133 E3
Ingleton *Dur* 212 A5
Ingleton *NYorks* 200 B5
Inglewhite 192 B4
Ingliston 235 F2
Ingmire Hall 200 B3
Ingoe 220 C4
Ingoldisthorpe 177 E4
Ingoldmells 177 D1
Ingoldsby 175 F4
Ingon 147 E2
Ingram 229 E5
Ingrave 137 F3
Ingrow 193 G4
Ings 199 F3
Ingst 131 E4
Ingworth 178 C3
Inhurst 119 G1
Inistrynich 240 D2
Injebreck 190 B3
Inkberrow 146 C2
Inkpen 119 E1
Inkstack 275 H1
Inmarsh 118 A1
Innellan 232 C3
Innergellie 245 D4
Innerhadden 250 B4
Innerleithen 227 E2
Innerleven 244 B4
Innermessan 214 B4
Innerwick *ELoth* 237 E2
Innerwick *P&K* 250 A5
Inninbeg 247 F5
Innsworth 146 A5
Insch 260 E2
Insh 259 F4
Inshore 273 F2
Inskip 192 A4
Instow 113 E2
Intake 186 C2
Intech, Winchester *Hants*
SO21 1HX 119 G5
International Centre, The,
Telford *Tel&W*
TF3 4JH 157 G2
Intwood 178 C5
Inver *A&B* 248 B5
Inver *Aber* 259 K5
Inver *High* 267 F3
Inver *High* 275 G5
Inver *P&K* 251 F5
Inver Mallie 248 D1
Inveraldie 244 C1
Inverailort 247 G1
Inverallligin 264 E6
Inverallochy 269 J4

Inveran 266 C2
Inveraray
(Inbhir Aora) 240 C4
Inverardoch Mains 242 C4
Inverardran 241 F2
Inverarish 256 B1
Inveranty 252 C5
Inverarnan
(Inbhir Àirnein) 241 F3
Inverasdale 264 E3
Inverbain 264 D6
Inverbeg 241 F5
Inverbervie 253 G2
Inverbroom 265 H3
Inverbrough 259 F2
Invercassley 266 B1
Inverchaolain 232 B2
Invercharnan 248 D5
Inverchorachan 241 E3
Inverchoran 265 J6
Invercreran 248 C5
Inverdruie 259 G3
Inverebrie 261 H1
Invereen 258 E1
Invererne 267 H5
Inveresk 236 A2
Inverey 251 F1
Inverfarigaig 258 C2
Invergarry
(Inbhir Garadh) 257 K4
Invergelder 259 K5
Invergeldie 242 C2
Inverglory 249 E1
Invergordon 266 E5
Invergowrie 244 B1
Inverguseran 256 D3
Inverharroch Farm 260 B1
Inverherive 241 F2
Inverhope 273 G2
Inverie 256 D4
Inverinan 240 C3
Inverinate 257 F2
Inverkeilor 253 E5
Inverkeithing 235 F1
Inverkeithny 268 E6
Inverkip 232 D2
Inverkirkaig 272 C7
Inverlael 265 H3
Inverlauren 233 E1
Inverliever 240 A4
Inverliver 240 C1
Inverlochlarig 241 H3
Inverlochy 241 D2
Inverlussa 231 E1
Invermay 243 F3
Invermoriston (Inbhir
Moireasdan) 258 B3
Invernaver 274 C2
Inverneil 231 G1
Inverness
(Inbhir Nis) 266 D7
Inverness Airport 266 E6
Invernettie 269 K6
Invernoaden 240 D5
Inveroran Hotel (Inbhir
Orain) 249 G5
Inverquharity 252 C4
Inverquhomery 269 J6
Inverroy 249 E1
Inversanda 248 B4
Invershiel 257 F3
Invershore 275 H5
Inversnaid Hotel 241 F4
Invertrossachs 242 A4
Inveruglas (Inbhir
Dhubhghlais) 241 F4
Inveruglass 259 F4
Inverurie 261 F2
Invervar 250 B5
Invervegain 232 B2
Invery House 260 E5
Inverythan 269 F6
Inwardleigh 99 F1
Inworth 138 C1
Iochdar 262 C7
Iping 121 D5
Ipplepen 101 E1
Ipsden 134 B4
Ipstones 172 B3
Ipswich 152 C3
Irby 183 D4
Irby Hill 183 D4
Irby in the Marsh 176 C1
Irby upon Humber 188 B2
Irchester 149 E1
Irchester Country
Park *N'hants*
NN29 7DL 149 E1
Ireby *Cumb* 209 F3
Ireby *Lancs* 200 B5
Ireland *Ork* 277 C7
Ireland *Shet* 279 C10
Ireland's Cross 171 E3
Ireleth 198 D5
Ireshopeburn 211 E4
Irlam 184 B3
Irnham 175 F5
Iron Acton 131 F4
Iron Cross 146 C2
Ironbridge 157 F2
Ironbridge Gorge *Tel&W*
TF8 7DQ 157 F2
Irons Bottom 122 B4
Ironside 269 G5
Ironville 173 F2
Irstead 179 E3
Irthington 210 A1
Irthlingborough 161 E5
Irton 204 D4
Irvine 224 B2
Isauld 274 E2
Isbister *Ork* 277 C6
Isbister *Ork* 276 B5
Isbister *Shet* 279 E6
Isbister *Shet* 278 C3
Isfield 109 G2
Isham 161 D5
Ishriff 239 F1
Isington 120 C3
Island of Stroma 275 J1

Islawr-dref 154 C1
Islay 230 A3
Islay Airport 230 B4
Islay House 230 B3
Isle Abbotts 116 A5
Isle Brewers 116 A5
Isle of Lewis (Eilean
Leodhais) 271 F3
Isle of Man 190 B3
Isle of Man Airport 190 A5
Isle of May 245 E5
Isle of Noss 279 E8
Isle of Sheppey 124 B1
Isle of Walney 191 E1
Isle of Whithorn 207 E6
Isle of Wight 107 D4
Isle of Wight Pearl *IoW*
PO30 4DD 106 D4
Isle of Wight (Sandown)
Airport 107 E4
Isle of Wight Zoo *IoW*
PO36 8QB 107 E4
Isleham 163 E5
Isleornsay (Eilean
Iarmain) 256 C3
Isles of Scilly
(Scilly Isles) 96 B1
Islesburgh 279 C6
Isleworth 136 A5
Isley Walton 173 F5
Islibhig 270 B5
Islip *N'hants* 161 E5
Islip *Oxon* 134 A1
Isombridge 157 F1
Istead Rise 123 F2
Itchen 106 D1
Itchen Abbas 119 G4
Itchen Stoke 119 G4
Itchen Valley Country Park
Hants SO30 3HQ 4 C2
Itchingfield 121 G5
Itchington 131 F4
Itteringham 178 C2
Itton *Devon* 99 G1
Itton *Mon* 131 D3
Itton Common 131 D3
Ivegill 210 A3
Ivelet 201 E3
Iver 135 F4
Iver Heath 135 F4
Iveston 212 A2
Ivetsey Bank 158 A1
Ivinghoe 135 E1
Ivinghoe Aston 135 E1
Ivington 145 D2
Ivington Green 145 D2
Ivy Hatch 123 E3
Ivy Todd 163 G2
Ivychurch 111 F1
Iwade 124 B2
Iwerne Courtney
(Shroton) 105 E1
Iwerne Minster 105 E2
Ixworth 164 A4
Ixworth Thorpe 164 A4

J
Jack Hill 194 A2
Jackfield 157 F2
Jacksdale 173 F2
Jackstown 261 F1
Jackton 233 G4
Jacobstow 98 B1
Jacobstowe 113 F5
Jacobswell 121 E2
James Hamilton
Heritage Park *SLan*
G74 5LB 31 E5
James Pringle Weavers
of Inverness *High*
IV2 4RB 266 D7
Jameston 127 D3
Jamestown *D&G* 218 B2
Jamestown *High* 266 B6
Jamestown *WDun* 233 E1
Janefield 266 E6
Janetstown *High* 275 F2
Janetstown *High* 275 J3
Jarrow 212 C1
Jarvis Brook 123 E5
Jasper's Green 151 F5
Jawcraig 234 C2
Jawyck 139 E4
Jayes Park 121 G3
Jealott's Hill 135 D5
Jeater Houses 202 D3
Jedburgh 228 A4
Jeffreyston 127 D2
Jemimaville 266 E5
Jephson Gardens *Warks*
CV32 4ER 16 B6
Jericho 184 C1
Jersey 100 C5
Jersey Airport 100 B5
Jersey Marine 128 D3
Jerviswood 234 C5
Jesmond 212 B1
Jevington 110 A3
Jinney Ring Craft Centre,
The *Worcs*
B60 4BU 146 B1
Jockey End 135 F1
Jodrell Bank *Ches*
CW4 9DU 184 B5
Jodrell Bank Observatory &
Arboretum *ChesE*
SK11 9DL 184 B5
John Muir Country Park
ELoth
EH42 1UW 236 D2
John o' Groats 275 J1
John o' Gaunts 110 C1
Johnby 210 A4
Johnshaven 253 F2
Johnson Street 179 E4
Johnston 126 C1
Johnston Mains 253 F2
Johnstone 233 F3
Johnstone Castle 233 F3

Johnstonebridge 217 E1
Johnstons Cashmere Visitor
Centre *Moray*
IV30 4AF 267 K5
Johnstown *Carmar* 127 G1
Johnstown *Wrex* 170 A3
Joppa 224 C2
Jordans 135 E3
Jordanston 140 C4
Jordanstone 252 A5
Jorvik YO1 9WT 90 York
Jorvik Glass *NYorks*
YO60 7DA 195 G1
Joy's Green 131 F1
Jumpers Common 106 A3
Juniper Green 235 F3
Juniper Hill 148 A4
Jura 231 D1
Jura House 230 C3
Jurby East 190 B2
Jurby West 190 B2

K
Kaber 200 C1
Kaimes 235 G3
Kames *A&B* 232 A2
Kames *A&B* 240 A3
Kames *EAyr* 225 E3
Kathellan *Fife*
KY4 0JR 243 G5
Kea 96 C5
Keadby 187 F1
Keal Cotes 176 B1
Kearsney 184 B2
Kearstwick 200 B5
Kearton 201 F3
Kearvaig 272 E1
Keasden 192 D1
Kebholes 268 E5
Keckwick 183 G4
Keddington 188 D4
Keddington Corner 189 D4
Kedington 151 F3
Kedleston 173 E3
Keelby 188 B1
Keele 171 F3
Keeley Green 149 F3
Keeres Green 137 E1
Keeston 126 B1
Keevil 118 A1
Kegworth 173 F5
Kehelland 96 A5
Keig 260 E3
Keighley 193 G3
Keighley & Worth Valley
Railway *W.Yorks*
BD22 8NJ 193 G3
Keil *A&B* 222 B5
Keil *High* 248 B4
Keilhill 269 F5
Keillmore 231 E1
Keillor 252 A5
Keillour 243 E2
Keills 230 C3
Keils 230 C3
Keinton Mandeville 116 C4
Keir House 242 C5
Keir Mill 216 C1
Keisby 175 F5
Keisley 210 D5
Keiss 275 J2
Keith 268 C5
Keithick 244 A1
Keithmore 260 B1
Keithock 253 E3
Kelbrook 193 F3
Kelby 175 F3
Keld *Cumb* 199 G3
Keld *NYorks* 201 D2
Keldholme 203 G4
Keldy Castle 203 G3
Kelfield *NLincs* 187 F2
Kelfield *NYorks* 195 E4
Kelham 174 C2
Kella 190 B2
Kellacott 99 E2
Kellan 247 E5
Kellas *Angus* 244 C1
Kellas *Moray* 267 J6
Kellaton 101 D4
Kellaways 132 B5
Kelleth 200 B2
Kelleythorpe 196 C2
Kelling 178 B1
Kellington 195 E5
Kelloe 212 C4
Kelloholm 225 F4
Kelly *Corn* 97 E2
Kelly *Devon* 99 D3
Kelly Bray 99 D3
Kelmarsh 160 C5
Kelmscott 133 E3
Kelsale 153 E1
Kelsall 170 C1
Kelsay 230 A4
Kelshall 150 B4
Kelsick 209 E1
Kelso 228 B3
Kelstedge 173 E1
Kelstern 188 C3
Kelston 117 E1
Keltneyburn 250 C5
Kelton 217 D3
Kelton Hill
(Rhonehouse) 216 B5
Kelty 243 G5
Kelvedon 138 B1
Kelvedon Hatch 137 E3
Kelvingrove Art Gallery &
Museum *Glas*
G3 8AG 38 B2
Kelvinside 233 G3
Kelynack 94 A4
Kemacott 113 G1
Kemback 244 C3
Kemberton 157 G2
Kemble 132 B3
Kemerton 146 B4
Kemeys
Commander 130 C2

Kemeys Inferior 130 C3
Kemnay 261 F3
Kemp Town 109 F3
Kempe's Corner 124 C4
Kempley 145 F5
Kempley Green 145 F5
Kemps Green 158 D5
Kempsey 146 A3
Kempsford 133 D3
Kempshott 119 G3
Kempston 149 F3
Kempston Hardwick 149 F3
Kempston West End 149 E3
Kempton 156 C4
Kemsing 123 E3
Kemsley 124 B2
Kenardington 124 B5
Kenchester 144 D3
Kencot 133 E2
Kendal 199 G3
Kenderchurch 144 D5
Kendleshire 131 F5
Kenfig 129 D4
Kenfig Hill 129 E4
Kenidjack 94 A3
Kenilworth 159 F5
Kenilworth Castle *Warks*
CV8 1NE 16 A4
Kenknock *P&K* 250 A5
Kenknock *Stir* 241 G1
Kenley *GtLon* 122 C2
Kenley *Shrop* 157 E2
Kenmore *A&B* 240 C4
Kenmore *High* 264 D6
Kenmore *P&K* 250 C5
Kenn *Devon* 102 C4
Kenn *NSom* 116 B1
Kennacley 263 G2
Kennacraig 231 G3
Kennards House 97 G1
Kennavay 263 H2
Kenneggy Downs 94 C4
Kennerleigh 102 B2
Kennerty 260 E5
Kennet 243 E5
Kennethmont 260 D2
Kennett 151 E1
Kennford 102 C4
Kenninghall 164 B3
Kennington *Kent* 124 C4
Kennington *Oxon* 134 A2
Kennoway 244 B4
Kenny 103 G1
Kennyhill 163 E5
Kennythorpe 195 G1
Kensaleyre 263 K6
Kensington 136 B4
Kensington Palace *GtLon*
W8 4PX 10 F2
Kenstone 170 C5
Kensworth 135 F1
Kent & East Sussex Railway
Kent TN30 6HE 124 A5
Kent International
Airport 125 F2
Kent Street *ESuss* 110 C1
Kent Street *Kent* 123 F3
Kentallen (Ceann an t-
Sàilein) 248 C4
Kentchurch 144 D5
Kentisbeare 103 D2
Kentisbury 113 G1
Kentisbury Ford 113 G1
Kentish Town 136 B4
Kentmere 199 F2
Kenton *Devon* 102 C4
Kenton *Suff* 152 C1
Kenton *T&W* 212 B1
Kenton Corner 152 D1
Kentra 247 F3
Kents Bank 199 E5
Kent's Green 145 G5
Kent's Oak 119 E5
Kenwick 170 B4
Kenwood House *GtLon*
NW3 7JR 10 F2
Kenwyn 96 C5
Kenyon 184 A3
Keoldale 273 F2
Keose (Ceòs) 271 F5
Keppanach 248 C3
Keppoch *A&B* 233 E2
Keppoch *High* 256 E2
Keprigan 222 B4
Kepwick 203 D3
Keresley 159 F4
Kernborough 101 D3
Kerne Bridge 145 F5
Kerrera 240 A2
Kerridge 184 D5
Kerris 94 B4
Kerry (Ceri) 156 A3
Kerrycroy 232 C3
Kerry's Gate 144 C4
Kerrysdale 264 E4
Kersall 174 C1
Kersey 152 B3
Kersey Vale 152 B3
Kershopefoot 218 C3
Kerswell 103 D2
Kerswell Green 146 A3
Kerthen Wood 94 C3
Kesgrave 152 D3
Kessingland 165 G3
Kessingland Beach 165 G3
Kestle 97 D5
Kestle Mill 96 C4
Keston 122 D2
Keswick *Cumb* 209 F4
Keswick *Norf* 178 D5
Keswick *Norf* 179 E3
Ketley Bank 157 F1
Ketsby 189 D5
Kettering 161 D5
Ketteringham 178 C5
Kettins 244 A1
Kettle Corner 123 G3
Kettlebaston 152 A2
Kettlebridge 244 B4
Kettlebrook 159 E2

Kettleburgh 153 D1
Kettlehill 244 B4
Kettleholm 217 F3
Kettleness 204 B1
Kettleshulme 185 D5
Kettlesing 194 B2
Kettlesing Bottom 194 B2
Kettlesing Head 194 B2
Kettlestone 178 A2
Kettlethorpe 187 F5
Kettletoft 276 F4
Kettlewell 201 E5
Ketton 161 E2
Kevington 123 D2
Kew 136 A5
Kewstoke 116 A1
Kexbrough 186 A2
Kexby *Lincs* 187 F4
Kexby *York* 195 G2
Key Green 171 F1
Keyham 160 B2
Keyhaven 106 C3
Keyingham 197 E5
Keymer 109 F2
Keynsham 117 D1
Key's Toft 176 C2
Keysoe 149 F1
Keysoe Row 149 F1
Keyston 161 F5
Keyworth 174 B4
Kibblesworth 212 B2
Kibworth
Beauchamp 160 B3
Kibworth Harcourt 160 B3
Kidbrooke 136 D5
Kiddemore Green 158 A5
Kidderminster 158 A5
Kiddington 147 G5
Kidlington 133 G1
Kidmore End 134 B5
Kidnal 170 B3
Kidsdale 207 E3
Kidsgrove 171 F2
Kidstones 201 E4
Kidwelly (Cydweli) 128 A2
Kiel Crofts 240 A1
Kielder 219 E2
Kielder Forest *N'umb*
NE48 1ER 219 E2
Kielder Water *N'umb*
NE48 1BX 219 F3
Kilbarchan 233 F3
Kilbeg 256 C4
Kilberry 231 F3
Kilbirnie 233 E4
Kilblaan 240 D3
Kilbrennan 246 D5
Kilbride *A&B* 240 A2
Kilbride *A&B* 232 B3
Kilbride *High* 256 B2
Kilbride Farm 232 A3
Kilbridemore 240 C5
Kilburn *Derbys* 173 E3
Kilburn *GtLon* 136 B4
Kilburn *NYorks* 203 E5
Kilby 160 B3
Kilchattan Bay 232 C4
Kilchenzie 222 B3
Kilcheran 240 A1
Kilchiaran 230 A3
Kilchoan *A&B* 239 G3
Kilchoan *High* 247 D3
Kilchoman 230 A3
Kilchrenan
(Cill Chrèanain) 240 C2
Kilchrist 222 B4
Kilconquhar 244 C4
Kilcot 145 F5
Kilcoy 266 C6
Kilcreggan 232 D1
Kildale 203 F2
Kildary 266 E4
Kildavie 222 C4
Kildermorie Lodge 266 C4
Kildonan *NAyr* 223 F3
Kildonan (Cilldonnain)
WIsles 254 C1
Kildonan Lodge 274 E6
Kildonnan 247 D1
Kildrochet House 214 B5
Kildrummy 260 C3
Kildwick 193 G3
Kilfinan 232 A2
Kilfinnan 257 J5
Kilgetty 127 E2
Kilgwrrwg Common 131 D3
Kilham *ERid* 196 C1
Kilham *N'umb* 228 C3
Kilkenneth 246 A2
Kilkenny 132 C1
Kilkerran *A&B* 222 C4
Kilkerran *SAyr* 224 B5
Kilkhampton 112 C4
Killamarsh 186 B4
Killay 128 C3
Killbeg 247 F5
Killean *A&B* 231 E5
Killean *A&B* 240 C4
Killearn 233 G1
Killellan 222 B4
Killen 266 D6
Killerby 212 A5
Killerton *Devon*
EX5 3LE 102 C2
Killichonan 250 A4
Killiechronan 247 E5
Killiecrankie 251 E3
Killiehuntly 258 E5
Killiemor 239 D1
Killilan 257 F1
Killimster 275 J3
Killin *High* 267 F1
Killin *Stir* 242 A1
Killinallan 230 B2
Killinghall 194 B2
Killington *Cumb* 200 B4
Killington *Devon* 113 G1
Killingworth 221 E4
Killochyett 236 B5

Killocraw 222 B2
Killunaig 239 D2
Killundine 247 E5
Kilmacolm 233 E3
Kilmaha 240 B4
Kilmahog 242 B4
Kilmalieu 248 A4
Kilmaluag 263 K4
Kilmany 244 B2
Kilmarie 256 B3
Kilmarnock 224 C2
Kilmartin 240 A5
Kilmaurs 233 F5
Kilmelford 240 A3
Kilmeny 230 B3
Kilmersdon 117 D2
Kilmeston 119 G5
Kilmichael 222 B3
Kilmichael
  Glassary 240 A5
Kilmichael of
  Inverlussa 231 F1
Kilmington Devon 103 F3
Kilmington Wilts 117 E4
Kilmington
  Common 117 E4
Kilmorack 266 B7
Kilmore (A' Chille Mhòr)
  A&B 240 A1
Kilmore High 256 B3
Kilmory A&B 231 F1
Kilmory A&B 231 F2
Kilmory High 255 J4
Kilmory High 247 E2
Kilmory NAyr 223 E3
Kilmote 274 E7
Kilmuir High 263 H7
Kilmuir High 266 D7
Kilmuir High 266 K4
Kilmuir High 263 J4
Kilmun 232 C1
Kilmux 244 B4
Kiln Green Here 131 F1
Kiln Green W'ham 134 D5
Kiln Pit Hill 211 G2
Kilnave 230 A2
Kilncadzow 234 C5
Kilnhurst 186 B3
Kilninian 246 D5
Kilninver 240 A2
Kilnsea 189 F1
Kilnsey 193 F1
Kilnwick 196 B3
Kilnwick Percy 196 A2
Kiloran 238 C5
Kilpatrick 223 E3
Kilpeck 144 D4
Kilphedir 274 E7
Kilpin 195 G5
Kilpin Pike 195 G5
Kilrenny 245 D4
Kilsby 160 A5
Kilspindie 244 A2
Kilstay 206 B3
Kilsyth 234 B2
Kiltarlity 266 C7
Kilton Notts 186 C5
Kilton R&C 203 F1
Kilton Som 115 E3
Kilton Thorpe 203 F1
Kiltyrie 242 B1
Kilvaxter 263 J5
Kilve 115 E3
Kilverstone 163 G4
Kilvington 174 D3
Kilwinning 233 E5
Kimberley Norf 178 B5
Kimberley Notts 173 G3
Kimberworth 186 B3
Kimble Wick 134 D2
Kimblesworth 212 B3
Kimbolton Cambs 149 F1
Kimbolton Here 145 E1
Kimbridge 119 E5
Kimcote 160 A4
Kimmeridge 105 F5
Kimmerston 229 D3
Kimpton Hants 119 D3
Kimpton Herts 136 A1
Kinaldy 244 D3
Kinblethmont 253 E5
Kinbrace 274 D5
Kinbreack 257 G5
Kinbuck 242 C4
Kincaldrum 252 C5
Kincaple 244 C3
Kincardine Fife 234 D1
Kincardine High 266 D3
Kincardine O'Neil 260 D5
Kinclaven 243 G1
Kincorth 261 H4
Kincraig Aber 261 H2
Kincraig High 259 F4
Kincraigie 251 E5
Kindallachan 251 E4
Kindrogan Field
  Centre 251 F3
Kinellar 261 G3
Kineton Glos 146 C5
Kineton Warks 147 F2
Kineton Green 158 D4
Kinfauns 243 G2
King Sterndale 185 E5
Kingarth 232 B4
Kingcoed 130 D2
Kingerby 188 A3
Kingham 147 E5
Kingholm Quay 217 D3
Kinghorn 235 G1
Kinglassie 244 A5
Kingoodie 244 B2
King's Acre 145 D3
King's Bank 111 D1
King's Bromley 158 D1
King's Caple 145 E5
King's Cliffe 161 F3
King's College Chapel,
  Cambridge Cambs
  CB2 1ST 150 C2
King's Coughton 146 C2
King's Green 145 G4

King's Heath 158 C4
Kings Hill Kent 123 F3
King's Hill Warks 159 F5
King's Hill WMid 158 B3
Kings Langley 135 F2
King's Lynn 177 E5
King's Meaburn 210 C5
Kings Mills 101 E5
King's Moss 183 G2
King's Muir 227 D2
King's Newnham 159 G5
King's Newton 173 E5
King's Norton Leics 160 B2
King's Norton
  WMid 158 C5
Kings Nympton 113 G4
King's Pyon 144 D2
Kings Ripton 162 A5
King's Somborne 119 E4
King's Stag 104 D1
King's Stanley 132 A2
King's Sutton 147 G4
King's Tamerton 100 A2
King's Walden 149 G5
Kings Worthy 119 F4
Kingsand 100 A2
Kingsbarns 245 D3
Kingsbridge Devon 100 D3
Kingsbridge Som 114 C4
Kingsburgh 263 J6
Kingsbury GtLon 136 A4
Kingsbury Warks 159 E3
Kingsbury Episcopi 116 B5
Kingsbury Water Park
  Warks B76 0DY 159 E3
Kingscavil 235 E2
Kingsclere 115 G1
Kingscote 132 A3
Kingscott 113 F4
Kingscross 223 F3
Kingsdale 244 B4
Kingsdon 116 C5
Kingsdown Kent 125 F4
Kingsdown Swin 133 D4
Kingsdown Wilts 117 F1
Kingseat 243 G5
Kingsey 134 C2
Kingsfold Pembs 126 C3
Kingsfold WSuss 121 G4
Kingsford Aber 269 F6
Kingsford Aber 260 D3
Kingsford
  Aberdeen 261 G4
Kingsford EAyr 233 F5
Kingsford Worcs 158 A4
Kingsgate 125 F1
Kingshall Street 152 A1
Kingsheanton 113 F2
Kingshouse 242 A2
Kingshouse Hotel 249 E4
Kingshurst 159 D4
Kingskerswell 101 E1
Kingskettle 244 B4
Kingsland Here 144 D1
Kingsland IoA 180 A4
Kingsley ChesW&C 183 G5
Kingsley Hants 120 C4
Kingsley Staffs 172 B3
Kingsley Green 121 D4
Kingsley Holt 172 B3
Kingslow 157 G3
Kingsmoor 136 D2
Kingsmuir Angus 252 C5
Kingsmuir Fife 244 D4
Kingsnorth 124 C5
Kingsnorth Power
  Station 124 A1
Kingstanding 158 C3
Kingsteignton 102 B5
Kingsteps 267 G6
Kingsthorne 145 D4
Kingsthorpe 148 C1
Kingston Cambs 150 B2
Kingston Corn 99 D3
Kingston Devon 100 D4
Kingston Devon 103 D4
Kingston Dorset 104 D2
Kingston Dorset 105 F5
Kingston ELoth 236 C1
Kingston GtMan 184 D3
Kingston Hants 106 A2
Kingston IoW 107 E4
Kingston Kent 125 D3
Kingston MK 149 E4
Kingston Moray 268 B4
Kingston Bagpuize 133 G3
Kingston Blount 134 C3
Kingston by Sea 109 E3
Kingston Deverill 117 F4
Kingston Gorse 108 C3
Kingston Lacy Dorset
  BH21 4EA 3 A1
Kingston Lisle 133 F4
Kingston Maurward 104 D3
Kingston near
  Lewes 109 F3
Kingston on Soar 173 G5
Kingston Russell 104 B3
Kingston St. Mary 115 F5
Kingston Seymour 116 B1
Kingston Stert 134 C2
Kingston upon Hull 196 D5
Kingston upon
  Thames 121 G1
Kingston Warren 133 F4
Kingstone Here 144 D3
Kingstone Here 145 F5
Kingstone Som 103 G1
Kingstone Staffs 172 B5
Kingstone Winslow 133 E4
Kingstown 209 G1
Kingswear 101 E2
Kingswell 233 G5
Kingswinford 158 A4
Kingswood Bucks 134 B1
Kingswood Glos 131 G3
Kingswood Here 144 B2
Kingswood Kent 124 A3
Kingswood Powys 156 B5
Kingswood SGlos 131 F5

Kingswood Som 115 E4
Kingswood Surr 122 B3
Kingswood Warks 159 D5
Kingthorpe 188 B5
Kington Here 144 B2
Kington Worcs 146 B2
Kington Langley 132 B5
Kington Magna 117 E5
Kington St. Michael 132 B5
Kingussie 258 E4
Kingweston 116 C4
Kinharrachie 261 H1
Kinharvie 216 D4
Kinkell 234 A2
Kinkell Bridge 243 E3
Kinknockie 269 J6
Kinlet 157 G4
Kinloch Fife 244 A3
Kinloch High 273 F5
Kinloch High 247 F4
Kinloch High 255 K5
Kinloch High 266 C4
Kinloch P&K 252 A5
Kinloch P&K 251 G5
Kinloch Hourn (Ceann Loch
  Shubhairne) 257 F4
Kinloch Laggan 250 A1
Kinloch Rannoch 250 B4
Kinlochan 248 A3
Kinlochard 241 G4
Kinlocharkaig 257 F5
Kinlochbeoraid 248 A1
Kinlochbervie 272 E3
Kinlocheil 248 B2
Kinlochetive 248 D5
Kinlochewe 265 G5
Kinlochlaich 248 B5
Kinlochleven (Ceann Loch
  Liobhann) 249 D3
Kinlochmoidart 247 G2
Kinlochmorar 256 E5
Kinlochmore 249 D3
Kinlochroag (Ceann
  Lochroag) 270 D5
Kinlochspelve 239 F2
Kinloss 267 H5
Kinmel Bay
  (Bae Cinmel) 182 A4
Kinmuck 261 G3
Kinnaber 253 F3
Kinnadie 269 H6
Kinnaird 244 A2
Kinneff 253 G2
Kinnelhead 226 B3
Kinnell Angus 253 E4
Kinnell Stir 242 A1
Kinnerley 170 A5
Kinnersley Here 144 C3
Kinnersley Worcs 146 A3
Kinnerton 144 B1
Kinnerton Green 170 A1
Kinnesswood 243 G4
Kinnettles 252 C5
Kinninvie 211 G5
Kinnordy 252 B4
Kinoulton 174 B4
Kinrara 259 F4
Kinross 243 G4
Kinrossie 243 G1
Kinsbourne Green 136 A1
Kinsham Here 144 C1
Kinsham Worcs 146 B4
Kinsley 186 B1
Kinson 105 G3
Kintarvie 270 E6
Kintbury 119 F1
Kintessack 267 G5
Kintillo 243 G3
Kintocher 260 D4
Kinton Here 156 D5
Kinton Shrop 156 C1
Kintour 230 C4
Kintra A&B 230 C4
Kintra A&B 238 C2
Kintradwell 267 G1
Kintraw 240 A4
Kinuachdrachd 239 G5
Kinveachy 259 G3
Kinver 158 A4
Kinwarton 146 D2
Kiplaw Croft 261 J1
Kipp 242 A3
Kippax 194 D4
Kippen P&K 243 F3
Kippen Stir 242 B5
Kippenross House 242 C4
Kippford (Scaur) 216 C5
Kipping's Cross 123 F4
Kippington 123 E3
Kirbister Ork 277 C7
Kirbister Ork 276 F5
Kirbuster 276 B5
Kirby Bedon 179 D5
Kirby Bellars 160 C1
Kirby Cane 165 E2
Kirby Corner 159 E5
Kirby Cross 165 D5
Kirby Fields 160 A2
Kirby Green 165 E2
Kirby Grindalythe 196 B1
Kirby Hill NYorks 202 A2
Kirby Hill NYorks 194 C1
Kirby Knowle 203 D4
Kirby le Soken 152 D5
Kirby Misperton 203 G5
Kirby Muxloe 160 A2
Kirby Row 165 E2
Kirby Sigston 202 D3
Kirby Underdale 196 A2
Kirby Wiske 202 C4
Kirdford 121 F5
Kirk 275 H3
Kirk Bramwith 186 D1
Kirk Deighton 194 C2
Kirk Ella 196 C5
Kirk Hallam 173 F3
Kirk Hammerton 195 D2
Kirk Ireton 173 D3
Kirk Langley 173 D4
Kirk Merrington 212 B4
Kirk Michael 190 B2

Kirk of Shotts 234 C3
Kirk Sandall 186 D2
Kirk Smeaton 186 C1
Kirk Yetholm 228 C4
Kirkabister 279 D9
Kirkandrews 207 G2
Kirkandrews-upon-
  Eden 209 G1
Kirkbean 217 D5
Kirkbride 209 F1
Kirkbuddo 252 D5
Kirkburn ERid 196 B2
Kirkburn ScBord 227 D2
Kirkburton 185 F1
Kirkby Lincs 188 A3
Kirkby Mersey 183 F3
Kirkby NYorks 203 E2
Kirkby Fleetham 202 B3
Kirkby Green 175 F2
Kirkby in Ashfield 173 F2
Kirkby la Thorpe 175 F3
Kirkby Lonsdale 200 B5
Kirkby Malham 193 E1
Kirkby Mallory 159 G2
Kirkby Malzeard 202 B5
Kirkby on Bain 176 A1
Kirkby Overblow 194 C3
Kirkby Stephen 200 C3
Kirkby Thore 210 C5
Kirkby Underwood 175 F5
Kirkby Wharfe 195 E3
Kirkby Woodhouse 173 F2
Kirkby-in-Furness 198 D4
Kirkbymoorside 203 F4
Kirkcaldy 244 A5
Kirkcambeck 210 B1
Kirkcolm 214 B4
Kirkconnel 225 F4
Kirkconnell 217 D4
Kirkcowan 215 E4
Kirkcudbright 216 A5
Kirkdale House 215 G5
Kirkdean 235 F5
Kirkfieldbank 234 C5
Kirkgunzeon 216 C4
Kirkham Lancs 192 A4
Kirkham NYorks 195 G1
Kirkhamgate 194 C5
Kirkharle 220 C3
Kirkhaugh 210 C3
Kirkheaton N'umb 220 C4
Kirkheaton WYorks 185 F1
Kirkhill Angus 253 E3
Kirkhill High 266 C7
Kirkhill Moray 268 D5
Kirkhope 227 E3
Kirkibost High 256 B3
Kirkibost (Circebost)
  WIsles 270 D4
Kirkinch 252 B5
Kirkinner 215 F5
Kirkintilloch 234 A2
Kirkland Cumb 210 C4
Kirkland Cumb 209 D5
Kirkland D&G 216 C1
Kirkland D&G 225 F4
Kirkland D&G 217 E2
Kirkland of
  Longcastle 207 D2
Kirkleatham 213 E5
Kirklevington 202 D1
Kirkley 165 G2
Kirklington Notts 174 B2
Kirklington NYorks 202 C4
Kirklinton 210 A1
Kirkliston 235 F2
Kirkmaiden 206 B3
Kirkmichael P&K 251 F3
Kirkmichael SAyr 224 B5
Kirkmuirhill 234 B5
Kirknewton N'umb 228 D3
Kirknewton WLoth 235 F3
Kirkney 260 D1
Kirkoswald Cumb 210 B3
Kirkoswald SAyr 224 A4
Kirkpatrick Durham 216 B3
Kirkpatrick-Fleming 218 A4
Kirksanton 198 C4
Kirkstall 194 B4
Kirkstead 175 G1
Kirkstile Aber 260 D1
Kirkstile D&G 218 B2
Kirkstyle 275 J1
Kirkthorpe 194 C5
Kirkton A&B 239 G4
Kirkton Aber 260 D4
Kirkton Aber 268 E5
Kirkton Aber 260 E3
Kirkton Angus 252 C5
Kirkton D&G 217 D2
Kirkton Fife 244 B2
Kirkton High 258 D1
Kirkton High 266 E6
Kirkton High 266 E6
Kirkton High 274 D2
Kirkton High 256 D2
Kirkton P&K 243 E3
Kirkton ScBord 227 G4
Kirkton Manor 226 D2
Kirkton of Airlie 252 B4
Kirkton of
  Auchterhouse 244 B1
Kirkton of Barevan 267 F7
Kirkton of Bourtie 261 G2
Kirkton of Collace 243 G1
Kirkton of Craig 253 F4
Kirkton of
  Culsalmond 260 E1
Kirkton of Durris 261 F5
Kirkton of
  Glenbuchat 260 B3
Kirkton of Glenisla 252 A3
Kirkton of
  Kingoldrum 252 B4
Kirkton of Lethendy 251 G5
Kirkton of Logie
  Buchan 261 H2
Kirkton of
  Maryculter 261 G5
Kirkton of Menmuir 252 D3
Kirkton of Monikie 244 D1

Kirkton of Rayne 260 E1
Kirkton of Skene 261 G4
Kirkton of Tealing 244 C1
Kirktonhill Aber 253 E3
Kirktonhill WDun 233 E2
Kirktown 269 J5
Kirktown of Alvah 268 E4
Kirktown of
  Auchterless 269 F6
Kirktown of
  Deskford 268 D4
Kirktown of
  Fetteresso 253 G1
Kirktown of Slains 261 J2
Kirkwall 277 D6
Kirkwall Airport 277 D7
Kirkwhelpington 220 B3
Kirmington 188 B1
Kirmond le Mire 188 B3
Kirn 232 C2
Kirriemuir 252 B4
Kirstead Green 165 D2
Kirtlebridge 218 A4
Kirtleton 218 A3
Kirtling 151 E2
Kirtling Green 151 E2
Kirtlington 134 A1
Kirtomy 274 D2
Kirton Lincs 176 B4
Kirton Notts 174 B1
Kirton Suff 153 D4
Kirton End 176 A3
Kirton Holme 176 A3
Kirton in Lindsey 187 G3
Kiscadale 223 F3
Kislingbury 148 B2
Kismeldon Bridge 113 D4
Kit Hill Country Park
  Corn PL17 8AX 99 D3
Kites Hardwick 147 G1
Kitley 100 D2
Kittisford 115 D5
Kittisford Barton 115 D5
Kittle 128 B4
Kitt's End 136 B3
Kitt's Green 159 D4
Kitwood 120 B4
Kivernoll 145 D4
Kiveton Park 186 B4
Klibreck 273 H5
Knabbygates 268 D5
Knaith 187 F4
Knaith Park 187 F4
Knap Corner 117 F5
Knaphill 121 E2
Knaplock 114 B4
Knapp P&K 244 A1
Knapp Som 116 A5
Knapthorpe 174 C2
Knaptoft 160 B4
Knapton Norf 179 E2
Knapton York 195 E2
Knapton Green 144 D2
Knapwell 150 B1
Knaresborough 194 C2
Knarsdale 210 C2
Knarston 276 C5
Knaven 269 G6
Knayton 202 D4
Knebworth 150 A4
Knebworth House Herts
  SG3 6PY 150 A4
Knedlington 195 G5
Kneesall 174 C1
Kneesworth 150 B3
Kneeton 174 C3
Knelston 128 A4
Knenhall 171 G4
Knettishall 164 A3
Knettishall Heath Country
  Park Suff
  IP22 2TQ 164 A3
Knightacott 113 G2
Knightcote 147 G2
Knightley 171 F5
Knightley Dale 171 F5
Knighton Devon 100 B3
Knighton Dorset 104 C1
Knighton Leic 160 A2
Knighton Poole 105 F3
Knighton (Tref-y-clawdd)
  Powys 156 B5
Knighton Som 115 E3
Knighton Staffs 171 E5
Knighton Staffs 171 E3
Knighton Wilts 133 E5
Knighton on Teme 157 F5
Knightswood 233 G3
Knightwick 145 G2
Knill 144 B1
Knipoch 240 A2
Knipton 174 D4
Knitsley 212 A3
Kniveton 172 D2
Knock A&B 239 E1
Knock Cumb 210 C5
Knock High 256 C4
Knock Moray 268 D5
Knock of
  Auchnahannet 259 H1
Knockalava 240 B5
Knockally 275 G6
Knockan 272 E7
Knockando 267 J7
Knockandhu 259 K2
Knockarthur 266 E1
Knockbain 266 D6
Knockban 265 J5
Knockbreck 266 E3
Knockbrex 207 G2
Knockdamph 265 J2
Knockdee 275 G2
Knockdow 232 C2
Knockdown 132 A4
Knockenkelly 223 F3
Knockentiber 224 B2
Knockfin 257 K2
Knockgray 215 G2
Knockholt 123 D3
Knockholt Pound 123 D3
Knockin 170 A5

Knockinlaw 224 C2
Knockintorran (Cnoc an
  Torrain) 262 C5
Knocklearn 216 B3
Knockmill 123 E2
Knocknaha 222 B4
Knocknain 214 A4
Knocknalling 215 G2
Knockrome 231 D2
Knocksharry 190 A3
Knockville 215 E3
Knockvologan 238 C3
Knodishall 153 F1
Knodishall Common 153 F1
Knodishall Green 153 F1
Knole 116 B5
Knolls Green 184 C5
Knolton 170 A4
Knook 118 A3
Knossington 160 D2
Knott End-on-Sea 191 G3
Knotting 149 F1
Knotting Green 149 F1
Knottingley 195 E5
Knotts 193 D3
Knotty Green 135 E3
Knowbury 157 E5
Knowe 215 E3
Knowes of Elrick 268 E5
Knowesgate 220 B3
Knoweside 224 A4
Knowetownhead 227 G4
Knowhead 269 H5
Knowl Green 151 F3
Knowl Hill 134 D5
Knowl Wall 171 F4
Knowle Bristol 131 F5
Knowle Devon 102 A2
Knowle Devon 113 E2
Knowle Devon 103 D4
Knowle Shrop 157 E5
Knowle Som 114 C3
Knowle WMid 159 D5
Knowle Cross 102 D3
Knowle Green 192 C4
Knowle Hall 116 A3
Knowle St. Giles 103 G1
Knowlton Dorset 105 G1
Knowlton Kent 125 E3
Knowsley 183 F3
Knowsley Safari Park
  Mersey L34 4AN 23 E2
Knowstone 114 B5
Knox Bridge 123 G4
Knucklas (Cnwclas) 156 B5
Knutsford 184 B5
Knypersley 171 F2
Krumlin 185 E1
Kuggar 95 E5
Kyle of Lochalsh (Caol
  Loch Aillse) 256 D2
Kyleakin
  (Caol Acain) 256 D2
Kylerhea
  (Ceol Reatha) 256 D2
Kyles Scalpay (Caolas
  Scalpaigh) 263 H2
Kylesbeg 247 F2
Kylesknoydart 256 E5
Kylesmorar 256 E5
Kylestrome 272 E5
Kyloag 266 D2
Kynaston 170 A5
Kynnersley 157 F1
Kyre Park 145 F1

L
Labost 270 E3
Lacasaigh 271 F5
Lace Market Centre
  NG1 1HF 80 Nottingham
Laceby 188 C2
Lacey Green 134 D2
Lach Dennis 184 B5
Lackford 163 F4
Lacklee (Leac a' Li) 263 G2
Lacock 118 A1
Ladbroke 147 G2
Laddingford 123 F4
Lade Bank 176 B2
Ladies Hill 192 A3
Ladock 96 C4
Lady Hall 198 C4
Lady Lever Art Gallery
  Mersey
  CH62 5EQ 22 B4
Ladybank 244 B3
Ladycross 98 D2
Ladyfield 240 C3
Ladykirk 237 F5
Ladysford 269 H4
Ladywood 146 A1
Laga 247 F3
Lagalochan 240 A3
Lagavulin 230 C5
Lagg A&B 231 D2
Lagg NAyr 223 E3
Lagg SAyr 224 A4
Laggan A&B 230 A4
Laggan (An Lagan)
  High 257 J5
Laggan High 258 D5
Laggan Moray 260 B1
Laggan Stir 242 A4
Lagganulva 247 D5
Lagganvoulin 259 J3
Laglingarten 240 D4
Lagnalean 266 D7
Lagrae 225 F4
Laguna 243 G1
Laid 273 G3
Laide 265 F2
Laig 247 D1
Laight 225 E4
Lainchoil 259 H3
Laindon 137 F4
Laing Art Gallery T&W
  NE1 8AG
  79 Newcastle upon Tyne
Lair 251 G3
Lairg 266 C1

Lairg Lodge 266 C1
Lairigmor 248 D3
Laisterdyke 194 A4
Laithers 268 E6
Laithes 210 A4
Lake Devon 113 F2
Lake Devon 100 B1
Lake IoW 107 E4
Lake Wilts 118 C4
Lake District Visitor Centre
  at Brockhole Cumb
  LA23 1LJ 199 E2
Lakenham 178 D5
Lakenheath 163 F4
Lakes Aquarium Cumb
  LA12 8AS 199 E4
Lakes End 162 D3
Lakes Glass Centre,
  Ulverston Cumb
  LA12 7LY 199 D5
Laleham 121 F1
Laleston 129 E5
Lamancha 235 G4
Lamarsh 151 G4
Lamas 178 D3
Lamb Corner 152 B4
Lamb Roe 192 D4
Lambden 237 E5
Lamberhurst 123 F5
Lamberhurst
  Quarter 123 F5
Lamberton 237 G4
Lambfell Moar 190 A3
Lambley N'umb 210 C2
Lambley Notts 174 B3
Lambourn 133 F4
Lambourn
  Woodlands 133 F5
Lambourne End 137 D3
Lambs Green 122 B5
Lambston 126 C1
Lambton 212 B2
Lamellion 97 G3
Lamerton 99 E3
Lamesley 212 B2
Lamington High 266 E4
Lamington SLan 226 A2
Lamlash 223 F2
Lamloch 215 G1
Lamonby 210 A4
Lamorna 94 B4
Lamorran 96 C5
Lampert 219 E4
Lampeter (Llanbedr Pont
  Steffan) 142 B3
Lampeter Velfrey 127 E1
Lamphey 126 D2
Lamplugh 209 D4
Lamport 160 C5
Lamyatt 117 E4
Lana Devon 98 D1
Lana Devon 112 D5
Lanark 234 C5
Lanarth 95 E4
Lancaster 192 A1
Lancaster Leisure Park
  Lancs LA1 3LA 192 A1
Lancaster Priory Lancs
  LA1 1YZ 192 A1
Lanchester 212 A3
Lancing 109 D3
Landbeach 150 C1
Landcross 113 E3
Landerberry 261 G4
Landewednack 95 E5
Landford 106 B1
Landhallow 275 G5
Landican 183 D4
Landimore 128 A3
Landkey 113 F2
Landmoth 202 D3
Landore 128 C3
Landrake 99 D4
Land's End Corn
  TR19 7AA 94 A4
Land's End Airport 94 A4
Landscove 101 D1
Landshipping 126 D1
Landulph 100 A1
Landwade 151 E1
Landywood 158 B2
Lane Bottom 193 E4
Lane End Bucks 134 D3
Lane End Cumb 198 C3
Lane End Derbys 173 F1
Lane End Dorset 105 E3
Lane End Hants 119 G5
Lane End Here 131 F1
Lane End Kent 137 E5
Lane End Wilts 117 F3
Lane Ends Derbys 172 D4
Lane Ends GtMan 185 D4
Lane Ends Lancs 193 D4
Lane Ends NYorks 193 F4
Lane Green 158 A2
Lane Head Dur 202 A1
Lane Head Dur 211 G5
Lane Head GtMan 184 A3
Lane Head WYorks 185 F2
Lane Heads 192 A4
Lane Side 193 D5
Laneast 97 G1
Laneham 187 F5
Lanehead Dur 211 E3
Lanehead N'umb 219 F3
Lanesend 127 D2
Lanesfield 158 B3
Laneshawbridge 193 F3
Langais 262 D5
Langamull 246 C4
Langar 174 C4
Langbank 233 E2
Langbar 193 G2
Langbaurgh 203 E1
Langcliffe 193 E1
Langdale End 204 C3

Langdon *Corn* 98 C1
Langdon *Corn* 98 D2
Langdon Beck 211 E4
Langdon Hills 137 F4
Langdon Hills Country Park *Essex* SS17 9NH 137 F4
Langdon House 102 C5
Langdyke 244 B4
Langford *CenBeds* 149 G3
Langford *Essex* 138 B2
Langford *Notts* 174 D2
Langford *Oxon* 133 E2
Langford Budville 115 E5
Langham *Essex* 152 B4
Langham *Norf* 178 B1
Langham *Rut* 160 D1
Langham *Suff* 145 E5
Langham Moor 152 B4
Langho 192 C4
Langholm 218 B3
Langland 128 C4
Langlands 216 A5
Langlee 228 A5
Langleeford 228 D4
Langley *ChesE* 184 D5
Langley *Derbys* 173 F3
Langley *Essex* 150 C4
Langley *Glos* 146 C5
Langley *GtMan* 184 C2
Langley *Hants* 106 D2
Langley *Herts* 150 A5
Langley *Kent* 123 G3
Langley *N'umb* 211 E1
Langley *Oxon* 133 F1
Langley *Slo* 135 E4
Langley *Som* 115 D5
Langley *Warks* 147 D1
Langley *WSuss* 120 C5
Langley Burrell 132 B5
Langley Corner 135 F4
Langley Green *Derbys* 173 D4
Langley Green *Warks* 147 E1
Langley Green *WSuss* 122 B5
Langley Heath 124 A3
Langley Marsh 115 D5
Langley Mill 173 F3
Langley Moor 212 B3
Langley Park 212 B3
Langley Park *Bucks* SL3 6DW 135 F4
Langley Street 179 E5
Langney 110 B3
Langold 186 C4
Langore 97 G1
Langport 116 B5
Langrick 176 A3
Langrick Bridge 176 A3
Langridge *B&NESom* 117 E1
Langridge *Devon* 113 F3
Langridgeford 113 F3
Langrigg 209 E2
Langrish 120 C5
Langsett 185 G2
Langshaw 227 G2
Langshawburn 227 D5
Langside *Glas* 233 G3
Langside *P&K* 242 C3
Langskaill 276 D3
Langstone *Hants* 107 G2
Langstone *Newport* 130 C3
Langthorne 202 B3
Langthorpe 194 C1
Langthwaite 201 F2
Langtoft *ERid* 196 C1
Langtoft *Lincs* 161 G1
Langton *Dur* 202 A1
Langton *Lincs* 189 D5
Langton *Lincs* 176 A1
Langton *NYorks* 195 G1
Langton by Wragby 188 B5
Langton Green *Kent* 123 E5
Langton Green *Suff* 164 C4
Langton Herring 104 C4
Langton Long Blandford 105 E2
Langton Matravers 105 F5
Langtree 113 E4
Langtree Week 113 E4
Langwathby 210 B4
Langwell 266 B1
Langwell House 275 G6
Langwith 186 C5
Langworth 188 A5
Lanhydrock *Corn* PL30 5AD 97 E3
Lanivet 97 E3
Lank 97 E2
Lanlivery 97 E4
Lanner 96 B5
Lanoy 97 G2
Lanreath 97 F4
Lansallos 97 F4
Lansdown 117 E1
Lanteglos 97 E1
Lanteglos Highway 97 F4
Lanton *N'umb* 228 D3
Lanton *ScBord* 228 A4
Lanvean 96 C3
Lapford 102 A2
Laphroaig 230 B5
Lapley 158 A1
Lapworth 159 D5
Larach na Gaibhre 231 F2
Larachbeg 247 F5
Larbert 234 C1
Larbreck 192 A3
Larden Green 170 C2
Larg 215 E3
Largie 260 E1
Largiemore 232 A1
Largoward 244 C4
Largs 232 D4
Largue 268 E6
Largybaan 222 B4
Largybeg 223 F3
Largymore 223 F3

Lark Hall 151 D2
Larkfield 232 B2
Larkhall 234 B4
Larkhill 118 C3
Larklands 173 F3
Larling 164 A3
Larriston 218 E2
Lartington 201 F1
Lary 260 B4
Lasborough 132 A3
Lasham 120 B3
Lashbrook 113 E5
Lashenden 124 A4
Lassington 145 G5
Lassintullich 250 C4
Lassodie 243 G5
Lasswade 236 A3
Lastingham 203 G3
Latchford 184 A4
Latchingdon 138 B2
Latchley 99 E3
Lately Common 184 A3
Lathbury 148 D3
Latheron 275 G5
Latheronwheel 275 G5
Lathockar 244 C3
Lathones 244 C4
Lathrisk 244 A4
Latimer 135 F3
Latteridge 131 F4
Lattiford 117 D5
Latton 132 C3
Lauchentyre 215 G5
Lauchintilly 261 F3
Lauder 236 C4
Laugharne (Lacharn) 127 G1
Laughterton 187 F5
Laughton *ESuss* 110 A2
Laughton *Leics* 160 B4
Laughton *Lincs* 175 F4
Laughton *Lincs* 187 F3
Laughton en le Morthen 186 C4
Launcells 112 C5
Launcells Cross 112 C5
Launceston 98 D2
Launde Abbey 160 C2
Launton 148 B5
Laurencekirk 253 F2
Laurieston *D&G* 216 A4
Laurieston *Falk* 234 D2
Lavendon 149 E2
Lavenham 152 A3
Laverhay 217 F1
Lavernock 115 E1
Laversdale 210 A1
Laverstock 118 C4
Laverstoke 119 F3
Laverton *Glos* 146 C4
Laverton *NYorks* 202 B5
Laverton *Som* 117 E2
Lavister 170 A2
Law 234 C4
Lawers *P&K* 242 C2
Lawers *P&K* 242 B1
Lawford *Essex* 152 B4
Lawford *Som* 115 E4
Lawhitton 99 D2
Lawkland 193 D1
Lawkland Green 193 D1
Lawley 157 F2
Lawnhead 171 F5
Lawrence Weston 131 E5
Lawrenny 126 D2
Laws 244 C1
Lawshall 151 G2
Lawshall Green 151 G2
Lawton 144 D2
Laxdale (Lacasdal) 271 G4
Laxey 190 C3
Laxfield 165 D4
Laxfirth *Shet* 279 D7
Laxfirth *Shet* 279 D8
Laxford Bridge 272 E4
Laxo 279 D6
Laxton *ERid* 195 G5
Laxton *N'hants* 161 E3
Laxton *Notts* 174 C1
Laycock 193 G3
Layer Breton 138 C1
Layer de la Haye 138 C1
Layer Marney 138 C1
Layham 152 B3
Laymore 103 G2
Layter's Green 135 E3
Laytham 195 G4
Layton 191 G4
Lazenby 213 E5
Lazonby 210 B4
Lea *Derbys* 173 E2
Lea *Here* 145 F5
Lea *Lincs* 187 F4
Lea *Shrop* 156 C4
Lea *Shrop* 156 D2
Lea *Wilts* 132 B4
Lea Bridge 173 E2
Lea Green 145 F1
Lea Marston 159 E3
Lea Town 192 A4
Lea Yeat 200 C4
Leachd 240 C5
Leachkin (An Leacainn) 266 D7
Leadburn 235 G4
Leaden Roding 137 E1
Leadenham 175 E2
Leaderfoot 227 G2
Leadgate *Cumb* 210 D3
Leadgate *Dur* 212 A2
Leadgate *N'umb* 212 A2
Leadhills 225 G4
Leadingcross Green 124 A3
Leafield 133 F1
Leagrave 149 F5
Leake Commonside 176 B2
Leake Hurn's End 176 C3
Lealands 110 A2
Lealholm 203 G2
Lealt *A&B* 239 F5
Lealt *High* 264 B5

Leam 185 G5
Leamington Hastings 147 G1
Leamington Spa 147 F1
Leamington Spa Art Gallery & Museum *Warks* CV32 4AA 16 B6
Leamoor Common 156 D4
Leanach *A&B* 240 C5
Leanach *High* 266 E7
Leanaig 266 C6
Leanoch 267 J6
Leargybreck 230 D2
Leasgill 199 F4
Leasingham 175 F3
Leask 261 J1
Leason 128 A3
Leasowe 183 D3
Leat 98 D2
Leatherhead 121 G2
Leathley 194 B3
Leaton *Shrop* 157 D1
Leaton *Tel&W* 157 F1
Leaveland 124 C3
Leavenheath 152 A4
Leavening 195 G1
Leaves Green 122 D2
Leavesden Green 136 A2
Lebberston 205 D4
Lechlade-on-Thames 133 E3
Leck 200 B5
Leckford 119 E4
Leckfurin 274 C3
Leckgruinart 230 A3
Leckhampstead *Bucks* 148 C4
Leckhampstead *WBerks* 133 G5
Leckhampstead Thicket 133 G5
Leckhampton 145 D2
Leckie *High* 265 G5
Leckie *Stir* 242 B5
Leckmelm (Leac Mailm) 265 H3
Leckroy 257 K5
Leckuary 240 A5
Leckwith 130 A5
Leconfield 196 C3
Ledaig (Leideag) 240 B1
Ledard 241 E5
Ledbeg 272 E7
Ledburn 149 D5
Ledbury 145 G4
Ledcharrie 242 A2
Ledgemoor 144 D2
Ledicot 144 D1
Ledmore *A&B* 247 E5
Ledmore *High* 272 E7
Lednagullin 274 C2
Ledsham *ChesW&C* 183 E5
Ledsham *WYorks* 195 D5
Ledston 194 D5
Ledstone 100 D3
Ledwell 147 G5
Lee *Devon* 113 E1
Lee *Hants* 106 C1
Lee *Lancs* 192 B2
Lee *Shrop* 170 B4
Lee Brockhurst 170 C5
Lee Chapel 137 F4
Lee Clump 135 E2
Lee Mill Bridge 100 B2
Lee Moor 100 B1
Lee Valley Park *Essex* EN9 1XQ 136 C2
Leebotten 279 D10
Leebotwood 157 D3
Leece 191 F1
Leeds *Kent* 124 A3
Leeds *WYorks* 194 B4
Leeds Art Gallery *WYorks* LS1 3AA 40 E3
Leeds Bradford International Airport 194 B3
Leeds Castle & Gardens *Kent* ME17 1PL 124 A3
Leedstown 94 D3
Leegomery 157 F1
Leek 171 G2
Leek Wootton 147 E1
Leekbrook 171 G2
Leeming *NYorks* 202 B4
Leeming *WYorks* 193 G4
Leeming Bar 202 B4
Lees *Derbys* 173 D4
Lees *GtMan* 185 D2
Leeswood 169 F2
Leftwich 184 A5
Legars 237 E5
Legbourne 189 D4
Legerwood 236 C5
Legoland Windsor *W&M* SL4 4AY 135 E5
Legsby 188 B4
Leicester 160 A2
Leicester Forest East 160 A2
Leideag 254 B5
Leigh *Dorset* 104 C2
Leigh *Dorset* 105 D2
Leigh *GtMan* 184 A2
Leigh *Kent* 123 E4
Leigh *Shrop* 156 C2
Leigh *Surr* 122 B4
Leigh *Wilts* 132 C3
Leigh *Worcs* 145 G2
Leigh Beck 138 B4
Leigh Common 117 E5
Leigh Delamere 132 A5
Leigh Green 124 B5
Leigh Park 107 G2
Leigh Sinton 145 G2
Leigh upon Mendip 117 E2
Leigh Woods 131 E5
Leigham 100 B2
Leighland Chapel 114 D4
Leigh-on-Sea 138 B4
Leighterton 132 A3

Leighton *NYorks* 202 A5
Leighton (Tre'r Llai) *Powys* 156 B2
Leighton *Shrop* 157 F2
Leighton *Som* 117 E3
Leighton Bromswold 161 G5
Leighton Buzzard 149 E5
Leinthall Earls 144 D1
Leinthall Starkes 144 D1
Leintwardine 156 D5
Leire 160 A4
Leirinmore 273 G2
Leiston 153 F1
Leith 235 G2
Leitholm 237 E5
Lelant 94 C3
Lelley 197 E4
Lem Hill 157 G5
Lemington 212 A1
Lemnas 269 G4
Lempitlaw 228 B3
Lemreway 271 K5
Lemsford 136 B1
Lenchwick 146 C3
Lendalfoot 214 C1
Lendrick Lodge 242 A4
Lenham 124 A3
Lenham Heath 124 B4
Lenie 258 C2
Lenimore 231 G5
Lennel 237 F5
Lennox Plunton 216 A5
Lennoxtown 234 A2
Lent Rise 135 E4
Lenton *Lincs* 175 F4
Lenton *Nott* 173 G4
Lenton Abbey 173 G4
Lenwade 178 B4
Lenzie 234 A2
Leoch 244 B1
Leochel-Cushnie 260 D3
Leominster 145 D2
Leonard Stanley 132 A2
Leorin 230 B5
Lepe 106 D3
Lephin 263 G7
Lephinchapel 240 B5
Lephinmore 240 B5
Leppington 195 G1
Lepton 185 G1
Lerags 240 B2
Lerryn 97 F4
Lerwick 279 D8
Lesbury 229 G5
Leschangie 261 F3
Leslie *Aber* 260 D2
Leslie *Fife* 244 A4
Lesmahagow 225 G2
Lesnewth 98 B1
Lessendrum 268 D6
Lessingham 179 E3
Lessness Heath 137 D5
Lessonhall 209 F1
Leswalt 214 B4
Letchmore Heath 136 A3
Letchworth Garden City 150 A4
Letcombe Bassett 133 F4
Letcombe Regis 133 F4
Leth Meadhanach 254 C3
Letham *Angus* 252 D5
Letham *Falk* 234 C1
Letham *Fife* 244 A3
Lethanhill 224 C4
Lethenty 269 G6
Letheringham 153 D2
Letheringsett 178 B2
Lettaford 102 A4
Letter Finlay 257 J5
Letterewe 265 F4
Letterfearn (Leitir Fheàrna) 256 E2
Lettermorar 247 G4
Lettermore *A&B* 247 D5
Lettermore *High* 273 J4
Letters 265 H3
Lettershaws 225 G3
Letterston 140 C5
Lettoch *High* 259 H3
Lettoch *High* 259 J1
Letton *Here* 156 C3
Letton *Here* 144 C3
Letty Green 136 B1
Letwell 186 C4
Leuchars 244 C2
Leumrabhagh 271 F6
Leurbost (Liurbost) 271 F5
Leusdon 102 A5
Levedale 158 A1
Level's Green 150 C5
Leven *ERid* 196 D3
Leven *Fife* 244 B4
Levencorroch 223 F3
Levenhall 236 A2
Levens 199 F4
Levens Green 150 B5
Levenshulme 184 C3
Levenwick 279 D10
Leverburgh (An T-Òb) 263 F3
Leverington 162 C1
Leverstock Green 135 F2
Leverton 176 B3
Leverton Lucasgate 176 C3
Leverton Outgate 176 C3
Levington 152 D4
Levisham 204 B3
Levishie 258 B3
Lew 133 F2
Lewannick 97 G1
Lewcombe 104 B2
Lewdown 99 E2
Lewes 109 G2
Leweston 140 C5
Lewisham 136 C5
Lewiston (Blàr na Maigh) 258 C2
Lewistown 129 F4
Lewknor 134 C3
Leworthy 113 G2
Lewson Street 124 B3
Lewth 192 A4

Lewtrenchard 99 E2
Ley *Aber* 260 D3
Ley *Corn* 97 F3
Ley Green 149 G5
Leybourne 123 F3
Leyburn 202 A3
Leyland 192 B5
Leylodge 261 F3
Leymoor 185 F1
Leys *Aber* 269 J5
Leys *Aber* 260 C4
Leys *P&K* 244 A1
Leys of Cossans 252 B5
Leysdown-on-Sea 124 C1
Leysmill 253 E5
Leysters 145 E1
Leyton 136 C4
Leytonstone 136 C4
Lezant 99 D3
Lezerea 95 D3
Lhanbryde 267 K5
Liatrie 257 J1
Libanus 143 F5
Libberton 235 D5
Liberton 235 G3
Liceasto 263 G2
Lichfield 158 D1
Lichfield Cathedral *Staffs* WS13 7LD 158 D2
Lickey 158 B5
Lickey End 158 B5
Lickey Hills Country Park *Worcs* B45 8ER 14 C2
Lickfold 121 E5
Liddaton Green 99 E2
Liddel 277 D9
Liddesdale 247 G4
Liddington 133 E4
Lidgate *Derbys* 186 A5
Lidgate *Suff* 151 F2
Lidgett 174 B1
Lidlington 149 E4
Lidsey 108 B3
Lidsing 123 G2
Lidstone 147 F5
Lienassie 257 F2
Lieurary 275 F2
Liff 244 B1
Lifton 99 D2
Liftondown 99 D2
Lightcliffe 194 A5
Lighthorne 147 F2
Lighthorne Heath 147 F2
Lighthouse, The, Glasgow *Glas* G1 3NU 39 F4
Lighthouse, The - Poole's Centre for the Arts *Poole* BH15 1UG 3 B4
Lightwater 121 E1
Lightwater Valley Park *NYorks* HG4 3HT 202 B5
Lightwood 171 G3
Lightwood Green *ChesE* 170 D3
Lightwood Green *Wrex* 170 A3
Lilbourne 160 A5
Lilburn Tower 229 E4
Lillesdon 116 A5
Lilleshall 157 G1
Lilley *Herts* 149 G5
Lilley *WBerks* 133 G5
Lilliesleaf 227 G3
Lilling Green 195 F1
Lillingstone Dayrell 148 C4
Lillingstone Lovell 148 C3
Lillington *Dorset* 104 C3
Lillington *Warks* 147 F1
Lilliput 105 G4
Lilly 113 F2
Lilstock 115 E3
Lilyhurst 157 G1
Limbury 149 F5
Lime Side 184 D2
Limefield 184 C1
Limehillock 268 D5
Limehurst 184 D2
Limekilnburn 234 B4
Limekilns 235 E1
Limerigg 234 C2
Limerstone 106 D4
Limington 116 D5
Limpenhoe 179 E5
Limpley Stoke 117 E1
Limpsfield 122 D3
Limpsfield Chart 122 D3
Linacre (Lionacleit) 262 C7
Linacre Reservoirs *Derbys* S42 7JW 186 A5
Linbriggs 220 A1
Linby 173 G2
Linchmere 121 D4
Lincluden 217 D3
Lincoln 187 G5
Lincoln Castle *Lincs* LN1 3AA 77 Lincoln
Lincoln Cathedral *Lincs* LN2 1PL 77 Lincoln
Lincomb 146 A1
Lincombe *Devon* 100 D2
Lincombe *Devon* 100 D3
Lindal in Furness 199 D5
Lindale 199 F4
Lindean 227 F2
Lindertis 252 B4
Lindfield 109 F1
Lindford 120 D4
Lindifferon 244 B3
Lindisfarne (Holy Island) 229 F2
Lindley 194 B3
Lindores 244 A3
Lindow End 184 C5
Lindridge 145 F1
Lindsaig 232 A2
Lindsell 151 E5
Lindsey 152 A3
Lindsey Tye 152 A3
Linfitts 185 D2

Linford *Hants* 106 A2
Linford *Thur* 137 F5
Linford Wood 148 D3
Lingague 190 A4
Lingards Wood 185 E1
Lingdale 203 F1
Lingen 144 C1
Lingfield 122 C4
Lingfield Green 183 G4
Lingwood 179 E5
Linhead 268 E5
Linhope 227 F5
Linicro 263 J5
Linkend 146 A4
Linkenholt 119 E2
Linkhill 110 D1
Linkinhorne 98 D3
Linklater 277 D9
Linksness *Ork* 277 B7
Linksness *Ork* 277 E6
Linktown 244 A5
Linley *Shrop* 156 C3
Linley *Shrop* 157 F3
Linley Green 145 F2
Linlithgow 235 E2
Linlithgow Bridge 235 D2
Linn of Muick Cottage 252 B1
Linnels 211 F1
Linney 126 B3
Linshiels 220 A1
Linsiadar 270 E4
Linsidemore 266 C2
Linslade 149 E5
Linstead Parva 165 E4
Linstock 210 A2
Linthwaite 185 F1
Lintlaw 237 F4
Lintmill 268 D4
Linton *Cambs* 151 D3
Linton *Derbys* 159 E1
Linton *Here* 145 F5
Linton *Kent* 123 G3
Linton *NYorks* 193 F1
Linton *ScBord* 228 B4
Linton *WYorks* 194 C3
Linton-on-Ouse 195 D1
Lintzford 212 A2
Linwood *Hants* 106 A2
Linwood *Lincs* 188 B4
Linwood *Renf* 233 F3
Lionel (Lional) 271 H1
Liphook 120 D4
Lipley 171 E4
Liscard 183 E3
Liscombe 114 B4
Liskeard 97 G3
L'Islet 101 F4
Lismore 240 A1
Liss 120 C5
Liss Forest 120 C5
Lissett 196 D2
Lissington 188 B4
Liston 151 G3
Lisvane 130 A4
Liswerry 130 C4
Litcham 163 G1
Litchborough 148 B2
Litchfield 119 F2
Litherland 183 E3
Litlington *Cambs* 150 B3
Litlington *ESuss* 110 A3
Little Abington 150 D3
Little Addington 161 E5
Little Alne 146 D1
Little Altcar 183 E2
Little Amwell 136 C1
Little Ann 119 E3
Little Asby 200 B2
Little Assynt 272 D6
Little Aston 158 C2
Little Atherfield 107 D5
Little Ayton 203 E1
Little Baddow 137 G2
Little Badminton 132 A4
Little Ballinluig 251 E4
Little Bampton 209 F1
Little Bardfield 151 E4
Little Barford 149 G2
Little Barningham 178 C2
Little Barrow 170 B1
Little Barugh 203 G5
Little Bavington 220 B4
Little Bealings 152 D3
Little Bedwyn 119 D1
Little Beeby 160 B2
Little Bentley 152 C5
Little Berkhamsted 136 B2
Little Billing 148 D1
Little Birch 145 E4
Little Bispham 191 G3
Little Blakenham 152 C3
Little Bloxwich 158 C2
Little Bollington 184 B4
Little Bookham 121 G2
Little Bourton 147 G3
Little Bowden 160 C4
Little Bradley 151 E2
Little Brampton 156 C4
Little Braxted 138 B1
Little Brechin 253 D3
Little Brickhill 149 E4
Little Bridgeford 171 F5
Little Brington 148 B1
Little Bromley 152 B5
Little Broughton 209 D3
Little Budworth 170 C1
Little Burdon 202 C1
Little Burstead 137 F3
Little Burton 196 D3
Little Bytham 161 F1
Little Canford 105 G3
Little Carlton *Lincs* 189 D4
Little Carlton *Notts* 174 C2
Little Casterton 161 F2
Little Catwick 196 D3
Little Catworth 161 F5
Little Cawthorpe 189 D4
Little Chalfield 117 F1
Little Chalfont 135 E3
Little Chart 124 B4

Little Chesterford 150 D3
Little Chesterton 148 A5
Little Cheverell 118 A2
Little Clacton 139 E1
Little Clanfield 133 E2
Little Clifton 209 D4
Little Coates 188 C2
Little Comberton 146 B3
Little Common 110 C3
Little Compton 147 E4
Little Corby 210 A2
Little Cornard 151 G4
Little Cowarne 145 F2
Little Coxwell 133 E3
Little Crakehall 202 B3
Little Cransley 160 D5
Little Crawley 149 E3
Little Creaton 160 C5
Little Creich 266 D3
Little Cressingham 163 G3
Little Crosby 183 E2
Little Crosthwaite 209 F4
Little Cubley 172 C4
Little Dalby 160 C1
Little Dens 269 J6
Little Dewchurch 145 E4
Little Ditton 151 E5
Little Doward 131 E1
Little Down 119 E2
Little Downham 162 D4
Little Drayton 171 D4
Little Driffield 196 C2
Little Dunham 163 G1
Little Dunkeld 251 F5
Little Dunmow 151 E5
Little Durnford 118 C4
Little Easton 151 E5
Little Eaton 173 E3
Little Eccleston 192 A4
Little Ellingham 164 A2
Little End 137 E2
Little Everdon 148 A2
Little Eversden 150 B2
Little Faringdon 133 E2
Little Fencote 202 B3
Little Fenton 195 E4
Little Finborough 152 B2
Little Fransham 178 A4
Little Gaddesden 135 E1
Little Garway 144 D5
Little Gidding 161 G4
Little Glemham 153 E2
Little Glenshee 243 F1
Little Gorsley 145 F5
Little Gransden 150 A2
Little Green *Cambs* 150 A3
Little Green *Notts* 174 C3
Little Green *Suff* 164 B4
Little Green *Suff* 164 B4
Little Green *Wrex* 170 B3
Little Grimsby 188 D3
Little Gringley 187 E4
Little Gruinard 265 F3
Little Habton 203 G5
Little Hadham 150 C5
Little Hale 175 G3
Little Hallingbury 137 D1
Little Hampden 135 D2
Little Haresfield 132 A2
Little Harrowden 161 D5
Little Haseley 134 B2
Little Hatfield 197 D3
Little Hautbois 179 D3
Little Haven *Pembs* 126 B1
Little Haven *WSuss* 121 G4
Little Hay 158 D2
Little Hayfield 185 E4
Little Haywood 172 B5
Little Heath 159 F4
Little Hereford 145 E1
Little Hockham 164 A2
Little Horkesley 152 A4
Little Hormead 150 C5
Little Horsted 109 G2
Little Horton 118 B1
Little Horwood 148 C4
Little Houghton 148 D2
Little Hucklow 185 F5
Little Hulton 184 B2
Little Hungerford 134 A5
Little Hutton 203 D5
Little Irchester 149 E1
Little Keyford 117 E3
Little Kimble 134 D2
Little Kineton 147 F2
Little Kingshill 135 D3
Little Langdale 199 E2
Little Langford 118 B4
Little Laver 137 E2
Little Lawford 159 G5
Little Leigh 184 A5
Little Leighs 137 G1
Little Lever 184 B2
Little Ley 260 E3
Little Linford 148 D3
Little Linton 151 D3
Little London *Bucks* 134 B1
Little London *Essex* 150 C5
Little London *ESuss* 110 A2
Little London *Hants* 119 E3
Little London *Hants* 120 B2
Little London *IoM* 190 B3
Little London *Lincs* 176 C5
Little London *Lincs* 176 A5
Little London *Lincs* 188 D5
Little London *Lincs* 188 B4
Little London *Norf* 177 D5
Little London *Norf* 163 F3
Little London *Oxon* 134 A2
Little London *Powys* 155 G4
Little London *Suff* 152 B2
Little London *WYorks* 194 B4
Little Longstone 185 F5
Little Lyth 157 D2

Little Malvern **145** G3
Little Maplestead **151** G4
Little Marcle **145** F4
Little Marland **113** F4
Little Marlow **135** D4
Little Marsden **193** E4
Little Massingham **177** F5
Little Melton **178** D5
Little Milford **126** C1
Little Mill **130** C2
Little Milton **134** B2
Little Missenden **135** E3
Little Musgrave **200** C1
Little Ness **158** D1
Little Newcastle **140** C5
Little Newsham **202** A1
Little Oakley *Essex* **152** D5
Little Oakley
 N'hants **161** D4
Little Odell **161** D4
Little Offley **149** G5
Little Onn **158** A1
Little Ouseburn **194** D1
Little Overton **170** A3
Little Packington **159** E4
Little Parndon **136** D1
Little Paxton **149** G3
Little Petherick **96** D2
Little Plumpton **191** F4
Little Plumstead **179** E4
Little Ponton **175** E4
Little Posbrook **107** E2
Little Potheridge **113** F4
Little Preston **148** A2
Little Raveley **162** A4
Little Ribston **194** C2
Little Rissington **133** D1
Little Rogart **266** E2
Little Rollright **147** E4
Little Ryburgh **178** A3
Little Ryle **229** E5
Little Ryton **157** D2
Little Salkeld **210** B4
Little Sampford **151** E4
Little Saxham **151** G1
Little Scatwell **265** K6
Little Shelford **150** C2
Little Shrawardine **156** C1
Little Silver **102** C2
Little Singleton **191** G4
Little Smeaton
 NYorks **186** C1
Little Smeaton
 NYorks **202** C2
Little Snoring **178** A2
Little Sodbury **131** G4
Little Sodbury End **131** G4
Little Somborne **119** E4
Little Somerford **132** B4
Little Soudley **171** E5
Little Stainforth **193** E1
Little Stainton **202** C1
Little Stanney **183** E5
Little Staughton **149** G1
Little Steeping **176** C1
Little Stoke **171** G4
Little Stonham **152** D4
Little Street **162** D4
Little Stretton *Leics* **160** B2
Little Stretton
 Shrop **156** D3
Little Strickland **199** G1
Little Stukeley **162** A5
Little Sugnall **171** F4
Little Sutton **183** E5
Little Swinburne **220** B4
Little Tarrington **145** F3
Little Tew **147** F5
Little Tey **151** G2
Little Thetford **162** D5
Little Thornage **178** B2
Little Thornton **191** G3
Little Thorpe **212** D3
Little Thurlow **151** E2
Little Thurlow
 Green **151** E2
Little Thurrock **137** F5
Little Torboll **266** E2
Little Torrington **113** F4
Little Tosson **220** C1
Little Totham **138** B1
Little Town *Cumb* **209** F5
Little Town *Lancs* **192** C4
Little Town *Warr* **184** A3
Little Twycross **159** F2
Little Urswick **199** D5
Little Wakering **138** C4
Little Walden **150** D3
Little Waldingfield **152** A3
Little Walsingham **178** A2
Little Waltham **137** G1
Little Warley **137** F3
Little Washbourne **146** B4
Little Weighton **196** B4
Little Welland **146** A4
Little Welnetham **151** G1
Little Wenham **152** B4
Little Wenlock **157** F2
Little Whittington **211** F1
Little Wilbraham **150** D2
Little Wishford **118** B4
Little Witcombe **132** B1
Little Witley **145** G1
Little Wittenham **134** A3
Little Wittingham
 Green **165** D4
Little Wolford **147** E4
Little Woodcote **122** B2
Little Wratting **151** E3
Little Wymington **149** E1
Little
 Wymondley **150** A5
Little Wyrley **158** C2
Little Wytheford **157** E1
Little Yeldham **151** F4
Littlebeck **204** B4
Littleborough
 Devon **102** B1

Littleborough
 GtMan **184** D1
Littleborough
 Notts **187** F4
Littlebourne **125** E3
Littlebredy **104** B4
Littlebury **150** D4
Littlebury Green **150** C4
Littledean **131** E1
Littleferry **267** F2
Littleham *Devon* **113** E3
Littleham *Devon* **102** D4
Littlehampton **108** C3
Littlehempston **101** E1
Littlehoughton **229** G5
Littlemill *EAyr* **224** C4
Littlemill *High* **267** G6
Littlemoor *Derbys* **173** E1
Littlemoor *Dorset* **104** C4
Littlemore **134** A2
Littlemoss **184** D3
Littleover **173** E4
Littleport **163** D4
Littlestead Green **134** C5
Littlestone-on-Sea **111** F1
Littlethorpe **194** C1
Littleton *ChesW&C* **170** B1
Littleton *Hants* **119** F4
Littleton *P&K* **244** A1
Littleton *Som* **116** B4
Littleton *Surr* **121** F1
Littleton Drew **132** A4
Littleton Panell **118** B2
Littleton-on-Severn **131** E3
Littletown *Dur* **212** C3
Littletown *IoW* **107** E3
Littlewick Green **134** D5
Littlewindsor **104** A2
Littleworth *Glos* **146** B4
Littleworth *Oxon* **133** F3
Littleworth *Staffs* **158** C1
Littleworth *SYorks* **186** D3
Littleworth *Worcs* **146** A3
Littley Green **137** F1
Litton *Derbys* **185** F5
Litton *NYorks* **201** E5
Litton *Som* **116** C2
Litton Cheney **104** B3
Liverpool **183** E3
Liverpool Cathedral
 Mersey L1 7AZ **42** E6
Liverpool John Lennon
 Airport **183** E4
Liverpool Metropolitan
 Cathedral (RC) *Mersey*
 L3 5TQ **43** E4
Liversedge **194** B5
Liverton *Devon* **102** B5
Liverton *R&C* **203** G1
Liverton Street **124** A4
Living Coasts, Torquay
 Torbay TQ1 2BG **101** F1
Livingston **235** E3
Livingston Village **235** E3
Lixwm **182** C5
Lizard **95** E5
Llaingarreglwyd **142** A2
Llaingoch **180** A4
Llaithddu **155** G4
Llampha **129** F5
Llan **155** E2
Llanaber **154** C1
Llanaelhaearn **166** C3
Llanaeron **142** A2
Llanafan **154** B5
Llanafan-fawr **143** F2
Llanafan-fechan **143** F2
Llanallgo **180** C4
Llanarmon Dyffryn
 Ceiriog **169** E4
Llanarmon-yn-Ial **169** E2
Llanarth *Cere* **142** A2
Llanarth *Mon* **130** C1
Llanarthney **142** B5
Llanasa **182** C4
Llanbabo **180** B4
Llanbadarn Fawr **154** B4
Llanbadarn Fynydd **155** G5
Llanbadarn-y-
 garreg **144** A3
Llanbadoc **130** C2
Llanbadrig **180** B3
Llanbeder **130** C3
Llanbedr *Gwyn* **167** E5
Llanbedr *Powys* **144** B5
Llanbedr *Powys* **144** A3
Llanbedr-Dyffryn-
 Clwyd **169** E2
Llanbedrgoch **180** D4
Llanbedrog **166** C4
Llanberis **167** E2
Llanbethery **114** D1
Llanblethian **129** F5
Llanboidy **141** F5
Llanbradach **130** A3
Llanbryn-mair **155** E2
Llancadle **114** D1
Llancarfan **129** G5
Llancayo **130** C2
Llancynfelyn **154** C3
Llandaff **130** A5
Llandaff North **130** A5
Llandanwg **167** E5
Llandawke **127** F1
Llanddaniel Fab **180** C5
Llanddarog **128** A1
Llanddeiniol **154** B5
Llanddeiniolen **167** E1
Llanddderfel **168** C4
Llanddeusant
 Carmar **143** D5
Llanddeusant *IoA* **180** B4
Llanddew **143** G4
Llanddewi **128** A2
Llanddewi
 Rhydderch **130** C1
Llanddewi
 Skirrid **130** C1

Llanddewi Velfrey **127** E1
Llanddewi
 Ystradenni **144** A1
Llanddewi-Brefi **142** C2
Llanddewi'r Cwm **143** G3
Llanddoged **168** B1
Llanddona **181** D5
Llanddowror **127** F1
Llanddulas **182** A5
Llanddwywe **167** E5
Llandefaelog Fach **143** G4
Llandefaelog-
 tre'r-graig **144** A5
Llandefalle **144** A4
Llandegfan **181** D5
Llandegfedd Reservoir
 Mon NP4 0TA **130** C3
Llandegla **169** E2
Llandegley **144** A1
Llandegveth **130** C3
Llandeilo **142** C5
Llandeilo
 Abercywyn **127** G1
Llandeilo Graban **143** G3
Llandeilo'r-Fan **143** E4
Llandeloy **140** B5
Llandenny **130** D2
Llandevaud **130** D3
Llandevenny **130** D4
Llandinabo **145** E5
Llandinam **155** G4
Llandissilio **141** E5
Llandogo **131** E2
Llandough *VGlam* **130** A5
Llandough *VGlam* **129** F5
Llandovery
 (Llanymddyfri) **143** D4
Llandow **129** F5
Llandre *Carmar* **142** C3
Llandre *Carmar* **141** E5
Llandre *Cere* **154** C4
Llandrillo **168** D4
Llandrindod Wells **143** G1
Llandrinio **156** B1
Llandudno **181** F4
Llandudno Junction **181** F5
Llandwrog **167** D2
Llandybie **128** C1
Llandyfaelog **128** C1
Llandyfan **128** C1
Llandyfriog **141** G3
Llandyfrydog **180** C4
Llandygai **181** F3
Llandygwydd **141** F3
Llandynog **169** E1
Llandysilio **156** B1
Llandyssil **156** A3
Llandysul **142** A3
Llanedeyrn **130** B4
Llanedy **128** B2
Llaneglwys **143** G4
Llanegryn **154** C2
Llanegwad **142** B5
Llaneilian **180** C3
Llanelian-yn-Rhos **181** G5
Llanelidan **169** E2
Llanelieu **144** A4
Llanellen **130** C2
Llanelli **128** B2
Llanelli Millennium Coastal
 Park *Carmar*
 SA15 2LF **128** A3
Llanelltyd **154** D1
Llanelly **130** B1
Llanelly Hill **130** B1
Llanelwedd **143** G2
Llanenddwyn **167** E5
Llanengan **166** B5
Llanerfyl **155** G2
Llaneuddog **180** C4
Llanfachraeth **180** B4
Llanfachreth **154** D1
Llanfaelog **180** B5
Llanfaelrhys **166** B5
Llanfaenor **130** D1
Llan-faes *IoA* **181** E5
Llanfaes *Powys* **143** G5
Llanfaethlu **180** B4
Llanfaglan **167** D1
Llanfair **167** E5
Llanfair Caereinion **156** A2
Llanfair Clydogau **142** C2
Llanfair Dyffryn
 Clwyd **169** E2
Llanfair Talhaiarn **182** A5
Llanfair Waterdine **156** B5
Llanfairfechan **181** E5
Llanfair-Nant-Gwyn **141** E4
Llanfair-Orllwyn **141** G3
Llanfairpwllgwyngyll
 180 D5
Llanfairynghornwy **180** B3
Llanfair-yn-neubwll **180** B5
Llanfallteg **127** E1
Llanfaredd **143** G2
Llanfarian **154** B5
Llanfechain **156** A1
Llanfechell **180** B3
Llanfendigaid **154** B2
Llanferres **169** E1
Llanfflewyn **180** B4
Llanfigael **180** B4
Llanfihangel Glyn
 Myfyr **168** C3
Llanfihangel Nant
 Bran **143** F4
Llanfihangel
 Rhydithon **144** A1
Llanfihangel
 Tal-y-llyn **144** A5
Llanfihangel-
 ar-arth **142** A3
Llanfihangel-nant-
 Melan **144** A2
Llanfihangel-uwch-
 Gwili **142** A5
Llanfihangel-y-
 Creuddyn **154** C5

Llanfihangel-yng-
 Ngwynfa **155** G1
Llanfihangel-yn-
 Nhwyn **180** B5
Llanfihangel-y-pennant
 Gwyn **167** E3
Llanfihangel-y-pennant
 Gwyn **154** C2
Llanfilo **144** A4
Llanfoist **130** B1
Llanfor **168** C4
Llanfrechfa **130** C3
Llanfrothen **167** E4
Llanfrwog *Denb* **169** E2
Llanfwrog *IoA* **180** B4
Llanfyllin **156** A1
Llanfynydd *Carmar* **142** B5
Llanfynydd *Flints* **169** F2
Llanfyrnach **141** F4
Llangadog **142** D5
Llangadwaladr *IoA* **166** C1
Llangadwaladr
 Powys **169** E4
Llangaffo **180** C5
Llangain **127** G1
Llangammarch
 Wells **143** F3
Llangan **129** F5
Llanganten **143** F2
Llangar **145** E5
Llangarron **145** E5
Llangasty-Talyllyn **144** A5
Llangathen **142** B5
Llangattock **130** B1
Llangattock
 Lingoed **130** C1
Llangattock-Vibon-
 Avel **131** D1
Llangedwyn **169** E5
Llangefni **180** C5
Llangeinor **129** F4
Llangeitho **142** C1
Llangeler **141** G4
Llangelynin **154** B2
Llangendeirne **128** A1
Llangennech **128** B2
Llangenny **130** B1
Llangernyw **168** B1
Llangian **166** B5
Llangiwg **128** D2
Llangloffan **140** C4
Llanglydwen **141** E5
Llangoed **181** E5
Llangoedmor **141** E3
Llangollen **169** F3
Llangollen Railway *Denb*
 LL20 8SN **169** F3
Llangolman **141** E5
Llangorse **144** A5
Llangorwen **154** C4
Llangovan **131** D2
Llangower **168** C4
Llangrannog **141** G2
Llangristiolus **180** C5
Llangrove **131** E1
Llangua **144** C5
Llangunllo **156** B5
Llangunnor **142** A5
Llangurig **155** F5
Llangwm *Conwy* **168** C3
Llangwm *Mon* **130** D2
Llangwm *Pembs* **126** C2
Llangwnnadl **166** B4
Llangwyfan **169** E1
Llangwyllog **180** C5
Llangwyryfon **154** C5
Llangybi *Cere* **142** C2
Llangybi *Gwyn* **166** D3
Llangybi *Mon* **130** C3
Llangyfelach **128** C3
Llangynhafal **169** E1
Llangynidr **130** A1
Llangyniew **156** A2
Llangynin **127** F1
Llangynllo **141** G3
Llangynog *Carmar* **127** G1
Llangynog *Powys* **169** D5
Llangynwyd **129** E4
Llanhamlach **143** G5
Llanharan **129** G4
Llanharry **129** G4
Llanhennock **130** C3
Llanhilleth **130** B2
Llanidloes **155** F4
Llaniestyn **166** B4
Llanigon **144** B4
Llanilar **154** C5
Llanilid **129** F4
Llanishen *Cardiff* **130** A4
Llanishen *Mon* **131** D2
Llanllawddog **142** A5
Llanllechid **167** F1
Llanllugan **155** G2
Llanllugan **155** G2
Llanllwch **127** G1
Llanllwchaiarn **156** A3
Llanllwni **142** A3
Llanllyfni **167** D2
Llanllywel **130** C3
Llanmadoc **128** A3
Llanmaes **114** C1
Llanmartin **130** C4
Llanmerewig **156** A3
Llanmihangel **129** F5
Llan-mill **127** E1
Llanmiloe **127** F2
Llanmorlais **128** B3
Llannefydd **182** A5
Llannerch Hall **182** B5
Llannerch-y-medd **180** C4
Llannerch-y-Môr **182** A5
Llannon *Carmar* **128** B2
Llan-non *Cere* **142** B1
Llannor **166** C4
Llanover **130** C2
Llanpumsaint **142** A5
Llanreithan **140** B5
Llanrhaeadr **169** D1
Llanrhian **140** B4

Llanrhidian **128** A3
Llanrhyddlad **180** B4
Llanrhystud **142** B1
Llanrothal **131** D1
Llanrug **167** E1
Llanrumney **130** B4
Llanrwst **168** A1
Llansadurnen **127** F1
Llansadwrn *Carmar* **142** C4
Llansadwrn *IoA* **181** D5
Llansaint **127** G2
Llansamlet **128** C3
Llansanffraid **142** B1
Llansanffraid Glan
 Conwy **181** G5
Llansannan **168** C1
Llansannor **129** F5
Llansantffraed **144** A5
Llansantffraed-
 Cwmdeuddwr **143** F1
Llansantffraed-in-
 Elwel **143** G1
Llansantffraid-ym-
 Mechain **156** A1
Llansawel **142** C4
Llansilin **169** F5
Llansoy **130** D2
Llanspyddid **143** G5
Llanstadwell **126** C2
Llansteffan **144** A3
Llanteg **127** G1
Llanthony **144** B5
Llantilio Crossenny **130** C1
Llantilio Pertholey **130** C1
Llantood **141** E3
Llantrisant *IoA* **180** B4
Llantrisant *Mon* **130** C3
Llantrisant *RCT* **129** G4
Llantrithyd **129** G5
Llantwit Fardre **129** G4
Llantwit Major **114** C1
Llantysilio **169** E3
Llanuwchllyn **168** B5
Llanvaches **130** D3
Llanvair-Discoed **130** D3
Llanvapley **130** C1
Llanvetherine **130** C1
Llanveynoe **144** C4
Llanvihangel
 Gobion **130** C2
Llanvihangel-Ystern-
 Llewern **130** D1
Llanvithyn **129** G5
Llanwarne **145** E5
Llanwddyn **155** G1
Llanwenog **142** A2
Llanwern **130** C4
Llanwinio **141** F5
Llanwnda *Gwyn* **167** D2
Llanwnda *Pembs* **140** C4
Llanwnnen **142** B3
Llanwnog **155** G3
Llanwonno **129** G3
Llanwrda **142** D4
Llanwrin **155** D2
Llanwrthwl **143** F1
Llanwrtyd **143** E3
Llanwrtyd Wells **143** E3
Llanwyddelan **155** G2
Llanyblodwel **169** F5
Llanybri **127** G1
Llanybydder **142** B3
Llanycefn **141** E5
Llanychaer
 Bridge **140** C4
Llanycil **168** C4
Llanycrwys **142** C3
Llanymawddwy **155** E1
Llanymynech **169** F5
Llanynghenedl **180** B4
Llanynys **169** E1
Llan-y-pwll **170** A2
Llanyre **143** G1
Llanystumdwy **167** D4
Llanywern **144** A5
Llawhaden **127** D1
Llawndy **182** C4
Llawnt **169** F4
Llawr-y-dref **166** B5
Llawryglyn **155** F2
Llay **170** A2
Llechcynfarwy **180** B4
Llecheiddior **167** D3
Llechfaen **143** G5
Llechryd *Caerp* **130** A2
Llechryd *Cere* **141** E3
Llechrydau **169** F4
Llechwedd Slate Caverns
 Gwyn LL41 3NB **168** A3
Lledrod *Cere* **154** C5
Lledrod *Powys* **169** F5
Llethryd **128** B3
Llidiad-Nenog **142** A4
Llidiardau **168** B4
Llithfaen **166** C3
Lloc **182** C5
Llong **169** F1
Llowes **144** A3
Lloyney **156** B5
Llundain-fach **142** B2
Llwydcoed **129** F2
Llwydiarth **155** G1
Llwyn **156** B4
Llwyncelyn **142** A2
Llwyn-croes **142** A5
Llwyndafydd **141** G2
Llwynderw **156** B2
Llwyn-du **130** B1
Llwyndyrys **166** C3
Llwyneinion **169** F3
Llwyngwril **154** B2
Llwynhendy **128** B3
Llwyn-Madoc **143** F2
Llwynmawr **169** F4
Llwyn-onn *Cere* **142** A2
Llwyn-onn *MTyd* **129** G1
Llwyn-y-brain
 Carmar **127** E1

Llwyn-y-brain
 Carmar **142** D4
Llwyn-y-groes **142** B2
Llwynypia **129** F3
Llyn Brenig *Conwy*
 LL21 9TT **168** C2
Llynclys **169** F5
Llynfaes **180** C5
Llysfaen **181** G5
Llyswen **144** A4
Llysworney **129** F5
Llys-y-frân **140** D5
Llywel **143** E4
Load Brook **185** G4
Loandhu **267** G6
Loanhead *Aber* **261** H1
Loanhead *Midlo* **235** G3
Loans **224** B2
Lobb **113** E2
Lobhillcross **99** E2
Loch a Charnain **262** D7
Loch an Eilein Visitor Centre
 & Forest Trail *High*
 PH22 1QT **259** F4
Loch Choire Lodge **273** J5
Loch Eil Outward
 Bound **248** C2
Loch Head *D&G* **206** D2
Loch Head *D&G* **215** F1
Loch Lomond Shores &
 Gateway Centre *WDun*
 G83 8QL **233** E1
Loch Ness Exhibition Centre
 High IV63 6TU **258** C2
Loch Sgioport **254** C1
Lochailort (Ceann Loch
 Ailleart) **247** G1
Lochaline
 (Loch Àlainn) **247** F5
Lochans **214** B5
Locharbriggs **217** D2
Lochawe
 (Loch Obha) **240** D2
Lochboisdale (Loch
 Baghasdail) **254** C3
Lochbuie **239** F2
Lochcarron
 (Loch Carrann) **264** E7
Lochdon **239** G1
Lochdrum **265** J4
Lochearnhead (Ceann Loch
 Èireann) **242** A2
Lochee **244** B1
Lochend *High* **275** H2
Lochend (Ceann Loch)
 High **258** C1
Lochfoot **216** D3
Lochgair **240** B5
Lochgarthside **258** C3
Lochgelly **243** F5
Lochgilphead (Ceann Loch
 Gilb) **231** G1
Lochgoilhead **241** E4
Lochgoyn **233** G3
Lochhill *EAyr* **225** D4
Lochhill *Moray* **267** K5
Lochinch Castle **214** C4
Lochinver
 (Loch an Inbhir) **272** C6
Lochlair **252** D5
Lochlane **242** D5
Lochlea **224** C2
Lochluichart **265** K5
Lochmaben **217** E2
Lochmaddy (Loch na
 Madadh) **262** D5
Lochore **243** G5
Lochore Meadows Country
 Park *Fife*
 KY5 8BA **243** G5
Lochportain **262** E4
Lochranza **232** A4
Lochside *Aber* **253** F3
Lochside *High* **273** G3
Lochside *High* **274** D5
Lochside *High* **275** H2
Lochslin **267** F3
Lochton **215** D2
Lochty **244** D4
Lochuisge **247** G3
Lochurr **216** B2
Lochussie **266** B6
Lochwinnoch **233** E4
Lockengate **97** E3
Lockerbie **217** F2
Lockeridge **118** C1
Lockerley **119** D5
Lockhills **210** B3
Locking **116** A2
Lockington *ERid* **196** B3
Lockington *Leics* **173** F5
Locklewood **171** D5
Locks Heath **107** E2
Locksbottom **122** D2
Locksgreen **106** D3
Lockton **204** B4
Locomotion: The National
 Railway Museum at
 Shildon *Dur*
 DL4 1PQ **212** B5
Loddington
 Leics **160** C2
Loddington
 N'hants **160** D5
Loddiswell **100** D3
Loddon **165** E2
Lode **150** D1
Loders **104** A3
Lodsworth **121** E5
Lofthouse *NYorks* **202** A5
Lofthouse *WYorks* **194** C5
Loftus **203** G1
Logan *D&G* **206** A2
Logan *EAyr* **225** D3
Loganlea **235** D3
Loggerheads **171** E4

Loggerheads Country Park
 Denb CH7 5LH **169** E1
Loggie
 (An Lagaidh) **265** H2
Logie *Angus* **253** E3
Logie *Angus* **252** B4
Logie *Fife* **244** C2
Logie *Moray* **267** H6
Logie Coldstone **260** C4
Logie Hill **266** E4
Logie Newton **260** D6
Logie Pert **253** E3
Logierait **251** E4
Login **141** E5
Lolworth **150** B1
Lonbain **264** C6
Londesborough **196** A3
London **136** C4
London Apprentice **97** E5
London Aquarium *GtLon*
 SE1 7PD **45** F5
London Ashford
 Airport **111** F1
London Beach **124** A5
London Biggin Hill
 Airport **122** D2
London City Airport **136** D4
London Colney **136** A2
London Eye *GtLon*
 SE1 7PB **45** F5
London Gatwick
 Airport **122** B4
London Heathrow
 Airport **135** F4
London Luton
 Airport **149** G4
London Minstead **106** B1
London Southend
 Airport **138** B4
London Stansted
 Airport **150** D4
London Transport Museum
 GtLon WC2E 7BB **45** E3
London Wetland Centre
 GtLon SW13 9WT **11** E6
London Zoo *GtLon*
 NW1 4RY **12** A3
Londonderry **202** B4
Londonthorpe **175** E4
Londubh **264** E3
Lonemore **266** E3
Long Ashton **131** E5
Long Bank **157** G5
Long Bennington **174** D3
Long Bredy **104** B3
Long Buckby **148** B1
Long Clawson **174** C5
Long Compton
 Staffs **171** F5
Long Compton
 Warks **147** E4
Long Crendon **134** B2
Long Crichel **105** F1
Long Dean **132** A5
Long Downs **95** E3
Long Drax **195** F5
Long Duckmanton **186** B5
Long Eaton **173** F4
Long Gill **193** D2
Long Green
 ChesW&C **183** E5
Long Green *Essex* **152** A5
Long Green *Worcs* **146** A4
Long Hanborough **133** G1
Long Itchington **147** G1
Long Lane **157** F1
Long Lawford **159** G5
Long Load **116** B5
Long Marston
 Herts **135** D1
Long Marston
 NYorks **195** E2
Long Marston
 Warks **147** D3
Long Marton **210** C5
Long Meadowend **156** D4
Long Melford **151** G3
Long Newton **132** B3
Long Preston **193** E2
Long Riston **196** D3
Long Stratton **164** C2
Long Street **148** C3
Long Sutton *Hants* **120** C3
Long Sutton *Lincs* **176** C5
Long Sutton *Som* **116** B5
Long Thurlow **152** B1
Long Whatton **173** F5
Long Wittenham **134** A3
Longbenton **212** B1
Longborough **147** D5
Longbridge *Plym* **100** B2
Longbridge *Warks* **147** E1
Longbridge *WMid* **158** C5
Longbridge Deverill **117** F3
Longburgh **209** G1
Longburton **104** C1
Longcliffe **172** D2
Longcombe **101** E2
Longcot **133** E3
Longcroft **234** B2
Longcross *Devon* **99** E3
Longcross *Surr* **121** E1
Longden **156** D2
Longdon *Staffs* **158** C1
Longdon *Worcs* **146** A4
Longdon Green **158** C1
Longdon upon Tern **157** F1
Longdown **102** B3
Longdowns **261** H3
Longfield **123** F2
Longfield Hill **123** F2
Longfleet **105** G3
Longford *Derbys* **172** D4
Longford *Glos* **146** A5
Longford *GtLon* **135** F5
Longford *Shrop* **170** D3
Longford *Tel&W* **157** G2
Longford *WMid* **159** F4
Longforgan **244** B2
Longformacus **237** D4
Longframlington **220** D1
Longham *Dorset* **105** G3

Lon - Mar

Longham Norf 178 A4
Longhill 269 H5
Longhirst 221 E3
Longhope Glos 131 F1
Longhope Ork 277 C8
Longhorsley 220 D2
Longhoughton 229 G5
Longlands Aber 260 C2
Longlands Cumb 209 F3
Longlands GtLon 136 D5
Longlane Derbys 173 D4
Longlane WBerks 133 G5
Longleat House Wilts BA12 7NW 117 F3
Longleat Safari Park Wilts BA12 7NW 117 F3
Longlevens 132 A1
Longley 185 F2
Longley Green 145 G2
Longmanhill 269 F4
Longmoor Camp 120 C4
Longmorn 267 K6
Longnewton ScBord 227 G3
Longnewton Stock 202 C1
Longney 131 G1
Longniddry 236 B2
Longniddry Bents ELoth EH32 0PX 236 B2
Longnor Shrop 157 D2
Longnor Staffs 172 B1
Longparish 119 F3
Longridge Lancs 192 C4
Longridge Staffs 158 B1
Longridge WLoth 235 D3
Longridge End 146 A5
Longridge Towers 237 G4
Longriggend 234 C2
Longrock 94 C3
Longsdon 171 G2
Longshaw 183 G2
Longside 269 J6
Longslow 171 D4
Longsowerby 209 G1
Longstanton 150 C1
Longstock 119 E4
Longstone 94 C3
Longstowe 150 B2
Longstreet 118 C2
Longthorpe 161 G3
Longton Lancs 192 A5
Longton Stoke 171 G3
Longtown Cumb 218 B5
Longtown Here 144 C5
Longville in the Dale 157 E3
Longwell Green 131 F5
Longwick 134 C2
Longwitton 220 C3
Longworth 133 F3
Longyester 236 C3
Lonmay 269 J5
Lonmore 263 H7
Looe 97 G4
Look Out Discovery Park, Bracknell BrackF RG12 7QW 121 D1
Loose 123 G3
Loosebeare 102 A2
Loosegate 176 B5
Loosley Row 134 D2
Lopcombe Corner 119 D4
Lopen 104 A1
Loppington 170 B5
Lorbottle 220 C1
Lorbottle Hall 220 C1
Lordington 107 G2
Lord's Cricket Ground & Museum GtLon NW8 8QN 10 F4
Lord's Hill 106 C1
Lorgill 263 G7
Lorn 233 E1
Lornty 251 G5
Loscoe 173 F3
Loscombe 104 A3
Losgaintir 263 F2
Lossiemouth 267 K4
Lossit 230 A4
Lost Gardens of Heligan Corn PL26 6EN 97 D5
Lostock Gralam 184 A5
Lostock Green 184 A5
Lostock Junction 184 A2
Lostwithiel 97 F4
Loth 276 F4
Lothbeg 274 E7
Lothersdale 193 F3
Lotherton Hall Estate WYorks LS25 3EB 195 D4
Lothmore 274 E7
Loudoun Castle Park EAyr KA4 8PE 224 D2
Loudwater 135 E3
Loughborough 160 A1
Loughor 128 B3
Loughton Essex 136 D3
Loughton MK 148 D4
Loughton Shrop 157 F4
Louis Tussaud's Waxworks FY1 5AA 64 Blackpool
Lound Lincs 161 F1
Lound Notts 187 D4
Lound Suff 165 G2
Lount 159 F1
Lour 252 C5
Louth 188 D4
Love Clough 193 E5
Lovedean 107 F1
Lover 106 B1
Loversall 186 C3
Loves Green 137 F2
Lovesome Hill 202 C3
Loveston 127 D2
Lovington 116 C4
Low Ackworth 186 B1
Low Angerton 220 C3
Low Ballevain 222 B3
Low Barlay 215 G5
Low Barlings 188 A5
Low Bentham (Lower Bentham) 192 C1
Low Bolton 201 F3
Low Bradfield 185 G3
Low Bradley (Bradley) 193 G3
Low Braithwaite 210 A3
Low Brunton 220 B4
Low Burnham 187 E2
Low Burton 202 B4
Low Buston 221 E1
Low Catton 195 G2
Low Coniscliffe 202 B1
Low Craighead 224 A5
Low Dinsdale 202 C1
Low Ellington 202 B4
Low Entercommon 202 C2
Low Etherley 212 A5
Low Fell 212 B2
Low Gate 211 F1
Low Grantley 202 B5
Low Green 151 G1
Low Habberley 158 A5
Low Ham 116 B5
Low Hawsker 204 C2
Low Haygarth 200 B3
Low Hesket 210 A3
Low Hesleyhurst 220 C2
Low Hutton 195 G1
Low Kingthorpe 204 B4
Low Laithe 194 A1
Low Langton 188 B5
Low Leighton 185 E4
Low Lorton 209 E4
Low Marishes 204 B5
Low Marnham 174 D1
Low Middleton 229 F3
Low Mill 203 F3
Low Moor Lancs 192 D3
Low Moor WYorks 194 A5
Low Moorsley 212 C3
Low Moresby 208 C4
Low Newton-by-the-Sea 229 G4
Low Row Cumb 210 B1
Low Row NYorks 201 E3
Low Stillaig 232 A3
Low Street 178 B5
Low Tharston 164 C2
Low Torry 235 E1
Low Town 220 D1
Low Toynton 188 C5
Low Wood 199 E4
Low Worsall 202 C2
Lowbands 145 G4
Lowdham 174 B3
Lowe 170 C4
Lowe Hill 171 G2
Lower Achachenna 240 C2
Lower Aisholt 115 F4
Lower Apperley 146 A5
Lower Arncott 134 B1
Lower Ashtead 121 G2
Lower Ashton 102 B4
Lower Assendon 134 C4
Lower Auchalick 232 A2
Lower Ballam 191 G4
Lower Barewood 144 C2
Lower Bartle 192 A4
Lower Bayble (Pabail Iarach) 271 H4
Lower Beeding 109 E1
Lower Benefield 161 E4
Lower Bentham (Low Bentham) 192 C1
Lower Bentley 146 B1
Lower Berry Hill 131 E1
Lower Birchwood 173 F2
Lower Boddington 147 G2
Lower Boscaswell 94 A3
Lower Bourne 120 D3
Lower Brailes 147 F4
Lower Breakish 256 C2
Lower Bredbury 184 D3
Lower Broadheath 146 A2
Lower Brynamman 128 D1
Lower Bullingham 145 E4
Lower Bullington 119 F3
Lower Burgate 106 A1
Lower Burrow 116 B5
Lower Burton 144 D2
Lower Caldecote 149 G3
Lower Cam 131 G2
Lower Cambourne 150 B2
Lower Camster 275 H4
Lower Chapel 143 G4
Lower Cheriton 103 E2
Lower Chicksgrove 118 A4
Lower Chute 119 E2
Lower Clent 158 B4
Lower Creedy 102 B2
Lower Cumberworth 185 G2
Lower Darwen 192 C5
Lower Dean 149 F1
Lower Diabaig 264 D5
Lower Dicker 110 A2
Lower Dinchope 157 D4
Lower Down 156 C4
Lower Drift 94 B4
Lower Dunsforth 194 D1
Lower Earley 134 C5
Lower Edmonton 136 C3
Lower Elkstone 172 B2
Lower End Bucks 134 B2
Lower End MK 149 E4
Lower End N'hants 149 D1
Lower Everleigh 118 C2
Lower Eythorne 125 E4
Lower Failand 131 E5
Lower Farringdon 120 C4
Lower Fittleworth 108 C2
Lower Foxdale 190 A4
Lower Freystrop 126 C1
Lower Froyle 120 C3
Lower Gabwell 101 F1
Lower Gledfield 266 C2
Lower Godney 116 B3
Lower Gravenhurst 149 G4
Lower Green Essex 150 C4
Lower Green Herts 149 G4
Lower Green Kent 123 F4
Lower Green Norf 178 A2
Lower Green Staffs 158 B2
Lower Green Bank 192 B2
Lower Halstock Leigh 104 B2
Lower Halstow 124 A2
Lower Hardres 124 D3
Lower Harpton 144 B1
Lower Hartshay 173 E2
Lower Hartwell 134 C1
Lower Hawthwaite 198 D4
Lower Haysden 123 E4
Lower Hayton 157 E4
Lower Heath 171 F1
Lower Hergest 144 B2
Lower Heyford 147 G5
Lower Higham 137 G5
Lower Holbrook 152 C4
Lower Hopton 185 G1
Lower Hordley 170 A5
Lower Horncroft 108 C2
Lower Horsebridge 110 A2
Lower Houses 185 F1
Lower Howsell 145 G3
Lower Kersal 184 C2
Lower Kilchattan 238 C5
Lower Kilcott 131 G4
Lower Killeyan 230 A5
Lower Kingcombe 104 B3
Lower Kingswood 122 B3
Lower Kinnerton 170 A1
Lower Langford 116 B1
Lower Largo 244 C4
Lower Leigh 172 B4
Lower Lemington 147 E4
Lower Lovacott 113 F3
Lower Loxhore 113 G2
Lower Lydbrook 131 E1
Lower Lye 144 D1
Lower Machen 130 B4
Lower Maes-coed 144 C4
Lower Mannington 105 G2
Lower Middleton Cheney 148 A3
Lower Milton 116 C3
Lower Moor 146 B3
Lower Morton 131 F3
Lower Nash 126 D2
Lower Nazeing 136 C2
Lower Netchwood 157 F3
Lower Nyland 117 E5
Lower Oddington 147 E5
Lower Ollach 256 B1
Lower Penarth 130 A5
Lower Penn 158 A3
Lower Pennington 106 C3
Lower Peover 184 B5
Lower Pollicott 134 C1
Lower Quinton 147 D3
Lower Race 130 B2
Lower Rainham 124 A2
Lower Roadwater 114 D4
Lower Sapey 145 F1
Lower Seagry 132 B4
Lower Shelton 149 E3
Lower Shiplake 134 C5
Lower Shuckburgh 147 G1
Lower Slaughter 147 D5
Lower Soothill 194 B5
Lower Stanton St. Quintin 132 B4
Lower Stoke 124 A1
Lower Stondon 149 G4
Lower Stone 131 F3
Lower Stonnall 158 C2
Lower Stow Bedon 164 A2
Lower Street Dorset 105 E3
Lower Street ESuss 110 C2
Lower Street Norf 179 D2
Lower Street Norf 178 C2
Lower Street Suff 152 C2
Lower Stretton 184 A4
Lower Sundon 149 F5
Lower Swanwick 107 D2
Lower Swell 147 D5
Lower Tadmarton 147 G4
Lower Tale 103 D2
Lower Tean 172 B4
Lower Thurlton 165 F2
Lower Thurnham 192 A2
Lower Town Corn 95 D4
Lower Town Devon 102 A5
Lower Town IoS 96 B1
Lower Town Pembs 140 C4
Lower Trebullett 98 D3
Lower Tysoe 147 F3
Lower Upcott 102 B4
Lower Upham 107 E1
Lower Upnor 137 G5
Lower Vexford 115 E4
Lower Wallop 156 C2
Lower Walton 184 A4
Lower Waterhay 132 C3
Lower Weald 148 C4
Lower Wear 102 C4
Lower Weare 116 B2
Lower Welson 144 B2
Lower Whatley 117 E3
Lower Whitley 184 A5
Lower Wick 146 A2
Lower Wield 120 B3
Lower Winchendon (Nether Winchendon) 134 C1
Lower Withington 171 F1
Lower Woodend 134 D4
Lower Woodford 118 C4
Lower Wyche 145 G3
Lowerhouse 193 E4
Lowertown 277 D8
Lowesby 160 C2
Lowestoft 165 G2
Loweswater 209 E4
Lowfield Heath 122 B4
Lowgill Cumb 200 B3
Lowgill Lancs 192 C1
Lowick Cumb 199 D4
Lowick N'hants 161 E4
Lowick N'umb 229 E3
Lowick Bridge 199 D4
Lowick Green 199 D4
Lownie Moor 252 C5
Lowry, The GtMan M50 3AZ 24 D3
Lowsonford 147 D1
Lowther 210 B5
Lowther Castle 210 B5
Lowthorpe 196 C1
Lowton Devon 113 G5
Lowton GtMan 184 A3
Lowton Som 103 E1
Lowton Common 184 A3
Loxbeare 102 C1
Loxhill 121 F4
Loxhore 113 G2
Loxley 147 E2
Loxley Green 172 B4
Loxton 116 A2
Loxwood 121 F4
Lubachoinnich 266 B2
Lubcroy 265 K1
Lubenham 160 C4
Lubfearn 265 K4
Lubmore 265 G6
Lubreoch 249 G5
Luccombe 114 C3
Luccombe Village 107 E4
Lucker 229 F3
Luckett 99 D3
Luckington 132 A4
Lucklawhill 244 C2
Luckwell Bridge 114 C4
Lucton 144 D1
Lucy Cross 202 B1
Ludag 254 C3
Ludborough 188 C3
Ludbrook 100 C2
Ludchurch 127 E1
Luddenden 193 G5
Luddenden Foot 193 G5
Luddenham Court 124 B2
Luddesdown 123 F2
Luddington NLincs 187 F1
Luddington Warks 147 D2
Luddington in the Brook 161 G4
Ludford Lincs 188 B4
Ludford Shrop 157 E5
Ludgershall Bucks 134 B1
Ludgershall Wilts 119 D2
Ludgvan 94 C3
Ludham 179 E4
Ludlow 157 E5
Ludney 189 D3
Ludstock 145 F4
Ludstone 158 A3
Ludwell 118 A5
Ludworth 212 C3
Luffincott 98 D1
Luffness 236 B1
Lufton 104 B1
Lugar 225 D3
Luggate 236 C2
Luggate Burn 236 D2
Luggiebank 234 B2
Lugton 233 F4
Lugwardine 145 E3
Luib 256 B2
Luibeilt 249 E3
Luing 239 G3
Lulham 144 D3
Lullington Derbys 159 E1
Lullington Som 117 E2
Lulsgate Bottom 116 C1
Lulsley 145 G2
Lulworth Camp 105 E4
Lulworth Cove & Heritage Centre Dorset BH20 5RQ 105 E5
Lumb Lancs 193 E5
Lumb WYorks 193 G5
Lumbutts 193 F5
Lumby 195 D4
Lumphanan 260 D4
Lumphinnans 243 G5
Lumsdaine 237 F3
Lumsdale 173 E1
Lumsden 260 C2
Lunan 253 E4
Lunanhead 252 C4
Luncarty 243 F2
Lund ERid 196 B3
Lund NYorks 195 F4
Lund Shet 278 E2
Lundale 270 D4
Lundavra 248 C3
Lunderston Bay Invclyd PA16 0DN 232 D2
Lunderton 269 K6
Lundie Angus 244 A1
Lundie High 257 H3
Lundin Links 244 C4
Lundwood 186 A2
Lundy 112 B1
Lunga 240 A4
Lunna 279 D6
Lunning 279 E6
Lunnon 128 B4
Lunsford's Cross 110 C2
Lunt 183 E2
Luntley 144 C2
Luppitt 103 E2
Lupset 186 A1
Lupton 199 G4
Lurgashall 121 E5
Lurignich 248 B4
Lusby 176 B1
Luss 241 F5
Lussagiven 231 E1
Lusta 263 H6
Lustleigh 102 A4
Luston 145 D1
Luthermuir 253 E3
Luthrie 244 B3
Luton Devon 103 D2
Luton Devon 102 C5
Luton Luton 149 F5
Luton Med 123 G2
Luton Airport 149 G5
Lutterworth 160 A4
Lutton Devon 100 B2
Lutton Dorset 105 F4
Lutton Lincs 176 C5
Lutton N'hants 161 G4
Luxborough 114 C4
Luxulyan 97 E4
Lybster High 275 F2
Lybster High 275 H5
Lydacott 113 E5
Lydbury North 156 C4
Lydcott 113 G2
Lydd 111 F1
Lydden 125 E4
Lyddington 161 D3
Lydd-on-Sea 111 F1
Lyde Green 131 F5
Lydeard St. Lawrence 115 E4
Lydford 99 F2
Lydford-on-Fosse 116 C4
Lydgate GtMan 185 D1
Lydgate GtMan 185 D2
Lydgate WYorks 193 F5
Lydham 156 C3
Lydiard Millicent 132 C4
Lydiard Tregoze 132 D4
Lydiate 183 E2
Lydlinch 104 D1
Lydney 131 F2
Lydstep 127 D3
Lye 158 B4
Lye Cross 116 B1
Lye Green Bucks 135 E2
Lye Green ESuss 123 E5
Lye Green Warks 147 D1
Lye's Green 117 F3
Lyford 133 F3
Lymbridge Green 124 D4
Lyme Regis 103 G3
Lymekilns 234 A4
Lyminge 125 D4
Lymington 106 C3
Lyminster 108 C3
Lymm 184 A4
Lymore 106 B3
Lympne 124 D5
Lympsham 116 A2
Lympstone 102 C4
Lynaberack 258 E5
Lynch 114 B3
Lynch Green 178 C5
Lynchat 258 E4
Lyndale House 263 J6
Lyndhurst 106 B2
Lyndon 161 E2
Lyne Aber 261 F4
Lyne ScBord 235 G5
Lyne Surr 121 F1
Lyne Down 145 F4
Lyne of Gorthleck 258 C2
Lyne of Skene 261 F3
Lyne Station 235 G5
Lyneal 170 B4
Lynegar 275 H3
Lyneham Oxon 147 E5
Lyneham Wilts 132 C5
Lyneholmeford 218 D4
Lynemore High 259 H2
Lynemore Moray 259 J1
Lynemouth 221 E2
Lyness 277 C8
Lynford 163 G3
Lyng 178 B4
Lyngate 179 E3
Lynmouth 114 A3
Lynn 157 G1
Lynsted 124 B2
Lynstone 112 C5
Lynton 114 A3
Lynton & Lynmouth Cliff Railway Devon EX35 6EP 114 A3
Lyon's Gate 104 C2
Lyonshall 144 C2
Lyrabus 230 A3
Lytchett Matravers 105 F3
Lytchett Minster 105 F3
Lyth 275 H2
Lytham 191 G5
Lytham St. Anne's 191 G5
Lythe 204 B1
Lythe Hill 121 E4
Lythes 277 D9
Lythmore 275 F2

M

M.V. Princess Pocahontas Kent DA11 0BS 137 F5
Mabe Burnthouse 95 E3
Mabie 217 D3
Mablethorpe 189 F4
Macclesfield 184 D5
Macclesfield Forest 185 D5
Macduff 269 F4
Macedonia 244 A4
Machan 234 B4
Machany 243 D3
Macharioch 222 C5
Machen 130 B4
Machrie A&B 230 A3
Machrie A&B 230 B5
Machrie NAyr 223 D2
Machrihanish 222 B3
Machrins 238 C5
Machynlleth 154 D2
McInroy's Point 232 D2
Mackerye End 136 A1
Mackworth 173 E4
Macmerry 236 B2
Macterry 269 F6
Madame Tussauds GtLon NW1 5LR 12 A4
Madderty 243 E2
Maddiston 234 D2
Madehurst 108 B2
Madeley Staffs 171 E3
Madeley Tel&W 157 G2
Madeley Heath 171 E3
Maders 98 D3
Madford 103 E1
Madingley 150 B1
Madjeston 117 F5
Madley 144 D4
Madresfield 146 A3
Madron 94 B3
Maenaddwyn 180 C4
Maenclochog 141 D5
Maendy Cardiff 130 A5
Maendy VGlam 129 G5
Maenporth 95 E4
Maentwrog 167 F3
Maen-y-groes 141 G2
Maer Corn 112 C5
Maer Staffs 171 E4
Maerdy Carmar 142 C5
Maerdy Carmar 142 C5
Maerdy Conwy 168 D3
Maerdy RCT 129 F3
Maesbrook 169 F5
Maesbury Marsh 170 A5
Maes-glas 130 B4
Maesgwynne 141 F5
Maeshafn 169 F1
Maesllyn 141 G3
Maesmynis 143 G3
Maesteg 129 E3
Maes-Treylow 144 B1
Maesybont 128 B1
Maesycrugiau 142 A3
Maesycwmmer 130 A3
Magdalen Laver 137 E2
Maggieknockater 268 B6
Maggots End 150 C5
Magham Down 110 B2
Maghull 183 E2
Magna Centre, Rotherham SYorks S60 1DX 21 C1
Magna Park 160 A4
Magor 130 D4
Magpie Green 164 B4
Maiden Bradley 117 E4
Maiden Head 116 C1
Maiden Law 212 A3
Maiden Newton 104 B3
Maiden Wells 126 C3
Maidencombe 101 F1
Maidenhayne 103 F3
Maidenhead 135 D4
Maidens 224 A5
Maiden's Green 135 D5
Maidensgrove 134 C4
Maidenwell Corn 97 F2
Maidenwell Lincs 188 D5
Maidford 148 B2
Maids' Moreton 148 C4
Maidstone 123 G3
Maidwell 160 C5
Mail 279 D10
Maindee 130 C4
Mainland Ork 277 B6
Mainland Shet 279 C7
Mains of Ardestie 244 D1
Mains of Balgavies 252 D4
Mains of Balhall 252 D3
Mains of Ballindarg 252 C4
Mains of Burgie 267 H6
Mains of Culsh 269 G6
Mains of Dillavaird 253 F1
Mains of Drum 261 G4
Mains of Dudwick 261 H1
Mains of Faillie 258 E1
Mains of Fedderate 269 G6
Mains of Glack 261 F2
Mains of Glassaugh 268 D4
Mains of Glenbuchat 260 B3
Mains of Linton 261 F3
Mains of Melgund 252 D4
Mains of Pitfour 269 H6
Mains of Pittrichie 261 G2
Mains of Sluie 267 H6
Mains of Tannachy 268 B4
Mains of Thornton 253 E2
Mains of Tig 214 C2
Mains of Watten 275 H3
Mainsforth 212 C4
Mainsriddle 216 D5
Mainstone 156 B4
Maisemore 146 A5
Major's Green 158 D5
Makendon 220 A1
Makeney 173 E3
Makerstoun 228 A3
Malacleit 262 C4
Malborough 100 D4
Malden Rushett 121 G1
Maldon 138 B2
Malham 193 F1
Maligar 263 K5
Malinbridge 186 A4
Mallaig (Malaig) 256 C5
Mallaigmore 256 C5
Mallaigvaig 256 C5
Malleny Mills 235 F3
Malletsheugh 233 G4
Malling 242 A4
Mallows Green 150 C5
Malltraeth 166 D1
Mallwyd 155 E1
Malmesbury 132 B4
Malmsmead 114 A3
Malpas ChesW&C 170 B3
Malpas Corn 96 C5
Malpas Newport 130 C3
Maltby Lincs 188 D4
Maltby Stock 203 D1
Maltby SYorks 186 C3
Maltby le Marsh 189 E4
Malting End 151 F2
Malting Green 138 C1
Maltman's Hill 124 A4
Malton 203 G5
Malvern Link 145 G3
Malvern Wells 145 G3
Mambeg 232 D1
Mamble 157 F5
Mamhead 102 C4
Mamhilad 130 C2
Manaccan 95 E4
Manadon 100 A2
Manafon 156 A2
Manaton 102 A4
Manby 189 D4
Mancetter 159 F3
Manchester 184 C3
Manchester Airport 184 C4
Manchester Apollo GtMan M12 6AP 47 H6
Manchester Art Gallery GtMan M2 3JL 47 E4
Manchester Central GtMan M2 3GX 46 D5
Manchester Craft & Design Centre GtMan M4 5JD 47 F3
Manchester Museum GtMan M13 9PL 47 F7
Manchester United Museum & Stadium Tour Centre GtMan M16 0RA 24 D3
Mancot Royal 170 A1
Mandally (Manndalaidh) 257 J4
Manea 162 C4
Maneight 224 D5
Manfield 202 B1
Mangaster 278 C5
Mangerton 104 A3
Mangotsfield 131 F5
Mangrove Green 149 G5
Mangurstadh 270 C4
Manish (Manais) 263 G3
Mankinholes 193 F5
Manley 183 G5
Manmoel 130 A2
Mannal 246 A2
Manningford Abbots 118 C2
Manningford Bohune 118 C2
Manningford Bruce 118 C2
Manningham 194 A4
Mannings Amusement Park Suff IP11 2DW 153 D4
Mannings Heath 109 E1
Mannington 105 G2
Manningtree 152 C4
Mannofield 261 H4
Manor Farm Country Park Hants SO30 2ER 4 D3
Manor Park 135 E4
Manorbier 127 D3
Manorbier Newton 126 D2
Manordeifi 141 F3
Manordeilo 142 C5
Manorowen 140 C4
Mansell Gamage 144 C3
Mansell Lacy 144 D3
Mansergh 200 B4
Mansfield 173 G1
Mansfield Woodhouse 173 G1
Manson Green 178 B5
Mansriggs 199 D4
Manston Dorset 105 E1
Manston Kent 125 F2
Manston WYorks 194 C4
Manswood 105 F2
Manthorpe Lincs 161 F1
Manthorpe Lincs 175 E4
Manton NLincs 187 G2
Manton Notts 186 C5
Manton Rut 161 D2
Manton Wilts 118 C1
Manuden 150 C5
Manwood Green 137 E1
Maolachy 240 A3
Maperton 117 D5
Maple Cross 135 F3
Maplebeck 174 C1
Mapledurham 134 B5
Mapledurwell 120 B2
Maplehurst 121 G5
Maplescombe 123 E2
Mapleton 172 C3
Mapperley Derbys 173 F3
Mapperley Notts 173 G3
Mapperton Dorset 104 B3
Mapperton Dorset 105 F3
Mappleborough Green 146 C1
Mappleton 197 E3
Mapplewell 186 A2
Mappowder 104 D2
Mar Lodge 259 H5
Maraig (Maaruig) 270 E7
Marazion 94 C3
Marbhig 271 G6
Marbury 170 C3
Marbury Country Park ChesW&C CW9 6AT 184 A5
March 162 C3
Marcham 133 G3
Marchamley 170 C5
Marchamley Wood 170 C4
Marchington 172 C4
Marchington Woodlands 172 C5
Marchwiel 170 A3
Marchwood 106 C1
Marcross 114 C1
Marcus 252 D4
Marden Here 145 E3
Marden Kent 123 G4
Marden T&W 221 F4
Marden Wilts 118 B2
Marden Ash 137 E2
Marden Beech 123 G4
Marden Thorn 123 G4
Marden's Hill 123 D5
Mardon 228 D3
Mardy 130 C1
Mare Green 116 A5
Marefield 160 C2
Mareham le Fen 176 A1
Mareham on the Hill 176 A1
Maresfield 109 G1
Marfleet 196 D4
Marford 170 A2
Margam 129 D4
Margam Country Park NPT SA13 2TJ 129 E4
Margaret Marsh 105 E1
Margaret Roding 137 E1
Margaretting 137 F2
Margaretting Tye 137 F2
Margate 125 F1
Margnaheglish 223 F2

Margreig 216 C3
Margrove Park 203 F1
Marham 163 F2
Marhamchurch 112 C5
Marholm 161 G2
Marian Cwm 182 B5
Mariandyrys 181 E4
Marian-glas 180 D4
Mariansleigh 114 A5
Marine Town 124 B1
Marishader 263 K5
Maristow House 100 A1
Mark 116 A3
Mark Causeway 116 A3
Mark Cross 123 E5
Markbeech 123 D4
Markby 189 E5
Markdhu 214 C3
Markeaton 173 E2
Markeaton Park Craft Village Derby DE22 3BG 18 A3
Market Bosworth 159 G2
Market Bosworth Country Park Leics CV13 0LP 159 G2
Market Deeping 161 G1
Market Drayton 171 D4
Market Harborough 160 C4
Market Lavington 118 C2
Market Overton 161 D1
Market Rasen 188 B4
Market Stainton 188 C5
Market Street 179 D3
Market Warsop 173 G1
Market Weighton 196 A3
Market Weston 164 A4
Markethill 244 A1
Markfield 159 G1
Markham 130 A2
Markham Moor 187 E5
Markinch 244 A4
Markington 194 B1
Marks Gate 137 D3
Marks Tey 152 A5
Marksbury 117 D1
Markwell 99 D5
Markyate 135 F1
Marl Bank 145 G3
Marland 184 C1
Marlborough 118 C1
Marlbrook 158 B5
Marlcliff 146 C2
Marldon 101 E1
Marle Green 110 A2
Marlesford 153 E2
Marley Green 170 C3
Marley Hill 212 B2
Marlingford 178 C5
Marloes 126 A1
Marlow Bucks 134 C4
Marlow Here 156 D5
Marlpit Hill 122 D4
Marlpool 173 F3
Marnhull 105 D1
Marnoch 268 D5
Marple 185 D4
Marple Bridge 185 D4
Marr 186 C2
Marrel 275 F7
Marrick 201 F3
Marrister 279 E6
Marros 127 F2
Marsden T&W 212 C1
Marsden WYorks 185 E1
Marsett 201 E4
Marsh 103 F1
Marsh Baldon 134 A3
Marsh Benham 119 F1
Marsh Farm Country Park Essex CM3 5WP 138 B3
Marsh Gibbon 148 B5
Marsh Green Devon 102 D3
Marsh Green GtMan 183 G2
Marsh Green Kent 122 D4
Marsh Green Tel&W 157 F1
Marsh Lane 186 B5
Marsh Street 114 C3
Marshall Meadows 237 G4
Marshalsea 103 G2
Marshalswick 136 A2
Marsham 178 C3
Marshaw 192 B2
Marshborough 125 F3
Marshbrook 156 D4
Marshchapel 189 D3
Marshfield Newport 130 B4
Marshfield SGlos 131 G5
Marshgate 98 B1
Marshland St. James 162 D2
Marshside 183 E1
Marshwood 103 G3
Marske 202 A2
Marske-by-the-Sea 213 F5
Marsland Green 184 A3
Marston ChesW&C 184 A5
Marston Here 144 C2
Marston Lincs 175 D3
Marston Oxon 134 A2
Marston Staffs 171 G5
Marston Staffs 158 A1
Marston Wilts 118 A2
Marston Warks 159 E3
Marston Doles 147 G2
Marston Green 158 D4
Marston Magna 116 C5
Marston Meysey 132 D3
Marston Montgomery 172 C4
Marston Moretaine 149 E3
Marston on Dove 172 D5
Marston St. Lawrence 148 A3
Marston Stannett 145 E2
Marston Trussell 160 B4
Marston Vale Millennium Country Park CenBeds MK43 0PR 149 F3

Marstow 131 E1
Marsworth 135 E1
Marten 119 D1
Marthall 184 B5
Martham 179 F4
Martin Hants 105 G1
Martin Lincs 175 G2
Martin Lincs 176 A1
Martin Drove End 118 B5
Martin Hussingtree 146 A1
Martin Mere Lancs L40 0TA 183 F1
Martinhoe 113 G1
Martinscroft 184 A4
Martinstown 104 C4
Martlesham 152 D3
Martlesham Heath 152 D3
Martletwy 126 D1
Martley 145 G1
Martock 104 A1
Marton ChesE 171 F1
Marton Cumb 198 D5
Marton ERid 197 D4
Marton ERid 197 E1
Marton Lincs 187 F4
Marton Middl 203 E1
Marton NYorks 194 D1
Marton NYorks 203 G4
Marton Shrop 156 B3
Marton Shrop 170 B5
Marton Warks 147 G1
Marton Abbey 195 E1
Marton-in-the-Forest 195 E1
Marton-le-Moor 202 C5
Martyr Worthy 119 G4
Martyr's Green 121 F2
Marwell Zoo Hants SO21 1JH 4 D1
Marwick 276 B5
Marwood 113 F2
Mary Rose PO1 3LX 82 Portsmouth
Mary Tavy 99 F3
Marybank (An Lagaidh) High 266 B6
Marybank Wisles 271 G4
Maryburgh (Baile Mairi) 266 C6
Maryfield Corn 100 A2
Maryfield Shet 279 D8
Marygold 237 F4
Maryhill Aber 269 G6
Maryhill Glas 233 G3
Marykirk 253 E2
Marylebone GtLon 136 B4
Marylebone GtMan 183 G2
Marypark 259 J1
Maryport Cumb 208 D3
Maryport D&G 206 B3
Marystow 99 E2
Maryton 253 E4
Marywell Aber 261 H5
Marywell Aber 260 H5
Marywell Angus 253 E5
Masham 202 B4
Mashbury 137 F1
Masongill 200 B5
Mastin Moor 186 B5
Mastrick 261 H4
Matchborough 146 C1
Matching 137 E1
Matching Green 137 E1
Matching Tye 137 E1
Matfen 220 C4
Matfield 123 F4
Mathern 131 E3
Mathon 145 G3
Mathry 140 B4
Matlaske 178 C2
Matlock 173 E1
Matlock Bank 173 E1
Matlock Bath 173 D2
Matson 131 G1
Matterdale End 209 G4
Mattersey 187 D4
Mattersey Thorpe 187 D4
Mattingley 120 C2
Mattishall 178 B4
Mattishall Burgh 178 B4
Mauchline 224 C3
Maud 269 H6
Maudlin 100 C2
Maugersbury 147 D5
Maughold 190 C2
Mauld 257 K1
Maulden 149 F4
Maulds Meaburn 200 B1
Maunby 202 C4
Maund Bryan 145 E2
Maundown 115 D5
Mautby 179 F4
Mavesyn Ridware 158 C1
Mavis Enderby 176 B1
Maw Green 171 E2
Mawbray 209 D2
Mawdesley 183 F1
Mawdlam 129 E4
Mawgan 95 E4
Mawgan Porth 96 C3
Mawla 96 B5
Mawnan 95 E4
Mawnan Smith 95 E4
Mawsley 160 D5
Mawthorpe 189 E5
Maxey 161 G2
Maxstoke 159 E4
Maxted Street 124 D4
Maxton Kent 125 F4
Maxton ScBord 228 A3
Maxwellheugh 228 B3
Maxwelltown 217 D3
Maxworthy 98 C1
May Hill 145 G5
Mayals 128 C3
Maybole 224 B5
Maybury 121 F2
Mayen 268 D6
Mayfair 136 B4
Mayfield ESuss 110 A2
Mayfield Midlo 236 A3

Mayfield Staffs 172 C3
Mayford 121 E2
Mayland 138 C2
Maylandsea 138 C2
Maynard's Green 110 A2
Maypole IoS 96 B1
Maypole Kent 125 D2
Maypole Mon 131 D1
Maypole Green Essex 152 A5
Maypole Green Norf 165 F2
Maypole Green Suff 153 D1
Maypole Green Suff 152 A2
May's Green NSom 116 A1
Mays Green Oxon 134 C4
Maywick 279 C10
Mead 112 C4
Mead End 118 B5
Meadgate 117 D2
Meadle 134 D2
Meadow Green 145 G2
Meadowhall 186 A3
Meadowmill 236 B2
Meadowtown 156 C2
Meadwell 99 E2
Meaford 171 F4
Meal Bank 199 G3
Mealabost 271 G4
Mealasta 270 C5
Meals 189 E3
Mealsgate 209 F2
Meanley 192 D3
Meanwood 194 B4
Mearbeck 193 E1
Meare 116 B3
Meare Green 115 F5
Mearns 234 B4
Mears Ashby 148 D1
Measham 159 F1
Meath op 199 F4
Meavy 100 B1
Medbourne 160 D3
Meddon 112 C4
Meden Vale 173 G1
Medlar 192 A4
Medmenham 134 D4
Medomsley 212 A2
Medstead 120 B4
Meer Common 144 C2
Meer End 159 E5
Meerbrook 171 G1
Meesden 150 C4
Meeson 171 D5
Meeth 113 F5
Meeting House Hill 179 E3
Meggethead 226 C3
Meidrim 141 F5
Meifod Denb 168 D2
Meifod Powys 156 A1
Meigle 252 A5
Meikle Earnock 234 B4
Meikle Grenach 232 B3
Meikle Kilmory 232 B3
Meikle Rahane 232 D1
Meikle Strath 253 E2
Meikle Tarty 261 H2
Meikle Wartle 261 F1
Meikleour 243 G1
Meikleyard 224 D2
Meinciau 128 A1
Meir 171 G3
Meirheath 171 G3
Melbost 271 G4
Melbost Borve (Mealabost) 271 G2
Melbourn 150 B3
Melbourne Derbys 173 E5
Melbourne ERid 195 G3
Melbury 113 D4
Melbury Abbas 105 E1
Melbury Bubb 104 B2
Melbury Osmond 104 B2
Melbury Sampford 104 B2
Melby 279 A7
Melchbourne 149 F1
Melcombe Bingham 105 D2
Melcombe Regis 104 C4
Meldon Devon 99 F1
Meldon N'umb 220 D3
Meldreth 150 B3
Meledor 96 D4
Melfort 240 A3
Melgarve 258 B5
Melgum 260 C4
Meliden (Gallt Melyd) 182 B4
Melincourt 129 E2
Melin-y-coed 168 B1
Melin-y-ddol 155 G2
Melin-y-grug 155 G2
Melin-y-Wig 168 D3
Melkinthorpe 210 B5
Melkridge 210 D1
Melksham 118 A1
Melksham Forest 118 A1
Melldalloch 232 A2
Melling Lancs 199 G5
Melling Mersey 183 E2
Melling Mount 183 F2
Mellis 164 B4
Mellon Charles 264 E2
Mellon Udrigle 264 E2
Mellor GtMan 185 D4
Mellor Lancs 192 C4
Mellor Brook 192 C4
Mells 117 E3
Melmerby Cumb 210 C4
Melmerby NYorks 201 F4
Melmerby NYorks 202 C5
Melplash 104 A3
Melrose Aber 269 F4
Melrose ScBord 227 G2
Melsetter 277 B9
Melsonby 202 A2
Meltham 185 D2
Melton ERid 196 B5
Melton Suff 153 D2
Melton Constable 178 B2

Melton Mowbray 160 C1
Melton Ross 188 A1
Meltonby 195 G2
Melvaig 264 D3
Melverley 156 C1
Melverley Green 156 C1
Melvich 274 D2
Membury 103 F2
Memsie 269 H4
Memus 252 C4
Menabilly 97 E4
Menai Bridge (Porthaethwy) 181 D5
Mendham 165 D3
Mendlesham 152 C1
Mendlesham Green 152 B1
Menethorpe 195 G1
Menheniot 97 G3
Menie House 261 H2
Menithwood 145 G1
Mennock 225 A3
Menston 194 A3
Menstrie 242 D5
Mentmore 135 E1
Meoble 247 G1
Meole Brace 157 D1
Meonstoke 107 E1
Meon 107 E2
Meopham 123 F2
Meopham Green 123 F2
Mepal 162 C4
Meppershall 149 G4
Merbach 144 C3
Mercaston 173 D3
Mere ChesE 184 B4
Mere Wilts 117 F4
Mere Brow 183 F1
Mere Green 158 D3
Mere Heath 184 A5
Mereclough 193 E4
Mereside 191 G4
Meretown 171 E5
Mereworth 123 F3
Mergie 253 F1
Meriden 159 E4
Merkadale 255 J1
Merkinch 266 D7
Merkland 216 B3
Merley 105 G3
Merlin's Bridge 126 C1
Merridge 115 F4
Merrifield 101 E3
Merrington 170 B5
Merrion 126 C3
Merriott 104 A1
Merrivale 99 F3
Merrow 121 F2
Merry Hill Herts 136 A3
Merry Hill WMid 158 B4
Merry Hill WMid 158 A3
Merrymeet 97 G3
Mersea Island 138 D1
Mersey Ferries Mersey CH44 6QY 42 A4
Merseyside Maritime Museum Mersey L3 4AQ 42 B5
Mersham 124 C5
Merstham 122 B3
Merston 108 A3
Merstone 107 E4
Merther 96 C5
Merthyr 141 G5
Merthyr Cynog 143 F4
Merthyr Dyfan 115 E1
Merthyr Mawr 129 E5
Merthyr Tydfil 129 G2
Merthyr Vale 129 G3
Merton Devon 113 F4
Merton Norf 164 A2
Merton Oxon 134 A1
Mervinslaw 228 A5
Meshaw 102 A1
Messing 138 C1
Messingham 187 F2
Metcombe 103 D3
Metfield 165 D3
Metherell 100 A1
Metheringham 175 F1
Methil 244 B5
Methlem 166 A4
Methley 194 C5
Methley Junction 194 C5
Methlick 261 G1
Methven 243 F2
Methwold 163 F3
Methwold Hythe 163 F3
Mettingham 165 E3
Metton 178 C2
Mevagissey 97 E5
Mewith Head 192 D1
Mexborough 186 B3
Mey 275 H1
Meysey Hampton 132 D2
Miabhag Wisles 263 G2
Miabhag Wisles 270 C7
Mial 264 D4
Miavaig (Miabhaig) 270 C4
Michaelchurch 145 E5
Michaelchurch Escley 144 C4
Michaelchurch-on-Arrow 144 B2
Michaelston-le-Pit 130 A5
Michaelston-super-Ely 130 A5
Michaelston-y-Fedw 130 B4
Michaelstow 97 E2
Michelcombe 100 C1
Micheldever 119 G4
Michelmersh 119 E5
Mickfield 152 C1
Mickle Trafford 170 B1
Micklebring 186 C3
Mickleby 204 B1
Micklefield 194 D4
Micklefield Green 135 F3
Mickleham 121 G2
Micklehurst 185 D2
Mickleover 173 E4

Micklethwaite Cumb 209 F1
Micklethwaite WYorks 193 G3
Mickleton Dur 211 F5
Mickleton Glos 147 D3
Mickletown 194 C5
Mickley Derbys 186 A5
Mickley NYorks 202 B5
Mickley Green 151 G2
Mickley Square 211 G1
Mid Ardlaw 269 H4
Mid Beltie 260 E4
Mid Calder 235 E3
Mid Clyth 275 H5
Mid Lambrook 104 A1
Mid Lavant 108 A3
Mid Letter 240 C4
Mid Lix 242 A1
Mid Mossdale 200 D3
Mid Yell 278 E3
Midbea 276 D3
Middle Assendon 134 C4
Middle Aston 147 G5
Middle Barton 147 G5
Middle Bickenhill 159 E4
Middle Bockhampton 106 A3
Middle Claydon 148 C5
Middle Drift 97 F3
Middle Drums 253 D4
Middle Duntisbourne 132 B2
Middle Handley 186 B5
Middle Harling 164 A3
Middle Kames 232 A1
Middle Littleton 146 C3
Middle Maes-coed 144 C4
Middle Marwood 113 F2
Middle Mill 140 B5
Middle Quarter 124 A5
Middle Rasen 188 A4
Middle Rigg 243 F4
Middle Salter 192 C1
Middle Sontley 170 A3
Middle Stoford 115 E5
Middle Taphouse 97 F3
Middle Town 96 A1
Middle Tysoe 147 F3
Middle Wallop 119 D4
Middle Winterslow 118 D4
Middle Woodford 118 C4
Middlebie 218 A4
Middlecliff 186 B2
Middlecott 113 E5
Middleham 202 A4
Middlehill Aber 269 G6
Middlehill Corn 97 G3
Middlehope 157 E4
Middlemarsh 104 C2
Middlemoor 99 E3
Middlequarter (Ceathramh Meadhanach) 262 D4
Middlesbrough 213 D5
Middlesceugh 210 A3
Middleshaw 199 G4
Middlesmoor 201 F5
Middlestone 212 B4
Middlestone Moor 212 B4
Middlestown 185 G1
Middlethird 228 A4
Middleton Aber 261 G3
Middleton Angus 253 D5
Middleton Cumb 200 B4
Middleton Derbys 173 D2
Middleton Derbys 172 C1
Middleton Essex 151 G3
Middleton GtMan 184 C2
Middleton Hants 119 F3
Middleton Here 145 E1
Middleton Lancs 192 A2
Middleton Midlo 236 A4
Middleton N'hants 160 D4
Middleton N'umb 220 D3
Middleton N'umb 229 E3
Middleton Norf 163 E1
Middleton NYorks 203 G4
Middleton P&K 243 F4
Middleton P&K 251 G5
Middleton Shrop 156 B3
Middleton Shrop 157 E5
Middleton Shrop 170 A5
Middleton Suff 153 F1
Middleton Swan 128 A4
Middleton Warks 159 D3
Middleton WYorks 194 A3
Middleton WYorks 194 C5
Middleton Baggot 157 F3
Middleton Bank Top 220 D3
Middleton Cheney 147 G3
Middleton Green 171 G3
Middleton Hall 229 D4
Middleton Moor 153 F1
Middleton of Potterton 261 H3
Middleton on the Hill 145 E1
Middleton One Row 202 C1
Middleton Park 261 H3
Middleton Priors 157 F4
Middleton Quernhow 202 C5
Middleton St. George 202 C1
Middleton Scriven 157 F4
Middleton Stoney 148 A5
Middleton Tyas 202 B2
Middleton-in-Teesdale 211 F5
Middleton-on-Leven 203 D1
Middleton-on-Sea 108 B3
Middleton-on-the-Wolds 196 B3
Middletown Cumb 198 A2
Middletown Powys 156 C1
Middlewich 171 E1
Middlewood ChesE 184 D4
Middlewood SYorks 186 A3
Middlewood Green 152 B1
Middlezoy 116 A4

Middridge 212 B5
Midfield 273 H2
Midford 117 D1
Midge Hall 192 B5
Midgeholme 210 C2
Midgham 119 G1
Midgley WYorks 185 G1
Midgley WYorks 193 G5
Midhurst 121 D5
Midland Railway Centre Derbys DE5 3QZ 173 F2
Midlem 227 G3
Midloe Grange 149 G1
Midpark 232 B3
Midsomer Norton 117 D2
Midthorpe 188 C5
Midtown High 273 H2
Midtown High 264 E3
Midtown of Barras 253 G2
Midville 176 B2
Midway 173 E5
Migdale 266 D2
Migvie 260 C4
Milarrochy 241 G5
Milber 102 B5
Milbethill 268 E5
Milborne Port 104 C1
Milborne St. Andrew 105 D3
Milborne Wick 117 D5
Milbourne N'umb 220 D4
Milbourne Wilts 132 B4
Milburn 210 C5
Milbury Heath 131 F3
Milcombe 147 G4
Milden 152 A3
Mildenhall Suff 163 F5
Mildenhall Wilts 118 D1
Mile Elm 118 A1
Mile End Essex 152 A5
Mile End Glos 131 E1
Mile End Park GtLon E3 4HL 12 D4
Mile Oak 123 E2
Mile Town 124 B1
Milebrook 156 C5
Milebush 123 G4
Mileham 178 A4
Miles Green 171 F3
Miles Hope 145 E1
Milesmark 235 E1
Mile's Green 119 G1
Milfield 228 D3
Milford Derbys 173 E3
Milford Devon 112 C3
Milford Shrop 170 B5
Milford Staffs 171 G5
Milford Surr 121 E3
Milford Haven (Aberdaugleddau) 126 B2
Milford on Sea 106 A3
Milkwall 131 E2
Milky Way Adventure Park Devon EX39 5RY 112 D3
Mill Bank 193 G5
Mill Brow 185 D4
Mill End Bucks 134 C4
Mill End Cambs 151 E2
Mill End Herts 150 B4
Mill End Green 151 E5
Mill Green Cambs 151 E3
Mill Green Essex 137 F2
Mill Green Herts 136 B2
Mill Green Norf 164 C3
Mill Green Shrop 171 D5
Mill Green Staffs 172 B5
Mill Green Suff 153 E1
Mill Green Suff 152 C2
Mill Green Suff 152 A2
Mill Green WMid 158 C2
Mill Hill B'burn 192 C5
Mill Hill Cambs 150 A2
Mill Hill GtLon 136 B3
Mill Houses 192 C1
Mill Lane 120 C2
Mill of Camsail 233 D1
Mill of Colp 269 F6
Mill of Elrick 269 H6
Mill of Fortune 242 C2
Mill of Kingoodie 261 G2
Mill of Monquich 261 G5
Mill of Uras 253 G1
Mill Side 199 F4
Mill Street Kent 123 F3
Mill Street Norf 178 B4
Milland 120 D5
Millbank 269 J6
Millbeck 209 F4
Millbounds 276 E4
Millbreck 269 J6
Millbridge 120 D3
Millbrook CenBeds 149 F4
Millbrook Corn 100 A2
Millbrook Devon 103 G3
Millbrook Soton 106 C1
Millburn Aber 260 E1
Millburn Aber 260 E2
Millcombe 101 E3
Millcorner 110 D1
Milldale 172 C2
Millden 261 H3
Milldens 252 D4
Millearne 243 E2
Millend 147 F5
Millenheath 170 C4
Millennium Seed Bank, Wakehurst Place WSuss RH17 6TN 122 C5
Millerhill 236 A3
Miller's Dale 185 F5
Millers Green Derbys 173 D2
Miller's Green Essex 137 E1
Millgate 193 E5
Millhalf 144 B3
Millhayes Devon 103 E1
Millhayes Devon 103 F2
Millholme 199 G3

Millhouse A&B 232 A2
Millhouse Cumb 209 G3
Millhouse Green 185 G2
Millhousebridge 217 F2
Millikenpark 233 F3
Millin Cross 126 C1
Millington 196 A2
Millington Green 173 D3
Millmeece 171 F4
Millness 257 K1
Millom 198 C3
Millow 150 A3
Millpool 97 F3
Millport 232 C4
Millthorpe 186 A5
Milltimber 261 G4
Milltown Aber 259 K4
Milltown Corn 97 F4
Milltown D&G 218 B4
Milltown Derbys 173 E1
Milltown Devon 113 F2
Milltown High 267 G7
Milltown of Aberdalgie 243 F2
Milltown of Auchindoun 260 B1
Milltown of Craigston 269 F5
Milltown of Edinvillie 267 K7
Milltown of Kildrummy 260 C3
Milltown of Rothiemay 268 D6
Milltown of Towie 260 C3
Milnathort 243 G4
Milners Heath 170 B1
Milngavie 233 G2
Milnrow 184 D1
Milnsbridge 185 F1
Milnthorpe 199 F4
Milovaig 263 G6
Milrig 224 D2
Milson 157 F5
Milstead 124 B3
Milston 118 C3
Milton Angus 252 B5
Milton Cambs 150 C1
Milton Cumb 210 B1
Milton D&G 216 C3
Milton D&G 216 C3
Milton D&G 214 D5
Milton Derbys 173 E5
Milton High 265 K6
Milton High 266 E4
Milton High 267 G6
Milton High 266 C7
Milton High 275 F3
Milton (Baile a' Mhuilinn) High 258 B1
Milton Moray 268 D4
Milton Newport 130 C4
Milton Notts 187 E5
Milton NSom 116 A1
Milton Oxon 147 G4
Milton Oxon 133 G3
Milton P&K 243 E1
Milton Pembs 126 D2
Milton Ports 107 F3
Milton Som 116 B5
Milton Stir 171 G2
Milton Stoke 171 G2
Milton WDun 233 F2
Milton Abbas 105 D2
Milton Abbot 99 E3
Milton Bridge 235 G3
Milton Bryan 149 E4
Milton Clevedon 117 D4
Milton Combe 100 A1
Milton Country Park Cambs CB24 6AZ 150 C1
Milton Damerel 113 D4
Milton End 131 G1
Milton Ernest 149 F2
Milton Green 170 B2
Milton Hill 133 G3
Milton Keynes 149 D4
Milton Keynes Village 149 D4
Milton Lilbourne 118 C1
Milton Malsor 148 C2
Milton Morenish 242 B1
Milton of Auchinhove 260 D4
Milton of Balgonie 244 B4
Milton of Buchanan 241 G5
Milton of Cairnborrow 268 C6
Milton of Callander 242 A4
Milton of Campfield 260 E4
Milton of Campsie 234 A2
Milton of Coldwells 261 H1
Milton of Cullerlie 261 F4
Milton of Cushnie 260 D3
Milton of Dalcapon 251 E4
Milton of Inveramsay 261 F2
Milton of Noth 260 D2
Milton of Tullich 260 B5
Milton on Stour 117 E5
Milton Regis 124 B2
Milton Street 110 A3
Miltonduff 267 J5
Miltonhill 267 H5
Miltonise 214 C3
Milton-Lockhart 234 C5
Milton-under-Wychwood 133 E1
Milverton Som 115 E5
Milverton Warks 147 F1
Milwich 171 G4
Mimbridge 121 E1
Minack Theatre Corn TR19 6JU 94 A4
Minard 240 B4
Minard Castle 240 B5
Minchington 105 F1
Minchinhampton 132 A2
Mindrum 228 C3
Mindrummill 228 C3

Minehead **114** C3
Minera **169** F2
Minety **132** C3
Minety Lower Moor **132** C3
Minffordd *Gwyn* **154** D1
Minffordd *Gwyn* **167** E4
Minffordd *Gwyn* **181** D5
Miningsby **176** B1
Minions **97** G2
Minishant **224** B4
Minley Manor **120** D2
Minllyn **155** E1
Minnes **261** H2
Minngearraidh **254** C2
Minnigaff **215** F4
Minnonie **269** F4
Minskip **194** C1
Minstead **106** B1
Minsted **121** D5
Minster *Kent* **124** B1
Minster *Kent* **125** F2
Minster Lovell **133** F1
Minsteracres **211** G2
Minsterley **156** C2
Minsterworth **131** G1
Minterne Magna **104** C2
Minterne Parva **104** C2
Minting **188** B5
Mintlaw **269** J6
Minto **227** G3
Minton **156** D3
Minwear **126** D1
Minworth **159** D3
Miodar **246** B1
Mirbister **277** C6
Mirehouse **208** C5
Mireland **275** J2
Mirfield **194** B5
Miserden **132** B2
Miskin *RCT* **129** G4
Miskin *RCT* **129** G3
Misselfore **118** B5
Misson **187** D3
Misterton *Leics* **160** A4
Misterton *Notts* **187** E3
Misterton *Som* **104** A2
Mistley **152** C4
Mitcham **122** B2
Mitchel Troy **131** D1
Mitcheldean **131** F1
Mitchell **96** C4
Mitchelland **199** F3
Mitcheltroy
   Common **131** D2
Mitford **221** D3
Mithian **96** B4
Mitton **158** A1
Mixbury **148** B4
Mixenden **193** G5
Moar **250** A5
Moat **218** C4
Moats Tye **152** B2
Mobberley *ChesE* **184** B5
Mobberley *Staffs* **172** B3
Moccas **144** C3
Mochdre *Conwy* **181** G5
Mochdre *Powys* **155** G4
Mochrum **206** D2
Mockbeggar *Hants* **106** A2
Mockbeggar *Kent* **123** G4
Mockerkin **209** D4
Modbury **100** C2
Moddershall **171** G4
Modern Art Oxford *Oxon*
   OX1 1BP **80** Oxford
Modsarie **273** J2
Moel Famau Country Park
   Denb LL15 1US **169** E1
Moelfre *IoA* **180** D4
Moelfre *Powys* **169** E5
Moffat **226** B5
Mogerhanger **149** G3
Moin'a'choire **230** B3
Moine House **273** H3
Moira **159** F1
Molash **124** C3
Mol-chlach **255** K3
Mold (Yr Wyddgrug) **169** F1
Molehill Green
   Essex **151** D5
Molehill Green
   Essex **151** F5
Molescroft **196** C3
Molesden **221** D3
Molesworth **161** F5
Mollance **216** B4
Molland **114** B5
Mollington
   ChesW&C **183** E5
Mollington *Oxon* **147** G3
Mollinsburn **234** B2
Monach Islands (Heisker
   Islands) **262** B5
Monachty **142** B1
Monachyle **241** G3
Monevechadan **241** D4
Monewden **152** D2
Moneydie **243** F2
Moneyrow Green **135** D5
Moniaive **216** B1
Monifieth **244** D1
Monikie Country Park
   Angus DD5 3QN **244** C1
Monimail **244** A3
Monington **141** E3
Monk Bretton **186** A2
Monk Fryston **195** E5
Monk Hesleden **213** D4
Monk Sherborne **120** B2
Monk Soham **152** D1
Monk Soham Green **152** D1
Monk Street **151** E5
Monken Hadley **136** B3
Monkerton **102** C3
Monkey Mates *W'ham*
   RG41 1JA **134** C5
Monkey World, Wareham
   Dorset
   BH20 6HH **105** E4
Monkhide **145** F3
Monkhill **209** G1

Monkhopton **157** F3
Monkland **145** D2
Monkleigh **113** E3
Monknash **129** F5
Monkokehampton **113** F5
Monks Eleigh **152** A3
Monks Eleigh Tye **152** A3
Monk's Gate **109** E1
Monks' Heath **184** C5
Monk's Hill **124** A4
Monks Kirby **159** G4
Monks Risborough **134** D2
Monkscross **99** D3
Monkseaton **221** F4
Monkshill **269** F6
Monksilver **115** D4
Monkstadt **263** J5
Monkswood **130** C2
Monkton *Devon* **103** E2
Monkton *Kent* **125** E2
Monkton *Pembs* **126** C2
Monkton *SAyr* **224** B3
Monkton *T&W* **212** C1
Monkton *VGlam* **129** F5
Monkton Combe **117** E1
Monkton Deverill **117** F2
Monkton Farleigh **117** F1
Monkton Heathfield **115** F5
Monkton Up
   Wimborne **105** G1
Monkton Wyld **103** G3
Monkwearmouth **212** C2
Monkwood **120** B4
Monmouth
   (Trefynwy) **131** E1
Monnington Court **144** C4
Monnington on
   Wye **144** C3
Monreith **207** D2
Montacute **104** B1
Montacute House *Som*
   TA15 6XP **104** B1
Monteach **269** G6
Montford **156** D1
Montford Bridge **156** D1
Montgarrie **260** D3
Montgomery
   (Trefaldwyn) **156** B3
Montgreenan **233** E5
Montpellier Gallery *Warks*
   CV37 6EP
   85 Stratford-upon-Avon
Montrave **244** B4
Montrose **253** F4
Monxton **119** E3
Monyash **172** C1
Monymusk **260** E3
Monzie **243** D2
Moodiesburn **234** A2
Moons Moat North **146** C1
Moonzie **244** B3
Moor Allerton **194** C4
Moor Cock **192** A1
Moor Crichel **105** F3
Moor End *Bed* **149** F2
Moor End *CenBeds* **149** E5
Moor End *Cumb* **199** G5
Moor End *ERid* **196** A4
Moor End *Lancs* **191** G4
Moor End *NYorks* **195** E4
Moor End *WYorks* **193** G5
Moor Green *Wilts* **117** F1
Moor Green *WMid* **158** C4
Moor Head **194** A4
Moor Monkton **195** E2
Moor Row **208** D5
Moor Side *Cumb* **198** D5
Moor Side *Lancs* **192** A4
Moor Side *Lancs* **192** A4
Moor Side *Lincs* **176** A2
Moor Street **124** A4
Moorby **176** A1
Moorcot **144** C2
Moordown **105** G3
Moore **183** G4
Moorend **209** G1
Moorends **187** D1
Moorfield **185** E1
Moorgreen **173** F3
Moorhall **186** A5
Moorhampton **144** C3
Moorhouse *Cumb* **209** G1
Moorhouse *Notts* **174** C1
Moorland (Northmoor
   Green) **116** A4
Moorlinch **116** A4
Moors Centre, Danby
   NYorks
   YO21 2NB **203** G2
Moors Valley Country Park
   Dorset
   BH24 2ET **106** A2
Moors Valley Railway
   Dorset
   BH24 2ET **106** A2
Moorsholm **203** F4
Moorside *Dorset* **105** D1
Moorside *GtMan* **185** D2
Moorside *WYorks* **194** B4
Moorthorpe **186** B1
Moortown *IoW* **106** D4
Moortown *Lincs* **188** A3
Moortown *Tel&W* **157** F2
Morangie **266** E3
Morar **256** C5
Morborne **161** G3
Morchard Bishop **102** A2
Morcombelake **104** A3
Morcott **161** E2
Morda **169** F5
Morden *Dorset* **105** F3
Morden *GtLon* **122** B2
Morden Hall Park *GtLon*
   SM4 5JD **11** F8
Morden Park **122** B2
Mordiford **145** E4
Mordington
   Holdings **237** G4
Mordon **212** C4
More **156** C3
Morebath **114** C5
Morebattle **228** B4

Morecambe **192** A1
Morefield **265** H2
Moreleigh **101** D2
Morenish **242** B1
Moresby Parks **208** C5
Morestead **119** G3
Moreton *Dorset* **105** E4
Moreton *Essex* **137** E2
Moreton *Here* **145** E1
Moreton *Mersey* **183** D4
Moreton *Oxon* **134** B2
Moreton *Staffs* **157** G1
Moreton *Staffs* **172** C4
Moreton Corbet **170** C5
Moreton Jeffries **145** F3
Moreton Mill **170** C5
Moreton Morrell **147** F2
Moreton on Lugg **145** E3
Moreton Paddox **147** F2
Moreton Pinkney **148** A3
Moreton Say **170** D4
Moreton Valence **131** G2
Moretonhampstead **102** A4
Moreton-in-Marsh **147** F4
Morfa *Carmar* **128** B1
Morfa *Cere* **141** G2
Morfa Bychan **167** E4
Morfa Glas **129** E5
Morfa Nefyn **166** B3
Morgan's Vale **118** C5
Morganstown **130** A4
Mork **131** E2
Morland **210** B5
Morley *Derbys* **173** E3
Morley *Dur* **212** A5
Morley *WYorks* **194** B5
Morley Green **184** C4
Morley St. Botolph **164** B2
Mornick **98** D3
Morningside *Edin* **235** G2
Morningside *NLan* **234** C4
Morningthorpe **164** D2
Morpeth **221** E3
Morphie **253** F3
Morrey **158** D1
Morridge Side **172** B2
Morriston *SAyr* **224** B5
Morriston *Swan* **128** C3
Morristown **130** A5
Morston **178** B1
Mortehoe **113** E1
Morthen **186** B4
Mortimer **120** B1
Mortimer West End **120** B1
Mortimer's Cross **144** D1
Mortlake **136** B5
Morton *Derbys* **173** F1
Morton *Lincs* **175** F5
Morton *Lincs* **187** F3
Morton *Lincs* **175** D1
Morton *Notts* **174** C1
Morton *SGlos* **131** F3
Morton *Shrop* **169** F5
Morton Bagot **146** D1
Morton on the Hill **178** C4
Morton Tinmouth **212** A5
Morton-on-Swale **202** C3
Morvah **94** B3
Morval **97** G4
Morvich (A'Mhormhaich)
   High **257** F2
Morvich *High* **266** E1
Morvil **140** D4
Morville **157** F3
Morwellham **100** A1
Morwellham Quay Museum
   Devon PL19 8JL **99** G3
Morwenstow **112** C4
Morwick Hall **221** E1
Mosborough **186** B4
Moscow **233** F5
Mosedale **209** G3
Moselden Height **185** E1
Moseley *WMid* **158** B3
Moseley *Worcs* **146** A2
Moses Gate **184** B2
Moss *A&B* **246** A2
Moss *SYorks* **186** C1
Moss *Wrex* **170** A2
Moss Bank **183** G3
Moss Houses **184** C5
Moss Nook **184** C4
Moss of Barmuckity **267** K5
Moss Side *GtMan* **184** C3
Moss Side *Lancs* **191** G4
Moss Side *Mersey* **183** E2
Mossat **260** C3
Mossbank **278** D5
Mossblown **224** C3
Mossbrownford **228** A5
Mossdale **216** A3
Mossend **234** B3
Mosser **209** E4
Mossgiel **224** C3
Mosshead **260** D1
Mosside of
   Ballinshoe **252** C4
Mossley *ChesE* **171** F1
Mossley *GtMan* **185** D2
Mossley Hill **183** E4
Mosspaul Hotel **218** B2
Moss-side *High* **267** F6
Moss-side *Moray* **268** D3
Mosstodloch **268** B4
Mosston **252** D5
Mossy Lea **183** G1
Mosterton **104** A2
Moston *GtMan* **184** C2
Moston *Shrop* **170** C5
Moston Green **171** E1
Mostyn **182** C4
Motcombe **117** F3
Mothecombe **100** C3
Mother Shipton's Cave
   NYorks
   HG5 8DD **194** C2
Motherby **210** A5
Motherwell **234** B4
Mottingham **136** D5
Mottisfont **119** E5

Mottisfont Abbey *Hants*
   SO51 0LP **119** E5
Mottistone **106** D4
Mottram in
   Longdendale **185** D3
Mottram
   St. Andrew **184** C5
Mouldsworth **183** G5
Moulin **251** F4
Moulsecoomb **109** F3
Moulsford **134** A4
Moulsham **137** G2
Moulsoe **149** E3
Moulton *Aber* **260** D3
Moulton *ChesW&C* **171** D1
Moulton *Lincs* **176** B5
Moulton *N'hants* **148** C1
Moulton *NYorks* **202** B2
Moulton *Suff* **151** E1
Moulton *VGlam* **129** G5
Moulton Chapel **162** A1
Moulton St. Mary **179** E5
Moulton Seas End **176** B5
Mounie Castle **261** F2
Mount *Corn* **96** B4
Mount *Corn* **97** F3
Mount *High* **267** G7
Mount *Kent* **125** D4
Mount *WYorks* **185** F1
Mount Ambrose **96** B5
Mount Bures **152** A4
Mount Charles **97** E4
Mount Edgcumbe Country
   Park *Corn*
   PL10 1HZ **2** B3
Mount Hawke **96** B5
Mount Manisty **183** E5
Mount Oliphant **224** B4
Mount Pleasant
   ChesE **171** F2
Mount Pleasant
   Derbys **173** E3
Mount Pleasant
   Derbys **159** E1
Mount Pleasant
   ESuss **109** G2
Mount Pleasant
   Flints **182** D5
Mount Pleasant
   GtLon **135** D4
Mount Pleasant
   Hants **106** C3
Mount Pleasant
   Norf **164** A2
Mount Pleasant
   Suff **151** F3
Mount Sorrel **118** B5
Mount Tabor **193** G5
Mountain **193** G4
Mountain Ash
   (Aberpennar) **129** G3
Mountain Cross **235** F5
Mountain Water **140** C5
Mountbenger **227** E2
Mountblairy **268** E5
Mountblow **233** F2
Mountfield **110** C1
Mountgerald **266** C5
Mountjoy **96** D3
Mountnessing **137** F2
Mounton **131** E3
Mountsorrel **160** A1
Mousa **279** D10
Mousehole **94** B4
Mouswald **217** E3
Mow Cop **171** F2
Mowden **202** B1
Mowhaugh **228** C4
Mowsley **160** B4
Moxley **158** B3
Moy *High* **249** D1
Moy *High* **249** G1
Moy *High* **258** E1
Moy House **267** H6
Moylgrove **141** E3
Muasdale **231** E5
Much Birch **145** E4
Much Cowarne **145** F3
Much Dewchurch **145** D4
Much Hadham **136** D1
Much Hoole **192** A5
Much Hoole Town **192** A5
Much Marcle **145** F4
Much Wenlock **157** F2
Muchalls **261** H5
Muchelney **116** B5
Muchelney Ham **116** B5
Muchlarnick **97** G4
Muchra **226** D4
Muchrachd **257** J1
Muck **246** D2
Muckle Roe **279** C6
Muckleford **104** C3
Mucklestone **171** E4
Muckleton **170** C5
Muckletown **260** D2
Muckley **157** F3
Muckley Corner **158** C2
Muckton **189** D4
Mudale **273** H5
Muddiford **113** F2
Muddles Green **110** A2
Muddleswood **109** E2
Mudeford **106** A4
Mudford **104** B1
Mudgley **116** B3
Mugdock Country Park
   Stir G62 8EL **30** C1
Mugeary **255** K1
Mugginton **173** D2
Muggintonlane
   End **173** D2
Muggleswick **211** G3
Mugswell **122** B3
Muie **266** D1
Muir **251** F1
Muir of Fowlis **260** D3
Muir of Lochs **268** B4
Muir of Ord
   (Am Blàr Dubh) **266** C6

Muiravonside Country Park
   Falk EH49 6LW **235** D2
Muirden **269** F5
Muirdrum **245** D1
Muiredge **244** B5
Muirhead *Aber* **260** D3
Muirhead *Angus* **244** B1
Muirhead *Fife* **244** A4
Muirhead *Moray* **267** H5
Muirhead *NLan* **234** A3
Muirhouses **235** E1
Muirkirk **225** E3
Muirmill **234** B1
Muirtack *Aber* **261** H1
Muirtack *Aber* **269** G6
Muirton *High* **266** E5
Muirton *P&K* **243** F2
Muirton *P&K* **243** G2
Muirton of Ardblair **251** G5
Muirton of Ballochy **253** E3
Muirtown **267** G6
Muiryfold **269** F5
Muker **201** E3
Mulbarton **178** C5
Mulben **268** B5
Mulhagery **271** F7
Mull **239** G7
Mullach
   Chàrlabhaigh **270** E3
Mullacott Cross **113** F1
Mullion **95** D5
Mullion Cove **95** D5
Mumby **189** F5
Munderfield Row **145** F2
Munderfield Stocks **145** F2
Mundesley **179** E2
Mundford **163** G3
Mundham **165** E2
Mundon **138** B2
Mundurno **261** H3
Munerigie **257** J4
Mungasdale **265** F2
Mungoswells **236** B2
Mungrisdale **209** G3
Munlochy **266** D6
Munnoch **232** D5
Munsley **145** F3
Munslow **157** E4
Murchington **99** G2
Murcott *Oxon* **134** A1
Murcott *Wilts* **132** B3
Murdostoun **234** C4
Murieston **235** E3
Murkle **275** G2
Murlaganmore **242** A1
Murlaggan *High* **257** G5
Murlaggan *High* **249** F1
Murra **277** B7
Murrell Green **120** C2
Murroes **244** C1
Murrow **162** B2
Mursley **148** D5
Murston **124** B2
Murthill **252** C4
Murthly **243** F1
Murton *Cumb* **210** D5
Murton *Dur* **212** C3
Murton *N'umb* **237** G5
Murton *Swan* **128** B4
Murton *York* **195** F2
Musbury **103** F3
Muscliff **105** G3
Musdale (Musdàl) **240** B2
Museum in Docklands
   GtLon E14 4AL **12** D4
Museum of Childhood,
   Edinburgh *Edin*
   EH1 1TG **37** B2
Museum of Childhood,
   London *GtLon*
   E2 9PA **12** C4
Museum of Flight *ELoth*
   EH39 5LF **236** C2
Museum of Garden History,
   London *GtLon*
   SE1 7LB **45** F7
Museum of London *GtLon*
   EC2Y 5HN **45** J2
Museum of Science &
   Industry, Manchester
   GtMan M3 4FP **46** C4
Museum of Transport,
   Glasgow *Glas*
   G3 8DP **38** A2
Musselburgh **236** A2
Mustard Hyrn **179** F4
Mustard Shop *Norf*
   NR2 1NQ **79** Norwich
Muston *Leics* **174** D4
Muston *NYorks* **205** E4
Mustow Green **158** A5
Mutford **165** F2
Muthill **243** D3
Mutley **100** A2
Mutterton **102** D2
Muxton **157** G1
Mybster **275** G3
Myddfai **143** D4
Myddle **170** B5
Mydroilyn **142** A2
Myerscough
   College **192** A4
Myerscough Smithy **192** C4
Mylor **95** F3
Mylor Bridge **95** F3
Mynachdy **130** A5
Myndtown **156** C4
Mynydd Llandygai **167** E1
Mynydd Mechell **180** B4
Mynydd-bach *Mon* **131** D3
Mynydd-bach
   Swan **128** C3
Mynytho **166** C4
Myrebird **261** F5
Mytchett **121** D2
Mytholm **193** F5
Mytholmroyd **193** G5
Mythop **191** G4
Myton-on-Swale **194** D1

Mytton **156** D1

N

Naast **264** E3
Nab's Head **192** C5
Na-Buirgh **263** F2
Naburn **195** E3
Nackington **125** D3
Nacton **152** D3
Nadderwater **102** B3
Nafferton **196** C2
Nailbridge **131** F1
Nailsbourne **115** F5
Nailsea **131** D5
Nailstone **159** G2
Nailsworth **132** A3
Nairn **267** F6
Nancegollan **94** C3
Nancekuke **96** A5
Nancledra **94** B3
Nanhoron **166** B4
Nannau **168** A5
Nannerch **169** E1
Nanpantan **160** A1
Nanpean **97** D4
Nanstallon **97** E3
Nant Peris **167** E2
Nant-ddu **129** G1
Nanternis **141** G2
Nantgaredig **142** A5
Nantgarw **130** A4
Nant-glas **143** F1
Nantglyn **168** D1
Nantgwyn **155** F5
Nantlle **167** E2
Nantmawr **169** F5
Nantmel **143** G1
Nantmor **167** F3
Nantwich **170** D2
Nantycaws **128** A1
Nant-y-derry **130** C2
Nant-y-dugoed **155** F1
Nantyffyllon **129** E3
Nantyglo **130** B1
Nant-y-Gollen **169** F5
Nant-y-groes **143** G1
Nant-y-moel **129** F3
Nant-y-Pandy **181** E5
Naphill **135** D3
Napley Heath **171** E4
Nappa **152** B2
Napton on the Hill **147** G1
Narberth (Arberth) **127** E1
Narborough *Leics* **160** A3
Narborough *Norf* **163** F1
Narkurs **98** C5
Narrachan **240** B3
Nasareth **167** D3
Naseby **160** A5
Nash *Bucks* **148** C4
Nash *Here* **144** C1
Nash *Newport* **130** C4
Nash *Shrop* **157** F5
Nash *VGlam* **129** F5
Nash Street **123** F2
Nassington **161** F3
Nasty **150** B5
Nateby *Cumb* **200** C2
Nateby *Lancs* **192** A3
Nately Scures **120** C2
National Agricultural Centre,
   Stoneleigh *Warks*
   CV8 2LZ **16** B5
National Army Museum
   GtLon
   SW3 4HT **13** A3
National Botanic Garden
   of Wales *Carmar*
   SA32 8HG **128** B1
National Coal Mining
   Museum for England
   WYorks
   WF4 4RH **27** F6
National Exhibition Centre
   WMid B40 1NT **15** H4
National Fishing Heritage
   Centre, Grimsby *NELincs*
   DN31 1UZ **188** C2
National Gallery *GtLon*
   WC2N 5DN **44** D4
National Gallery of Scotland
   Edin EH2 2EL **37** D4
National Indoor Arena,
   Birmingham
   WMid B1 2AA **34** D4
National Marine Aquarium
   PL4 0LF **81** Plymouth
National Maritime Museum
   Cornwall *Corn*
   TR11 3QY **95** F3
National Maritime Museum,
   Greenwich *GtLon*
   SE10 9NF **13** D5
National Media Museum
   WYorks BD1 1NQ
   65 Bradford
National Memorial
   Arboretum, Alrewas
   Staffs
   DE13 7AR **159** D1
National Motorcycle
   Museum, Solihull *WMid*
   B92 0EJ **159** E4
National Museum Cardiff
   CF10 3NP
   67 Cardiff
National Museum of
   Scotland *Edin*
   EH1 1JF **37** D5
National Portrait Gallery
   GtLon
   WC2H 0HE **44** D4
National Railway Museum
   YO26 4XJ **90** York
National Sea Life Centre,
   Birmingham
   WMid B1 2JB **34** D4
National Seal Sanctuary
   Corn TR12 6UG **95** E4
National Slate Museum,
   Llanberis *Gwyn*
   LL55 4TY **167** E2

National Space Centre,
   Leicester *Leic*
   LE4 5NS **17** C4
National Wallace Monument
   Stir FK9 5LF **242** D5
National War Museum,
   Edinburgh *Edin*
   EH1 2NG **37** A4
National Waterfront
   Museum SA1 3RD
   86 Swansea
National Wildflower Centre,
   Liverpool *Mersey*
   L16 3NA **22** D3
Natland **199** G4
Natural History Museum
   at Tring *Herts*
   HP23 6AP **135** E1
Natural History Museum,
   London *GtLon*
   SW7 5BD **11** F5
Natureland Seal
   Sanctuary *Lincs*
   PE25 1DB **177** D1
Naughton **152** B3
Naunton *Glos* **146** D5
Naunton *Worcs* **146** A4
Naunton
   Beauchamp **146** B2
Navenby **175** E2
Navestock **137** E3
Navestock Side **137** E3
Navidale **275** F7
Navity **266** E5
Nawton **203** F4
Nayland **152** A4
Nazeing **136** D2
Neacroft **106** A3
Neal's Green **159** F4
Neap **279** E7
Neap House **187** F1
Near Sawrey **199** F3
Nearton End **148** D5
Neasden **136** B4
Neasham **202** C1
Neat Enstone **147** F5
Neath
   (Castell-nedd) **129** D3
Neatham **120** B3
Neatishead **179** E3
Nebo *Cere* **142** B1
Nebo *Conwy* **168** B2
Nebo *Gwyn* **167** D2
Nebo *IoA* **180** C3
Necton **163** G2
Nedd **272** D5
Nedderton **221** E3
Nedging **152** A3
Nedging Tye **152** B3
Needham **163** D3
Needham Lake *Suff*
   IP6 8NU **152** B2
Needham Market **152** B2
Needham Street **151** F1
Needingworth **162** B5
Needles Pleasure Park *IoW*
   PO39 0JD **106** C4
Needwood **172** C5
Neen Savage **157** F5
Neen Sollars **157** F5
Neenton **157** F4
Nefyn **166** C3
Neighbourne **116** D3
Neilston **233** F4
Neithrop **147** G3
Nelson *Caerp* **130** A3
Nelson *Lancs* **193** E4
Nelson Village **221** E4
Nemphlar **234** C5
Nempnett
   Thrubwell **116** C1
Nenthall **211** D3
Nenthead **211** D3
Nenthorn **228** A3
Neopardy **102** A3
Nerabus **230** A4
Nercwys **169** F1
Neriby **230** B3
Nerston **234** A4
Nesbit **229** D3
Nesfield **193** G3
Ness **183** E5
Ness Botanic Gardens
   ChesW&C
   CH64 4AY **183** E5
Ness of Tenston **277** B6
Nesscliffe **156** C1
Neston *ChesW&C* **183** D5
Neston *Wilts* **117** F1
Nether Alderley **184** C5
Nether
   Auchendrane **224** B4
Nether Barr **215** F4
Nether Blainslie **236** C5
Nether Broughton **174** B5
Nether Burrow **200** B4
Nether Cerne **104** C3
Nether Compton **104** B1
Nether Crimond **261** G2
Nether Dalgliesh **227** D5
Nether Dallachy **268** B4
Nether Edge **186** A4
Nether End **185** G5
Nether Exe **102** C3
Nether Glasslaw **269** G5
Nether Handwick **252** B5
Nether Haugh **186** B3
Nether Heage **173** E2
Nether Heselden **201** D5
Nether Kellet **192** B1
Nether Kinmundy **269** J6
Nether Langwith **186** C5
Nether Lenshie **268** E6
Nether Loads **173** E1
Nether Moor **173** E1
Nether Padley **185** G5
Nether Pitforthie **253** G2
Nether Poppleton **195** E2
Nether Silton **203** D3
Nether Skyborry **156** B5
Nether Stowey **115** E4

Nether Urquhart 243 G4
Nether Wallop 119 E4
Nether Wasdale 198 C2
Nether Welton 209 G2
Nether Westcote 147 E5
Nether Whitacre 159 E3
Nether Winchendon (Lower Winchendon) 134 C1
Nether Worton 147 G5
Netheravon 118 C3
Netherbrae 269 F5
Netherbrough 277 C6
Netherburn 234 C5
Netherbury 104 A3
Netherby Cumb 218 B4
Netherby NYorks 194 C3
Nethercott 147 G5
Netherfield ESuss 110 C2
Netherfield Notts 174 B3
Netherfield SLan 234 B5
Netherhall 232 D3
Netherhampton 118 C5
Netherhay 104 A2
Netherland Green 172 C4
Netherley 261 G5
Nethermill 217 E2
Nethermuir 269 H6
Netherseal 159 E1
Nethershield 225 D3
Netherstreet 118 A1
Netherthird D&G 217 E3
Netherthird EAyr 225 D4
Netherthong 185 F2
Netherthorpe 186 C4
Netherton Angus 252 D4
Netherton ChesW&C 183 G5
Netherton Devon 102 B5
Netherton Hants 119 E2
Netherton Mersey 183 E2
Netherton N'umb 220 B1
Netherton NLan 234 B4
Netherton Oxon 133 G2
Netherton P&K 251 G4
Netherton SLan 234 B5
Netherton WMid 158 B4
Netherton Worcs 146 B3
Netherton WYorks 185 G1
Netherton WYorks 185 F1
Netherton Burnfoot 220 B1
Netherton Northside 220 B1
Nethertown Cumb 198 A2
Nethertown Ork 277 E7
Nethertown Staffs 158 D1
Netherwitton 220 D2
Netherwood D&G 217 D3
Netherwood EAyr 225 E3
Nethy Bridge 259 H2
Netley Abbey 107 D2
Netley Marsh 106 C1
Nettlebed 134 B4
Nettlebridge 116 D3
Nettlecombe Dorset 104 B3
Nettlecombe IoW 107 E5
Nettlecombe Som 115 D4
Nettleden 135 F1
Nettleham 188 A5
Nettlestead Kent 123 F3
Nettlestead Suff 152 B3
Nettlestead Green 123 F3
Nettlestone 107 F3
Nettlesworth 212 B3
Nettleton Lincs 188 B2
Nettleton Wilts 132 A5
Nettleton Hill 185 E1
Netton Devon 100 B3
Netton Wilts 118 C4
Neuadd Cere 142 A2
Neuadd IoA 180 B3
Neuadd Powys 143 F3
Nevendon 137 G3
Nevern 141 D4
Nevill Holt 160 D3
New Abbey 217 D4
New Aberdour 269 G4
New Addington 122 C2
New Alresford 119 G4
New Alyth 252 A5
New Arley 159 E3
New Arram 196 C3
New Ash Green 123 F2
New Balderton 174 D2
New Barn 123 F2
New Belses 227 G3
New Bewick 229 E4
New Bolingbroke 176 B2
New Boultham 187 G5
New Bradwell 148 D3
New Brancepeth 212 B3
New Bridge D&G 216 D3
New Bridge Devon 102 A5
New Brighton Flints 169 F1
New Brighton Hants 107 G2
New Brighton Mersey 183 E3
New Brighton Wrex 169 F2
New Brighton WYorks 194 B5
New Brinsley 173 F2
New Broughton 170 A2
New Buckenham 164 B2
New Byth 269 G5
New Cheriton 119 G5
New Cross Cere 154 C5
New Cross GtLon 136 C5
New Cumnock 225 E4
New Deer 269 G6
New Duston 148 C1
New Earswick 195 F2
New Edlington 186 C3
New Elgin 267 K5
New Ellerby 197 D4
New Eltham 136 D5
New End 146 C1
New England 161 G2
New Farnley 194 B4

New Ferry 183 E4
New Galloway 216 A3
New Gilston 244 C4
New Greens 136 A2
New Grimsby 96 A1
New Hartley 221 F4
New Haw 121 F1
New Hedges 127 E2
New Heaton 228 C3
New Herrington 212 C2
New Hinksey 134 A2
New Holland 196 C5
New Houghton Derbys 173 G4
New Houghton Norf 177 F5
New Houses 200 D5
New Hunwick 212 A4
New Hutton 199 G3
New Hythe 123 F3
New Inn Carmar 142 A4
New Inn Fife 244 A4
New Inn Mon 131 D2
New Inn Torfaen 130 B3
New Invention Shrop 156 B5
New Invention WMid 158 B2
New Kelso 265 F7
New Lanark 234 C5
New Lanark World Heritage Site SLan ML11 9DB 234 C5
New Lane 183 F1
New Lane End 184 A3
New Leake 176 C2
New Leeds 269 H5
New Leslie 260 D2
New Lodge 186 A2
New Longton 192 B5
New Luce 214 C4
New Mains 225 D3
New Mains of Ury 253 G1
New Malden 122 B2
New Marske 213 F5
New Marton 170 A4
New Mill Corn 94 B3
New Mill Herts 135 E1
New Mill WYorks 185 F2
New Mill End 136 A1
New Mills Corn 96 C4
New Mills Derbys 185 E4
New Mills Glos 131 F2
New Mills Mon 131 D2
New Mills (Y Felin Newydd) Powys 155 G2
New Milton 106 B3
New Mistley 152 C4
New Moat 141 D5
New Ollerton 174 B1
New Orleans 222 C4
New Oscott 158 C3
New Palace & Adventureland, New Brighton Mersey CH45 2JX 22 A2
New Park Corn 97 F1
New Park NYorks 194 B2
New Pitsligo 269 G5
New Polzeath 96 D2
New Quay (Ceinewydd) 141 G1
New Rackheath 179 D4
New Radnor (Maesyfed) 144 B1
New Rent 210 A4
New Ridley 211 G1
New Road Side 193 F3
New Romney 111 F1
New Rossington 186 D3
New Row Cere 154 C5
New Row Lancs 192 C4
New Sawley 173 F3
New Shoreston 229 F3
New Silksworth 212 C2
New Stevenson 234 B4
New Swannington 159 G1
New Totley 186 A5
New Town CenBeds 149 G3
New Town Cere 141 E3
New Town Dorset 105 F1
New Town Dorset 105 F2
New Town ELoth 236 B2
New Town ESuss 109 G1
New Town Glos 146 C4
New Tredegar 130 A2
New Tupton 173 E1
New Ulva 231 F1
New Valley 271 G4
New Village 186 C2
New Walk Museum & Art Gallery LE1 7EA 77 Leicester
New Walsoken 162 C2
New Waltham 188 C2
New Walton Pier Essex CO14 8ES 153 D5
New Winton 236 B2
New World 162 B3
New Yatt 133 F1
New York Lincs 176 A2
New York T&W 221 F4
Newall 194 B3
Newark Ork 276 G3
Newark Peter 162 A2
Newark Castle, Newark-on-Trent Notts NG24 1BG 174 C2
Newark-on-Trent 174 D2
Newarthill 234 B4
Newball 188 A5
Newbarn 125 D5
Newbarns 198 D5
Newbattle 236 A3
Newbiggin Cumb 210 A5
Newbiggin Cumb 210 C5
Newbiggin Cumb 210 B3
Newbiggin Cumb 191 E1
Newbiggin Cumb 198 B5
Newbiggin Dur 211 E5
Newbiggin N'umb 211 F1

Newbiggin NYorks 201 F4
Newbiggin NYorks 201 E3
Newbiggin-by-the-Sea 221 F3
Newbigging Aber 261 G5
Newbigging Aber 251 G1
Newbigging Angus 244 C1
Newbigging Angus 244 C1
Newbigging Angus 252 A5
Newbigging SLan 235 E5
Newbold Derbys 186 A5
Newbold Leics 159 G1
Newbold on Avon 159 G5
Newbold on Stour 147 E3
Newbold Pacey 147 E2
Newbold Verdon 159 G2
Newborough (Niwbwrch) IoA 166 D1
Newborough Peter 162 A2
Newborough Staffs 172 C5
Newbottle N'hants 148 A4
Newbottle T&W 212 C2
Newbourne 153 D3
Newbridge (Cefn Bychan) Caerp 156 B5
Newbridge Corn 94 B3
Newbridge Corn 98 D4
Newbridge Edin 235 G2
Newbridge ESuss 123 G5
Newbridge Hants 106 B1
Newbridge IoW 106 D4
Newbridge NYorks 204 D4
Newbridge Oxon 133 G2
Newbridge Pembs 140 C4
Newbridge Wrex 169 F3
Newbridge Green 146 A4
Newbridge on Wye 143 G3
Newbridge-on-Usk 130 C3
Newbrough 211 E1
Newbuildings 102 A2
Newburgh Aber 269 H5
Newburgh Aber 261 H2
Newburgh Fife 244 A3
Newburgh Lancs 183 F1
Newburgh ScBord 227 E3
Newburn 212 A1
Newbury Som 117 D2
Newbury WBerks 119 F1
Newbury Park 136 D4
Newby Cumb 210 B5
Newby Lancs 193 E3
Newby NYorks 203 E1
Newby NYorks 192 D1
Newby NYorks 204 D4
Newby Bridge 199 E4
Newby Cote 200 C5
Newby Cross 209 G1
Newby East 191 E1
Newby Hall NYorks HG4 5AE 194 C1
Newby West 209 G1
Newby Wiske 202 C4
Newcastle Bridgend 129 E5
Newcastle Mon 130 D1
Newcastle Shrop 156 B4
Newcastle Emlyn (Castell Newydd Emlyn) 141 G3
Newcastle International Airport 221 D4
Newcastle upon Tyne 212 B1
Newcastleton 218 C3
Newcastle-under-Lyme 171 F3
Newchapel Pembs 141 F4
Newchapel Staffs 171 F2
Newchapel Surr 122 C4
Newchurch Carmar 141 G5
Newchurch IoW 107 E4
Newchurch Kent 124 C5
Newchurch Lancs 193 E5
Newchurch Lancs 193 E4
Newchurch Mon 131 D3
Newchurch Powys 144 B2
Newchurch Staffs 172 C5
Newcott 103 F2
Newcraighall 236 A2
Newdigate 121 G3
Newell Green 135 D5
Newenden 110 D1
Newent 145 G5
Newerne 131 F2
Newfield Dur 212 B4
Newfield Dur 212 B2
Newfield High 266 E4
Newfound 119 G2
Newgale 140 B5
Newgate 178 B1
Newgate Street 136 C2
Newgord 278 E2
Newhall ChesE 170 D3
Newhall Derbys 173 D5
Newham 229 F4
Newham Hall 229 F4
Newhaven 109 G3
Newhey 184 D1
Newholm 204 B3
Newick 109 G1
Newingreen 124 D5
Newington Edin 235 G2
Newington Kent 125 D5
Newington Kent 124 A2
Newington Notts 187 D3
Newington Oxon 134 B3
Newington Bagpath 132 A3
Newland Glos 131 E2
Newland Hull 196 C4
Newland NYorks 195 F5
Newland Oxon 133 F1
Newland Worcs 145 G3
Newlandrig 236 A3
Newlands Cumb 209 G3
Newlands Essex 138 B4
Newlands N'umb 211 G2
Newlands ScBord 218 C2
Newland's Corner 121 F3

Newlands of Geise 275 F2
Newlands of Tynet 268 B4
Newlyn 94 B4
Newmachar 261 G3
Newmains 234 C4
Newman's End 137 E1
Newman's Green 151 G3
Newmarket Suff 151 E1
Newmarket WIsles 271 G4
Newmill Aber 253 F1
Newmill Aber 269 G6
Newmill Aber 261 G2
Newmill Moray 268 C5
Newmill ScBord 227 F4
Newmill of Inshewan 252 C3
Newmillerdam 186 A1
Newmillerdam Country Park WYorks WF2 6QP 27 H6
Newmills 266 D5
Newmiln P&K 243 G1
Newmiln P&K 243 F1
Newmilns 224 D2
Newney Green 137 F2
Newnham Glos 131 F1
Newnham Hants 120 C2
Newnham Herts 150 A4
Newnham Kent 124 B3
Newnham N'hants 148 A2
Newnham Bridge 145 F1
Newnham Paddox 159 G4
Newnoth 260 D1
Newport Corn 98 D2
Newport Devon 113 F2
Newport ERid 196 A4
Newport Essex 150 D4
Newport Glos 131 F3
Newport High 275 G5
Newport IoW 107 E4
Newport (Casnewydd) Newport 130 C4
Newport Norf 179 G3
Newport (Trefdraeth) Pembs 141 D4
Newport Som 116 A5
Newport Tel&W 157 G1
Newport Pagnell 149 D3
Newport-on-Tay 244 C2
Newpound Common 121 F5
Newquay 96 C3
Newquay Cornwall International Airport 96 C3
Newquay Zoo Corn TR7 2LZ 96 C3
Newsbank 171 F1
Newseat 261 F1
Newsells 150 B4
Newsham Lancs 192 B4
Newsham NYorks 202 A1
Newsham NYorks 202 A1
Newsholme ERid 195 G5
Newsholme Lancs 193 E2
Newsome 185 F1
Newstead N'umb 229 E1
Newstead Notts 173 G2
Newstead ScBord 227 G2
Newstead Abbey Notts NG15 8NA 173 G2
Newthorpe N'umb 173 F3
Newthorpe NYorks 195 E5
Newtoft 188 A4
Newton A&B 240 C5
Newton Aber 268 C6
Newton Aber 269 J6
Newton Bridgend 129 E5
Newton Cambs 162 C1
Newton Cambs 150 C3
Newton Cardiff 130 B5
Newton ChesW&C 170 C2
Newton ChesW&C 183 G5
Newton Cumb 198 D5
Newton D&G 217 F1
Newton Derbys 173 F1
Newton GtMan 185 D3
Newton Here 144 C1
Newton Here 145 E3
Newton Here 145 E4
Newton High 275 J3
Newton High 266 D3
Newton High 275 H3
Newton High 272 E5
Newton High 266 C6
Newton High 266 E5
Newton Lancs 192 C2
Newton Lancs 199 G5
Newton Lancs 191 G4
Newton Lincs 175 E4
Newton Moray 268 B4
Newton N'hants 161 D4
Newton N'umb 211 G1
Newton N'umb 220 B1
Newton NAyr 232 A4
Newton Norf 163 G1
Newton Notts 174 B3
Newton P&K 243 D1
Newton Pembs 140 C4
Newton Pembs 126 C1
Newton ScBord 227 G3
Newton SGlos 131 F3
Newton Shrop 170 C5
Newton SLan 226 A2
Newton Som 115 F4
Newton Staffs 172 B5
Newton Suff 152 A3
Newton Swan 128 C4
Newton Warks 160 A5
Newton Wilts 118 D5
Newton WLoth 235 E2
Newton WYorks 194 D5
Newton Abbot 102 B5
Newton Arlosh 209 F1
Newton Aycliffe 212 B5
Newton Bewley 213 D5
Newton Blossomville 149 E2
Newton Bromswold 149 E1
Newton Burgoland 159 F2
Newton by Toft 188 A4
Newton Ferrers 100 B3
Newton Flotman 164 D2

Newton Green 131 E3
Newton Harcourt 160 B3
Newton Kyme 195 D3
Newton Longville 148 D4
Newton Mearns 233 G4
Newton Morrell NYorks 202 B2
Newton Morrell Oxon 148 B5
Newton Mountain 126 C2
Newton Mulgrave 203 G1
Newton of Affleck 244 C1
Newton of Ardtoe 247 F2
Newton of Balcanquhal 243 G3
Newton of Dalvey 267 H6
Newton of Falkland 244 A4
Newton of Leys 258 D1
Newton on the Hill 170 B5
Newton Poppleford 103 D4
Newton Purcell 148 B4
Newton Regis 159 E2
Newton Reigny 210 A4
Newton St. Cyres 102 B3
Newton St. Faith 178 D4
Newton St. Loe 117 E1
Newton St. Petrock 113 E4
Newton Solney 173 D5
Newton Stacey 119 F3
Newton Stewart 215 F4
Newton Tony 118 D3
Newton Tracey 113 F3
Newton under Roseberry 203 E1
Newton Underwood 221 D3
Newton upon Derwent 195 G3
Newton Valence 120 C4
Newton with Scales 192 A4
Newtongrange 236 A3
Newtonhill H5
Newton-le-Willows Mersey 183 G3
Newton-le-Willows NYorks 202 B4
Newtonmill 253 E3
Newtonmore (Baile Ùr an t-Sleibh) 258 D5
Newton-on-Ouse 195 E2
Newton-on-Rawcliffe 204 B3
Newton-on-the-Moor 221 D1
Newtown Bucks 135 E2
Newtown ChesW&C 170 C2
Newtown Corn 97 G2
Newtown Corn 94 C3
Newtown Cumb 210 B1
Newtown Derbys 185 D4
Newtown Devon 114 A5
Newtown Devon 103 D3
Newtown Dorset 104 A2
Newtown Glos 131 F2
Newtown GtMan 183 G2
Newtown GtMan 184 B2
Newtown Hants 107 F1
Newtown Hants 119 F1
Newtown Hants 106 B1
Newtown Hants 119 E5
Newtown Hants 107 E1
Newtown Here 145 F3
Newtown Here 145 D2
Newtown High 257 K4
Newtown IoM 190 B4
Newtown IoW 106 D3
Newtown N'umb 229 E4
Newtown Oxon 134 C3
Newtown (Y Drenewydd) Powys 156 A3
Newtown RCT 129 G3
Newtown Shrop 170 B4
Newtown Som 115 F4
Newtown Som 103 F1
Newtown Staffs 171 G1
Newtown Staffs 172 B1
Newtown Staffs 158 B2
Newtown Wilts 118 A5
Newtown Wilts 119 E1
Newtown Linford 160 A2
Newtown St. Boswells 227 G2
Newtown Unthank 159 G2
Newtown-in-Saint-Martin 95 A3
Newtyle 252 A5
Newyears Green 135 F4
Neyland 126 C2
Nibley Glos 131 F4
Nibley SGlos 131 F4
Nibley Green 131 G3
Nicholashayne 103 E1
Nicholaston 128 B4
Nidd 194 C1
Nigg Aberdeen 261 H4
Nigg High 267 F4
Nightcott 114 B5
Nilig 168 D2
Nilston Rigg 211 E1
Nimlet 131 G5
Nine Ashes 137 E2
Nine Elms 132 D4
Nine Mile Burn 235 F4
Ninebanks 211 D2
Ninemile Bar (Crocketford) 216 C2
Nineveh 145 F1
Ninfield 110 C1
Ningwood 106 D4
Niton 107 E5
Nitshill 233 G3
Nizels 123 E3
No Man's Heath ChesW&C 170 C3
No Man's Heath Warks 159 F2
No Man's Land 97 G4

Noah's Ark 123 E3
Noak Hill 137 E3
Nobland 187 D3
Noblethorpe 185 G2
Nobottle 148 B1
Nocton 175 G5
Noddsdale 232 D3
Nogdam End 179 E5
Noke 134 A1
Nolton 126 B1
Nolton Haven 126 B1
Nomansland Devon 102 B1
Nomansland Wilts 106 B1
Noneley 170 B5
Nonington 125 E3
Nook Cumb 218 C4
Nook Cumb 199 G3
Noonsbrough 279 B7
Norbreck 191 G3
Norbury ChesE 170 C3
Norbury Derbys 172 C3
Norbury GtLon 136 C5
Norbury Shrop 156 C3
Norbury Staffs 171 E5
Norbury Common 170 C3
Norbury Junction 171 E5
Norchard 127 D3
Norcott Brook 184 A4
Nordelph 163 D2
Norden Dorset 105 F4
Norden GtMan 184 C1
Nordley 157 F3
Norham 237 G5
Norland Town 193 G5
Norley 183 G5
Norleywood 106 C3
Norman Cross 161 G3
Normanby NLincs 187 F1
Normanby NYorks 203 G4
Normanby R&C 203 E1
Normanby by Stow 187 F4
Normanby Hall Country Park NLincs DN15 9HU 187 F4
Normanby le Wold 188 B3
Normandy 121 E2
Norman's Bay 110 C3
Norman's Green 103 D2
Normanston 165 G2
Normanton Derby 173 E4
Normanton Leics 174 D4
Normanton Lincs 175 E3
Normanton Notts 174 C2
Normanton Rut 161 E2
Normanton WYorks 194 C5
Normanton le Heath 159 F1
Normanton on Soar 173 G5
Normanton on Trent 174 C1
Normanton-on-the-Wolds 174 B4
Normoss 191 G4
Norrington Common 117 F1
Norris Green 100 A1
Norris Hill 159 F1
Norristhorpe 194 B5
North Acton 136 B4
North Anston 186 C4
North Ascot 121 E1
North Aston 147 G5
North Baddesley 106 C1
North Ballachulish (Baile a' Chaolais a Tuath) 248 C3
North Balloch 215 E1
North Barrow 116 D5
North Barsham 178 A2
North Bay Miniature Railway NYorks YO12 6PF 204 D3
North Benfleet 137 G4
North Bersted 108 B3
North Berwick 236 C1
North Boarhunt 107 F1
North Bogbain 268 B5
North Bovey 102 A4
North Bradley 117 F2
North Brentor 99 E3
North Brewham 117 E4
North Bridge 121 E4
North Buckland 113 E1
North Burlingham 179 E4
North Cadbury 116 C5
North Cairn 214 A3
North Camp 121 D2
North Carlton Lincs 187 G5
North Carlton Notts 186 C4
North Cave 196 A4
North Cerney 132 C2
North Chailey 109 F1
North Charford 106 A1
North Charlton 229 E4
North Cheriton 117 D5
North Chideock 104 A3
North Cliffe 196 A4
North Clifton 187 F5
North Cockerington 189 D3
North Coker 104 B1
North Collafirth 278 C4
North Common SGlos 131 F5
North Common Suff 164 A4
North Commonty 269 G6
North Connel 240 B1
North Coombe 102 B2
North Cornelly 129 E4
North Corner 131 F4
North Cotes 188 D2

North Cove 165 F3
North Cowton 202 B2
North Crawley 149 E3
North Creake 177 G4
North Curry 116 A5
North Dallens 248 B5
North Dalton 196 B2
North Dawn 277 D7
North Deighton 194 C2
North Dell (Dail Bho Thuath) 271 G1
North Duffield 195 F4
North Elkington 188 C3
North Elmham 178 A3
North Elmsall 186 B1
North End Bucks 148 D5
North End Dorset 117 F5
North End ERid 197 D2
North End ERid 197 D3
North End ERid 197 E4
North End Essex 137 F1
North End Hants 119 G5
North End Hants 106 A1
North End Leics 160 A1
North End N'umb 220 D1
North End Norf 164 A3
North End NSom 116 B1
North End Ports 107 F2
North End WSuss 108 C4
North End WSuss 108 B3
North Erradale 264 D3
North Essie 269 J5
North Fambridge 138 B3
North Ferriby 196 B5
North Frodingham 196 D2
North Gluss 278 C5
North Gorley 106 A1
North Green Norf 164 D3
North Green Suff 165 E4
North Green Suff 153 E1
North Green Suff 153 E1
North Grimston 196 A1
North Halling 123 G2
North Harby 187 F5
North Hayling 107 G2
North Hazelrigg 229 E3
North Heasley 114 A4
North Heath WBerks 133 G5
North Heath WSuss 121 F5
North Hill 97 G2
North Hillington 135 F4
North Hinksey 133 G2
North Holmwood 121 G3
North Houghton 119 E4
North Huish 100 D3
North Hykeham 175 E1
North Johnston 126 C1
North Kelsey 188 A2
North Kessock 266 D7
North Killingholme 188 B1
North Kilvington 202 C4
North Kilworth 160 B4
North Kingston 106 A2
North Kyme 175 G2
North Lancing 109 D3
North Lee 134 D2
North Leigh 133 F1
North Leverton with Habblesthorpe 187 E4
North Littleton 146 C3
North Lopham 164 B3
North Luffenham 161 E2
North Marden 108 A2
North Marston 148 C5
North Middleton Midlo 236 A4
North Middleton N'umb 229 E4
North Millbrex 269 G6
North Molton 114 A5
North Moreton 134 A4
North Mundham 108 A3
North Muskham 174 C2
North Newbald 196 B4
North Newington 147 G4
North Newnton 118 C2
North Newton 115 F4
North Nibley 131 G3
North Norfolk Railway Norf NR26 8RA 178 C1
North Oakley 119 G2
North Ockendon 137 E4
North Ormesby 203 E1
North Ormsby 188 C3
North Otterington 202 C4
North Owersby 188 A3
North Perrott 104 A2
North Petherton 115 F4
North Petherwin 97 G1
North Pickenham 163 G2
North Piddle 146 B2
North Plain 217 F3
North Pool 101 D3
North Poorton 104 B3
North Quarme 114 C4
North Queensferry 235 F1
North Radworthy 114 A4
North Rauceby 175 F3
North Reston 189 D4
North Riding Forest Park NYorks YO18 7LT 204 B3
North Rigton 194 B3
North Rode 171 F1
North Roe 278 C4
North Ronaldsay 276 G2
North Ronaldsay Airfield 276 G2
North Runcton 163 E1
North Sandwick 278 E3
North Scale 191 E1
North Scarle 175 D1
North Seaton 221 E3
North Shian (Sithean a Tuath) 248 B5
North Shields 212 C1
North Shoebury 138 C4
North Side 162 A3

North Skelton **203** F1
North Somercotes **189** E3
North Stainley **202** B5
North Stainmore **200** D1
North Stifford **137** F4
North Stoke
  B&NESom **117** E1
North Stoke *Oxon* **134** B4
North Stoke *WSuss* **108** C2
North Stoneham **106** D1
North Street *Hants* **120** B4
North Street *Kent* **124** C3
North Street *Med* **124** A1
North Street
  WBerks **134** B5
North Sunderland **229** G3
North Tamerton **98** D1
North Tarbothill **261** H3
North Tawton **113** G5
North Third **234** B1
North Thoresby **188** C3
North Tidworth **118** D3
North Togston **221** E1
North Town *Devon* **113** F5
North Town *Hants* **121** D2
North Town *W&M* **135** D4
North Tuddenham **178** B4
North Uist (Uibhist a
  Tuath) **262** D4
North Walsham **179** D2
North Waltham **119** G3
North
  Warnborough **120** C2
North Water Bridge **253** E3
North Watten **275** H3
North Weald
  Bassett **137** D2
North Wembley **136** A4
North Wheatley **187** E4
North Whilborough **101** E1
North Wick **116** C1
North Widcombe **116** C2
North Willingham **188** B4
North Wingfield **173** F4
North Witham **175** E5
North Wootton
  Dorset **104** C1
North Wootton
  Norf **177** E5
North Wootton
  Som **116** C3
North Wraxall **132** A5
North Wroughton **132** D4
North Yardley **220** B1
North Yorkshire Moors
  Railway *NYorks*
  YO18 7AJ **204** B4
Northacre **164** A2
Northall **149** E5
Northall Green **178** A4
Northam *Devon* **113** E3
Northam *Soton* **106** D1
Northam Burrows Country
  Park *Devon*
  EX39 1XR **113** E2
Northampton **148** C1
Northaw **136** B2
Northay *Devon* **103** G2
Northay *Som* **103** F1
Northbay **254** C4
Northbeck **175** F3
Northborough **161** G2
Northbourne *Kent* **125** F3
Northbourne *Oxon* **134** A4
Northbridge Street **110** C1
Northbrook *Hants* **119** G4
Northbrook *Oxon* **147** G5
Northburnhill **269** G6
Northchapel **121** E5
Northchurch **135** E2
Northcote Manor **113** G4
Northcott **98** D1
Northcourt **134** A3
Northdyke **276** B5
Northedge **173** E1
Northend
  B&NESom **117** E1
Northend *Bucks* **134** C3
Northend *Warks* **147** F2
Northend House **227** F5
Northfield *Aber* **269** G4
Northfield
  Aberdeen **261** H4
Northfield *High* **275** J4
Northfield *Hull* **196** C5
Northfield *ScBord* **237** G3
Northfield *Som* **115** F4
Northfield *WMid* **158** C5
Northfields **161** F2
Northfleet **137** F5
Northhouse **227** F5
Northiam **110** D1
Northill **149** G3
Northington *Glos* **131** G2
Northington
  Hants **119** G4
Northlands **176** B2
Northleach **132** C2
Northleigh *Devon* **103** E3
Northleigh *Devon* **113** G2
Northlew **99** F1
Northmoor **133** G2
Northmoor Green
  (Moorland) **116** A4
Northmuir **252** B4
Northney **107** G2
Northolt **136** A4
Northop
  (Llaneurgain) **169** F1
Northop Hall **169** F1
Northorpe *Lincs* **176** A3
Northorpe *Lincs* **187** F3
Northorpe *Lincs* **161** F1
Northover *Som* **116** C5
Northover *Som* **116** B5
Northowram **194** A5
Northport **105** F4
Northpunds **279** D10
Northrepps **178** D2
Northton
  (Taobh Tuath) **262** E3
Northtown **277** D8

Northumbria Craft Centre,
  Morpeth *N'umb*
  NE61 1PD **221** E3
Northway *Glos* **146** B4
Northway *Som* **115** E5
Northwich **184** A5
Northwick *SGlos* **131** E4
Northwick *Som* **116** A3
Northwick *Worcs* **146** A2
Northwold **163** F3
Northwood *GtLon* **135** F3
Northwood *IoW* **107** D3
Northwood *Kent* **125** F2
Northwood *Mersey* **183** F3
Northwood *Shrop* **170** B3
Northwood Green **131** G1
Northwood Hills **136** A3
Norton *Glos* **146** A5
Norton *Halton* **183** G4
Norton *Herts* **150** A4
Norton *IoW* **106** C4
Norton *Mon* **144** D5
Norton *N'hants* **148** B1
Norton *Notts* **186** C5
Norton *NSom* **116** A1
Norton *NYorks* **203** G5
Norton *Powys* **144** C1
Norton *Shrop* **157** E2
Norton *Shrop* **157** G2
Norton *Shrop* **157** D4
Norton *Stock* **212** D5
Norton *Suff* **152** A1
Norton *Swan* **128** C4
Norton *SYorks* **186** A5
Norton *SYorks* **186** C4
Norton *VGlam* **129** E5
Norton *Wilts* **132** A4
Norton *WMid* **158** A4
Norton *Worcs* **146** A2
Norton *Worcs* **146** C3
Norton *WSuss* **108** B3
Norton *WSuss* **108** A4
Norton Bavant **118** A3
Norton Bridge **171** F4
Norton Canes **158** C2
Norton Canon **144** C3
Norton Disney **175** D2
Norton Ferris **117** E4
Norton Fitzwarren **115** E5
Norton Green
  Herts **150** A4
Norton Green *IoW* **106** C4
Norton Green
  Stoke **171** G2
Norton Hawkfield **116** C1
Norton Heath **137** F2
Norton in Hales **171** E4
Norton in the
  Moors **171** F2
Norton Lindsey **147** E1
Norton Little Green **152** A1
Norton Malreward **116** D1
Norton Mandeville **137** E2
Norton St. Philip **117** E2
Norton Subcourse **165** F2
Norton Wood **144** C3
Norton Woodseats **186** A4
Norton-Juxta-
  Twycross **159** F2
Norton-le-Clay **202** D5
Norton-sub-
  Hamdon **104** A1
Norwell **174** C1
Norwell Woodhouse **174** C1
Norwich **178** D5
Norwich Castle Museum &
  Art Gallery *Norf*
  NR1 3JU **79** Norwich
Norwich Cathedral *Norf*
  NR1 4DH **79** Norwich
Norwich International
  Airport **178** D4
Norwick **278** F1
Norwood End **137** E2
Norwood Green
  GtLon **136** A5
Norwood Green
  WYorks **194** A5
Norwood Hill **122** B4
Norwood Park **116** C3
Noseley **160** C3
Noss Mayo **100** B3
Nosterfield **202** B4
Nosterfield End **151** E3
Nostie **256** E2
Notgrove **146** D5
Nottage **129** E5
Notting Hill **136** B4
Nottingham *High* **275** J4
Nottingham *Nott* **173** G3
Nottingham Castle Museum
  & Art Gallery NG1 6EL
  80 Nottingham
Nottington **104** C4
Notton *Wilts* **118** A1
Notton *WYorks* **186** A1
Nottswood Hill **131** G1
Nounsley **137** G1
Noutard's Green **145** G1
Nowton **151** G1
Nowton Park *Suff*
  IP29 5LU **151** G1
Nox **156** D1
Noyadd Trefawr **141** F3
Nuffield **134** B4
Nun Monkton **195** E2
Nunburnholme **196** A3
Nuneaton **159** F3
Nuneham
  Courtenay **134** A3
Nunney **117** E3
Nunnington
  Here **145** E3
Nunnington
  NYorks **203** F5
Nunnington Park **115** D5
Nunnykirk **220** C2
Nunsthorpe **188** C2
Nunthorpe *Middl* **203** E1
Nunthorpe *York* **195** E2
Nunton **118** C5
Nunwick *N'umb* **220** A4
Nunwick *NYorks* **202** C5

Nup End **136** B1
Nupend **131** G2
Nursling **106** C1
Nursted **120** C5
Nurton **158** A3
Nutbourne *WSuss* **108** C2
Nutbourne *WSuss* **107** G2
Nutfield **122** C3
Nuthall **173** G2
Nuthampstead **150** C4
Nuthurst *Warks* **159** D5
Nuthurst *WSuss* **121** G5
Nutley *ESuss* **109** G1
Nutley *Hants* **120** B3
Nutwell **186** D2
Nyadd **242** C5
Nybster **275** J2
Nyetimber **108** A4
Nyewood **120** C5
Nymans *WSuss*
  RH17 6EB **109** E1
Nymet Rowland **102** A2
Nymet Tracey **102** A2
Nympsfield **132** A2
Nynehead **115** E5
Nythe **116** B4
Nyton **108** B3

O

O2, The *GtLon*
  SE10 0BB **13** C4
Oad Street **124** A2
Oadby **160** B2
Oak Cross **99** F1
Oak Tree **202** C1
Oakamoor **172** B3
Oakbank *A&B* **239** G1
Oakbank *WLoth* **235** E3
Oakdale *Caerp* **130** A3
Oakdale *Poole* **105** G3
Oake **115** E5
Oaken **158** A2
Oakenclough **192** B3
Oakengates **157** G1
Oakenhead **267** K5
Oakenholt **183** D5
Oakenshaw *Dur* **212** B4
Oakenshaw
  WYorks **194** A5
Oakerthorpe **173** E2
Oakes **185** F1
Oakfield *IoW* **107** E3
Oakfield *Torfaen* **130** B3
Oakford *Cere* **142** A2
Oakford *Devon* **114** C5
Oakfordbridge **114** C5
Oakgrove **171** G1
Oakham **161** D2
Oakhanger **120** C4
Oakhill **116** D3
Oakington **150** C1
Oaklands *Conwy* **168** B2
Oaklands *Herts* **136** B1
Oakle Street **131** G1
Oakley *Bed* **149** F2
Oakley *Fife* **235** E1
Oakley *Hants* **119** G3
Oakley *Oxon* **134** C2
Oakley *Poole* **105** G3
Oakley *Suff* **164** C4
Oakley Green **135** E5
Oakley Park **155** F4
Oakridge Lynch **132** B2
Oaks **156** D2
Oaks Green **172** C4
Oaksey **132** B3
Oakshaw Ford **218** D4
Oakshott **120** C5
Oakthorpe **159** F1
Oaktree Hill **202** C3
Oakwell Hall & Country Park
  WYorks
  WF17 9LG **27** E4
Oakwood Leisure Park
  Pembs
  SA67 8DE **127** D1
Oakwoodhill **121** G4
Oakworth **193** G4
Oare *Kent* **124** C2
Oare *Som* **114** B3
Oare *Wilts* **118** C1
Oasby **175** F4
Oatfield **222** B4
Oath **116** A5
Oathlaw **252** C4
Oatlands **194** C2
Oban (An t-Òban) **240** A2
Obley **156** C5
Oborne **104** C1
Obthorpe **161** F1
Occlestone Green **171** D1
Occold **164** C4
Occumster **275** H5
Oceanarium *BH2 5AA*
  64 Bournemouth
Ochiltree **224** D3
Ochr-y-foel **182** B5
Ochtermuthill **242** D3
Ochtertyre *P&K* **242** D2
Ochtertyre *Stir* **242** C5
Ockbrook **173** F4
Ockeridge **145** G1
Ockham **121** F2
Ockle **247** F2
Ockley **121** G4
Ocle Pychard **145** E3
Octon **204** D5
Odcombe **104** B1
Odd Down **117** E1
Oddendale **200** B1
Oddingley **146** B2
Oddington **134** A1
Odds Farm Park *Bucks*
  HP10 0LX **135** E4
Oddsta **278** E3
Odell **149** E2
Odham **113** E5
Odie **276** F5
Odiham **120** C2
Odsey **150** A4
Odstock **118** C5

Odstone **159** F2
Offchurch **147** F1
Offenham **146** C3
Offerton **184** D4
Offham *ESuss* **109** F2
Offham *Kent* **123** F3
Offham *WSuss* **108** C3
Offley Hoo **149** G5
Offleymarsh **171** E5
Offord Cluny **150** A1
Offord D'Arcy **150** A1
Offton **152** B3
Offwell **103** E3
Ogbourne Maizey **133** D5
Ogbourne
  St. Andrew **133** D5
Ogbourne
  St. George **133** D5
Ogden Water *WYorks*
  HX2 8YA **26** A3
Ogil **252** C3
Ogle **220** D4
Oglet **183** F4
Ogmore **129** E5
Ogmore Vale **129** F3
Ogmore-by-Sea **129** E5
Ogston Reservoir *Derbys*
  DE55 6EL **173** E1
Oil Terminal **277** C8
Okeford Fitzpaine **105** E1
Okehampton **99** F1
Okehampton Camp **99** F1
Okraquoy **279** D9
Olchard **102** B5
Olchfa **128** C3
Old **160** C5
Old Aberdeen **261** H4
Old Alresford **119** G4
Old Arley **159** E3
Old Basford **173** G3
Old Basing **120** B2
Old Belses **227** G3
Old Bewick **229** E4
Old Blacksmith's Shop,
  Gretna Green *D&G*
  DG16 5DY **218** B5
Old Blair **251** E3
Old Bolingbroke **176** B1
Old Bramhope **194** B3
Old Brampton **186** A5
Old Bridge of Urr **216** B4
Old Buckenham **164** B2
Old Burdon **212** C2
Old Burghclere **119** F2
Old Byland **203** E4
Old Cassop **212** C4
Old Church Stoke **156** B3
Old Cleeve **114** D3
Old Clipstone **174** B1
Old Colwyn **181** G5
Old Craig **261** H2
Old Craighall **236** A2
Old Crombie **268** D5
Old Dailly **214** D1
Old Dam **185** F5
Old Deer **269** H6
Old Dilton **117** F3
Old Down *SGlos* **131** F4
Old Down *Som* **116** D2
Old Edlington **186** C3
Old Eldon **212** B5
Old Ellerby **197** D4
Old Felixstowe **153** E4
Old Fletton **161** G3
Old Ford **136** C4
Old Glossop **185** E3
Old Goginan **154** C4
Old Goole **195** G5
Old Gore **145** F5
Old Grimsby **96** A1
Old Hall **188** C1
Old Hall Green **150** B5
Old Hall Street **179** E2
Old Harlow **137** D1
Old Heath **152** B5
Old Heathfield **110** A1
Old Hill **158** B4
Old Hurst **162** B5
Old Hutton **199** G4
Old Kea **96** C5
Old Kilpatrick **233** F2
Old Kinnernie **261** F4
Old Knebworth **150** A5
Old Leake **176** C1
Old Leslie **260** D2
Old Malton **204** B5
Old Milton **106** B3
Old Milverton **147** E1
Old Montsale **138** D3
Old Netley **107** D1
Old Newton **152** B1
Old Philpstoun **235** E2
Old Poltalloch **240** A4
Old Radnor
  (Pencraig) **144** B2
Old Rattray **269** J5
Old Rayne **260** E2
Old Romney **111** F1
Old Scone **243** G2
Old Shields **234** C2
Old Sodbury **131** G4
Old Somerby **175** E4
Old Station, The, Tintern
  Parva *Mon*
  NP16 7NX **131** E2
Old Stratford **148** C3
Old Sunderlandwick **196** C2
Old Swarland **221** D1
Old Swinford **158** B4
Old Thirsk **202** D4
Old Town *Cumb* **199** G4
Old Town *IoS* **96** B1
Old Town Farm **220** A2
Old Tupton **173** E1
Old Warden **149** G3
Old Weston **161** F5
Old Windsor **135** E5
Old Wives Lees **124** C3

Old Woking **121** F2
Old Woodhall **176** A1
Old Woods **170** B5
Oldberrow **146** D1
Oldborough **102** A2
Oldbury *Kent* **123** F3
Oldbury *Shrop* **157** G3
Oldbury *WMid* **158** B4
Oldbury Court Estate
  Bristol BS16 2JH **8** D2
Oldbury Naite **131** F3
Oldbury on the Hill **132** A4
Oldbury-on-Severn **131** F3
Oldcastle *Bridgend* **129** F5
Oldcastle *Mon* **144** D4
Oldcastle Heath **170** B3
Oldcotes **186** C4
Oldcroft **131** F2
Oldeamere **162** B3
Oldfield **146** A1
Oldford **117** E2
Oldhall *Aber* **260** C5
Oldhall *High* **275** H3
Oldham **184** D2
Oldham Edge **184** D2
Oldhamstocks **237** E2
Oldland **131** F5
Oldmeldrum **261** G2
Oldmill **260** D4
Oldpark **157** F2
Oldridge **102** B3
Oldshore Beg **272** D3
Oldshoremore **272** E3
Oldstead **203** E5
Oldtown **266** C3
Oldtown of Aigas **266** B7
Oldtown of Ord **268** E5
Oldwalls **128** A3
Oldways End **114** B5
Oldwhat **269** G5
Oldwich Lane **159** E5
Olgrinmore **275** G3
Oliver **226** C3
Oliver's Battery **119** F5
Ollaberry **278** C4
Ollerton *ChesE* **184** B5
Ollerton *Notts* **174** B1
Ollerton *Shrop* **170** D5
Olmstead Green **151** E3
Olney **149** D2
Olrig House **275** G2
Olton **158** D4
Olveston **131** F4
Ombersley **146** A1
Ompton **174** B1
Onchan **190** B4
Onecote **172** B2
Onehouse **152** B2
Ongar Hill **177** D5
Ongar Street **144** C1
Onich
  (Omhanaich) **248** C3
Onllwyn **129** E1
Onneley **171** E3
Onslow Green **137** F1
Onslow Village **121** E3
Onibury **157** D5
Opinan *High* **264** C5
Opinan *High* **264** D4
Orange Lane **237** E5
Orasaigh **271** F6
Orbliston **268** B5
Orbost **263** H7
Orby **176** C1
Orcadia **232** C3
Orchard **232** C1
Orchard Portman **115** F5
Orcheston **118** B3
Orcop **145** D5
Orcop Hill **145** D5
Ord **256** C3
Ordhead **260** E3
Ordie **260** C4
Ordiequish **268** B5
Ordsall **187** D5
Ore **110** D2
Oreham Common **109** E2
Oreston **100** B2
Oreton **157** F5
Orford *Suff* **153** E2
Orford *Warr* **184** A3
Organford **105** F3
Orgreave **158** D1
Orkney Islands **276** C5
Orlestone **124** B5
Orleton *Here* **145** D1
Orleton *Worcs* **145** F1
Orleton Common **145** D1
Orlingbury **161** D5
Ormacleit **254** C1
Ormesby **203** E1
Ormesby
  St. Margaret **179** F4
Ormesby
  St. Michael **179** F4
Ormidale **232** B1
Ormiscaig **264** E2
Ormiston **236** B3
Ormlie **275** G2
Ormsaigmore **247** D3
Ormsary **231** F2
Ormskirk **183** F2
Oronsay **230** B1
Orphir **277** C7
Orpington **123** C7
Orrell *GtMan* **183** G2
Orrell *Mersey* **183** E3
Orrisdale **190** B2
Orrok House **261** H3
Orroland **208** A2
Orsett **137** F4
Orsett Heath **137** F4
Orslow **158** A1
Orston **174** C3
Orton *Cumb* **200** B2
Orton *N'hants* **160** D5
Orton Longueville **161** G3
Orton Rigg **209** G1
Orton Waterville **161** G3

Old Woking **121** F2
Orton-on-the-Hill **159** F2
Orwell **150** B2
Osbaldeston **192** C4
Osbaldwick **195** F2
Osbaston *Leics* **159** G2
Osbaston *Shrop* **170** A5
Osbaston *Tel&W* **157** E1
Osbaston Hollow **159** G2
Osborne **107** E3
Osborne House *IoW*
  PO32 6JX **107** E3
Osbournby **175** F4
Oscroft **170** C1
Ose **263** J7
Osgathorpe **159** G1
Osgodby *Lincs* **188** A3
Osgodby *NYorks* **195** F4
Osgodby *NYorks* **205** D4
Oskaig **256** B1
Osleston **172** D4
Osmaston *Derby* **173** E4
Osmaston *Derbys* **172** C3
Osmington **104** C4
Osmington Mills **104** D4
Osmondthorpe **194** C4
Osmotherley **203** D3
Osnaburgh (Dairsie) **244** C3
Ospringe **124** C2
Ossett **194** B5
Ossett Street Side **194** B5
Ossington **174** C1
Ostend **138** C3
Osterley **136** A5
Osterley Park & House
  GtLon TW7 4RB **11** B5
Oswaldkirk **203** F5
Oswaldwistle **192** D5
Oswestry **169** F5
Oteley **170** B4
Otford **123** E3
Otham **123** G3
Otherton **158** B1
Othery **116** A4
Otley *Suff* **152** D2
Otley *WYorks* **194** B3
Otter **232** A2
Otter Ferry **232** A1
Otterbourne **119** F5
Otterburn *N'umb* **220** A2
Otterburn *NYorks* **193** E2
Otterburn Camp **220** A2
Otterden Place **124** B3
Otterham **98** B1
Otterham Quay **124** A2
Otterhampton **115** F3
Ottershaw **121** F1
Otterswick **278** E4
Otterton **103** D4
Otterton Mill *Devon*
  EX9 7HG **103** D4
Otterwood **106** D2
Ottery St. Mary **103** D3
Ottinge **125** D4
Ottringham **197** E5
Oughterby **209** G1
Oughtershaw **201** D4
Oughterside **209** E2
Oughtibridge **186** A3
Oulston **203** E5
Oulton *Cumb* **209** F1
Oulton *Norf* **178** C3
Oulton *Staffs* **171** G4
Oulton *Staffs* **171** E5
Oulton *Suff* **165** G2
Oulton *WYorks* **194** C5
Oulton Broad **165** G2
Oulton Grange **171** G4
Oulton Street **178** C3
Oultoncross **171** G4
Oundle **161** F4
Our Dynamic Earth *Edin*
  EH8 8AS **37** J4
Ousby **210** C4
Ousdale **275** F6
Ousden **151** F2
Ousefleet **196** A5
Ouston *Dur* **212** B2
Ouston *N'umb* **220** C4
Out Newton **197** F5
Out Rawcliffe **192** A3
Out Skerries Airstrip **278** F5
Outcast **199** E5
Outchester **229** F3
Outertown **277** B7
Outgate **199** E3
Outhgill **200** C2
Outlands **171** E5
Outlane **185** E1
Outwell **162** D2
Outwood *Surr* **122** C4
Outwood *WYorks* **194** C5
Outwoods **157** G2
Ouzlewell Green **194** C5
Ovenden **193** G5
Over *Cambs* **162** B5
Over *ChesW&C* **170** D1
Over *Glos* **132** A1
Over *SGlos* **131** E4
Over Burrows **173** D4
Over Compton **104** B1
Over Dinsdale **202** C1
Over End **185** G5
Over Green **159** D3
Over Haddon **172** D1
Over Hulton **184** A2
Over Kellet **192** B1
Over Kiddington **147** G5
Over Monnow **131** D1
Over Norton **147** F5
Over Peover **184** B5
Over Rankeilour **244** B3
Over Silton **203** D3
Over Stowey **115** E4
Over Stratton **104** A1
Over Tabley **184** B4
Over Wallop **119** D4
Over Whitacre **159** E3
Over Winchendon (Upper
  Winchendon) **134** C1
Over Worton **147** G5
Overbister **276** F3

Overbrae **269** G5
Overbury **146** B4
Overcombe **104** C4
Overgreen **186** A5
Overleigh **116** B4
Overpool **183** E5
Overscaig Hotel **273** G6
Overseal **159** E1
Overslade **159** G5
Oversland **124** C3
Oversley Green **146** C2
Overstone **148** D1
Overstrand **178** D1
Overthorpe **147** G3
Overton *Aber* **261** F3
Overton *ChesE* **183** G5
Overton *Hants* **119** G3
Overton *Lancs* **192** A2
Overton *NYorks* **195** F3
Overton *Shrop* **157** E5
Overton *Swan* **128** A4
Overton (Owrtyn)
  Wrex **170** A3
Overton *WYorks* **185** G1
Overton Bridge **170** A3
Overtown *Lancs* **200** B5
Overtown *NLan* **234** C4
Overtown *Swin* **133** D5
Overy **134** A3
Oving *Bucks* **148** C5
Oving *WSuss* **108** B3
Ovingdean **109** F3
Ovingham **211** G1
Ovington *Dur* **202** A1
Ovington *Essex* **151** F3
Ovington *Hants* **119** G4
Ovington *N'umb* **211** G1
Ovington *Norf* **178** A5
Ower *Hants* **106** C1
Ower *Hants* **107** D2
Owermoigne **105** D4
Owler Bar **185** G5
Owlpen **131** G3
Owl's Green **153** D1
Owlswick **134** C2
Owmby **188** A2
Owmby-by-Spital **188** A4
Owslebury **119** G5
Owston **160** C3
Owston Ferry **187** F2
Owstwick **197** E4
Owthorpe **174** B4
Oxborough **163** F2
Oxcliffe Hill **192** A1
Oxcombe **188** D5
Oxen End **151** E5
Oxen Park **199** E4
Oxencombe **102** B4
Oxenhall **145** G5
Oxenholme **199** G3
Oxenhope **193** G4
Oxenpill **116** B3
Oxenton **146** B4
Oxenwood **119** E2
Oxford **134** A2
Oxford Cathedral *Oxon*
  OX1 1AB **80** Oxford
Oxford Story *Oxon*
  OX1 3AJ **80** Oxford
Oxford University Museum
  of Natural History
  Oxon OX1 3PW
  80 Oxford
Oxhey **136** A3
Oxhill **147** F3
Oxley *Green* **138** C3
Oxley's Green **110** B1
Oxnam **228** B5
Oxnead **178** D3
Oxnop Ghyll **201** E3
Oxshott **121** G1
Oxspring **185** G2
Oxted **122** C3
Oxton *Mersey* **183** E4
Oxton *Notts* **174** B2
Oxton *ScBord* **236** B4
Oxwich **128** A4
Oxwich Green **128** A4
Oxwick **178** A3
Oykel Bridge **265** K1
Oyne **260** E2
Ozleworth **131** G3

P

Pabbay **262** D3
Packington **159** F1
Packwood **159** D5
Padanaram **252** C4
Padarn Country Park
  Gwyn
  LL55 4TY **167** E1
Padbury **148** C4
Paddington **136** B4
Paddlesworth **125** D4
Paddock **124** B3
Paddock Wood **123** F4
Paddockhaugh **267** K6
Paddockhole **218** A3
Paddolgreen **170** C4
Padeswood **169** F1
Padfield **185** E3
Padiham **193** D4
Padside **194** A2
Padstow **96** D2
Padworth **120** B1
Paganhill **132** A2
Pagham **108** A4
Paglesham
  Churchend **138** C3
Paglesham
  Eastend **138** C3
Paible **263** F2
Paignton **101** E1
Paignton & Dartmouth
  Steam Railway
  Torbay
  TQ4 6AF **101** E1
Paignton Pier
  Torbay
  TQ4 6BW **101** E1

307

Paignton Zoo
  Torbay
  TQ4 7EU **101** E2
Pailton **159** G4
Paine's Corner **110** B1
Painscastle **144** A3
Painshawfield **211** G1
Painswick **132** A2
Pairc **270** E3
Paisley **233** F3
Pakefield **165** G2
Pakenham **152** A1
Palace of Holyroodhouse
  Edin EH8 8DX **37** J4
Palacerigg Country Park
  NLan G67 3HU **234** B4
Pale **168** C4
Palehouse
  Common **109** G2
Palestine **119** D3
Paley Street **135** D5
Palgowan **215** E2
Palgrave **164** C4
Pallinsburn House **228** C3
Palmarsh **124** D5
Palmers Cross **121** F3
Palmers Green **136** C3
Palmerscross **267** K5
Palmerstown **130** A5
Palnackie **216** C5
Palnure **215** F4
Palterton **173** F1
Pamber End **120** B2
Pamber Green **120** B2
Pamber Heath **120** B1
Pamington **146** B4
Pamphill **105** F2
Pampisford **150** C3
Pan **277** C8
Panborough **116** B3
Pancrasweek **112** C5
Pancross **114** D1
Pandy Gwyn **154** C2
Pandy Mon **144** C5
Pandy Powys **155** F2
Pandy Wrex **169** E4
Pandy Tudur **168** B1
Pandy'r Capel **169** D2
Panfield **151** F5
Pangbourne **134** B5
Pannal **194** B3
Pannal Ash **194** B2
Panshanger **136** B1
Pant **169** F5
Pant Glas **167** D3
Pant Gwyn **168** B5
Pant Mawr **155** E4
Pantasaph **182** C5
Panteg **130** C3
Pantglas **155** D3
Pantgwyn Carmar **142** B5
Pantgwyn Cere **141** F3
Pant-lasau **128** C2
Panton **188** B5
Pant-pastynog **168** D1
Pantperthog **154** D2
Pant-y-dwr **155** F5
Pantyffrdd **169** F2
Pant-y-ffridd **156** A2
Pantyffynnon **128** C1
Pantygasseg **130** B3
Pantygelli **130** C1
Pantymwyn **169** E1
Panxworth **179** E4
Papa Stour **279** A6
Papa Stour Airstrip **279** A6
Papa Westray **276** D2
Papa Westray
  Airfield **276** D2
Papcastle **209** E3
Papil **279** C9
Papple **236** C2
Papplewick **173** G2
Papworth Everard **150** A1
Papworth St. Agnes **150** A1
Par **97** E4
Paradise Park, Newhaven
  ESuss BN9 0DH **109** G3
Paradise Wildlife Park,
  Broxbourne Herts
  EN10 7QA **136** C2
Parbold **183** F1
Parbrook Som **116** C4
Parbrook WSuss **121** F5
Parc **168** B4
Parcllyn **141** F2
Parc **268** C2
Parcrhydderch **142** C2
Parc-Seymour **130** D3
Pardshaw **209** D4
Parham **153** E1
Parish Holm **225** F3
Park **268** C2
Park Close **193** E3
Park Corner ESuss **123** E5
Park Corner Oxon **134** B4
Park End N'umb **220** A4
Park End Staffs **171** E2
Park End Worcs **157** G5
Park Gate Hants **107** E3
Park Gate Worcs **158** B5
Park Gate WYorks **194** A3
Park Gate WYorks **185** G1
Park Green **152** C1
Park Hill **186** A4
Park Lane **170** B4
Park Langley **122** C2
Park Rose Pottery & Leisure
  Park ERid
  YO15 3QF **196** D1
Parkend Cumb **209** G3
Parkend Glos **131** F2
Parker's Green **123** F4
Parkeston **152** D4
Parkfield Corn **98** D4
Parkfield SGlos **131** F5
Parkfield WMid **158** B3
Parkford **252** C4
Parkgate ChesW&C **183** D5
Parkgate D&G **217** E2
Parkgate Kent **124** A5
Parkgate Surr **122** B4
Parkgate SYorks **186** B3
Parkham **113** D3
Parkham Ash **113** D3
Parkhead Angus **253** E5
Parkhill P&K **251** G5
Parkhouse **131** D2
Parkhurst **107** D3
Parkmill **128** B4
Parkmore **268** B6
Parkneuk **253** F2
Parkside **170** A2
Parkstone **105** G3
Parkway **116** C3
Parley Cross **105** G3
Parley Green **106** A3
Parlington **194** D4
Parracombe **113** G1
Parrog **140** D4
Parson Cross **186** A3
Parson Drove **162** B2
Parsonage Green **137** F1
Parsonby **209** E3
Partick **233** G3
Partington **184** B3
Partney **176** C1
Parton Cumb **208** B5
Parton D&G **216** A3
Partridge Green **109** D2
Parwich **172** C2
Paslow Wood
  Common **137** E2
Passenham **148** C4
Passfield **120** D4
Passingford Bridge **137** E3
Paston **179** E2
Paston Street **179** E2
Pasturefields **171** G5
Patcham **109** F3
Patchacott **99** E1
Patching **108** C3
Patchole **113** F4
Patchway **131** F4
Pateley Bridge **194** A1
Path of Condie **243** F3
Pathe **116** A4
Pathfinder Village **102** B3
Pathhead Aber **253** F2
Pathhead EAyr **225** E4
Pathhead Fife **244** A5
Pathhead Midlo **236** A3
Pathlow **147** D2
Patmore Heath **150** C5
Patna **224** C4
Patney **118** B1
Patrick **190** A3
Patrick Brompton **202** B3
Patrington **197** F5
Patrington Haven **197** F5
Patrishow **144** B5
Patrixbourne **125** D3
Patterdale **209** G5
Pattingham **158** A3
Pattishall **148** B2
Pattiswick **151** G5
Paul **94** B4
Paulerspury **148** C3
Paull **197** D5
Paull Holme **197** D5
Paul's Green **94** D3
Paulton **117** D2
Paultons Park Hants
  SO51 6AL **106** C1
Pauperhaugh **220** D1
Pave Lane **157** G1
Pavenham **149** E2
Pavilion Gardens, Buxton
  Derbys
  SK17 6XN **185** E5
Pawlett **116** A3
Pawston **228** C3
Paxford **147** E4
Paxhill Park **109** F1
Paxton **237** G4
Payden Street **124** B3
Payhembury **103** D2
Paythorne **193** E2
Peacehaven **109** G3
Peacemarsh **117** F5
Peachley **146** A2
Peak Dale **185** E5
Peak Forest **185** F5
Peakirk **161** G2
Pean Hill **124** D2
Pear Tree **173** E4
Pearsie **252** B4
Pearson's Green **123** F4
Peartree **136** B1
Peartree Green
  Essex **137** E3
Peartree Green
  Here **145** F4
Pease Pottage **122** B5
Peasedown St. John **117** E2
Peasehill **173** F3
Peaseland Green **178** B4
Peasemore **133** G5
Peasenhall **153** E1
Peaslake **121** F3
Peasley Cross **183** G3
Peasmarsh ESuss **111** D1
Peasmarsh Surr **121** E3
Peaston **236** B3
Peastonbank **236** B3
Peat Inn **244** C4
Peathill **269** H4
Peathrow **212** A1
Peatling Magna **160** A3
Peatling Parva **160** A4
Peaton **157** E4
Pebble Coombe **122** B3
Pebmarsh **151** G4
Pebworth **146** D3
Pecket Well **193** F5
Peckforton **170** C2
Peckham **136** C5
Peckleton **159** G2
Pedham **179** E4
Pedmore **158** B4
Pedwell **116** B4
Peebles **235** G5
Peel IoM **190** A3
Peel Lancs **191** G4
Peening Quarter **111** D1
Peggs Green **159** G1
Pegsdon **149** G4
Pegswood **221** E3
Pegwell **125** F2
Peighinn nan
  Aoireann **254** C1
Peinchorran **256** B1
Peinlich **263** K6
Pelaw **212** B1
Pelcomb **126** C1
Pelcomb Bridge **126** C1
Pelcomb Cross **126** C1
Peldon **138** C1
Pellon **193** G5
Pelsall **158** C2
Pelton **212** B2
Pelutho **209** E2
Pelynt **97** G4
Pemberton **183** G2
Pembrey (Pen-bre) **128** A2
Pembrey Country Park
  Carmar
  SA16 0EJ **128** A2
Pembridge **144** C2
Pembroke (Penfro) **126** C2
Pembroke Dock
  (Doc Penfro) **126** C2
Pembury **123** F4
Penallt **131** E1
Penally **127** E3
Penalt **145** E5
Penare **97** D5
Penarron **156** A1
Penarth **130** A5
Pen-bont
  Rhydybeddau **154** C4
Penboyr **141** G4
Penbryn **141** F2
Pencader **142** A4
Pen-cae **142** A2
Pen-cae-cwm **168** C1
Pencaenewydd **166** D3
Pencaitland **236** B3
Pencarnisiog **180** B5
Pencarreg **142** B3
Pencarrow **97** F1
Pencelli **143** E4
Pen-clawdd **128** B3
Pencoed **129** F4
Pencombe **145** E2
Pencoyd **145** E5
Pencraig Here **145** E5
Pencraig Powys **168** C5
Pendeen **94** A3
Penderyn **129** F2
Pendine
  (Pentywyn) **127** F2
Pendlebury **184** B2
Pendleton **193** D4
Pendock **145** G4
Pendoggett **97** E2
Pendomer **104** B1
Pendoylan **129** G5
Penegoes **155** D2
Pen-ffordd **141** D5
Pengam **130** A3
Penge **136** C5
Pengenffordd **144** A5
Pengorffwysfa **180** C3
Pengover Green **97** G3
Pen-groes-oped **130** C2
Pengwern **182** B5
Penhale **95** D5
Penhallow **96** B4
Penhalvean **95** E3
Penhill **154** C3
Penhow **130** D3
Penhurst **110** B2
Peniarth **154** C2
Penicuik **235** G3
Peniel **142** A5
Penifiler **263** K7
Peninver **222** C3
Penisa'r Waun **167** E1
Penisarcwm **155** G1
Penishawain **143** E3
Penistone **185** G2
Penjerrick **95** E3
Penketh **183** G4
Penkill **214** D5
Penkridge **158** B1
Penlean **98** C1
Penley **170** B4
Penllech **166** B4
Penllergaer **128** C3
Pen-llyn IoA **180** B4
Penllyn VGlam **129** F5
Pen-lôn **166** D1
Penmachno **168** A2
Penmaen **128** B4
Penmaenan **181** F5
Penmaenmawr **181** F5
Penmaenpool (Llyn
  Penmaen) **154** C1
Penmaen-Rhôs **181** G5
Penmark **115** D1
Penmon **181** E4
Penmorfa **167** E3
Penmynydd **180** D5
Penn Bucks **135** E3
Penn WMid **158** A3
Penn Street **135** E3
Pennal **154** C2
Pennal-isaf **154** D2
Pennan **269** G4
Pennance **96** B5
Pennant Cere **142** B1
Pennant Powys **155** E3
Pennant Melangell **168** D5
Pennar **126** C2
Pennard **128** B4
Pennerley **156** C3
Penninghame **215** E4
Pennington Cumb **199** D5
Pennington Hants **106** C3
Pennington Flash Country
  Park GtMan
  WN7 3PA **184** A3
Pennington Green **184** A2
Pennorth **144** A5
Pennsylvania **131** G5
Penny Bridge **199** E4
Pennycross **100** A2
Pennyfuir **240** A1
Pennygate **179** E3
Pennyghael **239** E2
Pennyglen **224** A4
Pennygown **247** F5
Pennymoor **102** B1
Penny's Green **164** C2
Pennyvenie **224** C5
Penparc Cere **141** F3
Penparc Pembs **140** B4
Penparcau **154** B4
Penpedairheol **130** C2
Penpethy **97** E1
Penpillick **97** E4
Penpol **95** F3
Penpoll **97** F4
Penponds **94** D3
Penpont D&G **216** C1
Penpont Powys **143** F5
Penprysg **129** F4
Penquit **100** C2
Penrherber **141** F4
Penrhiw **141** F3
Penrhiwceiber **129** G3
Penrhiwgoch **128** B1
Penrhiw-llan **141** G3
Penrhiw-pâl **141** G3
Penrhiwtyn **128** D3
Penrhos Gwyn **166** C4
Penrhos IoA **180** A4
Penrhos Mon **130** D1
Penrhos Powys **129** E1
Penrhos-garnedd **181** D5
Penrhyn Bay
  (Bae Penrhyn) **181** G4
Penrhyn Castle Gwyn
  LL57 4HN **181** D5
Penrhyn-coch **154** C4
Penrhyndeudraeth **167** F4
Penrhyn-side **181** G4
Penrhys **129** G3
Penrice **128** A4
Penrith **210** B5
Penrose Corn **96** C2
Penrose Corn **97** G1
Penruddock **210** A5
Penryn **95** E3
Pensarn Carmar **128** A1
Pensarn Conwy **182** A5
Pen-sarn Gwyn **167** E5
Pen-sarn Gwyn **166** D3
Pensax **145** G1
Pensby **183** D4
Penselwood **117** E4
Pensford **116** D1
Pensham **146** B3
Penshaw **212** C2
Penshurst **123** E4
Pensilva **97** G3
Pensnett **158** B4
Penston **236** B2
Pentewan **97** E5
Pentir **167** E1
Pentire **96** B3
Pentireglaze **96** D2
Pentlepoir **127** E2
Pentlow **151** G3
Pentlow Street **151** G3
Pentney **163** F1
Penton Mewsey **119** E3
Pentonville **136** C4
Pentraeth **180** D5
Pentre Powys **169** D5
Pentre Powys **155** G4
Pentre Powys **144** B1
Pentre Powys **156** B3
Pentre Powys **156** A4
Pentre RCT **129** F3
Pentre Shrop **156** C1
Pentre Shrop **156** C5
Pentre Wrex **169** F3
Pentre Wrex **170** B4
Pentre Berw **180** C5
Pentre Ffwrndan **183** D5
Pentre Galar **141** E4
Pentre Gwenlais **128** C1
Pentre Gwynfryn **167** E5
Pentre Halkyn **182** C5
Pentre Isaf **168** B1
Pentre Llanrhaeadr **169** D1
Pentre Maelor **170** B3
Pentre Meyrick **129** F5
Pentre Poeth **128** C3
Pentre Saron **168** D1
Pentre-bach Cere **142** B3
Pentre-bach MTyd **129** G2
Pentre-bach Powys **143** F4
Pentrebach RCT **129** G4
Pentrebach Swan **128** B2
Pentre-bont **168** A2
Pentre-bwlch **169** E5
Pentrecagal **141** G3
Pentre-celyn
  Denb **169** E2
Pentre-celyn
  Powys **155** E2
Pentre-chwyth **128** C3
Pentreclwydau **129** E2
Pentre-cwrt **141** G4
Pentre-Dolau-
  Honddu **143** F3
Pentredwr Denb **169** E3
Pentre-dwr Swan **128** C3
Pentrefelin Carmar **142** C5
Pentrefelin Cere **142** C3
Pentrefelin Conwy **181** G5
Pentrefelin Gwyn **167** E4
Pentrefelin Powys **169** E5
Pentrefoelas **168** B2
Pentregat **141** G2
Pentreheyling **156** B3
Pentre-llwyn-
  llwyd **143** F2
Pentre-llyn **154** C5
Pennington Flash Country
Pennine
Pentre-llyn-
  cymmer **168** C2
Pentre-piod **168** B4
Pentre-poeth **130** B4
Pentre'r beirdd **156** A1
Pentre'r Felin **168** B1
Pentre'r-felin **143** F4
Pentre-tafarn-y-
  fedw **168** A2
Pentre-ty-gwyn **143** E4
Pentrich **173** E2
Pentridge **105** G1
Pentwyn Caerp **130** A2
Pen-twyn Caerp **130** B2
Pentwyn Cardiff **130** B4
Pen-twyn Mon **131** E2
Pentwyn-mawr **130** A3
Pentyrch **130** A4
Penuwch **142** B1
Penwithick **97** E4
Penwood **119** F1
Penwyllt **129** E1
Pen-y-banc **142** C5
Pen-y-bont
  Carmar **143** D4
Pen-y-bont
  Carmar **141** G5
Pen-y-bont Powys **155** G1
Pen-y-bont Powys **169** F5
Penybont Powys **144** A1
Pen-y-bryn Gwyn **154** C1
Pen-y-bryn Pembs **141** E3
Pen-y-bryn Wrex **169** F3
Pen-y-cae Powys **129** F3
Penycae Wrex **169** F3
Pen-y-cae-mawr **130** D3
Pen-y-cefn **182** C5
Pen-y-clawdd **130** D2
Pen-y-coedcae **129** G4
Penycwm **140** B5
Pen-y-Darren **129** G2
Pen-y-fai **129** E5
Penyffordd Flints **170** A1
Penyffridd **167** E2
Pen-y-gaer **144** A5
Pen-y-garn Carmar **142** B4
Pen-y-garn Cere **154** C4
Penygarn Torfaen **130** B2
Penygarnedd **143** G3
Pen-y-garreg **143** G3
Pen-y-Graig Gwyn **166** B4
Penygraig RCT **129** G3
Penygroes Carmar **128** B1
Penygroes Gwyn **167** D2
Pen-y-Gwryd Hotel **167** F2
Pen-y-lan **130** A5
Pen-y-Mynydd
  Carmar **128** A2
Penymynydd
  Flints **170** A1
Pen-y-parc **169** F1
Pen-y-Park **144** B3
Pen-yr-englyn **129** F3
Pen-yr-heol Mon **130** D1
Penyrheol Swan **128** B3
Pen-y-sarn **180** C3
Pen-y-stryt **169** E2
Penywaun **129** F2
Penzance **94** B3
Penzance Heliport **94** B3
People's Palace & Winter
  Gardens Glas
  G40 1AT **39** H6
Peopleton **146** B2
Peover Heath **184** B5
Peper Harow **121** E3
Peplow **170** D5
Pepper Arden **202** B2
Pepper's Green **137** F1
Perceton **233** E5
Percie **260** E5
Percyhorner **269** H4
Periton **114** C3
Perivale **136** A4
Perkhill **260** D4
Perkins Beach **156** C2
Perkin's Village **102** D3
Perlethorpe **186** D5
Perran Downs **94** C3
Perranarworthal **95** E3
Perranporth **96** A4
Perranuthnoe **94** C4
Perranzabuloe **96** B4
Perrott's Brook **132** C2
Perry Barr **158** C3
Perry Crofts **159** E2
Perry Green
  Essex **151** G5
Perry Green Herts **136** D1
Perry Green Wilts **132** B4
Perry Street **137** F5
Perrymead **117** E1
Pershall **171** F5
Pershore **146** B3
Persie House **251** G4
Pert **253** E3
Pertenhall **149** F1
Perth (Peairt) **243** G2
Perthcelyn **129** G3
Perthy **170** A4
Perton **132** B4
Pestalozzi Children's
  Village **110** C2
Peter Tavy **99** F3
Peterborough **161** G3
Peterburn **264** D3
Peterchurch **144** C4
Peterculter **261** G4
Peterhead **269** K6
Peterlee **212** D3
Peter's Green **136** A1
Peters Marland **113** E4
Peters Port
  (Port Pheadair) **262** D7
Petersfield **120** C5
Petersfinger **118** C5
Peterstone
  Wentlooge **130** B4
Peterston-super-
  Ely **129** G5
Peterstow **145** E5
Petham **124** D3
Petrockstowe **113** F5
Pett **111** D2
Pettaugh **152** C2
Petterill Green **210** A3
Pettinain **235** D5
Pettistree **153** D2
Petton Devon **114** D5
Petton Shrop **170** B5
Petts Wood **122** D2
Petty **261** F1
Petty France **131** G4
Pettycur **235** G1
Pettymuick **261** H2
Petworth **121** E5
Pevensey **110** B3
Pevensey Bay **110** B3
Peverell **100** A2
Pewsey **118** C1
Pheasant's Hill **134** C4
Phesdo **253** E2
Philham **112** C4
Philharmonic Hall, Liverpool
  Mersey L1 9BP **43** E5
Philiphaugh **227** F3
Phillack **94** C3
Phille
Philleigh **95** F3
Philpstoun **235** E2
Phocle Green **145** F5
Phoenix Green **120** C3
Phones **258** C5
Phorp **267** H6
Photographer's Gallery, The,
  London GtLon
  WC2H 7HY **44** E3
Pibsbury **116** B5
Pica **208** D4
Piccadilly Corner **165** D3
Pickerells **137** E2
Pickering **203** G4
Pickering Nook **212** A2
Picket Piece **119** E3
Picket Post **106** A2
Pickford Green **159** E4
Pickhill **202** C4
Picklescott **156** D3
Pickletillem **244** C2
Pickmere **184** A5
Pickney **115** E5
Pickstock **171** E5
Pickston **243** E2
Pickup Bank **192** D5
Pickwell Devon **113** E1
Pickwell Leics **160** C1
Pickworth Lincs **175** F4
Pickworth Rut **161** E1
Picton ChesW&C **183** F5
Picton NYorks **202** D2
Piddinghoe **109** G3
Piddington
  N'hants **148** D2
Piddington Oxon **134** B1
Piddlehinton **104** D3
Piddletrenthide **104** D3
Pidley **162** B5
Piece Hall, Halifax WYorks
  HX1 1RE **26** B4
Piercebridge **202** B1
Pierowall **276** D3
Pigdon **221** D3
Pike Hill **193** E4
Pikehall **172** C2
Pikeshill **106** B2
Pilgrims Hatch **137** E3
Pilham **187** F3
Pill **131** E5
Pillaton Corn **99** D4
Pillaton Staffs **158** B1
Pillerton Hersey **147** E3
Pillerton Priors **147** E3
Pilleth **144** B1
Pilley Hants **106** C3
Pilley SYorks **186** A2
Pilling **192** A3
Pilling Lane **191** G4
Pillowell **131** F2
Pilning **131** E4
Pilsbury **172** C1
Pilsdon **104** A3
Pilsgate **161** F2
Pilsley Derbys **173** F1
Pilsley Derbys **185** G5
Pilson Green **179** E4
Piltdown **109** G1
Pilton Devon **113** F2
Pilton N'hants **161** F4
Pilton Rut **161** E2
Pilton Som **116** D3
Pilton Swan **128** A4
Pilton Green **128** A4
Pimhole **184** C1
Pimlico **173** E2
Pimperne **105** F2
Pin Mill **152** D4
Pinchbeck **176** A5
Pinchbeck Bars **176** A5
Pinchbeck West **176** A5
Pincheon Green **187** D1
Pinchinthorpe **203** E1
Pindon End **148** C3
Pinehurst **132** D4
Pinfold **183** E1
Pinged **128** A2
Pinhay **103** G3
Pinhoe **102** C3
Pinkneys Green **135** D4
Pinley Green **147** E1
Pinminnoch **214** C5
Pinmore **214** D1
Pinn **103** E4
Pinner **136** A4
Pinner Green **136** A3
Pinvin **146** B3
Pinwherry **214** C2
Pinxton **173** F2
Pipe & Lyde **145** E3
Pipe Gate **171** E3
Pipe Ridware **158** C1
Pipehill **158** C2
Piperhall **232** B4
Piperhill **267** F6
Pipers Pool **97** G1
Pipewell **160** D4
Pippacott **113** F2
Pipton **144** A4
Pirbright **121** E2
Pirnmill **231** F5
Pirton Herts **149** G4
Pirton Worcs **146** A3
Pisgah **242** C4
Pishill **134** C4
Pistyll **166** C3
Pitagowan **250** D3
Pitblae **269** H4
Pitcairngreen **243** F2
Pitcairns **243** F3
Pitcaple **261** F2
Pitch Green **134** C2
Pitch Place Surr **121** E2
Pitch Place Surr **121** D4
Pitchcombe **132** A2
Pitchcott **148** C1
Pitchford **157** E2
Pitcombe **117** D4
Pitcot **129** E5
Pitcox **236** D2
Pitcur **244** A1
Pitfichie **260** E3
Pitgrudy **266** E2
Pitinnan **261** F1
Pitkennedy **252** D4
Pitkevy **244** A4
Pitlessie **244** B4
Pitlochry **251** E4
Pitman's Corner **152** C1
Pitmedden **261** G2
Pitminster **103** F1
Pitmuies **253** D5
Pitmunie **260** E3
Pitnacree **251** E4
Pitney **116** B5
Pitroddie **244** A2
Pitscottie **244** C3
Pitsea **137** G4
Pitsford **148** C1
Pitsford Hill **115** D4
Pitstone **135** E1
Pitt Devon **102** D1
Pitt Hants **119** F5
Pitt Rivers Museum Oxon
  OX1 3PP **80** Oxford
Pittendreich **267** J5
Pittentrail **266** E1
Pittenweem **244** D4
Pitteuchar **244** A5
Pittington **212** C3
Pittodrie House **260** E2
Pitton Swan **128** A4
Pitton Wilts **118** D4
Pittulie **269** H4
Pittville **146** B5
Pity Me **212** B3
Pityme **96** D2
Pixey Green **164** D4
Pixley **145** F4
Place Newton **204** B5
Plaidy **269** F5
Plain Dealings **127** D1
Plainfield **220** B4
Plains **234** B3
Plainsfield **115** E4
Plaish **157** E3
Plaistow GtLon **136** C4
Plaistow WSuss **121** F4
Plaitford **106** B2
Plaitford Green **119** D5
Plas **142** A5
Plas Gwynant **167** F2
Plas Isaf **169** D3
Plas Llwyd **182** A5
Plas Llwyngwern **155** D2
Plas Llysyn **155** F3
Plas Nantyr **169** E4
Plashett **127** F2
Plasisaf **168** C1
Plas-rhiw-Saeson **155** F2
Plastow Green **119** G1
Plas-yn-Cefn **182** B5
Platt **123** F3
Platt Bridge **184** A2
Platt Lane **170** C4
Platt's Heath **124** A3
Plawsworth **212** B3
Plaxtol **123** F3
Play Hatch **134** C5
Playden **111** E1
Playford **152** D3
Playing Place **96** C5
Playley Green **145** G4
Plealey **156** D2
Plean **234** C1
Pleasance **244** A3
Pleasant Valley **150** D4
Pleasington **192** C5
Pleasley **173** F1
Pleasleyhill **173** G1
Pleasure Beach, Great
  Yarmouth Norf
  NR30 3EH **179** G5
Pleasure Island Theme Park
  NELincs
  DN35 0PL **188** D2
Pleasurewood Hills Theme
  Park Suff
  NR32 5DZ **165** G2
Pleck Dorset **104** D1
Pleck WMid **158** B3
Pledgdon Green **151** D5
Pledwick **186** A1
Plemstall **183** F5
Plenmeller **210** D1
Pleshey **137** F1
Plessey Woods Country
  Park N'umb
  NE22 6AN **221** E3
Plockton (Am Ploc) **256** E1
Plocropol **263** G2
Plomer's Hill **135** D3

Plot Gate 116 C4
Plough Hill 159 F3
Plowden 156 C4
Ploxgreen 156 C2
Pluckley 124 B4
Pluckley Thorne 124 B4
Plucks Gutter 125 E2
Plumbland 209 E3
Plumbley 186 B4
Plumley 184 B5
Plumpton Cumb 210 A4
Plumpton ESuss 109 F2
Plumpton N'hants 148 B3
Plumpton Green 109 F2
Plumpton Head 210 B4
Plumstead GtLon 137 D5
Plumstead Norf 178 C2
Plumtree 174 B4
Plungar 174 C4
Plush 104 D2
Plusha 97 G1
Plushabridge 98 D3
Plwmp 141 G2
Plym Bridge 100 B2
Plymouth 100 A2
Plymouth City
  Airport 100 B1
Plymouth Pavilions
  PL1 3LF 81 Plymouth
Plympton 100 B2
Plymstock 100 B2
Plymtree 103 D2
Pockley 203 F4
Pocklington 196 A3
Pockthorpe 178 B3
Pocombe Bridge 102 B3
Pode Hole 176 A5
Podimore 116 C5
Podmore 171 E4
Podsmead 132 A1
Poffley End 133 F1
Point Clear 139 D1
Pointon 175 G4
Polanach 248 B4
Polapit Tamar 98 D2
Polbae 215 D3
Polbain 272 B7
Polbathic 98 D5
Polbeth 235 E3
Poldean 217 F1
Pole Moor 185 E1
Polebrook 161 F4
Polegate 110 A3
Poles 266 E2
Polesden Lacey Surr
  RH5 6BD 121 G2
Polesworth 159 E2
Polglass 265 G1
Polgooth 97 D4
Polgown 225 F5
Poling 108 C3
Poling Corner 108 C3
Polkemmet Country Park
  WLoth
  EH47 0AD 234 D3
Polkerris 97 E4
Poll a' Charra 254 C3
Polla 273 F3
Pollardras 94 D4
Polldubh 248 D3
Pollie 274 C7
Pollington 186 D1
Polloch 247 G2
Pollok 233 G3
Pollokshaws 233 G3
Pollokshields 233 G3
Polmassick 97 D5
Polmont 234 D2
Polnoon 233 G4
Polperro 97 G4
Polruan 97 F4
Polsham 116 C3
Polstead 152 A4
Polstead Heath 152 A3
Poltalloch 240 A5
Poltimore 102 C3
Polton 235 G3
Polwarth 237 E4
Polyphant 97 G1
Polzeath 96 D2
Pomphlett 100 B2
Pond Street 150 C4
Ponders End 136 C3
Pondersbridge 162 A3
Ponsanooth 95 E3
Ponsonby 198 B2
Ponsongath 95 E5
Ponsworthy 102 A5
Pont Aber 142 D5
Pont Aberglaslyn 167 E3
Pont ar Hydfer 143 E5
Pont Crugnant 155 E3
Pont Cyfyng 168 A2
Pont Dolgarrog 168 A1
Pont Pen-y-benglog 167 F1
Pont Rhyd-sarn 168 B5
Pont Rhyd-y-cyff 129 E4
Pont Walby 129 E2
Pont yr Alwen 168 C2
Pontamman 128 C1
Pontantwn 128 A1
Pontardawe 128 C2
Pontarddulais 128 B2
Pontargothi 142 B5
Pont-ar-llechau 142 D5
Pontarsais 142 A5
Pontblyddyn 169 F1
Pontbren Llwyd 129 F2
Pontefract 195 D5
Ponteland 221 D4
Pontesbury 156 D2
Pontesbury Hill 156 C2
Pontesford 156 D2
Pontfadog 169 F4
Pontfaen Pembs 140 D4
Pont-faen Powys 143 F4
Pontgarreg 141 G2
Pont-Henri 128 A2
Ponthir 130 C3
Ponthirwaun 141 F3

Pontllanfraith 130 A3
Pontlliw 128 C2
Pontllyfni 166 D2
Pontlottyn 130 A2
Pontneddfechan 129 F2
Pontrhydfendigaid 142 D1
Pontrhydyfen 129 D3
Pont-rhyd-y-groes 154 D5
Pontrilas 144 C5
Pontrobert 156 A1
Pont-rug 167 E1
Ponts Green 110 B2
Pontshill 145 F5
Pont-siân 142 A3
Pontsticill 129 G1
Pontwelly 142 A4
Pontyates
  (Pont-iets) 128 A2
Pontyberem 128 B1
Pont-y-blew 170 A4
Pontybodkin 169 F2
Pontyclun 129 G4
Pontycymer 129 F3
Pontygwaith 129 G3
Pontymoel 130 B2
Pontypool 130 B2
Pontypridd 129 G3
Pont-y-rhyl 129 F4
Pontywaun 130 B3
Pooksgreen 106 C1
Pool Corn 96 A5
Pool WYorks 194 B3
Pool Bank 199 F4
Pool Green 158 C2
Pool Head 145 E2
Pool of Muckhart 243 F4
Pool Quay 156 B1
Pool Street 151 F4
Poole 105 G3
Poole Keynes 132 B3
Poole Pottery Poole
  BH15 1HJ 3 B4
Poolend 171 F3
Poolewe 264 E3
Pooley Bridge 210 A5
Pooley Street 164 B3
Poolfold 171 F2
Poolhill 145 G5
Poolsbrook 186 B5
Poolthorne Farm 188 A2
Pope Hill 126 C1
Popeswood 120 D1
Popham 119 G3
Poplar 136 C4
Porchfield 106 D3
Porin 265 K6
Poringland 179 D5
Porkellis 95 D3
Porlock 114 B3
Porlock Weir 114 B3
Port Allen 244 A2
Port Appin (Port na
  h-Apainn) 248 B5
Port Askaig 230 C3
Port Bannatyne 232 B3
Port Carlisle 218 A5
Port Charlotte 230 A4
Port Clarence 213 E5
Port Driseach 232 A2
Port e Vullen 190 C2
Port Ellen 230 B5
Port Elphinstone 261 F3
Port Erin 190 A5
Port Eynon 128 A4
Port Gaverne 97 E1
Port Glasgow 233 E2
Port Henderson 264 D4
Port Isaac 97 D1
Port Logan 206 A2
Port Lympne Wild Animal
  Park Kent
  CT21 4PD 124 D5
Port Mòr 246 D2
Port Mulgrave 203 G1
Port na Craig 251 E4
Port nan Long 262 D4
Port of Menteith 242 A4
Port of Ness
  (Port Nis) 271 H1
Port o'Warren 216 C5
Port Penrhyn 181 D5
Port Quin 97 D1
Port Ramsay 248 A5
Port St. Mary 190 A5
Port Solent 107 F2
Port Sunlight 183 E4
Port Talbot 129 D4
Port Tennant 128 C3
Port Wemyss 230 A4
Port William 206 D2
Portachoillan 231 F4
Portavadie 232 A3
Portbury 131 E5
Portchester 107 F2
Portencross 232 C5
Portesham 104 B4
Portessie 268 C4
Portfield A&B 239 G2
Portfield WSuss 108 A3
Portfield Gate 126 C1
Portgate 99 E2
Portgordon 268 B4
Portgower 275 F7
Porth Corn 96 C3
Porth RCT 129 G3
Porth Colmon 166 A4
Porth Navas 95 E4
Porthallow Corn 95 E4
Porthallow Corn 97 G4
Porthcawl 129 E5
Porthcothan 96 C2
Porthcurno 94 A4
Porthgain 140 B4
Porthill 171 F3
Porthkerry 115 D1
Porthkerry Country Park
  VGlam
  CF62 3BY 115 D1

Porthleven 94 D4
Porthmadog 167 E4
Porthmeor 94 B3
Portholland 97 D5
Porthoustock 95 F4
Porthpean 97 E4
Porthtowan 96 A5
Porthyrhyd
  Carmar 142 D4
Porthyrhyd
  Carmar 128 B1
Porth-y-waen 169 F5
Portincaple 241 E1
Portington 195 G4
Portinnisherrich 240 B3
Portinscale 209 F4
Portknockie 268 C4
Portland Basin Museum
  GtMan
  OL7 0QA 25 H3
Portlethen 261 H5
Portlethen Village 261 H5
Portloe 95 G3
Portlooe 97 F4
Portmahomack 267 G3
Portmeirion 167 E4
Portmeirion Village Gwyn
  LL48 6ET 167 E4
Portmellon 97 E5
Portmore 106 C3
Port-na-Con 273 G2
Portnacroish
  (Port na Croise) 248 B5
Portnaguran (Port nan
  Giùran) 271 H4
Portnahaven 230 A4
Portnalong 255 J1
Portnaluchaig 247 F1
Portobello 236 A2
Porton 118 C4
Portpatrick 214 B5
Portreath 96 A5
Portree (Port Righ) 263 K7
Portscatho 95 F3
Portsea 107 F2
Portskerra 274 D2
Portskewett 131 E4
Portslade 109 E3
Portslade-by-Sea 109 E3
Portslogan 214 A5
Portsmouth 107 F3
Portsmouth Guildhall
  PO1 2AB
  82 Portsmouth
Portsmouth Historic
  Dockyard PO1 3LJ
  82 Portsmouth
Portsonachan 240 C2
Portsoy 268 D4
Portuairk 246 D3
Portvoller 271 H4
Portway Here 144 C3
Portway Here 145 D3
Portway Here 145 D4
Portway Worcs 158 C5
Portwrinkle 99 D5
Portyerrock 207 E3
Posenhall 157 F2
Poslingford 151 F3
Postbridge 99 G3
Postcombe 134 C3
Postling 124 D5
Postwick 179 D5
Potarch 260 E5
Potsgrove 149 E5
Pott Row 177 F5
Pott Shrigley 184 D5
Potten End 135 F2
Potter Brompton 204 C5
Potter Heigham 179 F4
Potter Street 137 D2
Pottergate Street 164 C2
Potterhanworth 175 F1
Potterhanworth
  Booths 175 F1
Potteries Museum & Art
  Gallery ST1 3DW
  85 Stoke-on-Trent
Potterne 118 A2
Potterne Wick 118 B2
Potternewton 194 C4
Potters Bar 136 B2
Potters Crouch 136 A2
Potter's Green 159 F4
Potters Marston 159 G3
Potterspury 148 C3
Potterton Aber 261 H3
Potterton WYorks 194 D4
Pottle Street 117 F3
Potto 203 D2
Potton 150 A3
Pott's Green 152 A5
Poughill Corn 112 C5
Poughill Devon 102 B2
Poulshot 118 A2
Poulton 132 D2
Poulton-le-Fylde 191 G4
Pound Bank 145 G3
Pound Green ESuss 110 A1
Pound Green Suff 151 F2
Pound Green
  Worcs 157 G5
Pound Hill 122 B5
Pound Street 119 F1
Poundbury 104 C3
Poundffald 128 B3
Poundfield 123 E5
Poundgate 109 G1
Poundland 214 C2
Poundon 148 B5
Poundsbridge 123 E4
Poundsgate 102 A5
Poundstock 98 C1
Povey Cross 122 B4
Pow Green 145 G3
Powburn 229 E5
Powderham 102 C4
Powderham Castle Devon
  EX6 8JQ 102 C4
Powerstock 104 B3
Powfoot 217 F4

Powick 146 A2
Powis Castle & Garden
  Powys
  SY21 8RG 156 B2
Powler's Piece 113 D4
Powmill 243 F5
Poxwell 104 D4
Poyle 135 F5
Poynings 109 E2
Poyntington 117 D5
Poynton ChesE 184 D4
Poynton Tel&W 157 E1
Poynton Green 157 E1
Poyntzfield 266 E5
Poys Street 165 E4
Poyston 126 C1
Poyston Cross 126 C1
Poystreet Green 152 A2
Praa Sands 94 C4
Pratis 244 B4
Pratt's Bottom 123 D2
Praze-an-Beeble 94 D3
Predannack Wollas 95 D5
Prees 170 C4
Prees Green 170 C4
Prees Heath 170 C4
Prees Higher Heath 170 C4
Prees Lower Heath 170 C4
Preesall 191 G3
Preesgweene 169 F4
Prenbrigog 169 F1
Prendergast 126 C1
Prendwick 229 E5
Pren-gwyn 142 A3
Prenteg 167 E3
Prenton 183 E4
Prescot 183 F3
Prescott Devon 103 D1
Prescott Shrop 170 B5
Presley 267 H6
Pressen 228 C3
Prestatyn 182 B4
Prestbury ChesE 184 D5
Prestbury Glos 146 B5
Presteigne
  (Llanandras) 144 C1
Presthope 157 E3
Prestleigh 116 D3
Prestolee 184 B2
Preston B&H 109 F3
Preston Devon 102 B5
Preston Dorset 104 D4
Preston ELoth 236 B2
Preston ERid 197 D4
Preston Glos 145 F4
Preston Glos 132 C2
Preston Herts 149 G5
Preston Kent 124 C2
Preston Kent 125 E2
Preston Lancs 192 B5
Preston N'umb 229 F4
Preston Rut 161 D2
Preston ScBord 237 E5
Preston Shrop 157 D1
Preston Som 115 D4
Preston Suff 152 A2
Preston Torbay 101 E1
Preston Wilts 132 C4
Preston Wilts 133 E5
Preston Bagot 147 D1
Preston Bissett 148 B4
Preston Bowyer 115 E5
Preston Brockhurst 170 C5
Preston Brook 183 G4
Preston Candover 120 B3
Preston Capes 148 A2
Preston Deanery 148 C2
Preston Gubbals 157 D1
Preston Guildhall Lancs
  PR1 1HT 82 B5
Preston on Stour 147 E3
Preston on the Hill 183 G4
Preston on Wye 144 C3
Preston Plucknett 104 B1
Preston upon the Weald
  Moors 157 F1
Preston Wynne 145 E3
Preston-le-Skerne 212 C5
Prestonpans 236 A2
Preston-under-Scar 201 F3
Prestwich 184 C2
Prestwick N'umb 221 D4
Prestwick SAyr 224 B3
Prestwold 173 G5
Prestwood Bucks 135 D2
Prestwood Staffs 172 C3
Price Town 129 F3
Prickly Ball Farm &
  Hedgehog Hospital
  Devon
  TQ12 6BZ 101 E1
Prickwillow 163 D4
Priddy 116 C2
Priest Hill 192 C4
Priest Hutton 199 G5
Priest Weston 156 B3
Priestcliffe 185 F5
Priestland 225 D2
Priestwood 123 F2
Primethorpe 160 A3
Primrose Green 178 B4
Primrose Hill 136 B4
Princes End 158 B3
Princes Gate 127 E1
Princes Risborough 134 D2
Princethorpe 159 G5
Princetown Caerp 130 A1
Princetown Devon 99 F3
Prior Muir 244 D3
Prior's Frome 145 E4
Priors Halton 157 D5
Prior's Norton 146 A5
Priors Park 146 A4
Priorslee 157 G1
Priory Country Park Bed
  MK41 9SH 149 F3
Priory Wood 144 B3
Priston 117 D1
Pristow Green 164 C3
Prittlewell 138 B4
Privett 120 B5

Prixford 113 F3
Proaig 230 C4
Probus 97 F4
Protstonhill 269 G4
Provand's Lordship Glas
  G4 0RH 39 H3
Prudhoe 211 G1
Prussia Cove 94 C4
Pubil 249 G1
Publow 116 D1
Puckeridge 150 B5
Puckington 103 G1
Pucklechurch 131 G5
Pucknall 119 E5
Puckrup 146 A4
Puddinglake 171 E1
Puddington
  ChesW&C 183 E5
Puddington Devon 102 B1
Puddlebrook 131 F1
Puddledock 164 B2
Puddletown 105 D3
Pudleston 145 E2
Pudsey 194 B4
Pugneys Country Park
  WYorks
  WF2 7EQ 27 G6
Pulborough 108 C3
Pulborough Brooks RSPB
  Nature Reserve WSuss
  RH20 2EL 108 C3
Puldagon 275 J4
Puleston 171 E5
Pulford 170 A2
Pulham 104 D2
Pulham Market 164 C3
Pulham St. Mary 164 D3
Pulley 157 D2
Pulloxhill 149 F4
Pulrossie 266 E3
Pulverbatch 156 D2
Pumpherston 235 E3
Pumsaint 142 C3
Puncheston 140 D5
Puncknowle 104 B4
Punnett's Town 110 B1
Purbrook 107 F2
Purewell 106 A3
Purfleet 137 E5
Puriton 116 A3
Purleigh 138 B2
Purley 122 C2
Purley on Thames 134 B5
Purlogue 156 B5
Purlpit 117 F1
Purls Bridge 162 C4
Purse Caundle 104 C1
Purslow 156 C4
Purston Jaglin 186 B1
Purtington 103 G2
Purton Glos 131 F2
Purton Glos 131 F2
Purton Wilts 132 C4
Purton Stoke 132 C3
Purves Hall 237 E5
Pury End 148 C3
Pusey 133 F3
Putley 145 F4
Putley Green 145 F4
Putney 136 B5
Putsborough 113 E1
Puttenham Herts 135 D1
Puttenham Surr 121 E3
Puttock End 151 G3
Putts Corner 103 E3
Puxton 116 B1
Pwll 128 A2
Pwllcrochan 126 C2
Pwlldefaid 166 A5
Pwll-glas 169 E2
Pwllgloyw 143 G4
Pwllheli 166 C4
Pwll-Mawr 130 B5
Pwllmeyric 131 E3
Pwll-trap 127 F1
Pwll-y-glaw 129 D3
Pye Corner Herts 137 D1
Pye Corner Kent 124 A4
Pye Corner
  Newport 130 C4
Pye Green 158 B1
Pyecombe 109 E2
Pyle Bridgend 129 E5
Pyle IoW 107 D5
Pyleigh 115 E4
Pylle 116 D3
Pymore (Pymore) 162 C4
Pymore (Pymoor)
  Cambs 162 C4
Pymore Dorset 104 A3
Pyrford 121 F2
Pyrford Green 121 F2
Pyrton 134 B3
Pytchley 161 D4
Pyworthy 112 D5

Powick 146 A2
Prixford 113 C3
Proaig 230 C4

Prickly Ball Farm &
  Hedgehog Hospital

Quabbs 156 B4
Quadring 176 A4
Quadring Eaudike 176 A4
Quainton 148 C5
Quarff 279 D9
Quarley 119 D3
Quarndon 173 E3
Quarr Hill 107 E5
Quarrier's Village 233 E3
Quarrington 175 F3
Quarrington Hill 212 C4
Quarry Bank 158 B4
Quarry Bank Mill & Styal
  Estate ChesE
  SK9 4LA 184 C4
Quarrybank 171 D1
Quarrywood 267 J5
Quarter 234 B4
Quatford 157 G3
Quatt 157 G4
Quebec 212 A3
Quedgeley 132 A1
Queen Adelaide 163 D4
Queen Camel 116 C5
Queen Charlton 116 D1

Prixford 113 C3
Proaig 230 C4
Probus 97 F4
Protstonhill 269 G4

Provand's Lordship Glas
Prudhoe 211 G1

Queen Dart 102 B1
Queen Elizabeth Country
  Park, Petersfield Hants
  PO8 0QE 107 F2
Queen Elizabeth Forest Park
  Stir FK8 3SX 241 G5
Queen Elizabeth Hall
  GtLon SE1 8XX 45 F4
Queen Elizabeth II
  Conference Centre GtLon
  SW1P 3EE 44 D6
Queen Elizabeth II Country
  Park, Ashington N'umb
  NE63 9YF 221 E3
Queen Oak 117 E4
Queen Street 123 F4
Queenborough 124 B1
Queen's Bower 107 E4
Queen's Gallery,
  Buckingham Palace
  GtLon SW1A 1AA 44 B6
Queen's Hall, Edinburgh
  Edin EH8 9JG 37 H6
Queen's Head 170 A5
Queen's View Centre P&K
  PH16 5NR 251 E3
Queensbury
  WYorks 194 A4
Queensferry (South
  Queensferry)
  Edin 235 F2
Queensferry Flints 170 A1
Queenswood Country Park
  Here HR6 0PY 145 D2
Queenzieburn 234 A2
Quemerford 118 A1
Quendale 279 F9
Quendon 150 D4
Quenington 132 D2
Queniborough 160 B1
Quenington 132 D2
Quernmore 192 B1
Queslett 158 C3
Quethiock 98 D4
Quholm 277 B6
Quick's Green 134 A5
Quidenham 164 B3
Quidhampton 119 G2
Quidinish
  (Cuidhtinis) 263 G2
Quilquox 261 H1
Quina Brook 170 C4
Quindry 277 D8
Quine's Hill 190 B4
Quinhill 231 F4
Quinton N'hants 148 C2
Quinton WMid 158 B4
Quinton Green 148 C2
Quintrell Downs 96 C3
Quixhill 172 C3
Quoditch 99 E1
Quoig 242 D2
Quoiggs House 242 D4
Quoisley 170 C3
Quorn (Quorndon) 160 A1
Quorndon (Quorn) 160 A1
Quothquan 226 A2
Quoyloo 276 B5
Quoys 278 F1
Quoys of Reiss 275 J3

R
R.A.F. Museum, Cosford
  Shrop
  TF11 8UP 157 G2
R.A.F. Museum, Hendon
  GtLon
  NW9 5LL 10 D1
R.H.S. Garden Harlow Carr
  NYorks
  HG3 1QB 194 B2
R.H.S. Garden Hyde Hall
  Essex
  CM3 8ET 137 G3
R.H.S. Garden Rosemoor
  Devon
  EX38 8PH 113 F4
R.H.S. Garden Wisley Surr
  GU23 6QB 121 F2
Raasay 264 B7
Raby 183 E5
Rachan 226 C2
Rachub 167 F1
Rackenford 102 B1
Rackham 108 C2
Rackheath 179 D4
Racks 217 E3
Rackwick Ork 277 B8
Rackwick Ork 276 D3
Radbourne 173 E3
Radcliffe GtLon 184 B2
Radcliffe N'umb 221 E1
Radcliffe on Trent 174 B4
Radclive 148 B4
Radcot 133 E3
Raddington 114 D5
Radernie 244 C4
Radford B&NESom 117 D2
Radford Nott 173 G3
Radford Oxon 147 G5
Radford WMid 159 F4
Radford Semele 147 F1
Radipole 104 C4
Radlett 136 A2
Radley 134 A3
Radley Green 137 F2
Radmore Green 170 C2
Radnage 134 C3
Radstock 117 D2
Radstone 148 A3
Radway 147 F3
Radway Green 171 E2
Radwell Bed 149 F2
Radwell Herts 150 A4
Radwinter 151 E4
Radyr 130 A4
Raecheon 220 B3
Raemoir House 260 E5
Raffin 272 C5
Rafford 267 H6
Ragdale 160 B1
Ragged Appleshaw 119 E3

Raglan 130 C2
Ragnall 187 F5
Rahoy 247 F4
Rain Shore 184 C1
Rainford 183 F2
Rainham GtLon 137 E4
Rainham Med 124 A2
Rainhill 183 F3
Rainhill Stoops 183 G3
Rainow 185 D5
Rainsough 184 B1
Rainton 202 C5
Rainworth 173 G2
Raisbeck 200 B2
Raise 210 C2
Rait 244 A2
Raithby Lincs 176 B1
Raithby Lincs 188 D4
Rake 120 D5
Raleigh's Cross 114 D4
Ram 142 B3
Ram Alley 118 D1
Ram Lane 124 B4
Ramasaig 263 G7
Rame Corn 95 E3
Rame Corn 100 A3
Rampisham 104 B2
Rampside 191 E2
Rampton Cambs 150 C1
Rampton Notts 187 F5
Ramsbottom 184 B1
Ramsbury 133 E5
Ramscraigs 275 G6
Ramsdean 120 C5
Ramsdell 119 G2
Ramsden 133 F1
Ramsden Bellhouse 137 G3
Ramsden Heath 137 G3
Ramsey Cambs 162 A4
Ramsey Essex 152 D4
Ramsey IoM 190 C2
Ramsey Forty Foot 162 B4
Ramsey Heights 162 A4
Ramsey Island
  Essex 138 C2
Ramsey Island
  Pembs 140 A5
Ramsey Mereside 162 A4
Ramsey St. Mary's 162 A4
Ramsgate 125 F2
Ramsgate Street 178 B2
Ramsgill 202 A5
Ramsholt 153 E3
Ramshorn 172 B3
Ramsnest Common 121 E4
Ranachan 247 G3
Ranby Lincs 188 C5
Ranby Notts 187 D4
Rand 188 B5
Rand Farm Park Lincs
  LN8 5NJ 188 B5
Randwick 132 A2
Rangemore 172 C5
Rangeworthy 131 F4
Ranish (Ranais) 271 G5
Rankinston 224 C4
Rank's Green 137 G1
Ranmoor 186 A4
Rannoch School 250 A4
Ranochan 248 A1
Ranscombe 114 C3
Ranskill 187 D4
Ranton 171 F5
Ranton Green 171 F5
Ranworth 179 E4
Rapness 276 E3
Rapps 103 G1
Rascarrel 208 A2
Rash 200 B4
Rashwood 146 B2
Raskelf 203 D5
Rassau 130 A1
Rastrick 194 A5
Ratagan 257 F3
Ratby 160 A2
Ratcliffe Culey 159 F3
Ratcliffe on Soar 173 F5
Ratcliffe on the
  Wreake 160 B1
Ratford Bridge 126 C2
Ratfyn 118 C3
Rathen 269 H4
Rathillet 244 B2
Rathliesbeag 249 E1
Rathmell 193 E1
Ratho 235 F2
Ratho Station 235 F2
Rathven 268 C4
Ratley 147 F3
Ratling 125 E3
Ratlinghope 156 D3
Ratsloe 102 C3
Rattar 275 H1
Ratten Row Cumb 209 G2
Ratten Row Lancs 192 A3
Rattery 100 D1
Rattlesden 152 A2
Rattray 251 G5
Raughton Head 209 G2
Raunds 161 E5
Ravenfield 186 B3
Ravenglass 198 B3
Ravenglass & Eskdale
  Railway Cumb
  CA18 1SW 198 C3
Raveningham 165 E2
Raven's Green 152 C5
Ravenscar 204 C2
Ravensden 149 F2
Ravenshaw 193 F3
Ravenshayes 102 C2
Ravenshead 173 G2
Ravensmoor 170 D2
Ravensthorpe
  N'hants 160 B5
Ravensthorpe
  WYorks 194 B5
Ravenstone Leics 159 G1
Ravenstone MK 149 D2
Ravenstonedale 200 C2
Ravenstruther 234 D5

309

...sworth 202 A2
... 204 C2
...cliffe ERid 195 F5
...wcliffe York 195 E2
...awcliffe Bridge 195 F5
Rawdon 194 B4
Rawmarsh 186 B3
Rawnsley 158 C1
Rawreth 137 G3
Rawridge 103 F2
Rawson Green 173 E3
Rawtenstall 193 E5
Rawyards 234 B3
Raxton 261 G1
Raydon 152 B2
Raylees 220 B2
Rayleigh 138 B3
Raymond's Hill 103 G3
Rayne 151 F5
Rayners Lane 136 A4
Raynes Park 122 B2
Reach 151 D1
Read 193 D4
Reading 134 C5
Reading Green 164 C4
Reading Street 124 B5
Reagill 200 B1
Real Mary King's Close, The
  Edin EH1 1PG 37 F4
Rearquhar 266 E2
Rearsby 160 B1
Rease Heath 170 D2
Reaster 275 H2
Reaveley 229 E5
Reawick 279 C8
Reay 274 E2
Reculver 125 E2
Red Ball 103 D1
Red Bull 171 F2
Red Dial 209 F2
Red Hill Hants 107 G1
Red Hill Warks 146 D2
Red Lodge 163 E5
Red Lumb 184 C1
Red Oaks Hill 151 D4
Red Point 264 D5
Red Post Corn 112 C5
Red Post Devon 101 E1
Red Rail 145 E5
Red Rock 183 G2
Red Roses 127 F1
Red Row 221 E2
Red Street 171 F2
Red Wharf Bay
  (Traeth Coch) 180 D4
Redberth 127 D2
Redbourn 136 A1
Redbourne 187 G3
Redbrook Glos 131 E1
Redbrook Wrex 170 C3
Redbrook Street 124 B5
Redburn High 266 C5
Redburn High 267 G7
Redburn N'umb 211 D1
Redcar 213 F5
Redcastle Angus 253 E4
Redcastle High 266 C7
Redcliff Bay 130 D5
Redcloak 253 G1
Reddingmuirhead 234 D2
Reddish 184 C3
Redditch 146 C1
Rede 151 G2
Redenhall 165 D3
Redesmouth 220 A3
Redford Aber 253 F2
Redford Angus 253 D5
Redford Dur 211 G4
Redford WSuss 121 D5
Redgrave 164 B4
Redheugh 252 C3
Redhill Aber 260 E1
Redhill Aber 261 F4
Redhill Moray 268 D6
Redhill Notts 173 G3
Redhill NSom 116 B1
Redhill Surr 122 B3
Redhill Aerodrome &
  Heliport 122 B4
Redhouse A&B 231 G3
Redhouse Aber 260 D5
Redhouses 230 B3
Redisham 165 F3
Redland Bristol 131 E5
Redland Ork 276 C5
Redlingfield 164 C4
Redlynch Som 117 E4
Redlynch Wilts 118 D5
Redmarley D'Abitot 145 G4
Redmarshall 212 C5
Redmile 174 C4
Redmire 201 F3
Redmoor 97 E3
Rednal 170 A5
Redpath 227 G2
Redruth 96 A5
Redscarhead 235 G5
Redshaw 225 G3
Redstone Bank 127 E1
Redwick Newport 130 D4
Redwick SGlos 131 E4
Redworth 212 B5
Reed 150 B4
Reed End 150 B4
Reedham 179 F5
Reedley 193 E4
Reedness 195 G5
Reef (Riof) 270 D4
Reegaby 190 C2
Regil 116 C1
Regoul 267 F6
Reiff 272 B7
Reigate 122 B3
Reighton 205 E5
Reisgill 275 H5
Reiss 275 J3
Rejerrah 96 C4
Releath 95 F4
Relubbus 94 C3
Relugas 267 G7
Remenham 134 C4
Remenham Hill 134 C4
Remony 250 C3
Rempstone 173 G5
Rendcomb 132 C1
Rendham 153 E1
Rendlesham 153 F5
Renfrew 233 G3
Renhold 149 F2
Renishaw 186 B5
Rennington 229 G5
Renton 233 E2
Renwick 210 B3
Repps 179 F4
Repton 173 E5
Rescobie 252 D4
Rescorla 97 E4
Resipole 247 G3
Resolis 266 D5
Resolven 129 E2
Resourie 248 A2
Respryn 97 F3
Reston 237 F3
Restormel 97 F3
Reswallie 252 D4
Reterth 96 D3
Retew 96 D4
Retford
  (East Retford) 187 E4
Rettendon 137 G3
Rettendon Place 137 G3
Retyn 96 C4
Revesby 176 A1
Revesby Bridge 176 B1
Rew 102 A5
Rew Street 107 D3
Rewe Devon 102 C3
Rewe Devon 102 B3
Reybridge 118 A1
Reydon 165 F4
Reydon Smear 165 G4
Reymerston 178 B5
Reynalton 127 D2
Reynoldston 128 A4
Rezare 99 D3
Rhadyr 130 C2
Rhandirmwyn 143 D3
Rhaoine 266 D1
Rhayader
  (Rhaeadr Gwy) 143 F1
Rhedyn 166 B4
Rheged - the Village in the
  Hill Cumb
  CA11 0DQ 210 A5
Rhegreanoch 272 C7
Rheindown 266 C7
Rhelonie 266 C2
Rhemore 247 E4
Rhenigidale
  (Reinigeadal) 270 E7
Rheola 129 E2
Rhes-y-cae 169 E1
Rhewl Denb 169 E1
Rhewl Denb 169 E1
Rhewl Shrop 170 A4
Rhian 273 H7
Rhicarn 272 C6
Rhiconich 272 E3
Rhicullen 266 D4
Rhidorroch 265 H2
Rhifail 274 C4
Rhigos 129 F2
Rhilochan 266 E1
Rhinduie 266 C7
Rhireavach 265 G2
Rhiroy 265 H3
Rhiston 156 B3
Rhiw 166 B5
Rhiwargor 168 C5
Rhiwbina 130 A4
Rhiwbryfdir 167 F3
Rhiwderin 130 B4
Rhiwinder 129 G4
Rhiwlas Gwyn 167 E1
Rhiwlas Gwyn 168 C4
Rhiwlas Powys 169 F4
Rhode 115 F4
Rhodes 184 C2
Rhodes Minnis 124 D4
Rhodesia 186 C5
Rhodiad-y-brenin 140 A5
Rhodmad 154 B5
Rhonadale 222 C2
Rhonehouse
  (Kelton Hill) 216 B5
Rhoose 115 D1
Rhos Carmar 141 G4
Rhos NPT 128 D2
Rhos Common 156 B1
Rhosaman 128 D1
Rhoscolyn 180 A5
Rhoscrowther 126 C2
Rhosesmor 169 F1
Rhos-fawr 166 C4
Rhosgadfan 167 E2
Rhos-goch IoA 180 C4
Rhosgoch Powys 144 A3
Rhos-hill 141 E3
Rhoshirwaun 166 A5
Rhoslan 167 D3
Rhoslefain 154 B2
Rhosllanerchrugog 169 F3
Rhoslligwy 180 C4
Rhosmaen 142 C5
Rhosmeirch 180 C5
Rhosneigr 180 B5
Rhosnesni 170 A2
Rhôs-on-Sea 181 G4
Rhossili 128 A4
Rhosson 140 A5
Rhostrehwfa 180 C5
Rhostryfan 167 D2
Rhostyllen 170 A3
Rhos-y-bol 180 C4
Rhos-y-brithdir 169 E5
Rhosycaerau 140 C4
Rhos-y-gwaliau 168 C5
Rhos-y-llan 166 B4
Rhos-y-mawn 168 B1
Rhos-y-Meirch 144 B1
Rhu 233 D1
Rhuallt 182 B5
Rhubodach 232 B2
Rhuddall Heath 170 C1
Rhuddlan 182 B5
Rhue 265 H2
Rhulen 144 A3
Rhumach 247 F1
Rhunahaorine 231 F5
Rhyd Gwyn 167 F3
Rhyd Powys 155 F2
Rhydargaeau 142 A5
Rhydcymerau 142 B4
Rhyd-Ddu 167 E2
Rhydding 128 D2
Rhydgaled 168 C1
Rhydlanfair 168 B2
Rhydlewis 141 G3
Rhydlios 166 A4
Rhydlydan Conwy 168 B2
Rhydlydan Powys 155 G3
Rhydolion 166 B5
Rhydowen 142 A3
Rhyd-Rosser 142 B1
Rhydspence 144 B3
Rhydtalog 169 F2
Rhyd-uchaf 168 B4
Rhyd-wen 168 B5
Rhyd-wyn 180 B4
Rhyd-y-ceirw 169 F2
Rhyd-y-clafdy 166 C4
Rhydycroesau 169 F4
Rhydyfelin Cere 154 B5
Rhydyfelin RCT 129 G4
Rhyd-y-foel 182 A5
Rhyd-y-fro 128 D2
Rhyd-y-groes 167 E1
Rhydymain 168 B5
Rhydymwyn 169 F1
Rhyd-yr-onnen 154 C2
Rhyd-y-sarn 167 F3
Rhydywrach 127 E1
Rhyl 182 B4
Rhyl Sun Centre Denb
  LL18 3AQ 182 B4
Rhymney 130 A2
Rhyn 170 A2
Rhynd 243 G2
Rhynie Aber 260 C3
Rhynie High 267 F4
Ribbesford 157 G5
Ribchester 192 C4
Ribigill 273 H3
Riby 188 B2
Riccall 195 F4
Riccarton 224 C2
Richards Castle 145 D1
Richings Park 135 F5
Richmond GtLon 136 A5
Richmond NYorks 202 A2
Richmond SYorks 186 B4
Rich's Holford 115 E4
Rickarton 253 G1
Rickford 116 B2
Rickinghall 164 B4
Rickleton 212 B2
Rickling 150 C4
Rickling Green 150 D5
Rickmansworth 135 F3
Riddell 227 G3
Riddings 173 F2
Riddlecombe 113 G4
Riddlesden 193 G3
Ridge Dorset 105 F4
Ridge Herts 136 B2
Ridge Wilts 118 A4
Ridge Green 122 C4
Ridge Lane 159 F3
Ridgebourne 143 G1
Ridgeway 186 B3
Ridgeway Cross 145 G3
Ridgeway Moor 186 B4
Ridgewell 151 F3
Ridgewood 109 G1
Ridgmont 149 E4
Ridham Dock 124 B2
Riding Gate 117 E5
Riding Mill 211 G1
Ridley 123 F2
Ridleywood 170 A2
Ridlington Norf 179 E2
Ridlington Rut 160 D2
Ridsdale 220 B3
Riechip 251 F5
Rievaulx 203 E4
Rift House 213 D4
Rigg D&G 218 A5
Rigg High 264 B6
Riggend 234 B3
Rigifa 275 J1
Rigmaden Park 200 B4
Rigsby 189 E5
Rigside 225 G2
Riley Green 192 C5
Rileyhill 158 D1
Rilla Mill 97 G2
Rillaton 97 G2
Rillington 204 B5
Rimington 193 E3
Rimpton 116 D5
Rimswell 197 D5
Rinaston 140 C5
Ring o' Bells 183 F1
Ringford 216 A5
Ringinglow 185 G4
Ringland 178 C4
Ringles Cross 109 G1
Ringmer 109 G2
Ringmore Devon 100 C3
Ringmore Devon 102 C5
Ringorm 267 K7
Ring's End 162 B2
Ringsfield 165 F3
Ringsfield Corner 165 F3
Ringshall Herts 135 F1
Ringshall Suff 152 B2
Ringshall Stocks 152 B2
Ringstead N'hants 161 E5
Ringstead Norf 177 F3
Ringwood 106 A2
Ringwould 125 F4
Rinloan 259 K4
Rinmore 260 C3
Rinnigill 277 C8
Rinsey 94 C4
Ripe 110 A3
Ripley Derbys 173 E2
Ripley Hants 106 A3
Ripley NYorks 194 B1
Ripley Surr 121 F2
Riplingham 196 B4
Ripon 202 C5
Rippingale 175 G5
Ripple Kent 125 F4
Ripple Worcs 146 A4
Ripponden 185 E1
Risabus 230 B5
Risbury 145 E2
Risby ERid 196 C4
Risby Suff 151 F1
Risca 130 B3
Rise 197 D3
Riseden 123 G5
Riseholme 187 G5
Risegate 176 A5
Riseley Bed 149 F1
Riseley W'ham 120 C1
Rishangles 164 C4
Rishton 192 D4
Rishworth 185 E1
Risinghurst 134 A2
Risley Derbys 173 F3
Risley Warr 184 A3
Risplith 194 B1
Rispond 273 G2
Rivar 119 E1
Rivenhall 138 B1
Rivenhall End 138 B1
River Kent 125 E4
River WSuss 121 E5
River Bank 150 D1
River Bridge 116 A3
River Link Boat Cruises
  Devon TQ6 9AJ 101 E3
Riverford Bridge 101 D4
Riverhead 123 E3
Riverside 130 A4
Riverside Country Park Med
  ME7 2XH 124 A2
Riverview Park 137 F5
Riverton 113 G2
Riviera International Centre
  Torbay TQ2 5LZ
  87 Torquay
Rivington 184 A1
Roa Island 191 F1
Roach Bridge 192 B5
Road Green 165 D2
Road Weedon 148 B2
Roade 148 C2
Roadhead 218 D4
Roadside High 275 G2
Roadside Ork 276 F3
Roadside of Kinneff 253 G2
Roadwater 114 D4
Roag 263 H7
Roast Green 150 C4
Roberton ScBord 227 F4
Roberton SLan 226 A3
Robertsbridge 110 C1
Robertstown
  Moray 267 K7
Robertstown RCT 129 G2
Roberttown 194 A5
Robeston Cross 126 B2
Robeston Wathen 127 D1
Robeston West 126 B2
Robin Hill Countryside
  Adventure Park IoW
  PO30 2NU 107 E4
Robin Hood
  Derbys 185 G5
Robin Hood
  Lancs 183 G1
Robin Hood
  WYorks 194 C5
Robin Hood Doncaster
  Sheffield Airport 187 D3
Robin Hood's Bay 204 C2
Robinhood End 151 F4
Robins 120 D5
Robinswood Hill Country
  Park Glos
  GL4 6SX 132 A1
Roborough Devon 113 F4
Roborough Plym 100 B1
Roby 183 F3
Roby Mill 183 G2
Rocester 172 C4
Roch 140 B5
Roch Bridge 140 B5
Roch Gate 140 B5
Rochallie 251 G4
Rochdale 184 C1
Roche 97 D3
Rochester Med 123 G2
Rochester N'umb 220 A2
Rochester Cathedral Med
  ME1 1SX 123 G2
Rochford Essex 138 B3
Rochford Worcs 145 F1
Rock Corn 96 D2
Rock N'umb 229 G4
Rock Worcs 157 G5
Rock Ferry 183 E4
Rockbeare 102 D3
Rockbourne 106 A1
Rockcliffe Cumb 218 B5
Rockcliffe D&G 216 C5
Rockcliffe Cross 218 B5
Rockfield A&B 231 D1
Rockfield High 267 G3
Rockfield Mon 131 D1
Rockford 106 A2
Rockhampton 131 F3
Rockhead 97 E1
Rockingham 161 D3
Rockland All Saints 164 A2
Rockland St. Mary 179 E5
Rockland St. Peter 164 A2
Rockley 133 D5
Rockside 230 A3
Rockwell End 134 C4
Rinmore 260 C3
Rockwell Green 103 E5
Rodborough 132 A2
Rodbourne 132 B4
Rodbridge Corner 151 G3
Rodd 144 C1
Roddam 229 E4
Rodden 104 C4
Rode 117 F2
Rode Heath 171 F2
Rodeheath 171 F1
Rodel (Roghadal) 263 F3
Roden 157 E1
Rodington 157 E1
Rodington Heath 157 E1
Rodley 131 G1
Rodmarton 132 B2
Rodmell 109 G3
Rodmersham 124 B2
Rodmersham Green 124 B2
Rodney Stoke 116 B2
Rodsley 172 D3
Rodway 115 F3
Roe Cross 185 D3
Roe Green 150 B4
Roecliffe 194 C1
Roehampton 136 B5
Roesound 279 C6
Roffey 121 G4
Rogart 266 E1
Rogate 120 D5
Rogerstone 130 B4
Rogiet 131 D4
Rokemarsh 134 B3
Roker 212 D1
Rollesby 179 F4
Rolleston Leics 160 C2
Rolleston Notts 174 C2
Rollestone 118 B3
Rolleston-on-Dove 172 D5
Rolston 197 E3
Rolstone 116 A1
Rolvenden 124 A5
Rolvenden Layne 124 A5
Romaldkirk 211 F5
Roman Baths & Pump Room
  B&NESom BA1 1LZ
  63 Bath
Romanby 202 C3
Romannobridge 235 F5
Romansleigh 114 A5
Romesdal 263 K6
Romford Dorset 105 G2
Romford GtLon 137 E4
Romiley 184 D3
Romney, Hythe &
  Dymchurch Railway
  Kent TN28 8PL 124 D5
Romney Street 123 F2
Romsey 119 E5
Romsley Shrop 157 G4
Romsley Worcs 158 B5
Rona 264 C6
Ronachan 231 F4
Ronague 190 A4
Ronnachmore 230 B4
Rood End 158 C4
Rookhope 211 F3
Rookley 107 E4
Rookley Green 107 E4
Rooks Bridge 116 A2
Rook's Nest 115 D4
Rookwith 202 B4
Roos 197 E4
Roose 191 F1
Roosebeck 191 F1
Roosecote 191 F1
Rootham's Green 149 F2
Rootpark 235 D4
Ropley 120 B4
Ropley Dean 120 B4
Ropley Soke 120 B4
Ropsley 175 F4
Rora 269 J5
Rorandle 260 E3
Rorrington 156 C2
Rosarie 268 B6
Rose 96 B4
Rose Ash 114 A5
Rose Green Essex 152 A3
Rose Green WSuss 108 B4
Rose Hill 109 G2
Roseacre Kent 123 G3
Roseacre Lancs 192 A4
Rosebank 234 C5
Rosebrough 229 F4
Rosebush 140 D5
Rosecare 98 B1
Rosecliston 96 C4
Rosedale Abbey 203 G3
Roseden 229 E4
Rosehall 266 B1
Rosehearty 269 H4
Rosehill Aber 260 D5
Rosehill Shrop 157 D1
Roseisle 267 J5
Roselands 110 B3
Rosemarket 126 C2
Rosemarkie 266 E6
Rosemary Lane 103 E1
Rosemount P&K 251 G5
Rosemount SAyr 224 B3
Rosenannon 97 D3
Rosenithon 95 F4
Rosepool 126 B1
Rosevean 97 E4
Roseville 158 B3
Roseworth 212 D5
Rosgill 199 G1
Roshven 247 G2
Roskhill 263 H7
Roskorwell 95 E4
Rosley 209 G2
Roslin 235 G3
Rosliston 159 E1
Rosliston Forestry Centre
  Derbys
  DE12 8JX 159 E1
Rosneath 233 D1
Ross D&G 207 G2
Ross N'umb 229 F3
Ross P&K 242 C2
Ross Priory 233 F1
Rossdhu House 233 E1
Rossett 170 A2
Rossett Green 194 C2
Rosside 199 D5
Rossie Farm School 253 E4
Rossie Ochill 243 F3
Rossie Priory 244 A1
Rossington 186 D3
Rosskeen 266 D5
Rosslyn Chapel Midlo
  EH25 9PU 32 D4
Rossmore 105 G3
Ross-on-Wye 145 F5
Roster 275 H5
Rostherne 184 B4
Rosthwaite Cumb 209 F5
Rosthwaite Cumb 198 D4
Roston 172 C3
Rosudgeon 94 C4
Rosyth 235 F1
Rothbury 220 C1
Rother Valley Country Park
  SYorks S26 5PQ 21 C4
Rotherby 160 B1
Rotherfield 123 E5
Rotherfield Greys 134 C4
Rotherfield Peppard 134 C4
Rotherham 186 B3
Rothersthorpe 148 C2
Rotherwick 120 C2
Rothes 267 K7
Rothesay 232 B3
Rothiebrisbane 261 F1
Rothiemurchus High
  PH22 1QH 259 H4
Rothienorman 261 F1
Rothiesholm 276 F5
Rothley Leics 160 A1
Rothley N'umb 220 C3
Rothney 260 E2
Rothwell Lincs 188 B3
Rothwell N'hants 160 D4
Rothwell WYorks 194 C5
Rotsea 196 C3
Rottal 252 B3
Rotten Row Bucks 134 C4
Rotten Row WMid 159 D5
Rottingdean 109 F3
Rottington 208 C5
Roud 107 E4
Roudham 164 A3
Rough Close 171 G4
Rough Common 124 D3
Rougham Norf 177 G5
Rougham Suff 152 A1
Roughburn 249 E1
Roughlee 193 E3
Roughley 158 D3
Roughton Lincs 176 A1
Roughton Norf 178 D2
Roughton Shrop 157 G3
Round Bush 136 A3
Roundbush Green 137 E1
Roundham 104 A2
Roundhay 194 C4
Roundstreet
  Common 121 F5
Roundway 118 B1
Rous Lench 146 C2
Rousay 276 D4
Rousdon 103 F3
Rousham 147 G5
Rousham Gap 147 G5
Routenburn 232 C3
Routh 196 C3
Rout's Green 134 C3
Row Corn 97 E2
Row Cumb 199 F4
Row Cumb 210 C4
Row Heath 139 E4
Row Town 121 F1
Rowanburn 218 C4
Rowardennan
  Lodge 241 F5
Rowarth 185 E4
Rowbarton 115 F5
Rowberrow 116 B2
Rowchoish 241 F4
Rowde 118 A1
Rowden 99 G1
Rowen 181 F5
Rowfields 172 C3
Rowfoot 210 C1
Rowhedge 152 B5
Rowhook 121 G4
Rowington 147 E1
Rowland 185 G5
Rowland's Castle 107 G1
Rowlands Gill 212 A2
Rowledge 120 D3
Rowlestone 144 C5
Rowley Devon 102 A1
Rowley Dur 211 G3
Rowley Shrop 156 C2
Rowley Park 171 G5
Rowley Regis 158 B4
Rowly 121 F3
Rowner 107 E2
Rowney Green 158 C5
Rownhams 106 C1
Rowrah 209 D5
Rowsham 135 D1
Rowsley 173 D1
Rowstock 133 G4
Rowston 175 F2
Rowthorne 173 F1
Rowton
  ChesW&C 170 B1
Rowton Shrop 156 C1
Rowton Tel&W 157 F1
Roxburgh 228 B3
Roxby NLincs 187 G1
Roxby NYorks 203 G1
Roxton 149 G2
Roxwell 137 F2
Royal Academy of Arts
  GtLon W1J 0BD 44 C4
Royal Albert Hall GtLon
  SW7 2AP 11 F5
Royal Albert Memorial
  Museum & Art Gallery
  Devon EX4 3RX
  72 Exeter
Royal Armouries Museum,
  Leeds WYorks
  LS10 1LT 41 G5
Royal Bath & West
  Showground Som
  BA4 6QN 16 B4
Royal Botanic Garden,
  Edinburgh Edin
  EH3 5LR 36 D1
Royal Botanic Gardens,
  Kew GtLon
  TW9 3AB 11 C6
Royal British Legion
  Village 123 G3
Royal Centre NG1 5ND
  80 Nottingham
Royal Cornwall Museum
  Corn TR1 2SJ 96 C5
Royal Festival Hall GtLon
  SE1 8XX 45 E4
Royal Highland Showground
  Edin EH28 8NB 32 B2
Royal Horticultural Halls
  GtLon SW1P 2PB 44 D7
Royal Hospital Chelsea
  GtLon SW3 4SR 13 A5
Royal Leamington
  Spa 147 F1
Royal Mews, Buckingham
  Palace GtLon
  SW1W 0QH 44 B6
Royal Naval Museum
  PO1 3NH
  82 Portsmouth
Royal Oak 183 F1
Royal Observatory
  Greenwich GtLon
  SE10 8XJ 13 D5
Royal Opera House GtLon
  WC2E 9DD 45 E3
Royal Pavilion B&H
  BN1 1EE 65 Brighton
Royal Scots Regimental
  Museum, The Edin
  EH1 2YT 37 E5
Royal Scottish Academy
  Edin EH2 2EL 37 F4
Royal Tunbridge
  Wells 123 E5
Royal Victoria Country Park
  Hants SO31 5GA 4 C4
Royal Welch Fusiliers
  Regimental Museum
  Gwyn
  LL55 2AY 167 D1
Royal Yacht Britannia
  Edin EH6 6JJ 32 C1
Roybridge (Drochaid
  Ruaidh) 249 E1
Roydon Essex 136 D1
Roydon Norf 164 C3
Roydon Norf 177 F5
Roydon Hamlet 136 D2
Royston Herts 150 B3
Royston SYorks 186 A1
Royton 184 D2
Rozel 100 C5
Ruabon (Rhiwabon) 170 A3
Ruaig 246 B2
Ruan Lanihorne 96 C5
Ruan Major 95 D5
Ruan Minor 95 E5
Ruanaich 238 B2
Ruardean 131 F1
Ruardean Hill 131 F1
Ruardean Woodside 131 F1
Rubery 158 B5
Ruckcroft 210 B3
Ruckinge 124 C5
Ruckland 188 D5
Rucklers Lane 135 F2
Ruckley 157 E2
Rudbaxton 140 C5
Rudby 203 D2
Rudchester 212 A1
Ruddington 173 G4
Ruddlemoor 97 E4
Rudford 145 G5
Rudge 117 F2
Rudgeway 131 F4
Rudgwick 121 F4
Rudhall 145 F5
Rudheath 184 A5
Rudley Green 138 B2
Rudloe 117 F1
Rudry 130 A4
Rudston 196 C1
Rudyard 171 G2
Rudyard Lake Staffs
  ST13 8RT 171 G2
Rufford 183 F1
Rufford Country Park Notts
  NG22 9DF 174 B1
Rufforth 195 E2
Ruffside 211 F2
Rugby 160 A5
Rugby Football Union,
  Twickenham GtLon
  TW1 1DZ 11 B6
Rugeley 158 C1
Ruilick 266 C7
Ruisigearraidh 262 E3
Ruislip 136 A4
Ruislip Gardens 136 A4
Ruislip Manor 136 A4
Rum 255 J5
Rumbling Bridge 243 F5
Rumburgh 165 E3
Rumford 96 C2
Rumleigh 100 A1
Rumney 130 B5
Rumwell 115 E5
Runacraig 242 A3
Runcorn 183 G4
Runcton 108 A3
Runcton Holme 163 E2
Rundlestone 99 F3

Runfold 121 D3
Runhall 178 B5
Runham Norf 179 F4
Runham Norf 179 G5
Runnington 115 E5
Runsell Green 137 G2
Runshaw Moor 183 G1
Runswick Bay 204 B1
Runtaleave 252 A3
Runwell 137 G3
Ruscombe Glos 132 A2
Ruscombe W'ham 135 D5
Rush Green GtLon 137 E4
Rush Green Herts 150 A5
Rushall Here 145 F4
Rushall Norf 164 C5
Rushall Wilts 118 C2
Rushall WMid 158 C2
Rushbrooke 151 G1
Rushbury 157 E3
Rushden N'hants 149 E1
Rushden Herts 150 B4
Rushford Devon 99 E3
Rushford Norf 164 A3
Rushgreen 184 A4
Rushlake Green 110 C4
Rushmere 165 F1
Rushmere
   St. Andrew 152 D3
Rushmoor 121 D3
Rushock 158 A5
Rusholme 184 C3
Rushton ChesW&C 170 C1
Rushton N'hants 160 D4
Rushton Shrop 157 E2
Rushton Spencer 171 G1
Rushwick 146 A2
Rushy Green 109 G2
Rushyford 212 B5
Ruskie 242 B4
Ruskington 175 F2
Rusko 215 G5
Rusland 199 E4
Rusper 122 B5
Ruspidge 131 F1
Russ Hill 122 B4
Russel 264 E7
Russell Green 137 G1
Russell's Green 110 C2
Russel's Green 165 D4
Russel's Green 185 D4
Rusthall 123 E5
Rustington 108 C3
Ruston 204 C4
Ruston Parva 196 C1
Ruswarp 204 B2
Rutherend 234 A4
Rutherford 228 A3
Rutherglen 234 A3
Ruthernbridge 97 E3
Ruthers of Howe 275 J2
Ruthin (Rhuthun)
   Denb 169 E2
Ruthin VGlam 129 F5
Ruthrieston 261 H4
Ruthven Aber 268 D6
Ruthven Angus 252 A5
Ruthven High 259 F1
Ruthven High 258 E5
Ruthvoes 96 D3
Ruthwaite 209 F3
Ruthwell 217 E4
Rutland Water Rut
   LE15 8QL 161 D2
Ruyton-XI-Towns 170 A5
Ryal 220 C4
Ryal Fold 192 C5
Ryall Dorset 104 A3
Ryall Worcs 146 A3
Ryarsh 123 F3
Rydal 199 E2
Ryde 107 E3
Rydon 112 D5
Rye 111 E1
Rye Foreign 111 D1
Rye Harbour 111 E2
Rye Park 136 C2
Rye Street 145 G4
Ryebank 170 C4
Ryeford 145 F5
Ryehill Aber 260 E2
Ryehill ERid 197 E5
Ryhall 161 F1
Ryhill 186 A1
Ryhope 212 D2
Rylands 173 G4
Rylstone 193 F2
Ryme Intrinseca 104 B1
Ryther 195 E4
Ryton Glos 145 G4
Ryton NYorks 203 G5
Ryton Shrop 157 G2
Ryton T&W 212 A1
Ryton-on-
   Dunsmore 159 F5

S

S.S. Great Britain Bristol
   BS1 6TY 8 B3
Saasaig 256 C4
Sabden 193 D4
Sabden Fold 193 E4
Sackers Green 152 A4
Sacombe 136 C1
Sacombe Green 136 C1
Sacriston 212 B3
Sadberge 202 C1
Saddell 222 C2
Saddington 160 B3
Saddle Bow 163 E1
Sadgill 199 F2
Saffron Walden 150 D4
Sageston 127 D2
Saham Hills 178 A5
Saham Toney 163 G2
Saighdinis 262 D5
Saighton 170 B1
St. Abbs 237 G3
St. Agnes 96 B4
St. Aidan's Winery N'umb
   TD15 2RX 229 F2
St. Albans 136 A2

St. Albans Cathedral Herts
   AL1 1BY 136 A2
St. Allen 96 C4
St. Andrews 244 D3
St. Andrew's & Blackfriars
   Halls Norf NR3 1AU
   79 Norwich
St. Andrews Major 130 A5
St. Anne 101 G4
St. Anne's 191 G5
St. Ann's 217 E1
St. Ann's Chapel
   Corn 99 E3
St. Ann's Chapel
   Devon 100 C3
St. Anthony 95 F3
St. Anthony-in-
   Meneage 95 E4
St. Anthony's Hill 110 B3
St. Arvans 131 E3
St. Asaph
   (Llanelwy) 182 B5
St. Athan 114 D1
St. Aubin 100 C5
St. Audries 115 E3
St. Austell 97 E4
St. Bees 208 C5
St. Blazey 97 E4
St. Blazey Gate 97 E4
St. Boswells 227 G2
St. Botolph's Church, Boston
   Lincs PE21 6NP 176 B3
St. Brelade 100 B5
St. Breock 97 D2
St. Breward 97 E2
St. Briavels 131 E2
St. Brides 126 B1
St. Brides Major 129 E5
St. Bride's
   Netherwent 130 D4
St. Brides
   Wentlooge 130 B4
St. Bride's-super-
   Ely 129 G5
St. Budeaux 100 A2
St. Buryan 94 B4
St. Catherine 117 E1
St. Catherines 240 D4
St. Clears (Sanclêr) 127 F1
St. Cleer 97 G3
St. Clement Chanl 100 C5
St. Clement Corn 96 C5
St. Clether 97 G1
St. Colmac 232 B3
St. Columb Major 96 D3
St. Columb Minor 96 C3
St. Columb Road 96 D4
St. Combs 269 J4
St. Cross South
   Elmham 165 D3
St. Cyrus 253 F3
St. Davids Fife 235 F1
St. David's P&K 243 E2
St. David's (Tyddewi)
   Pembs 140 A5
St. David's Hall Cardiff CF10 1AH
   67 Cardiff
St. Day 96 B5
St. Decumans 115 D3
St. Dennis 97 D4
St. Denys 106 D1
St. Dogmaels
   (Llandudoch) 141 E3
St. Dogwells 140 C5
St. Dominick 100 A1
St. Donats 114 C1
St. Edith's Marsh 118 A1
St. Endellion 97 D1
St. Enoder 96 C4
St. Erme 96 C5
St. Erney 99 D5
St. Erth 94 C3
St. Erth Praze 94 C3
St. Ervan 96 C2
St. Eval 96 C3
St. Ewe 97 D5
St. Fagans 130 A5
St. Fagans National History
   Museum Cardiff
   CF5 6XB 7 A4
St. Fergus 269 J5
St. Fillans 242 B2
St. Florence 127 D2
St. Gennys 98 B1
St. George Bristol 131 F5
St. George Conwy 182 A5
St. Georges NSom 116 A1
St. George's Tel&W 157 G1
St. George's VGlam 129 G5
St. George's Hall, Liverpool
   Mersey L1 1JJ 42 D3
St. Germans 99 D5
St. Giles' Cathedral,
   Edinburgh Edin
   EH1 1RE 37 F4
St. Giles in the
   Wood 113 F2
St. Giles on the
   Heath 99 D1
St. Harmon 155 F5
St. Helen Auckland 212 A5
St. Helena 178 D4
St. Helen's ESuss 110 D2
St. Helens IoW 107 F4
St. Helens Mersey 183 G3
St. Helier Chanl 100 C5
St. Helier GtLon 122 B2
St. Hilary Corn 94 C3
St. Hilary VGlam 129 G5
St. Hill 122 C5
St. Ibbs 149 G5
St. Illtyd 130 B2
St. Ippollitts 149 G5
St. Ishmael 127 G2
St. Ishmael's 126 B2
St. Issey 96 D2
St. Ive 98 D4
St. Ives Cambs 162 B5
St. Ives Corn 94 C2
St. Ives Dorset 106 A2
St. James South
   Elmham 165 E3

St. John Chanl 100 C4
St. John Corn 100 A2
St. John the Baptist Church,
   Cirencester Glos
   GL7 2NX 132 C2
St. John's GtLon 136 C5
St. John's IoM 190 A3
St. John's Surr 121 E2
St. John's Worcs 146 A2
St. John's Chapel
   Devon 113 F3
St. John's Chapel
   Dur 211 E4
St. John's Fen End 162 D1
St. John's Hall 211 G4
St. John's Highway 162 D1
St. John's Kirk 226 A2
St. John's Town of
   Dalry 216 A1
St. Judes 190 B2
St. Just 94 A3
St. Just in Roseland 95 F3
St. Katherines 261 F1
St. Keverne 95 E4
St. Kew 97 E2
St. Kew Highway 97 E2
St. Keyne 97 G3
St. Lawrence Corn 97 E3
St. Lawrence Essex 138 C2
St. Lawrence IoW 107 E2
St. Lawrence's Church,
   Eyam Derbys
   S32 5QH 185 G5
St. Leonards
   Bucks 135 E2
St. Leonards
   Dorset 106 A2
St. Leonards
   ESuss 110 D3
St. Leonards
   Grange 106 D3
St. Leonard's Street 123 F3
St. Levan 94 A4
St. Lythans 130 A5
St. Mabyn 97 E2
St. Madoes 243 G2
St. Margaret South
   Elmham 165 E3
St. Margarets
   Here 144 C4
St. Margarets
   Herts 136 C1
St. Margarets
   Wilts 118 D1
St. Margaret's at
   Cliffe 125 F3
St. Margaret's Hope 277 D8
St. Mark's 190 A4
St. Martin Chanl 101 F5
St. Martin Chanl 100 C5
St. Martin Corn 97 G4
St. Martin Corn 95 F4
St. Martin-in-the-Fields
   Church GtLon
   WC2N 4JH 44 E4
St. Martin's IoS 96 B1
St. Martins P&K 243 G1
St. Martin's Shrop 170 A4
St. Mary 100 C5
St. Mary Bourne 119 F2
St. Mary Church 130 A5
St. Mary Cray 123 D2
St. Mary Hill 129 F5
St. Mary Hoo 137 G5
St. Mary in the
   Marsh 111 F1
St. Mary Magdalene Chapel,
   Sandringham Norf
   PE35 6EH 177 E5
St. Mary the Virgin Church,
   Holy Island N'umb
   TD15 2RX 229 F2
St. Mary the Virgin Church,
   Oxford Oxon
   OX1 4AH 134 A2
St. Mary the Virgin Church,
   Rye ESuss
   TN31 7HE 111 E2
St. Marychurch 101 F1
St. Mary's IoS 96 B1
St. Mary's Ork 277 D7
St. Mary's Airport 96 B1
St. Mary's Bay 111 F1
St. Mary's Church, Whitby
   NYorks
   YO22 4JT 204 C1
St. Mary's Croft 214 B4
St. Mary's Grove 116 B1
St. Maughans
   Green 131 D1
St. Mawes 95 F3
St. Mawgan 96 C3
St. Mellion 99 D4
St. Mellons 130 B4
St. Merryn 96 C2
St. Mewan 97 D4
St. Michael Caerhays 97 D5
St. Michael Church 116 A4
St. Michael Penkevil 96 C5
St. Michael South
   Elmham 165 E3
St. Michaels Fife 244 C2
St. Michaels Kent 124 A5
St. Michaels Worcs 145 E1
St. Michael's Church,
   Hathersage Derbys
   S32 1AJ 185 G4
St. Michael's Mount Corn
   TR17 0HT 94 C3
St. Michael's on
   Wyre 192 A3
St. Mildred's Church,
   Whippingham IoW
   PO32 6LP 107 E3
St. Minver 97 D2
St. Monans 244 D4
St. Mungo Museum of
   Religious Life & Art
   Glas G4 0RH 39 H3
St. Mungo's Cathedral,
   Glasgow Glas
   G4 0QZ 39 J3

St. Neot 97 F3
St. Neots 149 G1
St. Newlyn East 96 C4
St. Nicholas Pembs 140 C4
St. Nicholas VGlam 129 G5
St. Nicholas at
   Wade 125 E2
St. Ninians 242 C5
St. Osyth 139 E1
St. Ouen 100 B5
St. Owen's Cross 145 E5
St. Paul's Cathedral,
   London GtLon
   EC4M 8AD 45 J3
St. Paul's Cray 123 D2
St. Paul's Walden 149 G5
St. Peter 100 C5
St. Peter Port 101 F5
St. Peter's 125 F2
St. Petrox 127 D3
St. Pinnock 97 G3
St. Quivox 224 B3
St. Ruan 95 E5
St. Sampson 101 F4
St. Saviour Chanl 101 E5
St. Saviour Chanl 100 C5
St. Stephen 96 D4
St. Stephens Corn 100 A2
St. Stephens Corn 98 D2
St. Stephens Herts 136 A2
St. Teath 97 E1
St. Thomas 102 C3
St. Tudy 97 E2
St. Twynnells 126 C3
St. Veep 97 F4
St. Vigeans 253 E5
St. Wenn 97 D3
St. Weonards 145 D5
St. Winnow 97 F4
St. Winwaloe's Church,
   Gunwalloe Corn
   TR12 7QE 95 D4
Saintbury 146 C4
Salachail 248 C4
Salcombe 100 C4
Salcombe Regis 103 E4
Salcott 138 C1
Sale 184 B4
Sale Green 146 B2
Saleby 189 E5
Salehurst 110 C1
Salem Carmar 142 C5
Salem Cere 154 C4
Salem Gwyn 167 E2
Salen A&B 247 E5
Salen High 247 F3
Salendine Nook 185 F1
Salesbury 192 C4
Saleway 146 B2
Salford CenBeds 149 E4
Salford GtMan 184 C3
Salford Oxon 147 E5
Salford Priors 146 C2
Salfords 122 B4
Saline 243 F5
Salisbury 118 C5
Salisbury Cathedral
   Wilts SP1 2EF
   83 Salisbury
Salkeld Dykes 210 B4
Sallachan 248 B3
Sallachy Arg 240 C3
Sallachy High 266 C1
Sallachy High 257 F1
Salle 178 C3
Sally Lunn's House
   B&NESom BA1 1NX
   63 Bath
Salmonby 188 D5
Salmond's Muir 245 D1
Salperton 146 C5
Salph End 149 F2
Salsburgh 234 C3
Salt 171 G5
Salt Hill 135 E4
Salt Holme 213 D2
Saltaire 194 A4
Saltash 100 A2
Saltburn 266 E4
Saltburn-by-the-
   Sea 213 F5
Saltburn's Inclined
   Tramway R&C
   TS12 1DP 213 F5
Saltby 175 D5
Saltcoats Cumb 198 B3
Saltcoats NAyr 232 D5
Saltcotes 191 G5
Saltdean 109 F3
Salterbeck 208 C4
Salterforth 193 E3
Saltergate Dend 204 C2
Salterhill 267 K5
Salterswall 170 D1
Saltfleet 189 E3
Saltfleetby All
   Saints 189 E3
Saltfleetby
   St. Clements 189 E3
Saltfleetby St. Peter 189 E4
Saltford 117 D1
Salthaugh Grange 197 E5
Salthouse 178 B1
Saltley 158 C4
Saltmarshe 195 G5
Saltness 277 B8
Saltney 170 A1
Salton 203 G4
Saltrens 113 E3
Saltwell Park, Gateshead
   T&W NE9 5AX 28 B3
Saltwick 221 D4
Saltwood 125 D5
Salum 246 B2
Salvington 108 D3
Salwarpe 146 A1
Salwayash 104 A3
Salween 277 B8
Salwick 192 A4
Sambourne 146 C1
Sambrook 171 E5
Samhla 262 C5
Samlesbury 192 C4

Sampford Arundel 103 E1
Sampford Brett 115 D3
Sampford
   Courtenay 113 G5
Sampford Moor 103 E1
Sampford Peverell 102 D1
Sampford Spiney 99 F3
Samuelston 236 B2
Sancreed 94 B4
Sancton 196 B4
Sand Shet 279 C8
Sand Som 116 B3
Sand Hutton 195 F2
Sandaig A&B 246 A2
Sandaig High 256 D4
Sandaig High 256 D3
Sandal Magna 186 A1
Sanday 276 F3
Sanday Airfield 276 F3
Sandbach 171 E1
Sandbank 232 C1
Sandbanks 105 G4
Sandend 268 D4
Sanderstead 122 C2
Sandford Cumb 200 C1
Sandford Devon 102 B2
Sandford Dorset 105 F4
Sandford IoW 107 E4
Sandford NSom 116 B2
Sandford Shrop 170 C4
Sandford Shrop 170 A5
Sandford SLan 234 B5
Sandford Orcas 116 D5
Sandford St. Martin 147 G5
Sandfordhill 269 K6
Sandford-on-
   Thames 134 A2
Sandgarth 277 E6
Sandgate 125 E5
Sandgreen 215 G5
Sandhaven 269 H4
Sandhead 214 B5
Sandhills Dorset 104 C1
Sandhills Dorset 104 B2
Sandhills Surr 121 E4
Sandhills WYorks 194 C4
Sandhoe 211 F1
Sandholme ERid 196 A4
Sandholme Lincs 176 B4
Sandhurst BrackF 120 D1
Sandhurst Glos 146 A5
Sandhurst Kent 110 C1
Sandhurst Cross 110 C1
Sandhutton 202 C4
Sandiacre 173 F4
Sandilands 189 F4
Sandiway 184 A5
Sandleheath 106 A1
Sandleigh 133 G2
Sandling 123 G3
Sandlow Green 171 E1
Sandness 279 A7
Sandon Essex 137 G2
Sandon Herts 150 B4
Sandon Staffs 171 G5
Sandown 107 F4
Sandplace 97 G4
Sandquoy 276 G3
Sandridge Devon 101 E2
Sandridge Herts 136 A1
Sandridge Wilts 118 A1
Sandringham 177 E5
Sandrocks 109 F1
Sandsend 204 B1
Sandside 199 F4
Sandside House 274 C2
Sandsound 279 C8
Sandtoft 187 E2
Sanduck 102 A4
Sandway 124 A3
Sandwell 158 C4
Sandwell Park Farm WMid
   B71 4BG 14 D2
Sandwell Valley Country
   Park WMid
   B71 4BG 14 D2
Sandwich 125 F3
Sandwick Cumb 199 F1
Sandwick Shet 279 D10
Sandwick (Sanndabhaig)
   WIsles 271 G4
Sandwith 208 B5
Sandy Carmar 128 A2
Sandy CenBeds 149 G3
Sandy Bank 176 A2
Sandy Haven 126 B2
Sandy Lane Wilts 118 A1
Sandy Lane Wrex 170 B3
Sandy Lane
   WYorks 194 A4
Sandy Way 107 D4
Sandycroft 170 A1
Sandygate Devon 102 B5
Sandygate IoM 190 B2
Sandyhills 216 C5
Sandylands 192 A1
Sandypark 102 A4
Sandyway 145 D5
Sangobeg 273 G2
Sankyn's Green 145 G1
Sanna 247 D3
Sannaig 230 D3
Sannox 232 B5
Sanquhar 225 F5
Santon Bridge 198 C2
Santon Downham 163 G4
Sant-y-Nyll 129 G5
Sapcote 159 G3
Sapey Common 145 G1
Sapiston 164 A4
Sapperton Derbys 172 C4
Sapperton Glos 132 B2
Sapperton Lincs 175 F4
Saracen's Head 176 B5
Sarclet 275 J4
Sardis 126 C2
Sarisbury 107 E2
Sark 101 G5
Sarn Bridgend 129 F4
Sarn Powys 156 B3
Sarn Bach 166 C5

Sarn Meyllteyrn 166 B4
Sarnau Carmar 127 G3
Sarnau Cere 141 G2
Sarnau Gwyn 168 C4
Sarnau Powys 156 B5
Sarnau Powys 143 G4
Sarnesfield 144 C2
Saron Carmar 128 C3
Saron Carmar 141 G5
Saron Gwyn 167 E1
Saron Gwyn 167 D2
Sarratt 135 F3
Sarre 125 E2
Sarsden 147 E5
Sarsgrum 273 F2
Sartfield 190 B2
Satley 212 A3
Satron 201 E3
Satterleigh 113 G3
Satterthwaite 199 E3
Satwell 134 C5
Sauchen 260 E3
Saucher 243 G1
Sauchie 243 D5
Sauchieburn 253 E3
Sauchrie 224 B4
Saughall 183 E5
Saughall Massie 183 D4
Saughtree 219 D2
Saul 131 G2
Saundby 187 E4
Saundersfoot 127 E2
Saunderton 134 C2
Saunton 113 E2
Sausthorpe 176 B1
Saval 266 C1
Savalbeg 266 C1
Saverley Green 171 G4
Savile Town 194 B5
Sawbridge 148 A1
Sawbridgeworth 137 D2
Sawdon 204 C4
Sawley Derbys 173 F4
Sawley Lancs 193 D3
Sawley NYorks 194 B1
Sawston 150 C3
Sawtry 161 G4
Saxby Leics 160 D1
Saxby Lincs 188 A4
Saxby All Saints 187 G1
Saxelbye 174 B5
Saxham Street 152 B1
Saxilby 187 F5
Saxlingham 178 B2
Saxlingham Green 164 D2
Saxlingham
   Nethergate 164 D2
Saxlingham Thorpe 164 D2
Saxmundham 153 E1
Saxon Street 151 E2
Saxstead 153 D1
Saxtead Green 153 D1
Saxtead Little
   Green 153 D1
Saxthorpe 178 C2
Saxton 195 D4
Sayers Common 109 E2
Scackleton 203 F5
Scadabhagh 263 G2
Scaftworth 187 D3
Scagglethorpe 204 B5
Scaitcliffe 193 E4
Scalasaig 238 C5
Scalby ERid 196 A5
Scalby NYorks 204 D3
Scaldwell 160 C5
Scale Houses 210 B3
Scaleby 210 A1
Scalebyhill 210 A1
Scales Cumb 209 G4
Scales Cumb 199 D5
Scalford 174 B5
Scaling 203 G1
Scallasaig 256 E3
Scallastle 239 G1
Scalloway 279 C9
Scalpay (Eilean
   Scalpaigh) 263 H2
Scambesby 188 C5
Scammadale 240 A2
Scamodale 248 A1
Scampston 204 B5
Scampton 187 G5
Scaniport 258 D1
Scapa 277 D7
Scapegoat Hill 185 E1
Scar 276 F2
Scarborough 204 D3
Scarborough Sea Life &
   Marine Sanctuary
   NYorks
   YO12 6RP 204 D3
Scarcewater 96 D4
Scarcliffe 173 F1
Scarcroft 194 C3
Scardroy 265 J6
Scarff 278 B4
Scarfskerry 275 H1
Scargill 201 F1
Scarinish 246 B2
Scarisbrick 183 E1
Scarning 178 A4
Scarrington 174 C3
Scarrowhill 210 B2
Scarth Hill 183 F2
Scarthingwell 195 D4
Scartho 188 C2
Scarwell 276 B5
Scatraig 258 E1
Scaur (Kippford)
   D&G 216 C5
Scaur D&G 216 C3
Scawby 187 G2
Scawby Brook 187 G2
Scawton 203 E4
Scayne's Hill 109 F1
Scealascro 270 D5
Scethrog 144 A5
Schaw 224 C3
Scholar Green 171 F2
Scholes SYorks 186 A3
Scholes WYorks 194 C4

Scholes WYorks 185 ...
Scholes WYorks 194 A...
School Green 170 D1
School Green 103 D2
Schoose 208 D4
Sciberscross 266 E1
Science Museum GtLon
   SW7 2DD 11 F5
Scilly Isles
   (Isles of Scilly) 96 B1
Scissett 185 G1
Scleddau 140 C4
Sco Ruston 179 D3
Scofton 186 D4
Scole 164 C3
Scolpaig 262 C4
Scone 243 G2
Scones Lethendy 243 G2
Sconser 256 B1
Scoor 238 D3
Scopwick 175 F2
Scoraig 265 G2
Scorborough 196 C3
Scorrier 96 B5
Scorriton 100 D1
Scorton Lancs 192 B3
Scorton NYorks 202 B2
Scottow 179 D3
Scotby 210 A2
Scotch Corner 202 B2
Scotch Whisky Heritage
   Centre Edin
   EH1 2NE 37 F4
Scotforth 192 A2
Scothern 188 A5
Scotland 175 F4
Scotland End 147 F4
Scotland Street School
   Museum of Education
   Glas G5 8QB 38 C6
Scotlandwell 243 G4
Scotnish 231 F1
Scots' Gap 220 C3
Scotsburn 266 E4
Scotston Aber 253 F2
Scotston P&K 251 E5
Scotstoun 233 G2
Scotstown 248 A3
Scott Willoughby 175 F4
Scotter 187 F2
Scotterthorpe 187 F2
Scottlethorpe 175 F5
Scotton Lincs 187 F3
Scotton NYorks 202 A3
Scotton NYorks 194 A3
Scottow 179 D3
Scoughall 236 D1
Scoulton 178 A5
Scounslow Green 172 B5
Scourie 272 D4
Scourie More 272 D4
Scousburgh 279 F9
Southead 185 D2
Scrabster 275 G1
Scrafield 176 B1
Scrainwood 220 B1
Scrane End 176 B3
Scraptoft 160 B2
Scratby 179 G4
Scrayingham 195 G2
Scredington 175 F3
Scremby 176 B1
Scremerston 229 E2
Screveton 174 C3
Scriven 194 C2
Scronkey 192 A3
Scrooby 187 D3
Scropton 172 C4
Scruton 202 C3
Scrub Hill 176 A2
Sculthorpe 177 G4
Scunthorpe 187 F1
Scurlage 128 A4
Sea 103 G1
Sea Life Centre, Blackpool
   FY1 5AA
   64 Blackpool
Sea Life Centre, Brighton
   B&H BN2 1TB
   65 Brighton
Sea Life Centre, Great
   Yarmouth Norf
   NR30 3AH 179 G5
Sea Life Sanctuary,
   Hunstanton Norf
   PE36 5BH 177 E3
Sea Mills 131 E5
Sea Palling 179 F3
Seabank 248 B5
Seaborough 104 A2
Seaburn 212 D2
Seacombe 183 E3
Seacroft Lincs 177 D1
Seacroft WYorks 194 C4
Seadyke 176 B4
Seafield A&B 231 F1
Seafield SAyr 224 B3
Seafield WLoth 235 E3
Seaford 109 G4
Seaforth 183 E3
Seagrave 160 B1
Seagry Heath 132 B4
Seaham 212 D3

Seaham Grange **212** D2
Seahouses **229** G3
Seal **123** E3
Sealand **170** A1
Seale **121** D3
Sea-Life Adventure,
  Southend-on-Sea *S'end*
  SS1 2ER **138** B4
Sealham **140** C5
Seamer *NYorks* **203** D1
Seamer *NYorks* **204** D4
Seamill **212** D4
SeaQuarium, Rhyl *Denb*
  LL18 3AF **182** B4
Searby **188** A2
Seasalter **124** C2
Seascale **198** B2
Seathorne **177** D1
Seathwaite *Cumb* **209** F5
Seathwaite *Cumb* **198** D3
Seatle **199** E4
Seatoller **209** F5
Seaton *Corn* **98** D5
Seaton *Cumb* **208** D3
Seaton *Devon* **103** F3
Seaton *Dur* **212** C2
Seaton *ERid* **197** D3
Seaton *N'umb* **221** F4
Seaton *Rut* **161** E3
Seaton Burn **221** E4
Seaton Carew **213** E5
Seaton Delaval **221** F4
Seaton Junction **103** F3
Seaton Ross **195** G3
Seaton Sluice **221** F4
Seaton Tramway *Devon*
  EX12 2NQ **103** F3
Seatown *Aber* **269** J5
Seatown *Dorset* **104** A3
Seatown *Moray* **268** D4
Seave Green **203** D3
Seaview **107** F3
Seaville **209** E1
Seavington
  St. Mary **104** A1
Seavington
  St. Michael **104** A1
Seawick **139** E1
Sebastopol **130** B3
Sebergham **209** G2
Seckington **159** E2
Second Coast **265** F2
Sedbergh **200** B3
Sedbury **131** E3
Sedbusk **201** D3
Seddington **149** G3
Sedgeberrow **146** C4
Sedgebrook **175** D4
Sedgefield **212** C5
Sedgeford **177** F4
Sedgehill **117** F5
Sedgemere **159** E5
Sedgley **158** B3
Sedgwick **199** G4
Sedlescombe **110** C2
Sedlescombe
  Street **110** C2
Seend **118** A1
Seend Cleeve **118** A1
Seer Green **135** E3
Seething **165** E2
Sefton **183** E2
Seghill **221** E4
Seifton **157** D4
Seighford **171** F5
Seil **239** G3
Seilebost **263** F2
Seion **167** E1
Seisdon **158** A3
Seisiadar **271** H4
Seized! Revenue & Customs
  Uncovered *Mersey*
  L3 4AQ **42** B5
Selattyn **169** F4
Selborne **120** C4
Selby **195** F4
Selham **121** E5
Selhurst **122** C2
Selkirk **227** F3
Sellack **145** E5
Sellafirth **198** B2
Sellafield Visitors Centre
  Cumb
  CA20 1PG **198** B2
Sellafirth **278** E3
Sellindge **124** D5
Selling **124** C3
Sells Green **118** A1
Selly Oak **158** C4
Selmeston **110** A3
Selsdon **122** C2
Selsey **108** A4
Selsfield Common **122** C5
Selside *Cumb* **199** G3
Selside *NYorks* **200** C5
Selsley **132** A2
Selstead **125** E4
Selston **173** F2
Selworthy **114** C3
Semblister **279** C7
Semer **152** A3
Semington **117** F1
Semley **117** F5
Send **121** F2
Send Marsh **121** F2
Senghenydd **130** A3
Sennen **94** A4
Sennen Cove **94** A4
Sennybridge **143** F5
Senwick **207** F5
Sequer's Bridge **100** C3
Serlby **186** D4
Serpentine Gallery *GtLon*
  W2 3XA **11** G7
Serrington **118** B4
Sessay **203** D5
Setchey **163** E1
Setley **106** C2
Setter *Shet* **279** E8
Setter *Shet* **279** C7
Settiscarth **277** C6
Settle **193** E1

Settrington **204** B5
Seven Ash **115** E4
Seven Bridges **132** D3
Seven Kings **137** D4
Seven Sisters **129** E2
Seven Springs **132** B1
Sevenhampton
  Glos **146** C5
Sevenhampton
  Swin **133** E3
Sevenoaks **123** E3
Sevenoaks Weald **123** E3
Seven Beach **131** E4
Seven Stoke **146** A3
Sewerby **197** D1
Sewerby Hall & Gardens
  ERid
  YO15 1EA **197** D1
Seworgan **95** E3
Sewstern **175** D5
Seymour Villas **113** E1
Sezincote **147** D4
Sgarasta Mhòr **263** F2
Sgiogarstaigh **271** H1
Sgodachail **266** B2
Shabbington **134** B2
Shackerley **158** A2
Shackerstone **159** F2
Shackleford **121** E3
Shadfen **221** E3
Shadforth **212** C3
Shadingfield **165** F3
Shadoxhurst **124** B5
Shadsworth **192** D5
Shadwell *Norf* **164** A3
Shadwell *WYorks* **194** C3
Shaftenhoe End **150** C4
Shaftesbury **117** F5
Shafton **186** A1
Shakespeare's Birthplace
  Works CV37 6QW
  85 Stratford-upon-Avon
Shakespeare's Globe Theatre
  GtLon SE1 9DT **45** J4
Shalbourne **119** E1
Shalcombe **106** C4
Shalden **120** B3
Shalden Green **120** C3
Shaldon **102** C5
Shalfleet **106** D4
Shalford *Essex* **151** F5
Shalford *Surr* **121** F3
Shalford Green **151** F5
Shallowford *Devon* **114** A3
Shallowford *Staffs* **171** G5
Shalmsford Street **124** C3
Shalmstry **275** G2
Shalstone **148** B4
Shalunt **232** B2
Shambellie **217** D4
Shamley Green **121** F3
Shandon **233** D1
Shandwick **267** F4
Shangton **160** C3
Shankend **227** G5
Shankhouse **221** E4
Shanklin **107** E4
Shanklin Chine *IoW*
  PO37 6BW **107** E4
Shannochie **223** E3
Shantron **233** E1
Shantullich **266** D6
Shanzie **252** A4
Shap **199** G1
Shapinsay **277** E6
Shapwick *Dorset* **105** F2
Shapwick *Som* **116** B4
Sharcott **118** C2
Shard End **159** D4
Shardlow **173** F4
Shareshill **158** B2
Sharlston **186** A1
Sharlston Common **186** A1
Sharnal Street **137** G5
Sharnbrook **149** E2
Sharneyford **193** E5
Sharnford **159** G3
Sharnhill Green **104** D2
Sharow **202** C5
Sharp Street **179** E3
Sharpenhoe **149** F4
Sharperton **220** B1
Sharpham House **101** E2
Sharpness **131** F2
Sharpthorne **122** C5
Sharrington **178** B2
Shatterford **157** G4
Shatterling **125** E3
Shaugh Prior **100** B1
Shave Cross **104** A3
Shavington **171** E2
Shaw *GtMan* **184** D2
Shaw *Swin* **132** D4
Shaw *WBerks* **119** F1
Shaw *Wilts* **117** F1
Shaw *Herts* **150** A4
Shaw Green
  NYorks **194** B2
Shaw Mills **194** B1
Shaw Side **184** D2
Shawbost
  (Siabost) **270** E3
Shawbury **170** C5
Shawell **160** A4
Shawfield *GtMan* **184** C1
Shawfield *Staffs* **172** B1
Shawford **119** F5
Shawforth **193** E5
Shawhead **216** C3
Shawtonhill **234** A5
Sheanachie **222** C4
Sheandow **259** K1
Shearington **217** E3
Shearsby **160** B3
Shebbear **113** E5

Shebdon **171** E5
Shebster **275** F2
Shedfield **107** E1
Sheen **172** C1
Sheepridge **185** F1
Sheepscombe **132** A1
Sheepstor **100** B1
Sheepwash *Devon* **113** E5
Sheepwash *N'umb* **221** E3
Sheepway **131** D5
Sheepy Magna **159** F2
Sheepy Parva **159** F2
Sheering **137** E1
Sheerness **124** B1
Sheet **120** C5
Sheffield **186** A4
Sheffield Botanic Gardens
  SYorks S10 2LN **21** B3
Sheffield Bottom **120** B1
Sheffield Green **109** G1
Sheffield Park Garden
  ESuss
  TN22 3QX **109** G1
Shefford **149** G4
Shefford Woodlands **133** F5
Sheigra **272** D2
Sheinton **157** F2
Shelderton **156** D5
Sheldon *Derbys* **172** C1
Sheldon *Devon* **103** E2
Sheldon *WMid* **158** D4
Sheldwich **124** C3
Sheldwich Lees **124** C3
Shelf *Bridgend* **129** F4
Shelf *WYorks* **194** A5
Shelfanger **164** C3
Shelfield *Works* **146** D1
Shelfield *WMid* **158** C2
Shelfield Green **146** D1
Shelford **173** G2
Shellachan *A&B* **240** A2
Shellachan *A&B* **240** A2
Shellbrook **159** F1
Shellbrook Hill **170** A3
Shellingford **133** F3
Shellow Bowells **137** F2
Shelsley
  Beauchamp **145** G1
Shelsley Walsh **145** G1
Shelswell **148** B4
Shelthorpe **160** A1
Shelton *Beds* **149** F1
Shelton *Norf* **164** D2
Shelton *Notts* **174** C3
Shelton *Shrop* **157** D1
Shelve **156** C3
Shelwick **145** E3
Shelwick Green **145** E3
Shenfield **137** F3
Shenington **147** F3
Shenley **136** A2
Shenley Brook End **148** D4
Shenley Church
  End **148** D4
Shenleybury **136** A2
Shenmore **144** C4
Shennanton **215** E4
Shenstone *Staffs* **158** D2
Shenstone *Worcs* **158** A5
Shenstone
  Woodend **158** D2
Shenton **159** F2
Shenval **259** H2
Shepeau Stow **162** B1
Shephall **137** E1
Shepherd's Bush **136** B5
Shepherd's Green **134** C4
Shepherd's Patch **131** G2
Shepherdswold
  (Sibertswold) **125** E4
Shepley **185** F2
Sheppardstown **275** H5
Shepperdine **131** F3
Shepperton **121** F1
Shepreth **150** C3
Shepreth Wildlife Park
  Cambs SG8 6PZ **150** B3
Shepshed **159** G1
Shepton
  Beauchamp **104** A1
Shepton Mallet **116** D3
Shepton Montague **117** D4
Shepway **123** G3
Sheraton **212** D4
Sherborne *Dorset* **104** C1
Sherborne *Glos* **133** D1
Sherborne St. John **120** B2
Sherbourne **147** E1
Sherbourne Street **152** A3
Sherburn *Dur* **212** C3
Sherburn *NYorks* **204** C5
Sherburn Hill **212** C3
Sherburn in Elmet **195** D4
Shere **121** F3
Shereford **177** G5
Sherfield English **119** D5
Sherfield on
  oddon **120** B2
Sherford *Devon* **101** D3
Sherford *Som* **115** F5
Sheriff Hutton **195** F1
Sheriffhales **157** G1
Sheringham **178** C1
Sheringham Park *Norf*
  NR26 8TL **178** C1
Sherington **149** D3
Shernal Green **146** B1
Shernborne **177** F4
Sherramore **258** C5
Sherrington **118** A4
Sherston **132** A4
Sherwood **173** G3
Sherwood Forest Country
  Park *Notts*
  NG21 9HN **174** B1
Sherwood Forest Fun Park
  Notts
  NG21 9QA **174** B1
Sherwood Green **113** F3

Sherwood Pines Forest
  Park *Notts*
  NG21 9JL **174** B1
Shetland Islands **279** B7
Shevington **183** G2
Shevington Moor **183** G1
Sheviock **99** D5
Shide **107** E4
Shidlaw
  (Drochaid Sheile) **257** F3
Shieldaig *High* **264** E6
Shieldaig *High* **264** K6
Shieldhill **234** C2
Shielfoot **247** F2
Shielhill **252** C2
Shiels **260** E4
Shifford **133** F2
Shifnal **157** G2
Shilbottle **221** E1
Shildon **212** B5
Shillingford
  Devon **114** C3
Shillingford *Oxon* **134** A3
Shillingford Abbot **102** C4
Shillingford
  St. George **102** C4
Shillingstone **105** E1
Shillington **149** G4
Shillmoor **220** A1
Shilstone **113** F5
Shilton *Oxon* **133** E2
Shilton *Warks* **159** F4
Shimpling *Norf* **164** C3
Shimpling *Suff* **151** G2
Shimpling Street **151** G2
Shincliffe **212** B3
Shiney Row **212** C2
Shinfield **120** C1
Shingay **150** B3
Shingham **163** F2
Shingle Street **153** E3
Shinness Lodge **273** H7
Shipbourne **123** E3
Shipbrookhill **184** A5
Shipdham **178** A5
Shipham **116** B2
Shiphay **101** E1
Shiplake **134** C5
Shiplake Row **134** C5
Shipley *N'umb* **229** F5
Shipley *Shrop* **158** A3
Shipley *WSuss* **121** G5
Shipley *WYorks* **194** A4
Shipley Bridge
  Devon **100** C1
Shipley Bridge *Surr* **122** C4
Shipley Common **173** F3
Shipley Country Park
  Derbys
  DE75 7GX **18** D2
Shipmeadow **165** E2
Shippea Hill **163** E4
Shippon **133** G3
Shipston on Stour **147** E3
Shipton *Glos* **132** C1
Shipton *NYorks* **195** E2
Shipton Bellinger **118** D3
Shipton Gorge **104** A3
Shipton Green **108** A3
Shipton Moyne **132** A4
Shipton Oliffe **132** C1
Shipton Solers **132** C1
Shipton-on-
  Cherwell **133** G1
Shiptonthorpe **196** A3
Shipton-under-
  Wychwood **133** E1
Shira **241** D3
Shirburn **134** B3
Shirdley Hill **183** E1
Shire Hall Gallery, Stafford
  Staffs ST16 2LD **171** G5
Shire Oak **158** C2
Shirebrook **173** G1
Shirecliffe **186** A3
Shiregreen **186** A3
Shirehampton **131** E5
Shiremoor **221** F4
Shireoaks **186** C4
Shirl Heath **144** D2
Shirland **173** E2
Shirley *Derbys* **172** D3
Shirley *GtLon* **122** C2
Shirley *Hants* **106** A3
Shirley *Soton* **106** D1
Shirley *WMid* **158** D5
Shirley Heath **158** D5
Shirley Warren **106** C1
Shirleywich **171** G5
Shirrell Heath **107** E1
Shirwell **113** F2
Shirwell Cross **113** F2
Shiskine **223** E3
Shittlehope **211** G4
Shobdon **144** C1
Shobley **106** A2
Shocklach **170** B3
Shocklach Green **170** B3
Shoeburyness **138** C4
Sholden **125** F3
Sholing **107** D1
Shoot Hill **156** D1
Shooter's Hill **136** D5
Shop *Corn* **96** C5
Shop *Corn* **112** C4
Shop Corner **153** E2
Shopnoller **115** E4
Shore **101** D1
Shoreditch **136** C4
Shoreham **123** E2
Shoreham Airport **109** D3
Shoreham-by-Sea **109** E3
Shoremill **266** D5
Shoresdean **237** G5
Shoreswood **237** G5
Shoreton **266** D5
Shorley **119** G5
Shorncote **132** C3
Shorne **137** F5

Shorne Ridgeway **137** F5
Short Cross **156** B2
Short Green **164** B3
Short Heath
  Derbys **159** F1
Short Heath *WMid* **158** C3
Shortacombe **99** F2
Shortbridge **109** G1
Shortfield Common **120** D3
Shortgate **109** G2
Shortgrove **150** D4
Shorthampton **147** F5
Shortlands **122** C2
Shortlanesend **96** C5
Shorton **101** E1
Shorwell **107** D4
Shoscombe **117** E2
Shotatton **170** A5
Shotesham **164** D2
Shotgate **137** G3
Shotley *N'hants* **161** E3
Shotley *Suff* **152** D4
Shotley Bridge **211** G2
Shotley Gate **152** D4
Shotleyfield **211** G2
Shottenden **124** C3
Shottermill **121** D4
Shottery **147** D2
Shotteswell **147** G3
Shottisham **153** E3
Shottle **173** E2
Shottlegate **173** E3
Shotton *Dur* **212** D4
Shotton *Dur* **212** C5
Shotton *Flints* **170** A1
Shotton *N'umb* **228** C3
Shotton Colliery **212** C3
Shotts **234** C3
Shotwick **183** E5
Shouldham **163** E2
Shouldham Thorpe **163** E2
Shoulton **146** A2
Shover's Green **123** F5
Shrawardine **156** C1
Shrawley **146** A1
Shreding Green **135** F4
Shrewley **147** E1
Shrewsbury **157** D1
Shrewton **118** B3
Shri Venkateswara (Balaji)
  Temple of the United
  Kingdom *WMid*
  B69 3DU **14** D3
Shrine of Our Lady of
  Walsingham (Anglican)
  Norf NR22 6EF **178** A2
Shripney **108** B3
Shrivenham **133** E4
Shropham **164** A2
Shroton (Iwerne
  Courtney) **105** E1
Shrub End **152** A5
Shucknall **145** E3
Shudy Camps **151** E3
Shugborough Estate *Staffs*
  ST17 0XB **171** G5
Shurdington **132** B1
Shurlock Row **134** D5
Shurnock **146** C1
Shurrery **275** F3
Shurrery Lodge **275** F3
Shurton **115** F3
Shustoke **159** E3
Shut Heath **171** F5
Shute *Devon* **103** F3
Shute *Devon* **102** B2
Shutford **147** F3
Shuthonger **146** A4
Shutlanger **148** C3
Shutt Green **158** A2
Shuttington **159** E2
Shuttlewood **186** B5
Shuttleworth **184** B1
Siabost Bho Dheas **270** E3
Siabost Bho Thuath **270** E3
Siadar Iarach **271** F2
Siadar Uarach **271** F2
Sibbaldie **217** F2
Sibbertoft **160** B4
Sibdon Carwood **156** D4
Sibertswold
  (Shepherdswell) **125** E4
Sibford Ferris **147** F4
Sibford Gower **147** F4
Sible Hedingham **151** F4
Sibley's Green **151** E5
Sibsey **176** B2
Sibson *Cambs* **161** F3
Sibson *Leics* **159** F2
Sibster **275** J3
Sibthorpe **174** C3
Sibton **153** E1
Sibton Green **165** E4
Sicklesmere **151** G1
Sicklinghall **194** C3
Sid **103** E3
Sidbury *Devon* **103** E3
Sidbury *Shrop* **157** F4
Sidcot **116** B2
Sidcup **137** D5
Siddal **194** A5
Siddington *ChesE* **184** C5
Siddington *Glos* **132** C3
Sidemoor **158** B5
Sidestrand **179** D2
Sidford **103** E3
Sidlesham **108** A4
Sidley **110** C3
Sidlow **122** B4
Sidmouth **103** E4
Sigford **102** A5
Sigglesthorne **197** D3
Sigingstone **129** F5
Signet **133** E1
Silchester **120** B1
Sildinis **270** E6
Sileby **160** B1
Silecroft **198** C4
Silfield **164** C2
Silian **142** B2
Silk Willoughby **175** F3
Silksworth **212** C2
Silkstead **119** F5
Silkstone **185** G2

Silkstone Common **185** G2
Sill Field **199** G4
Silloth **209** E1
Sills **220** A1
Sillyearn **268** C5
Silpho **204** C3
Silsden **193** G3
Silsoe **149** F4
Silver End *CenBeds* **149** G3
Silver End *Essex* **151** G5
Silver Green **165** D2
Silver Street *Kent* **124** A2
Silver Street *Som* **116** C4
Silverburn **235** G3
Silvercraigs **231** G1
Silverdale *Lancs* **199** F5
Silverdale *Staffs* **171** F3
Silvergate **178** C3
Silverhill **110** C2
Silverlace Green **153** E2
Silverley's Green **165** D4
Silvermoss **261** G1
Silverstone **148** B3
Silverton **102** C2
Silvington **157** F5
Silwick **279** B8
Simister **184** C2
Simmondley **185** E3
Simonburn **220** A4
Simonsbath **114** A4
Simonside **212** C1
Simonstone
  Bridgend **129** F4
Simonstone *Lancs* **193** D4
Simprim **237** F5
Simpson **149** D4
Sinclair's Hill **237** F4
Sinclairston **224** C4
Sinderby **202** C5
Sinderhope **211** E2
Sindlesham **120** C1
Sinfin **173** E4
Singdean **227** G5
Singleton *Lancs* **191** G4
Singleton *WSuss* **108** A2
Singlewell **137** F5
Singret **170** A2
Sinkhurst Green **124** A4
Sinnahard **260** C3
Sinnington **203** G4
Sinton Green **146** A1
Sipson **135** F5
Sirhowy **130** A1
Sirhowy Valley Country
  Park *Caerp*
  NP11 7BD **130** A3
Sisland **165** E2
Sissinghurst **123** G5
Sissinghurst Castle Garden
  Kent TN17 2AB **124** A5
Siston **131** F5
Sithney **94** D4
Sittingbourne **124** B2
Siulaisiadar **271** H4
Six Ashes **157** G4
Six Hills **174** B5
Six Mile Bottom **151** D2
Six Roads End **172** C5
Sixhills **188** B4
Sixmile **124** D4
Sixpenny Handley **105** G1
Sizewell **153** F1
Skail **274** C4
Skaill *Ork* **277** B6
Skaill *Ork* **277** E7
Skaill *Ork* **276** D4
Skares *Aber* **260** E1
Skares *EAyr* **224** D4
Skarpigarth **279** A7
Skateraw **237** E2
Skaw **279** E6
Skeabost **263** K7
Skeabrae **276** B5
Skeeby **202** B2
Skeffington **160** C2
Skeffling **189** D1
Skegby **173** G1
Skegness **177** D1
Skegness Water Leisure
  Park *Lincs*
  PE25 1JF **177** D1
Skelberry *Shet* **279** F9
Skelberry *Shet* **279** D6
Skelbo **266** E2
Skelbo Street **266** E2
Skelbrooke **186** C1
Skeld (Easter Skeld) **279** C8
Skeldon **224** B4
Skeldyke **176** B4
Skellingthorpe **187** G5
Skellister **279** D7
Skellow **186** C1
Skelmanthorpe **185** G1
Skelmersdale **183** F2
Skelmonae **261** G1
Skelmorlie **232** C3
Skelmuir **269** H6
Skelpick **274** C3
Skelton *Cumb* **210** A4
Skelton *ERid* **195** D5
Skelton *NYorks* **201** F2
Skelton (Skelton-in-
  Cleveland) R&C **203** F1
Skelton *York* **195** E2
Skelton-in-Cleveland
  (Skelton) **203** F1
Skelton-on-Ure **194** C1
Skelwick **276** D3
Skelwith Bridge **199** E2
Skendleby **176** C1
Skendleby Psalter **189** E5
Skenfrith **145** D5
Skerne **196** C2
Skeroblingarry **222** C3
Skerray **273** J2
Skerton **192** A1
Sketchley **159** G3
Sketty **128** C3
Skewen **128** D3
Skewsby **203** F5
Skeyton **179** D3
Skeyton Corner **179** D3

Skidbrooke **189** E3
Skidbrooke North
  End **189** E3
Skidby **196** C4
Skilgate **114** C5
Skillington **175** D5
Skinburness **209** E1
Skinflats **234** C1
Skinidin **263** H7
Skinnet **275** C2
Skinningrove **203** G1
Skipness **231** G4
Skippool **191** G3
Skipsea **197** D2
Skipsea Brough **197** D2
Skipton **193** F2
Skipton Castle *NYorks*
  BD23 1AW **193** F2
Skipton-on-Swale **202** C5
Skipwith **195** F3
Skirbeck **176** B3
Skirbeck Quarter **176** B3
Skirethorns **193** F1
Skirlaugh **196** D4
Skirling **226** B2
Skirmett **134** C4
Skirpenbeck **195** G2
Skirwith *Cumb* **210** C4
Skirwith *NYorks* **200** C5
Skirza **275** J2
Skittle Green **134** C2
Skomer Island **126** A2
Skulamus **256** C2
Skullomie **273** J2
Skye **255** K1
Skye Green **151** G5
Skye of Curr **259** G2
Skyreholme **193** G1
Slack *Aber* **260** D1
Slack *Derbys* **173** D1
Slack *WYorks* **193** F5
Slackhall **185** E4
Slackhead **268** C4
Slad **132** A2
Slade *Devon* **113** F1
Slade *Devon* **103** E2
Slade *Pembs* **126** C1
Slade *Swan* **128** A4
Slade Green **137** E5
Slade Hooton **186** C4
Sladesbridge **97** E2
Slaggyford **210** C2
Slaidburn **192** D3
Slains Park **253** G2
Slaithwaite **185** E1
Slaley **211** F2
Slamannan **234** C2
Slapton *Bucks* **149** E5
Slapton *Devon* **101** E3
Slapton *N'hants* **148** B3
Slate Haugh **268** C4
Slatepit Dale **173** E1
Slattadale **264** E4
Slaugham **109** E1
Slaughden **153** F2
Slaughterford **132** A5
Slawston **160** C3
Sleaford *Hants* **120** D4
Sleaford *Lincs* **175** F3
Sleagill **199** G1
Sleap **170** B5
Sledge Green **146** A4
Sledmere **196** B1
Sleights **204** B2
Slepe **105** F2
Slerra **112** D3
Slickly **275** H2
Sliddery **223** E3
Sliemore **259** H2
Sligachan **255** K2
Slimbridge **131** G2
Slimbridge Wildfowl &
  Wetlands Trust *Glos*
  GL2 7BT **131** G2
Slindon *Staffs* **171** F4
Slindon *WSuss* **108** B3
Slinfold **121** G4
Sling **131** E2
Slingsby **203** F5
Slioch **260** D1
Slip End *CenBeds* **135** F1
Slip End *Herts* **150** A4
Slipper Chapel, Houghton
  St. Giles *Norf*
  NR22 6AL **178** A2
Slipton **161** E5
Slitting Mill **158** C1
Slochd **259** F2
Slockavullin **240** A5
Slogarie **216** A4
Sloley **179** D3
Slongaber **216** C2
Sloothby **189** E5
Slough **135** E4
Slough Green
  Som **115** F5
Slough Green
  WSuss **109** E1
Sluggan **259** F2
Slyne **192** A1
Smailholm **228** A3
Small Dole **109** E2
Small Hythe **124** A5
Smallbridge **184** D1
Smallbrook **102** B3
Smallburgh **179** E3
Smallburn *Aber* **269** J6
Smallburn *EAyr* **225** E3
Smalldale **185** E5
Smalley **173** F3
Smallfield **122** C4
Smallford **136** A2
Smallridge **103** F2
Smallthorne **171** F2
Smallworth **164** B3
Smannell **119** E3
Smardale **200** C3
Smarden **124** A4
Smaull **230** A3
Smeatharpe **103** E1
Smeeth **124** C5

Smeeton Westerby 160 B3
Smerclet 254 C3
Smestow 158 A3
Smethwick 158 C4
Smethwick Green 171 F1
Smirisary 247 F2
Smisby 159 F1
Smith End Green 145 G2
Smithfield 210 A2
Smithies 158 A2
Smithincott 103 D1
Smith's End 150 B4
Smith's Green Essex 151 D5
Smith's Green Essex 151 E5
Smithstown 264 D4
Smithton 266 E7
Smithy Green 184 B5
Smockington 159 G4
Smugglers Adventure ESuss TN34 3HY 75 Hastings
Smyrton 214 C2
Smythe's Green 138 C1
Snailbeach 156 C2
Snainton 204 C4
Snailwell 151 E1
Snaith 195 F5
Snape NYorks 202 B4
Snape Suff 153 E2
Snape Green 183 E1
Snape Watering 153 E2
Snarestone 159 F2
Snarford 188 A4
Snargate 111 E1
Snave 111 F1
Sneachill 146 B2
Snead 156 C3
Snead's Green 146 A1
Sneath Common 164 C3
Sneaton 204 B2
Sneatonthorpe 204 C2
Snelland 188 A4
Snellings 198 A2
Snelston 172 C3
Snetterton 164 A2
Snettisham 177 E4
Snipeshill 124 B2
Snishival (Sniseabhal) 254 C1
Snitter 220 C1
Snitterby 187 G3
Snitterfield 147 E2
Snitterton 173 D1
Snittlegarth 209 F3
Snitton 157 E5
Snodhill 144 C3
Snodland 123 G2
Snow End 150 C4
Snow Street 164 B3
Snowden Hill 185 G2
Snowdon Mountain Railway Gwyn LL55 4TY 167 E2
Snowshill 146 C4
Snowshill Manor Glos WR12 7JU 146 C4
Soar Cardiff 129 G4
Soar Carmar 142 C5
Soar Devon 100 D4
Soay 255 K3
Soberton 107 F1
Soberton Heath 107 F1
Sockbridge 210 B5
Sockburn 202 C2
Sodom 128 B5
Sodylt Bank 170 A4
Softley 211 G5
Soham 163 D5
Soham Cotes 163 D5
Soldon 112 D4
Soldon Cross 112 D4
Soldridge 120 B4
Sole Street Kent 124 C4
Sole Street Kent 123 F2
Soleburn 214 B4
Solihull 159 D5
Solihull Lodge 158 C5
Sollas (Solas) 262 C3
Sollers Dilwyn 144 D2
Sollers Hope 145 F4
Sollom 183 E1
Solomon's Tump 131 G1
Solsgirth 243 E5
Solva 140 A5
Solwaybank 218 B4
Somerby Leics 160 C1
Somerby Lincs 188 A2
Somercotes 173 F2
Somerford 158 B2
Somerford Keynes 132 C3
Somerley 108 A4
Somerleyton 165 F2
Somersal Herbert 172 C4
Somersby 188 D5
Somerset House GtLon WC2R 1LA 45 F3
Somersham Cambs 162 B5
Somersham Suff 152 B3
Somerton Newport 130 C4
Somerton Oxon 147 G5
Somerton Som 116 B5
Somerton Suff 151 G2
Sompting 109 D3
Sompting Abbotts 109 D3
Sonning 134 C5
Sonning Common 134 C4
Sonning Eye 134 C5
Sontley 170 A3
Sookholme 173 G1
Sopley 106 A3
Sopworth 132 A4
Sorbie 207 E2
Sordale 275 G2
Sorisdale 246 B3
Sorn 225 D3
Sornhill 225 D2
Soroba 240 A2
Sortat 275 H2
Sotby 188 C5

Sots Hole 175 G1
Sotterley 165 F3
Soudley 171 E5
Soughton 169 F1
Soulbury 149 D5
Soulby 200 C1
Souldern 148 A4
Souldrop 149 E1
Sound ChesE 170 D3
Sound Shet 279 D8
Sound Shet 279 C7
Sourhope 228 C4
Sourin 276 D4
Sourton 99 F2
Soutergate 198 D4
South Acre 163 G1
South Acton 136 A5
South Alkham 125 E4
South Allington 101 D4
South Alloa 243 D5
South Ambersham 121 E5
South Anston 186 C4
South Ascot 121 E5
South Baddesley 106 C3
South Ballachulish (Baile a' Chaolais a Deas) 248 C4
South Balloch 215 E1
South Bank 213 E5
South Barrow 116 D5
South Bellsdyke 234 D1
South Benfleet 137 G4
South Bersted 108 B3
South Blackbog 261 F1
South Bockhampton 106 A3
South Bowood 104 A3
South Brent 100 C1
South Brentor 99 E2
South Brewham 117 E4
South Broomhill 221 E2
South Burlingham 179 E5
South Cadbury 116 D1
South Cairn 214 A4
South Carlton 187 G5
South Cave 196 B4
South Cerney 132 C3
South Chard 103 G2
South Charlton 229 F4
South Cheriton 117 D5
South Church 212 B5
South Cliffe 196 A4
South Clifton 187 F5
South Cockerington 189 D4
South Collafirth 278 C4
South Common 109 F2
South Cornelly 129 E4
South Corriegills 223 F2
South Cove 165 F3
South Creagan 248 B5
South Creake 177 G4
South Crosland 185 F1
South Croxton 160 B1
South Croydon 122 C2
South Dalton 196 B3
South Darenth 137 E5
South Dell (Dail Bho Dheas) 271 G1
South Duffield 195 F4
South Elkington 188 C4
South Elmsall 186 B1
South End Bucks 149 D5
South End Cumb 191 F1
South End Hants 106 A1
South End NLincs 196 D5
South Erradale 264 C4
South Fambridge 138 B3
South Fawley 133 F4
South Fernby 196 B5
South Field 196 C5
South Flobbets 261 F1
South Garth 278 E3
South Godstone 122 C4
South Gorley 106 A1
South Green Essex 137 F3
South Green Essex 138 D1
South Green Norf 178 B4
South Green Suff 164 C4
South Gyle 235 F2
South Hall 232 B2
South Hanningfield 137 G3
South Harefield 135 F4
South Harting 107 G1
South Hayling 107 G3
South Hazelrigg 229 E3
South Heath 135 E2
South Heighton 109 G3
South Hetton 212 C3
South Hiendley 186 A1
South Hill 98 D3
South Hinksey 134 A2
South Hole 112 C4
South Holme 203 F5
South Holmwood 121 G3
South Hornchurch 137 E4
South Hourat 233 D4
South Huish 100 C3
South Hykeham 175 E1
South Hylton 212 C2
South Kelsey 188 A3
South Kessock (Ceasag a Deas) 266 D7
South Killingholme 188 B1
South Kilvington 202 D4
South Kilworth 160 B4
South Kirkby 186 B1
South Kirkton 261 F4
South Knighton 102 B5
South Kyme 175 G3
South Lakes Wild Animal Park Cumb LA15 8JR 198 D5
South Lancing 109 D3
South Ledaig 240 B1
South Leigh 133 F2
South Leverton 187 E4
South Littleton 146 C3
South Lopham 164 B3
South Luffenham 161 E2
South Malling 109 G2
South Marston 133 D4
South Middleton 229 D4
South Milford 195 D4

South Milton 100 C3
South Mimms 136 B2
South Molton 114 A5
South Moor 212 A2
South Moreton 134 A4
South Mundham 108 A3
South Muskham 174 C2
South Newbald 196 B4
South Newington 147 G4
South Newton 118 B4
South Normanton 173 F2
South Norwood 122 C2
South Nutfield 122 C4
South Ockendon 137 E4
South Ormsby 189 D5
South Ossett 185 G1
South Otterington 202 C4
South Owersby 188 A3
South Oxhey 136 A3
South Park 122 B4
South Parks 244 A5
South Perrott 104 A2
South Petherton 104 A1
South Petherwin 98 D2
South Pickenham 163 G2
South Pool 101 D3
South Queensferry (Queensferry) 235 F2
South Radworthy 114 A4
South Rauceby 175 F3
South Raynham 177 G5
South Redbriggs 269 F6
South Reston 189 E4
South Ronaldsay 277 D9
South Ruislip 136 A4
South Runcton 163 E2
South Scarle 174 D1
South Shian (Sithean a Deas) 248 B5
South Shields 212 C1
South Shields Museum & Art Gallery T&W NE33 2JA 28 E2
South Somercotes 189 E3
South Somercotes Fen Houses 189 E3
South Stainley 194 C1
South Stoke B&NESom 117 E1
South Stoke Oxon 134 B4
South Stoke WSuss 108 C3
South Street ESuss 109 F2
South Street GtLon 123 F2
South Street Kent 123 F2
South Street Kent 124 D2
South Street Kent 124 A2
South Tawton 99 G1
South Thoresby 189 D5
South Tidworth 118 D3
South Tottenham 136 C4
South Town Devon 102 C4
South Town Hants 120 B4
South Uist (Uibhist a Deas) 254 C1
South Upper Barrack 269 H6
South View 120 B2
South Walsham 179 E4
South Warnborough 120 C3
South Weald 137 E3
South Weston 134 C3
South Wheatley Corn 98 C1
South Wheatley Notts 187 E4
South Whiteness 279 C8
South Wigston 160 A3
South Willingham 188 B4
South Wingfield 173 E2
South Witham 161 E1
South Wonston 119 F4
South Woodham Ferrers 138 B3
South Wootton 177 E5
South Wraxall 117 F1
South Yardle 158 D4
South Zeal 99 G1
Southall 136 A4
Southam Glos 146 B5
Southam Warks 147 G1
Southampton 106 D1
Southampton Airport 107 D1
Southbar 233 F3
Southborough GtLon 122 D2
Southbourne Bourne 106 A3
Southbourne WSuss 107 G2
Southbrook 102 D3
Southburgh 178 B5
Southburn 196 B2
Southchurch 138 C4
Southcott Devon 99 F1
Southcott Wilts 118 C2
Southcourt 134 D1
Southdean 219 E1
Southdene 183 F1
Southease 109 G3
Southend A&B 222 B5
Southend Aber 269 F6
Southend Bucks 134 C4
Southend (Bradfield Southend) WBerks 134 A5
Southend Wilts 133 D5
Southend Airport 138 B4
Southend Pier S'end SS1 1EE 138 C4
Southend-on-Sea 138 B4
Southerfield 209 E2
Southerly 99 F2
Southern Green 150 B4
Southerndown 129 E5
Southerness 217 D5
Southery 163 E3
Southfield 244 A5
Southfields 136 B5
Southfleet 137 F5

Southgate Cere 154 B4
Southgate GtLon 136 C3
Southgate Norf 178 C3
Southgate Norf 177 E4
Southgate Swan 128 B4
Southill 149 G3
Southington 119 G3
Southleigh 103 F3
Southmarsh 117 E4
Southminster 138 C3
Southmoor 133 F3
Southmuir 252 B4
Southoe 149 G1
Southolt 152 C1
Southorpe 161 F2
Southowram 194 A5
Southport 183 E1
Southport Pier Mersey PR8 1QX 183 E1
Southrepps 179 D2
Southrey 175 G1
Southrop 133 D2
Southrope 120 B3
Southsea Ports 107 F3
Southsea Wrex 169 F2
Southtown Norf 179 G5
Southtown Ork 277 D8
Southwaite Cumb 200 C2
Southwaite Cumb 210 A3
Southway 116 C3
Southwell Dorset 104 D5
Southwell Notts 174 B2
Southwell Minster Notts NG25 0HD 174 B2
Southwick D&G 216 D5
Southwick Hants 107 F3
Southwick N'hants 161 F3
Southwick Som 116 A3
Southwick T&W 212 C1
Southwick Wilts 117 F2
Southwick WSuss 109 E3
Southwold 165 G4
Southwood 116 C4
Sowden 102 C4
Sower Carr 191 G3
Sowerby NYorks 202 D4
Sowerby WYorks 193 G5
Sowerby Bridge 193 G5
Sowerby Row 209 G2
Sowerhill 114 A5
Sowley Green 151 F2
Sowood 185 E1
Sowton 102 C3
Soyal 266 C2
Spa Common 179 D2
Spa Complex NYorks YO11 2HD 83 Scarborough
Spadeadam 219 D4
Spalding 175 F5
Spaldington 195 G4
Spaldwick 161 G5
Spalefield 245 D4
Spalford 174 D1
Spanby 175 F4
Sparham 178 B4
Spark Bridge 199 E4
Sparkford 116 D5
Sparkhill 158 C4
Sparkwell 100 B2
Sparrow Green 178 A4
Sparrowpit 185 E4
Sparrow's Green 123 F5
Sparsholt Hants 119 F4
Sparsholt Oxon 133 F4
Spartylea 211 E3
Spath 172 B4
Spaunton 203 G4
Spaxton 115 F4
Spean Bridge (Drochaid an Aonachain) 249 E1
Spean Bridge Woollen Mill High PH34 4EP 249 E1
Spear Hill 108 D2
Speddoch 216 C2
Speedwell 131 F5
Speen Bucks 134 D2
Speen WBerks 119 F1
Speeton 205 E5
Speke 183 F4
Speldhurst 123 E4
Spellbrook 137 D1
Spelsbury 147 F5
Spen Green 171 F1
Spencers Wood 120 C1
Spennithorne 202 A4
Spennymoor 212 B4
Spernall 146 C2
Spetchley 146 A2
Spetisbury 105 F2
Spexhall 165 E3
Spey Bay 268 B4
Speybridge 259 H2
Speyview 267 K7
Spilsby 176 B1
Spindlestone 229 F3
Spinkhill 186 B5
Spinnaker Tower PO1 3TN 82 Portsmouth
Spinningdale 266 D3
Spirthill 132 B5
Spital High 275 G2
Spital W&M 135 E5
Spital in the Street 187 G3
Spitalbrook 136 C2
Spitfire & Hurricane Memorial, R.A.F. Manston Kent CT12 5DF 125 F2
Spithurst 109 G2
Spittal D&G 215 F5
Spittal D&G 215 E5
Spittal ELoth 236 B2
Spittal N'umb 229 G5
Spittal Pembs 140 C5
Spittal of Glenmuick 252 B1
Spittal of Glenshee 251 G3
Spittalfield 251 G5

Spixworth 178 D4
Splayne's Green 109 G1
Splott 130 B5
Spofforth 194 C2
Spondon 173 F4
Spooner Row 164 B2
Spoonley 171 D4
Sporle 163 G1
Sportsman's Arms 168 C2
Spott 237 D2
Spratton 160 C5
Spreakley 120 D3
Spreyton 99 G1
Spriddlestone 100 B2
Spridlington 188 A4
Spring Grove 136 A5
Spring Vale 107 F3
Springburn 234 A3
Springfield A&B 232 B2
Springfield D&G 218 B5
Springfield Fife 244 B3
Springfield Moray 267 H6
Springfield P&K 243 F2
Springfield WMid 158 C4
Springhill Staffs 158 C2
Springhill Staffs 158 B2
Springholm 216 C4
Springkell 218 A4
Springleys 261 F1
Springside 224 B2
Springthorpe 187 F4
Springwell 212 B2
Sproatley 197 D4
Sproston Green 171 E1
Sprotbrough 186 C2
Sproughton 152 C3
Sprouston 228 B3
Sprowston 178 D4
Sproxton Leics 175 D5
Sproxton NYorks 203 F4
Sprytown 99 E2
Spurlands End 135 D3
Spurstow 170 C2
Spyway 104 B3
Square Point 216 B3
Squires Gate 191 G4
Sròndoire 231 G2
Sronphadruig Lodge 250 C2
Stableford Shrop 157 G3
Stableford Staffs 171 F4
Stacey Bank 185 G3
Stackhouse 193 E1
Stackpole 126 C3
Stacksteads 193 E5
Staddiscombe 100 B2
Staddlethorpe 196 A5
Staden 185 E5
Stadhampton 134 B3
Staffield 210 B3
Staffin 263 K5
Stafford 171 G5
Stagden Cross 137 F1
Stagsden 149 E2
Stagshaw Bank 211 F1
Stain 275 J2
Stainburn Cumb 208 D4
Stainburn NYorks 194 B3
Stainby 175 D5
Staincross 186 A1
Staindrop 212 A5
Staines 135 F5
Stainfield Lincs 175 F5
Stainfield Lincs 188 B5
Stainforth NYorks 193 E1
Stainforth SYorks 186 D1
Staining 191 G4
Stainland 185 E1
Stainsacre 204 C2
Stainsby Derbys 173 F1
Stainsby Lincs 188 D5
Stainton Cumb 199 G4
Stainton Cumb 210 A5
Stainton Dur 201 F1
Stainton Middl 203 D1
Stainton NYorks 202 A3
Stainton SYorks 186 C3
Stainton by Langworth 188 A5
Stainton le Vale 188 B3
Stainton with Adgarley 198 D5
Staintondale 204 C3
Stair Cumb 209 F4
Stair EAyr 224 C3
Stairfoot 186 A2
Staithes 203 G1
Stake Pool 192 A3
Stakeford 221 E3
Stakes 107 F2
Stalbridge 104 D1
Stalbridge Weston 104 D1
Stalham 179 E3
Stalham Green 179 E3
Stalisfield Green 124 B3
Stalling Busk 201 F4
Stallingborough 188 B1
Stallington 171 G4
Stalmine 191 G3
Stalybridge 185 D3
Stambourne 151 F4
Stamford Lincs 161 F2
Stamford N'umb 229 G5
Stamford Bridge ChesW&C 170 B1
Stamford Bridge ERid 195 G2
Stamfordham 220 C4
Stanah 191 G3
Stanborough 136 B1
Stanborough Park Herts AL8 6XF 136 B1
Stanbridge CenBeds 149 E5
Stanbridge Dorset 105 G2
Stanbridge Earls 119 E5
Stanbury 193 G4
Stand 234 B3
Standalone Farm, Letchworth Garden City Herts SG6 4JN 150 A4
Standburn 234 D2

Standeford 158 B2
Standen 124 A5
Standen Street 124 A5
Standerwick 117 F2
Standford 120 D4
Standford Bridge 171 E5
Standish Glos 132 A2
Standish GtMan 183 G1
Standlake 133 F2
Standon Hants 119 F5
Standon Herts 150 B5
Standon Staffs 171 F4
Standon Green End 136 C1
Stane 234 C4
Stanecastle 224 B2
Stanfield 178 A3
Stanford CenBeds 149 G3
Stanford Kent 124 D5
Stanford Shrop 156 C1
Stanford Bishop 145 F2
Stanford Bridge 145 G1
Stanford Dingley 134 A5
Stanford End 120 C1
Stanford in the Vale 133 F3
Stanford on Avon 160 A5
Stanford on Soar 173 G5
Stanford on Teme 145 G1
Stanford Rivers 137 E2
Stanford-le-Hope 137 F4
Stanfree 186 B5
Stanghow 203 F1
Stanground 162 A3
Stanhoe 177 G4
Stanhope Dur 211 F4
Stanhope ScBord 226 C3
Stanion 161 E4
Stanklyn 158 A5
Stanley Derbys 173 F3
Stanley Dur 212 A2
Stanley Notts 173 F1
Stanley P&K 243 G1
Stanley Shrop 157 G4
Stanley Staffs 171 G2
Stanley Wilts 132 B5
Stanley WYorks 194 C5
Stanley Common 173 F3
Stanley Crook 212 A4
Stanley Gate 183 F2
Stanley Hill 145 F3
Stanleygreen 170 C4
Stanlow ChesW&C 183 F5
Stanlow Shrop 157 G3
Stanmer 109 F3
Stanmore GtLon 136 A3
Stanmore WBerks 133 G5
Stannersburn 219 F3
Stanningfield 151 G2
Stannington N'umb 221 E4
Stannington SYorks 186 A4
Stansbatch 144 C1
Stansfield 151 F2
Stanshope 172 C2
Stanstead 151 G3
Stanstead Abbotts 136 C1
Stansted 123 F2
Stansted Airport 150 D5
Stansted Mountfitchet 150 D5
Stanton Derbys 159 E1
Stanton Glos 146 C4
Stanton N'umb 220 D2
Stanton Staffs 172 C3
Stanton Suff 164 A4
Stanton by Bridge 173 E5
Stanton by Dale 173 F4
Stanton Drew 116 C1
Stanton Fitzwarren 133 D3
Stanton Harcourt 133 G2
Stanton Hill 173 F1
Stanton in Peak 172 D1
Stanton Lacy 157 D5
Stanton Lees 173 D1
Stanton Long 157 E3
Stanton Prior 117 D1
Stanton St. Bernard 118 B1
Stanton St. John 134 A2
Stanton St. Quintin 132 B5
Stanton Street 152 A1
Stanton under Bardon 159 G1
Stanton upon Hine Heath 170 C5
Stanton Wick 116 D1
Stanton-on-the-Wolds 174 B4
Stanwardine in the Fields 170 B5
Stanwardine in the Wood 170 B5
Stanway Essex 152 A5
Stanway Glos 146 C4
Stanway Green Essex 152 A5
Stanway Green Suff 164 D4
Stanwell 135 F5
Stanwell Moor 135 F5
Stanwick 161 F5
Stanwix 210 A2
Stanydale 279 B7
Staoinebrig 254 C1
Stapeley 171 D2
Stapeley Water Gardens ChesE CW5 7LH 171 D2
Stapenhill 173 D5
Staple Kent 125 E3
Staple Som 115 E3
Staple Cross 114 D5
Staple Fitzpaine 103 F1
Staplecross 110 C1
Staplefield 109 E1
Stapleford Cambs 150 C2
Stapleford Herts 136 C1
Stapleford Leics 160 D1
Stapleford Lincs 175 D2
Stapleford Notts 173 F4
Stapleford Wilts 118 B4

Standedge Tunnel & Visitor Centre WYorks HD7 6NQ 185 E1
Stapleford Abbotts 137 D3
Stapleford Tawney 137 E3
Staplegrove 115 F5
Staplehay 115 F5
Staplehurst 123 G4
Staplers 107 E4
Staplestreet 124 C2
Stapleton Cumb 218 D4
Stapleton Here 144 C1
Stapleton Leics 159 G3
Stapleton NYorks 202 B3
Stapleton Shrop 157 D2
Stapleton Som 116 B5
Stapley 103 E3
Staploe 149 G1
Staplow 145 F3
Star Fife 244 B4
Star Pembs 141 F4
Star Som 116 B2
Starbotton 201 E5
Starcross 102 C4
Stareton 159 F5
Starkholmes 173 E2
Starling 184 B1
Starling's Green 150 C4
Starr 215 F1
Starston 164 D3
Startforth 201 F1
Startley 132 B4
Statham 184 A4
Stathe 116 A5
Stathern 174 C4
Station Town 212 D4
Staughton Green 149 G1
Staughton Highway 149 G1
Staunton Glos 131 E1
Staunton Glos 145 G5
Staunton Harold Hall 173 E5
Staunton Harold Reservoir Derbys DE73 8DN 173 E5
Staunton in the Vale 174 D3
Staunton on Arrow 144 C1
Staunton on Wye 144 C3
Staveley Cumb 199 F3
Staveley Derbys 186 B5
Staveley NYorks 194 C1
Staveley-in-Cartmel 199 F4
Staverton Devon 101 D1
Staverton Glos 146 A5
Staverton N'hants 148 A1
Staverton Wilts 117 F1
Staverton Bridge 146 A5
Stawell 116 A4
Stawley 115 D5
Staxigoe 275 J3
Staxton 204 D5
Staylittle (Penffordd-las) 155 E3
Staynall 191 G3
Staythorpe 174 C2
Stean 201 F5
Steane 148 A4
Stearsby 203 F5
Steart 115 F3
Stebbing 151 E5
Stebbing Green 151 E5
Stechford 158 D4
Stedham 121 D5
Steel Cross 123 E5
Steel Green 198 C5
Steele Road 218 D2
Steen's Bridge 145 E2
Steep 120 C5
Steep Marsh 120 C5
Steeple Dorset 105 F4
Steeple Essex 138 C2
Steeple Ashton 118 A2
Steeple Aston 147 G5
Steeple Barton 147 G5
Steeple Bumpstead 151 E3
Steeple Claydon 148 B5
Steeple Gidding 161 G4
Steeple Langford 118 B4
Steeple Morden 150 A3
Steeraway 157 F2
Steeton 193 G3
Stein 263 H6
Steinis 271 G4
Steinmanhill 269 F6
Stella 212 A1
Stelling Minnis 124 D4
Stembridge 116 B5
Stemster High 275 G2
Stemster High 275 G4
Stemster House 275 G2
Stenalees 97 E4
Stenhill 103 E1
Stenhousemuir 234 C1
Stenigot 188 C4
Stenness 278 B5
Stenscholl 263 K5
Stenson 173 E5
Stenton ELoth 236 D2
Stenton P&K 251 F5
Stepaside Pembs 127 E2
Stepaside Powys 155 G4
Stepney 136 C4
Steppingley 149 F4
Stepps 234 A3
Sternfield 153 E1
Sterridge 113 F1
Stert 118 B2
Stetchworth 151 E2
Stevenage 150 A5
Stevenston 233 D5
Steventon Hants 119 G3
Steventon Oxon 133 G3
Steventon End 151 D3
Stevington 149 E2
Stewart Park, Middlesbrough Middl TS7 8AR 29
Stewartby 149 F3
Stewarton D&G 207 E2
Stewarton EAyr 233 F5
Stewkley 149 D5
Stewley 103 G1
Stewton 189 D4
Steyning 109 D2

Steynton 126 C2
Stibb 112 C4
Stibb Cross 113 E4
Stibb Green 118 D1
Stibbard 178 A3
Stibbington 161 F3
Stichill 228 B3
Sticker 97 D4
Stickford 176 B1
Sticklepath *Devon* 99 G1
Sticklepath *Som* 103 G1
Stickling Green 150 C4
Stickney 176 B2
Stiff Street 124 A2
Stiffkey 178 A1
Stifford's Bridge 145 G3
Stileway 116 B3
Stilligarry
(Stadhlaigearraidh) 254 C1
Stillingfleet 195 E3
Stillington *NYorks* 195 E1
Stillington *Stock* 212 C5
Stilton 161 G4
Stinchcombe 131 G3
Stinsford 104 D3
Stirchley *IoT* 157 G2
Stirchley *WMid* 158 C4
Stirkoke House 275 J3
Stirling *Aber* 269 K6
Stirling (Sruighlea)
Stir 242 C5
Stirling Castle *Stir*
FK8 1EJ 242 C5
Stirling Visitor Centre *Stir*
FK8 1EH 242 C5
Stirton 193 F2
Stisted 151 G5
Stitchcombe 118 D1
Stithians 95 E3
Stittenham 266 D4
Stivichall 159 F5
Stix 250 C5
Stixwould 175 G1
Stoak 183 F5
Stobo 226 C2
Stoborough 105 F4
Stoborough Green 105 F4
Stobwood 235 D4
Stock 137 F3
Stock Green 146 B2
Stock Lane 133 E5
Stock Wood 146 C2
Stockbridge *Hants* 119 E4
Stockbridge *Stir* 242 C4
Stockbridge *WSuss* 108 A3
Stockbury 124 A2
Stockcross 119 F1
Stockdale 95 E3
Stockdalewath 209 G2
Stockerston 160 D3
Stockgrove Country Park
CenBeds
LU7 0BA 149 E5
Stocking Green *Essex* 151 D4
Stocking Green *MK* 148 D3
Stocking Pelham 150 C5
Stockingford 159 F3
Stockinish (Stocinis) 263 G2
Stockland *Cardiff* 130 A5
Stockland *Devon* 103 F2
Stockland Bristol 115 F3
Stockleigh English 102 B2
Stockleigh Pomeroy 102 B2
Stockley 118 B1
Stocklinch 103 G1
Stockport 184 C3
Stocksbridge 185 G3
Stocksfield 211 G2
Stockton *Here* 145 E1
Stockton *Norf* 165 E2
Stockton *Shrop* 157 G3
Stockton *Shrop* 156 D2
Stockton *Tel&W* 157 G1
Stockton *Warks* 147 G1
Stockton *Wilts* 118 A4
Stockton Heath 184 A4
Stockton on Teme 145 G1
Stockton on the
Forest 195 F2
Stockton-on-Tees 202 D1
Stockwell *Bristol* 116 D1
Stockwell Heath 172 B5
Stockwood *Bristol* 116 D1
Stockwood *Dorset* 104 B2
Stodday 192 A2
Stodmarsh 125 E2
Stody 178 B2
Stoer 272 C6
Stoford *Som* 104 B1
Stoford *Wilts* 118 B4
Stogumber 115 D4
Stogursey 115 F3
Stoke *Devon* 112 C4
Stoke *Hants* 119 F2
Stoke *Hants* 107 G2
Stoke *Med* 124 A1
Stoke *Plym* 100 A2
Stoke *WMid* 159 F5
Stoke Abbott 104 A2
Stoke Albany 160 D4
Stoke Ash 164 C4
Stoke Bardolph 174 B3
Stoke Bishop 131 E5
Stoke Bliss 145 F1
Stoke Bruerne 148 C3
Stoke by Clare 151 F3
Stoke Canon 102 C3
Stoke Charity 119 F4
Stoke Climsland 99 D3
Stoke D'Abernon 121 G2
Stoke Doyle 161 F4
Stoke Dry 161 D3
Stoke Edith 145 F3
Stoke Farthing 118 B5
Stoke Ferry 163 F2
Stoke Fleming 101 E3
Stoke Gabriel 101 E2
Stoke Gifford 131 F5
Stoke Golding 159 F3
Stoke Goldington 148 D3
Stoke Green 135 E4

Stoke Hammond 149 D5
Stoke Heath *Shrop* 171 D5
Stoke Heath *Worcs* 146 B1
Stoke Holy Cross 178 D5
Stoke Lacy 145 F3
Stoke Lyne 148 A5
Stoke Mandeville 134 D1
Stoke Newington 136 C4
Stoke on Tern 170 D5
Stoke Orchard 146 B5
Stoke Pero 114 B3
Stoke Poges 135 E4
Stoke Pound 146 B1
Stoke Prior *Here* 145 E2
Stoke Prior *Worcs* 146 B1
Stoke Rivers 113 G2
Stoke Rochford 175 E5
Stoke Row 134 B4
Stoke St. Gregory 116 A5
Stoke St. Mary 115 F5
Stoke St. Michael 117 D3
Stoke St. Milborough 157 E4
Stoke sub Hamdon 104 A1
Stoke Talmage 134 B3
Stoke Trister 117 E5
Stoke Villice 116 C1
Stoke Wake 105 D2
Stokeford 105 E4
Stokeham 187 E5
Stokeinteignhead 102 C5
Stokenham 101 E3
Stoke-on-Trent 171 F3
Stokesay 156 D4
Stokesley 203 E2
Stolford 117 F3
Ston Easton 116 D2
Stonar Cut 125 F2
Stondon Massey 137 E2
Stone *Bucks* 134 C1
Stone *Glos* 131 F3
Stone *Kent* 137 E5
Stone *Kent* 111 E1
Stone *Som* 116 C4
Stone *Staffs* 171 G4
Stone *SYorks* 186 C4
Stone *Worcs* 158 A5
Stone Allerton 116 B2
Stone Cross *Dur* 201 F1
Stone Cross *ESuss* 110 A1
Stone Cross *ESuss* 110 B3
Stone Cross *Kent* 124 C5
Stone Cross *Kent* 125 E5
Stone House 200 C4
Stone Street *Kent* 123 E3
Stone Street *Suff* 165 E3
Stone Street *Suff* 152 A4
Stonea 162 C3
Stonebridge *ESuss* 110 A1
Stonebridge *NSom* 116 A2
Stonebridge *Warks* 159 E4
Stonebroom 173 F2
Stonecross Green 151 G2
Stonefield *A&B* 231 G2
Stonefield *Staffs* 171 G4
Stonegate *ESuss* 110 B1
Stonegate *NYorks* 203 G2
Stonegrave 203 F5
Stonehaugh 219 F4
Stonehaven 253 G1
Stonehenge *Wilts*
SP4 7DE 118 C3
Stonehill 121 E1
Stonehouse
ChesW&C 183 G5
Stonehouse *D&G* 216 C4
Stonehouse *Glos* 132 A2
Stonehouse *N'umb* 210 C2
Stonehouse *Plym* 100 A2
Stoneleigh *Surr* 122 B2
Stoneleigh *Warks* 159 F5
Stonely 149 G1
Stoner Hill 120 C5
Stones 193 F3
Stones Green 152 C5
Stonesby 174 D5
Stonesfield 133 F1
Stonestreet Green 124 C5
Stonethwaite 209 F5
Stoney Cross 106 B1
Stoney Middleton 185 G5
Stoney Stanton 159 G3
Stoney Stoke 117 E4
Stoney Stratton 117 D4
Stoney Stretton 156 C2
Stoneyburn 235 D3
Stoneyford 103 D4
Stoneygate 160 B2
Stoneyhills 138 C3
Stoneykirk 214 B5
Stoneywood 261 G3
Stonganess 278 E2
Stonham Aspal 152 C2
Stonham Barns *Suff*
IP14 6AT 152 C2
Stonnall 158 C2
Stonor 134 C4
Stonton Wyville 160 C3
Stony Houghton 173 F1
Stony Stratford 148 C3
Stonybreck 278 A1
Stoodleigh *Devon* 102 B1
Stoodleigh *Devon* 113 G2
Stopham 108 C2
Stopsley 149 G5
Stoptide 96 D2
Storeton 183 E4
Stormontfield 243 G2
Stornoway
(Steornabhagh) 271 G4
Stornoway Airport 271 G4
Storridge 145 G3
Storrington 108 C2
Storrs 185 G4
Storth 199 F4
Storwood 195 G3
Storybook Glen *Aber*
AB12 5FT 261 G5

Stotfield 267 K4
Stotfold 150 A4
Stottesdon 157 F4
Stoughton *Leics* 160 B2
Stoughton *Surr* 121 E2
Stoughton *WSuss* 107 G1
Stoughton Cross 116 B3
Stoul 256 D5
Stoulton 146 B3
Stour Provost 117 E5
Stour Row 117 F5
Stourbridge 158 A4
Stourhead *Wilts*
BA12 6QD 117 E4
Stourpaine 105 E2
Stourport-on-Severn 158 A5
Stourton *Staffs* 158 A4
Stourton *Warks* 147 E4
Stourton *Wilts* 117 E4
Stourton Caundle 104 D1
Stove 276 F4
Stoven 165 F3
Stow *Lincs* 187 F4
Stow *ScBord* 236 B5
Stow Bardolph 163 E2
Stow Bedon 164 A2
Stow cum Quy 150 D1
Stow Longa 161 G4
Stow Maries 138 B3
Stow Pasture 187 F4
Stowbridge 163 E2
Stowe *Glos* 131 E2
Stowe *Shrop* 156 C5
Stowe *Staffs* 158 D1
Stowe Landscape Gardens
Bucks
MK18 5DQ 148 B4
Stowe-by-Chartley 172 B5
Stowehill 148 B2
Stowell *Glos* 132 C1
Stowell *Som* 117 D5
Stowey 116 C2
Stowford *Devon* 99 E2
Stowford *Devon* 113 G2
Stowford *Devon* 103 E4
Stowlangtoft 152 A1
Stowmarket 152 B2
Stow-on-the-Wold 147 D5
Stowting 124 D4
Stowupland 152 B2
Straad 232 B3
Strachan 260 E5
Strachur (Clachan
Strachur) 240 C4
Stradbroke 164 D4
Stradishall 151 F2
Stradsett 163 E2
Stragglethorpe 175 E2
Straight Soley 133 F5
Straiton *Edin* 235 G3
Straiton *SAyr* 224 B5
Straloch *Aber* 261 G2
Straloch *P&K* 251 F3
Stramshall 172 B4
Strands 198 C4
Strang 190 B4
Strangford 145 E5
Stranna 263 F3
Stranraer 214 B4
Strata Florida 142 D1
Stratfield Mortimer 120 B1
Stratfield Saye 120 B1
Stratfield Turgis 120 B2
Stratford *CenBeds* 149 G3
Stratford *Glos* 146 A4
Stratford *GtLon* 136 C4
Stratford St. Andrew 153 E2
Stratford St. Mary 152 B4
Stratford sub Castle 118 C4
Stratford Tony 118 B5
Stratford-upon-Avon 147 E2
Stratford-upon-Avon Butterfly
Farm *Warks* CV37 7LS
85 Stratford-upon-Avon
Strath 275 H3
Strathan *High* 272 C6
Strathan *High* 257 F5
Strathaven 234 B5
Strathblane 233 G2
Strathcanaird 265 H1
Strathcarron 265 F7
Strathclyde Country Park
NLan ML1 3ED 31 G5
Strathdon 260 B3
Strathgirnock 260 B5
Strathkinness 244 C3
Strathmiglo 244 A3
Strathpeffer (Strath
Pheofhair) 266 B6
Strathrannoch 265 K4
Strathtay 251 E4
Strathwhillan 223 F2
Strathy 274 D2
Strathyre 242 A3
Stratton *Corn* 112 C5
Stratton *Dorset* 104 C3
Stratton *Glos* 132 C2
Stratton Audley 148 B5
Stratton Hall 152 D4
Stratton St. Margaret 133 D4
Stratton St. Michael 164 D2
Stratton Strawless 178 D3
Stratton-on-the-Fosse 117 D2
Stravanan 232 B4
Stravithie 244 D3
Strawberry Hill 136 A5
Stream 115 D4
Streat 109 F2
Streatham 136 B5
Streatham Vale 136 B5
Streatley *CenBeds* 149 F5
Streatley *WBerks* 134 A4
Street *Devon* 103 E4
Street *Lancs* 192 B2
Street *NYorks* 203 G2
Street *Som* 116 B4
Street *Som* 103 G2
Street Ashton 159 G4
Street Dinas 170 A4
Street End 108 A4
Street Gate 212 B2

Street Houses 195 E3
Street Lane 173 E3
Street on the Fosse 116 D4
Streethay 158 D2
Streethouse 194 C5
Streetlam 202 C3
Streetly 158 C3
Streetly End 151 E3
Strefford 156 D4
Strelley 173 G3
Strensall 195 F1
Strensham 146 B3
Stretcholt 115 F3
Strete 101 E3
Stretford *GtMan* 184 B3
Stretford *Here* 144 D2
Stretford *Here* 145 E2
Strethall 150 C4
Stretham 162 D5
Strettington 108 A3
Stretton *ChesW&C* 170 B2
Stretton *Derbys* 173 E1
Stretton *Rut* 161 E1
Stretton *Staffs* 158 A1
Stretton *Staffs* 173 D5
Stretton *Warr* 184 A4
Stretton en le Field 159 F1
Stretton Grandison 145 F3
Stretton Heath 156 C1
Stretton Sugwas 145 D3
Stretton under Fosse 159 G4
Stretton Westwood 157 E3
Stretton-on-
Dunsmore 159 G5
Stretton-on-Fosse 147 E4
Stribers 199 E4
Strichen 269 H5
Strines 185 D4
Strinesdale Countryside
Area *GtMan*
OL4 2JJ 25 H1
Stringston 115 E3
Strixton 149 E1
Stroat 131 E3
Stromeferry 256 E7
Stromemore 256 E7
Stromness 277 B7
Stronaba 249 E1
Stronachlachar 241 G3
Stronchrubie 272 E7
Stronlonag 232 C1
Stronmilchan (Sròn nam
Mialchon) 241 D2
Stronsay 276 F4
Stronsay Airfield 276 F5
Strontian (Sròn an
t-Sithein) 248 A3
Strontoiller 240 B2
Stronvar 242 A2
Strood 123 G2
Strood Green *Surr* 122 B4
Strood Green *WSuss* 121 F5
Strood Green *WSuss* 121 G5
Stroquhan 216 C2
Stroud *Glos* 132 A2
Stroud *Hants* 120 C5
Stroud Common 121 F3
Stroud Green *Essex* 138 B3
Stroud Green *Glos* 132 A2
Stroude 121 F1
Stroul 232 D1
Stroxton 175 E4
Struan *High* 255 J1
Struan *P&K* 250 C3
Strubby *Lincs* 189 E4
Strubby *Lincs* 188 B5
Strumpshaw 179 E5
Struthers 244 B4
Struy 258 B2
Stryd y Facsen 180 B4
Stryt-issa 169 F1
Stuart & Waterford Crystal
Factory Shop, Crieff *P&K*
PH7 4HQ 243 D2
Stuart Line Cruises, Exmouth
Devon EX8 1EJ 102 C4
Stuartfield 269 H6
Stub Place 198 B3
Stubber's Green 158 C2
Stubbington 107 E2
Stubbins 184 B1
Stubbs Green 165 E2
Stubhampton 105 F1
Stubley 186 A5
Stubshaw Cross 183 G2
Stubton 175 D2
Stuck *A&B* 232 A1
Stuck *A&B* 240 D5
Stuckbeg 241 E5
Stuckgowan 241 F4
Stuckindroin 241 F3
Stuckreoch 240 D5
Stuckton 106 A1
Stud Green 135 D5
Studdon 211 E2
Studfold 200 D5
Studham 135 F1
Studholme 209 F1
Studland *Dorset*
BH19 3AX 105 G4
Studland & Godlingston Heath
NNR *Dorset*
BH19 3AX 105 G4
Studley *Warks* 146 C1
Studley *Wilts* 132 B5
Studley Common 146 C1
Studley Green 134 C3
Studley Roger 202 B5
Studley Royal Park & ruins of
Fountains Abbey *NYorks*
HG4 3DY 194 B1
Stuggadhoo 190 B4
Stump Cross *Essex* 150 D3
Stump Cross *Lancs* 192 B4
Stuntney 163 D5
Stunts Green 110 B2
Sturbridge 171 F4
Sturgate 187 F4

Sturmer 151 E3
Sturminster Common 105 D1
Sturminster Marshall 105 F2
Sturminster Newton 105 D1
Sturry 125 D2
Sturton by Stow 187 F4
Sturton le Steeple 187 E4
Stuston 164 C3
Stutton *NYorks* 195 D3
Stutton *Suff* 152 C4
Styal 184 C4
Styrrup 186 D3
Suardail 271 G4
Succoth *A&B* 241 E4
Succoth *Aber* 260 C1
Succothmore 240 D4
Suckley 145 G2
Suckley Green 145 G2
Suckley Knowl 145 G2
Sudborough 161 E4
Sudbourne 153 F2
Sudbrook *Lincs* 175 E3
Sudbrook *Mon* 131 E4
Sudbrooke 188 A5
Sudbury *Derbys* 172 C4
Sudbury *GtLon* 136 A4
Sudbury *Suff* 151 G3
Sudbury Hall *Derbys*
DE6 5HT 172 C4
Sudden 184 C1
Sudgrove 132 B2
Suffield *Norf* 178 D2
Suffield *NYorks* 204 C3
Sugarloaf 124 B5
Sugnall 171 E4
Sugwas Pool 145 D3
Suie Lodge Hotel 241 G2
Suisnish 256 B3
Sulby *IoM* 190 B2
Sulby *IoM* 190 B4
Sulgrave 148 A3
Sulham 134 A5
Sulhamstead 120 B1
Sullington 108 C2
Sullom 278 C5
Sullom Voe Oil
Terminal 278 C5
Sully 115 E1
Sumburgh 279 F10
Sumburgh Airport 279 F9
Summer Bridge 194 B1
Summer Isles 265 F1
Summer Lodge 201 E3
Summercourt 96 C4
Summerfield *Norf* 177 F3
Summerfield *Worcs* 158 A5
Summerhill 170 A2
Summerhouse 202 B1
Summerlands 199 G4
Summerleaze 130 D4
Summit 184 D1
Sun Green 185 D3
Sunadale 231 G5
Sunbiggin 200 B1
Sunbury 121 G1
Sundaywell 216 C2
Sunderland *Cumb* 209 E3
Sunderland *Lancs* 192 A2
Sunderland *T&W* 212 C2
Sunderland Bridge 212 B4
Sunderland Museum & Winter
Gardens *T&W* SR1 1PP
86 Sunderland
Sundhope 227 E3
Sundon Park 149 F5
Sundown Adventure Land
Notts DN22 0HX 187 E5
Sundridge 123 D3
Sundrum Mains 224 C3
Sunhill 132 D2
Sunipol 246 C4
Sunk Island 188 C1
Sunningdale 121 E1
Sunninghill 121 E1
Sunningwell 133 G2
Sunniside *Dur* 212 A4
Sunniside *T&W* 212 B2
Sunny Bank 199 D3
Sunny Brow 212 A4
Sunnylaw 242 C5
Sunnyside *Aber* 261 G5
Sunnyside *N'umb* 211 F1
Sunnyside *SYorks* 186 B3
Sunnyside *WSuss* 122 C5
Sunton 118 D2
Surbiton 121 G1
Surfleet 176 A5
Surfleet Seas End 176 A5
Surlingham 179 E5
Sustead 178 C2
Susworth 187 F2
Sutcombe 112 D4
Sutcombemill 112 D4
Suton 164 B2
Sutors of Cromarty 267 F5
Sutterby 189 D5
Sutterton 176 A4
Sutton *Cambs* 162 C5
Sutton *CenBeds* 150 A3
Sutton *Devon* 102 A2
Sutton *Devon* 100 D3
Sutton *GtLon* 122 B2
Sutton *Kent* 125 F4
Sutton *Lincs* 175 D2
Sutton *Norf* 179 E3
Sutton *Notts* 174 C5
Sutton *Notts* 187 D4
Sutton *Oxon* 133 G2
Sutton *Pembs* 126 C1
Sutton *Peter* 161 F3
Sutton *Shrop* 157 G4
Sutton *Shrop* 171 D4
Sutton *Shrop* 157 E1
Sutton *Shrop* 170 A5
Sutton *Staffs* 171 E5
Sutton *Suff* 153 E3
Sutton *SYorks* 186 C1
Sutton *WSuss* 108 B2
Sutton Abinger 121 G3
Sutton at Hone 137 E5

Sutton Bank National Park
Centre *NYorks*
YO7 2EH 203 E4
Sutton Bassett 160 C4
Sutton Benger 132 B5
Sutton Bingham 104 B2
Sutton Bonington 173 G5
Sutton Bridge 176 C5
Sutton Cheney 159 G2
Sutton Coldfield 158 D3
Sutton Courtenay 134 A3
Sutton Crosses 176 C5
Sutton Grange 202 B5
Sutton Green *Oxon* 133 G2
Sutton Green *Surr* 121 F2
Sutton Green *Wrex* 170 B3
Sutton Holms 105 G2
Sutton Howgrave 202 C5
Sutton in Ashfield 173 F2
Sutton in the Elms 160 A3
Sutton Ings 196 D4
Sutton Lane Ends 184 D5
Sutton le Marsh 189 F4
Sutton Leach 183 G3
Sutton Maddock 157 G2
Sutton Mallet 116 A4
Sutton Mandeville 118 A5
Sutton Montis 116 D5
Sutton on Sea 189 F4
Sutton on the Hill 172 D4
Sutton on Trent 174 C1
Sutton Poyntz 104 D4
Sutton St. Edmund 162 B1
Sutton St. James 162 C1
Sutton St. Nicholas 145 E3
Sutton Scarsdale 173 F1
Sutton Scotney 119 F4
Sutton upon Derwent 195 G3
Sutton Valence 124 A4
Sutton Veny 117 F3
Sutton Waldron 105 E1
Sutton Weaver 183 G5
Sutton Wick
B&NESom 116 C2
Sutton Wick *Oxon* 133 G3
Sutton-in-Craven 193 G3
Sutton-on-Hull 196 D4
Sutton-on-the-Forest 195 E1
Sutton-under-Brailes 147 F4
Sutton-under-
Whitestonecliffe 203 D4
Swaby 189 D5
Swadlincote 159 F1
Swaffham 163 G2
Swaffham Bulbeck 151 D1
Swaffham Prior 151 D1
Swafield 179 D2
Swainbost
(Suaineabost) 271 H1
Swainby 203 D2
Swainshill 145 D3
Swainsthorpe 178 D5
Swainswick 117 E1
Swalcliffe 147 F4
Swalecliffe 124 D2
Swallow 188 B2
Swallow Beck 175 E1
Swallow Falls *Conwy*
LL24 0DW 168 A2
Swallowcliffe 118 A5
Swallowfield 120 C1
Swallows Cross 137 F3
Swampton 119 F2
Swan Green
ChesW&C 184 B5
Swan Green *Suff* 165 D4
Swan Street 151 G5
Swanage 105 G5
Swanage Railway *Dorset*
BH19 1HB 105 G4
Swanbach 171 D3
Swanbourne 148 D5
Swanbridge 115 E1
Swancote 157 G3
Swanland 196 B5
Swanlaws 228 B5
Swanley 123 E2
Swanley Village 123 E2
Swanmore *Hants* 107 E1
Swanmore *IoW* 107 E3
Swannington *Leics* 159 G1
Swannington *Norf* 178 C4
Swanscombe 137 F5
Swansea (Abertawe) 128 C3
Swansea Museum SA1 1SN
86 Swansea
Swanston 235 G3
Swanton Abbot 179 D3
Swanton Morley 178 B4
Swanton Novers 178 B2
Swanton Street 124 A3
Swanwick *Derbys* 173 F2
Swanwick *Hants* 107 E2
Swanwick Green 170 C3
Swarby 175 F3
Swardeston 178 D5
Swarkestone 173 E5
Swarland 221 D1
Swarraton 119 G4
Swarthmoor 199 D5
Swaton 175 G4
Swavesey 150 B1
Sway 106 B3
Swayfield 175 E5
Swaythorpe 196 C1
Sweetham 102 B3
Sweethay 115 F5
Sweetshouse 97 E3
Sweffling 153 E1
Swell 116 A5
Swepstone 159 F1
Swerford 147 F4
Swettenham 171 F1
Swffryd 130 B3
Swift's Green 124 A4
Swiftsden 110 C1
Swilland 152 C2
Swillington 194 C4
Swimbridge 113 G3
Swimbridge Newland 113 F2
Swinbrook 133 E1

Swincliffe 194 B2
Swincombe 113 G1
Swinden 193 E2
Swinderby 175 D1
Swindon *Staffs* 158 A3
Swindon *Swin* 133 D4
Swindon Village 146 B5
Swine 196 D4
Swinefleet 195 G5
Swineford 117 D1
Swineshead *Bed* 149 F1
Swineshead *Lincs* 176 A3
Swineshead Bridge 176 A3
Swineside 201 F4
Swiney 275 H5
Swinford *Leics* 160 A5
Swinford *Oxon* 133 G2
Swingate 173 G3
Swingfield Minnis 125 E4
Swingleton Green 152 A3
Swinhoe 229 G4
Swinhope 188 C3
Swining 279 D6
Swinithwaite 201 F4
Swinscoe 172 C3
Swinside Hall 228 B5
Swinstead 175 F5
Swinton *GtMan* 184 B2
Swinton *Lincs* 203 G5
Swinton *NYorks* 202 B5
Swinton *NYorks* 203 F5
Swinton *ScBord* 237 F5
Swinton *SYorks* 186 B3
Swinton Quarter 237 F5
Swintonmill 237 F5
Swithland 160 A1
Swordale 266 C5
Swordland 256 D5
Swordle 247 E2
Swordly 274 C2
Sworton Heath 184 A4
Swyddffynnon 142 C1
Swyncombe 134 B3
Swynnerton 171 F4
Swyre 104 B4
Sychnant 155 F5
Syde 132 B1
Sydenham *GtLon* 136 C5
Sydenham *Oxon* 134 C2
Sydenham Damerel 99 E3
Syderstone 177 F3
Sydling St. Nicholas 104 C3
Sydmonton 119 F2
Sydney 171 E2
Syerston 174 C3
Sykehouse 186 D1
Sykes 192 C3
Sylen 128 B2
Symbister 279 E6
Symington *SAyr* 224 B2
Symington *SLan* 226 A2
Symonds Yat 131 E1
Symondsbury 104 A3
Synod Inn
(Post-mawr) 142 A2
Syre 273 J4
Syreford 146 C5
Syresham 148 B3
Syston *Leics* 160 B1
Syston *Lincs* 175 E3
Sytchampton 146 A1
Sywell 148 D1
Sywell Country Park *N'hants*
NN6 0QX 148 D1

T

Taagan 265 G5
Tableyhill 184 B5
Tabost 271 F6
Tachbrook Mallory 147 F1
Tacher 275 G4
Tackley 147 G5
Tacolneston 164 C2
Tadcaster 195 D3
Tadden 105 F2
Taddington *Derbys* 185 F5
Taddington *Glos* 146 C4
Taddiport 113 E4
Tadley 120 B1
Tadlow 150 A3
Tadmarton 147 F4
Tadpole Bridge 133 G2
Tadworth 122 B3
Tafarnaubach 130 A1
Tafarn-y-bwlch 141 D5
Tafarn-y-Gelyn 169 E1
Taff Merthyr Garden
Village 130 A3
Taff's Well
(Ffynnon Taf) 130 A4
Tafolwern 155 E2
Taibach *NPT* 129 D4
Tai-bach *Powys* 169 E5
Taicynhaeaf 154 C1
Tain *High* 275 H2
Tain *High* 266 E3
Tai'n Lôn 166 D3
Tai'r Bull 143 F5
Tairgwaith 128 C3
Tai'r-heol 130 A3
Tairlaw 224 C5
Tai'r-ysgol 128 C3
Takeley 151 D5
Takeley Street 150 D5
Talachddu 143 G4
Talacre 182 C4
Talardd 168 B5
Talaton 103 D3
Talbenny 126 B1
Talbot Green 129 G4
Talbot Village 105 G3
Talerddig 155 F2
Talgarreg 142 A2
Talgarth 144 A4
Taliesin 154 C3
Talisker 255 J1
Talke 171 F2
Talke Pits 171 F2
Talkin 210 B2
Talla Linnfoots 226 C4
Talladale 265 F4
Talladh-a-Bheithe 250 A4

Talland 97 G4
Tallarn Green 170 B3
Tallentire 209 E3
Talley (Talyllychau) 142 C4
Tallington 161 F2
Talog 141 G5
Tal-sarn 142 B2
Talsarnau 167 F4
Talskiddy 96 D3
Talwrn IoA 180 C5
Talwrn Wrex 169 F3
Talwrn Wrex 170 A3
Talybont Cere 154 C4
Tal-y-bont Conwy 168 A1
Tal-y-bont Gwyn 167 G3
Tal-y-bont Gwyn 181 E5
Talybont-on-Usk 144 A5
Tal-y-Cae 167 F1
Tal-y-cafn 181 F5
Tal-y-coed 130 D1
Talygarn 129 G4
Tal-y-llyn Gwyn 154 D2
Talyllyn Powys 144 A5
Talysarn 167 D2
Tal-y-wern 155 E2
Tamavoid 242 A5
Tamerton Foliot 100 A1
Tamworth 159 E2
Tamworth Green 176 B3
Tan Office Green 151 F2
Tandem 185 F1
Tandridge 122 C3
Tanerdy 142 A5
Tanfield 212 A2
Tanfield Lea 212 A2
Tang 194 B2
Tang Hall 195 F2
Tangiers 126 C1
Tanglandford 261 G1
Tangley 119 E2
Tangmere 108 B3
Tangwick 278 B5
Tangy 222 B3
Tank Museum, Bovington Dorset BH20 6JG 105 E4
Tankerness 277 E7
Tankersley 186 A4
Tankerton 124 D2
Tan-lan 167 F3
Tannach 275 J4
Tannachie 253 F1
Tannachy 266 E1
Tannadice 252 C4
Tannington 152 D1
Tannochside 234 A3
Tansley 173 E2
Tansley Knoll 173 E2
Tansor 161 F3
Tantobie 212 A2
Tanton 203 E1
Tanworth in Arden 158 D5
Tan-y-fron 168 C1
Tan-y-graig 166 C4
Tanygrisiau 167 F3
Tan-y-groes 141 F3
Tan-y-pistyll 169 D5
Tan-yr-allt 182 B4
Taobh a' Deas Loch Baghasdail 254 C3
Taobh Siar 270 D7
Tapeley 113 E3
Taplow 135 E4
Tapton Grove 186 B5
Taransay (Tarasaigh) 270 C7
Taraphocain 248 C5
Tarbat House 266 E4
Tarbert A&B 231 G3
Tarbert A&B 231 E4
Tarbert A&B 231 F3
Tarbert High 247 F3
Tarbert (Tairbeart) WIsles 270 D7
Tarbet (An Tairbeart) A&B 241 F4
Tarbet High 256 D5
Tarbet High 272 D4
Tarbock Green 183 F4
Tarbolton 224 C3
Tarbrax 235 E4
Tardebigge 146 B1
Tardy Gate 192 B5
Tarfside 252 C2
Tarland 260 C4
Tarleton 192 A5
Tarlscough 183 F1
Tarlton 132 B3
Tarnbrook 192 B2
Tarnock 116 A2
Tarporley 170 C1
Tarr 115 E4
Tarrant Crawford 105 F2
Tarrant Gunville 105 F1
Tarrant Hinton 105 F1
Tarrant Keyneston 105 F2
Tarrant Launceston 105 F2
Tarrant Monkton 105 F2
Tarrant Rawston 105 F2
Tarrant Rushton 105 F2
Tarrel 267 F3
Tarring Neville 109 G3
Tarrington 145 F3
Tarrnacraig 223 E2
Tarsappie 243 G2
Tarskavaig 256 B4
Tarves 261 G1
Tarvie (Tairbhidh) High 266 B6
Tarvie P&K 251 F3
Tarvin 170 B1
Tarvin Sands 170 B1
Tasburgh 164 D2
Tasley 157 F3
Taston 147 F5
Tate Britain GtLon SW1P 4RG 13 B5
Tate Liverpool Mersey L3 4BB 42 B5

Tate St. Ives Corn TR26 1TG 94 C2
Tatenhill 172 D5
Tathall End 148 D3
Tatham 192 C1
Tathwell 188 D4
Tatsfield 122 D3
Tattenhall 170 B2
Tattenhoe 148 D4
Tatterford 177 G5
Tattersett 177 G4
Tattershall 176 A2
Tattershall Bridge 175 G2
Tattershall Thorpe 176 A2
Tattingstone 152 C4
Tatton Park ChesE WA16 6QN 184 B4
Tatworth 103 G2
Tauchers 268 B5
Taunton 115 F5
Tavelty 261 F3
Taverham 178 C4
Tavernspite 127 E1
Tavistock 99 E3
Taw Bridge 113 G5
Taw Green 99 G1
Tawstock 113 F3
Taxal 185 E5
Tayburn 233 G5
Taychreggan 240 C2
Tayinloan 231 E5
Taylors Cross 112 C4
Taynafead 240 C3
Taynish 231 F1
Taynton Glos 145 G5
Taynton Oxon 133 E1
Taynuilt (Taigh an Uillt) 240 C1
Tayock 253 E4
Tayovullin 230 A2
Tayport 244 C2
Tayvallich 231 F1
Tea Green 149 G5
Tealby 188 B3
Tealing 244 C1
Team Valley 212 B1
Teanamachar 262 C5
Teangue 256 C4
Teasses 244 C4
Tebay 200 B2
Tebworth 149 E5
Techniquest, Cardiff Cardiff CF10 5BW 7 B4
Tedburn St. Mary 102 B3
Teddington Glos 146 B4
Teddington GtLon 136 A5
Tedstone Delamere 145 F2
Tedstone Wafre 145 F2
Teeton 160 B5
Teffont Evias 118 A4
Teffont Magna 118 A4
Tegryn 141 F4
Tehidy Country Park Corn TR14 0HA 96 A5
Teigh 161 D1
Teign Village 102 B4
Teigngrace 102 B5
Teignmouth 102 C5
Telford 157 F2
Telham 110 C2
Tellisford 117 F2
Telscombe 109 G3
Telscombe Cliffs 109 G3
Tempar 250 B4
Templand 217 E2
Temple Corn 97 F2
Temple Midlo 236 A4
Temple Balsall 159 E5
Temple Bar 142 B2
Temple Cloud 116 D2
Temple End 151 E2
Temple Ewell 125 E4
Temple Grafton 146 C2
Temple Guiting 146 C5
Temple Herdewyke 147 F2
Temple Hirst 195 F5
Temple Newsam WYorks LS15 0AE 27 H2
Temple Normanton 173 F2
Temple Sowerby 210 C5
Templecombe 117 E5
Templeton Devon 102 B1
Templeton Pembs 127 E1
Templeton Bridge 102 B1
Templewood 253 E3
Tempsford 149 G2
Ten Mile Bank 163 E3
Tenbury Wells 145 E1
Tenby (Dinbych-y-pysgod) 127 E2
Tendring 152 C5
Tendring Green 152 C5
Tenga 247 E5
Tenterden 124 A5
Terally 206 B2
Terling 137 G1
Tern 157 E2
Ternhill 170 D4
Terregles 216 D3
Terriers 135 D3
Terrington 203 F5
Terrington St. Clement 177 D5
Terrington St. John 162 D1
Terry's Green 158 D5
Tervieside 259 K1
Teston 123 G3
Testwood 106 C1
Tetbury 132 A3
Tetbury Upton 132 A3
Tetchill 170 A4
Tetcott 99 D1
Tetford 188 D5
Tetney 188 D2
Tetney Lock 188 D2
Tetsworth 134 B2
Tettenhall 158 A3
Tettenhall Wood 158 A3
Tetworth 150 A2

Teuchan 261 J1
Teversal 173 F1
Teversham 150 C2
Teviot Water Gardens ScBord TD5 8LE 227 F5
Teviothead 227 F5
Tewel 253 G1
Tewin 136 B1
Tewkesbury 146 A4
Tewkesbury Abbey Glos GL20 5RZ 146 A4
Teynham 124 B2
Thackley 194 A4
Thainston 253 E2
Thainstone 261 F3
Thakeham 108 D2
Thame 134 C2
Thames Ditton 121 G1
Thames Haven 137 G4
Thamesmead 137 D4
Thanington 124 D2
Thankerton 226 A2
Tharston 164 C2
Thatcham 119 G1
Thatto Heath 183 G3
Thaxted 151 E4
The Apes Hall 163 D3
The Bage 144 B3
The Balloch 242 D3
The Banking 261 F1
The Bar 121 G5
The Birks 261 F4
The Bog 156 C3
The Bourne 120 D3
The Bratch 158 A3
The Broad 145 D1
The Bryn 130 C2
The Burf 146 A1
The Burn 253 D2
The Butts 117 E3
The Camp 132 B2
The Chequer 170 B3
The City Bucks 134 C3
The City Suff 165 E3
The Common Wilts 118 D4
The Common Wilts 132 C4
The Craigs 266 B2
The Cronk 190 B2
The Delves 158 C3
The Den 233 E4
The Dicker 110 A3
The Down 157 F3
The Drums 252 B3
The Eaves 131 F2
The Flatt 219 D4
The Folly 136 A1
The Forge 144 C2
The Forstal ESuss 123 E5
The Forstal Kent 124 C5
The Grange Lincs 189 F5
The Grange Shrop 170 A4
The Grange Surr 122 C4
The Green A&B 246 A2
The Green Cumb 198 C4
The Green Essex 137 G3
The Green Flints 169 F5
The Green Wilts 117 F4
The Grove 146 A3
The Haven 121 F4
The Headland 213 E4
The Heath 172 B4
The Herberts 129 F5
The Hill 146 A4
The Hermitage 122 B3
The Holme 194 B2
The Howe 190 A5
The Isle 157 D1
The Laurels 165 E2
The Leacon 124 B5
The Lee 135 E2
The Leigh 146 A5
The Lhen 190 B1
The Lodge 241 D5
The Marsh 156 C3
The Moor ESuss 110 D2
The Moor Kent 110 C1
The Mumbles 128 C4
The Murray 234 A4
The Mythe 146 A4
The Narth 131 E2
The Neuk 261 F5
The Node 136 B1
The Oval 117 E1
The Polchar 259 G4
The Quarter 124 A4
The Reddings 146 B5
The Rhos 126 C5
The Rookery 171 F2
The Rowe 171 F4
The Sale 159 D1
The Sands 223 D1
The Shoe 132 A5
The Slade 134 A4
The Smithies 157 F3
The Stocks 111 E1
The Swillett 135 F3
The Thrift 150 B4
The Vauld 145 E3
The Wern 169 F2
The Wyke 157 G2
Theakston 202 C4
Thealby 187 F1
Theale Som 116 B4
Theale WBerks 134 B5
Thearne 196 C4
Theberton 153 F1
Thedden Grange 120 B4
Theddingworth 160 B4
Theddlethorpe All Saints 189 E4
Theddlethorpe St. Helen 189 E4
Thelbridge Barton 102 A1
Thelbridge Cross 102 A1
Thelnetham 164 B4
Thelveton 164 C3
Thelwall 184 A4
Themelthorpe 178 B3
Thenford 148 A3
Therfield 150 B4
Thermae Bath Spa B&NESom BA1 1SJ 63 Bath

Thetford Lincs 161 G1
Thetford Norf 163 G4
Thetford Forest Park Norf IP27 0TJ 163 G4
Thethwaite 209 G2
Theydon Bois 136 D3
Theydon Garnon 137 D2
Theydon Mount 137 D3
Thickwood 132 A5
Thimbleby Lincs 176 A1
Thimbleby NYorks 202 D3
Thingley 137 E5
Thirkleby 203 D5
Thirlby 203 D4
Thirlestane 236 C5
Thirn 202 B4
Thirsk 202 D4
Thirston New Houses 221 D2
Thirtleby 197 D4
Thistleton Lancs 192 A4
Thistleton Rut 161 E1
Thistley Green 163 E5
Thixendale 196 A1
Thockrington 220 B4
Tholomas Drove 162 B2
Tholthorpe 195 D1
Thomas Chapel 127 E2
Thomas Close 210 A3
Thomastown 260 D1
Thompson 164 A2
Thomshill 267 K6
Thong 137 F5
Thongsbridge 185 F2
Thoralby 201 F4
Thoresby 186 C5
Thoresthorpe 189 E5
Thoresway 188 B3
Thorganby Lincs 188 C3
Thorganby NYorks 195 F3
Thorgill 203 G3
Thorington 165 F4
Thorington Street 152 B4
Thorley 137 D1
Thorley Houses 150 C5
Thorley Street Herts 137 D1
Thorley Street IoW 106 C4
Thormanby 203 D5
Thornaby-on-Tees 203 D1
Thornage 178 B2
Thornborough Bucks 148 C4
Thornborough NYorks 202 B5
Thornbury Devon 113 D5
Thornbury Here 145 F2
Thornbury SGlos 131 F3
Thornbury WYorks 194 A4
Thornby 160 B5
Thorncliff 172 B1
Thorncliffe 172 B2
Thorncombe 103 G2
Thorncombe Street 121 F3
Thorncote Green 149 G3
Thorncross 106 D4
Thorndon 152 C1
Thorndon Country Park Essex CM13 3RZ 137 F3
Thorndon Cross 99 F1
Thorne 187 D1
Thorne St. Margaret 115 D5
Thorner 194 C3
Thorney Bucks 135 F5
Thorney Notts 187 F5
Thorney Peter 162 A2
Thorney Som 116 B5
Thorney Close 212 C2
Thorney Hill 106 B3
Thornfalcon 115 F5
Thornford 104 C1
Thorngrafton 211 D1
Thorngrove 116 A4
Thorngumbald 197 E5
Thornham 177 F3
Thornham Magna 164 C4
Thornham Parva 164 C4
Thornhaugh 161 F2
Thornhill Cardiff 130 A4
Thornhill Cumb 198 B2
Thornhill D&G 216 C1
Thornhill Derbys 185 F4
Thornhill Soton 107 D1
Thornhill Stir 242 B4
Thornhill WYorks 185 G1
Thornhill Lees 185 G1
Thornholme 196 D1
Thornicombe 105 E2
Thornley Dur 212 C4
Thornley Dur 212 A4
Thornley Gate 211 E2
Thornliebank 233 G4
Thornroan 261 G1
Thorns 151 F2
Thorns Green 184 B4
Thornsett 185 E4
Thornton Angus 252 B5
Thornton Bucks 148 C4
Thornton ERid 195 G3
Thornton Fife 244 A5
Thornton Lancs 191 G3
Thornton Leics 159 G2
Thornton Lincs 176 A1
Thornton Mersey 183 E2
Thornton Middl 203 D1
Thornton N'umb 237 G5
Thornton Pembs 126 C2
Thornton WYorks 194 A4
Thornton Bridge 202 D5
Thornton Curtis 188 A1
Thornton Heath 122 C2
Thornton Hough 183 E4
Thornton in Lonsdale 200 B5
Thornton le Moor 188 A3
Thornton le-Moor 202 C3
Thornton Park 237 G5
Thornton Rust 201 E4
Thornton Steward 202 A4
Thornton Watlass 202 B4
Thorntonhall 233 G4
Thornton-in-Craven 193 F3
Thornton-le-Beans 202 D3

Thornton-le-Clay 195 F1
Thornton-le-Dale 204 B4
Thornton-le-Moor 202 C4
Thornton-le-Moors 183 F5
Thornton-le-Street 202 D4
Thornwood 137 D2
Thornydykes 236 D5
Thornyhill 253 D2
Thornylee 257 F2
Thoroton 174 D3
Thorp Arch 194 D3
Thorpe Derbys 172 C2
Thorpe ERid 196 B3
Thorpe Lincs 189 E4
Thorpe Norf 165 F2
Thorpe Notts 174 C2
Thorpe NYorks 193 G1
Thorpe Surr 121 F1
Thorpe Abbotts 164 C3
Thorpe Acre 173 G5
Thorpe Arnold 174 C5
Thorpe Audlin 186 B1
Thorpe Bassett 204 B5
Thorpe Bay 138 C4
Thorpe by Water 161 D3
Thorpe Constantine 159 E2
Thorpe Culvert 176 C1
Thorpe End 179 D4
Thorpe Green Essex 152 C5
Thorpe Green Lancs 192 B5
Thorpe Green Suff 152 A2
Thorpe Hall 203 E5
Thorpe Hesley 186 A3
Thorpe in Balne 186 C1
Thorpe in the Fallows 187 G4
Thorpe Langton 160 C3
Thorpe Larches 212 C5
Thorpe le Street 196 A3
Thorpe Malsor 160 D5
Thorpe Mandeville 148 A3
Thorpe Market 178 D2
Thorpe Morieux 152 A2
Thorpe on the Hill Lincs 175 E1
Thorpe on the Hill WYorks 194 B1
Thorpe Park Surr KT16 8PN 121 F1
Thorpe Row 178 A5
Thorpe St. Andrew 179 D5
Thorpe St. Peter 176 C1
Thorpe Salvin 186 C4
Thorpe Satchville 160 C1
Thorpe Street 164 B4
Thorpe Thewles 212 D5
Thorpe Tilney Dales 175 G2
Thorpe Underwood N'hants 160 C4
Thorpe Underwood NYorks 195 D2
Thorpe Waterville 161 F4
Thorpe Willoughby 195 E4
Thorpefield 202 D5
Thorpe-le-Soken 152 C5
Thorpeness 153 F2
Thorpland 163 E2
Thorrington 152 B5
Thorverton 102 C2
Thrandeston 164 C4
Thrapston 161 E5
Threapland 193 F1
Threapwood 170 B3
Threapwood Head 172 B3
Three Ashes 131 E4
Three Bridges 122 B5
Three Burrows 96 B5
Three Chimneys 124 A5
Three Cocks (Aberllynfi) 144 A4
Three Counties Showground Worcs WR13 6NW 145 G3
Three Crosses 128 B3
Three Cups Corner 110 B1
Three Hammers 97 G1
Three Holes 162 D2
Three Leg Cross 123 F5
Three Legged Cross 105 G2
Three Mile Cross 120 C1
Three Oaks 110 D2
Threehammer Common 179 E4
Threekingham 175 F4
Threemilestone 96 B5
Threlkeld 209 G4
Threshfield 193 F1
Threxton Hill 163 G2
Thrieplely 244 B1
Thrigby 179 F4
Thrigby Hall Wildlife Gardens Norf NR29 3DR 179 F4
Thringarth 211 F5
Thringstone 159 G1
Thrintoft 202 C3
Thriplow 150 C3
Throapham 186 C4
Throckenholt 162 B2
Throcking 150 B4
Throckley 212 A1
Throckmorton 146 B3
Throop 105 G3
Throphill 220 D3
Thropton 220 C1
Througham 132 B2
Throwleigh 99 G1
Throwley 124 B3
Throws 151 E5
Thrumpton Notts 173 G4
Thrumpton Notts 187 E5
Thrumster 275 J4
Thruxton Hants 119 D3
Thruxton Here 144 D4
Thrybergh 186 B3
Thrybergh Country Park SYorks S65 4NU 186 B3
Thulston 173 F4

Thunder Bridge 185 F1
Tilney High End 163 D1
Tilney St. Lawrence 162 D1
Thundergay 231 G5
Thundersley 138 B4
Thunderton 269 J6
Thurcaston 160 A1
Thurcroft 186 B4
Thurdistoft 275 H2
Thurdon 112 C4
Thurgarton Norf 178 C2
Thurgarton Notts 174 B3
Thurgoland 185 G2
Thurlaston Leics 160 A3
Thurlaston Warks 159 G5
Thurlbear 115 F5
Thurlby Lincs 161 G1
Thurlby Lincs 175 E1
Thurlby Lincs 189 E5
Thurleigh 149 F2
Thurlestone 100 C3
Thurloxton 115 F4
Thurlstone 185 G2
Thurlton 165 F2
Thurlwood 171 F2
Thurmaston 160 B2
Thurnby 160 B2
Thurne 179 F4
Thurnham 124 A3
Thurning N'hants 161 F4
Thurning Norf 178 B3
Thurnscoe 186 B2
Thursby 209 G1
Thursden 193 F4
Thursford 178 A2
Thursford Collection Norf NR21 0AS 178 A2
Thursley 121 E4
Thurso (Inbhir Theòrsa) 275 G2
Thurstaston 182 D4
Thurston 152 A1
Thurston Clough 185 D2
Thurstonfield 209 G1
Thurstonland 185 F1
Thurton 179 E5
Thurvaston Derbys 172 D4
Thurvaston Derbys 172 C5
Thuster 275 H3
Thuxton 178 B5
Thwaite NYorks 201 D3
Thwaite Suff 152 C1
Thwaite Head 199 E3
Thwaite St. Mary 165 E2
Thwaites 193 G3
Thwaites Brow 193 G3
Thwing 205 D5
Tibbermore 243 F2
Tibberton Glos 145 G5
Tibberton Tel&W 171 D5
Tibberton Worcs 146 B2
Tibbie Shiels Inn 226 D3
Tibenham 164 C2
Tibertich 240 A4
Tibshelf 173 F1
Tibthorpe 196 B2
Ticehurst 123 F5
Tichborne 119 G4
Tickencote 161 E2
Tickenham 131 D5
Tickford End 149 D3
Tickhill 186 C3
Ticklerton 157 D3
Tickton 196 C3
Tidbury Green 158 D5
Tidcombe 119 D2
Tiddington Oxon 134 B2
Tiddington Warks 147 E2
Tiddleywink 132 A5
Tidebrook 110 B1
Tideford 98 D5
Tideford Cross 98 D4
Tidenham 131 E3
Tidenham Chase 131 E3
Tideswell 185 F5
Tidmarsh 134 B5
Tidmington 147 E4
Tidpit 105 G3
Tidworth 118 D3
Tiers Cross 126 C1
Tiffield 148 B2
Tifty 269 F6
Tigerton 252 D3
Tigh a' Gearraidh 262 C4
Tighachnoic 247 F5
Tighnablair 242 D3
Tighnabruaich 232 A2
Tighnacomaire 248 B3
Tigley 101 D1
Tilbrook 149 F1
Tilbury 137 F5
Tilbury Green 151 F4
Tile Hill 159 E5
Tilehurst 134 B5
Tilford 121 D3
Tilgate 122 B5
Tilgate Forest Row 122 B5
Tilgate Park WSuss RH10 5PQ 122 B5
Tillathrowie 260 C1
Tillers' Green 145 F4
Tillery 261 H2
Tilley 170 C5
Tillicoultry 243 E5
Tillietudlem 225 G1
Tillingham 138 C2
Tillington Here 145 D3
Tillington WSuss 121 E5
Tillington Common 145 D3
Tillyarblet 252 D3
Tillybirloch 260 E4
Tillycairn Castle 260 E3
Tillycorthie 261 H2
Tillydrone 261 H4
Tillyfar 269 G6
Tillyfour 260 D3
Tillyfourie 260 E3
Tillygarmond 260 E5
Tillygreig 261 G2
Tillyprone 260 C4
Tilmanstone 125 E3
Tiln 187 E4
Tilney All Saints 163 D1

Tilney Fen End 162 D1
Tilney High End 163 D1
Tilney St. Lawrence 162 D1
Tilshead 118 B3
Tilstock 170 C4
Tilston 170 B2
Tilstone Fearnall 170 C1
Tilsworth 149 E5
Tilton on the Hill 160 C2
Tiltups End 132 A3
Timberland 175 G2
Timberland Dales 175 G1
Timbersbrook 171 F1
Timberscombe 114 C3
Timble 194 A2
Timewell 114 C5
Timperley 184 B4
Timsbury B&NESom 117 D2
Timsbury Hants 119 E5
Timsgearraidh 270 C4
Timworth 151 G1
Timworth Green 151 G1
Tincleton 105 D3
Tindale 210 C2
Tindon End 151 E4
Tingewick 148 B4
Tingley 194 B1
Tingrith 149 F4
Tingwall (Lerwick) Airport 279 D8
Tinhay 99 D2
Tinney 98 C1
Tinshill 194 B4
Tinsley 186 B3
Tinsley Green 122 B5
Tintagel 97 E1
Tintagel Castle Corn PL34 0HE 97 E1
Tintern Parva 131 E2
Tintinhull 104 A1
Tintwistle 185 E3
Tinwald 217 E2
Tinwell 161 F2
Tippacott 114 A3
Tipperty Aber 253 F1
Tipperty Aber 261 H2
Tipps End 162 C3
Tiptoe 106 B3
Tipton 158 B3
Tipton St. John 103 D3
Tiptree 138 B1
Tiptree Heath 138 B1
Tiptree Museum Essex CO5 0RF 138 C1
Tirabad 143 F3
Tiree 246 B2
Tiree Airport 246 B2
Tirindrish 249 E1
Tirley 146 A5
Tirphil 130 A2
Tirril 210 B5
Tir-y-dail 128 C1
Tisbury 118 A5
Tisman's Common 121 F4
Tissington 172 C2
Tister 275 G2
Titchberry 112 C3
Titchfield 107 E2
Titchmarsh 161 F5
Titchwell 177 F3
Titchwell Marsh Norf PE31 8BB 177 F3
Tithby 174 B4
Titley 144 C1
Titlington 229 F5
Titmore Green 150 A5
Titsey 122 D3
Titson 112 C5
Tittensor 171 F4
Tittleshall 177 G5
Tiverton ChesW&C 170 C1
Tiverton Devon 102 C1
Tivetshall St. Margaret 164 C3
Tivetshall St. Mary 164 C3
Tivington 114 C3
Tixall 171 G5
Tixover 161 E2
Toab Ork 277 E7
Toab Shet 279 F9
Tobermory 247 E4
Toberonochy 239 G4
Tobson 270 D4
Tocher 260 E1
Tockenham 132 C5
Tockenham Wick 132 C4
Tockholes 192 C5
Tockington 131 F4
Tockwith 195 D2
Todber 117 E5
Toddington CenBeds 149 F5
Toddington Glos 146 C4
Todenham 147 E4
Todhills Angus 244 C1
Todhills Cumb 218 B5
Todlachie 260 E3
Todmorden 193 F5
Todwick 186 B4
Toft Cambs 150 B2
Toft Lincs 161 F1
Toft Shet 278 D5
Toft Hill 212 A5
Toft Monks 165 F2
Toft next Newton 188 A4
Toftcarl 275 J4
Toftrees 177 G5
Tofts 275 J2
Toftwood 178 A4
Togston 221 E1
Tokavaig 256 C3
Tokers Green 134 B5
Tolastadh a' Chaolais 270 D4
Tolastadh Ur 271 H3
Toll Bar 186 C2
Tolland 115 E4
Tollard Farnham 105 F1

Tollard Royal **105** F1
Tollcross **234** A3
Toller Down Gate **104** B2
Toller Fratrum **104** B3
Toller Porcorum **104** B3
Toller Whelme **104** B3
Tollerton *Notts* **174** B4
Tollerton *NYorks* **195** E1
Tollesbury **138** C1
Tollesby **203** E1
Tolleshunt D'Arcy **138** C1
Tolleshunt Knights **138** C1
Tolleshunt Major **138** B1
Tolmachan **270** C7
Tolpuddle **105** D3
Tolvah **259** F5
Tolworth **121** G1
Tom an Fhuadain **271** F6
Tomatin **259** F2
Tombreck **258** D2
Tomchrasky
   (Tom Chrasgaidh) **257** J3
Tomdon **257** H4
Tomdow **267** H7
Tomich *High* **257** K2
Tomich *High* **266** E4
Tomich *High* **266** D1
Tomintoul **259** J3
Tomnacross **266** C7
Tomnamoon **267** H6
Tomnaven **260** C1
Tomnavoulin **259** K2
Tomvaich **259** H1
Ton Pentre **129** F3
Tonbridge **123** E4
Tondu **129** E4
Tonedale **115** E5
Tonfanau **154** B2
Tong *Kent* **124** A4
Tong *Shrop* **157** G2
Tong *WYorks* **194** B4
Tong Norton **157** G2
Tong Street **194** A4
Tonge **173** F5
Tongham **121** D3
Tongland **216** A5
Tongue **273** H3
Tongue House **273** H3
Tongwynlais **130** A4
Tonna **129** D3
Tonwell **136** C1
Tonypandy **129** F3
Tonyrefail **129** F4
Toot Baldon **134** A2
Toot Hill **137** E2
Toothill *Hants* **106** C1
Toothill *Swin* **132** D4
Tooting Graveney **136** B5
Top End **149** F1
Top of Hebers **184** C2
Topcliffe **202** B5
Topcroft **165** D2
Topcroft Street **165** D2
Toppesfield **151** F4
Toppings **184** B1
Toprow **164** C2
Topsham **102** C4
Topsham Bridge **100** D2
Torastan **246** B3
Torbain **259** J3
Torbeg *Aber* **260** B4
Torbeg *NAyr* **223** E3
Torbothie **234** C4
Torbryan **101** E1
Torcastle **248** D2
Torcross **101** E3
Tordarroch **258** D1
Tore (An Todhar) **266** D6
Toredduff **267** J5
Toremore *High* **259** J1
Toremore *High* **275** G5
Torfrey **97** F4
Torgyle **257** K3
Torksey **187** F5
Torlum **262** C6
Torlundy
   (Tòrr Lunndaidh) **248** D2
Tormarton **131** G5
Tormisdale **230** A4
Tormore **223** D2
Tormsdale **275** G3
Tornagrain **266** E6
Tornahaish **259** K4
Tornaveen **260** E4
Torness **258** C2
Toronto **212** A4
Torpenhow **209** F3
Torphichen **235** D2
Torphins **260** E4
Torpoint **100** A2
Torquay **101** F1
Torquhan **236** B5
Torr **100** B2
Torran *A&B* **240** A4
Torran *High* **266** E4
Torran *High* **264** B7
Torrance **234** A2
Torrance House **234** A4
Torrancroy **260** B2
Torre *Som* **114** D3
Torre *Torbay* **101** F1
Torrich **267** F6
Torridon **264** E6
Torrin **256** B2
Torrisdale *A&B* **222** C2
Torrisdale *High* **273** J2
Torrish **274** E7
Torrisholme **192** A1
Torroble **266** C1
Torry *Aber* **268** C6
Torry *Aberdeen* **261** H4
Torryburn **235** E1
Torsonce **236** B5
Torterston **269** J6
Torthorwald **217** E3
Tortington **108** B3
Torton **158** A5
Tortworth **131** G3
Torvaig **263** K7
Torver **199** D3
Torwood **234** B1

Torworth **187** D4
Tosberry **112** C3
Toscaig **256** D1
Toseland **150** A1
Tosside **193** D2
Tostarie **246** C5
Tostock **152** A1
Totaig **263** G6
Totamore **246** A4
Tote **263** K7
Tote Hill **121** D5
Totegan **274** E2
Totford **119** G4
Tothom Hill **138** B1
Tothill **189** E4
Totland **106** C4
Totley **186** A5
Totnes **101** E2
Totronald **246** A4
Totscore **263** J5
Tottenham **136** C3
Tottenhill **163** E1
Tottenhill Row **163** E1
Totteridge *Bucks* **135** D3
Totteridge *GtLon* **136** B3
Totternhoe **149** E5
Tottington *GtMan* **184** B1
Tottington *Norf* **163** G3
Totton **106** C1
Toulton **115** E4
Tournaig **264** E3
Toux **269** H5
Tovil **123** G4
Tow Law **212** A4
Towan Cross **96** B5
Toward **232** C3
Towcester **148** B3
Towednack **94** B4
Tower Bridge Exhibition
   GtLon SE1 2UP **12** C4
Tower End **163** E1
Tower of London *GtLon*
   EC3N 4AB **12** C4
Towersey **134** C2
Towie *Aber* **269** G4
Towie *Aber* **260** D2
Towie *Aber* **260** C4
Towiemore **268** B6
Town End *Cambs* **162** C3
Town End *Cumb* **199** F4
Town End *Mersey* **183** F4
Town Green *Lancs* **183** E2
Town Green *Norf* **179** E4
Town of Lowton **184** A3
Town Row **123** E5
Town Street **163** F4
Town Yetholm **228** C4
Towneley Hall Art Gallery &
   Museum *Lancs*
   BB11 3RQ **193** E4
Townfield **211** F3
Townhead *D&G* **207** G2
Townhead *SYorks* **185** F2
Townhead of
   Greenlaw **216** B4
Townhill *Fife* **235** F1
Townhill *Swan* **128** C3
Towns End **119** G4
Towns Green **170** D1
Townshend **94** C3
Towthorpe *ERid* **196** B4
Towthorpe *York* **195** F2
Towton **195** D4
Towyn **182** A5
Toynton All Saints **176** B1
Toynton Fen Side **176** B1
Toynton St. Peter **176** C1
Toy's Hill **123** D3
Trabboch **224** C3
Traboe **95** E4
Tradespark *High* **267** F6
Tradespark *Ork* **277** D7
Trafford Centre **184** B3
Trafford Park **184** B3
Trago Mills, Newton Abbot
   Devon TQ12 6JD **102** B5
Trallong **143** F5
Trallwn **128** C3
Tram Inn **145** D4
Tranent **236** B2
Tranmere **183** E4
Trantlebeg **274** D3
Trantlemore **274** D3
Tranwell **221** D3
Trap **128** C1
Trap Street **171** F1
Traprain **236** C2
Traquair **227** E2
Trawden **193** F4
Trawscoed
   (Crosswood) **154** C5
Trawsfynydd **168** A4
Trealaw **129** G3
Treales **192** A4
Trearddur **180** A5
Treaslane **263** J6
Tre-Aubrey **129** G5
Trebah Garden *Corn*
   TR11 5JZ **95** E4
Trebanog **129** G3
Trebanos **128** D2
Trebarrow **98** C1
Trebartha **97** G2
Trebarvah **97** E5
Trebarwith **97** E1
Trebeath **97** G1
Trebetherick **96** D2
Trebister **279** D9
Tre-boeth **128** C3
Treborough **114** D4
Trebudannon **96** C3
Trebullett **98** D3
Treburley **98** D3
Treburrick **96** C2
Trebyan **97** E3
Trecastle **143** E5
Trecott **113** G5
Trecrogo **98** D3
Trecwn **140** C4
Trecynon **129** F2

Tredaule **97** G1
Tredavoe **94** B4
Treddiog **140** B5
Tredegar **130** A2
Tredington *Glos* **146** B5
Tredington *Warks* **147** E3
Tredinnick *Corn* **96** D3
Tredinnick *Corn* **97** G4
Tredogan **115** D1
Tredomen **144** A4
Tredrissi **141** D3
Tredunnock **130** C3
Tredworth **132** A1
Treen *Corn* **94** A4
Treen *Corn* **94** B3
Treesmill **97** E4
Treeton **186** B4
Trefasser **140** B4
Trefechan *Glos* **129** G3
Trefeglwys **155** F3
Trefenter **142** C1
Treffgarne **140** C5
Treffynnon **140** B5
Trefgarn Owen **140** B5
Trefil **130** A1
Trefilan **142** B2
Trefin **140** B4
Treflach **169** F5
Trefnanney **156** B1
Trefnant **182** B5
Trefonen **169** F5
Trefor *Gwyn* **166** C3
Trevaughan *Carmar* **127** E1
Treveighan **97** E2
Trevellas **96** B4
Trevelmond **97** G3
Trevenen **95** D4
Treverva **95** E3
Trevescan **94** A4
Trevethin **130** B2
Trevigro **98** D4
Trevine **240** C2
Treviscoe **96** D4
Trevivian **97** F1
Trevone **96** C2
Trevor **169** F3
Trewalder **97** E1
Trewarmett **97** E1
Trewarthenick **96** D5
Trewassa **97** F1
Trewellard **94** A3
Trewen *Here* **131** E1
Trewennack **95** D4
Trewent **126** D3
Trewern **156** B1
Trewethern **97** E1
Trewidland **97** G4
Trewilym **141** E3
Trewint *Corn* **98** B1
Trewint *Corn* **97** G1
Trewithian **95** F3
Trewoon **97** D4
Treworga **96** C5
Treworlas **95** F3
Treworman **97** D2
Treworthal **95** F3
Tre-wyn **144** C5
Treyarnon **96** C2
Treyford **108** A2
Trezaise **97** D4
Triangle **193** G5
Trickett's Cross **105** G2
Triermain **210** B1
Trimdon **212** C4
Trimdon Colliery **212** C4
Trimdon Grange **212** C4
Trimingham **179** D3
Trimley Lower Street **153** D4
Trimley St. Martin **153** D4
Trimley St. Mary **153** D4
Trimpley **158** A5
Trimsaran **128** A2
Trimstone **113** E1
Trinafour **250** C3
Trinant **130** B3
Tring **135** E1
Trinity *Angus* **253** E3
Trinity *Chanl* **100** C5
Trinity *Edin* **235** G2
Trisant **154** D5
Triscombe *Som* **114** C4
Triscombe *Som* **115** E4
Trislaig **248** C2
Trispen **96** C4
Tritlington **221** E2
Trochry **243** E1
Troedyraur **141** G3
Troedyrhiw **129** G2
Trofarth **181** G5
Trondavoe **278** C5
Troon *Corn* **95** D3
Troon *SAyr* **224** B2
Tropical Butterfly House,
   Wildlife & Falconry Centre
   SYorks S25 4EQ **21** F3
Tropical World, Roundhay
   WYorks LS8 2ER **27** G1
Trosairidh **254** C3
Troston **163** G5
Troswell **98** C1
Trottick **244** C1
Trottiscliffe **123** F2
Trotton **120** D5
Trough Gate **193** E5
Troughend **220** B2
Troustan **232** B2
Troutbeck *Cumb* **199** F2
Troutbeck *Cumb* **209** G4
Troutbeck Bridge **199** F2
Trow Green **131** E2
Troway **186** A5
Trowbridge *Cardiff* **130** B4
Trowbridge *Wilts* **117** F2
Trowell **173** F4
Trowle Common **117** F2
Trowley Bottom **135** F1
Trows **228** A3
Trowse Newton **178** D5
Troy **194** B4

Trescowe **94** C3
Tresean **96** B4
Tresham **131** G3
Treshnish **246** C5
Tresillian **96** C5
Tresinney **97** F1
Tresinwen **140** B3
Treslea **97** F3
Tresmeer **97** G1
Tresowes Green **94** D4
Tresparrett **98** B1
Tresparrett Posts **98** B1
Tressait **250** D3
Tresta *Shet* **278** F3
Tresta *Shet* **279** C7
Treswell **187** E5
Trethewey **94** A4
Trethomas **130** A4
Trethurgy **97** E4
Tretio **140** A5
Tretire **145** E5
Tretower **144** A5
Treuddyn **169** F2
Trevadlock **97** G2
Trevalga **98** A1
Trevalyn **170** A2
Trevanson **97** D2
Trevarnon **94** C3
Trevarrack **94** B3
Trevarren **96** D3
Trevarrian **96** C3
Trevarrick **97** D5
Tre-vaughan *Carmar* **141** G5
Trevaughan *Carmar* **127** E1

Trudernish **230** C4
Trudoxhill **117** E3
Trull **115** F5
Trumaisgearraidh **262** D4
Trumpan **263** H5
Trumpet **145** F4
Trumpington **150** C2
Trumps Green **121** E2
Trunch **179** D2
Trunnah **191** G3
Truro **96** C5
Truro Cathedral *Corn*
   TR1 2AF **96** C5
Truscott **98** D2
Trusham **102** B4
Trusley **173** E5
Trusthorpe **189** F4
Truthan **96** C4
Trysull **158** A3
Tubney **133** G3
Tuckenhay **101** E2
Tuckhill **157** G4
Tuckingmill **96** A5
Tuddenham *Suff* **152** C3
Tuddenham *Suff* **163** F5
Tudeley **123** F4
Tudeley Hale **123** F4
Tudhoe **212** B4
Tudweiliog **166** B4
Tuesley **121** E3
Tuffley **132** A1
Tufton *Hants* **119** F3
Tufton *Pembs* **140** D5
Tugby **160** C2
Tugford **157** E4
Tughall **229** G4
Tulchan **243** D2
Tullibardine Distillery *P&K*
   PH4 1QG **243** E4
Tullibody **243** D5
Tullich *A&B* **240** C3
Tullich *A&B* **240** A3
Tullich *High* **267** F4
Tullich *High* **258** D2
Tullich *Moray* **268** B6
Tullich *Stir* **242** A1
Tullich *Muir* **266** E4
Tullie House Museum & Art
   Gallery *Cumb* CA3 8TP
   68 Carlisle
Tulliemet **251** F4
Tulloch *Aber* **261** G1
Tulloch *High* **266** D2
Tulloch *Moray* **267** H6
Tullochgorm **240** B5
Tullochgribban High **259** G2
Tullochvenus **260** D4
Tulloes **252** C5
Tulse Hill **136** C5
Tumble (Y Tymbl) **128** B1
Tumby **176** A2
Tumby Woodside **176** A2
Tummel Bridge **250** C4
Tunbridge Wells **123** E5
Tundergarth Mains **217** F2
Tunga **271** G4
Tungate **179** D3
Tunley **117** D2
Tunstall *ERid* **197** F4
Tunstall *Kent* **124** A2
Tunstall *Lancs* **200** B5
Tunstall *Norf* **179** F5
Tunstall *NYorks* **202** B3
Tunstall *Stoke* **171** F2
Tunstall *Suff* **153** E2
Tunstall *T&W* **212** C2
Tunstead *GtMan* **185** E2
Tunstead *Norf* **179** E3
Tunstead Milton **185** E4
Tunworth **120** B3
Tupholme **175** G1
Tupsley **145** E4
Tupton **173** E1
Tur Langton **160** C3
Turbiskill **231** F1
Turclossie **269** G5
Turgis Green **120** B2
Turin **252** C4
Turkdean **132** D1
Turleigh **117** F2
Turn **184** C1
Turnastone **144** C4
Turnberry **224** A5
Turnchapel **100** A2
Turnditch **173** D3
Turner's Green **147** D1
Turners Hill **122** C5
Turners Puddle **105** E3
Turnford **136** C2
Turnworth **105** E2
Turret Bridge **257** K5
Turriff **269** F6
Turton Bottoms **184** B1
Turvey **149** E2
Turville **134** C3
Turville Heath **134** C3
Turweston **148** B4
Tutbury **172** D5
Tutbury Castle *Staffs* DE13
   9JF **172** D5
Tutnall **158** B5
Tutshill **131** E3
Tuttington **178** D3
Tutts Clump **134** A5
Tutwell **99** D3
Tuxford **187** E5
Twatt *Ork* **276** B5
Twatt *Shet* **279** C7
Twechar **234** B2
Tweedmouth **237** G4
Tweedsmuir **226** B3
Twelve Oaks **110** B1

Twelveheads **96** B5
Twemlow Green **171** E1
Twenty **175** G5
Twickenham **136** A5
Twigworth **146** A5
Twineham **109** E1
Twineham Green **109** E1
Twinhoe **117** E2
Twinstead **151** G4
Twiss Green **184** A3
Twiston **193** E3
Twitchen *Devon* **114** A4
Twitchen *Shrop* **156** C5
Twitton **123** D3
Twizell House **229** F4
Two Bridges *Devon* **99** G3
Two Bridges *Glos* **131** F2
Two Dales **173** D1
Two Gates **159** E2
Two Mills **183** E5
Twycross **159** F2
Twycross Zoo *Leics*
   CV9 3PX **159** F2
Twyford *Bucks* **148** B5
Twyford *Derbys* **173** E5
Twyford *Dorset* **105** E1
Twyford *Hants* **119** F5
Twyford *Leics* **160** C1
Twyford *Norf* **178** B3
Twyford *Oxon* **147** G4
Twyford *W'ham* **134** C5
Twyford Common **145** E4
Twyn Shôn-Ifan **130** A3
Twynholm **216** A5
Twyning **146** A4
Twynllanan **143** E5
Twyn-yr-odyn **130** A5
Twyn-y-Sheriff **130** D2
Twywell **161** E5
Ty Croes **180** B5
Ty Common **137** F3
Tycroes **128** C1
Tycrwyn **156** A1
Tydd Gote **162** C1
Tydd St. Giles **162** C1
Tydd St. Mary **162** C1
Tye **137** F3
Tye Green *Essex* **151** F5
Tye Green *Essex* **151** E5
Tye Green *Essex* **137** F1
Tye Green *Essex* **136** D2
Tyersal **194** A4
Ty-hen **166** A4
Tyldesley **184** A2
Tyle-garw **129** G4
Tyler Hill **124** D2
Tylers Green *Bucks* **135** E3
Tyler's Green *Essex* **137** E2
Tylorstown **129** G3
Tylwch **155** F5
Ty-Mawr *Conwy* **168** C3
Ty-mawr *Denb* **169** E2
Ty-nant *Conwy* **168** C3
Ty-nant *Gwyn* **168** C5
Tyndrum
   (Taigh an Droma) **241** F1
Tyne Green Country Park
   N'umb NE46 3RY **211** F1
Tyneham **105** E4
Tynehead **236** A4
Tynemouth **212** C1
Tynewydd **129** F3
Tyninghame **236** D2
Tynron **216** C1
Tyntesfield **131** E5
Tyn-y-cefn **169** D3
Ty'n-y-coedcae **130** A4
Tyn-y-cwm **155** E4
Tyn-y-ffridd **169** E4
Tyn-y-garn **129** E4
Tyn-y-gongl **180** D4
Tyn'y-groes **181** F5
Tyrie **269** H4
Tyringham **149** D3
Tyseley **158** D4
Tythegston **129** E5
Tytherington *ChesE* **184** D4
Tytherington *SGlos* **131** F4
Tytherington *Som* **117** E3
Tytherington *Wilts* **118** A3
Tytherleigh **103** F2
Tytherton Lucas **132** B5
Tyttenhanger **136** A2
Ty-uchaf **168** C5
Tywardreath **97** E4
Tywardreath Highway **97** E4
Tywyn **154** B2

U

Uachdar **262** D6
Uags **256** D1
Ubberley **171** G3
Ubbeston Green **165** E1
Ubley **116** C2
Uckerby **202** B2
Uckfield **109** G1
Uckinghall **146** A4
Uckington **146** B5
Uddingston **234** A3
Uddington **225** G2
Udimore **111** D2
Udley **116** B1
Udny Green **261** G2
Udny Station **261** H2
Udston **234** B4
Udstonhead **234** B5
Uffcott **132** D5
Uffculme **103** D1
Uffington *Lincs* **161** F2
Uffington *Oxon* **133** F4
Uffington *Shrop* **157** E1
Ufford *Peter* **161** F2
Ufford *Suff* **153** D2
Ufton **147** G1
Ufton Green **120** B1
Ufton Nervet **120** B1
Ugborough **100** C2
Ugford **118** B4
Uggeshall **165** F3
Ugglebarnby **204** B2
Ugley **150** D5

Ugley Green **150** D5
Ugthorpe **203** G1
Uidh **254** B5
Uig *A&B* **246** A4
Uig *A&B* **232** B2
Uig (Uige) *High* **263** J5
Uig *High* **263** G6
Uigen **270** C4
Uiginish **263** H7
Uigshader **263** K7
Uisken **238** C3
Uiskevagh
   (Uisgebhagh) **262** D6
Ulbster **275** J4
Ulcat Row **210** A5
Ulceby *Lincs* **189** E5
Ulceby *NLincs* **188** B1
Ulceby Cross **189** E5
Ulceby Skitter **188** B1
Ulcombe **124** A4
Uldale **209** F3
Uldale House **200** C3
Uley **131** G3
Ulgham **221** E2
Ullapool (Ullapul) **265** H2
Ullenhall **146** D1
Ullenwood **132** B1
Ulleskelf **195** E4
Ullesthorpe **160** A4
Ulley **186** A4
Ulley Reservoir Country Park
   SYorks S26 3XL **21** F3
Ullingswick **145** E3
Ullinish **255** J1
Ullock **209** D4
Ullswater Steamers *Cumb*
   CA11 0US **209** G5
Ulpha *Cumb* **198** C3
Ulpha *Cumb* **199** F4
Ulrome **197** D2
Ulsta **278** D4
Ulting **138** B2
Uluvalt **239** E1
Ulva **238** D1
Ulverston **199** D5
Ulwell **105** G4
Ulzieside **225** F5
Umberleigh **113** G3
Unapool **272** E5
Underbarrow **199** F3
Undercliffe **194** A4
Underhill **136** B3
Underhoull **278** E2
Underling Green **123** G4
Underriver **123** E3
Underwood *Newport* **130** C4
Underwood *Notts* **173** F2
Underwood *Plym* **100** B2
Undley **163** E4
Undy **130** D4
Ungisiadar **270** D5
Unifirth **279** B7
Union Croft **261** G5
Union Mills **190** B4
Union Street **123** G5
University of Glasgow Visitor
   Centre *Glas*
   G12 8QQ **38** B1
Unst **278** F1
Unst Airport **278** F2
Unstone **186** A5
Unstone Green **186** A5
Unsworth **184** C2
Unthank *Cumb* **210** A4
Unthank *Derbys* **186** A5
Up Cerne **104** C2
Up Exe **102** C2
Up Hatherley **146** B5
Up Holland **183** G2
Up Marden **107** G1
Up Mudford **104** B1
Up Nately **120** B2
Up Somborne **119** E4
Up Sydling **104** C2
Upavon **118** C2
Upchurch **124** A2
Upcott *Devon* **99** E1
Upcott *Devon* **113** F2
Upcott *Here* **144** C2
Upcott *Som* **114** C5
Upend **151** F2
Upgate **151** F2
Upgate Street *Norf* **164** B2
Upgate Street *Norf* **165** D2
Uphall *Dorset* **104** B2
Uphall *WLoth* **235** E2
Uphall Station **235** E2
Upham *Devon* **102** B2
Upham *Hants* **119** G5
Uphampton *Here* **144** C1
Uphampton *Worcs* **146** A1
Uphempston **101** E1
Uphill **116** A2
Uplands *Glos* **132** A2
Uplands *Swan* **128** C3
Uplawmoor **233** F4
Upleadon **145** G5
Upleatham **203** F1
Uplees **124** C2
Uploders **104** B3
Uplowman **102** D1
Uplyme **103** G3
Upminster **137** E4
Upottery **103** F2
Upper Affcot **156** D4
Upper Ardroscadale **232** B3
Upper Arley **157** G4
Upper Arncott **134** B1
Upper Astley **157** E1
Upper Aston **158** A3
Upper Astrop **148** A4
Upper Barvas **271** F2
Upper Basildon **134** B5
Upper Bayble
   (Pabail Uarach) **271** H4
Upper Beeding **109** D2
Upper Benefield **161** E4
Upper Bentley **146** B1
Upper Berwick **157** D1
Upper Bighouse **274** D3
Upper Boat **130** A4
Upper Boddam **260** E1

Upper Boddington **147** G2
Upper Borth **154** C4
Upper Boyndlie **269** H4
Upper Brailes **147** F4
Upper Breakish **256** C2
Upper Breinton **145** D3
Upper Broadheath **146** A2
Upper Broughton **174** B5
Upper Brynamman **128** D1
Upper Bucklebury **119** G1
Upper Burgate **106** A1
Upper Burnhaugh **261** G5
Upper Caldecote **149** G3
Upper Camster **275** H4
Upper Canada **116** A2
Upper Catesby **148** A2
Upper Catshill **158** B5
Upper Chapel **143** G3
Upper Cheddon **115** F5
Upper Chicksgrove **118** A4
Upper Chute **119** D2
Upper Clatford **119** E3
Upper Coberley **132** B1
Upper Colwall **145** G3
Upper Cotton **172** B3
Upper Cound **157** E2
Upper Cumberworth **185** G2
Upper Cwmbran **130** B3
Upper Dallachy **268** B4
Upper Dean **149** F1
Upper Denby **185** G2
Upper Denton **210** C1
Upper Derraid **259** H1
Upper Derwent Reservoirs
   Derbys S33 0AQ **185** F4
Upper Dicker **110** A2
Upper Diabaig **264** E5
Upper Dovercourt **152** D4
Upper Dunsforth **194** D1
Upper Dunsley **135** E1
Upper Eastern Green **159** E4
Upper Eathie **266** E5
Upper Egleton **145** F3
Upper Elkstone **172** B2
Upper End **185** E1
Upper Enham **119** E2
Upper Farringdon **120** C4
Upper Framilode **131** G1
Upper Froyle **120** C4
Upper Gills **275** J1
Upper Glendessarry **257** F5
Upper Godney **116** B3
Upper Gornal **158** B3
Upper Gravenhurst **149** G4
Upper Green Essex **150** C4
Upper Green Essex **151** D4
Upper Green Mon **130** C1
Upper Green WBerks **119** E1
Upper Grove Common **145** E5
Upper Gylen **240** C2
Upper Hackney **173** D1
Upper Halliford **121** F1
Upper Halling **123** F2
Upper Hambleton **161** E2
Upper Hardres Court **125** D3
Upper Hartfield **123** D5
Upper Hatton **171** F4
Upper Hawkhillock **261** J1
Upper Haysden **123** E4
Upper Hayton **157** E4
Upper Heath **157** E4
Upper Heaton **185** F1
Upper Hellesdon **178** D4
Upper Helmsley **195** F2
Upper Hengoed **169** F4
Upper Hergest **144** B2
Upper Heyford
   N'hants **148** B2
Upper Heyford Oxon **147** G5
Upper Hill Here **145** D2
Upper Hill SGlos **131** F3
Upper Horsebridge **110** A2
Upper Howsell **145** G5
Upper Hulme **172** B1
Upper Inglesham **133** E3
Upper Kilchattan **238** C5
Upper Killay **128** B3
Upper Knockando **267** J7
Upper Lambourn **133** F4
Upper Langford **116** B2
Upper Langwith **173** G1
Upper Largo **244** C4
Upper Leigh **172** B4
Upper Ley **131** G2
Upper Loads **173** E1
Upper Lochton **260** E5
Upper Longdon **158** C1
Upper Longwood **157** F2
Upper Ludstone **158** A3
Upper Lybster **275** H5
Upper Lydbrook **131** F1
Upper Lyde **145** D3
Upper Lye **144** C1
Upper Maes-coed **144** C4
Upper Midhope **185** G3
Upper Milovaig **263** G7
Upper Milton **133** E1
Upper Minety **132** C3
Upper Moor **146** B3
Upper Morton **131** F3
Upper Muirskie **261** G5
Upper Nash **126** D2
Upper Newbold **186** A5
Upper North Dean **135** D3
Upper Norwood **136** C5
Upper Obney **243** F1
Upper Oddington **147** E5
Upper Ollach **256** B1
Upper Padley **185** G5
Upper Pennington **106** B3
Upper Pollicott **134** C1
Upper Poppleton **195** E2
Upper Quinton **147** D3
Upper Ratley **119** E5
Upper Ridinghill **269** J5
Upper Rissington **147** E5
Upper Rochford **145** F1
Upper Sanday **277** E7
Upper Sapey **145** F1
Upper Scolton **140** C5
Upper Seagry **132** B4

Upper Shelton **149** E3
Upper Sheringham **178** C1
Upper Shuckburgh **147** G1
Upper Siddington **132** C3
Upper Skelmorlie **232** D3
Upper Slaughter **147** D5
Upper Sonachan **240** C2
Upper Soudley **131** F1
Upper Staploe **149** G2
Upper Stoke **179** D5
Upper Stondon **149** G4
Upper Stowe **148** B2
Upper Street Hants **106** A1
Upper Street Norf **179** E4
Upper Street Norf **164** C4
Upper Street Suff **152** D4
Upper Street Suff **152** C2
Upper Strensham **146** B4
Upper Sundon **149** F5
Upper Swanmore **107** E1
Upper Swell **147** D5
Upper Tean **172** B4
Upper Thurnham **192** A2
Upper Tillyrie **243** G4
Upper Tooting **136** B5
Upper Town Derbys **172** D1
Upper Town Derbys **173** D2
Upper Town Derbys **172** D2
Upper Town Here **145** E3
Upper Town NSom **116** C1
Upper Tysoe **147** F3
Upper Upham **133** E5
Upper Upnor **137** G5
Upper Victoria **244** D1
Upper Vobster **117** E3
Upper Wardington **147** G3
Upper Waterhay **132** C3
Upper Weald **157** E4
Upper Weedon **148** B2
Upper Welson **144** A4
Upper Weston **117** E1
Upper Whiston **186** B4
Upper Wick **146** A2
Upper Wield **120** B4
Upper Winchendon (Over
   Winchendon) **134** C1
Upper Witton **158** C3
Upper Woodford **118** C4
Upper Woolhampton **119** G1
Upper Wootton **119** G2
Upper Wraxall **132** A5
Upper Wyche **145** G3
Upperby **210** A2
Upperthong **185** F2
Upperton **121** E5
Uppertown Derbys **173** E1
Uppertown Ork **275** J1
Uppingham **161** D2
Uppington **157** E2
Upsall **203** D4
Upsettlington **237** F5
Upshire **136** D2
Upstreet **125** E2
Upthorpe **164** A4
Upton Bucks **134** C1
Upton Cambs **161** G5
Upton ChesW&C **170** B1
Upton Corn **97** G2
Upton Corn **112** C5
Upton Devon **103** D2
Upton Devon **101** D1
Upton Dorset **104** D4
Upton Dorset **105** F3
Upton ERid **196** D2
Upton Hants **119** E2
Upton Hants **106** C1
Upton Leics **159** F3
Upton Lincs **187** F4
Upton Mersey **183** D4
Upton N'hants **148** C1
Upton Norf **179** E4
Upton Notts **188** B5
Upton Notts **174** C2
Upton Oxon **134** A4
Upton Oxon **133** E1
Upton Pembs **126** D2
Upton Peter **161** G2
Upton Slo **135** E5
Upton Som **114** C5
Upton Som **116** B5
Upton Wilts **117** F4
Upton WYorks **186** B1
Upton Bishop **145** F5
Upton Cheyney **117** D1
Upton Country Park Poole
   BH17 7BJ **3** A2
Upton Cressett **157** F3
Upton Crews **145** F5
Upton Cross **97** G2
Upton End **149** G4
Upton Grey **120** B3
Upton Hellions **102** B2
Upton Lovell **118** A3
Upton Magna **157** E2
Upton Noble **117** E4
Upton Park **136** D4
Upton Pyne **102** C3
Upton St. Leonards **132** A1
Upton Scudamore **117** F3
Upton Snodsbury **146** B2
Upton upon Severn **146** A3
Upton Warren **146** B1
Upwaltham **108** B2
Upware **162** D5
Upwell **162** D2
Upwey **104** C4
Upwick Green **150** C5
Upwood **162** A4
Uradale **279** D9
Urafirth **278** C5

Urquhart Moray **267** K5
Urquhart Castle High
   IV63 6XJ **258** C2
Urra **203** D4
Urray **266** C6
Ushaw Moor **212** B3
Usher Hall, Edinburgh Edin
   EH1 2EA **36** E5
Usk (Brynbuga) **130** C2
Usselby **188** A3
Usworth **212** C2
Utley **193** G3
Utterby **188** D3
Uttoxeter **172** B4
Uwchmynydd **166** A5
Uxbridge **135** F4
Uyeasound **278** E2
Uzmaston **126** C1

V

Valley (Y Fali) **180** A5
Valley Truckle **97** F1
Valleyfield D&G **216** A3
Valleyfield Fife **235** E1
Valsgarth **278** F1
Vange **137** G4
Vardre **128** C2
Varteg **130** B2
Vatersay
   (Bhatarsaigh) **254** B5
Vatsetter **278** E4
Vatten **263** H7
Vaul **246** B2
Vaynor **129** G1
Vaynor Park **156** A2
Veaullt **144** A2
Veensgarth **279** D8
Velindre Pembs **141** D4
Velindre Powys **144** A4
Vellow **115** D4
Venn **100** D3
Venn Ottery **103** D3
Venngreen **113** D4
Vennington **156** C2
Venny Tedburn **102** B3
Venterdon **99** D3
Ventnor **107** E5
Ventnor Botanic Gardens IoW
   PO38 1UL **107** E5
Venton **100** B2
Vernham Dean **119** E2
Vernham Street **119** E2
Vernolds Common **157** D4
Verwood **105** G2
Veryan **95** G3
Veryan Green **96** D5
Vickerstown **191** E1
Victoria **97** D3
Victoria & Albert Museum
   GtLon SW7 2RL **44** A3
Victoria Art Gallery B&NESom
   BA2 4AT **63** Bath
Vidlin **279** D6
Viewfield **275** F2
Viewpark **234** B3
Vigo **158** C2
Vigo Village **123** F2
Villavin **113** F4
Vinehall Street **110** C1
Vine's Cross **110** A2
Viney Hill **131** F2
Virginia Water **121** E1
Virginstow **99** D1
Virley **138** C1
Vobster **117** E3
Voe Shet **279** D6
Voe Shet **278** C4
Vogrie Country Park Midlo
   EH23 4NU **32** F4
Voirrey Embroidery Mersey
   CH63 6JA **22** A5
Volks Electric Railway B&H
   BN2 1EN **109** F3
Vowchurch **144** C4
Voy **277** B6
Vron Gate **156** C2

W

W.R. Outhwaite & Son
   Ropemakers NYorks
   DL8 3NT **201** D3
Waberthwaite **198** C3
Wackerfield **212** A5
Wacton **164** C2
Wadbister **279** D8
Wadborough **146** B3
Waddesdon **134** C1
Waddesdon Manor Bucks
   HP18 0JH **134** C1
Waddeton **101** E2
Waddicar **183** E3
Waddingham **187** G3
Waddington Lancs **192** D3
Waddington Lincs **175** E1
Waddingworth **188** B5
Waddon Devon **102** B5
Waddon GtLon **122** C2
Wadebridge **97** D2
Wadeford **103** G1
Wadenhoe **161** F4
Wadesmill **136** C1
Wadhurst **123** F5
Wadshelf **186** A5
Wadworth **186** A3
Wadworth Hill **197** D5
Waen Denb **169** E1
Waen Denb **168** C1
Waen Aberwheeler **169** D1
Waen-fâch **156** B1
Waen-wen **167** E1
Wag **275** F6
Wainfleet All Saints **176** C2
Wainfleet Bank **176** C2
Wainfleet St. Mary **176** C2
Wainford **165** E2
Waingroves **173** F3
Wainhouse Corner **98** B1
Wainscott **137** G5

Wainstalls **193** G5
Waitby **200** C2
Wakefield **194** C5
Wakehurst Place WSuss
   RH17 6TN **122** C5
Wakerley **161** E3
Wakes Colne **151** G5
Walberswick **165** F4
Walberton **108** B3
Walbottle **212** A1
Walcot Lincs **175** F4
Walcot Lincs **175** G2
Walcot NLincs **196** A5
Walcot Shrop **156** C4
Walcot Tel&W **157** E1
Walcot Green **164** C3
Walcote Warks **146** D2
Walcote Leics **160** A4
Walcott **179** E2
Walcott Dales **175** G2
Walden **201** E3
Walden Head **201** E4
Walden Stubbs **186** A5
Walderslade **123** G2
Walderton **107** G1
Walditch **104** A3
Waldley **172** C4
Waldridge **153** D3
Waldringfield **153** D3
Waldron **110** A2
Wales **186** B4
Wales Millennium Centre,
   Cardiff Cardiff
   CF10 5AL **130** A5
Walesby Lincs **188** B3
Walesby Notts **187** D5
Waleswood **186** B4
Walford Here **156** C5
Walford Here **145** E5
Walford Shrop **170** B5
Walford Staffs **171** F4
Walford Heath **156** D1
Walgherton **171** D3
Walgrave **160** D5
Walhampton **106** C3
Walk Mill **193** E4
Walkden **184** B2
Walker **212** B1
Walker Art Gallery, Liverpool
   Mersey L3 8EL **42** D3
Walker Fold **192** C3
Walkerburn **227** E2
Walkeringham **187** E3
Walkerith **187** E3
Walkern **150** A5
Walker's Green **145** E3
Walkford **106** B3
Walkhampton **100** B1
Walkington Hill **194** C1
Walkington **196** B4
Walkwood **146** C1
Wall Corn **94** D3
Wall N'umb **211** F1
Wall Staffs **158** C1
Wall End **198** D4
Wall Heath **158** A4
Wall Houses **211** G1
Wall under Heywood **157** E3
Wallace Collection, London
   GtLon W1U 2BN **44** A2
Wallacehall **218** A4
Wallacetown **224** A5
Wallasey **183** D3
Wallaston Green **126** C2
Wallend **124** A1
Waller's Green **145** F4
Wallingford **134** A4
Wallington GtLon **122** B2
Wallington Hants **107** E2
Wallington Herts **150** A4
Wallingwells **186** C4
Wallis **140** D5
Wallisdown **105** G3
Walliswood **121** G4
Walls **279** B8
Wallsend **212** C1
Wallyford **236** A2
Walmer **125** F3
Walmer Bridge **192** A5
Walmersley **184** C1
Walmley **158** D3
Walmsgate **189** D5
Walpole **165** E5
Walpole Cross Keys **162** D1
Walpole Highway **162** D1
Walpole Marsh **162** C1
Walpole St. Andrew **162** D1
Walpole St. Peter **162** D1
Walrond's Park **116** A5
Walrow **116** A3
Walsall **158** C2
Walsall Arboretum
   Illuminations WMid
   WS1 2AB **14** D1
Walsall Wood **158** C2
Walsden **193** F5
Walsgrave on Sowe **159** F4
Walsham le Willows **164** B4
Walshford **194** D2
Walsoken **162** C1
Walston **235** E5
Walsworth **149** G4
Walter's Ash **134** D3
Walterston **129** G5
Walterstone **144** C5
Waltham Kent **124** D4
Waltham NELincs **188** C2
Waltham Abbey **136** C3
Waltham Chase **107** E1
Waltham Cross **136** C2
Waltham on the
   Wolds **174** C5
Waltham
   St. Lawrence **134** D5
Walthamstow **136** C4
Walton Bucks **134** D5
Walton Cumb **210** B1
Walton Derbys **173** E1
Walton Leics **160** A4
Walton Mersey **183** E3
Walton MK **149** D4

Walton Peter **161** G2
Walton Powys **144** B2
Walton Shrop **145** D1
Walton Som **116** B4
Walton Staffs **171** F4
Walton Suff **153** E4
Walton Tel&W **157** E1
Walton Warks **147** E2
Walton WYorks **186** A1
Walton WYorks **194** D3
Walton Cardiff **146** B4
Walton East **140** D5
Walton Elm **105** D1
Walton Hall Gardens Warr
   WA4 6SN **23** H4
Walton Highway **162** C1
Walton Lower Street **153** D4
Walton on the Hill **122** B3
Walton on the Naze **153** D5
Walton on the Wolds **160** A1
Walton Park D&G **216** C3
Walton Park NSom **130** D5
Walton West **126** A1
Walton-in-Gordano **130** D5
Walton-le-Dale **192** A5
Walton-on-Thames **121** G1
Walton-on-the-Hill **171** G5
Walton-on-Trent **159** E1
Walwen Flints **182** D5
Walwen Flints **182** D5
Walwick **220** B4
Walworth **202** B1
Walworth Gate **212** B5
Walwyn's Castle **126** B1
Wambrook **103** F2
Wanborough Surr **121** E3
Wanborough Swin **133** E4
Wandel **229** E4
Wandon **229** E4
Wandon End **149** G5
Wandsworth **136** B5
Wandylaw **229** F4
Wangford Suff **165** F4
Wangford Suff **163** F4
Wanlip **160** A1
Wanlockhead **225** G2
Wannock **110** A3
Wansbeck Riverside Park
   N'umb NE63 8TX **221** E3
Wansford ERid **196** C2
Wansford Peter **161** F3
Wanshurst Green **123** G4
Wanstrow **117** E3
Wanswell **131** F2
Wantage **133** F4
Wapley **131** G5
Wappenbury **147** F1
Wappenham **148** B3
Warbleton **110** B1
Warblington **107** G2
Warborough **134** A3
Warboys **162** B4
Warbreck **191** G3
Warbstow **98** C1
Warburton **184** A4
Warcop **200** C1
Ward End **158** D4
Ward Green **152** B1
Warden Kent **124** C1
Warden N'umb **211** F1
Warden Hill **146** B5
Warden Street **149** G3
Wardhouse **260** D1
Wardington **147** G3
Wardle ChesE **170** D2
Wardle GtMan **184** D1
Wardley GtMan **184** B2
Wardley Rut **160** D2
Wardley T&W **212** C1
Wardlow **185** F5
Wardsend **184** D4
Wardy Hill **162** C4
Ware Herts **136** C1
Ware Kent **125** E2
Wareham **105** F4
Warehorne **124** B5
Waren Mill **229** F3
Warenford **229** F4
Warenton **229** F3
Wareside **136** C1
Waresley Cambs **150** A2
Waresley Worcs **158** A5
Warfield **135** D5
Wargrave Mersey **183** G3
Wargrave W'ham **134** C5
Warham Here **145** D4
Warham Norf **178** A1
Wark N'umb **220** A4
Wark N'umb **228** C3
Warkleigh **113** G3
Warkton **161** D5
Warkworth N'hants **147** G3
Warkworth N'umb **221** E1
Warland **193** F5
Warleggan **97** F3
Warley Essex **137** E3
Warley WMid **158** C4
Warley Town **193** G5
Warlingham **122** C3
Warmfield **194** C5
Warmingham **171** E1
Warminghurst **108** D2
Warmington N'hants **161** F3
Warmington Warks **147** G3
Warminster **117** F3
Warmlake **124** A4
Warmley **131** F5
Warmley Hill **131** F5
Warmsworth **186** C2
Warmwell **105** D4
Warndon **146** A2
Warners End **135** F2
Warnford **120** B5
Warnham **121** G4
Warningcamp **108** C3
Warninglid **109** E1
Warren ChesE **184** C5
Warren Pembs **126** C3
Warren House **99** G2
Warren Row **134** C4
Warren Street **124** B3

Warrenby **213** E5
Warren's Green **150** A5
Warrington MK **149** D2
Warrington Warr **184** A4
Warroch **243** F4
Warsash **107** D2
Warslow **172** B2
Warsop Vale **173** G1
Warter **196** A2
Warthill **195** F2
Wartle **260** D4
Wartling **110** B3
Wartnaby **174** C5
Warton Lancs **199** G5
Warton Lancs **192** A5
Warton N'umb **220** C1
Warton Warks **159** E2
Warton Bank **192** A5
Warwick **147** E1
Warwick Bridge **210** A2
Warwick Castle Warks
   CV34 4QU **16** A6
Warwick Wold **122** C3
Warwick-on-Eden **210** A2
Wasbister **276** C4
Wasdale Head **198** C2
Wash **185** E4
Wash Common **119** F1
Washall Green **150** C4
Washaway **97** E3
Washbourne **101** D2
Washbrook **116** B3
Washfield **102** C1
Washfold **201** E3
Washford Som **114** D3
Washford Warks **146** C1
Washford Pyne **102** B1
Washingborough **188** A5
Washington T&W **212** C2
Washington WSuss **108** D2
Washmere Green **152** A3
Wasing **119** G1
Waskerley **211** G3
Wasperton **147** E2
Wasps Nest **175** F1
Wass **203** D5
Wat Tyler Country Park Essex
   SS16 4UH **137** G4
Watchet **115** D3
Watchfield Oxon **133** E3
Watchfield Som **116** A3
Watchgate **199** G3
Watcombe **101** F1
Watendlath **209** F5
Water Devon **102** A1
Water Eaton MK **149** D4
Water Eaton Oxon **134** A1
Water End Bed **149** G3
Water End CenBeds **149** F4
Water End ERid **195** F4
Water End Essex **151** D3
Water End Herts **136** B2
Water End Herts **135** F1
Water Newton **161** G3
Water Orton **159** D4
Water Stratford **148** B4
Water Yeat **199** D4
Waterbeach **150** C1
Waterbeck **218** A4
Watercombe **105** D4
Waterden **134** C3
Waterfall **172** B2
Waterfoot ERenf **233** G4
Waterfoot Lancs **193** E5
Waterford **136** C1
Watergate **97** F1
Waterhead Cumb **199** E2
Waterhead D&G **216** B2
Waterheath **165** F2
Waterhill of Bruxie **269** H6
Waterhouses Dur **212** A3
Waterhouses Staffs **172** B2
Wateringbury **123** F3
Waterlane **132** B2
Waterloo Aber **261** J1
Waterloo Derbys **173** F1
Waterloo GtMan **184** D2
Waterloo High **256** C2
Waterloo Mersey **183** E3
Waterloo NLan **234** C4
Waterloo Norf **178** D4
Waterloo P&K **243** F1
Waterloo Pembs **126** C2
Waterloo Poole **105** G3
Waterloo Cross **103** D1
Waterloo Port **167** D1
Waterlooville **107** F1
Watermead Country Park
   Leics LE7 4PF **17** C3
Watermeetings **226** A4
Watermillock **210** A5
Watermouth Castle Devon
   EX34 9SL **113** F1
Waterperry **134** B2
Waterperry Oxon
   OX33 1JZ **134** B2
Waterrow **115** D5
Waters Upton **157** F1
Watersfield **108** C2
Watershed Mill Visitor Centre,
   Settle NYorks
   BD24 9LR **193** E1
Watersheddings **184** D2
Waterside Aber **260** B3
Waterside Aber **261** J2
Waterside B'burn **192** D5
Waterside Bucks **135** E2
Waterside EAyr **225** D1
Waterside EAyr **233** F5
Waterside EDun **234** A2
Waterstock **134** B2
Waterston **126** C2
Waterthorpe **186** B4
Waterworld, Hanley ST1 5PU
   85 Stoke-on-Trent
Watford Herts **136** A3
Watford N'hants **148** B1
Watford Park **130** A4

Wath NYorks **202** C5
Wath NYorks **194** A1
Wath Brow **208** D5
Wath upon Dearne **186** B2
Watley's End **151** F4
Watlington Norf **163** E1
Watlington Oxon **134** B3
Watnall **173** G3
Watten **275** H3
Wattisfield **164** B4
Wattisham **152** B2
Watton Dorset **104** A3
Watton ERid **196** C2
Watton Norf **178** A5
Watton at Stone **136** C1
Watton Green **178** A5
Watton's Green **137** E3
Wattston **234** B3
Wattstown **129** G3
Wattsville **130** B3
Waughtonhill **269** H5
Waun Fawr **154** C4
Waun y Clyn **128** A3
Waunarlwydd **128** C3
Waunclunda **142** C3
Waunfawr **167** E2
Waun-Lwyd **130** A2
Wavendon **149** E4
Waverbridge **209** F2
Waverton ChesW&C **170** B1
Waverton Cumb **209** F2
Wavertree **183** E4
Wawne **196** C4
Waxham **179** F3
Waxholme **197** F5
Way Gill **193** F3
Way Village **102** B1
Way Wick **116** A1
Wayford **104** A2
Waytown **104** A3
Weachyburn **268** E5
Weacombe **115** D3
Weald **133** G2
Weald & Downland Open Air
   Museum WSuss
   PO18 0EU **108** A2
Weald Country Park Essex
   CM14 5QS **137** E3
Wealdstone **136** A4
Weardley **194** B3
Weare **116** B2
Weare Giffard **113** E3
Wearhead **211** E4
Wearne **116** B5
Weasenham
   All Saints **177** G5
Weasenham St. Peter **177** G5
Weathercote **200** C5
Weatheroak Hill **158** C5
Weaverham **184** A5
Weaverthorpe **204** C5
Webheath **146** C1
Webton **144** D4
Wedderlairs **261** G1
Weddington **159** F3
Wedhampton **118** B2
Wedmore **116** B3
Wednesbury **158** B3
Wednesfield **158** B3
Weedon **134** D1
Weedon Bec **148** B2
Weedon Lois **148** B3
Weeford **158** D2
Week Devon **102** A1
Week Devon **101** D1
Week Som **114** C4
Week Orchard **112** C5
Week St. Mary **98** C1
Weeke **119** F4
Weekley **161** D4
Weel **196** C4
Weeley **152** C5
Weeley Heath **152** C5
Weem **250** C4
Weeping Cross **171** G5
Weethley **146** C2
Weeting **163** F4
Weeton ERid **197** F5
Weeton Lancs **191** G4
Weeton NYorks **194** B3
Weetwood **194** B4
Weir Essex **138** B4
Weir Lancs **193** E5
Weir Quay **100** A1
Weirbrook **170** A5
Weisdale **279** C7
Welbeck Abbey **186** C5
Welborne **178** B5
Welbourn **175** E2
Welburn NYorks **195** G1
Welburn NYorks **203** F4
Welbury **202** C2
Welby **175** E4
Welches Dam **162** C4
Welcombe **112** C4
Weldon **161** E4
Welford N'hants **160** B4
Welford WBerks **133** G5
Welford-on-Avon **146** D2
Welham Leics **160** C3
Welham Notts **187** E4
Welham Green **136** B2
Well Hants **120** C3
Well Lincs **189** E5
Well NYorks **202** B5
Well End Bucks **135** D4
Well End Herts **136** B3
Well Hill **123** D2
Well Street **123** F3
Well Town **102** C2
Welland **145** G3
Wellbank **244** C1
Wellesbourne **147** E2
Wellhill **267** G5
Wellhouse WBerks **134** A5
Wellhouse WYorks **185** E1
Welling **137** D5
Wellingborough **149** D1
Wellingham **177** G5
Wellingore **175** E2
Wellington Cumb **198** B2
Wellington Here **145** D3

Wellington *Som* 115 E5
Wellington *Tel&W* 157 F1
Wellington Heath 145 B4
Wellow *B&NESom* 117 E2
Wellow *IoW* 106 C4
Wellow *Notts* 174 B1
Wells 116 C3
Wells Cathedral *Som*
  BA5 2UE 116 C3
Wells Green 158 D4
Wellsborough 159 F2
Wellstye Green 137 F1
Wellwood 235 E1
Welney 162 D3
Welsh Bicknor 131 E1
Welsh End 170 C4
Welsh Frankton 170 A4
Welsh Hook 140 C5
Welsh Mountain Zoo *Conwy*
  LL28 5UY 181 G5
Welsh Newton 131 D1
Welsh St. Donats 129 G5
Welshampton 170 B4
Welshpool
  (Y Trallwng) 156 B2
Welton *B&NESom* 117 D2
Welton *Cumb* 209 G2
Welton *ERid* 196 B5
Welton *Lincs* 188 A5
Welton *N'hants* 148 A1
Welton le Marsh 176 C1
Welton le Wold 188 C4
Welwick 197 F5
Welwyn 136 B1
Welwyn Garden City 136 B1
Wem 170 C5
Wembdon 115 F4
Wembley 136 A4
Wembley *GtLon*
  HA9 0WS 10 C3
Wembley Park 136 A4
Wembury 100 B3
Wemworthy 113 G4
Wemyss Bay 232 C3
Wenallt *Cere* 154 C5
Wenallt *Gwyn* 168 C3
Wendens Ambo 150 D4
Wendlebury 134 A1
Wendling 178 A4
Wendover 135 D2
Wendover Dean 135 D2
Wendron 95 D3
Wendy 150 B3
Wenfordbridge 97 E2
Wenhaston 165 F4
Wenlli 168 B3
Wennington *Cambs* 162 A5
Wennington *GtLon* 137 F4
Wennington *Lancs* 200 B5
Wensley *Derbys* 173 D1
Wensley *NYorks* 201 F4
Wensleydale Cheese Visitor
  Centre, Hawes *NYorks*
  DL8 3RN 201 D4
Wentbridge 186 B1
Wentnor 156 C3
Wentworth *Cambs* 162 C5
Wentworth *SYorks* 186 A3
Wenvoe 130 A5
Weobley 144 C2
Weobley Marsh 144 D2
Weoley Castle 158 C4
Wepham 108 C3
Wepre 169 F1
Wepre Country Park *Flints*
  CH5 4HL 169 F1
Wereham 163 E2
Wergs 158 A2
Wern *Gwyn* 167 E4
Wern *Powys* 156 B1
Wern *Powys* 130 A1
Wern *Shrop* 169 F4
Wernffrwd 128 B3
Wern-olau 128 B3
Wernrheolydd 130 C2
Wern-y-cwrt 130 C2
Werrington *Corn* 98 D2
Werrington *Peter* 161 G2
Werrington *Staffs* 171 G3
Wervil Grange 141 G2
Wervin 183 F5
Wesham 192 A4
Wessington 173 E2
West Aberthaw 114 D1
West Acre 163 F1
West Acton 136 A4
West Allerdean 237 G5
West Alvington 100 D3
West Amesbury 118 C3
West Anstey 114 B5
West Ashby 188 C5
West Ashford 113 F2
West Ashling 108 A3
West Ashton 117 F2
West Auckland 212 A5
West Ayton 204 C4
West Bagborough 115 E4
West Barkwith 188 B4
West Barnby 204 B1
West Barns 237 D2
West Barsham 178 A2
West Bay 104 A3
West Beckham 178 C2
West Benhar 234 C3
West Bergholt 152 A5
West Bexington 104 B4
West Bilney 163 F1
West Blatchington 109 E3
West Boldon 212 C1
West Bourton 117 E5
West Bowling 194 A4
West Brabourne 124 C4
West Bradford 192 D3
West Bradley 116 C4
West Bretton 185 G1
West Bromwich 158 C3
West Buckland
  Devon 113 G2
West Buckland *Som* 115 E5

West Burrafirth 279 B7
West Burton *NYorks* 201 F4
West Burton *WSuss* 108 B2
West Butsfield 211 G3
West Butterwick 187 F2
West Byfleet 121 F1
West Cairncake 269 G6
West Caister 179 G4
West Calder 235 E3
West Camel 116 C5
West Carbeth 233 G2
West Carr Houses 187 F2
West Cauldcoats 234 A5
West Chaldon 105 D4
West Challow 133 F4
West Charleton 101 D3
West Chevington 221 E2
West Chiltington 108 C2
West Chiltington
  Common 108 C2
West Chinnock 104 A1
West Chisenbury 118 C2
West Clandon 121 F2
West Cliffe 125 E4
West Clyne 267 F1
West Coker 104 B1
West Compton
  Dorset 104 B3
West Compton *Som* 116 C3
West Cowick 195 F5
West Cross 128 C4
West Crudwell 132 B3
West Curry 98 C1
West Curthwaite 209 G2
West Dean *Wilts* 119 D5
West Dean *WSuss* 108 A2
West Deeping 161 G2
West Derby 183 E3
West Dereham 163 E2
West Ditchburn 229 F5
West Down 113 F1
West Drayton *GtLon* 135 F5
West Drayton *Notts* 187 E5
West Dullater 242 A4
West Dunnet 275 H1
West Edington 221 D3
West Ella 196 C5
West End *Bed* 149 E2
West End *BrackF* 135 D5
West End *Caerp* 130 B3
West End *Cambs* 162 C3
West End *ERid* 196 C1
West End *Hants* 107 D1
West End *Herts* 136 B2
West End *Kent* 125 D3
West End *Lancs* 192 A1
West End *Lincs* 189 D3
West End *Norf* 179 F4
West End *Norf* 178 A5
West End *NSom* 116 B4
West End *NYorks* 194 A2
West End *Oxon* 133 G2
West End *Oxon* 134 A4
West End *Slan* 128 D5
West End *Suff* 165 F3
West End *Surr* 121 G1
West End *Surr* 121 E1
West End *Wilts* 118 A5
West End *Wilts* 118 A5
West End *Wilts* 118 A5
West End Green 120 B1
West Farleigh 123 G3
West Farndon 148 A2
West Felton 170 A5
West Firle 109 G3
West Fleetham 229 F4
West Flotmanby 205 D5
West Garforth 194 C4
West Ginge 133 G4
West Glen 232 A2
West Grafton 118 D1
West Green *GtLon* 136 C4
West Green *Hants* 120 C2
West Grimstead 118 D5
West Grinstead 121 G5
West Haddlesey 195 E5
West Haddon 160 B5
West Hagbourne 134 A4
West Hagley 158 B4
West Hall 210 B1
West Hallam 173 F3
West Halton 196 B5
West Ham 136 C4
West Handley 186 A5
West Hanney 133 G3
West Hanningfield 137 G3
West Hardwick 186 B1
West Harnham 118 C5
West Harptree 116 C2
West Harrow 136 A4
West Hatch *Som* 115 F5
West Hatch *Wilts* 118 A5
West Head 163 E2
West Heath *ChesE* 171 F1
West Heath *GtLon* 137 D5
West Heath *Hants* 121 D2
West Heath *Hants* 119 D2
West Heath *WMid* 158 C5
West Helmsdale 275 F7
West Hendon 136 B4
West Hendred 133 G4
West Heslerton 204 C5
West Hewish 116 A4
West Hill *Devon* 103 D3
West Hill *ERid* 197 D4
West Hill *NSom* 131 D5
West Hoathly 110 B3
West Holme 105 E4
West Horndon 137 F4
West Horrington 116 C3
West Horsley 121 F2
West Horton 229 E3
West Hougham 125 E5
West Howe 105 G3
West Howetown 114 C4
West Huntspill 116 A3
West Hyde 135 F3
West Hythe 124 D5
West Ilsley 133 G4
West Itchenor 107 G3
West Keal 176 B1

West Kennett 118 C1
West Kilbride 232 D5
West Kingsdown 123 E2
West Kington 132 A5
West Kington Wick 132 A5
West Kirby 182 D4
West Knapton 204 B5
West Knighton 104 D4
West Knoyle 117 F4
West Kyloe 229 E2
West Lambrook 104 A1
West Langdon 125 F4
West Langwell 266 D1
West Lavington
  Wilts 118 B2
West Lavington
  WSuss 121 D5
West Layton 202 A2
West Leake 173 G4
West Learmouth 228 C3
West Lees 203 D2
West Leigh *Devon* 113 G5
West Leigh *Devon* 101 D2
West Leigh *Som* 115 E4
West Leith 135 E1
West Lexham 163 G1
West Lilling 195 F1
West Linton 235 F4
West Lingo 244 C5
West Liss 120 C5
West Littleton 131 G5
West Lockinge 133 G4
West Looe 97 G4
West Lulworth 105 E4
West Lutton 196 B1
West Lydford 116 C4
West Lyn 114 A3
West Lyng 116 A5
West Lynn 163 E1
West Mains 229 E2
West Malling 123 F3
West Malvern 145 G3
West Marden 107 G1
West Markham 187 E5
West Marsh 188 C2
West Marton 193 E2
West Melbury 117 F5
West Melton 186 B2
West Meon 120 B5
West Meon Hut 120 B5
West Mersea 138 D5
West Midland Safari Park &
  Leisure Park *Worcs*
  DY12 1LF 158 A5
West Milton 104 A3
West Minster 124 B1
West Molesey 121 G1
West Monkton 115 F5
West Moors 105 G2
West Morden 105 F3
West Morriston 236 D5
West Morton 193 G3
West Muir 253 D2
West Ness 203 F5
West Newbiggin 202 C1
West Newton *ERid* 197 D4
West Newton *Norf* 177 E5
West Norwood 136 C5
West Ogwell 101 E1
West Orchard 105 E1
West Overton 118 C1
West Panson 98 D1
West Park *Aber* 261 F5
West Park *Mersey* 183 G3
West Parley 105 G3
West Peckham 123 F3
West Pelton 212 B2
West Pennard 116 C4
West Pentire 96 B3
West Perry 149 G1
West Porlock 114 B3
West Prawle 101 D4
West Preston 108 C3
West Pulham 104 D2
West Putford 113 E4
West Quantoxhead 115 E3
West Raddon 102 B2
West Rainton 212 C3
West Rasen 188 A4
West Raynham 177 G5
West Retford 187 D4
West Rounton 202 D2
West Row 163 E5
West Rudham 177 G5
West Runton 178 C1
West Saltoun 236 B3
West Sandford 102 B2
West Sandwick 278 D4
West Scrafton 201 F4
West Shepton 116 D3
West Shinness
  Lodge 273 H7
West Somerton 179 F4
West Stafford 104 D4
West Stockwith 187 E3
West Stoke 108 A3
West Stonesdale 201 D3
West Stoughton 116 B3
West Stour 117 E5
West Stourmouth 125 E2
West Stow 163 G5
West Stow Country Park *Suff*
  IP28 6HG 163 F5
West Stowell 118 C1
West Stratton 119 G3
West Street *Kent* 124 B3
West Street *Med* 137 G3
West Street *Suff* 164 A4
West Tanfield 202 B5
West Taphouse 97 F3
West Tarbert 231 G3
West Tarring 108 D3
West Thirston 221 D1
West Thorney 107 G3
West Thurrock 137 F5
West Tilbury 137 G5
West Tisted 120 B5
West Tofts *Norf* 163 G3

West Tofts *P&K* 243 G1
West Torrington 188 B4
West Town *B&NESom* 116 C1
West Town *Hants* 107 G3
West Town *NSom* 116 B1
West Town *Som* 116 C4
West Tytherley 119 D5
West Walton 162 C1
West Wellow 106 B1
West Wemyss 244 B5
West Wick 116 A1
West Wickham
  Cambs 151 E3
West Wickham *GtLon* 122 C2
West Williamston 126 D2
West Winch 163 E1
West Winterslow 118 D4
West Wittering 107 G3
West Witton 201 F4
West Woodburn 220 A3
West Woodhay 119 E1
West Woodlands 117 E3
West Worldham 120 C4
West Worlington 102 A1
West Worthing 108 D3
West Wratting 151 E3
West Wycombe 134 D3
West Yatton 132 A5
West Yell 278 D4
West Youlstone 112 C4
Westbere 125 D2
Westborough 174 D3
Westbourne *Bourne* 105 G3
Westbourne *WSuss* 107 G3
Westbourne Green 136 B4
Westbrook *Kent* 125 F1
Westbrook *WBerks* 133 G5
Westbrook *Wilts* 118 A1
Westbury *Bucks* 148 B4
Westbury *Shrop* 156 C2
Westbury *Wilts* 117 F2
Westbury Leigh 117 F2
Westbury on Trym 131 E5
Westbury-on-Severn 131 G1
Westbury-sub-Mendip 116 C3
Westby *Lancs* 191 G4
Westby *Lincs* 175 E5
Westcliff-on-Sea 138 B4
Westcombe 117 D4
Westcot 133 F4
Westcott *Bucks* 134 C1
Westcott *Devon* 102 D2
Westcott *Surr* 121 G3
Westcott Barton 147 G5
Westcourt 118 D1
Westcroft 148 D4
Westdean 110 A4
Westdowns 97 E1
Westend Town 131 G5
Wester Aberchalder 258 C2
Wester Badentyre 269 F5
Wester Balgedie 243 G4
Wester Culbeuchly 268 E4
Wester Dechmont 235 E2
Wester Fintray 261 G3
Wester Foffarty 252 C5
Wester Greenskares 269 F4
Wester Gruinards 266 C2
Wester Hailes 235 G3
Wester Lealty 266 D4
Wester Lonvine 266 E4
Wester Newburn 244 C4
Wester Ord 261 G4
Wester Quarff 279 D9
Wester Skeld 279 B8
Westerdale *Highld* 275 G3
Westerdale *NYorks* 203 F2
Westerfield *Shet* 279 C7
Westerfield *Suff* 152 C3
Westergate 108 B3
Westerham 122 D3
Westerhope 212 A1
Westerleigh 131 F5
Westerloch 275 J3
Westerton *Aber* 261 F5
Westerton *Angus* 253 E4
Westerton *Dur* 212 B4
Westerton *P&K* 243 D3
Westerwick 279 B8
Westfield *Cumb* 208 C4
Westfield *ESuss* 110 D2
Westfield *High* 275 F2
Westfield *NLan* 234 B2
Westfield *Norf* 178 A5
Westfield *WLoth* 234 C2
Westfield *WYorks* 194 B5
Westfield Sole 123 G2
Westgate *Dur* 211 F4
Westgate *N'umb* 220 D4
Westgate *NLincs* 187 E2
Westgate *Norf* 178 A1
Westgate Hill 194 B5
Westgate on Sea 125 F1
Westhall *Aber* 260 E2
Westhall *Suff* 165 F3
Westham *Dorset* 104 D5
Westham *ESuss* 110 B3
Westham *Som* 116 B3
Westhampnett 108 A3
Westhay *Devon* 103 G2
Westhay *Som* 116 B3
Westhead 183 F2
Westhide 145 E3
Westhill *Aber* 261 G4
Westhill *High* 266 E7
Westhope *Here* 145 D3
Westhope *Shrop* 157 D2
Westhorp 148 A2
Westhorpe *Lincs* 176 A4
Westhorpe *Notts* 174 B2
Westhorpe *Suff* 152 B1
Westhoughton 184 A2
Westhouse 200 B5
Westhouses 173 F2
Westhumble 121 G2
Westing 278 E2
Westlake 100 C3
Westlands 171 F3
Westlea 132 D4
Westleigh *Devon* 113 E3
Westleigh *Devon* 103 D1

Westleigh *GtMan* 184 A2
Westleton 153 F1
Westley *Shrop* 156 C2
Westley *Suff* 151 G1
Westley Heights 137 F4
Westley Waterless 151 E2
Westlington 134 C1
Westlinton 218 B5
Westloch 235 G4
Westmancote 146 B4
Westmarsh 125 E2
Westmeston 109 F2
Westmill 150 B5
Westminster 136 B5
Westminster Abbey *GtLon*
  SW1P 3PA 44 E6
Westminster Abbey - Chapter
  House & Pyx Chamber
  GtLon SW1P 3PA 44 E6
Westminster Cathedral
  GtLon SW1P 2QW 44 C7
Westmuir 252 B4
Westness 276 C4
Westnewton *Cumb* 209 E2
Westnewton *N'umb* 228 D3
Westoe 212 C1
Weston *B&NESom* 117 E1
Weston *ChesE* 171 E2
Weston *Devon* 103 E4
Weston *Devon* 103 E2
Weston *Dorset* 104 C5
Weston *Halton* 183 G4
Weston *Hants* 120 C5
Weston *Here* 144 C3
Weston *Herts* 150 A4
Weston *Lincs* 176 A4
Weston *Moray* 268 E4
Weston *N'hants* 148 A3
Weston *NYorks* 194 A3
Weston *Shrop* 170 C5
Weston *Shrop* 157 E3
Weston *Shrop* 156 C2
Weston *Soton* 107 D1
Weston *Staffs* 171 G5
Weston *WBerks* 133 G5
Weston Bampfylde 116 D5
Weston Beggard 145 E3
Weston by Welland 160 C3
Weston Colville 151 E2
Weston Corbett 120 B3
Weston Coyney 171 G3
Weston Favell 148 C1
Weston Green *Cambs* 151 E2
Weston Green *Norf* 178 C4
Weston Heath 157 G1
Weston Hills 176 A5
Weston in Arden 159 F4
Weston Jones 171 E5
Weston Longville 178 C4
Weston Lullingfields 170 B5
Weston Park *Staffs*
  TF11 8LE 158 A1
Weston Patrick 120 B3
Weston Point 183 F4
Weston Rhyn 169 F4
Weston Subedge 146 D3
Weston Town 117 E3
Weston Turville 135 D1
Weston under
  Penyard 145 F5
Weston under
  Wetherley 147 F1
Weston Underwood
  Derbys 173 D3
Weston Underwood
  MK 149 D2
Westoning 149 F4
Weston-in-Gordano 131 D5
Weston-on-Avon 147 D2
Weston-on-the-Green 134 A1
Weston-on-Trent 173 E5
Weston-super-Mare 116 A1
Weston-under-Lizard 158 A1
Westonzoyland 116 A4
Westow 195 G1
Westpoint Arena, Clyst St.
  Mary *Devon*
  EX5 1DJ 102 C3
Westport *A&B* 222 B3
Westport *Som* 116 A5
Westra 130 A5
Westray 276 C3
Westray Airfield 276 D2
Westridge Green 134 A5
Westrigg 234 D3
Westruther 236 D5
Westry 162 B3
Westside 261 G5
Westvale 183 F3
Westville 173 G3
Westward 209 F2
Westward Ho! 113 E3
Westwell *Kent* 124 B4
Westwell *Oxon* 133 E2
Westwell Leacon 124 B4
Westwick *Cambs* 150 C1
Westwick *Dur* 201 F1
Westwick *Norf* 179 D3
Westwick *NYorks* 194 C1
Westwood *Devon* 102 D3
Westwood *SLan* 234 A4
Westwood *Wilts* 117 F2
Westwood Heath 159 E5
Westwoodside 187 E3
Wetham Green 124 A3
Wetheral 210 A2
Wetherby 194 D3
Wetherden 152 B1
Wetherden Upper
  Town 152 B1
Wetheringsett 152 C1
Wethersfield 151 F4
Wethersta 279 C6
Wetherup Street 152 C1
Wetley Abbey 171 G3
Wetley Rocks 171 G3

Westleigh *GtMan* 184 A2
Wettenhall 170 D1
Wettenhall Green 170 D1
Wetton 172 C2
Wetwang 196 B2
Wetwood 171 E4
Wexcombe 119 D2
Wexham Street 135 F4
Weybourne *Norf* 178 C1
Weybourne *Surr* 121 D3
Weybread 164 D3
Weybread Street 165 D4
Weybridge 121 F1
Weycroft 103 G2
Weydale 275 G2
Weyhill 119 E3
Weymouth 104 C5
Weymouth Sea Life Adventure
  Park & Marine Sanctuary
  Dorset DT4 7SX 104 C4
Whaddon *Bucks* 148 D4
Whaddon *Cambs* 150 B3
Whaddon *Glos* 131 G1
Whaddon *Glos* 146 B5
Whaddon *Wilts* 118 C5
Whaddon *Wilts* 117 F1
Whaddon Gap 150 B3
Whale 210 B5
Whaley 186 C5
Whaley Bridge 185 E4
Whaley Thorns 186 C5
Whaligoe 275 J4
Whalley 192 D3
Whalsay 279 E6
Whalsay Airport 279 E6
Whalton 220 D3
Wham 193 D1
Whaplode 176 B5
Whaplode Drove 162 B1
Whaplode
  St. Catherine 162 B1
Wharfe 193 D1
Wharles 192 A4
Wharley End 149 E3
Wharncliffe Side 185 G3
Wharram le Street 196 A1
Wharram Percy 196 A1
Wharton
  ChesW&C 171 D1
Wharton *Here* 145 E2
Whashton 202 A2
Whatcote 147 F3
Whateley 159 E3
Whatfield 152 B3
Whatley 117 E3
Whatlington 110 C2
Whatsole Street 124 D4
Whatstandwell 173 E2
Whatton 174 C4
Whauphill 207 E2
Whaw 201 E3
Wheatacre 165 F2
Wheatcroft 173 E2
Wheatenhurst 131 G2
Wheathampstead 136 A1
Wheathill *Shrop* 157 E4
Wheathill *Som* 116 C4
Wheatley *Hants* 120 C4
Wheatley *Oxon* 134 B2
Wheatley *WYorks* 193 G5
Wheatley Hill 212 C4
Wheatley Lane 193 E4
Wheatley Park 186 C2
Wheaton Aston 158 A1
Wheddon Cross 114 C4
Wheedlemont 260 C2
Wheelerstreet 121 E3
Wheelock 171 E2
Wheelock Heath 171 E2
Wheelton 192 C5
Wheen 252 B2
Wheldale 195 D5
Wheldrake 195 F3
Whelford 133 D3
Whelley 183 G2
Whelpley Hill 135 F2
Whelpo 209 G3
Whelston 182 D5
Whenby 195 F1
Whepstead 151 G2
Wherstead 152 C3
Wherwell 119 E3
Wheston 185 F5
Whetley Cross 104 A2
Whetsted 123 F3
Whetstone *GtLon* 136 B3
Whetstone *Leics* 160 A3
Whicham 198 C4
Whichford 147 F4
Whickham 212 B1
Whiddon 113 E5
Whiddon Down 99 G1
Whifflet 234 B3
Whigstreet 252 C5
Whilton 148 B1
Whim 235 G5
Whimble 112 D5
Whimple 102 D3
Whimpwell Green 179 E3
Whin Lane End 191 G3
Whinburgh 178 B5
Whinny Hill 202 C1
Whinnyfold 261 J1
Whippingham 107 E3
Whipsnade 135 F1
Whipsnade Zoo *CenBeds*
  LU6 2LF 135 F1
Whipton 102 C3
Whirlow 186 A4
Whisby 175 E1
Whissendine 160 D1
Whissonsett 178 A3
Whisterfield 184 C5
Whistley Green 134 C5
Whiston *Mersey* 183 F3
Whiston *N'hants* 148 C1
Whiston *Staffs* 172 B3
Whiston *Staffs* 158 A1
Whiston *SYorks* 186 B3
Whiston Cross 157 G2

Whiston Eaves 172 B3
Whitacre Fields 159 E3
Whitacre Heath 159 E3
Whitbeck 198 C4
Whitbourne 145 G2
Whitburn *T&W* 212 D1
Whitburn *WLoth* 234 D3
Whitby *ChesW&C* 183 E5
Whitby *NYorks* 204 B1
Whitby Abbey *NYorks*
  YO22 4JT 204 C1
Whitby Lifeboat Museum
  NYorks YO21 3PU 204 B1
Whitbyheath 183 E5
Whitchurch
  B&NESom 116 D1
Whitchurch *Bucks* 148 D5
Whitchurch *Cardiff* 130 A4
Whitchurch *Devon* 99 E3
Whitchurch *Hants* 119 F3
Whitchurch *Here* 131 E1
Whitchurch *Pembs* 140 A5
Whitchurch *Shrop* 170 C3
Whitchurch *Warks* 147 E3
Whitchurch
  Canonicorum 103 G2
Whitchurch Hill 134 B5
Whitchurch-on-
  Thames 134 B5
Whitcombe 104 D4
Whitcott Keysett 156 B4
White Ball 103 D1
White Colne 151 G5
White Coppice 184 A1
White Cross *Corn* 96 C4
White Cross *Here* 145 D3
White Cross *Wilts* 117 E5
White Cube *GtLon*
  N1 6PB 12 C4
White End 146 A5
White Hill 117 F4
White Houses 187 E5
White Kirkley 211 G4
White Lackington 104 D3
White Ladies Aston 146 B2
White Lund 192 A1
White Mill 142 A5
White Moor 173 E3
White Notley 137 G1
White Ox Mead 117 E2
White Pit 189 D5
White Post Farm Centre,
  Farnsfield *Notts*
  NG22 8HL 174 B2
White Rocks 144 D5
White Roding 137 E1
White Waltham 134 D5
Whiteacen 267 K7
Whiteash Green 151 G4
Whitebirk 192 D5
Whitebog 269 H5
Whitebridge *High* 275 H1
Whitebridge (An Drochaid
  Bhàn) *High* 258 C3
Whitebrook 131 E2
Whiteburn 236 C5
Whitecairn 214 D5
Whitecairns 261 H3
Whitecastle 235 E5
Whitechapel 192 B3
Whitechurch 141 E4
Whitecote 194 B4
Whitecraig 236 A2
Whitecroft 131 F2
Whitecross *Corn* 94 C3
Whitecross *Corn* 97 D2
Whitecross *Dorset* 104 A3
Whitecross *Falk* 235 D2
Whiteface 266 E3
Whitefarland 223 D1
Whitefaulds 224 B5
Whiteley 107 E2
Whiteley Bank 107 E4
Whiteley Green 184 D5
Whiteley Village 121 F1
Whiteleys 214 B5
Whitemans Green 109 F1
Whitemire 267 G6
Whitemoor 97 D4
Whiteness 279 C8
Whiteoak Green 133 F1
Whiteparish 118 D5
Whiterashes 261 G2
Whiterow 275 J4
Whiteshill 132 A2
Whiteside *N'umb* 210 D1
Whiteside *WLoth* 235 D3
Whitesmith 110 A2
Whitestaunton 103 F1
Whitestone *A&B* 222 C2
Whitestone *Aber* 260 E5
Whitestone *Devon* 102 B3
Whitestreet Green 152 A4
Whitestripe 269 H5

Whiteway 132 B1
Whitewell Aber 269 H4
Whitewell Lancs 192 C3
Whitewell Wrex 170 B3
Whiteworks 99 G3
Whitewreath 267 K6
Whitfield Here 144 D4
Whitfield Kent 125 F4
Whitfield N'hants 148 B4
Whitfield N'umb 211 D2
Whitfield SGlos 131 F3
Whitford Devon 103 F3
Whitford (Chwitffordd) Flints 182 C5
Whitgift 196 A5
Whitgreave 171 F5
Whithorn 207 E2
Whiting Bay 223 F3
Whitkirk 194 C4
Whitlam 261 G2
Whitland (Hendy-Gwyn) 127 F1
Whitland Abbey 127 F1
Whitleigh 100 A1
Whitletts 224 B3
Whitley NYorks 195 E5
Whitley Read 120 C1
Whitley Wilts 117 F1
Whitley WMid 159 F5
Whitley Bay 221 F4
Whitley Chapel 211 F2
Whitley Heath 171 F5
Whitley Lower 185 G1
Whitley Row 123 D3
Whitlock's End 158 D5
Whitminster 131 G2
Whitmore Dorset 105 G2
Whitmore Staffs 171 F3
Whitnage 102 D1
Whitnash 147 F1
Whitnell 115 F3
Whitney-on-Wye 144 B3
Whitrigg Cumb 209 F1
Whitrigg Cumb 209 F3
Whitsbury 106 A1
Whitsome 237 F4
Whitson 130 C4
Whitstable 124 D2
Whitstone 98 C1
Whittingham 229 E5
Whittingslow 156 D4
Whittington Derbys 186 A5
Whittington Glos 146 C5
Whittington Lancs 200 B5
Whittington Norf 163 F3
Whittington Shrop 170 A4
Whittington Staffs 158 A4
Whittington Staffs 159 D2
Whittington Worcs 146 A2
Whittlebury 148 B3
Whittle-le-Woods 192 B5
Whittlesey 162 A3
Whittlesford 150 C3
Whittlestone Head 184 B1
Whitton GtLon 136 A5
Whitton N'umb 220 C1
Whitton NLincs 196 B5
Whitton Powys 144 B1
Whitton Shrop 157 E5
Whitton Stock 212 C5
Whitton Suff 152 C3
Whittonditch 133 E5
Whittonstall 211 G2
Whitway 119 F2
Whitwell Derbys 186 C5
Whitwell Herts 149 G5
Whitwell IoW 107 E5
Whitwell NYorks 202 B3
Whitwell Rut 161 E2
Whitwell Street 178 C3
Whitwell-on-the-Hill 195 G1
Whitwick 159 G1
Whitwood 194 D5
Whitworth 184 C1
Whitworth Art Gallery, Manchester GtMan M15 6ER 25 E4
Whixall 170 C4
Whixley 194 D2
Whorlton Dur 202 A1
Whorlton NYorks 203 D2
Whygate 219 F4
Whyle 145 E1
Whyteleafe 122 C3
Wibdon 131 E3
Wibsey 194 A4
Wibtoft 159 G4
Wichenford 145 G1
Wichling 124 B3
Wick Bourne 106 A3
Wick Devon 103 E2
Wick (Inbhir Ùige) High 275 J3
Wick SGlos 131 G5
Wick Som 115 F3
Wick Som 116 C4
Wick VGlam 129 F5
Wick Wilts 118 C5
Wick Worcs 146 B3
Wick WSuss 108 C3
Wick Airport 275 J3
Wick Hill Kent 124 A4
Wick Hill W'ham 120 C1
Wick St. Lawrence 116 A1
Wicken Cambs 163 D5
Wicken N'hants 148 C4
Wicken Bonhunt 150 C4
Wickenby 188 A4
Wicker Street Green 152 A3
Wickerslack 200 B1
Wickersley 186 B3
Wicketwood Hill 174 B3
Wickford 137 G3
Wickham Hants 107 E1
Wickham WBerks 133 F5
Wickham Bishops 138 B1
Wickham Heath 119 F1
Wickham Market 153 E2
Wickham St. Paul 151 G4
Wickham Skeith 152 B1
Wickham Street Suff 151 F2
Wickham Street Suff 152 B1
Wickhambreaux 125 E3
Wickhambrook 151 F2
Wickhamford 146 C3
Wickhampton 179 F5
Wicklewood 178 B5
Wickmere 178 C2
Wicksteed Park N'hants NN15 6NJ 161 D5
Wickstreet 110 A3
Wickwar 131 G4
Widcombe 117 E1
Widdington 150 D4
Widdop 193 F4
Widdrington 221 E2
Widdrington Station 221 E2
Wide Open 221 E4
Widecombe in the Moor 102 A5
Widegates 97 G4
Widemouth Bay 112 C5
Widewall 277 D8
Widford Essex 137 F2
Widford Herts 136 D1
Widford Oxon 133 E1
Widgham Green 151 E2
Widmer End 135 D3
Widmerpool 174 B5
Widnes 183 G4
Widworthy 103 F3
Wigan 183 G2
Wigan Pier GtMan WN3 4EU 183 G2
Wiganthorpe 203 F5
Wigborough 104 A1
Wiggaton 103 E3
Wiggenhall St. Germans 163 D1
Wiggenhall St. Mary Magdalen 163 D1
Wiggenhall St. Mary the Virgin 163 D1
Wiggenhall St. Peter 163 E1
Wiggens Green 151 E3
Wigginton Herts 135 E1
Wigginton Oxon 147 F4
Wigginton Shrop 170 A4
Wigginton Staffs 159 E2
Wigginton York 195 F2
Wigglesworth 193 E2
Wiggonby 209 G1
Wiggonholt 108 C2
Wighill 195 D3
Wighton 178 A2
Wightwizzle 185 G3
Wigley 106 C1
Wigmore Here 144 D1
Wigmore Med 124 A2
Wigsley 187 F5
Wigsthorpe 161 F4
Wigston 160 B3
Wigston Parva 159 G4
Wigthorpe 186 C4
Wigtoft 176 A4
Wigton 209 F2
Wigtown 215 F5
Wike 194 C3
Wilbarston 160 D4
Wilberfoss 195 G2
Wilburton 162 C5
Wilby N'hants 149 D1
Wilby Norf 164 B2
Wilby Suff 164 D4
Wilcot 118 C1
Wilcott 156 C1
Wilcrick 130 D4
Wilday Green 186 A5
Wildboarclough 171 G1
Wilde Street 163 F5
Wilden Bed 149 F2
Wilden Worcs 158 A5
Wildhern 119 E2
Wildhill 136 B2
Wildmoor 158 B5
Wildsworth 187 F3
Wilford 173 G4
Wilkesley 170 D3
Wilkhaven 267 G3
Wilkieston 235 F3
Wilksby 176 A1
Willand Devon 102 D1
Willand Som 103 E1
Willaston ChesE 171 D2
Willaston ChesW&C 183 E5
Willaston Shrop 170 C4
Willen 149 D3
Willen Lakeside Park MK MK15 9HQ 9 D2
Willenhall WMid 158 B3
Willenhall WMid 159 F5
Willerby ERid 196 C5
Willerby NYorks 204 D5
Willersey 146 D4
Willersley 144 C3
Willesborough 124 C4
Willesborough Lees 124 C4
Willesden 136 B4
Willesleigh 113 F2
Willesley 132 A4
Willett 115 E4
Willey Shrop 157 F3
Willey Warks 159 G4
Willey Green 121 E2
William's Green 152 A3
Williamscot 147 G3
Williamson Park, Lancaster Lancs LA1 1UX 192 A1
Williamthorpe 173 F1
Willian 150 A4
Willimontswick 211 D1
Willingale 137 E2
Willingdon 110 A3
Willingham 162 C5
Willingham by Stow 187 F4
Willingham Green 151 E2
Willington Bed 149 G2
Willington Derbys 173 D5
Willington Dur 212 A4
Willington Kent 123 G3
Willington T&W 212 C1
Willington Warks 147 E4
Willington Corner 170 C1
Willisham 152 B2
Willitoft 195 G4
Williton 115 D3
Willoughbridge 171 E3
Willoughby Lincs 189 E5
Willoughby Warks 148 A1
Willoughby Waterleys 160 A3
Willoughby-on-the-Wolds 174 B5
Willoughton 187 G3
Willow Green 184 A5
Willows Farm Village Herts AL2 1BB 136 A2
Willows Green 137 G1
Willsbridge 131 F5
Willslock 172 B4
Willsworthy 99 F2
Willtown 116 A5
Wilmcote 147 D2
Wilmington B&NESom 117 D1
Wilmington Devon 103 F2
Wilmington ESuss 110 A3
Wilmington Kent 137 E5
Wilmslow 184 C4
Wilnecote 159 E2
Wilney Green 164 B3
Wilpshire 192 C4
Wilsden 193 G4
Wilsford Lincs 175 F3
Wilsford Wilts 118 C4
Wilsford Wilts 118 C2
Wilsham 114 A3
Wilshaw 185 F2
Wilsill 194 A1
Wilsley Green 123 G5
Wilsley Pound 123 G5
Wilson 173 F5
Wilstead 149 F3
Wilsthorpe ERid 197 D1
Wilsthorpe Lincs 161 F1
Wilstone 135 E1
Wilton Cumb 208 D5
Wilton Here 145 E5
Wilton NYorks 204 B4
Wilton R&C 203 E1
Wilton ScBord 227 F4
Wilton Wilts 119 D1
Wilton Wilts 118 B4
Wilton House Wilts SP2 0BJ 118 B4
Wiltown 103 E1
Wimbish 151 D4
Wimbish Green 151 E4
Wimblebury 158 C1
Wimbledon 136 B5
Wimbledon All England Lawn Tennis & Croquet Club GtLon SW19 5AG 11 E7
Wimblington 162 C3
Wimborne Minster 105 G2
Wimborne Minster Dorset BH21 1HT 3 B2
Wimborne St. Giles 105 G1
Wimbotsham 163 E2
Wimpole 150 B2
Wimpole Home Farm Cambs SG8 0BW 150 B3
Wimpole Lodge 150 B3
Wimpstone 147 E3
Wincanton 117 E5
Winceby 176 B1
Wincham 184 A5
Winchburgh 235 E2
Winchcombe 146 C5
Winchelsea 111 E2
Winchelsea Beach 111 E2
Winchester 119 F5
Winchester Cathedral Hants SO23 9LS 89 Winchester
Winchet Hill 123 G4
Winchfield 120 C2
Winchmore Hill Bucks 135 E3
Winchmore Hill GtLon 136 C3
Wincle 171 G1
Wincobank 186 A3
Windermere 199 F3
Windermere Lake Cruises Cumb LA12 8AS 199 E3
Winderton 147 F3
Windhill 266 C7
Windle Hill 183 E5
Windlehurst 185 D4
Windlesham 121 E1
Windley 173 E3
Windmill 185 F5
Windmill Hill ESuss 110 B2
Windmill Hill Som 103 G1
Windmill Hill Worcs 146 B3
Windrush 133 D1
Windsor 135 E5
Windsor Castle W&M SL4 1NJ 89 Windsor
Windsor Green 151 G2
Windy Nook 212 B1
Windygates 244 B4
Windy-Yett 233 F4
Wineham 109 E1
Winestead 197 E5
Winewall 193 F4
Winfarthing 164 C3
Winford IoW 107 E4
Winford NSom 116 C1
Winforton 144 B3
Winfrith Newburgh 105 E4
Wing Bucks 149 D5
Wing Rut 161 D2
Wingate 212 C4
Wingates GtMan 184 A2
Wingates N'umb 220 C2
Wingerworth 173 E1
Wingfield CenBeds 149 F5
Wingfield Suff 164 D4
Wingfield Wilts 117 F2
Wingfield Green 164 D4
Wingham 125 E3
Wingham Well 125 E3
Wingmore 125 D4
Wingrave 135 D1
Winkburn 174 C2
Winkfield 135 E5
Winkfield Row 135 D5
Winkhill 172 B2
Winkleigh 113 G5
Winksley 202 B5
Winkton 106 A3
Winlaton 212 A1
Winlaton Mill 212 A1
Winless 275 J3
Winmarleigh 192 A3
Winnard's Perch 96 D3
Winnersh 134 C5
Winnington 184 A5
Winscombe 116 B2
Winsford ChesW&C 171 D1
Winsford Som 114 C4
Winsham Devon 113 E2
Winsham Som 103 G2
Winshill 173 D5
Winsh-wen 128 C3
Winskill 210 B4
Winslade 120 B3
Winsley 117 F1
Winslow 148 C5
Winson 132 C2
Winsor 106 C1
Winster Cumb 199 F3
Winster Derbys 172 D1
Winston Dur 202 A1
Winston Suff 152 C1
Winston Green 152 C1
Winstone 132 B2
Winswell 113 E4
Winter Gardens FY1 1HW 64 Blackpool
Winter Gardens NSom BS23 1AJ 88 Weston-super-Mare
Winterborne Came 104 D4
Winterborne Clenston 105 E2
Winterborne Herringston 104 C4
Winterborne Houghton 105 E2
Winterborne Kingston 105 E3
Winterborne Monkton 104 C4
Winterborne Stickland 105 E2
Winterborne Whitechurch 105 E2
Winterborne Zelston 105 E3
Winterbourne SGlos 131 F4
Winterbourne WBerks 133 G5
Winterbourne Abbas 104 C3
Winterbourne Bassett 132 D5
Winterbourne Dauntsey 118 C4
Winterbourne Earls 118 C4
Winterbourne Gunner 118 C4
Winterbourne Monkton 132 D5
Winterbourne Steepleton 104 C4
Winterbourne Stoke 118 B3
Winterbrook 134 B4
Winterburn 193 F2
Wintercleugh 226 A4
Winteringham 196 B5
Winterley 171 E2
Wintersett 186 A1
Wintershill 107 E1
Winterslow 118 D4
Winterton 187 G1
Winterton-on-Sea 179 F4
Winthorpe Lincs 177 D1
Winthorpe Notts 174 D2
Winton Bourne 105 G3
Winton Cumb 200 C1
Wintringham 204 B5
Winwick Cambs 161 G4
Winwick N'hants 160 B5
Winwick Warr 184 A3
Wirksworth 173 D2
Wirksworth Moor 173 E2
Wirral Country Park Mersey CH61 0HN 182 D4
Wirswall 170 C3
Wisbech 162 C2
Wisbech St. Mary 162 C2
Wisborough Green 121 F5
Wiseton 187 E4
Wishaw NLan 234 B4
Wishaw Warks 159 D3
Wisley 121 F2
Wispington 188 C5
Wissett 165 E4
Wissington 152 A4
Wistanstow 156 D4
Wistanswick 171 D5
Wistaston 171 D2
Wiston Pembs 126 D1
Wiston SLan 226 A2
Wiston WSuss 108 D2
Wistow Cambs 162 A4
Wistow NYorks 195 E4
Wiswell 192 D4
Witcham 162 C5
Witchampton 105 F2
Witchburn 222 C3
Witchford 162 D5
Witcombe 116 B5
Witham 138 B1
Witham Friary 117 E3
Witham on the Hill 161 F1
Withcall 188 C4
Withcote 160 C2
Withdean 109 F3
Witherenden Hill 110 B1
Witherhurst 110 B1
Witheridge 102 B1
Witherley 159 F3
Withern 189 E4
Withernsea 197 F5
Withernwick 197 D3
Withersdale Street 165 D3
Withersfield 151 E3
Witherslack 199 F4
Witherslack Hall 199 F4
Withiel 97 D3
Withiel Florey 114 C4
Withielgoose 97 E3
Withington Glos 132 C1
Withington GtMan 184 C3
Withington Here 145 E3
Withington Shrop 157 E1
Withington Staffs 172 B4
Withington Green 184 C5
Withington Marsh 145 E3
Withleigh 102 C1
Withnell 192 C5
Withnell Fold 192 C5
Withybrook Som 117 D3
Withybrook Warks 159 G4
Withycombe 114 D3
Withycombe Raleigh 102 D4
Withyham 123 D5
Withypool 114 B4
Witley 121 E4
Witnesham 152 C2
Witney 133 F2
Wittering 161 F2
Wittersham 111 D1
Witton Angus 253 D2
Witton Norf 179 E5
Witton Worcs 146 A1
Witton Bridge 179 E2
Witton Gilbert 212 B3
Witton Park 212 A4
Witton-le-Wear 212 A4
Wiveliscombe 115 D5
Wivelsfield 109 F1
Wivelsfield Green 109 F2
Wivenhoe 152 B5
Wiveton 178 B1
Wix 152 C5
Wixford 146 C2
Wixhill 170 C5
Wixoe 151 F3
Woburn 149 E4
Woburn Safari Park CenBeds MK17 9QN 9 F3
Woburn Sands 149 E4
Wokefield Park 120 B1
Woking 121 F2
Wokingham 120 D1
Wolborough 102 B5
Wold Newton ERid 204 D5
Wold Newton NELincs 188 C3
Woldingham 122 C3
Wolds Village, Bainton ERid YO25 9EF 196 B2
Wolfelee 227 G5
Wolferlow 145 F1
Wolferton 177 E5
Wolfhampcote 148 A1
Wolfhill 243 G1
Wolfpits 144 B2
Wolf's Castle 140 C5
Wolfsdale 140 C5
Woll 227 F3
Wollaston N'hants 149 E1
Wollaston Shrop 156 C1
Wollaston WMid 158 A4
Wollaton 173 G4
Wollerton 170 D5
Wollescote 158 B4
Wolsingham 211 G4
Wolston 159 G5
Wolsty 209 E1
Wolvercote 134 A2
Wolverhampton 158 B3
Wolverhampton Art Gallery WMid WV1 1DU 14 A1
Wolverley Shrop 170 B4
Wolverley Worcs 158 A5
Wolvers Hill 116 A1
Wolverton Hants 119 G2
Wolverton MK 148 D3
Wolverton Warks 147 E1
Wolverton Wilts 117 E4
Wolverton Common 119 G2
Wolvesnewton 131 D3
Wolvey 159 G4
Wolvey Heath 159 G4
Wolviston 213 D5
Womaston 144 B1
Wombleton 203 F4
Wombourne 158 A3
Wombwell 186 A2
Womenswold 125 E3
Womersley 186 C1
Wonastow 131 D1
Wonersh 121 F3
Wonford 102 C3
Wonson 99 G2
Wonston 119 F4
Wooburn 135 E4
Wooburn Green 135 E4
Wood Bevington 146 C2
Wood Burcote 148 B3
Wood Dalling 178 B3
Wood Eaton 158 A1
Wood End Bed 149 F3
Wood End Bed 149 F1
Wood End Bucks 148 C4
Wood End Herts 150 B5
Wood End Warks 159 E3
Wood End Warks 158 D5
Wood End Warks 159 E4
Wood End WMid 158 B2
Wood Enderby 176 A1
Wood Green GtLon 136 C3
Wood Green Norf 164 D2
Wood Green Animal Shelter, Godmanchester Cambs PE29 2NH 150 A1
Wood Lane 170 B4
Wood Norton 178 B3
Wood Seats 186 A3
Wood Stanway 146 C4
Wood Street 179 E3
Wood Street Village 121 E2
Woodacott 113 D5
Woodale 201 F5
Woodall 186 B4
Woodbastwick 179 E4
Woodbeck 187 E5
Woodborough Notts 174 B3
Woodborough Wilts 118 C2
Woodbridge Devon 103 E3
Woodbridge Dorset 104 D1
Woodbridge Suff 153 D3
Woodbury Devon 102 D4
Woodbury Som 116 C3
Woodbury Salterton 102 D4
Woodchester 132 A2
Woodchurch Kent 124 B5
Woodchurch Mersey 183 D4
Woodcombe 114 C3
Woodcote Oxon 134 B4
Woodcote Tel&W 157 G1
Woodcote Green 158 B5
Woodcott 119 F2
Woodcroft 131 E3
Woodcutts 105 F1
Woodditton 151 E2
Woodeaton 134 A1
Woodend Aber 260 E3
Woodend Cumb 198 C3
Woodend High 258 E2
Woodend High 247 G3
Woodend N'hants 148 B3
Woodend P&K 250 C5
Woodend WSuss 108 A3
Woodend Green 151 D5
Woodfalls 118 C5
Woodfield Oxon 148 A5
Woodfield SAyr 224 B3
Woodfoot 200 B1
Woodford Corn 112 C4
Woodford Devon 101 D2
Woodford Glos 131 F3
Woodford GtLon 136 D3
Woodford GtMan 184 C4
Woodford N'hants 161 E5
Woodford Som 115 D4
Woodford Bridge 136 D3
Woodford Green 136 D3
Woodford Halse 148 A2
Woodgate Devon 103 E1
Woodgate Norf 178 B4
Woodgate WMid 158 B4
Woodgate Worcs 146 B1
Woodgate WSuss 108 B3
Woodgreen 106 A1
Woodhall Invcly 233 E2
Woodhall NYorks 201 E3
Woodhall Hills 194 A4
Woodhall Spa 175 G1
Woodham Bucks 134 B1
Woodham Dur 212 B5
Woodham Surr 121 F1
Woodham Ferrers 137 G3
Woodham Mortimer 138 B2
Woodham Walter 138 B2
Woodhaven 244 C2
Woodhead Aber 261 F1
Woodhead Staffs 172 B3
Woodhey 183 E4
Woodhey Green 170 C2
Woodhill Shrop 157 G4
Woodhill Som 116 A5
Woodhorn 221 E3
Woodhouse Cumb 199 G4
Woodhouse Leics 160 A1
Woodhouse SYorks 186 B4
Woodhouse WYorks 194 B4
Woodhouse WYorks 194 C5
Woodhouse WYorks 194 A5
Woodhouse Down 131 F4
Woodhouse Eaves 160 A1
Woodhouse Green 171 G1
Woodhouses GtMan 184 C2
Woodhouses Staffs 159 D1
Woodhouses Staffs 158 C2
Woodhuish 101 F2
Woodhurst 162 B5
Woodingdean 109 F3
Woodington 119 E5
Woodland Devon 101 D1
Woodland Dur 211 G5
Woodland Kent 124 D4
Woodland Head 102 A3
Woodlands Dorset 105 G2
Woodlands Hants 106 C1
Woodlands NYorks 194 C2
Woodlands Shrop 157 G4
Woodlands Som 115 E3
Woodlands Leisure Park, Dartmouth Devon TQ9 7DQ 101 E2
Woodlands Park 135 D5
Woodlands St. Mary 133 F5
Woodlane 172 C5
Woodleigh 100 D3
Woodlesford 194 C5
Woodley GtMan 184 D3
Woodley W'ham 134 C5
Woodmancote Glos 132 C2
Woodmancote Glos 146 B5
Woodmancote Glos 131 G3
Woodmancote WSuss 109 E2
Woodmancote WSuss 107 G2
Woodmancott 119 G3
Woodmansey 196 C4
Woodmansterne 122 B3
Woodmanton 102 D4
Woodmill 172 C5
Woodminton 118 B5
Woodmoor 156 B2
Woodnesborough 125 F3
Woodnewton 161 F3
Woodperry 134 A1
Woodplumpton 192 B4
Woodrising 178 A5
Woodrow 105 D1
Wood's Corner 110 B2
Woods Eaves 144 B3
Wood's Green 123 F5
Woodseaves Shrop 171 D4
Woodseaves Staffs 171 E5
Woodsend 133 E5
Woodsetts 186 C4
Woodsford 105 D3
Woodside Aberdeen 261 H4
Woodside BrackF 135 E5
Woodside CenBeds 135 F1
Woodside Cumb 208 D3
Woodside D&G 217 E3
Woodside Fife 244 C4
Woodside Fife 244 A4
Woodside GtLon 122 C2
Woodside Hants 106 C3
Woodside Herts 136 B2
Woodside NAyr 233 E4
Woodside P&K 243 G1
Woodside Shrop 156 C4
Woodside WMid 158 B4
Woodside Animal Farm & Leisure Park CenBeds LU1 4DG 135 F1
Woodside Green 124 B3
Woodstock Oxon 133 G1
Woodstock Pembs 140 D5
Woodthorpe Derbys 186 B5
Woodthorpe Leics 160 A1
Woodthorpe Lincs 189 E4
Woodthorpe SYorks 186 A4
Woodthorpe York 195 E3
Woodton 165 D2
Woodtown 113 E3
Woodvale 183 E1
Woodville 159 F1
Woodwall Green 171 E4
Woodwalton 162 A4
Woodwick 276 C5
Woodworth Green 170 C2
Woodyates 105 G1
Woofferton 145 E1
Wookey 116 C3
Wookey Hole 116 C3
Wookey Hole Caves & Papermill Som BA5 1BB 116 C3
Wool 105 E4
Woolacombe 113 E1
Woolage Green 125 E4
Woolage Village 125 E3
Woolaston 131 E2
Woolaston Slade 131 E2
Woolavington 116 A3
Woolbeding 121 D5
Woolcotts 114 C4
Wooldale 185 F2
Wooler 229 D4
Woolfardisworthy Devon 102 B2
Woolfardisworthy Devon 112 D3
Woolfold 184 B1
Woolfords Cottages 235 E4
Woolgarston 105 F4
Woolgreaves 186 A1
Woolhampton 119 G1
Woolhope 145 F4
Woolland 105 D2
Woollard 116 D1
Woollaton 113 E4
Woollensbrook 136 C2
Woolley B&NESom 117 E1
Woolley Cambs 161 G5
Woolley Corn 112 C4
Woolley Derbys 173 E1
Woolley WYorks 186 A1
Woolley Green W&M 135 D5
Woolley Green Wilts 117 F1
Woolmer Green 136 B1
Woolmere Green 146 B1
Woolmersdon 115 F4
Woolpit 152 A1
Woolpit Green 152 A1
Woolscott 147 G1
Woolsgrove 102 A2
Woolstaston 157 D3
Woolsthorpe 174 D4
Woolsthorpe by Colsterworth 175 E5
Woolston Devon 100 D3
Woolston Shrop 170 A5
Woolston Shrop 156 D4
Woolston Soton 106 D1
Woolston Warr 184 A4
Woolston Green 101 D1
Woolstone Glos 146 B4
Woolstone MK 149 D4
Woolstone Oxon 133 E4
Woolton 183 F4
Woolton Hill 119 F1
Woolverstone 152 C4
Woolverton 117 E2
Woolwich 136 D5
Woonton 144 C2
Wooperton 229 E5
Woore 171 E3
Wootten Green 164 D4
Wootton Bed 149 F3
Wootton Hants 106 B3
Wootton IoW 107 E3
Wootton Kent 125 E4
Wootton N'hants 148 C2
Wootton NLincs 188 A1
Wootton Oxon 133 G1
Wootton Oxon 133 G2
Wootton Shrop 157 D5
Wootton Shrop 170 A5
Wootton Staffs 171 F5
Wootton Staffs 172 C3
Wootton Bassett 132 C4
Wootton Bridge 107 E3
Wootton Common 107 E3
Wootton Courtenay 114 C3
Wootton Fitzpaine 103 G3
Wootton Green 149 F3
Wootton Rivers 118 C1
Wootton St. Lawrence 119 G2
Wootton Wawen 147 D1
Worcester 146 A2
Worcester Cathedral Worcs WR1 2LH 90 Worcester
Worcester Park 122 B2
Worcester Woods Country Park Worcs WR5 2LG 146 A2
Wordsley 158 A4
Wordwell 163 G5
Worfield 157 G3
Worgret 105 F4
Work 277 D6
Workhouse End 149 G2
Workington 208 D4
Worksop 186 C5
Worlaby Lincs 188 D5
Worlaby NLincs 188 A1
World Museum Liverpool Mersey L3 8EN 42 D3
World of Beatrix Potter Attraction Cumb LA23 3BX 199 F3

World of James Herriot, Thirsk
  NYorks YO7 1PL **202** D4
World's End *Bucks* **135** D2
Worlds End *Hants* **107** F1
World's End *WBerks* **133** G5
Worlds End *WMid* **158** D4
Worle **116** A1
Worleston **171** D2
Worlingham **165** F3
Worlington **163** E5
Worlingworth **152** D1
Wormald Green **194** C1
Wormbridge **144** D4
Wormegay **163** E1
Wormelow Tump **145** D4
Wormhill **185** F5
Wormingford **152** A4
Worminghall **134** B2
Wormington **146** C4
Worminster **116** C3
Wormiston **245** E4
Wormit **244** B2
Wormleighton **147** G2
Wormley *Herts* **136** C2
Wormley *Surr* **121** E4
Wormley West End **136** C2
Wormshill **124** A3
Wormsley **144** D3
Worplesdon **121** E2
Worrall **186** A3
Worsbrough **186** A2
Worsley **184** B2
Worstead **179** E3
Worsted Lodge **150** D2
Worsthorne **193** E4
Worston **193** D3
Worswell **100** B3
Worth *Kent* **125** F3
Worth *WSuss* **122** B5
Worth Matravers **105** F5
Wortham **164** B4
Worthen **156** C2
Worthenbury **170** B3
Worthing *Norf* **178** A4
Worthing *WSuss* **108** D3
Worthington **173** F5
Worting **120** B2
Wortley *Glos* **131** G3
Wortley *SYorks* **186** A3
Wortley *WYorks* **194** B4
Worton *NYorks* **201** E4
Worton *Wilts* **118** A2
Wortwell **165** D3
Wothersome **194** D3
Wotherton **156** B2
Wotter **100** B1
Wotton **121** G3
Wotton Underwood **134** B1
Wotton-under-
  Edge **131** G3
Woughton on the
  Green **149** D4
Wouldham **123** G2
Wrabness **152** C4
Wrae **269** F5
Wrafton **113** E2
Wragby **188** B5
Wragholme **189** D3
Wramplingham **178** C5
Wrangaton **100** C2
Wrangham **260** E1
Wrangle **176** C2
Wrangle Lowgate **176** C2
Wrangway **103** E1
Wrantage **116** A5
Wrawby **188** A2
Wraxall *NSom* **131** D5
Wraxall *Som* **116** D4
Wray **192** C1
Wray Castle **199** E2
Wrays **122** B4
Wraysbury **135** F5
Wrayton **200** B5
Wrea Green **191** G4
Wreay *Cumb* **210** A5
Wreay *Cumb* **210** A3
Wrecclesham **120** D3
Wrekenton **212** B2
Wrelton **203** G4
Wrenbury **170** C3
Wrench Green **204** C4
Wreningham **164** C2
Wrentham **165** F3
Wrenthorpe **194** C5
Wrentnall **156** D2
Wressle *ERid* **195** G4
Wressle *NLincs* **187** G2
Wrestlingworth **150** A3
Wretham **164** A2
Wretton **163** E2
Wrexham (Wrecsam) **170** A3
Wrexham Arts Centre *Wrex*
  LL11 1AU **170** A2
Wrexham Industrial
  Estate **170** A3
Wribbenhall **157** G5
Wrightington Bar **183** G1
Wrightpark **242** B5
Wright's Green **137** E1
Wrinehill **171** E3
Wrington **116** B1
Writhlington **117** D2
Writtle **137** F2
Wrockwardine **157** F1
Wroot **187** E2
Wrose **194** A4
Wrotham **123** F3
Wrotham Heath **123** F3
Wrotham Hill Park **123** F2
Wrottesley **158** A2
Wroughton **132** D4
Wroxall *IoW* **107** E5
Wroxall *Warks* **159** E5
Wroxeter **157** E2
Wroxham **179** E4
Wroxham Barns *Norf*
  NR12 8QU **179** E3
Wroxton **147** G3
Wstrws **141** G3
Wyaston **172** C3
Wyberton **176** B3
Wyboston **149** G2

Wybunbury **171** D3
Wych Cross **122** D5
Wychbold **146** B1
Wychnor **159** D1
Wychnor Bridges **159** D1
Wyck **120** C4
Wyck Rissington **147** D5
Wycliffe **202** A1
Wycoller **193** F4
Wycoller Country Park
  Lancs BB8 8SY **193** F4
Wycomb **174** C5
Wycombe Marsh **135** D3
Wyddial **150** B4
Wye **124** C4
Wyesham **131** E1
Wyfordby **160** C1
Wyke *Devon* **102** B3
Wyke *Dorset* **117** E5
Wyke *Shrop* **157** F2
Wyke *Surr* **121** E2
Wyke *WYorks* **194** A5
Wyke Champflower **117** D4
Wyke Regis **104** C5
Wykeham *NYorks* **204** C4
Wykeham *NYorks* **204** B5
Wyken *Shrop* **157** G3
Wyken *WMid* **159** F4
Wykey **170** A5
Wylam **212** A1
Wylde Green **158** D3
Wyllie **130** A3
Wylye **118** B4
Wymering **107** F2
Wymeswold **174** B5
Wymington **149** E1
Wymondham *Leics* **161** D1
Wymondham *Norf* **178** C5
Wyndham **129** F3
Wynford Eagle **104** B3
Wynnstay Park **170** A3
Wynyard **212** B2
Wynyard Woodland Park
  Stock TS21 3JG **212** C5
Wyre Forest *Worcs*
  DY14 9XQ **157** G5
Wyre Piddle **146** B3
Wyresdale Tower **192** C2
Wysall **174** B5
Wyson **145** E1
Wythall **158** C5
Wytham **133** G2
Wythburn **209** G5
Wythenshawe **184** C4
Wyton *Cambs* **162** A5
Wyton *ERid* **197** D4
Wyverstone **152** B1
Wyverstone Street **152** B1
Wyville **175** D5
Wyvis Lodge **266** B4

X

Xscape Castleford *WYorks*
  WF10 4DA **194** D5

Y

Y Bryn **168** B5
Y Fan **155** F4
Y Felinheli **167** E1
Y Ffôr **166** C4
Y Fron (Upper
  Llandwrog) **167** E2
Yaddlethorpe **187** F2
Yafford **106** D4
Yafforth **202** C3
Yalberton **101** E2
Yalding **123** F4
Yanley **116** C1
Yanwath **210** B5
Yanworth **132** C1
Yapham **195** G2
Yapton **108** B3
Yarburgh **188** D3
Yarcombe **103** F2
Yardley **158** D4
Yardley Gobion **148** C3
Yardley Hastings **149** D2
Yardro **144** B2
Yarford **115** F5
Yarkhill **145** F3
Yarlet **171** G5
Yarley **116** C3
Yarlington **117** D5
Yarm **202** D1
Yarmouth **106** C4
Yarnacott **113** G2
Yarnbrook **117** F2
Yarnfield **171** F4
Yarnscombe **113** F3
Yarnton **133** G1
Yarpole **145** D1
Yarrow *ScBord* **227** E3
Yarrow *Som* **116** A3
Yarrow Feus **227** E3
Yarrowford **227** F3
Yarsop **144** D3
Yarwell **161** F3
Yate **131** G4
Yatehouse Green **171** E1
Yateley **120** D1
Yatesbury **132** C5
Yattendon **134** A5
Yatton *Here* **144** D1
Yatton *NSom* **116** B1
Yatton Keynell **132** A5
Yaverland **107** F4
Yawl **103** G3
Yaxham **178** B4
Yaxley *Cambs* **161** G3
Yaxley *Suff* **164** C4
Yazor **144** D3
Ye Olde Pork Pie Shoppe,
  Melton Mowbray *Leics*
  LE13 1NW **160** C1
Yeabridge **104** A1
Yeading **136** A4
Yeadon **194** B3
Yealand Conyers **199** G5
Yealand Redmayne **199** G5
Yealand Storrs **199** G5
Yealmbridge **100** B2
Yealmpton **100** B2

Yearby **213** F5
Yearsley **203** E5
Yeaton **156** D1
Yeaveley **172** C3
Yeavering **228** C4
Yedingham **204** B5
Yelford **133** F2
Yell **278** D4
Yelland *Devon* **113** E2
Yelland *Devon* **99** F1
Yelling **150** A3
Yelvertoft **160** A5
Yelverton *Devon* **100** B1
Yelverton *Norf* **179** D5
Yenston **117** E5
Yeo Mill **114** B5
Yeo Vale **113** E3
Yeoford **102** A3
Yeolmbridge **98** D2
Yeomadon **112** D5
Yeovil **104** B1
Yeovil Country Park *Som*
  BA20 1QZ **104** B1
Yeovil Marsh **104** B1
Yeovilton **116** C5
Yerbeston **127** D2
Yesnaby **277** B6
Yesterday's World, Battle
  ESuss TN33 0AQ **110** C2
Yetholm Mains **228** C4
Yetlington **229** E5
Yetminster **104** B1
Yettington **103** D4
Yetts o'Muckhart **243** F4
Yew Green **147** E1
Yielden **149** F1
Yieldshields **234** C4
Ynys **167** E4
Ynys Tachwedd **154** C3
Ynysboeth **129** G3
Ynysddu **130** A3
Ynyshir **129** G3
Ynyslas **154** C3
Ynysmaerdy **129** G4
Ynysmeudwy **128** D2
Ynystawe **128** C2
Ynyswen **129** F3
Ynysybwl **129** G3
Yockenthwaite **201** E5
Yockleton **156** C1
Yokefleet **196** A5
Yoker **233** G3
Yonder Bognie **268** E6
York **195** F2
York Castle Museum
  YO1 9SA **90** York
York Dungeon
  YO1 9RD **90** York
York Minster
  YO1 7HH **90** York
Yorkletts **124** C2
Yorkley **131** F2
Yorkshire Museum
  YO1 7FR **90** York
Yorkshire Sculpture Park
  WYorks WF4 4LG **185** G1
Yorton **170** C5
Yorton Heath **170** C5
Youldon **112** D5
Youldonmoor Cross **112** D5
Youlgreave **172** D1
Youlthorpe **195** G2
Youlton **195** D1
Young's End **137** G1
Yoxall **158** D1
Yoxford **153** E1
Ysbyty Cynfyn **155** D5
Ysbyty Ifan **168** B3
Ysbyty Ystwyth **154** D5
Ysceifiog **182** C5
Ysgubor-y-coed **154** C3
Ystalyfera **129** D2
Ystrad **129** F3
Ystrad Aeron **142** B2
Ystrad Meurig **142** D1
Ystrad Mynach **130** A3
Ystradfellte **129** F1
Ystradffin **143** D3
Ystradgynlais **129** D1
Ystradowen *Carmar* **128** D1
Ystradowen *VGlam* **129** G5
Ystumtuen **154** D5
Ythanwells **260** E1
Ythsie **261** G1

Z

Zeal Monachorum **102** A2
Zeals **117** E4
Zelah **96** C4
Zennor **94** B3
Zouch **173** G5